ARABIC—ENGLISH
AND
ENGLISH—ARABIC
DICTIONARY

JOHN WORTABET, M. D.
AND
HARVEY PORTER, Ph.D.

With a Supplement of
Modern Science Terminology
English-Arabic and Arabic-English

Prepared by
the Dictionaries Dept., Librairie du Liban

LIBRAIRIE DU LIBAN
P O B 945, Beirut, Lebanon

INTERNATIONAL BOOK CENTRE
P O B 295, Troy, Michigan, U S A

New Impression 1984

طبع في لبنان

Printed in Lebanon, by Typopress

ARABIC—ENGLISH
AND
ENGLISH—ARABIC
DICTIONARY

JOHN WORTABET, M. D.

AND

HARVEY PORTER, Ph.D.

With a Supplement of

Modern Science Terminology

English-Arabic and Arabic-English

Prepared by

the Dictionaries Dept., Librairie du Liban

LIBRAIRIE DU LIBAN
P O B 945, Beirut, Lebanon

INTERNATIONAL BOOK CENTRE
P O B 295, Troy, Michigan, U S A

قاموس عربي وانكليزي

ARABIC-ENGLISH DICTIONARY.

ا

أ	As a numerical sign = 1.
أ	Particle of interrogation.
أَبٌ مث أَبَوَانِ ج آبَاء	Father.
آبٌ	Month of August.
أَبَوِيٌّ	Fatherly, paternal.
أُبُوَّةٌ	Fatherhood.
أَبَدٌ	Time, eternity (future).
أَبَدَ الآبِدِينَ	For ever.
أَبَداً	Ever ; always.
أَبَدِيٌّ وَمُؤَبَّدٌ	Eternal.
أَبَدِيَّةٌ	Eternity, perpetuity.
إِبْرَةٌ ج إِبَرٌ	Needle.
مِئْبَرٌ ج مَآبِرُ	Needle-case.
إِبْرِيزٌ	Pure gold.
أَبْرَشِيَّةٌ	Diocese.
إِبْرِيقٌ ج أَبَارِيقُ	Water-jug.
إِبْزِيمٌ ج أَبَازِيمُ	Buckle, clasp.
إِبْطٌ ج آبَاطٌ	Arm-pit.
أَبَقَ يَأْبِقُ	To run away.
آبِقٌ	Runaway (slave).
إِبِلٌ	Camels (coll noun).
إِبْلِيسٌ ج أَبَالِسَةٌ	Satan.
أَبَّنَ	To praise the dead.
إِبَّانَ	Time or season of a thing.
اِبْنٌ ج أَبْنَاء وَبَنُونَ	Son.
اِبْنَةٌ أَوْ بِنْتٌ ج بَنَاتٌ	Daughter.
أَبَنُوسٌ	Ebony.
أُبَّهَةٌ	Beauty. Greatness,
أَبَى يَأْبَى	To refuse, refrain.
أَبِيٌّ	Refusing, disdaining.

إِباءٌ	Refusal, rejection.
أَتانٌ ج أُتُنٌ وَأُتْنٌ	She-ass.
أَتونٌ ج أُتُنٌ	Oven, furnace.
أَتَى يأتِي	To come, arrive.
آتَى إِيتاءً	To give ; requite.
تأَتَّى	To happen.
إِتْيانٌ	Arrival, coming.
آتٍ	Comer, one who arrives.
أَلآتِي	The future ; coming next.
أَثَّ يَئِثُّ	To abound.
أَثاثٌ	Household furniture.
أَثِرَ يأْثَرُ	To choose.
أَثَّرَ فِي	To impress.
آثَرَ	To choose, prefer.
تأَثَّرَ	To follow one's tracks
أَثَرٌ ج آثارٌ	Trace, impression.
تأْثيرٌ	Influence ; impression.
مأْثُرةٌ ج مآثِرُ	Memorable deed.
مؤَثِّرٌ	Impressive.
أَثْلٌ	A kind of tamarisk.
أَثِمَ يأْثَمُ	To sin.
أَثَّمَ	To accuse of sin.
إِثْمٌ ج آثامٌ	Sin, crime.
أَثِيمٌ ج أُثَماءُ	Guilty.
مأْثَمةٌ ومأْثَمٌ ج مآثِمُ	Sin, crime.
أَجَّ يَؤُجُّ أَجيجاً	To burn, blaze.
أَجَرَ يأْجِرُ	To pay ; let on hire.
آجَرَ	To pay, let for money.
إِستأْجَرَ	To hire, take on hire.
أَجْرٌ ج أُجورٌ	Recompense.
أُجْرٌ وأُجْرةٌ	Wages, salary.
آجُرٌّ	Baked bricks.
إِيجارٌ	Lease, hire, rent.
أَجيرٌ ج أُجَراءُ	Hired labourer.
مُؤْجِرٌ ومُؤَاجِرٌ	Landlord.
مُسْتأْجِرٌ	Tenant.
إِجّاصٌ وإِنْجاصٌ	Pear (fruit).
أَجِلَ يأْجَلُ	To delay, tarry.

أَجَّلَ To grant a delay.

الأَجَل Appointed time.

أَجْلٌ Cause, reason, sake.

آجِلٌ Postponed, future.

أَجَمٌ ج آجَامٌ Thicket, jungle.

آحَّدَ ووَحَّدَ To unify.

إِتحَدَ بِ To unite with ; join.

أحَدٌ م إِحْدَى ج آحَادٌ One.

الأَحَدُ Sunday.

آحَادٌ Units.

إِتِّحادٌ Union ; agreement.

اخَذَ يأخذُ To take.

أَخَذَ يَقولُ To begin, to say.

أَخَذَ بِ To seize, take hold of.

أَخَذَ بِيَدِهِ To aid, assist.

آخَذَ مُؤَاخَذَةً بِ أوْ على To blame.

إِتَّخَذَ To take to himself.

مَأْخَذٌ ج. مآخذٌ Source. Way.

أَخَّرَتا خيراً To postpone.

تَأَخَرَ To tarry, delay.

آخَرُ م اخرَى Other, another.

آخِرٌ ج أَوَاخِرُ End, last.

الآخِرَةَ The future life.

أَخِيرٌ ج أَخِيرُون Last, extreme.

أَخيراً At the end, finally, lastly.

مُؤَخَّر Posterior part.

إِخَاءٌ وَاخوَّة Brotherhood.

أَخٌ ج إِخْوَةٌ وإِخْوَانٌ Brother.

أختٌ ج أَخَوَاتٌ Sister.

أَخَوِيٌّ Fraternal, brotherly.

أَخُورٌ Stable.

أَدُبَ يأدُبُ To be educated.

أَدَبَ يأدِبُ To invite to a meal.

أَدَّبَ To discipline, chastise.

تَأَدَّبَ Become well-educated.

أَدَبٌ ج آدَابٌ Liberal education.

عِلْمُ الأَدَبِ Polite literature.

تَأْدِيبٌ Chastisement.

Moral. Polite. أَدَبِيٌّ

Literary, learned. أَدِيبٌ ج أُدَبَاءُ

Condiment, seasoning. إِدَامٌ

Human skin. أَدَمَةٌ

Dark or tawny colour. أُدْمَةٌ

Human being. آدَمِيٌّ

To give up, deliver. أَدَّى

To bring to أَدَّى إِلَى

Payment, discharge. أَدَاءٌ

Tool, utensil. أَدَاةٌ ج أَدَوَاتٌ

When. Lo. إِذْ

Behold! When. إِذَا

Therefore. إِذًا وإِذَنْ

March (month). آذَارُ

To give leave to. أَذِنَ لِ يأذَن

To call to prayer. أَذَّنَ

To ask permission. إِسْتَأْذَنَ

Permission, leave. اِذْنٌ

Ear. Handle. اُذْنٌ واُذُنٌ ج آذَانٌ

The Moslem call to prayer. أَذَانٌ

Minaret. مِئْذَنَةٌ ومَأْذَنَةٌ ج مَآذِنُ

One who calls to prayer. مُؤَذِّنٌ

To injure, annoy. آذَى إِيذَاءً

Injury, damage. أَذًى وأَذِيَّةٌ

Hurtful, harmful. مُؤْذٍ

Need, want. أَرَبٌ ج آرَابٌ

In pieces, limb by limb. إِرْبًا إِرْبًا

Groin. اربِيَّةٌ

Purpose. مَأْرَبَةٌ ومَأْرَبٌ ج مَآرِبُ

Europe. اورُبَّا

European. أُورُبِّيٌّ

Inheritance. (*See* وَرِثَ) إِرْثٌ

Purple (*n*). أُرْجُوَانٌ

Purple (*adj*). ارْجُوَانِيٌّ

To date ; write a history. أَرَّخَ

Epoch. history. تَأْرِيخٌ ج تَوَارِيخُ

Historian. مُؤَرِّخٌ

Dated مُؤَرَّخٌ

Ardeb, (corn measure).	إِرْدَبٌّ
Cedar or pine (tree).	أَرْزٌ
Rice.	أُرْزٌ وَأُرُزٌّ وَرُزٌ
Earth, soil, land.	أَرْضٌ
Terrestrial.	أَرْضِيٌّ
To be sleepless.	أَرِقَ يَأْرَقُ
Wakefulness; insomnia.	أَرَقٌ
Hare, rabbit	ارنبٌ ج أَرَانِبُ
To flow.	أَزَبَ يَأْزِبُ أَزْباً
Drain.	مِيزَابٌ ج مَيَازِيبُ
To assist, strengthen.	أَزَرَ
A long wrapper, veil.	إِزَارٌ
Succour, assistance.	مُؤَازَرَةٌ
An apron.	مِئْزَرٌ ج مَآزِرُ
Eternity.	أَزَلٌ وَأَزَلِيَّةٌ
Eternal (of past time).	ازَلِيٌّ
Distress; draught.	أَزْمَةٌ
In front, opposite to.	إِزَاءَ
To found.	أَسَّسَ
To be founded, built.	تَأَسَّسَ
Foundation.	اسَاسٌ ج أُسُسٌ
Fundamental.	اسَاسِيٌّ
Founder.	مُؤَسِّسٌ
Founded, established.	مُؤَسَّسٌ
Spinach, spinage.	أَسْبَانَخ
Master, professor.	اسْتَاذٌ ج أَسَاتِذَةٌ وَأَسَاتِيذُ
Lion.	اسَدٌ ج اسُودٌ
To take captive.	اسَرَ يَأْسِرُ
To submit as a captive.	إِسْتَأْسَرَ
All, the whole of.	بِأَسْرِهِ
Captivity, retention.	أَسْرٌ
Near relations.	اسْرَةٌ
Captive.	أَسِيرٌ ج اسَرَاءُ وَأَسْرَى
Stable.	إِسْطَبْلٌ ج إِسْطَبْلاتٌ
Fleet.	أُسْطُولٌ ج اسَاطِيلُ
To regret.	أَسِفَ وَتَأَسَّفَ
Sorrow, grief, regret.	أَسَفٌ
Oh! Alas!	اسَفِيٌّ وَيَا أَسَفاً

إِسفِنجٌ	Sponge.
إِسكِلَةٌ ج أَساكِلُ	Harbour.
إِسْمٌ ج أَسماء	Name ; noun.
أَسِيَ يَأْسَى	To be grieved.
أَسًى وَأَساً	Grief, sorrow.
أَصُلَ يَأْصُلُ	To be firmly rooted.
تَأَصَّلَ	To be firmly rooted.
إِستَأْصَلَ	To extirpate.
أَصْلٌ ج أُصُولٌ	Root ; principle.
أَصْلِيٌّ	Radical, original.
أَصِيلٌ	Noble ; judicious.
أَلأَصِيلُ	Evening.
إِفرَنجٌ وَإِفْرَنجَةٌ	Franks.
إِفرَنجِيٌّ	A European.
أُفُقٌ ج آفَاقٌ	Horizon ; region.
أَفَكَ يَأْفِكُ	To tell a lie.
إِفْكٌ وَإِفْكَةٌ	A lie.
أَفَلَ يَأْفُلُ	To disappear, set.
أَفْيُونٌ	Opium.
أُقحُوَانٌ	Camomile.
أُقَّةٌ ج أُقَقٌ وَأُقَاتٌ	Oke.
أَكَّدَ	To assure.
تَأَكَّدَ	To be assured.
أَكِيدٌ	Firm ; certain.
تَأْكِيدٌ	Assurance, certitude,
أَكَلَ يَأْكُلُ	To eat.
أُكْلَةٌ	A morsel, mouthful.
آكِلَةٌ وَأَكَلَةٌ	Corroding ulcer.
أَكِيلٌ وَأَكُولٌ	Glutton.
مَأْكَلٌ ج مَآكِلُ	Food.
أَكَمَةٌ ج آكَامٌ	Hill. Mound.
أَلْ	The (definite article).
أَلاَ	Is it not so ? Surely.
أَلاَّ أَنْ لا	That-not.
إِلاَّ	Unless, except.
أَلَّذِي مث أَللذَانِ ج أَلَّذِينَ	Who, which (*Masc*).
أَلَّتِي ج أَللَّوَاتِي	Who, Which (*Fem*).

أَلِفَ يَأْلَفُ To be accustomed
آلَفَ To be friendly.
أَلَّفَ To compile a book.
تَأَلَّفَ To be united.
إِلْفٌ وَأَلِيفٌ Friend, companion.
أَلْفٌ ج اُلُوفٌ وآلافٌ Thousand.
أُلْفَةٌ Friendship, alliance.
إِئْتِلافٌ Accord, harmony.
تَأْلِيفٌ ج تَآلِيفُ Compilation.
مَأْلُوفٌ Customary, usual.
مُؤَالَفَةٌ Friendship, familiarity.
مُؤَلِّفٌ Author (of a book).
مُؤَلَّفٌ Book. Composed.
أَلِمَ يَأْلَم To suffer, feel pain.
أَلَّمَ وآلَمَ To pain, cause pain.
تَأَلَّمَ To feel pain, ache.
أَلَمٌ ج آلامٌ Pain, grief, ache.
أَلِيمٌ ومُؤْلِمٌ Painful.
أَلْمَاسٌ Diamond.

إِلٰهٌ ج آلِهَةٌ A god, divinity.
اللّٰه God ; the One True God.
أَلَّهَ To deify.
اللّٰهُمَّ O God !
اُلُوهَةٌ وَالوهية Divinit y.
أَلْيَةٌ ج الايَا وَأَلَيَاتٌ Rump.
الآيٌ ج الآيَاتٌ Regiment.
إِلَى To, unto, until.
إِلَى أَنْ Until, till.
إِلَى مَتَى Until when ? How long ?
أَمَّ يَؤُمُّ To seek ; lead.
اُمٌّ ج اماتٌ وَاُمَّهَاتٌ Mother.
أَمَامَ Before, in-front.
إِمَامٌ ج أَئِمَّة Imam, leader.
اُمَّةٌ ج اُمَمٌ Nation, people.
اُمِّيٌّ Maternal, Illiterate.
أَمَّا But, but as to.
إِمَّا — وَإِمَّا Either, or.
أَمَدٌ ج آمَادٌ Limit, end, term

أَمَرَ يَأْمُرُ	To order, command.
آمَرَ مُؤَامَرَةً فِي	To consult.
أَمْرٌ ج أَوَامِرُ	Command, order.
أَمْرٌ ج أُمُورٌ	Matter, affair.
إِمَارَةٌ	Prefecture, power.
أَمِيرٌ ج أُمَرَاءُ	Chief, prince.
أَمِيرُ الآيِ	Colonel.
أَمِيرُ ٱلْبَحْرِ	Admiral.
أَمِيرُ ٱلْمُؤْمِنِينَ	Caliph.
أَمِيرِيٌّ	Princely.
أَلْمَالُ ٱلأَمِيرِيُّ	Taxes.
مَأْمُورٌ	Sub-governor.
أَمْسِ	Yesterday.
أَمَلَ يَأْمُلُ	To hope, hope for.
تأَمَّلَ	To meditate, reflect upon.
أَمَلٌ ج آمَالٌ	Hope, desire.
مَأْمُولٌ	Hoped, expected.
أَمُنَ يَأْمُنُ	To be faithful.
أَمِنَ يَأْمَنُ	To be or feel safe.
أَمَّنَ وآمَنَهُ عَلَى	To entrust.
آمَنَ إِيمَاناً بِ	To believe in.
أَمَّنَهُ	To protect
إِئْتَمَنَ	To trust, rely upon.
أَمْنٌ وأَمَانٌ	Safety, protection.
آمِنٌ	Safe, secure.
أَمَانَةٌ	Faithfulness, fidelity.
أَمِينٌ ج أُمَنَاءُ	Faithful.
أَمِينُ ٱلصُّنْدُوقِ	Treasurer.
آمِينَ وأَمِينَ	Amen ; so be it.
إِيمَانٌ	Creed, belief.
مَأْمُونٌ	Trustworthy.
مُؤْمِنٌ	Believer, faithful.
أَمَةٌ ج إِمَاءٌ	Female slave.
أَنْ وأَنْ	That (*particle*).
إِنْ	If. Not.
أَنَّ وإِنَّ	Certainly, truly.
إِنَّمَا	Only , but. Verily.
أَنَّ يَئِنُّ أَنِيناً	To groan ; moan.

أنا ج نحن — I, we.

أنتَ ج أنتم م أنتِ ج أنتنّ — Thou.

أنتما — You two, both of you.

أنثى ج إناث وأناثى — Female.

مؤنّث — Feminine, effeminate.

ألإنجيل — The Gospel.

أنِسَ يأنَسُ — To be polite, affable.

آنسَ مؤانسة — To be sociable.

آنسَ إيناساً — To cheer.

أنس — Social life. Cheerfulness.

إنس — Mankind.

إنسان ج أناس — Man.

إنسانيّ — Human ; polite.

إنسانيّة — Humanity ; politeness.

أنيس ومؤانس — Friendly, gentle.

أنِفَ يأنَفُ — To hate, disdain.

إستأنفَ — To recommence; appeal.

أنف ج آناف وأنوف — Nose.

آنفاً — Little while age.

أنفة — Dislike. Scorn.

أنوف — Disdainful.

مجلس الاستئناف — Court of appeal

أنِقَ بِ يأنَق — To be pleased.

تأنّق — To be dainty.

أنام وآنام — Men, mankind.

تأنّى — To act deliberately.

أناة — Patience, deliberateness.

إناء ج آنية وأوان — Vessel.

تأنّ — Deliberateness.

متأنّ — Deliberate, careful.

أنيسون — Anise.

أنّى = من أين — Whence ?

آه وآها — Ah ! Alas !

أهّبَ — To equip, get one ready.

تأهّبَ لِ — To get ready.

أهبة ج أهب — Apparatus, tools.

أهّلَ لِ — To render fit for.

أهّلَ به — To bid welcome.

تَأَهَّلَ To marry.

إِسْتَأْهَلَ To deserve, merit.

أَهْلاً وَسَهْلاً Welcome !

أَهْلٌ ج أَهَالٍ Family ; relations.

أَهْلٌ لِ Worthy of, fit for.

أَهْلِيٌّ Domestic.

اهْلِيَّةٌ Aptitude, fitness.

مُسْتَأْهِلٌ Deserving, meriting.

أَو Or, unless.

آبَ يَؤُوبُ إِيَاباً To return.

إِوَز Geese.

آسٌ Myrtle.

آفَةٌ ج آفَاتٌ Injury, damage.

آلَ يَؤُولُ To result in.

أَوَّلَ To explain, make clear.

آلٌ Family ; kinsfolk.

آلَةٌ ج آلاَتٌ Instrument.

آلِيٌّ Organic.

أَوَّلُ ج أَوَائل First, beginning.

أَوَّلاً Firstly, in the first place.

أَوَّلاً فَاوَّلاً Successively.

اولئِكَ Those, these.

إِيَالَة ج إِيَالاَتٌ Province.

تَاوِيلٌ Interpretation.

مَآلٌ End, result, issue.

آنٌ وَاوَانٌ Time.

أَلآنَ Now at present.

إِيوَانٌ إِيوَانَاتٌ Porch, hall.

أَوَى يَأْوِي To resort for shelter.

مَأْوًى ج مَآوٍ Abode shelter.

إِبْنُ آوى Jackal.

أَيْ That is to say; namely.

أَيٌّ Whoever, whichever.

آيَةٌ ج آيَاتٌ Sign ; miracle.

إِيَّاهُ Him.

إِيَّاي Me.

ايَّدَ To strengthen, aid.

ايَّار May (month).

أَيِسَ يأيسُ	To despair.
إِيَاسٌ	Despair.
أَيِسٌ وآئِسٌ	Despairing.
أَيَّلٌ وإِيَّلٌ	Deer, stag.
أَيْلُولُ	September.
آنَ يَئِينُ	Its time comes.
أَيْنَ	Where ? whither ?
أَيْنَمَا	Whither ; everywhere.
إِلَى أَيْنَ	Whither ? where ?
مِنْ أَيْنَ	From whence ?

ب

ب	As a numerical sign 2.
بِ	With, during, by, at, in.
بِٱللهِ	By God !
بِمَا أَنْ	By reason of, inasmuch.
بابا ج باباوات	Pope ; father.
بابَوِيٌّ وبَاباوِيّ	Papal.
بُؤْبُؤُ ٱلعَيْنِ	Pupil of the eye.
بابُوجٌ ج بَوَابِيجُ	Slipper.
بابُونَجٌ	Camomile.
بَاذِنْجانٌ	Egg-plant.
بِئْرٌ ج آبَارٌ	Well, cistern.
بارَةٌ ج بارات	Para (coin).
بَارُودٌ	Gunpowder.
بَارُودَةٌ ج بَوَارِيد	Gun.
بَازٌ	Falcon, hawk.
بَازَارٌ	Market.
بَازِرْگَانٌ	Cloth-merchant.
بِئْسَ	Evil ! Bad, very bad. !
بَأْسٌ	Courage , boldness.
بَأْسٌ وَبُؤْسٌ	Misfortune.

اَلبأْسَاء Misfortune, distress.
بائِسٌ Unfortunate, poor.
بَاشَا ج بَاشاوَاتٌ Pasha.
بَاشَقٌ ج بَواشِق Sparrow-hawk.
بَاقَةٌ Bunch of flowers, bouquet.
بَالَةٌ Bale (of merchandise).
بَامِيَا وَبَامِيَةٌ Okra.
بَبْغَاء ج ببغَاوَاتٌ Parrot.
بَتَّ يَبتُّ To cut off ; decide.
اَلْبَتَّةَ وَبَتَّةً Irrevocably; not at all.
بَتَرَ يبتُر To cut off; amputate.
بَتُولٌ Virgin.
بَتُولِيَّةٌ Virginity.
بَثَّ يَبثُّ To disperse, publish.
إِنْبَثَّ To be divulged, spread.
بَثْرٌ ج بُثُورٌ Pustule.
بَثَقَ يبثق To break out.
إِنْبَثَقَ من To proceed from.
إِنْبَثَقَ ٱلْفجر To dawn.

بَجَعٌ Stork.
بَجُلَ يَبْجُلُ بَجَالَةً To be great.
بَجَّلَ To honour, praise.
بَحَّ يبَحُّ بَحًّا To be hoarse.
بُحَّةٌ Hoarseness ; rough voice.
أَبَحُّ وَمَبْحُوحٌ Hoarse.
بَحَثَ عَنْ To investigate.
بَاحَثَ وتَبَاحَثَ To discuss.
بَحْثٌ Examination, enquiry.
مَبْحَثٌ ج مَبَاحِثُ Research.
مُبَاحَثَةٌ Discussion, controversy.
بَحْثَرَ To scatter.
بَحْرٌ ج أَبْحُرٌ وَبُحُورٌ Sea.
بَحْرُ ٱلظُّلُمَاتِ The Atlantic Ocean.
اَلْبَحْرُ ٱلأَحْمَرُ The Red Sea.
اَلْبَحْرُ ٱلاسْوَدُ The Black Sea.
بَحْرُ ٱلْخَزَرِ The Caspian Sea.
اَلْبَحْرُ ٱلْمحيط The Pacific Ocean.
اَلْبَحْرُ ٱلْمتَوسِّطُ او بَحْرُ ٱلرُّومِ The Mediterranean.

To disperse ; squander.	بَدَّد
To be dispersed.	تَبَدَّدَ
To be arbitrary.	إِستَبَدَّ
By all means, necessarily.	لاَبُدَّ
To begin ; create.	بَدَأَ يَبدَأُ
To give precedence.	بَدَّأَ
To create ; produce.	أَبْدَأَ
To begin, commence.	إِبتَدَأَ ب
Beginning.	بَدْءٌ وَبَدَاءَةٌ
Initial, primary.	إِبتِدَائِيٌّ
Principle.	مَبْدَأٌ ج مَبَادِئُ
Dissipation ; pride.	بَذَخ
To hasten towards.	بَدَرَ إِلَى
To hasten.	بَادَرَ وَابتَدَرَ
Full moon.	بَدْرٌ ج بدورٌ
Thrashing-floor.	بَيْدَرٌ ج بَيَادِرُ
To originate.	بَدَعَ يَبْدَعُ
To originate.	أَبْدَعَ وَابتَدَعَ
Innovation.	بِدْعَة ج بِدَعٌ

Basin, pool.	بَحْرَةٌ ج بِحَارٌ
Lake.	بُحَيْرَةٌ ج بُحَيْرَاتٌ
Nautical.	بَحْرِيٌّ
Sailor.	بَحْرِيٌّ ج بَحْرِيَّةٌ
Fortune, good luck.	بَخْتٌ
To swagger.	بَخْتَرَ وَتَبَخْتَرَ
To steam.	بَخَرَ يَبْخُرُ بَخْراً
To fumigate, steam.	بَخَّرَ
Steamship.	بَاخِرَةٌ ج بَوَاخِر
Vapour steam.	بُخَارٌ ج أَبْخِرَةٌ
Incense.	بَخُورٌ
Cyclamen (plant).	بَخُورُ مَرْيَمَ
Having a foul breath.	أَبْخَرُ
Censer.	مِبْخَرَةٌ ج مَبَاخِر
To diminish.	بَخَسَ يَبْخَسُ
Defective, low price.	بَخْسٌ
To be miserly.	بَخِلَ يَبْخَلُ
Avarice, stinginess.	بُخْلٌ
Miser ; miserly.	بَخِيلٌ ج بُخَلاءُ

بَدِيعٌ	Astonishing.
عِلْمُ ٱلْبَدِيعِ	Rhetoric.
إِبْدَاعٌ وَٱبْتِدَاعٌ	Invention.
مُبْدِعٌ	Inventor. Creator.
بَدَّلَ يُبَدِّلُ	To change, exchange.
تَبَدَّلَ	To be changed or altered.
إِسْتَبْدَلَ	To take in exchange.
بَدَلٌ وَبَدِيلٌ	Substitute.
بَدَلَ أَنْ	Instead of.
بَدَلاً مِنْ	In exchange for.
تَبَادُلٌ	Reciprocity.
مُتَبَادِلٌ	Reciprocal
بَدَنٌ ج أَبْدَانٌ	Body, trunk.
بَدَهَ يَبْدَهُ	To come suddenly.
بَدَاهَةٌ	Intuitive knowledge.
بَدِيهًا. عَلَى ٱلْبَدِيهَةِ	Intuitively.
بَدِيهِيَّةٌ	Axiom.
بَدَا يَبْدُو	To appear.
أَبْدَى	To make plain, reveal.

أَلْبَدْو	Nomads, bedouins.
بَادِيَةٌ ج بَوَادٍ	Desert.
بَدَاوَةٌ	Desert life ; desert.
بَدَوِيٌّ	Beduin ; nomad.
بَذِخَ يَبْذَخُ	To be proud.
بَذَخٌ	Pride, haughtiness.
بَذَرَ يَبْذُرُ	To sow ; disperse.
بَذْرٌ ج بِذَارٌ	Seed, grain.
تَبْذِيرٌ	Dissipation, prodigality.
مُبَذِّرٌ	Prodigal.
بَذَلَ يَبْذِلُ	To give.
بَذْلٌ	Generous gift, present.
بَرَّرَ	To justify.
تَبَرَّرَ	To be justified.
بِرٌّ	Goodness, piety.
بُرٌّ	Wheat.
بَرٌّ	Land as opposed to sea.
بَرًّا وَبَحْرًا	By land and by sea.
بَارٌّ ج أَبْرَارٌ	Just, pious.

بَرّانِيّ ج بَرّانِيُّون	External.
بَرِّيّ	Wild (tree or animal).
بَرِيَّة ج بَرارِيّ	Desert, waste.
تَبْرِير	Justification.
بَرَأ يَبرأ	To create.
بَرَأ وبَرِئَ يَبْرأ	To be innocent of. Recover from an illness.
بَرَّأ مِن	To acquit.
بُرْء وبَرْء	Recovery, cure.
بَرِيء ج ابرياء	Innocent.
براءَة	Immunity. Document.
أَلْبارِئ	Creator (God).
بَرِيَّة ج برايا	Creature, creation.
بَرْبَرِيّ	Native of Barbary.
بُرْتُقان وبردقان	Oranges.
بُرْج ج بروج	Tower, castle.
بروج الأفلاكِ	Signs of zodiac.
بارِجَة ج بوارِج	Man-of-war.
بَرِح يَبْرَح	To part from.
ما بَرِح	To continue, persevere.
بَرَّح	To cause pain.
البارِحُ والبارحةُ	Yesterday.
البارحةَ الاولى / اوّل البارحةِ	Day before yesterday.
بَرَدَ يَبرِدُ	To become cold.
بَرَدَ	To file (iron).
بَرَّدَ	To make cool or cold.
بَرْد	Cold.
بَرَد	Hail ; hail stones.
بُرَداء وبردِيَّة	Fever and ague.
بَرْدِيّ	Reed, papyrus reed.
بارِد	Cold.
برودة	Freshness, coolness.
بَرِيد ج بُرُد	Courier, post.
مِبْرَد ج مبارِدُ	File.
بَرْذَعَة	Donkey-saddle.
بَرَزَ يَبرز	To appear, issue.
بارَزَ	To go to battle.

أَبْرَزَ To publish, bring out.

بِرَاز وَمُبَارَزَة Combat, duel.

بُرُوز Appearance.

مُبَارِز Champion ; fighter.

بَرْزَخ ج بَرَازِخ Isthmus.

بِرْسِيم Alexandrian clover.

بَرْش Stramonium.

أَبْرَش م بَرْشَاء Piebald, spotted.

بِرِشْت Soft-boiled egg.

بَرْشَان Wafer.

بَرَص Leprosy.

أَبْرَص م بَرْصَاء ج بُرْص Leper.

بَرْطَلَ بَرْطَلَة To bribe.

بِرْطِيل ج بَرَاطِيل Bribe.

بَرَعَ يَبْرَع To excel.

تَبَرَّعَ ب To bestow of free will.

بَارِع Distinguished ; perfect.

بَرَاعَة Distinction ; elegance.

بُرْعُم ج بَرَاعِم Bud.

بُرْغُوث ج بَرَاغِيث Flea.

بَرْغَش Small flies ; gnats.

بَرْغَشَة A small fly ; gnat.

بُرْغُل Wheat coarsely ground.

بُرْغِيّ ج بَرَاغِيّ Screw.

بَرَقَ يَبْرُق To flash, lighten.

أَبْرَقَ To flash, gleam.

بَرْق ج بُرُوق Lightning.

بُورَق Borax.

بَرْقَعَ To veil the face.

بُرْقُع ج بَرَاقِع A lady's veil.

بَرْقُوق Yellow plum ; apricot.

إِبْرِيق ج أَبَارِيق Ewer.

بَرَكَ يَبْرُك To kneel.

بَارَكَ فِي أَوْ عَلَى To bless.

تَبَرَّكَ بِ To seek blessing.

تَبَارَكَ To be blessed.

بَرَكَة ج بَرَكَات Blessing.

بِرْكَة ج بِرَك Pool, pond ; tank.

Blessed. مُبارَك

Compasses. بِرْكارٌ وبيكارٌ

Volcano. بُرْكانٌ ج براكِين

To twist. بَرَمَ يَبْرُمُ

To make firm. أَبْرَمَ

Gimlet; augur. بِيْرَمٌ وبَرِيمةٌ

Affirmed, assured. مُبْرَمٌ

Twisted cord. مَبْرُومٌ

Barrel ; cask. بَرْمِيلٌ ج بَرَامِيلُ

A kind of cloak. بُرْنُسٌ

Hat. بُرْنَيطَةٌ

Space of time. بُرْهَةٌ

To prove بَرْهَنَ عَلَى أو عَنْ

To be demonstrated. تَبَرْهَنَ

Proof, evidence. بُرْهانٌ ج بَرَاهِينُ

Demonstrated, proved. مُبَرْهَنٌ

Frame. بِرْوازٌ ج بَرَاوِيزُ

To pare ; emaciate. بَرَى يَبْرِي

To vie with. بارَى وَانْبَرَى

Creation, universe. بَرِيَّةٌ ج بَرَايَا

Mended or cut (pen). مَبْرِيٌّ

Linen or cotton clothes. بَزٌّ

Udder, nipple. بِزٌّ ج أَبْزاز

Seed, grain. بِزْرٌ ج بُزُورٌ

A grain or seed. بِزْرَةٌ

To peep forth (sun). بَزَغَ يَبْزُغُ

Rising of sun or moon. بُزُوغٌ

To spit. بَزَقَ يَبْزُقُ بَزْقاً

Spittle, saliva. بُزَاقٌ

Snail. بَزَّاقَةٌ (*coll.* بَزاقٌ)

Spittoon. مِبْزَقَةٌ

To split. Tap a cask. بَزَلَ يَبْزُلُ

Perforator. بِزَالٌ وَمِبْزَلٌ

Buckle. إِبْزِيمٌ

Bath-tub. أَلإِبْزَنُ ج ابَازِنُ

Cat. بَسٌّ م بَسَّةٌ (بُسَينٌ م بسَيْنَةٌ)

Garden ; orchard. بُسْتَانٌ ج بَسَاتِين

Gardener. بُسْتانيٌّ

Piles. بَاسورٌ

To spread out ; cheer. بَسَطَ يبسُطُ

To be cheerful, merry. إنبَسَطَ

Carpet. بِساط ج بُسُطٌ

Simple. بَسيط ج بُسطاء

The Earth. ألبَسِيطة

Cheerfulness. إنبِساط وبسْطٌ

Extended ; happy. مبْسوطٌ

To spit. بَسَقَ يبْسق بَسقاً

To be brave. بَسُل يبْسل

Bold, brave. بَاسِل ج بسلاء

Bravery ; heroism. بسالَةٌ

To smile. بَسَمَ يَبْسِم وتَبَسَّم وا بْتَسَم

Smile. تبَسُّمٌ وا بْتِسامٌ

To be cheerful. بَشّ

Cheerfulness of face, gentleness. بَشَاشَة

To rejoice at. بَشَرَ يبشِرُ

To announce good news. بَشَّرَ

To manage an affair. باشَرَ

Epidermis ; cuticle. بَشَرةٌ

Man ; mankind ; humanity. بَشَرٌ

Mankind, men. ألبَشَر

Good news. بشرى

Human. بَشَريٌّ

Good news ; gospel. بِشارة ج بشائر

Bearer of good news. بَشيرٌ

Announcer of news ; preacher. مُبَشِّرٌ

To be ugly, deformed. بَشِعَ يَبْشع

Bad taste (food); ugliness. بشاعة

Ugly ; repulsive. بَشِعٌ وبَشِيعٌ

Indigestion. بَشَم

Lotus (plant). بشنينٌ

To shine, glitter. بَصَّ يبِصُّ

A live coal. بَصّةٌ

Spy. بَصّاصٌ ج بَصّاصون

To see. بصر يبصر بصر يبصر

To consider, observe. تبَصَّر

Sight. بَصَرٌ ج أبصارٌ

Intelligent.	بَصِيرٌ ج بُصَراء
Consideration ; reflection.	تَبَصُّرٌ
To spit.	بَصق يَبْصُق بَصْقاً
Spittle, saliva.	بُصَاق
Onion ; bulb.	بَصَلٌ
To cut, incise.	بَضَعَ يَبضَع
A small number.	بِضْعٌ وبِضْعَةٌ
A few days.	بِضعة أيام
Merchandise.	بِضاعة ج بَضائِع
Knife ; lancet.	مِبضَعٌ ج مباضِع
To lance a tumour.	بطَّ يَبطُّ
Duck.	بَطَّة ج بَطٌّ
Bottle.	بَطَّةٌ ج بُطَطٌ
To linger.	بَطُؤَ يَبْطُو
To be slow, dally.	تَبَاطَأَ فِي
Slowness.	بطاء و بطءٌ وبطوءٌ
Slow, tardy, dilatory.	بَطِيءٌ
Water-course.	بطحاء وبَطيحة
Water-melon.	بِطِّيخٌ أحمَر

Musk-melon.	بَطِّيخٌ أَصْفَر
To exult.	بطِرَ يَبطِر بَطَراً
Exultation. Wantonness.	بَطَرٌ
Toshoe animals	بَيْطَرَ
Farrier.	بَيْطارٌ ج بَيَاطِرة
Veterinary art .	بَيطَرَةٌ
Battery (of cannons).	بَطَّارِيَّةٌ
Patriarch.	بطْرِكٌ ج بطارِكَةٌ
Patriarchate.	بَطْرِيَرْكِيَّةٌ وبَطْرِكِيَّةٌ
To assault.	بَطَش يَبطِش ب
Power ; violence.	بَطْشٌ
A marked ticket.	بِطَاقَةٌ
To cease.	بطَل يَبطل
To repeal, abolish.	بطل وأبْطَل
Vanity ; lie.	بطْلٌ وبطْلان
Hero.	بطَلٌ ج أَبْطَالٌ
False, vain, useless.	بَاطِلٌ
Lazy, idle ; useless.	بَطَّالٌ
Idleness ; holidays.	بِطالَة

Abolition, repeal. إِبْطَالٌ

Marine muscle. بَطْلَينُوسٌ

Terebinth. بُطْمٌ

To line (clothes). بطَنَ وأَبْطَنَ

Belly, abdomen. بَطْنٌ ج بُطونٌ

Inner lining. بطانَةٌ

Inner, hidden. بَاطِنٌ ج بواطِن

Internally, secretly. باطناً

To send. بعثَ يَبْعَثُ إلى

To raise the dead. بعَثَ

Cause, motive. باعِثٌ

Sent. Envoy. مَبعوثٌ

To scatter, uncover. بعثَرَ

To be far distant. بعُدَ يبعُدُ

To make distant. بَعَّدَ وأَبْعَدَ

To be far from. تَبَاعَدَ عَن

To go far from. إبتعَدَ عَن

To regard improbable. إستَبعَدَ

Distance ; interval. بُعْدٌ

Then ; afterwards ; after. بَعْدَ

Distant ; far. بعيدٌ

Camel. بَعِيرٌ ج بعرانٌ

To scatter, dissipate. بعزق

Portion, part ; some. بَعضٌ

Gnats, mosquitoes. بعوضٌ

A gnat or mosquito. بعوضةٌ

Husband, wife. بَعلٌ ج بعولٌ

Unwatered land. بَعْلٌ

To take by surprise. بَغَتَ يبغَتُ وباغَتَ

Surprise. بَغْتَةٌ ج بغتات

Suddenly, unexpectedly. بغتَةً

Strait. بوغازٌ ج بَوَاغيزُ

To hate, detest. أَبغَضَ

Hatred ; enmity. بُغْضٌ

Violent hatred. بغضةٌ وبَغضاءُ

One who hates. مُبْغِضٌ

Mule. بغلٌ ج بِغال وأبغال

Muleteer. بَغّالٌ

بَغمة	Necklace.
بَغَى يَبغِي	To seek ; desire.
بَغَى عَلَى	To be unjust ; oppress.
يَنبغِي أن	It is desirable.
بَغْي	Injustice ; aggression.
بُغاء وابتغاء	Wish, desire.
بُغْيَة وبِغْيَة	Anything wished for or sought.
بَاغٍ ج بُغاة	Unjust aggressor.
بُقجة ج بُقَج	Bundle of clothes.
بَقدونس	Parsley.
بَقَر ج أبقار	Oxen.
بَقَرة ج بَقَرات	Cow.
بَقْس	Box-tree.
بَقِعَ يَبْقَع بَقَعاً	To be spotted.
بَقَع	Spots, stains.
بُقعة ج بُقَع وبِقاع	Piece of land.
بَقْل ج بُقول	Vegetables, herbs.
بَقّال	Green-grocer.
بَقَّم	Logwood.

بَقِيَ يَبقَى	To remain ; continue.
أَبقَى وَاستَبقَى	To preserve.
تَبَقَّى	To be left.
بَقَاء	Continuance, uration.
بَقِيَّة ج بَقَايَا	Remainder.
بَاقٍ ج بَاقُون	Remaining.
الباقِي	The Everlasting (God).
بَاقِيَّة	Vetch.
أَبقَى	More enduring.
بَكَّت	To reprove, scold.
بَكَّرَ وبَاكَرَ	To come early.
بِكْر ج أبكار	First-born ; virgin.
بُكْرَة	Dawn ; to-morrow.
بَكَرة ج بَكَر	Pulley.
بَكارة	Virginity.
بَاكِرًا	Early.
بَاكُورَة	First fruits.
بَكِمَ يَبكَمُ	To be dumb
أَبكَمَ	To cause to be silent.

بَكَمٌ	Dumbness.
أبكَم ج بُكْمٌ	Dumb ; mute.
بَكَى يَبْكِي	To weep.
بكَّى وأبكَى	To cause to weep.
بُكَاءٌ وبُكًى	Weeping.
بَلْ	But ; nay but.
بَلَّ يَبُلُّ	To wet, moisten.
تَبَلَّلَ وابْتَلَّ	To become wet
مَبْلُولٌ ومُبَلَّلٌ	Wet, moistened.
بَلْبَلَ	To mix, confound.
بُلْبُلٌ ج بَلابِلُ	Nightingale.
بَلْبَالٌ	Intense anxiety.
بَلَحٌ	Dates (*Coll.*)
بَلُدَ يَبْلُدُ	To be stupid.
بَلَدٌ ج بِلادٌ وبُلْدانٌ	Town ; land.
بَلَدِيٌّ	Native ; urban.
بَلادة	Stupidity ; dullness.
بَلِيدٌ وأبْلَد	Imbecile, stupid.
بلُّورٌ وبِلَّوْرٌ	Crystal.

ابْلِيسٌ ج أبَالِسَةٌ	Devil, Satan.
بَلَسَمٌ	Balsam, balm.
بَلَسَانٌ	Elder-tree.
بَلَصَ يَبْلُصُ	To tax illegally.
بَلْصٌ	Oppressive taxation.
بلَّط	To pave with flage-stones.
بَلْطَة	Axe, battle-axe.
بَلاَط	Flag-stones ; pavement.
بلُّوطٌ	Oak-tree, acron.
بَلْطَجِيٌّ	Sapper, executioner.
تَبْلِيطٌ	Act of paving.
مُبَلِّطٌ	Paver.
مُبَلَّطٌ	Paved.
بَلَعَ يَبْلَعُ	To swallow.
بَلْعٌ وابْتِلاعٌ	Swallowing.
بَالُوعَة	Sink, sewer, gutter.
بلْعومٌ	Gullet.
بَلَغَ يَبْلُغُ بُلوغاً	To reach, attain.
بَلَّغَ	To inform.

بالَغَ فِي	To exaggerate.
بالِغٌ	Mature ; of full age.
بَلاغٌ	Message.
بَلاغة	Elegance of style.
علم البَلاغَة	Rhetoric.
بُلوغٌ	Arrival, maturity.
بَلِيغٌ	Eloquent efficacious.
مَبْلَغٌ ج مَبالِغُ	Sum, amount.
مُبالَغَة	Exaggeration.
بَلْغَمٌ ج بلاغِمُ	Phlegm.
بلغَمِيٌّ	Phlegmatic.
أَبْلَقُ م بَلْقاء ج بُلْقٌ	Spotted.
بَلانٌ	A thorny plant.
بَلَهٌ وبَلاهَة	Stupidity, idiocy.
أَبْلَهُ م بَلْهاء ج بُلْهٌ	Stupid ; simpleton, idiot.
بَلا يَبْلو	To test, try ; afflict.
بَلِيَ يَبْلَى	To decay.
بالَى بِ	To be attentive to.
بِلًى	Decay ; rottenness.
بَلَى	Yes, certainly.
بَلاءٌ	Trial. Grief ; calamity.
بلوى ج بَلايا	Affliction.
بالٍ	Used up ; rotten.
بِمَ	Wherewith ?
بِما ان	Because, inasmuch as
بُنٌّ	Coffee-berries ; coffee.
بَنانٌ	Fingers.
بَنَّجَ	To drug, stupefy.
بَنْجٌ	Henbane, Hyoscyamus.
بَنْدٌ ج بنودٌ	Section. Banner.
بَنْدورةٌ	Tomatoes.
بَنْدَيرةٌ	Flag, banner.
بُنْدُقةٌ وبُنْدُق	Hazel-nut.
بُنْدُقِيَّةٌ	Musket, gun.
بُنْدُوقٌ ج بَنادِيقُ	Bastard.
بَنَفْسَجٌ	Violet (*plant*).
بَنَفْسَجِيٌّ	Violet (*colour*).
بِنْصِرٌ ج بَناصِرُ	Ring-finger.

To be dazzled.	بَهَرَ
Beautiful, admirable.	باهِرٌ
Heavy, distressing.	باهِظٌ
To supplicate.	إِبْتَهَلَ إِلى
Supplication.	إِبْتِهالٌ
Rope-dancer.	بَهْلَوانٌ
To be doubtful.	أُبْهِمَ وَٱسْتَبْهَمَ
Brute, beast.	بَهِيمَةٌ ج بَهائِمُ
Doubt ; ambiguity.	إِبْهامٌ
Thumb.	إِبْهامٌ ج أَباهِمُ
Ambiguous ; doubtful.	مُبْهَمٌ
To be beautiful.	بَهَا يَبْهُو
To rival in beauty.	باهَى
Beauty, brilliancy.	بَهاءٌ
Beautiful splendid.	بَهِيٌّ
Door. Chapter.	بابٌ ج أَبْوابٌ
The Sublime Porte.	أَلْبابُ ٱلعالِي
Door-keeper.	بَوَّابٌ
Large door, gate.	بَوَّابَةٌ

Seat. Bank.	بَنْكٌ ج بُنُوكَةٌ
To construct, build.	بَنَى يَبْنِي
To adopt a son.	تَبَنَّى
Building, edifice.	بِناءٌ وَبِنايَةٌ
In consequence of.	بِناءً على
Mason.	بَنّاءٌ ج بَنّاؤُونَ
Form ; constitution.	بِنْيَةٌ
Son, boy.	إِبْنٌ ج بَنُونَ وَأَبْناءٌ
Daughter.	إِبْنَةٌ وَبِنْتٌ ج بَناتٌ
Traveller, wayfarer.	إِبْنُ ٱلسَّبِيلِ
Built. Indeclinable.	مَبْنِيٌّ
To be astonished ; faded.	بَهِتَ يَبْهَتُ
To astonish, perplex.	بَهَتَ يَبْهَتُ
Lie ; slander.	بُهْتانٌ
To rejoice, cheer.	بَهَجَ وَأَبْهَجَ
To rejoice at.	بَهِجَ وَٱبْتَهَجَ
Joy, gladness ; beauty	بَهْجَةٌ
Cheering ; causing joy.	مُبْهِجٌ
To shine.	بَهَرَ يَبْهَرُ

باحَ يبُوح	To be known.
باحَ بِ	To divulge.
أَباحَ	To allow.
إستَباحَ	To consider lawful.
إِباحة	Revealing, licence.
مُباحٌ	Permissable; lawful.
باخَ يبُوخ	To abate ; fade.
بارَ يبور	To perish.
بور	Uncultivated land.
بَوارٌ	Destruction, ruin.
بُورَق	Borax ; natron.
بازٌ ج بيزان	Falcon, hawk.
باسَ يبُوس بَوْساً	To kiss.
بُوسطةٌ	Post ; mail.
بوسطجي	Postman.
باعٌ ج أبْوَاعٌ	A fathom.
طَوِيل ٱلباعِ	Generous. Able.
بوَّق	To blow a trumpet.
بوقٌ ج أبْوَاقٌ	Trumpet; shell.
بائِكةٌ ج بوَائِك	Storehouse.
بالَ يبُولُ	To micturate. Melt ; flow.
بالٌ	Condition ; mind ; thought.
خطر ببِال	To occur to mind
بالَةٌ	Bale.
بَوْلٌ	Urine.
بُولاَدٌ (فولاَذٌ)	Steel.
بُومةٌ	An owl.
بولِيصةٌ ج بوَالِص	Bill ; order ; receipt.
بانٌ	The Egyptian willow.
بَوْنٌ	Distance ; difference.
بَاتَ يَبِيت	To pass the night.
بَيْتٌ ج بيوتٌ وَأَبيَاتٌ	House, room. Verse of poetry.
بَيْتُ ٱلمَاءِ / بيْتُ ٱلخَلاَءِ / بَيْتُ ٱلقضاءِ	Water-closet ; latrine ; privy.
بيتُ ٱلمَال	Public treasury.
بَيت ٱلعنكَبوت	Cobweb.
بيتُ ٱلمقدِس	Jerusalem.

اَلْبَيْتُ اَلْحَرَام	The Kaaba in Mecca.
مَبِيت	House, night's lodging.
بَادَ يَبِيدُ	To perish, vanish.
أَبَادَ	To destroy, annihilate.
بَيْدَاءُ ج بِيدٌ	Desert.
بَيَّادِيٌّ بَيَّادَة	Foot-soldier.
بَيْدَ أَنْ	But, although.
بَيْدَرٌ	Thrashing-floor.
بِئْرٌ	Well of water.
بَيْرَقٌ بَيَارِق	Banner.
بَاضَ يَبِيضُ	To lay eggs.
بَيَّضَ	To whiten, bleach.
إِبْيَضَّ	To become white.
بَيْضٌ ج بُيُوضٌ	Eggs.
بَيْضَة	An egg. Testicle.
بَيْضِيٌّ	Oval, ovate ; elliptical.
بَيَاضٌ	Whiteness.
أَبْيَضُ م بَيْضَاءُ ج بِيضٌ	White.
مُبَيِّضٌ	Tinner; white-washer.
بَيْطَرَ	To shoe a horse.
بَاعَ يَبِيعُ	To sell.
بَايَعَ مُبَايَعَة	To swear fealty.
إِبْتَاعَ مِنْ	To buy from.
بَيْعٌ	Selling, sale.
بِيعَةٌ ج بِيَعٌ	Church, synagogue.
بَائِعٌ ج بَاعَة	Seller.
بَيَّاع	Seller.
مَبِيع	Sale ; place of sale.
بَيْكٌ وَبَك	Bey.
بِيكَارٌ	Pair of compasses.
بَيْلَسَانٌ	Elder (tree).
بِيمَارِسْتَان	Hospital.
بَانَ يَبِينُ	To be distinct, separate.
بَيَّنَ	To render clear ; explain.
بَايَنَ	To quit, abandon.
تَبَيَّنَ	To be clear, lucid.
بَيْنَ	Between, among.
بَيْنَ بَيْنَ	Middling.

بَيْنَا وبَيْنَمَا Whilst, while.

بَيَان Explanation.

عِلْم ٱلبَيَان A branch of Rhetoric.

بائِنٌ وبيِّنٌ Distinct, evident.

بيِّنةٌ ج بَيِّنَاتٌ Evidence.

تبَاين Difference ; contrast.

مبِيْنٌ و بيّن Clear, evident.

ت

ت As a numeral sign=400

تَاللّٰه I swear by God.

تَابوت ج توابِيت Chest. Coffin.

تارةً Once ; sometimes.

تَوأَمةٌ ج توَائِمُ Twin.

تَوأمٌ Twins ; double.

أَلتوأَمَان The sign of Gemini.

تَب يَتبُّ To suffer loss.

إِستَتَب To be established.

تَبًّا لهُ Evil be to him !

تبْرٌ Native gold.

تَبِع يتبَعُ وٱتَّبَعَ To follow.

أَتْبَعَ To cause to follow.

تَابع متابعَةً علَى To follow.

تتبع To follow up.

تَتَابع To follow consecutively.

تبَعٌ ج اتبَاعٌ Follower.

متَتَابِعٌ Successive.

تَبْغٌ Tobacco.

تبّل وتَابَلَ To season (a dish).

توَابلُ Condiments.	تخم يتخم تخمًا To confine, limit.
متبَلَ Seasoned (dish.)	تاخم Adjoin, border upon.
تبن Straw.	أتخم To cause indigestion.
تترٌ Tartars (*coll.*)	تَخْمٌ ج تخومٌ Boundary.
تتريٌّ A Tartar.	متاخمٌ Adjoining.
تَتْرى One after another.	تخمة Indigestion.
تُتنٌ Tobacco	ترب To cover with earth.
تجَر يتجر وتاجَر To trade.	ترابٌ ج أتْربَة Earth, dust.
تجارَةٌ Commerce, trade.	تربَةٌ ج تربٌ Cemetery. Soil.
تاجرٌ ج تجّارٌ Merchant.	اترجٌّ واترْنجٌ Citron.
مَتْجَرٌ ج متَاجر Commerce.	ترجم To translate.
تُجَاه In front of, opposite to.	ترجمةٌ Translation.
تحْتَ Under, below, beneath.	ترجمانٌ Dragoman, interpreter.
تحْتانيٌّ Inferior, placed below.	مُترجمٌ Translator, interpreter.
أتْحَف ب To present with.	مُترجَمٌ Translated, interpreted.
تحفَةٌ Precious object, gift.	تَرَحٌ ج أتْراحٌ Sorrow, grief.
تَخْتٌ ج تُخوتٌ Bench ; bedstead.	ترسٌ ج أتراسٌ Shield.
تختروان Palanquin.	مْتراسٌ ج متاريس Bulwark.
تختُ الملْكِ Capital of a kingdom.	ترسانَةٌ وتَرْسخانَة Arsenal.

تُرْعَةٌ ج تُرَع	Channel, canal.
تَرَفٌ وتُرْفَةٌ	Luxury ; ease.
تَرْقُوَةٌ	Collar-bone, clavicle.
تَرَكَ يَتْرُكُ	To abandon, allow.
تَرَكَ لِ	To leave to, bequeath.
تَرْكٌ	Abandoning leaving.
تُرْكٌ ج أَتْرَاكٌ	Turk.
تُرْكِيٌّ	A turk ; Turkish.
تِرْكَةٌ وتَرِكَةٌ	Estate of one dead.
مَتْرُوكٌ	Abandoned, omitted.
تُرْمُسٌ	Lupine.
تِرْيَاقٌ	Theriac ; antidote.
تِسْعَةٌ م تِسْعٌ	Nine.
تُسْعٌ	A ninth (part).
تَاسِعٌ	Ninth (*ord. num.*)
تِسْعُونَ	Ninety, ninetieth.
تِشْرِينُ الأَوَّلُ	October.
تِشْرِينُ الثَّانِي	November.
تَعَالَ	Come !
تَعِبَ يَتْعَبُ	To become tired.
أَتْعَبَ	To give trouble ; tire.
تَعَبٌ ج أَتْعَابٌ	Fatigue, toil.
تَعِبٌ	Tired, fatigued.
مُتْعِبٌ	Toilsome, fatiguing.
مُتْعَبٌ	Fatigued.
تَعِسَ يَتْعَسُ	To stumble
تَعْسٌ وتَعَاسَةٌ	Misfortune.
تَعِسٌ	Unhappy, unlucky.
تُفَّاحٌ	Apple.
تُفَّاحَةٌ	An apple, apple-tree.
تَفَلَ يَتْفُلُ	To spit.
تُفْلٌ	Spittle, saliva.
مَتْفَلَةٌ	Spittoon.
تَفِهَ يَتْفَهُ	To be mean, foolish.
تَفَاهَةٌ	Insipidity.
أَتْقَنَ	To arrange skilfully.
تَقَانَةٌ	Perfection (of a work).
إِتْقَانٌ	Skilful elaboration.

مُتْقَن	Skilfully made.
تَقِيّ	Pious.
تَقْوَى	Piety.
تَلٌّ ج تِلَالٌ	Small hill.
تَلِفَ يَتْلَفُ تَلَفًا	To perish.
أَتْلَفَ	To ruin.
تَلَفٌ	Destruction.
مُتْلِفٌ	Destroyer, waster.
مِتْلَافٌ	Squanderer.
تِلْكَ	That (*fem.*)
تَلَمٌ ج أَتْلَامٌ	Furrow, rut.
تَلْمَذَ	To be a pupil.
تِلْمِيذٌ ج تَلَامِيذ	Disciple, pupil.
تَلَا يَتْلُو تُلُوًّا	To follow ; succeed.
تَلَا يَتْلُو تِلَاوَةً	To read ; recite.
تِلَاوَة	Reading, recitation.
تَال	Following, next.
تَمَّ يَتِمّ	To be complete.
تَمَّمَ وأَتَمَّ	To complete, finish.

تَمَامٌ	Completion, end.
تَمَامًا وبالتَّمَام	Completely.
تَمِيمَةٌ ج تَمَائِم	Talisman, amulet
تَامٌّ م تَامَّة	Perfect, complete.
تَتِمَّة	Complement.
تَمْتَامٌ	Stammerer.
تَمْرٌ ج تُمُورٌ	Ripe dates.
تَمْرٌ هِنْدِيٌّ	Tamarind (*fruit*).
تَمُوز وتَمُّوز	July.
تِمْسَاحٌ ج تَمَاسِيحُ	Crocodile.
تِنِّينٌ ج تَنَانِين	Dragon.
تَنْبَكٌ	Persian tobacco.
تَنْبَلٌ ج تَنَابِلُ	Idler, lazy.
تَنُّورٌ ج تَنَانِيرُ	Oven-pit.
تَنَكٌ	Tin.
أَتْهَمَ واتَّهَمَ	To suspect, accuse.
تُهَمَة	Suspicion. Accusation.
تَابَ يَتُوبُ	To repent.
تَوْبَةٌ	Repentence ; penitence.

تائِبٌ Repentant, penitent.

تُوتٌ White mulberry.

تُوتٌ شَامِيٌّ Black mulberry.

تُوتُ ٱلعُلَّيقِ Blackberry.

تُوتِيَاء Zinc.

تَوَّجَ To crown.

تَتَوَّجَ To be crowned.

تَاجٌ ج تِيجانٌ Crown, diadem.

تَوْرَاةٌ Pentateuch. Bible.

تَارَةٌ One time.

تَاقَ يَتُوقُ إِلَى To long for, desire.

تَوْقٌ وَتَوَقَانٌ Passion, desire.

تَائِقٌ Yearning, desiring.

تَاهَ يَتُوهُ To lose one's way.

تَيَّارٌ A strong, deep current.

تَاحَ وَأَتَاحَ لِ To be appointed, decreed to.

تَيْسٌ ج تُيُوسٌ He-goat.

تِينٌ Figs ; fig-trees.

تِينَةٌ A fig, a fig tree.

تَاهَ يَتِيهُ To be proud. Wander.

تِيهٌ Desert. Pride.

تَائِهٌ Lost, wandering. Proud.

ث

ث As a numeral sign = 500

تَثَاءَبَ تَثَاؤُباً To yawn.

ثَأْرٌ ثَارٌ ج اثَارٌ Revenge.

ثُؤْلُولٌ ج ثَآلِيلُ Wart.

ثَبَتَ يَثْبُتُ To stand firm.

ثَبَتَ عِنْدَ To be certain, assured.

ثَبَّتَ وَأَثْبَتَ	To prove.
ثَبَاتٌ وَثُبُوتٌ	Firmness. Reality.
ثَابِتٌ	Firm ; certain sure.
ثَابِتَةٌ ج ثَوَابِتُ	Fixed star.
مُثْبَتٌ وَثَابِتٌ	Firm ; proved.
ثَابَرَ عَلَى مُثَابَرَةً	To persevere in.
مُثَابِرٌ	Assiduous, persevering.
ثَخُنَ يَثْخُنُ	To be thick.
أَثْخَنَ	To make slaughter
ثُخْنٌ وَثُخُونَةٌ	Thickness; hardness.
ثَخِينٌ ج ثِخَانٌ	Thick, firm.
ثَدْيٌ ج ثُدِيٌّ	Breast (mamma).
ثَرْبٌ ج ثُرُوبٌ	Omentum, caul.
ثَرِيد	Bread with broth.
ثَرِيَ وَأَثْرَى	To abound in wealth.
ثَرَاءٌ وَثَرْوَةٌ	Wealth, riches.
ثُرَيَّا	The Pleiades.
ثَرًى ج أَثْرَاءٌ	Moisture ; earth.
ثُعْبَان ج ثَعَابِين	Large serpent.
ثَعْلَبٌ ج ثَعَالِبُ	Fox.
دَاءُ الثَّعْلَبِ	Alopecia, falling of hair.
ثَغَرَ يَثْغَرُ	To make a breach.
ثَغْرٌ ج ثُغُورٌ	Frontier. Mouth.
ثُغْرَةٌ ج ثُغُورٌ	Opening ; breach.
ثُفْلٌ	Sediment, dregs.
ثَقَبَ يَثْقُبُ ثَقْبًا	To pierce.
تَثَقَّبَ وَانْثَقَبَ	To be pierced.
ثَقْبٌ ج ثُقُوبٌ	Hole.
ثَاقِبٌ	Penetrating.
مِثْقَبٌ ج مَثَاقِبُ	Gimlet, drill.
مَثْقُوبٌ	Pierced, perforated.
ثَقِفَ يَثْقَفُ	To be skilful.
ثَقَافَةٌ	Sagacity, intelligence.
مُثَقَّفٌ	Well-made; educated.
ثَقُلَ يَثْقُلُ	To be heavy.
ثَقَّلَ	To make heavy.
ثَقُلَ عَلَى	To burden, annoy.
إِسْتَثْقَلَ	To deem heavy

ثِقْلٌ ج أَثْقَالٌ	Weight, burden.
أَلثَّقَلَانِ	Mankind and geni.
ثَقِيلٌ ج ثُقَلَاءُ وَثِقَالٌ	Heavy.
مُثَقَّلٌ	Overburdened.
مِثْقَالٌ ج مَثَاقِيلُ	$1\frac{3}{7}$ dirhems.
ثَاكِلٌ وَثَكْلَى	Mother bereft of children.
ثَلَبَ يَثْلِبُ	To blame, censure.
ثَلْبٌ	Censure, reproach.
مَثْلَبَةٌ ج مَثَالِبُ	Fault, vice.
ثَلَّثَ	To make three.
أَثْلَثَ	To become three.
ثُلْثٌ وَثُلُثٌ	Third part, third.
ثَالِثٌ	Third.
ثَالِثًا	Thirdly.
ثَلَاثًا	Thrice, three times.
اَلثُّلَاثَاءُ وَالثَّلَثَاءُ	Tuesday.
ثَلَاثَةٌ اوْ ثَلٰثَةٌ م ثَلَاثٌ	Three.
ثُلَاثِيٌّ	Triliteral.
ثَلَاثُونَ وَثَلٰثُونَ	Thirty.

مُثَلَّثٌ	Triangular ; triangle.
ثَالُوثٌ	Trinity.
عِلْمُ ٱلْمُثَلَّثَاتِ	Trigonometry.
ثَلَجَ يَثْلُجُ وَأَثْلَجَ	To snow.
ثَلْجٌ ج ثُلُوجٌ	Snow.
ثَلِجٌ	Icy cold.
ثَلَمَ يَثْلِمُ ثَلْمًا وَثَلَّمَ	To blunt.
ثَلِمَ وَتَثَلَّمَ وَٱنْثَلَمَ	To be blunted.
ثَلْمٌ	Furrow ; breach.
ثَمَّ	Yonder ; there.
ثُمَّ وَثُمَّتَ	Then ; moreover.
إِثْمِدٌ	Antimony.
ثَمَرَ يَثْمُرُ وَأَثْمَرَ	To bear fruit.
ثَمَرٌ ج أَثْمَارٌ وَثِمَارٌ	Fruit.
ثَمَرَةٌ ج ثَمَرٌ وَثَمَرَاتٌ	A fruit.
مُثْمِرٌ	Productive, fruitful.
ثَمَلٌ	Intoxication.
ثَمَّنَ	To value, estimate.
ثَمَنٌ ج أَثْمَانٌ	Price, value.

ثُمْنٌ ج أَثْمَانٌ Eighth part.

ثَامِنٌ Eighth.

ثَمَانِيَةٌ م ثَمَانٍ Eight.

ثَمَانُونَ Eighty.

ثَمِينٌ وَمُثْمِنٌ Costly, precious.

تَثْمِينٌ Valuation, estimation.

مُثَمِّنٌ Estimator appraiser.

مُثَمَّنٌ Octagon. Estimated.

ثَنَى يَثْنِي ثَنْيًا To fold, double.

ثَنَى عَنْ To dissuade.

ثَنَّى To make two.

أَثْنَى عَلَى To praise a person.

إِنْثَنَى To be bent, folded.

إِنْثَنَى عَنْ To desist from.

إِسْتَثْنَى مِنْ To exclude.

ثَنَاءٌ ج أَثْنِيَةٌ Praise, eulogy.

ثَانٍ م ثَانِيَةٌ Second.

ثَانِيًا وَثَانِيَةً Secondly.

فِي إِثْنَاءِ ج ثَوَانٍ Second, (time).

ثَانِيَةٌ ذَلِكَ Meanwhile.

إِثْنَانِ م ثِنْتَانِ وَآثْنَتَانِ Two.

يَوْمُ ٱلإِثْنَيْنِ Monday.

إِسْتِثْنَاءٌ Exception, exclusion.

إِسْتِثْنَائِيٌّ Exceptional.

ثَنَّى Put in the dual, (noun).

أَلْمُثَنَّى The dual.

مُسْتَثْنَى Excpeted, excluded.

ثَوَّبَ To reward, recompense.

أَثَابَ إِثَابَةً To reward.

ثَوْبٌ ج ثِيَابٌ وَأَثْوَابٌ Garment.

ثَوَابٌ Reward, recompense.

ثَارَ يَثُورُ To rise up ; break out.

ثَوَّرَ وَأَثَارَ To stir up ; rouse.

ثَوْرٌ ج أَثْوَارٌ وَثِيرَانٌ Bull, ox.

ثَوْرَةٌ Excitement. Mutiny.

ثُومٌ Garlic.

ثَوَى يَثْوِي To abide. To die.

مَثْوًى ج مَثَاوٍ Abode.

ثَيِّبٌ ج ثَيِّبَاتٌ Woman freed from her husband

ج

ج	As a numeral sign = 3.
جَاثَلِيقٌ	Primate of Christians.
جَاشٌ	Agitation, commotion.
جَبَّ يَجُبُّ	To lop ; cut off.
جُبٌّ ج أَجْبَابٌ	A deep well.
جُبَّةٌ ج جُبَبٌ	A long coat.
جَبَرَ يَجْبُرُ	To set a broken bone. To repair.
جَبَرَ على	To force, compel.
جَبَّرَ	To set a broken bone.
أَجْبَرَ على	To constrain, force.
تَجَبَّرَ عَلَى	To be haughty.
جَبْرٌ	Compulsion.
أَلْجَبْرُ	Algebra.
جَبِيرَةٌ ج جَبَائِرُ	Bandage ; splint.
جَبَّارٌ ج جَبَابِرَةٌ	Strong, Proud.
أَلْجَبَّارُ	God. Orion.
مُجَبِّرٌ	Bone-setter.
مَجْبُورٌ	Set (bone) ; constrained.
جِبْرِيلُ	The Angel Gabriel.
جِبْسٌ	Gypsum.
جَبَلَ يَجْبُلُ	To form, knead.
جَبَلٌ ج أَجْبَالٌ وَجِبَالٌ	Mountain.
جِبِلَّةٌ وَجِبْلَةٌ	Natural temper.
جَبَلِي	Mountainous.
جِبِلِّيٌّ	Natural, inborn.
مَجْبُولٌ	Kneaded ; formed.
جَبُنَ يَجْبُنُ	To be timid, cowardly.
تَجَبَّنَ	To become curdled.
جُبْنٌ وَجَبَانَةٌ	Cowardice.
جُبْنٌ وَجُبُنٌ	Cheese.
جَبِينٌ	Brow forehead.
جَبَانٌ ج جُبَنَاءُ	Coward.
جَبَّانَةٌ	Burying-ground.
جَبْهَةٌ	Brow, forehead.
جَبَا يَجْبُو وَيَجْبِي	To gather taxes.
إِجْتَبَى	To choose.

جبايَةٌ ج جبايَاتٌ — Tribute, tax.

جَابٍ — Tax-gatherer.

جثةٌ ج جثثٌ — Corpse ; body.

جثَا يجثو جثُوًّا — To kneel.

جحدَ يجحدُ — To deny ; disbelieve.

جاحدٌ — Denying. An apostate.

جحودٌ — Unbelief ; denial.

جحرٌ ج أجحارٌ وأجحِرَةٌ — Den, hole.

جحشٌ ج جِحَاشٌ — Foal of an ass.

جحظ ـَ جحوظًا — To protrude (eye).

جَحطَ إِلى — To look sharply at.

أجحَفَ بِـ — To injure ; oppress.

إِجحافٌ — Damage ; injury.

جَحِيمٌ — Large fire ; hell.

جدَّ يَجِدُّ — To exert oneself.

جَدَّ جدةً — To be new.

جددَ — To renew ; restore.

تجَدد — To be renewed, restored.

إستَجَدَّ — To become new.

جَدٌّ — Fortune, success.

جِدٌّ — Exertion, seriousness.

جِدًّا — Much ; very ; seriously.

جدٌّ ج جدودٌ — Grandfather.

جَدَّةٌ ج جَدَّات — Grandmother.

جدِيدٌ ج جددٌ — New, recent.

جدبٌ — Drought ; dearth.

أجدَب م جدباء — Sterile, bare.

مجذوبٌ — Imbecile, idiot.

جدَثٌ ج أجدَاثٌ — Grave.

جِدَارٌ ج جدُرٌ — Wall, enclosure.

جَدَرِيٌّ — Small-box.

جدِيرٌ بـ — Fit, worthy of.

أجدَر — More worthy, fitted.

جدَعَ يجدَع — To cut off, main.

جَدْعٌ — Mutilation.

أجدَع — Maimed, mutilated.

جدف — To row.

جدفَ عَلَى — To blaspheme.

تَجْدِيفٌ ج تَجَادِيفُ	Blasphemy.
مِجْدَافٌ ج مَجَادِيفُ	Oar, paddle.
جَدَلَ يَجْدِلُ جَدْلاً	To twist.
جَدَّلَ	To braid the hair.
جَادَلَ	To contend, dispute.
جِدَالٌ وَمُجَادَلَةٌ	Contention, dispute.
جَدْوَلٌ ج جَدَاوِلُ	Brook. List.
مَجْدُولٌ	Plaited, twisted.
أَجْدَى	To be useful, profitable.
جَدْوَى	Gift. Benefit.
جَدْيٌ ج جِدَاءٌ	Kid. Capricorn.
جَذَبَ يَجْذِبُ	To draw ; attract.
اِنْجَذَبَ	To be drawn, attracted.
قُوَّةٌ جَاذِبَةٌ	Power of attraction.
جَذَرَ يَجْذِرُ	To lop, cut off.
جِذْرٌ ج جُذُورٌ	Root, origin. Root of number.
جَذَعٌ وَجُذْعَانٌ	Lad, youth.
جِذْعٌ	Trunk of tree.
جَذَفَ يَجْذِفُ	To row (a boat).
مِجْذَافٌ مَجَاذِيفُ	Oar.
جَذَمَ يَجْذِمُ وَجَذَمَ	To cut off.
جُذَامٌ	Leprosy.
أَجْذَمُ ج جَذْمَى	Leper.
جَرَّ يَجُرُّ جَرًّا	To draw, drag.
اِنْجَرَّ	To be pulled, drawn.
اِجْتَرَّ	To chew the cud.
هَلُمَّ جَرًّا	And so on, et cetera.
حُرُوفُ ٱلْجَرِّ	Prepositions.
جَرُّ ٱلأَثْقَالِ	Mechanics.
جَرَّةٌ ج جِرَارٌ	Earthen jar.
جَارٌّ وَمَجْرُورٌ	Preposition and case governed by it.
جَيْشٌ جَرَّارٌ	Large army.
جَرِيرَةٌ ج جَرَائِرُ	Sin, crime.
أَلْمَجَرَّةُ	Milky-way.
جَرُؤَ يَجْرُؤُ جَرَاءَةً	To be bold.
جَرَّأَ	To embolden, encourage.
اِجْتَرَأَ	To bare, venture.
جُرْأَةٌ وَجَرَاءَةٌ	Boldness, courage.

جَرِبَ يَجْرَبُ	To have the itch.
جَرَّبَ	To put to the test, try.
جَرَبٌ	Itch, scabies.
جِرَابٌ ج أَجْرِبَةٌ	Leathern sack.
أَجْرَبُ	Suffering from itch.
جَرِيبٌ ج أَجْرِبَةٌ	A corn-measure.
تَجْرِبَةٌ ج تَجَارِبُ	Trial, experiment; temptation.
مُجَرَّبٌ	Tried, tested.
جُرْثُومَةٌ ج جَرَاثِيمُ	Root; germ.
جَرْجِيرٌ	Cress, water-cress.
جَرَحَ يَجْرَحُ	To wound, hurt.
جُرْحٌ ج جُرُوحٌ	Wound, cut.
جِرَاحَةٌ ج جِرَاحٌ	Wound.
عِلْمُ ٱلْجِرَاحَةِ	Surgery.
جَرَّاحٌ وَجَرَاحِيٌّ	Surgeon.
جَرِيحٌ ج جَرْحَى	Wounded.
جَارِحَةٌ ج جَوَارِحُ	Beast of prey.
مَجْرُوحٌ ج مَجَارِيحُ	Wounded.
مُجَرَّحٌ	Covered with wounds.

جَرَّدَ	To strip, abstract.
تَجَرَّدَ	To be stripped, bared.
جَرَادٌ	Locusts.
جَرِيدٌ	Branch of palm-tree.
أَجْرَدُ م جَرْدَاءُ	Naked, hairless.
مُجَرَّدٌ	Separated; bare, naked.
مُجَرَّدًا لِ	Solely for.
مُجَرَّدَاتٌ	Abstractions.
جُرَذٌ ج جِرْذَانٌ	Field-rat.
جُرْزَةٌ	Bundle of sticks.
جَرَسٌ ج أَجْرَاسٌ	Bell.
جَرَشَ يَجْرُشُ	To bruise; bray.
جَارُوشٌ ج جَوَارِيشُ	Hand-mill.
جَرَعَ يَجْرَعُ وَٱجْتَرَعَ	To swallow.
جُرْعَةٌ	Draught of water.
جَرَفَ يَجْرُفُ	To sweep away.
مِجْرَفَةٌ	Shovel; hoe.
جَرَمَ وَأَجْرَمَ	To commit a crime.
تَجَرَّمَ	To impute a crime falsely.

جُرْمٌ ج جُرُومٌ وَأَجْرَامٌ Sin, crime.

جُرْمٌ ج أَجْرَامٌ Body, bulk.

الأجرام الفَلَكِيَّةُ The celestial bodies.

جُرْمٌ ج جُرُومٌ Boat, lighter.

لَاجَرَمَ Verily, truly.

جَرِيمَةٌ ج جَرَائِمُ Sin, guilt, crime.

مُجْرِمٌ Criminal, guilty.

جُرْنٌ ج أَجْرَانٌ Mortar, basin.

جَرْوٌ ج أَجْرِيَةٌ Cub, whelp.

جَرَى يَجْرِي جَرْيًا وَجَرَيَانًا To flow.

جَرَّى وَأَجْرَى To cause to flow.

أَجْرَى To carry out, execute.

جَارَى فِي To agree with.

جِرَايَةٌ Rations of a soldier.

جَارٍ Running ; current.

جَارِيَةٌ Slave-girl, girl.

إِجْرَاءٌ Execution of an order.

مَجْرًى ج مَجَارٍ Course ; duct.

جَزَّ يَجُزُّ To shear, cut, mow.

جِزَّةٌ Fleece, shorn wool.

جَزَّازٌ Shearer.

مِجَزٌّ Shears, scissors.

مَجْزُوزٌ Shorn, cut.

جَزَّأَ To divide into portions.

تَجَزَّأَ To be divided into parts.

جُزْءٌ ج أَجْزَاءٌ Part, portion.

جُزْئِيٌّ Partial, particular.

جُزْئِيَّةٌ Particular proposition.

جُزْئِيَّاتٌ Details, parts ; trifles.

أَجْزَائِيٌّ Apothecary, druggist.

أَجْزَائِيَّة Pharmacy.

مُتَجَزِّئٌ Divided into parts.

جَزَرَ يَجْزُرُ To slaughter, kill.

جَزَرَ يَجْزُرُ جَزْرًا To ebb (sea).

جَزْرٌ Slaughter. Ebb.

جَزَرٌ Carrots.

جَزَّارٌ Butcher ; slaughterer.

جَزِيرَةٌ ج جَزَائِرُ وَجُزُرٌ Island.

Peninsula.	شِبْهُ جَزِيرَةٍ
Algiers.	أَلْجَزَائِر
Slaughter-house.	مَجْزَرٌ ج مَجَازِر
To grow impatient.	جَزِعَ يَجْزَعُ
Impatience, grief.	جَزَعٌ وَجُزُوعٌ
Impatient.	جَزِعٌ وَجَزُوعٌ
At random, by conjecture.	جِزَافٌ وَمُجَازَفَةٌ وَجِزَافًا
To abound.	جَزُلَ يَجْزُلُ جَزَالَةً
To give largely.	أَجْزَلَ
Abundant ; much.	جَزِيلٌ
Very venerable.	جَزِيلُ ٱلْاحْتِرَامِ
To decide ; make binding.	جَزَمَ يَجْزِمُ جَزْمًا
Boot.	جَزْمَةٌ ج جَزَمَات
Decisive.	جَازِمٌ ج جَوَازِمُ
To recompense.	جَزَى يَجْزِي
To reward.	جَازَى
To be rewarded or punished.	تَجَازَى
Requital, reward.	جَزَاءٌ وَمُجَازَاةٌ
Tax on a tributary ; land tax.	جِزْيَةٌ
To touch.	جَسَّ يَجُسُّ وَٱجْتَسَّ
To spy out.	جَسَّ وَتَجَسَّسَ
Spy.	جَاسُوسٌ ج جَوَاسِيسُ
To assume a body.	تَجَسَّدَ
Body, flesh.	جَسَدٌ ج أَجْسَادٌ
Corporeal.	جَسَدِيٌّ وَجُسْدَانِيٌّ
Incarnation.	تَجَسُّدٌ
To dare venture.	جَسَرَ يَجْسُرُ
To venture boldly.	تَجَاسَرَ
Bridge. Dike.	جِسْرٌ ج أَجْسُرٌ
Courage, audacity.	جَسَارَةٌ
Bold, courageous.	جَسُورٌ
Courage, audacity.	تَجَاسُرٌ
To be large.	جَسُمَ جَسَامَةً
To assume a form.	تَجَسَّمَ
Body.	جِسْمٌ ج أَجْسَامٌ
Bodily ; material.	جُسْمَانِيٌّ
Importance.	جَسَامَةٌ

Large. Important. جَسِيمٌ

Solid, corporeal, bulky. مُجَسَّمٌ

To belch, eruct. جَشَأَ وَتَجَشَّأَ

Eructation. جُشَاءٌ

To undertake a difficult task. جَشِمَ وَتَجَشَّمَ

Gypsum ; mortar. جَصٌّ

Quiver. جَعْبَةٌ ج جِعَابٌ

To be curly (hair). جَعُدَ يَجْعُدُ

To be curly, wrinkled. تَجَعَّدَ

Buffoon ; low fellow. جُعَيْدِيٌّ

To put, place, make. جَعَلَ يَجْعَلُ

He began to weep. جَعَلَ يَبْكِي

Pay, wages; bribe. جَعَالَةٌ وَجُعْلٌ

To become dry. جَفَّ يَجِفُّ جَفَافًا

To dry cause to dry. جَفَّفَ

To become dry. تَجَفَّفَ

Dry, withered, جَافٌّ وَجَفِيفٌ

To be frightened, shy. جَفَلَ وَأَجْفَلَ

To put to flight ; frighten. جَفَّلَ

Eyelid. جَفْنٌ ج جُفُونٌ وَأَجْفَانٌ

To treat rudely. جَفَا يَجْفُو جَفَاءً

To shun, turn away from. جَافَى

Harshness. جِفْوَةٌ وَجَفَاءٌ

Thick, coarse, rude. جَافٍ

To be great. جَلَّ يَجِلُّ جَلَالًا

To disdain. جَلَّ وَتَجَالَّ عَنْ

To honour, magnify. أَجَلَّ

Pack-saddle. جُلٌّ ج أَجْلَالٌ

The gist of a matter. جُلُّ الأَمْرِ

Splendour, majesty. جَلَالٌ

Maker of pack-saddles. جَلَالَاتِيٌّ

Human greatness ; majesty. جَلَالَةٌ

Great. جَلِيلٌ ج أَجِلَّاءُ

Book ; review. مَجَلَّةٌ

To gather ; bring. جَلَبَ يَجْلُبُ

To be led, imported. إِنْجَلَبَ

Importation, import. جَلْبٌ

Camlour, noise, tumult. جَلَبٌ

Imported slaves, cattle.	جَلَبٌ
Scab. Hunger, distress.	جُلْبَةٌ
Clamour, tumult.	جَلَبَةٌ
Cattle or slave-dealer.	جَلَّابٌ
Julep, raisin-water.	جُلَّابٌ
Drawn ; imported.	مَجْلُوبٌ
Little bell.	جُلْجُلٌ ج جَلَاجِلُ
Baldness on the temples.	جَلَحَةٌ
Bald on the temples.	أَجْلَحُ
To whet (a razor).	جَلَخَ وَجَلَّخَ
Grindstone.	جَلْخٌ
To scourge.	جَلَدَ يَجْلِدُ جَلْدًا
To be frozen.	جَلِدَ يَجْلَدُ جَلَدًا
To bind a book.	جَلَّدَ
To bear patiently.	تَجَلَّدَ
Endurance. Firmament.	جَلَدٌ
Skin, hide, leather.	جِلْدٌ ج جُلُودٌ
Endurance.	جَلَادَةٌ وَجُلُودَةٌ
Executioner.	جَلَّادٌ
Hoar-frost, ice.	جَلِيدٌ
Book-binder.	مُجَلِّدٌ
Bound in leather, book.	مُجَلَّدٌ
To sit, sit up.	جَلَسَ يَجْلِسُ
To sit in company with.	جَالَسَ
To cause to sit.	أَجْلَسَ
A single sitting ; session.	جَلْسَةٌ
Sitting. Straight.	جَالِسٌ
Act of sitting.	جُلُوسٌ
Companion.	جَلِيسٌ ج جُلَسَاءُ
Council.	مَجْلِسٌ ج مَجَالِسُ
Council of ministers.	مَجْلِسُ ٱلْوُزَرَاءِ
Court of the First Instance.	ألْمَجْلِسُ ٱلابْتِدَائِيُّ
Court of Appeal.	مَجْلِسُ ٱلاسْتِئْنَافِ
Mixed Tribunal.	أَلْمَجْلِسُ ٱلْمُخْتَلَطُ
Council of war.	مَجْلِسٌ حَرْبِيٌّ
To tear, scrape.	جَلَفَ يَجْلُفُ جَلْفًا
Large sack.	جُوَالِقُ ج جَوَالِيقُ
Catapult.	مَنْجَلِيقٌ وَمَنْجَنِيقٌ

جَلَا يَجْلُو	To polish ; remove.
جَلَا لِ	To become evident.
جَلَا عَن	To depart.
أَجْلَى	To emigrate.
تَجَلَّى لِ	To appear.
إِنْجَلَى	To be disclosed.
جَلَاءٌ	Clearness. Emigration.
جَلِيٌّ	Clear, evident, manifest.
جَلِيًّا	Clearly, evidently.
أَلتَّجَلِّي (عيد)	Transfiguration.
مَجْلُوٌّ وَمَجْلِيٌّ	Polished, planed.
جَلَى يَجْلِي جَلْيًا	To polish.
جَمٌّ غَفِيرٌ	Great number, crowd.
جُمْجُمَةٌ ج جَمَاجِم	Skull.
جَمَحَ يَجْمَحُ	To be restive, run-away (horse).
جَامِحٌ وَجَمُوحٌ	Refractory.
جَمَدَ يَجْمُدُ	To congeal, harden.
جَامِدٌ ج جَوَامِد	Underived word.
أَلْجَوَامِد	The mineral kingdom

جَمَادٌ	Mineral, solid.
جُمَادَى ٱلاولَى و ٱلآخِرَة	The fifth and sixth months of the Mohammedan year.
جَمْرَةٌ ج جَمْرٌ	Live coal. Tribe.
جَمْرَةٌ	Carbuncle (*disease*).
مِجْمَرَةٌ ج مَجَامِر	Censer ; fire-pan.
جُمَّيْزٌ وَجُمَّيْزَى	Sycamore.
جَامُوسٌ ج جَوَامِيس	Buffalo.
جَمَعَ يَجْمَعُ	To gather, add.
جَمَعَ بَيْنَ	To bring together.
أَجْمَعُوا عَلَى	To agree upon.
تَجَمَّعَ وَاجْتَمَعَ	To assemble, be gathered.
جَمْعٌ ج جُمُوع	Assembly ; plural.
أَلْجَمْعُ ٱلسَّالِم	Whole plural.
جَمْعُ ٱلتَّكْسِير	Broken plural.
جُمْعَةٌ ج جُمَع	Week.
أَلْجُمْعَةُ	Friday.
جَمَاعَةٌ	Party ; community.
جَامِعٌ	Collector ; comprehensive.

Mosque. جامع ج جوامع

All, the whole of. جميع

All; altogether. جميعاً

Company ; committee. جمعية

All, whole. أجمع ج أجمعون

Unanimity. إجماع

Assembly, gathering. إجتماع

Confluence. Society of learned men. مجمع ج مجامع

United, total. مجموع ج مجاميع

Pay, salary. جامكية

To embellish, adorn. جمل

To treat with affability. جامل

Camel. جمل ج جمال

Sum, total. Sentence, phrase, paragraph. جملة ج جمل

In the aggregate. بالجملة

Beauty, grace. جمال

Camel-driver. جمال

Handsome, good deed. جميل

Generally speaking. بالإجمال

Sum, total; summary. مجمل

Multitude. جمهور ج جماهير

Republican. جمهوري

Republic. جمهورية

To be dark (night). جن يجن

To become mad. جن

To madden. جنن وأجن

Demons, genii. جن وجان وجنة

Garden, paradise. جنة ج جنات

Heart, mind. جنان ج أجنان

Madness, insanity. جنون

Embryo, fœtus. جنين ج أجنة

Small garden. جنينة

Shield. مجن ج مجان

Mad, insane. مجنون ج مجانين

To shun, avoid. تجنب واجتنب

Side, flank. جنب ج جنوب

Pleurisy. ذات الجنب

Flank, part. جانب ج جوانب

لينُ الجانبِ Mild, gentle.

جنابٌ Title of respect.

جنوبٌ South ; south wind.

جنوبيٌّ Southern.

أجنبيٌّ ج أجانبُ Foreign.

إجتنابٌ وتجنُّبٌ Act of avoiding.

جنحَ يجنحُ To incline towards.

جناحٌ ج أجنحة Wing.

جُناحٌ Sin, crime, guilt.

جنَّدَ To levy troops.

تجنَّدَ To be enlisted, enrolled.

جُندٌ ج جُنودٌ Army.

جُنديٌّ A soldier.

جُندبٌ ج جنادِبُ Grasshopper.

جندلَ To throw a man down.

جنريك A kind of plum.

جَنازةٌ ج جنائز Funeral, corps.

جُنازٌ ج جنانيز Funeral rites.

جنزارٌ Verdigris.

جنَّسَ To make similar.

جانَسَ To appear similar.

جِنسٌ ج أجناس Genus, kind, race, sex ; nationality.

إسمُ جنسٍ Generic noun.

جنسيَّة Nationality.

مُجانِس Of the same kind.

جنَفَ وأجنَفَ To act unjustly.

جنَفٌ Wrong, injustice.

جنفاصٌ وجنفيصٌ Coarse linen.

منجنيقٌ ج مجانِق ومجانيقُ Catapult.

جنى ـ واجتنى To gather (fruit).

جنى جِنايَةً To commit a crime.

تجنّي على To accuse falsely.

جانٍ A gatherer. Criminal.

جِنايَةٌ Crime ; sin.

جهُد To toil.

جهَّدَ To weary, fatigue.

جاهَدَ مجاهَدَةً وجِهاداً To struggle.

إجتهَدَ في To strive after.

Exertion, effort. جُهْدٌ

He did his best. أفرغ جَهْدَهُ

Combat, struggle. جِهادٌ

Military. جِهَادِيٌّ

Diligence, effort. إجتِهَادٌ

Champion. مجَاهِدٌ

To publish. جَهَرَ بِ

To be dazzled. جَهِرَ يَجْهَرُ

To declare publicly. جَاهَرَ بِ

To appear in public. تَجاهَرَ

Publicly, openly. جَهْراً وَجِهاراً

Day-blind. اجْهَرُ م جَهْرَاءُ

Microscope. مِجْهَرٌ

To equip, fit out. جَهَّزَ

To get ready. تَجَهَّزَ

Trousseau. Requisites, apparatus. جَهَازٌ ج أجْهِزَةٌ

Equipment, expedition. تَجْهِيزٌ

To be ignorant. جَهِلَ يَجْهَلُ

To impute ignorance. جَهَّلَ

To affect ignorance. تَجَاهَلَ

To deem one ignorant. إِسْتَجْهَلَ

Ignorance. Folly. جَهْلٌ وَجَهَالَةٌ

Ignorant, fool. جاهِلٌ

Pre-islamic age. أَلْجاهِلِيَّةُ

Unknown. Passive verb. مَجْهُولٌ

Hell. جَهَنَّمُ

Hellish, infernal. جَهَنَّمِيٌّ

Sky, atmosphere. جَوٌّ

To travel. جَابَ يَجُوبُ

To answer, reply. جَاوَبَ

To answer, respond. أَجَابَ

To answer ; listen to. إِسْتَجَابَ

Answer reply. جَوَابٌ ج أَجْوِبَةٌ

Compliance. إِجَابَةٌ وَاسْتِجَابَةٌ

Answerer. مجيبٌ وَمستَجِيبٌ

Answered (prayer). مُسْتَجَابٌ

Broadcloth. جُوْخٌ ج أجْوَاخٌ

Cloth-maker or dealer. جَوَّاخٌ

جَادَ يَجُودُ جُودَةً To excel.
جَادَ جُوداً To give abundantly.
جَوَّدَ To make good.
جُودٌ Liberality, generosity.
جُودَةٌ Goodness, excellence.
جَوَادٌ ج أَجْوَادٌ Generous.
جَوَادٌ ج جِيَاد Fleet (horse).
جَيِّدٌ ج جِيَادٌ Good, excellent.
جَيِّداً Very well.
جَارَ يَجُورُ عَلَى To oppress.
جَاوَرَ To be contiguous.
أَجَارَ إِجَارَةً To save; protect.
تَجَاوَرَ To be neighbours.
إِسْتَجَارَ To seek protection.
جَارٌ ج جِيرَانٌ Neighbour.
جَوْرٌ Oppression, tyranny.
جِوَارٌ Neighbourhood, vicinity.
مُجَاوِرٌ Neighbour; contiguous.
مُجِيرٌ Protector, defender.

جَوْرَبٌ ج جَوَارِبُ Stocking.
جَازَ يَجُوزُ To pass, travel.
جَازَ جَوَازاً To be allowable.
جَوَّزَ To allow; permit.
جَاوَزَ مُجَاوَزَةً To exceed.
أَجَازَ إِجَازَةً To allow; permit.
تَجَاوَزَ To exceed the bounds.
تَجَاوَزَ عَنْ To overlook.
إِجْتَازَ بِ To pass by.
جَوْزٌ Nut, nut-tree. Walnut.
جَوْزٌ هِنْدِيٌّ Cocoa-nut.
جَوْزُ ٱلطِّيبِ Nutmeg.
الجَوْزَاءُ Twins. Orion.
جَائِزٌ Passing; lawful.
جَوَازٌ Lawfulness; passage.
جَائِزَةٌ ج جَوَائِزُ Present, prize.
إِجَازَةٌ Permission; licence.
مَجَازٌ Passage. Figurative.
مَجَازِيٌّ Metaphoric.

جَوْشَنٌ ج جَوَاشِن Coat of mail.

جَاعَ يَجُوعُ To be hungry.

جَوَّعَ وَأَجَاعَ To starve.

جُوعٌ Hunger.

جَائِعٌ ج جِيَاعٌ Hungry.

مَجَاعَةٌ Famine ; hunger.

جَوَّفَ To hollow.

جَوْفٌ ج أَجْوَافٌ Cavity. Belly.

اجْوَف Empty, hollow.

تَجْوِيفٌ ج تَجَاوِيف Cavity.

مُجَوَّفٌ Hollow, empty.

جَوْقَة ج جَوْقَاتٌ Crowd.

جَالَ يَجُول To travel.

جَائِلٌ Travelling roaming.

جَوَلَانٌ Act of travelling about.

مَجَالٌ Range ; sphere of action.

جَامٌ ج جَامَاتٌ Vessel, tray.

جَاهٌ Honour, rank, dignity

جَوْهَرٌ ج جَوَاهِر Jewels, pearls, Essence, nature element.

أَلْجَوْهَر ٱلْفَرْدُ Atom ; monad.

جَوْهَرَةٌ A jewel, pearl.

جَوْهَرِيٌّ Jeweller. Essential.

جَوَّانِيٌّ Interior, inward.

جَاءَ يَجِيءُ To come, arrive.

جَاءَ ب To bring.

مَجِيءٌ Act of coming, arrival.

جَيْبٌ ج جُيُوبٌ Pocket, Sinus.

جِيدٌ ج أَجْيَادٌ وَجُيُود Neck.

جِيرٌ Gypsum ; quicklime.

جَيَّشَ To collect an army.

جَأْشٌ وجَاشٌ The soul.

جَيْشٌ ج جُيُوشٌ Army.

جِيفَةٌ ج جِيَفٌ Corpse, carcass.

جِيلٌ ج أَجْيَالٌ Race ; generation.

ح

ح — As a numeral sign = 8.

حَبَّ يَحِبُّ حِبًّا وَحُبًّا — To love.

حَبَّبَ إِلَى — To make lovable.

أَحَبَّ — To love ; like.

تَحَبَّبَ — To show love.

إِسْتَحَبَّ عَلَى — To prefer.

حَبٌّ ج حُبُوبٌ — Grain ; seed ; berry; pill ; pustule.

حُبٌّ وَمَحَبَّةٌ — Love, friendship.

حَبَّةٌ ج حَبَّاتٌ — A grain.

حَبِيبٌ ج احِبَّاء — Lover ; beloved.

حُبًّا وَكَرَامَةً — With all my heart.

أَحَبُّ — Dearer ; preferable.

مُحِبٌّ — Lover ; friend.

مَحْبُوبٌ — Beloved ; liked.

حَبَّذَا . يا حَبَّذَا — Well done.

حَبِرَ يَحْبَرُ حُبُوراً — To be glad.

حِبْرٌ ج أَحْبَارٌ — Learned, good man.

الْحَبْرُ الأَعْظَمُ — High priest, the Pope.

حِبْرٌ — Ink.

حُبُورٌ — Joy, gladness, happiness.

مَحْبَرَةٌ ج مَحَابِرُ — Inkstand.

حَبَسَ يَحْبِسُ — To imprison.

حَبَسَ عَنْ — To restrain.

حَبْسٌ ج حُبُوسٌ — Prison.

حَبْسٌ وَٱحْتِبَاسٌ — Imprisonment.

إِحْتِبَاسٌ — Retention.

مَحْبُوسٌ — Imprisoned ; arrested.

حَبَشٌ وَحَبَشَةٌ — The Abyssinians.

حَبَشِيٌّ — An Abyssinian.

بِلَادُ ٱلْحَبَشِ وَٱلْحَبَشَةِ — Abyssinia.

حَبَطَ يَحْبَطُ — To fail ; perish.

حُبُوطٌ — Failure.

حَبَقٌ — Basil, penny-royal.

حَبَكَ يَحْبُكُ — To weave ; unite.

محبُوكٌ Well woven ; strong.

حبِلَتْ تحبَلُ To conceive (woman).

تَحَبَّلَ To be entangled.

حَبْلٌ ج حِبَالٌ Rope, cable.

حَبْلُ ٱلْوَرِيد Jugular vein.

حَبَل Pregnancy, conception.

أُحْبُولَةٌ ج حَبَائِل Net, snare.

حُبلَى ج حَبَالى Pregnant (woman).

حبَّالٌ Rope-maker.

حَبَا يحْبو To creep, crawl.

حابى To be partial to.

مُحَاباة Partiality, favour.

مُحَاب Partial.

حَتَّ يحُتُّ حتًّا To rub off.

حتَّةٌ ج حتَتٌ Bit of anything.

حتَّى Until, to, as far as, even.

حتَّى أَن So that.

حَتْفٌ ج حتوفٌ Death.

حتفَ أَنفِهِ Natural death.

حَتَمَ يحتِمُ To decide, decree.

حَتَمَ ب To decide ; order.

حَتَمَ على To compel.

حتْمٌ ج حتومٌ Final decision.

محتومٌ Decided, fixed.

حَثَّ يحُثُّ To exhort, instigate.

حَثٌّ وإحْثَاثٌ Instigation.

حَجَّ يحِجُّ To go as a pilgrim to Mecca.

حَجَّهُ To overcome in argument.

حَاجَّ To dispute, contend with.

إِحْتَجَّ ب To offer as a proof.

إِحْتَجَّ عَلَى To argue against.

حَجٌّ وحِجَّةٌ Pilgrimage to Mecca.

حُجَّةٌ ج حُجَجٌ Proof ; title, deed. Pretext, excuse.

ذو ٱلْحِجَّة The last month of the Mohammedan year.

حَاجٌّ ج حُجَّاجٌ Pilgrim to Mecca.

حجَبَ يحْجُب To hide, cover.

حَجَبَ عَنْ To prevent.

إِحْتَجَبَ To conceal one's self.

Partition; veil. حِجَابٌ ج حُجُبٌ

Diaphragm. اَلْحِجَابُ ٱلْحَاجِزُ

Chamberlain. Door-keeper. حَاجِبٌ ج حُجَّابٌ

Eye-brow. حَاجِبٌ ج حَوَاجِبُ

To prevent, restrain. حَجَرَ يَحْجُرُ

To be turned into stone. تَحَجَّرَ

Prevention, prohibition. حَجْرٌ

Stone. حَجَرٌ ج أَحْجَارٌ وَحِجَارَةٌ

Nitrate of silver. حَجَرُ جَهَنَّمَ

Chamber; sepulchre. حُجْرَةٌ

Stone-cutter. حَجَّارٌ ج حَجَّارُونَ

Larynx. حَنْجَرَةٌ ج حَنَاجِرُ

To prevent, hinder. حَجَزَ يَحْجُزُ

To separate. حَجَزَ بَيْنَ

To sequester goods. حَجَزَ عَلَى

Prevention, restraint. حَجْزٌ

Arabia Petrœa, Hijas. أَلْحِجَازُ

A barrier. حَاجِزٌ ج حَوَاجِزُ

Hindered, prevented. مَحْجُوزٌ

To hop, leap. حَجَلَ يَحْجِلُ

Partridge. حَجَلٌ ج حِجْلَانٌ

Having white foot, or feet, (horse). مُحَجَّلٌ

To cup, scarify. حَجَمَ يَحْجُمُ

To be cupped. إِحْتَجَمَ

Bulk; size. حَجْمٌ ج حُجُومٌ

Art of cupping, cupping. حِجَامَةٌ

Cupper. حَجَّامٌ

Cupping instrument. مِحْجَمٌ

To propose riddles. تَحَاجَى

Intelligence. حِجًى ج أَحْجَاءٌ

Enigma; riddle. أُحْجِيَّةٌ ج أَحَاجِيُّ

To confine, define. حَدَّ يَحُدُّ

To go into mourning. حَدَّ حِدَادًا

To confine; define; sharpen. حَدَّدَ

To look sharply. أَحَدَّ ٱلنَّظَرَ

To be limited; defined. تَحَدَّدَ

To be excited. إِحْتَدَّ

Limit, boundary. حَدٌّ ج حُدُودٌ

Impetuosity ; acerbity. حِدَّةٌ

Sharp, pointed ; pungent. حَادٌّ

Acute angle. زَاوِيَة حَادَّةٌ

Mourning. حِدَادٌ

Blacksmith. حَدَّادٌ

Iron. حَدِيدٌ

A piece of iron. حَدِيدَةٌ

Demarcation. تَحْدِيدٌ

Limited ; bounded. مَحْدُودٌ

Kite (hawk). حِدَأَةٌ ج حِدَاء

To become convex. تَحَدَّبَ

To be hump-backed. إِحْدَوْدَبَ

Hump-backed. أَحْدَب م حَدْبَاء

Convex ; bulging. مُحَدَّبٌ

To happen, occur. حَدَثَ يَحْدُثُ

To tell ; relate. حَدَّثَ

To converse. حَادَثَ مُحَادَثَةً

To cause to exist. أَحْدَثَ

To converse together. تَحَادَثَ

Event. حَادِثَةٌ ج حَوَادِثُ

Newness, youth. حَدَاثَةٌ

New, recent. حَدِيث

Story, tale.
Mohammedan tradition. حَدِيث ج أَحَادِيثُ

Tale. اُحْدُوثَةٌ ج أَحَادِيثُ

Conversation. مُحَادَثَةٌ

To descend. إِنْحَدَرَ

Descent. حُدُورٌ وَٱنْحِدَارٌ

To surmise. حَدَسَ يَحْدِسُ فِي

Conjecture; guess. حَدْسٌ

Hypotheses. حَدَسِيَّاتٌ

To surround, enclose. أَحْدَقَ بِ

To look sharply at. حَدَّقَ إِلَى

The pupil of the eye. حَدَقَةٌ

Garden. حَدِيقَةٌ ج حَدَائِقُ

Glow (of a fire). حَدْمٌ وَحَدَمٌ

Growing with heat. مُحْتَدِمٌ

Camel-driver. حَادٍ ج حُدَاةٌ

حَادِي عَشَرَ The eleventh.

حَذِرَ يَحْذَرُ To be cautious.

حَذَّرَ To warn.

تَحَذَّرَ وَٱحْتَذَرَ To be cautious.

حِذْرٌ وَحَذَرٌ Caution ; distrust.

حَذِرٌ ج حَذِرُون Cautious.

حَذَارِ Take care !

مَحْذُورٌ A thing to be avoided.

حَذَفَ يَحْذِفُ To cut off ; drop.

حَذَفَ ب To throw at.

حَذْفٌ Elision ; suppression.

مَحْذُوفٌ Cut off ; suppressed.

حَذَقَ يَحْذِقُ To be skilful.

حِذْقٌ Sharpness, skill.

حاذِقٌ ج حُذَّاقٌ Sharp ; clever.

حَذَا يَحْذُو حَذْواً To imitate, emulate.

حَاذَى To be opposite to.

حِذَاءَ Opposite to ; vis-à-vis.

حِذَاءٌ ج أَحْذِيَةٌ Shoe, sandal.

مُحَاذٍ Placed opposite ; vis-a-vis.

حَرَّ يَحِرُّ To be hot.

حَرَّرَ To set free, free (a slave).

تَحَرَّرَ To be set free, freed.

حَرٌّ Heat.

حُرٌّ ج أَحْرَارٌ Freeman ; noble.

حَرَارَةٌ Heat warmth.

حُرِّيَّةٌ Liberty, freedom.

حَرِيرٌ Silk ; silk-stuff.

تَحْرِيرٌ ج تَحَارِيرُ Letter, note.

حَارٌّ Hot, burning ; fervent.

مُحَرَّرٌ Liberated ; set free.

مَحْرُورٌ Heated (with anger, etc.)

حَارَبَ مُحَارَبَةً To fight.

تَحَارَبَ To fight one another.

حَرْبٌ ج حُرُوبٌ War, battle.

دَارُ ٱلْحَرْبِ Enemy's territory.

حِرْبَاءُ ج حَرَابِيُّ Chameleon.

حَرْبَةٌ ج حِرَابٌ Lance ; bayonet.

Place of prayer.	مِحْرَابٌ
To till.	حَرَثَ يَحْرِثُ حَرْثًا
Agriculture.	حِرَاثَةٌ
Ploughman.	حَارِثٌ وَحَرَّاثٌ
A plough.	مِحْرَثٌ وَمِحْرَاثٌ
To be in difficulty.	حَرِجَ يَحْرَجُ
To be forbidden.	حَرِجَ عَلَى
Narrow. Forbidden.	حَرِجٌ
No blame or sin.	لاَ حَرَجَ
Auction.	حَرَاجٌ
To be angry.	حَرِدَ يَحْرَدُ
Anger, grudge, hatred.	حَرَدٌ
Lizard.	حِرْذَوْنٌ ج حَرَاذِينَ
To guard carefully.	حَرَزَ يَحْرُزُ
To guard. Obtain.	أَحْرَزَ
To guard against.	تَحَرَّزَ وَٱحْتَرَزَ
Caution ; amulet.	حِرْزٌ
Fortified ; valued.	حَرِيزٌ
To guard, watch.	حَرَسَ يَحْرُسُ
To be cautioned.	تَحَرَّسَ وَٱحْتَرَسَ
Watch, guard.	حِرَاسَةٌ
Watchman, guard.	حَارِسٌ ج حُرَّاسٌ
To excite discord.	حَرَّشَ بَيْنَ
To meddle with.	تَحَرَّشَ بِ
Wood, thicket.	حُرْشٌ ج أَحْرَاشٌ
To covet eagerly.	حَرَصَ يَحْرِصُ
Greed, cupidity.	حِرْصٌ
Covetous.	حَرِيصٌ ج حُرَصَاءُ
To incite, instigate.	حَرَّضَ عَلَى
To turn from.	حَرَفَ يَحْرِفُ عَنْ
To falsify, garble.	حَرَّفَ
To deviate from.	إِنْحَرَفَ عَنْ
To earn sustenance.	إِحْتَرَفَ
Edge, border.	حَرْفٌ ج حِرَفٌ
Letter, particle (in grammer).	حَرْفٌ ج حُرُوفٌ وَأَحْرُفٌ
Literal.	حَرْفِيٌّ
Trade, craft.	حِرْفَةٌ ج حِرَفٌ

حَرافة	Pungency.
حَرِّيفٌ	Sharp, pungent.
مُحَرَّفٌ	Falsified.
مُنحَرِفٌ	Oblique ; trapezium
حَرَقَ يَحرِقُ وَأَحرَقَ	To burn.
اِحتَرَقَ وَتَحَرَّقَ	To be burned.
حُرقَةٌ	Heat, burning pain.
حَرِيقٌ	Heat, conflagration.
حَرَّاقَةٌ ج حَرَّاقَات	Blister ; tinder
حَرقَفَةٌ ج حَرَاقِف	Hip-bone.
حَرُكَ يَحرُكُ	To be in motion.
حَرَّكَ	To move a thing
تَحَرَّكَ	To be moved.
حَرِكٌ	Brisk, nimble.
حَرَكَةٌ ج حَرَكَاتٌ	Motion ; gesture.
(ـَ ـُ ـِ)	Vowel-point.
حِرَاكٌ	Motion.
حَارِك	Withers of a horse.
تَحرِيكٌ	Act of moving.
حَرَمَ يَحرِمُ	To refuse, forbid.
حَرُمَ يَحرُمُ	To be unlawful.
حَرَّمَ	To forbid.
تَحَرَّمَ	To be forbidden.
إِحتَرَمَ	To honour, venerate.
إِستَحرَمَ	To hold as unlawful.
حِرمٌ	Excommunication.
حَرَمٌ	Sacred (territory).
الحَرَم	Sacred territory at Mecca.
الحَرَمَان	Mecca and Medina.
حُرمَةٌ ج حُرَمٌ	Sacredness. Wife.
حَرَامٌ	Unlawful, sacred.
أَلمَسجِدُ ٱلحَرَامِ	El Kaaba.
الشَّهرُ ٱلحَرَام . مُحَرَّمٌ	The month.
حَرَامِيٌّ ج حَرَامِيَةٌ	Robber, thief.
حَرِيمٌ	Women of a household.
مُحَرَّمٌ	Unlawful ; first month of the Moslem year.
مَحرُومٌ	Denied, refused. Excommunicated.
مُحتَرَمٌ	Venerable, respected.

حَرَنَ يَحْرُنُ To rear and kick.

حَرُونٌ Restive, refractory.

حَرِيَ بِ To be adapted to.

تَحَرَّى To seek, aim at.

حَرِيٌّ بِ Suitable, proper for.

أَحْرَى More suited, better.

كَمْ بِالْحَرِيّ How much more.

بِالأَحْرَى Rather.

حَزَّ يَحُزُّ To cut, incise, notch.

حَزَازٌ وَحَزَازَة Dandruff, scurff.

حزبَ To collect parties.

حِزْبٌ ج أَحْزَابٌ Troop ; party.

مُتَحَزِّبٌ Leagued ; partisan.

حَزَرَ يَحْزِرُ To guess, compute.

حزيرَانُ June (month).

حَزَمَ يَحْزِمُ To tie together.

حَزُمَ يَحْزُمُ To be firm, prudent.

حُزْمَةٌ ج حُزَمٌ Bundle, parcel.

حَزْمٌ Firmness, resolution, discretion.

حِزَامٌ ج أَحْزِمَةٌ Belt, girth.

حَازِمٌ Prudent, resolute.

مِحْزَمٌ ج مَحَازِمُ Belt, girth.

حَزِنَ يَحْزَنُ To grieve.

حَزِنَ يَحْزَنُ To be grieved.

أَحْزَنَ To grieve another.

حُزْنٌ ج أَحْزَانٌ Sadness.

حَزِينٌ Sad, sorrowful.

مُحْزِنٌ Sad thing, sorrowful.

مَحْزُونٌ Saddened, grieved.

حَسَّ يَحِسُّ To feel ; perceive.

أَحَسَّ بِ To feel ; perceive.

حِسٌّ Perception, sense.

حِسِّيٌّ ومَحْسُوسٌ Perceptible.

حَاسَّةٌ ج حَوَاسُّ Faculty of each of the five senses ; feeling.

اَلْحَوَاسُّ اَلْخَمْسُ The five senses.

مِحَسَّةٌ Curry-comb.

حَسَبَ يَحْسُبُ To count.

To suppose, consider.	حَسِبَ يَحْسِبُ
To account with.	حَاسَبَ
To settle an account.	تَحَاسَبَ
Sufficient ; sufficiency.	حَسْبٌ
According to.	بِحَسَبِ
Honour ; pedigree.	حَسَبٌ
Account, calculation.	حِسَابٌ
Arithmetic.	عِلْمُ ٱلْحِسَابِ
Noble	حَسِيبٌ ج حُسَبَاءُ
Counted, calculated.	مَحْسُوبٌ
To envy.	حَسَدَ يَحْسُدُ
Envy, grudge.	حَسَدٌ
Envious.	حَاسِدٌ وَحَسُودٌ ج حُسَّادٌ
Envied ; object of envy.	مَحْسُودٌ
To grieve for.	حَسِرَ يَحْسَرُ عَلَى
To feel regret.	تَحَسَّرَ عَلَى
Grief.	حَسْرَةٌ ج حَسَرَاتٌ
Alas !	يَا حَسْرَتِي . وَاحَسْرَتَاهُ
Hatred. Thistle.	حَسَكٌ

To cut off ; stop.	حَسَمَ يَحْسِمُ
Sharp sword.	حُسَامٌ
To be handsome.	حَسُنَ يَحْسُنُ
To embellish, adorn.	حَسَّنَ
To treat well.	حَاسَنَ
To do a thing well.	أَحْسَنَ
To confer a benefit.	أَحْسَنَ إِلَى
To approve.	إِسْتَحْسَنَ
Beauty ; good.	حُسْنٌ ج مَحَاسِنُ
Beautiful ; good.	حَسَنٌ ج حِسَانٌ
Good deed.	حَسَنَةٌ ج حَسَنَاتٌ
Goldfinch.	حَسُّونٌ
More beautiful, better.	أَحْسَنُ
How beautiful.	مَا أَحْسَنَ
Benefit, beneficence.	إِحْسَانٌ
Good deeds or qualities.	مَحَاسِنُ
To cut hay.	حَشَّ يَحُشُّ حَشًّا
Smoker of hashish.	حَشَّاشٌ
Grass; hay. Hashish.	حَشِيشٌ

Part, share.	حِصَّةٌ ج حِصَصٌ
Stones, firewood.	حَصَبٌ
Measles.	حَصْبَةٌ
To mow, reap.	حَصَدَ يَحْصُدُ
Mower, reaper.	حَاصِدٌ وَحَصَّادٌ
Harvest, harvest-time.	حَصَادٌ
Mown, reaped.	حَصِيدٌ وَمَحْصُودٌ
To confine, restrict.	حَصَرَ يَحْصُرُ
To besiege.	حَاصَرَ مُحَاصَرَةً
Restriction ; confinement.	حَصْرٌ
Strictly speaking.	بِالْحَصْرِ
Siege, blockade.	حِصَارٌ وَمُحَاصَرَةٌ
Maker or seller of mats.	حُصْرِيٌّ
Mat.	حَصِيرٌ وَحَصِيرَةٌ ج حَصَائِرُ
Besieger ; blockader.	مُحَاصِرٌ
Besieged ; restricted.	مَحْصُورٌ
Green grapes.	حِصْرِمٌ
Sound judgment.	حَصَافَةٌ
To happen to one.	حَصَلَ - لِ

To assemble, *v. t.*	حَشَدَ يَحْشُدُ
To be assembled.	إِحْتَشَدَ
Troop, assembly.	حَشْدٌ
Places of assembling.	مَحَاشِد
To assemble.	حَشَرَ يَحْشُرُ حَشْرًا
Day of Judgment.	يَوْمُ الْحَشْرِ
Place of gathering.	مَحْشَرٌ ج مَحَاشِرُ
Insect.	حَشَرَةٌ ج حَشَرَاتٌ
To stand in awe or shame.	إِحْتَشَمَ
Attendants, retinue.	حَشَمٌ
Reverence ; modesty.	حِشْمَةٌ
Reverence ; modesty.	اِحْتِشَامٌ
To stuff, cram.	حَشَا يَحْشُو
To be filled.	إِحْتَشَى وَانْحَشَى
Viscera, bowels.	حَشًا ج أَحْشَاءٌ
Stuffing, wadding.	حَشْوٌ
To abstain, disdain.	تَحَاشَى عَنْ
Except. God forbid!	حَاشَا
Annotation. Followers.	حَاشِيَةٌ ج حَوَاشٍ

حَصَلَ عَلَى	To obtain, acquire.
تَحَصَّلَ	To be obtained.
حَاصِلٌ ج حَوَاصِلُ	Result.
الحَاصِلُ	The result ; in short.
تَحْصِيلٌ	Acquisition.
مَحْصُولٌ ج مَحَاصِيل	Result, produce.
حَصُنَ يَحْصُنُ	To be fortified.
حَصَّنَ	To fortify.
تَحَصَّنَ	To be entrenched.
حِصْنٌ ج حُصُونٌ	Fortress.
حِصَانٌ ج حُصُنٌ وَأَحْصِنَةٌ	Horse.
حَصِينٌ	Strongly fortified.
أَبُو الحُصَيْنِ	Fox.
احْصَى	To count, number.
حَصًى	Small pebbles.
حَصَاةٌ	Small pebble.
غَيْرُ مُحْصًى	Innumerable.
حَضَّ يَحُضُّ	To instigate, incite.
حَضِيضٌ	Foot of a mountain.

حَضَرَ يَحْضُرُ	To be present.
حَضَرَ إِلَى	To come.
حَضَّرَ وَأَحْضَرَ	To bring.
تَحَضَّرَ	To be ready.
إِسْتَحْضَرَ	To cause to come.
حَضَرٌ	Towns, cultivated land.
حَضْرَةٌ	Presence. Highness.
حَاضِرٌ	Present, ready.
أَلْحَاضِرُ	Present tense.
مُحْتَضَرٌ	Approach of death.
حَضَنَ يَحْضُنُ	To embrace.
حِضْنٌ ج حُضُونٌ	Bosom.
حِضَانَةٌ	Nursing ; incubation.
حَطَّ يَحُطُّ	To fall, go down.
حط	To put down.
انْحَطَ	To descend, fall.
إِنْحِطَاطٌ	Falling.
مَحَطٌّ وَمحطةٌ	Railway station.
مُنْحَطّ	Fallen, depressed.

مَحْطُوطٌ	Placed, laid, deposited.
إِحْتَطَبَ	To collect fire-wood.
حَطَبٌ	Fuel, wood.
حَطَّابٌ	Wood-cutter.
حَطَمَ يَحْطِمُ وَحَطَّمَ	To break.
تَحَطَّمَ وَآنْحَطَمَ	To crumble.
حِطْمَةٌ وَحُطَامٌ	Piece, fragment.
حُطَامُ ٱلدُّنْيَا	Goods or vanities of this world.
حَظَّ يَحُظُّ	To be fortunate.
حَظٌّ ج حُظُوظٌ	Happiness.
مَحْظُوظٌ	Happy.
حَظَرَ يَحْظُرُ عَلَى	To forbid.
حَظِيرَةٌ ج حَظَائِرُ	Enclosure.
مَحْظُورَاتٌ	Prohibited things.
حَظِيَ يَحْظَى بِ	To obtain.
حَفَّ بِ	To encompass.
خُبْزٌ حَافٌّ	Dry bread.
حَافَّةٌ	Edge, rim, border.
مِحَفَّةٌ	Kind of litter.
مَحْفُوفٌ	Surrounded.
حَفِيدٌ ج حَفَدَةٌ	Grandson.
حَفَرَ يَحْفِرُ وَآحْتَفَرَ	To dig.
حُفْرَةٌ ج حُفَرٌ	Ditch, pit.
حَافِرٌ ج حَوَافِرُ	Hoof.
حَفَّارٌ	Grave-digger.
مَحْفُورٌ	Dug, dug out.
حَفِظَ يَحْفَظُ	To guard, keep.
حَافَظَ عَلَى	To be careful of.
تَحَفَّظَ	To be watchful.
حِفْظٌ	Guard ; careful watch.
حِفَاظٌ	Truss.
(ٱلْقُوَّةُ) ٱلْحَافِظَةُ	Memory.
مُحَافِظٌ	Guardian, keeper.
مُحَافَظَةٌ	Guardianship.
مَحْفُوظٌ	Guarded, preserved.
حَفَلَ يَحْفِلُ	To gather, assemble.
إِحْتَفَلَ لَهُ	To receive with houour.
إِحْتَفَلَ بِ	To give attention to.

حَفْلٌ Large assembly ; care.

حَافِلٌ Entirely full (hall &c.)

إِحْتِفَالٌ Celebration ; pomp.

مَحْفِلٌ ج مَحَافِلُ Assembly.

مُحْتَفَلٌ Place of assembly.

حَفْنَةٌ ج حَفَنَاتٌ Handful.

حَفِيَ يَحْفَى To go bare-foot.

حَفِيَ وَاحْتَفَى بِ To show joy and honour.

حَفَاءٌ وَحُفُوَّةٌ Bare-footedness.

حَافٍ Bare-foot ; unshod.

حَقَّ يَحِقُّ To be true, right.

حَقَّقَ To verify, confirm.

تَحَقَّقَ To assure one's self.

إِسْتَحَقَّ To deserve ; fall due.

حَقٌّ ج حُقُوقٌ Right ; truth ; obligation, worth ; true ; truthful.

حَقٌّ عَلَى Duty.

حَقٌّ بِ Worthy of.

حَقًّا وَبِالْحَقِّ Truly, indeed.

حُقٌّ ج حِقَاقٌ Socket.

حُقَّةٌ ج حُقَقٌ Case, casket.

حَقِيقَةٌ ج حَقَائِقُ Reality, truth. ssence.

حَقِيقَةً وَفِي ٱلْحَقِيقَةِ Truly.

حَقِيقِيٌّ Real ; proper (sense).

أَحَقُّ بِ More worthy of.

إِسْتِحْقَاقٌ ج إِسْتِحْقَاقَاتٌ Merit.

تَحْقِيقٌ Verification.

مُحَقَّقٌ Verified, confirmed.

مُسْتَحِقٌّ Worthy of, deserving.

حُقْبٌ ج أَحْقَابٌ A long time.

حَقِيبَةٌ Saddle-bag.

حَقَدَ يَحْقِدُ To bear spite.

حِقْدٌ Hatred, grudge, spite.

حَاقِدٌ وَحَقُودٌ Spiteful.

حَقَرَ يَحْقِرُ وَاحْتَقَرَ To despise.

حَقُرَ يَحْقُرُ To be contemptible.

حَقَارَةٌ Contempt ; vileness.

حَقِيرٌ Despised ; mean ; paltry.

حَقْلٌ ج حُقُولٌ — Field.

حَقَنَ يَحْقُنُ — To retain. Inject.

إِحْتَقَنَ — To be congested.

حُقْنَةٌ ج حُقَنٌ — Clyster ; syringe.

حَقْوٌ ج حِقَاءٌ — Waist ; loins.

حَكَّ يَحُكُّ — To rub, scrape.

إِحْتَكَّ بِ — To rub against.

حَكٌّ — Rubbing ; scratching.

حُكٌّ — Magnetic compass.

حِكَّةٌ وَحُكَاكٌ — An itching.

مِحَكٌّ — Touchstone.

تَحَكَّرَ وَٱحْتَكَرَ — To withhold grain for sale at high prices.

حُكْرَةٌ — Usurious grain-trade.

حَكَمَ يَحْكُمُ — To give judgment.

حَكَمَ لِ — To judge in favour of.

حَكَمَ عَلَى — To judge against.

حَكَّمَ — To appoint one to judge.

حَاكَمَ — To contest in law.

أَحْكَمَ — To do a thing well.

تَحَاكَمَ — To go together to law.

حُكْمٌ ج أَحْكَامٌ — Judgment ; government ; authority, rule.

حِكْمَةٌ ج حِكَمٌ — Wisdom.

حَاكِمٌ — Judge ; governor.

حُكُومَةٌ — Judgment ; government.

حَكِيمٌ ج حُكَمَاءُ — Wise.

مُحْكَمٌ — Well made.

مَحْكَمَةٌ ج مَحَاكِمُ — Tribunal.

حَكَى يَحْكِي — To tell, relate.

حَـكَى وَحَاكَى — To resemble.

حِكَايَةٌ — Story, tale, narrative.

حَلَّ يَحُلُّ — To alight, abide.

حَلَّ يَحُلُّ حَلًّا — To solve (a problem) dissolve (a solid) ; loosen.

حَلَّ عَلَى — To come upon one.

حَلَّ يَحِلُّ — To be lawful.

حَلَّلَ — To permit. Analyze.

أَحَلَّ — To allow, permit.

إِسْتَحَلَّ	To deem lawful.
حَلٌّ	A solving, dissolving.
حِلٌّ	Lawful.
حُلَّةٌ ج حُلَلٌ	Garment.
حَلَالٌ	Lawful ; right.
حُلُولٌ	An alighting, abiding.
حَلِيلٌ م حَلِيلَةٌ	Husband ; wife.
إِسْتِحْلَالٌ	Deeming lawful.
تَحْلِيلٌ	Dissolving ; analysis.
مَحَلٌّ ج مَحَالّ	Place ; quarter.
مَحَلَّةٌ	Inn ; stopping-place.
حَلَبَ يَحْلُبُ	To milk.
تَحَلَّبَ وَٱنْحَلَبَ	To flow ; exude.
حَلَبُ	Aleppo.
حُلْبَةٌ	Fenugreek.
حَالِبٌ وَحَلَّابٌ	Milkman.
حَلِيبٌ	Fresh milk.
مُسْتَحْلَبٌ	Emulsion.
حِلْتِيتٌ	Assafoetida.
حَلَجَ يَحْلِجُ	To card cotton.
حِلَاجَةٌ	Carding of cotton.
حَلَّاجٌ	Cotton-carder.
مِحْلَجٌ	Instrument for carding.
حَلَزُونٌ	Snail.
حَلَزُونِيٌّ	Spiral.
حَلَفَ يَحْلِفُ	To swear.
حَلَّفَ وَٱسْتَحْلَفَ	To make swear.
حَالَفَ	To be in league with.
تَحَالَفَ	To confederate.
حِلْفٌ	Oath ; league.
حَلِيفٌ ج حُلَفَاءُ	Confederate.
تَحَالُفٌ وَمُحَالَفَةٌ	Alliance.
حَلَقَ يَحْلِقُ	To shave.
حَلْقٌ ج حُلُوقٌ	Throat, palate.
حُرُوفُ ٱلْحَلْقِ	Guttural letters.
حَلَقَةٌ	Circle ; link, ear-ring.
حَلَّاقٌ	Barber.
حِلَاقَةٌ	Barber's trade.

Shaved, shorn. حَلِيقٌ ج حَلْقَى

Shaved. مَحْلُوقٌ

Throat. حُلْقُومٌ ج حَلَاقِيم

Intense blackness. حَلَكٌ

Very black. حَالِكٌ

To dream. حَلَمَ يَحْلُمُ

To be gentle, mild. حَلُمَ يَحْلُمُ

Gentleness, clemency. حِلْمٌ

Dream, vision. حُلْمٌ ج أَحْلَامٌ

Teat, nipple. حَلَمَةٌ

Gentle, mild. حَلِيمٌ ج حُلَمَاءُ

To be sweet. حَلَا يَحْلُو

To sweeten. حَلَّى تَحْلِيَةً

To find sweet. إِسْتَحْلَى

Sweet, agreable. حُلْوٌ

Present ; gratuity. حُلْوَانٌ

Confectioner. حَلَوَانِيٌّ

Sweetmeats. حَلْوَى

Sweetness. حَلَاوَةٌ

Sweetened, sugared. مُحَلًّى

To be adorned. حَلِيَ يَحْلَى

To adorn (with jewels). حَلَّى

To gild. حَلَّى بِذَهَب

To be adorned. تَحَلَّى

Jewels ; ornaments. حَلْيٌ ج حُلِيٌّ

Adornment. حِلْيَةٌ ج حِلًى

To have fever. حُمَّ

To take a bath. إِسْتَحَمَّ

Fever. حُمَّى ج حُمَّيَاتٌ

Thermal spring. حَمَّةٌ

Fate ; death. حِمَامٌ

Dove ; pigeon. حَمَامَةٌ ج حَمَامٌ

Bath. حَمَّامٌ ج حَمَّامَاتٌ

Suffering from fever. مَحْمُومٌ

To praise ; thank. حَمِدَ يَحْمَدُ

Praise ; thanks. حَمْدٌ

Praise be to God. أَلْحَمْدُ لِلّٰهِ

Praised. حَمِيدٌ

مَحْمُودٌ	Praised, praiseworthy.
حَمَّرَ	To dye red ; redden.
إِحْمَرَّ	To become red; blush.
حُمَّرٌ	Bitumen.
حُمْرَةٌ	Redness. Erysipelas.
حِمَارٌ ج حَمِيرٌ	Ass, donkey.
حِمَارُ ٱلْوَحْشِ	Wild ass.
حَمَّارٌ ج حَمَّارَةٌ	Ass-driver.
أَحْمَرُ م حَمْرَاءُ ج حُمْرٌ	Red.
مُحَمِّرٌ	Rubefacient.
حَمِسَ يَحْمَسُ	To be hard in religion, etc.
حَمَّسَ وَأَحْمَسَ	To irritate.
حَمَاسَةٌ	Bravery energy.
حَمَّصَ	To roast, toast.
تَحَمَّصَ	To be roasted.
حِمْصُ	Hems (city).
حِمِّصٌ	Chick-peas.
حَمِضَ يَحْمَضُ	To be sour, acid.
حَامِضٌ	Acid ; sour.
حُمُوضَةٌ	Acidity ; sourness.
حُمَاضٌ وَحُمَّيْضٌ	Sorrel (plant).
مُحَمَّضٌ	Acidulated, acid, sour.
حَمِقَ يَحْمَقُ	To be foolish.
حُمْقٌ وَحَمَاقَةٌ	Stupidity, folly.
حُمَاقٌ	Chicken-pox.
أَحْمَقُ	Stupid, foolish.
حَمَلَ يَحْمِلُ	To carry, lift.
حَمَلَتْ	To conceive (woman).
حَمَلَ على	To attack, charge.
حَمَلَ يَحْمِلُ	To bear fruit.
حَمَلَ ٱلنَّهْرُ	To overflow (river).
حَمَّلَ	To burden, load.
تَحَمَّلَ	To suffer patiently.
إِحْتَمَلَ	To bear, suffer.
إِحْتَمَلَ أَنْ	To be possible.
حَمْلٌ	Carrying. Pregnancy.
حِمْلٌ ج أَحْمَالٌ	Burden, load.
حَمَلٌ ج حُمْلَانٌ	Lamb.

أَلحَمَلُ	Sign of the Ram (Aries).
حَمْلَةٌ	Attack ; charge in battle.
حَمَّالٌ	Porter.
إِحْتِمَالٌ	Patience ; endurance.
مَحْمِلٌ ج مَحَامِل	Litter.
مَحْمُولٌ	Borne ; suffered.
مُحْتَمَلٌ	Bearable. Possible.
حَمُو ج أَحْمَاء	Father-in-law.
حَمَاةٌ ج حَمَوَاتٌ	Mother-in-law.
حَمَى يَحْمِي	To protect, defend.
حَمِيَ يَحْمَى	To be very hot.
أَحْمَى إِحْمَاءً	To make hot.
حَامَى عَنْ	To defend.
إِحْتَمَى	To protect one's self.
حِمًى ج أَحْمَاء	Interdicted place.
حِمْيَة	Care of diet.
حَمِيَّة	Anger, rage. Disdain.
حُمَة	Venom, sting.
حَامٍ	Protector. Hot.
حَامِيَةٌ	Guard, garrison.
حِمَايَة	Protection. Protégé.
مُحْمًى	Heated.
مُحَامٍ	Protector ; advocate.
حَنَّ يَحِنُّ إِلَى	To yearn.
تَحَنَّنَ عَلَى	To have compassion.
حَنَّانٌ وَحَنُونٌ	Compassionate, tender.
حَنَّأَ	To dye with *Henna*.
حِنَاء	The plant *henna*.
حَانُوتٌ ج حَوَانِيتُ	Shop.
حَنِثَ يَحْنَثُ	To break an oath.
حِنْثٌ	Perjury. Sin, crime.
حَانِثٌ	A perjurer.
حَنَشٌ ج أَحْنَاشٌ	Snake.
حَنَطَ وَأَحْنَطَ	To embalm.
حِنْطَةٌ	Wheat.
حَنْظَلٌ	Colocynth.
حَنَفِيَّة	Tap.
حَنِقَ يَحْنَقُ	To be enraged.

Leather. Poplar tree. حَوَرٌ

Disciple of a prophet. حَوَارِيٌّ

A quarter of a town. حَارَةٌ

Panier. Oyster. مَحَارَةٌ

Pivot. مِحْوَرٌ ج مَحَاوِر

Conversation ; debate. مُحَاوَرَة

To get ; possess. حازَ يَحُوز

To drow aside from. إِنْحَازَ عَنْ

To turn to and join. إِنْحَازَ إِلَى

Space occupied by a body. حَيِّزٌ

To gather, collect. حَوَّش

To be taken in. إِنْحَاشَ

Fold ; court. حَوْشٌ ج احْوَاشٌ

Mixed people ; rabble. حَوَشٌ

Saddle-girth, girdle. حِيَاصَةٌ

Stomach of a bird. حَوْصَلَة

Reservoir, tank. حَوْضٌ ج أَحْوَاضٌ

To surround ; enclose. حَوَّطَ

To invest, surround. احَاطَ ب

Violent anger ; spite. حَنَق

To make wise. حَنَكَ وَأَحْنَكَ

Palate. حَنَكٌ ج احْنَاكٌ

Experienced. مُحَنَّكٌ

To bend, incline. حَنَى يَحْنِي

To be bent. تَحَنَّى وَانْحَنَى

Tenderness, compassion. حُنُوٌّ

Wine-house, tavern. حَانِيَةٌ

Bent, crooked ; inclined. مُنْحَنٍ

Large fish. Whale. حُوتٌ ج حِيتَانٌ

To compel. أَحْوَجَ

To want, need, require. إِحْتَاجَ

Want ; need ; necessity ; object ; desire. حَاجَةٌ ج حَاجَات وَحَوَائِجُ

Want ; having need. إِحْتِيَاجٌ

In want or need of مُحْتَاجٌ إِلَى

To overcome. اسْتَحْوَذَ عَلَى

Coachman, cabman. حُوذِيٌّ

To be bewildered. حَارَ يَحَارُ

To converse, debate. حَاوَرَ

Wall. حَائِطٌ ج حِيطَانٌ

Investment. Caution. إِحتِيَاطٌ

Circumference. مُحِيطٌ

The ocean. أَلْبَحْرُ ٱلْمُحِيطُ

Edge, border. حَافَةٌ ج حَافَاتٌ

To surround. حَاقَ يَحُوق بِ

To strike out, erase. حَوَّقَ

To weave. حَاكَ يَحُوكُ

Weaver. حَائِكٌ ج حَاكَةٌ

The art of weaving. حِيَاكَةٌ

To be changed. حَالَ وَتَحَوَّلَ

To come between. حَالَ بَيْنَ

To change, alter. حَوَّلَ إِلَى

To attempt. حَاوَلَ

To use stratagem. احْتَالَ

To be changed. Absurd. إِسْتَحَالَ

State, condition. حَالٌ ج أَحوَالٌ

Immediately. حالاً وَفي ٱلْحال

As soon as. حَالمَا

State, condition. حَالَةٌ ج حَالاَتٌ

Power. Year. حَوْلٌ ج احْوَالٌ

All around, around. حَوْلَ

Squint. حَوَلٌ

Transfer of a debt. حَوَالَةٌ

Stratagem ; means. حِيلَةٌ ج حِيَلٌ

Mechanics. عِلْمُ ٱلْحِيَلِ

In front of, opposite to. حِيَالَ

Squint-eyed. أَحْوَل م حولاء

More cunning, crafty. أَحْيَلَ

Transferring. تَحْوِيلٌ

Absurd, unreasonable. مُحَالٌ

Undoubtedly. لاَ مُحالَةَ

Cunning, sly, wily. مُحْتَالٌ

Impossible ; absurd. مستَحِيلٌ

To run around ; hover. حامَ يَحُوم

Wine-shop. حَانَةٌ وَحَانُوتٌ

Eve (mother of mankind). حَوَّاءُ

To possess ; contain. حَوَى يَحْوِي

إِحْتَوَى عَلَى	To comprise.
حَاوٍ	Snake-charmer. Containing.
حَيْثُ	Where, where there.
حَيْثُمَا	Wherever.
مِنْ حَيْث	In respect of, since.
بِحَيْثُ انْ	So that.
حَادَ يَحِيدُ	To deviate ; turn aside.
حَايَدَ مُحَايَدَةً	To avoid, shun.
حَارَ يَحَارُ	To be bewildered.
حَيَّرَ	To bewilder, perplex.
تَحَيَّرَ فِي	To be perplexed.
حَيْرَةٌ وَتَحَيُّرٌ	Perplexity.
حَارَةٌ ج حَارَاتٌ	Street ; quarter.
حَائِرٌ	Confused, perplexed.
مُتَحَيِّرَةٌ ج مُتَحَيِّرَاتٌ	Planet.
حَيِّزٌ	Space occupied by a body.
حَاضَتْ تَحِيضُ	To menstruate.
حَيْضٌ	Menstruation ; menses.
حَافَ يَحِيفُ	To be unjust.
حَيْفٌ	Injustice, oppression.
حَاقَ يَحِيقُ ب	To surround, befall.
حَيْلٌ	Strength, power, might.
حَانَ يَحِينُ	To draw near (time).
حَانٌ وَحَانَةٌ	Wine-house, tavern.
حِينٌ ج أَحْيَانٌ	Time, season.
لِلْحِين	Instantaneously ; at once.
أَحْيَانًا	From time to time.
حِينَئِذٍ	Then ; at that time.
حَيِيَ يَحْيَا حَيَاةً	To live.
حَيِيَ حَيَاءً مِنْ	To be ashamed of.
حَيَّا تَحِيَّةً	To salute, greet.
أَحْيَا	To bring to life.
اِسْتَحْيَا	To spare one's life.
إِسْتَحْيَا وَآسْتَحَى	To be ashamed.
حَيَّ	Come ! come quickly !
حَيَاءٌ	Shame ; modesty.
حَيَاةٌ أَوْحَيَوةٌ	Life : life-time.
حَيٌّ ج أَحْيَاءٌ	Alive. Tribe. Quarter of a town.

حَيَّةٌ ج حَيَاتٌ Snake.

حَيَوَانٌ ج حَيَوَانَاتٌ Animal.

عِلْمُ ٱلْحَيَوَانِ Zoology.

حَيَوَانِيٌّ Animal (*Adj.*)

حَيَوِيٌّ Vital.

تَحِيَّةٌ ج تَحِيَاتٌ Greeting.

مُحَيًّا Face.

مُحْيٍ Vivifying, giving life.

خ

خ As a numeral sign =600.

خَبَّ يَخُبُّ To trot, amble.

خَبَبٌ Ambling pace, trot.

خَبَأَ يَخْبَأُ وَخَبَّأَ To conceal, hide.

إِخْتَبَأَ وَتَخَبَّأَ To be concealed.

خِبَاءٌ ج أَخْبِئَةٌ Small tent.

خَابِيَةٌ ج خَوَابٍ Large jug.

مَخْبَأٌ ج مَخَابِئُ A hiding place.

خَبُثَ يَخْبُثُ To be corrupt.

خُبْثٌ وَخَبَاثَةٌ Wickedness.

خَبِيثٌ ج خُبَثَاءُ Vile, malicious.

خَبَائِثُ Infamous actions.

مَخْبَثَةٌ A cause of evil.

خَبَرَ يَخْبُرُ To test, try, prove.

خَابَرَ To negotiate.

خَبَّرَ وَأَخْبَرَ بِ To inform.

إِخْتَبَرَ To learn by experience.

إِسْتَخْبَرَ To ask for information

خَبَرٌ ج اخْبَارٌ New report.

خُبْرَةٌ Knowledge ; experience.

خَبَرِيَّةٌ Report ; story.

خَبِيرٌ ج خُبَرَاءُ Well informed.

أَخْبَرُ Better informed.

خَبَزَ يَخْبِزُ To bake bread.

خُبْزٌ Bread.

خُبْزَةٌ Loaf of bread.

خِبَازَةٌ Baker's trade.

خَبَّازٌ م خَبَّازَةٌ Baker.

خُبَّازَى وَخُبَّيْزَةٌ Mallow (plant).

مَخْبُوزٌ وَخَبِيزٌ Any thing baked.

خَبَصَ يَخْبِصُ To mix ; bungle.

خَبَّاصٌ Rash bungler.

خَبَطَ يَخْبِطُ To strike.

خَبْطُ عَشْوَاءَ At random.

خَبَلَ يَخْبِلُ To be or make insane.

خَبِلٌ وَأَخْبَلُ وَمُخَبَّلٌ Mad, insane.

مَخْبُولٌ Fatigued ; weakened.

خِبَاءٌ ج أَخْبِيَةٌ Tent of wool.

خَابِيَةٌ ج خَوَابٍ Large jug, jar.

خَتَلَ يَخْتِلُ وَخَاتَلَ To cheat.

مُخَاتَلَةٌ Fraud, deceit.

خَتَمَ يَخْتِمُ To seal, stamp.

خَتَمَ To conclude, terminate.

خَاتَمٌ ج خَوَاتِمُ Seal-ring, signet.

خَاتِمَةٌ End, conclusion.

خِتَامٌ ج خُتُمٌ End, conclusion.

مَخْتُومٌ Sealed ; closed.

خَتَنَ يَخْتِنُ To circumcise.

اِخْتَتَنَ To be circumcised.

خَتَنٌ Any relation on side of wife.

خَاتُونٌ ج خَوَاتِينُ Noble lady.

خِتَانٌ وَخِتَانَةٌ Circumcision.

خَثَرَ يَخْثُرُ وَتَخَثَّرَ To coagulate.

خَثَّرَ وَأَخْثَرَ To thicken.

خُثَارَةٌ Sediment, dregs.

خَاثِرٌ Coagulated ; thickened.

خَجِلَ يَخْجَلُ To be ashamed, blush.

خَجَّلَ وَأَخْجَلَ To put to shame.

خَجَلٌ Shame, confusion.

خَجْلَانُ وَمَخْجُولٌ Modest, bashful.

خَدٌّ ج خُدُودٌ Cheek.

خَدٌّ وَأُخْدُودٌ Furrow, pit.

خُدَّةٌ ج خُدَدٌ Furrow, track.

خُدَيْدِيَةٌ Small cushion.

Cushion, pillow. مِخَدَّةٌ

To be benumbed. خَدِرَ يَخْدَرُ

To benumb. خَدَّرَ

Curtain, veil. خِدْرٌ ج خُدُورٌ

Numbness ; stupefaction. خَدَرٌ

Sedative, anæsthetic. مُخَدِّرٌ

Girl kept in seclusion. مُخَدَّرَةٌ

To scratch. خَدَشَ يَخْدِشُ خَدْشاً

To deceive. خَدَعَ يَخْدَعُ وَخَادَعَ

Deceit, guile. خدعة

To be deceived. إِنْخَدَعَ

Deceit. خَدِيعَةٌ ج خَدَائِعُ

Impostor ; deceitful. خَادِعٌ

Impostor, great cheat. خَدَّاعٌ

Chamber. مُخْدَعٌ ج مَخَادِعُ

Deceived, deluded. مَخْدُوعٌ

To serve. خَدَمَ يَخْدُمُ خِدْمَةً

To employ. إِسْتَخْدَمَ

Service ; official duty. خِدْمَةٌ

Servant. خَادِمٌ ج خَدَمٌ وَخُدَّامٌ

Friend. خِدْنٌ ج أَخْدَانٌ

Prince, viceroy. خُدَيْوِيٌّ

To forsake. خَذَلَ يَخْذُلُ خَذْلاً

To be forsaken. إِنْخَذَلَ

Forsaken, unaided. مَخْذُولٌ

To gurgle, rumble. خَرَّ يَخِرُّ

To prostrate one's self. خَرَّ لِ

Gurgling, murmur. خَرِيرٌ

To ease the bowels. خَرِئَ يَخْرَأُ

Excrement. خُرْءٌ وَخِرَاءٌ

To be ruined. خَرِبَ يَخْرَبُ

To demolish, ruin. خَرَّبَ يُخَرِّبُ

To be destroyed. تَخَرَّبَ

A ruin, waste. خِرْبَةٌ ج خِرَبٌ

Devastation ; ruin. خَرَابٌ

Carob-tree. خَرُّوبٌ وَخُرْنُوبٌ

Devastation, destruction. تَخْرِيبٌ

To scratch a writing. خَرْبَشَ

Hellebore. خَرْبَقٌ

To get out ; emerge. خَرَجَ يَخْرُجُ

To take out ; expel. أَخْرَجَ

To be well trained. تَخَرَّجَ

To draw out, extract. إِسْتَخْرَجَ

Expenditure. خَرْجٌ

Saddle-bags. خُرْجٌ ج أَخْرَاجٌ

Exterior, quotient. خَارِجٌ

Fareign affairs. الأُمُورُ ٱلْخَارِجِيةُ

Land-tax ; tribute, tax. خَرَاجٌ

Abscess. خُرَاجٌ ج خُرَاجَاتٌ

Outlet ; issue. مَخْرَجٌ

Skilful, well-trained. مُخَرَّجٌ

To rattle, snore. خَرْخَرَ

Small shot. خُرْدُقٌ

Mustard. خَرْدَلٌ

To pierce ; bore. خَرَزَ يَخْرِزُ

Small shells, beads. خَرَزٌ

Vertebræ of the back. خَرَزَاتُ ٱلظَّهْرِ

Awl. مِخْرَزٌ مَخَارِزُ

To be dumb. خَرِسَ يَخْرَسُ

Dumbness. خَرَسٌ

Dumb. أَخْرَسُ

Ear-ring. خُرْصٌ ج خِرْصَانٌ

To turn on a lathe. خَرَطَ يَخْرِطُ

To unsheathe a sword. إِخْتَرَطَ

Trade of a turner. خِرَاطَةٌ

Shavings of a lathe. خُرَاطَةٌ

Turner. Liar. خَرَّاطٌ

Lathe. مِخْرَطَةٌ ج مَخَارِطُ

Cone. مَخْرُوطٌ

Conical. مَخْرُوطِيٌّ

Snout. خُرْطُومٌ ج خَرَاطِيمُ

To invent, devise. إِخْتَرَعَ

Castor-oil-plant. خِرْوَعٌ

Invention. إِخْتِرَاعٌ ج إِخْتِرَاعَاتٌ

To dote from old age. خَرِفَ يَخْرَفُ

Dotage. خَرَفٌ وَخَرَافَةٌ

Doting, idiotic. خَرِفٌ وَخَرْفَانٌ

Fictitious tale, fable. خُرَافَةٌ

Lamb, sheep. خَرُوفٌ ج خِرَافٌ

Autumn. خَرِيفٌ

To pierce. خَرَقَ يَخْرُقُ خَرْقًا

To be pierced. إِنْخَرَقَ

To traverse. إِخْتَرَقَ

Rent, hole. خَرْقٌ ج خُرُوقٌ

Stupid, awkward. خَرِقٌ وَأَخْرَقُ

Rag, tatter. خِرْقَةٌ ج خِرَقٌ

Unusual. خَارِقٌ ج خَوَارِقُ

To slit. Fail. خَرَمَ يَخْرِمُ

To embroider. خَرَّمَ

To be torn, slit, pierced. إِنْخَرَمَ

Bore. خُرْمٌ ج خُرُومٌ

Acromion (anatomy). أَلأَخْرَمُ

Embroidery. تَخْرِيمٌ

Embroidered, chased. مُخَرَّمٌ

To scratch. خَرْمَشَ

See. خَرُّوبٌ خُرْنُوبٌ

Silk-stuff. خَزٌّ ج خُزُوزٌ

Caspian Sea. بَحْرُ ٱلْخَزَرِ

Ratan, Bamboo. خَيْزُرَانٌ

A fable. خُزَعْبَلَةٌ ج خُزَعْبَلَاتٌ

Earthenware, pottery. خَزَفٌ

Potter. خَزَفِيٌّ وَخَزَّافٌ

To penetrate; tear. خَزَقَ يَخْزِقُ

To impale. خَوْزَقَ

To cut off. خَزَلَ يَخْزِلُ خَزْلاً

To pierce the nose. خَزَمَ يَخْزِمُ

Nose-ring. خِزَامٌ

Lavender. Hyacinth. خُزَامَى

To store, hoard. خَزَنَ يَخْزُنُ

Treasury. خَزْنَةٌ وَخِزَانَةٌ

Treasure. خِزْنَةٌ وَخَزِينَةٌ ج خَزَائِنُ

Library. خِزانَةُ ٱلْكُتُبِ

Armoury. خِزَانَةُ ٱلسِّلَاحِ

Treasurer. خَازِنٌ ج خَزَنَةٌ

Magazine.	مَخْزَنٌ ج مَخَازِنُ
To subdue.	خَزَا يَخْزُو خَزْواً
To be despised.	خَزِيَ يَخْزَى
To be ashamed of.	خَزِيَ مِن
Shame, disgrace.	خِزْيٌ
Shameful thing.	خِزْيَةٌ
To be mean.	خَسَّ يَخِسُّ خَسَاسَةً
Lettuce.	خَسٌّ
Vile, mean (miserly).	خَسِيسٌ
To lose.	خَسِرَ يَخْسَرُ
To cause loss, damage.	خَسَّرَ
Loss.	خُسْرٌ وخَسَارَةٌ وخُسْرَانٌ
Losing, loser.	خَاسِرٌ
To sink into the earth and vanish. Be eclipsed.	خَسَفَ يَخْسِفُ
To be eclipsed.	إِنْخَسَفَ
Eclipse.	خُسُوفٌ
Eclipsed.	مَخْسُوفٌ
To enter, penetrate.	خَشَّ يَخُشُّ

Timber-wood.	خَشَبٌ
A piece of wood.	خَشَبَةٌ
Coarse ; hard.	خَشِبٌ
Wood-seller.	خَشَّابٌ
To rustle ; clink.	خَشْخَشَ
Poppy.	خَشْخَاشٌ
Charnel-house.	خَشْخَاشَةٌ
Refuse.	خُشَارٌ وخُشَارَةٌ
Te be submissive.	خَشَعَ يَخْشَعُ
To humble one's self.	تَخَشَّعَ
Lowliness ; humility.	خُشُوعٌ
Humble.	خَاشِعٌ ج خاشِعُون
Young gazelle.	خِشْفٌ وخِشْفَةٌ
Bat (animal).	خُشَّافٌ
Nose.	خَشْمٌ . خَيْشُومٌ ج خَيَاشِيمُ
To be rough.	خَشُنَ يَخْشُنُ
To treat one harshly.	خَاشَنَ
Roughness.	خُشْنَةٌ وخُشُونَةٌ
Rough.	خَشِنٌ ج خِشَانٌ

خَشِيَ يَخْشَى	To fear, dread.
خَشْيَةٌ وَخِشْيَانٌ	Fear.
خَشْيَةَ أَنْ	For fear that.
خَاشٍ وَخَشْيَانُ	Fearful.
خَصَّ يَخُصُّ بِ	To distinguish by
خَصَّ خُصُوصاً	To be special to.
خَصَّصَ بِ	To assign.
إِخْتَصَّ بِ	To be one's property.
خُصٌّ ج خِصَاصٌ	Hut, booth.
خَاصٌّ لِ وبِ	Special to.
خَاصَّةٌ ج خَوَاصُّ	Quality, property.
خَاصَّةً	Particularly.
اَلْخَاصَّةُ والخَوَاصُّ	The notables.
خَاصِّيَّةٌ	Particular property.
عَلَى ٱلْخُصُوصِ وَخُصُوصاً	Especially.
خُصُوصِيٌّ	Special, particular.
خَصِبَ يَخْصَبُ	To be fertile.
خِصْبٌ	Fertility.
خَصِبٌ وَمُخْصِبٌ	Fertile.

إِخْتَصَرَ	To abridge
خَصْرٌ ج خُصُورٌ	Waist.
خَاصِرَةٌ ج خَوَاصِرُ	Side ; flank.
إِخْتِصَارٌ	Abridgment.
بِالإِخْتِصَارِ	In short ; briefly.
مِخْصَرَةٌ ج مَخَاصِرُ	Whip, staff.
مُخْتَصَرٌ	Abridged ; compend.
خَصْلَةٌ ج خِصَالٌ	Habit, quality.
خُصْلَةٌ ج خُصَلٌ	Lock of hair. Bunch.
خَاصَمَ	To dispute, contend with.
خَصْمٌ ج خُصُومٌ	Adversary.
خَصِيمٌ ج خُصَمَاءُ	Adversary.
خِصَامٌ	Dispute, quarrel.
خَصَى يَخْصِي	To geld, castrate.
خَصِيٌّ ج خِصْيَانٌ	Eunuch.
خُصْيَةٌ ج خُصًى	Testicle.
خَضَّ وَخَضْخَضَ	To stir (water).
خَضَبَ يَخْضِبُ	To dye.
تَخَضَّبَ وَاخْتَضَبَ	To be dyed.

خِضَابٌ	Dye, colour.
خَضِرَ يَخْضَرُ	To be green.
خَضَّرَ	To become green.
خُضْرَةٌ ج خُضَرٌ	Greenness. Vegetables.
أَخْضَرُ م خَضْرَاءُ ج خُضْرٌ	Green.
خِضْرَاوَاتٌ	Fruits ; herbs.
خَضَعَ يَخْضَعُ	To submit ; obey.
خَضَّعَ وَأَخْضَعَ	To subdue.
تَخَضَّعَ	To humble one's self.
خَاضِعٌ وَخَضُوعٌ	Submissive.
خُضُوعٌ	Submission.
خَطَّ يَخُطُّ	To trace ; write.
خَطَّطَ	To mark with lines.
خَطٌّ ج خُطُوطٌ	Line, streak.
خَطُّ ٱلْاسْتِوَاءِ	Equator.
خَطُّ ٱلْاعْتِدَالِ	Equinoctial line.
خَطُّ نِصْفِ ٱلنَّهَارِ	Meridian.
خَطٌّ شَرِيفٌ	Imperial edict.
خُطَّةٌ	Affair. Line of action.
خَطِئَ يَخْطَأُ	To err, sin.
خَطَّأَ	To charge with mistake.
أَخْطَأَ	To err, transgress ; miss one's aim.
خَطَأٌ وَخَطَاءٌ	Error ; sin, mistake.
خَطِيئَةٌ ج خَطَايَا	Sin.
خَاطِئٌ ج خُطَاةٌ وَخُطَاةٌ	Sinner.
مُخْطِئٌ	Erring, missing.
خَطَبَ يَخْطُبُ	To make a speech.
خَطَبَ يَخْطُبُ	To betroth, ask in marrigae.
خَاطَبَ	To talk or converse with.
خَطْبٌ ج خُطُوبٌ	Calamity.
خُطْبَةٌ وَخِطَابٌ	Address, speech.
خِطْبَةٌ	Betrothal.
خَطِيبٌ ج خُطَبَاءُ	Preacher.
مُخَاطَبٌ	Second person, (*Gram.*)
خَطَرَ لَهُ	To occur to his mind.
خَاطَرَ بِ	To expose to danger.
خَطَرٌ ج أَخْطَارٌ	Danger, risk.
خَاطِرٌ ج خَوَاطِرُ	Thought, idea.

إِخْطَارٌ Admonition, warning.

خَطِيرٌ Great ; important.

مُخْطِرٌ وَخَطِرٌ Dangerous.

مَخَاطِرُ Risks, dangers, perils.

خَطَفَ يَخْطَفُ To seize, abduct.

إِخْتَطَفَ To snatch away, rob.

خَطْفٌ Robbery ; abduction.

خَاطِفٌ Seizing with violence.

خُطَّافٌ ج خَطَاطِيفُ Swallow (bird).

خَطَمَ يَخْطِمُ To muzzle.

خِطْمِيٌّ Marsh-mallow.

خَطَا يَخْطُو To step, walk.

تَخَطَّى To pass beyond.

خُطْوَةٌ ج خُطُوَاتٌ Step, pace.

خَطِيئَةٌ Sin, transgression.

خَفَّ يَخِفُّ To be light (in weight).

خَفَّفَ To make light, ease.

إِسْتَخَفَّ To make light of.

خُفٌّ ج أَخْفَافٌ Boot, shoe.

خِفَّةٌ Lightness ; agility.

خَفِيفٌ Light (in weight) ; quick.

إِسْتِخْفَافٌ Slighting, despising.

تَخْفِيفٌ Alleviating, lightening.

خَفَرَ يَخْفُرُ To protect, guard.

خَفَرٌ Sentry, guard.

خَفِيرٌ ج خُفَرَاءُ Sentry, escort.

خُفَّاشٌ ج خَفَافِيشُ Bat (animal).

خَفَضَ يَخْفِضُ To depress, lower.

خَفَّضَ To let down, lower.

إِنْخَفَضَ To become low.

خَفْضٌ Abasement.

خَفَقَ يَخْفِقُ To beat. Flutter.

أَخْفَقَ To fail, miss.

خَفَقَانٌ Palpitation.

خَفِيَ يَخْفَى خَفَاءً To be hidden.

خَفِيَ خُفْيَةً To go out of sight.

أَخْفَى إِخْفَاءً To conceal.

تَخَفَّى To be concealed.

To disappear.	إِختَفَى مِن
Secret ; unperceived.	خَفَا وَخَفَاء
Cocealed, secret.	خَفًا ج خَفَايَا
Secretly ; in secret.	خُفْيَةً
King.	خَاقَانٌ ج خَوَاقِينُ
To become vinegar.	خَلَّ
To be remiss in, neglect.	اَخَلَّ بِ
To penetrate, enter.	تَخَلَّلَ فِي
To be shaky, faulty.	اِخْتَلَّ
Vinegar. Slit, rent.	خَلٌّ
Intimate friend.	خِلٌّ ج أَخْلَالٌ
Defect ; injury.	خَلَلٌ
Quality, habit.	خلةٌ ج خلالٌ
Friend.	خَلِيل ج أَخِلَاء وَخِلانٌ
Mental disorder ; fault.	إِخْتِلَالٌ
Leading to disorder.	مُخِلٌّ
Claw, talon.	مِخْلَبٌ ج مَخَالِبُ
To quiver.	خَلَجَ يَخْلُجُ خَلْجاً
To contend with.	خَالَجَ
To tremble, quiver.	إِخْتَلَجَ
Bay, gulf; canal.	خَلِيجٌ ج خُلْجَانٌ
To be displaced.	تَخَلْخَلَ
Ankle-ring.	خَلْخَالٌ ج خلاخيلُ
To be eternal.	خَلَدَ يَخْلُدُ
Eternity ; immortality.	خُلُودٌ
Mole (animal).	خُلْدٌ ج مناجذ
Everlasting.	خَالِدٌ وَ مُخلدٌ
To steal.	خَلَسَ يَخْلِسُ وَاخْتَلَسَ
Theft, robbery.	إِختِلَاسٌ
Thief, robber.	مُختَلِسٌ وخَالسٌ
To be pure. Escape.	خلَصَ يَخْلُص
To deliver, rescue, save.	خَلَّصَ
To be sincere.	أَخلَصَ
To be saved ; escape.	تَخَلَّصَ
Rescue ; salvation.	خَلَاصٌ
Essence ; extract.	خُلَاصَةٌ
Pure, unmixed ; free.	خَالِصٌ
Sincerity.	إِخْلَاصٌ وَخلوصٌ

Sincere. مُخْلِصٌ

The Saviour. اَلْمُخَلِّصُ

To mix, mingle. خَلَطَ يَخْلِطُ

To confuse, disorder. خَلَّطَ

To associate with. خَالَطَ وَتَخَالَطَ

To be mixed, mingled. إِخْتَلَطَ

Mixture. خِلْطٌ ج أَخْلَاطٌ

Social intercourse. خُلْطَةٌ

To cast off, strip. Depose ; unhinge ; dislocate. خَلَعَ يَخْلَعُ

To disjoint, pull to pieces. خَلَّعَ

To be removed ; dislocated. إِنْخَلَعَ

Dislocation. Deposition. خَلْعٌ

Robe of honour. خِلْعَةٌ ج خِلَعٌ

Disorderly life. Vice. خَلَاعَةٌ

Unhinged ; feeble, weak. مُخَلَّعٌ

To succeed ; replace. خَلَفَ يَخْلُفُ

To leave behind. خَلَّفَ

To oppose. خَالَفَ مُخَالَفَةً وَخِلَافًا

To break one's promise. اخْلَفَ الْوَعْدَ

To remain behind. تَخَلَّفَ عَنْ

To disagree. تَخَالَفَ واخْتَلَفَ

Behind, after. خَلْفَ

Successor, descendant. خَلَفٌ

Difference. خُلْفَةٌ واخْتِلَافٌ

Disagreement. خِلَافٌ

Contrary to that. خِلَافًا لِذَلِكَ

Caliphate. Succession. خِلَافَةٌ

Successor. Caliph. خَلِيفَةٌ ج خُلَفَاءُ

Opposition. مُخَالَفَةٌ

Varied, different. مُخْتَلِفٌ

To create. خَلَقَ يَخْلُقُ خَلْقًا

To be worn out. خَلُقَ يَخْلُقُ

To be adapted to. خَلُقَ بِ ولِ

To invent, forge lies. إِخْتَلَقَ

To affect, feign. تَخَلَّقَ بِ

Creation ; creatures. Mankind. خَلْقٌ

Natural shape. خِلْقَةٌ ج خِلَقٌ

Inbron quality. خُلْقٌ ج اخلاقٌ

خلقيٌّ	Congenital.
خَالِقٌ وَخَلَّاقٌ	Creator (God).
خليقٌ ج خُلَقَاء بِ	Fit, suitable.
خَلِيقَةٌ ج خلائقُ	Creature.
أَلْمَخْلُوقَاتُ	Created things.
خلا يَخْلُو	To be vacant ; alone.
خَلَا مِنْ وَعَنْ	To be free from.
خَلَا بِ	To meet privately.
خَلَّى	To leave, let alone.
اخْلاهُ	To vacate a place.
تَخَلَّى عَنْ	To withdraw from.
تَخَلَّى لِ	To confine himself to.
خَلَاءٌ	Empty space ; solitude.
بَيْتُ ٱلْخَلَاءِ	Water-closet.
خَلَا وَمَا خَلَا	Except.
خُلُوٌّ	Emptiness.
خَلْوَة	Privacy, solitude.
عَلَى خَلْوَةٍ	Aside, apart.
خَلِيَةٌ ج خَلَايَا	Bee-hive ; cell.
خَالٍ	Empty, vacant. Free.
أَلْقُرُونُ ٱلْخَالِيَةُ	Past ages.
مِخْلَاةٌ	Feed-bag (for animals).
خَمَّ يَخِمُّ	To be putrid.
خَمَّ يَخُمُّ خَمًّا	To examine a country.
خُمٌّ	Hen-coop.
خَمَدَ يَخْمُدُ	To subside ; abate.
خَامِدٌ	Silent ; dead.
خُمُودٌ	Abatement, subsidence.
خَمَرَ يَخْمُرُ	To veil, conceal.
خَمَّرَ	To conceal. Leaven.
خَامَرَ	To be mixed with.
تَخَمَّرَ	To veil the head, face.
إِخْتَمَرَ	To ferment ; rise (dough).
خَمْرٌ وَخَمْرَةٌ	Wine.
خِمَارٌ ج خُمُر	Covering ; veil.
خَمِيرٌ وَخَمِيرَة	Leaven.
خَمَّار	Wine-merchant.
خَمَّارَة	Wine-shop.

Fermented.	مُخَمَّرٌ
To be the fifth.	خَمَسَ يَخْمُسُ
To make pentagonal.	خَمَّسَ
The fifth part.	خُمْسٌ ج أَخْمَاسٌ
Five.	خَمْسَةٌ م خَمْسٌ
Fifth.	خَامِسٌ
Fifty, fiftieth.	خَمْسُونَ
Thursday.	يَوْمُ ٱلْخَمِيسِ
Pentagon. Pentagonal.	مُخَمَّسٌ
To scratch.	خَمَشَ يَخْمِشُ
Hollow of the foot.	أَلأَخْمَصُ
To limp.	خَمَعَ يَخْمَعُ
Nap of cloth.	خَمْلٌ
To be obscure (man).	خَمَلَ يَخْمُلُ
Villi of stomach.	خَمَلُ ٱلْمِعْدَةِ
Velvet.	مُخَمَّلٌ
To surmise.	خَمَنَ يَخْمُنُ وخَمَّنَ
By supposition.	عَلَى ٱلتَّخْمِينِ
To snuffle.	خَنَّ يَخِنُّ خَنِينًا
Nasal twang.	خُنَّةٌ
Sunffles (disease).	خُنَانٌ
To be effeminate.	خَنِثَ يَخْنَثُ
Hermaphrodite.	خُنْثَى
Poniard.	خَنْجَرٌ ج خَنَاجِرُ
Trench, moat.	خَنْدَقٌ ج خَنَادِقُ
Canals of the Nile.	خَنَادِلُ
Hog, pig.	خِنْزِيرٌ ج خَنَازِيرُ
Wild boar.	خِنْزِيرٌ بَرِّيٌّ
Scrofula.	دَاءُ ٱلْخَنَازِيرِ
The stars.	أَلْخُنَّسُ
Satan.	أَلْخَنَّاسُ
Fern (plant).	خِنْشَارٌ
Sucking, pig.	خِنَّوْصٌ ج خَنَانِيص
The little finger.	خِنْصِرٌ ج خَنَاصِر
Black beetle	خُنْفُسَاءُ ج خَنَافِس
To strangle.	خَنَقَ يَخْنُقُ
To be strangled.	إِخْتَنَقَ وٱنْخَنَقَ
Quinsy (disease).	خُنَّاقٌ

Strangled. خنِقٌ وَمَخْنوقٌ

Foul words. انْخَنَى

Suffocation ; asphyxia. إِخْتِنَاقٌ

(Mister, Mr. خَوَاجَه خَوَاجَاتٌ (

(Teacher. خوجَه ج خوجَات(

Plum ; peach. خَوْخٌ

Helmet. خُوذَةٌ ج خُوَذٌ

To bellow. خارَ يَخُورُ

To fail (strength). خارَ خُؤُوراً

Bellowing of cattle. خُوَارٌ

Curate, person. خُورِيٌّ ج خَوَارِنَةٌ

To be unsaleable. خاسَ يَخُوسُ

Leaves of the plam-tree. خوصٌ

Having a deformed eye. أَخْوَصُ

To wade ; ford. خَاضَ يَخُوضُ

Ford. مَخَاضَةٌ ج مَخَاوِضُ

To fear, be afraid of. خافَ يَخَافُ

To frighten. خَوَّفَ وَأَخَافَ

Fear, fright. خوفٌ وَمَخَافة وَخِيفَةٌ

Timid, fearing. خَائِفٌ

Intimidation. تَخْوِيفٌ

Fearful, perilous. مَخُوِّفٌ

Terrible, inspiring fear. مَخِيفٌ

Cause of fear. مَخَافَةٌ ج مَخَاوِفُ

To bestow upon. خَوَّلَ

Maternal uncle. خَالٌ ج أَخْوَالٌ

Mole on the face. خَالٌ ج خِيلانٌ

Maternal aunt. خَالَةٌ ج خَالاتٌ

Steward. خَوَلِيٌّ ج خَوَلٌ

Calico. خَامٌ

To be unfaithful. خانَ يَخُونُ

To accuse of treachery. خوَّنَ

Inn (Prince). خانٌ ج خَانَاتٌ

Deceit, treachery. خَوْنٌ وَخِيَانَةٌ

Table for food. خِوَانٌ ج أَخْوِنَةٌ

Unfaithful, traitor. خَائِنٌ

Treacherous. خَوُونٌ وَخَوَّانٌ

To be waste, empty. خَوَى يَخْوِي

خاوٍ Empty, hollow ; void.

خَابَ يَخِيبُ To be disappointed.

خَيَّبَ وَاخَابَ To disappoint.

خَيْبَةٌ Failure, disappointment.

خَائِبٌ Frustrated.

خَيَّرَ عَلَى To deem better ; prefer.

خَيَّرَ To give one a choice.

إِخْتَارَ To choose, select, prefer.

خَيْرٌ ج خِيَارٌ A good thing.

خَيْرٌ مِنْ Better than.

خَيْرُ النَّاسِ The best of men.

خَيْرِيٌّ Good, benevolent.

خِيَارٌ Choice. Cucumber.

خَيِّرٌ Good, liberal.

خَيْرٌ (اخير) Better ; preferable.

اخْتِيَارٌ Choice, election.

اخْتِيَارِيٌّ Voluntary.

مُخَيَّرٌ Free to choose.

مُخْتَارٌ Preferred.

خَارَصِينِي Zinc.

خَيْشٌ Coarse canvas.

خَيْشَةٌ ج خَيْشَاتٌ Large sack.

خَاطَ يَخِيطُ وَخَيَّطَ To sew.

خَيْطٌ ج خُيُوطٌ وَخِيطَانٌ Thread.

خِيَاطَة Needle-work, sewing.

خَيَّاط Tailor.

مَخِيطٌ وَمَخْيُوطٌ Sewn, stitched.

خَالَ يَخَالُ To conceive; imagine.

خُيِّلَ لَ وَإِلَى To seem to.

تَخَيَّلَ To imagine, fancy.

خَيْلٌ ج خُيُول Horse ; cavalry.

خَيَالٌ ج اخْيِلَة Spectre, phantom.

خَيَالِيٌّ Imaginary ideal.

اَلْمُخَيِّلَة Faculty of imagination.

خَيَّالٌ ج خَيَّالَة Horseman.

خَيَّمَ To pitch a tent ; abide.

خَامٌ Unbleached cloth.

خَيْمَةٌ ج خِيَامٌ Tent ; booth.

د

د	As a numerical sign=4.
دَأْبٌ	State, condition ; habit.
دَبَّ يَدِبُّ	To crawl, creep.
دُبٌّ ج أَدْبَابٌ	Bear (animal).
دَابَّةٌ ج دَوَابُّ	Animal ; beast.
دُوَيْبَّةٌ	Little animal ; reptile.
دِيبَاجٌ	Silk brocade.
دِيبَاجَةٌ	Introduction, preface.
دَبْدَبَ	To tread, crawl.
دَبَّرَ	To plan ; manage well.
أَدْبَرَ	To go back, retreat.
تَدَبَّرَ	To regard attentively.
دُبْرٌ ج أَدْبَارٌ	Back, hind part.
تَدْبِيرٌ ج تَدَابِيرُ	Management.
مُدْبِرٌ	One who turns back.
مُدَبِّرٌ	Administrator ; director.
دِبْسٌ	Thick juice of grapes.
دَبُّوسٌ ج دَبَابِيس	Mace. Pin.
دَبَغَ يَدْبُغُ	To tan (leather).
دِبَاغَةٌ	Trade of a tanner.
دَبَّاغٌ	Tanner.
مَدْبَغَةٌ ج مَدَابِغ	Tannery.
مَدْبُوغٌ	Tanned.
دَبِقَ يَدْبَقُ ب	To adhere to.
دِبْقٌ	Glue, bird-lime.
دَثَرَ يَدْثُرُ	To be effaced.
دَثَّرَ	To cover with a blanket.
إِنْدَثَرَ	To be destroyed.
دَاثِرٌ	That which perishes.
دُجَاجٌ	Poultry.
دُجَاجَةٌ	A hen.
دُجَاجُ ٱلْهِنْدِ	Turkey.

Woodcock.	دُجَاجُ ٱلأَرْضِ
Partridge.	دُجَاجُ ٱلْبَرِّ
Completely armed.	مُدَجَّجٌ
To lie ; cheat.	دَجَلَ يَدْجُلُ
Liar ; imposter ; quack.	دَجَّالٌ
Tigris (river).	دِجْلَة
To be cloudy, dark. To become tame.	دَجَنَ يَدْجُنُ
To abide.	دَجَنَ دُجُونًا بِ
Darkness.	دُجْنَّةٌ ج دُجَنٌ
Tame animal.	دَاجِنٌ ج دَوَاجِنُ
Darkness.	دُجًى
To drive away.	دَحَرَ يَدْحَرُ
To roll down (*tran*).	دَحْرَجَ
To be rolled.	تَدَحْرَجَ
Lucern.	دُحَيْرِجَة
Whitlow.	دَاحِسٌ
To force into.	دَحَشَ يَدْحَشُ
To rebut, refute.	أَدْحَضَ
To be refuted, rebutted.	إِنْدَحَضَ

To enter.	دَخَلَ يَدْخُلُ
To be included.	دَخَلَ تَحْتَ وَفِي
To cause to enter.	أَدْخَلَ
To intermeddle.	تَدَاخَلَ فِي
Income, revenue.	دَخْلٌ
I beseech you.	دَخْلَكَ وَدَخِيلَكَ
Interior, inside.	دَاخِلٌ
Home Secretary.	وَزِيرُ ٱلدَّاخِلِيَّةِ
Stranger. Guest.	دَخِيلٌ ج دُخَلَاءُ
Door ; access.	مَدْخَلٌ ج مَدَاخِلُ
Revenue.	مَدْخُولٌ ج مَدَاخِيلُ
To smoke.	دَخَنَ وَدَخَّنَ وَأَدْخَنَ
Millet.	دُخْنٌ
Smoke. Tobacco.	دُخَانٌ
Chimney.	مَدْخَنَةٌ ج مَدَاخِنُ
To flow copiously.	دَرَّ يَدِرُّ
Copious flow of milk.	دَرٌّ
How exquisite !	لِلّٰهِ دَرُّهُ
Pearl. Parrot.	دُرَّةٌ ج دُرَّاتٌ

Copious flow.	مدْرَارٌ
To guide, direct.	دَرَّبَ
To be practised in.	تَدَرَّبَ
Path ; way.	دَرْبٌ ج دُروبٌ
Training ; drill.	تَدْرِيبٌ
Trained ; excercised.	مُدَرَّبٌ
Balustrade.	دَرَبزِينٌ وَدَرَابِزُون
To proceed gradually.	دَرَجَ يَدْرُجُ
To introduce.	أَدْرَجَ وَدَرَّجَ في
To proceed by degrees.	تَدَرَّجَ
Roll of Paper.	دَرْجٌ ج أَدْرَاجٌ
Box, case.	دُرْجٌ ج أَدْرَاجٌ
Road, path.	دَرْجٌ ج ادرَاجٌ وَدِرَاجٌ
Step; degree.	درجَةٌ ج دَرَجَاتٌ
Gradually.	تَدْرِيجاً وَبِالتَّدْرِيجِ
Common, current.	دَارِجٌ
Francolin.	دُرَّاجٌ
To lie unconscious.	انْدَرَجَ
Elm.	دَرْدَارٌ

To sew, stitch.	دَرَزَ يَدْرُزُ
Seam.	دَرْزٌ ج دُرُوزٌ
Druze.	دُرْزِيٌّ ج دُرُوزٌ
To efface.	دَرَسَ يَدْرُسُ
To read, study.	دَرَسَ يَدْرِسُ
To tread out corn, thresh.	دَرَسَ
To study or read under a teacher.	دَرَسَ عَلَى
To teach, lecture.	دَرَّسَ
To be effaced.	إِنْدَرَسَ
Lesson. study.	دَرْسٌ ج دُرُوسٌ
Threshing.	دِرَاسٌ وَدِرَاسَةٌ
School.	مَدْرَسَةٌ ج مَدَارِسُ
Teacher, professor.	مُدَرِّسٌ
To put on a coat of mail.	إِدَّرَعَ وَتَدَرَّعَ
Coat of mail.	دِرْعٌ ج دُرُوعٌ
Armoured.	مُدَرَّعٌ
Water jug.	دَوْرَقٌ ج دَوَارِقُ
Peach.	دُرَاقِنٌ وَدُرَّاقٌ
To make responsible for.	دَرَّكَ

To overtake. دَارَكَ

To reach ; comprehend. أَدْرَكَ

To overtake ; rectify. تَدَارَكَ

To seek to obviate. إِسْتَدْرَكَ

Comprehension. إِدْرَاكٌ

To be filthy. دَرِنَ يَدْرَنُ

Dirt, Tubercle. دَرَنٌ ج أَدْرَانٌ

Polluted, dirty, دَرِنٌ

Drachm ; money. دِرْهَمٌ ج دَرَاهِمُ

Dervish. دَرْوِيشٌ ج دَرَاوِيشُ

To know. دَرَى يَدْرِي

To treat kindly, cajole. دَارَى

To acquaint, inform. أَدْرَى بِ

Knowledge. دِرَايَةٌ

To hide, insert. دَسَّ يَدُسُّ

To plot against. دَسَّ عَلَى

To be hidden, concealed. إِنْدَسَّ

Spy. داسوسٌ ج دَوَاسِيسُ

Intrigue. دَسِيسَةٌ ج دَسَائِسُ

A game. Copper pot, دَسْتٌ ج دُسُوتٌ

Rule, regulation. دُسْتُورٌ

Town, village. دَسْكَرَةٌ ج دَسَاكِرُ

To be fatty. دَسِمَ يَدْسَمَ

Fat, grease. دَسَمٌ وَدُسُومَةٌ

To dismiss ; leave. دَشَرَ

Let ! (*imp. from* وَدَعَ) دَعْ

To sport, jest with. دَعَبَ وَدَاعَبَ

Wickedness. دَعَرٌ وَدَعَارَةٌ

To tread under foot. دَعَسَ يَدْعَسُ

A track, foot-print. دِعْسَةٌ

To rup. دَعَكَ يَدْعَكُ

To contend with. دَاعَكَ مُدَاعَكَةً

To prop. دَعَمَ يَدْعَمُ دَعْماً

Support, prop. دِعَامَةٌ ج دَعَائِمُ

To call ; pray, دَعَا يَدْعُو

To invite. دَعَا دَعْوَةً

To pray for. دَعَا لِ

To invoke a curse upon. دَعَا عَلَى

إدَّعى بِ	To claim ; pretend.
إدَّعى على	To claim against.
إستدعى	To call, invite.
دُعاءٌ ج ادعية	Call ; prayer.
دَعوةٌ	Invocation ; invitation. Imprecation.
دعوى ج دَعاوٍ	Claim ; law-suit.
دَاعٍ ج دعاة	Calling. Preacher.
داعيةٌ ج دَواعٍ	Cause ; motive.
إدعاءٌ	Claim, pretention.
مُدَّعٍ	Pretender ; plaintiff.
مُدَّعًى عليه	Defendant.
دَغدَغ دَغدغة	To tickle.
دَغَشٌ	Darkness ; nightfall.
دَغَل ج أدغالٌ	Corruption. Thicket.
دَفٌّ ج دفوفٌ	Tambourine.
دَفّةٌ	Side. Rudder.
دَفِئَ يَدفأ	To be warm.
دَفَّأَ وَأدفأ	To warm.
تدفّأ	To warm one's self.
دِفءٌ	Heat, warmth.
دَفتَرٌ ج دفاتِرُ	Register. Account-book.
دَفتردارٌ	Minister of Finances.
دَفَرَ يَدفُرُ	To push back.
دِفرانٌ	Juniper tree.
دَفَشَ يَدفش	To push.
دَفَعَ يَدفَعُ	To push back, repel.
دَفَعَ إلى ول	To hand over to.
دَافَعَ	To contend with. Defer.
دَافَعَ عَن	To protect, defend.
إندَفَعَ	To be thrust back.
دَفعٌ	Pushing back. Payment.
قُوّةٌ دَافِعةٌ	Expulsive force.
مِدفعٌ ج مَدافِعُ	Cannon.
دَفَقَ يَدفُقُ	To pour forth (water).
تدفّقَ وَآندفقَ	To be poured out.
مُتَدَفِّقٌ	Overflowing.
دِفلٌ وَدِفلى	Oleander.
دَفَنَ يَدفِنُ	To bury ; conceal.

To be buried.	إِندَفَنَ
Burying, burial.	دَفْنٌ
Buried treasure.	دَفِينَةٌ ج دَفَائِنُ
Tomb.	مَدْفَنٌ ج مَدَافِنُ
To be fine, thin.	دقَّ يَدِقُّ
To crush ; knock.	دَقَّ يَدُقُّ
To ring the bell.	دق الْجرَس
To be precise.	دَقَّقَ
To examine minutely.	دَقَّقَ النظرَ
Exactness, accuracy.	دِقَّةٌ
Pestle.	مِدَقٌّ وَمِدَقَّةٌ
Fine : thin. Fine flour.	دَقِيقٌ ج أَدِقَّةٌ وَدِقَاقٌ
Minute (time).	دَقِيقَةٌ ج دَقَائِقُ
Exactness, precision.	تَدْقِيقٌ
Exact, precise.	مُدَقَّقٌ
To demolish. To charge a gun.	دَكَّ يَدُكُّ
Wide bench, seat.	دَكَّةٌ
Ramrod.	مِدَكٌّ
Loaded (gun).	مَدْكُوكٌ
To be blackish.	دَكِنَ يَدْكَنُ
Blackish colour.	دُكْنَةٌ
Shop.	دُكَّانٌ ج دَكَاكِينُ
Shop-keeper.	دُكَّنْجِيٌّ
Blackish.	أَدْكَنُ م دَكْنَاءُ
To point out, show.	دَلَّ يَدُلُّ على
To spoil (a child).	دَلَّلَ
To sell at auction.	دَلَّلَ على
To be coquettish.	تَدَلَّلَ
To seek, or to find a proof.	إِستَدَلَّ على
Coquetry.	دَلَالٌ
Broker, auctioneer.	دَلَّالٌ
Sign, proof.	دَلِيلٌ ج أَدِلَّةٌ
Guide.	دَلِيلٌ ج أَدِلَّاءُ
Plane-tree.	دُلْبٌ
Water-wheel.	دُولَابٌ ج دَوَالِيبُ
Deceit.	دَلَسٌ وَدُلْسَةٌ
To loll the tongue.	دَلَعَ لِسَانَهُ
To leak.	دَلَفَ يَدْلِفُ دَلْفًا

دُلْفِينٌ ج دَلَافِينُ	Dolphin.
دَلَقَ يَدْلُقُ	To pour out (a liquid).
دَلَكَ يَدْلُكُ دَلْكاً ب	To rub.
مَدْلَكٌ وَمَدْلَكَةٌ	Rubbing stone.
ادْلَهَمَّ	To be very dark.
مُدْلَهِمٌّ	Very black.
دَلَا يَدْلُو	To draw a bucket.
دَلَّى وَادْلَى	To let down.
تَدَلَّى	To be let down.
دَلْوٌ ج دِلَاءٌ	Bucket.
الدَّلْوُ	Aquarius.
دَالِيَةٌ ج دَوَالٍ	Grape-vine.
دَمٌ	Blood.
دَمَوِيٌّ	Bloody.
دَمُثَ يَدْمُثُ	To be gentle.
دَمْثٌ وَدَمِيثٌ	Mild, soft.
دَمَاثَةٌ	Gentleness, delicacy.
دَمَجَ يَدْمُجُ وَانْدَمَجَ	To be joined.
مُدْمَجٌ وَمُنْدَمِجٌ	Compact.

دَمْدَمَ عَلَى	To murmur against.
دَمَرَ يَدْمُرُ	To perish utterly.
دَمَرَ وَدَمَّرَ	To annihilate, destroy.
دَمَارٌ	Destruction, annihilation.
تَدْمُرُ	Palmyra.
دَمَسَ يَدْمُسُ	To be dense, (darkness).
دَمَسَ يَدْمِسُ	To conceal, bury.
دَامِسٌ	Dark, (night).
دِمَشْقُ	Damascus.
دَمَعَ يَدْمَعُ	To shed tears, (eyes).
دَمْعٌ ج دُمُوعٌ وَأَدْمُعٌ	Tears.
دَمْعَةٌ	A tear, a drop.
دَمَغَ يَدْمَغُ	To mark by branding.
دَمْغَةٌ	Mark, brand.
دِمَاغٌ ج أَدْمِغَةٌ	Brain.
دَمَلَ يَدْمُلُ	To manure land.
دَمَلَ يَدْمُلُ وَانْدَمَلَ	To be healed.
دُمَّلٌ ج دَمَامِلُ	Pustule, boil.
دَمَالٌ	Manure.

Bracelet.	دُمْلُجٌ ج دَمالِجُ
To manure land.	دَمَنَ وَدَمَّنَ
To be permanent.	دَمِنَ يَدْمَنُ
To persevere in, cleave to.	أَدْمَنَ
Constant practice.	إِدْمَانٌ
Addicted to.	مُدْمِنٌ
To bleed, flow (blood).	دَمِيَ يَدْمِي
To cause to bleed.	دَمَّى وَأَدْمَى
Blood.	دَمٌ ج دِمَاءٌ
Bloody.	دَمِيٌّ وَدَمَوِيٌّ
Large wine-jar.	دَنٌّ ج دِنَانٌ
To be low, vile.	دَنَا يَدْنَا
Meanness; weakness.	دَنَاءَةٌ
Low; worthless.	دَنِيءٌ ج أَدْنِيَاءُ
A gold coin.	دِينَارٌ ج دَنَانِيرُ
To be defiled.	دَنِسَ يَدْنَسُ
To stain, pollute.	دَنَّسَ
To be defiled.	تَدَنَّسَ
Filth, pollution.	دَنَسٌ ج أَدْنَاسٌ

Soiled, foul.	دَنِسٌ ج أَدْنَاسٌ
To be near death.	أَدْنَفَ
To perish with cold.	دَنِقَ يَدْنَقُ
Small coin.	دَانِقٌ ج دَوَانِقُ
To approach.	دَنَا يَدْنُو
Nearness; proximity.	دَنَاوَةٌ
Meanness, baseness.	دَنَايَةٌ
Vile. Near.	دَنِيءٌ ج أَدْنِيَاءُ
Anything base.	دَنِيَّةٌ ج دَنَايَا
The (present) world.	دُنْيَا
Worldly.	دُنْيَوِيٌّ
Nearer. Viler, worse.	أَدْنَى
Time; age.	دَهْرٌ ج دُهُورٌ
For ever and ever.	دَهْرُ الدَّاهِرِينَ
To be bewildered.	دَهِشَ يَدْهَشُ
To perplex.	دَهَّشَ وَأَدْهَشَ
Astounded.	دَهِشٌ وَمَدْهُوشٌ
Confusion; perplexity.	دَهْشَةٌ
Vestibule.	دِهْلِيزٌ ج دَهَالِيزُ

دَهَكَ يَدْهَكُ دَهْكاً	To scatter.
دَهَمَ يَدْهَمُ	To come unexpectedly.
دُهْمَةٌ	Blackness.
أَدْهَمُ	Black (horse).
دَهَنَ يَدْهَنُ	To anoint, paint.
دَاهَنَ	To beguile ; coax.
تَدَهَّنَ	To be anointed.
دُهْنٌ ج أَدْهَانٌ	Oil, grease.
دِهَانٌ وَدَهُونٌ	Paint. Ointment.
دَهَّانٌ	Painter.
مُدَاهَنَةٌ	Dissimulation ; flattery.
مُدَهَّنٌ وَمَدْهُونٌ	Painted.
دَهِيَ يَدْهَى	To be sly, subtle.
دَهَاءٌ	Cunning, craft.
دَاهِيَةٌ ج دَوَاهٍ	Calamity.
دَاهٍ وَدَاهِيَةٌ	Sagacious, cunning.
دَهْوَرَ	To throw down.
تَدَهْوَرَ	To tumble down.
دَاءٌ ج أَدْوَاءٌ	Illness, disease.

دَاءُ ٱلْمُلُوكِ	Gout.
دَاءُ ٱلْكَلَبِ	Hydrophobia.
دَاءُ ٱلْفِيلِ	Elephantiasis.
دَاخَ يَدُوخُ	To be giddy, sea sick.
دَوَّخَ	To subdue, conquer.
دَوْخَةٌ	Giddiness.
دُودَةٌ ج دِيدَانٌ وَدُودٌ	A worm.
دُودَةُ ٱلْقَزِّ	Silk-worm.
دَاوُدُ	David.
دَارَ يَدُورُ	To revolve, circulate.
أَدَارَ	To set going ; administer.
تَدَوَّرَ وَٱسْتَدَارَ	To be round.
دَارٌ ج دُورٌ وَدِيَارٌ	House.
دَارُ ٱلْبَقَاءِ	The world to come.
دَارُ ٱلْفَنَاءِ	The world that is.
أَلدَّارَانِ	The two worlds (of time and eternity).
دَوْرٌ ج أَدْوَارٌ	Turn ; age, period.
دَوَرَانٌ	Rotation, circulation.
دُورِيٌّ	Sparrow.

Revolving ; roaming.	دَائِرٌ
Circle; or bit of a planet. Calamity. Department.	دَائِرَةٌ ج دَوَائِرُ
Encyclopedia.	دَائِرَةُ ٱلْعُلُومِ
Giddiness.	دُوَارٌ
Convent.	دَيْرٌ ج أَدْيِرَةٌ
Administration.	إِدَارَةٌ
Circular form.	إِسْتِدَارَةٌ
Pivot, axis.	مَدَارٌ
Round, circular.	مُدَوَّرٌ وَمُسْتَدِيرٌ
Inspector ; director.	مُدِيرٌ
Territory of a Mudir.	مُدِيرِيَّةٌ
To tread, trample.	دَاسَ يَدُوسُ
To be trodden upon.	إِنْدَاسَ
Shoe, sandal.	مَدَاسٌ
To alternate.	دَاوَلَ مُدَاوَلَةً
To do by turns.	تَدَاوَلَ
Dynasty ; empire.	دَوْلَةٌ ج دُوَلٌ
Vine, grapes.	دَوَالِيٌّ
By turns, alternately.	مُدَاوَلَةٌ
Used, employed commonly.	مُتَدَاوَلٌ
To continue ; endure.	دَامَ يَدُومُ
As long as it stands.	مَادَامَ قَائِمًا
To persist in.	دَاوَمَ عَلَى
To prolong.	أَدَامَ
To continue.	إِسْتَدَامَ
Continuance.	دَوَامٌ وَدَيْمُومَةٌ
The ban palm.	دَوْمٌ
Continually ; for ever.	عَلَى ٱلدَّوَامِ
Spinning-top.	دُوَّامَةٌ
Continuing, lasting.	دَائِمٌ
Always.	دَائِمًا
Wine.	مُدَامٌ وَمُدَامَةٌ
Perseverance.	مُدَاوَمَةٌ
To write out.	دَوَّنَ
Beneath. Before, behind.	دُونَ
Except.	دُونَ أَنْ

بِدُونِ وَمِنْ دُونِ	Without.
دُونٌ	Low, mean, vile, bad.
دُونَكَ	Take it !
دِيوَانٌ ج دَوَاوِينُ	Court of justice ; tribunal Poems.
مُدَوَّنٌ	Inserted, registered.
دَاوَى	To treat medically.
دَوَاءٌ ج أَدْوِيَةٌ	Medicine, remedy.
دَوَاةٌ وَدَوَايَةٌ	Inkstand.
دَوِيٌّ	Hum, buzz; rustling.
مُدَاوَةٌ	Treatment, cure.
مُدَاوٍ	Physician.
دِيكٌ ج دُيُوكٌ	Cock.
دَانَ يَدِينُ	To borrow ; lend.
دَانَ دِيناً	To judge, requite. Follow a religion.
دانَ لِ	To submit, yield to.
دَيَّنَ وَأَدَانَ	To lend money.
تَدَيَّنَ وَٱسْتَدَانَ مِنْ	To borrow.
تدَيَّنَ ب	To follow a religion.
دَيْنٌ ج دُيُونٌ	Debt, loan.
دَيْنٌ ج ادْيَانٌ . ديَانَةٌ ج دِيَانَاتٌ	Religion ; belief.
يومُ ٱلدِّينِ	The Judgment Day.
دَيْنُونَةٌ	Judgment.
دَائِنٌ	Debtor ; creditor.
دَيَّانٌ	Judge.
مَدِينَةٌ	City. (*see* مدن)
مَدْيُونٌ ج مَدْيُونون	Debtor.

ذ

ذ As a numeral sign=700.

ذا ج اولاء This, this one.

ذاكَ ج اولئكَ That, that one.

ذلك ج اولائكَ That, that one.

لماذا What? ماذا Why?

كذا Thus, like this.

هذا مث هذانِ ج هؤلاء This.

هكذا Thus, like this.

ذِئبٌ ج ذئابٌ Wolf.

ذبَّ يَذُبُّ عنْ To repel; defend.

ذُبابٌ ج ذِبّانٌ Fly.

ذُبابةٌ A fly.

ذبَحَ يذبَحُ To slaughter, slay.

تَذابَحَ To kill one another.

ذَبْحٌ Act of slaughtering.

ذبحة Angina, croup.

ذبيحٌ Slaughtered.

ذبيحةٌ ج ذبائحُ Sacrifice.

مذبَحٌ ج مَذابِحُ Alter.

مذبوحٌ Slaughtered, immolated.

ذَبْذَبَ To swing to and fro.

مُذَبْذَبٌ ومُتَذَبْذِبٌ Wavering.

ذَبُلَ يَذْبُلُ ذُبولاً To wither.

أَذْبَلَ To cause to wither, dry up.

ذابلٌ Withered, withering.

ذَخَرَ يذخَرُ وادَّخَرَ To treasure up.

ذُخرٌ ج أَذْخارٌ وذَخيرةٌ ج ذخائِر Treasure; stores.

ذَرَّ يَذُرُّ ذَرّاً To scatter, sprinkle.

ذرٌّ Young or small ants.

ذرَّةٌ An atom.

ذُرِّيةٌ ج ذراريُّ Descendants.

ذَرَّاحٌ ج ذَرَارِيحُ Spanish fly.
ذَرْذَرَ To scatter, strew.
ذَرْعٌ Power, capacity.
ضَاقَ ذَرْعًا To be unable.
ذِرَاعٌ ج أَذْرُعٌ Arm ; cubit.
ذَرِيعٌ Sudden, rapid.
ذَرَفَ يَذْرِفُ To flow; shed (tears).
ذَرَى يَذْرِي To winnow ; scatter.
ذَرَّى وَأَذْرَى To winnow.
ذَرَّى وَاسْتَذْرَى To seek shelter.
ذُرَةٌ A kind of millet.
ذُرَةٌ صَفْرَاءُ Maize.
ذَرًى Dispersed dust. Shelter.
ذَرْوَةٌ ج ذُرًى Summit.
مِذْرًى Winnowing fork.
ذَعَرَ يَذْعَرُ وَأَذْعَرَ To frighten.
ذُعِرَ وَانْذَعَرَ To be terrified.
ذُعْرٌ Fright, terror.
ذَعَرٌ Bewilderment.

مَذْعُورٌ Bewildered ; frightened.
ذَعِنَ يَذْعَنُ وَأَذْعَنَ لِ To obey.
اذْعَنَ بِ To confess, submit.
إِذْعَانٌ Submission.
مُذْعِنٌ Obedient, submissive.
ذَفَرٌ Strong odour.
ذَقْنٌ ج ذُقُونٌ Chin ; beard.
ذَكَرَ يَذْكُرُ To remember.
ذَكَرَ To mention, relate.
ذَكَّرَ وَأَذْكَرَ To remind of
ذَاكَرَ فِي To confer with.
تَذَكَّرَ To remember, think of.
تَذَاكَرَ فِي To confer together.
ذِكْرٌ Memory ; praise. Mention.
ذَكَرٌ ج ذُكُورٌ Male. Male organ.
ذِكْرَى Remembrance.
ذَاكِرَةٌ Faculty of memory.
تَذْكِرَةٌ ج تَذَاكِرُ Permit, passport.
تَذْكَارٌ Remembrance.

Frequent remembrance.	تَذَكُّرٌ
Conference.	مُذَاكَرَةٌ
Masculine, (word).	مُذَكَّرٌ
Mentioned. Praised.	مَذْكُورٌ
To be quick, (in intellect).	ذَكِيَ يَذْكَى
Quick understanding.	ذَكَاءٌ
Intelligent.	ذَكِيٌّ ج أَذْكِيَاء
Quicker in perception.	أَذْكَى
To be low ; submissive.	ذَلَّ يَذِلُّ
To humble, humiliate.	ذَلَّلَ وَأَذَلَّ
To render tractable.	ذَلَّلَ
To humble one's self.	تَذَلَّلَ
Submissiveness.	ذُلٌّ
Humiliation.	ذُلٌّ وَمَذَلَّةٌ
Low, abject.	ذَلِيلٌ ج أَذِلَّاء
This ; that. (*see* ذَا)	ذَلِكَ
To blame, censure.	ذَمَّ يَذُمُّ
Blame, rebuke.	ذَمٌّ وَمَذَمَّةٌ
Covenant ; security.	ذِمَّةٌ ج ذِمَمٌ
Protected tributaries.	أَهْلُ ٱلذِّمَّةِ
Conscience ; moral sense.	ذِمَّةٌ
Blamed ; censured.	ذَمِيمٌ
Blameworthy action.	مَذَمَّةٌ
Blamed ; censured.	مَذْمُومٌ
To murmur against.	تَذَمَّرَ عَلَى
To be guilty.	أَذْنَبَ
Crime guilt.	ذَنْبٌ ج ذُنُوبٌ
Tail, extremity.	ذَنَبٌ ج أَذْنَابٌ
Comet.	نَجْمٌ ذُو ذَنَبٍ
Guilty ; criminal.	مُذْنِبٌ
To go, depart.	ذَهَبَ يَذْهَبُ
To think, believe.	ذَهَبَ إِلَى
To gild.	ذَهَّبَ وَأَذْهَبَ
To cause to disappear.	أَذْهَبَ
Gold.	ذَهَبٌ
Golden, of gold.	ذَهَبِيٌّ
Nile-boat.	ذَهَبِيَّةٌ
Going ; passing.	ذَاهِبٌ

Departure. ذهابٌ

Gilt. مذهَّبٌ

Way. Creed. مَذْهبٌ ج مَذَاهِبُ

To embrace a creed. تمَذْهَبَ

Gold powder. ماء ٱلذهَب

To forget, neglect. ذَهَلَ يَذهَلُ عَن

To be astonished. ذَهَلَ وٱنْذَهَلَ

To cause to forget. أذهل عن

Astonishment. إِنْذِهالٌ

Astonished, bewildered. مُنذَهِلٌ

Mind, intellect. ذِهْنٌ ج أذْهانٌ

Intellectual, subjective. ذِهنِيٌّ

Master, possessor. ذو ج ذَوُو

Essence; person, self. ذاتٌ

To the right. ذاتَ ٱليمينِ

On a certain day. ذاتَ يَوْمٍ

In person. بذاتِهِ

In itself. في ذَاتِهِ

Essential, personal. ذَاتِيٌّ

Selfishness. محبة ٱلذاتِ

To dissolve, melt. ذَابَ يذُوبُ

To cause to melt. ذوَّب وَاذابَ

Melting, in a fluid state. ذائبٌ

Manager. مِذْوَدٌ ج مَذَاوِد

To taste; try. ذَاقَ يذُوقُ

To give to taste. أذاقَ

Taste, sense of taste. ذَوْقٌ

Sound taste. ذَوْقٌ سَلِيمٌ

Flavour. مَذاقٌ

That, yonder. (*See* اذا) ذاكَ

To wither, (plant). ذَوَى يَذْوِي

This, (*fem. of* دا) ذِي وَهذِي

To be public, (news). ذَاعَ يذِيعُ

To make public. اذاعَ وَبَ

Publication. إِذَاعة

To add an appendix. ذَيَّلَ

Tail, skirt. Fringes. Appendix. ذَيْلٌ ج ذُيُولٌ

Appendix, supplement. تَذْييل

ر

ر	As a numeral sign=200.
رَاتِينَجٌ	Resin.
رَأَسَ يَرْأَسُ	To be a chief.
رَأَّسَ	To make one a leader.
تَرَأَّسَ	To become a chief.
رَأْسٌ ج رُؤُوسٌ	Head ; peak ; cape ; chief, leader ; principal part.
رَأْساً	Directly ; completely.
عَلَى ٱلرَّأْسِ وَٱلْعَيْنِ	Most willingly.
رَأْسُ ٱلْمَالِ	Capital ; stock.
رِآسَةٌ وَرِيَاسَةٌ	Headship, authority.
رَئِيسٌ ج رُؤَسَاءُ	President, chief.
أَلْأَعْضَاءُ ٱلرَّئِيسَةُ	The vital organs.
مَرْؤُوسٌ	Under authority.
رَأَفَ يَرْأَفُ	To show pity.
رَأْفَةٌ	Compassion, pity, mercy.
رَؤُوفٌ وَرَئِفٌ	Compassionate.
رِئْمٌ ج آرَامٌ	White antelope.
رَأَى يَرَى	To see, perceive ; judge.
رَأَى رُؤْيَا	To have a vision.
رَاءَى مُرَاءَاةً	To dissemble.
يَا تُرَى	Do you suppose ?
أَرَى إِرَاءَةً	To show.
تَرَأَّى وَتَرَاءَى لِ	To appear to.
إِرْتَأَى	To consider.
رَأْيٌ ج آرَاءٌ	Opinion ; view.
رَايَةٌ	Military banner.
رِيَاءٌ	Hypocrisy.
رِئَةٌ ج رِئَاتٌ	Lung.
ذَاتُ ٱلرِّئَةِ	Inflammation of lung.
رُؤْيَا ج رُؤًى	Dream, vision.
رُؤْيَةٌ ج رُؤًى	Act of seeing.

مِرْآةٌ ج مَرَايَا	Mirror.
مُرَاءٍ	Hypocrite.
مُرَاءَاة	Hypocrisy.
رَبٌّ ج أَرْبَابٌ	Lord, master.
أَلرَّبُّ	The Lord.
رُبٌّ ج رِبَابٌ	Syrup.
رُبَّ وَرُبَّمَا	Often. Seldom.
رَبَّانِيٌّ	Divine. Rabbi.
رَبَابٌ	A kind of violoncello.
رُبَّانٌ	Captain of ship ; chief.
رَبِحَ يَرْبَحُ رِبْحًا	To gain.
رَبَّحَ	To cause one to gain.
رِبْحٌ ج أَرْبَاحٌ	Profit, gain.
رِيبَاسٌ	A kind of sorrel (plant).
تَرَبَّصَ	To wait, expect.
رُوبَاصٌ	Pure, refined, (silver).
رَبَضَ يَرْبِضُ	To lie in wait.
رَبَضٌ ج أَرْبَاضٌ	Suburb.
مَرْبِضٌ ج مَرَابِضُ	Enclosure.
رَبَطَ يَرْبُطُ	To tie, bind, fasten.
تَرَابَطَ	To agree upon.
إِرْتَبَطَ	To be tied.
رَبْطَةٌ ج رَبْطَاتٌ	Bundle, parcel.
رَابِطُ ٱلدَّرْبِ	Highway-robber.
رِبَاطٌ ج رُبُطٌ	Bond, rope.
رَابِطَةٌ	Connective, copula.
مَرْبَطٌ ج مَرَابِطُ	Stable.
مِرْبَطٌ	Cord, rope ; halter.
رَبَعَ بِ	Pasture freely in.
رَبَّعَ	To square.
تَرَبَّعَ	To sit cross-legged.
رُبْعٌ ج ارْبَاعٌ	Fourth part.
رَبْعَةٌ	Medium in stature.
رَابِعٌ رَابِعَةٌ	Fourth.
رُبَاعِيٌّ	Quadrilateral.
رَبِيعٌ	Spring-time.
رَبِيعُ ٱلأَوَّلُ	The third month of the Mohammedan year.

The fourth month. رَبِيعُ ٱلْآخِرُ
Four. أَرْبَعَةٌ م أَرْبَعُ
Quadrupeds. ذَوَاتُ ٱلْأَرْبَعِ
Wednesday. اَلْأَرْبِعَاءُ
Forty. أَرْبَعُونَ
Square form or number. مُرَبَّعٌ
Of medium stature. مَرْبُوعٌ
Jerboa. يَرْبُوعٌ ج يَرَابِيعُ
To entangle, bind. رَبَقَ يَرْبُقُ رَبْقًا
Loop, noose. رِبْقٌ وَرِبْقَةٌ
To mix, confuse. رَبَكَ يَرْبُكُ
To be entangled. رَبِكَ وَٱرْتَبَكَ
Confused, entangled. مُرْتَبِكٌ
Captain of a ship. رُبَّانٌ
To increase ; grow. رَبَا يَرْبُو
To nourish ; train up. رَبَّى
To take usury. رَابَى مُرَابَاةً
To increase *v. t.* أَرْبَى
To be brought up. تَرَبَّى

Usury, interest. رِبًا وَرِبَاءٌ
Asthma, panting. رَبْوٌ
Hill, height. رَبْوَةٌ ج رُبًى
Ten thousand. رَبْوَةٌ ج رَبَوَاتٌ
Hill, height. رَابِيَةٌ ج رَوَابٍ
Education, training. تَرْبِيَةٌ
Groin. اُرْبِيَّةٌ
Usurer. مُرَابٍ
Educator, trainer. مُرَبٍّ
Educated, trained up. مُرَبًّى
To set in order. رَتَّبَ
To be arranged. تَرَتَّبَ
To result from. تَرَتَّبَ عَلَى
Rank, position. رُتْبَةٌ ج رُتَبٌ
Salary, pension. رَاتِبٌ
Arrangement, order. تَرْتِيبٌ
Grade, rank. مَرْتَبَةٌ ج مَرَاتِبُ
To live in abundance. رَتَعَ يَرْتَعُ
To repair. رَتَقَ يَرْتُقُ رَتْقًا

رَتَّلَ	To sing.
رُتَيْلاَءُ ج رُتَيْلاَوَاتٌ	Large spider.
تَرْتِيلٌ ج تَرَاتِيلُ	Singing, chanting.
رَثَّ يَرِثُّ	To be ragged.
رَثٌّ	Worn out. Rags.
رَثَاثَةٌ	Squalor, raggedness.
رَثَى يَرْثِي	To bewail (the dead).
رَثَى لِ	To sympathize with, pity.
رِثَاءٌ	Elegy.
مَرْثِيَةٌ وَمَرْثَاةٌ ج مَرَاثٍ	Elegy.
رَجَّ يَرُجُّ	To move, shake.
إِرْتِجَاجٌ	Agitation, trembling.
أَرْجَأَ	To put off, defer.
رَجَبٌ	The seventh month of the Moslem year.
رَجَحَ يَرْجَحُ	To over-weigh.
رَجَّحَ عَلَى	To prefer.
تَرَجَّحَ	To be more probable.
رَاجِحٌ	Outweighing, preferable.
أَرْجَحُ	Preferable, more probable.
أُرْجُوحَةٌ	Swing.
تَرْجِيحٌ	Preference, probability.
رَجَزٌ	A poetical metre.
أُرْجُوزَةٌ	Poem of رَجَز metre.
رَجَسَ يَرْجُسُ	To defile one's self.
رِجْسٌ وَرَجَسٌ وَرَجَاسَةٌ	Pollution.
رَجِسٌ	Dirty, foul.
رَجَعَ يَرْجِعُ	To return.
رجعَ إِلَى	To have recourse to.
رَجَعَ عَن	To renounce.
رَجَّعَ	To restore.
رَاجَعَ	To review.
أَرْجَعَ	To restore.
إِسْتَرْجَعَ	To reclaim.
رُجُوعٌ	Return.
مُرَاجَعَةٌ	Review, repetition.
رَجَفَ يَرْجُفُ	To quake, tremble.
أَرْجَفَ	To shake, agitate.
إِرْتَجَفَ	To tremble.

رَجْفَةٌ	Trembling, shaking.
أَرَاجِيفُ	Seditious rumours.
رَجَلَ يَرْجَلُ	To go on foot.
تَرَجَّلَ	To dismount.
إِرْتَجَلَ	To speak extempore.
رِجْلٌ ج أَرْجُلٌ	Foot, leg.
رَجُلٌ ج رِجَالٌ	A man.
رَجِلٌ وَرَاجِلٌ	Pedestrain.
رُجُولِيَّةٌ	Manliness ; virility.
إِرْتِجَالٌ	Extemporizing.
مِرْجَلٌ ج مَرَاجِلُ	Caldron.
مُرْتَجَلٌ	Improvised (speech).
رَجَمَ يَرْجُمُ	To stone ; kill.
رَجَمَ بِٱلْغَيْبِ	To guess.
إِرْتَجَمَ	To be heaped up.
رَجَمٌ ج رِجَامٌ	Heap of stones.
رُجْمَةٌ ج رُجَمٌ	Tomb-stone.
رَجِيمٌ	Stoned, killed. Cursed.
مَرْجَانٌ	Coral.
رَجَا يَرْجُو	To hope, expect.
تَرَجَّى وَٱرْتَجَى	To hope for.
تَرَجَّى	To beg, entreat.
أَرْجَأَ	To put off, defer.
رَجَاءٌ	Hope.
رَحُبَ يَرْحُبُ	To be spacious (place).
رَحَّبَ وَأَرْحَبَ	To make wide.
رَحَّبَ وَتَرَحَّبَ بِ	To welcome.
رَحْبٌ وَرَحِيبٌ	Ample, spacious.
تَرْحَابٌ	Welcome.
مَرْحَبًا بِكَ	Welcome !
رَحَضَ يَرْحَضُ	wash.
مِرْحَاضٌ ج مَرَاحِيضُ	Wash-tub, water, closet.
رُحَاقٌ وَرَحِيقٌ	Choice wine.
رَحَلَ يَرْحَلُ وَٱرْتَحَلَ	To depart, migrate.
رَحْلٌ ج رِحَالٌ	Pack-saddle.
رِحْلَةٌ وَٱرْتِحَالٌ	Journey.
رَحِيلٌ وَٱرْتِحَالٌ	Migration.
رَاحِلٌ ج رُحَّلٌ	Traveller.

Great traveller. رَحَّالٌ وَرَحَّالَةٌ

Day's journey. مَرْحَلَةٌ ج مَرَاحِلُ

To pity, to be merciful. رَحِمَ يَرْحَمُ

To have, or pray for, pity for one. تَرَحَّمَ عَلَى

To implore pity. إِسْتَرْحَمَ

Uterus, womb. رَحِمٌ ج أَرْحَامٌ

Pity, compassion. رَحْمَةٌ

Compassion. رَحِيمٌ ج رُحَمَاءُ

The Merciful. اَلرَّحْمٰنُ اَلرَّحِيمُ

Act of mercy. مَرْحَمَةٌ ج مَرَاحِمُ

Deceased (person). مَرْحُومٌ

Mill-stone. رَحًى ج أَرْحَاءٌ

A fabulons bird. رُخٌّ

Saddle. رَخْتٌ ج رُخُوتٌ

To be cheap. رَخُصَ يَرْخُصُ

To be soft, supple. رَخُصَ رَخَاصَةً

To lower the price. رَخَّصَ

To allow, permit. رَخَّصَ لِ

To consider a thing cheap. To ask leave. إِسْتَرْخَصَ

Soft, tender. رَخْصٌ م رَخْصَةٌ

Cheapness of price. رُخْصٌ

Cheap. Soft, tender. رَخِيصٌ

To be soft (voice). رَخُمَ يَرْخُمُ

Marble. رُخَامٌ

Soft (voice). رَخِيمٌ وَرَخِمٌ

Elision of last letter of a word. تَرْخِيمٌ

To be soft, flaccid. رَخِيَ يَرْخَى

To loosen, let down. أَرْخَى

To flag, be slow. تَرَاخَى

To become lax. إِرْتَخَى وَاسْتَرْخَى

Relaxation ; abundance. رَخَاءٌ

Lax, soft, loose. رَخْوٌ

Softness, slackness. رَخَاوَةٌ

Free from care. رَخِيُّ ٱلْبَالِ

Relaxation. إِرْتِخَاءٌ وَاسْتِرْخَاءٌ

To return, send back, turn away. Refer. رَدَّ يَرُدُّ

To ponder ; repeat. رَدَّدَ

To frequent (a place). تَرَدَّدَ إِلَى

To waver ; hesitate. تَرَدَّدَ فِي

To go back, retreat, revert. إِرْتَدَّ

To be converted to. إِرْتَدَّ إِلَى

To depart from. إِرْتَدَّ عَنْ

To reclaim ; revoke. اِسْتَرَدَّ

Repulse. Return. Reply. رَدٌّ

Conversion to. إِرْتِدَادٌ إِلَى

Apostasy. إِرْتِدَادٌ عَنْ

Reclamation, recovery. اِسْتِرْدَادٌ

Frequenting. Wavering. تَرَدُّدٌ

Setting aside, repelling. مَرَدٌّ

Convert ; apostate. مُرْتَدٌّ

Vacillating, hesitating. مُتَرَدِّدٌ

Rejected ; refuted. مَرْدُودٌ

Divorced woman. مَرْدُودَةٌ

Evil, malice. رَدَاءَةٌ وَرَدَاوَةٌ

Bad, wicked. رَدِيءٌ ج أَرْدِيَاء

Worse, more wicked. أَرْدَأُ

Corn measure. أَرْدَبٌّ

Restrain, prevent. رَدَعَ يَرْدَعُ عَنْ

To be restrained. إِرْتَدَعَ عَنْ

To follow. رَدَفَ يَرْدُفُ

To be synonymous, (words). تَرَادَفَ

The reserves, (soldiers). رَدِيفٌ

Synonymous (words). مُتَرَادِفٌ

To stop, fill up. رَدَمَ يَرْدِمُ

To be stopped up. إِرْتَدَمَ

Ruins of a wall, debris. رَدْمٌ

To spin. Purr (cat). رَدَنَ يَرْدُنُ

Sleeve. رُدْنٌ ج أَرْدَان

The Jordan. الأُرْدُنّ

Spindle. مِرْدَنٌ ج مَرَادِن

A large hall. رَدْهَةٌ ج رِدَاه

To perish. رَدِيَ يَرْدَى رَدًى

To put on a mantle. تَرَدَّى

Mantle, cloak. رِدَاءٌ ج أَرْدِيَة

Enveloped in a mantle. مُتَرَدٍّ

To be mean, base. رَذَلَ يَرْذُلُ

To reject.	رَذَلَ يَرْذُلُ رَذْلاً
Ignoble, base.	رَذِيلٌ ج رُذَلاء
Vileness.	رَزَالَةٌ ج رَزَالاَتٌ
Vice.	رَذِيلَةٌ ج رذَائِلُ
Rice.	رزٌّ (for أُرزٌّ)
Iron peg.	رزَّةٌ ج رزَّاتٌ
To diminish. Afflict.	رَزَأَ يَرْزَأُ
Misfortune.	رَزِيئَةٌ ج رَزَايَا
Iron rod.	إِرْزَبَّةٌ ومِرْزَبَةٌ
Satrap.	مَرْزُبَانٌ ج مَرَازِبَةٌ
To fall from fatigue.	رَزَحَ يَرْزَحُ
Extreme fatigue.	رُزُوحٌ
Fatigued, exhausted.	رَازِحٌ
District.	رُزْدَاقٌ ج رُزْدَاقات
To grant, bestow.	رَزَقَ يَرْزُقُ
To receive means of life.	إِرْتَزَقَ
To seek means of life.	إِسْتَرْزَقَ
Means of living.	رِزْقٌ ج أَرْزَاقٌ
God.	اَلرَّازِقُ وٱلرَّزَّاقُ
Blessed with worldly goods.	مَرْزُوقٌ
To wrap up a package.	رَزَمَ يَرْزِمُ
Package, bale.	رِزْمَةٌ ج رِزَمٌ
To be grave, dignified.	رَزُنَ يَرْزُنُ
Gravity, dignity.	رَزَانَةٌ
Weighty, grave, calm.	رَزِينٌ
Almanac.	رُزْنَامَةٌ
To settle down. (liquid).	رَسَبَ يَرْسُبُ
Sediment.	رُسُوبٌ ورُسَابَةٌ
Theatre.	مَرْسَحٌ ج مَرَاسِحُ
To be firm, stable.	رَسَخَ يرسَخُ
Firm, stable.	رَاسِخٌ ج رَاسِخُونَ
Well instructed.	رَاسِخٌ فِي ٱلْعِلْمِ
The ankle, wrist.	رسغٌ ج أَرْسَاغٌ
To correspond about.	رَاسَلَ
To dismiss, send.	أَرْسَلَ
To hang loose, (hair).	إِسْتَرْسَلَ
Message, letter, epistle. Mission.	رِسَالَةٌ ج رَسَائِلُ
Messenger, apostle.	رَسُولٌ ج رُسُلٌ

مُرْسَلٌ	One sent, missionary.
مُرَاسِلٌ	Correspondent.
مُرَاسَلَةٌ	Correspondence.
رَسَمَ يَرْسُمُ عَلَى	To trace ; design.
رَسَمَ لِ	To prescribe, enjoin.
رَسَمَ رِسَامَةً	To ordain to a sacred office.
رَسْمٌ ج رُسُومٌ	Trace ; sign. Tax.
رَسْمِيّ	Official, authoritative.
مَرْسُومٌ	Marked. Ordained.
رَسَنٌ ج أَرْسُنٌ وَأَرْسَانٌ	Halter.
رَسَا يَرْسُو	To be firm.
أَرْسَى إِرْسَاءً	To cast anchor.
رَاسٍ	At anchor, (ship).
مَرْسًى ج مَرَاسٍ	Port. Anchorage.
مِرْسَاةٌ ج مَرَاسٍ	Anchor.
رَشَّ يَرُشُّ	To sprinkle.
مِرَشَّةٌ ج مِرَشَّاتٌ	Watering-pot.
رَشَحَ يَرْشَحُ رَشْحًا	To exude, ooze.
رَشَّحَ لِ	To train, bring up.
تَرَاشَحَ لِ	To be trained for.
رَشْحٌ	Cold in the heat.
مُرَشَّحٌ	Trained. Candidate.
أَرْشَدَ	To direct, guide.
إِسْتَرْشَدَ	To ask for guidance.
رُشْدٌ	Rectitude. Maturity.
رَشَادٌ	Cress, pepperwort.
رَاشِدٌ وَرَشِيدٌ	Follower of right way.
رَشَفَ يَرْشُفُ	To sip. suck.
رَشَقَ يَرْشُقُ	To hurl (a weapon).
رَشِيقٌ	Fine, elegant form.
رَشَاقَةٌ	Elegance of from.
رَوْشَنٌ ج رَوَاشِنُ	Window.
رَشَا يَرْشُو رَشْوًا	To bribe.
إِرْتَشَى	To receive a bribe.
إِسْتَرْشَى	To ask for a bribe.
رَشْوَةٌ ج رُشًى	Bribe.
رَصَّ يَرُصُّ	To press, squeeze.
رَصَّصَ	To overlay with lead.

رَصَاصٌ Lead.
رَصَاصَةٌ Piece of lead ; bullet.
رَصَاصِيٌّ Lead-colour.
مَرْصُوصٌ Firm, compact.
رَصَدَ يَرْصُدُ To watch for.
رَصَدَ لِ To lie in wait for.
تَرَصَّدَ To observe, watch.
رَصْدٌ Watching, observation.
رَصِيدٌ Balance of account.
مَرْصَدٌ ج مَرَاصِدُ Observatory.
مِرْصَادٌ Highway, lurking-place.
رَصَّعَ To set with jewels
مُرَصَّعٌ Inlaid with gold-work.
رَصَفَ يَرْصُفُ رَصْفًا To pave.
رَصَافَةٌ Firmness, solidity.
رَصِيفٌ Firm. Paved road.
رَصُنَ يَرْصُنُ To be solid, grave.
رَصَانَةٌ Gravity, sedateness.
رَصِينٌ Firm, dignified, grave.

رَضَّ يَرُضُّ To pound, bruise.
تَرَضَّضَ وَآرْتَضَّ To be bruised.
رَضٌّ وَرَضَّةٌ Bruise, contusion.
رُضَابٌ Saliva.
رَضَخَ يَرْضَخُ رَضْخًا لِ To submit.
رَضِعَ يَرْضَعُ To nurse (infant).
أَرْضَعَ To nurse, (mother).
رَضِيعٌ Infant at the breast.
إِرْضَاعٌ Act of nursing a child.
مُرْضِعَةٌ ج مُرْضِعَاتٌ Wet-nurse.
رَضِيَ يَرْضَى To be pleased.
رَضِيَ بِ To consent to.
رَاضَى To satisfy, conciliate.
أَرْضَى إِرْضَاءً To satisfy, please.
إِرْتَضَى To be content with.
رِضًى وَرِضْوَانٌ Satisfaction.
رَاضٍ ج رَاضُونَ Satisfied, content.
عِيشَةٌ رَاضِيَةٌ Comfortable life.
تَرَاضٍ Mutual agreement.

مُرْضٍ Satisfying, pleasing.

رَطِبَ يَرْطَبُ To be moist, damp.

رَطَّبَ To moisten ; cool.

تَرَطَّبَ To be moistened.

رُطَبٌ Fresh, ripe dates.

رُطُوبَةٌ Moisture ; humidity.

رَطْلٌ ج أَرْطَالٌ 449.28 grammes.

إِرْتَطَمَ To stick in mire.

رَعَاعٌ The rabble, dregs of men.

رَعَبَ يَرْعَبُ To frighten.

رَعَّبَ وَأَرْعَبَ To terrify.

إِرْتَعَبَ To be frightened.

رُعْبٌ وَرُعُبٌ Fright, fear.

رَاعِبٌ وَمُرْعِبٌ Causing fear.

رَعَدَ يَرْعُدُ To thunder.

إِرْتَعَدَ To tremble, be afraid.

رَعْدٌ ج رُعُودٌ Thunder.

رَعَشَ يَرْعَشُ وَآرْتَعَشَ To tremble.

رَعَّشَ To cause to tremble.

رَعْشٌ A trembling, shaking.

رَعِفَ يَرْعَفُ To bleed, (nose).

رُعَافٌ Bleeding from the nose.

رَعْنٌ Sun-stroke.

رَعْنٌ وَرُعُونَةٌ Stupidity

رَعَى يَرْعَى To graze ; tend (cattle). Rule (subjects). Have regard to.

رَاعَى To have regard for.

إِرْتَعَى وَتَرَعَّى To pasture, graze.

رِعَايَةٌ Guarding ; pasturing.

رَعِيَّةٌ ج رَعَايَا Subjects (of a ruler).

رَاعٍ ج رُعَاةٌ Shepherd. Pastor.

مَرْعًى ج مَرَاعٍ Pasturage, pasture.

مَرْعِيٌّ Observed, regarded.

مُرَاعَاةً لِ Out of regard for.

رَغِبَ يَرْغَبُ فِي To desire, long for.

رَغِبَ عَنْ To have no desire for, refrain from.

رَغِبَ إِلَى To implore, entreat.

رَغَّبَ To inspire with desire.

Strong desire, eagerness. رَغْبَة

A desired object. رَغِيبَة ج رَغَائِبُ

Comfortable, easy. رَغْد وَرَغِيد

Loaf (of bread). رَغِيف ج أَرْغِفَة

To humiliate, vex ; force. أَرْغَمَ

In spite of him. رَغْماً عَنْهُ

To effervesce, froth. رَغَا يَرْغُو

Foam, froth, cream. رَغْوَة

To shine ; flutter. رَفَّ يَرِفُّ

Flock. Shelf. رَفّ ج رُفُوف

To mend (a garment). رَفَأَ يَرْفَأ

To make peace between. رَفَأَ بَين

Peace, concord, accord. رَفَاء

Harbour for ships. مَرْفَأ

To refuse, reject. رَفَتَ يَرْفُتُ

Permit (for goods). رَفْتِيَّة

To rise, swell (dough). رَفَخَ

To aid. Dress (a wound). رَفَدَ يَرْفِدُ

To ask help. إِسْتَرْفَدَ

Assistance. رِفْد ج أَرْفَاد

Cushion ; bandage. رِفَادَة

To flap the wings. رَفْرَفَ

To kick. رَفَسَ يَرْفِسُ

A kick. رَفْسَة

To shovel. رَفَشَ يَرْفُشُ رَفْشاً

Winnowing-shovel. رَفْش

To leave, reject. رَفَضَ يَرْفُضُ

To be separated, disperse. إِرْفَضَّ

One who rejects. رَافِض ج رَفَضَة

A fanatic. مُتَرَفِّض

Rejected. مَرْفُوض

To raise ; take away. رَفَعَ يَرْفَعُ

To be exalted. رَفُعَ يَرْفُعُ

To present to ; inform. رَفَعَ إِلَى

To cite before a judge. رَافَعَ إِلَى

To bring a cause together before a judge. تَرَافَعَ

To rise high ; carried off. إِرْتَفَعَ

Act of raising, elevating. رَفْع

رِفعة	High rank, dignity.
رَفِيعٌ	High, elevated.
إِرْتِفاعٌ	Elevation, height.
مَرْفَعٌ ج مَرَافِعُ	Carnival.
مَرْفُوعٌ	Raised up. Carried off.
رَفِقَ يَرْفُقُ بِ	To be gentle towards.
رَافَقَ	To accompany one.
تَرَفَّقَ بِ	To treat with kindness.
تَرَافَقَ	To be companions.
رِفْقٌ	Kindness, compassion.
رِفْقَةٌ ج رُفَقٌ	Company.
رَفِيقٌ ج رُفَقَاءُ	Companion.
مِرْفَقٌ وَمَرْفِقٌ ج مَرَافِقُ	Elbow.
مُرْتَفَقٌ	Water-closet
رَفِهَ يَرْفَهُ	To live in luxury.
رَفُهَ يَرْفُهُ	To be comfortable, (life).
رَفَاهَةٌ وَرَفَاهِيَةٌ	Good living.
رَقَّ يَرِقُّ	To be thin, fine.
رَقَّ لَهُ	To pity one.

رَقَّ رِقًّا	To become a slave.
رَقَّقَ وَارَقَّ	To make thin, fine.
إِسْتَرَقَّ	To enslave.
رِقٌّ	Slavery.
رَقٌّ ج رُقُوقٌ	Parchment ; paper.
رِقَّةٌ	Fineness. Compassion.
رِقَّةُ ٱلْقَلْبِ	Tender-heartedness.
رُقَاقٌ ج رِقَاقٌ	Thin bread.
رَقِيقٌ ج رِقَاقٌ	Thin. Slave.
رَقِيقُ ٱلحَالِ	Not rich.
رَقَبَ يَرْقُبُ	To watch, observe.
رَاقَبَ	To guard, keep. Observe.
تَرَقَّبَ	To expect, look for.
رَقَبَةٌ ج رِقَابٌ	Neck. Slave.
رَقِيبٌ ج رُقَبَاءُ	Guardian.
مَرْقَبٌ ج مَرَاقِبُ	Watch-tower.
مِرْقَبٌ	Telescope.
رَقَدَ يَرْقُدُ	To sleep.
أَرْقَدَ	To put to sleep.

Sleep.	رُقَاد
Bed ; dormitory.	مَرْقِدٌ ج مَرَاقِدُ
To variegate.	رَقَشَ يَرْقُشُ وَرَقَّشَ
To be embellished.	تَرَقَّشَ
Variegated.	ارْقَشُ رَقْشَاءُ ج رُقْشٌ
To dance.	رَقَصَ يَرْقُصُ رَقْصاً
To cause to dance.	رَقَّصَ وَأَرْقَصَ
Dancing, leaping.	رَقْصٌ
Dancer. Pendulum.	رَقَّاصٌ
To be spotted.	تَرَقَّطَ
Spotted.	ارْقَطُ رَقْطَاءُ ج رُقْطٌ
To patch.	رَقَعَ يَرْقَعُ وَرَقَّعَ
To be foolish.	رَقُعَ يَرْقُعُ رَقَاعَةً
Patch scrap.	رُقْعَةٌ ج رِقَاعٌ
Folly, stupidity.	رَقَاعَةٌ
Firmament.	رَقِيعٌ
Patched, mended.	مُرَقَّعٌ
To write.	رَقَمَ يَرْقُمُ رَقْماً
To mark with stripes.	رَقَّمَ وَرَقَمَ
Numerical sign.	رَقْمٌ ج ارْقَامٌ
Indian numerals.	الرَّقْمُ ٱلْهِنْدِيُّ
Written. Embroidered.	مَرْقُومٌ
Clavicle. collar-bone.	تَرْقُوَةٌ
To ascend, rise.	رَقِيَ يَرْقَى
To use magic.	رَقَى يَرْقِي رُقْيَةً
To raise high, elevate.	رَقَّى
To rise high.	تَرَقَّى وَٱرْتَقَى فِي وَإِلى
Magic, incantation.	رُقْيَةٌ
Charmer, magician.	رَاقٍ ج رُقَاةٌ
Rising, progress.	تَرَقٍّ وَٱرْتِقَاءٌ
Ladder, stairs.	مَرْقًى وَمِرْقَاةٌ ج مَرَاقٍ
To be weak.	رَكَّ يَرِكُّ رَكَاكَةً
To make a foundation.	رَكَّ يَرُكُّ
Rubble used in masonry.	رَكَّةٌ
Weak.	رَكِيكٌ ج رِكَاكٌ
Pressed.	مَرْكُوكٌ
To ride ; embark.	رَكِبَ يَرْكَبُ
To follow one's fancy.	رَكِبَ هَوَاهُ

رَكِبَ اَللَّيلَ	To brave danger.
رَكَّبَ	To compose, mix.
تَرَكَّبَ	To be constructed, mixed.
إِرْتَكَبَ	To commit a crime.
رَكْبٌ	Band of horsemen.
رُكْبَةٌ ج رُكَبٌ	Knee.
رِكَابٌ ج رُكُبٌ	Stirrup.
رَاكِبٌ ج رُكَّابٌ	Rider. Passenger.
تَرْكِيبٌ	Composition, structure.
مَرْكَبٌ ج مَرَاكِبُ	Ship, vessel.
مَرْكَبَةٌ	Carriage.
مَرْكُوبٌ ج مَرَاكِيبُ	Shoes.
مُرَكَّبٌ	Compound. Joined.
رَكَدَ يَرْكُدُ	To be still, motionless.
رَاكِدٌ	Still, stagnant.
رَكَزَ يَرْكُزُ	To fix in (the ground).
رَكِيزَةٌ ج رَكَائِزُ	Prop, buttress.
مَرْكَزٌ ج مَرَاكِزُ	Centre.
رَكَضَ يَرْكُضُ رَكْضاً	To run.
رَاكَضَ	To vie with in running.
رَكُوضٌ	Good runner.
رَكَعَ يَرْكَعُ	To bow (in prayer); kneel.
رَكَّعَ وَأَرْكَعَ	To cause one to bow.
رَكْعَةٌ ج رَكَعَاتٌ	Bowing in (prayer).
رَكَمَ يَرْكُمُ رَكْماً	To heap up.
تَرَاكَمَ وَٱرْتَكَمَ	To be heaped up.
رَكْمٌ وَرُكَامٌ	Heap, pile.
رَكَنَ يَرْكُنُ إِلَى	To rely upon.
أَرْكَنَ إِلَى	To trust in.
أُرْكِنَ إِلَى ٱلفِرَارِ	To take to fight.
رُكْنٌ ج أَرْكَانٌ	Support, prop.
الأَرْكَانُ	The elements (of things).
رُكُونَةٌ وَرَكَانَةٌ	Firmness; gravity.
تَرَكَّى وَٱرْتَكَى عَلَى	To rely upon.
رَكْوَةٌ ج رِكَوَةٌ	Small vessel.
رَكِيَّةٌ ج رَكَايَا	Well.
رَمَّ يَرُمُّ وَرَمَّمَ	To mend, restore.
رَمَّ وَأَرَمَّ	To become decayed.

To be repaired by degrees. تَرَمَّم

Altogether. بِرُمَّتِه

Decayed bones. رِمَّة ج رِمَم

Decayed (bone). رَمِيم

Lance, spear. رُمْحٌ ج رِمَاحٌ

Lancer, spearman. رَامِحٌ

To have sore eyes. رَمِدَ يَرْمَدُ

Ophthalmia. رَمَدٌ

Ashes. رَمادٌ

Having ophthalmia. رَمْدَانٌ

Grey, ash-coloured. رَمادِيٌّ

To indicate by a sign. رَمَزَ يَرْمِزُ

To be intelligent. رَمُزَ يَرْمُز رَمَازَةً

Sign. Allegory. رَمْزٌ ج رُمُوزٌ

Model, specimen. رَامُوزٌ ج رَوَامِيزُ

Alluded to. مَرْمُوزٌ إِلَيْه

To conceal; bury. رَمَسَ يَرْمُسُ

Tomb, grave. رَمْسٌ ج رُمُوسٌ

Lupine (herb). تُرْمُسٌ

To be very hot. رَمِضَ يَرْمَض

Intense heat. رَمْضَاء

The ninth month of the Moslem year. رَمَضَان

To glance furtively. رَمَقَ يَرْمُقُ

The last breath of life. رَمَقٌ

To put sand into. رَمَلَ

To become sandy. أَرْمَلَ

To become a widow or widower. أَرْمَلَ وَتَرَمَّلَ

Sand. رَمْلٌ ج رِمَالٌ وَارْمَالٌ

Hour-glass. سَاعَة رَمْلِيَّةٌ

Widower; widow. أَرْمَلٌ ج أَرْمَلَةٌ

Pomegranate. رُمَّانٌ

The Armenians. أَلْأَرْمَن

Armenian. أَرْمَنِيٌّ

To throw; hit; accuse. رَمَى يَرْمِي

To be thrown. إِرْتَمَى ارْتِمَاءً

Throw, hit. رَمْيَة ج رميات

Archer, slinger. رَامٍ ج رُمَاةٌ

Sagittarius (of the Zodiac). الرَّامِي

مِرْمًى ج مَرَامٍ	Instrument for throwing (projectile, arrow).
مِرْماةٌ ج مَرامٍ	Arrow, missile.
رَنَّ يَرِنُّ رَنِيناً	To twang, ring.
رَنِينٌ وَرَنَّةٌ	Sound, tone, echo.
أَرْنَبٌ ج أَرَانِبُ	Hare.
رَنَّحَ	To make giddy, (wine).
تَرَنَّحَ	To stagger.
رَوْنَقٌ	Lustre, brilliancy.
رَنِمَ يَرْنَمُ ورَنَّمَ وَتَرَنَّمَ	To sing.
تَرْنِيمَةٌ	Poem. Hymn.
تَرَنُّمٌ	Singing, psalmody.
رَهِبَ يَرْهَبُ رَهْبَةً	To fear, dread.
رَهَّبَ وَارْهَبَ	To frighten.
تَرَهَّبَ	To become a monk.
رَهْبَةٌ	Fear.
رَهْبَنَةٌ ورَهْبَانِيَّةٌ	Monachism.
راهِبٌ ج رُهْبَانٌ	Monk.
راهِبَةٌ ج راهِبَاتٌ	Nun.
رَهِيبٌ	Fearful, awful.
رَهَجٌ	Dust. Excitement.
إِرْتَهَطَ	To assemble, congregate.
رَهْطٌ ج أَرْهُطٌ	Company of men.
رَهُفَ يَرْهُفُ	To be thin, sharp.
رَهِيفٌ وَمُرْهَفٌ	Thin, slender.
رَاهَقَ	To approach puberty.
مُرَاهِقٌ	Boy at puberty.
مَرْهَمٌ ج مَرَاهِمُ	Ointment.
رَهَنَ يَرْهَنُ رَهْناً	To be firm.
رَهَنَ عِنْدَ	To pledge with.
رَاهَنَ	To bet, lay a wager.
تَرَاهَنَ	To bet together.
إِرْتَهَنَ	To receive a pledge.
إِسْتَرْهَنَ	To require a pledge.
رَهْنٌ ج رِهَانٌ	Pledge, mortgage.
رَاهِنٌ	Fixed, stable, durable.
رَهِينٌ وَمُرْتَهَنٌ ومَرْهُونٌ	Pledged.
رَهِينَةٌ ج رَهَائِنُ	Pledge, security.

Long-suffering. طَوِيلُ ٱلرُّوحِ	Ambling-horse. رهْوَانٌ
Spiritual, incorporeal. رُوحَانِيٌّ	To curdle, (milk.) رَابَ يَرُوبُ
Wind. Odour. رِيحٌ ج رِيَاحٌ	Curdled ; churned. رَائِبٌ وَمُرَوَّبٌ
Whitlow. رِيحُ ٱلشَّوْكَةِ	Ferment of; milk. رَوْبَةٌ
Odour. Puff of wind. رِيحَةٌ	To void excrement, (horse). رَاثَ يَرُوثُ رَوْثًا
Myrtle. رَيْحَانٌ ج رَيَاحِينُ	To be current. رَاجَ يَرُوجُ
Odour. رَائِحَةٌ ج رَوَائِحُ	To put in circulation. رَوَّجَ
Generous, liberal. أَرْيَحِيٌّ	Currency. Good market. رَوَاجٌ
Cattle-fold. مُرَاحٌ	Selling well. Current. رَائِجٌ
Fan. مِرْوَحٌ وَمِرْوَحَةٌ ج مَرَاوِحُ	To go, depart. رَاحَ يَرُوحُ
Water-closet. مُسْتَرَاحٌ	To give rest. أَرَاحَ إِرَاحَةً
To ask for. Seek (food). رَادَ يَرُودُ	To be pleased. إِرْتَاحَ
To beguile, seduce ; entice. رَاوَدَ	To rest. إِسْتَرَاحَ
To wish, desire. أَرَادَ	Wine. Mirth. رَاحٌ
To mean, intend. أَرَادَ بِ	Rest ease, quietude. رَاحَةٌ
Slowly, gently. رُوَيْدًا	Palm of the hand. رَاحَةٌ رَاحَاتٌ
Will ; volition. إِرَادَةٌ	Water-closet. بَيْتُ ٱلرَّاحَةِ
Voluntary. إِرَادِي	Breath, spirit. رُوحٌ ج أَرْوَاحٌ
Desired. Purpose · meaning. مُرَادٌ	The Holy Spirit. رُوحُ ٱلْقُدُسِ

To train, discipline. رَوَّضَ

Garden, flower-bed. رَوْضٌ

Meadow. رَوْضَةٌ ج رِيَاضٌ

Exercise, training. رِيَاضَةٌ

Mathematics. عِلْمُ ٱلرِّيَاضَاتِ

To fear. رَاعَ يَرُوعُ وَٱرْتَاعَ

To frighten. رَاعَ وَرَوَّعَ وَأَرَاعَ

Fear, fright. رَوْعٌ وَرَوْعَةٌ

To act slyly. رَاغَ يَرُوغُ رَوْغًا

To employ a ruse. رَاوَغَ

Ruse, trick. مُرَاوَغَةٌ

To be clear, limpid. رَاقَ يَرُوقُ

To render clear, clarify. رَوَّقَ

To pour out or forth. أَرَاقَ

To breakfast. اتروَّقَ

Tent, portico. رِوَاقٌ ج أَرْوِقَةٌ

Clear, limpid, pure. رَائِقٌ

To desire strongly. رَامَ يَرُومُ

Roman. Greek. رُومٌ ج أَرْوَامٌ

Mediterranean Sea. بَحْرُ ٱلرُّومِ

Rafter. رُومِيَّةٌ ج رَوَامِيُّ

Desire, purpose. مَرَامٌ

Rhubarb. رَوَنْدٌ وَرَاوَنْدٌ

To report, quote. رَوَى يَرْوِي رِوَايَةً

To quench one's thirst. رَوِيَ يَرْوَى

To consider attentively. تَرَوَّى

To quench thirst. أَرْوَى إِرْوَاءً

Narration, tale. رِوَايَةٌ

Narrator. رَاوٍ ج رُوَاةٌ وَرَاوُونَ

Rain ; irrigation. رِيٌّ

Well watered. رَيَّانُ

Well watered. Cited. مَرْوِيٌّ

To make doubtful. رَابَ يَرِيبُ

To trouble, disquiet. أَرَابَ

To have doubts. إِرْتَابَ

Doubt. رَيْبٌ وَرَيْبَةٌ ج رِيَبٌ

Doubt, hesitation. ارْتِيَابٌ

Causing, doubt. مُرِيبٌ

رَيْثَمَا	As long as ; while.
رِيشٌ ج رِيَاش	Feathers.
رِيشَةٌ	A feather.
رِيَاشٌ	Furniture, goods.
رَيْعَانٌ	The best part.
رِيفٌ ج أَرْيَافٌ	A fertile land along the banks of a river.
رِيفُ الْبَحْرِ	Sea-coast.

رَاقَ يَرِيقُ	To pour out.
أَرَاقَ	To pour out a liquid.
رِيقٌ	Saliva.
عَلَى الرِّيقِ	Before breakfast.
رَالَ يَرِيلُ رَيْلاً	To droll (child).
رِيَالٌ	Saliva. Dollar.
رِيمٌ	White gazelle or antelope.
رَايَةٌ ج رَايَاتٌ	Flag ; standard.

ز

	As a numeral sign=7.
زَوْبَرٌ وَزِوِبْرٌ	Nap of cloth.
زِئْبَقٌ	Mercury, quicksilver.
زَأَرَ يَزْأَرُ وَزَئِرَ	To roar (lion).
زَائِرٌ	Roaring ; angry ; enemy.
زُوَانٌ	Tares, (seed and plant).
زَبَبٌ	Hairiness, Down.

زَبِيبٌ	Raisins, dried figs.
أَزَبُّ م زَبَّاءُ	Hairy.
عَامٌ أَزَبُّ	Fertile year.
زَبَدَ يَزْبُدُ	To churn (butter).
زَبَّدَ وَازْبَدَ	To foam, froth.
زَبَدٌ	Foam, froth.
زُبْدٌ وَزُبْدَةٌ	Butter.

زُبْدَةٌ Cream.

زَبَادٌ A kind of perfume ; civet.

مُزْبِدٌ Foaming. Enraged.

زَبُورٌ ج زُبُرٌ Psalms of David.

زِبِّيرٌ Powerful man.

زَبَرْجَدٌ Chrysolite.

زَوْبَعَةٌ ج زَوَابِعُ A whirlwind.

زَبَلَ يَزْبُلُ وَزَبَّلَ To manure.

زِبْلٌ وَزِبْلَةٌ Manure.

زُبَالَةٌ Dirt ; sweepings.

زَبَّالٌ Manure-gatherer.

زَنْبِيلٌ ج زَنَابِيل Basket, pannier.

مَزْبَلَةٌ ج مَزَابِلُ Dung-hill.

زَبُونٌ ج زَبَائِنُ Customer.

زَجَّ يَزُجُّ زَجًّا To thrust with a lance.

زُجٌّ ج زِجَاجٌ Point of a spear.

زُجَاجٌ Glass ; glass vessels.

زُجَاجَةٌ Piece, or cup, of glass.

زَجَّاجٌ Glass-manufacturer.

زُجَاجِيٌّ Glass-merchant.

أَزَجُّ م زَجَّاءُ Having long eyebrows.

زَجَرَ يَزْجُرُ To forbid. Rebuke.

اِنْزَجَرَ To be forbidden.

زَجَلٌ Play. Uproar.

حَمَامُ ٱلزَّاجِلِ Carrier-pigeons.

زَحَّ يَزُحُّ To remove a thing.

زَحَرَ يَزْحِرُ To strain in breathing.

زَحِيرٌ Straining. Dysentery.

زَحْزَحَ عَنْ To remove a thing.

زَحَفَ يَزْحَفُ To march. Creep.

زَحْفٌ Marching. An army.

ٱلزَّحَّافَةُ وَٱلزَّحَّافَاتُ Reptiles.

زَحَلَ يَزْحَلُ عَنْ To depart ; retire.

زَحَّلَ وَأَزْحَلَ To move a thing.

زُحَلُ The planet Saturn.

زَحَمَ يَزْحَمُ وَزَاحَمَ To crowd ; press.

تَزَاحَمَ وَٱزْدَحَمَ To be crowded.

زَحْمَةٌ وَزِحَامٌ Pressure ; throng.

زَاخِرٌ	Full ; copious.
زَخِيرَةٌ ج زَخَائِرُ	Munitions of war.
زَخْرَفَ زَخْرَفَةً	To adorn.
زُخْرُفٌ ج زَخَارِفُ	Vain show.
مُزَخْرَفٌ	Adorned with tinsel.
زَخْمَةٌ	Whip of thong. Strap.
زَرَّ يَزُرُّ زَرًّا وَزَرَّرَ	To button.
زِرٌّ ج أَزْرَارٌ	Button. Knob.
زَرَبَ يَزْرُبُ	To make a sheep-fold.
زَرِبَ يَزْرَبُ زَرَبًا	To flow ; leak.
زِرَابَةٌ	Payment for stabling.
زَرِيبَةٌ ج زَرَائِبُ	Flod for cattle ; lurking place.
زَارُوبٌ ج زَوَارِيبُ	Narrow street.
مِزْرَابٌ ج مَزَارِيبُ	Water-course.
زَرِدَ يَزْرُدُ وَازْدَرَدَ	To swallow.
زَرَدٌ ج زُرُودٌ	Coat of mail.
زَرَدَةٌ	Ring, or link of a chain.
زُرْدِي	A kind of pudding.
زُرْزُورٌ ج زَرَازِيرُ	Starling.

زَرَعَ يَزْرَعُ	To sow ; plant.
زَارَعَ مُزَارَعة	To sow in shares.
زَرْعٌ ج زُرُوعٌ	Seed. Off-spring.
زَارِعٌ ج زُرَّاعٌ	Husbandman.
زِرَاعَةٌ	Seed. Agriculture.
مَزْرَعَة ج مَزَارِعُ	Plantation.
زرافةٌ ج زَرَافى	Giraffe.
زَرَقَ يَزْرِقُ	To thrust ; dung, (bird).
إِزْرَقَّ ازْرِقَاقًا	To become blue.
زُرْقَةٌ	Blue (colour).
أَلزَّرْقَاء	Sky ; heavens.
زُرَيق	A black singing bird.
زُرَيْقَا	A kind of bread-salad.
أَزْرَقُ م زَرْقَاء ج زُرْق	Blue.
عَدُوٌّ ازْرَق	Bitter enemy.
مِزْرَاقٌ ج مَزَارِيقُ	Short spear.
زَرَكَ يَزْرُكُ	To press, vex.
زَرْكَةٌ	Crowd, throng.
زَرْكَشَ	To embroider.

Brocade of silk. زَرْكَشٌ

Arsenic. زِرْنِيخٌ

To reproach. زَرَى يَزْرِي عَلَى

To despise. ازْدَرَى إِزْدِرَاءٌ ب

Contemptible. زَرِيٌّ

Despiser. مُزْدَرٍ

To cheat by tricks. زَعْبَرَ زَعْبَرَةً

Juggler. مُزَعْبِرٌ

Thyme. (see صَعْتَر) زَعْتَرٌ

To disturb. زَعَجَ يَزْعَجُ وَأَزْعَجَ

To be troubled. إِنْزَعَجَ

Agitation ; trouble. زَعْجٌ وَانْزِعَاجٌ

Medlar (tree and fruit). زُعْرُورٌ

Thin haired. Thief. أَزْعَرُ ج زُعْرَانٌ

To shake ; move. زَعْزَعَ

To be shaken ; moved. تَزَعْزَعَ

Violent wind. زَعْزَعٌ ج زَعَازِعُ

Inconstant ; unstable. مُتَزَعْزِعٌ

Quick in killing. زُعَافٌ

Saffron. زَعْفَرَانٌ

To cry out, shout. زَعَقَ يَزْعَقُ

To frighten. زَعَقَ ب وَأَزْعَقَ

Thunderbolt. (see صَاعِقَةٌ) زَاعِقَةٌ

To be angry ; bored. زَعِلَ يَزْعَلُ

Angry, bored. زَعْلَانُ

To assert. زَعَمَ يَزْعَمُ زَعْماً

Assertion. زَعْمٌ وَزَعْمَةٌ

Honour. Authority. زَعَامَةٌ

Chief. Spokesman. زَعِيمٌ

Fin. زَعْنِفَةٌ ج زَعَانِفُ

Down ; fine hair, feathers. زَغَبٌ

Nap of cloth. زِغْبِرٌ وَزِغْبَرٌ

To adulterate. زَغَلَ يَزْغَلُ زَغْلاً

Young pigeon. زُغْلُولٌ ج زَغَالِيلُ

To lead a bride home. زَفَّ يَزِفُّ

Procession of joy. زِفَّةٌ

To cover with pitch. زَفَتَ

Pitch. زِفْتٌ

مزفّت — Covered with pitch.

زفر يزفر — To expire breath.

زفرة ج زفرات — Deep sigh.

زفير — Expiration. Deep sigh.

زيزفون — Oleaster.

زقّ ج زقاق — Water-skin.

زُقاق ج ازقّة — Street, lane.

زكيبة — A sack made of hair.

زُكْرة ج زُكَر — A wine-skin.

زكزك — To tickle.

زكِم — To have a cold in the head.

زُكام وزُكمة — A cold in the head; catarrh.

زكن يزكن — To consider.

زكا يزكو — To be pure.

زكّى — To give alms. Justify.

تزكّى — To be justified.

زكوة (زكاة) ج زكا — Alms.

زكيّ ج أزكياء — Pure; just.

زلّ يزلّ زلاً — To stumble; slip.

زلل — A slip; fault.

زلّة ج زلات — A fault, fall.

زُلال — Clear, pure, cool (water). (White of an egg).

(زلحفة زلاحف) — Tortoise.

زلزل زلزلة وزلزالاً — To shake.

زلزلة ج زلازل — Earth-quake.

(تزلط) — To strip one's self.

زلعوم ج زلاعيم — Throat.

زلّف — To exaggerate.

أزلف — To bring near.

زلفة وزلفى — Nearness.

زلق يزلق زلقاً — To slip, glide.

زلق ومزلقة — Slippery (place).

زلق الامعاء — Diarrhœa.

زليق — A kind of fish.

زلم ج أزلام — Arrow for devining.

(زلمة ج زلم) — Man. Footman.

زمّ يزمّ زماً — To tighten. Strap.

زمام ج ازمّة — Halter. Shoe-strap.

To shout ; roar.	زَمْجَرَ زَمْجَرَةً
To play on a reed.	زَمَّرَ يُزَمِّرُ
Musical reed.	زَمْرٌ ج زُمُورٌ
Group ; party.	زُمْرَةٌ ج زُمَرٌ
A piper.	زَمَّارٌ
A pipe.	زَمَّارَةٌ ومِزْمَارٌ ج مَزَامِيرُ
Epiglottis.	لِسَانُ ٱلْمِزْمَارِ
Psalm.	مَزْمُورٌ ج مَزَامِيرُ
Emerald.	زُمُرُّدٌ
To be about to happen.	أَزْمَعَ
About to happen.	مُزْمِعٌ
Beast of burden.	زَامِلَةٌ ج زَوَامِلُ
Comrade ; companion.	زَمِيلٌ ج زُمَلَاءُ
Chisel.	إِزْمِيلٌ ج أَزَامِيلُ
To continue a long time.	أَزْمَنَ
Time.	زَمَنٌ وزَمَانٌ ج أَزْمِنَةٌ
Temporal ; transient.	زَمَنِيٌّ
Chronic disease.	زَمِنٌ (مَرَضٌ)
To be inflamed.	زَمْهَرَ وازْمَهَرَّ
Intense cold.	زَمْهَرِيرٌ
To scorn ; frown.	تَزَنْبَرَ عَلَى
Wasp ; hornet.	زُنْبُورٌ ج زَنَابِيرُ
Spring of a watch.	زُنْبُرُكٌ
Lily. Iris, (flower and plant).	زَنْبَقٌ
The black races.	زِنْجٌ ج زُنُوجٌ
A black ; negro.	زِنْجِيٌّ
Ginger.	زَنْجَبِيلٌ
To bind with a chain.	زَنْجَرَ
Verdigris.	زِنْجَارٌ
Chain.	زِنْجِيرٌ (جنزيرٌ) ج زناجير
Book-keeping.	حِسَابُ ٱلزِّنْجِيرِ
Cinnabar.	زُنْجُفْرٌ وزِنْجَفْرٌ
To become rancid.	زَنِخَ يَزْنَخُ
Ulna (bone).	زَنْدٌ ج زِنَادٌ
Steel for atriking fire.	زِنَادٌ
To disbelive religion.	تَزَنْدَقَ
Unbeliever.	زِنْدِيقٌ ج زَنَادِقَةٌ
To gird one's self.	تَزَنَّرَ

Girdle.	زُنَّارٌ ج زَنانِيرُ
Melia (tree).	زَنْزَلَختٌ (أَزْدَرَخْتٌ)
Necklace. Shackle.	زِنَاقٌ
To commit adultery.	زَنَى يَزْنِي
Adulterer.	زانٍ ج زُنَاةٌ
Munition.	(رَهْبٌ ورَهْبَةٌ)
To renounce.	زَهِدَ يَزْهَدُ (فِي وعَن)
To become an ascetic.	تَزَهَّدَ
Indifference.	زُهْدٌ
Ascetic ; indifferent.	زَاهِدٌ ج زُهَّادٌ
Little. Insignificant.	زَهِيدٌ
To shine.	زَهَرَ يَزْهَرُ زُهُوراً
To blossom ; flourish.	أَزْهَرَ
Flower.	زَهْرَةٌ ج أَزْهَارٌ
Dice.	زَهْرُ ٱلنَّرْدِ
The planet Venus.	أَلزُّهَرَةُ
A Mosque in Cairo.	أَلْجَامِعُ ٱلأَزْهَرُ
A graduate of	أَزْهَرِيٌّ الأَزْهَرِ
In blossom ; flourishing.	مُزْهِرٌ
Lute. Timbrel.	مِزْهَرٌ ج مَزَاهِرُ
To vanish.	زَهَقَ يَزْهَقُ زُهُوقاً
To blossom.	زَهَا يَزْهُو زَهْواً وازْهَى
Pomp of this world.	زَهَا ٱلدُّنْيَا
Quantity ; number.	زُهَاءٌ
About a hundred.	زُهَاءَ مِئَةٍ
Beautiful ; bright.	زَاهٍ
To give in marriage.	زَوَّجَ
To marry a woman.	تَزَوَّجَ
Copperas ; vitriol.	زَاجٌ
Husband. Pair.	زَوْجٌ ج أَزْوَاجٌ
Pair, couple.	زَوْجَانِ
Wife.	زَوْجَةٌ ج زَوجَاتٌ
Marriage.	زَوَاجٌ وزِيجَةٌ
Married.	مُزَوَّجٌ ومُتَزَوِّجٌ
Double ; doubled.	مُزْدَوِجٌ
To leave its place.	زَاحَ يَزُوحُ
To move from its place.	أَزَاحَ
To provide food for journey.	زَوَّدَ

To take provisions. تَزَوَّدَ

Food for the journey. زَادٌ

Sack for food. مِزْوَدٌ ج مَزَاوِدُ

Water-skin. مَزَادٌ ج مَزَاوِدُ

To visit. زَارَ يَزُورُ زِيَارَةً وَمَزَاراً

To falsify ; forge. زَوَّرَ

Falsehood. زُورٌ

Visitor. Pilgrim. زَائِرٌ ج زُوَّارٌ

Baghdad. ألزَوْرَاء

Visit. Pilgrimage. زِيَارَة

Crooked. أزْوَر

Falsification ; forgery. تَزْوِير

Shrine. مَزَارٌ ج مَزَارَاتٌ

Falsifier ; counterfeiter. مُزَوِّرٌ

Falsified ; conterfeited. مُزَوَّرٌ

Small boat. زَوْرَقٌ ج زَوَارِق

To deviate. زَاغَ يَزُوغُ زَوْغَاً

Hyssop (plant). زُوفَا وَزُوفى

To embellish. زَوَّقَ تَزْوِيقاً

Embellished, decorated. مُزَوَّقٌ

To pass away ; cease. زَالَ يَزُولُ

To continue. مَا زَالَ وَلَا يَزَالُ

To remove. زَوَّلَ وَأَزَالَ

To strive, prevail. زَاوَلَ مُزَاوَلَةً

Disappearance. Cessation. زَوَالٌ

Vanishing ; transient. زَائِلٌ

Juice. زُومٌ

To be apart ; removed. إِنْزَوَى

Tares. زُوَانٌ

Angle, corner. زَاوِيَةٌ ج زَوَايَا

Acute angle. زَاوِيَةٌ حَادَّةٌ

Obtuse angle. زَاوِيَةٌ مُنْفَرِجَة

Right anlge. زَاوِيَةٌ قَائِمَةٌ

Quicksilver. زِيْبَقٌ وَزِئْبَق

To oil. زَيَّتَ

Oil. زَيْتٌ ج زُيُوت

Olive (tree and fruit). زَيْتُون

Olive-coloured. زَيْتُونِيٌّ

زِيجٌ	Astronomical tables. Plumb-line.
زَاحَ يَزِيحُ	To depart ; deviate.
أَزَاحَ	To move away ; remove.
زِيحٌ ج أَزْيَاحٌ	Line.
زَادَ يَزِيد	To increase, (*v. t. & i.*)
زَادَ عَنْ وَعَلَى	To exceed.
زَايَدَ	To bid higher.
تَزَايَدَ	To increase gradually.
إِزْدَادَ	To be increased.
زِيَادَةٌ ج زِيَادَاتٌ	An increase.
زَائِدٌ	In excess ; superfluous.
أَزْيَدُ	More ; more abundant.
مَزَادٌ ج مَزَادَاتٌ	Auction.
مَزِيدٌ ج مَزِيدَاتٌ	Increased.

زِيرٌ ج أَزْيَارٌ	Large water-jar.
زِيرٌ	A kind of cricket.
زَاغَ يَزِيغُ زَيَغَانًا وَزِيغًا	To deviate.
أَزَاغَ	To cause to deviate.
زَاغٌ ج زِيغَانٌ	A kind of crow.
زَافَ يَزِيفُ	To be counterfeit.
زَيَّفَ	To counterfeit money.
زَائِفٌ ج زُيُوفٌ	Counterfeit.
زَانَ يَزِينُ وَزَيَّنَ	To adorn.
تَزَيَّنَ تَزَيُّنًا وَازْدَانَ	To be adorned.
زِينَةٌ ج زِيَنٌ	Ornament ; finery.
مُزَيِّنٌ	Barber ; hair-dresser.
تَزَيَّا	To assume the costume, or habits of others.
زِيٌّ ج أَزْيَاءٌ	Form. Costume.

س

س As a numeral sign=60.

سَائِرٌ Remaining; the rest; all.

سَأَلَ يَسْأَلُ To ask; request.

تَسَآلَ وَتَسَوَّلَ To beg (alms).

سُؤَالٌ Question, request.

سَائِلٌ Questioner. Beggar.

مَسْأَلَةٌ ج مَسَائِلُ Question; request.

مَسْؤُولٌ Questioned. Responsible.

مَسْؤُولِيَّة Responsibility.

سَئِمَ يَسْأَمُ مِن To loathe.

سَبَّ يَسِبُّ To revile, defame.

سَبَّبَ To cause, occasion.

تَسَبَّبَ To be caused.

تَسَبَّبَ بِ To live by.

سَبٌّ Abuse, invective.

سَبَبٌ ج أَسْبَابٌ Cause, reason; means; means of living.

سَبَبِيَّة Causality.

سَبَّابَة Forefinger, index.

مُسَبَّبٌ وَمُتَسَبَّبٌ عَنْ Caused.

مُتَسَبِّبٌ Trader.

سَبْتٌ ج سُبُوتٌ Sabbath. Saturday.

سُبَاتٌ Heavy sleep, lethargy.

سَبَحَ يَسْبَحُ سِبَاحَةٌ To swim, float.

سَبَّحَ To praise, magnify God.

سُبْحَانَ آللهِ Praise be to God!

سُبْحَةٌ ج سُبَحٌ وَسُبُحَاتٌ Rosary.

سِبَاحَةٌ Swimming floating.

سَابِحَاتٌ Ships. Stars.

سَوَابِحُ Fleet horses

Heptagon. مُسَبَّعٌ

To give abundantly. أَسْبَغَ عَلى

To go before, precede. سَبَق يسبِقُ

To go hastily to one. سَبَق إِلى

To try to precede. سَابَقَ سِبَاقاً

To contend for precedence. تَسابَقَ

Previous, former. سَابِقٌ

Formerly, before, of old. سَابِقاً

Antecedent. سَابِقَةٌ ج سَوابق

Racing ; a race. سِبَاقٌ ومُسَابَقَةٌ

To melt metals ; cast into a mould. سَبَكَ يَسْبُكُ سَبْكاً

Melted; moulded. سَبِيكٌ ومَسْبُوكٌ

Ingot. سَبِيكَةٌ ج سَبائِك

Foundery. مَسْبَكٌ ج مسابِك

To lower the veil ; let fall. اسبَلَ

To put forth ears, (grains). أَسْبَلَ الزرعُ

Ears of grain. سَبَلٌ

Road, way ; manner; means. Public fountain. سَبِيلٌ ج سبل

Hymn. تَسْبِحَةٌ ج تَسابِيحُ

Act of praising God. تَسْبِيحٌ

Rosary. مِسْبَحَةٌ ج مَسابِحُ

Salty, marshy (sod). سَبِخٌ

Salty, marsh. سَبِخَةٌ ج سِبَاخٌ

To probe. Try, test. سَبَرَ يسبُرُ

Probing, sounding. سَبْرٌ

Surgeon's probe. مِسْبَرٌ ج مَسَابِرُ

Tribe Jewish). سِبْطٌ ج أَسْبَاطٌ

February (month). شُبَاطُ

To make (in) seven. سَبَّعَ

To become seven. أَسْبَعَ

Seven. سَبْعَةٌ م سَبْعٌ

Seventh part. سُبْعٌ ج اسْبَاعٌ

Beast of prey. سَبُعٌ ج سِبَاعٌ

Seventh. سَابِعٌ

Composed of seven. سُبَاعِيٌّ

Seventy ; seventieth. سَبْعُونَ

Week. أُسْبُوعٌ ج أَسَابِيعُ

Traveller, wayfarer. إِبْنُ آلسَّبِيلِ
Spinage. سَبَانِخُ وَاسْبَانَاخُ
To take prisoner, captivate. سَبَى يَسْبِي
Captives. Booty. سَبْيٌ وَسَبِيٌّ ج سَبَايَا
Six. سَتَّة م سِت
Lady. (سِتٌّ ج سِتَّاتٌ)
Sixty ; sixtieth. سِتُّون
To cover, veil. سَتَرَ يَسْتُرُ
To be covered. تَسَتَّرَ وَاسْتَتَرَ
Veil, curtain, cover. سِتْرٌ ج سُتُور
Veil, cover. سِتَارٌ ج سُتُرٌ
God who covers sins. أَلسَّتَّار
Concealed. Understood, (pronoun). مُسْتَتِرٌ
Constantinople. أَلْإِسْتَانَةُ
Anus, podex. إِسْتٌ ج أَسْتَاهٌ
To worship, adore. سَجَدَ يَسْجُدُ
Worshipper. سَاجِدٌ ج سُجَّدٌ
Prayer-carpet. سَجَّادَة
Prostration, adoration. سُجُود

Mosque. مَسْجِدٌ ج مَسَاجِدُ
Turbidness ; agitation. سَجَسٌ
To coo ; rhyme. سَجَعَ يَسْجَعُ
Rhymed prose. سَجْعٌ وَتَسْجِيعٌ
Rhymed (prose). مُسَجَّعٌ وَمَسْجُوعٌ
Curtain, veil. سَجْفٌ ج سُجُوفٌ
To register, record. سَجَّلَ
Record ; scroll. سِجِلٌّ سِجِلَّاتٌ
To flow, stream. سَجَمَ يَسْجُمُ وَآنْسَجَمَ
To shed. سَجَمَ يَسْجُمُ وَأَسْجَمَ
Flowing effusion. إِنْسِجَامٌ
To imprison. سَجَنَ يَسْجُنُ سَجْنًا
Prison. سِجْنٌ ج سُجُونٌ
Jailor. سَجَّانٌ
Imprisoned. سَجِينٌ ج سُجَنَاءُ
Natural disposition. سَجِيَّةٌ ج سَجَايَا
To flow. سَحَّ يَسُحُّ سَحًّا
To drag, trail. سَحَبَ يَسْحَبُ سَحْبًا
To be dragged, drawn. إِنْسَحَبَ

Cloud. سَحَابٌ وَسَحَابَةٌ ج سُحُبٌ

To scratch, rub off. سَحَجَ يَسْحَجُ

To be rubbed off. تَسَحَّجَ وَانْسَحَجَ

Dysentery. سَحَجٌ

To bewitch, fascinate. سَحَرَ يَسْحَرُ

To take a morning meal. تَسَحَّرَ

Magic, enchantment. سِحْرٌ

Early daybreak. سَحَرٌ ج أَسْحَارٌ

Sorcerer, magician. سَاحِرٌ ج سَحَرَةٌ

Wooden box. سَحَّارَةٌ

Meal before daybreak. سُحُورٌ

To pound, crush. سَحَقَ يَسْحَقُ

To be crushed. تَسَحَّقَ وَانْسَحَقَ

Bruised, powdered. مَسْحُوقٌ

Contrition. إِنْسِحَاقُ ٱلْقَلْبِ

Shore ; coast. سَاحِلٌ ج سَوَاحِلُ

To break, crush. سَحَنَ يَسْحَنُ

Aspect ; complexion. سَحْنَةٌ

Tanned leather. سِخْتِيَانٌ

To compel to labour without wages. سَخَرَ يَسْخَرُ وَسَخَّرَ

To laugh at, mock. سَخِرَ يَسْخَرُ مِنْ

Compulsory labour. سُخْرَةٌ

To be angry. سَخِطَ يَسْخَطُ وَتَسَخَّطَ

To provoke to anger. أَسْخَطَ

Anger, displeasure. سُخْطٌ وَسَخَطٌ

To be weak. سَخُفَ يَسْخُفُ سَخَافَةً

Shallowness, weakness. سَخَافَةٌ

To blacken with soot. سَخَّمَ

Soot, crock. سُخَامٌ

To be hot ; have fever. سَخُنَ يَسْخُنُ

To warm, heat. سَخَّنَ وَأَسْخَنَ

Heat. Fever ; illness. سُخُونَةٌ

Warm, hot. سُخْنٌ

Hot ; sick, ill. سَاخِنٌ ج سُخَّانٌ

So be liberal. سَخَا يَسْخُو وَسَخِيَ يَسْخَى

Generosity. سَخَاءٌ وَسَخَاوَةٌ

Generous, liberal. سَخِيٌّ ج أَسْخِيَاءُ

To close, stop up. سَدَّ يَسُدُّ سَدّاً

To take the place of. سَدَّ مَسَدّاً

Balance, pay an account. سَدَّدَ

To be stopped. إِنْسَدَّ وَاسْتَدَّ

To collect a debt. إِسْتَدَّ

Barrier ; dam. سَدّ ج أَسْدَادٌ

Vestibule, porch. سُدَّة

A stopper, a cork. سِدَادَةٌ

Right, true. سَدّ وَسَدِيدٌ

Stopped, corked. مَسْدُودٌ

Simplicity of mind. سَدَاجَة

A species of lotus. سِدْرٌ ج سُدُورٌ

To be the sixth. سَدَسَ يَسْدِسُ

To make six. سَدَّسَ

Sixth part. سُدْسٌ ج أَسْدَاسٌ

Sixth. سَادِسٌ

Consisting of six. سُدَاسِيٌّ

Hexagon. مُسَدَّسٌ

To let down. سَدَلَ يَسْدِلُ وَأَسْدَلَ

To be let down. تَسَدَّلَ وَانْسَدَلَ

Mist. Nebula: سَدِيمٌ

In vain, to no purpose. سُدًى

Warp (of cloth). سُدَاةٌ ج أَسْدِيَةٌ

Rue-plant. سَذَابٌ

To gladden, cheer. سَرَّ يَسُرُّ

To rejoice at. سُرَّ سُرُوراً بِ

To cheer, gladden. أَسَرَّ

To impart a secret. سَارَّ مُسَارَّةً

To keep secret, conceal. أَسَرَّ

To confide a secret to. أَسَرَّ إِلَى

Secret, mystery. سِرٌّ ج أَسْرَارٌ

Secretary. كَاتِمُ الْأَسْرَارِ

Navel. سُرَّةٌ ج سُرَّاتٌ وَسُرُورٌ

Happy state of life. سَرَّاءُ

Mysterious, secret. سِرِّيٌّ

Joy, pleasure. سُرُورٌ وَمَسَرَّةٌ

Bed, cradle ; throne. سَرِيرٌ ج أَسِرَّةٌ

Hidden thought. سَرِيرَةٌ ج سَرَائِرُ

Concubine. سُرِّيَّةٌ ج سَرَارِيُّ

Joy, pleasure. مَسَرَّةٌ ج مَسَرَّاتٌ

Happy, pleased. مَسْرُورٌ

To drive to pasture. سَرَّبَ

Troop, flock. سِرْبٌ ج أَسْرَابٌ

Aqueduct, canal. سَرَبٌ ج أَسْرَابٌ

Mirage. سَرَابٌ

Shirt; dress. سِرْبَالٌ ج سَرَابِيلُ

To saddle (a horse). سَرَجَ يَسْرِجُ

Saddle. سَرْجٌ ج سُرُوجٌ

Dung, manure. سِرْجِين

Lamp, torch. سِرَاجٌ ج سُرُجٌ

Glow-worm. سِرَاجُ ٱللَّيْلِ

Glanders. Saddlery. سِرَاجَةٌ

Saddler. سَرَّاجٌ وَسُرُوجِيٌّ

Sesame oil. سِيرَجٌ وَشِيرَجٌ

Lamp-stand. مِسْرَجَةٌ ج مَسَارِجُ

To pasture at will. سَرَحَ يَسْرَحُ

To send away; set free. سَرَّحَ

Pasture. مَسْرَحٌ ج مَسَارِحُ

Comb. مِسْرَحٌ ج مَسَارِحُ

Cellar, vault. سِرْدَابٌ ج سَرَادِيبُ

Strip of leather. سَرِيدَةٌ ج سَرَائِدُ

Awning. سُرَادِقٌ ج سُرَادِقَاتٌ

Sticking-paste. (*for* شِرَاسٌ) سِرَاسٌ

Way, street, road. سِرَاطٌ وَصِرَاطٌ

Crab. Cancer. سَرَطَانٌ

Cancer (of the Zodiac). ٱلسَّرَطَانُ

To hasten, hurry. سَرُعَ يَسْرُعُ

To hasten to do. أَسْرَعَ فِي

Quickness, haste, speed. سُرْعَةٌ

Quick, rapid, swift. سَرِيعٌ

To be extravagant, act immoderately. أَسْرَفَ

Extravagance. سَرَفٌ وَإِسْرَافٌ

A spendthrift. مُسْرِفٌ

To steal, rob. سَرَقَ يَسْرِقُ

To steal away. إِنْسَرَقَ

Theft, robbery. سِرْقَةٌ وَسَرِقَةٌ

Thing stolen. سَرِقَةٌ وَسُرَاقَةٌ

Thief. سَارِقٌ ج سُرَّاقٌ وَسَرَقَةٌ

Great thief. سَرَّاقٌ

Dung. سَرْقِينٌ

Continuing endlessly. سَرْمَدٌ

Eternal. سَرْمَدِيٌّ

Cypress (tree). سَرْوٌ

Liberal, noble. سَرِيٌّ ج سَرَاةٌ

Trowsers. سِرْوَالٌ ج سَرَاوِيلُ

To travel. سَرَى يَسْرِي

To cause to travel. أَسْرَى بِ

Night-journey. سُرَى

Night-traveller. سَارٍ ج سُرَاةٌ

Column ; mast. سَارِيَةٌ ج سَوَارٍ

Palace. سَرَايَا ج سَرَايَاتٌ

The Syriac language. السُّرْيَانِيَّةُ

To spread out. سَطَحَ يَسْطَحُ وَسَطَّحَ

To be spread out. تَسَطَّحَ

Surface ; terrace. سَطْحٌ ج سُطُوحٌ

Flat, plane, even. مُسَطَّحٌ

To write. سَطَرَ يَسْطُرُ

Line ; row. سَطْرٌ ج أَسْطُرٌ وَسُطُورٌ

Large knife. سَاطُورٌ ج سَوَاطِيرُ

Fable, legend. أُسْطُورَةٌ ج أَسَاطِيرُ

Ruler (for lines). Sample. مَسْطَرَةٌ

New wine. مُسْطَارٌ

Authority, guardianship. سَيْطَرَةٌ

To rise ; gleam. سَطَعَ يَسْطَعُ

Pail, bucket. سَطْلٌ

Ship of war. Fleet. أُسْطُولٌ

To stop up, bar. سَطَمَ يَسْطُمُ

Cork, stopper ; bolt. سِطَامٌ

Cylinder. أُسْطُوَانَةٌ ج أَسَاطِينُ

Cylindrical. أُسْطُوَانِيٌّ

To attack ; assail. سَطَا يَسْطُو على

Attack ; power. سَطْوَةٌ ج سَطَوَاتٌ

Thyme (plant). سَعْتَرٌ (أَوْ صَعْتَرٌ)

To be fortunate. سَعِدَ يَسْعَدُ

To help, assist. سَاعَدَ

To make happy. أَسْعَدَ

Luck, success. سَعْدٌ ج سُعُودٌ

Monkey. سَعْدَانٌ ج سَعَادِينُ

Fore-arm. سَاعِدٌ ج سَوَاعِد

Happiness, felicity. سَعَادَةٌ

Your Excellency. سَعَادَتُكَ

Fortunate. سَعِيدٌ ج سُعَدَاءُ

To light a fire. سَعَرَ يَسْعَرُ

To fix, estimate a price. سَعَّرَ

To be fixed, (price). تَسَعَّرَ

To blaze, spread. إِسْتَعَرَ

Price. سِعْرٌ ج أَسْعَارٌ

Flame, blaze. Fire. سَعِيرٌ

Snuff. سَعُوطٌ

To assist. سَعَفَ يَسْعَفُ وأَسْعَفَ بِ

To assist, help. سَاعَفَ

Branches of palm-tree. سَعَفٌ

To cough. سَعَلَ يَسْعُلُ سُعَالاً

Cough. سُعَالٌ

To run. Seek. سَعَى يَسْعَى سَعْياً

To calumniate. سَعَى بِ

Effort, exertion. سَعْيٌ

Messenger. سَاعٍ ج سُعَاةٌ

Effort ; enterprise. مَسْعًى ج مَسَاعٍ

Medicine (in powder). سَفُوفٌ

Bill of exchange. سُفْتَجَةٌ ج سَفَاتِجُ

To shed. سَفَحَ يَسْفَحُ سُفُوحاً وسَفْحاً

To fornicate. سَافَحَ

Foot of a mountain. سَفْحٌ

Fornication. سِفَاحٌ

Roasting-fork. سَفُودٌ ج سَفَافِيدُ

To travel. سَفِرَ يَسْفُرُ سَفَراً

To send on a journey. سَفَّرَ

To depart, travel. سَافَرَ

To shine, (dawn). أَسْفَرَ

Written book. سِفْرٌ ج أَسْفَارٌ

Journey. سَفَرٌ ج أَسْفَارٌ

سَفْرَةٌ ج سَفَرَاتٌ	A journey.
سُفْرَةٌ	Table-cloth ; table.
مُسَافِرٌ	Traveller.
سِفَارَةٌ	Embassy.
سَفِيرٌ ج سُفَرَاءُ	Ambassador.
سَفَرْجَلٌ ج سَفَارِجُ	Quince.
سَفْسَطَةٌ وَسِفْسِطَةٌ	Sophism.
سَفْسَطِيٌّ	Sophistical ; sophist.
سَفَقَ يَسْفِقُ	To shut, slap.
سَفِيقٌ	Thick, compact.
سَفِيقُ ٱلْوَجْهِ	Impudent, insolent.
سَفَكَ يَسْفُكُ سَفْكًا .	To shed.
إِنْسَفَكَ	To be shed.
سَفَّاكٌ لِلدِّمَاءِ	Blood-shedder.
مَسْفُوكٌ	Shed, (blood, &c.)
سَفَلَ يَسْفُلُ	To be low, sink.
سَفُلَ سَفَالَةً	To be mean.
سُفْلٌ	The lowest part, bottom.
سُفْلِيٌّ	The lower part.
سَفَالَةٌ	Baseness, vileness.
سَافِلٌ ج سَفَلَةٌ	Low, vile.
اسْفَلُ	The lowest part.
سَفِينٌ وَإِسْفِينٌ	Wedge.
سَفِينَةٌ ج سُفُنٌ	Ship, boat.
سَفَنْجٌ وَسِفَنْجٌ	Sponge.
سَفِهَ يَسْفَهُ سَفَهًا	To be foolish.
تَسَفَّهَ عَلَى	To revile.
سَفَهٌ وَسَفَاهَةٌ	Stupidity.
سَفِيهٌ ج سُفَهَاءُ	Stupid, foolish.
سَقَطَ يَسْقُطُ	To fall, fall down.
أَسْقَطَ	To cause to fall, let fall. Discount. Subtract.
تَسَاقَطَ	To fall by degrees.
سَقَطٌ ج أَسْقَاطٌ	Refuse. Defect.
سَقْطَةٌ	Fall, slip, fault, error.
سَاقِطٌ ج سُقَّاطٌ	Low, worthless.
سُقَاطَةٌ	Refuse, what is rejected.
سقاطةٌ	Door-latch.
سُقُوط	Falling, downfall.

إِسْقَاطٌ Discount. Subtraction.

مَسْقَطُ ٱلرَّأْسِ Native place.

سَقَفَ يَسْقُفُ سَقْفاً وَسَقَّفَ To roof.

سَقْفٌ ج سُقُوفٌ Roof ; ceiling.

سَقِيفَةٌ ج سَقَائِفُ Porch, roof.

أُسْقُفٌ ج أَسَاقِفَةٌ Bishop.

أُسْقُفِيَّةٌ Bishopric.

سَقْلَبِيٌّ ج سَقَالِبَةٌ A Slavonian.

سَقِمَ يَسْقَمُ To be weak, diseased.

أَسْقَمَ To make ill.

سُقْمٌ ج أَسْقَامٌ Disease, illness.

سَقِيمٌ ج سُقَمَاءُ Diseased, weak.

سَقَمُونِيَا Scammony, (plant).

سَقَى يَسْقِي To give to drink, irrigate.

إِسْتَقَى To draw water ; ask for water.

إِسْتَسْقَى To be dropsical.

سَقْيٌ Giving to drink, watering.

سِقَاءٌ ج أَسْقِيَةٌ Water-skin.

سَقَّاءٌ ج سَقَّاؤُونَ Water-carrier.

سَاقٍ Cup-bearer.

سَاقِيَةٌ ج سَوَاقٍ Water-wheel. Irrigation-canal.

إِسْتِسْقَاءٌ Dropsy.

مُسْتَسْقٍ Dropsical.

سَكَّ ٱلنُّقُودَ To coin money.

سِكَّةٌ ج سِكَكٌ Ploughshare. Road, high road. Coined money.

سِكَّةُ حَدِيدٍ Railway.

سَكَبَ يَسْكُبُ To pour out ; melt.

سَكَبَ سُكُوباً وَٱنْسَكَبَ To flow.

سَكْبٌ Melting, flowing.

سَكَتَ يَسْكُتُ To be silent, still.

سَكَّتَ وَأَسْكَتَ To silence, still.

سَكْتٌ وَسُكُوتٌ Silence ; pause.

سَكْتَةٌ Apoplexy. A pause.

سَكُوتٌ Silent, reserved.

سَكِرَ يَسْكَرُ To become intoxicated.

سَكَّرَ وَأَسْكَرَ To intoxicate.

سُكْرٌ Drunkenness.

سَكْرَةُ ٱلْمَوْتِ Agony of death.
سَكَرَةٌ Wooden lock to a door.
سُكَّرٌ Sugar.
سَكْرَانُ ج سُكَارَى Intoxicated.
سِكِّيرٌ Habitual drunkard.
سِكَافَة Trade of a shoemaker.
إِسْكَافٌ ج أَسَاكِفَةٌ Shoemaker.
أُسْكُفَّةٌ Threshold.
سَكَنَ يَسْكُنُ سُكُونًا To subside.
سَكَنَ سَكَنًا وفِي To dwell in.
سَكَنَ إِلَى To rely upon, trust in.
سَكَّنَ To calm, pacify, quiet.
أَسْكَنَ To make to dwell.
سَكَنٌ Habitation.
سَاكِنٌ ج سُكَّانٌ An inhabitant.
سُكُونٌ Rest, quiescence.
سِكِّينٌ ج سَكَاكِينُ Knife.
سَكِينَةٌ Quiet.
مَسْكَنٌ ج مَسَاكِنُ House. abode.

مَسْكَنَةٌ Poverty ; lowliness.
مَسْكُونٌ Inhabited; possessed.
أَلْمَسْكُونَةُ The world.
مِسْكِينٌ ج مَسَاكِينُ Poor ; lowly.
سَلَّ يَسُلُّ وَٱسْتَلَّ To draw a sword.
تَسَلَّلَ وَٱنْسَلَّ To slip away.
سَلٌّ وَسَلَّةٌ ج سِلَالٌ Basket.
دَاءُ ٱلسُّلِّ Consumption, (disease).
سُلَالَةٌ Offspring, progeny.
سَلِيلٌ Child ; male offspring.
مِسَلَّةٌ Large needle. Obelisk.
مَسْلُولٌ Unsheathed. Phthisical.
سَلَأَ يَسْلَأُ To melt, clarify (butter).
سَلَبَ يَسْلُبُ وَٱسْتَلَبَ To rob. Seize.
سَلْبٌ Robbery. Negation.
مَسْلُوبٌ Robbed, plundered.
أُسْلُوبٌ ج أَسَالِيبُ Method, way.
سَلَّحَ بِ To arm equip.
تَسَلَّحَ To arm one's self.

Sultan.	سُلْطَانٌ ج سَلاَطِينُ
Imperial.	سُلْطَانِيٌّ
High road.	طَرِيقٌ سُلْطَانِيٌّ
Article for sale.	سِلْعَةٌ ج سِلَعٌ
To pass away ; precede.	سَلَفَ يَسْلُفُ
To give in advance.	سَلَّفَ وَأَسْلَفَ
To borrow ; receive payment in advance.	تَسَلَّفَ وَاسْتَسْلَفَ
Payment in advance.	سَلَفٌ
Predecessor.	سَلَفٌ ج أَسْلَافٌ
Vanguard of army.	سُلَافُ ٱلْعَسْكَرِ
Preceding ; former.	سَالِفٌ
To boil.	سَلَقَ يَسْلُقُ سَلْقًا
To scale or climb a wall.	تَسَلَّقَ
Ulceration of eye-lids.	سُلَاقٌ
Greyhound.	سَلُوقِيٌّ
Natural trait.	سَلِيقَةٌ ج سَلَائِقُ
Naturally, instinctively.	بِٱلسَّلِيقَةِ
Boiled.	مَسْلُوقٌ

Arms, weapons.	سِلَاحٌ ج أَسْلِحَةٌ
Tortoise.	سُلَحْفَاةٌ ج سَلَاحِفُ
To skin, flay.	سَلَخَ يَسْلَخُ سَلْخًا
To be stripped off.	انْسَلَخَ
End of (the month).	سَلْخٌ وَمُنْسَلَخٌ
Slaughter-house.	مَسْلَخٌ مَسَالِخُ
To be loose, docile.	سَلِسَ يَسْلَسُ
Docility.	سَلَسٌ وَسَلَاسَةٌ
Docile ; compliant.	سَلِسٌ
To chain.	سَلْسَلَ
To trace a pedigree.	سَلْسَلَ إِلَى
Chain.	سِلْسِلَةٌ ج سَلَاسِلُ
Artificial fountain.	سَلْسَبِيلٌ
A continued series.	تَسَلْسُلٌ
To make one a ruler.	سَلَّطَهُ
To overcome ; rule.	تَسَلَّطَ عَلَى
Rule, dominion.	سَلْطَةٌ وَتَسَلُّطٌ
Power, dominion.	سَلْطَنَةٌ
Absolute power.	سُلْطَانٌ

سلكَ يسلُكُ	To travel, enter. Behave.
أسلكَ	To make to enter.
سِلكٌ ج أسلاكٌ	String ; wire.
سُلوكٌ	Conduct, behaviour.
علمُ السُّلوك	Good manners.
سالِك	Ordinary, usual, current.
مَسلَك ج مَسالِكُ	Path road.
سَلِمَ يسلَمُ	To be sound, safe.
سلِمَ مِنْ	To be free from.
سَلَّمَ مِنْ	Tsave ; preser ove.
سلمَ بِ	To admit.
سلمَ لِ	To surrender, yield.
سلَّم إلى	To give over, hand to.
سلم على	To salute, greet.
سَالَمَ	To keep peace with.
اسْلمَ	To deliver up.
أسْلَمَ	To profess Islâm.
تَسلم	To take possession of.
إستَسلمَ	To yield, surrender.

سِلْمٌ	Peace, reconciliation.
سُلمٌ ج سَلَالِمُ	Ladder, stairs.
سَلَامٌ وَسَلَامَةٌ	Peace, well-being.
سَلَامٌ	Greeting ; salutation.
سَالِمٌ	Sound and safe.
ألجمعُ السالمُ	Sound plural.
سَلِيمٌ ج سُلَمَاء	Sound, safe.
سُلَيْمَانِيٌّ	Corrosive sublimate.
أَسْلَمُ	More secure, safer.
الإِسْلَامُ	Religion of Islâm.
تَسْلِيمٌ	Delivery ; surrender.
مُسْلِمٌ ج مُسْلِمُونَ	Moslem.
مُسَلمٌ	Delivered ; conceded.
سُلَا يَسلو	To forget.
سَلَّى	To divert, cheer, amuse.
تَسَلى	To be diverted.
سُلْوَةٌ وَتَسْلِيَة وَتسَلٍّ	Diversion.
سَلْوَى	Quail. Consolation.
سُلْوَانٌ	Consolation.

To poison. سَمَّ يَسُمُّ سَمًّا

Hole. Poison. سُمٌّ ج سُمُومٌ

Arsenic ; ratsbane. سَمُّ ٱلْفَارِ

Poisonous. سامٌّ

Hot wind. سَمُومٌ

Holes ; pores. مسامٌّ

Poisoned. مسمومٌ

Way ; manner. سَمْتٌ

Azimuth. أَلسَّمْتُ ج سُمُوتٌ

Zenith. سَمْتُ ٱلرَّاسِ

To be ugly. سَمِجَ يَسْمَجُ سَمَاجَةً

Ugly, horrid ; foul. سَمْجٌ وَسَمِيجٌ

To grant, permit ; pardon. سَمَحَ يَسْمَحُ

To pardon, excuse. سَامَحَ

Kindness ; grace. سَمَاحٌ وَسَمَاحَةٌ

Allowed ; permitted. مَسْمُوحٌ بِهِ

Periosteum. سِمْحَاقٌ

To manure the soil. سَمَّدَ

Manure. سَمَادٌ

Semolino. سَمِيذٌ وَسَمِيدٌ

To be brownish. سَمُرَ يَسْمُرُ وَاسْمَرَّ

To nail. سَمَرَ وَسَمَّرَ

To converse with. سَامَرَ وَتَسَامَرَ

Brownish colour. سُمْرَةٌ

Samaria (in Palestine). السَّامِرَةُ

Samaritan. سَامِرِيٌّ

Sable (animal). سَمُّورٌ

Brownish. أَسْمَرُ سَمْرَاءُ ج سُمْرٌ

Nail. Foot-corn. مِسْمَارٌ ج مَسَامِيرُ

To act as a broker. سَمْسَرَ

Brokerage ; fee of a broker. سَمْسَرَةٌ

Broker. سِمْسَارٌ ج سَمَاسِرَةٌ

Sesame. سِمْسِمٌ

Sesamoid bone. سُمْسُمَانِيٌّ

To strap with thongs. سَمَّطَ

Thong. سِمْطٌ ج سُمُوطٌ

Table-cloth. سِمَاطٌ ج أَسْمِطَةٌ

To hear, listen. سَمِعَ يَسْمَعُ وَاسْتَمَعَ

To hear of.	سَمِعَ ب
To accept, obey.	سَمِعَ لِ ومن
Sense of hearing.	سَمْعٌ
You shall be obeyed.	سَمْعًا وَطَاعَةً
Report, fame.	سُمْعَةٌ
Irregular, traditional.	سَمَاعِيٌّ
The hearer of all (God).	السَّمِيعُ
Sumach, (tree and fruit).	سُمَّاقٌ
To become thick.	سَمُكَ سَمَاكَةً
To thicken, make thick.	سَمَّكَ
Depth, thickness.	سَمْكٌ وسَمَاكَةٌ
Fish.	سَمَكٌ ج اسْمَاكٌ
A fish.	سَمَكَةٌ
Deep, thick.	سَمِيكٌ
To grow fat.	سَمِنَ يَسْمَنُ سِمَنًا
To butter; fatten.	سَمَّنَ
Clarified butter.	سَمْنٌ
Seller of butter. Grocer.	سَمَّانٌ
Quail.	سُمَنَةٌ ج سُمَّنٌ وَسَمَامِنُ)
Fat, corpulent.	سَمِينٌ ج سِمَانٌ
To be high ; rise high.	سَمَا يَسْمُو
Give a name ; name.	سَمَّى
To be named ; mentioned.	تَسَمَّى
Name ; noun.	إِسْمٌ ج أَسْمَاءٌ
The name of God.	إِسْمُ ٱلْجَلَالَةِ
Height ; greatness.	سُمُوٌّ
Heaven.	سَمَاءٌ ج سَمَوَاتٌ
Heavenly.	سَمَاوِيٌّ وَسَمَائِيٌّ
High ; sublime.	سَامٍ ج سُمَاةٌ
Grand vizierial order.	أَمْرٌ سَامٍ
Named, determined.	مُسَمًّى
To sharpen, whet.	سَنَّ يَسُنُّ
To introduce a law.	سَنَّ سُنَّةً
To become aged.	اسَنَّ
Tooth. Age in life.	سِنٌّ ج اسْنَانٌ
To become old.	طَعَنَ فِي ٱلسِّنِّ
Law ; usage.	سُنَّةٌ ج سُنَنٌ
Head of a spear.	سِنَانٌ ج أَسِنَّةٌ

سُنّيّ ج سُنّيّة	A Sunnite.
مِسَنّ	Whet-stone.
مُسِنّ	Advanced in age.
سُنْبُوق	Skiff, small boat.
سُنْبُلَة ج سَنَابِل	An ear of corn.
السُّنْبُلَة	Virgo (of the Zodiac).
سِنْجَاب	Squirrel.
سِنْجَق ج سَنَاجِق	Standard, flag.
سَنَحَ يَسْنَحُ	To occur to the mind.
سَنَحَ عَن	To dissuade.
سِنْخ ج أَسْنَاخ	Socket of a tooth.
سَنَدَ يَسْنُدُ وَٱسْتَنَدَ إِلى	To lean upon.
سَنَّدَ	To support firmly.
أَسْنَدَ إِلَى	To ascribe, trace up.
سَنَد ج أَسْنَاد	Support; refuge.
سَنْدَان ج سَنَادِين	Anvil.
سِنْدِيَان	Evergreen oak; ilex.
مِسْنَد ج مَسَانِدُ	Cushion, pillow.
مُسْتَنَد	Supported, propped.
المُسْنَد	Predicate.
أَلْمُسْنَدُ إِلَيْهِ	Subject.
سِنْدَرُوس	Sandarach.
سُنْدُس	Silk brocade; fine silk.
سِنَّوْر ج سَنَانِير	Cat.
سَنْط	Acacia (*Nilotica*).
سِنْطِير وَسَنْطُور	A kind of harp.
سَنْكَرِيّ ج سَنَاكِرَة	Tinker.
سَنَام ج أَسْنِمَة	Hump of camel.
مُسْنَم	Raised; convex.
تَسَنَّى	To ascend. Be easy.
سَنًى	Brightness, gleaming.
سَنَاء	Sublimity; high rank.
سَنَا مَكَّة	Senna, (plant).
سَنَة سِنُون وَسَنَوَات	Year.
سَنِيّ	High, sublime, noble.
سَنَوِيّ	Annual, yearly.
سُنُونُو	Swallow.
أَسْهَبَ	To be lengthy, prolix.

To give largely.	اسْهَبَ فِي ٱلْعَطَاءِ
Prolixity ; amplification.	اسْهَابٌ
Loquacious ; diffuse.	مُسْهِبٌ
To be sleepless.	سَهِدَ يَسْهَدُ
To deprive of sleep.	سَهَّدَ
Sleeplessness.	سُهْدٌ وَسُهَادٌ
To keep awake.	سَهِرَ يَسْهَرُ
Awake.	سَاهِرٌ وَسَهْرَان
To be level ; easy.	سَهُلَ يَسْهُلُ
To smooth ; facilitate.	سَهَّلَ
To be level ; become easy.	تَسَهَّلَ
To be accommodating.	تَسَاهَلَ
To regard as easy.	إِسْتَسْهَلَ
Plain ; level.	سَهْلٌ ج سُهُولٌ
Gentle.	سَهْلُ ٱلْخُلُقِ
Easy ; smooth, soft.	سَهْلٌ
Ease, facility. Evenness.	سُهُولَةٌ
Canopus, (star).	سُهَيْلٌ
Diarrhœa.	إِسْهَال
Purgative, laxative.	مُسْهِلٌ
Arrow.	سَهْمٌ ج سِهَامٌ
Lot, share.	سَهْمٌ ج اسْهُمٌ
Sagittarius.	سَهْمُ ٱلرَّامِي
To overlook, neglect.	سَهَا يَسْهُو عَنْ
Oversight, forgetfulness.	سَهْوٌ
Thoughtlessly.	سَهْواً
Forgetful, negligent.	سَاهٍ
To be evil, bad.	سَاءَ يَسُوءُ
To treat badly ; offend.	سَاءَ سُوءاً
To be evil to ; offend.	أَسَاءَ إِلى
To suspect evil.	أَسَاءَ ٱلظَّنَّ
Evil.	سُوءٌ ج أَسْوَاءٌ وَمَسَاوِئُ
Evil, bad.	سَيِّئٌ م سَيِّئَةٌ
Sin ; calamity.	سَيِّئَةٌ ج سَيِّئَاتٌ
Teak-tree.	سَاجٌ
See under. سيح	سَاحَ يَسُوحُ
Court ; yard.	سَاحَةٌ ج سَاحَاتٌ
Traveller.	سَائِحٌ ج سُيَّاحٌ

To rule a people. To groom a horse. ساسَ يَسُوس

To be moth-eaten. سوَّسَ

Moth, worm. Liquorice. سُوسٌ

Political administration. سِيَاسَةٌ

Groom. سَائِسٌ ج سَاسَةٌ وَسُوَّاسٌ

Lily. سُوسَنٌ وَسُوسَانٌ

To whip. سَاطَ يَسُوط سَوْطاً

Whip, lash. سَوْطٌ ج سِيَاطٌ

Hour. Watch. سَاعَةٌ ج سَاعَاتٌ

Sun-dial. سَاعَةٌ شَمْسِيَّةٌ

Hour-glass. سَاعَةٌ رَمْلِيَّةٌ

Watch-maker. سَاعَاتِيٌّ

To be permitted, lawful. سَاغَ لَ

To allow, permit. سَوَّغَ لَ

Lawful, allowable. سَائِغٌ

To put off, defer. سَوَّفَ

Row, course. سَافٌ ج سَافَاتٌ

A particle which changes the *present* tense into a future; *e.g.* Thou shalt see. سَوْفَ ترَى سوفَ

To rule. سَادَ يَسُودُ سِيَادَةً

To become black. إِسْوَدَّ

To blacken; write a rough draft. سَوَّدَ

To be blackened. تَسَوَّدَ

Dominion; honour. سُؤْدُدٌ وَسِيَادَةٌ

Black bile. Melancholy. سَوْدَاءُ

Sudan (country). بِلَادُ ٱلسُّودَانِ

Blackness. Large number. سَوَادٌ

Power, authority. سِيَادَةٌ

Master, lord. سَيِّدٌ ج سَادَةٌ

Black. أَسْوَدُ م سَوْدَاءُ ج سُودٌ

First copy, rough draft. مُسَوَّدَةٌ

Glass bottle. مُسَوَّدَةٌ ج مُسَوَّدَاتٌ

To wall in a town. سَوَّرَ

Wall, ramparts. سُورٌ ج أَسْوَارٌ

Chapter of Koran. سُورَةٌ ج سُوَرٌ

Syria. سُورِيَّةُ

Bracelet. سُوَارٌ وَإِسْوَارٌ ج أَسْوِرَةٌ

Surrounded with walls. مُسَوَّرٌ

مَسَافَةٌ Distance.

سَاقَ يَسُوقُ To drive, urge on.

سَاقَ إِلى To lead to.

إِنْسَاقَ To be driven, urged on.

سَاقٌ ج سُوقٌ وسِيقَانٌ Leg. Stem (of a plant). Side of a triangle.

سُوقٌ ج أَسْوَاق Market.

سَوِيقٌ Fine flour.

سِيَاقٌ Logical connection.

سَائِقٌ Driver, driving.

تَسَوَّكَ To clean one's teeth.

سِوَاكٌ وَمِسْوَاكٌ Toothpick.

سَوَّلَ لِ To deceive, incite to evil.

سَامَ يَسُومُ To compel.

سَاوَمَ مُسَاوَمَةً To bargain.

سِيمَةٌ وَسِيمَاء Sign, mark.

سَوِيَ يَسْوَى وَسَاوَى To be worth.

سَوَّى تَسْوِيَةً To adjust, rectify.

سَاوَى وَٱسْتَوَى To be equal.

إِسْتَوَى To be ripe, well cooked.

إِسْتَوَى عَلَى To sit upon.

سَوَاءٌ Just, right. Same, alike.

عَلَى حَدٍّ سَوَاء Alike, equally.

سَوِيَّةً وَسَوَاءً Equally ; together.

لَاسِيَّمَا Chiefly, principally.

هُمَاسِيَّان Equally, alike, (both).

خَطُّ الإِسْتِوَاء Equator.

مُسَاوَاةٌ Equaliy. Moderation.

مُسَاوٍ وَمُتَسَاوٍ Equal.

مُسْتَوٍ Common gender.

سَيَّبَ To set free.

سَائِبٌ Left free, at liberty.

مُسَيَّبٌ Unguarded ; free.

سَيَّجَ To hedge in, enclose.

سِيَاجٌ ج سِيَاجَاتٌ Hedge.

مُسَيَّجٌ Surrounded by a hedge.

سَاحَ يَسِيحُ To travel. Flow.

سِيَاحَة Long journery.

سَائِحٌ ج سيَّاح	Traveller.
سَيَّاحٌ	Great traveller.
مَسَاحَةٌ	Area.
عِلْمُ ٱلْمَسَاحَة	Land surveying.
سِيخٌ ج أَسْيَاخٌ	Large knife.
سَارَ يَسير	To go ; travel.
سَارَ بِ	To carry away.
سَيْرٌ ج سيور	Journey. Thong.
سيرَةٌ ج سِيَرٌ	Conduct. Biography.
سَائِرٌ	Current, customary.
سَيَّارَةٌ ج سَيَّارَات	Planet.
مَسِيرٌ	Journey, road.
سَيْفٌ ج سُيُوفٌ	Sword.
سَالَ يَسيلُ	To flow ; become liquid.
سَيَّلَ وَأَسَالَ	To liquify.
سَيْلٌ ج سُيُولٌ	Stream ; torrent.
سَيَلَانٌ	Flow ; flux.
سَيْلَانُ	Ceylon.
سَيْلَانٌ	Ruby ; carbuncle.
سَائِلٌ ج سَوَائِلُ	Liquid, fluid.
مَسِيلٌ	Water-course.

ش

As a numeral sign=300.	ش
To be inauspicious.	شُؤُمَ وَشَئِمَ
To take as a bad omen.	تَشَاءَمَ
Evil omen, ill luck.	شُؤْمٌ
Syria. Damascus.	الشَّامُ
Syrian. Damascene.	شَامِيٌّ
Nature, disposition.	شِيمَةٌ
Inauspicious, unlucky.	مَشُومٌ
Thing ; state ; honour.	شَأْنٌ
Of great importance.	عَظِيمُ ٱلشَّأْنِ
White falcon.	شَاهِينٌ ج شَوَاهِينُ
To grow up, (youth).	شَبَّ يَشِبُّ
To blaze (fire, war).	شَبَّ يَشُبُّ
Vitriol. Alum.	شَبٌّ
Young man.	شَابٌّ ج شُبَّانٌ

Young woman.	شَابَّةٌ ج شَابَّاتٌ
Youth.	شَبَابٌ وَشَبِيبَةٌ
A reed or musical pipe.	شَبَّابَةٌ
To take firm hold.	تَشَبَّثَ بِ
Dill (plant).	شِبِتٌّ
Object of vision.	شَبَحٌ ج أَشْبَاحٌ
A horse's shackle.	شِبْحَةٌ
Span.	شِبْرٌ ج أَشْبَارٌ
To scarify.	شَبَّطَ
February.	شُبَاطُ وَسُبَاطُ
To be satiated.	شَبِعَ يَشْبَعُ
To satiate, satisfy.	أَشْبَعَ
Satiety, satiation.	شِبَعٌ
Satiated, satisfied.	شَبْعَانُ
To entwine, entangle.	شَبَكَ يَشْبِكُ

تَشَبَّكَ وَٱشْتَبَكَ	To be entangled.
شَبَكَةٌ ج شَبَكٌ	Fishing-net.
شُبَّاكٌ ج شَبَابِيكُ	Window.
شِبْلٌ ج أَشْبَالٌ	Cub of a lion.
شَبِينٌ م شَبِينَةٌ	Groomsman.
شَبَّهَ بِ	To liken, compare.
شَابَهَ وَأَشْبَهَ	To resemble.
تَشَبَّهَ بِ	To imitate.
تَشَابَهَ	To resemble one another.
إِشْتَبَهَ	To be obscure.
إِشْتَبَهَ فِي	To be in doubt.
شِبْهٌ	A similar person or thing.
شَبَهٌ	Similarity; likeness.
وَجْهُ ٱلشَّبَهِ	Point of resemblance.
شُبْهَةٌ ج شُبُهَاتٌ	Doubt, suspicion.
شَبِيهٌ	Resembling, like.
اِشْتِبَاهٌ	Ambiguity; doubt.
تَشْبِيهٌ	Comparison; metaphor.
مُشْتَبِهٌ	Doubtful, obscure.
مُشَابَهَةٌ	Resemblance.
شَتَّ يَشِتُّ	To be scattered.
شَتَّ وَشَتَّتَ وَأَشَتَّ	To scatter.
تَشَتَّتَ	To be dispersed.
شَتٌّ وَشَتَاتٌ	Disunion.
شَتَّانَ	Great is the difference!
أَشْيَاءُ شَتَّى	Various things.
شَتْلَةٌ	Nursery-plant.
مَشْتَلٌ	Plant-nursery.
شَتَمَ يَشْتُمُ شَتْمًا	To revile.
شَتِيمَةٌ ج شَتَائِمُ	Defamation.
شَتِيمٌ وَمَشْتُومٌ	Reviled.
شَتَا يَشْتُو وَشَتَّى	To pass the winter.
شِتَاءٌ	Winter; rain.
شَتَوِيٌّ	Pertaining to winter.
شَاتٍ	Wintry; rainy.
مَشْتًى	Winter abode.
شَجَّ يَشُجُّ	To wound the head.
شَجَّةٌ	Wound in the head.

To become woody. شَجَّرَ

To quarrel with. شَاجَرَ مُشَاجَرَةً

To abound in trees. شَجَرَ

To dispute, quarrel. تَشَاجَرَ

Tree; shrub, bush. شَجَرٌ ج أَشْجَارٌ

A tree. شَجَرَةٌ

Abounding in trees. شَجِرٌ وَمُشْجِرٌ

Dispute, contest. مُشَاجَرَةٌ

To be brave. شَجُعَ يَشْجُعُ شَجَاعَةً

To encourage, embolden. شَجَّعَ

To take courage. تَشَجُّعٌ

Courage, bravery. شَجَاعَةٌ

Brave, bold. شُجَاعٌ ج شُجْعَانٌ

To grieve. Coo. شَجَنَ يَشْجُنُ شَجَنًا

Grief. شَجَنٌ ج شُجُون

To cause anguish. شَجَا يَشْجُو

To be grieved. شَجِيَ يَشْجَى شَجًا

Anxiety, grief. شَجًا وَشَجْوٌ

Grieved, anxious, sad. شَجٍ وَشَجِيٌّ

To be niggardly. شَحَّ يَشُحُّ شَحًّا

To contend together. تَشَاحَّ

Avarice, covetousness. شُحٌّ

Avaricious. شَحِيحٌ ج شِحَاحٌ

Incontestable. لا مُشَاحَّةَ في

To ask for alms, beg. شَحَذَ يَشْحَذُ

Mendicity. شِحَاذَةٌ

Importunate beggar. شَحَّاذٌ

Stye on the eyelid. شَحَّاذُ ٱلْعَيْنِ

To drag along. شَحَطَ يَشْحَطُ

Grease, lard, fat. شَحْمٌ ج شُحُومٌ

Lobe of the ear. شَحْمَةُ ٱلْأُذُنِ

To fill, load. شَحَنَ يَشْحَنُ وأَشْحَنَ بِ

To treat with enmity. شَاحَنَ

Freight, cargo. شَحْنٌ وَشَحْنَةٌ

Hatred, enmity. شَحْنَاءُ وَشَحِنَةٌ

Garrison. شِحْنَةٌ

Hatred, enmity. مُشَاحَنَةٌ

To micturate. شَخَّ يَشِخ شَخًّا

Urine.	شِخَاخٌ
To snore ; snort.	شخَرَيشخِرُ شَخِيراً
To gaze at.	شَخَصَ بِبَصَرِهِ إِلَى
To go from . . to . .	شَخَصَ مِنْ وَإِلَى
To distinguish.	شَخَصَ
To be distinct.	تَشَخَّصَ
Person, individual.	شَخْصٌ ج أَشْخَاصٌ
Diagnosis of (disease).	تَشخِيصٌ
To strap, bind.	شَدَّ يَشُدُّ شَدًّا
To bind fast, strengthen.	شَدَّدَ
To treat with severity.	شَدَّدَ عَلَى
To be strengthened.	تَشَدَّدَ وَٱشْتَدَّ
To be strong, intense.	إِشْتَدَّ
Violence, intensity.	شِدَّةٌ
Hardship, distress.	شِدَّةٌ ج شَدَائِدُ
Name of the sign (ّ).	شَدَّةٌ
Violent, strong.	شَدِيدٌ ج اشِدَّاءُ
Courageous, brave.	شَدِيدُ ٱلْبَأْسِ
More intense, stronger.	أَشَدُّ
Blacker.	أَشَدُّ سَوَاداً
More or most angry.	أَشَدُّ غَضَباً
Violence. Strength.	إِشْتِدَادٌ
Cheek.	شِدْقٌ
Deacon	شَدْيَاقٌ ج شَدَايِقَة
Diffuse in speech.	مُتَشَدِّقٌ
A young gazelle.	شَادِنٌ
To sing.	شَدَا يَشْدُو وَأَشْدَى
To be exceptional.	شَذَّ يَشُذُّ
Irregular, rare.	شَاذٌّ ج شَوَاذ
Irregularity ; rarity.	شُذُوذٌ
Anything bad, evil.	شَرٌّ ج شُرُورٌ
Wicked. Worse.'	شَرٌّ ج أَشْرَارٌ
A spark.	شَرَارَةٌ
Bad, wicked.	شَرِيرٌ ج أَشْرَارٌ
Very wicked.	شِرِّيرٌ ج شِرِّيرونَ
The Evil One, Satan.	أَلشِّرِّيرُ
To drink, swallow.	شَرِبَ يَشْرَبُ
To smoke tobacco.	شَرِبَ ٱلدخَّانَ

To saturate. شَرَّبَ

To absorb, imbibe. تَشَرَّبَ

Act of drinking. شِرْبٌ

Draught. Water-jug. شَرْبَةٌ

Drink, beverage. شَرَابٌ ج أَشْرِبَةٌ

Syrup. شَرَابٌ

Tassel. شَرَّابَةٌ ج شَرَارِيبُ

Moustache. شَارِبٌ ج شَوَارِبُ

Addicted to drink. شِرِّيبٌ

Inclination. مَشْرَبٌ ج مَشَارِبُ

To entangle, confuse. شَرْبَكَ

A species of fir. شَرْبِينٌ

To baste. شَرَّجَ

Sesame-oil. شِيرَجٌ وَسِيرَجٌ

To explain. شَرَحَ يَشْرَحُ

To dissect. شَرَّحَ

To be enlarged. Happy. إِنْشَرَحَ

Commentary. شَرْحٌ ج شُرُوحٌ

Commentator. شَارِحٌ ج شُرَّاحٌ

Long slice of meat. شَرِيحٌ وَشَرِيحَةٌ

Dissection. تَشْرِيحٌ

Anatomy. عِلْمُ ٱلتَّشْرِيحِ

Anatomist. مُشَرِّحٌ ج مُشَرِّحُونَ

Prime of youth. شَرْخٌ

To flee, take fright. شَرَدَ يَشْرُدُ

To depart from. شَرَدَ عَنْ

Roaming, fugitive. شَارِدٌ

Strange, unusual. شَوَارِدُ

Small number of men. شِرْذِمَةٌ

To be ill-natured. شَرِسَ يَشْرَسُ

Ill-natured. شَرِسٌ

Sticking-paste. شِرَاسٌ وَسِرَاسٌ

Extremity of a rib. شُرْسُوفٌ

Epigastric region. أَلْقِسْمُ ٱلشَّرَاسِيفِيُّ

Root. شِرْسٌ ج شُرُوسٌ

A fringe. شَرْشَرَةٌ ج شَرَاشِرُ

Bed-sheet. شَرْشَفٌ ج شَرَاشِفُ

To stipulate. شَرَطَ يَشْرُطُ وَٱشْتَرَطَ

شَرَطَ وشَرَّطَ	To make incisions.
شَارَطَ وتَشَارَطَ	To stipulate with.
شَرْطٌ ج شُرُوطٌ	Condition, stipulation, contract.
شَرْطِيٌّ ج شُرْطَةٌ	Guard's-man.
شَرِيطٌ ج شُرُط	Wire ; tape.
مِشْرَط ج مَشَارِط	Bistoury.
مُشَارَطَةٌ	Stipulation. Betting.
شَرَعَ يَشْرَعُ واشْتَرَعَ	To make a law.
شَرَعَ شُرُوعاً	To begin.
شَرَعَ يَقُولُ	He began to say.
شَرَعَ فِي	To engage in an affair.
شَرْعٌ	Divine or religious law.
شَرْعِيٌّ	Legitimate, legal.
شَارِعٌ ج شَوَارِعُ	Main street. Legislator.
شِرَاعٌ ج أَشْرِعَةٌ	A sail.
شَرِيعَةٌ ج شَرَائِعُ	Law, statute.
أَلشَّرِيعَةُ	Jordan (river).
تَثْنِيَةُ الاشْتِرَاعِ	Deuteronomy.
مُشْتَرِعٌ	Legislator.
شَرُفَ يَشْرُفُ	To be noble.
شَرَفَ يَشْرُفُ شَرَفاً	To be high.
شَرَّفَ	To exalt, honour.
أَشْرَفَ عَلَى	To be near to ; overtop.
تَشَرَّفَ	To be honoured.
شَرَفٌ ج أَشْرَافٌ	Elevated place. Eminence.
شَرَفٌ	Honour, nobility ; height.
شُرْفَةٌ ج شُرُفَاتٌ	Battlement.
شَرِيفٌ ج أَشْرَافٌ	Noble.
أَلْخَطُّ الشَّرِيفُ	An edict by the Sultan's own hand.
مُشْرِفٌ	Projecting, overlooking.
شَرَقَ يَشْرُقُ	To rise (sun).
شَرَّقَ	To go eastward.
أَشْرَقَ	To rise, shine, beam.
شَرْق	East ; Orient.
شَرْقِيٌّ	Eastern ; Oriental.
مَشْرِقٌ ج مَشَارِق	East ; Orient. Levant.
شَارَكَ مُشَارَكَةً	To share with.
أَشْرَكَ فِي	To take a partner.

To be a polytheist. أَشْرَكَ بِاللهِ

To share. شَارَكَ وَٱشْتَرَكَ

Polytheism. شِرْكٌ

Snare. شَرَكٌ ج أَشْرَاكٌ

Company; partnership. شُرْكَةٌ

Shoe-string. شِرَاكٌ ج شُرُكٌ

Partner. شَرِيكٌ ج شُرَكَاءُ

Polytheist, idolater. مُشْرِكٌ

Associate. Subscriber. مُشْتَرِكٌ

Common to several. مُشْتَرَكٌ

To split, slit. شَرَمَ يَشْرُمُ شَرْماً

To be split. شَرِمَ وَتَشَرَّمَ وَٱنْشَرَمَ

Split, rent. شَرْمٌ ج شُرُومٌ

Cocoon. شَرْنَقَةٌ ج شَرَانِقُ

To be greedy for. شَرِهَ يَشْرَهُ إِلَى

Inordinate desire. شَرَهٌ وَشَرَاهَةٌ

Greedy. Glutton. شَرِهٌ وَشَرْهَانُ

Trowsers. شِرْوَالٌ وَسِرْوَالٌ

To buy. شَرَى يَشْرِي شِرَاءً وَشِرًى

To buy. إِشْتَرَى

Purchase. شِرَاءٌ وَشِرًى

Nettle-rash; urticaria. شَرًى

Artery. شِرْيَانٌ ج شَرَايِينُ

Buyer. شَارٍ وَمُشْتَرٍ ج شُرَاةٌ

Jupiter (planet). أَلْمُشْتَرِي

To look askance at. شَزَرَ يَشْزُرُ شَزْراً إِلَى

To be distant. شَسَعَ يَشْسَعُ شُسُوعاً

Very remote, distant. شَاسِعٌ

Water-closet. (شِشْمَةٌ)

Sample. (شِشْنَةٌ)

Fish-hook. شِصٌّ ج شُصُوصٌ

To go beyond bounds. شَطَّ فِي

Shore, bank. شَطٌّ ج شُطُوطٌ

Excess. Injustice. شَطَطٌ

Shore. Coast. شَاطِئٌ ج شَوَاطِئُ

To cut into strips. Deviate. شَطَبَ يَشْطُبُ

To divide, halve. شَطَرَ يَشْطُرُ

To balve with another. شَاطَرَ

شَطْرٌ ج شُطُورٌ	Half ; part.
شَاطِرٌ ج شُطَّارٌ	Wicked ; sharper.
مَشْطُورٌ	Divided into halves.
مُشَاطِرٌ	Adjacent, neighbouring.
شَطْرَنْجٌ	Chess.
شَطَفَ يَشْطُفُ شَطْفًا	To wash ; rinse.
شَيْطَنَ وَتَشَيْطَنَ	To be rebellious.
شَيْطَنَةٌ	Devilishness.
شَيْطَانٌ ج شَيَاطِينُ	Satan, devil.
شَظِيَّةٌ ج شَظَايَا	Splinter. Fibula.
شَعَّ يَشُعُّ شَعَاعًا	To disperse.
شَعَّ يَشِعُّ	To be dispersed.
أَشَعَّ	To emit rays.
شُعَاعٌ ج أَشِعَّةٌ وَشُعَاعٌ	Sun-beam.
تَشَعَّبَ وَٱنْشَعَبَ	To ramify.
شِعْبٌ ج شِعَابٌ	Mountain-pass.
شَعْبٌ ج شُعُوبٌ	People, nation.
شُعْبَةٌ ج شُعَبٌ	Branch. Portion.
شَعْبَانُ	The eighth lunar month.
مُتَشَعِّبٌ	Ramified.
شَعْبَذَ	To juggle.
مُشَعْبِذٌ	Juggler.
شَعِثَ وَتَشَعَّثَ	To be dishevelled.
شَعَرَ يَشْعُرُ بِ	To know ; feel.
أَشْعَرَهُ بِ	To inform.
شِعْرٌ ج أَشْعَارٌ	Poetry, verse.
شَعْرٌ ج شُعُورٌ	Hair.
شَعْرَةٌ ج شَعَرَاتٌ	A hair.
شِعْرِيٌّ	Poetical.
أَلشِّعْرَى	Sirius, Dog-Star.
لَيْتَ شِعْرِي	Would that I knew !
أَشْعَرُ ج شُعْرٌ	Hairy, shaggy.
شِعَارٌ وَشَعَائِرُ	Rites.
شَعْرِيَّةٌ ج شَعْرِيَّاتٌ	Trellis-work.
شَاعِرٌ ج شُعَرَاءُ	Poet.
شُعُورٌ	Knowing, perceiving.
شَعِيرٌ	Barley.
مَشْعَرٌ ج مَشَاعِرُ	Sense (sight, &c.)

To kindle. شَعَلَ يَشْعَلُ وَشَعَّلَ وَاشْعَلَ

To be kindled. شَعَلَ وَاَشْتَعَلَ

To be enraged. إِشْتَعَلَ غَضَبًا

Firebrand, flame. شُعْلَةٌ ج شُعَلٌ

Burning wick. شَعِيلَةٌ ج شُعُلٌ

Conflagration. إِشْتِعَالٌ

Lamp ; torch. مِشْعَلٌ ج مَشَاعِلُ

Palm-Sunday. عِيدُ ٱلشَّعَانِينِ

To juggle. شَعْوَذَ

Jugglery. شَعْوَذَةٌ

Juggler. مُشَعْوِذٌ

To stir up discord, evil. شَغَبَ يَشْغَبُ

Discord, tumult ; revolt. شَغْبٌ

To inflame with love. شَغَفَ حُبًّا

To be smitten. شَغِفَ بِ

Passionate love. شَغَفٌ

Passionately taken up. مَشْغُوفٌ

To occupy. شَغَلَ يَشْغَلُ

To divert from. شَغَلَ عَنْ

To busy, occupy much. شَغَّلَ

To be occupied. To act. إِشْتَغَلَ

Occupation, work. شُغْلٌ ج أَشْغَالٌ

Busying affair. شَاغِلٌ ج شَوَاغِلُ

Occupation. إِشْتِغَال

Occupied ; busy. مَشْغُولٌ

To be very fine, transparent. شَفَّ يَشِفُّ

Thin, fine dress. شَفٌّ ج شُفُوفٌ

Transparent. شَفَّافٌ

Transparency. شُفُوفٌ

Edge, border. شُفْرٌ ج أَشْفَارٌ

Blade. شَفْرَةٌ ج شِفَارٌ

Border of a valley. شَفِيرُ ٱلْوَادِي

To plead, intercede. Couple, double. شَفَعَ يَشْفَعُ

To make double. شَفَّعَ

Right of pre-emption. شُفْعَةٌ

Intercession, mediation. شَفَاعَةٌ

Intercessor. شَافِعٌ وَشَفِيعٌ ج شُفَعَاءُ

To pity. شَفَقَ يَشْفِقُ وَأَشْفَقَ عَلَى

شَفَقٌ	Evening twilight.
شَفَقَة	Compassion ; tenderness.
شَفُوق وَشَفِيق	Compasionate.
شافَهَ	To speak mouth to mouth.
شَفَةٌ ج شَفَاةٌ وَشَفَهَاتٌ وَشَفَوَات	Lip.
شَفَهِيٌّ وَشَفَوِيٌّ	Labiat.
مشافهةً وَشفاهاً	By word of mouth.
شَفَى يَشْفِي شِفَاءً مِن	To cure, heal.
اشْفَى على	To be very near.
اشْفَى	To recover (one's health).
إِسْتَشْفَى	To seek a cure.
شِفَاءٌ	Cure, recovery.
شَفَا	Brink, edge, extremity.
شَافٍ	Curing, healing.
جَوَابٌ شَافٍ	A clear answer.
مستَشْفي وَدَارُ الشِّفَاءِ	Hospital.
شَقَّ يَشُقُّ شَقًّا	To split, cleave.
شَقَّ مَشَقَّةً على	To trouble, distress.
شَقَّ الْعَصَا	To rebel.
شَقَّقَ	To split into pieces
إِنشَقَّ	To be split or separated.
شَقٌّ ج شُقُوق	Split, rent ; crack.
شَقٌّ و مَشَقَّة	Great hardship.
شِق	Half, one side of a thing.
شِقَّةٌ ج شِقَق	Piece of cloth.
شَاقٌّ	Troublesome, hard.
شِقَاق	Separation, discord.
شَقِيقٌ ج اشقّاء	Full brother.
شَقَائِقُ النُّعْمَانِ	Red anemone.
إِشْتِقَاق	Derivation of a word.
إِنْشِقَاقٌ	Separation, division.
مَشَقَّةٌ ج مَشَاقّ	Great hardship.
مُشْتَقّ	Derived (word).
شُقْرَةٌ	Light red, sorrel colour.
أَشْقَرُ	Of fair complexion, sorrel.
شَقِرَّاق	The green wood pecker.
شَقْشَقَةُ اللّسان	Verbosity.

To pile up.	شَقَعَ يَشْقَعُ شَقْعاً
To split, cut into pieces.	شَقَّفَ
Earthen pot ; piece.	شَقَفَةٌ ج شَقَفٌ
To lift up.	شَقَلَ يَشْقُلُ شَقْلاً
To be miserable.	شَقِيَ يَشْقَى
To labour, toil.	شَقِيَ فِي
To struggle with.	شَاقَى
To make miserable.	أَشْقَى
Misery.	شَقَا وَشَقَاء وَشَقَاوَةٌ
Miserable.	شَقِيٌّ ج أَشْقِيَاء
To doubt.	شَكَّ يَشُكُّ وَتَشَكَّكَ فِي
To pierce through.	شَكَّ
To throw into doubt.	شَكَّكَ فِي
Uncertainty, doubt.	شَكٌّ ج شُكُوكٌ
Thrust (of a lance, &c.)	شَكَّةٌ
Armed.	شَاكُّ السِّلَاحِ
Doubtful, uncertain.	مَشْكُوكٌ فِيهِ
To thank.	شَكَرَ يَشْكُرُ وَتَشَكَّرَ لِ
Thanks.	شُكْرٌ وَشُكْرَانٌ ج شُكُورٌ
Thankful.	شَاكِرٌ وَشَكُورٌ
Hemlock.	شَوْكَرَانٌ وَشَيْكَرَانٌ
To be stubborn.	شَكُسَ يَشْكُسُ
Refractory.	شَكْسٌ وَشَكِسٌ
To be obscure.	شَكَلَ يَشْكُلُ وَاشْكَلَ عَلَى
To tether, tie up.	شَكَلَ وَشَكَّلَ
To resemble.	شَاكَلَ
To be fashioned, shaped.	تَشَكَّلَ
To resemble one another.	تَشَاكَلَ
To be ambiguous.	إِشْتَكَلَ
To deem dubious.	إِسْتَشْكَلَ
Likeness ; form. Fashion. Kind, sort. Vowel point.	شَكْلٌ ج أَشْكَالٌ
Tether.	شِكَالٌ ج شُكُلٌ
Side. Way.	شَاكِلَةٌ ج شَوَاكِلُ
Resemblance.	مُشَاكَلَةٌ وَتَشَاكُلٌ
Difficulty.	مُشْكِلٌ ج مَشَاكِلُ
Mouth-bit.	شَكِيمَةٌ
To complain to.	شَكَا يَشْكُو إِلَى

To complain of pain. شكا ألماً

To complain. تشكّى وآشتكى إلى

Complaint ; accusation. شكاية

Plaintiff. شاكٍ ومشتكٍ

Accused. مشكوٌّ ومُشتكى عليه

To be paralyzed. شلَّ يشلُّ وشلَّ

To paralyze, disable. أشلّ

Paralysis. شلل

Cataract. شلّالٌ ج شلّالاتٌ

To strip, undress. شلَح يشلَحُ

To strip, plunder. شلّح

Mantle. مَشلَحٌ

Body after decay. شِلْوٌ ج أشلاءٌ

Darnel-grass. شيلَمٌ

To smell. شمّ يشمّ شمّاً

To make one smell. شمّمَ وأشمّ

Sense of smell. شمّ

A fragrant, striped melon. شمّامٌ

To rejoice شمِتَ يشمت شماتة ب
at the affliction of an enemy.

To disappoint. شمّتَ

To be high, lofty. شمخ يشمخ

To be high ; be proud. تشامخ

High ; proud. شامخ ج شُمَّخ

Pride, haughtiness. تشامُخٌ

Proud, haughty. مُتشامِخٌ

To tuck up a garment. شمَر يشمُرُ

To be ready for. تشمّرَ وآنشمرَ ل

Fennel. شمْرة وشمارٌ

To abhor. شمز يشمز من

To shrink from. اشمأزّ آشمئزازاً

To be sunny. شمِس يشمُسُ وأشمس

To be restive. شمَس يشمُسُ

To expose in the sun. شمّس

Sun. شمسٌ ج شموسٌ

Solar. شمسيٌّ

Umbrella ; sun-shade. شمسيّة

Deacon. شمّاسٌ ج شمامِسة

Restive, refractory. شمُوسٌ

مُشَمَّس	Exposed to the sun.
شَمَطٌ	Whiteness, hoariness.
أَشْمَطُ	Gray-haired, graizzled.
شَمَّعَ	To wax ; cover with wax.
شَمْعٌ ج شُمُوعٌ	Wax.
شَمْعَةٌ ج شَمَعَاتٌ	Wax-candle.
مُشَمَّعٌ	Waxed. Oil-cloth.
شَمَعْدَانٌ	Candlestick.
شَمَلَ يَشْمُلُ	To shift to north.
شَمَلَ يَشْمُلُ	To take the left side.
شَمَلَ يَشْمُلُ	To include, contain.
إِشْتَمَلَ عَلَى	To comprise, contain.
شَمْلٌ	Union.
شَامِلٌ	Comprehensive ; general.
شَمَالٌ	Left side ; north.
شَمَالِيٌّ	Northern, northerly.
مَشْمُولٌ	Endowed. Included.
شَمَنْدَرٌ وَشَمَنْدُرٌ	Beet (root).
شَنَّ وَأَشَنَّ ٱلْغَارَةَ عَلَى	To attack.
شَنَأَ وَشَنِئَ يَشْنَأُ	To hate, detest.
شَنْءٌ	Hatred, detestation.
شَانِئٌ ج شُنَاءٌ	Hater, enemy.
مَشْنُوءٌ	Hated ; hateful.
شَنَبٌ ج اشْنَابٌ	Moustache.
شُنْبُلٌ ج شَنَابِلُ	A grain-measure.
تَشَنُّجٌ	Spasmodic contraction.
شِنْشِنَةٌ ج شَنَاشِنُ	Nature, disposition.
شَنُعَ يَشْنُعُ شَنَاعَةً	To be bad.
شَنَّعَ شَنْعاً	To disgrace, revile.
شَنَّعَ عَلَيْهِ	To accuse him of evil.
إِسْتَشْنَعَ	To regard as foul.
شُنْعَةٌ وَشَنَاعَةٌ	Infamy, ugliness.
شَنِعٌ شَنِيعٌ وَأَشْنَعُ	Foul, ugly.
شَنَّفَ	To embellish.
شَنْفٌ ج شُنُوفٌ	Ear-ring.
شَنَقَ يَشْنِقُ شَنْقاً	To hang.
شَنْقٌ	Hanging.
شَنِقٌ وَشَانِقٌ	Longing, yearning.

Cord, rope.	شِنَاقٌ ج أَشْنِقَة
Gibbet, gallows.	مِشْنَقَةٌ ج مَشَانِقُ
Hanged.	مَشْنُوق
Gray colour.	شُبْهَةٌ وَشَهَبٌ
Meteor.	شِهَابٌ ج شُهُبٌ
Gray.	أَشْهَبُ م شَهْبَاء ج شُهْبٌ
Aleppo.	أَلشَّهْبَاء
To witness, be present.	شَهِدَ يَشْهَدُ
To witness against.	شَهِدَ يَشْهَدُ على
To bear witness to.	شَهِدَ بِ
To be an eye-witness ; see.	شَاهَدَ
Call to witness.	أَشْهَدَ وَٱسْتَشْهَدَ
To die as a martyr.	أُسْتُشْهِدَ
Honeycomb.	شُهْدٌ ج شِهَادٌ
Eye-witness.	شَاهِدٌ ج شُهُودٌ
Testimony. Diploma.	شَهَادَةٌ
Martyrdom.	شَهَادَةٌ وَٱسْتِشْهَادٌ
Witness. Martyr.	شَهِيدٌ ج شُهَدَاء
Assembly. Aspect.	مَشْهَدٌ
Vision, sight, scene.	مُشَاهَدَة
To make public.	شَهَرَ يَشْهَرُ
To make known, publish.	أَشْهَرَ
To become known ; be celebrated ; notorius.	إِشْتَهَرَ
Month.	شَهْرٌ ج شُهُورٌ وَأَشْهُرٌ
Celebrity, fame, repute.	شُهْرَة
Celebrated, notorious.	شَهِيرٌ
Well-known.	مَشْهُورٌ ج مَشَاهِيرُ
According to usage.	على ٱلْمَشْهُورِ
To draw the breath.	شَهَقَ يَشْهَقُ
A single cry.	شَهْقَةٌ
High, lofty.	شَاهِقٌ ج شَوَاهِقُ
Inspiration and expiration in breathing.	أَلشَّهِيقُ وَٱلزَّفِيرُ
A mixture of two colours.	شَهَلٌ
To be sagacious.	شَهُمَ يَشْهُمُ
Honourable.	شَهْمٌ ج شِهَامٌ
Sagacity. Honour.	شَهَامَةٌ
Falcon.	شَاهِين ج

شَهَا يَشْهُو	To crave for.
شَهَّى	To excite a desire.
إِشْتَهَى	To desire eagerly.
شَهْوَةٌ ج شَهَوَات	Strong desire, appetite, passion, lust.
شَهِيٌّ وَمُشْتَهًى	Desired, pleasant.
شَهَوَانِيٌّ	Sensual.
أَشْهَى	More desirable, delicious.
إِشْتِهَاء	Desire, craving.
مُشْتَهًى ج مُشْتَهَيَاتٌ	Craved.
شَابَ يَشُوبُ شَوْبًا	To mix.
شَائِبَةٌ ج شَوَائِب	Blemish.
شُوحَةٌ	A species of kite.
أَشَارَ إِلَى	To point out or at.
أَشَارَ عَلَى ب	To counsel, advise.
شَاوَرَ وَاسْتَشَارَ	To consult.
تَشَاوَرَ عَلَى	To consult together.
مَشْوَرَةٌ وَمَشُورَةٌ	Consultation.
أَهْلُ ٱلشُّورَى	Councillors.
مَجْلِسُ ٱلشُّورَى	Council.
إِشَارَةٌ	Sign ; signal ; allusion.
إِسْمُ الإِشَارَةِ	Demonstrative pronoun.
مُشَارٌ إِلَيْهِ	Indicated, referred to.
مُشِيرٌ	Councillor ; minister.
مُسْتَشَارٌ	Councillor.
شَوْرَبَةٌ	Soup.
شَوَّشَ	To trouble, confuse.
تَشَوَّشَ	To be confused ; sick.
شَاشٌ	Thin muslin.
شَاوِيشٌ (جَاوِيشٌ)	Sergeant.
شُوَشَةٌ	Hair of head.
تَشْوِيشٌ	Confusion. Sickness.
مُشَوَّشٌ	Confused. Ill.
أَشْوَصُ م شَوْصَاء	Squint-eyed.
شَافَ يَشُوفُ شَوْفًا	To see.
شَوَّفَ	To show.
شَاقَ وَشَوَّقَ إِلَى	To fill with longing.
تَشَوَّقَ وَاشْتَاقَ إِلَى	To long for.

شَوْقٌ ج أَشْوَاق Strong desire.
شَائِقٌ Desirable, charming.
مُشْتَاقٌ Ardently longing.
شَاكَ وَشَوَّكَ To pierce with a thorn.
شَوْكٌ ج أَشْوَاكٌ Thorns, prickles.
شَوْكَةٌ A thorn, sting.
شَالٌ ج شَالَاتٌ Shawl.
شَوْلٌ ج أَشْوَالٌ Desert.
شُوَالٌ ج شُوَالَاتٌ Large sack.
شَوَّالٌ The tenth lunar month.
شُونَةٌ ج شُوَن Watch-tower. Barn.
شَوَّهَ To disfigure.
تَشَوَّهَ To be ugly, disfigured.
شَوَهٌ Deformity, ugliness.
أَشْوَهُ م شَوْهَاء Deformed ugly.
شَاهٌ King ; Shah, (*Persian*).
شَاهَانِيٌّ Royal, imperial.
شَاةٌ ج شَاء وشِيَاهٌ Sheep, lamb.
شَوٌّ Ugly, deformed. Stupid.

شَوَى يَشْوِي To roast, broil (meat).
إِنْشَوَى To be roasted, grilled.
شِوِي وَمَشْوِيٌّ Roasted, grilled.
مِشْوًى ومِشْوَاةٌ Gridiron.
شَاءَ يَشَاءُ To will, wish, desire.
شَيْءٌ ج أَشْيَاءُ Thing, something.
شَيْئاً فشيئاً Gradually.
(شُوَيَّة) A small thing ; a little.
مَشِيئَةٌ Will, wish, desire.
شَابَ يَشِيبُ To become gray.
أَشَابَ وَشَيَّبَ To make gray.
شَيْبٌ وَمَشِيبٌ Old age.
شَيْبَةٌ White or hoary beard.
شَائِبٌ وأَشْيَبُ Hoary ; old.
شيت Cotton-prints.
شِيحٌ Artemesia ; wormwood.
شَاخَ يَشِيخُ وَشَيَّخَ To grow old.
شَيْخٌ ج شُيُوخ Old man, Sheikh.
شَيْخُ الإِسْلَامُ Religious Chief of the Moslems.

Old age.	شَيْخُوخَةٌ
Republic. Senate.	مشيَخَةٌ
To build up.	شادَ يَشِيدُ وَشَيَّدَ
High, elevated.	مَشِيدٌ وَمُشَيَّدٌ
To be slightly burnt.	شَاطَ يَشِيطُ
To get angry.	إِسْتَشاطَ عَلَى
Satan, devil.	شَيْطانٌ
Inflamed by anger.	مُسْتَشِيطٌ
To be spread abroad.	شاعَ يَشِيعُ
To publish.	شاعَ ب وَأَشَاعَ
To see a guest off.	شَيَّعَ
To escort, follow.	شَايَعَ
To publish the news.	أَشاعَ آلْخَبَرَ
Party, sect ; the Shites.	شِيعة
A Shite.	شِيعِيٌّ
Public ; common.	شَائِعٌ وَمُشاعٌ
Partisan of.	مُشايِعٌ لِ
To lift up, carry.	شَالَ يَشِيلُ شَيْلاً
To trade of a porter.	شِيَالَةٌ
A porter.	شَيَّالٌ
Black spot ; mole.	شَامَةٌ ج شَامَاتٌ
Syria.	أَلشَّامُ
Character, nature.	شِيمَةٌ ج شِيَمٌ
Of noble qualities.	كَرِيمُ آلشِّيَمِ
To disgrace.	شَانَ يَشِينُ شَيْناً
A disgraceful thing.	شَيْنٌ
Tea.	شَايٌ

ص

ص	As a numeral sign=90.
صَبَّ يَصُبُّ صبًّا	To pour out.
صَبَّ عَلَى	To dart or rush upon.
صَبَّ يَصَبُّ صَبَابَةً	To be in love.
أَصَبَّ	To descend.
إِنْصَبَّ	To be poured out. Incline.
صَبٌّ	Longing lover.
صَبَّةٌ	Catarrh of the nose.
صَبَابَةٌ	Excessive love or desire.
صَبِيبٌ	Poured forth.
مَصَبٌّ	Mouth of a river.
صَابِئٌ ج صَابِئُونَ	Sabian.
صَبُحَ يَصْبُحُ	To be handsome.
صَبَّحَ	To bid good morning.
أَصْبَحَ	To rise in the morning.
أَصْبَحَ عَالِمًا	He became learned.
أَصْبَحَ يَفْعَلُ	To take to doing.
صُبْحٌ ج أَصْبَاحٌ	Dawn. Morning.
صُبْحَةٌ	Early part of forenoon.
صَبَاحٌ	Morning.
صَبَاحَةٌ	Beauty, comeliness.
صَبِيحَةٌ	Morning.
مِصْبَاحٌ ج مَصَابِيحُ	Lamp.
صَبَرَ يَصْبِرُ	To be patient. Confine.
صَبَّرَ	To ask one to be patient. Embalm Ballast.
تَصَبَّرَ وَاصْطَبَرَ	To be patient.
صَبْرٌ	Patience, endurance.
صَبِرٌ وَصَبْرٌ	Aloe. Aloe-plant.
صَابِرٌ ج صَابِرُونَ	Patient.
صَبَّارٌ وَصَبُورٌ	Very patient.

Cactus.	صُبَّيْرٌ
Ballast (of a ship).	صَابُورَةٌ
A kind of basket.	صَابُورِيَّةٌ
Finger, toe.	أُصْبُعٌ ج أَصَابِعُ
Gridiron.	مِصْبَعٌ
To dye, colour.	صَبَغَ يَصْبِغُ
To be baptized ; dyed.	إِصْطَبَغَ
Dye ; paint.	صِبْغٌ وَصِبَاغٌ
Dye. Religion. Baptism.	صِبْغَةٌ
Dyer.	صَبَّاغٌ
Art of dyeing.	صِبَاغَةٌ
A dye-house.	مَصْبَغَةٌ
To wash with soap.	صَبَنَ وَصَوْبَنَ
Soap-maker.	صَبَّانٌ
Soap.	صَابُونٌ
Soap factory.	مَصْبَنَةٌ
To incline to, long for.	صَبَا ـُ إِلَى
Light east-wind.	ألصَّبَا
Youth, boyhood. Love.	ألصِّبَا
Youth.	صَبْوَةٌ
Boy, youth.	صَبِيٌّ ج صِبْيَانٌ
Young woman.	صَبِيَّةٌ ج صَبَايَا
To recover from disease. To be sound ; true.	صَحَّ يَصِحُّ
To cure a sick person. Correct ; render sound.	صَحَّحَ تَصْحِيحًا
Health. Soundness. Truth.	صِحَّة
Healthy, sound. True.	صَحِيحٌ ج أَصِحَّاءُ
Chapter.	إِصْحَاحٌ ج إِصْحَاحَاتٌ
Correction.	تَصْحِيحٌ
To accompany.	صَحِبَ يَصْحَبُ وَصَاحَبَ
To take the part of.	تَصَحَّبَ لِ
To associate with.	تَصَاحَبَ مَعَ
To associate together.	إِصْطَحَبَ
Companionship.	صُحْبَةٌ
Friend. Owner.	صَاحِبٌ ج أَصْحَابٌ
Wealthy.	صَاحِبُ مَالٍ
Accompanied.	مَصْحُوبٌ
Desert.	صَحْرَاءُ ج صَحْرَاوَاتٌ

To alter a word. صحّفَ تَصْحِيفاً
Large plate. صَحْفَةٌ ج صِحَافٌ
A written page. صَحِيفَةٌ ج صَحَائِفُ
The Koran. مُصْحَفٌ ج مَصَاحِفُ
Plate (for food). صحْنٌ ج صحونٌ
Court (of a house). صحْنُ الدَّار
To become clear (sky) صَحَا يَصْحُو وَصَحِيَ يَصْحَى
To recover consciousness after intoxication or sleep.
To rouse. أصحى
Fair weather ; clear sky. صَحْوٌ
Mental clearness. صَحْوَةٌ
Clear (sky) ; conscious. صَاحٍ
To shout, clamour. صخبَ
Clamourous. صخِبٌ وَصَخُوبٌ
Rock. صخْرٌ وَصَخْرَةٌ ج صُخُورٌ
Rocky ; stony. صخِرٌ وَمُصْخِرٌ
To turn away from. صَدَّ يَصُدُّ عَنْ
To oppose ; prevent. صَدَّ صَدًّا
Aversion ; opposition. صَدٌّ

Subject in hand. صَدَدٌ
Pus ; matter. صَدِيدٌ
To become rusty. صَدِئَ يَصْدَأُ
To confront ; face. تصدَّى لِ
Rust. صَدَأٌ
To sing. صَدَحَ يَصْدَحُ
Singer. صَادِحٌ
To take place ; occur. صَدَرَ ـُ
To proceed from. صَدَرَ مِنْ
To arise, result from. صَدَرَ عَنْ
To go to. صَدَرَ إِلَى
To begin (a book) with. صَدَّر بِ
To show forth ; issue. أَصْدَرَ
Chest ; bosom. صَدْرٌ ج صُدُورٌ
The first part. Chief.
Prime Minister. اَلصَّدْرُ الأَعْظَم
Vest. صُدْرِيَّةٌ صَدَارَةٌ
The office of Prime Minister. صَدَارَة
Going out. صَادِرٌ
(*opp. to* وارد coming in).

Origin ; source. Noun of action. مَصْدَرٌ ج مَصَادِرُ

To have a sprain. صَدِعَ وَصُدِّعَ

To trouble ; annoy. صَدَّعَ

To be sprained. إِنْصَدَعَ

Fissure. Sprain. صَدْعٌ ج صُدُوعٌ

Headache. صُدَاعٌ

To incline to. صَدَغَ يَصْدَغُ إِلَى

Temple ; temporal region. صُدْغٌ ج أَصْدَاغٌ

To meet by chance. صَدَفَ يَصْدُفُ

To encounter. صَادَفَ مُصَادَفَةً

To happen by chance. تَصَدَّفَ

To meet together. تَصَادَفَ

Sea-shells. صَدَفٌ

A see-shell. صَدَفَةٌ ج صَدَفَاتٌ

Chance. صُدْفَةٌ ج صُدَفٌ

To say the truth. صَدَقَ يَصْدُقُ

It applies correctly to. يَصْدُقُ عَلَى

To believe. Verify. صَدَّقَ

To treat as a friend. صَادَقَ

To ratify, confirm. صَادَقَ عَلَى

To give alms, charity. تَصَدَّقَ

Truth; veracity ; sincerity. صِدْقٌ

Alms ; charity. صَدَقَةٌ ج صَدَقَاتٌ

Dower given to a wife. صَدَاقٌ

True friendship. صَدَاقَةٌ

True, sincere. صَادِقٌ

True friend. صَدِيقٌ ج أَصْدِقَاءُ

Righteous. صِدِّيقٌ ج صِدِّيقُونَ

More, most, true. أَصْدَقُ

Belief ; faith. Verification. تَصْدِيقٌ

Believer. Verifying. Confirming. مُصَدِّقٌ

One who gives alms. مُتَصَدِّقٌ

An apothecary's trade. صَيْدَلَةٌ

Druggist. صَيْدَلَانِيٌّ ج صَيَادِلَةٌ

A pharmacy. صَيْدَلِيَّةٌ

To strike ; repel. صَدَمَ يَصْدِمُ

To dash against ; thrust. صَادَمَ

To collide. تَصَادَمَ وَٱصْطَدَمَ

Shock, collision. صَدْمَةٌ

To return an echo. أَصْدَى إِصْدَاءً

Echo ; sound. صَدًى ج أَصْدَاءٌ

To tie up. صَرَّ يَصُرُّ صَرًّا

Creak ; chirp ; tingle. صَرَّ يَصِرُّ

To persist in. أَصَرَّ عَلَى

Parcel ; packet. صُرَّةٌ ج صُرَرٌ

Persistence. إِصْرَارٌ

Grating noise. صَرِيرٌ

To be pure, clear. صَرُحَ يَصْرُحُ

To make clear proclaim. صَرَّحَ

Pure, clear. Explicit. صَرِيحٌ

Clearness. Purity. صَرَاحَةٌ

Clear expression. تَصْرِيحٌ

To cry out. صَرَخَ يَصْرُخُ

A loud cry. صَرْخَةٌ

Cries, screams. صُرَاخٌ وَصَرِيخٌ

Crying out. صَارِخٌ

Intense cold. صَرْصَرٌ

A cockroach. صُرْصُرٌ وَصُرْصُورٌ

Violent, cold wind. رِيحٌ صَرْصَرٌ

Way ; path. صِرَاطٌ

To strike down. صَرَعَ يَصْرَعُ

To have a fit. صُرِعَ

To wrestle. صَارَعَ وَتَصَارَعَ

To be thrown down. إِنْصَرَعَ

Epilepsy. صَرْعٌ

Epileptic. صَرِيعٌ وَمَصْرُوعٌ

Hemistich. مِصْرَاعٌ ج مَصَارِيعُ
Half of a folding door.

Wrestler, combatant. مُصَارِعٌ

To send away ; صَرَفَ يَصْرِفُ
change or spend (money).

To avert from. صَرَفَ عَنْ

To turn him to. صَرَفَهُ إِلَى

To conjugate, decline. صَرَّفَ

To commit to. صَرَّفَ فِي

To be inflected. تَصَرَّفَ

Severity.	صَرامَةٌ
Shoe.	(صُرْمَايَةٌ ج صَرَامِيٌّ)
The past year.	اَلْعَامُ ٱلْمُنْصَرِمُ
Mast.	صَارٍ وَصَارِيَةٌ ج صوَارٍ
Platform.	مِصْطَبَةٌ ج مَصَاطِبُ
To be difficult.	صَعُبَ يَصْعُبُ
To make difficult.	صَعَّبَ وَتَصَعَّبَ
To find difficult.	إِسْتَصْعَبَ
To be difficult.	تَصَعَّبَ وَاسْتَصْعَبَ
Difficult, hard.	صَعْبٌ ج صِعَابٌ
Difficulty.	صُعُوبَةٌ
Difficulties, troubles.	مَصَاعِبُ
Thyme.	صَعْتَرٌ (أَوْ سَعْتَرٌ)
To ascend.	صَعِدَ يَصْعَدُ صُعُوداً
To take or carry up.	صَعِدَ بِ
To cause to ascend.	أَصْعَدَ
Distress, calamity.	صَعْدَاءُ
Sighing, deep sigh.	صُعَدَاءُ
Henceforth.	مِنَ ٱلآنَ فَصَاعِداً

To carry out.	تَصَرَّفَ فِي
To depart; be inflected.	إِنْصَرَفَ
Etymology.	صَرْفٌ
Pure, unmixed.	صِرْفٌ
Evils of fortune.	صُرُوفُ ٱلدَّهْرِ
Broker's trade ; brokerage.	صِرَافَةٌ
Money-changer.	صَرَّافٌ ج صَيَارِفَةٌ
Departing, going off.	إِنْصِرَافٌ
Freedom of action.	تَصَرُّفٌ
Inflection of words.	تَصْرِيفٌ
Vicissitudes of time.	تَصَارِيفُ ٱلدَّهْرِ
Expense.	مَصْرُوفٌ مَصَارِيفُ
Having free action. Inflected word. Governor.	مُتَصَرِّفٌ
A governor's district.	مُتَصَرِّفِيَّةٌ
A word capable of inflection.	مُتَصَرِّفٌ
To cut off, sever.	صَرَمَ يَصْرِمُ
To cease.	تَصَرَّمَ وَٱنْصَرَمَ
Sharp severe.	صَارِمٌ ج صَوَارِمُ

Earth. Elevated land.	صَعِيدٌ
Upper Egypt.	صَعِيدُ مِصْرَ
Place of ascent.	مَصْعَدٌ ج مَصَاعِدُ
Vehement sound, cry.	صَعَقٌ
Thunderbolt.	صَاعِقَةٌ ج صَوَاعِقُ
Poor, pauper.	صُعْلُوكٌ ج صَعَالِيكُ
To be small.	صَغِرَ يَصْغَرُ
To be base.	صَغُرَ يَصْغُرُ
To make small.	صَغَّرَ وَأَصْغَرَ
To change a noun into the diminutive form.	صَغَّرَ ٱلْإِسْمَ
To become small, or base.	تَصَاغَرَ
To esteem as little.	إِسْتَصْغَرَ
Smallness.	صِغَرٌ وصَغَارَةٌ
Adject.	صَاغِرٌ ج صَاغِرُونَ
Little, small.	صَغِيرٌ ج صِغَارٌ
A small sin.	صَغِيرَةٌ ج صَغَائِرُ
Smaller, younger; least.	أَصْغَرُ
The minor proposition of a syllogism.	اَلصُّغْرَى
Act of diminishing.	تَصْغِيرٌ
Noun in the diminutive form.	مُصَغَّرٌ
To incline to.	صَغَا يَصْغُو إِلَى
To listen to.	صَغَا وَأَصْغَى إِلَى
Attention, listening.	إِصْغَاءٌ
To set in a line.	صَفَّ يَصُفُّ
To take position in line.	إِصْطَفَّ
Row, line, class.	صَفٌّ ج صُفُوفٌ
Line of battle.	مَصَفٌّ ج مَصَافُّ
To consider, examine.	صَفَحَ ـَ
To turn away from, leave. Pardon, forgive.	صَفَحَ ـَ عَنْ
To cover with plates (metal).	صَفَّحَ
To clap the hands.	صَفَّحَ بِالْيَدِ
To take by the hands (in saluting).	صَافَحَ مُصَافَحَةً وصِفَاحًا
To examine attentively.	تَصَفَّحَ
Forgiveness.	صَفْحٌ
To disregard.	ضَرَبَ عَنْهُ صَفْحًا
Page of a book.	صَفْحَةٌ ج صَفَحَاتٌ
Generous, forgiving.	صَفُوحٌ

Plate of metal. صفيحة ج صفائح

Grasp of the hand. مصافحة

Broad, flat. Plated. مصفّح

To shackle, fetter. صفد يصفد

Bond, fetter. صفد ج أصفاد

To whistle. صفر يصفر صفيراً

To be empty. صفر يصفر صفراً

To make, or dye, yellow. صفّر

To make vacant. صفّر وأصفر

To become poor. أصفر

To become yellow, pale. إصفرّ

Empty. صفر ج أصفار

Having nothing. صفر اليدين

Zero. صفر وسفر ج أصفار

Second month of lunar year. صفر

Yellowness, paleness. صفرة

Whistle. صافورة وصفيرة

Yolk of an egg. صفار البيض

Golden oriole. صفارية

Yellow. أصفر م صفراء ج صفر

(Yellow) bile. صفراء

A poor man, destitute. مصفر

Desert, plain. صفصف

Willow, osier. صفصاف

To slap. صفع يصفع صفعاً

A slap. صفعة

To strike ; flap. صفق يصفق صفقاً

To be strong. صفق يصفق صفاقة

To clap the hands. صفّق

To agree upon. اصفق على

They ratified a compact. تصافقوا

Side, flank, face. صفق ج صفوق

Contract, bargain. صفقة

Fascia ; aponeurosis. صفاق

Thick, firm (texture). صفيق

Scrotum. صفن ج أصفان

Saphena vein. صافن ج صوافن

To be clear. صفا يصفو

To purify, filter. صَفَّى وَأَصْفَى

To be sincere. صَافَى وَأَصْفَى ٱلْوُدَّ

To choose, select. إِصْطَفَى

Smooth stone. صَفًا ج أَصْفَاءٌ

Serenity of life, pleasure. صَفَاءٌ

Clearness. صَفْوٌ وَصَفَاءٌ وَصَفْوَةٌ

Pure ; chosen. صَفِيٌّ ج أَصْفِيَاء

Pure, lear, climpid. صَافٍ

Strainer. مِصْفَاةٌ ج مَصَافٍ

Purified, filtered. مُصَفًّى

Chosen. مُصْطَفَى

To strike. صَقَرَ يَصْقُرُ

Hawk. صَقْرٌ ج أَصْقُرٌ

Hell. صَقَرُ

A pickaxe. صَاقُورٌ

To be covered with frost. صُقِعَ

To be cold, icy. صَقَعَ

Region, district. صُقْعٌ ج أَصْقَاعٌ

Intenseness of cold. صَقْعَةٌ

Hoar-frost. صَقِيعٌ

To polish, give lustre. صَقَلَ يَصْقُلُ

Staging. صَقَالَةٌ ج صَقَائِل

Polisher. صَقَّالٌ ج صَيَاقِلَةٌ

Polished. Sword. صَقِيلٌ

Sclav. صَقْلَبِيٌّ ج صَقَالِبَةٌ

To strike coin (money). صَكَّ يَصُكُّ

To trip, stumble. صَكَّ يَصُكُّ

To strike each other. إِصْطَكَّ

A legal deed. صَكٌّ ج صُكُوكٌ

Deadly serpent. صِلٌّ ج أَصْلَالٌ

To crucify. صَلَبَ يَصْلُبُ صَلْبًا

To become hard, tough. صَلُبَ يَصْلُبُ

To render hard. To make the sign of the cross. صَلَّبَ

To become hard, firm. تَصَلَّبَ

Crucifixion. صَلْبٌ وَتَصْلِيبٌ

The loins. صُلْبٌ ج أَصْلَابٌ

Hardness, firmness. صَلَابَةٌ

Cross. صَلِيبٌ ج صُلْبَانٌ

Crusader.	صَلِيبِيٌّ ج صَلِيبِيَّة
Crosswise.	مُصَالَبَةً
Crossing at right angles.	مُصَلَّبٌ
Crucified.	مَصْلُوبٌ ج مَصَالِيبُ
Fair ; wide.	صَلْتٌ
Sceptre.	صَوْلَجَان وَصَوْلَجَانَة
To be good, right.	صَلَحَ يَصْلُحُ
To be suitable, good for.	صَلَحَ لِ
To make peace.	صَالَحَ مُصَالَحَةً
To agree upon.	صَالَحَ عَلَى
To repair, improve.	أَصْلَحَ
To make peace between (two parties).	أَصْلَحَ بَيْنَ
To be reconciled.	تَصَالَحَ وَاصْطَلَحَ
To become better.	إِصْطَلَحَ
To agree upon. ...	إِصْطَلَحَ عَلَى
Peace, reconciliation.	صُلْحٌ
Good ; fit ; just. (one's good, self-interest).	صَالِحٌ
A good deed.	صَالِحَةٌ ج صَالِحَاتٌ
Goodness, virtue.	صَلَاحٌ
Reformation ; improvement.	إِصْلَاحٌ
Technical use.	إِصْطِلَاحٌ
Conventional.	إِصْطِلَاحِيٌّ
Peacemaker, reformer.	مُصْلِحٌ
Advantage. Department.	مَصْلَحَةٌ ج مَصَالِحُ
Reconciliation.	مُصَالَحَةٌ
To be hard.	صَلَدَ يَصْلُدُ صَلْداً
To sound.	صَلْصَلَ وَتَصَلْصَلَ
Clay.	صِلْصَالٌ
Baldness of the head.	صَلَعٌ
Bald spot.	صَلْعَةٌ وَصُلْعَةٌ
Bald.	أَصْلَعُ م صَلْعَاءُ ج صُلْعٌ
Abbreviation of the formula: صَلَّى ٱللّٰهُ عَلَيْهِ وَسَلَّم	صلعم
To boast.	صَلَفَ يَصْلَفُ وَتَصَلَّفَ
Boasting.	صَلَفٌ
To pray.	صَلَّى صَلَاةً أَوْ صَلْوَةً
To pray for ; bless.	صَلَّى عَلَى
Prayer. Mercy.	صَلَاةٌ ج صَلَوَاتٌ

Place of prayer.	مُصَلًّى
One who prays.	مصلّ
To roast, broil.	صَلَى يصلي
To put into the fire.	أصلى
To warm one's self by the fire.	تصلّى وٱصطلى بالنار
Fuel ; fire.	صلاء
To stop (a flask).	صَمَّ يصم صمًّا
To become deaf.	صمّ وأصمّ
To determine upon.	صَمَّم على
Deafness.	صَمَم
Stopper, cork. Valve.	صمام
Most sincerely.	من صميم القلب
Deaf.	أصمّ م صمّاء ج صمّ
Hard stone.	حجر أصمّ
A surd root.	جذر أصمّ
To be silent.	صمت يصمت صمتًا
To silence.	صمّت وأصمت
Silence.	صمت وصمات وصموت
Solid (not hollow).	مصمت
Canal of the ear.	صماخ ج أصمخة
To arrange ; adorn.	صمد يصمد صمدًا
To lay up, save.	صمّد
Solid ; not hollow.	صمد
The Eternal (God).	الصمد
Cell of a recluse.	صومعة ج صوامع
To gum, put gum into.	صمّغ
Gum.	صمغ ج صموغ
Gum Arabic.	الصمغ العربي
To have a fetid odour.	أصنّ
Stench.	صنّة وصنان
Tube, pipe.	صنبور
Pine tree.	صنوبر
Cone-shaped.	صنوبري
Cymbal.	صنج ج صنوج
Valiant.	صنديد ج صناديد
Chest, trunk.	صندوق ج صناديق
Sandal-wood.	صندل
Fish-hook.	صنّارة ج صنانير

To make; construct.	صَنَعَ يَصنَعُ
To arrange skilfully.	صَنَّعَ
To coax, flatter.	صَانَعَ مُصَانَعَةً
To effect good manners.	تَصَنَّعَ
To make ; have made.	إِصْطَنَعَ
Act of making ; deed.	صُنْع
Good deed ; benefit.	صُنْع
Work. Carft, trade.	صَنْعَة
Craft, trade, industry. Art.	صِنَاعَة ج صِنَاعَاتٌ
Artisans.	أَصْحَابُ ٱلْحِرَفَ
Maker, artisan.	صَانِعٌ ج صُنَّاعٌ
Artificial.	صِنَاعِي
Deed. Good deed.	صَنِيعَةٌ ج صَنَائِعُ
Affectation.	تَصَنُّع
Factory.	مَصْنَع وَمَصْنَعَةٌ ج مَصَانِعُ
Affected ; artificial.	مُصَنَّع
Made. Fabricated.	مَصْنُوع
To assort ; compose.	صَنَّفَ
Sort, kind.	صِنْفٌ ج صُنُوفٌ
Literary work.	مُصَنَّفٌ ج مُصَنَّفَاتٌ
Author.	مُصَنِّفٌ
Idol. Camel's hump.	صَنَمٌ ج أَصْنَامٌ
Hush ! Be silent !	صَهْ
A reddish colour.	صَهَبٌ وَصُهْبَةٌ
Reddish.	أَصْهَبُ م صَهْبَاءُ ج صُهْبٌ
A very cold day.	يَوْمٌ أَصْهَبُ
(Red) wine.	أَلصَّهْبَاءُ
To melt. Smite.	صَهَرَ يَصْهَرُ
To become related to by marriage.	صَاهَرَ
Son-in-law, brother-in-law.	صِهْرٌ ج أَصْهَارٌ
Water-tank.	صِهْرِيجٌ ج صَهَارِيجُ
To neigh (horse).	صَهَلَ يَصْهِلُ
Neighing.	صَهِيلٌ وَصُهَالٌ
To hit the mark.	صَابَ ـ وَأَصَابَ
To approve. Point, aim.	صَوَّبَ
To attain one's purpose.	أَصَابَ

To be right.	أَصَابَ فِي قَوْلِهِ
To do right.	أَصَابَ فِي عَمَلِهِ
To assail, smite.	أَصَابَ
To descend, (rain).	أَنْصَابَ
To hold to be right.	إِسْتَصْوَبَ
Side, course, direction.	صَوْبٌ
Right, correct.	صَائِبٌ وَمُصِيبٌ
What is right, correct.	صَوَابٌ
Struck, stricken.	مُصَابٌ
Affliction.	مُصِيبَةٌ ج مَصَائِبُ
To make a noise.	صَاتَ يَصُوتُ وَصَوَّتَ
Sound, voice.	صَوْتٌ ج أَصْوَاتٌ
Reputation, fame.	صِيتٌ
To fashion, shape, picture.	صَوَّرَ
To imagine.	صُوِّرَ لَهُ
To be formed. To imagine.	تَصَوَّرَ
Tyre (city). Horn, trumpet.	صُورٌ
Picture, form.	صُورَةٌ ج صُوَرٌ
Imagination, idea.	تَصَوُّرٌ

Sculptor. Painter.	مُصَوِّرٌ
Young chick.	صُوصٌ ج صِيصَانٌ
To measure grain.	صَاعَ يَصُوعُ
A measure for grain.	صَاعٌ
To form, fashion.	صَاغَ يَصُوغُ صَوْغًا
Pure, unmixed.	صَاغٌ
Money at its legal value.	صَاغٌ
Grammatical form.	صِيغَةٌ ج صِيَغٌ
Goldsmith.	صَائِغٌ ج صَاغَةٌ وَصُيَّاغٌ
Goldsmith's art.	صِيَاغَةٌ
Jewelry.	مَصَاغٌ
To become a *Sûfi*.	تَصَوَّفَ
Wool.	صُوفٌ ج أَصْوَافٌ
A tuft of wool.	صُوفَةٌ
Tinder, agaric.	صُوفَانٌ
Religious mystic ; *Sûfi*.	صُوفِيٌّ
To overpower, subdue.	صَالَ يَصُولُ عَلَى
To clean wheat.	صَوَّلَ ٱلْحِنْطَةَ
To soak, slake.	صَوَّلَ

Power ; rule ; force. صَوْلَةٌ

Rubbish, refuse matter. صُوَالَةٌ

Implement for cleaning wheat ; trough. مِصْوَلٌ ج مَصَاوِلُ

Sceptre. صَوْلَجَانٌ

To fast. صَامَ يَصُومُ صَوْمًا وَصِيَامًا

To abstain from. صَامَ عَنْ

To cause to fast. صَوَّمَ

Fast ; abstinence. صَوْمٌ وَصِيَامٌ

Fasting. صَائِمٌ ج صُوَّامٌ وَصُيَّمٌ

Hermit's cell. صَوْمَعَةٌ ج صَوَامِعُ

To keep, preserve, guard. صَانَ يَصُونُ

To enclose with a wall. صَوَّنَ

Act of preserving. صَوْنٌ وَصِيَانَةٌ

Flint, flint-stone. صَوَّانَةٌ ج صَوَّانٌ

Guarded, preserved. مَصُونٌ

To cry out ; crow, (cock). صَاحَ يَصِيحُ

To call out to. صَاحَ بِ

To cry out against. صَاحَ عَلَى

Cry ; crowing of a cock. صِيَاحٌ

Cry, shout. صَيْحَةٌ

Clamorous (man). صَيَّاحٌ

To hunt; trap, snare ; catch fish صَادَ يَصِيدُ وَتَصَيَّدَ وَٱصْطَادَ

Hunting, fishing ; game. صَيْدٌ

Hunter, fisherman. صَيَّادٌ

Sidon (city). صَيْدَاءُ

Trap, snare. مَصْيَدَةٌ ج مَصَايِدُ

Prey taken in hunting. مَصِيدٌ

Pharmacy. صَيْدَلَةٌ

Druggist. صَيْدَلَانِيٌّ

To become ; change into. صَارَ يَصِيرُ

To happen to, befall. صَارَ لَهُ

To begin to do. صَارَ يَفْعَلُ

To arrive at. صَارَ مَصِيرًا إِلَى

To cause to become. صَيَّرَ

Fold (for sheep). صِيرَةٌ ج صِيَرٌ

Act of becoming. صَيْرُورَةٌ

مَصِيرٌ Destination, end, result.

صَافَ يَصِيفُ To pass the summer.

صَيْفٌ Summer.

صَيْفِيٌّ Belonging to summer.

يَوْمٌ صَائِفٌ A hot day.

مَصِيفٌ Summer residence.

أَلصِّينُ China.

صِينِيٌّ Chinese, Chinese porcelain.

صِينِيَّةٌ Tray.

صِيوَانٌ Large tent. Pavilion.

صِيوَانُ ٱلأُذُنِ External ear.

ض

ض As a numeral sign=800.

ضَاضَأَ To shout in battle.

ضَوْضَى وَضَوْضَاءُ Shouts of war.

ضَئِيلٌ ج ضُؤَلَاءُ Thin ; small.

ضَأْنٌ Sheep, (*coll noun*).

ضَبَّ وَأَضَبَّ عَلَى To grasp, keep.

ضَبٌّ ج ضِبَابٌ Lizard.

ضَبَابَةٌ ج ضَبَابٌ Mist ; thin cloud.

ضَبَطَ يَضْبِطُ ضَبْطاً To guard. Do a thing well ; perfect.

ضَبَطَ عَلَى To withhold, restrain.

ضَبْطٌ Exactness, correctness.

ضَابِطٌ ج ضَوَابِطُ Rule ; canon.

ضَابِطٌ ج ضُبَّاطٌ Military officer.

ضَابِطُ ٱلْكُلِّ Almighty (God).

ضَابِطِيٌّ ج ضَابِطِيَّةٌ Policeman.

Written sentence, decision. (*law*). مَضْبَطَةٌ ج مَضَابِطُ

Well-regulated ; exact. مَضْبُوطٌ

Hyena. ضَبْعٌ وَضَبُعٌ ج ضِبَاعٌ

To cry, shout. ضَجَّ يَضِجُّ وَأَضَجَّ

To contend with. ضَاجَّ

Tumult, cry. ضَجَّةٌ وضَجِيجٌ

To be irritated, impatient, bored. ضَجِرَ يَضْجَرُ وَتَضَجَّرَ من

To bore, vex, distress. أَضْجَرَ

Uneasiness. ضَجَرٌ وَضَجْرَةٌ

Uneasy ; irritable. ضَجِرٌ وَمُتَضَجِّرٌ

Vexing, distressing. مُضْجِرٌ

To lie down. ضَجعَ يَضْجَعُ وَاضْجَعَ

To lie with (a woman). ضَاجَعَ

To make one to lie down. أَضْجَعَ

Bed-fellow. ضَجِيعٌ

Bed, bed-chamber. مَضْجَعٌ ج مَضَاجِعُ

To laugh. ضَحِكَ يَضْحَكُ ضَحِكاً

To laugh at. ضَحِكَ من وَعَلَى

To make one laugh. أَضْحَكَ

Pleasantry. ضُحْكَةٌ وَاضْحُوكَةٌ

Comic, causing laughter. مُضْحِكٌ

To appear. ضَحَا يَضْحُو ضَحْواً

To come in the morning. ضَحَّى

To sacrifice an animal. ضَحَّى ب

To show, reveal. أَضْحَى وَضَحَّى عَنْ

He took to laughing. أَضْحَى يَضْحَكُ

ضَحَاءٌ وَضَحْوَةٌ وَضحًى وَضَحِيَّةٌ

Early morning after sunrise.

Sacrifice. ضَحِيَّةٌ ج ضَحَايَا

Suburb, region. ضَاحِيَةٌ ج ضَوَاحٍ

Bright ; cloudless. أَضْحَى م ضَحْيَاءُ

Day of sacrifice. يَوْمُ ٱلأَضْحَى

(tenth of the month. ذُو ٱلْحِجَّةِ)

To be large. ضَخُمَ يَضْخُمُ

Large bulk ; corpulence. ضَخَامَةٌ

Large ; heavy. ضَخْمٌ ج ضِخَامٌ

To overcome. ضَدَّ يَضُدُّ

Injurious, harmful. مُضِرٌّ

Injury ; means of harm. مَضَرَّةٌ

To strike. ضَرَبَ يَضْرِبُ ضَرْباً

Multiply, (*Arith*). Pitch (tent). Strike (money).

To impose a tax. ضَرَبَ عَلَى

To overlook. ضَرَبَ عَنْهُ صَفْحاً

To incline to blackness. ضَرَبَ إِلَى ٱلسَّوَادِ

To blow a trumpet. ضَرَبَ فِي ٱلْبُوق

To travel. ضَرَبَ فِي ٱلأَرْضِ

To give a parable. ضَرَبَ مَثَلاً

To be silent. أَضْرَبَ

To quit, cease. أَضْرَبَ عَنْ

To speculate. ضَارَبَ مُضَارَبَةً

To fight together. تَضَارَبَ

To be agitated. إِضْطَرَبَ

To be confused. إِضْطَرَبَ ٱلأَمْرُ

Multiplication. (*Arith*). ضَرْبٌ

Kind, form. ضَرْبٌ ج ضُرُوبٌ

To oppose. ضَادَّ مُضَادَّةً

To disagree. تَضَادَّ تَضَادّاً

Contrary ; enemy. ضِدٌّ ج أَضْدَادٌ

Two opposites. ضِدَّان

Contrast ; opposition. تَضَادٌّ

To injure. ضَرَّ يَضُرُّ وَأَضَرَّ بِ

To receive an injury. تَضَرَّرَ

To force, compel. إِضْطَرَّ إِلَى

To be forced. اضْطُرَّ إِلَى

Harm ; evil. ضُرٌّ وَضَرَرٌ

Adversity. ضَرَّاء

A fellow-wife to a woman's husband. ضَرَّةُ ٱلْمَرْأَةِ ج ضَرَائِرُ

Necessity. ضَرُورَةٌ ج ضَرُورَاتٌ

Necessarily. بِالضَّرُورَةِ وَضَرُورَةً

Indispensable. ضَرُورِيٌّ

Necessary things. ضَرُورِيَّاتٌ

Blind. ضَرِيرٌ ج أَضِرَّاء

Necessity. إِضْطِرَارٌ

A blow, stroke. ضَرْبَةٌ ج ضَرَبَاتٌ

Striking. Multiplier. ضَارِبٌ

Impost, tax. ضَرِيبَةٌ ج ضَرَائِبُ

Agitation. إِضْطِرَابٌ

Large tent. مَضْرَبٌ ج مَضَارِبُ

Struck. Multiplicand. مَضْرُوب

Sharer in traffic. مُضَارِب

Agitated, confused. مُضْطَرِبٌ

To smear. ضَرَجَ يَضْرِجُ ضَرْجًا

To dye red. Adorn. ضَرَّجَ

Grave. ضَرِيحٌ ج ضَرَائِحُ

To be set on edge (teeth). ضَرِسَ يَضْرَسُ

To contend with. ضَارَسَ

Molar tooth. ضِرْسٌ ج أَضْرَاسٌ

Wisdom teeth. أَضْرَاسُ ٱلْعَقْلِ

Experienced man. مُضَرَّسٌ

To beseech. ضَرَعَ يَضْرَعُ إِلى

To resemble. ضَارَعَ مُضَارَعَةً

To beseech. تَضَرَّعَ إِلى

Udder. ضَرْعٌ ج ضُرُوعٌ

Prayer with humility. تَضَرُّعٌ

Present-future tense. مُضَارِعٌ
of verbs; (*e.g.* يَضْرِبُ)

Lion. Brave man. ضِرْغَامٌ

To burn, blaze. ضَرِمَ يَضْرَمُ وَاضْطَرَمَ

To kindle a fire. أَضْرَمَ

To be kindled. إِضْطَرَمَ

Firewood. Blazing. ضِرَامٌ

Blazing. مُضْطَرِمٌ

Rapacious animal. ضَارٍ ج ضَوَارٍ

Humiliation, (*from* وَضَعَ). ضَعَةٌ

To pull down, rase. ضَعْضَعَ ضَعْضَعَةً

To be weak, feeble. ضَعُفَ يَضْعُفُ

Te double. ضَعَّفَ يُضَعِّفُ وضَاعَفَ

To weaken, enfeeble. أَضْعَفَ

To be doubled. تَضَاعَفَ

Weakness, feebleness. ضُعْفٌ

Double. ضِعْفٌ ج أَضْعَافٌ

ضَعِيفٌ ج ضُعَفَاءُ Weak, feeble.

ضَغَثَ يَضْغَثُ To mix, confuse.

ضَغَطَ يَضْغَطُ ضَغْطًا To press, squeeze.

إِنْضَغَطَ To be pressed.

ضَغْطَةٌ Pressure. Compulsion.

ضَاغُوطٌ Night-mare.

ضَغِنَ يَضْغَنُ عَلَى To bear malice.

تَضَاغَنَ To bear malice or hatred against each other.

ضَغِنٌ Spiteful, malevolent.

ضِغْنٌ ج أَضْغَانٌ Hatred, malice.

ضَغِينَةٌ ج ضَغَائِنُ Malice, spite.

ضِفَّةٌ Side of a river.

ضِفْدَعٌ ج ضَفَادِعُ Frog.

ضَفَرَ يَضْفِرُ وَضَفَّرَ To braid, plait.

إِنْضَفَرَ To be braided, twisted.

ضَفِيرَةٌ ج ضَفَائِرُ Braid; tress.

ضَفَا يَضْفُو To be ample.

ضَلَّ يَضِلُّ To err; wander from.

أَضَلَّ إِضْلَالًا To lead into error.

ضَلٌّ وَضَلَالٌ وَضَلَالَةٌ Error.

ضَالٌّ ج ضَالُّونَ Strayed; erring.

ضَالَّةٌ A stray animal.

أُضْلُولَةٌ ج أَضَالِيلُ Error.

مُضِلٌّ Leading astray.

مَضَلَّةٌ Cause of error.

ضَلُعَ يَضْلُعُ ضَلَاعَةً To be strong.

تَضَلَّعَ To be full, strong.

ضِلْعٌ ج ضُلُوعٌ وَأَضْلَاعٌ وَأَضْلُعٌ (م) Rib. Side of a triangle, &c.

ضَلِيعٌ Strong, powerful; large.

مُضَلَّعٌ Ribbed; striped.

ضَمَّ يَضُمُّ ضَمًّا To join, add. To vocalize a letter with (ُ).

ضَمَّ عَلَى To grasp, seize.

إِنْضَمَّ To be joined, annexed.

ضَمٌّ وَضَمَّةٌ The vowel-point (ُ).

مَضْمُومٌ Collected, joined. Having the vowel-point.

إِضْمَحَلَّ To vanish.

To be avaricious.	ضَنَّ يَضِنُّ ضَنًّا
A prized thing.	ضِنٌ ج ضَنَائِن
Avaricious, stingy.	ضَنِين
To be larrow ; feebne.	ضَنَكَ يَضْنُكُ
Distress. Narrowness.	ضَنْكٌ
To be sickly.	ضَنِيَ يَضْنَى ضَنًى
To suffer, endure.	ضَانَى مُضَانَاةً
To consume (disease).	أَضْنَى
To be consumed slowly.	إِنْضَنَى
Disease ; weakness.	ضَنًى
Sickly, emaciated.	مُضْنَى
To overcome.	ضَهَدَ يَضْهَدُ
To maltreat ; persecute	إِضْطَهَدَ
Presecution.	إِضْطِهَادٌ
Persecutor.	مُضْطَهِدٌ
To resemble.	ضَاهَى مُضَاهَاةً
To shine ; glitter.	ضَاءَ يَضُوءُ
To illuminate.	ضَوَّأَ تَضْوِئَةً
To shine.	أَضَاءَ اضَاءَةً

To dress a wound.	ضَمَدَ يَضْمِدُ وَضَمَّدَ
Dressing for a wound.	ضِمَادٌ
Bandage.	ضِمَادَةٌ
To be thin, emaciated.	ضَمَرَ يَضْمُرُ
To conceal, hide.	أَضْمَرَ
To resolve.	أَضْمَرَ فِي نَفْسِهِ
To be shrivelled.	تَضَمَّرَ وَٱنْضَمَرَ
Emaciation, atrophy.	ضُمُورٌ
Secret thought. Heart, Conscience. Pronoun.	ضَمِيرٌ ج ضَمَائِرُ
Secret; understood. (*Gram*).	مُضْمَرٌ
To stand surety. To farm or rent.	ضَمِنَ يَضْمَنُ
To make one responsible for. To put in ; inclose.	ضَمَّنَ
To include, comprise.	تَضَمَّنَ
Within. Inclosed.	ضِمْنَ
Suretyship. Responsibility.	ضَمَانٌ
Responsible for.	ضَامِنٌ وَضَمِينٌ
Sense ; meaning. Ensured ; assured.	مَضْمُونٌ ج مَضَامِين

To seek light. إِستَضَاءَ

Light. ضِيَاءٌ وضَوْءٌ ج أَضْوَاءٌ

Light-giving ; brilliant. مُضِيءٌ

Tumult of war. ضَوْضَى وَضَوْضَاءٌ

To injure. ضَارَ يَضِيرُ ضَيْراً

To suffer pain. تَضَوَّرَ

To be lost ; perish. ضَاعَ يَضِيعُ

To lose. Destroy. ضَيَّعَ وَأَضَاعَ

Lost. Neglected. ضَائِعٌ

Unmissed. ضَيَاعاً

Village. ضَيْعَةٌ ج ضِيَعٌ وَضِيَاعٌ

To be a guest. ضَافَ يَضِيفُ

To treat with hospitality. أَضَافَ

To join, add. To put a noun in the construct state. أَضَافَ إِلَى

To be joined. إِنْضَافَ إِلَى

To seek hospitality. إِسْتَضَافَ

Guest. ضَيْفٌ ج أَضْيَافٌ وَضُيُوفٌ

Entertainment. ضِيَافَةٌ

Annexation. إِضَافَةٌ

Two nouns in the construct state (e.g. كِتَابُ زَيْدٍ) أَلْمُضَافُ وَٱلْمُضَافُ إِلَيْهِ

Host. مُضِيفٌ

Hospitable. مِضْيَافٌ

To be narrow. ضَاقَ يَضِيقُ ضِيقاً

To be inabequate. ضَاقَ عَنْ

To make narrow. ضَيَّقَ

To annoy ; oppress. ضَايَقَ

To feel oppressed. تَضَايَقَ

Narrowness. Distress. ضِيقٌ

Poverty. Misery. ضِيقَةٌ

Narrow ; contracted. ضَيِّقٌ

Narrower. أَضْيَقُ

Narrowplace. مَضِيقٌ ج مَضَايِقُ

To oppress. ضَامَ يَضِيمُ ضَيْماً

Wrong ; injury. ضَيْمٌ

ط

ط	As a numeral sign=9.
طَاطَا	To bend down.
تَطَاطَا	To be depressed, abased.
طَبَّ تَطْبِيباً	To treat the sich.
طِبٌّ	Medical treatment.
عِلْمُ ٱلطِّبِّ	The science of medicine.
طِبِّيٌّ	Medical.
طَبِيبٌ ج أَطِبَّاء	Physician.
طَبَخَ يَطْبُخُ طَبْخاً	To cook.
اِنْطَبَخَ	To be cooked.
طَبْخٌ	Cooking. Food cooked.
طَبَّاخٌ	Cook.
طِبَاخَةٌ	Art of cookery.
طَبِيخٌ	Cooked food.
مَطْبَخٌ ج مَطَابِخُ	Kitchen.

مَطْبُوخٌ	Cooked.
طَبَرِيَّة	Tiberias.
طَابُورٌ	Battalion.
طَبَاشِير	Chalk.
طَبَعَ يَطْبَعُ	To stamp. Print.
طَبَّعَ	To break in (a horse).
تَطَبَّعَ	To assume a character.
إِنْطَبَعَ	To be imprinted.
طَبْعٌ ج طِبَاعٌ	Natural disposition.
طِبَاعَة	Art of printing.
طَبِيعَةٌ ج طَبَائِعُ	Nature.
طَبِيعِيٌّ	Natural. Naturalist.
عِلْمُ ٱلطَّبِيعِيَّاتِ	Physics.
مَطْبَعَةٌ ج مطابِعُ	Printing-press.
مَطْبُوعٌ	Impressed, printed.

To fit, suit. طَابَقَ مطَابَقَةً

To make to agree. طبّقَ وطَابَق بَيْنَ

To cover, close, shut. أطْبَقَ

To agree upon. أطْبَقَ على

To agree. تَطَابَقَ

To apply to something. إنْطَبَقَ على

Suitable, conformable to. طِبْقٌ

Cover. Tray. طَبَقٌ ج أطْبَاقٌ

Layer ; stratum. طَبَقَةٌ ج طَبَقَاتٌ

Class ; Grade. Stage.

A hard year سَنَةٌ مُطْبِقَةٌ

Conformable to. مُطَابِقٌ

Agreement, accord. مطَابقَةٌ

To beat the drum. طبّلَ

Drum. طَبْلٌ ج طُبُولٌ

Drummer. طَبَّالٌ

Pistol. طَبَنْجَةٌ ج طَبَنْجَاتٌ

To fry. طَجَنَ يَطْجُنُ طَجْناً

Frying-pan. طَاجِنٌ ج طَوَاجِنُ

To strain in breathing. طَحَرَ يَطْحِرُ

Straining. طحارٌ وَطحيرٌ

Spleen. طحالٌ ج طحلٌ

Water-moss. طُحْلُبٌ وَطِحْلِبٌ

To rush upon. طَحَمَ يَطْحَمُ عَلَى

Impetuous ; violent. طَحُومٌ

To grind (flour). طَحَنَ يَطْحَنُ طَحْناً

Miller. طَحّانٌ

Mill. طَاحُونٌ وَطَاحُونَةٌ ج طَوَاحِينُ

Grinders, (teeth). طَوَاحِنُ

Flour. طَحِينٌ

Dregs of sesame-oil. طَحِينَةٌ

Mill-machine. مِطْحَنَةٌ

Mill. مِطْحَنَةٌ ج مطاحِنُ

All ; every one. طُرّاً

To happen to. طَرَأَ يَطْرَأُ على

To overwhelm with praise. اطْرَأَ

Fresh, juicy, moist. طَرِيءٌ

Unexpected calamity. طَارِئَةٌ

Exaggerated praise. إِطْرَاءٌ

To be joyful. طَرِبَ يَطْرَبُ طَرَباً

To sing, chant, trill. طَرَّبَ

To gladden. طَرَّبَ وَأَطْرَبَ

Mirth, glee. طَرَبٌ

One who feels merry. طَرِبٌ

Exciting mirth or delight. مُطْرِبٌ

Red cap, fez. طَرْبُوشٌ ج طَرَابِيشُ

To throw. Subtract. طَرَحَ يَطْرَحُ

Casting. Subtraction. طَرْحٌ

Abortion, miscarriage. طِرْحٌ

Veil worn by a female. طَرْحَةٌ

Sheet of paper. طَرْحِيَّةُ وَرَق

Cushion to sit on. طَرَّاحَةٌ

Cast down. طَرِيحَةٌ ج طَرْحَى

Place. مَطْرَحٌ ج مَطَارِحُ

Tarragon. طَرْخُونٌ (نَبَاتٌ)

To drive awry ; chase. طَرَدَ يَطْرُدُ

To attack, charge, assault. طَارَدَ

To be sent away. انْطَرَدَ

To follow regularly. إِطَّرَدَ

To digress. إِسْتَطْرَدَ اسْتِطْرَاداً

Bale of goods. طَرْدٌ ج طُرُودٌ

Attack ; charge ; pursuit. طِرَادٌ

Expelled, outcast. طَرِيدٌ

Chased game. طَرِيدَةٌ ج طَرَائِدُ

Having no exception. مُطَّرِدٌ

To embroider. طَرَّزَ

Form, shape, manner. طَرْزٌ

Mode, manner. طِرَازٌ

Embroiderer. طَرَّازٌ وَمُطَرِّزٌ

Embroidered. مُطَرَّزٌ

To be deaf. طَرِشَ يَطْرَشُ

To whitewash. (طَرَشَ يَطْرُشُ)

Deafness. طَرَشٌ

Lime for whitewashing. (طَرْشٌ)

Whitewasher. (طَرَّاشٌ)

Deaf. اطْرَشُ م طَرْشَاء ج طُرْشٌ

A high pointed cap. طَرْطُورٌ

طَرَفَ يَطْرِفُ To hurt the eye.

تَطَرَّفَ To go to an extreme.

طَرْفٌ The eye.

طَرْفُ ٱلْعَيْنِ The eyelid.

طَرَفٌ ج أَطْرَافٌ Side. End part.

ألاطْرَافُ Limbs, extremities.

أَطْرَافُ ٱلْحَدِيثِ Choice subjects of conversation.

أَطْرَافُ ٱلنَّاسِ The lower classes.

طَرْفَةٌ Twinkling of an eye.

طَرْفَاءُ Tamarisk (tree).

طَرَقَ يَطْرُقُ طَرْقاً To strike, knock.

أَطْرَقَ To be silent.

تَطَرَّقَ إِلى To find or seek a way.

إِسْتَطْرَقَ To take a way.

طَارِقَةٌ ج طَوَارِقُ Calamity ; evil.

طَرِيقٌ ج طُرُقٌ Way ; road, path.

طَرِيقَةٌ ج طَرَائِقُ Way ; manner.

مِطْرَقَةٌ ج مَطَارِقُ Hammer.

مَطْرُوقٌ وَمُسْتَطْرَقٌ Beaten (road).

طَارِمَةٌ Cabin of a ship.

طَرَّى To soften, moisten.

أَطْرَى إِطْرَاءً To praise highly.

طَرِيٌّ Tender ; fresh ; juicy.

طَسْتٌ وَطَشْتٌ ج طُسُوتٌ وَطُشُوتٌ Basin for washing.

طَعَّمَ To graft. Vaccinate.

أَطْعَمَ To give food.

تَطَعَّمَ To be grafted, inoculated.

إِسْتَطْعَمَ To taste.

طَعْمٌ ج طُعُومٌ Taste ; flavour.

طُعْمٌ Bait thrown to fish.

طَعَامٌ ج أَطْعِمَةٌ Food.

مَطْعَمٌ ج مَطَاعِمُ Food. Place of food.

طَعَنَ يَطْعَنُ بِ Thrust, pierce.

طَعَنَ فِي وَعَلَى To defame.

طَعَنَ فِي ٱلسِّنِّ To become old.

طَعْنَةٌ A thrust.

طَاعُونٌ ج طَوَاعِينُ Plague.

The Turkish Imperial cypher. طُغْرَاءٌ ج طُغْرَاءَاتٌ
A company ; order. طُغْمَةٌ
To overflow. طغَا يطغو
Highly wicked. طَاغٍ ج طُغَاةٌ
Idol. Tempter. الطَّاغُوتُ
To look down upon. أَطَفَّ عَلَى
Small quantity. طَفِيفٌ
To put out (fire) ; allay. أَطْفَأَ
To be extinguished. انْطَفَأَ انْطِفَاءً
To be full ; overflow. طَفَحَ يَطْفَحُ
To fill to overflowing. طَفَّحَ وأَطْفَحَ
Ove flowing. طفْحانُ وَطَافِحٌ
To jump, leap. طَفَرَ يطفِرُ طَفْراً
A leap. Eruption. طَفْرَةٌ
To commence to do. طَفِقَ يَفْعَلُ
To have a child, (woman). أَطْفَلَ
To approach setting. أَطْفَلَتِ ٱلشَّمْسُ
To intrude. تَطفَّلَ

Time before sunset. طَفَلٌ
Infant. طِفْلٌ ج أطْفَالٌ
Infancy. Childhood. طُفُولِيَّةٌ
Intruder. طُفَيْلِيٌّ
To rise high, (water). طَفَا يَطْفُو
To float. طَفَا فَوْقَ ٱلْمَاءِ
Scum. طُفَاوَةٌ
To make a sound. طَقَّ يَطُقُّ
Weather. Religious rite. طَقْسٌ ج طُقُوسٌ
To make a noise. طَقْطَقَ طَقْطَقَةً
Suit of clothes. Set. طَقْمٌ ج طُقُومَةٌ
To look down upon. أَطَلَّ عَلَى
Finest rain ; dew. طَلٌّ
Overlooking place. مطَلٌّ
To seek ; ask ; desire. طَلَبَ يطْلُبُ
To beseech ; pray. طلَبَ إِلَى
To demand ; claim. طَالَبَ
To demand repeatedly. تَطَلَّبَ
Desire. Request. طَلَبٌ وطِلْبَةٌ

طَالِبٌ ج طُلَّابٌ وطَلَبَةٌ Seeker.

طَالِبُ عِلْمٍ A student.

مَطْلَبٌ ج مَطَالِبُ Demand ; desire.

مَطْلُوبٌ ج مَطَالِيبُ Claim. Object sought or desired.

طَلَحَ يَطْلَحُ طَلَاحًا To be wicked.

طَلْحٌ A kind of thorny acacia.

طَالِحٌ ج طُلَّحٌ وطَالِحُونَ Wicked.

طَلَاحٌ Wickedness.

طَلْحِيَّةٌ ج طَلَاحِيُّ Sheet of paper.

طَلَسَ يَطْلِسُ To blot. Obliterate.

أَطْلَسُ Satin. Atlas.

طَيْلَسَانٌ ج طَيَالِسَةٌ A particular robe worn by learned men.

طَلْسَمَ To write a talisman.

طَلْسَمٌ ج طَلَاسِمُ Talisman.

طَلَعَ يَطْلُعُ To rise, (sun). Sprout.

طَلَعَ وطَلِعَ يَطْلَعُ To ascend.

طَالَعَ مُطَالَعَةً To study ; read.

أَطْلَعَ To appear. Sprout.

أَطْلَعَ على To inform.

تَطَلَّعَ إلى To look at, or for.

إِطَّلَعَ على To know, see.

إِسْتَطْلَعَ To examine.

طَلْعٌ Spadix, spathe.

طَلْعَةٌ Face. Aspect.

طَالِعٌ ج طَوَالِعُ Star (of fortune).

طُلُوعٌ Rising ; appearance.

طَلِيعَةٌ ج طَلَائِعُ Vanguard.

مَطْلَعٌ First line of a poem.

طَلُقَ يَطْلُقُ To be freed.

طَلُقَ يَطْلُقُ To have a cheerful face.

طَلَّقَ To divorce (his wife).

أَطْلَقَ To free, liberate.

أَطْلَقَ القَوْلَ To generalize.

أَطْلَقَ لَهُ To permit him.

أُطْلِقَ To be applied ; apply.

إِنْطَلَقَ To go, depart.

طَلْقٌ Pains of childbirth.

طَلْقُ ٱلْيَدَيْنِ	Liberal.
طَلْقُ ٱلْوَجْهِ	Cheerful.
طَلْقُ ٱللِّسَانِ	Eloquent.
طَلَاقٌ	Divorce.
طَالِقٌ وَطَالِقَةٌ	Divorced (woman).
عَلَى ٱلْإِطْلَاقِ وَمُطْلَقًا	Absolutely.
مُطْلَقٌ	Free. Absolute.
طُلْمَةٌ ج طُلَمٌ	Loaf of bread.
طَلَاوَةٌ	Beauty ; grace.
طَلَى يَطْلِي	To anoint ; cover with.
طِلَاءٌ	Ointment ; tar ; plaster.
مَطْلِيٌّ	Smeared, covered.
طَامَّةٌ	Calamity.
طَمَّ يَطُمُّ طَمًّا	To cover up.
إِنْطَمَّ	To be filled, covered up.
طَمْثٌ	Menstruation ; menses.
طَمَحَ يَطْمَحُ إِلى	To gaze at.
طَامِحٌ وَطَمُوحٌ	Aspring. Proud.
طَمَرَ يَطْمِرُ	To bury, conceal.
مُطَمَّرٌ	Accumulated.
طَمَسَ يَطْمُسُ وَطَمَّسَ	To efface.
تَطَمَّسَ وَٱنْطَمَسَ	To be effaced.
طَمِيسٌ وَمَطْمُوسٌ	Obliterated.
طَمِعَ يَطْمَعُ فِي وَبِ	To covet, hope.
طَمَعٌ	Covetousness ; avidity.
طَمَعٌ ج أَطْمَاعٌ	A coveted object.
طَامِعٌ وَطَمِعٌ وَطَمَّاعٌ	Covetous.
مَطْمَعٌ ج مَطَامِعُ	Thing coveted.
طَمْأَنَ	To tranquillize ; reassure.
إِطْمَأَنَّ	To be low, (land). To be free fro.n disquietude.
إِطْمَأَنَّ بِٱلْمَوْضِعِ	To abide, dwell.
إِطْمَأَنَّ إِلى	To trust implicitly.
طُمَأْنِينَةٌ وَٱطْمِئْنَانٌ	Tranquility.
مُطْمَئِنٌّ	Tranquil ; composed.
طَمَا يَطْمُو	To rise high, (water).
طَامٍ	High (water, sea).
طَنَّ يَطِنُّ طَنِينًا	To buzz ; ring.
طَنِينٌ	Humming ; ringing.

طَنَّانٌ Sonorous. Wide-spread.

أَطْنَبَ فِي To be eloquent ; exert one's self in.

طُنُبٌ ج أَطْنَابٌ Tent-rope.

إِطْنَابٌ Superfluity, prolixity.

مُطْنِبٌ An immoderate praiser.

مُطَنَّبٌ Made fast with ropes.

طُنْبُورٌ ج طَنَابِيرُ Tambour.

طَنْجَرَةٌ ج طَنَاجِرُ A cooking pan.

طَنْطَنَ طَنْطَنَةً To hum, ring.

طَنَفٌ ج أَطْنَافٌ Peak.

طَنْفَسَةٌ ج طَنَافِسُ A carpet.

طَهُرَ يَطْهُرُ To be clean, pure.

طَهَّرَ To cleanse. Circumcise.

تَطَهَّرَ To be cleansed, purified.

طَهَارَة Purity. Holiness.

طَاهِرٌ ج أَطْهَارٌ Pure. Holy.

مَطْهَرٌ Purgatory.

مُطَهَّرٌ Purified.

طَاهٍ ج طُهَاة A cook.

طُوبٌ Brick, canon.

طُوبْجِيٌّ Gunner ; artillery-man.

طُوبَى Blessedness.

طَاحَ يَطُوحُ To perish.

طَوَّحَ وأَطَاحَ To mislead.

تَطَوَّحَ To wander ; perish.

طَوَائِحُ وَمَطَاوِحُ Adversities.

طَوْدٌ ج أَطْوَادٌ High mountain.

مُنْطَادٌ Lofty ; rising high.

طَوْراً بَعْدَ طَوْرٍ Time after time.

طَوْرٌ ج أَطْوَارٌ State, manner.

طُورٌ Mountain.

أَلطُّورُ Mount Sinai.

طَاسٌ ج طَاسَاتٌ Drinking-cup.

طَاوُوسٌ ج طَوَاوِيسُ Peacock.

طَوْشٌ Frivolity.

طَوَاشٍ ج طَوَاشِيَةٌ Eunuch; gelding.

طَاعَ يَطُوعُ وَأَطَاعَ To obey.

طَاوَعَ مُطَاوَعَة To consent; follow.

تطوَّعَ	To volunteer.
إِسْتَطَاعَ	To be able.
طَوْعٌ وطَائِعٌ	Obedient.
طَوْعاً	Voluntarily ; willingly.
طَاعة	Obedience ; submission.
أَطْوَعُ	More submissive.
إِسْتِطَاعَةٌ	Ability ; power.
تَطَوُّعٌ	Voluntary action.
مُطَاعٌ	Obeyed. Accepted.
طَافَ يَطُوفُ حَوْلَ وفِي	To go around. To travel. Circumambulate.
طَوَّفَ	To lead around.
أَطَافَ ب	To surround.
طَوْفٌ	Night-police. Raft.
طُوفَانٌ	Flood ; deluge.
طَائِفَةٌ ج طَوَائِفُ	Party, sect.
طَوَافٌ	Circumambulation.
مُطَوِّفٌ	A Mecca guide.
طَاقَ يَطُوقُ وَأَطَاقَ	To be able.
طَوَّقَ	To put a collar on.
طَاقٌ ج طَاقَاتٌ	Window.
طَوْقٌ ج أَطْوَاقٌ	Collar.
طَاقَةٌ	Ability. Window.
إِطَاقَةٌ	Ability ; power.
طَالَ يَطُولُ طُولاً	To be long.
طَوَّلَ وأَطَالَ	To lengthen.
طَاوَلَ فِي	Defer, put off.
تطَاوَلَ عَلَى	To wrong.
إِسْتَطَالَ	To be long, extend.
طَالَمَا	During a long time.
طُولٌ	Length. Duration.
خطوطُ الطُّول	Longitude.
طَائِلٌ	Advantage ; benefit.
طَاوِلَة	Table.
طَوِيلٌ ج طِوَالٌ	Long. Tall.
طَوِيلُ الْبَاعِ	Competent.
أَطْوَلُ	Longer.
تَطْوِيلٌ	Lengthening.

مستطيلٌ Parallelogram.
طَوَى يَطْوِي طَيًّا To fold, fold up.
طَوِيَ يطْوَى To suffer hunger.
إنْطَوَى To be folded up.
طَيٌّ Folding. Traversing.
فِي طَيِّهِ Within it.
طَوًى Hunger.
مطْوِيٌّ Folded up.
طَابَ يَطِيبُ طِيبًا To be good.
طَابَتْ نَفسهُ To be cheerful.
طَيَّبَ To perfume.
تَطَيَّبَ To be perfumed.
إِستَطَابَ وَاستَطْيَبَ To find good.
طِيبٌ ج أَطْيَابٌ Perfume.
(طَابَةٌ) Ball used in play.
طَيِّبٌ Good. In good health
طَيِّبُ النفْسِ Cheerful, happy.
طَيِّبَةٌ ج طَيِّبَاتٌ A good thing.
(طَابُو) A tax on houses, &c.
مَا أَطْيَبَهُ How good it is !

طُوبَى Blessedness.
طَارَ يطِيرُ طَيَرَانًا To fly, (bird).
طَارَ الى To hasten to...
طَيَّرَ أَو أَطَارَ To make to fly.
تَطَيَّرَ To draw a bad omen.
تَطَايَرَ تَطَايُرًا To be dispersed.
طَيَرَ Evil augury or omen.
طَيَرَانٌ Flight (of birds, &c.)
طَائِرٌ ج طَيْرٌ وَطُيُورٌ Bird.
طَيَّارَاتٌ Paper-kite.
مُستَطِيرٌ Spreading.
طَاشَ يَطِيشُ To be light-headed.
طَاشَ عَنْ To miss, (an arrow).
طَيْشٌ وَطَيْشَانٌ Frivolity.
طَائِشٌ Light, fickle, frivolous.
طَيْفٌ Apparition ; spectre.
طَيَّنَ To plaster with clay.
طِينٌ ج أَطْيَانٌ Clay ; mortar.
طِينَةٌ A lump of clay.
طَيَّانٌ Plasterer.

ظ

ظ As a numeral sign=900.

ظَبْيٌ م ظَبْيَةٌ ج ظِبَاء Gazelle.

ظَرَّفَ To adorn, embellish.

إِسْتَظْرَفَ To deem beautiful.

ظَرْفٌ ج ظُرُوفٌ Vessel, receptacle. Adverbial noun of time or place.

ظَرِيفٌ ج ظُرَفَاء Beautiful. Witty.

ظَعَنَ يَظْعَنُ ظَعْنًا To travel.

ظَعُونٌ ج ظُعُنٌ Camel.

ظَعِينَةٌ ج أَظْعَانٌ Litter for woman.

ظَفَرَ يَظْفِرُ To scratch with the nail.

ظَفِرَ بِ وعَلَى To obtain. Overcome.

ظَفَّرَ وَأَظْفَرَ To give victory.

ظِفْرٌ ج اظْفَار Nail ; claw ; hoof.

ظَفْرٌ وظَفَرَة Pterygium.

ظَفَرٌ Success ; victory.

مُظَفَّرٌ Victorious ; conqueror.

ظَلَّ يَظَلُّ To continue.

ظَلَّ يَفْعَلُ To continue to act.

ظَلَّلَ وَأَظَلَّ To cover ; shade.

تَظَلَّلَ بِ To be in the shade of.

إِسْتَظَلَّ بِ To seek the shade.

ظِلٌّ ج أَظْلَالٌ Shade ; protection.

ظُلَّةٌ ج ظِلَالٌ Cover. Cloud.

ظَلَالٌ وَظِلَالٌ وظِلَالَةٌ Cloud.

ظَلِيلٌ ومُظِلٌّ Giving shade.

مُظِلٌّ وَمُظَلَّلٌ Shady. Cloudy.

مَظَلَّةٌ ج مَظَالٌّ Tent. Umbrella.

ظِلْفٌ ج ظُلُوفٌ وأَظْلَافٌ Hoof.

ظَلَمَ يَظْلِمُ To wrong ; oppress.

ظَلِمَ يَظْلُمُ وَأَظْلَمَ — To be dark.

ظَلَّمَ — To accuse of injustice.

تَظَلَّمَ مِنْ — To accuse of injustice.

انظَلَمَ — To suffer injustice.

ظُلْمٌ — Injustice ; oppression.

ظُلْمَةٌ ج ظُلُمَاتٌ — Darkness.

بَحْرُ ٱلظُّلُمَاتِ — Atlantic Ocean.

ظَالِمٌ ج ظَالِمُونَ وَظَلَمَةٌ — Tyrant.

ظَلَامٌ وَظَلْمَاءُ — Darkness.

ظَلَّامٌ وَظَلُومٌ — Great tyrant.

مَظْلَمَةٌ ج مَظَالِمُ — Wrong ; injustice.

مَظْلُومٌ وَظَلِيمٌ — Wronged.

ظَلِمٌ — Dark ; obscure.

ظَمِئَ يَظْمَأُ — To be thirsty.

ظَمْءٌ ج أَظْمَاءٌ — Thirst. Longing.

ظَمِئٌ وَظَمْآنُ — Thirsty ; desirous.

ظَنَّ يَظُنُّ ظَنًّا — To suppose.

ظَنَّ وَاظَّنَّ وأَظَنَّ بِ — To-suspect.

ظَنٌّ ج ظُنُونٌ — Supposition

ظِنَّةٌ ج ظِنَنٌ — Suspicion.

مَظِنَّةٌ — Presumption.

مَظْنُونٌ — Supposed.

مَظْنُونَاتٌ — Probable propositions.

ظَهَرَ يَظْهَرُ ظُهُوراً — To appear.

ظَهَرَ عَلَى — To overcome, subdue.

ظَاهَرَ مُظَاهَرَةً — To aid, assist.

أَظْهَرَ — To show, manifest.

تَظَاهَرَ بِ — To show forth.

إِسْتَظْهَرَ بِ — To seek help or aid.

إِسْتَظْهَرَ عَلَى — To overcome.

ظَهْرٌ ج ظُهُورٌ — Back.

عَنْ ظَهْرِ ٱلْقَلْبِ — From memory.

ظُهْرٌ ج أَظْهَارٌ — Mid-day ; noon.

ظَاهِرٌ — Clear ; evident. External.

فِي ٱلظَّاهِرِ — Apparently.

ظَاهِرَةٌ ج ظَوَاهِرُ — Phenomenon.

ظُهُورٌ — Appearance.

ظَهِيرَةٌ — Mid-day ; hour of noon.

إِظْهَارٌ — Disclosure, manifestation.

ع

ع	As a numeral sign=70.
عُبٌّ ج عِبَابٌ	Covering of bosom.
عُبَابٌ	Torrent, billows.
عَبَأَ يَعْبَأُ عَبْأً	To care for.
عَبَاءٌ وَعَبَاءَةٌ ج أَعْبِئَةٌ	Woollen cloak.
عَبِثَ يَعْبَثُ عَبَثًا	To play.
عَبَثٌ	Play, sport. Useless.
عَبَثًا	To no purpose, in vain.
عَبَدَ يَعْبُدُ	To worship, adore.
تَعَبَّدَ	To take one as a slave.
تَعَبَّدَ لِ	To devote one's self to ...
إِسْتَعْبَدَ	To enslave.
عَبْدٌ ج عَبِيدٌ	Servant, slave.
أَلْعِبَادُ	Mankind.
عَابِدٌ ج عَبَدَةٌ وَعُبَّادٌ	Worshipper.
عِبَادَةٌ	Religious worship.
عُبُودِيَّةٌ	Slavery, servitude.
تَعَبُّدٌ	Self-consecration to God.
مَعْبَدٌ ج معَابِدُ	Place of worship.
معْبُودٌ	Object of worship.
عَبَرَ يَعْبُرُ	To pass; pass away.
عَبَّرَ	To cause to pass over.
عَبَّرَ عَنْ	To explain.
إِعْتَبَرَ	To consider.
اِعْتَبَرَ بِ	To take warning from.
عِبْرٌ	On the other side.
عَبْرَةٌ ج عَبَرَاتٌ	Tear; sobbing.
عِبْرَةٌ ج عِبَرٌ	Admonition.
عِبْرِيٌّ وَعِبْرَانِيٌّ	Hebrew.
عابِر سَبيل	Awayfarer.

Fine, excellent. عَبْقَرِيٌّ

To pack (goods). عَبَا يعبُو وَعَبّى

To be filled ; arranged. تَعَبّى

To importune ; rebuke. عَتَّ يعتُّ

To blame, censure. عَتَبَ يعتُبُ عَلى

To blame, censure. عَاتَبَ مُعاتَبَةً

Threshold. عَتَبَةٌ ج عَتَبَاتٌ

Blame. عِتابٌ وَمَعْتَبَةٌ ج مَعَاتِبُ

To be ready. عَتُدَ يعتُدُ عَتَاداً

About to happen ; ready. عَتِيدٌ

To become old. عَتَقَ يعتِق عِتْقاً

To set free. عَتَّقَ يُعتِّق

To make old, let grow old. عَتَّقَ

To set free, emancipate. أَعْتَقَ

Antiquity, oldness. عِتقٌ

Emancipation. عَتْقٌ وَعَتاقٌ

Shoulder. عاتِقٌ ج عَوَاتِقُ

Old. Emancipated. عَتِيقٌ ج عِتاقٌ

Kept long, made old. مُعَتَّقٌ

Expression. Style, diction. عِبارَةٌ

This means. هذا عِبارَةٌ عَنْ

Act of passing over. عُبُورٌ

Perfume. عَبِيرٌ

Consideration, regard. إعْتِبارٌ

Explanation. تَعْبِيرٌ

Ferry, passage. مَعْبَرٌ ج مَعَابِرُ

Esteemed ; important. مُعْتَبَرٌ

To frown. عَبَسَ يَعْبِسُ

Austere, stern. عابِسٌ وَعَبُوسٌ

Very stern. Lion. عَبَّاسٌ

Frowning, sternness. عُبُوسٌ

To injure. عَبَطَ يَعْبِطُ عَبْطاً

To carry off in the flower of one's age, (death). أَعْبَطَ وَاعْتَبَطَ

A pure lie. عَبْطٌ

An act without reason. إعْتِباطٌ

To be diffused, (perfume). عَبِقَ ـَ

Sense of suffocation. عَبْقَةٌ

Freed, emancipated. مَعْتُوقٌ

Shoulder-pole. عَتَلَةٌ

Porter. عَتَّالٌ ج عَتَّالَةٌ

Porterage. عِتَالَةٌ

To become dark. عَتَمَ يَعْتِمُ وَعَتَّمَ

Darkness of night. عَتْمٌ وَعَتَمَةٌ

Obscure, dark. مُعْتِمٌ وَمُعَتِّمٌ

To be idiotic. عَتِهَ عَتَاهَةً

Idiocy, stupidity. أَعْتَهُ وَعَتَاهَة

Idiot ; mad. مَعْتُوهٌ

To be proud, rebel. عتا يَعْتُو عُتُوًّا

Proud rebellious. عاتٍ ج عُتَاةٌ

Moth-worm. عُثَّةٌ ج عُثٌّ

To stumble, trip. عَثَرَ يَعْثُرُ عَثْراً

To stumble upon. عَثَرَ يَعْثُرُ عَلَى

To cause to stumble. عَثَّرَ وَأَعْثَرَ

A false step. عَثْرَةٌ ج عَثَرَاتٌ

Young bastard. Serpent. عُثْمَانُ

To do evil, mischief. عثا يعثو عثوًّا

Acting corruptly. عاثٍ ج عُثَاةٌ

To cry out. عَجَّ يَعُجُّ عَجًّا وَعَجِيجاً

To raise the dust, (wind). عَجَّ

Outcry, clamour. عَجٌّ وَعَجِيجٌ

Omelet. (عُجَّةٌ)

Dust, smoke. عَجَاجٌ وَعَجَاجَةٌ

عجب يَعْجَبُ عَجَباً مِنْ وَلِ وَتَعَجَّبَ

To wonder at. وَاسْتَعْجَبَ مِنْ

To cause to wonder. عَجَّبَ وَأَعْجَبَ

To please. أَعْجَبَ

To be vain, conceited. اعْجَبَ بِنَفْسِهِ

Pride, vanity, self-conceit. عُجْبٌ

Astonishment. عَجَبٌ

Very wonderful. عَجَبٌ وعَجَابٌ

O wonderful يا لِلعَجَبِ

Wonderful, extraordinary. عجيبٌ

عَجِيبَةٌ ج عَجَائِبُ وَأُعْجُوبَةٌ ج أَعَاجِيبُ

Wonderful thing, marvel.

More wonderful. أَعْجَبُ

تَعَجُّبٌ Wonder, astonishment.
مُعْجَبٌ بِنَفْسِهِ Vain, self-conceited.
عُجْرَةٌ ج عُجَر Knot, knob.
عَجُورٌ A kind of melon.
تَعَجْرَفَ عَلَى To act haughtily.
عَجْرَفَةٌ Coarseness, rudeness.
عَجَزَ يَعْجِزُ عَجْزاً To lack strength.
عَجَّزَ وأَعْجَزَ To render unable.
عَجْزٌ Weakness, impotence.
Second hemistich of a verse.
عَجُزٌ ج أَعْجَازٌ The posterior part.
عَاجِزٌ ج عَوَاجِزُ Feeble.
عَجُوزٌ ج عَجَائِزُ Old woman.
مُعْجِزَةٌ ج مُعْجِزَاتٌ Miracle.
عَجِفَ يَعْجَفُ عَجَفاً To be lean.
عَجِفٌ م عَجْفَاءُ ج عِجَافٌ Very lean.
عَجِلَ يَعْجَلُ وَاسْتَعْجَلَ To hasten.
عَجَّلَ وَاسْتَعْجَلَ To press one on.
عَجَلٌ وَعَجَلَةٌ وَاسْتِعْجَالٌ Haste.
عِجْلٌ ج عُجُولٌ Calf.

عَجَلَةٌ ج عَجَلٌ Cart ; wheel.
عَجُولٌ Hasty, quick.
أَعْجَلُ More hasty, expeditious.
مُعَجَّلٌ Hastened, accelerated.
عَجَمٌ Foreigners. *sp.* Persians.
أَلْعَجَمُ وَبِلَادُ ٱلْعَجَمِ Persia.
عُجْمَةٌ Foreign origin of a word.
أَعْجَمِيٌّ ج أَعْجَامٌ Foreigner.
مُعْجَمٌ Marked with vowel-points (letters). Obscure.
عَجَنَ يَعْجِنُ عَجْناً To knead (dough).
عِجَانٌ The perinæum.
عَجِينٌ Kneaded ; dough.
مِعْجَنٌ ج مَعَاجِنُ Kneading-trough.
مُعَجَّنَاتٌ Pastry.
مَعْجُونٌ ج مَعَاجِينُ Electuary.
عَجْوَةٌ Pressed dates.
عَدَّ يَعُدُّ To number ; regard.
أَعَدَّ To prepare, make ready.
تَعَدَّدَ To be multiplied.

لا يُعتَدُّ بِهِ Of no account.

اِسْتَعَدَّ To be ready, prepare.

عَدَدٌ ج أَعْدَادٌ Number.

عُدَّةٌ ج عُدَدٌ Implements.

عَدِيدٌ Numerous.

إِسْتِعْدَادٌ Preparation.

تَعْدَادٌ Enumeration.

مُعَدٌّ Reday, prepared.

مُعتَدٌّ بِهِ Important.

مَعْدُودٌ Numbered, counted.

مُسْتَعِدٌّ Reday, prepared.

عَدَسٌ Lentils.

عَدَسَةٌ Lens. A small pustule.

عَدَسِيٌّ Lenticular.

عَدَلَ يَعْدِلُ عَدْلاً To act justly.

عَدَلَ عُدُولاً عَنْ To deviate.

عَدَلَ بَيْن To act with equity.

عَدَّلَ To make just, equal.

عادَلَ مُعادَلَة To be equal to.

تَعَدَّلَ To be valued at.

تَعادَلَ To be equal, (two things).

إِنْعَدَلَ عَنْ To turn aside from.

إِعْتَدَلَ To become right.

عَدْلٌ Equity, justice.

عادِلٌ ج عُدولٌ Just, equable.

عَدالَةٌ Justice, equity.

عَدِيلٌ وَعِدْلٌ Like, equal.

عَدِيلَةٌ Bag, sack.

إِعْتِدالٌ Equality, equity. Moderation. Equinox.

إِعْتِدالِيٌّ Equinoctial.

مُعادِلٌ Equal, like.

مُعادَلَةٌ Equation. Equilibrium.

مُعَدَّلٌ Average.

مُعتَدِلٌ Temperate, moderate.

عَدِمَ يَعْدَمُ عَدَماً To lack, want.

أَعْدَمَ To deprive of ; annihilate.

إِنْعَدَمَ To cease to exist.

عَدَمٌ Non-existence.

عَدِيمٌ ج عُدَمَاء	Lacking.
مَعْدُومٌ	Non-existent.
عَدَنَ وَعَدَّنَ	To manure land.
عدْنٌ	Eden. Abode.
جَنات عَدْنٍ	Paradise.
مَعْدِنٌ ج مَعَادِنُ	Mine. Metal, mineral. Origin, source.
مَعْدِنِيٌّ	Mineral, metallic.
عَدَا يَعْدُو عَدْواً	To run.
عَدَاهُ	To pass beyond it.
عَدَّى	To cause to go beyond.
عَادَى	To treat with enmity.
أَعْدَى	To infect (disease).
تَعَدَّى	To pass the limit ; transgress. Be transitive (verb).
إِعْتَدَى عَلَى	To be hostile toward.
عَدَا وَمَا عَدَا	Except.
عِدًى (قَوْمٌ)	Hostile party.
عَدْوَى	Infection or contagion.
عُدْوَانٌ	Gross injustice.
عَدَاوَةٌ	Hostility, enmity.
عَدُوٌّ ج أَعْدَاء وَأَعَادٍ وعِدًى	Enemy.
إِعْتِدَاء وتَعَدٍّ	Injustice.
مُعْدٍ	Infectious, contagious.
مُتَعَدٍّ وَمُعْتَدٍ عَلَى	Unjust.
مُتَعَدٍّ	Transitive (verb).
عذب يَعْذُبُ عُذُوبَةً	To be sweet.
عذّب	To punish, torment.
تعذّب	To be punished ; suffer.
عَذْبٌ	Sweet, (water).
عَذَابٌ	Punishment ; torment.
عُذُوبَةٌ	Sweetness, agreableness.
عَذَرَ يَعْذِرُ	To excuse.
تَعَذَّرَ وَأَعْتَذَرَ	To apologize.
تَعَذَّرَ عَلَى	To be impossible.
إِسْتَعْذَرَ	To ask to be excused.
عُذْرٌ ج أَعْذَارٌ	Excuse, apology.
عَذْرَاء ج عَذَارَى	Virgin.
اَلْعَذْرَاء	The sign Virgo.

Halter. Cheek.	عِذَارٌ ج عُذُرٌ
To throw off restraint.	خَلَعَ ٱلْعِذَارَ
Excuse pretext.	إِعْتِذَارٌ
Difficulty, impossibility.	تَعَذُّرٌ
Excuse.	مَعْذِرَةٌ ج مَعَاذِرُ
Excused, excuseable.	مَعْذُورٌ
To blame.	عَذَلَ يَعْذِلُ عَذْلاً
To blame one's self.	إِعْتَذَلَ وَتَعَذَّلَ
Censure, blame.	عَذْلٌ وَعَذَلٌ
One who blames.	عَاذِلٌ ج عُذَّالٌ
Salubrious, (land).	عَذِيَةٌ (أَرْضٌ)
To arabicize a foreign word.	عَرَّبَ
To speak clearly.	أَعْرَبَ
To become an Arab.	تَعَرَّبَ وَٱسْتَعْرَبَ
The Arabs.	أَلْعَرَبُ وَعُرْبَانٌ
The pure Arabs.	أَلْعَرَبُ أَلْعَرْبَاءُ
Carriage, coach.	عَرَبَةٌ وَعَرَبَانَةٌ
Arabic; An Arabian.	عَرَبِي
The Arabic language.	أَلْعَرَبِيَّةُ
Coachman.	عَرْبَجِيٌّ
Syntax; parsing.	إِعْرَابٌ
Bedouin.	أَعْرَابِيٌّ ج أَعْرَابٌ
Declinable, capable of receiving all the vowel-points.	مُعْرَبٌ
Arabicized.	مُعَرَّبٌ
To embroil, trouble.	عَرْبَسَ
To give a pledge.	عَرْبَنَ
Pledge.	عُرْبُونٌ ج عَرَابِينُ
To ascend, mount.	عَرَجَ يَعْرُجُ فِي
To be taken up.	عُرِجَ بِهِ
To limp, be lame.	عَرَجَ عَرَجاً
To halt, stop at.	عَرَّجَ وَتَعَرَّجَ عَلى
To incline, decline.	إِنْعَرَجَ
Lameness.	عَرَجٌ وَعَرَجَانٌ
Lame.	أَعْرَجُ م عَرْجَاءُ ج عُرْجٌ
Sloping. Bend.	مُنْعَرَجٌ
Booth.	عِرْزَالٌ ج عَرَازِيلُ
Husband, wife.	عِرْسٌ ج أَعْرَاسٌ

Wedding. عِرْسٌ ج أَعْرَاسٌ

Weasel. إِبْنُ عِرْسٍ

Bridegroom. عَرِيسٌ ج عُرْسٌ

Bride. عَرُوسٌ ج عَرَائِسُ

Throne. Booth. عَرْشٌ ج عُرُوشٌ

Grape-vine. عَرِيشٌ ج عَرَائِشُ

Court of a house. عَرْصَةٌ ج أَعْرَاصٌ

To happen. عَرَضَ يَعْرِضُ

To offer. عَرَضَ عَلَى

To be wide, broad. عَرُضَ يَعْرُضُ

To make broad. عَرَّضَ

To expose to. عَرَّضَ لِ

To oppose ; contradict. عَارَضَ

To turn away from. أَعْرَضَ عَنْ

To be exposed. تَعَرَّضَ وَاعْتَرَضَ

To interfere in. تَعَرَّضَ لَ

To review an army. إِعْتَرَضَ الْجُنْدَ

To be in the way of. إِعْتَرَضَ دُونَ

To oppose, object to. اعْتَرَضَ عَلَى

Breadth, width. عَرْضٌ ج عُرُوضٌ

Latitude. خُطُوطُ ٱلْعَرْضِ

Day of Judgment. يَوْمُ ٱلْعَرْضِ

Petition. عَرْضُحَالٌ ج عَرْضُحَالاَتٌ

Honour. عِرْضٌ ج أَعْرَاضٌ

Accident. عَرَضٌ ج اعْرَاضٌ

By chance, accidentally. عَرَضاً

Accidental. عَرَضِيٌّ

Cross-beam. عَارِضَةٌ ج عَوَارِضُ

Science of prosody. عِلْمُ ٱلْعَرُوضِ

Broad. عَرِيضٌ ج عِرَاضٌ

Opposition, objection. إِعْتِرَاضٌ

Exposition. مَعْرِضٌ

Opposition, contradiction. مُعَارَضَةٌ

Offered, presented. مَعْرُوضٌ

Transverse; obstructing. مُعْتَرِضٌ

Parenthetic clause. جُمْلَةٌ مُعْتَرِضَةٌ

Juniper-tree. عَرْعَرٌ

To know. عَرَفَ يَعْرِفُ

To sweat.	عَرِقَ يعْرَق عَرَقًا	To make known. Define.	عَرَّفَ
To cause to sweat.	عَرَّقَ	To be known.	تَعَرَّفَ
Extend its roots, (tree).	أَعْرَقَ	To acknowledge.	إِعْتَرَفَ ب
Sweat. Distilled spirits.	عَرَقٌ	Odour, (*sp*. fragrant).	عَرْفٌ
Root. Vein.	عِرْقٌ ج عُروقٌ	Comb of a cock.	عرفٌ
Sweating, perspiring.	عَرْقَانُ	Cock's-comb, (plant).	عرفُ ٱلدّيكِ
Irak.	بِلَادُ ٱلعِرَاقِ	Common usage.	عُرْفِيٌّ
Rooted. Noble.	عَرِيقٌ	Mount Arafât.	عَرَفَاتٌ
Diaphoretic.	مُعَرِّقٌ	Knowing. Skilled.	عَارِفٌ
To hamstring (a beast).	عَرْقَبَ	The diviner's art.	عِرَافَةٌ
Hamstring.	عُرْقوبٌ ج عَرَاقِيبُ	Diviner, astrologer.	عَرَّافٌ
To confuse, complicate.	عَرْقَلَ	Overseer.	عَرِيفٌ ج عُرَفَاءُ
To be dangled, confused.	تَعَرْقَلَ	Confession.	إِعْتِرَافٌ
Difficulties.	عَرَاقِيلُ	Tariff. Defining.	تَعْرِيفٌ ج تَعْرِيفَاتٌ
To rub.	عَرَكَ يَعْرُكُ عَرْكًا	The definite article.	حرفُ ٱلتعريفِ
To fight.	عَارَكَ مُعَارَكَةً وَعِرَاكًا	Knowledge.	مَعْرِفَةٌ ج مَعَارِفُ
Nature.	عَرِيكَةٌ ج عَرَائِكُ		Determinate, noun.
Gentle, tractable.	لَيِّنُ ٱلعَرِيكَةِ	Determinate, definite.	مُعَرَّفٌ
Battle.	مَعْرَكَةٌ ج مَعَارِكُ	Known. Kindness.	مَعْرُوفٌ

A heap. عُرْمَةٌ ج عُرَمٌ

Numerous, (army). عَرَمْرَمٌ

Covert, lair. عَرِينٌ وَعَرِينَةٌ

To be fall. عَرَا — وَٱعْتَرَى

Loop, button-loop. عُرْوَةٌ ج عُرًى

The firmest support. اَلْعُرْوَةُ ٱلْوُثْقَى

Overtaken (by). مُعْتَرًى

To be naked ; free from. عَرِيَ يَعْرَى

To strip, denude. عَرَّى وَأَعْرَى

To be stripped. تَعَرَّى

Nakedness. عُرْيٌ وَعُرْيَةٌ

Naked ; free from. عَارٍ ج عُرَاةٌ

Naked. عُرْيَانٌ ج عُرْيَانُونَ

Naked, denuded. مُعَرًّى

To be mighty, noble. عَزَّ يَعِزُّ

To be distressing to. عَزَّ عَلَيْهِ

God, exalted and magnified (be His name!). أَللّٰهُ عَزَّ وَجَلَّ

To render powerful. عَزَّزَ

To love. أَعَزَّ

To become powerful. تَعَزَّزَ

To overcome. إِعْتَزَّ وَٱسْتَعَزَّ عَلَى

Might. Honour. عِزٌّ وَعِزَّةٌ

Self-respect. عِزَّةُ ٱلنَّفْسِ

Mighty ; noble ; dear. عَزِيزٌ ج أَعِزَّاءُ

The mighty God. أَلْعَزِيزُ

Governor of Egypt. عَزِيزُ مِصْرَ

Dear, or dearer. أَعَزُّ

Celibacy. عُزْبَةٌ وَعُزُوبَةٌ

To be celibate. عَزَبَ يَعْزُبُ

Unmarried. أَعْزَبُ م عَزْبَاءُ ج عُزْبٌ

To punish ; reprove. عَزَّرَ

Punishment. تَعْزِيرٌ

The angel of death. عِزْرَائِيل

To play upon a musical instrument. عَزَفَ يَعْزِفُ

To furrow (the earth). عَزَقَ يَعْزِقُ عَزْقًا

A hoe. مِعْزَقٌ وَمِعْزَقَةٌ ج مَعَازِقُ

To set aside ; depose. عَزَلَ يَعْزِلُ

عَزَّلَ	To clean out.
إِعْتَزَلَ	To separate one's self.
عَزْلٌ	Removal (of an officer).
عُزْلَةٌ	Retirement. seclusion.
إِعْتِزَالٌ وآنْعِزَالٌ	Retirement.
معزل	Place of seclusion.
بِمَعْزِلٍ عَنْ	Away, aloof from.
مُعْتَزِلٌ	Seceder.
مَعْزُولٌ	Removed, separated.
عَزَمَ يَعْزِمُ عَلَى	To resolve to do.
عَزَّمَ	To invite. Recite charms.
عَزْمٌ	Resolution, firm purpose.
عَازِمٌ ج عَزَمَةٌ	Firm, resolute.
عَزَّامٌ ومُعَزِّمٌ	Magician, charmer.
عَزُومٌ	Determined, resolute.
عَزَّى تَعْزِيَةً	To comfort.
تَعَزَّى	To be comforted.
عَزَاءٌ	Patience. Mourning.
مُعَزٍّ	Comforter, consoler.
مُعَزًّى	Consoled, comforted.
عَزَى يَعْزُو	To ascribe, attribute.
عَسَّ يَعُسُّ وآعْتَسَّ	To patrol.
عَسٌّ وعَسَسٌ	Night-patrol.
يَعْسُوبٌ	Male-bee. Chief.
عَوْسَجٌ	Bax-thorn.
عَسْجَدٌ	Gold. Gem.
عَسُرَ يَعْسُرُ عُسْراً عَلَى	To be difficult for.
عَسَّرَ	To make difficult.
عَاسَرَ	To treat harshly.
أَعْسَرَ	To become poor.
تَعَسَّرَ	To become difficult.
إِسْتَعْسَرَ	To find difficult.
عُسْرٌ وعُسْرَى ومَعْسُرَةٌ	Difficulty.
عَسِرٌ وعَسِيرٌ	Difficult, hard.
أَعْسَرُ م عَسْرَاءُ	Left-handed.
مُعْسِرٌ	Poor, indigent.
عَسَفَ يَعْسِفُ	To treat unjustly.
عَسْفٌ	Injustice, oppression.

To form a camp.	عَسْكَرَ
Army, troops.	عَسْكَرٌ ج عَسَاكِرُ
Soldier.	عَسْكَرِيٌّ ج عَسَاكِرُ
Military service.	عَسْكَرِيَّةٌ
Military camp.	مُعَسْكَرٌ
Honey.	عَسَلٌ
To make honey, (bees).	عَسَّلَ
Tender shoot.	عُسْلُجٌ ج عَسَالِجُ
Stiffness of the wrist.	عَسَمٌ
Having stiff wrist or ankle.	أَعْسَمُ
To become hard.	عَسَا يَعْسُو
Thick, coarse, rough.	عَاسٍ
It may be that, perhaps.	عَسَى أَنْ
To make a nest.	عَشَّشَ وَأَعْشَشَ
Bird's nest.	عُشٌّ ج أَعْشَاشٌ
To produce herbage.	أَعْشَبَ
Green herb.	عُشْبٌ ج اعشَابٌ
To take tithes.	عَشَرَ وَعَشَّرَ
To consort with.	عَاشَرَ
To associate together.	تَعَاشَرَ
Tithe ; a tenth.	عُشْرٌ ج أَعْشَارٌ
Social intercourse.	عِشْرَةٌ ومُعَاشَرَةٌ
Ten.	عَشَرَةٌ م عَشْرٌ ج عَشَرَاتٌ
Twenty.	عِشْرُونَ
Tenth.	عَاشِرٌ
Tithe-gatherer.	عَشَّارٌ ج عَشَّارُونَ
Associate, friend.	عَشِيرٌ ج عُشَرَاءُ
Kinsfolk.	عَشِيرَةٌ ج عَشَائِرُ
Decimal. (*arith.*)	أَعْشَارِيٌّ
Community.	مَعْشَرٌ ج مَعَاشِرُ
Familiar friend.	مُعَاشِرٌ
Companionship.	مُعَاشَرَةٌ
To love passionately.	عَشِقَ يَعْشَقُ
Passionate love.	عِشْقٌ وَمَعْشَقٌ
Beloved one.	عَشِيقٌ وَمَعْشُوقٌ
Passionate lover.	عَاشِقٌ ج عُشَّاقٌ
To sup.	عَشَا يَعْشُو وَتَعَشَّى
Weakness of sight.	عَشاً وَعَشَاوَةٌ
Supper.	عَشَاءٌ

The Eucharist. اَلْعَشَاءُ ٱلسِّرِّيُّ

Evening. عَشِيَّةٌ ج عَشَايَا

Yesterday evening. عَشِيَّةَ أَمْسِ

Darkness of night. عَشْوَةٌ وَعَشْوَاءُ

Cook. عَشِّيٌّ

To bind up. عَصَبَ وَعَصَّبَ

To defend a cause. تَعَصَّبَ فِي

To take the part of. تَعَصَّبَ لِ

To league against. تَعَصَّبَ عَلَى

To be leagued. اِعْتَصَبَ

Sinew. Nerve. عَصَبٌ ج أَعْصَابٌ

Male relations. عَصَبَةٌ ج عَصَبَاتٌ

Troop, band. عُصْبَةٌ ج عُصَبٌ

Nervous. عَصَبِيٌّ

Partisanship. Male relations. عَصَبِيَّةٌ

Bandage. Troop. عِصَابَةٌ ج عَصَائِبُ

Obstinacy, fanaticism. تَعَصُّبٌ

A zealous partisan. مُتَعَصِّبٌ

Bound, tied. مَعْصُوبٌ

To press, squeeze. عَصَرَ يَعْصِرُ

To be contemporary with. عَاصَرَ

To be pressed. تَعَصَّرَ وَٱنْعَصَرَ

A time, period. عَصْرٌ ج أَعْصُرٌ

Latter part of the day. عَصْرٌ

The afternoon prayer. صَلَاةُ ٱلْعَصْرِ

Juice, extract. عَصِيرٌ وَعُصَارَةٌ

A press. مَعْصَرَةٌ ج مَعَاصِرُ

Contemporary. مُعَاصِرٌ

Tail-bone. عُصْعُصٌ ج عَصَاعِصُ

To blow violently. عَصَفَ يَعْصِفُ

Hurricane. عَاصِفَةٌ ج عَوَاصِفُ

Chaff, straw. عُصَافَةٌ

Safflower. عُصْفُرٌ

Small bird. عُصْفُورٌ ج عَصَافِيرُ

To prevent ; defend. عَصَمَ يَعْصِمُ

To take refuge. اِعْتَصَمَ وَٱسْتَعْصَمَ

Prevention, defence. عِصْمَةٌ

Capital of a country. عَاصِمَةٌ

Wrist. مِعْصَمٌ ج مَعَاصِمُ

Preserved, protected. مَعْصُومٌ

Staff, rod, cane. عَصًا ج عُصِيٌّ

Knot-grass. عَصَا الرَّاعِي

To disobey, rebel. عَصَى يَعْصِي

Rebellious. عَاصٍ ج عُصَاةٌ

The river Orontes. نَهْرُ الْعَاصِي

Disobedience. عِصْيَانٌ وَمَعْصِيَةٌ

To bite. عَضَّ يَعَضُّ عَضًّا

To defame. عَضَّ بِلِسَانِهِ

To aid, assist. عَضَدَ يَعْضُدُ وَعَاضَدَ

To aid one another. تَعَاضَدَ

To seek assistance of. إِعْتَضَدَ ب

Aid Assistance. عَضْدٌ ج أَعْضَادٌ

The upper arm. عِضْدٌ ج أَعْضَادٌ

Side, side-post. عِضَادَةٌ

To be difficult. عَضَلَ وَأَعْضَلَ

Muscular. عَضِلٌ

Muscle. عَضَلَةٌ ج عَضَلٌ وَعَضَلَاتٌ

Severe; difficult. عُضَالٌ وَمُعْضِلٌ

Difficult case. مُعْضِلَةٌ ج مُعْضِلَاتٌ

Member, limb. عِضْوٌ ج أَعْضَاءٌ

To perish. عَطِبَ يَعْطَبُ عَطَبًا

To destroy. Damage. أَعْطَبَ

To perfume. عَطَّرَ

To perfume one's self. تَعَطَّرَ

Perfume. عِطْرٌ ج أَعْطَارٌ

Ottar of roses. عِطْرُ الْوَرْدِ

Aromatic. عَطِرٌ م عَطِرَةٌ

Grocer. عَطَّارٌ ج عَطَّارُونَ

Grocery. عِطَارَةٌ

The planet Mercury, عُطَارِدُ

To sneeze. عَطَسَ يَعْطُسُ

To make one sneeze. عَطَّسَ

A sneezing. عَطْسَةٌ وَعُطَاسٌ

Snaff. عَطُوسٌ

To thirst. عَطِشَ يَعْطَشُ عَطَشًا

عَطَّشَ وَأَعْطَشَ To cause to thirst.
عَطَشٌ Thirst.
عَطْشَانُ ج عَطَاشَى Thirsty.
عَطَفَ يَعْطِفُ إِلى To incline towards.
عَطَفَ وَتَعَطَّفَ عَلى To be kind to.
عَطَفَ كَلِمَةً To join one word to another by a conjunction.
عَطَفَ عَنْ To turn away from.
إِنْعَطَفَ To be bent, inclined.
إِسْتَعْطَفَ To seek favour.
حَرْفُ عَطْفٍ A conjunction.
عِطْفٌ ج أَعْطَافٌ Side, flank.
عَاطِفٌ Conjunctive particle.
عَاطِفَةٌ ج عَوَاطِفُ Kindness, pity.
مَعْطُوفٌ Joined ; inclined.
مَعْطُوفٌ عَلَيْهِ A word to which another is joined by a conjunction.
مُنْعَطَفٌ A bend.
عَطِلَ وَتَعَطَّلَ To be without work. Be spoiled.
عَطَّلَ To leave unemployed. Ruin.

عُطْلٌ وَضَرَرٌ Damage and loss.
عُطْلُ ٱلْمَالِ Interest on money.
عُطْلَةٌ وَعَطَالَةٌ Vacant time.
عَاطِلٌ Spoiled, useless.
مُعَطَّلٌ Without work ; useless.
عَطَنٌ وَعَطْنَةٌ Mouldiness.
عَطِنٌ وَمُعَطَّنٌ Mouldy.
أَعْطَى To give present, offer.
تَعَطَّى وَٱسْتَعْطَى To beg.
تَعَاطَى To engage in.
عَطًا وَعَطَاءٌ وَعَطِيَّةٌ Gift.
مُعْطٍ Giver.
عَظُمَ يَعْظُمُ To be great, large.
عَظُمَ عَلَى To be hard upon.
عَظَّمَ To make large ; magnify.
تَعَظَّمَ To be great ; proud.
تَعَاظَمَ To magnify one's self.
إِسْتَعْظَمَ To regard as great.
عَظْمٌ ج عِظَامٌ Bone.

Pride; majesty. عِظَمٌ وَعَظَمَةٌ

Great. عَظِيمٌ ج عُظَمَاءُ وَعِظَامٌ

The Great (God). أَلْعَظِيمُ

A great thing. عَظِيمَةٌ ج عَظَائِمُ

Greater. أَعْظَمُ م عُظْمَى

Greater, or chief part. مُعْظَمٌ

Exalted, made great. مُعَظَّمٌ

To abstain from wrong. عَفَّ يَعِفُّ عَنْ

Virtuous. عَفِيفٌ ج أَعِفَّاءُ

Continence, chastity. عِفَّةٌ

To cover with dust. عَفَرَ يَعْفِرُ

Dust. عَفْرٌ وَعَفَرٌ

Demon. عِفْرِيتٌ ج عَفَارِيتُ

To heap up. عَفَشَ يَعْفِشُ

Trash. Baggage. عَفْشٌ

Galls. عَفْصٌ

To become decayed, rotten, mouldy. عَفِنَ يَعْفَنُ وَعَفَّنَ وتَعَفَّنَ

Mildew. وعُفُونَةٌ

Decayed. عَفِنٌ وَمَعْفُونٌ ومُعَفَّنٌ

Putrid, mouldy. مُتَعَفِّنٌ

To pardon, forgive. عَفَا يَعْفُو عَنْ

To restore to health. عَافَى

Bravo! Well done. عَافَاكَ

To exempt, excuse. أَعْفَى من

To be restored to health. تَعَافَى

To ask to be released. إِسْتَعْفَى

Pardon, amnesty. Young ass. عَفْوٌ

Spontaneously; easily. عَفْواً

Health. عَافِيَةٌ ج عَوَافٍ وَعَافِيَاتٌ

Resignation. إِسْتِعْفَاءٌ

Restoration to health. مُعَافَاةٌ

Convalescent. مُتَعَافٍ

Cornelian. عَقِيقٌ

To succeed. عَقَبَ ـُ عُقْبًا

To follow. عَقَبَ وَأَعْقَبَ وَٱعْتَقَبَ

To punish. عَاقَبَ

To follow out. تَعَقَّبَ

To follow (one another). تَعَاقَبَ

Heel of foot. عَقِبٌ ج أَعْقَابٌ

Mountain road. عَقَبَةٌ ج عِقَابٌ

End, issue. عُقْبَى

End, result. عَاقِبَةٌ ج عَوَاقِبُ

Punishment. عِقَابٌ وَمُعَاقَبَةٌ

Eagle. عُقَابٌ ج أَعْقُبٌ وعِقْبَانٌ

That which follows. عَقِيبٌ

To tie, knot. Conclude. Ratify. عَقَدَ يَعْقِدُ

To determine upon. عَقَدَ عَلَى

To make a contract with. عَاقَدَ

To be complicated. تَعَقَّدَ

To unite in a contract. تَعَاقَدَ

To believe firmly. إِعْتَقَدَ

Contract. Vault. عَقْدٌ ج عُقُودٌ

Necklace. عِقْدٌ ج عُقُودٌ

Knot. Joint. عُقْدَةٌ ج عُقَدٌ

Maker of silk-cord. عَقَّادٌ

Ally, confederate. عَقِيدَةٌ

Article of faith. عَقِيدَةٌ ج عَقَائِدُ

Belief, creed. إِعْتِقَادٌ

Bond, contract, union. إِنْعِقَادٌ

Obscurity, complexity. تَعْقِيدٌ

Very knotty ; tangled. مُعَقَّدٌ

Doctrine, belief. مُعْتَقَدٌ

To cut, wound. عَقَرَ يَعْقِرُ عَقْراً

To persevere in. عَاقَرَ

To be wounded. إِنْعَقَرَ

Wounding, wound. عَقْرٌ

Barrenness. عُقْرٌ وعُقْرَةٌ وَعَقَارَةٌ

Barren. عَاقِرٌ ج عَوَاقِرُ

Real estate. عَقَارٌ ج عَقَارَاتٌ

A drug. عَقَّارٌ ج عَقَاقِيرُ

Scorpion. عَقْرَبٌ ج عَقَارِبُ

Scorpion (of the zodiac). أَلْعَقْرَبُ

To plait (the hair). عَقَصَ يَعْقِصُ

To sting. (عَقَصَ يَعْقِصُ وَعَقْصَ)

Plait (of hair). عَقِيصَةٌ ج عَقَائِصُ

عِقاصٌ	Hair-filet.
عقَفَ يعقِفُ	To crook, bend.
تعقَّفَ وانعقَفَ	To become bent.
أعقفُ ومعقوفٌ	Bent, hooked.
عقَلَ يعقِلُ واعتقَلَ	To bind.
عقَلَ معقولاً	To understand.
تعقَّلَ	To conceive, know.
إعتقَلَ	To withhold, restrain.
عَقلٌ ج عقولٌ	Mind, intellect.
عقليٌّ	Rational ; mental.
عاقِلٌ ج عُقالٌ وعُقلاءُ	Intelligent.
عِقالٌ ج عُقُلٌ	Rope cord.
عقيلةٌ ج عقائلُ	A noble woman.
معقِلٌ ج معاقِلُ	Fortress, refuge.
معقولٌ	Intelligible, reasonable.
عِلمُ المعقولاتِ	Mental science.
عقَمَ يعقُمُ	To be barren.
عقَّمَ وأعقَمَ	To render barren.
عُقمٌ	Barrenness.

عقيمٌ ج عُقُمٌ	Barren, sterile.
عكَّةُ وعكَّاءُ	Acre, (town).
عكِرَ يعكَرُ وتعكَّرَ	To become turbid.
عكَّرَ وأعكَرَ	To render turbid.
عكَرٌ	Dregs, lees, sediment.
عكِرٌ ومُعكَّرٌ	Troubled, turbid.
عكَزَ وتعكَّزَ على	To lean upon (a staff.)
عُكَّازٌ ج عكاكيزُ	Staff ; crosier.
عكَسَ يعكِسُ	To reverse, invert.
عاكَسَ	To invert, oppose.
إنعكَسَ	To be inverted, reflected.
إنعِكاسٌ	Inversion, reflection.
بالعكسِ	On the contrary.
عكِشٌ	Thick, dense.
عكَفَ يعكُفُ عكفاً	To detain.
عكَفَ على	To persevere in.
عكَفَ واعتكَفَ في	To abide in.
عاكِفٌ	Keeping to.
إعتِكافٌ	Religious seclusion.

To tie up. Muzzle.	عكَمَ يَعْكِمُ
To become ill.	عَلَّ علة
To Divert. Account for.	علَّلَ بِ
To offer excuses.	تعَلَّلَ
To divert one's self.	تعَلَّلَ بِ
To become diseased, sick.	إِعْتَلَّ
May-be, perhaps.	علَّ ولَعلَّ
Cause. Malady.	علةٌ ج عِلَلٌ
The weak letters.	حُرُوفُ العِلة
Upper chamber.	علِيَّةٌ ج عَلالِيُّ
Sick, diseased.	عَليلٌ ومَعْلُولٌ
Assignment of a cause.	تعليلٌ
Ill, diseased. Containing one of the weak letters.	مُعْتَلٌّ
Small box.	عُلْبَةٌ ج عُلَبٌ
To work at. Treat (a disease).	عَالَجَ
To take medical treatment.	تعَالَجَ
To strive with one another.	تعَالَجَ
Treatment of disease. Remedy, cure,	عِلاَجٌ ومُعَالَجَةٌ
Dispute, contention.	مُعَالَجَةٌ
To feed (a beast).	عَلَفَ يَعْلِفُ
Fodder (for beasts).	عَلَفٌ
Seller of provender.	عَلاَّفٌ
Manger.	مَعْلَفٌ ج مَعالِفُ
Fattened (animal),	مُعَلَّفٌ
To hang to.	عَلِقَ يَعلقُ وٱعْتَلَقَ بِ
To conceive, (woman).	عَلِقَ عُلُوقًا
To love.	عَلِقَ عُلُوقًا بِهِ
To begin to do.	عَلِقَ يَعْلَقُ
To attach.	عَلَّقَ
To note down.	عَلَّقَ فِي
To be attached to.	تَعَلَّقَ بِ
Leech.	عَلَقَةٌ ج عَلَقَاتٌ وعَلَقٌ
Connection.	عَلاَقَةٌ ج عَلاَئِقُ
Forage, for animals.	عَلِيقٌ
Climbing plant ; brier.	عُلَّيْقٌ
Connection.	تعَلُّقٌ
Attached, suspended.	مُعَلَّقٌ

مُتَعَلِّقٌ بِ	Attached to.
عَلْقَمٌ	Very bitter plant.
عَلَكَ يَعْلُكُ عَلْكاً	To chew.
عَلِمَ يَعْلَمُ	To know, perceive.
عَلَّمَ	To teach. To mark.
أَعْلَمَ	To inform.
تَعَلَّمَ	To learn.
إِسْتَعْلَمَ	To desire to know ; ask.
عَلَمٌ ج أَعلامٌ	Sign. Banner.
إِسْمُ عَلَمٍ	Proper name.
عِلْمٌ ج عُلُومٌ	Science, knowledge.
عِلْمِيٌّ	Scientific.
عالِمٌ ج عُلَماءُ	Knowing ; learned.
عالَمٌ ج عَوالِمُ وعالَمُونَ	World.
عالَمُ الْحَيَوانِ	The animal kingdom.
عالَمُ النَّباتِ	The vegetable kingdom.
عالَمُ الْمَعادِنِ	The mineral kingdom.
عَلّامٌ وعَلّامَةٌ	Very learned.
عَلامَةٌ	Sign, mark.
عَلِيمٌ ج عُلَماءُ	Learned, savant.
إِعْلامٌ	Announcement, notice.
تَعْلِيمٌ	Instruction. Doctrine.
تَعْلِيماتٌ	Instructions ; orders.
مُعَلَّمٌ	Taught. Marked.
مُعَلِّمٌ	Teacher, master.
مَعْلُومٌ	Known. Active voice (verb). Certainly, of course.
عَلَنَ يَعْلُنُ	To be open, manifest.
أَعْلَنَ	To publish, reveal.
إِعْتَلَنَ وَاسْتَعْلَنَ	To be manifest.
عَلَنٌ وَعالَنٌ	Manifest, open.
عَلانِيَةً	Openly, publicly.
إِعْلانٌ	Manifestation, announcement. Advertisement.
عَلا يَعْلُو	To be high ; ascend.
عَلا عَلى	To overcome.
عَلَّى وَأَعْلَى	To elevate.
تَعَلَّى وَتَعالَى	To be elevated.
اللّهُ تَعالَى	God, the exalted one.

Come ! come here !	تَعَالَ
To rise high.	عْتَلَى وَٱسْتَعْلَى
Nobility ; eminence.	عَلَاء وَعُلَى
Height. Grandeur.	عُلُوّ
In addition to.	عِلَاوَة
High ; elevated ; noble.	عَلِيّ ج عَلِيُّونَ
God, the most High.	ٱلْعَلِيّ
Upper chamber.	عِلِّيَّة ج عَلَالِي
High, sublime.	عَالٍ
The Sublime Porte.	ٱلْبَاب ٱلْعَالِي
Higher, nobler.	أَعْلَى ج أَعَالٍ
The exalted, (God).	ٱلْمُتَعَالِي
To address a letter.	عَلْوَنَ
Address ; title.	عُلْوَان
To ascend.	عَلِيَ يَعْلَى عَلْيًا وَعُلِيًّا
Upon, with, for, at.	عَلَى
You ought to do ...	عَلَيْكَ أَنْ تَفْعَلَ...
He is in debt.	عَلَيْهِ دَيْنٌ
In his time.	عَلَى عَهْدِهِ
By means of.	عَلَى يَدِ فُلَانٍ
To be general ; include.	عَمَّ يَعُمُّ
To generalize.	عَمَّمَ
Paternal uncle.	عَمّ ج أَعْمَام
Paternal aunt.	عَمَّة ج عَمَّات
Cousin on the father's side. Husband.	إِبْنُ ٱلْعَمِّ
Cousin on the father's side. Wife.	بِنْتُ ٱلْعَمِّ
For what ?	عَمَّ (عَنْ مَا)
For whom ?	عَمَّنْ (عَنْ مَنْ)
General, universal.	عَامّ
The common people.	ٱلْعَامَّة
They all came.	جَاءَ ٱلْقَوْمُ عَامَّةً
To common people.	ٱلْعَوَامّ
Vulgar, common.	عَامِّيّ
Turban.	عِمَامَة ج عَمَائِم
Universality, totality.	عُمُوم
Ingeneral, universally.	عُمُومًا

General, universal.	عُمُومِيّ
More common or general.	أَعَمّ
Turbaned.	مُعَمَّم وَمُتَعَمِّم
To prop up, support.	عَمَدَ يَعْمِدُ
To intend, purpose.	عَمَدَ وَتَعَمَّدَ
To aim at, seek, repair to.	عَمَدَ إِلَى
To baptize.	عَمَدَ وَعَمَّدَ
To be baptized.	تَعَمَّدَ وَٱعْتَمَدَ
To depend upon.	اعْتَمَدَ عَلَى
Intentionally.	عَمْداً وَتَعَمُّداً
Prop. Committee.	عُمْدَة
Column, pillar.	عَمُود ج أَعْمِدَة
Perpendicular line.	خَطّ عَمُودِيّ
Representative.	مُعْتَمَد
Baptism.	مَعْمُودِيَّة
To live a long time.	عَمَرَ يَعْمُرُ
To be inhabited.	عَمَرَ يَعْمُرُ
To inhabit.	عَمَرَ عِمَارَةً
To build.	عَمَرَ عِمَارَة
To make inhabited.	أَعْمَرَ
To be flourishing.	عَمَرَ يَعْمَرُ
To build, construct.	عَمَّرَ
To colonize.	أَعْمَرَ وَٱسْتَعْمَرَ
Life-time ; age.	عُمْر ج أَعْمَار
By my life!	لَعَمْرِي
Prosperity of a land. Civilization.	عُمْرَان
Edifice. Cultivation.	عِمَارَة ج عَمَائِر
Inhabited.	عَامِر وَعَمِير وَمَعْمُور
Mason.	مِعْمَار وَمِعْمَارِيّ ج مِعْمَارِيَّة
Colony.	مُسْتَعْمَرَة
Weakness of sight.	عَمَش
Weak in sight.	أَعْمَش
To be deep.	عَمُقَ يَعْمُقُ
To make deep.	عَمَّقَ وَأَعْمَقَ
To go deeply into.	تَعَمَّقَ فِي
Depth.	عَمْق وَعُمْق ج أَعْمَاق
Deep, profound.	عَمِيق
To work, do, make.	عَمِلَ يَعْمَلُ

To act upon. عَمِلَ فِي

To deal with. Treat. عَامَلَ

To employ, use, exert. اعْمَلَ

To deal with one another. تَعَامَلَ

To labour, work. إِعْتَمَلَ

To use ; employ. إِسْتَعْمَلَ

Work, service, deed, action ; occupation. عَمَلٌ ج اعْمَال

An evil deed. عَمْلَة

Money. عُمْلَة

Practical. Artificial. عَمَلِي

Operation. عَمَلِيَّة

Workman, doer. عَامِلٌ ج عُمَّالٌ

A word that governs another (*in gram.*) عَامِلٌ ج عَوَامِلُ

Commercial agent. عَمِيلٌ

Use, employment. إِسْتِعْمَالٌ

Mill, factory. مَعْمَلٌ ج مَعَامِلُ

Transaction. Manner of treatment. مُعَامَلَةٌ ج مُعَامَلَاتٌ

Made. Governed (word). مَعْمُولٌ

To become blind. عَمِيَ يَعْمَى

To be blind to. عَمِيَ عَنْ

To be obscure to. عَمِيَ ٱلْأَمْرُ عَلَى

To render blind. اعْمَى

To feign blindness. تَعَامَى

Blindness. عَمًى

Blind. أَعْمَى م عَمْيَاءُ ج عُمْيٌ

For, from, at. عَنْ

He left us. ذَهَبَ عَنَّا

After a little while. عَنْ قَلِيلٍ

To the last man. عَنْ آخِرِهِمْ

At his right hand. عَنْ يَمِينِهِ

Life for life. نَفْسٌ عَنْ نَفْسٍ

Because of a promise. عَنْ وَعْدٍ

To appear. عَنَّ يَعِنُّ عَنًّا

Clouds. عَنَانٌ

Reins. عِنَانٌ ج اعِنَّة

Grapes. عِنَبٌ

Jujube tree and fruit. عتابٌ

Ambergris. Ship-hold. A kind of Mimosa. عَنْبَرٌ

To treat with rigour. عَنَّتَ

At, near, with, on. عِنْدَ

I came from him. جِئْتُ مِنْ عِنْدِهِ

At sunrise. عِنْدَ طُلُوعِ ٱلشَّمْسِ

He sat with him. جَلَسَ عِنْدَهُ

I have property. عِنْدِي مَالٌ

Such is my opinion. عِنْدِي كَذَا

When it happened. عِنْدَ مَا صَارَ

Then ; thereupon. عِنْدَ ذٰلِكَ

To be obstinate. عَنَدَ يَعْنُدُ

To resist. عَانَدَ عِناداً وَمُعَانَدَةً

To oppose one another. تَعَانَدَ

Obstinate. عَنِيدٌ ج عُنُدٌ وَمُعَانِدٌ

She-goat. عَنْزٌ ج عُنُوزٌ وَعِنَازٌ

Element. Origin. عُنْصُرٌ ج عَنَاصِرُ

Feast of Pentecost. أَلْعَنْصَرَةُ

Simple, elemental. عُنْصُرِيٌّ

Wild onion ; squill. عَنْصُلٌ

To be harsh ; rude. عَنُفَ يَعْنُفُ

To upbraid. عَنَّفَ وَأَعْنَفَ

Roughness, harshness. عُنْفٌ

Violently. عُنْفاً

The first of a thing. عُنْفُوَانٌ

Prime of youth. عُنْفُوَانُ ٱلشَّبَابِ

Harsh, violent. عَنِيفٌ

To embrace. عَانَقَ وَٱعْتَنَقَ

Neck. عُنُقٌ ج أَعْنَاقٌ

Embrace. عِنَاقٌ وَمُعَانَقَةٌ

Fabulous bird ; griffin. أَلْعَنْقَاءُ

Bunch. عُنْقُودٌ ج عَنَاقِيدُ

Spider. عَنْكَبُوتٌ ج عَنَاكِبُ

To trouble, distress. عَنَا يَعْنُو

To submit to. عَنَا (ل)

To subdue. عَنَّى وَأَعْنَى

Force, violence. عَنْوَةٌ

Captive ; submissive. عَانٍ ج عُنَاةٌ

To address a letter. عَنْوَنَ

Title ; address. عُنْوَانٌ

To mean, intend. عَنَى يَعْنِي

To concern. عُنِيَ عِنَايَةً

To distress, afflict. عَنَّى وأَعْنَى

To suffer, endure. عَانَى

To care for, manage. إِعْتَنَى بِ

Difficulty, trouble. عَنَاء

Care, solicitude. عِنَايَةٌ وَآعْتِنَاء

Divine Providence. أَلْعِنَايَةُ ٱلإِلٰهِيَّةُ

Meaning, sense. مَعْنًى ج مَعَانٍ

Rhetoric. عِلْمُ ٱلْمَعَانِي

Ideal, mental. مَعْنَوِيٌّ

To know. عَهِدَ يَعْهَدُ عَهْداً

To enjoin, charge. عَهِدَ إِلَى

To make an agreement. عَاهَدَ

To swear to one. عَاهَدَه

To be careful of. تَعَهَّدَ وَتَعَاهَدَ

To make an engagement. تَعَاهَدَ

Covenant, agreement. Time, epoch. عَهْدٌ ج عُهُودٌ

The Old Testament. أَلْعَهْدُ ٱلْقَدِيمُ

The New Testament. أَلْعَهْدُ ٱلْجَدِيدُ

Presumptive heir. وَلِيُّ ٱلْعَهْدِ

Compact. Responsibility. عُهْدَةٌ

Treaty, alliance. مُعَاهَدَةٌ

Stipulated. Known. مَعْهُودٌ

Debauchery. عَهْرٌ وَعَهَارَةٌ

To stop ; pass by. عَاجَ يَعُوجُ

To crook, bend, contort. عَوَّجَ

To become bent. تَعَوَّجَ وَآعْوَجَّ

Ivory. عَاجٌ

Crookedness. عِوَجٌ وَآعْوِجَاجٌ

Crooked. أَعْوَجُ م عَوْجَاءُ ج عُوجٌ

Crooked, tortuous. مُعَوَّجٌ

To return to. عَادَ يَعُودُ إِلَى

To repeat. عَادَ وَأَعَادَ

To visit (the sick). عَادَ عِيَادَةً

عَوَّدَ To accustom.

أَعَادَ إِلَى To restore.

تَعَوَّدَ وَٱعْتَادَ To be accustomed.

عَادَةٌ ج عَادَاتٌ Custom.

عَادِيٌّ Old. Customary.

أَلْعَادِيَّاتُ Ancient monuments.

عَوْدٌ Return ; repetition.

عُودٌ ج عِيدَانٌ Stick. Lute.

أَلْعُودُ Aloes-wood.

عِيدٌ ج أَعْيَادٌ Festival, feast-day.

عَائِدٌ A visitor, (*sp*. of the sick).

عَائِدَةٌ ج عَوَائِدُ Benefit ; utility.

إِعَادَةٌ Repetition.

إِعْتِيَادِيٌّ Habitual, customary.

أَلْمَعَادُ The future life.

مُعَوَّدٌ وَمُعْتَادٌ Habituated.

عَاذَ يَعُوذُ بِ To seek protection.

عَوْذٌ وَعِيَاذٌ Taking refuge.

مَعَاذٌ وَمَعَاذَةٌ Refuge, asylum.

مَعَاذَ ٱللهِ God forbid !

عَوِرَ وَٱعْوَرَّ To lose one eye.

أَعَارَ To lend.

إِسْتَعَارَ To borrow.

عَوْرَةٌ ج عَوْرَاتٌ Private parts.

إِعَارَةٌ Loan ; act of lending.

إِسْتِعَارَةٌ Borrowing. Metaphor.

إِسْتِعَارِيٌّ Metaphorical.

أَعْوَرُ م عَوْرَاءُ ج عُورٌ One-eyed.

مُسْتَعَارٌ Borrowed. Metaphorical.

عَازَ يَعُوزُ وَأَعْوَزَ To want, lack.

أَعْوَزَهُ ٱلشَّيْءُ He needed it.

أَعْوَزَهُ ٱلدَّهْرُ Fortune has reduced him to poverty.

عَوَزٌ Poverty, need.

عَوِزٌ وَعَائِزٌ وَأَعْوَزُ وَمُعْوِزٌ Needy.

مَعَاوِزُ Wants.

عَوِصَ يَعْوَصُ To be difficult.

Difficulty, obscurity. عَوَصٌ

Difficult. عَوِيصٌ م عَوْصَاءُ

To give something in exchange. عَاضَ يَعُوضُ وَعَوَّضَ

To receive in compensation for. تَعَوَّضَ وَٱعْتَاضَ عَنْ أَوْ مِنْ

Thing in exchange. عِوَضٌ

Compensation. عِوَضٌ وَتَعْوِيضٌ

Instead of. عِوَضاً عَنْ أَوْ مِنْ

To hinder. عَاقَ يَعُوقُ وَعَوَّقَ وَأَعَاقَ

To be hindered. تَعَوَّقَ

Delay. عَاقَةٌ

Obstacle. عَائِقٌ وَعَائِقَةٌ ج عَوَائِقُ

Capella (star). أَلْعَيُّوقُ

Act of retarding. إِعَاقَةٌ وَتَعْوِيقٌ

To support ; nourish. عَالَ يَعُولُ

To be unfaithful in. عَالَ فِي

His patience was exhausted. عَالَ وَعِيلَ صَبْرُهُ

To wail. عَوَّلَ وَأَعْوَلَ وَٱعْتَوَلَ

To rely upon. عَوَّلَ عَلَى وَبِ

To sustain a family. أَعَالَ

Wailing. عَوْلٌ وَعَوْلَةٌ وَعَوِيلٌ

Family. عَائِلَةٌ ج عَائِلَاتٌ

A family, household. عِيَالٌ

Pickaxe. مِعْوَلٌ ج مَعَاوِلُ

To swim, float. عَامَ يَعُومُ عَوْماً

A year. عَامٌ ج أَعْوَامٌ

Swimming. عَائِمٌ

To aid, assist. عَاوَنَ وَأَعَانَ عَلَى

To give mutual aid. تَعَاوَنَ

To seek the aid of. إِسْتَعَانَ بِ

Aid, assistance. عَوْنٌ وَمَعُونَةٌ

Aider, assistant. عَوْنٌ ج أَعْوَانٌ

Aid, assistance. إِعَانَةٌ وَمُعَاوَنَةٌ

Assistant, coadjutor. مُعَاوِنٌ

Bane, pest, blight. عَاهَةٌ

To howl, bark. عَوَى يَعْوِي عُوَاءً

Howling, crying, barking.	عُوَاءٌ
To be faulty.	عَابَ يَعِيبُ
To find fault with.	عَابَ وَعَيَّبَ
Blemish ; shame.	عَيْبٌ ج عُيُوبٌ
Defective, faulty.	عَائِبٌ
Shameful.	مَعِيبٌ وَمَعْيُوبٌ
To act corruptly.	عَاثَ يَعِيثُ
To celebrate a feast.	عَيَّدَ
Feast, festival.	عِيدٌ ج أَعْيَادٌ
Christmas.	عِيدُ ٱلْمِيلَادِ
To go about ; journey.	عَارَ يَعِيرُ
To upbraid, reproach. To verify by weighing.	عَيَّرَ
Disgrace, shame.	عَارٌ
Standard of weight.	عِيَارٌ
Jesus (Christ).	عِيسَى
Christian.	عِيسَوِيٌّ
To live.	عَاشَ يَعِيشُ عَيْشًا
To nourish.	عَيَّشَ وَأَعَاشَ
To seek means of living.	تَعَيَّشَ
Life.	عَيْشٌ وَعِيشَةٌ
Wheat, bread, food.	عَيْشٌ
Living, living well.	عَائِشٌ
Means of living.	مَعَاشٌ وَمَعِيشَةٌ
To cry out, shout.	عَيَّطَ
Shouting.	عِيَاطٌ
To dislike.	عَافَ يَعَافُ وَيَعِيفُ
To become poor.	عَالَ يَعِيلُ
To have a large family.	أَعْيَلَ
Family.	عَائِلَةٌ ج عِيَالٌ
Having a large family.	مُعْيِلٌ
To appoint ; specify.	عَيَّنَ
To see.	عَايَنَ مُعَايَنَةً وَعِيَانًا
To be specified ; appointed.	تَعَيَّنَ
Eye. Self.	عَيْنٌ ج أَعْيُنٌ وَعُيُونٌ
The chief men, notables.	ٱلْأَعْيَانُ
Fountain	عَيْنٌ ج عُيُونٌ

It is he himself. هُوَ هُوَ عَيْنُهُ

Certain knowledge. عَيْنُ ٱلْيَقِين

Act of seeing. عِيَانٌ ومُعَايَنَةٌ

Clearly, evidently. عِيَانًا

Occular (witness). عِيَانِيٌّ

Spectacles, eye-glasses. عُوَيْنَاتٌ

Specification, designation. تَعْيِينٌ

Designated, appointed. مُعَيَّنٌ

A rhombus, (*geom.*). مُعَيَّنٌ

A rhomboid. الشَّبِيهُ بالمُعَيَّنِ

Designated, appointed. مُتَعَيِّنٌ

Bane, scourge, blight. عَاهَةٌ

To be unable. عَيِيَ يَعْيَى عَيًّا

To be disabled ; disable. أَعْيَا

Weakness, disease. عَيَاءٌ

Weak. عَيِيٌّ ج أَعْيَاءٌ

Weak, incapable, sick. عَيَّانٌ

غ

As a numeral sign=1000. غ

To visit at intervals. غَبَّ ـُ

At intervals. غِبًّا

After. غِبَّ

To raise the dust. غَبَّرَ وأَغْبَرَ

To become dusty. تَغَبَّرَ

To become dust-coloured. إِغْبَرَّ

Dust. غَبْرَةٌ وغُبْرَةٌ وَغُبَارٌ

Remaining. Passing away. غَابِرٌ

Dust-coloured. أَغْبَرُ م غَبْرَاءُ ج غُبْرٌ

Duskiness. غَبَسٌ وغُبْسَةٌ

Ash-coloured. أَغْبَسُ م غَبْسَاءُ

Small pistol. غَدَّارَةٌ ج غَدَّارَاتٌ

Pool of water. غَدِيرٌ ج غُدْرَانٌ

To go forth early. غَدَا يغدو

To breakfast. تَغَدَّى

To give breakfast. غَدَّى

To-morrow. غَداً وَفِي ٱلغَدِ

Day after to-morrow. بعدَ ٱلغَدِ

Morning meal ; lunch. غَدَاءٌ

Early morning. غُدُوٌّ وَغَدَاةٌ

To nourish (food). غَذَاـُ وَغَذَّى

To be fed. تَغَذَّى وَٱغْتَذَى

Food nutriment. غذاءٌ ج أَغْذِيَةٌ

Nourishing (food). مُغَذٍّ

To beguile. غَرَّ يَغُرُّ غُرُوراً

To be deceived. إِغْتَرَّ

White mark on the forehead of a horse. The new moon. The best of anything. غُرَّةٌ ج غُرَرٌ

Very deceitful. غَرَّارٌ وَغَرُورٌ

Unexperienced, ignorant. غِرٌّ ج أَغْرَارٌ

To be in a happy state. إِغْتَبَطَ

Happy state. غَبْطٌ وَغِبطَةٌ

Channel of water. غَبِيطٌ ج غُبُطٌ

Fortunate ; blessed. مَغْبُوطٌ

To cheat. غَبَنَ يَغْبِنُ غَبْناً

To conceal. غَبَنَ وَٱغْتَبَنَ

To be deceived, or cheated. إِنْغَبَنَ

Fraud, deceit. غَبْنٌ وَغَبِينَةٌ

To be hidden from. غَبِيَ عَلَى

Ignorance, heedlessness. غَبَاوَة

Ignorant, stupid. غَبِيٌّ ج أَغْبِيَاء

Lean, meagre. غَثٌّ وَغَثِيثٌ

Ash-colour. غُثْمَةٌ

To be nauseated. غثا يَغْثِي غَثَيَانَا

Wen ; gland. غُدَّةٌ ج غُدَدٌ

To deceive. غَدَرَ يَغْدِرُ غَدْراً بِ

To leave, abandon. غَادَرَ

Perfidy, treachery. غَدْرٌ

Treacherous. غَادِرٌ وَغَدَّارٌ

غُرُورٌ False things, vanities.

أَغَرُّ م غَرَّاءُ Beautiful. Noble.

مَغْرُورٌ Deceived, deluded.

غَرَبَ يَغْرُبُ To depart ; set (sun).

غَرَّبَ وَأَغْرَبَ To go west.

تَغَرَّبَ To go to a strange land.

إِسْتَغْرَبَ To regard as strange.

غَرْبٌ The west.

غُرْبَةٌ وتَغَرُّبٌ وَٱغْتِرَابٌ Travelling in a foreign land.

غُرَابٌ ج غِرْبَانٌ A crow.

غَرَابَةٌ Strangeness, obscurity.

غُرُوبٌ Setting, sun-set.

غَرِيبٌ ج غُرَبَاءُ A stranger.

غَرِيبَةٌ ج غَرَائِبُ Strange event.

مَغْرِبٌ ج مَغَارِبُ The west.

مَغْرِبُ ٱلشَّمْسِ Hour of sun-set.

مَغْرِبِيٌّ ج مَغَارِبَةٌ Moor, Arab of N. W. Africa.

غَرْبَلَ To sift ; disperse.

غِرْبَالٌ ج غَرَابِيلُ Sieve.

غَرَدَ يَغْرِدُ وَغَرَّدَ To warble.

غَرَزَ يَغْرِزُ غَرْزاً ب To prick.

غَرَزَ وَغَرَّزَ وَأَغْرَزَ To insert.

غَرِيزَةٌ ج غَرَائِزُ Nature ; natural, innate quality.

غَرِيزِيٌّ Natural, innate.

غَرَسَ يَغْرِسُ غَرْساً To plant.

إِنْغَرَسَ To be planted.

غَرْسٌ ج أَغْرَاسٌ Planted tree.

مَغْرِسٌ ج مَغَارِسُ Plantation.

مَغْرُوسٌ Planted (tree).

غِرْشٌ ج غُرُوشٌ Piastre.

غَرَضٌ ج أَغْرَاضٌ Aim, object.

غَرْغَرَ To gargle.

غَرْغَرَةٌ A gargle.

غَرَفَ يَغْرُفُ وَٱغْتَرَفَ To dip out with a ladle.

غُرْفَةٌ ج غُرَفٌ Upper chamber.

غُرْفَةٌ ج غِرَافٌ Handful.

Ladle.	مِغْرَفَةٌ ج مَغَارِفُ
To sink, be drowned.	غَرِقَ يَغْرَقُ
To drown.	غَرَّقَ وَأَغْرَقَ
To take in, comprise.	إِسْتَغْرَقَ
Drowning, sinking.	غَرَقٌ
Drowned.	غَرِيقٌ ج غَرْقَى
To pay a tax, fine.	غَرِمَ يَغْرَمُ
To impose a fine.	غَرَّمَ وَأَغْرَمَ
To be very fond of.	اغْرِمَ بِ
To pay a tax ; fine.	تَغَرَّمَ
Fine, tax ; loss.	غَرَامَةٌ
Fond attachment.	غَرَامٌ
Debtor ; litigant.	غَرِيمٌ ج غُرَمَاءُ
Eagerly desirous.	مُغْرَمٌ
Crane ; stork.	غُرْنُوقٌ ج غَرَانِقُ
To glue.	غَرَا يَغْرُو وَغَرَّى
To incite, urge.	أَغْرَى
To be glued.	تَغَرَّى
Glue.	غِرَاءٌ
No wonder !	لَا غَرْوَ
Incitement, instigation.	إِغْرَاءٌ
Glue pot.	مِغْرَاةٌ
To prick.	غَزَّ يَغُزُّ بِ
Gaza, (town).	غَزَّةُ
To be copious.	غَزُرَ يَغْزُرُ
Abundance.	غَزَارَةٌ
Abundant.	غَزِيرٌ ج غِزَارٌ
To spin.	غَزَلَ يَغْزِلُ غَزْلاً
To say amatory words.	تَغَزَّلَ
Spun thread or yarn.	غَزْلٌ
Amatory words.	غَزَلٌ وَتَغَزُّلٌ
Gazelle.	غَزَالٌ ج غِزْلَانٌ
Female gazelle. The sun.	غَزَالَةٌ
Spindle.	مِغْزَلٌ ج مَغَازِلُ
Spun.	مَغْزُولٌ
To wage war, invade the enemy's country.	غَزَا يَغْزُو
Military expedition.	غَزْوٌ

غَزْوَةٌ ج غَزَوَاتٌ	An incursion.
غَازٍ ج غُزَاةٌ	Warrior ; invader.
مَغْزَى ٱلْكَلَامِ	Sense, meaning.
غَسَقَ يَغْسِقُ	To become very dark.
غَسَقٌ	Early darkness of night.
غَسَلَ يَغْسِلُ وَغَسَّلَ	To wash.
إِنْغَسَلَ	To be washed.
إِغْتَسَلَ	To wash one's self.
غُسْلٌ	Washing, ablution.
غَسَّالَةٌ	Washerwoman.
غَسِيلٌ	Clothes that are washed.
غَشَّ يَغُشُّ	To deceive, falsify.
إِنْغَشَّ	To be deceived.
غِشٌّ	Deceit, dishonesty, fraud.
غَاشٌّ وَغَشَّاشٌ	Deceitful.
مَغْشُوشٌ	Deceived ; falsified.
غُشْمٌ	Inexperience.
غَشِيمٌ ج غُشَمَاءُ	Inexperienced.
غَشَاوَةٌ	Film (on the eyes)
غَشِيَ يَغْشَى	To cover, conceal.
غَشِيَ وَأَغْشَى	To be dark, (night).
غُشِيَ عَلَيْهِ غَشَيَانًا	He swooned.
غَشَّى	To put a covering upon.
غِشَاءٌ ج أَغْشِيَةٌ	Cover ; membrane.
غَشْيَةٌ وَغَشَيَانٌ	Swoon.
مُغْشًى وَمَغْشًى	Covered, enveloped.
مَغْشِيٌّ عَلَيْهِ	Swooning, senseless.
غَصَّ يَغَصُّ	To be choked.
أَغَصَّ	To choke. Grieve.
غُصَّةٌ ج غُصَصٌ	Choking. Grief.
غَصَبَ يَغْصِبُ غَصْبًا عَلَى	To force. To take by violence.
غَصَبَ وَٱغْتَصَبَ مِنْ	To violate.
غَصْبٌ	Violence.
غَصْبًا عَنْهُ	In spite of him.
غَاصِبٌ وَمُغْتَصِبٌ	Oppressor.
إِغْتِصَابٌ	Violence, tyranny.
مَغْصُوبٌ وَمُغْتَصَبٌ	Forced.

غُصْنٌ ج أَغْصَانٌ Branch, twig.

غَضَّ يَغِضُّ To be fresh (plant).

غَضَّ ٱلطَّرْفَ To take no notice.

غَضٌّ Fresh, juicy, luxuriant.

غَضِبَ يَغْضَبُ To be angry.

غَاضَبَ وَأَغْضَبَ To make angry.

تَغَضَّبَ To be angry.

غَضَبٌ Anger, rage, passion.

غَضْبَانُ ج غَضْبَى Angry, enraged.

غَضُوبٌ Stern, austere, angry.

مَغْضُوبٌ عَلَيْهِ Object of anger.

غَضَارَةٌ Ease of life, affluence.

غُضْرُوفٌ ج غَضَارِيفُ Cartilage.

غَضْنٌ Wrinkle, fold.

فِي غُضُونِ كَذَا During.

غَضَا يَغْضُو To become dark.

أَغْضَى عَنْهُ To close the eyes to.

تَغَاضَى عَنْ To neglect, disregard.

غَطَّ يَغِطُّ غَطًّا To immerse, dip.

غَطَّ يَغِطُّ غَطِيطًا To snore.

إِنْغَطَّ To be plunged, immersed.

غَطْرَسَ غَطْرَسَةً To be proud.

غَطَسَ يَغْطِسُ غَطْسًا فِي To immerse. To plunge.

غَطَّسَ To immerse.

عِيدُ ٱلْغِطَاسِ Feast of Epiphany.

غَطَّاسٌ Diver.

مِغْطَسٌ ج مَغَاطِسُ Bath-tub.

مَغْنَطِيسٌ وَمَغْنَاطِيسٌ Magnet.

غَطَّى To cover up, conceal.

تَغَطَّى To be covered, concealed.

غِطَاءٌ ج أَغْطِيَةٌ Cover, covering.

غَفَرَ ـ وَغَفَّرَ To cover, veil.

غَفَرَ ـِ لِ To forgive, pardon.

إِسْتَغْفَرَ To ask for pardon.

غَفَرٌ Guard, escort.

غُفْرَانٌ Pardon, forgiveness.

غَفَّارٌ وَغَفُورٌ Forgiving, (God).

Guard, sentinel. غَفِيرٌ وَخَفِيرٌ

Pardon, forgiveness. مَغْفِرَةٌ

To be heedless of. غَفَلَ يَغْفُلُ عَنْ

To make one unmindful. أَغْفَلَ

Forget, disregard. أَغْفَلَ

To be unmindful of. تَغَافَلَ عَنْ

To watch for one's unmindfulness. إِسْتَغْفَلَ

Heedlessness. غَفْلٌ وَغَفْلَةٌ وَغُفُولٌ

Unawares. غَفْلَةً وَعَلَى غَفْلَةٍ

Unmindful, heedless. غَافِلٌ

Simpleton. مُغَفَّلٌ

To sleep. غَفَا يَغْفُو وَغَفِيَ يَغْفَى

Sleepy ; sleeping. غَافٍ

To fetter, shackle. غَلَّ يَغُلُّ

To yield income. أَغَلَّ وَغَلَّ

To take the proceeds. إِسْتَغَلَّ

Rancour, malice. غِلٌّ وَغَلِيلٌ

Manacle, shackle. غُلٌّ ج أَغْلَالٌ

Burning of love &c. غَلِيلٌ

Proceeds, غَلَّةٌ ج غَلَّاتٌ وَغِلَالٌ
revenue from land, crops.

Burning of love or grief. غَلِيلٌ

Fruitful, productive. مُغِلٌّ

Manacled, shackled. مَغْلُولٌ

To conquer, subdue. غَلَبَ يَغْلِبُ

To contend for victory. غَالَبَ

To prevail, overcome. تَغَلَّبَ عَلَى

To be overcome, defeated. إِنْغَلَبَ

Victory, conquest. غَلَبَةٌ

Victor, conqueror. غَالِبٌ ج غَلَبَةٌ

Usually. غَالِبًا وَفِي ٱلْغَالِبِ

Conquered, overcome. مَغْلُوبٌ

The last darkness of night. غَلَسٌ

At early dawn. غَلَسًا

To make a mistake. غَلِطَ يَغْلَطُ

To accuse one of mistake. غَلَّطَ

Mistake, error. غَلَطٌ ج أَغْلَاطٌ

غَلْطَةٌ — Single mistake, fault.

مغلَّط وَمَغْلوطٌ — Erroneous.

مغَالطَة — Sophism.

غَلُظَ يَغْلُظُ — To be thick, bulky.

غَلَّظَ على — To be hard, severe.

أَغْلَظَ لهُ — To be rough, uncivil.

غلاَظةٌ — Thickness, incivility.

غَلِيظٌ ج غِلاَظٌ — Thick ; rough.

غَلَّفَ — To put into an envelope.

تَغلَّفَ وَاغْتَلَفَ — To have a cover.

غِلاَفٌ ج غُلفٌ — Covering, sheath.

(مُغلَّفٌ ج مُغلَّفَاتٌ — Envelope.

أَغْلَفُ ج غُلفٌ — Uncircumcised.

أَغْلَقَ — To close, shut.

إِنغلَقَ — To be closed, shut.

غَلَقٌ ج أَغْلاَقٌ — Lock.

مُغلَقٌ — Closed, locked.

ـِقَة حِسَاب — Balance of account.

غُلاَمٌ ج غِلمَانٌ — Boy, youth.

غَيْلَمٌ — Tortoise.

غَلَّنَ — To become calm, (sea).

(غَلِّينَة) — Quiet, calmness of the sea.

غَلاَ يَغْلُو غُلُوًّا — To be excessive.

غَلاَ غَلاَءً — To be high in price.

غَلَّى — To make the price high.

غَالَى مُغَالاَةً في — To go too far.

إِستغلَى — To find it high-priced.

غَلاَءٌ — High price ; dearness.

غُلُوٌّ — Excess, exaggeration.

غَلْوَةٌ ج غَلَوَاتٌ — Furlong.

غَالٍ — High-priced, dear.

أَغْلَى — Of higher price, dearer.

غَلَى يَغْلِي — To boil (pot).

غَلَّى وَأَغْلَى — To cause to boil.

غَلْيٌ وَغَلَيَانٌ — Boiling, ebullition.

غَلْيُونٌ ج غلاَيِينُ — Tobacco-pipe.

غَلاَّيَةٌ — Vessel for heating water.

غَمَّ يَغُمُّ To cover, to grieve.

إِنْغَمَّ وَاغْتَمَّ To be grieved.

غَمٌّ ج غُمُومٌ Grief, sorrow.

غَمَامٌ ج غَمَائِمُ Clouds, (*coll*).

غَمَامَةٌ A cloud.

مُغِمٌّ Sorrowful, mournful.

مَغْمُومٌ Afflicted, grieved.

غَمَدَ يَغْمُدُ وَأَغْمَدَ To sheathe; cover.

غَمَّدَ وَتَغَمَّدَ To cover, veil.

غِمْدٌ ج أَغْمَادٌ Scabbard, sheath.

غَمَرَ يَغْمُرُ To submerge (water).

غَمُرَ يَغْمُرُ To be abundant.

إِنْغَمَرَ وَاغْتَمَرَ To be submerged.

غَمْرٌ Abundant (water).

غَمْرَةٌ Deep water. Difficulty.

غَمَرَاتُ ٱلْمَوْتِ Pangs of death.

غَمَزَ يَغْمُزُ غَمْزاً To wink. Press.

غَمْزَةٌ Sign made with the eye.

غَمَسَ يَغْمُسُ To immerse, dip.

إِنْغَمَسَ وَاغْتَمَسَ To be plunged.

غَمُضَ يَغْمُضُ To be obscure.

غَمَّضَ وَاغْمَضَ To shut (the eyes).

إِنْغَمَضَ To be closed, (eye).

غَامِضٌ ج غَوَامِضُ Obscure.

مُغَمَّضٌ Closed (eye). Obscure.

(غُمْقٌ) Depth.

(غَمِيقٌ) Deep.

غُمِيَ عَلَيْهِ وَاغْمِيَ عَلَيْهِ To swoon.

غَمْيٌ وَإِغْمَاءٌ Swooning, swoon.

مُغْمًى عَلَيْهِ In a swoon.

غَنِجَ To be coquettish.

غُنْجٌ وَغِنَاجٌ Coquetry.

غَنِجَةٌ وَغَنُوجَةٌ Coquette.

غَنِمَ يَغْنَمُ To plunder; obtain.

غَنَّمَ To give a free gift.

إِغْتَنَمَ To seize as spoil.

To seize the opportunity.	إِغْتَنَمَ وَٱسْتَغْنَمَ ٱلْفُرْصَةَ
Booty.	غُنْمٌ وَغَنِيمَةٌ ج غَنَائِمُ
Sheep (*coll.*).	غَنَمٌ ج أَغْنَامٌ
Shepherd.	غَنَّامٌ
Spoiler ; successful.	غَانِمٌ
To be rich.	غَنِيَ يَغْنَى
To be content with.	غَنِيَ بِ
To be in no need of.	غَنِيَ عَنْ
To sing, chant.	غَنَّى
To free from want.	أَغْنَى
To become rich.	إِغْتَنَى وَٱسْتَغْنَى
To be in no need of.	إِسْتَغْنَى عَنْ
Wealth, opulence.	غِنًى وَغَنَاءٌ
He cannot do without it.	مَا لَهُ عَنْهُ غِنًى
Song.	غِنَاءٌ وَأُغْنِيَّةٌ ج أَغَانٍ وَأَغَانِيُّ
Rich, opulent.	غَنِيٌّ ج أَغْنِيَاءُ
Beautiful woman.	غَانِيَةٌ ج غَوَانٍ
Singer.	مُغَنٍّ ج مُغَنِّيَةٌ
Very dark, black.	غَيْهَبٌ ج غَيَاهِبُ
To aid, succour.	غَاثَ يَغُوثُ وَأَغَاثَ
To seek aid.	إِسْتَغَاثَ وَبِ
Aid, succour.	غَوْثٌ وَإِغَاثَةٌ
Request of aid.	إِسْتِغَاثَةٌ
To sink deep.	غَارَ يَغُورُ
To attack, invade.	أَغَارَ عَلَى
Laurel (plant).	غَارٌ
Raid, incursion.	غَارَةٌ ج غَارَاتٌ
He made a raid.	شَنَّ ٱلْغَارَةَ
Bottom, depth. Low land.	غَوْرٌ
Cave, cavern.	مَغَارَةٌ ج مَغَائِرُ
To plunge into.	غَاصَ يَغُوصُ فِي
To plunge dip (*v.t.*).	غَوَّصَ
One who plunges.	غَائِصٌ
Diver, (*sp.* pearl-fisher).	غَوَّاصٌ
Deep.	(غَوِيصٌ)
To dig, excavate. Sink.	غَاطَ يَغُوطُ

To void excrement. تَغَوَّطَ

Low ground. غَوْطٌ وَغَوْطَةٌ

Excrement, fæces. غَائِطٌ

To destroy. غَالَ يَغُولُ وَٱغْتَالَ

To slay covertly. إِغْتَالَ

Goblin, demon. غُولٌ ج غِيلَانٌ

Evil, mischief. غَائِلَةٌ ج غَوَائِلُ

To err. غَوِيَ يَغْوَى غَوًى

To seduce. غَوَى وَأَغْوَى

To be led into error. إِنْغَوَى

Error, leading astray. غَيٌّ وَغَوَايَةٌ

Error. غَيَّةٌ ج غَيَّاتٌ

Erring; deceiver. غَاوٍ ج غُوَاةٌ

To be absent, distant. غَابَ يَغِيبُ

To set; disappear. غَابَ غِيَابًا

To lose one's reason. غَابَ عَنِ ٱلصَّوَابِ

To slander. غَابَ وَٱغْتَابَ

To go away, travel. غَابَ وَتَغَيَّبَ

To conceal from. غَيَّبَ عَنْ

Absence. غَيْبٌ وَغَيْبَةٌ وَغِيَابٌ

Hidden thing. غَيْبٌ ج غُيُوبٌ

From memory. غَيْبًا وَعَلَى ٱلْغَائِبِ

The unseen world. عَالَمُ ٱلْغَيْبِ

Forest. غَابَةٌ ج غَابَاتٌ

Calumny, backbiting. غِيبَة

Absent, hidden. غَائِبٌ

Time or place of the setting of the sun. مَغِيبُ ٱلشَّمْسِ

To water with rain. غَاثَ يَغِيثُ

Rain. غَيْثٌ ج غُيُوثٌ

Fresh, tender (woman) غَادَةٌ

Tender. أَغْيَدُ م غَيْدَاءُ ج غِيدٌ

To be jealous. غَارَ يَغَارُ

To alter, change. غَيَّرَ

To make jealous. أَغَارَ

To be changed. تَغَيَّرَ

To differ. غَايَرَ وَتَغَايَرَ

غَيْرُ Other ; another. Except.

وَغَيْرُ ذَلِكَ Et cætera.

غَيْرُ خَالِصٍ Not pure, impure.

مِنْ غَيْرِ ذَلِكَ Without that.

غَيْرَ أَنَّ Although.

لاَ غَيْرُ Nothing else.

غَيْرَةٌ Jealously ; zeal.

غَيُورٌ Very jealous.

(مِغْيَارٌ) Unhealthy (climate).

غَيْضَةٌ ج غِيَاضٌ Thicket, wood.

غَاظَ يَغِيظُ وَأَغَاظَ To anger, enrage.

إِغْتَاظَ وَتَغَيَّظَ To become angry.

غَيْظٌ Anger, rage, wrath.

مُغْتَاظٌ Angry, enraged.

غَاقٌ Crow, raven.

(غَالٌ ج غَالاَتٌ) Lock.

غِيلٌ ج أَغْيَالٌ Thicket, jungle.

غِيلَةٌ Subterfuge, deception.

غَائِلَةٌ Rancour, malice ; evil.

غَامَ وَأَغْيَمَ وَتَغَيَّمَ To be cloudy.

غَيْمٌ ج غُيُومٌ Clouds (*coll.*)

غَايَةٌ ج غَايَاتٌ Extremity, term. Ultimate object.

إِلَى ٱلْغَايَةِ Extremely.

ف

And ; then. As a numeral sign=80.	ف
Heart ; soul ; mind.	فُؤَادٌ ج أَفْئِدَةٌ
Rat ; mouse.	فَأْرٌ ج فِئْرَانٌ
A mouse.	فَأْرَةٌ ج فَأْرَاتٌ
Axe ; hatchet.	فَأْسٌ ج فُؤُوسٌ
To draw a favourable augury.	تَفَأَّلَ وَتَفَاءَلَ ب
Good or evil omen.	فَأْلٌ وَتَفَاؤُلٌ
Company, band.	فِئَةٌ ج فِئَاتٌ
To break in pieces.	فَتَّ يَفُتُّ
To be crumbled.	تَفَتَّتَ وَآنْفَتَّ
Small pieces ; crumbs.	فُتَاتٌ
Crumbled.	فَتِيتٌ وَمَفْتُوتٌ
To cease from.	فَتِئَ يَفْتَأُ عَنْ
He continued to do.	مَا فَتِئَ يَفْعَلُ
To open. Conquer (a country).	فَتَحَ يَفْتَحُ
To succour. Reveal.	فَتَحَ عَلَى
To address one first.	فَاتَحَ
To be opened.	تَفَتَّحَ وَآنْفَتَحَ
To open, commence. Attack and conquer (a land).	إِفْتَتَحَ
To begin. Seek succour.	إِسْتَفْتَحَ
Victory, conquest.	فَتْحٌ ج فُتُوحٌ
Conquered countries.	فُتُوحَاتٌ
The short vowel *fatha*. (َ)	فَتْحَةٌ
An opening.	فَتْحَةٌ
Conqueror. Light-coloured.	فَاتِحٌ
Introduction, preface.	فَاتِحَةٌ
First chapter of the Koran.	أَلْفَاتِحَةُ
He who opens, conquers.	فَتَّاحٌ

Introduction. Conquest. افتتَاحٌ

Introductory. افتتَاحِيٌّ

Key. مفتَاحٌ ج مفَاتِيحُ

Opened. Vocalized by the vowel *fatha*. مَفْتُوحٌ

To subside ; be tepid. فتَرَ يفتُرُ

To desist ; abate. فتَرَ عَنْ

To allay. Make tepid. فتَّرَ

Measure between extended thumb and index finger. فِتْرٌ

Intermission. فتْرَة ج فتَرَاتٌ

Languid ; lukewarm. فَاتِرٌ

Lukewarmness, languor. فُتُورٌ

To examine, investigate. فتَّشَ

Examination, inquest. تَفْتِيشٌ

Examiner, inspector. مفتِّشٌ

To crumble (*v.t.*). (فتَّفَتَ)

To cleave, slit, rip. فتَقَ يفتُقُ فتْقاً

To be split ; ripped. تَفَتَّقَ وَآنفتَقَ

Rupture, hernia. Rent. فَتْقٌ وَفِتَاقٌ

Ruptured, ripped. مَفْتُوقٌ

To assault ; kill. فَتَكَ بِ

Bold, daring. فَاتِكٌ ج فُتَّاكٌ

To twist. فتَلَ يفتِلُ فتْلاً وَفَتَّلَ

To be twisted. تَفَتَّلَ وَآنْفتَلَ

Twister (of rope, &c.) فَتَّالٌ

Twisted (rope, &c.) فتِيلٌ وَمفْتُولٌ

Wick of a lamp. فتِيلة ج فَتَائِل

To please ; infatuate. فتَنَ يفتِنُ

To please ; seduce. أَفْتَنَ

To lead, or to be led, into error. افتتَنَ

Seduction. Trial, affliction. Sedition. فِتْنَة

Seducer ; charmer. فَاتِنٌ ج فتَّانٌ

Infatuated ; seduced. مفتُونٌ

To be young. فتِيَ يفتَى فتًى وَفتَاءً

To answer أَفْتَى (ٱلعَالِمُ) فِي مَسْأَلةٍ a learned question.

To affect youth. تَفَتَّى

To ask the solution of a learned question, *sp.* judicial. إِستَفتَى

A young man. فَتًى ج فِتيَانٌ

A young woman. فَتَاةٌ ج فَتَيَاتٌ

Manliness, generosity. فُتُوَّةٌ

Judicial sentence. فَتوَى ج فَتَاوٍ

A lawyer. Mufti. مُفْتٍ (اَلْمُفْتِي)

Way, path. فَجٌّ ج فِجَاجٌ

Unripe (fruit). فِجٌّ وفَجٌّ

To attack or befall suddenly. فَجَأَ يَفْجَأُ وفَاجَأَ

Suddenly; unawares. فَجْأَةً

To give exit to water. فَجَرَ يَفْجُرُ

To live in open sin. فَجَرَ يَفْجُرُ

To flaw. Dawn. تَفَجَّرَ وَانْفَجَرَ

Dawn, day-break. فَجْرٌ

Wicked (man). فَاجِرٌ ج فُجَّارٌ

Great wickedness. فُجُورٌ

To give pain. فَجَعَ يَفْجَعُ فَجْعًا

To suffer pain from loss. فَجِعَ

To grieve, complain. تَفَجَّعَ

Calamitous. فَاجِعٌ وَفَجُوعٌ

Great calamity. فَاجِعَة ج فَوَاجِع

Radish (plant). فُجْلٌ

To notch, blunt. فَجَمَ يَفْجُمُ فَجْمًا

To be excessive; foul. فَحُشَ يَفْحُشُ

To use foul words. فَحَشَ وَأَفْحَشَ

Shameless evil. Excess. فُحْشٌ

Evil. Excessive. فَاحِشٌ

Atrocious sin. فَاحِشَةٌ ج فَوَاحِشُ

To examine. فَحَصَ ـَ وتَفَحَّصَ

Examination. (فَحْصٌ ج فُحُوصٌ)

To become formidable. اسْتَفْحَلَ

Male. Strong man. فَحْلٌ ج فُحُولٌ

Elites in science. فُحُول الْعُلَمَاءِ

To be silence. فَحَمَ يَفْحَمُ

To blacken. فَحَّمَ

أفْحَمَ To silence by argument.
فَحْمٌ Charcoal.
فَحْمُ ٱلحجرِ أو فَحْمٌ حَجَرِيٌّ Coal.
فَحَّامٌ ج فَحَّامَة Seller of charcoal.
فُحمَةٌ Blackness ; darkness.
مُفْحِمٌ (Answer) that silences.
فَحْوى وَفَحْوَاء Meaning ; sense.
فَخٌّ ج فِخاخٌ وفخوخٌ Trap, snare.
فختَ يفْخَتُ To break through.
إنفختَ To be perforated.
فخت Hole, break, perforation.
فخذٌ ج أفْخاذٌ Thigh. Sub-tribe.
فخرَ يفخرُ وَٱفتخر To glory, boast.
فخرَ وفخَّرَ وأفخرَ على To prefer.
فَاخرَ To compete or vie with.
فخرٌ Glory, excellence.
فاخِرٌ Glorious ; excellent.
فخَّارٌ Pottery ; earthen-ware.
فخَّارِيٌّ وَفاخُورِيٌّ Potter.

مفخرَةٌ ج مفَاخِر Glorious trait.
فَخُمَ يفخُم فخامة To be great.
فخّم To show great honour.
مُفَخَّمٌ Highly honoured.
أفْدَعُ ج فدعٌ Club-footed.
فَدَغَ يفْدَغ To wound the head.
فَدَّان وفَدَان ج فَدَادِين Yoke of oxen. Field-measure, acre.
فادِنٌ ج فَوَادِن Plum-line.
فَدى يفْدِي To redeem, ransom.
إفتدى To ransom.
فداء Ransom. Redemption.
فدَاكَ May it be a ransom to you !
الفَادِي The Redeemer.
فَذَّ يفذُّ To become apart.
فَذٌّ One alone, single.
فَذَاذى وَفُذاذاً One by one.
فَذْلَكَةٌ Resumé, gist.
فَرَّ يفرُّ فرّاً To flee ; escape.

فارّ وفرّار Fleeing, fugitive.

فُرِّيّ Snipe, quail.

فرارٌ Flight ; escape.

مَفَرٌّ Escape. Place of escape.

فرا وفراء Wildass ; onager.

ألفُرَات The Euphrates (river).

(فُرْتِيكَة) Fork.

فُرْتُونَة) Storm at sea.

فَرْث Excrement, fæces.

فَرَج يفرِج فَرْجًا To relieve.

أفرج بين To separate.

فرج لِ To make place for.

فرَّجَ To open ; widen. Relieve.

فرَّجَ على To show,

تفرَّجَ To see a new thing.

انفرج To be opened, separate ; to diverge. Be relieved.

فَرَجٌ Relief.

فُرْجة ج فُرَج Opening Show.

فَرَجِيَّة Over-garment.

فرُّوجٌ ج فرارِيجُ Chicken.

مَفْرُوجٌ Open. Relieved.

مُنفرِجٌ Diverging.

ألزَّاوِيَةُ ٱلمُنْفَرِجةُ Obtuse angle.

فرِح يفرَح فرحًا To rejoice.

فرَّح وأفرَح To make glad.

فَرَحٌ Joy, gladness, happiness.

فَرِحٌ ج فرِحون Happy, glad.

فَرْحانٌ م فرْحانة Glad, rejoicing.

فرَّخ وأفْرَخ To sprout ; hatch.

فَرْخٌ ج فروخ Sprout. Chick

فرّخة Chicken.

فرد عن To separate one's self.

افرَدَ To make single ; set apart.

تفرَّد وٱنفرَد To be alone.

إستفرَدَ To seek privacy.

فَرْدٌ ج أفْرَادٌ One ; one of a pair. Individual.

Atom ; monad.	اَلجَوْهَر آلفَرْد
Pistol.	فَرْدٌ ج فُرُودَة
Bale of goods.	فَرْدَةٌ
One by one.	فُرَاداً وَفُرَادَى
Unique, matchless.	فَرِيدٌ
Precious gem.	فَرِيدَةٌ ج فَرَائِدُ
Singular number (*gram.*).	مُفْرَدٌ
Alone; insolated.	مُنفَرِدٌ
Paradise.	فِرْدَوْسٌ ج فَرَادِيس
To set aside.	فَرَزَ يَفْرِزُ وَأَفْرَزَ
To go aside, or away.	إِنفَرَزَ
Cornice, frieze.	إِفْرِيزٌ ج أَفَارِيز
To perceive ; gaze	تَفَرَّسَ
To capture (prey).	أفْتَرَسَ
Horse.	فَرَسٌ ج أَفْرَاسٌ
Hippopotamus.	فَرَسُ ٱلبَحْرِ
Horseman.	فَارِسٌ ج فُرْسَان
Persia.	بِلَادُ فَارِسَ وبِلَادُ ٱلفُرْس
Persian.	فَارِسِيٌّ وَفُرْسِيٌّ ج فُرْسٌ

The Persian language.	أَلفَارِسِيَّةَ
Horsemanship.	فِرَاسَة وفُرُوسَةٌ
Skilful discernment.	فِرَاسة
Physiognomy.	علم الفِرَاسَةِ
Prey (of a lion).	فَرِيسَةٌ
Pharisee.	فَرِّيسِيّ ج فَرِّيسِيُّونَ
Parasang; league.	فَرْسَخٌ ج فَرَاسِخُ
To spread out.	فَرَشَ يَفْرُشُ
To be spread out.	إِفْتَرَشَ وَآنفَرَشَ
House-furniture.	فَرْشٌ وَمَفْرُوشٌ
Brush.	فُرْشَةٌ
Bed.	فِرَاشٌ وفَرْشَةٌ ج فُرُشٌ
Moth ; butterfly.	فَرَاشَةٌ ج فَرَاشٌ
Furnished (house).	مَفْرُوش
To separate the feet.	فَرْشَخَ
Occasion; chance.	فُرْصَةٌ ج فُرَصٌ
To avail one's self of an opportunity.	إِنتَهَزَ آلفُرْصَةَ
To appoint ; ordain. Estimate ; suppose. Allot.	فَرَضَ يَفْرِضُ

To notch, cut. فَرَضَ وفَرَّضَ

To impose. فَرَضَ وٱفتَرَضَ عَلَى

To enact (a law). إِفتَرَضَ

Decree. فَرْضٌ ج فُرُوضٌ
Supposition.

On the supposition. على فَرْضِ

Harbour. فُرْضَةٌ ج فُرَضٌ

Ordinance; duty. فَرِيضَةٌ ج فَرَائِضُ
Alloted portion.

The science of the laws of inheritance. عِلْمُ الفَرَائِض

Enactment. Supposition. إِفتِرَاضٌ

Supposed. Enacted. مَفْرُوضٌ

To lose an opportunity. فَرَطَ يَفْرُطُ

To do a thing hastily. فَرَطَ مِنْ

To miss; neglect. فَرَّطَ (في)

To go to excess. أَفْرَطَ افْرَاطًا

Excess. فَرْطٌ ج أَفْرَاط

Cheap. فرط

Excessive, immoderate. مُفْرِطٌ

To flatten; make broad. فَرْطَحَ

Broad; flattened. مُفَرْطَحٌ

To derive, deduce. فَرَّعَ مِنْ

To ramify; branch forth. تَفَرَّعَ

Branch. Derivative. فَرْعٌ ج فروع

Hatchet. فَرَّاعَةٌ

To be very proud. تَفَرْعَنَ

Pharaoh. فِرْعَوْنٌ ج فَرَاعِنَةٌ

To be empty, vacant. فَرَغَ يَفْرُغُ

To finish a thing. فَرَغَ مِنْ

To pour out. Empty. فَرَّغَ وأَفْرَغَ

To be free from, be at leisure. تَفَرَّغَ من

To devote one's self to. تَفَرَّغَ لِ

To exhaust; vomit. إِسْتَفْرَغَ

Empty, vacant. فَرِغٌ وفَارِغٌ

Emptiness; cessation. فَرَاغٌ

To flap the wings. فَرْفَرَ فَرْفَرَةً

Light-headed, noisy. فُرْفَارٌ

To divide. Distinguish. فَرَقَ يَفْرُقُ بَيْنَ

To scatter ; disperse. فَرَّقَ

To distribute among. فَرَّقَ عَلَى

To stir up dissention. فَرَّقَ بَيْنَ

To abandon. Die. فَارَقَ

To be separated. تَفَرَّقَ وَافْتَرَقَ

To leave one another. تَفَارَقَ

To be separated from. إِنْفَرَقَ عَنْ

Difference, distinction. فَرْقٌ

The Koran. اَلْفُرْقَانُ

Party of men. فِرْقَة ج فِرَقٌ

Separation. فُرْقَةٌ وَافْتِرَاقٌ

Separation. Death. فِرَاقٌ

General of a division. فَرِيقٌ

Africa. أَفْرِيقِيَةُ

Separation, dispersion. تَفْرِيقٌ

In parts, in detail. بِالتَّفْرِيقِ

A point from which a road branches. مَفْرَقٌ ج مَفَارِقُ

To rub. فَرَكَ يَفْرُكُ فَرْكًا

To be mature, (grain). أَفْرَكَ

To be rubbed and pressed. إِنْفَرَكَ

To become full (grain). إِسْتَفْرَكَ

Act of rubbing ; friction. فَرْكٌ

Rubbed soft grain. فَرِيكٌ

To mince. فَرَمَ يَفْرِمُ فَرْمًا

To change the teeth, (child). فَرَّمَ

A small piece. (فَرْمَةٌ)

Firman. فَرَمَانٌ

Oven. فُرْنٌ ج أَفْرَانٌ

Baker. فَرَّانٌ

Europeans. Franks. إِفْرَنْجٌ وَفِرِنْجٌ

France. فَرَنْسَا

French. فَرَنْسِيٌّ فَرَنْسَاوِيٌّ

To line with fur. فَرَّى تَفْرِيَةً

Garment of fur. فَرْوٌ ج فِرَاءٌ

Scalp. Fur-cloak. فَرْوَةٌ

Furrier. فَرَّاءٌ

To fabricate a lie.	إفترى الكذب
Wilful lie.	فرية ج فرى
Unusual thing.	فريّ
To be excited.	فرّ ـ
To frighten, disturb.	فزّ وأفزّ
To excite, incite.	إستفزّ
To cut ; break.	فزر يفزر فزراً
To be afraid.	فزع يفزع فزعاً
To flee for help to.	فزع الى
To frighten.	فزّع وافزع
Fear ; fright.	فزع
Frightened, afraid.	فزع
Refuge. Succour.	مفزع
Pistachio (tree and fruit).	فستق
Basin ; reservoir.	فسقيّة
Female gown.	فستان ج فساتين
To make place for ; permit.	فسح يفسح وأفسح له في
To be spacious, (place).	فسح يفسح
To make roomy, wide.	فسّح
His bosom was dilated (with joy).	إنفسح صدره
Space ; court-yard.	فسحة ج فسح
Spaciousness, width.	فساحة
Spacious, roomy, ample.	فسيح
To annul, abrogate.	فسخ يفسخ
To split.	فسّخ
To be annulled, split.	إنفسخ
Abrogation. Separation.	فسخ
A part, a piece.	فسخة
Salted fish.	فسيخ
To become corrupt.	فسد يفسد
To corrupt.	فسّد وأفسد
To stir up strife.	أفسد بين
To be corrupted, bad.	إنفسد
Corruption, mischief. Invalidity. Decomposition.	فساد
Bad. Invalid. Spoilt.	فاسد
Causing mischief or strife.	مفسد

Cause of evil. مَفْسَدَةٌ ج مَفَاسِد

To make plain ; explain. فَسَّرَ

To seek an explanation. إِسْتَفْسَرَ

Explanation. تَفْسِيرٌ ج تَفَاسِير

Pavilion ; tent. فُسْطَاطٌ

Phosphorus. فُسْفُورٌ وَفُصْفُورٌ

Bugs ; bed-bugs. فَسَافِس

Mosaic-pavement. فُسَيْفِسَاء

To be impious. فَسَقَ يَفْسِق

Impiety. فِسْقٌ وَفُسُوقٌ

Impious, dissolute. فَاسِقٌ

Adulteress. فَاسِقَة

To pick a lock. فَشَّ يَفُشُّ فَشًّا

To vent one's anger. فَشَّ خُلْقَهُ

Do take a wide step. فَشَخَ يَفْشَخ

A step. فَشْخَةٌ

To talk incoherently. فَشَرَ وَفَشَّرَ

Incoherent talk ; babbling. فَشَارٌ

Cartridge. فَشَكَةٌ ج فَشَكٌ)

To be faint-hearted. فَشِلَ يَفْشَل

To fail, be disappointed. تَفَشَّلَ

Disappointment. فَشَلٌ

To be spread. فَشَا يَفْشُو فَشْوًا

To spread. Divulge. أَفْشَى

To become wide ; extend. تَفَشَّى

Stone or gem of a signet-ring. Lobe. فَصٌّ ج فُصُوص

A species of clover. فِصَّةٌ

To break forth, (light). فَصَحَ يَفْصَح

To appear clearly. أَفْصَحَ

To affect eloquence. تَفَاصَحَ

Passover ; Easter. فِصْحٌ

Lucidity ; eloquence. فَصَاحَةٌ

Elegant speaker. فَصِيحٌ ج فُصَحَاء

To open a vein. فَصَدَ يَفْصِد فَصْدًا

To be bled. إِنْفَصَدَ

Bleeder, phlebotomist. فَصَّادٌ

Cut out. Detailed. مُفَصَّل	A person who is bled. مَفْصُود
In detail. مُفَصَّلاً	Lancet. مِفْصَد
Hinge. مَفَصَّلَة ج مُصَّلات	To cut off ; separate. فَصَلَ يَفْصِلُ
Detached. مَفْصُول ومُنفَصِل	Decide a disputed point.
To break, crack. فَصَمَ يَفْصِم	To divide into parts. فَصَّلَ
To be broken, cracked. إِنفَصَم	To bargain for a price. فَاصَل
To break open. فَضَّ يَفُضّ فَضًّا	To expire ; die. أَفْصَلَ
To cover with silver. فَضَّض	To be separated ; detatched. إِنفَصَل
To be dispersed. إِنفَضّ	To go away from. إِنْفَصَلَ عَنْ
Silver. Para. فِضَّة	Separation. Chapt er. فَصْلٌ ج فُصُول
To divulge, disgrace. فَضَحَ يَفْضَح	A season of the year.
Disgrace. فَضِيحَة ج فَضَائِح	That which separates. فَاصِل
To remain over. فَضَلَ يَفْضَل	Decisive judgment. حُكْمٌ فَاصِلٌ
To excel, surpass. فَضَلَ وَعَلَى	Family ; species. فَصِيلَة ج فَصَائِل
To prefer. فَضَّلَ عَلَى	Judge, arbiter. فَيْصَلٌ ج فَيَاصِل
To show favour. أَفْضَلَ وَتَفَضَّلَ	Detailed statement. تَفْصِيلٌ ج تَفَاصِيل
Do me the favour. تَفَضَّلْ	In detail. بِالتَّفْصِيل
To leave a part. إِسْتَفْضَلَ مِنْ	Joint. مَفْصِلٌ ج مَفَاصِل
	Rheumatism. دَاءُ المَفَاصِل

Excess Favour. فَضْلٌ ج فُضُولٌ
Superiority, excellence.

Besides. فَضْلاً عَن

Portion remaining. فَضْلَةٌ

Superior; excellent. فَاضِلٌ وَفَضِيلٌ

Officiousness. فُضُولٌ

Meddlesome. فُضُولِيٌّ

Virtue. Excellence. فَضِيلَةٌ ج فَضَائِلُ

Better. أَفْضَلُ ج أَفَاضِلُ

The best. اَلأَفْضَلُ

Calculus (integral and differential). حِسَابُ ٱلتَّمَامِ وَٱلتَّفَاضُلِ

Preference. تَفْضِيلٌ

Adjective in the comparative degree, *as* : أَكْبَرُ إِسْمُ ٱلتَّفْضِيلِ

Preferable. مُفَضَّلٌ

Distinguished for excellence. مِفْضَالٌ

To be empty. فَضَا يَفْضُو فَضَاءً

To empty, turn out. فَضَّى

To reach. Lead to. أَفْضَى إِلَى

To have leisure for. تَفَضَّى لِ

Open space. فَضَاءٌ

Empty; unoccupied. فَاضٍ

To create, (God). فَطَرَ

To break one's fast. فَطَرَ وَأَفْطَرَ

To be broken. تَفَطَّرَ وَٱنْفَطَرَ

Fungus. فُطْرٌ

Feast of Ramadan. عِيدُ ٱلْفِطْرِ

Innate quality. فِطْرَةٌ ج فِطَرٌ

Creator. فَاطِرٌ

Midday, meal. فُطُورٌ

Unleavened. فَطِيرٌ

Jewish feast of unleavened bread. عِيدُ ٱلْفِطْرِ

Pastry-cake. فَطِيرَةٌ ج فَطَائِرُ

To die. فَطَسَ يَفْطِسُ فُطُوساً

To be suffocated. فَطِسَ يَفْطَسُ

To kill. Suffocate. فَطَّسَ

Flat-nosed. أَفْطَسُ م فَطْسَاءُ ج فُطْسٌ

فطم يفطم To wean (an infant).

إنفطم To be weaned.

إنفطم عن To cease from.

فطام Weaning.

فطيم ومفطوم Weaned (child).

فطن يفطن ب To remember ; consider. Understand.

فطّن ب To remind.

تفطّن ل To understand. Remember.

فطنة Understanding ; sagacity.

فطن وفطين Intelligent.

فظ يفظ فظاظة To be rough, rude.

فظ ج فظاظ Rough, rude.

فظع يفظع فظاعة To be horrid.

فظع وفظيع Atrocious ; horrid.

فعل يفعل To do ; perform ; act.

إنفعل To be affected. Be done.

افتعل To forge ; invent.

فعل ج افعال Act, deed. Verb.

فاعل ج فعلة Doer. Agent or subject of the verb.

إسم الفاعل Noun of agent.

نائب الفاعل Agentor subject of the passive verb.

فعّال Effective, efficient.

إنفعال ج إنفعالات Influence, impression.

إنفعال نفساني Emotion.

تفعيل ج تفاعيل Foot (*in prosody*).

مفعول ج مفاعيل Something done. Impression ; influence.

مفعول به Object of transitive verb.

إسم المفعول Noun of patient.

مفتعل Invented. Done purposely.

فعم يفعم To fill (a vessel).

فعم يفعم فعومة To be full.

مفعم Filled, full.

أفعى وافعوان ج افاعٍ Viper.

فغر يفغر To open (the mouth).

فغر وانفغر To open.

فقأ يفقأ To open (an abscess). Put out an eye.

To burst ; break. تَفَقَّأَ وَآنْفَقَأَ

To lose. فَقَدَ يَفْقِدُ فَقْداً وَفِقْدَاناً

To deprive of, cause to lose. أَفْقَدَ

To seek a lost object. تَفَقَّدَ

To miss, fail to find. Visit a sick person. إِفْتَقَدَ

Lost object. Dead. فَقِيدٌ وَمَفْقُودٌ

To slit, perforate. فَقَرَ يَفْقُرُ

To impoverish. أَفْقَرَ

To become poor. إِفْتَقَرَ

To need. إِفْتَقَرَ إِلى

Poverty ; need. فَقْرٌ

Vertebra. فِقْرَةٌ ج فِقَرٌ

Poor ; needy. فَقِيرٌ ج فُقَرَاءُ

To hatch eggs (bird). فَقَسَ يَفْقِسُ فَقْساً

To be hatched. تَفَقَّسَ وَآنْفَقَسَ

Small melon. فَقُّوسٌ

To break open. فَقَشَ يَفْقُشُ فَقْشاً

Only. فَقَطْ

To die from heat or grief. فَقَعَ

To be cleft or rent. إِنْفَقَعَ

Very bright-coloured. فَاقِعٌ

Bubble of air. فُقَّاعَةٌ ج فَقَاقِيعُ

Unripe figs. (فُقَّيْعٌ)

Excessive poverty. فَقْرٌ مُفْقِعٌ

To be full, (vessel). فَقِمَ يَفْقَمُ

To become very serious. تَفَاقَمَ

Seal. (sea-animal). فُقْمَةٌ وَفُقَّمَةٌ

To understand. فَقِهَ يَفْقَهُ فِقْهاً

To be skilled in the Law. فَقُهَ يَفْقُهُ

To teach. فَقَّهَ وَأَفْقَهَ

To understand ; learn. تَفَقَّهَ

Knowledge ; intelligence. فِقْهٌ

Science of Law. عِلْمُ ٱلْفِقْهِ

Understanding ; learning. فَقَاهَةٌ

Skilled in Law. فَقِيهٌ ج فُقَهَاءُ

فَكَّ يَفُكُّ فَكًّا To separate; untie.

فَكَّكَ To separate; disentangle.

إِنْفَكَّ To be separated; untied.

مَا ٱنْفَكَّ Not to cease.

إِسْتَفَكَّ To seek redemption.

فَكٌّ ج فُكُوكٌ Jaw-bone.

فَكَّرَ يَفْكِرُ وَفَكَّرَ وَتَفَكَّرَ وَٱفْتَكَرَ فِي To think of; consider.

(فَكَّرَ) To remind.

فِكْرٌ ج أَفْكَارٌ Thought; reflection.

فِكِّيرٌ Very thoughtful.

(فَاكُورَةٌ ج فَوَاكِير) Latch.

فَكِهَ يَفْكَهُ فَكَاهَةً To be gay.

فَكَّهَ To cheer by wit.

تَفَكَّهَ بِ To enjoy.

تَفَاكَهَ To jest with another.

فَكِهٌ ج فَكِهُونَ Merry; cheerful.

فَاكِهَةٌ ج فَوَاكِهُ Fruit.

فُكَاهَةٌ Jesting; merriment.

فَلَّ يَفُلُّ فَلًّا To blunt or notch.

فُلٌّ Arabian Jasmine.

فَلَتَ يَفْلِتُ To free, liberate.

أَفْلَتَ وَتَفَلَّتَ وَٱنْفَلَتَ To escape

تَفَلَّتَ عَلَى To spring on.

فَلْتٌ Escape.

فَلْتَةٌ Sudden event.

فَلْتَةً Suddenly. Undesignedly.

(فَلَتِيٌّ) Vagabond.

فَالِتٌ Loose, free.

(كَلَامٌ فَالِتٌ) Improper language.

فُلِجَ وَٱنْفَلَجَ To be paralyzed.

انْفَلَجَ To shine, (day break).

فَالِجٌ Paralysis; palsy.

مَفْلُوجٌ Paralysed; paralytic.

فَلَحَ يَفْلَحُ To plough; till.

أَفْلَحَ To prosper; be successful.

فَلْحٌ ج فُلُوحٌ Furrow.

فَلَاحٌ Prosperity; success.

فَلاَحَةٌ Agriculture.

فَلاَّحٌ ج فَلاَّحُونَ Farmer, peasant.

فِلذة ج أَفْلاَذ A piece.

فَالُوذ وَفَالُوذَجٌ A sweet pastry.

فُولاَذٌ (بُولاَدٌ) Steel.

فِلِزٌّ Bronze. Metal.

فَلَّسَ To proclaim bankrupt.

أَفْلَسَ To become bankrupt.

فَلْسٌ ج فُلُوسٌ A small coin.
Pl. scales of fish. Money.

إِفْلاَسٌ Insolvency, bankruptcy.

مُفْلِسٌ Bankrupt; penniless.

فِلَسْطِين Palestine.

تَفَلْسَفَ To philosophize.

فَلْسَفَةٌ Philosophy.

أَلْفَلْسَفَةُ الطَّبِيعِيَّةُ Physics.

أَلْفَلْة الْعَقْلِيَّةُ Psychology.

فَلْسَفِيٌّ Philosophical.

فَيْلَسُوفٌ ج فَلاَسِفَة Philosopher.

(فَلَشَ) To spread out.

(إِنْفَلَشَ) To be spread out.

(فَلَصَ يَفْلُصُ مِنْ) To escape from.

افلص وتَفَلَّصَ وَانْفَلَصَ To escape.

فَلْطَحَ To flatten, make broad.

مُفَلْطَحٌ Flattened; broad.

فَلْفَلَ To pepper.

فُلْفُلٌ وفِلْفِلٌ Pepper (tree or fruit).

فُلَيْفِلَةٌ Pepper plant.

مُفَلْفَلٌ Peppered.

فَلَقَ يَفْلِقُ To cleave; split.

أَفْلَقَ وَافْتَلَقَ To be skilled in.

تَفَلَّقَ وَانْفَلَقَ To be split, cleft.

انْفَلَقَ الصُّبْحُ The dawn broke.

فَلَقٌ ج أَفْلاَقٌ Dawn. Stocks.

فِلْقَةٌ ج فِلَقٌ Lobe. Cotyledon.

مُفْلِقٌ Distinguished (poet).

فَلَّكَ وتَفَلَّكَ To augur or predict.

فُلْكٌ Ship. Noah's ark.

فَلَكٌ ج أَفْلَاكٌ Celestial sphere.

عِلْمُ ٱلْفَلَك Astronomy.

فَلَكِيٌّ Astronomer.

(فُلوكَةٌ) Small ship; boat.

فُلَانٌ A certain person.

فُلَانِيٌّ Such and such.

(فَلَا) Open space; the open air.

فِلْوٌ ج فَلَاوى وأَفْلَاءٌ Foal.

فَلَاةٌ ج فَلَوَاتٌ Open country.

فَلَّى To clean from lice.

فِلِّينٌ Cork. Bottle-cork.

فَلْيونٌ God-son.

فَمٌ وفَمٌّ Mouth. (*see* فوه)

فَنٌّ ج فُنُونٌ Form; kind. Art.

تَفَنَّنَ To be accomplished.

مُتَفَنِّنٌ Accomplished; skilful.

فِنجَانٌ ج فَنَاجِينُ Small cup.

فَنَّدَ To state in detail. Accuse of untruth or error.

فَنَدٌ فُنُودٌ Branch. Taper.

فُنْدُقٌ ج فَنَادِقُ Inn; hotel.

فَنَارٌ ج فنارَاتٌ Lantern. Light-house.

فَانُوسٌ ج فوانيسُ Lantern. Lamp.

فَنِيَ يفنى To perish.

أَفْنَى To annihilate; destroy.

فَنَاءٌ Destruction. Vanishing.

فَانٍ Transient; perishing.

فَهْدٌ ج فُهُود Panther; lynx.

فَهْرَسَ To make index.

فِهْرِس وفِهْرِسْتٌ ج فَهَارِس Catalogue. Index, table of contents.

فَهِمَ يَفْهَمُ To understand.

فَهَّمَ وأَفْهَمَ To make understand.

إِنْفَهَمَ To be understood.

إِسْتَفْهَمَ To seek to know.

فَهْمٌ Understanding.

فَهِيمٌ وفَهَّامَة Very intelligent.

إِسْتِفْهَامٌ Interrogation.

إِسْمُ ٱستفهَامٍ Interrogative pronoun.

مَفْهُومٌ	Understood. Meaning.
فَاتَ يَفُوتُ	To pass. Miss.
فَوَّتَ	To make pass ; omit.
تَفَاوَتَ	To differ ; be dissimilar.
فَوْتٌ وفوات	Passing ; missing.
تَفَاوُتٌ	Dissimilarity ; difference.
فَوْجٌ ج أَفْوَاجٌ	Troop ; company.
افواجًا أفواجًا	In troops, crowds.
فَاحَ يَفُوحُ	To be diffused, (odour).
فَارَ يَفُورُ فَوْرًا وفَوَرَانًا	To boil.
أَفَارَ وفَوَّرَ	To make boil.
فَارٌ ج فِيرَانٌ	Mice.
فَارَةٌ	Mouse. Carpenter's plane.
عَلَى ٱلفَوْرِ	Immediately ; at once.
فَوَّارَةٌ	Jet d'eau ; fountain.
فَازَ يَفُوزُ	To win, succeed.
فَازَ بِ	To obtain ; attain.
فَوْزٌ	Success. Escape.
مَفَازَةٌ ج مفازاتٌ ومَفَاوِزُ	Desert.
فَاشَ يَفُوشُ فَوْشًا	To float.
فَوَّضَ إِلَى	To commit to.
فَاوَضَ	To converse with.
تَفَاوَضَ	To converse together.
فَوْضَى	Anarchy.
مُفَاوَضَةٌ	Conversation.
فُوطَةٌ ج فُوَطٌ	Napkin ; towel.
فَاقَ يَفُوقُ	To surpass; excel.
فَاقَ فُوَاقًا	To hiccough.
أَفَاقَ وَٱستَفَاقَ مِن	To awake.
فَوْقُ	Above ; upon ; beyond.
إِلَى فوقُ	Upwards.
فَمَا فوقُ	And upwards.
فَاقَةٌ	Poverty ; want ; need.
فَوْقَانِيٌّ	What is above.
فُوَاقٌ	Hiccough.
فَائِقٌ	Surpassing, excelling.
فَائِقُ ٱلوَصْفِ	Beyond description.
فُولٌ (فولَة *sing.*)	Horse-beans.

فوّالٌ Cook or seller of beans.

فومٌ Garlic.

فَاه يفوهُ وتفوّه To speak ; utter.

فوهٌ وفمٌ ج أفواهٌ وأفمَامٌ Mouth,

فوّةٌ وفوّةٌ Madder-root.

فوّهةٌ ج فوّهاتٌ وأفواهٌ Opening.

في In, among, with, at.

فَاءَ وفيّأَ To shade.

تفيّأَ To shade one's self.

فيءٌ ج أفياءٌ Shadow.

فئةٌ ج فئاتٌ Party ; company.

فاحَ يفيح فيحًا وفيحَانًا To flow.

أفَاحَ To spill, shed.

أفيَح م فيحاء Wide ; extensive.

أفَاد To benefit ; serve ; mean.

إستفاد To be benefited ; acquire.

فَائدةٌ ج فوائد Benefit ; use ; profit. Interest (on money).

إفَادةٌ Bestowal of benefit.

مفيدٌ Beneficial ; useful.

فيروزٌ Turquoise (stone).

فيصلٌ *See under.* فَصْلٌ

فَاضَ يَفيض فيضَانًا To abound ; overflow, (river.) Be full, (vessel).

أفَاض To pour (water) ; fill.

فَيْضٌ ج فيوضٌ Abundance.

فيضَانُ النيل Periodic overflow or inundation of the Nile.

فيفَاءُ ج فيَاف Waterless desert.

فيلٌ ج أفيالٌ وفيلَة Elephant.

فيْلقٌ ج فيالق An army-corps.

فيمَ (في ما) Why? Wherefore ?

فَان يَفين فينًا To be niggardly.

ق

ق As a numeral sign=100.

قَبَّبَ To make convex.

(قَبَّةٌ) Collar (to a shirt, &c.).

قُبَّةٌ ج قُبَبٌ Cupola, dome.

قَبَّانٌ ج قَبَابين Large steelyard.

مقبب Surmounted with a dome.

قَبح يقبحُ To be ugly, vile.

قَبَّح To render, or deem ugly.

قابَح To revile, insult.

اقبح To act meanly, shamefully.

إستقبح To detest, abhor.

قُبْحٌ وقَبَاحةٌ Ugliness, foulness.

قبحاً له Fie on him!

قبيحٌ ج قباحٌ Ugly, infamous.

قَبيحةٌ ج قبائح Vile action.

قَبَرَ يقبر قبْراً To bury, inter.

قبْرٌ ج قُبورٌ Grave, sepulchre.

قنبرةٌ ج قنَابر Sky-lark, lark.

قُبَّارٌ Capers.

مقبرةٌ ج مقَابر Cemetery.

مقبورٌ Interred, buried.

قُبرس Cyprus (island).

قُبرسيٌّ Of Cyprus; Cypriote.

قَبَس يقبس واقتَبَس من To seek fire, or knowledge, from.

إقتَبَس من To quote an author.

قَبْسةٌ A coal, a fire-brand.

قبض يقبض To seize, grasp; arrest. To contract.

قَبَض To receive (money).

قَبَضَهُ God caused him to die.

قُبِضَ To die.

قَبَّضَ To make a payment to.

تَقَبَّضَ وٱنقَبَضَ To shrink.

قَبْضٌ Grasping, taking possession. Constipation.

قَبْضَةٌ A grasp ; handful.

قُبْضَةٌ Handle, haft, hilt.

قَابِضٌ Astringent.

إِنقِبَاضٌ Contraction, constipation.

مَقْبَضٌ ج مَقَابِض Handle, hilt.

مَقبوضٌ Seized ; received. Dead.

قِبْطٌ وأَقبَاط Copts.

قِبْطِيٌّ A Copt ; Coptic.

قُبَعٌ وقُبَّعَة Hood, cowl.

قَبْقَابٌ ج قَبَاقِيب Clogs.

قَبِلَ يَقبَلُ قبولاً To receive, accept, admit ; consent, agree to.

أَقبَلَ عَلَى To take up.

أَقبَلَ To approach, be near.

قَبَّلَ To kiss.

قَابَلَ To correspond to ; meet.

قَابَلَ بِ To compare, collate.

تَقَبَّلَ To receive, accept.

تَقَابَلَ To meet ; be compared.

إِستَقبل To go to meet, receive.

قبلُ وقَبْلاً ومِن قَبْلُ Previously.

قِبَلٌ Side, direction.

مِنْ قِبَله With respect to ; from.

قِبلةٌ Direction of Mecca. South.

قُبلةٌ ج قُبَلٌ. وتَقْبيلٌ Kiss.

قِبليٌّ Southern.

قَابِلٌ ل Capable of, subject to.

قَابِلةٌ ج قوابِلُ Midwife. Receiver.

قَابِليَّةٌ Capacity ; appetite.

قِبَالةٌ Over against.

قِبالة Midwifery.

قبولٌ Consent ; reception.

مِنْ هذا القبيل As regards this.

قَبِيلَةٌ ج قَبَائِل — Tribe.

إِقْبَالٌ — Approach. Prosperity.

إِسْتِقْبَالٌ — The future. Reception.

مُقَابَلَةٌ — Meeting. Collation (of two texts). Antithesis.

مُقْبِلٌ — Coming, approaching.

مُقَابِلٌ — Opposite to, in front of.

مَقْبُولٌ — Accepted ; received.

مُسْتَقْبَلٌ — The future ; Facing.

قَبَّنَ — To weigh with steelyard.

قَبَّانٌ — Steelyard.

قِبَانَة — Trade of a weigher.

قَبَّانِيٌّ — One who weighs.

قَبُونَةٌ — Weighing.

قَبَا يَقْبُو قَبْواً — To bend, curve.

قَبَاءٌ ج أَقْبِيَةٌ — Outer garment.

قَبْوٌ ج أَقْبِيَةٌ — Vault.

قَتَبٌ ج أَقْتَابٌ — Small pack-saddle.

قَتَرَ وأَقْتَرَ عَلَى — To be niggardly.

قَتْرٌ وتَقْتِيرٌ — Avarice, economy.

قَاتِرٌ ومُقَتِّرٌ — Parsimonious, economical.

قَتَلَ يَقْتُلُ — To kill, murder.

قَاتَلَ مُقَاتَلَةً — To fight against.

تَقَاتَلَ واقْتَتَلَ — To combat with one another, fight.

إِسْتَقْتَلَ — To seek death, stake one's life.

قَتْلٌ — Murder ; execution.

قَاتِلٌ ج قَتَلَةٌ — Murderer, assassin.

قِتَالٌ ومُقَاتَلَة — Battle, combat.

قَتَّالٌ — Deadly, causing death.

قَتِيلٌ ج قَتْلَى . ومَقْتُول — Killed.

مَقْتَلٌ — Vital part (of the body).

مُقَاتِلٌ — Warrior, combatant.

قَتَامٌ — Darkness.

قَاتِمٌ وأَقْتَمُ — Dark-coloured.

قِثَّاء — Cucumber.

قِثَّاءُ الحِمَار — *Elaterium.*

(قَحَّ يَقِحُّ) — To cough.

قُحٌّ ج أَقْحَاحٌ — Pure, unmixed.

A cough.	(قَحَّة)
Cough. Prostitute.	قَحْبَةٌ ج قِحَابٌ
To be rainless.	قَحِطَ يَقْحَطُ وأَقْحَطَ
Drought, famine.	قَحْطٌ
Year of drought.	عَامٌ مُقْحِطٌ
To sweep away.	قَحَفَ يَقْحَفُ
Skull.	قِحْفٌ ج أَقْحَافٌ
What is swept away.	قُحَافَة
Winnowing-fan; dust-pan.	مِقْحَفَة
To dry up, wither.	قَحِلَ يَقْحَلُ قَحْلاً
To dry, cause to wither.	أَقْحَلَ
Dryness, aridity.	قُحُولَة
To rush.	قَحَمَ يَقْحُمُ قُحُوماً في
To draw near to.	قَحَمَ إِلَى
To rush upon.	إِقْتَحَمَ
Anthemis, camomile.	أُقْحُوان
Particle, e. g. Zeid has *just* risen.	قد. قَدْ قَامَ زَيْدٌ
The liar *sometimes* speaks the truth.	قَدْ يَصْدُقُ الكَذُوب
Verily he prospers.	قَدْ أَفْلَحَ
To cut, cleave.	قَدَّ يَقُدُّ قَدًّا
To cut and dry (meat).	قَدَّدَ
To be cut and dried.	تَقَدَّدَ
To be cut, slit, divided.	إِنْقَدَّ
Stature, size.	قَدٌّ ج قُدُودٌ
Equal to in measure.	عَلَى قَدِّهِ
Goodly in form.	حَسَنُ القَدِّ
Cured meat.	قَدِيدٌ ومُقَدَّدٌ
To bore, pierce.	قَدَحَ يَقْدَحُ
To strike fire.	قَدَحَ واقْتَدَحَ
To revile, censure.	قَدَحَ فِي
Drinking-cup.	قَدَحٌ ج أَقْدَاحٌ
Slanderer, calumniator.	قَادِحٌ
Gimlet.	مِقْدَحٌ ومِقْدَاحٌ
To be able.	قَدَرَ يَقْدِرُ عَلَى
To measure; compute.	قَدَرَ وقَدَّرَ
To decree for.	قَدَرَ وقَدَّرَ عَلَى
To prepare, assign.	قدر لِ

To put a value upon. قدَّر

To enable. قَدَرعلى

To be preordained. تقدَّر

To be powerful, or rich. اقتَدر

Quantity, measure. قَدْرٌ

Fate ; divine decree. Powder, position. قَدَرٌ ج أقْدار

Cooking-pot. قِدْرٌ ج قُدورٌ

Might, power, authority. قُدرةٌ

Powerful ; able. قادرٌ وقديرٌ

The Omnipotent. ألقدير

Predestination. Suppositon. Implied meaning. Evaluation. تقديرٌ ج تقادير

Hypothetically. تقدِيراً

Quantity, fixed measure. مقدارٌ

As much as. بِمِقْدارما

Power, ability. مقدرةٌ

Valuer, estimator. مقدِّرٌ

Predestinated. مقدَّرٌ ومقدورٌ

To hallow ; sanctify. قَدَّس

To be purified, sanctified. تَقَدَّس

Holiness. قُدْسٌ وقداسةٌ

Jerusalem. القُدْس

The Holy Ghost. (ألروح القدس)

Mass, liturgy. قداسٌ ج قداديس

The All-Holy (God). القدوس

Saint. قدّيسٌ ج قدّيسونَ

Sanctification. تقدِيسٌ

Jerusalem. بيت المَقدس

Sanctified. مقدسٌ ومُتقدّسٌ

The Holy Bible. ألكتاب المقدَّس

To arrive from. قدِم يقدُم من

To be old. قدم يقدم . وتقادم

To prefer (a thing). قدَّمهُ علَى

To present, offer to. قَدم ل

To undertake boldly. اقْدم على

To advance, lead. تقدَّم

To advance towards. تقدَّم إِلى

To surpass.	تقدّم على
Antiquity.	قدْمٌ وقِدْمة
Precedence.	قِدم
Foot.	قدمٌ ج أقدامٌ
Priority, precedence.	قُدْمةٌ
Comer ; coming.	قادمٌ
In front of, before.	قُدّام
Courageous, bold.	قدومٌ ج قُدُمٌ
Hatchet, adze.	قدومٌ وقدُّومٌ
Ancient, old.	قديمٌ ج قدماء
The Eternal (God).	ألقديم
Formerly.	قديمًا وفي القديم
In olden times.	من القديم
More ancient.	أقدم ج أقدمون
The ancients.	ألأقدمون
Boldness ; diligence.	إقدامٌ
Present ; offering.	تقدمةٌ ج تقادم
Presenting, offering.	تقديم
Pre-eminence ; progress.	تقدُّم
Antiquity, oldness, &c.	تقادُمٌ
Front part, fore part.	مُقدَّم
Advance guard of (an army). Preface ; premise.	مقدَّمةٌ
One who is in advance.	متقدّمٌ
Afore-mentioned.	متقدّمٌ ذكره
Courageous, energetic.	مقدامٌ
To imitate, emulate.	اقتدى ب
Model for imitation.	قُدوةٌ
Way, manner.	قِدْيةٌ
Imitation.	اقتِداء
To be unclean.	قَذُر يقذُر وقذر يقذر
To foul, render unclean.	قذّر
Filth.	قذر ج أقذارٌ وقاذورةٌ
Dirty, filthy ; unclean.	قذرٌ
To throw. Row.	قذف يقذف
To accuse of.	قذف بِ
Throwing ; abusing.	قذف
Rower.	قذّافٌ

Oar. مقذافٌ ومقذفٌ ج مقاذيف

Mote, or small particle. قَذًى

To stay, dwell. قَرَّ يقِرُّ

To persist, persevere in. قَرَّ على

He was content. قَرَّ عيناً

To settle, fix, establish. قَرَّر

To cause one to stay. قَرَّر وأقرَّ

To cause one to confess. To settle, fix. قَرَّر

To decide upon. قَرَّر في نفسِه أن

To confess, avow. أقرَّ ب

To refresh, console. أقرَّ عينَه

To be stated, determined. تقرَّر

To dwell, inhabit. إستقرَّ في

Water-cress. Darling. قُرَّةُ العَين

Dwelling ; stability. قَرارٌ

Refrain, (music). قَرارٌ

Continent, firm-land. قَارةٌ

Glass bottle. قَارورةٌ ج قوارير

Consoled, content. قريرُ العَين

Affirmation ; confession. إقرارٌ

Report. تقريرٌ

Residence. مقرٌّ ومستقَرٌّ

To read. قَرأ يَقرأُ قراءةً

To study with (a teacher). قرأ على

To send, or deliver, a greeting. أقرأه السلام

To investigate. إستقرأ

Act of reading. قِراءةٌ ج قراءات

The Coran. ألقرآن

Reader, reciter. قارئٌ ج قرّاء

Read, recited. مقروءٌ ومقريٌّ ومقروٌّ

To approach. قرب يقرب الى ومن

To bring near ; offer. قرَّب

To be near to. قاربَ

To be on the point of. قَاربَ أن

To approach. تقرَّب تقرباً إلى

To be near one another. تقارب

To approach. إقترب

Nearness.	قربٌ
Near ; soon.	عن قُرب
In the vicinity of.	بالقربِ مِن
Skin-bag.	قِربةٌ ج قِرَباتٌ وقِرَبٌ
Offering to God.	قربانٌ ج قَرَابين
Sheath, scabbard.	قِرَابٌ ج اقربةٌ
Kinship ; relations.	قرابةٌ وقُربَى
Boat, skiff.	قَاربٌ ج قَوَارب
Near ; related ; neighbour, followman ; relation.	قريبٌ ج أقرباء
Shortly, soon.	عن قريب
Nearer ; more probable.	أقربُ
Approximation.	تقريبٌ
Approximately.	تقريبًا وبالتقريب
Pommel.	قَربُوسٌ ج قَرَابِيس
To wound.	قرح يقرح قرحًا
To finish teething (horse).	قرح يقرَح
To invent ; improvise. Demand.	إقترحَ
A wound ; an ulcer.	قرحةٌ

Pure (water).	قَرَاحٌ
Talent, genius.	قريحةَ ج قرائح
Ape, monkey.	قردٌ ج قرودٌ
Tick, (insect).	قرادٌ ج أقردةٌ
To burn, blaze (coal).	قردح
Armourer.	قرداحيٌّ وقَرْدَحجيٌّ
To freeze.	قرس يقرس قرسًا
Intense cold.	قَارِسٌ وقريس
A kind of plum.	(قراسيَا)
To curdle (milk).	قرش الحليب
Piastre.	قرشٌ ج قروشٌ
Tribe of Koreish.	قُرَيْشٌ
Sweet curd.	قريشة
Rich.	(مقُرشٌ)
To pinch.	قَرص يقرُص قَرصًا
To cut out (dough).	قرَّص
Disc ; cake.	قُرصٌ ج أقرَاصٌ
Nettle (plant).	(قرّاصٌ وَ قُرَيْصٌ)
Corsairs, pirates.	قُرصانٌ

قَرَضَ يَقْرِضُ To cut ; nibble.

أَقْرَضَ To lend one money.

إِنْقَرَضَ To die out, perish.

إِقْتَرَضَ وَاسْتَقْرَضَ To borrow.

قَرْضٌ ج قُرُوضٌ Loan, debt.

قُرَاضَةٌ Cuttings, clippings.

قَرِيضٌ Poetry.

مِقْرَاضٌ ج مَقَارِيضُ Scissors.

قَرَطَ يَقْرِطُ To cut.

قَرَّطَ عَلَى To give little to.

قُرْطٌ ج أَقْرَاطٌ Ear-ring. Cluster.

قِيرَاطٌ ج قَرَارِيطُ Carat, inch.

قُرْطُبَة Cordova (in Spain).

قِرْطَاسٌ ج قَرَاطِيسُ Paper.

قِرْطَلٌ ج قَرَاطِلُ Reed-basket.

قَرَّظَ To laud, eulogize.

تَقْرِيظٌ Eulogy. Panegyric.

قَرَعَ يَقْرَعُ قَرْعاً To knock, rap.

قَرَّعَ To scold, rebuke.

قَارَعَ مُقَارَعَةً وَقِرَاعاً To fight.

تَقَارَعَ To cast lots, or play dice.

إِقْتَرَعَ فِي وَعَلَى To cast lots for.

قَرْعٌ Knocking. Gourd.

قَرَعَةٌ Baldness ; scald-head.

قَرْعَةٌ A gourd, Chemical retort.

قُرْعَةٌ ج قُرَعٌ Lot. Ballot.

أَلْقُرْعَةُ لَهُ He wins.

اَلْقُرْعَةُ عَلَيْهِ He loses.

قَارِعَةٌ Middle part of the way.

اَلْقَارِعَةُ Day of judgement.

أَقْرَعُ Bald, scald-headed. Bare.

مِقْرَعَةٌ ج مَقَارِعُ Whip, knocker.

قَرَفَ وَقَرَّفَ بِ To suspect, blame.

قَرِفَ يَقْرَفُ قَرَفاً To loathe.

أَقْرَفَ To cause disgust.

إِقْتَرَفَ To commit (a crime).

قَرَفٌ Disgust, loathing.

قِرْفَةٌ Suspicion. Cinnamon.

Disgusting. مُقرِف

To cluck, (hen). قَرَقَ يقرق قَرَقًا

Hernia in the scrotum. (قُرقٌ)

Sitting-hen. (قُرَقَةٌ)

To dry, become hard. (قَرقَدَ)

Squirrel. قَرقذانٌ وقَرَقْذَونٌ

To rumble, (stomach). قَرْقَرَ

Rumbling. قَرقَرَةٌ ج قَرَاقِر

Lamb. (قَرقورٌ)

To gnaw at. (قَرقَشَ)

To cut into small pieces. (قَرْقَطَ)

To rumble, clatter (قَرقَعَ)

A rattling, rumbling. (قَرقَعَةٌ)

To gnaw off. قَرَمَ يقرُم قَرماً

The Crimea. أَلْقَرَم

Stump of a tree. قرمةٌ ج قرمٌ

Tile, brick. قرميدٌ

Cochineal ; crimson. قِرْمِز

Of a crimson colour. قرمزيٌّ

A Karmathian. قرمطيٌّ

Sect of Karmathians. قَرَامِطَةٌ

To join. قرنَ يقرن قرنًا بِ

To join together. أَقرن

To be joined ; married. إِقترن ب

Horn. Century, age. قَرْنٌ ج قرونٌ

Alexander the Great. ذو القَرْنَين

Rhinoceros. وحيد القَرن

One's equal. قِرْنٌ ج أقرَانٌ

Projecting angle or corner. قُرنَةٌ

Close union. قِرانٌ ومقَارَنَةٌ

Comrade ; husband. قَرِينٌ ج قُرَنَاءُ

Wife. Context. قَرِينَة ج قَرَائِنُ

Horned ; angled. مُقَرَّنٌ

Joined, yoked. مقرونٌ ومقْتَرِنٌ

Cauliflower. قَرْنَبيطٌ (قُنَّبيطٌ)

Cloves. Carnation (plant). قَرَنفلٌ

Cloves. كَبْش القرنفل

قرنفلة A pink, carnation.

قراب. واستقرى To follow out.

إستقراء (See إستقراً) Analogy.

قرا يقري To receive hospitably.

قرى Entertainment ; feasting.

قرية ج قرى Village.

قزّ يقزّ عن To feel aversion to.

قزّ Raw-silk, floss silk.

دود القز Silk-worm.

قزاز (زجاج) Glass, glass-ware.

قزّاز Silk, or glass merchant.

قزحية Iris (of the eye).

قزدير (عوض: قصدير) Tin.

قزل يقزل قزلاً To limp.

قزل Limping.

أقزل قزلاء ج قزل Lame.

قزم يقزم To be small, mean.

قزم وقزم Mean, dwarfish.

قس ج قسوس. وقسّيس ج قسّيسون Clergyman, minister.

مقساس Sebesten plum. *Cordia Myxa L.*

قسر يقسر To force, compel.

قسر Violence, compulsion.

قسراً By force.

قسط يقسط قسطاً وقسوطاً To act unjustly, swerve from what is right, to separate, distribute.

قسط يقسط وأقسط To do justice.

قسّط To pay by instalments.

تقسّط بين To divide equally.

قسط Justice ; just, equitable.

قسط ج اقساط Part, portion.

قسطل ج قساطل Pipe, conduit.

قسم يقسم قسماً وقسّم To divide.

قاسم To share mutually.

أقسم بالله To swear by God.

تقسّم To be divided, separated.

تقاسم واقتسم To share.

تقاسم — To take mutual oaths.
إنقسم — To be divided.
قَسَمٌ ج أَقسَامٌ — Oath.
قِسمٌ ج أَقسَامٌ — Part; share.
قِسمَةٌ ج قِسَمٌ — Division, share, lot.
خَارِج القِسمَة — Quotient, (*arith.*).
قَسِيمٌ ج أَقسِمَاء — Sharer ; lot.
مُقَسَّمٌ — Divided, distributed.
مقسومٌ — Dividend (*arith.*).
مقسومٌ عليه — Divisor, (*arith.*).
قسا يَقسُو — To be hard, unyielding.
قَسَّى وأَقسى — To harden.
قاسى — To endure, suffer.
قَساوة — Hard-heartedness.
قاس ج قُسَاة — Hard, severe.
قَش يَقُشُّ — To gather, collect. Sweep. Skim.
قَشٌّ — Straw.
قشّة — A single straw.

قَشَّاشٌ — Cleaner (sweeper).
مِقَشَّةٌ — Broom.
مُقَشَّشَةٌ — Demijohn.
قَشَبٌ — Chapped skin.
قِشدةٌ — Cream.
قَشَرَ يقشر قَشْراً — To peel, skin.
تَقَشَّرَ وانقَشَرَ — To be peeled.
قِشرٌ ج قشورٌ — Rind, bark, shell.
قِشرةٌ وقشارةٌ — A rind, bark, shell.
مُقَشَّرٌ — Peeled.
قَشَطَ يقشط قَشْطاً عن — To strip off.
قَشَّط — To strip; rob.
تَقَشَّطَ وانقشط — To be stripped.
(قِشْطَةٌ) — Sugar-candy. Cream.
(قِشَاطٌ) — Leather strap.
(قشع يقشَعُ) — To see.
أَقشع — To be dispersed, (clouds).
أَقشَعَ عن — To be dispelled.

انْشَعَ To be seen. Dispelled.

إِقْشَعَرَّ To shudder, shiver.

قُشَعْرِيرَةٌ Shudder ; shivering.

قَشِفَ يَقْشَفُ قَشَافَةً To be wretched.

تَقَشَّفَ To lead an ascetic life.

قَشَفٌ Life in misery.

مُتَقَشِّفٌ Ascetic.

(قُشْلَةٌ) Barrack.

قَصَّ يَقُصُّ قَصًّا To out off, clip.

قَصَّ يَقُصُّ عَلَى To tell ; narrate.

قَاصَّ مُقَاصَّةً وَقِصَاصاً To punish.

انْقَصَّ To be clipped, cut off.

اقْتَصَّ To take vengeance. Tell.

قَصٌّ Sternum.

قِصَّةٌ ج قِصَصٌ Tale, story.

قِصَاصٌ Punishment.

قُصَاصَةٌ Cuttings ; parings.

مِقَصٌّ ج مَقَاصٌّ Scissors.

قَصَبٌ Reeds. Thread of gold.

قَصَبُ ٱلسُّكَّرِ Sugar-cane.

قَصَبَةٌ ج قَصَبٌ A reed or cane. City ; capital.

قَصَبَةُ ٱلْمَرِيءِ Œsophagus.

قَصَبَةُ ٱلرِّئَةِ Windpipe.

قَصَبَةُ ٱلْأَنْفِ Bone of the nose.

قِصَابَةٌ Butcher's trade.

قَصَّابٌ Butcher.

مَقْصَبَةٌ Slaughter-house.

قَصَدَ يَقْصِدُ To purpose; repair to.

قَصَدَ وَٱقْتَصَدَ فِي To economise.

قَصْدٌ Intention, purpose, aim.

قَاصِدٌ ج قُصَّادٌ Visitor. Legate.

مَقْصُودٌ Intended, desired.

قَصِيدَةٌ ج قَصَائِدُ A poem.

إِقْتِصَادٌ Moderation ; economy.

مَقْصِدٌ ج مَقَاصِدُ Intention, aim.

قَصْدِيرٌ Tin.

قَصُرَ يَقْصُرُ To be short.

قَصَرَ وَقَصَّرَ عَنْ To lack power.

قَصَّرَ وأَقْصَرَ To shorten.

قصر قَصْراً وقِصارة To bleach.

قَصَرَهُ في To shut up, confine.

قَصَرَ على To limit, restrict.

قَصَّرَ في To lag, fall short of.

اقصَرَ عن To desist from.

تقصَّرَ To shrink, contract.

إقتصَرَ على To limit one's self to.

قِصْرٌ وقِصَر Shortness.

قصورٌ Remissness.

قُصارى End (of an affair).

قَصْرٌ ج قصورٌ Castle, palace.

قاصرٌ Minor, under age.

قاصِرُ اليد Powerless.

قَصَّارٌ Fuller, bleecher.

قِصارَةٌ Art of bleaching.

قَيْصَرٌ ج قَياصِرةٌ Cæsar, emperor.

قَصيرٌ ج قِصارٌ Short; small.

أَقْصَرُ م قُصرى ج أَقاصِرُ Shorter.

تقصيرٌ Abbreviation ; neglect.

مَقصورٌ Limited. Bleached.

مقصورةٌ ج مقاصير A large room.

قَصْعَةٌ ج قِصَعٌ قَصَعاتٌ Large dish.

قَصَفَ يقصِفُ قَصْفاً To break.

قَصَفَ يقصِف To roar, (thunder).

تَقَصَّفَ وانقصَفَ To be broken.

قَصِفٌ Brittle, easily broken.

قاصِفٌ Breaking, roaring.

مَقصَفٌ Pleasure-house.

قَصَلَ يقصِلُ قَصْلاً To cut off, mow.

قَصَلٌ وقُصالة Stubble, chaff.

قَصيل Green food for animals.

قَصَمَ يقصِمُ قَصْماً To break in pieces.

تقصَّمَ وانقصمَ To be broken.

قَصِمٌ Brittle, fragile.

قصيمٌ ومقصوم Broken shattered.

قَصا يقصو To be very distant.

تقصَّى واستقصى في To penetrate deeply ; follow out to the end.

قَصًا وَقَصَاء Distance.

قَاصٍ ج أَقْصَاء Very distant.

إِسْتِقْصَاء Investigation.

أَقْصَى م قُصْوَى ج أَقَاصٍ More distant.

الغَايَةُ القُصْوَى The extreme end ; highest purpose.

أَقَاصِي الأَرْض The uttermost parts of the earth.

قَضَّ يَقُضُّ قَضًّا To break, crush.

إِنقَضَّ To swoop down (bird). To fall.

قَضَبَ وَاقْتَضَبَ To cut off, prune.

تَقَضَّبَ وَانْقَضَبَ To be pruned.

قُضَابَة Prunings.

قَضِيبٌ ج قُضْبَانٌ Rod, stick.

مُقْتَضَبٌ Improvised (speech).

قَضِمَ يَقْضَمُ To nibble at, gnaw.

(قَضَامَة أَوْ قَضَامِيٌّ) Roasted peas.

قَضَى يَقْضِي To decide, fulfil (a duty) ; satisfy (a want) ; execute (an order).

قَضَى بَيْنَ يَقْضِي To judge.

قَضَى عَلَى To require.

قَضَى أَوْ قَضَى أَجلهُ أَوْ نَحْبَهُ To die.

قَضَى الزَّمَان To spend the time.

قَضَى الدَّيْن To pay a debt.

قَضَى ل To judge in favour of.

قَضَى الوَطَر To fulfil a purpose.

قَضَّى To execute, carry out.

قَاضَى To summon before a judge.

إِنقَضَى To be carried out ; cease.

تَقَاضَيَا They had a law-suit.

إِقْتَضَى To be required ; necessary.

قَضَى وَقَضَاء ج أَقْضِيَة Judgment.

قَضِيَّة ج قَضَايَا Event ; fact, matter ; question, proposition.

قَاضٍ ج قُضَاة A judge.

قَاضِي القُضَاة Supreme Judge.

القَاضِيَة Death.

إِنْقِضَاء End ; completion.

إِقْتِضَاء Exigency ; requisite.

Accomplished. مَقْضِيٌّ

Required, necessary. مُقْتَضَى

In conformity with. بِمُقْتَضَى

To cut (a reed-pen). قَطَّ يَقُطُّ

Never, not at all. قَطُّ وَقَطْ

I never saw him. مَا رَأَيْتُهُ قَطُّ

Tom-cat, cat. قِطٌّ ج قِطَاطٌ

Female cat. قِطَّة

To frown. قَطَبَ يَقْطِبُ قَطْبًا . وَقَطَّبَ

Axis, pivot. قُطْبٌ ج قُطُوبٌ

Pole, pole-star. Leader. قُطْبٌ

Pole-star. نَجْمَةُ ٱلْقُطْبِ

One of the earth's poles. قُطْبَةٌ

Polar. قُطْبِيٌّ

One who frowns. قَاطِبٌ وَقَطُوبٌ

All together. قَاطِبَةً

To trickle. قَطَرَ يَقْطُرُ قَطْرًا

To place in line or file. قَطَرَ يَقْطُرُ

To fall in drops. تَقَطَّرَ

To come from all sides. تَقَاطَرَ

To distil. إِسْتَقْطَرَ

Dropping. قَطْرٌ وَقَطَرَانٌ

Rain; drops. قَطْرٌ

Side, region. قُطْرٌ ج أَقْطَار
Diameter.

Diameter of a circle. قُطْرُ ٱلدَّائِرَةِ

Diagonal قُطْرُ ٱلْمُرَبَّعِ اوْ ٱلْمُسْتَطِيلِ
of a square or parallelogram.

A drop. Collyrium. قَطْرَةٌ

Liquid pitch; tar. قَطْرَانٌ

File or string; train. قِطَارٌ

Distillation. تَقْطِيرٌ

Hand-cuffs; stocks. مِقْطَرَةٌ

To cut off, cross. قَطَعَ يَقْطَعُ قَطْعًا

To carry on highway robbery. قَطَعَ ٱلطَّرِيقَ

To sever; prevent. قَطَعَ عَنْ

To assign a portion. قَطَعَ لَهُ

To speak decisively. قَطَعَ فِي ٱلْقَوْلِ

To cut off entirely. قَطَّعَ

قَطَّعَ ٱلشِّعْرَ To scan poetry.

قَطَّعَ ٱلزَّمَانَ To while away time.

قَاطَعَ To separate from.

أَقْطَعَ To take across (a river). Give land as a fief.

تَقَطَّعَ وَانْقَطَعَ To be cut off.

إِنْقَطَعَ To be interrupted ; cease.

إِنْقَطَعَ إِلَى To be devoted to.

إِقْتَطَعَ مِنْ To cut off a part.

قَطْعٌ Amputation. Section. Size.

قَطْعٌ زَائِدٌ Hyperbola.

قَطْعٌ نَاقِصٌ Ellipse.

قَطْعٌ مُكَافِئٌ Parabola.

قَطْعُ ٱلْمَخْرُوطِ Conic section.

قَطْعًا Certainly ; not at all.

قِطْعَةٌ ج قِطَعٌ A part, piece.

قَاطِعٌ Sharp ; decisive.

(قَاطِعُ ٱلنَّهْرِ) Opposite side of a river.

قَاطِعُ ٱلطَّرِيقِ Highway-man.

قَطَاعَةٌ ج قَطَائِعُ Lent.

قَطِيعٌ ج قُطْعَانٌ Herd, flock.

قَطِيعَةٌ ج قَطَائِعُ Fief-land. Tax.

إِنْقِطَاعٌ Separation ; interruption.

تَقْطِيعٌ تَقَاطِيعُ Scanning.

مَقْطَعٌ ج مَقَاطِعُ Syllable.

مَقْطَعُ ٱلنَّهْرِ Ford of a river.

مُقَاطَعَةٌ ج مُقَاطَعَاتٌ Province.

(بِٱلْمُقَاطَعَةِ) Work by the job.

مُقَطَّعٌ Cut into pieces.

مُنْقَطِعٌ Separated, detached.

مَقْطُوعٌ Cut off ; amputated.

قَطَفَ يَقْطِفُ وَٱقْتَطَفَ To cull, pluck, gather.

قَطْفٌ Act of gathering fruit.

قِطَافٌ Time of gathering.

قَطَائِفُ A kind of sweet cake

مِقْطَفٌ Basket, panier.

قَطَمَ يَقْطِمُ قَطْمًا To cut off.

Piece, fragment. قُطَيْمَة

To inhabit (a place). قَطَنَ يَقْطُنُ فِي

Loins ; lumbar region. قَطْنٌ

Cotton. قُطْنٌ ج أَقْطَانٌ

Settled inhabitant. قَاطِنٌ ج قُطَّانٌ

Pumpkin, squash. يَقْطِينٌ

A kind of snipe. قَطَاةٌ ج قَطًا

To sit down ; dwell. قَعَدَ يَقْعُدُ

To lie in wait for. قَعَدَ لِ

To desist from. قَعَدَ عَنْ

To cause to sit, seat. أَقْعَدَ

To be unable to walk. أُقْعِدَ

To neglect. تَقَعَّدَ وَتَقَاعَدَ عَنْ

Eleventh month of the Arabian year. ذُو ٱلْقَعْدَةِ

Foundation, base; rule, canon ; model. قَاعِدَةٌ ج قَوَاعِدُ

Capital of a country. قَاعِدَةُ ٱلْبِلَادِ

Sitting ; inactivity. قُعُودٌ

A place of sitting. مَقْعَدٌ ج مَقَاعِدُ

Infirm ; cripple. مُقْعَدٌ

Pensioner. Neglectful. مُتَقَاعِدٌ

To be deep. قَعُرَ يَقْعُرُ قَعَارَةً

To make concave. قَعَّرَ

To dig deep. قَعَّرَ وَأَقْعَرَ

Bottom ; depth. قَعْرٌ ج قُعُورٌ

Dug ; hollow ; concave. مُقَعَّرٌ

To clatter, rattle. قَعْقَعَ ج قَعْقَعَةً

Magpie. قَعْقَعٌ وَقُعْقُعٌ ج قُعْقُعَانٌ

Large basket, panier. قُفَّةٌ ج قُفَفٌ

To track. قَفَرَ يَقْفُرُ قَفْرًا وَتَقَفَّرَ وَٱقْتَفَرَ

To be waste, deserted. أَقْفَرَ

Desert, waste (land). قَفْرٌ ج قِفَارٌ

Bee-hive ; basket. قَفِيرٌ ج قُفْرَانٌ

To jump, leap. قَفَزَ يَقْفِزُ قَفْزًا

Jump, leap. قَفْزَةٌ ج قَفَزَاتٌ

A certain measure. قَفِيزٌ ج أَقْفِزَةٌ

Bird-cage ; coop. قَفَصٌ ج أَقْفَاصٌ

To shiver from cold. قَفْقَفَ

To return. قَفَلَ يَقفُلُ قُفُولاً

To guard, lock up. قَفَلَ يَقفِلُ قَفْلاً

To lock, shut. قَفَّلَ وَأَقْفَلَ

To cause to return. أَقْفَلَ عَنْ

To be locked, bolted. إِنْقَفَلَ

Lock, bolt. Caravan. قُفْلٌ ج أَقْفَالٌ

Caravan. قَافِلَةٌ ج قَوَافِلُ

Vein in the arm. قِيفَالٌ

To walk behind, follow. قَفَا يَقفُو

To send after. قَفَّى ب

To follow, imitate. تَقَفَّى وَاقْتَفَى

To prefer, select, chose. اقْتَفَى

Back side, reverse. قَفًا وَقَفَاءٌ

Rhyme, (final word). قَافِيَةٌ ج قَوَافٍ

Imitation ; preference. إِقْتِفَاءٌ

Rhymed prose. أَلْكَلَامُ المُقَفَّى

Cardamon. قَاقُلَّة

To be little in quantity, be scarce, happen rarely. قَلَّ يَقِلُّ

Rarely, قَلَّمَا (قَلَّ مَا)

To bear, carry. قَلَّ قَلاًّ وَأَقَلَّ

To diminish, lessen. قَلَّلَ وَأَقَلَّ

To have little property. أَقَلَّ

To find small, paltry. إِسْتَقَلَّ

To be independent. إِسْتَقَلَّ ب

Earthen water-jug. قُلَّةٌ ج قُلَلٌ

Littleness, small quantity. قِلَّة

Plural which signifies from 3 to 10 objects. جَمْعُ القِلَّةِ

A (monk's) cell. قِلِّيَّةٌ وَقِلاَّيَةٌ

Few, little, scarce. قَلِيلٌ ج قَلِيلُونَ

Rarely, seldom, slightly. قَلِيلاً

Less, rarer. أَقَلُّ

Least, rarest. أَلأَقَلُّ

Poor, having but little. أَقَلُّ وَمُقِلٌّ

Diminishing, lessening. تَقْلِيلٌ

Independence. إِسْتِقْلَالٌ

Independent.	مُستَقِلّ
To change, alter. To overturn ; overthrow.	قَلَبَ يَقلِبُ
To manipulate ; prove.	قلّب
To be turned ; be fickle.	تقَلّب
To be turned upside down.	انقَلَبَ
To return to.	إنقَلَبَ إلى
Change of letters (*in gram*).	قَلْبٌ
Heart, mind, thought ; centre, core.	قَلْبٌ ج قُلوبٌ
Sincere, earnest, hearty.	قَلْبيٌّ
Mould, cast, last.	قَالِبٌ ج قوَالِب
Loaf of sugar.	قَالِبُ سُكَّرٍ
Revolution ; overthrow.	إنقِلابٌ
Solstice.	إنقِلَابُ الشَّمْسِ
Change ; inconstancy.	تَقَلُّبٌ
Vicissitudes.	تقَلُّباتٌ
Turned, turned over.	مقلُوبٌ
Final resting place.	مُنقَلَبٌ
To wind round ; adorn. Imitate.	قَلَّدَ
To undertake an affair.	تقَلَّدَ الأَمْرَ
To put on the sword.	تقَلَّدَ السَّيفَ
Necklace ; collar.	قِلَادَةٌ ج قَلائِدُ
Imitation. Church tradition.	تقليدٌ ج تَقَالِيدُ
Imitator, counterfeiter.	مُقَلِّدٌ
Imitated, counterfeited.	مُقَلَّدٌ
Management of affairs.	مقَاليدُ الامُورِ
Red Sea.	بَحْرُ القُلْزُمِ
Hood, cap.	قَلَنسُوَةٌ
Eel.	أَنقَلِيس وَإِنقِلِيس
To contract, shrink.	قَلَصَ يَقلُصُ
To be wrinkled, shrunk.	تقَلَّصَ
To tear from its place, pull out, uproot.	قَلَعَ يَقلَعُ
To set sail.	أَقلَعَ
To withdraw from.	أَقلَعَ عَنْ
To be taken away.	إنقَلَعَ
To pull out, uproot.	إقْتَلَعَ

Sail.	قِلْعٌ ج قُلُوعٌ
Castle, fortress.	قَلْعَة ج قِلَاعٌ
Sores in the mouth, (aphthæ).	قُلَاعٌ
Stone-quarry.	مَقْلَع ج مَقَالِعُ
Sling.	مِقْلَاع ج مَقَالِيعُ
Uprooted, pulled out.	مَقْلُوعٌ
To circumcise.	قَلَفَ يَقْلُفُ
To calk a ship.	قَلَفَ وَقَلَّفَ
Prepuce.	قَلَفَة وَقُلْفَة ج قُلَفٌ
Trade of calking ships.	قِلَافَة
Uncircumcised.	أَقْلَفُ
To be agitated.	قَلِقَ يَقْلَقُ قَلَقًا
To agitate, disturb.	أَقْلَقَ
Disquietude, trouble.	قَلَقٌ
Disturbed ; restless.	قَلِق
Colocassia (plant).	قُلْقَاس
To move, shake.	قَلْقَلَ قِلْقَالاً
To be moved, shaken.	تَقَلْقَلَ
Agitation.	قَلْقَلَة
To pare (the nails).	قَلَمَ ـ وَقَلَّمَ
Pen ; handwriting. Style.	قَلَم ج أَقْلَامٌ
Pencil.	قَلَم رُصَاص
Slate-pencil.	قَلَم حَجَرٍ
Parings (of nails &c.).	قُلَامَة
Region, tract, province ; climate.	إِقْلِيم ج أَقَالِيمُ
Cut, pared.	مُقَلَّم
Pen-case.	مَقْلَمَة
Cowl, cap.	قَلَنْسُوَة ج قَلَانِسُ
To fry.	قَلَا يَقْلُو قَلْوًا وَقَلَى يَقْلِي قَلْيًا
Ash of alkaline plants.	قِلًى وَقِلْي
Cell of a monk.	قِلَّايَة
Fried food.	قَلِيَّة
A frying-pan.	مِقْلًى وَمِقْلَاة
Fried, roasted.	مَقْلِيٌّ وَمُقْلًى
Summit, top.	قِمَّة ج قِمَم
Wheat.	قَمْح
Grain of wheat; grain (weight).	قَمْحَه

قَمَرَ يَقْمِرُ To play a game of chance.

قَامَرَ مُقَامَرَةً وَقِمَاراً To gamble.

أَقْمَرَ To be moonlight.

تَقَامَرَ To play at dice.

قَمَرٌ ج أَقْمَار Moon.

قَمْرَة Moonlit (night).

قَمَرِيّ Lunar ; moonlike.

قَمَرِيَّة Small window.

قِمَار Gambling.

مُقْمِرَة Moonlit (night).

مُقَامِر Gambler.

قَمَزَ يَقْمُزُ قَمْزاً To jump.

قَمَسَ يَقْمُسُ قَمْساً To dive.

قَامُوسٌ ج قَوَامِيسُ Dictionary.

قَمْشَة Whip.

قُمَاشٌ ج أَقْمِشَة Woven stuff.

قُمَاشُ البَيْتِ Household things.

قَمَصَ يَقْمِصُ To jump, leap.

تَقَمَّصَ To transmigrate (soul).

قَمِيصٌ ج أَقْمِصَة وَقُمْصَانٌ Shirt.

تَقَمُّصٌ Transmigration (soul).

قَمَطَ وَقَمَّطَ To bind ; swaddle.

قِمَاطٌ ج قُمُطٌ Swaddling-cloth.

مُقَمَّط Bound up, swaddled.

قَمَعَ يَقْمَعُ وَأَقْمَعَ To tame, subdue.

قَمَعَ وَأَقْمَعَ عَنْ To prevent.

إِنْقَمَعَ To be subdued, tamed.

قَمْعٌ وَإِقْمَاعٌ Subjugating.

قِمْعٌ ج أَقْمَاع Funnel.

تَقَمْقَمَ To murmur, find fault.

قُمْقُمٌ ج قَمَاقِمُ Jar, cup; flask.

قَمْلٌ Lice, vermin.

قَمِلٌ وَمُقَمَّلٌ Infested with lice.

قَمْلَة A louse.

قُمَّل Very small insects.

قَمِينٌ Oven to heat baths.

قُنٌّ Poultry-house, hen-coop.

قُنَّةٌ ج قُنَنٌ	Small mountain. Peak.
قَانُونٌ ج قَوَانِينُ	Rule, canon, law. Kind of harp.
قَانُونِيٌّ	Canonical, legal.
قَنِّينَةٌ ج قَنَانِيُّ	Glass bottle, phial.
قَنَأَ يَقْنَأُ قُنُوءًا	To be very red.
أَحْمَرُ قَانِئٌ	Very dark red.
قُنَّبٌ	Hemp ; coarse rope.
قُنْبَرَاءُ وَقُنْبُرَةٌ ج قَنَابِرُ	Lark.
قُنْبُرَةٌ ج قَنَابِرُ	Crest of a cock.
قُنَّبِيطٌ وَقَرْنَبِيطٌ	Cauliflower.
قُنْبُلَةٌ ج قَنَابِلُ	Bomb-shell.
قَنَتَ يَقْنُتُ وَأَقْنَتَ	To obey God.
قَنَتَ يَقْنُتُ قَنَاتَةً	To eat sparingly.
قَانِتٌ م قَانِتَةٌ	Pious.
قُنُوتٌ	Piety, submission to God.
قِنْدِيلٌ ج قَنَادِيلُ	Lamp.
قَنَصَ يَقْنِصُ وَاقْتَنَصَ	To hunt.
قَنْصٌ وَاقْتِنَاصٌ	Hunting.
قَنَصٌ وَقَنِيصٌ	Prey ; game.
قَانِصٌ وَقَنَّاصٌ	Hunter.
قَانِصَةٌ ج قَوَانِصُ	Crop, gizzard.
قُنْصُلٌ ج قَنَاصِلُ	Consul.
قُنْصُلِيَّةٌ وَقُنْصُلاَتُو	Consulate.
قَنَطَ يَقْنِطُ وَقَنُطَ يَقْنُطُ	To despair.
قَنَّطَ	To throw into despair.
قَنَطٌ وَقُنُوطٌ	Despair.
قَنِطٌ	Discouraged ; despairing.
قَنْطَرَ وتَقَنْطَرَ	To fall from a horse.
قَنْطَرَةٌ ج قَنَاطِرُ	Arch.
قِنْطَارٌ ج قَنَاطِيرُ	100 rottles.
قِنْطَارِيُونٌ	Centaury.
مُقَنْطَرٌ	Collected together.
قَنِعَ يَقْنَعُ	To be contented.
قَنَّعَ وَأَقْنَعَ	To convince, persuade.
تَقَنَّعَ	To veil one's self.
إِقْتَنَعَ بِ	To be content. To be persuaded, convinced.
قَنِعٌ وَقَنُوعٌ	Content, temperate.

قَانِعٌ Contented.

قِنَاعٌ ج قُنُعٌ Veil for the head.

قَنَاعَةٌ وقُنُوعٌ Contentedness.

مُقَنَّعٌ Wearing an iron helmet.

قِنفِذٌ ج قَنَافِذُ Porcupine.

قَنَا يَقْنُو وَاقْتَنَى To acquire.

قَنَّى To dig a canal.

أَقْنَى To give one possession.

قُنْوَةٌ Acquisition ; possession.

قَنَاةٌ ج قَنَوَاتٌ Canal. Lance.

قِنْيَةٌ ج قِنًى That which is acquired.

قَانٍ Possessor, proprietor, owner.

أَقْنَى Having an aquiline nose.

قَهَرَ يَقْهَرُ To subdue, oppress.

قَاهَرَ To treat with violence.

قَهْرٌ Violence ; oppression.

قَهْرًا By force, inspite of.

قَاهِرٌ Victor, conqueror.

القَاهِرَةُ Cairo, *i.e. Viclirx.*

أَلْقَهَّارُ God, the Almighty.

مَقْهُورٌ Forced, conquered.

قَهْرَمَانٌ ج قَهَارِمَةٌ Steward.

قَهْقَرَ وَتَقَهْقَرَ To go backwards.

قَهْقَرَى Retrograde movement.

قُهْقُورٌ (وَقَعْقُورٌ) Pile of stones.

قَهْقَهَ To laugh immoderately.

قَهْقَهَةٌ Immoderate laughter.

قَهْوَةٌ Coffee. Wine.

قَهْوَةٌ ج قَهَوَاتٌ Coffee-house ; café.

(قَهْوَجِيٌّ) Coffee-house keeper.

قَابَ قَوْسٍ A bow's length.

قُوبَاءُ Ring-worm, tetter.

قَاتَ يَقُوتُ To nourish, feed.

تَقَوَّتَ وَاقْتَاتَ To be nourished.

قُوتٌ ج أَقْوَاتٌ Food, victuals.

مُقِيتٌ Sustainer, guardian.

قادَ يقودُ واَقتادَ To lead, guide.

إنقادَ واَقتادَ To be guided, led.

إنقادَ ل To obey.

قَوْدٌ وقِيادَةٌ Leading, guiding.

قائِدٌ ج قُوّادٌ Guide ; leader.

مِقوَدٌ ج مَقاوِدُ Halter.

مَقُودٌ ومَقوُودٌ Led, guided.

قارةٌ ج قاراتٌ Small, isolated mountain.

مُقوَّرٌ A thing with a hole in its middle.

قاسَ يقوسُ واَقتاسَ To measure.

قَوِسَ يقوَسُ وتَقوَّسَ To be bent.

(قوَّسَ) To shoot with a gun.

(تقوَّسَ) To be shot, fired.

قَوْسٌ ج قِسِيٌّ واَقواسٌ Bow, arc.

قوسُ قُزَحَ Rainbow.

قوّاسٌ ج قوّاسةٌ Cavass ; archer.

قُوَيْسَةٌ Sage (plant).

قُوشٌ ج أقواشٌ) Crupper.

قاضَ وقوَّضَ To demolish.

قَوْضٌ Exchange.

قاعٌ ج قِيعٌ Plain ; bottom-land.

قاعةٌ ج قاعاتٌ Courtyard. Hall.

قاقَ يقوقُ قَوْقاً To cackle (hen).

قاوُوقٌ ج قواويقُ Cylindrical hat.

قالَ يقولُ To speak, say, propose.

قالَ ب To give as an opinion.

قالَ على To speak against.

قِيلَ It is said, has been said.

قاوَلَ To argue, bargain with.

تقوَّلَ To make a false report.

تقاوَلَ To converse together.

قالٌ وقِيلٌ Talk.

قَوْلٌ ج أقوالٌ وأقاوِيلُ Saying, word, speech ; promise.

قائِلٌ Author of a saying.

مقالةٌ Treatise ; chapter ; article.

مقُولٌ Said ; word, sentence.

Conference. Contract. مُقاوَلَةٌ
Colic. قُولَنْجٌ
Colon (intestine). أَلقُولُونُ
To rise ; stand. قَامَ يَقُومُ
To rise against, revolt. قَامَ عَلَى
To rise to honour one. قَامَ لِ
To take one's place. قَامَ مَقَامهُ
To carry on (a matter). قَامَ بِ
To keep a promise. قَامَ بِوَعْدِهِ
She began to cry. قَامَتْ تَنُوحُ
To erect ; straighten. قَوَّمَ
To oppose, dispute with. قَاوَمَ
To set up ; establish. أَقَامَ
To stay (in a place). أَقَامَ بِ
To persevere in. اقَامَ عَلَى
To appoint to. أَقَامَهُ عَلَى
He brought a charge against him. أَقَامَ عَلَيْهِ الدَّعْوَى
To be straightened. تَقَوَّمَ

To be upright, straight. إِسْتَقَامَ
People ; company. قَوْمٌ ج أَقْوَامٌ
The enemy. أَلقَوْمُ
Consistence. قَوَامٌ
Support ; sustenance. قِوَامٌ
Stature ; fathom. قَامَةٌ ج قَامَاتٌ
Price, value, worth. قِيمَةٌ ج قِيَمٌ
Upright, vertical ; firm. قَائِمٌ
Governor. Lt.-Colonel. قَائِمَقَام
Right-angled. قَائِمُ الزَّاوِيَةِ
Right angle. زَاوِيَةٌ قَائِمَةٌ
Foot of a quadruped. قَائِمَةٌ ج قَوَائِمُ
List, catalogue. قَائِمَةٌ ج قَوَائِمُ
Resurrection. قِيَامَةٌ
Manager ; agent. قَيِّمٌ
Straight ; true. قَوِيمٌ ج قِيَامٌ
The Self-Existent (God) أَلقَيُّومُ
Abiding ; preforming. إِقَامَةٌ

Uprightness ; rectitude. إِسْتِقَامَةٌ

Calendar. تَقْوِيمُ ٱلسَّنَةِ

Valuation of a country for purposes of taxation. تَقْوِيمُ ٱلْبِلَادِ

Place, rank, office. مُقَامٌ

Resisting ; adversary. مُقَاوِمٌ

Resistance, opposition. مُقَاوَمَةٌ

Straight. Upright. مُسْتَقِيمٌ

To be, or grow, strong. قَوِيَ يَقْوَى

To be able to do it. قَوِيَ عَلَى ٱلْأَمْرِ

To strengthen. قَوَّى

To grow strong. تَقَوَّى وَٱسْتَقْوَى

Strength, faculty, ability ; potentiality. قُوَّةٌ ج قُوَّات وَقُوًى

The mental faculties. أَلْقُوَى ٱلْعَقْلِيَّةُ

Perception. أَلْقُوَّةُ ٱلنَّظَرِيَّةُ

Reasoning. أَلْقُوَّةُ ٱلْعَمَلِيَّةُ

Memory. أَلْقُوَّةُ ٱلْحَافِظَةُ

Strong, powerful. قَوِيٌّ ج أَقْوِيَاءُ

Act of strengthening. تَقْوِيَةٌ

Strengthening, fortifying. مُقَوٍّ

To vomit. قَاءَ يَقِي قَيْئًا

To make vomit. قَيَّأَ تَقْيِئَة وَأَقَاءَ

Act of vomiting. قَيْءٌ

Emetic. مُقَيِّئٌ

Guitar. قِيثَارٌ ج قَيَاثِيرُ

To suppurate. قَاحَ يَقِيحُ وَقَيَّحَ وَتَقَيَّحَ

Pus, suppuration. قَيْحٌ

To bind. Register. To restrict. (the sense of a word). قَيَّدَ

To be bound, registered. تَقَيَّدَ

To be bound to. تَقَيَّدَ بِ

Fetter, chain, limit. قَيْدٌ ج قُيُودٌ

Limitation, restriction. Registration. تَقْيِيدٌ

Bound ; Registered. مُقَيَّدٌ

Pitch, tar. قِيرٌ وَقَارٌ

Cyrene. أَلْقَيْرَوَانُ

To measure, compare. قَاسَ يَقِيسُ

To measure. قايَسَ مُقَايَسَة

To compare a thing with another. قايَسَ بَيْنَ

To be measured. انْقَاسَ

Measure ; rule, analogy. Syllogism. قِيَاسٌ ج أَقْيِسَةٌ

According to rule. قِيَاسِيٌّ

Estimate by analogy. مُقَايَسَةٌ

A measure. مِقْيَاس ج مَقَايِيسُ

Nilometer. مِقْيَاس النِّيلِ

To exchange for. قاضَ ـ مِن

To exchange with. قَايَضَ مُقَايَضَةً

To be broken down. تَقَيَّضَ

Exchange. قِيَاضٌ وَمُقَايَضَةٌ

Silk-cord. (قَيْطَانٌ)

To be very hot. قَاظَ يَقِيظ قَيْظًا

Heat of summer. Drought. قَيْظ

Maple (tree). قَيْقَبٌ

To take a siesta. قَالَ يَقِيلُ

To abrogate a sale. أَقَالَ

To seek abrogation. إِسْتَقَالَ

Hydrocele. قِيلَةٌ

Mid-day nap, siesta. قَيْلُولَةٌ

Annulment of a bargain. إِقَالَةٌ

Place of a mid-day nap. مَقِيلٌ

Maid-servant. Female singer. قَيْنَةٌ

ك

As a numeral sign=20.	ك
Pronominal suffix.	كَ وكِ
He struck thee.	ضَرَبَكَ
Thy book.	كِتابُكِ
As, like.	كَ
Like a lion.	كالاسَدِ
To be sad.	كَئِبَ يَكْأَبُ وٱكْتَأَبَ
Grief, sorrow.	كَأْبٌ وكَآبَةٌ
Grieved.	كَئِبٌ وكَئِيبٌ ومُكْتَئِبٌ
Cup.	كَأْسٌ ج كَاسَاتٌ وكُؤُس
Death.	كَأْسُ ٱلْمَنِيَّةِ
As if, as though.	كَأَنَّ وكَأَنْ
As if Zeid were a lion.	كَأَنَّ زَيْداً أَسَدٌ
To invert; overthrow.	كَبَّ يَكُبُّ كَبًّا
To be intent upon.	أَكَبَّ عَلَى
To fall prostrate.	إِنْكَبَّ
Ball of thread.	كُبَّةٌ ج كُبَبٌ
Broiled bits of meat.	كَبَاب
Cubeb.	كَبَابَةٌ (نبات)
Hedge-hog.	كَبَابَةُ ٱلشَّوْكِ
Thread-reel.	مِكَبٌّ ج مِكَبَّات
Over-coat.	كَبُّوتٌ ج كَبَابِيتُ
To pull in a horse.	كَبَحَ يَكْبَحُ
To restrain, prevent.	كَبَحَ عَنْ
To be in the zenith.	كَبَّدَ وتَكَبَّدَ
To suffer, endure.	كابَدَ

The middle of the sky. كَبْدٌ

Liver. كَبْدٌ وَكِبْدٌ ج أَكْبَادٌ وَكُبُودٌ

Interior ; middle. كَبَدٌ

Citron. كُبَّادٌ

To be advanced in age. كَبِرَ يَكْبَرُ

To be large ; grow. كَبُرَ يَكْبُرُ

It became formidable to him. كَبُرَ عَلَيهِ الأَمْرُ

To enlarge ; magnify. كَبَّرَ

To grow proud. تَكَبَّرَ وَاسْتَكْبَرَ

To deem great. إِسْتَكْبَرَ

Greatness, glory, pride. كُبْرٌ

Greatness, advanced age. كِبَرٌ

Caper-bush. كَبَرٌ وَ(كَبَّارٌ وَقَبَّارٌ)

Major proposition, (*logic*). كُبْرَى

Greatness ; pride. كِبْرِيَاءُ

Great, large. كَبِيرٌ ج كِبَارٌ وَكُبَرَاءُ

Great crime. كَبِيرَةٌ ج كَبَائِرُ

Greater ; older. أَكْبَرُ

God is great ! أَللّٰهُ أَكْبَرُ

The grandees. الأَكَابِرُ

Pride, haughtiness. تَكَبُّرٌ

Magnifying God. تَكْبِيرٌ

Proud, haughty. مُتَكَبِّرٌ

Sulphur ; matches. كِبْرِيت

Sulphuretted. مُكَبْرَتٌ

To press. Surprise. كَبَسَ يَكْبِسُ

To train an animal. كَبَّسَ

To be pressed, squeezed. تَكَبَّسَ

Assault. Pressure. كَبْسٌ

A sudden attack. كَبْسَةٌ

Nightmare. كَابُوس ج كَوَابِيسُ

Pickles. كبيس

Leap year. سَنَةٌ كَبِيسَةٌ

Hand-press. مِكْبَسٌ ج مَكَابِسُ

Assailed, pressed. Pickled. مَكْبُوسٌ

To grasp. كَبَشَ يَكْبُشُ كَبْشًا

Ram, male sheep.	كَبْشٌ ج كِبَاشٌ
Mulberry-fruit.	كَبْشُ ٱلتُّوتِ
Cloves.	كَبْشُ ٱلْقَرُنْفُلِ
A handful.	(كَبْشَةٌ)
To bind, fetter.	كَبَلَ يَكْبِلُ وَكَبَّلَ
To be fettered.	تَكَبَّلَ
Heavy fetter.	كَبْلٌ ج كُبُولٌ
Fettered.	مُكَبَّلٌ وَمَكْبُولٌ
Horse-blanket.	(كَوبَانٌ)
To fall, trip.	كَبَا يَكْبُو كَبْواً
Trip, stumble.	كَبْوَةٌ
Charpie, lint.	كَتِيتٌ
To write.	كَتَبَ يَكْتُبُ كِتَابَةً
To prescribe, appoint.	كَتَبَ عَلَى
To arrange troops in order.	كَتَّبَ
To correspond with.	كَاتَبَ
To assemble in squadrons.	تَكَتَّبَ
To write to one another.	تَكَاتَبَ
To enrol one's self.	إِكْتَتَبَ
To ask to write.	إِسْتَكْتَبَ
Book-seller.	كُتُبِيٌّ
Writer, clerk.	كَاتِبٌ ج كُتَّابٌ
Writing, book.	كِتَابٌ ج كُتُبٌ
Christians. Jews.	أَهْلُ ٱلْكِتَابِ
School.	كُتَّابٌ ج كَتَاتِيبُ
Writing; calligraphy.	كِتَابَةٌ
Squadron.	كَتِيبَةٌ ج كَتَائِبُ
School. Office.	مَكْتَبٌ ج مَكَاتِبُ
Library; study.	مَكْتَبَةٌ ج مَكَاتِبُ
Correspondent.	مُكَاتِبٌ
Correspondence by letter.	مُكَاتَبَةٌ
Inscribed, registered.	مُكْتَتِبٌ
Written; letter.	مَكْتُوبٌ ج مَكَاتِيبُ
Crippled. Whole.	أَكْتَعُ م كَتْعَاءُ ج كُتْعٌ
To tie the hands back.	كَتَفَ
To cross the arms.	تَكَتَّفَ

Shoulder. كَتِفٌ ج أَكْتَافٌ

Heap, lump. كُتْلَةٌ ج كُتَلٌ

Catholic. كَاثُولِيكِيٌّ ج كَاثُولِيكُ

To conceal, hide. كَتَمَ يَكْتُمُ

To be concealed, hidden. إِنْكَتَمَ

To confide a secret. إِسْتَكْتَمَ

Concealing. كَتْمٌ وَكِتْمَانٌ

Private secretary. كَاتِمُ ٱلْأَسْرَارِ

Constipation, costiveness. كُتَامٌ

Kept secret. مَكْتُومٌ وَمُكْتَتَمٌ

Flax, linen. كَتَّانٌ

Linseed. بِزْرُ كَتَّانٍ

Thick, dense. كَثٌّ وَكَثِيثٌ

To be much, many ; increase, multiply. كَثُرَ يَكْثُرُ

To increase ; do too much. كَثَّرَ

To be rich ; increase, grow. أَكْثَرَ

To speak much. أَكْثَرَ فِي ٱلْكَلَامِ

To increase multiply. تَكَاثَرَ

To regard as much. إِسْتَكْثَرَ

To thank. إِسْتَكْثَرَ بِخَيْرِهِ

Great number, plenty, abundance كُثْرٌ وَكَثْرَةٌ

Much, many ; abundant. كَثِيرٌ

Abundantly, often, very. كَثِيرًا

Tragacanth, goat's thorn. كَثِيرَاءُ

More, more frequent. أَكْثَرُ

Most people. أَكْثَرُ ٱلنَّاسِ

Growth, increase. تَكَاثُرٌ

Rich. مُكْثِرٌ

To be thick, dense. كَثُفَ يَكْثُفُ

Thickness, denseness. كَثَافَةٌ

Thick, dense, compact. كَثِيفٌ

To apply collyrium, or paint, to one's eyes. تَكَحَّلَ وَٱكْتَحَلَ

An eye-salve or paint. كُحْلٌ

Black antimony-powder. كُحَالٌ

Horse of best breed. كَحِيلٌ ج كَحَائِلُ

Having the eye-lashes black. أَكْحَلُ م كَحْلَاءُ ج كُحْلٌ

Pencil with which the *kohl* is applied. مُكْحُلٌ وَمِكْحَالٌ

Vessel containing the *kohl*. مُكْحُلَةٌ ج مَكَاحِلُ

Secretary. كَاخِيَةٌ ج كَوَاخٍ

To toil hard. To weary. كَدَّ يَكُدُّ

Toil ; effort, exertion. كَدٌّ

Laborious. كَدُودٌ

To be muddy, turbid. كَدِرَ يَكْدَرُ

To trouble ; make turbid. كَدَّرَ

To be troubled ; muddy. تَكَدَّرَ

Turbidness ; vexation. كَدَرٌ

Troubled ; turbid. كَدِرٌ وَمُكَدَّرٌ

To heap reaped grain. كَدَسَ يَكْدِسُ

Heap of grain. كُدْسٌ ج أَكْدَاسٌ

To bite (horse). كَدَشَ يَكْدِشُ

Pack-horse. كَدِيشٌ ج كُدْشٌ

To bite. كَدَمَ يَكْدُمُ كَدْماً

Scar. كَدْمٌ ج كُدُومٌ

To yoke oxen. كَدَنَ يَكْدُنُ

Thus, like this. كَذَا وَكَذَلِكَ

So and so. كَذَا وَكَذَا

To lie, speak falsely. كَذَبَ يَكْذِبُ

To accuse of lying. كَذَّبَ

To discredit a thing. كَذَّبَ

To contradict one's self ; belie one's self. كَذَّبَ وَأَكْذَبَ نَفْسَهُ

Lie, fraud. كِذْبٌ وَأُكْذُوبَةٌ ج أَكَاذِيبُ

Liar. كَذُوبٌ وَكَاذِبٌ وَكَذَّابٌ

More false. أَكْذَبُ

Falsely accused. مَكْذُوبٌ عَلَيْهِ

Falsehood. مَكْذَبَةٌ ج مَكَاذِبُ

To return. كَرَّ يَكُرُّ كُرُوراً

To return against. كَرَّ كَرّاً

To repeat. Purify, refine. كَرَّرَ

To be repeated. تَكَرَّرَ

Return, return to attack. كَرٌّ

Turn, time. كَرَّةٌ ج كَرَّاتٌ

Globe, ball. كُرَةٌ ج كُرَاتٌ

Succession of ages. كُرُورُ ٱلدُّهُورِ

Repetition. تِكْرَارٌ وَتَكْرِيرٌ

Repeatedly. تَكْرَاراً

Repeated. Refined. مُكَرَّر

To grieve. كَرَبَ يَكْرُبُ كَرْباً

To offect with sorrow. أَكْرَبَ

To be in distress, grief. إِكْتَرَب

Grief, sorrow. كَرْبٌ ج كُرُوبٌ

Cherub. كَرُوبٌ

Grieved. كَرِيبٌ وَمَكْرُوبٌ

Horse-whip. كَرْبَاجٌ ج كَرَابِيجُ

To impose a quarantine. كَرْتَنَ

To be kept in quarantine. تَكَرْتَنَ

Quarantine. كَرَنْتِينَةٌ

Paste-board. كَرْتُونٌ

To look after. إِكْتَرَثَ لِ وَبِ

Leek. كُرَّاثٌ

Georgia. بِلَادُ ٱلْكُرْجِ

Georgian. كُرْجِيٌّ

Kurd. كُرْدٌ وَأَكْرَادٌ

A Kurd. كُرْدِيٌّ

Neck chain. (كُرْدَانٌ)

To divide into squadrons. كَرْدَسَ

The Kurds country. كُرْدِسْتَانُ

Squardon. كُرْدُوسَةٌ ج كَرَادِيس

To preach. كَرَزَ يَكْرِزُ كَرْزاً

Preaching. كَرْزٌ وَكِرَازَةٌ

Cherry, cherry tree. كَرَزٌ

The leading ram. كَرَّازٌ

Earthen flask. كُرَازٌ وَكَرَّارٌ

To consecrate. (كَرَّسَ)

To be devoted to God. تَكَرَّسَ

Pamphlet. كُرَّاسَةٌ ج كَرَارِيس

Chair. كُرْسِيٌّ ج كَرَاسِيٌّ وَكَرَاسٍ

Carriage. (كَرُّوسَةٌ ج كَرُّوسَاتٌ)

Consecration, dedication. (تَكْرِيسٌ)

Vetch. كِرْسِنَّةٌ

To be wrinkled. كَرِشَ يَكْرَشُ وَتَكَرَّشَ

Stomach. كِرْشٌ ج كُرُوشٌ

To sip water. كَرَعَ يَكْرَعُ

Celery. كَرَفْسٌ

Distilling-retort. كَرَكَةٌ

Crane (bird). كُرْكِيٌّ ج كَرَاكِيُّ

To disarrange, confuse. كَرْكَبَ

Rhinoceros. كَرْكَدَّنٌ

To laugh loud. كَرْكَرَ

Saffron. كُرْكُمٌ

To be generous, noble. كَرُمَ يَكْرُمُ

To exalt, honour. كَرَّمَ وَأَكْرَمَ

How generous he is ! مَا أَكْرَمَهُ

To act generously. تَكَرَّمَ

Grace, liberality. كَرَمٌ

Vine (grape). كَرْمٌ ج كُرُومٌ

A vine-tree. كَرْمَةٌ

Vine-dresser. كَرَّامٌ

Generosity ; honour. كَرَامَةٌ

Most gladly ! حُبًّا وَكَرَامَةً

Noble, liberal. كَرِيمٌ ج كِرَامٌ

Precious object. كَرِيمَةٌ

More noble, or generous. أَكْرَمُ

Respect, reverence. إِكْرَامٌ

For the sake of. إِكْرَامًا لِ

Honouring, honour. تَكْرِيمٌ

Honoured. مُكْرَمٌ وَمُكَرَّمٌ

Noble action. مَكْرُمَةٌ ج مَكَارِمُ

Cabbage. كُرُنْبٌ وَكَرَنْبٌ

To loathe, abhor. كَرِهَ يَكْرَهُ

To be loathsome. كَرُهَ يَكْرُهُ

To render hateful. كَرَّهَ

أَكْرَهَ على To force one to . .
تَكَرَّهَ وتَكَارَهَ To loathe.
إِسْتَكْرَهَ To find loathsome.
كُرْهٌ وَكَرَاهَةٌ Aversion, disgust.
كَرِهٌ وَكَرِيهٌ Detestable.
كَرِيهَةٌ ج كَرَائِهُ Adversity.
إِكْرَاهٌ Compulsion.
مَكْرُوهٌ Abhorred, detested.
كَرَوْيَا وَكَرَاوِيَا Caraway.
كَرِيَ يَكْرَى كَرًى To slumber.
كَارَى وأَكْرَى To let, rent.
إِكْتَرَى وَآسْتَكْرَى To hire, rent.
كِرَاءٌ وَكِرْوَةٌ Hire, wages; rent.
كُرَةٌ ج كُرَاتٌ وَكُرًى Globe, ball.
كُرَةُ ٱلأَرْضِ Terrestrial globe.
كُرَوِيٌّ Globular, spherical.
إِكْرَاءٌ Act of renting, letting.
إِكْتِرَاءٌ Act of hiring.

مُكَارٍ ج مُكَارُونَ Muleteer.
مُكْرٍ Hirer out, letter.
مُكْرًى Hired, rented, let.
كَزَّ يَكَزُّ To dry up; become rigid.
كُزَازٌ وَكُزَّازٌ Tetanus.
كُزْبُرَةٌ وَكُزَبُرَةٌ Coriander.
كَسَبَ يَكْسِبُ To earn ; acquire.
كَسَّبَ وأَكْسَبَ To bestow; give.
إِكْتَسَبَ To seek gain ; acquire.
كَسْبٌ Earnings, gain.
إِكْتِسَابٌ Acquiring, earning.
إِكْتِسَابِيٌّ Acquired.
مَكْسَبٌ ج مَكَاسِبُ Gain, profit.
مَكْسُوبٌ وَمُكْتَسَبٌ Acquired.
(كَسْتَنَا) Chestnut.
كَسَحَ يَكْسَحُ كَسْحًا To cut off.
كَسِحَ يَكْسَحُ كَسَحًا To be crippled.
كُسَاحَةٌ Rickets. Sweepings.

Lame, crippled. كَسِيحٌ ج كُسْحَانٌ

A cripple. أَكْسَحُ م كَسْحَاءُ ج كُسْحٌ

To sell badly. كَسَدَ يَكْسُدُ

Worthless ; selling badly. كَاسِدٌ

To break ; rout, defeat. كَسَرَ يَكْسُرُ

To break into pieces. كَسَّرَ

To seek an abatement. كَاسَرَ

To be broken into pieces. تَكَسَّرَ

To be broken ; routed ; become a bankrupt, fail. إِنْكَسَرَ

Breach, fracture. كَسْرٌ

Fraction (*arith*). كَسْرٌ ج كُسُورٌ

Fragment. كِسْرَةٌ ج كِسَرٌ

The vowel. (ِ) A fracture ; defeat. كَسْرَةٌ ج كَسَرَاتٌ

Chosroes. كِسْرَى ج أَكَاسِرَةٌ

Bird of prey. كَاسِرَةٌ ج كَوَاسِرُ

A fragment. كُسَارَةٌ

Elixir. إِكْسِيرٌ

Defeat ; bankruptcy. إِنْكِسَارٌ

Broken plural. جَمْعُ ٱلتَّكْسِيرِ

Broken into pieces. مُكَسَّرٌ

Routed ; bankrupt. مَكْسُورٌ

To be eclipsed. كَسَفَ وَٱنْكَسَفَ

Eclipse. كُسُوفٌ وَٱنْكِسَافٌ

Heavy-hearted. كَاسِفُ ٱلْبَالِ

Eclipsed. مَكْسُوفٌ وَمُنْكَسِفٌ

To be lazy. كَسِلَ يَكْسَلُ وَتَكَاسَلَ

Laziness, idleness. كَسَلٌ وَتَكَاسُلٌ

Lazy, idle. كَسْلَانُ ج كَسَالَى

Mode, fashion. كَسْمٌ

To clothe. كَسَا يَكْسُو وَأَكْسَى

To be dressed, clothed. إِكْتَسَى

Garment, dress. كِسَاءٌ ج أَكْسِيَةٌ

Clothing, dress. كُسْوَةٌ ج كُسًى

To frown. Chase away. (كَشَّ)

Lock of hair. كَشَّةٌ

A thimble. (كِشْتُبَانٌ)

كَشَحَ ـَ To disperse.

إِنكَشَحَ عَنْ To retire from.

كَشْحٌ ج كُشُوحٌ Flank ; waist.

كَشَرَ عَنْ نَابِهِ To snarl (beast).

كَشَطَ يَكْشِطُ To strip ; scrape.

تَكَشَّطَ To be dispersed (clouds).

إِنْكَشَطَ To be taken off.

كَشَفَ يَكْشِفُ وَكَشَّفَ To uncover.

كَاشَفَ بِ To reveal, disclose.

إِنْكَشَفَ To be uncovered.

إِكْتَشَفَ To discover ; find out.

إِسْتَكْشَفَ To try to discover.

كَشْفٌ Unveiling, revealing.

(كَاشِفٌ ج كَشَفَةٌ) Overseer. Test.

مَكْشُوفٌ Uncovered, disclosed.

إِكْتِشَافٌ ج إِكْتِشَافَاتٌ Discovery.

مُكْتَشِفٌ Discoverer.

كَشْكَشٌ Ruffle of a garment.

كَشْكُولٌ A beggar's bag.

كِشْمِشٌ Currants.

كَظَّ يَكُظُّ To surfeit (food).

كِظَّةٌ Indigestion ; surfeit.

كَظَمَ يَكْظِمُ To shut ; restrain.

كَاظِمٌ Silent, speechless.

كَظِيمٌ Suppressing anger.

كَعَّبَ To cube (a number).

كَعْبٌ Ankle. Cube, (*arith*).

أَلْكَعْبَةُ *The kaba* in Mecca.

مُكَعَّبٌ Cubic ; cube.

كُعْبُرَةٌ The radius (bone).

كَعْكٌ Biscuit, cake, bun.

كَعَمَ يَكْعَمُ To muzzle.

كِعَامٌ Muzzle of the camel.

كَعِيمٌ وَمَكْعُومٌ Muzzled.

كَعَا يَكْعُو To be timid.

(كَعَّى) To defy.

Paper. كَاغِدٌ

To hem, seam. كَفَّ يَكُفُّ كَفًّا

To prevent. To cease. كَفَّ عَنْ

To become blind. كُفَّ بَصَرُهُ

To abstain from. إِنْكَفَّ عَنْ

Palm of hand. كَفٌّ ج كُفُوفٌ

Scale (of a balance). كَفَّةٌ

Silk handkerchief. كَفِيَّةٌ

All. كَافَّةً

Equal ; daily bread. كَفَافٌ

Blind. كَفِيفٌ وَمَكْفُوفٌ ج مَكَافِيفُ

To reward. كَافَأَ مُكَافَأَةً وَكِفَاءً

To retreat ; turn back. إِنْكَفَأَ

Equality, likeness. كَفَأٌ وَكَفَاءَةٌ

Equal, like. كَفَاءٌ وَكُفْوءٌ

To face. كَفَحَ يَكْفَحُ وَكَافَحَ

To fight for, defend. كَافَحَ عَنْ

To drive back. أَكْفَحَ عَنْ

To encounter one another. تَكَافَحَ

Battle, combat. كِفَاحٌ وَمُكَافَحَةٌ

To cover. كَفَرَ يَكْفُرُ وَكَفَّرَ

To be an infidel. كَفَرَ يَكْفُرُ

To renounce, deny. كَفَرَ بِ

To expiate. كَفَّرَ

Village, hamlet. كَفْرٌ ج كُفُورٌ

Unbelief ; infidelity. كُفْرٌ

Infidel. كَافِرٌ ج كُفَّارٌ وَكَفَرَةٌ

Camphor. كَافُورٌ

Atonement ; expiation. كَفَّارَةٌ

Atonement ; expiation. تَكْفِيرٌ

To take charge of. كَفَلَ يَكْفُلُ

To stand security. كَفَلَ يَكْفِلُ

To make one give bail. كَفَّلَ

To guarantee. تَكَفَّلَ لَهُ بِ

Buttocks. كَفَلٌ ج أَكْفَالٌ

One who stands bail. كَافِلٌ

أَلْـكافِلُ	God.
كَفَالَةٌ	Bail, security, pledge.
كَفِيلٌ كُفَلاءُ	A surety.
مكْفُولٌ	Guaranteed.
إِكْفَهَرَّ	To be very dark (night)
كَفَنَ	To shroud the dead.
كَفَنٌ ج أَكْفَانٌ	Shroud.
كَفَى يكْفِي	To suffice ; satisfy.
كَفَاهُ الشَّرَّ	To prevent evil.
كَافَى بِـ	To recompense.
إِكْتَفَى	To be contented.
كَفِيٌّ وكَافٍ	Sufficient.
كِفَايَةٌ	Sufficient quantity.
مـكَافَاةٌ	Recompense, requital.
كَلَّ يَكِلُّ	To be tired, weary.
كَلَّ و كَلَّلَ	To be dim, dull.
كَلَّلَ	To crown. To join in wedlock, marry.
أَكَلَّ	To fatigue ; to dim.
تـكَلَّلَ	To be crowned.
كَلٌّ وَكَلَالٌ	Weariness ; dulness.
كَلٌّ وَكَلِيلٌ	Blunt ; dim.
كُلٌّ	All ; each, every.
كِلاَ (كِلْتَا dual fem	Both of.
كَلاَّ	No ! by no means.
كُلَّةٌ ج كُلَلٌ	Cannon ball.
كُلَّمَا	As often as, whenever.
كُلِّيٌّ م كُلِّيَّةٌ	Universal, general.
أَلْـكُلِّيَّةُ	General term, (*logic*).
بالْـكُلِّيَّةِ	Altogether, entirely.
كَالٌّ	Fatigued ; dim ; blunt.
إِكْلِيلٌ ج أَكالِيلُ	Crown ; umbel.
مُـكَلَّلٌ	Crowned.
كَلَأٌ	Forage ; herbage.
كَلِبَ ـَ	To have hydrophobia.
كَلْبٌ ج كِلاَبٌ	Dog.
كَلْبُ ٱلْبَحْرِ	Shark.

Beaver. كَلْبُ ٱلمَاءِ

Canis major. أَلْـكَلْبُ ٱلأَكْبَرُ

Canis minor. أَلْـكَلْبُ ٱلأَصْغَرُ

Hydrophobia. كَلِبٌ

Seized with hydrophobia. كَلِبٌ

Female dog, bitch. كَلْبَةٌ

Tongs, forceps. كلبتان

Hook ; grapnel. كُلَّابٌ ج كَلَالِيبُ

See : كِلَا Both, (*fem*). كلتا

To frown. كَلَحَ يَكْلَحُ وأَكْلَحَ وتكلَّحَ

Austere, severe. كَالِحٌ

To plaster with lime. كَلَّسَ

Lime mortar. كِلْسٌ

Sock, stocking. (كَلْسَةٌ)

Lime-kiln. كَلَّاسَةٌ

Lime-burner; plasterer. مُكَلِّسٌ

Plastered with lime. مُكَلَّسٌ

Eel. أَنْكَلِيسٌ

To be freckled. كَلِفَ يَكْلَفُ كَلَفًا

To be devoted to. كَلِفَ بِ

To impose a difficult matter upon one. كَلَّفَ وإِلى

To cost. كَلَّفَ

To take the trouble (to do anything). كَلَّفَ خَاطِرَهُ

Please do this ! كَلِّفْ خَاطِرَكَ

To take pains. تَكَلَّفَ

Ardent love. Freckles. كَلَفٌ

Trouble, labour, hardship. Cost, expense. كُلْفَةٌ ج كُلَفٌ

Freckled ; maculated. أَكْلَفُ

Trouble. تَكْلِيفٌ ج تَكَالِيفُ

Without ceremony. بِلَا تَكْلِيف

Expensive. مُكْلِفٌ وَمُكَلِّفٌ

Responsible agent. مُكَلَّفٌ

Intruder. متكلِّفٌ

Raft. كَلَكٌ

To wound. كَلَمَ يَكْلِمُ وَكَلَّمَ

To speak ; speak to.	كَلَّمَ
To converse with.	كَالَمَ
To talk, converse.	تكَلَّمَ
Wound.	كَلْمٌ ج كُلُومٌ وَكِلَامٌ
Incomplete sentence.	كَلِمٌ
Word, sentence.	كَلِمَةٌ ج كَلِمَاتٌ
Speech, saying.	كَلَامٌ
Talking, speech.	تَكَلُّمٌ
Speaker, 1st person, (*gram*).	مُتَكَلِّمٌ
Wounded.	مَكْلُومٌ وَكَلِيمٌ
Both. (*dual*).	كِلَا م كِلْتَا
Kidney.	كُلْيَةٌ ج كُلًى
How much ? How many ?	كَمْ
How many men ?	كَمْ رَجُلاً
Pronominal suffix.	كُمْ
Your book (*pl. m.*).	كِتَابُكُمْ
Your book (*dual*).	كِتَابُكُمَا
As, even as, just as.	كَمَا
To muzzle (an animal).	كَمَّ
Quantity.	كَمٌّ وَكَمِّيَّةٌ ج كَمِّيَّاتٌ
Calyx, spathe.	كِمٌّ ج أَكْمَامٌ
Sleeve.	كُمٌّ ج أَكْمَامٌ
Muzzle.	كِمَامَةٌ وَكِمَامٌ
Muzzled.	مَكْمُومٌ
Truffle.	كَمْءٌ وَكَمْأَةٌ
Bill ; cheque.	كَمْبِيَالَةٌ
Rate, or bill of exchange.	كَمْبِيُو
Dark brown, bay.	كُمَيْتٌ
Pear.	كُمَّثْرَى
A pear.	كُمَّثْرَاةٌ ج كُمَّثْرَيَاتٌ
Scum ; film.	كَمْخَةٌ
To be sad.	كَمِدَ يَكْمَدُ كَمَداً
To make sad.	أَكْمَدَ
Change of colour. Concealed grief.	كَمَدٌ وَكُمْدَةٌ
A kind of belt.	كَمَرٌ ج أَكْمَارٌ
Duty ; custom-house.	كُمْرُكٌ

كُمْرُكْجِيٌّ Receiver of customs.

كَيْمُوسٌ Chyme.

(كَمَشَ) To grasp.

إِنْكَمَشَ وَتَكَمَّشَ To be wrinkled.

(كَمْشَةٌ) A handful.

(كَمَّاشَةٌ) Carpenter's pincers.

كَمَلَ يَكْمُلُ وَتَكَمَّلَ وَتَكَامَلَ وَاكْتَمَلَ To be complete, finished.

كَمَّلَ وَأَكْمَلَ To finish, complete.

كَامِلٌ Entire, complete.

كَمَالٌ Perfection.

تَكْمِيلٌ Finishing ; perfecting.

مُكَمَّلٌ Completed, finished.

كَمَنَ ـُ وَاكْتَمَنَ To hide ; hide one's self.

اكْمَنَ ل To lie in ambush.

كَمْنَةٌ ج كِمَانٌ Ambush.

كُمُونٌ State of being hidden.

كَمُّونٌ Cumin.

كَمِينٌ ج كُمَنَاءُ Hidden ; ambush.

مَكْمَنٌ ج مَكَامِنُ Place of ambush.

مُكْتَمِنٌ Hidden, concealed.

كَمَنْجَةٌ Violin.

كَمَهٌ Blindness.

أَكْمَهُ م كَمْهَاءُ ج كُمْهٌ Blind.

كُنَّ *Pronominal suffix.*

كِتَابُكُنَّ Your book, (*fem*).

كَنَّ يَكُنُّ To conceal, secrete.

إِكْتَنَّ To be concealed.

إِسْتَكَنَّ To retire ; be quiet.

كِنٌّ ج أَكْنَانٌ Cover, shelter.

كَنَّةٌ ج كَنَائِنُ Son's wife.

كُنَّةٌ ج كِنَانٌ Roof for shelter.

كَانُونٌ ج كَوَانِينُ Hearth, stove.

كَانُونُ الأَوَّل December.

كَانُونُ الثَّانِي January.

كَنِينٌ وَمَكْنُونٌ Concealed.

كَنَبٌ Callousness (of hand).

Ingratitude. كُنُودٌ

Frankincense. كُنْدُرٌ

Shoe. (كُنْدُرَةٌ ج كَنَادِرُ)

Hem, border. كِنَارٌ

Canary bird. كَنَارِيٌّ

Lute, harp. كِنَّارَةٌ ج كِنَّارَاتٌ

To treasure, store. كَنَزَ يَكْنِزُ

To be firm, hard. إِكْتَنَزَ

Treasure. كَنْزٌ ج كُنُوزٌ

Firm and compact. مُكْتَنِزٌ

Hidden, buried (treasure). مَكْنُوزٌ

To sweep. كَنَسَ يَكْنِسُ كَنْسًا وكَنَّسَ

Sweeper. كَنَّاسٌ

Sweepings. كُنَاسَةٌ

Synagogue. كَنِيسٌ

Church. كَنِيسَةٌ ج كَنَائِسُ

Ecclesiastical. كَنَائِسِيٌّ وكَنَسِيٌّ

Broom. مِكْنَسَةٌ ج مَكَانِسُ

Canaan. كَنْعَانُ

The Canaanites. اَلْكَنْعَانِيُّونَ

To shelter. كَنَفَ يَكْنُفُ كَنْفًا

To surround. تَكَنَّفَ واكْتَنَفَ

Refuge. كَنَفٌ ج أَكْنَافٌ

A kind of sweet pastry. كُنَافَةٌ

Privy, sewer. كَنِيفٌ ج كُنُفٌ

Substance, essence. كُنْهٌ

To hint at. كَنَى يَكْنِي كِنَايَةً عَنْ

To give a surname. كَنَّى بِ

To take a surname. تَكَنَّى بِ

Surname. Epithet. كُنْيَةٌ

Metaphor, metonomy. كِنَايَةٌ

Instead or in place of. كِنَايَةً عَنْ

To electrify. كَهْرَبَ

Yellow amber. كَهْرَبَاءُ

Electric. كَهْرَبَائِيٌّ

Electricity. كَهْرَبَائِيَّةٌ

Electrified.	مُكَهْرَبٌ
Cavern, cave.	كَهْفٌ ج كُهُوفٌ
To be middle-aged.	كَهَلَ يَكْهَلُ
Middle-aged.	كَهْلٌ ج كُهُولٌ
Mature age.	كُهُولَةٌ وَكُهُولِيَّةٌ
To divine, foretell.	كَهَنَ يَكْهَنُ
Soothsayer ; priest.	كَاهِنٌ ج كَهَنَةٌ
Soothsaying ; divination.	كَهَانَةٌ
Priesthood.	كَهْنُوتٌ
A large cup.	كُوبٌ ج أَكْوَابٌ
A horse cloth.	(كُوبَانٌ)
Stern of ship ; helm.	كَوْثَلٌ
Hut.	كُوخٌ ج أَكْوَاخٌ
To restrain, hinder.	كَادَ يَكُودُ كَوْداً
He almost did.	كَادَ يَفْعَلُ
He hardly did.	مَا كَادَ يَفْعَلُ
Art, profession.	كَارٌ ج كَارَاتٌ
Furnace, forge.	كُورٌ ج أَكْوَارٌ
Small district.	كُورَةٌ ج كُوَرٌ
Bee-hive	كُوارَةُ نَحْلٍ
Quarantine.	كُورَنْتِينا
Petroleum. Gas.	كازٌ
Drinking-mug.	كُوزٌ ج أَكْوازٌ
Drinking-cup.	كاسٌ ج كُؤُوسٌ
Vegetable marrow.	كُوسا
Elbow.	كُوعٌ ج أَكْواعٌ
Kufa (city).	اَلْكُوفَةُ
Kufic (writing) ; of Kufa.	كُوفِيٌّ
Head-wrapper.	كُوفِيَّةٌ
Planet, star.	كَوْكَبٌ ج كَوَاكِبُ
A party ; assembly.	كَوْكَبَةٌ
To make a heap.	كَوَّمَ
A heap.	كُومَةٌ ج كُوَمٌ وأَكْوامٌ
To be, exist.	كانَ يَكُونُ
He had wealth.	كانَ لَهُ مالٌ
He was standing.	كانَ قائِماً

كَانَ يَفعَلُ He was doing.

كانَ قدْ قَالَ He had said.

كَوَّنَ To create, form.

تَـكَوَّنَ To be created, formed.

كِيَانٌ Existence, nature.

كَوْنٌ ج أَكْوَان Nature ; universe.

كَائِنٌ Being ; creature.

كَائِنةٌ ج كَائِنَاتٌ Incident, event.

أَلْـكَائِنَاتُ All created things.

تَـكْوِينٌ Formation, creation.

سِفْرُ ٱلتَّـكْوِينِ Book of Genesis.

مكَانٌ ج أَمْكِنَةٌ وَأَمَاكِنُ Place.

ظَرْفُ ٱلْمَكَانِ Adverb of place.

مَكَانَةٌ ج مَكَانَاتٌ Place ; rank.

مُكَوِّنٌ Creator.

كُوَّةٌ ج كُوَّات وَكُوًى Window.

كَوَى يَكْوِي To burn, cauterise.

كَوَى (To iron clothes).

إِكْتَوَى To be cauterised.

كَيٌّ Cauterisation, ironing.

مِكْوَاةٌ ج مَكَاوٍ Smoothing-iron.

مَكْوِيٌّ Cauterised ; ironed.

كَيْ وَلِـكَيْ In order that.

كَيْ لاَ وَلِكَيْ لاَ In order not...

كَيْتَ وَكَيْتَ So and so.

كَادَ يَكِيدُ كَيْداً وَكَايَدَ To deceive...

كَيْدٌ Stratagem, guile.

مَكِيدَةٌ ج مَكَائِدُ. *Same as.* كَيْدٌ

كَاسَ يَكِيسُ To be shrewd.

كَيَّسَ To put into a bag.

كَيْس وَكِيَاسَةٌ Intelligence.

كِيسٌ ج أَكْيَاسٌ Bag, purse.

كَيِّسٌ Clever ; handsome.

(كُوَيِّس) Handsome, pretty.

أَكْوَسُ More handsome.

تَـكَيَّفَ To take a special form.

How ; in what way? كَيْفَ

Enjoyment. Quality. (كَيْف)

Howsoever. كَيفما كَانَ

Quality ; form. كَيفِيَّة ج كَيفِيَّاتٌ

To measure. كالَ يَكِيلُ وَكَيْلٌ

To measure out. إِكْتالَ

Measure of grains كَيْلٌ ج أَكْيَال

= 6 *mudds*. (٦ أَمْدَادٍ)

A small measure. كَيلَة ج كَيلاَت

Measuring, weighing. كِيَالة

One who measures. كَيَّالٌ

Measure of capacity. مِكْيَلٌ

Measured. مَكيلٌ وَمَكْيُولٌ

Chyle. كَيْلُوسٌ

In order that. كَيْمَا (كَيْ مَا)

Chemistry. كيمـيا وكِيمِيَاء

Chemist ; chemical. كِيمِيٌّ

Quinine. كِينا

Cinchona bark. خَشَبُ ٱلْكِينا

ل

As a numeral sign=30. ل

To, for. لِ

Let him write. لِيكْتُبْ

By thy life! لَعَمْرُكَ

No; not. لاَ

Neither, nor. لا وَلاَ

لَاتَ	No, there is not or no...
أللاَّتُ	An Arabian godess.
لازَوَرْدُ	Lapis lazuli.
لازَوَرْدِيٌّ	Azure-blue.
مَلَأكٌ وَمَلَكٌ ج مَلائكَةٌ	Angel.
لألأَ وَتَلالأَ	To shine, glitter.
لُؤْلُؤٌ	Pearls.
لُؤْلُؤَةٌ ج لآلِئُ	A pearl.
لُؤْلُؤِيٌّ	Pearl-coloured.
لأَمَ يَلأَمُ	To bind up a wound.
لَؤُمَ	To be of a low character.
لاءَمَ	To agree with.
لاءَمَ بَيْنَ	To reconcile.
إِلْتَأَمَ	To assemble. Unite. *v. i.*
لُؤْمٌ	Avarice, meanness.
لَئِيمٌ ج لِئامٌ	Base, sordid.
مُلائِمٌ	Convenient ; suitable.
مُلاءَمَةٌ	Suitableness.
مُلْتَئِمٌ	Assembled, gathered.
الَبَّ بِ	To stay in.
لُبٌّ ج لُبُوبٌ	Marrow, pith.
لبٌّ ج أَلْبابٌ	Heart ; mind.
لَبِيبٌ ج أَلِبَّاء	Intelligent.
لبَاء	First milk.
لَبُؤَةٌ ج لَبُؤَاتٌ	Lioness.
لَبِثَ يَلْبَثُ ب	To tarry, abide in.
مَالَبِثَ أَنْ فعلَ	He did not delay to do.
لبثٌ وَلُبْثٌ وَلَبَاثٌ	A tarrying.
لُبْثَةٌ	A short stay, delay.
لبَخَ يلْبَخُ	To beat. To abuse.
لَبَخ (وَلَبْخُ)	Persea (tree).
لَبْخةٌ ج لَبخاتٌ	Poultice, cataplasm.
لَبَدَ وَأَلْبدَ بِ	To abide, dwell in.
لَبَّدَ	To cram, compress.
تلبَّدَ	To be compact together.
تلبَّدَ ب	To stick to, cleave to.

إِلْتَبَدَ To be pressed closely.

لِبَّادَةٌ Cap of cloth or felt.

لَبِسَ يَلْبَسُ عَلَى To make obscure.

لَبِسَ يَلْبَسُ To put on a dress.

لَبَّسَ To render obscure. To clothe.

أَلْبَسَ To cover, clothe.

إِلْتَبَسَ To be dark, obscure.

إِلْتَبَسَ بِ To be confused with.

لَبْسٌ وَٱلْتِبَاسٌ Ambiguity.

لُبْسٌ ج لُبُوسٌ Clothing, dress.

لِبَاسٌ ج أَلْبِسَةٌ Garment.

مَلْبَسٌ ج مَلَابِسُ Clothing.

مُلْتَبِسٌ Obscure; doubtful.

(مُلَبَّسٌ) Sugar-plums.

مَلْبُوسٌ ج مَلَابِيسُ Garment.

(لَبَّشَ) To collect pell-mell.

لَبَشٌ Baggage, chattels.

لَبَطَ يَلْبُطُ لَبْطًا To kick.

لَبْطَةٌ A kick.

لَبِقَ بِ To fit, become one.

لَبَقٌ وَلَبَاقَةٌ Wit and cleverness.

لَبِقٌ وَلَبِيقٌ Skilful, clever.

لَبَكَ يَلْبُكُ وَلَبَّكَ To mix; confuse.

تَلَبَّكَ وَٱلْتَبَكَ To be confused, embarrassed.

لَبْكٌ وَلَبْكَةٌ Confused affair.

مُلْتَبِكٌ وَمَلْبُوكٌ Embarrassed.

لَبْلَابٌ Egyptian bean.

لَبَنٌ ج أَلْبَانٌ Milk; sour milk. Sap.

لَبِنٌ وَلِبْنٌ Brick, tile.

لَبِنَةٌ A brick.

لُبْنَانُ Mount Lebanon.

لُبْنَانِيٌّ Of Mount Lebanon.

لُبَانٌ Frankincence. Pine.

لَبَّانٌ Brick-maker. Milk-man.

لَبْوَةٌ ج لَبَوَاتٌ Lioness.

لَبَّى To obey, respond.

Here I am! لَبَّيْكَ	To take refuge in, repair to. لَجَأَ يَلْجَأُ وَلَجِئَ يَلْجَأُ والْتَجَأَ إِلى
To speak nonsense. لَتَّ يَلُتُّ لَتًّا	To force, compel. لَجَّأَ وأَلْجَأَ إِلى
Two idols. أللاَّتُ والْعُزَّى	To defend, protect. أَلْجَأَ
Who, which (fem). الَّتِي مث اللَّتَانِ ج اللَّوَاتِي	Refuge. لَجَأٌ ومَلْجَأٌ ج ملاجِئُ
To stammer, lisp. لَثِغَ يَلْثَغُ	Seeking shelter. لاجِئٌ ومُلْتَجِئٌ
Stammering, lisping. لَثْغٌ ولُثْغَةٌ	To stammer. لَجْلَجَ وَتَلَجْلَجَ
Lisper. أَلْثَغُ م لَثْغَاءُ ج لُثْغٌ	One who stutters. لَجْلاجٌ
To kiss. لَثَمَ يَلْثُمُ وَلَثِمَ يَلْثَمُ لَثْمًا	To bridle (a horse). لَجَمَ وَأَلْجَمَ
To muffle the mouth. لَجَمَ ولَثَّمَ	To be bridled. اِلْتَجَمَ
A kiss. لَثْمَةٌ	Bridle, curb. لِجَامٌ ج أَلْجِمَةٌ وَلُجُمٌ
Veil لِثَامٌ	Bridled. مُلْجَمٌ
Gums (of the teeth). لِثَةٌ ج لِثَاتٌ	Committee. لَجْنَةٌ
To persist, persevere. لَجَّ يَلَجُّ	To be close, near. لَحَّ يَلُحُّ لَحًّا
To importune. لَجَّ عَلى	To persist in one's demands. أَلَحَّ في السُّؤال
To wrangle with. لاجَّ	To importune, press. أَلَحَّ عَلَيْهِ
High sea; the deep. لُجَّة ج لُجَجٌ	Importunity; persistence. إِلْحَاحٌ
Pertinacious. لاجٌّ ولَجُوجٌ	One who insists. مُلِحٌّ وَمِلْحَاحٌ
Pertinacity. لَجَاجٌ وَلَجَاجَةٌ	

لَحَدَ يَلْحَدُ لَحْداً وَأَلْحَدَ To bury.
أَلْحَدَ عن To swerve from.
أَلْحَدَ وَٱلْتَحَدَ To apostatize.
لَحْدٌ ج أَلْحَادٌ وَلُحُودٌ A grave.
إِلْحَادٌ Apostasy ; heresy.
مُلْحِدٌ ج مُلْحِدُون An apostate.
لَحَسَ ـَ لَحْساً To lick.
لَحَظَ يَلْحَظُ لَحْظاً To regard, observe.
لَاحَظَ To look at attentively.
لَحْظَةٌ Glance, moment.
مُلَاحَظَةٌ Observation.
مَلْحُوظٌ ج مَلْحُوظَاتٌ Regarded.
لَحَفَ يَلْحَفُ To wrap up
إِلْتَحَفَ To wrap one's self up.
لَحْفُ Foot of a mountain.
لِحَافٌ ج لُحُفٌ Cover, blanket.
مِلْحَفَةٌ ج مَلَاحِفُ An outer dress.
لَحِقَ يَلْحَقُ To reach, overtake.

لَاحَقَ To pursue, follow.
أَلْحَقَ ب To annex, join to.
إِلْتَحَقَ بِ To reach ; be annexed.
لَاحِقٌ Overtaking, reaching.
إِلْحَاقٌ Adding ; annexing.
مُلْحَقٌ Appendix ; supplement.
لَحِمَ يَلْحَمُ لَحْماً To be fleshy.
لُحِمَ لَحْماً To be killed, massacred.
لَحَمَ يَلْحُمُ لَحْماً To solder.
لَاحَمَ وَأَلْحَمَ ب To join, unite.
تَلَاحَمَ To kill one another.
إِلْتَحَمَ To be soldered, united.
اِلْتَحَمَ To grow bloody, (combat).
لَحْمٌ ج لُحُومٌ Flesh, meat.
لَحْمَةٌ ج لُحَمٌ Woof (of a stuff).
لِحَامٌ Solder.
لَحَّامٌ Butcher ; flesh-monger.
إِلْتِحَامٌ Union ; alliance.

Combat, battle. مَلْحَمَةٌ ج مَلَاحِمُ

To make grammatical mistakes in speaking. لَحَنَ يَلْحَنُ

To chant. لَحَّنَ فِي ٱلْقِرَاءَةِ

Tone; chant, air. لَحْنٌ ج أَلْحَانٌ

Error of pronunciation.

Musical art. صِنَاعَةُ ٱلْأَلْحَانِ

Chanting. تَلْحِينٌ

To let one's beard grow. إِلْتَحَى

Jaw-bone. لَحْيٌ مث لَحْيَانِ ج لُحِيٌّ

Bark, (*sp.* inner bark). لِحَاءٌ

Beard. لِحْيَةٌ ج لُحًى

Wild salsify. لِحْيَةُ ٱلتَّيْسِ

Obscurity in speech. لَخَّةٌ

To extract; sum up. لَخَّصَ

Abstract. Explanation. تَلْخِيصٌ

Summary, abstract مُلَخَّصٌ

To quarrel; oppose. لَدَّ يَلُدُّ لَدًّا

Violent in opposition. أَلَدُّ

To sting, bite. لَدَغَ يَلْدَغُ لَدْغًا

Sting, poisonous bite. لَدْغَةٌ

To be pliable, flexible. لَدُنَ يَلْدُنُ

Soft; supple. لَدْنٌ ج لُدْنٌ

At, by, to, with, near to. لَدُنْ

Softness, flexibility. لَدَانَةٌ وَلُدُونَةٌ

At, by, to, with. لَدَى

Near or by thee; to thee. لَدَيْكَ

To be sweet, agreeable. لَذَّ يَلَذُّ

To enjoy. لَذَّ وَٱلْتَذَّ وَٱسْتَلَذَّ بِ

To delight. تَلَذَّذَ

Pleasure, delight. لَذَّةٌ ج لَذَّاتٌ

Sweet, pleasant. لَذِيذٌ

Delight, pleasure. مَلَذَّةٌ ج مَلَاذُّ

To burn, brand. لَذَعَ يَلْذَعُ لَذْعًا

To feel a burning pain. إِلْتَذَعَ

A burn. لَذْعَةٌ

Stinging pungent. لَذَّاعٌ

Ingenious; witty. لَوْذَعٌ وَلَوْذَعِيٌّ

أَللاذِقِيـة Latakia (*city*).

أَلَّذِي مث اَللَّذانِ ج اَلَّذِينَ Who, which.

لَزَّ يَلُزُّ لَزًّا To press.

اِلْتَزَّ بِهِ To adhere to it.

لازِبٌ Necessary; constant.

لَزِجَ يَلْزَجُ To stick, adhere.

لَزِجٌ Viscid, sticky, cohesive.

لُزُوجَةٌ Viscidity, stickiness.

لَزِقَ يَلْزَقُ وَاِلْتَزَقَ بِ To stick to.

لازَقَ To adhere to another.

أَلْزَقَ وَلَزَّقَ To glue together.

لِزْقٌ That which adjoins.

لَزْقَةٌ وَلَزُوقٌ Poultice, plaster.

لَزِمَ يَلْزَمُ To adhere to; persist in; be necessary, follow of necessity.

لازَمَ To cling to, persevere in.

أَلْزَمَ إِلْزَامًا To impose as a duty, compel.

إِلْتَزَمَ To be responsible; be forced. To farm taxes.

اِسْتَلْزَمَ To find necessary.

لازِمٌ Necessary, unavoidable. Intransitive verb (*Gram.*).

لُزُومٌ Necessity.

إِلْزَامٌ Compulsion.

إِلْتِزَامٌ ج إِلْتِزَامَاتٌ Necessity; obligation. Renting; farming

(مِلْزَمَةٌ ج. مَلازِمُ) Hand-vice; press.

مُلازِمٌ Lieutenant (*mil.*).

مُلازَمَةٌ Assiduity, application.

مَلْزُومٌ Obliged, compelled.

مُلْتَزِمٌ Farmer of revenues.

لَسَعَ يَلْسَعُ لَسْعًا To sting.

لَسِنَ يَلْسَنُ لَسَنًا To be eloquent.

لَسِنٌ ج لُسْنٌ Eloquent.

لِسَانٌ ج أَلْسُنٌ Tongue; language. Cape of land.

لِسَانُ ٱلْمِزْمَار Epiglottis.

لِسَانُ ٱلْحَال Speaking for itself.

لِسَانًا By word of mouth.

ذُو لِسَانَيْنِ Double dealer, false.

لِسَانِيٌّ Lingual.

لاشى	To destroy, annihilate.
تلاشى	To vanish, perish.
مُلاشاة وتلاشٍ	Annihilation.
لصّ ج لُصوص	Thief, robber.
لُصوصيّة	Robbery, thieving.
لصِق يلصَق والتصق بِ	To stick to.
لاصق	To cling to, be devoted to
ألصق ب	To fasten, join.
لُصوق	A dressing (for wounds).
مُلاصِق	Contiguous.
مُلاصقة	Contiguity, adherence.
لطخ يلطخ ولطّخ بِ	To soil with.
تلطّخ بِ	To be soiled with.
لُطخة	A soil, stain.
لطف يلطُف بِ	To be kind.
لطّف	To soften, mitigate.
لاطف	To treat with kindness.
تلطّف لِ	To be polite, courteous to.
إستلطف	To find pretty or nice.
لُطف	Friendliness. Favour.
حركة لُطفٍ	Light illness.
لطافة	Delicacy. Tenuity.
لطيف ج لطفاء	Graceful ; kind. Rare (not dense).
اللطيف	God.
لطيفة ج لطائف	Witty saying.
تلطُّف	Friendliness ; courtesy.
مُلاطفة	Friendly treatment.
لطم يلطُم لطماً	To slap.
تلاطم والتطم	To clash, collide.
لطمة ج لطمات	Slap on the face.
لطا يلطو	To take shelter.
لظّ يلظ	To cleave to.
لظي يلظى لظًى	To blaze (fire).
تلظّى والتظى	To be enflamed.
لظى	Fire; flame
لعِب لعِباً	To play, sport, jest.

لاَعَب To play, sport with.

لَعْبٌ ولَعِبٌ Play, sport.

لعبُ آلقِمَار Gambling.

لُعْبَةٌ ج لُعَبٌ A game, sport.

لُعَابٌ Saliva, spittle. Mucilage.

لُعَابِيٌّ Mucilaginous, slimy.

لَعَّابٌ ولَعِّيبٌ Professional player.

أُلْعُوبَةٌ Play, pleasantry.

تلاعُبٌ Sporting, jesting.

ملْعبٌ ج مَلاَعبُ Place to play in.

مَلْعَبَةٌ Toy, plaything.

(مَلْعُوبٌ ج ملاَعيبُ) A trick in play.

لعج يَلْعَجُ لَعْجاً To pain, burn.

لاَعِجٌ ج لوَاعِج Burning pain.

لعق يَلْعَقُ لعقاً To lick.

لَعُوقٌ Electuary.

مِلْعَقَةٌ ج ملاَعِقُ Spoon.

لعلَّ وَعَلَّ Perhaps, may be.

لعلَّ زَيْداً قائِمٌ It may be that Zeid is standing.

لَعْلَعَ وتَلَعْلَعَ To shine, gleam.

لعن يَلْعَنُ لعناً To curse.

تلاَعَن To curse one another.

لَعْنٌ ولعنَةٌ ج لعَنَاتٌ Imprecation.

أَللَّعِينُ Satan.

ملعُونٌ ج ملاَعِينُ Cursed.

لغَبَ — To be very tired.

تلَغَّبَ To chase long.

لُغْزٌ ج أَلْغَازٌ Riddle ; enigma.

مُلْغَزٌ Enigmatic, ambiguous.

لغط يَلْغَطُ To speak indistinctly.

لَغْطٌ ج أَلْغَاطٌ Noise ; sound.

لُغْمٌ ج لُغُومٌ Mine, blast.

لُغْمَجِيٌّ Miner ; blaster.

لغَا يَلْغُو To speak.

أَلْغَى To exclude, abolish.

لُغَةٌ ج لُغَات Language, dialect ; idiom, expression.

Lexicography. عِلْمُ ٱللُّغَةِ

Lexicographers. أَهْلُ ٱللُّغَةِ

Faulty language, nonsense. لَغْوٌ

Etymological ; linguistic. لُغَوِيٌّ

Abolishing, annulling. إِلْغَاءٌ

Suppressed, abolished. مُلْغًى

To wrap up, roll. لَفَّ يَلُفُّ لَفًّا

To wrap one's self up. اِلْتَفَّ

To be entwined. إِلْتَفَّ

A turban. (لَفَّةٌ ج لَفَّاتٌ)

Bandage. لِفَافَةٌ ج لَفَائِفُ

Mixed crowd. لَفِيفٌ

Wrapped up. Cabbage. مَلْفُوفٌ

To twist, turn. لَفَتَ يَلْفِتُ لَفْتًا

To consider, regard. إِلْتَفَتَ إِلَى

Turnip, rape. لِفْتٌ

Side-glance. لَفْتَةٌ ج لَفَتَاتٌ

Attention ; favour. إِلْتِفَاتٌ

To burn, scorch. لَفَحَ يَلْفَحُ لَفْحًا

Scorching. لَفُوحٌ وَلَافِحٌ ج لَوَافِحُ

Mandrake (plant). لُفَّاحٌ

To pronounce. Dei. لَفَظَ يَلْفِظُ

To utter. لَفَظَ وَتَلَفَّظَ بِ

Utterance ; word. لَفْظٌ ج أَلْفَاظٌ

As regards the wording and the meaning. لَفْظًا وَمَعْنًى

A word ; an utterance. لَفْظَةٌ ج لَفَظَاتٌ

Verbal. لَفْظِيٌّ

To seam. لَفَقَ يَلْفِقُ لَفْقًا

To interpolate, falsify, lie. لَفَّقَ

Embellished by falsehood. مُلَفَّقٌ

To wrap up, envelop. لَفْلَفَ

Convolutions of the brain. تَلَافِيفُ ٱلدِّمَاغِ

To find. أَلْفَى إِلْفَاءٌ

To mend ; take up. تَلَافَى

To give a title لَقَّبَ بِ

Surname ; title. لَقَبٌ ج أَلْقَابٌ

مُلَقَّبٌ Surnamed; having a title.

لَقَحَ يَلْقَحُ لَقْحاً To fecundate.

لَقِحَ يَلْقَحُ لَقَحاً To be fecundated.

لَقَّحَ وَأَلْقَحَ To fecundate.

لَقْحٌ Fecundation.

لِقَاحٌ Pollen.

(تَلَقَّسَ) To delay, be late.

لَقَطَ يَلْقُطُ To pick up; glean.

تَلَقَّطَ وَٱلْتَقَطَ To glean. Catch.

لَاقِطٌ م لَاقِطَةٌ Freed slave.

لِقَاطٌ Picking up; gleaning.

لُقَاطَةٌ What is picked up.

لَقِيطٌ ج لُقَطَاءُ Foundling.

مِلْقَطٌ ج مَلَاقِطُ Pincers; tongs.

لَقَفَ وَٱلْتَقَفَ To snatch away.

لَقْلَقٌ وَلَقْلَاقٌ ج لَقَالِقُ Stork.

لَقِمَ يَلْقَمُ لَقْماً To swallow.

لَقَّمَ وَٱلْقَمَ To feed.

تَلَقَّمَ وَٱلْتَقَمَ To swallow.

لُقْمَةٌ ج لُقَمٌ Morsel, mouthful.

لَقِنَ يَلْقَنُ To understand readily.

لَقَّنَ To instruct, teach.

تَلَقَّنَ To learn.

لَقِنٌ Of quick understanding.

لَقْوَةٌ Facial paralysis.

لَقِيَ يَلْقَى To meet; see, find.

لَاقَى لِقَاءً To go to meet, meet.

أَلْقَى بِ To throw away, fling.

أَلْقَى عَنْ To cast away from.

أَلْقَى عَلَى To propound, propose.

تَلَقَّى To receive. To encounter.

تَلَاقَى وَٱلْتَقَى To meet one another.

إِسْتَلْقَى عَلَى To lie on one's back.

تِلْقَاءَ Towards.

مِنْ تِلْقَاءِ نَفْسِهِ Spontaneously.

تَلَاقٍ Mutual encounter.

Was it not? أَلَمْ وأَفَلَمْ وأَوَلَمْ	The day of resurrection. يَوْمُ ٱلتَّلَاقِي
To gather, amass. لَمَّ يَلُمُّ لَمًّا	Leaning or resting upon. ملتقًى عَلَى
To come upon, befall. أَلَمَّ بـ	Meeting-place. مُلْقًى ومُلْتَقًى
When. Not yet. لَمَّا	Meeting. مُلاقَاةٌ
Inasmuch as... لَمَّا كَانَ	Lac (resin); sealing wax. لَكٌّ
Why? لِمَاذَا (لِمَا ـ ذَا)	Ten millions. Lac. لَكٌّ ج أَلْكَاكٌ
Calamity; misfortune. لَمَّةٌ	To push, thrust. لَكَزَ يَلْكُزُ لَكْزًا
Lock of hair. لِمَّةٌ ج لِمَمٌ ولِمَامٌ	To be vile. لَكِعَ يَلْكَعُ لَكَعًا ولَكَاعَة
Slight madness. لَمَمٌ	Dirty, vile, abject. لَكِعٌ م لَكَاعِ
Knowledge, experience. إِلْمَامٌ	To strike with the fist. لَكَمَ يَلْكُمُ لَكْمًا
Calamity; chance. مُلِمَّةٌ ج مُلِمَّاتٌ	Boxing, fighting. مُلاكَمَةٌ
Collected. Slightly mad. مَلْمُومٌ	But, yet, however. لَكِنْ ولَكِنَّ
Light meal before lunch. لُمْجَةٌ	Large copper basin. (لَكَنٌ ج أَلْكَانٌ)
To glance at. لَمَحَ يَلْمَحُ إِلَى	Stammerer. أَلْكَنُ م لَكْنَاءُ ج لُكْنٌ
To direct the sight. لَمَحَ بِالْبَصَر	In order that. لِكَيْ ولِكَيْمَا
To shine, gleam. لَمَحَ يَلْمَحُ	Not, not yet. لَمْ
To hint at, suggest. لَمَّحَ إِلَى	He has not eaten. لَمْ يَأْكُل
A glance resemblance. لَمْحَةٌ	Why? (for لِمَا) لِمَ

Gleaming, shining. لَامِحٌ ولُمُوحٌ

Allusion, hint. تَلْمِيحٌ

Points of resemblance. مَلَامِحُ

To touch. لَمَسَ يَلْمِسُ لَمْسًا وَلَامَسَ

To seek for repeatedly. تَلَمَّسَ

To entreat, ask for. إِلْتَمَسَ مِنْ

Touch, feeling. لَمْسٌ ومَلْمَسٌ

Entreaty supplication. إِلْتِمَاسٌ

Touched. مَلْمُوسٌ

To shine, flash. لَمَعَ يَلْمَعُ وَٱلْتَمَعَ

To beckon with. أَلْمَعَ بِ

Flash, brightness. لَمْعٌ ولَمَعَان

A small quantity. لُمْعَةٌ ج لُمَعٌ

That which shines. لَامِعٌ ج لُمَّعٌ

Having a sharp genius. أَلْمَعِيٌّ

Genius, wit. أَلْمَعِيَّةُ

Mottled, spotted. مُلَمَّعٌ

To gather, get together. لَمْلَمَ

To be gathered. تَلَمْلَمَ

A numerous army. لَمْلَمٌ

Not. By no means. لَنْ

To flame, blaze(fire). لَهِبَ يَلْهَبُ

To make to blaze. لَهَّبَ وَأَلْهَبَ

To flame, blaze. تَلَهَّبَ وَٱلْتَهَبَ

Flame. لَهَبٌ ولَهِيبٌ

Inflammation. إِلْتِهَابٌ ج إِلْتِهَابَات

The divine nature. أَللَّاهُوت

Theology. عِلْمُ ٱللَّاهُوت

Theologian. لَاهُوتِيٌّ

To pant. Thirst. لَهَثَ يَلْهَثُ

Thirsty; out of breath. لَهْثَانُ

To be addicted to. لَهِجَ يَلْهَجُ بِ

To be taken up with. أَلْهِجَ بِ

Voice, tone. لَهْجَةٌ

To regret. لَهِفَ يَلْهَفُ وتَلَهَّفَ عَلَى

Regret, grief, sadness. لَهْفٌ

Oh ! Alas ! يا لَهفاهُ ويا لهفي على

Grieved. لَهفانُ م لهفى

To swallow at one gulp. لَهِم يَلْهَمُ والْتَهَم

To inspire. أَلْهَم

Greedy, voracious. لَهِمٌ

Divine guidance. إِلْهَام ج إِلْهَامَاتٌ

To play. لَها يَلْهُو لَهْواً

To be infatuated with. لَهَا بِ

To forget ; neglect. (لها عنْ)

To preoccupy. لَهَّى وأَلْهى (عنْ)

To be diverted. تلاهَى والْتهَى

Amusement ; diversion. لَهْوٌ

Soft palate. لُهاةٌ ج لَهَواتٌ

Palatial. لَهَوِيٌّ

Diverted, thoughtless. لاهٍ

Amusement. مَلْهًى ج مَلاهٍ

If. O that. لَوْ

Although, though. ولَوْ

Unless ; if not. لَوْ لَمْ

Were it not for... لَوْلا ولَوْ ما

To thirst. Be restless. لاَبَ يَلُوبُ

Beans. لُوباء ولُوبِيَا

Pl. of. ٱلَّتِي أَللوَاتِي

To stain ; soil. Mix. لَوَّثَ

To be soiled. تَلَوَّثَ تَلَوُّثاً

To glimmer ; appear. لاَحَ يَلُوحُ

Plate ; tablet. Shoulder-blade. لَوْحٌ ج أَلْوَاحٌ

Schedule. لاَئِحَةٌ ج لَوَائِح

Appearances. لَوائِح

To take refuge in لاَذَ يَلُوذُ (ب)

Refuge ; fortress. مَلاَذٌ

Almond (tree and fruit). لَوْزٌ

The tonsils. (أَللَّوزتَانِ)

To taste. لاَسَ يَلُوسُ لَوْساً

To be impatient. لاَعَ يَلُوعُ

To torture. لَوَّعَ تَلْوِيعاً

Pain ; anguish ; torture.	لَوْعَةٌ
A plant, the Arum.	لُوفٌ
To masticate.	لاكَ يَلُوكُ لوْكًا
Hotel (*Ital*).	(لُوكَنْدَةٌ)
Were it not for....	لوْلاَ
Screw.	لوْلبٌ ج لَوَالِبُ
Spiral.	لوْلَبِيٌّ
To blame censure.	لاَمَ يَلُومُ لَوْماً
To blame ; one another.	تلاَوَمَ
Blame ; censure.	لوْمٌ
Blamer ; censurer.	لاَئِمٌ
Blame ; censure.	ملاَمٌ وَمَلاَمةٌ
Blamable ; reprehensible.	ملُومٌ
Hyoid bone.	أَلْعَظْمُ ٱللاَّمِيُّ
State-prison.	(لُومانٌ)
To colour.	لوَّن تَلْوِيناً
To be coloured.	تلوَّن
Colour. Kind.	لوْنٌ ج أَلْوَانٌ
Changeful.	متلَوِّنٌ
Lavander.	(لَوَنْدَا)
To twist.	لَوَى يلْوِي ليًّا
To bend.	لوَّى وَأَلْوَى
To be bent, deflected.	إِلْتوَى
Flag, standard. District.	لِواءٌ ج أَلوِيَةٌ
A general of the army.	أَمِيرُ ٱللِّوَاءِ
Curvature.	إِلْتِوَاءٌ
O that ! Would that !	لَيْتَ
Would that Zeid were going !	لَيْتَ زَيْدًا ذَاهِبٌ
Would that I had done it !	لَيْتَنِي فَعَلْتُهُ
Lion.	لَيْثٌ ج لُيُوثٌ
Not.	لَيْسَ
God is not unjust.	لَيْسَ ٱللّٰهُ بِظَالِمٍ
Fiber of palm, &c.	لِيفٌ
To be fit, suitable.	لاقَ يَلِيقُ
Suitable, proper.	لائِقٌ
Night.	لَيْلٌ ج لَيَالٍ . ولَيْلَةٌ ج لَيْلاَتٌ

لئلاَّ (لِأَنْ.لَا *From*) Lest.

لِئَلاَّ يَقُولَ Lest he should say.

ليمُونٌ Lemon.

لانَ يَلِين To be soft, tender.

لَيَّنَ تَلْيِيناً وأَلانَ إِلاَنَة To soften.

لاينَ مُلاَيَنَة To conciliate.

تَلَيَّنَ To become soft, tender.

تلَيَّنَ لَهُ To coax, conciliate.

لَيِّنٌ ج لَيِّنُونَ Tender, flexible.

لِينٌ Softness. Diarrhœa.

لُيُونَةٌ Softness, pliability.

مُلَيِّنٌ Laxative, aperient.

(لِيوَانٌ) إِيوَانٌ Portico.

م

م As a numeral sign=40.

مَا What?

ما فعلَ What has he done?

ما صَنَعَ What he has done.

أَمْرٌ مَا A certain affair.

ما دُمْتُ حَيًّا As long as I live.

ما أَجْمَلَهُ How beautiful!

مَا أَدْرِي I do not know.

ماذا What?

مَاذَا تَفْعَل What art thou doing?

لِمَاذا جِئْتَ Why hast thou come?

مَاهِيَّةٌ Nature, essence.

مَاهِيه ج مَاهِيات — Wages, pay.

مَاء ج مِياه — Water (see موه)

مُوق — Inner angle of the eye.

مأَن يَمأَن مَأْنًا — To provide.

مؤونة ومؤنة ج مؤن — Provisions.

مِئَة ومائة ج مِئات — One hundred.

مِئوي — Centenary.

مِتر ج امتار — Metre (measure).

مَتَّع وأَمتَع ب — To grant.

تمتَّع بِ ومِن — To enjoy.

مُتعة ج مُتَع — Enjoyment, privilege.

مَتاع ج امتِعة — Furniture, effects.

تمتُّع واستِمتاع — Enjoyment, privilege.

مَتُن يَمتُن مَتانة — To be firm.

مَتن — Text of a book.

مَتانة — Solidity, firmness.

مَتِين — Strong, solid, robust.

مَتى — When? When.

مَتى ما — When, at the time when.

مَثَل يَمثُل وماثَل — To resemble.

مَثَّل وماثَل بِ — To compare to.

مَثُل يَمثُل بَين يدَيه — To stand before someone.

تَمَثَّل لَهُ — He imagined (a thing).

تمثَّل بِ — To imitate.

تماثَل — To resemble each other.

تماثَل مِن علّته — To be nearly convalescent.

إِمتَثَل الأَمر — To obey order.

مِثل ج أَمثال — Similar, like.

مِثلما — As well as.

مَثَل ج أَمثال — Proverb; a saying.

ضَرَب مَثَلاً — To give an example.

مِثال ج امثِلة — Model. Example.

(مَثالة ج مثالات ومَثائِل) — Lesson.

مَثِيل ج مُثُل — Resembling.

أَمثَل م مُثلى ج اماثِل — The best.

أُمثولة — Example. Lesson.

تِمْثَالٌ ج تَمَاثِيلُ Image, figure.

تَمْثِيلُ Assimilation. Analogy.

مَثَانَةٌ ج مَثَانَاتٌ Bladder.

مَجَّ يَمُجُّ مَجًّا To spit ; reject.

مَجُدَ يَمْجُدُ To be great, glorious.

مَجَّدَ To glorify ; exalt, honour.

تَمَجَّدَ To be glorified, praised.

مَجْدٌ ج أَمْجَادٌ Glory, praise.

تَمْجِيدٌ Glorification, praising.

مَجِيدٌ وَمَاجِدٌ Noble, glorious.

أَلْمَجِيدُ The Glorious (God).

أَمْجَدُ ج أَمَاجِدُ More glorious.

مَجَرٌ Hungarian.

بِلَادُ ٱلْمَجَرِ Hungary.

مَجُوسٌ Magians.

أَلْمَجُوسِيَّةُ Creed of the Magians.

مَجَلَّةٌ Code, book, (*see* جل)

مَجَنَ يَمْجُنُ مُجُونًا To jest.

مُجَّانٌ Buffoon, jester.

مَجَّانًا Gratuitously ; freely.

مُحٌّ Yolk of an egg.

مَحَّارَةٌ Litter, panier.

مَحَصَ يَمْحَصُ مَحْصًا بِ To purify.

مَحَّصَ To purify. To try, prove.

مَحَضَ يَمْحَضُ مَحْضًا لَهُ To be sincere.

مَحْضٌ Pure, unmixed.

مَحَقَ يَمْحَقُ مَحْقًا To blot out, efface.

إِمْتَحَقَ وَٱمَّحَقَ To be effaced.

مَحْقٌ Perdition, annihilation.

مُحَاقٌ Waning of the moon.

مَحَكَ يَمْحَكُ مَحْكًا To brawl, dispute.

مَاحَكَهُ To quarrel with one.

مُمَاحَكَةٌ A quarrel, brawl.

مَحِكٌ وَمَاحِكٌ Quarrelsome.

مَحَلَ يَمْحَلُ وَأَمْحَلَ To be sterile.

مَحْلٌ Sterility, barrenness.

Cunning, deceitful. مَحَّالٌ

Barren, unfruitful. ماحِلٌ وَمُمْحِلٌ

To try, test. مَحَنَ يَمْحَنُ مَحناً

To try, examine. إِمتحن

Trial, affliction. مِحنةٌ ج مِحَن

Experience; examination. إِمْتِحانٌ

To efface, blot out. مَحا يَمحو مَحْواً

To be blotted out. امّحى (إِنمحى)

Effected; blotted out. ممحوٌّ

A wiper. مِمحاة

Marrow; brain. مُخٌّ ج مِخاخٌ

To plough the water. مَخَرَ يَمْخُرُ

A ship. ماخِرةٌ ج مَواخِرُ

Wine shop. House of ill-fame. ماخُورٌ

To churn. مَخَضَ يَمخضُ مَخضاً

To suffer the pains of childbirth. مَخَضَتْ تَمْخَضُ وتَمَخَّضَتْ

To be churned. تَمَخَّضَ وَامتخض

Labour of childbirth. مَخاضٌ

Butter-milk. مَخيضٌ

A churning-vessel. مِمْخَضٌ

To blow the nose. مَخَطَ يَمْخُطُ

Mucus. مُخاطٌ

Gossamar. مُخاطُ ٱلشَّيْطانِ أَوِ ٱلشَّمْسِ

Mucous. مُخاطِيٌّ

Lever. مُخْلٌ ج أَمخالٌ ومُخُولٌ

To rinse the mouth. (مَخْمَضَ فاهُ وتَمَخْمَضَ)

To spread, extend. مَدَّ يَمُدُّ مَدّاً

To dip the pen in ink. مَدَّ ٱلقَلَمَ

To help, aid, assist. مَدَّ وَأَمَدَّ

To reach; extend to. إِمْتَدَّ إِلى

To be extended, lie down. تمدَّدَ

To seek help. إِستمَدَّ

Tide; flux. مَدٌّ ج مُدُودٌ

The sign. (آ) مَدٌّ ومدَّةٌ

A dry measure. مُدٌّ ج أَمدادٌ

Period; while. مُدَّةٌ ج مُدَدٌ

Assistance.	مَددٌ وإمدادٌ
Ink. Oil (f a lamp).	مدادٌ
Matter.	مَادَّةٌ ج مَوادُّ
Material.	مادِّيٌّ
Long.	مديدٌ
Extensin ; dilatati n.	تَمدُّدٌ
Prolonged ; extended.	مُمْتدٌّ
A letter with. (آ) مَدة	ممدودٌ
To braise, extol.	مَدَحَ يمدحُ
To praise, Be extended.	إمتدحَ
Eulogy.	مَدحٌ .ومَديحٌ ج مَدَائحُ
Panegyrist.	مادِحٌ ومَدَّاحٌ
Village, town, city.	مدَرٌ
Inhabitants of towns.	أَهْلُ آلْمدَرِ
To build cities ; civilize.	مَدَّنَ
To become civilized.	تمدَّنَ
Refinement, civilizati n.	تمدُّنٌ
City, town.	مَدِينَة ج مُدنٌ ومَدائِنُ
Medina (in Arabia).	أَلْمدِينَة
Bagdad.	مَدينةُ السَّلام
Citizen, townsman.	مَدَنِيٌّ
To grant one a delay.	مادى
To take a long time.	تمادى
Distance, extent ; end.	مدًى
Large knife.	مُدْيَة ج مدى
Since.	مُذْ
To become rotten.	مَذِرَ يمذَرُ
To disperse, scatter.	مَذَّرَ
Hither and thither.	شَذَرَ مَذَرَ
Spoilt, rotten (egg) ; foul.	مذِرٌ
Insincere, dissembler.	مُماذِق
To pass, pass by.	مَرَّ يمُرُّ
To embitter, make bitter.	مَرَّرَ
He caused him to pass.	أَمرَّهُ
To continue ; last.	إستمرَّ
Course, succession.	مَرٌّ ومُرُور

Bitter. Myrrh (plant). مُرٌّ

Once. مَرَّةٌ ج مِرارٌ ومَرَّاتٌ

Several times, often. مَرارًا

Gall ; bile. امَرَّةٌ ج مِرَرٌ

Aforesaid. أَلْمارُّ ذِكْرُهُ

Bitterness. Gall-bladder. مَرارَةٌ

More bitter. أَمَرُّ

Passage ; pathway. مَمَرٌّ

Continued, continual. مُسْتَمِرٌّ

To be healthy (food). مَرِئَ يَمْرَأُ

Man. مَرْءٌ وامْرُؤٌ

Woman. مَرْأَةٌ وامْرَأَةٌ

Courage, bravery. مُرُوءَةٌ ومُرُوَّةٌ

Gullet, œsophagus. مَرِيءٌ

To moisten, soak. مَرَثَ يَمْرُثُ

Meadow, pasture. مَرْجٌ ج مُرُوجٌ

Confusion, disorder. هَرْجٌ وَمَرْجٌ

Coral. مَرْجانٌ

To be very gay. مَرِحَ يَمْرَحُ

Very gay. مَرِحٌ ج مَرْحَى ومَراحَى

(See رحب) مَرْحَبًا

To anoint. مَرَخَ يَمْرُخُ مَرْخًا

Liniment. مَرُوخٌ

Mars (planet). أَلْمِرِّيخُ

To rebel, revolt. مَرَدَ يَمْرُدُ وتَمَرَّدَ

To be proud, insolent. تَمَرَّدَ عَلَى

Rebellious. مارِدٌ ج مَرَدَةٌ

Beardless (youth). أَمْرَدُ ج مُرْدٌ

Marjoram. مَرْدَقُوشٌ ومَرْزَنْجُوشٌ

To steep, soak. مَرَسَ يَمْرُسُ

To exercise, practice. مارَسَ

Rope, cord. مَرَسَةٌ ج مَرَسٌ وأَمْراس

Exercise, practice. مُمارَسَةٌ

Myrtle-tree. مَرْسِين

Hospital. مارِسْتانٌ

To fall ill, be sick. مَرِضَ يَمْرَضُ

To nurse the sick. مرَّضَ

To make ill, or sick. أَمْرَضَ

To feign illness. تمارَضَ

Disease, illness. مَرَضٌ ج أمْراضٌ

Sick, ill. مَرِيضٌ ج مَرْضَى

To pull out (hair). مرطَ يَمْرُطُ مَرْطاً

Scanty-haired. أَمْرَطُ م مَرْطاء

To graze (cattle). مرعَ يَمْرَعُ مَرْعاً

To roll one in the dust. مرَّغ

To roll in the dust. تمرَّغ

To penetrate, pass. مرق يَمْرُقُ مِنْ

Broth ; gravy, sauce. مرقٌ ومَرَقَةٌ

A heretic. مارِقٌ

Marble. مَرْمَرٌ

To become elastic. مرن يَمْرُنُ

To be accustomed to. مرنَ على

To train, habituate. مرَّن عَلَى

To be habituated to. تمرَّنَ على

Elastic, flexible. مَرِنٌ

Elasticity, flexibility. مُرُونَةٌ

Maronite. مارُونِيٌّ ج مَوارِنَةٌ

Practice; exercise. تَمْرِينٌ وتَمَرُّنٌ

Trained ; inured. مُمَرَّنٌ

Ointment. مَرْهَمٌ ج مَراهِمُ

Saint *(Syriac)*. مار ومَاري

Dispute, quarrel. مِرْيَةٌ

To suck. مَزَّ يَمُزُّ مَزّاً

Sourish. Insipid. مُزٌّ ومُزَّةٌ

To mix. مزِجَ يَمْزُجُ مَزْجاً

To associate with. مازَجَ

To get mixed with... إِمْتَزَجَ ب

Mixture, amalgamation. إِمْتِزاجٌ

Mixture, alloy. مَزِيجٌ

Temperament. مِزاجٌ ج أمْزِجَة

To joke, jest. مزح يَمْزَحُ مَزْحاً

To jest together. تمازَحَ

مزاحٌ Jesting, bantering.

مِزْرٌ A kind of beer.

مَزَق يَمْزِق وَمَزَّق To tear to pieces.

مَزَّق To disperse (a crowd).

تَمَزَّق To be torn into pieces.

مَزِيَّةٌ ج مزايَا Merit; trait.

مَسّ يَمَسّ مَسًّا To touch.

تَماسّ To touch one another.

مَسٌّ Touch; contact. Insanity.

حاجةٌ مَاسَّةٌ Urgent business.

مُمَاسٌّ Tangent *(geom.)*.

مَمْسُوسٌ Touched. Insane.

مِسْتٌ ج مُسُوتٌ A kind of shoe.

مَسَح يَمْسَح مَسْحًا To wipe; anoint.

مَسَح الارْض To measure land.

مَسْحٌ Wiping. Anointing.

مِسْحٌ ج مُسُوحٌ Sack-cloth.

مِسَاحَةٌ Land-survey.

عِلْمُ ٱلْمِسَاحَةِ Mensuration.

مَسِيحٌ ج مُسَحاءُ وَمَسْحَى Anointed.

أَلْمَسِيحُ Christ, the Messiah.

أَلْمَسِيحُ ٱلدَّجَّالُ Antichrist.

مَسِيحِيٌّ ج مَسِيحِيُّونَ Christian.

أَلْمَسِيحِيَّةُ Christianity.

مَسَّاحٌ ج مَسَّاحُونَ Land-surveyor.

مَسْحَاءُ Flat barren land.

تِمْسَاحٌ ج تَمَاسِيحُ Crocodile.

مَسَخ يَمْسَخ مَسْخًا To change; distort.

مَسْخ Distorted, corrupted.

مَسَد يَمْسُدُ To plait or twist.

(مَسَّدَ) To rub with the hand.

مَسَدٌ ج مِسَادٌ Cord of fibres.

(تَمْسِيدٌ) Massage.

مَسَكَ يَمْسُكُ وَأَمْسَكَ To hold, seize.

أَمْسَكَ To retain, hold back.

أَمْسَكَ عن To refrain from.

Musk. مِسْكٌ

Avarice. Abstinence. إِمْسَاكٌ

Scented with musk. مُمَسَّكٌ

To wish one good evening. مَسَّى

To enter into the evening. أَمْسَى

Eve, evening. مَسَاءٌ

Good evening. مَسَاءَ ٱلْخَيْرِ

To comb (the hair). مَشَطَ يَمْشُطُ وَمَشَّطَ

Comb; rake. مِشْطٌ ج أَمْشَاطٌ

Instep of the foot. مِشْطُ ٱلرِّجْلِ

Hair-dresser. مَاشِطٌ م مَاشِطَةٌ

Slenderness. مَشْقٌ

The refuse of silk. مُشَاقَةٌ

Slim, Slender. مَمْشُوقٌ

Apricots. مِشْمِشٌ

An apricot. مِشْمِشَةٌ

To walk; go. مَشَى يَمْشِي وَتَمَشَّى

To cause to walk. مَشَّى وَأَمْشَى

To walk with one. مَاشَى

Walking, marching. مَشْيٌ

Walker on foot; foot-soldier. مَاشٍ ج مُشَاةٌ

Flocks, cattle. مَاشِيَةٌ ج مَوَاشٍ

Corridor. مَمْشًى ج مَمَاشٍ

To suck; sip. مَصَّ يَمُصُّ وَٱمْتَصَّ

To absorb. إِمْتَصَّ

What is sucked. مُصَّةٌ وَمُصَاصٌ

Sugar-cane. (قَصَبُ ٱلْمَصِّ)

Twine, pack-thread. خَيْطٌ مِصِّيصٌ

Siphon; sucking tube. مَمَصٌّ

Absorption. اِمْتِصَاصٌ

To build cities. مَصَّرَ

Egypt. Cairo. مِصْرُ

Great city. Limits. مِصْرٌ ج أَمْصَارٌ

Egyptian. مِصْرِيٌّ ج مِصْرِيُّونَ

Intestines. مُصْرَانٌ ج مَصَارِينُ

Mastic (kind of gum). مُصْطَكَى

To drop, trickle.	مَصَل يَمْصُلُ
Whey. Serum.	مَصْلٌ
To cause pain.	مَضَّ يَمُضُّ وَأَمَضَّ
Pain, grief.	مضٌّ ومَضَّةٌ ومَضَضٌ
To masticate, chew.	مضغ يَمْضَغُ
Mastication, chewing.	مَضْغٌ
Morsel.	مَضْغَةٌ ج مُضَغٌ
To rinse, wash.	مَضْمَضَ
To pass; go, depart.	مضى يَمْضِي
To sign (a letter).	مَضَى على
To take, carry off.	مضى بِ
To execute, accomplish.	أَمْضَى
To pass off, carried cut.	تَمَضَّى
Execution, Signature.	إِمْضَاءٌ
The past; past tense.	الْمَاضِي
Signer; subscriber.	مُمْضٍ
To draw; stretch.	مطَّ يَمُطُّ
To rain.	مطر يَمْطُرُ وَامطر
To pray for rain.	إِسْتَمْطَرَ
Rain; heavy rain.	مَطَرٌ ج امْطَارٌ
Rainy (weather).	مَاطِرٌ وَمُمْطِرٌ
A water-skin.	مَطَرَةٌ
Bishop.	مُطْرَانٌ ج مطارِنَةٌ
To defer, put off.	مَطَل وَمَاطَل
Delay, putting off.	مَطْلٌ وَمُمَاطَلَةٌ
One who puts off.	مُمَاطِلٌ
Deferred.	مَمْطُولٌ
To mount, ride.	أَمْطَى وَامْتَطَى
Beast of burden.	مطيّةٌ ج مَطَايَا
With, together with.	مع وَمَعَ
Nevertheless, yet.	مع ذَلِك
Although.	مع أَنَّ
Together, simultaneously.	مَعًا
Company, attendance.	معيّةٌ
Stomach.	معدةٌ وَمِعْدَةٌ ج مِعَدٌ
Goats (coll noun).	معزٌ ومعزى

A goat. ماعِزٌ ج مَواعِزُ

Goat-herd. مَعَّازٌ

To crush. (مَعَسَ يَمْعَسُ مَعْساً)

To pull out (hair). مَعَطَ يَمْعَطُ

Hairless. أَمْعَطُ م معطاء ج مُعْطٌ

To rub. مَعَكَ يَمْعَكُ مَعْكاً

To delay paying. ماعك بدينِهِ

Tumult of battle. مَعْمَعَةٌ ج مَعامِعُ

To consider. أَمْعَنَ ٱلنَّظرَ. وَ تَمَعَّنَ

Consideration. إِمْعانٌ وَتَمَعُّنٌ

Utensil ; boat. ماعُونٌ ج مَواعِينُ

Running water. مَعِينٌ ج مُعُنٌ

Intestine. مِعيٌ ومِعىً ج أَمْعاءٌ

Red earth for dyeing. مَغْرَة

To suffer from colic. مُغِصَ

Colic gripes. مَغْصٌ

To stretch. مَغَطَ يَمْغَطُ . وَمَغَّطَ

To be stretched. تَمَغَّطَ وَٱمْتَغَطَ

To draw (a sword). إِمْغَطَ

To speak indistinctly. مَغْمَغَ ٱلْكَلامَ

To magnetize. (مَغْطَسَ)

The magnet. مَغْنَطِيسٌ

To hate, detest. مَقَتَ يَمْقُتُ مَقْتاً

Hatred ; aversion. مَقْتٌ

Hated, detested. مَقِيتٌ وَمَمْقُوتٌ

Sebesten (*Cordia myxa*). مَقْساسٌ

To look at. مَقَلَ يَمْقُلُ مَقْلاً

The eye ; eye-ball. مُقْلَةٌ ج مُقَلٌ

Mecca (city in Arabia). مَكَّةُ

Meccan. مَكِّيٌّ وَمَكَّاوِيٌّ

Weaving-shuttle. مَكُّوكٌ

To abide, dwell. مَكَثَ يَمْكُثُ

Sojourn, stay. مَكْثٌ

To deceive. مَكَرَ يَمْكُرُ وَمَاكَرَ

Trick, deceit, fraud. مَكْرٌ

Cunning, deceitful. ماكِرٌ ج مَكَرَةٌ

مكّارٌ	Deceiver ; trickster.
مَكَسَ وَمَكَّسَ	To collect taxes.
مَكْسٌ ج مُكوسٌ	Custom duties.
ماكسٌ وَمَكّاسٌ	Tax-gatherer.
مَكُنَ يَمْكُنُ	To be strong.
مَكَّنَ	To strengthen.
مَكَّنَ وَأَمْكَنَ مِن	To enable.
أَمْكَنَهُ	To be possible for (him).
يُمْكِنُ أَنْ	It is possible that...
تَمَكَّنَ	To be stable, firm, solid.
تَمَكَّنَ مِنْ	To be able, overcome.
مَكْنَةٌ	Possibility. Power.
مَكان ج أَماكِن	Place ; station.
مَكانَةٌ	Influence ; power.
إِمْكانٌ	Possibility ; power.
مُمْكِنٌ	Possible.
مُتَمَكِّنٌ	Declinable noun.
مَلَّ يَمُلُّ مَلًّا	To tack, baste.
مَلَّ يَمَلُّ مِنَ	To tire of.
أَمَلَّ	To cause weariness.
تَمَلَّلَ	To be restless, tired.
مِلَّةٌ ج مِلَلٌ	A religion, creed.
مَلَلٌ وَمَلالٌ وَمَلالَةٌ	Weariness.
مُلّا	Mollah, a Turkish judge.
مَلُّولٌ	Acorn-tree ; kind of oak.
مَلَأَ يَمْلأُ مَلأً	To fill up.
مَلِئَ يَمْلأُ وَامْتَلأَ مِنْ	To be filled.
مَلَّأَ تَمْلِئَةً	To fill, fill up.
مِلْءٌ	Quantity which fills up.
مَلأٌ ج أَمْلاءٌ	An assembly.
مُلاءَةٌ وَمِلايَةٌ	A kind of garment.
مَلآنُ م مَلأَى وَمَلآنَةٌ	Full.
إِمْتِلاءٌ	Fullness Plethora.
مَمْلُوءٌ وَمَمْلُوٌّ وَمُمْتَلِئٌ	Full.
مَلَحَ يَمْلَحُ وَمَلَّحَ	To salt (food.)
مَلُحَ يَمْلُحُ مُلُوحَةٌ	To be salty. Be beautiful.

How handsome he is! ما أَمْلَحهُ

Salt. مِلْحٌ ج أَمْلاحٌ

Pleasant anecdote. مُلحةٌ ج مُلحٌ

Beauty, goodliness. مَلاحَةٌ

The art of navigation. مِلاحةٌ

Sailor. Salt merchant. مَلَّاحٌ

Salt-works, salt mine. مَلَّاحةٌ

Saltness. مُلوحةٌ

Goodly, pretty. مَليحٌ ج مِلاحٌ

Salted. مُملَّحٌ

Salt-cellar. مَمْلحةٌ ج ممالح

Jew's mallow. ملوخيةٌ وملُوخيا

To be smooth. مَلِسَ يَملُسُ

To make smooth. مَلَّسَ

Twilight, dawn. مَلَسُ آلظَّلام

Smoothness. مَلاسةٌ

Smooth. أَملسُ م مَلْساءُ ج مُلسٌ

To escape. ماصَ وَتَملَّصَ مِنْ

To plaster. مَلَطَ يَملطُ وَمَلَّطَ

Plaster. مِلاطٌ

Malta (Island). مالِطَةُ

Maltese. مالِطيٌّ

Scanty-haired. أَمْلَطُ م مَلْطاءُ

To flatter. مَلِقَ يَملَقُ. وَمالَقَ

To flatter, cajole. تَمَلَّقَ تَملقاً

Flattery. مَلَقٌ وَتَمْليقٌ وَتَملّقٌ

Adulator, flatterer. مَلِقٌ ومَلَّاقٌ

To possess. مَلَكَ يَمْلِكُ وتَمَلَّكَ

To reign or rule over. مَلَكَ على

To give in possession. مَلَّكَ

To rule, possess. تَمَلَّكَ

To abstain from. تَمالَكَ عَنْ

Property; goods. مِلْكٌ ج امْلاكٌ

Power, authority, reign. مُلْكٌ

Angle. مَلَكٌ ومَلاكٌ ج مَلائِكةٌ

King. مَلِكٌ ج مُلوكٌ

Queen. مَلِكة

Custom, habit. مَلَكةٌ ج مَلَكات

Royalty. Kingdom. مَلَكُوتٌ

Royal, Kingly. مَلَكِيٌّ وَمُلُوكِيٌّ

Possessor, proprietor. مالِكٌ

Heron (bird). مالِكُ ٱلْحزين

Possessor. King. مَلِيكٌ ج مُلَكاء

Kingdom. مَمْلَكةٌ ج ممالِكُ

Mamluk. مَمْلُوكٌ ج مَمَالِيكُ

To be restless. تَمَلْمَلَ

Melancholy; black bile. مَلَنْخوليا

To dictate a writing. أَمْلى عَلى

A long time. مَلِيًّا مِنَ الدهر

Dictation. إِمْلاءٌ ج أَمالٍ

Million. مِلْيُونٌ ج مَلايِين

For what? From what? مِمَّا (مِنْ ما)

Who? Whoever. مَنْ

From; of; for; than. مِنْ

Some *of* them say. مِنْهُمْ مَنْ يَقُولُ

He drew nigh *to* him. قَرُبَ مِنْهُ

Better *than*. أَفْضَلُ مِنْ

He came at once. جاءَ مِنْ ساعَتِهِ

To be gracious. مَنَّ يَمُنُّ وَٱمْتَنَّ

To reproach for benefits. مَنَّ وَمَنَّنَ

Gift, benefit. Manna. مَنٌّ

By the grace of God. بِمَنِّهِ تَعالى

Grace, bounty. مِنَّةٌ ج مِنَنٌ

Generous. مَنَّانٌ

God, the Giver of good. أَلْمَنَّانُ

Death. Ill-fortune. ٱلْمَنُونُ

Reproach for benefit. إِمْتِنانٌ

Under obligation. (مَمْنُونٌ)

Obligation. (مَمْنُونِيَّةٌ)

Battering-ram. مَنْجَنِيقٌ وَمَنْجَلِيقٌ

To give, grant. مَنَحَ يَمْنَحُ مَنْحًا

Gift, favour. مِنْحَةٌ ج مِنَحٌ

مُنْذُ وَمُذْ	Since.
مَنَعَ يَمْنَعُ عَنْ وَمِنْ	To refuse; prohibit.
مَنُعَ يَمْنُعُ	To be inaccessible.
مَانَعَ	To refuse; oppose.
تَمَنَّعَ عَنْ	To abstain from.
تَمَنَّعَ بِ	To intrench one's self.
إِمْتَنَعَ	To be impossible.
إِمْتَنَعَ وَتَمَنَّعَ	To refrain from.
مَنْعٌ	Prevention.
مَنِيعٌ	Impregnable, inaccessible.
مَانِعٌ	Something which prevents.
مُمْتَنِعٌ	Impossible.
مَمْنُوعٌ	Interdicted, prohibited.
مَنَّى تَمْنِيَة	To grant one's desire.
تَمَنَّى	To wish, desire.
مَنًا ج أَمْنَاء	A measure.
مَنِيَّةٌ ج مَنَايَا	Death. Destiny.
مُنْيَة ج مُنًى	Wish, desire.
أُمْنِيَّةٌ ج أَمَانِيُّ	Wish, vain wish.
مُهْجَةٌ ج مُهَجٌ	Soul, life.
مَهَدَ يَمْهَدُ وَمَهَّدَ	To level; prepare.
تَمَهَّدَ	To be made easy.
مَهْدٌ ج مُهُودٌ	Bed; child's cradle.
مَهَرَ يَمْهَرُ	To be skilful.
تَمَهَّرَ	To become skilful.
مَهْرٌ ج مُهُورٌ	Dowry.
مُهْرٌ ج مِهَارٌ	Foal. Signet.
مُهْرْدَارٌ	Seal-bearer, secretary.
مُهْرَةٌ ج مُهُرَاتٌ	Filly.
مَهَارَةٌ	Skilfulness, dexterity.
مَاهِرٌ ج مَهَرَةٌ	Skilful.
مَهَلَ يَمْهَلُ . وَتَمَهَّلَ	To act slowly.
مَهَّلَ وَأَمْهَلَ	To grant a delay.
إِسْتَمْهَلَ	To ask for a delay.
مَهْلٌ	Deliberate action.
مَهْلاً	Go slowly; softly!

إِمْهَالٌ Concession of a delay.

تَمَهُّلٌ Slowness, delay.

مَهْمَا Whatever.

مَهَنَ يَمْهَنُ To serve. Overwork.

إِمْتَهَنَ To employ. Despise.

مِهْنَةٌ ج مِهَنٌ Art, trade.

مَهَاةٌ ج مَهًا Antelope.

مَاتَ يَمُوتُ مَوْتًا To die, expire.

مَوَّتَ وَأَمَاتَ To kill.

تَمَاوَتَ To feign death.

اِسْتَمَاتَ To act desperately.

مَوْتٌ وَمَوْتَةٌ Death, decease.

مَوْتَانٌ وَمُوتَانٌ Cattle-plague.

مَائِتٌ ج مَائِتُونَ Dying.

مَيْتٌ وَمَيِّتٌ ج أَمْوَاتٌ Dead.

مِيتَةٌ Kind of death.

مَمَاتٌ Death, decease.

مُمِيتٌ Deadly, mortal, fatal.

مُسْتَمِيتٌ Bold, desperate.

مَاجَ يَمُوجُ وَتَمَوَّجَ To be agitated.

مَوْجٌ ج أَمْوَاجٌ Wave, billow.

تَمَوُّجٌ Commotion ; fluctuation.

مَارِسْتَانٌ A hospital; asylum.

مَوْزٌ Banana (tree or fruit).

مَاسٌ Diamond.

مُوسَى أَوْ مُوسًى و (مُوسٌ) ج مَوَاسٍ A razor.

مُوسَى Moses.

مُوسِيقَى Music.

مُوسِيقِيّ Musician. Musical.

مَاشٌ Indian peas.

مُوقٌ Inner angle of the eye.

مَالَ يَمُولُ To be wealthy, rich.

تَمَوَّلَ To become rich.

مَالٌ ج أَمْوَالٌ Goods, riches.

بَيْتُ ٱلْمَالِ Public Treasury.

مالِيٌّ	Financial ; pecuniary.
المالِيَّةُ	Finance; ministry of...
وزيرُ ٱلْمالِيَّة	Minister of Finance.
مُتَموِّلٌ	A wealthy man.
مومِيا	A kind of bitumen.
مومِيَةٌ ج مُومِياتٌ	Mummy.
مَانَ يَمُونُ . ومَوَّنَ	To furnish.
تَموَّنَ	To lay in a store.
مُونَةٌ (مؤُنةٌ)	Provisions.
بيْتُ ٱلْمُونَةِ	Store-room.
موَّهَ	To gild, or silver.
موَّهَ	To falsify (news).
ماءٌ ج امْواهٌ ومِياهٌ	Water.
مائِيٌّ	Watery; fluid. Aquatic.
ماهِيَّةٌ	Nature, essence. Salary.
مُموَّهٌ	Falsified (narrative).
تَمْويهٌ	Equivocation.
مَاحَ يَمِيحُ	To give a gift.
إِسْتِمَاحٌ	To seek a gift.
مَائِدةٌ ج مَائِداتٌ وموائِدُ	A table.
ميدانٌ ج مَيادِينُ	Race-field; arena.
مِيرِيٌّ أوْ مِيرةٌ (أميريٌّ)	Taxes.
مَيَّزَ	To detect, distinguish.
تَمَيَّزَ وٱمْتازَ	To be distinguished.
تَمْيِيزٌ	Separation ; distinction.
سِنُّ ٱلتَّمْيِيزِ	The age of reason.
إِمْتِيازٌ	Distinction; privilege ; preference.
مُتَمَيِّزٌ	Distinguishing.
مُتَمَيَّزٌ ومُمْتَازٌ	Distinguished.
مَيْسٌ	Hackberry tree.
مَاعَ يَمِيعُ	To flow (liquid).
مَيْعَةٌ	Incense, perfume. Balm.
مَائِعٌ	Fluid, liquid.
مالَ يَمِيلُ إِلى	To be inclined to.
مالَ عَنْ	To deviate from.
مالَ على	To be adverse to...

مَالَ يميلُ To decline, (sun).

تمَايَلَ To reel in walking.

إستمالَ To conciliate.

ميَّلَ وأمالَ To incline, bend.

ميْلٌ ج مُيُولٌ Inclination.

مِيلٌ ج أميَالٌ A probe. A mile.

مَائِلٌ Bent, inclined.

مَيَّالٌ Very much inclined.

مَانَ يَمِينُ To lie, tell a falsehood.

مَيْنٌ ج مُيُونٌ A lie, falsehood.

مِينَا A harbour, port. Enamel.

ن

ن As a numeral sign=50.

نَارْجِيلٌ وَنَارِجِيلٌ Cocoa-nut.

نأى ينأى عن To be far from.

انْتَأى عَن To go far from.

نَاءٍ One who is far away, remote.

أنبُوبٌ ج أنَابِيب A tube, pipe.

نبا عَلى To assault.

نَبَأَ ب To lead to.

نَبَّأَ وَأَنْبَأَ To announce, inform.

تَنَبَّأَ To prophesy; foretell.

إستَنبَأَ To seek information.

نَبَأٌ ج أنباء News; information.

نبُوءَة ونبُوَّة A prophecy.

نبَوِيٌّ Prophetic.

A prophet. نبيّ ج أنبياء ونبيّون

To sprout (plant). نبتَ ينبتُ

To cause to sprout. أنبتَ

A plant; herb; sprout. نبتٌ

Plant, vegetation. نباتٌ ج نباتات

Botany. علم النباتِ

The vegetable world. عالم النباتِ

Botanist. Vegetable. نباتيّ

Sprouting, germinating. نابتٌ

A club. نبّوتٌ ج نبابيت

Herbarium. Origin. منبتٌ ج منابِت

To bark (dog). نبحَ ينبحُ نبحاً

Barking. نباحٌ

To throw; give up. نبذَ ينبذ

The rabble, mob. أنباذ الناس

Section, article. نبذةٌ ج نبذ

Wine. نبيذٌ ج أنبذةٌ

To speak loud. نبرَ ينبرُ نبراً

A store; granary. نبرٌ ج أنابِر

Emphasis (in speaking). نبرة

Stage, pulpit. منبرٌ ج منابِرُ

A lamp. نبراسٌ ج نباريس

To unearth, dig up. نبشَ ينبشُ

Earth or pit dug out. نبيشةٌ

A digger. نبّاشٌ

To pulsate, throb. نبضَ ينبِضُ

Pulsation; pulse. نبضٌ

A throb, pulsation. نبضةٌ

To invent (something). إستنبطَ

The Nabathæns. نبطٌ ج أنباط

A vulgar word. كلمةٌ نبطيّةٌ

Discovery, invention. إستنباطٌ

To spring, gush (water). نبعَ ينبعُ

Spring of water. نبعٌ

Source, origin. منبعٌ ج منابِعُ

A fountain. ينبوعٌ ج ينابيع

نَبَغَ يَنْبُغُ To arise ; appear.

نَابِغَة ج نَوَابِغُ Distinguished.

انبيقٌ ج أَنَابِيقُ Chemical retrot.

نَبَلَ يَنْبُلُ نَبْلًا To shoot arrows.

نَبُلَ يَنْبُلُ To have genius, skill.

تَنَبَّلَ To become skilful.

نَبْلٌ ج نِبَالٌ Arrows, darts.

نَبِيلٌ ج نُبَالٌ Highly intelligent.

نَبْلَة An arrow, dart.

نَبَالَة Ability; ; superiority.

نَبِهَ يَنْبَهُ نَبْهًا لِ To perceive.

نَبِهَ نَبْهًا مِنَ ٱلنَّوْمِ To awake.

نَبَّهَهُ مِنَ النَّوْمِ To wake ; one up.

نَبَّهَ عَلَى أَوْ إِلَى To warn inform.

تَنَبَّهَ وَٱنْتَبَهَ To awake.

تَنَبَّهَ لِ To be awake to.

إِنْتَبَهَ لِ To perceive.

نَبَاهَة Celebrity. Intelligence.

إِنْتِبَاهٌ Attention; wakefulness.

تَنْبِيهٌ Warning. Notice.

مُتَنَبِّهٌ وَمُنْتَبِهٌ Awake, Attentive.

نَتَأَ يَنْتَأُ نُتُوءًا To project.

نَاتِئٌ Projecting; jutting out.

نَتَجَ يَنْتُجُ To bring forth.

نَتَجَ عَنْ To arise, result from...

إِسْتَنْتَجَ To deduce, infer.

نَتِيجَة ج نَتَائِجُ Conclusion. Result; consequence.

نَتَرَ يَنْتُرُ To pull, snatch.

نَتَشَ يَنْتِشُ نَتْشًا To snatch, pluck.

نَتَفَ يَنْتِفُ To pluck, pull out.

تَنَتَّفَ To be plucked off.

نُتْفَة ج نُتَفٌ A small quantity.

نَتَنَ يَنْتِنُ نَتْنًا وَأَنْتَنَ To stink.

نَتْنٌ وَنَتَانَةٌ Stench.

نَتِنٌ وَمُنْتِنٌ Stinking, putrid.

نُتُوءٌ ج نُتُوءَاتٌ Tuberosity.

نات	Swollen. Projecting.
نثر ينثر	To disperse, scatter.
تناثر وانتثر	To be scattered.
نثر. (opp. to نظم)	Prose,
منثور	Gilly-flower.
نجب ينجب	To be noble.
إنتجب	To choose, select.
نجابة	Nobility.
نجيب ج نجباء	Noble.
نجائب	The choicest parts.
نجح ينجح	To succeed, prosper.
نجّح وأنجح	To give success.
نجح ونجاح	Success, prosperity.
ناجح	Successful, thriving.
نجد ينجد. وأنجد	To help, aid.
نجّد	To upholster.
ناجد مناجدة	To bring help to.
إستنجد	To invoke assistance.
نجد ج أنجد	High land.
نجدة ج نجدات	Help, succour.
نجّاد ومنجد	An upholsterer.
نجر ينجر	To plane (wood).
نجارة	Carpentry.
نجارة	Shavings chips of wood.
نجّار ج نجّارون	Carpenter.
نجز ينجز ونجّز	To finish a thing.
نجز ينجز	To come to an end.
أنجز	To achieve; accomplish.
نجز ونجاز	Achievement.
ناجز ونجيز	Ready, present.
نجس ينجس نجساً	To be impure.
نجّس وأنجس	To defile, pollute.
تنجّس	To become polluted.
نجاسة	Filth. Legal impurity.
نجس ج أنجاس	Impure, filthy.
النّجاشي	Title of the Abyssinian kings.

نَجَعَ يَنْجَعُ	To benefit, profit.
نَجِيعٌ	Profitable, useful. Dark red blood.
نَجْلٌ ج أَنْجال	Child, son.
إِنْجِيلٌ ج أَنَاجِيلُ	Gospel.
إِنْجِيلِيٌّ	Evangelical ; evangelist.
مِنْجَلٌ ج مَنَاجِلُ	A sickle.
نَجَمَ يَنْجُمُ وَأَنْجَمَ	To appear.
نَجَمَ عَنْ	To arise, or result from.
نَجْمٌ ج أَنْجُمٌ وَنُجُومٌ	A star. Shrub.
عِلْمُ ٱلنُّجُومِ	Astronomy.
عِلْمُ ٱلتَّنْجِيمِ	Astrology.
مُنَجِّمٌ	Astronomer. Astrologer.
مَنْجَمٌ ج مَنَاجِم	Mine. Source.
نَجَا يَنْجُو نَجَاة	To escape.
نَاجَى	To confide a secret to.
نَجَّى وَأَنْجَى مِن	To save deliver.
تَنَاجَى	To commune secretly.
نَجَاة وَنَجَاء	Deliverance.
مَنْجًى ج مَنَاجٍ	An asylum.
مُنَاجَاة	Secret communication.
نَحَبَ يَنْحَبُ	To weep, cry, wail.
نَحْبٌ	Bitter weeping. Death.
قَضَى نَحْبَهُ	To die.
نَحِيبٌ	Wailing. Lamenation.
نَحَتَ يَنْحِتُ	To cut, hew, carve.
نُحَاتَةٌ	Fragments, chips.
نَحَّاتٌ	Stone-cutter. Sculptor.
نَحِيتٌ وَمَنْحُوت	Cut, hewed.
مِنْحَتٌ ج مَنَاحِتُ	Sculptor's chisel.
نَحَرَ يَنْحَرُ	To kill (an animal).
تَنَاحَرَ	To contend together.
إِنْتَحَرَ	To commit suicide.
نِحْرِيرٌ ج نَحَارِيرُ	Skilled.
نَحْرٌ ج نُحُورٌ	Lower part of neck.
مَنْحَرٌ	Throat.
نَحَسَ	To cover with copper.

Ill-luck. نحسٌ ج نحوسٌ

Unlucky. نَحْسٌ ومَنْحُوسٌ

Brass. نحاسٌ

Copper. نحاسٌ أحمر

A piece of copper. نحاسةٌ

A copper merchant. نحّاسٌ

To be slim. نحف يَنْحف نحافةً

To make thin. أنحف

Leanness ; slenderness. نحافةٌ

Thin, meagre. نحيفٌ ج نِحافٌ

To become thin. نحَلَ ينحل

To make thin. أنحل

To plagiarize. تنحل وانتحل

To embrace a religion. انتحل

Bees. نَحْلٌ

A bee. نَحْلة

A religious sect. نحلةٌ ج نِحَلٌ

Thinness, leanness. نحول

Thin, emaciated. نحيلٌ

We. نَحْنُ

To move towards. نحا يَنْحو

To send away. نحّى عَنْ

To go aside. تَنَحّى عَنْ

Towards. Nearly, about. For example. نَحْوَ

Region. Method. نَحْوٌ ج أنحاء

Grammar, *sp*. syntax. عِلْم النَّحْو

Grammarian. نَاحٍ ج نُحاةٌ

Grammatical. نَحْويٌّ

Side, direction. نَاحِيَة ج نَوَاحٍ

To select. نخب ينخب وانتخب

Choice, election. نخبٌ وانتخاب

Chosen. Choice. نُخْبةٌ ج نُخَبٌ

Elector. منتخِب

Chosen ; elected. منتخَبٌ

To snore ; snort. نخر ينخر

To be rotten. نخِر ينخَر نخراً

Pride. Sense of honour. نَخْوَةٌ	Rotten, decayed. نَخِرٌ وَناخِرٌ
To expose one's faults. نَدَّدَ بِ	Nostril ; nose. مِنْخَرٌ ج مَناخِيرُ
A kind of perfume. نِدٌّ	To prick with. نَخَرَ يَنْخُرُ بِ
Similar to, an equal. نِدٌّ ج أَندادٌ	To prick. نَخَسَ يَنْخُسُ نَخْساً
To weep, lament. نَدَبَ يَنْدُبُ	Cattle-trade ; slave-trade. نِخاسَةٌ
To call, appoint. نَدَبَ وَٱنْتَدَبَ	Cattle, or slave trader. نَخَّاسٌ
To be cicatrized. نَدِبَ يَنْدَبُ	A goad, spur. مَنْخَسٌ ج مَناخِسُ
To respond to a call. إِنْتَدَبَ لِ	To hawk, clear the throat. تَنَخَّعَ
Scar. نَدْبَةٌ ج نُدُوبٌ وَأَنْدابٌ	Marrow. Brain. نُخاعٌ ج نُخُعٌ
An elegy, a lamentation. نَدْبَةٌ	Phlegm, mucus. نُخاعَةٌ
A weeper, lamenter. نادِبٌ	To sift, bolt flour. نَخَلَ يَنْخُلُ
Mourned. Commissioner. مَندُوبٌ	The palm-tree. نَخْلٌ وَنَخِيلٌ
Liberty of action. مَندُوحَةٌ	A palm-tree. نَخْلَةٌ
To be rare. نَدَرَ يَنْدُرُ	Bran. نُخالَةٌ
Rarity ; infrequency. نَدْرَةٌ	A sieve. مُنْخُلٌ ج مَناخِلُ
A rare thing. نادِرٌ ج نَوادِرُ	To blow the nose. تَنَخَّمَ
Rarely, seldom. نادِراً أَوفي ٱلنَّادِرِ	Mucus ; phlegm. نُخامَةٌ
To card (cotton). نَدَفَ يَنْدِفُ	To incite, instigate. نخى وانْخى

نداقةٌ Trade of carding.
نَدَّافٌ Wool or cotton carder.
مَندوفٌ Carded.
مَنديلٌ ج مَنادِيلُ A towel. Veil.
ألأندلُسُ Andalusia. Spain.
اندلُسِيٌّ Andalusian.
نَدِمَ يَندَمُ. وتَندَّمَ على To regret
نَادَمَ مُنادَمَةً To associate with.
نَدَمٌ و نَدامَةٌ Regret, repentance.
نَادِمٌ Repentant contrite.
نَديمٌ ج نُدَماءُ Associate, friend.
نَدِيَ يَندَى To be wet.
نَدَّى تندِيَةً To dampen, wet.
نادَى مُناداةً وَنِداءً To call.
نادَى ب To proclaim ; publish.
أندَى إِنداءً To be liberal.
تَندَّى Ta become wet.
انتَدَى To assemble *v.i*

نَدًى ج أنداءٌ Moisture. Dew.
نِداءٌ Call. Proclamation.
حرفُ ٱلنِّدَاءِ Vocative particle.
نَدوَةٌ An assembly, a meeting.
نَادٍ ج أندِيَةٌ Place of assembly.
مُنادٍ A public crier.
منتدًى Assembly-hall.
نَذَرَ ـُ To make a vow; dedicate
أنذرَ إِنذاراً بِ To warn.
نَذْرٌ ج نُذُورٌ A vow.
إِنذارٌ A warning. Prognosis.
نَذيرٌ ج نُذُرٌ Vowed. Preacher.
مَنذُورٌ Vowed, consecrated.
نَذُلَ يَنذُلُ نَذالَةً To be abject.
نَذْلٌ ج أنذالٌ Vile, mean.
نرْجِسٌ Narcissus (plant).
نارِجيلٌ وَنَأرَجيلٌ Cocoa-nut.
نَارِجيلةٌ Nargileh.

نَرْدٌ Backgammon.

نَارَدِينٌ وَنَرْدِينٌ Spikenard.

نَارَنْجٌ Orange.

نَوْرَجٌ Thrashing-harrow.

نَزَّ يَنِزُّ نَزًّا To exude.

نَزٌّ نُزُوزٌ Leakage.

نَزَحَ يَنْزَحُ To exhaust a well.

نَزِحَ بِهِ وَانْتَزَحَ To emigrate.

نَازِحٌ وَنَزِيحٌ Distant, Emigrant.

نَزْرٌ Little ; mean.

نَزَعَ يَنْزَعُ وَانْتَزَعَ To remove.

نَازَعَ To fight, dispute with.

تَنَازَعَ To contend among themselves.

إِنْتَزَعَ To be taken away.

نَزْعٌ وَنِزَاعٌ Agony of death.

نِزَاعٌ وَمُنَازَعَةٌ Contention.

مَنْزُوعٌ Taken away, removed.

نُزِفَ ـــ To be exhausted (well).

نَزَفَ To have a flow of blood.

نَزْفُ ٱلدَّمِ Hemorrhage

نَزِقٌ Quick, hot-tempered.

نَيْزَكٌ ج نَيَازِكُ A falling star.

نَزَلَ يَنْزِلُ نُزُولاً To descend.

نَزَلَ فِي وَعَلَى To stop at a place.

نَزَّلَ وَأَنْزَلَ To bring down.

نَزَّلَ وَأَنْزَلَ عَلَى To reveal.

نَازَلَ To fight with.

تَنَزَّلَ عَنْ To renounce.

تَنَازَلَ To condescend.

اِسْتَنْزَلَ To seek or offer hospitaliy.

نَزْلٌ Place where men gather.

نُزُولٌ ج أَنْزَالٌ Guests.

نَزْلَةٌ A cold in the head.

نَازِلَةٌ ج نَوَازِلُ Calamity.

نَزِيلٌ ج نُزَلَاءُ A guest.

إِنْزَالٌ وَتَنْزِيلٌ A revelation.

تنازُلٌ Condescension, affability.

مَنْزِلٌ ج مَنَازِلُ Hostlery ; house.

تدبيرُ ٱلْمَنْزِلِ Domestic economy.

مَنْزِلَةٌ Degree, rank.

نَزِهَ يَنْزَهُ To abstain from evil.

تَنَزَّهَ To walk, divert one's self.

تَنَزَّهَ عَنْ To be free from.

نَزْهٌ وَنَزَاهَةٌ Purity of the soul.

نَزِيهٌ ج نُزَهَاءُ Pure, upright.

نُزْهَةٌ ج نُزَهٌ Amusement.

مُتَنَزَّهٌ Place of recreation.

نَسَبَ إِلَى To attribute, ascribe.

نَاسَبَ To resemble. Be suitable.

تَنَاسَبَ To correspond with.

إِنْتَسَبَ To trace one's genealogy.

إِسْتَنْسَبَ To approve.

نَسَبٌ ج أَنْسَابٌ Lineage.

نِسْبَةٌ Arithmetical proportion.

نِسْبَةٌ ج نِسَبٌ Relation, affinity.

نَسِيبٌ ج أَنْسِبَاءُ Kinsman.

مُنَاسَبَةٌ وَتَنَاسُبٌ Proportion.

مُنَاسِبٌ Suited to, convenient.

مُتَنَاسِبٌ Proportioned.

مَنْسُوبٌ إِلَى Ascribed, imputed.

نَاسُوتٌ Human nature.

نَسَجَ يَنْسُجُ نَسْجاً To weave.

إِنْتَسَجَ To be woven.

نِسَاجَةٌ The art of weaving.

نَسَّاجٌ Weaver.

نَسِيجٌ ج نُسُجٌ Woven tissue.

مِنْسَجٌ Loom.

مَنْسُوجٌ Woven ; tissue.

نَسَخَ يَنْسَخُ نَسْخاً To abrogate. abolish To copy, transcribe.

تَنَاسَخَ To follow successively.

إِنْتَسَخَ وَٱسْتَنْسَخَ To copy a (book).

إِنْتَسَخَ To annul, abrogate.

Abrogation. Transcribing. نَسْخٌ

Copy ; manuscript, نسخةٌ ج نُسَخٌ

Transmigration of souls. تَناسُخٌ

Abolished. Copied. مَنْسُوخٌ

An eagle ; vulture. نَسْرٌ ج نُسُورٌ

A fistula, sinus. نَاسُورٌ ج نَوَاسِيرُ

Beak of a bird. مِنْسَرٌ ج مَناسِيرُ

A scented white rose. نِسْرِينٌ

Nestorian. نَسْطُورِيٌّ ج نَساطِرَةٌ

To demolish winnow. نَسَفَ يَنْسِفُ

Chaff. Froth. نُسَافَةٌ

Winnowing-fan. مِنْسَفٌ ج مَناسِفُ

A razing machine. مِنْسَفَةٌ

To compose. نَسَقَ يَنْسُقُ نَسْقاً

To place in order; arrange. نَسَّقَ

To be arranged. تَنَسَّقَ وتَناسَقَ

Order ; system, method. نَسَقٌ

To lead an ascetic's life. نَسَكَ وتَنَسَّكَ

A hermit's life. نَسْكٌ وَنُسُكٌ

A hermit. نَاسِكٌ ج نُسَّاكٌ

To beget. نَسَلَ يَنْسُلُ نَسْلاً

To multiply (men). تَنَاسَلَ

Posterity, progeny. نَسْلٌ

Descent by generation. تَنَاسُلٌ

To blow gently. نَسَمَ يَنْسِمُ

To breathe. تَنَسَّمَ

Breath of life. Man. نَسَمَةٌ ج نَسَمَاتٌ

A soft breeze. نَسِيمٌ

An ape. نَسْنَاسٌ

Women. نُسْوَةٌ وَنِسَاءٌ وَنِسْوَانٌ

Sciatica. عِرْقُ ٱلنَّسَا

To forget. نَسِيَ يَنْسَى نَسْياً وَنِسْيَاناً

To cause to forget. نَسَّى وَأَنْسَى

To feign forgetfulness. تَنَاسَى

Forgetfulness. نَسْوَةٌ وَنِسْيَانٌ

Forgotten. مَنْسِيٌّ

To dry up ; ooze.	نَشَّ يَنِشُّ
Blotting-paper.	وَرَقٌ نَشَّاشٌ
To grow up. (child). To live, orginate. Rise.	نَشأَ يَنْشأُ وَنَشوَ يَنْشوُ
To follow, proceed from.	نَشأَ مِن
To create ; originate. Train up.	أَنْشأَ
He began to say.	أَنْشأَ يَقولُ
Growing, developing.	نُشوءٌ
Growing. Resulting.	نَاشِئٌ
Composition ; style. Origination.	إِنْشاءٌ
Native country. Source.	مَنْشأٌ
A creator. Author.	مُنْشِئٌ
To break out (war).	نَشبَ ـ بَيْنَ
An arrow (of wood).	نُشَّابٌ
An archer.	نَشَّابٌ
To seek a lost object.	نَشدَ يَنْشدُ
To abjure by God.	نَشدَهُ اللهَ
To cause to swear.	نَاشَدَ
To recite (verses).	أَنْشدَ
Chanting. Song.	نَشيدٌ
The Song of Songs.	نَشيدُ الأَنْشادِ
A poem. Song.	نَشيدةٌ ج نَشائدُ
Ammonia.	نَشادِرٌ ونُوشادِرٌ
To spread out. To saw.	نَشرَ يَنْشرُ
To publish.	نَشرَ يَنْشرُ
To resuscitate, raise to life.	نَشَرَ يَنْشرُ
To be extended.	تَنَشَّرَ وَانْتَشَرَ
To be published.	إِنْتَشرَ
Resurrection. Publication.	نَشْرٌ
ay of Resurrection.	يومُ النشورِ
written open paper.	نَشْرةٌ
havings, saw-dust.	نُشارةٌ
rt of sawing.	نِشارةٌ
issemination.	إِنْتِشارٌ
ispersed.	مَنْشورٌ وَمُنْتَشِرٌ
saw.	مِنْشارٌ ج مَناشِيرُ
rism. Circular.	مَنْشورٌ

مَنْشُورِيٌّ Prismatic form.

نَشِطَ يَنْشَطُ. وَتَنَشَّطَ To be active.

نَشَطَ يَنْشُطُ To knot (a cord).

نَشَّطَ إِلَى وَفِي To encourage in.

نَشَاطٌ Ardour, energy.

نَشِيطٌ ج نِشَاطٌ Active, energetic.

أُنْشُوطَةٌ ج أَنَاشِيط A knot, noose.

نَشِفَ يَنْشَفُ To become dry.

تَنَشَّفَ To dry, wipe (the body).

نَاشِفٌ Dry.

تَنْشِيفٌ Wiping, drying up.

مِنْشَفَةٌ ج مَنَاشِفُ A towel.

نَشِقَ يَنْشَقُ. وَٱسْتَنْشَقَ To inhale.

أَنْشَقَ To cause one to inhale.

نَشُوقٌ Snuff.

نَشَلَ يَنْشُلُ وَٱنْتَشَلَ To snatch; steal.

نَشَّالٌ A pickpocket.

مِنْشَلٌ وَمِنْشَالٌ ج مَنَاشِلُ A ladle.

نَشِيَ ـ نَشْوًا وَنَشْوَةً To be drunk.

نَشِيَ وَاسْتَنْشَى To smell. Be drunk.

نَشَّى To starch (linen).

نَشًا وَنَشَاءٌ Starch.

نَشْوَةٌ Odour. Exhilaration of wine.

نَشْوَانٌ م نَشْوَى ج نَشَاوَى Drunk.

نَصَّ ـ لِ To dictate a writing.

نَصٌّ ج نُصُوصٌ Text (of a book).

مَنْصُوصٌ عَلَيْهِ Clearly stated.

نَصَبَ يَنْصُبُ To fix, plant; raise.

نَصِبَ ـ نَصَبًا To strive, toil.

نَصَّبَ To appoint to an office.

نَاصَبَ To resist, oppose.

إِنْتَصَبَ To rise; stand erect.

نُصْبٌ ج أَنْصَابٌ Idol, statue.

نُصْبَ عَيْنِي Before my eye.

نِصَابٌ ج نُصُبٌ Origin Handle.

نَصَّابٌ Swindler.

Portion ; lot.	نَصِيبٌ ج أَنْصِبَةٌ
Fatiguing, toilsome.	نَاصِبٌ
Rank ; place.	مَنْصَبٌ ج مَنَاصِبُ
Elevated, erected.	مَنْصُوبٌ
To listen to	نَصَتَ يَنْصِتُ وأَنْصَتَ لَ
To silence.	أَنْصَتَ
To listen.	تَنَصَّتَ
To advise, counsel.	نَصَحَ يَنْصَحُ
To act sincerely.	نَصَحَ نُصْحاً
To receive advice.	إِنْتَصَحَ
A sincere adviser.	نَاصِحٌ
Sincere.	نَصُوحٌ وَنَصِيحٌ
Advice, counsel.	نَصِيحَةٌ ج نَصَائِحُ
To assist aid.	نَصَرَ يَنْصُرُ
To become a Christian.	تَنَصَّرَ
To strive to assist.	تَنَصَّرَ لَ
To help one another.	تَنَاصَرَ
To conquer, vanquish.	اِنْتَصَرَ عَلَى
To seek aid from.	إِسْتَنْصَرَ بِ
Help. Victory.	نَصْرٌ وَنُصْرَةٌ
A Christian.	نَصْرَانِيٌّ ج نَصَارَى
Christianity.	أَلنَّصْرَانِيَّةُ
Victory, triumph.	إِنْتِصَارٌ
Helper.	نَاصِرٌ ج نُصَّارٌ وأَنْصَارٌ
Helper.	نَصِيرٌ ج نُصَرَاءُ
Victorious, conquering.	مُنْتَصِرٌ
Aided Conqueror.	مَنْصُورٌ
To be pure, unmixed.	نَصَعَ يَنْصَعُ
Pure, unmixed (color)	نَاصِعٌ
To divide into two halves.	نَصَّفَ
To be just, equitable.	أَنْصَفَ
To get one's due.	إِنْتَصَفَ
To be mid-day.	إِنْتَصَفَ ٱلنَّهَارُ
Half. Middle.	نِصْفٌ ج أَنْصَافٌ
Justice, equity.	إِنْصَافٌ
Middle (of anything).	مُنْتَصَفٌ

To come out. (نَصَلَ يَنْصُلُ نُصُولاً)	To jump, skip. (نَطَّ يَنُطُّ نَطًّا)
Blade ; arrow-head. نَصْلٌ ج نِصَالٌ	To butt. نَطَحَ يَنْطَحُ نَطحاً
Forelock. نَاصِيَةٌ ج نَوَاصٍ	To butt one another. تَنَاطَحَ
To ooze, flow out. نَضَّ يَنِضُّ نَضًّا	Butted ; gored. نَطِيحٌ وَمَنْطُوحٌ
Remainder, rest. نُضَاضَةٌ	To guard. To wait. نَطَرَ يَنْطُرُ
To be well cooked ; ripe. نَضِجَ يَنْضَجُ	Keeper (of gardens). نَاطُورٌ ج. نَوَاطِيرُ
Cooked well, ripe. نَاضِجٌ	A watch-tower. مَنْطَرَةٌ ج مَنَاطِرُ
Of mature judgment. نَضِيجُ الرَّأْيِ	Very learned. نَطِسٌ وَنِطَاسِيٌّ
To ooze ; exude. نَضَحَ يَنْضَحُ نَضْحاً	To speak utter. نَطَقَ يَنْطِقُ
To sprinkle with. نَضَحَ بِ	To gird. نَطَّقَ
To pile up. نَضَدَ يَنْضِدُ . وَنَضَّدَ	To gird one's self. تَنَطَّقَ وَانْتَطَقَ
Laid in layers. نَضِيدٌ وَمَنْضُودٌ	To question, examine. إِسْتَنْطَقَ
To be soft. Blooming. نَضَرَ يَنْضُرُ	Speech ; articulation. نُطْقٌ
Bloom, freshness. نَضْرَةٌ وَنَضَارَةٌ	Belt, girdle. نِطَاقٌ ج نُطُقٌ
Blooming, verdant. نَضِرٌ وَنَضِيرٌ	Endowed with speech. نَاطِقٌ
To defend. نَاضَلَ عَنْ	The human soul. أَلنَّفْسُ النَّاطِقَةُ
Combat. نِضَالٌ وَمُنَاضَلَةٌ	Speech, language. Logic. مَنْطِقٌ
A horse-shoe. نَضْوَةٌ	Logical. Logician. مَنْطِقِيٌّ

A girdle, belt. مِنْطَقةٌ ج مَناطِقُ

The Zodiac. مِنْطَقةُ ٱلبُرُوجِ

Proper signification. مَنْطُوقٌ

Examiner *(law)*. مُستَنْطِقٌ

To foment. نَطَلَ يَنْطُلُ · ونطَّلَ

A fomentation. نَطُولٌ ج نُطُولاتٌ

To see, look at. نَظَرَ يَنظُرُ وإِلى

To consider. نظَرَ ينظُرُ في

To resemble ; rival. Debate. Superintend, inspect. نَاظَرَ

To debate with one another. تناظَرَ

To expect. إِنْتَظَرَ وَٱستَنْظَرَ

Vision. Favour. نَظَرٌ ج أَنْظارٌ

As regards. نَظَرًا وَ بِالنَّظَرِ إِلَى

A look, a glance. نَظْرَةٌ

Theoretical. Subjective. نَظَرِيٌّ

A problem. نظَرِيَّةٌ ج نَظَرِياتٌ

Inspector. Director. نَاظِرٌ ج نُظَّارٌ

Prime Minister. نَاظِرُ ٱلنظارِ

Minister of Works. ناظِرُ الاشغالِ

Minister of Public Instruction. نَاظِرُ ٱلمعارفِ العُمُوميةِ

Minister of Finance. نَاظِرُ ٱلماليةِ

Minister of Foreign Affairs. نَاظِرُ ٱلخارجية

Minister of the Interior. نَاظِرُ الدَّاخلية

Minister of War. نَاظِرُ الحربية

Minister of Justice. نَاظِرُ ٱلحَقَّانية

Administration. Ministry. نِظَارةٌ

A telescope. نَظَّارةٌ وَنَاظُورٌ

Spectacles. نَظَّارات

Similar, equal to. نَظِيرٌ ج نُظَراءُ

Expectation. إِنْتِظارٌ وَٱستِنْظارٌ

View. Aspect. مَنْظَرٌ ج مَناظِرُ

Speculum. مِنْظارٌ

Similar to. Inspector. مُناظِرٌ

Rivalry. Inspection. مُناظَرَةٌ

To be clean ; comely. نَظُفَ يَنْظُفُ

To cleanse, purify. نَظَّفَ

تَنَظَّفَ	To become clean.
نَظَافَةٌ	Cleanliness. Beauty.
نَظِيفٌ ج نظفاء	Clean; comely.
نَظَمَ ـِ	To arrange; compose (verses).
تَنَظَّمَ وَٱنْتَظَمَ	To be arranged.
نَظْمٌ	Arrangement. Poetry.
نِظَامٌ ج أَنْظِمَةٌ	System, method.
مُنَظَّمٌ	Well-arranged.
مَنْظُومٌ	Arranged, composed.
نَعَتَ يَنْعَتُ نَعْتًا	To describe.
نَعْتٌ	Qualification; attribute.
نَعْتٌ ج نُعُوت	Adjective.
مَنْعُوتٌ	A qualified noun.
نَعْجَةٌ ج نِعَاجٌ	A sheep, an ewe.
نَعَّارٌ	A kind of finch (bird).
(نَعَّارَةٌ ج نَعَائِرُ)	Earthen cooler.
نَاعُورَةٌ ج نَوَاعِير	Irrigating wheel.
نَعَسَ يَنْعَسُ	To grow sleepy.
أَنْعَسَ	To make sleepy.
تَنَاعَسَ	To feign sleep.
نُعَاسٌ	Sleepiness; drowsiness
نَاعِسٌ وَنَعْسَان ج نُعَّسٌ	Sleepy.
نَعَشَ يَنْعَشُ . وَأَنْعَشَ	To cheer, refresh.
إِنْتَعَشَ	To be revived, animated.
نَعْشٌ	Bier.
بنات نَعْشٍ الكبرى	Ursa Major.
نَعَقَ يَنْعَقُ	To croak, (crow).
نَعَلَ يَنْعَلُ نَعْلًا	To shoe (an animal).
نَعْلٌ ج نِعَالٌ	Shoe. Horse-shoe.
نَعِمَ يَنْعَمُ	To live in ease.
نَعُمَ يَنْعُمُ	To be soft to the touch.
نِعْمَ الرَّجُلُ	Excellent man!
نِعِمَّا	Excellent! Good!
نَعَّمَ	To make one easy in life.
أَنْعَمَ عَلَيْهِ	To bestow, confer on.
تَنَعَّمَ	To enjoy life; enjoy.

Yes, certainly, assuredly. نَعَمْ

Cattle, camles. نَعَمٌ ج أَنْعَامٌ

Blessing, favour. نِعْمَةٌ ج نِعَمٌ

Opulent, rich. وَاسِعُ ٱلنِّعْمَةِ

An ostrich. نَعَامَةٌ ج نَعَائِمُ وَنَعَامَاتٌ

Softness, smoothness. نُعُومَةٌ

Anemone. شَقَائِقُ ٱلنُّعْمَانِ

Soft, tender. نَاعِمٌ م نَاعِمَةٌ

Contented, tranquil. نَعِيمُ ٱلْبَالِ

Goodness, favour. إِنْعَامٌ ج إِنْعَامَاتٌ

Luxury; enjoyment. تَنَعُّمٌ

Benefactor; beneficent. مُنْعِمٌ

Mint (plant). نَعْنَعٌ وَنَعْنَاعٌ

To announce death. نَعَى يَنْعَى

News of death. نَعِيَّةٌ

Announcer of death. نَاعٍ ج نُعَاةٌ

To be troubled. نَغِصَ يَنْغَصُ نَغَصاً

To trouble, vex. نَغَّصَ وَأَنْغَصَ عَلَى

To be annoyed (in life). تَنَغَّصَ

To be inflamed, (wound). نَغِلَ يَنْغَلُ

Bastard. Hinny. نَغْلٌ

To sing softly. نَغَمَ يَنْغُمُ . وَنَغَّمَ

Melody, tune. نَغْمَةٌ ج نَغَمَاتٌ

To spit out. نَفَثَ يَنْفُثُ

Expectoration. Puff. نَفَثٌ

To blow (wind). نَفَحَ يَنْفَحُ نَفْحاً

A breath. A gift. نَفْحَةٌ ج نَفَحَاتٌ

To blow with the mouth. نَفَخَ يَنْفُخُ

To be puffed up proud. إِنْتَفَخَ

Breath, puff; blowing. نَفْخٌ

A water-bubble. Vesicle. نُفَاخَةٌ

Bellows. مِنْفَاخٌ وَمِنْفَخٌ ج مَنَافِخُ

Inflated, swollen. مَنْفُوخٌ

To be spent, consumed. نَفِدَ يَنْفَدُ

To consume. أَنْفَدَ وَٱسْتَنْفَدَ

To pierce through. نَفَذَ يَنْفُذُ مِنْ

نَفَذَ To be executed (an order).

نفذ إِلى To reach, arrive at.

نَفَّذَ وأَنفذ To send, execute.

نفاذٌ ونفوذٌ Execution; efficiency.

نافذ Efficacious, effective.

نافِذَةٌ ج نوافذ Window.

مَنفذٌ ج منافِذ Outlet, passage.

نفر ينفر مِن To turn away from.

نَفَّر To cause aversion.

تنافر To have mutual aversion.

نَفَرٌ ج أَنفار A number of men.

تَنَافُرٌ Contest, repulsion.

نفيرٌ A trumpet, bugle.

نفس ينفس To be precious.

نفست تنفس To give birth.

تَنَفَّسَ To breathe.

تَنَفَّسَ الصُّعداء To sigh deeply.

تَنافَسَ To contend together.

نفسٌ ج نفوسٌ وأَنفسٌ Soul, self.

جاء نفسُهُ He himself came.

نُفَساء A woman at child-birth.

نَفْسُ الشيءِ The thing itself.

نَفَسٌ ج أنفاس Breath. Style.

نفاسٌ Confinement, child-birth.

تَنَفُّسٌ Respiration, breathing.

نَفيسٌ ج نَفائِس A valuable thing.

أَنفَسُ More precious.

نفش ـ ونَفَّش To teaze (cotton).

تنفَّشَ To bristle (hair), ruffle (feathers).

نفض ـ ونفَّض To shake, shake off.

مِنفضة ج منافِض A plate for ashes.

نفط Matches.

نِفط Naptha, bitumen.

نفطة Pustule, vesicle.

مُنَفِّط A vesicating medicine.

نَفَعَ ينفع نفعًا To be useful.

To profit by. إنتفعَ بِ ومِنْ

To seek benefit. إستنفعَ

Advantage, benefit. نَفعٌ ومنفعةٌ

Useful, profitable. نافِعٌ

To have a brisk sale. To be exhausted. نفقَ ينفُقُ نفاقاً

To sell well. نفَّقَ وأنفقَ

To be hypocritical. نافَقَ

To exhaust one's means. انفقَ

Cost, expenses. نَفقةٌ ج نَفقاتٌ

Selling briskly. نافِقٌ

Hypocrisy. نفاقٌ ومُنافقةٌ

A hypocrite ; deceiver. مُنافِقٌ

A supererogatory deed. نفْلٌ

Booty. Present. نفلٌ ج أنفالٌ

Clover. نفلةٌ

To expel ; deny, exclude. نفى ينفِي

To banish, exile. نفى مِنْ

To oppose, be incompatible. نافى

To be excluded, rejected. إنتفى

Banishment. Negation. نَفيٌ

Particle of negation. حَرْفُ النفْيِ

Rejected as useless. نفاوةٌ ونُفايةٌ

Excluded. Exiled. مَنفِيٌّ

Incompatibility. تنافٍ ومنافاةٌ

Exile. مَنفًى ج مُنافٍ

To dig through. نقَبَ ينقُبُ نقباً

To travel over. نقَبَ في

To examine. نقَبَ عنْ

To put on a veil. تَنقبَ وانتقَبَ

A hole in a wall. نقبٌ ج انقابٌ

Veil of a woman. نِقابٌ ج نُقبٌ

Chief. Magistrate. نقيبٌ ج نقباء

Worthy deed. مَنقبةٌ ج مناقبُ

To revise, correct. نقَّحَ وأنقحَ

Revision, correction. تَنقيحٌ

To neck (bird). نقَدَ ينقُدُ نقداً

نَقَدَ لِ To pay in cash.

نَقَّدَ وتَنَقَّدَ To sort, pick out.

نَقْدٌ Ready money, cash.

نُقُودٌ ونَقْدِيَّةٌ Money, cash.

إِنْتِقَادٌ Testing ; criticism.

مِنْقَادٌ ج مَنَاقِيدُ Beak (of a bird).

نَقَذَ يَنْقُذُ وأَنْقَذَ To deliver, save.

نَقْذٌ Rescue, deliverance.

مُنْقِذٌ Deliverer.

نَقَرَ يَنْقُرُ To cut into (stone, wood) ; peck (bird).

نَقَّرَ ونَقَرَ عَنْ To examine.

نَاقَرَ مُنَاقَرَةً To dispute with.

نَقْرٌ Cavity. Carving.

نُقْرَةٌ ج نُقَرٌ Hollow, cavity.

نَقَّارٌ Sculptor, carver.

(نَقَّارَةٌ ونُقَيْرَةٌ) A small tambourine.

نَاقُورٌ ج نَوَاقِيرُ Hunting-horn.

مِنْقَارٌ ج مَنَاقِيرُ Beak of a bird.

نِقْرِسٌ Gout.

نَقَزَ يَنْقِزُ To skip.

نَاقُوسٌ ج نَوَاقِيسُ A church-bell.

نَقَشَ يَنْقُشُ To paint; sculpture.

نَاقَشَ مُنَاقَشَةً To reckon with.

نَقْشٌ ج نُقُوشٌ Painting. Tracing.

نِقَاشَةٌ Painting. Sculpture.

نَقَّاشٌ Painter. Engraver.

مِنْقَشٌ ومِنْقَاشٌ Brush. Chi sel.

نَقَصَ يَنْقُصُ To reduce, decrease.

تَنَاقَصَ To decrease gradually.

إِنْتَقَصَ To defame.

نَقْصٌ ونُقْصَانٌ Diminu tion ; loss.

نَاقِصٌ Diminished, defective.

نَقِيصَةٌ ج نَقَائِصُ Fault ; vice.

نَقَضَ يَنْقُضُ To demolish; annul.

نَاقَضَ To contradict.

إِنْتَقَضَ To be annulled.

Destruction, dissolution. نَقْضٌ

Beam, joist. نَقَضَةٌ

The contrary, opposite. نقيضٌ

Contrariety. تَنَاقُضٌ ومناقَضةٌ

To mark with dots. نَقَطَ يَنْقُطُ ونَقَّطَ

Dot of a letter. نُقْطَةٌ ج نُقَطٌ

Geometrical point. A drop.

Centre of a circle. نقطة الدَّائرة

Epilepsy. داء النقطة

To soak, macerate. نَقَعَ يَنقَعُ

To become stagnant. إِستنقع

Penetrating, pervading. ناقِعٌ

Infusion. نقيعٌ ومنقوعٌ

Dried apricots. (نقوعٌ)

A marsh, swamp. مُسْتَنْقَعٌ ونَقْعٌ

To take out. إِنتقف

To remove, transport. نَقَلَ يَنقل

To copy from ; quote. نَقَلَ عَنْ

To emigrate. انتقل من إلى

To die. إِنتقلَ إِلى رَحمةِ ٱللهِ

Transpsrt. Quotation. نَقْلٌ

Narrator. Bearer. Copyist. ناقِلٌ

Movable (estate). منتقِلٌ

Transferred ; quoted. مَنقولٌ

To punish, chastise. إِنتَقَمَ مِنْ

Vengeance. نقمةٌ وَٱنتقامٌ

An avenger. ناقِمٌ ومنتقِمٌ

To recover (from illness). نَقَهَ يَنقَهُ نَقْهاً

Convalescent. ناقِهٌ ونَقِهٌ ج نُقَّهٌ

To be pure. نَقِيَ يَنقى

To clean, purify. نَقَّى وَأَنقى

To choose, select. تَنَقَّى وَٱنتقى

To cleanse one's body. إِستنقى

Purity. Innocence. نَقاءٌ وَنَقاوةٌ

Pure. clean. Innocent. نقيٌّ

Purer, cleaner. أنقى

To afflict. نَكَبَ يَنكُبُ نَكْباً

To swerve from. نَكَبَ عَنْ

Adversity. نَكْبَةٌ ج نَكَبَاتٌ

Shoulder; side. مَنْكِبٌ ج مَنَاكِبُ

Afflicted, smitten. مَنْكُوبٌ

To find fault with. نَكَّتَ عَلَى

Speck. Witty saying. نُكْتَةٌ ج نُكَتٌ

Criticism. تَنْكِيتٌ

To break a compact. نَكَثَ يَنْكِثُ

To be broken (promise). إِنْتَكَثَ

Broken, violated. مَنْكُوثٌ

To marry. نَكَحَ يَنْكِحُ نِكَاحاً

To give in marriage. أَنْكَحَ

Marriage contract. نِكَاحٌ

To be hard. نَكِدَ ـ نَكَداً

To molest, annoy. نَكَّدَ وَنَاكَدَ

To molest each other. تَنَاكَدَ

Irritable, peevish. نَكِدٌ م نَكْدَاءُ

Annoyance, molestation. تَنْكِيدٌ

Unfortunate. مَنْكُودُ ٱلْحَظِّ

To be ignorant of. نَكِرَ يَنْكَرُ

To deny. أَنْكَرَ

To disapprove of. أَنْكَرَ عَلَى

To be disguised. تَنَكَّرَ

To deny. To censure. إِسْتَنْكَرَ

Cunning. نُكْرٌ وَنَكَارَةٌ

Indefinite noun. نَكِرَةٌ ج نَكِرَاتٌ

Denial. Repudiation. إِنْكَارٌ

Disguise. تَنَكُّرٌ

Illicit deed. مُنْكَرٌ ج مُنْكَرَاتٌ

Indeterminate noun. مُنَكَّرٌ

To push ; prick. نَكَزَ يَنْكُزُ نَكْزاً

To upset. نَكَسَ يَنْكُسُ وَنَكَّسَ

To be upset, inverted. تَنَكَّسَ

To have a relapse. نُكِسَ وَٱنْتَكَسَ

A relapse. نُكْسٌ وَٱنْتِكَاسٌ

Reversed. مَنْكُوسٌ وَمُنْتَكِسٌ

Ichneumon ; weasel.	نِمْس ج نُمُوسٌ
Law. Mosquito.	نَامُوس ج نَوَامِيسُ
Mosquito-net.	نَامُوسِيَّةٌ
Freckles.	نَمَشٌ
A straight sword.	نِمْشَةٌ
Freckled.	نَمِشٌ م نَمْشَاءُ ج نُمْشٌ
Cropped grass.	نَمِيصٌ
Manner ; fashion.	نَمَطٌ ج نِمَاطٌ
To write well, embellish.	نَمَّقَ
To be numb.	نَمِلَ ـ نَمَلاً
An ant. A pustule.	نَمْلَةٌ ج نَمْلٌ
Tip of the finger.	أَنْمُلَةٌ ج أَنَامِلُ
To embellish, adorn.	نَمْنَمَ
To grow, develop.	نَمَا يَنْمُو
To attribute, ascribe, to.	نَمَا إِلَى
Growth, increase.	نُمُوٌّ
Example.	نَمُوذَجٌ ج نَمُوذَجَاتٌ
To grow, increase.	نَمَى يَنْمِي

To exhaust. To dig.	نَكَشَ يَنْكُشُ
Pickaxe.	مِنْكَاشٌ ج مَنَاكِيشُ
To withdraw from.	نَكَصَ يَنْكُصُ عَنْ
To turn back.	نَكَصَ عَلَى عَقِبَيْهِ
To abstain from, reject.	نَكَفَ يَنْكُفُ عَنْ
To discuss, contend.	تَنَاكَفَ
To disdain, scorn.	إِسْتَنْكَفَ
To punish severely.	نَكَلَ وَنَكَّلَ بِ
A strong fetter.	نِكْلٌ ج أَنْكَالٌ
Chastisement ; warning.	نَكَالٌ
Smell of breath.	نَكْهَةٌ
To overcome ; vex.	نَكَى يَنْكِي نِكَايَةً
To make mischief.	نَمَّ ـ بَيْنَ
A calumniator.	نَمَّامٌ وَنَمُومٌ
Calumny, slander.	نَمِيمَةٌ ج نَمَائِمُ
To mark with numbers.	(نَمَّرَ)
Leopard ; panther. Tiger.	نِمْرٌ ج نُمُورَةٌ
Number *(For)*.	(نُمْرَةٌ ج نُمَرٌ)

To ascribe to one.	نمى إلى
To cause to grow.	أنمى
To trace one's origin to.	إنتمى إلى
Growing, increasing.	نامٍ
To plunder.	نَهَبَ يَنْهُبُ وانْتَهَبَ
Pillage, rapine.	نَهْبٌ
Booty, plunder, spoil.	نُهْبَةٌ
Pillager, depredator,	نَهّابٌ
Pillaged, plundered.	مَنْهُوبٌ
To follow (the way).	نَهَجَ يَنْهَجُ
To be out of breath:	نَهِجَ يَنْهَجُ
Rapid breathing, panting.	نَهَجٌ
A plain road. Way.	مَنْهَجٌ ومِنْهاجٌ ج مَناهِج
To contend with in battle.	ناهَدَ
To sigh, groan.	تَنَهَّدَ
To flow.	نَهَرَ يَنْهُرُ نَهْراً
To chide, check.	نَهَرَ وانْتَهَرَ
River.	نَهْرٌ ج أَنْهُرٌ وأَنْهارٌ
Day.	نَهارٌ ج نُهُرٌ
To be near.	نَهَزَ يَنْهَزُ نَهْزاً
To approach, be close to.	ناهَزَ
To seize an opportunity.	إنْتَهَزَ
Opportunity.	نُهْزَةٌ ج نُهَزٌ
To bite.	نَهَشَ يَنْهَشُ نَهْشاً
To rise, get up.	نَهَضَ يَنْهَضُ عَنْ
To revolt, rise against.	نَهَضَ على
To rush towards.	نَهَضَ إلى
To urge ; cause to rise,	أَنْهَضَ
To rise up.	إنْتَهَضَ
To urge, incite.	إسْتَنْهَضَ لِ
Lifting ; rising.	نُهُوضٌ
To bray.	نَهَقَ يَنْهَقُ نُهاقاً ونَهِيقاً
To overcome, wear out.	نَهَكَ يَنْهَكُ
To defame.	نَهَكَ عِرْضَهُ وانْتَهَكَ
To weaken.	نَهَكَ وانْتَهَكَ
Enfeebled, weakened.	مَنْهُوكٌ

To drink. نَهَلَ يَنْهَلُ نَهلاً

A watering place. مَنْهَلٌ ج مَناهِلُ

To be ravenous. نَهِمَ يَنْهَمُ

An insatiable avidity. نَهْمٌ

Greedy ; glutton. نَهِمٌ وَنَهِيمٌ

To prohibit. نَهَى يَنْهَى عَنْ

To accomplish, achieve. أَنْهَى

To inform. أَنْهَى إِلَى

To lead to. إِنتَهَى إِلَى

To be completed. تَناهَى وَٱنْتَهَى

To abstain from. تَناهَى وَٱنْتَهَى عَنْ

Prohibition, interdiction. نَهْيٌ

Intelligence. نُهًى

End, utmost. نِهايَةٌ ج نِهايَاتٌ

One who forbids. نَاهٍ

What a man ! نَاهِيكَ مِنْ رَجُلٍ

End, termination ; limit. إِنْتِهَاءٌ

Prohibited. مَنْهِيٌّ عَنْهُ

Prohibited things. أَلْمَناهِي

Infinite ; endless. غَيْرُ مُتَناهٍ

End, extremity ; limit. مُنْتَهًى

The final plural. مُنْتَهَى ٱلجُموعِ

Storm ; tempest. نَوْءٌ ج أَنْوَاءٌ

To take one's place. نَابَ يَنُوبُ عَنْ

To repent. نَابَ وَأَنَابَ إِلَى اللهِ

To overtake, befall. نَابَ وَٱنْتَابَ

To appoint a substitute. أَنَابَ

To do a thing in turn. تَناوَبَ عَلَى

The Nubians. نُوبٌ وَنُوبَةٌ

A Nubian. نُوبِيٌّ

A turn ; time. نَوْبَةٌ ج نُوَبٌ

Musical concert. نَوْبَةٌ ج نَوْبَاتٌ

Lieutenancy, vicarship. نِيابَةٌ

In place of, instead of. نِيابَةً عَنْ

Substitute, deputy. نائِبٌ ج نُوَّابٌ

The subject of a passive verb. نائِبُ ٱلفاعِلِ

Parliament. مَجْلِسُ ٱلنوَّاب

Misfortune. نائِبَةٌ ج نَوَائِبُ

Mariner, sailor. نُوتِيٌّ ج نوتِيَّة

To wail ; coo (pigeon). نَاحَ يَنوحُ

To bewail the dead. نَاحَ عَلَى

Lamentation. نَوْحٌ وَنُوَاحٌ وَنِيَاحٌ

A mourner, weeper. نائحٌ

Wailing women. نائِحَةٌ ج نَوَائِحُ وَنائِحات

To cause a camel to kneel. أَنَاخَ

To abide in a place. أَناخَ بِالْمَكان

Climate. مُنَاخٌ ج مُنَاخَات

To shine, sparkle. نَارَ يَنُورُ وَأَنَارَ

To flower, blossom (plant). نَوَّرَ وَأَنَارَ

To light up. نَوَّرَ وَأَنَارَ

To be enlightened by. إِسْتَنَارَ بِ

Fire. نَارٌ ج نِيرَانٌ

A volcano. جَبَلُ ٱلنَّار

A steam-ship. مَرْكَبُ ٱلنَّار

Light. نورٌ ج أنْوارٌ

Gipsy. نوريٌّ ج نَوَرٌ

Illumination. إِنَارَةٌ وَتَنْوِيرٌ

Shining, bright. نيِّرٌ م نيِّرَةٌ

Giving light ; shining. مُنِيرٌ

A light-house. Minaret. منارَةٌ

A threshing-harrow. نَوْرَجٌ

Men; people. (for أَنَاسٌ) نَاسٌ

Sarcophagus. نَاوُوسٌ ج نَوَاوِيس

To engage in a combat. نَاوَشَ

To attack one another. تَنَاوَشَ

To take out. إِنتَاشَ

To flee away. نَاصَ يَنُوصُ عَنْ

A refuge, an asylum. مَنَاصٌ

To suspend to. نَاطَ يَنُوطُ وَأَنَاطَ بِ

Dependent on. مَنُوطٌ بِ

To divide, classify, specify. نَوَّعَ

To be of different kinds. تَنوَّعَ

Kind, sort species. نَوْعٌ ج أنواع

Diversified ; diverse, متنوّعٌ

To overlook, surmount. نافَ على

More, upwards of. نَيّفٌ وَنَيْفٌ

Upwards of ten. عشرةٌ وَنيّفٌ

Water-lily. نوفرٌ

Jet d'eau. نوفرة

She-camel. ناقةٌ ج نوقٌ ونياقٌ

Dainty, fastidious. نَيّقٌ

To give to, hand over. ناوَلَ

To procure for one. نالَ

To obtain, receive. تناوَلَ

A loom. نَوْلٌ ج أنوال

Freight money. ناوُلونُ

Mode, manner, fashion. منوالٌ

To sleep. نامَ ينامُ نَوْماً وَنياماً

To put to sleep. نَوَّمَ وأَنامَ

To feign sleep تناوَمَ

Sleep, slumber. نَوْمٌ

Sleeping ; sleeper. نائِمٌ ج نيام

Sleep. A dream. مَنامٌ

A dormitory. مَنامٌ وَمَنامَةٌ

Hypnotic, soporific. مُنَوِّمٌ

To mark with the double vowels ( ) و ( ) ( ). نَوَّنَ تنويناً

A dimple on chin. نُونَةٌ

To purpose, resolve. نَوَى يَنْوِي

Distance, absence. نَوًى

A fruit stone. Nucleus. نَواةٌ ج نَوًى

Intention. نِيّةٌ ج نِيّاتٌ

Intended, purposed. مَنْوِيٌّ

Raw, underdone. نِيءٌ ونِيٌّ

Canine tooth ; tusk. نابٌ ج أنياب

To give rest. (نَيَّحَ)

To die. تَنَيَّحَ

Yoke. نيرٌ ج أنيارٌ وَنيرانٌ

نَيْرٌ ج أَنْيَارٌ	Woof.
نَيِّرَةٌ	Tooth-gum.
نِيسَانُ	April.
نِيشَانٌ ج نَيَاشِينُ	A decoration.
نَافَ يَنِيفُ عَلَى	To surpass, exceed.
نِيَافَةٌ	Eminence, (*title of honour*).
نَيِّفٌ وَنَيْفٌ . نُوف	*See under*
نَالَ يَنَالُ	To obtain, acquire.
نَالَ وَأَنَالَ	To cause to obtain.
نِيْلٌ	Indigo-plant ; indigo.
أَلنِّيلُ	The Nile.
نِيلُوفَرٌ وَنَيْنُوفَرٌ	Nenuphar, lotus.
نِينَوَى	Nineveh.
نَايٌ ج نَايَاتٌ	A kind of flute.

ه

ه	As a numeral sign = 5.
ه	His, him, it.
هَا	Her, it.
هَا	Lo ! Behold !
هاكَ	Take thou ! Here you are !
هَبْ . وَهَبْ	Grant ! (*Imp, of*
هَبْنِي قلت	Suppose I said.
هَبَّ يَهُبُّ	To blow (wind).
هَبَّ وَأَهَبَّ	To shake (a sword).
هَبَّ يَفْعَلُ	To begin to do.
هَبَّ مِنَ ٱلنَّوْمِ	To awake from sleep.
هَبَابٌ	Fine dust in the air.

Blowing (of wind). هُبُوبٌ	To defame, disgrace. هَتَكَ سِتره
Place of blowing of wind. مَهَبٌّ	To be disclosed, divulged. تَهَتَّك
Flesh, a piece of meat. هَبْرٌ	Solution of continuity. هَتْكٌ
A wind raising dust. رِيحٌ هَبَارِيَّةٌ	Disgrace, dishonour. (هَتِيكَةٌ)
Flakes. Scurf. هِبْرِيَةٌ	Rapid, quick (march). هَجَاجٌ
To descend ; fall. هَبَطَ يَهْبُطُ	To subside. هَجَأَ يَهْجَأُ هَجْأً
To cause to come down. أَهْبَطَ ه	To spell (a ward). تَهَجَّأَ
Fall ; abatement. هَبْطٌ وَهُبُوطٌ	To forsake, renounce. هَجَرَ يَهْجُرُ
A fall; a descent. هَبْطَةٌ	To emigrate. هَاجَرَ مِنْ
To take a vapour bath. (تَهَبَّلَ)	Forsaking. هَجْرٌ وَهِجْرَانٌ
Vapour; steam. (هَبْلَةٌ)	Separation; flight. هِجْرَةٌ
Fumigation. (تَهْبِيلٌ)	The Hegira, Moslem Era. أَلْهِجْرَةُ
Dust flying in the a ir. هَبَاءٌ	Hot mid-day. هَاجِرَةٌ وَهَجِيرَةٌ
To defame. هَتَرَ يَهْتِرُ هَتْراً	Emigrant. مُهَاجِرٌ
To be reckless; neglect. إِسْتَهْتَرَ	Emigration. مُهَاجَرَةٌ
To call, shout. هَتَفَ يَهْتِفُ هُتَافاً	Deserted, forsaken. مَهْجُورٌ
Call, cry, shauting. هُتَافٌ	To occur to the mind. هَجَسَ يَهْجِسُ
To tear off ; divulge. هَتَكَ يَهْتِكُ	A troubled though t. هَاجِسٌ

هَجَعَ يَهْجَعُ هُجُوعاً To sleep; subside.

هَجِيعٌ مِنَ ٱللَّيلِ Part of the night.

هَجَمَ يَهْجِمُ عَلَى To assail, surprise.

هَاجَمَ To attack suddenly.

هَجْمَةٌ A surprise, sudden attack.

هُجُومٌ Sudden attack or surprise.

هَجُنَ يَهْجُنُ هُجْنَةً To be low, vile.

إِسْتَهْجَنَ To consider mean.

هُجْنَةٌ Fault, meanness.

هَجِينٌ Fast dromedary.

هَجَا يَهْجُو هَجْواً To mock, ridicule.

هَجَا وَهَجَّى وَتَهَجَّى To spell.

هِجَاءٌ A satire, lampoon.

هِجَاءٌ وَتَهْجِيَةٌ وَتَهَجٍّ Spelling.

حُرُوفُ ٱلْهِجَاءِ The alphabet.

هُجُوَّةٌ وَأُهْجِيَّةٌ ج أَهَاجِي Satire.

هَدَّ يَهُدُّ To pull down, demolish.

هَدَّدَ وَتَهَدَّدَ To threaten, menace.

إِنْهَدَّ To be pulled down.

هَدٌّ Destruction, demolition.

تَهْدِيدٌ وَتَهَدُّدٌ Threatening.

مِهَدَّةٌ Sledge-hammer.

هَدَأَ يَهْدَأُ To subside, calm down.

هَدَّأَ تَهْدِئَةً To calm, appease.

هُدُوءٌ Rest, tranquillity, quiet.

هُدْبٌ ج أَهْدَابٌ Eye-lashes; fringe.

هَدَرَ يَهْدُرُ To be spent uselessly. Squander.

هَدِيرٌ Roaring (of waves, &c.)

هَدَفَ يَهْدُفُ إِلَى To approach.

هَدَفٌ ج أَهْدَافٌ Target, aim.

هَدَلَ ـ هَدْلاً To let down.

هَدِلَ وَتَهَدَّلَ To hang down.

أَبُو هَدْلَانَ A bovine epidemic. Rinderpest.

هَدَمَ يَهْدُمُ هَدْماً To pull down.

تَهَدَّمَ وَٱنْهَدَمَ To be destroyed.

هَدْمٌ Destruction, demolition.

Clothes, garments.	(هدوم)
Death.	هادِم اَللّذاتِ
Destroyed, demolished.	مهدوم
To come to an agreement.	هادَنَ
To make a truce.	تهادن
Armistice, truce.	هدنة ومهادنة
Hoopoo (bird).	هدْهد ج هداهد
To lead aright, guide.	هدى يهدي
To give a present.	أهدى
To make mutual presents.	تَهادى
To be rightly guided.	اهتدى
To ask for guidance.	إستهدى
The right path.	هداية وهُدى
A present, gift.	هَديّة ج هدايا
Guide, leader.	هادٍ ج هُداة
Rightly guided, offered.	مهديّ
To ponder over.	هذّ ـ هذيذاً في
This.	هَذا م هَذه وهَذي

Dual of هَذا	هذان
To trim; improve.	هذّب
To be educated; improved.	تَهذّب
Education. Correction.	تهذيب
Refined. polished.	مهذّب ومتهذب
To babble,	هَذر يهذر هَذْراً
Fem of. هذا	هَذه
To talk irrationally.	هَذى يهذي
Delirium.	هذاء وهَذيان
A cat.	هرّ ج هِررة
A she-cat.	هرّة ج هِرر
Whining, yelping.	هَرير
To become tattered,	هرئ يهرأ
To run away, flee.	هَرب يهرب
To put to flight; smuggle.	هرّب
Escape, flight.	هَرب
A fugitive.	هَارب
Place of refuge.	مَهرب ج مهارب

هَرَّجَ	To joke, jest.
هَرْجٌ	Agitation, tumult.
هَارِجٌ وَمُهَرِّجٌ	Jester ; buffoon.
هرس يهرس	To pound, crush.
هَرَّشَ بَيْنَ	To excite discord.
تَهَارَشَ وَاهترش	To sport.
هَرَاشٌ	Tumult, row.
هرطوقيٌّ ج هَراطقَةٌ	Heretic.
هرع يهرع هرعاً	To walk fast.
هَرَقَ يهرق. وهرَّقَ	To pour out.
إهراقٌ	Effusion, shedding.
هرقْلُ	Heraclius *(Emperor)*.
هرم يهرُمُ	To be decrepit.
هرم يهرِمُ . وهرَّمَ	To cut, hash.
هرَّمَ وأهرَمَ	To render one old.
هرمٌ	Decrepitude.
هَرَمٌ ج أهرامٌ	A pyramid.
هرِمٌ ج هَرِمُونَ	Very old.
هَرْوَلَ	To walk fast.
هِرَاوَةٌ ج هَرَاوَى	A cudgel.
(هَرَى يهري هَرْياً)	To wear out.
(إِهْتَرَى)	To get worn out.
هُرْيٌ ج أهراء	Granary.
هزَّ يهز هزًّا	To shake, brandish.
إِهْتَزَّ وانهزَّ	Ta be shaken.
هَزَّةٌ	Earthquake.
هزِيزٌ	Sound. Rustling.
هزَأَ وهزِئَ يهزأُ بِ	To mock at.
تهزَّأ واستهزأ بِ	To ridicule.
هزْء وهزُوء واستهزاء	Mockery.
هزِيجٌ من اللَّيْلِ	Part of the night.
أهزوجةٌ ج أهازيج	A song.
هزِيعٌ من اللَّيْلِ	Part of the night.
هَيْزَعَةٌ	Fear. Tumult.
هَزَلَ يهزِلُ هزْلاً	To joke, jest.
هَزَلَ هُزْلاً . وهزَّلَ	To emaciate.

هَزَلَ يَهزُلُ To be emaciated.

هَزْلٌ وهَزَالَةٌ Sport, jest, joke.

هُزالٌ Thinness, emaciation.

هَزِيل و مَهْزول Thin, meagre.

هَزَمَ يَهزِمُ To put to flight.

إِنهزام To be put to flight.

هَزْم و هَزِيمة Rout, defeat.

هَزِيم Thunder. Rain.

هَزْهَزَ To shake, agitate.

هَشَّ يَهِشُّ To be cheerful.

هَشٌّ Joyous cheerful.

هَشٌّ وهَشاشٌ Tender, soft.

(هَشَلَ يَهشِلُ هَشْلاً) To roam about.

(هَشَلَ) To drive away, expel.

هَشَمَ يَهشِمُ وهَشَّمَ To crush, break.

تَهَشَّمَ وانهَشَمَ To be crushed.

هَضْبَةٌ ج هِضابٌ A hill.

هَضَمَ يَهضِمُ To break. To digest.

هَضَمَ وتَهَضَّمَ واهتَضَمَ To oppress.

هَضَمَ حقَّهُ To wrong.

إِنهضَمَ To be digested (food).

هَضْم وانهِضام Digestion.

سُوءُ الهَضْمِ Indigestion.

هَضِيمة ج هَضائِمُ Injury, wrong.

هَطَلَ يَهطِلُ هَطْلاً To rain.

هَطَلٌ Fine but continuous rain.

هَفَّ يَهِفُّ To rustle; walk quickly.

هَفَّ إِلى To long for.

هَفَتَ يَهفِتُ To fly up and down.

تَهافَتَ عَلى To rush to, or into.

هَفْوة ج هَفَوات A slip, fault.

هافٍ Famished.

هَكذا Thus, so.

تَهَكَّمَ عَلى To mock at, deride.

تَهَكُّمٌ Mockery. Irony. Sarcasm.

هَلْ *Particle of Interrogation.*

Did you write ?	هَلْ كَتَبْتَ
Is not ? Why not ?	هَلاَّ
Come! Hasten!	حيَّ هلْ
To appear, (new moon).	هَلَّ يَهِلُّ
To praise God.	هلَّلَ
To exult, be joyous.	تهلَّلَ
To pour down (rain).	إِنهَلَّ
The new moon.	هِلٌّ وَهَلَّةٌ
New moon. Crescent.	هلال
Semi-lunar, crescentic.	هِلاَلِيٌّ
Act of parising God.	تَهْليلٌ
Elliptical. Oval.	أَهْليلجيٌّ
To perish, die.	هلكَ يَهْلِكُ
To ruin. destroy.	هلك وأَهْلَكَ
To squander, exhaust.	إِستهْلكَ
Ruin, loss. Death.	هلاَكٌ
Perishing, lost, dead.	هالِكٌ
Perdition, ruin.	تهْلُكَة
Dangerous place.	مَهْلَكَةٌ
Here ! Come here !	هَلُمَّ
And so on, *et cœtera*.	هَلُمَّ جرًّا
Jelly.	هُلاَمٌ
Jelly-like, gelatinous.	هُلاَمِيٌّ
They ; their ; them.	هُمْ
Their book.	كِتابُهُمْ
He struck them.	ضَرَبَهُمْ
To cause anxiety.	هَمَّ يَهُمُّ . وأَهَمَّ
To desire, seek.	هَمَّ يَهُمُّ هَمًّا ب
To be grieved.	إِهتمَّ
To take pains in...	إِهتمَّ بِ
To be solicitous about	إِهْتمَّ لِ
Care, anxiety.	همٌّ ج هُمومٌ
Concern ; energy.	هِمَّةٌ ج هِمَمٌ
Reptile, insect.	هَامَّةٌ ج هوامُّ
Energetic.	هُمامٌ
More important.	أَهَمُّ

Care, effort.	إِهْتِمامٌ
Important matter.	مُهِمٌّ ج مَهامُّ
Provisions, necessaries.	مُهِمّاتٌ
Preoccupied, anxious.	مَهْمومٌ
Stupid, savage people.	هَمَجٌ
To subside.	هَمَدَ يَهْمُدُ هُمُودًا
To extinguish ; clam.	هَمَّدَ وأَهْمَدَ
To pour out.	هَمَرَ يَهْمُرُ
To be poured out, flow.	إِنْهَمَرَ
To beat ; push.	هَمَزَ يَهْمِزُ هَمْزًا
A hemza = (ء)	هَمْزَةٌ ج هَمَزاتٌ
A spur, goad.	مِهْمازٌ ج مَهامِيزُ
Marked with a hemza.	مَهْمُوزٌ
To mumble.	هَمَسَ يَهْمِسُ هَمْسًا
Margin of a book.	هامِشٌ
To shed tears.	هَمَعَ يَهْمَعُ
To press, urge.	هَمَكَ يَهْمُكُ
To be engrossed in.	إِنْهَمَكَ فِي
To rain quietly.	هَمَلَ يَهْمُلُ
To neglect, forget.	أَهْمَلَ
To be negligent,	(تَهامَلَ في)
Negligence, carelessness.	(تَهامُلٌ)
Unused, obsolete (word).	مُهْمَلٌ
Neglected.	مُهْمَلٌ
To mumble, mutter.	هَمْهَمَ
To fall, flow, run.	هَمَا يَهْمُو
Belt.	هِمْيانٌ ج هَمايِينُ
Royal.	هَمايُونٌ وهَمايُونِيٌّ
They ; their · them, *fem.*	هُنَّ
To congratulate.	هَنَّأَ بِ
To enjoy, relish.	هَنِئَ يَهْنَأُ بِ
To enjoy, relish.	تَهَنَّأَ تَهَنُّؤًا بِ
Wholesome. Pleasant.	هَنِيءٌ
Congratulation.	تَهْنِئَةٌ
India, the Indies.	أَلْهِنْدُ
Cocoa-nut.	جَوْزُ الْهِنْدِ

هنديٌّ ج هنودٌ	An Indian.
هندباء	Endive, wild chicory.
هندَسَ	To make a plan.
هندَسةٌ	Engineering. Architecture.
علم الهندسةِ	Geometry.
هندسيٌّ	Geometrical.
مُهندِس	Geometrician. Architect. Engineer.
هندَمَ	To arrange, adorn.
هنا وهَهُنا	Here *(adv)*.
هنا وهُنالِكَ	There, yonder.
هنيّةٌ وهُنيهةٌ	A little while, trifle.
هُوَ	He, it.
هُوّةٌ ج هُوَتٌ	An abyss.
هادَ وتهوَّدَ	To become a Jew.
هاوَدَ	To abate price.
يهودُ	Jews.
يهوديٌّ	Jew.
يهوديّةٌ	Jewess. Judea.
هودَجٌ ج هوادِج	Camel-litter.
هُوذا	Lo ! Behold !
تهوَّرَ	To roll down, fall down.
تهوَّرَ	To rush imprudently.
تهوُّرٌ	Rashness. Collapse.
هَوَس	Folly. Passionate desire.
(هَوِيسٌ)	Scorched green wheat.
هاشَ يهوشُ	To be agitated ; (bark).
هوشةٌ ج هَوشاتٌ	Tumult.
هاعَ يهاعُ ويهوعُ هَوعاً	To vomit.
هالَ يهولُ	To frighten.
هوَّلَ عليهِ بِ	To threaten with.
إهتالَ	To be terrified.
هَولٌ ج أهوالٌ	Terror, fright.
أبو الهولِ	The sphinx.
هائلٌ ومَهولٌ	Frightful, terrible.
هالةٌ ج هالاتٌ	Halo (of moon).
هامةٌ ج هاماتٌ	Head. Chief.

To be easy. هَانَ يَهُونُ هَوْنًا عَلى

To be despised. هَانَ يَهُونُ هَوْنًا

To facilitate. هَوَّنَ عَلى

To despise. أَهَانَ

To neglect. تَهَاوَنَ بِ

Contemptibleness. هَوَانٌ

Disdain ; insult. إِهَانَةٌ ج إِهَانَاتٌ

Negligence ; idleness. تَهَاوُن

Mortar (for pounding). هَاوُنٌ

Light, easy to do. هَيْنٌ وَهَيِّنٌ

Lighter, easier. أَهْوَن

Disdained ; injured. مُهَانٌ

Contempt, shame. مَهَانَةٌ

To fall. هَوَى يَهْوِي هَوِيًّا

To love ; desire. هَوِيَ يَهْوَى

To ventilate. هَوَّى تَهْوِيَة

To fall down ; descend. أَهْوَى

Passionate desire. هَوًى ج أَهْوَاء

Ringing in the ears. هَوِيٌّ

Air, atmosphere. هَوَاءٌ ج أَهْوِيَةٌ

Atmospherical. هَوَائِيٌّ

The lower world ; hades. اَلْهَاوِيَةُ

She, it ; they. هِيَ ج هُنَّ

To prepare. هَيَّأَ تَهْيِئَةً

To be prepared for. تَهَيَّأَ لِ

Form, aspect. هَيْئَةٌ ج هَيْئَاتٌ

Astronomy. عِلْمُ ٱلْهَيْئَةِ

To fear ; revere. هَابَ يَهَابُ وَٱهْتَابَ

Imp. of هَابَ and وَهَبَ هَبْ

Respect, awe, veneration. هَيْبَةٌ

More respected. أَهْيَب

Venerable ; respected. مَهِيبٌ

Fear ; veneration, respect. مَهَابَة

Give ! هَاتِ ج هَاتُوا

To be agitated, excited. هَاجَ يَهِيجُ

To excite, agitate. هَاجَ وَهَيَّجَ

To be agitated. تهيَّج و اهْتاجَ

Agitation, excitement. هيجانٌ

Battle, combat ; strife. هيجاء

Agitated, excited. هائجٌ

Diarrhœa. هيضةٌ

Slim. أهْيفُ م هَيْفاء ج هِيفٌ

Temple ; alter, هيكل ج هياكل

The skeleton. الهيكل العظميُّ

Matter. هيولى

Material *(adj)*. هيوليٌّ و هَيُولانيٌّ

To love passionately. هام يَهيم

Passionate love. هُيامٌ

Love stricken. هائِمٌ ج هُيَّمٌ و هُيَّامٌ

Starless night. ليلٌ أهْيمُ

Heart lost in love. قلبٌ مُستهامٌ

God (the Protector), ألمُهَيْمِن

Easy. هَيْنٌ وهَيِّنٌ

Far ! Far away ! هَيْهاتَ

Come ! Quick ! هيّا وهيّ

و

As a numeral sign=6. و

And. و

By God ! والله

Oh ! Ah ! Alas ! وا

Shame. Dishonour. إِبَةٌ

Pestilence. وباء وَوَبَأ ج أوْبئةٌ وأوْباء

Epidemic ; pestiiential. وَبائيٌّ

Pestilential. وَبِيءٌ ومَوْبُوءٌ

To rebuke, reprimand. وَبَّخَ

Scolding, rebuking. تَوْبِيخٌ

Cony. وَبْرٌ ج وُبُورٌ وَوِبَارٌ

Soft hair (of animals). وَبْرٌ

Nomad people. أَهْلُ ٱلْوَبَرِ

Low people. وَبَشٌ ج أَوْبَاشٌ

To rain. وَبَلَ يَبِلُ وَبْلاً

To be unhealthy, (land). وَبُلَ يَوْبُلُ

A heavy shower. وَبْلٌ وَوَابِلٌ

Unhealthiness. Hardship. وَبَالٌ

Unhealthy. Hard. وَبِيلٌ

To make firm. وَتَدَ يَتِدُ وَوَتَّدَ

Wooden peg. A kind of foot *(Prosody)*. وَتِدٌ ج أَوْتَادٌ

Mountains. أَوْتَادُ ٱلْأَرْضِ

To string a bow. وَتَرَ وَوَتَّرَ وَأَوْتَرَ

To be strained hard. تَوَتَّرَ

To follow one another. تَوَاتَرَ

Single ; odd number. وِتْرٌ

Cord of a circle. وَتَرٌ وَوَتَرٌ

String of a bow, or musical instrument. Tendon وَتَرٌ ج أَوْتَارٌ

Succession. تَوَاتُرٌ

Repeated at intervals. مُتَوَاتِرٌ

Often, repeatedly. مُتَوَاتِراً

A bruise or wound. وَثْءٌ وَوَثَاءَةٌ

To leap. وَثَبَ يَثِبُ وَثْباً وَوُثُوباً

A leap, jump. An assault. وَثْبَةٌ

To rely upon. وَثِقَ يَثِقُ بِ

To be firm. وَثُقَ يَوْثُقُ وَثَاقَةً

To make firm. وَثَّقَ

To make a covenant with. وَاثَقَ

To fetter, tie fast. أَوْثَقَ بِٱلْوِثَاقِ

To trust, rely upon. إِسْتَوْثَقَ مِنْ

Confidence. ثِقَةٌ

A tie, fetter, rope, strap. وِثَاقٌ

Firm or solid. Reliable. وَثِيقٌ

Compact, alliance. وَثِيقَةٌ ج وَثَائِقُ

Firmer, firmest.	أوْثَق وُثْقَى
The strongest hold.	أَلعُرْوَةُ ٱلوُثْقَى
Covenant.	مِيثَاقٌ ج مَوَاثِيقُ
An idol.	وَثَنٌ ج أَوْثَانٌ
Idolater ; heathen.	وَثَنِيٌّ ج وَثَنِيُّون
A sprain.	وَثْيٌ
To be necessary, due.	وَجَبَ يَجِبُ
To make binding.	أَوْجَبَ
To be worthy of.	إِسْتَوْجَبَ
A set of the same kind.	وَجْبَةٌ
Necessity, duty.	وُجُوبٌ
Affirmation.	إِيجَابٌ
Affirmative, positive.	إِيجَابِيٌّ
Necessary, obligatory.	وَاجِبٌ
Duty.	وَاجِبٌ ج وَاجِبَاتٌ
Cause, motive, reason.	مُوجِبٌ
According to.	بِمُوجِبِ
To find.	وَجَدَ يَجِدُ
To be ; to exist.	وُجِدَ
To create, produce.	أَوْجَدَ إِيجَاداً
To be grieved for.	تَوَجَّدَ لِ
Wealth, competence.	جِدَةٌ
Love ; joy ; grief.	وَجْدٌ
Inner consciousness.	وِجْدَانٌ
Existence.	وُجُودٌ
Found ; existing.	مَوْجُودٌ
Existing things.	أَلْمَوْجُودَاتُ
Grotto, cave.	وَجْرٌ ج أَوْجَارٌ
Den, lair.	وِجَارٌ ج أَوْجِرَةٌ
To be brief in speech.	وَجَزَ يَجِزُ
To abbreviate, abridge.	أَوْجَزَ
Abridged, concise.	وَجِيزٌ ومُوجَزٌ
Conciseness, brevity.	إِيجَازٌ
To feel pain.	وَجِعَ يَوْجَعُ وَيَيْجَعُ
To cause or inflict pain.	أَوْجَعَ

توجَّعَ	To feel pain.
توجعَ لَ	To feel pain for.
جِعَةٌ	Beer, ale.
وَجَعٌ ج أَوْجَاعٌ	Pain. Disease.
وجيعٌ وَمُوجِعٌ	Painful ; sore.
وُجَاقٌ وأُوجَاقٌ	Fire-place, hearth.
وَجِلَ يَوْجَلُ	To fear.
وَجَلٌ ج أَوْجَالٌ	Fear, terror.
وجِلٌ ج وَجِلُون	Timorous.
وجنةٌ ج وَجَنَاتٌ	Cheek (face).
ميجنةٌ ج مَوَاجِنُ	Mallet.
وجُهَ يَوْجُهُ	To be respected.
وَجَّهَ	To turn a thing towards.
وَجَّهَ	To send.
واجَهَ مواجهةً	To meet one.
توجه نحوَ وإِلى	To repair to.
(تواجَهَ)	To have an interview.
	To turn towards.

وَجْهٌ ج أَوْجُهٌ وَوُجُوهٌ	Face. Chief. Manner. Aim. Surface.
عمله لِوجهِ اللّه	To do for God.
بوجهٍ	In some manner.
جِهةٌ ج جِهاتٌ	Side. Dimension. *(Geom).*
من جِهتِهِ	Concerning.
وَجاهةٌ	Consideration, position.
تجاهٌ	Opposite to, in front of.
وَجيهٌ ج وَجهاءُ	Chief, prince.
متوجّهٌ	Going, turning to.
وَحدَ يحدُ	To be alone.
وَحَّدَ	To reduce to one ; unify.
توحَّدَ	To be one, single, alone.
إِتّحد	To be united.
على حِدَةٍ	Separately.
وَحْدَهُ	Alone.
وَحْدانيّةٌ	Unity, being unique.
وَحْدَةٌ	Solitude, isolation.

وَاحِـدٌ	One; single; unique.
الوَاحِـد	The only one.
اَحدٌ م إِحْـدى ج آحادٌ	One.
الأَحد	Sunday.
وحيدٌ م وحيدةَ	Unique.
إتّحادٌ	Union ; harmony ; accord.
تَوْحيد	Unification. Belief in the unity of God.
تَوحُّد	Isolation, solitude.
تَوحّـد	A unitarian.
مُتوحّـدٌ	Isolated, alone. One.
وَحُشَ وَتَوَحَّش	To be unpeopled.
تَوَحَّش	To grow savage.
اِستَوْحَش	To feel lonely.
وَحْشٌ ج وحُوش	Wild beast.
حِمار وَحْش	Onager, wild ass.
وَحْشةٌ	Grief ; solitude.
وَحْشيٌّ	Wild, ferocious cruel.
تَوَحُّش	Savage state. Barbarity.

مُتوحّشٌ	Savage, brute-like.
وَحْلٌ ج وُحُول	Thin mud, mire.
وَحِلٌ	Muddy, miry.
وَحنَ يحِن	To be spiteful.
أَوْحى إِلى	To inspire. Send.
وَحيٌ	Divine inspiration.
وَحَى	Haste, hurry.
وَاَخذ مواَخذةً)	To find fault with.
(لاتُواخِذْني)	Excuse me.
وَخزَ يخز وخزاً	To prick.
وَخطه آلشّيْب	To be grizzled.
وَخُمَ يَوْخُمُ	To be unhealthy.
أَتخم	To surfeit (food).
إتّخم	To be ill (from food).
وَخِمٌ وَوخيم	Dirty unclean.
تخمة	Indigestion.
وَخّى وَتوخّى	To seek diligently.
(وَاَخى مُواَخاةً)	To fraternize with.

To love ; wish for.	وَدَّ يَوَدّ
To show love to.	تَوَدَّدَ إِلى
To have mutual love.	توادّ توادًّا
Love ; friendship.	ود ووِدادٌ
It is my wish.	بودي (بدّي)
Lover, affectionate.	ودّ ووَدُود
Affection, friendship.	مَوَدّة
Mutual, love.	موادّة وتَوادٌّ
Jugular vein.	وَداج مث وَداجان
To forsake, leave.	وَدَع يَدَع
Let me, allow me !	دَعْني
To take leave of.	وَدّعَ يودّع
To conciliate.	ودع وداعًا
To deposit with.	أَوْدع عِنْد
To bid farewell. Deposit.	إِسْتَوْدعَ
White shell.	وَدَعَةٌ ج وَدَعاتٌ
Bidding adieu, farewell.	وَداعٌ
Mildness, gentleness.	وَداعَة
Rest, quiet ; gentleness.	دعة
Quiet, gentle.	وديع ج ودعاء
Deposit ; trust, charge.	وَديعَةٌ
Depositor.	مستوْدِعٌ
Depository.	مستوْدَعٌ
Race-field.	ميدان ج مَيادين
To send.	وَدَّى
To perish.	أَوْدى إِيداءً
Blood-money.	دِيَة ج دِياتٌ
Valley.	وادٍ ج أَوْدِيَة
Let him alone,	وذَرَ — ذَرْهُ
Behind. Beyond.	وَرَاءَ
To equivocate.	وارب مُوارَبَة
Obliquity. Diagonal,	(وَرْبٌ)
To inherit.	وَرِثَ يرث إِرْثًا وَوِراثةً
To bequeath.	وَرَّث وَأَوْرَث
To bring on (an evil).	أَوْرَث

To throw into difficulty. وَرَّط

To fall into difficulty. تورَّط

Difficulty. ورْطةٌ ج وَرَطاتٌ

To be pious. وَرِعَ يَرِعُ

Fear of God. Piety. وَرَعٌ

A pious man. وَرِعٌ ج أَوْرَاعٌ

Foliage, paper. وَرَقٌ ج أَوْرَاق

To put forth leaves. أَوْرَقَ

A leaf (of a tree) ; a piece of paper ; ticket. وَرَقَةٌ

Stationer. Plasterer. مُوَرِّقٌ

Hip bone ; hip. وَرْكٌ وَوِرْكٌ

A large lizard. وَرَلٌ ج وِرْلانٌ

To swell. وَرِمَ يَرِمُ وَرَماً . وتورَّمَ

To cause to swell. وَرَّمَ

Swelling. Tumour. وَرَمٌ ج أَوْرَام

Bee-eater (bird). وَرْوَارٌ ج وَرَاوِير

To conceal. وَرَّى وَوَارَى

To hide one's self. تَوَارَى عَن

To inherit. توارَثَ

Inheritance. إِرْثٌ وَوِراثَةٌ

Heir. وارِثٌ ج وَرَثَةٌ وَوُرَّاثٌ

Inherited ; hereditary. مَوْرُوثٌ

Inheritance. مِيراثٌ ج مَوارِيث

To come, arrive. وَرَدَ يَرِدُ وُرُوداً

Flower. Rose. وَرْدٌ ج وُرُود

A rose. وَرْدَةٌ

Cockroach. بِنْتُ وَرْدَانَ

Red, rose-coloured. وَرْدِيٌّ

Coming, arriving. وارِد

Revenue. إِيرادات

Vein. وَرِيدٌ ج اوْرِدَةٌ

Jugular vein. حَبْلُ الوَرِيدِ

Access, entrance. مَوْرِدٌ ج مَوارِد

Of a rose colour, rosy. مُوَرَّدٌ

Brick, restless. وَرِش

Work-shop. (وَرْشَةٌ)

Creatures ; mankind. ورى

Behind, وراءَ

The Pentateuch. Bible. توْراةٌ

Using a word in a double sense. توْرِيَةٌ

Geese. وَزٌ (اوز)

A goose. وزَّةٌ

To flow. وزب يزب وزوبا

Water-drain. ميزابٌ ج ميازيب

To commit a sin. وزر يزر

To aid, help. وازر على

To become a vizier. توزَّر

To put on a وزرة . إِتّزر

Burden. Crime. وزْرٌ ج أوزار

Loin-cloth. وزرةٌ ج وزْرات

Office of a vizier. وزارةٌ

Vizier. وزير ج وزراء

Assistant. موازرٌ

To distribute. وزَّع وأوْزع بيْن

To be divided, distributed. توزَّع

Scotch broom. (وزّالٌ)

To weigh. وَزَنَ يزن وزناً وَزِنَةً

To compose (a verse) according to measure scan. وَزَنَ الشّعر

To be heavy. وَزُنَ يوْزُنُ وزانةً

To be equal in weight. وازن

To compare. وازن بيْن

To be equal in weight. توازن

Weighing ; weigh. وزن وزنةٌ

Weight; measure; metre of a verse. وزنٌ ج أوْزانٌ

A weight. Talent. وزنةٌ ج وزنات

A weigher. Of full weight. وازنٌ

Prudent, reflecting. وزينُ الرّأْي

Equal, equivalent to. موازن

Equilibrium. موازنةٌ

Weighed ; measured. موْزونٌ

Scales, balance. Standard. Measure. ميزانٌ ج موازينُ

Libra (zodiac). أَلميزانُ

وازَى	To correspond to, be parallel with.
تَوازَى	To correspond to,
مُوازاةٌ	Correspondence.
مُتَوازٍ	Parallel (line).
وَسِخَ يَوْسَخُ	To be foul, soiled,
وَسَّخَ وَأَوْسَخ	To soil.
وَسَخ ج أَوْساخٌ	Dirt, uncleanness.
وَسِخٌ	Dirty, unclean, soiled.
وسد	To prop with a pillow.
وِسادٌ ج وُسُد	A pillow, cushion.
وِسادَة ج وِسادات	A pillow.
وَسَّطَ	To put in the middle.
تَوَسَّطَ	To take a middle position.
تَوَسَّطَ بَيْن	To mediate between.
وَسْطٌ وَوَسَط	Middle, centre.
واسِطَةٌ ج وَسائِط	Means.
بِواسِطَة	By means of, through.
وَساطَة وَتَوَسُّط	Intermediation.
وَسِيط ج وُسَطاء	Mediator.
الْوُسْطَى	The middle finger.
مُتَوَسِّط	Intermediate. Mediator.
أَلْبَحْرُ الْمُتَوَسِّطُ	Mediterranean.
وَسِعَ يَوْسَعُ	To be spacious, wide.
وَسِعَ يَسَعُ سَعَةً	To contain, hold.
لا يَسَعُكَ انْ	Thou canst not.
وَسَّعَ وَأَوْسَعَ	To widen, enlarge.
وَسَّعَ وَأَوْسَعَ عَلى	To enrich (God).
تَوَسَّعَ في	To be at ease.
إِتَّسَعَ وَاسْتَوْسَعَ	To be enlarged.
وُسْعٌ وَسِعَةٌ	Power, ability.
سَعَة وَاتِّساع	Width ; capacity.
إِتِّساعٌ	Extent, dilatation.
واسِع وَوَسِيع وَمُتَّسِع	Spacious.
اوْسَعِ	Wider, more vast.
مُوسِعٌ	Rich, wealthy, opulent.
وَسَقَ يَسِقُ وَسْقًا	To load; to freight.

A load ; cargo.	وسْق ج أوْسَاق
Freighted, loaded.	مُوسوق
To implore, seek.	توسَّل إلى
Means.	وسيلة ج وَسَائِل
Supplication.	توسّل
To brand.	وَسَمَ يَسِمُ وَسْماً وَسِمَة
Sign, mark.	وَسْم ج وُسُوم. سِمَة ج سِمات
Badge of honour.	وِسَام
Season.	مُوسِم ج مَوَاسِم
Marked. Branded.	مَوْسُوم
To slumber.	وَسِنَ يَوْسَن
Slumber; unconsciousness.	سِنة
To suggest wicked things.	وَسْوَسَ لِ
Hallucination.	وسْوَاس ج وَسَاوِس
Satan.	الوَسْوَاس
A razor.	مُوسَى وَ (موس)
Moses.	مُوسَى
Mosaic; a Jew.	مُوسَوِيّ

To adorn.	وَشَّحَ
To put on.	تَوَشَّحَ وَآتَّشَحَ
A sash set with jewels.	وُشاح
Double-rhymed poetry.	موشَّحة
To saw (wood).	وَشَرَ يَشِر
A prism.	مَوْشُور ج مَوَاشِير
A saw.	مِيشار
To be quick.	وَشُكَ يَوْشُك وَشْكاً
To be on the point of.	أوْشك أنْ
Celerity ; haste, hurry.	وَشْك
Swift ; on the point of.	وَشِيك
To tattoo.	وشم يَشِم وَشْماً وَوشَّم
To whisper.	وشْوَشَ وَتَوَشْوَش
To embellish.	وَشَى يَشِي . وَوَشَى
To slander.	وشى بفلان إلى
Slanderer.	واشٍ ج وشاة وَوَاشون
Coloured ; embroiderd.	موشَّى
Illnes, pain.	وَصَب ج أوْصَاب

To shut, close (a door). أوْصَدَ

Shut, closed. موصَدٌ

To describe, qualify. وصَفَ يَصِفُ

To prescribe medicine وَصَفَ لِ
to a sick person, (physician).

To be qualified. إتَّصفَ

Description. وَصْفٌ ج أوْصَاف

Prescription of physician. وَصفةٌ

Descriptive. وَصفيٌّ

Quality ; adjective. صِفةٌ ج صِفات

Young servant. وصيف ج وصَفاء

Qualified noun. موْصُوف

To unite, join. وَصَل يَصِلُ ب

To reach, arrive at. وَصَلَ إلى

To give, bestow. وَصَلَ

To bring to. وَصَّلَ وَأوْصَلَ إلى

To persevere in. واصَلَ

To arrive at. تَوَصَّلَ إلى

To be joined. تَوَاصَلَ

To be continuous. إتَّصلَ

To arrive at, reach. إتَّصلَ إلى

To be united to. إتَّصلَ بِ

Connection, Receipt. وصلٌ

Junction, union. وصلةٌ وَاتّصال

Union of the friends. وِصَالٌ

Union. Gift. صِلةٌ ج صِلات

Arrival. وُصول ج وُصولات
Receipt.

Continuity ; connexion. إتِّصالٌ

Continuity. Union. مُواصَلة

Connective. مُوصِل

Joined. Continual. متَّصلٌ

Suffixed pronoun. الضمير المتَّصِل

United, joined. مَوْصول

Relative Pronoun. ألاسْمُ المَوْصول

Fault; shame. وَصْمٌ وَوَصْمةٌ

To peep through a hole. وصوصَ

To bequeath. وصى وأوْصَى

To recommend.	وَصّى إِلى بِ
To charge, commend.	وَصّى وَأَوْصى
A testator, Executor of a will. Guardian.	وَصيّ ج أَوْصِياء
An order, charge. Will, testament.	وَصِيّةٌ ج وَصايا
Testator.	مُوصٍ
What is bequeathed.	مُوصًى بِهِ
A legatee, legatory.	مُوصًى لَهُ
To be clean.	وَضُؤَ يَوْضُؤُ وَضُوءًا
To perform ablutions.	تَوَضَّأَ
Water for ablutions.	وَضُوء
Cleanliness ; beauty.	وَضاءَة
Ablutions before prayers.	تَوَضُّؤ
To be clear, evident.	وَضَحَ يَضِحُ
To explain clearly.	وَضَّحَ وَأَوْضَحَ
To become clear.	تَوَضَّحَ وَٱتَّضَحَ
To ask for explanation.	إِسْتَوْضَحَ
Distinctness.	وُضوحٌ وَٱتِّضاح
Clear, manifest, evident.	واضِحٌ
Clear exposition.	إِيضاحٌ وَتَوْضيحٌ
Evident, manifest, clear.	مُتَّضِحٌ
To lay put down.	وَضَعَ يَضَعُ
To give birth.	وَضَعَتْ تَضَعُ
To humiliate, abase.	وَضَعَ فُلانًا
To be humble.	تَواضَعَ وَٱتَّضَعَ
To be humbled.	إِتَّضَعَ
Position, site.	وَضْعٌ ج أَوْضاعٌ
Humiliation.	ضِعَةٌ
Laying down. Founder.	واضِعٌ
Humble, low.	وَضيعٌ ج وُضَعاء
Humility.	تَواضُعٌ وَٱتِّضاع
Place, site, spot.	مَوْضِعٌ ج مَواضِع
Humble, meek.	مُتَّضِعٌ وَمُتَواضِع
Object; subject.	مَوْضوعٌ ج مَواضيع
To tread upon.	وَطِئَ يَطَأُ
To mount.	وَطِئَ (ٱلفَرَسَ)
To prepare, render easy.	وَطَّأَ

To agree upon. واطأ وَتواطأ عَلى

Low ground. وَطاء وَوطء

Pressure, violence. وَطأةٌ

Low. واطِئ

Foot-stool. مَوْطِئ ج مَواطِئ

To fix, make firm. وطد يَطِد وَوَطَّد

To be made firm, fixed. تَوَطَّد

Mountains. أوْطاد

Firm, solid, immovable. وَطيدٌ

Object purpose. وَطرٌ ج أوْطار

To reside in. وَطَن يطِن. وَأوْطَن ب

To inhabit. وطَّن وَآستوطَن

To resolve. وطَّن نفسهُ

Native place. وَطنٌ ج أوْطانٌ

Abode, home. موطِن ج مَواطِن

A bat. وَطواطٌ ج وَطاويطُ

To lower, let down. وَطّى

وَظَبَ يَظبُ وظوبًا وَواظبَ على
To persevere in.

Perseverance, assiduity. مُواظبَةٌ

To give an office to one. وظَّفَ

To be employed. تَوظَّفَ

Pay, Office, function, employment. وَظيفةٌ ج وظائِفُ

Physiology. عِلمُ وَظائِفِ الأعْضاء

Functionary; official. مُتَوَظِّفٌ

To take up wholly. وَعَبَ يَعبُ

To fill up; complete. أوْعبَ إيعابًا

To contain, hold. إستوعَب

To promise. وَعَد يعدُ

To make an appointment. وَاعَدَ

To threaten. توَعَّدَ

To promise one another. تواعَد

A promise. عِدةٌ وَوَعدٌ ج وُعودٌ

Menaces, threats. وَعيدٌ

Appointed time مَوْعِدُ ج مَواعِدُ

Appointed time or place. ميعادٌ

Rugged place. وَعرٌ ج وُعورٌ

Rugged, difficult.	وعِرٌ
To intimate.	وَعزَ وَأَوْعزَ إليه في
To exhort, warn.	وَعظ يَعِظ
To listen to warning.	إتعظَ
Sermon ; exhortation.	وعظٌ وَعظةٌ وَموعِظةٌ
A preacher.	واعِظٌ ج وعَّاظٌ
To be ill, indisposed.	توَعَّكَ
An illness.	وَعْكةٌ
Antelope.	وعلٌ ج أوْعَالٌ
Good morning.	وَعِمَ — عِمْ صَباحاً
To gather ; contain.	وَعَى يَعي
To put into a vessel.	أوْعَى إِيعاء
To be careful.	توَعَّى وَاستوْعَى
Attention, care.	وَعيٌ
Vessel, receptacle.	وِعاءٌ ج أوْعيةٌ
Remembering. Cautious.	وَاعٍ
To be very hot.	وغر يَغِر وَغراً
Intense heat. Anger.	وغْرٌ
Tumult ; battle.	وَغى وَوَغيٌ
To come arrive.	وَفد يفِدُ على
To send (an envoy).	وَفد وأوْفد
A deputation.	وفدٌ ج وفُودٌ
Epidemic.	وَافِدٌ ج وفُودٌ
To increase, multiply.	وَفر يفِر
To economise ; save.	وَفَّرَ
Wealth, affluence.	وَفرٌ ج وفُورٌ
Economy ; saving.	وفرٌ وَتوْفِيرٌ
Abundant, plentiful.	وَافِرٌ
More abundant.	أوْفرُ
To make fit. To assist.	وَفَّقَ
To reconcile.	وفَّقَ وَوَافقَ بيْنَ
To agree or accord with.	وَافَقَ
To succeed.	توَفَّقَ
To agree together.	توَافَقَ في
To agree upon.	إتَّفقَ على أوْ في
To happen, occur.	إتفقَ لِ

Accord, agreement,	وفق وِفاقٌ
In accordance with.	وفقًا ل
Agreement, fitness.	مُوافقةٌ
Coincidence. Accord.	إتّفاقٌ
Accidental, by chance.	اتّفاقي
Success. Prosperity.	تَوفيقٌ
Convenient, suitable.	مُوافقٌ
Prosperous, successful.	مُتَوَفّقٌ
To keep one's promise. To pay a debt.	وفى يفي وأوْفى
To be perfect, complete.	وفى وَفيًا
To come to, meet.	وَافى
To pay the whole.	وَفى حقّهُ
To die.	تُوفّي وَتوفّاهُ الله
Payment of a dept.	وَفاء وإيفاء
Death, decease.	وَفاةُ ج وَفياتٌ
Complete.	وَاف
Cavity, hole.	وقبٌ ج أوْقابٌ
To appoint a time.	وقت وَوَقّتَ
Time, season,	وَقتٌ ج أوْقاتٌ
Then, at that time,	وقتئذٍ
Immediately.	لِلوقتِ وَلوقتِهِ
Temporal, provisional.	وَقتيٌّ
To be impudent.	وَقَحَ يَقِحُ وَتوَقّحَ
Impudent, brazen-faced.	وَقِحٌ
Impudence.	وَقاحةٌ وَقِحةٌ
To burn, blaze (a fire).	وَقَدَ يَقِدُ. وَتَوَقّدَ وَاتّقد
To kindle (a fire) : light.	أوْقَدَ
Fuel.	وَقودٌ وَوَقيدٌ
Fire-grate.	مَوْقَدٌ وَمَوْقدَةٌ
Lit, kindled.	مَوْقُودٌ ومُتَقِدٌ
To honour, respect.	وَقّرَ
To load (an animal).	أوْقرَ إيقارًا
Load, burden,	وِقرٌ ج أوْقارٌ
Dignified bearing.	وَقارٌ
Venerable.	وَقُورٌ
To fall, fall down.	وَقَعَ يَقَعُ

وقعَ لِ — To happen, occur to one.

وقعَ في — To slander, insult one.

وقعَ وَأوْقعَ ب — To attack, assail.

توقِّع — To let fall. Seal, sign.

واقِع — To charge, rush upon.

أوقع — To tune, put in tune.

توقَّع وَآستوْقعَ — To expect.

تواقَعَ — To fight together.

تَواقعَ عَلى — To beseech humbly.

وَقعة ج وَقعاتٌ — Event. Battle.

وقيعٌ — Imploring help.

في الوَاقع — Actually, in fact.

وَاقعةٌ — Event, catastrophe.

إيقاع — Harmony of sounds.

توقع — Expectation ; hope.

توقيع ج توَاقيع — Signature.

مَوقع ج مواقع — Place.

وَقفَ يَقِفُ — To stop ; stand.

وَقفَ ل وعلى — To endow.

وَقفَ وُقُوفًا على — To inform. Know.

وَقَّفَ وَأوْقف — To seize. To arrest.

وَاقفَ في — To contend with.

توقَّفَ في — To hesitate.

تَوَقَّف عَنْ — To abstain from.

تَوَقَّف عَلى — To depend on.

وَقفٌ ج أوْقاف — Endowment.

وَاقِفٌ ج وُقوف — Standing. Pause.

وُقُوف — Standing ; stopping.

تَوَقف — Hesitation ; arrest.

توْقيف — Suspension ; arrest.

مَوقِفٌ ج مَوَاقِف — A stand, station.

مَوقُوف — Dependent on, stopped. Endowed.

وقى يَقي — To guard, protect.

تَوقى وَآتقى — To be on one's guard.

إتقى يَتقي — To fear God.

وِقايَةٌ وَوِقاء — Protection.

Fear of God, piety. تقًى و تقوى

Pious, God-fearing. تقيٌّ ج أتقياء

Sixty drams. A pharmaceutical ounce. اوقيةٌ ج أواقٍ

A man who fears God. متّقٍ

To lean upon. توكّأ واتّكأ على

To sit leaning on the side. اتّكأ

A staff; a couch. متّكأٌ ج متّكآتٌ

To advance slowly. وكب يكب

A procession. موكبٌ ج مواكبُ

To affirm, confirm. وكّد وأكّد

To be confirmed. توكّد وتأكّد

Certain, affirmed. أكيدٌ ومؤكّدٌ

Affirmation, confirmation. Emphasis. توكيدٌ وتأكيدٌ

Certatinly. بالتأكيدِ

Nest of a bird. وكرٌ ج أوكارٌ

To push, thrust. وكز ـــ ِ

To be defective. وكس ـــ ِ

Diminution of value; loss. وكسٌ

To sell at a loss. بَاعَ بالوكس

To drop, trickle. وكف يكِف

Trickling, leaking. وكفٌ

To confide to. وكل يكلُ إلى

To appoint as an agent. وكّل

To trust in. توكّل واتّكل على

Agency. وكالةٌ ج وكالات

Substitute, agent. وكيلٌ ج وكلاء

Trust, confidence. إتّكالٌ

Committed to. موكول إلى

To enter. وَلجَ يلج ولوجا وفي

To commit to. ولّج وإلى

To beget bring, forth. ولد يلدُ

To act as a midwife. ولّد

To originate from. تولّد من

Child, son. ولدٌ ج أولادٌ

Birth, parturition. ولادةٌ

Midwifery. عِلمُ الولادَةِ

وَالد ج وَالدُون	Father ; sire.
والدةٌ ج وَالداتٌ	Mother ; dam.
ألوالدان	Father and mother.
مَولدٌ ج مَوالدُ	Generation.
ميلادٌ ج مَواليدُ	Birthday.
عيدُ ألميلادِ	Christmas.
مُوَنَّدةٌ	Unclassical (word)
مُوَلِّدةٌ	Midwife.
مَولُودٌ ج مَواليدُ	Born. Child.
وَلِعَ يَوْلعُ بِ	To be attached to.
وَلَّعَ	To light or kindle.
(وَلعةٌ)	Material for lighting with.
وَلَعٌ	Violent love, passion.
مُوْلعٌ بِ	Passionately addicted.
وَالفَ مُوالفةً	To associate with.
اوْلَمَ	To entertain.
وَليمةٌ ج وَلائِمُ	Entertainment.
وَلهَ يَلِهُ	To grieve much.
وَلهٌ	Grief, passion, love.
وَلهَانُ م وَلهَى	Overcome with grief.
وَلوَلَ وَلوَلةً	To wail, lament.
وَلِيَ وَوَلِيَ يَلِي	To follow.
وَلِيَ وِلايَةً وَعلى	To rule.
وَلّى	To make one a ruler.
وَلّى عَن	To turn away from.
وَلّى هَارِباً	He turned and fled.
وَلّى وَجْهَهُ	He turned his face.
وَالَى مُوالاةً	To help, protect.
أوْلى مَعرُوفاً	To do a good deed.
تَوَلّى	To take charge of.
تَوَالى	To follow one another.
إستولى	To take possession.
وَليٌّ ج أوْلياء	Master, lord.
وَليُّ الله	Friend of God.
وِلايَةٌ ج وِلايَاتٌ	Province. Rule.
وَليُّ العهد	Heir apparent.

Benefactor. ولِيُّ آلنعمِ

Ruler, governor. وَالٍ ج وُلاةٌ

More deserving, fit. أوْلى بِ

Master, lord. موْلى ج مَوَالٍ

Invested with power. متوَلٍّ

Successive. متوالٍ

A Sheïte. متوَالٍ ج متاولةٌ

To beckon to. وَمَا يَمأُ . وَأوْمَأَ إلى

Indication by sign. ومأٌ وَإيماء

Indicated. ألمُومَا إليهِ

A prostitute. مومِسةٌ ومومِسٌ

To flash. وَمَضَ يَمِضُ . وَأوْمَضَ

Lightning; flash; gleam. وميضٌ

To reprove, reprimand. ونب

To be faint, weak. ونى يَني . وَوَنيَ

To relax one's efforts. توانى في

Fatigue, faintness. ونًى وَوَناء

Slowness, slackness. توَانٍ

Lazy, languid; slow. متوَانٍ

Enamel. مينا

Port, harbour. مينا وَميناء ج مَوَانٍ

To grant, give. وَهَبَ يهَبُ

Grant ! (*Imp. of* وَهَبْ) هَبْ

To ask for a present. إستوْهَبَ

Gift, present. هِبةٌ ج هِباتٌ

Donation, gift. موْهِبةٌ ج مواهِبُ

Mohammedan Wahhabite. وهَّابيٌّ

To blaze, burn. وهَجَ يهِجُ

To kindle (a fire). أوْهجَ إيهاجاً

To glow burn. توهّجَ

Glow, heat (of fire, sun). وهَجٌ

Intensely glowing. وهَّاجٌ

Deep pit; abyss. وهدة ج وهَدٌ

To lead into evil. وهَّطَ وأوْهَطَ

To rush rashly into. توهَّطَ في

Precipice, abyss. وهْطةٌ ج وهْطٌ

وَهَلٌ وَوَهلةٌ	Terror, fear, fright.
أوَّل وهلةٍ	At first sight.
وَهِمَ يَهِمُ	To imagine, fancy.
وهَّمَ وأوهَمَ	To lead into error.
إتَّهَمَ بِ	To suspect, accuse.
توهَّمَ	To suppose, imagine.
اتُّهِم ب	To be suspected.
وَهْمٌ ج أوهامٌ	Opinion, idea.
ألقوَّة الوهمية	The imagination.
وهميٌّ	Imaginary, hypothetical.
إيهامٌ	Ambiguity. Misleading.
تُهمةٌ ج تُهَمٌ	Suspicion, charge.
مُتَّهَمٌ	Suspected person.
توهُّمٌ	Fanciful imagination.
وَهَنَ يهِنُ . وَوهِنَ ـ	To be weak.
وهَّنَ وأوْهَنَ	To weaken.
واهِنٌ ج وُهُنٌ	Weak, frail.
وَهَى وَوهِيَ يَهِي	To be weak.
أوْهَى	To weaken, break.
واهٍ مواهيهُ ج واهون	Feeble, frail.
واهاً ل	Wonderful! Alas!
ويلَك	Woe to you!
واحةٌ ج واحاتٌ	Oasis.
وَيْحٌ وَيلٌ	Woe to!
وَيلٌ	Disaster, calamity.
وَيلي	Woe to me!
وَيلةٌ ج وَيلاتٌ	Disgrace.

ي

ي	As a numeral sign=10.
ي	My, me, *e. g.*
كِتَابِي	My book.
مَعِي	With me.
ضَرَبَنِي	He struck me.
ي	*A particle of relation, e.g.*
مِصْرِيّ	Egyptian.
يا	*Interjection*, O *e.g.*
يا زَيْدُ	O Zeid !
يَئِسَ يَيْأَسُ ويَيْئِسُ مِنْ	To despair of,
يَأْسٌ	Despair, loss of hope.
يَؤُسٌ ويَؤُوس	Despairing.
يَبِسَ يَيْبَسُ	To dry up, wither.
يَبَّسَ وأَيْبَسَ	To cause to dry.
أليَبَس واليابسة	To dry land.
يابِس	Dry.
يُبُوسة	Dryness.
يَتَّمَ	To make one an orphan.
تَيَتَّمَ	To become an orphan
يُتْم	State of orphanage.
يَتِيمٌ ج يتامى وأيْتامُ	Orphan.
درة يتيمة	A rare pearl.
(يَخْنَةٌ)	A kind of stew.
يَدٌ ج أيدٍ وأيادٍ	Hand; arm. Power. Handle.
عن يَدٍ	By force.
بَيْنَ يديهِ	In his presence.
لهُ يدٌ بيضاء	He is well versed.
أليد الطولى	Power, influence.

Manual. يَدِيٌّ ويدويٌّ

Scattered. ايدِي سَبا

Jerboa (animal). يرْبوعٌ

Glow-worm. Reed-pen. يرَاعٌ

Jaundice. Blight. يرْقانٌ

To be easy. يسر ييسر يُسْرًا

To facilitate, make easy. يَسَّر

To become easy. تيسرَ وآستيسر

To be feasible to one. تيسَّرَ لَهُ

Facility, ease ; affluence. يُسْر

Left. side. Ease. يسارٌ ج يُسُر

Easy. Small quantity. يسيرٌ

More easy. أيسر

The left side. ألأيسر والْيُسرى

Rich, affluent. موسرٌ ج مَياسِير

Gambling. مَيْسِر

Ease, affluence, wealth. مَيْسُرة

Left side. ميسرةٌ ج مياسر

Feasible, easy مَيْسُورٌ ج مياسير

Arrest, interdicted. (يَسَقْ)

A cavass (*Turk*). (يسقجيٌّ)

Jasmine (jessamine). ياسمينٌ

Male bee. Chief. يَعسوبٌ

Fontanelle. يَافوخٌ

A young man. Lad. يافِعٌ ج يفَعَةٌ

Ruby. ياقُوتٌ

To be awake. يقِظَ ييقظُ

To awaken. يقَّظَ وأيقظَ

To wake up. تيقظ وآستيقظ

Wakefulness. Attention. يَقظَةٌ

Awake, watchful. يَقظٌ ويقظانُ

To be certain, sure. يَقِنَ ييقَنُ

To believe firmly. أيقن وآستيقنَ

To know, be sure of. تيقَّنَ

Certain belief, conviction. يَقِينٌ

He is sure of it. هوعلى يقِينٍ منهُ

Certainly, undoubtedly. يَقيناً

Certain knowledge. علمُ اليقِين

Fountain. يَنْبوعٌ
Anise. يانسُون (أنيسُون)
To ripen (fruit). يَنَعَ يَينع . وأينَع
Ripe (fruit). يانِع ويَنيعٌ ج يِنْعٌ
Jew (See هود) . يَهُوديٌّ ج يهود
Day. Time ; season يَوْمٌ ج أيّامٌ
Day by day. يوماً فيوماً
The same day. منْ يومِهِ
Once, some day. يوماً ما
On a certain day, once. ذات يوم
To-day. أليومُ
Daily. يوميٌّ
Day by day, daily. يومياً
On that day. يومئذٍ
Jonah. يُونس (يونانٌ)
The Greek nation. أليُونانُ
Greece. بلادُ اليُونان
Greek. Grecian· يونانيٌّ ج يُونانيُّون
The Greek language. أليُونانيّةُ

Indubitable truth. حقُّ اليقين
Certain truths ; axioms. يقينيّات
Confident, sure. مُوقِنٌ
Sea, ocean. يَمٌّ ج يُمومٌ
Wood-pigeon. يمامٌ ويمامةٌ
To go to the right. يمَّنَ ويامَنَ
To seek a blessing. تيمَّنَ ب
To exact an oath. إستيمن
Blessing, success, luck. يُمْنٌ
Right side or hand. يُمنةٌ
Yemen (Arabia Felix). اليمنُ
Right hand. يُمنى ج يمنيات
Right side, right hand. يَمينٌ
Oath. يمينٌ ج أيمُنٌ وأيمانٌ
By God. أيمُ وايمُ اللهِ
The South. التيمُّن
Right Side. Right wing of an army. ميمنةٌ ج ميامنُ
Fortunate. ميمونٌ ج ميامين
Auspicious. ميمونُ الطائر

Arabic-English

SUPPLEMENT

of Modern Science Terminology

In this Supplement the Arabic entries are listed in absolute alphabetical order—not according to their roots.

الهمزة

إبتلاع	ingestion
ابْتِناء	anabolism
إبراز	excretion
أَبْرَق	concrete
إبْصار	vision
إبْط	axil
إتّحاد	fusion
إتّحاد (كيماويّ)	combination
إتّزان	equilibrium
اتّصالٌ جِنسيّ	coition
إتّصال عَصَبيّ	synapse
إتّصال مَفْصِليّ	articulation
الإثْنا عَشَري	duodenum
أثير	ether
آح (بياضُ البَيض)	albumen
أحاديُّ الخليّة	unicellular
احتِراق	burning; combustion
احتِكاك	friction
إحراق	burning
أحشاء	viscera
أُحْفورة	fossil
أحْمَى	heat
إختبار	experiment
اختِزال	reduction
اختِلاف	variation
اختِلافُ المَنْظَر	parallax
اختِمار	fermentation
إخراجُ الفَضَلات	egestion

إخصاب	fertilization
أخمَدَ	extinguish
أخينيوم	achene
إدراك	consciousness
أَدْرَجَة	hydrogenation
أدرينالين	adrenalin
أَدَمة	dermis
اذَابَ	dissolve; melt
أُذُن	ear
أُذُيْنَة (السّماعة)	earpiece
ارتِباط	association
ارتِجاف	shivering
ارتِشاح	filtration
ارتِعاش	shivering
أَرجون	argon
إرساب	precipitation
أرض • أرضيّ	earth
أرغون	argon
أرومة	stock
إزاحة	displacement
أزال اللون	decolorize
إزالةُ الماء	dehydration
ازدِراد	ingestion
ازْهار • ازهرار	inflorescence
الأزُوت	nitrogen
أَسال	liquefy
أَسبَستُوس	asbestos
إسْت	anus
إستَبان	detect
استِجابة	response
استِحالة	change of state
استِحالة • تحوُّل	metamorphosis

استَحْجَر	petrify
استَخْرَج	extract
استخراج • استخلاص	extraction
استَخْلَص	extract
استرطابيّ	hygroscopic
استِضاءَة	illumination
استِعمـار	colonization
استَقْصَى	investigate
استِقطاب • استقطاب الخلايا	polarization
استِنْبـات	culture
أُسروع	caterpillar
الاسقربوط	scurvy
أَسَلَـة	barb
أُسلوب • طريقة	process
إسْمَنْت • اسمنتُ السِّنّ	cement
إسهاميّ الترابُط	covalent
أسِيتون	acetone
أسِيتيلين	acetylene
أشـابَة	alloy
إشْتِعـال	ignition
إشْعـاع	radiation
الإشعاعُ فوقَ البَنَفْسَجِي	ultra-violet radiation
الإشْعاعُ الكَوْنِيّ	cosmic radiation
إشْعـاعِيّ	radioactive
إشْعـال	ignition
أشِعَّة إكس • الاشعة السينيّة	X-rays
اشِعَّة غاما • الاشعة الجيمية	gamma rays
أُشْنـات • طَحَالِب	algae
أُشنَة • حَزاز	lichen
إصبَع	digit
إصْطِناعي	synthetic
إصْطَنع	synthesize
أَصْفَر	yellow
أَصْـل	origin
إضـاءَة	illumination
الأضراس	molars
إضْرام	ignition
إضْمِحْلال	decay
إطْراحُ (الفضلات)	excretion
أطفأ	extinguish
أطفأ اللَّمْعَة	tarnish
إطْلاق (الغاز)	evolution
إعادةُ تَوليد	regeneration
إعقـام	sterilization
أغار (آغار)	agar agar
الاغتـذاء	nutrition
آفَـة	blight
إفراز	excretion; secretion
إقْتِران	conjugation
أقصى	distal
أَكّـال	caustic; corrosive
إكْتَشَف	detect
إكْتِنـاز	turgor
أُكسجين	oxygen
أَكْسَـد	oxidize
أَكْسَـدَة	oxidation
أُكْسِيـد	oxide
أُكسيد قاعِديّ	basic oxide
أُكسيد الكالسيُوم	calcium oxide; quicklime
أُكسيد مائي	hydroxide
آكِلُ العُشب	herbivore
آكِلُ اللَّحم	carnivore
إكليل (الزَّهرة)	corolla
أكْمَـد	opaque

آلَـة	machine
آلَةُ تَصْوير	camera
إلتِصَاق	adhesion
ألَّف	synthesize
أُلْفَـة	affinity
ألَق	fluorescencc
إلقَـاح	fertilization
إلقاحٌ تَهْجينيّ	cross-pollination
إلِكترود	electrode
إلِكترونسكُوب	electroscope
إلِكْترُولِيت	electrolyte
إلِكْترُون	electron
ألوانٌ مُتَتَامَّة	complementary colours
ألومنيُوم	aluminium
آلِيَّة	mechanism
أمـاميّ	anterior
أمبير	ampere
أمبير سَاعَة	ampere-hour
أمبير متر • أمّيتر	ammeter
أمْبُولَة	ampulla
إمتِزَاز	adsorption
إمتِصاص	absorption
أمفوتَري	amphoteric
أملاحُ حامِض الكربونيك	carbonates
أمُونيـا	ammonia
أمّيتر	ammeter
إنـارة	illumination
إنْبَـات	germination
إنبجاس	effusion
إنبعـاث	evolution
إنْبَعَث	evolve
أُنبوب إختِبار	test tube
أُنبوب الأشِعَّة الكَاثُودِيَّة	cathode-ray tube
أُنبوبٌ شَعرِيّ	capillary tube
إنْبيق	retort; still
إنتِبـاش	germination
إنتـان	sepsis
إنتِحـاء	tropism
إنتِشـار	diffusion
إنتِشار الضَّوْء	diffusion of light
الانتشار الغشائي	osmosis
إنْتَشَر	diffuse
إنتِقاض	catabolism
إنحِراف	declination; deviation
إنحَلَّ (بالذَّوَبان)	dissociate
إنحِـلال	decomposition; disintegration; dissociation
انحِلال مائيّ	hydrolysis
أندريد	anhydride
إندِفـاق	effusion
إندمـاج	fusion
اندِماج • تلبُّد	flocculation
إندوسَبرم	endosperm
أَنزِيم	enzyme
إنسانُ العَيْن	pupil
إنْسِجام	coordination
أنسِجَـة	tissues; textiles
إنسِلاخ	moulting
إنْشَاءُ المُسْتَوْطَنَات	colonization
إنشِطـار	fission
إنشِطار خُلَويّ	cell division
إنشِطَـارِي	fissile
إنشِقَـاق	cleavage
أَنصَـلَ	decolorize

إنصهار	fusion
إنطَلَق	evolve
إنطِلاق (الغاز)	evolution
إنعِدامُ الوَزنِ	weightiessness
إنعِطاف	deviation
إنعِكاس	reflection
إنعِكاسي	reversible
إنفِجار	explosion
إنفِلاق	fission
إنفلُونزا	influenza
أنفي	nasal
إنقِسام الخَلِيَّة	cell division
إنكِسار	refraction
إنمِياع	deliquescence
أنُود	anode
أنهَيْدريد	anhydride
أنيمية	anaemia
آنيُون	anion
إهتِضام	digestion
الأوالي	protozoans
أوانٍ خَزَفيَّة	earthenware
أوْراقٌ كأسِيَّة	sepals
الأوزُون	ozone
الأوَّليات	protozoans
أُوَيْل · بُروتون	proton
إيثانُول	ethanol
إيثيلين	ethylene
إيدرُوجين	hydrogen
ايدرومتر	hydrometer
إيصال	conduction
أيض	metabolism
أيضٌ بِنائِيّ	anabolism
أيضٌ هَدْمِيّ	catabolism
إيقاد	ignition
أيونٌ سالِبُ الشِّحنَة	anion

ب

باردُ الدّم	cold-blooded
بارود	gunpowder
بارومِتر	barometer
باكليت	bakelite
البترول	petroleum
بَتلَة · تُويجِيّة	petal
بُخار	vapour
بُخارُ الماء	steam
بَخَّر	evaporate
بِذرة	seed
بَرّادٌ	refrigerator
بِراز	faeces
بُرَداء	malaria
بُرعُم	bud
بُرعُمٌ إنتِهائي	terminal bud
بُرعُمة	bud
بَرْمائِي	amphibious
بَرْمائِيّات	amphibia
بَرْنيق	varnish
البروتوبلازم	protoplasm
بُروتون	proton
البُرونز	bronze
بَريتون	peritoneum
بِريسكوب	periscope
بِزْرة	seed

بَسْتَرة	pasteurization
بُسَّـذ	coral
بَصَرِيّ	optic
بَصَلَة · بُصَيْلة	bulb
بَطَّارِيَّة	battery
بَطْن	abdomen
بُطَيْن	ventricle
بَعَثَ	evolve
بُعْدٌ بُؤرِيّ	focal length
بَقِيَّـة	residue
بَكَّـارة	block and tackle
بَكتيريا · بكتيريا	bacteria
بَكَرة	pulley
بَكَرَةٌ وحَبَل	block and tackle
ألبلاتين	platinum
بلازمـا	plasma
بلازْما خارِجيَّة	ectoplasm
بلازْما داخِليَّة	endoplasm
ألبلاسْتيك	plastics
بُلْعُوم	pharynx
بَلْوَر	crystallize
بَلُّورَة	crystal
بَلُّورِيّ	crystalline
بُلوغ	puberty
بَلِيَ	corrode
بليُون	billion
بَنْج	anaesthetic
بِنْزين	benzene; gas(oline); petrol
بِنْزين مُحَرِّكات	motor spirit
بَنـدول	pendulum
البَنْكرياس	pancreas
بُؤبؤ	pupil
ألبوتاسا الكاوية	caustic potash
البُوتاسيوم	potassium
بُوتَقَة · بودقة	crucible
بُؤْرة	focus
بَوْرَق	borax
بُوري	blowpipe
بُوصَلَة	compass
بُوصَلَة مغنطيسيَّة	magnetic compass
بَوغ · بُوغة	spore
بَول	urine
بُويـة	paint
بِيئـة	environment
بِيئَة طَبيعيَّة · مَوْطِن	habitat
بَيْضَـة	egg; ovum
بيكربونات الصودا	baking soda
بيُوتـان	butane
بيُولوجيَة	biology
بَيُوض	oviparous
بُيَيْضَـة	ovum; ovule

ت

تَأْبِير	pollination
تَارِيخُ الحَيَاةِ	life history
تَآصُـل	allotropy
تَأَكْسُد	oxidation
تَأَكْسَدَ	oxidize
تَآكُـل	corrosion
تَآكُلٌ بالصَّدأ · صدأ	rusting
تَأْليف	composition
تَامُور	pericardium

تأوُّد • انتحاء	tropism
تبايُن (وِراثي)	variation
تبخَّر	evaporate
تبخُّر • تبخير	evaporation
تبدُّل	variation
تبرُّز	defecation
تبلَّرَ • تبلْوَر	crystallize
تبييض	bleaching
تجاوُب	response
تجدُّد • تجديد	regeneration
تجرِبة	experiment
تجرِبةٌ حاكِمَةٌ أو مُقارِنة	control experiment
تجويفُ الحوض	pelvis
تجويفٌ خلويّ	vacuole
تجويفٌ عظميّ	sinus
تحاتّ	corrosion
تحت جِلديّ	subcutaneous
تحجَّر	petrify
تحرُّك	locomotion
تحلُّل	decomposition
التحلُّل بالماء	hydrolysis
التَّحلُّل بالكَهرباء	electrolysis
تحليل	analysis
التَّحليلُ الحَجْمي	volumetric analysis
التَّحليلُ الكَمّي	quantitative analysis
التَّحليلُ الكَهْربائي	electrolysis
التَّحليلُ النَّوعيّ	qualitative analysis
تحوُّل	metamorphosis
تحوُّل طارىء	mutation
تحويلة	shunt
تخثَّر	coagulate
تخصُّص	specialization

تخلخُل	rarefaction
تخلَّل	percolate
التخليقُ الضَّوئيّ	photosynthesis
تخليقي	synthetic
تخمُّر • تخمير	fermentation
تداخُل	interference
تداعٍ	association
تدرُّج	gradient
التَّدرُّن الرِّئوي	tuberculosis
تدفُّق	flux
تدمُّج	flocculation
تذبذُب	oscillation
ترابُط	association
ترابُطٌ كيماوي	linkage
ترجُّح	oscillation
تُربة	soil
تُربةٌ رَمْليَّة طِينيَّة	loam
تردُّد	frequency
ترسُّب • ترسيب	precipitation
ترشُّح • ترشيح	filtration
ترشَّح	filter
ترشَّح عبْر	percolate
ترقُوة	clavicle; collarbone
تركيب	composition; synthesis
تركيبة	assemblage
تركيبيّ	synthetic
تركيز	concentration
ترمُوس	thermos flask
ترمُوستات	thermostat
ترمُومِتر	thermometer
ترمُومِتر طِبّيّ	clinical thermometer
تزاوُج	conjugation

تَزاوَج	mate	تَعْجِيل	acceleration
تَزَهُّر	efflorescence	تَعْقِيم	pasteurization; sterilization
تَسارُع	acceleration	تَعْمِيَة · تَمْوِيه	camouflage
تَسامِي	sublime	التَّغْذِيَة	nutrition
التَّسامِي	sublimation	تَغَوُّط	defecation
تَسَلُّط	dominance	تَغَيُّر	variation
تَسَيُّل	deliquescence	تَغَيُّرات طَبِيعِيَّة	physical changes
تَسَيَّل	liquefy	تَغَيُّر الحالَة	change of state
تَشابُكٌ عَصَبِيٌّ	synapse	تَغَيُّر كِيمَاوِيّ	chemical change
تَشَتُّت	dispersion	تَفاعَل	react
تَشْذِيب	pruning	تَفاعُل تَعادُلِيّ	neutralization
تَشْرِيح	anatomy	تَفاعُل كِيمَاوِي	chemical reaction
تَشَعُّب عَصَبِيّ	dendron	تَفاعُل مُتَسَلْسِل	chain reaction
تَشَنُّج	cramp	تَفاعُلِيّ	reactive
تَصَعَّد	sublime	تَفَتُّت	disintegration
التَّصَعُّد (الحَرارِيّ)	convection	تَفَجُّر	explosion
التَّصعِيد	sublimation	تَفَكُّك	dissociation
ألتَّصفِيح	plating	تَفَكَّك (بالحَرارَة)	dissociate
التَّصفِيحُ الكَهْرُبائِيّ	electroplating	تَفَلُّج	cleavage
تَصْنِيف	classification	تَفَلْوُر	fluorescence
تَضَخُّمُ الغُدَّةُ الدَّرَقِيَّة	goitre	تَقاصُر	deceleration; retardation
تَضْخِيم	magnification	تَقَزُّح	dispersion
تَطْعِيم · تَلْقِيح	inoculation; vaccination	تَقْصِير (الألْوان)	bleaching
تَطْعِيم	graft	تَقَطَّر	distil
تَطَوُّر	evolution	تَقْطِير إتْلافِيّ	destructive distillation
تَعادُل	equilibrium	التَّقْطِير الهَدَّام	cracking
تَعاقُبُ الأَجْيال	alternation of generations	تَقْلِيم	pruning
تَعاقُبُ الزُّرُوع	crop rotation	تَكاثَر	propagate
ألتَّعايُش	symbiosis	تَكاثُر	reproduction
تَعَب	fatigue	التَّكاثُر الخُضَرِي	vegetative reproduction
تَعَدُّدُ الأشْكال المُتَأصِلَة	allotropy	التَّكاثُر الشِّقِيّ	sexual reproduction
تَعَرُّق · تَعْرِيق	venation	تَكاثُف	condensation

تَكَافُئِيَّة	valency
التَّكَافُل المَعيشِيّ	symbiosis
تَكَافُؤ	valency
تَكْبير	magnification
تَكَثُّف · تَكْثِيف	condensation
تَكَدُّر	tarnish
التَّكْسير	cracking
تَكْعِيبِي	cubic
تَكْوين	composition
تَكَيُّف · تَكْيِيف	accommodation
تَلْحيم	welding
تِلْقائِيّاً	spontaneously
تَلْقيح · إِخْصَاب	fertilization
تَلْقيح · تَأْبير	pollination
تَلْقيح · تَطْعيم	inoculation; vaccination
تَلْقيح مُخْتَلِط	cross-pollination
تِلِسْكُوب	telescope
تِلِسْكُوب فَلَكِيّ	astronomical telescope
تَـلاصُق	adhesion
تِلِفُون	telephone
تَماسُك	cohesion
تَمـايُز	differentiation
تَمَثُّل · تَمْثِيل	assimilation
التَّمْثِيل الضَّوْئِي	photosynthesis
تَمَفْصُـل	articulation
تَمَوُّج	wave
تَمْويـه	camouflage
تَمَيُّع	deliquescence
التَّنَاضُح	osmosis
تَناسُبِيّ	proportional
تَناسُـل	reproduction
التَّناسُل الجِنْسِي	sexual reproduction
تَنَاوُبُ الأَجْيالِ	alternation of generations
تَنَـدُّف	flocculation
تَنْسيق	coordination
تَنَفُّخ	turgor
تَنَفُّس	breathing; respiration
تَنَفُّس هَوَائِي	aerobic respiration
تَنَفُّسٌ لاَهَوَائِيٌّ	anaerobic respiration
تَنَقُّـل	locomotion
تَنْقِيَة بِالصَّهْر	smelting
التَّنَك ، القَصْدِير	tin
تَهَيُّجِيَّة	irritability
تَوَازُن	equilibrium
تَوَاتُر	frequency
تَوالُـد	reproduction
تَوْأَمـان	twins
التُّوتـة	thymus
تَوَتُّر	tension
ألتَّوَتُّر السَّطْحِيّ	surface tension
تَوْصِيـل	conduction
تَوْلِيف	synthesis
تَوْلِيفـة	blend
تُوَيْج (الزَّهْرَة)	corolla
تُوَيْجَة	petal
تَيـار	current
تَيَّارٌ كَهْرَبائي	electric current
تَيَّارٌ مُتَرَدِّد أو مُتَنَاوِب	alternating current
تَيَّار مُسْتَمِرّ أو مُطَّرِد	direct current
تِيلَـة	fibre
التِّيفُوئِيد	typhoid fever
التِّيفُوس	typhus

ث

ثابت	constant
ثاني أُكسيد الكَرْبُون	carbon dioxide
ثانيَة	second
ثديِيّ • لَبُون	mammal
ثِقْل • حِمْل	load
ثِقْل • وَزْن	weight
ثِقْلُ آلبَنْدُول	bob
الثِّقْل النَّوْعِي	specific gravity
ثُمالَة	residue
ثَمَرَة	fruit
ثَمَرَة عُصارِيَّة	succulent fruit
ثَمَرَة عِنَبِيَّة	berry
ثَمَرَةٌ فُقَيْرَة	achene
ثَمَرَةٌ لُبِّيَّة	berry
ثَمَرَةٌ مُتَجَمِّعَة	aggregate fruit
ثُنائِي	binary
ثُنائِي التَّحَدُّب	biconvex
ثُنائِي التَّقَعُّر	biconcave
ثُنائِي العُنْصُر	binary
ثَنِيَّة	incisor

ج

جاذِبِيَّة	gravity
جاذِبِيَّة الإلْتِصاق	adhesion
جاذِبِيَّة التَّماسُك	cohesion
جامِد	solid
جِبْس	gypsum
جِبْلَة	plasma
الجِبْلَة الأُولَى	protoplasm
جِبْلَة خارِجِيَّة	ectoplasm
جِبْلَة داخِلِيَّة	endoplasm
الجُدَرِي	smallpox
جُدَرِي آلبَقَر	cowpox
جَذْر	root
جَذْرٌ شَعْرِيّ	root hair
جَذْر وَتَدِيّ رَئِيسِيّ	taproot
جِذْع	stalk
جُذَيْر	radicle
جَرَاثِيم • بكتريا	bacteria
جرافيت	graphite
جُرْثُومَة	germ
جَرْس (الصوت)	timbre
جَرَسٌ كَهْرَبائي	electric bell
جِرْوٌ • عُلَيْبَة	capsule
جُزْءٌ قِوامِيّ	component; constituent
جُزْءٌ من مِئَة	centi-
جُزَيْء	molecule
جِسْمٌ مُضادّ	antibody
جُسَيْمٌ أَلْفِيّ	alpha particle
جُسَيْمٌ بائِيّ	beta particle
جَصّ	gypsum
جُفاء	slag
جِفْت	forceps
جَلَّط	coagulate
جِلْد	skin
جَلِيد	ice
جَلِيدٌ جافّ	dry ice
جِماع	coition

جُمْجُمَة	cranium; skull
جَمد • جَليد	ice
الجَمْرة	anthrax
جَناح	wing
جِنْث • جَذْرٌ وَتَدِيٌّ رَئِيسيّ	taproot
جِنْس	sex
جِنْس (تَصْنِيفِي)	genus
جَنِين	embryo
جَنِين ، حَمِيل	foetus
جِهاز تَكْثِيف ، مُكَثِّف	condenser
جِهازُ طَرْدٍ مَرْكَزِيّ	centrifuge
جِهازٌ عَصَبِيّ	nervous system
جُهْد	effort
جُهْدٌ كَهْرَبائِيّ	potential; voltage
جَوّ	atmosphere
جَوْف	coelom
جَوْف ، بَطْن	abdomen
جَوْهَرٌ فَرْد ، ذَرَّة	atom
جَيْب	sinus
جِير	lime
جِيرٌ حَيّ	calcium oxide; quicklime
جِيرٌ مُطْفَأ	slaked lime
جِينَة ، مُورِثَة	gene

ح

حَاتّ	corrosive
حَاثَّة	hormone
حَادّ	sharp
حَادّ (الرَّائِحَة)	pungent
حَاسَّة اللَّمْس	touch
حَاشِدَة • بَطَّارِيَّة	battery
حَاشِدَة كَهْرَبائِيَّة • مُرَكِّم	accumulator
حَافِز	stimulus; impulse
حَافِظَة المغنطيس	keeper
حَال • حَالَة	state
حَالَةُ انعِدَامِ الوَزْنِ	weightlessness
حَالِق	tendril
حَامِضُ الخَلّ	acetic acid
حَامِضُ الكَرْبُونِيك	carbonic acid
حَامِض اللَّيمُون	citric acid
حَامِضِيّ	acidic
حَامِلُ السِّمَة	style
حَامِلٌ ثُلاثِيّ	tripod
حَبَّة	seed
حَبَل	pregnancy
حَبْلٌ سُرِّي	umbilical cord
حَتّ	corrode
حَتٌّ كِيميائِيّ	corrosion
حِجَاج	orbit
حَجَّر	petrify
حَجَرٌ جِيرِيّ • حَجَرُ الكِلْس	limestone
حَجَرٌ طَبَاشِيرِيّ	chalk
حَجْم	volume
حُجَيْرَة	alveolus
الحَدِيد	iron
حَدِيدُ الزَّهر • حَدِيدُ الصَّبّ	cast iron
حَرَارَة	heat
حَرْشَفَة	scale
حَرِيرٌ اصطِنَاعِي	rayon
حَرِيرٌ صَخرِيّ	asbestos
حَزَاز	lichen
حِزَام	girdle

حُزْمَةُ اَشِعَّة	beam
حَسَّاسِيَّة	sensitivity
الحَسَر	myopia; short sight
حَشْوَة	cytoplasm
حَصَانَة	immunity
حَضَانَة	incubation
حَفَّاز	catalyst
الحَفَر	scurvy
حَقَّقَ فِي	investigate
حَقْل	field
حَقْنٌ باللِّقاح	vaccination
حُكّ	compass
حَلّ	dissociation
حَلَزُون الأُذُن البَاطِنِيَّة	cochlea
حَلَقَاتٌ حَوْلِيَّة أو سَنَوِيَّة	annual rings
حَلْقَة	annulus
حَلَّلَ بالكَهْرَباء	electrolyze
حُلْم	puberty
حَلْمأة	hydrolysis
حَلَمَة (الثّدي)	teat
حَلِيب	milk
حَمَّى ، سَخَّن	heat
حُمّى التِّيفوئيد	typhoid fever
حُمّى التِّيفوس	typhus
حَمَّام رَمْلِيّ	sand bath
حَمَّام مَائِيّ	water bath
حُمَة	virus
حَمْضِيّ	acidic
حَمْضِيٌّ قِلْوِيّ	amphoteric
حِمْل	load
حَمْل	pregnancy
الحَمْلُ (الحَرارِي)	convection
حِمْلاج	blowpipe
حَمِيل	foetus
حَنْجَرَة	larynx
حَنَك	palate
حَوامِض أمِينِيَّة	amino acids
حَوض ، طَسْت	trough
الحَوْض	pelvis
الحَوْلِيَّات	annuals
حُوَيْصِلَة	vacuole; alveolus
الحُوَيْصِلَة الصَّفْرَاوِيَّة	gall bladder
حَيَدان	deviation
الحَيْض	menstruation
الحَيَمينات	vitamins
حَيَوان	animal
حَيَوانٌ بَيُوض	oviparous
حَيَوان قَارِض	rodent
حَيَوان مُجْتَرّ	ruminant
حَيَوان مُفْتَرِس	predator
حَيَوانٌ من ذَوَاتِ الأَرْبَع	quadruped
حَيَوان مِن اللَّبُونَات	mammal
حَيَوانٌ مِنَ اللافَقارِيَّات	invertebrate
حُيَيٌّ مَنَوِيّ	sperm

خ

خَادِرَة	pupa
الخَارَصِين	zinc
خَاصَّة	property; characteristic
ألخَاصَّة الشَّعرِيَّة	capillarity
خَاصِّيَّة	property
خَالٍ مِنَ المَاءِ	anhydrous

خَام • خَامَة	ore
خَامِل	inert
خَانِق	choke
خِبَاء	carpel
خَبَث	slag
خَبَثُ الفَحْم	clinker
خَبْط	knocking
الخُثّ	peat
خَثَّر	coagulate
خُرْدَة	scrap metal
خَرَسَانَة	concrete
خُرطُوم	proboscis
خَزَف صِينِيّ	porcelain
خُسُوف (القَمَر)	eclipse
خَشَب	xylem
خُصْيَة	testis
خِضَاب • خِضْب	pigment
خَطٌّ بَيَانِيّ	graph
خَطُّ الزَّوَال • خَطُّ الطُّول	meridian
خَطُّ العَرضِ	latitude
خَطُّ المِحْوَر	axis
خَطُّ اللاَّإنْحِرَاف (المَغنطِيسيّ)	agonic line
خَفضُ الأَكْسَدَة • إخْتِزَال	reduction
خَلّ	vinegar
الخَلاَص	afterbirth
خِلْطٌ مَائِيّ	aqueous humour
خَلْفِيّ	posterior
خَلُّون	acetone
خَلِيَّة	cell
خَلِيَّة جَافَّة	dry cell
خَلِيَّة عَصَبِيَّة	neuron
خَلِيط مَعْدِنِيّ	alloy
خَلِيُّوز	cellulose
خَمَج	sepsis
خَمْلَة	villus
خَمِيرَة	yeast
خَمِيرَة إصْطِنَاعِيَّة	baking powder
خُنْثَى	hermaphrodite
خَوَاء	vacuum
خَيَال	image
خَيْشُوم	gill
خَيْطُ السَّدَاة • خُيَيْط	filament

د

دَاء	disease
الدَّاءُ السُّكَّرِيّ	diabetes
دَائِرَة	circuit
دَائِرَةُ قِصَر	short circuit
دَائِم	perennial
دَائِمُ الخُضْرَة	evergreen
دَارَة	circuit
دَافِع	impulse
دَايُود	diode
دُبَال	humus
دَرَّجَ	graduate; calibrate
دَرَجَةُ الحَرَارَة	temperature
دَرَجَةُ الحَرَارَة بِالمِيزَانِ المِئَوِيّ (السَّنتِيغرَاد)	centigrade temperature
دَرَجَةُ الحَرَارَةِ الحَرِجَة	critical temperature
دَرَجَةُ الحَرَارَةِ المُطْلَقَة	absolute temperature
دَرَجَةُ الصِّفْرِ المُطلَق	absolute zero
دَرَجَةُ الغَلَيَان	boiling point

دَبِق · لَزِج	viscous
دُخَان	smoke
الدَّرَقِيَّة	thyroid
دَرَنَة	tuber
دَسْر	thrust
دُعْمُوص · يَرَقانة	larva
دَفْع · دَفْعَة	thrust; impulse
دَفْعٌ تَعْوِيمِيّ	buoyancy
دَفْعٌ عُلْوِيّ	upthrust
دَفْق	flux
دَقّ	knocking
دَقِيقَةُ أَلْفَا	alpha particle
دَقِيقَةُ بِيتَا	beta particle
دَلِيل	indicator
دَلِيلُ الإِنْكِسَار	refractive index
دَم	blood
دِمَاغ	brain
دِنَمُو	dynamo
دِهَان	paint
دِهْلِيز (الأُذُن)	vestibule
دُهْن حَيَوَانِيّ	lard
دُهُون	fats
دَوَاء	drug
دَوْر · دَوْرَة	cycle
دَوْرَةُ الكَرْبُون (في الكَوْن)	carbon cycle
دُوَيْدَة شَرِيطِيَّة	fluke
دِيسِي	deci-
دِيكَا	deca-
دِيُوتِرِيُوم	deuterium
دِينَامُو	dynamo

ذ

ذَائِب	solute
ذَابَ	dissolve; melt
ذَاتُ الرَّأْسَيْن	biceps
ذَبْذَبَة	oscillation
ذَبْل	carapace
ذُبُول	wilting
ذُبُولٌ فُطْرِيّ	damping-off
ذَرَّة	atom
ذَرِّيّ	atomic
ذَكَاء	intelligence
ذَكَرُ النَّحل	drone
ذَنَب	tail
ذَنَبِيّ	caudal
الذَّهَب	gold
ذَوَّاب	soluble
ذُو أَرْبَع	quadruped
ذَوْب	melt
ذُو دَم حَار	warm-blooded
ذو شَرَفَتَيْن	bicuspid
ذو صِمَامَيْن	bivalve
ذو العَيْنَيْن	binoculars
ذو فِلْقَتَيْن	dicotyledon
ذو مَاء	aqueous
ذو نَشَاطٍ إِشْعَاعِيّ	radioactive
ذَيْل	tail
ذَيْلِيّ	caudal

ر

رَابِطٌ كِيمِيَائِيّ	bond
رِئَــة	lung
راتينات ・ راتينجات	resins
رَاتِينج أَصْفَر	amber
رَاسِب	deposit
رَاشِح	filtrate
رَافِدَةُ القَصّ	keel
رِئَوِيّ	pulmonary
رِبَـاط	ligament
رُبَاعِيّ السُّطوح المُثَلَّثِيَّة	tetrahedron
رَحِم	womb
رَحِيق	nectar
رُخَـام	marble•
رُزَام	beriberi
رُسَابَة	deposit; sediment
رُسْغ اليَد	wrist
رَسْمٌ بَيَانِيّ	graph
رُسُوب	sediment
رُشَاحَة	filtrate
رَشَّح	filter
الرَّصَاص	lead
رَضَفَة	patella
رَطْبٌ	humid; moist
رُطُوبَـة	humidity; moisture
الرُّطوبة المَائِيَّة (في العَيْن)	aqueous humour
رُعَـاش	shivering
الرُّغَامَى	trachea
رَغْوَة	lather
رُقَـاد	dormancy
رَقَّـاص	pendulum
رُقْعَـة	graft
رَقِيقَـة	lamina
رِكَـاز	ore
رَكَّب	synthesize
رَكَّز	concentrate
رَمَادُ العَظْم	bone ash
رَمْز	symbol
رَمْزٌ كِيمَاوِيّ	chemical symbol
رَمْـل	sand
رَنْح	cerebellum
رُؤْيَـة	vision
رِيشَـة	feather
رِيشِيّ	pinnate
رِيق	saliva

ز

زَائِدَة	appendix
زَائِدَة شَجَرِيَّة	dendrite
الزَّائِدَة الدُّودِيَّة	appendix
الزِّئْبَق	mercury
الزَّاج	vitriol
الزَّاجُ الأَزْرَق	copper sulphate
زَاحِف	reptile
زُبَانَى	antenna
زَبَـد	scum
زُجَـاج	glass
زَخْم	momentum
الزِّرَاعَة المَائِيَّة	hydroponics

الزُّرْب	diabetes
زَرْدَمَة	glottis
زَعَانِف	fins
زُغْبَة	villus
زِفْت	pitch
زَفْر · زَفِير	expiration
زُلَال	albumen
زُمْرَةُ الدَّم	blood group
زُنَّار	girdle
الزِّنْك ، الخَارِصِين	zinc
زَهْرَة	flower
زَوْرَق	boat
زَوْرَق التَّوِيج	keel
زَيْت	oil
زَيْتُ البِتْرُول	petroleum
زَيْتُ البَرَافِين	paraffin oil
زَيْتُ الدِّيزِل	diesel oil
زَيْتُ الزَّاج	vitriol
زَيْتُ الغَاز	gas oil
زَيْتٌ مَعْدَنِي	mineral oil
زَيْتٌ نَبَاتِيّ	vegetable oil
زَيْتُ الوُقُود	fuel oil
زَيْغ	aberration

س

سَائِل	liquid
سَائِلُ تَبْرِيد	coolant
سَاقٌ (نَبَاتِيَّة)	stem; stalk
سَامّ	toxic
سِبّ	gauze
سُبَات	dormancy
سَبْلَة ، كَأْسِيَّة	sepal
سَبِيكَة	alloy
سَبِيكَةُ لِحَام	solder
سَحَابَة	cloud
سَحَّاحَة	burette
سُخَام	soot
السُّخْد	placenta
السُّخْدُ وأغشِيَتُه	afterbirth
سَخَّن	heat
سَدَاة	stamen
سُدَاسِي · سُدَاسِيّ الأَضْلَاع	hexagonal
سَرْءٌ	spawn
سَرَاب	mirage
سُرْعَة	speed; velocity
سُرْعَةٌ إتِّجَاهِيَّة	velocity
سُرْعَة زَاوِيَّة	angular velocity
سُرْفَة	caterpillar
سَرِيعُ الإلْتِهَاب	inflammable; flammable
سَرِيعُ التَّبَخُّر	volatile
سَرِينَة	siren
سَطْح · وَجْه	face
سَطْحٌ مَائِل	inclined plane
سَطْحٌ هِلَالِيّ	meniscus
سُطَيْح	facet
سَعَة	amplitude
سُعْر	calorie
سَفَّاطَة	aspirator
سَقْفُ الحَلْق	palate
سَقَم	disease
سُقُوط ، وُرُود	incidence
السُّكَّر	sugar

سُكَّرُ البَنْجَر	beet sugar
سُكَّرُ العِنَب	glucose; grape sugar
سُكَّرُ القَصَب	cane sugar; sucrose
السُّل	tuberculosis
السَّلَى	amnion
سِلْسِلَة	chain
سَلْعَة	goitre
سَليب ، مُعبِل	deciduous
سِلْيُولوز	cellulose
سَماد	fertilizer
سِمَة	stigma
سَمْعِيّ	auditory
السَّمعِيّات	acoustics
سُمِّيّ	toxic
سِنّ	tooth
سِناج	soot
سَنْتي	centi-
سَنْتيمِتر مُكَعَّب ، مِلّيلِتر	millilitre
سَنْدان	anvil
سِنْفَة	legume
سَهمُ الرِيشَة	quill
السُّولار	gas oil
سُوَيْداءُ البِزْرَة	endosperm; albumen
سُوَيْداءُ الظِّلّ	umbra
سُوَيْقَة	stalk
سِيادَة	dominance
سَيّار	mobile
سَيّال	fluid
سيتوبلازم	cytoplasm
سِيرَة	life history
سِيفُون	siphon
سَيَّل	liquefy

ش

شَبَكَة (الِكتْرُود)	grid
شَبَكَةُ تَوزِيعِ القُدْرَة	grid
شَبَكَة سِلْكِيَّة	wire gauze
شَبَكِيَّة (العَيْن)	retina
شِبْهُ الظِّلّ	penumbra
شُبَيْكَة	lattice
شَجَرِيّ	arboreal
شَحْم	lard
شَحْمُ الحُوت	blubber
شِحْنَة كَهْرَبائِيَّة	electric charge
شُحُوم	fats
شَدّ	tension
شُدْفَة	segment
شَرَج	anus
شُرْغُوف	tadpole
شَرْنَقَة	cocoon
شِرْيان	artery
شِرْيان دَقِيق	arteriole
شِرْيانُ الوَتِين	aorta
شَرِيحَة ثُنائِيَّة المَعدِن	bimetallic strip
شُرَيِّين	arteriole
شَظِيَّة ، عَظْمُ الشَّظِيَّة	fibula
شُعْبَة	phylum
شُعْبَة هَوائِيَّة	bronchus
شَعْر	hair
شَعْرِيّ	capillary
شُعْلَة	flame
شُعَيْرَة	filament

شِغافُ القَلْب	pericardium
شُغْـل	work
شَفّ	translucent
شَفَّاطَة	aspirator
شفـاف	transparent
شَفِيف	transparent
شِقّ حَامِضِيّ	acid radical
شَكْل ، طَوْر	phase
شَكْلٌ مُتَآصِل	allotrope
شَمْعُ البَرَافِين	paraffin wax
شَهْـد	honey
شَهِيق	inspiration; inhalation
شوكَةٌ رَنَّانَة	tuning fork
شَيْئِيَّة	objective
الشِّلاك	shellac

ص

الصَّاءَة	amnion
صَـادِر	efferent
صَالِبُ العَظْم الزَّوْرَقِي	keel
صَالِحٌ لِلزِّرَاعَة	arable
صِبَـاغ	pigment; dye
صُبَّـة	ingot
صِبْغ ، صَبْغَة	dye; pigment
صِبْغَة اليُود	tincture of iodine
صِبْغُ عَبَّاد الشَّمْس	litmus
صِبْغِيَّـة	chromosome
صَدَأ	rust; rusting
صَدِئ	corrode; rust
صَـدَى	echo
صَـدْر	thorax
صَدِيد	pus
صَعَّـد	sublime
صَفَارُ البَيْض	yolk
صَفَّارَةُ إِنْذَار	siren
صِفَـاق	peritoneum
صِفَـة	character
صَفْحَةُ الرِّيشَة	vane
الصَّفْرَاء	bile
صَفَّق (السائِل)	decant
صَفِيحَةٌ رَقِيقَة	lamina
صُلْب	solid
الصُّلْب ، الفُولاَذ	steel
صُلْب ، عَمُود فِقَري	backbone
صُلَّجَـة	cocoon
صَلْصَال نَارِيّ	fireclay
صِمَام ، صِمَامٌ الِكترُونِي	valve
صِمَامٌ ثُنَائِيّ	diode
صِمَامٌ ذُو شَرَفَتَين	bicuspid valve
صَمْغُ اللّك	shellac
صَمْغٌ نَبَاتِيّ	mucilage
صُنْعِيّ	synthetic
صُهَـارَة	melt
صَهْر	fusion; smelting
صَهَر	melt
صَهُور	flux
صَهِيرَة	fuse
الصَّوْتِيَّات	acoustics
صُودا الخَبِيز	baking soda
الصُّودا الكَاوِيَة	caustic soda
الصواعِد والهوابِط	stalagmites and stalactites
الصُّوديُوم	sodium

صُورَة	image
صُوف	wool
صِيغَة	formula
صِينِيّ	porcelain

ض

ضَار	predator
ضَباب	fog; mist
ضَبابٌ دُخانِيّ	smog
ضِرس	tooth
ضَغْط	pressure
ضَغطُ البُخَار	vapour pressure
ضَغْطٌ جَوّي	atmospheric pressure
ضِلع	rib
ضَوء	light
ضَوءُ الشَّمس	sunlight
ضَواة	ganglion

ط

طَائِفَة	group; class
طَاحِنٌ أَمامِيّ	premolar
طَاقَة	energy
طَاقَةٌ حَرارِيَّة	heat energy
طَاقَةُ الحَرَكَة ، طَاقَةٌ حَرَكِيَّة	kinetic energy
الطَّاقَةُ الذَّرِّيَّة	atomic energy
طَاقَةٌ ضوئيَّة	light energy
طَاقَةٌ كامِنَة	potential energy
طَاقَةٌ مِيكانِيكيَّة	mechanical energy
طَاقَةُ الوَضْع	potential energy
طَباشِير	chalk
طَبْلَةُ الأُذن	eardrum
طِبْي	teat
طِحَال	spleen
طَحالِب	algae
طُحْلُب ، حزاز	moss
الطَّرَح	hypermetropia
طَرْحُ الرِّيش	moulting
طَرْحُ الفَضَلات	egestion
طَرُوق	malleable
طَسْت	trough
طُعْم	vaccine
طُعْم (رُقعي)	graft
طُفَال	fireclay; clay
طُفَالٌ رَمْلِيّ	loam
طَفْرة	mutation
طَفويَّة	buoyancy
طُفَيل ، طُفَيلِيّ	parasite
طَقْطَقَة	knocking
طِلاء	paint
طَلَى بالزِّنْك	galvanize
الطِّلاءُ بالكَهرباء	electroplating
الطَّمْث	menstruation
طَمْي	silt
الطَّواحِن	molars
طَوْر	phase
طَوْق	annulus
طُولٌ بُؤرِيّ	focal length
طُولُ البَصر	hypermetropia
طُولٌ مَوْجِيّ	wavelength
طَيَّار ، سَريعُ التَّبَخُّر	volatile

طَيْف — spectrum
طِين — clay
طِينٌ حَرَارِيّ — fireclay

ظ

ظَاهِرَة — phenomenon
ظِلّ — shadow; umbra
ظَهْرِيّ — dorsal

ع

عاتِقُ (الميزان) — beam
عَازِل — insulator
عَازِلٌ كَهْرَبَائِيّ — dielectric
عَاشِب — herbivorous
عَاشِبٌ لاَحِم — omnivorous
عَامِلٌ تَجْفِيف — drying agent
عَامِلٌ مُؤَكْسِد — oxidant
عَانَة — pubis
عاير ، يعاير — calibrate
عَتَلَة — lever
عَجِين — dough
العَدَدُ الذَّرِّيّ — atomic number
عَدَسَة — lens
عَدَسَةٌ أَكْرُومَاتِيَّة — achromatic lens
عَدَسَةٌ شَيْئِيَّة — objective
عَدَسَةٌ عَيْنِيَّة — eyepiece
عَدَسَةٌ لاَلَوْنِيَّة — achromatic lens
عَدَسَةٌ لاَمَّة أو مُجَمِّعَة — converging lens
عَدَسَةٌ مُفَرِّقَة — diverging lens
عَدَسَةٌ مُقَعَّرَة — diverging lens
عَدَسَةٌ مُكَبِّرَة — magnifying glass
عَدِيمُ الذَّوَبَان — insoluble
عَرَضِيّ — adventitious
عَرَق — perspiration; sweat
عِرْق — vein
عُسْقُول — tuber
عَسَل — honey
عُسْلُوج — twig
عُشْب ، عُشْبَة ضَارَّة — weed
عُشْبِيّ — herbaceous
عُشْر — deci-
عَشَرَة — deca-
عُصَارَة — sap
عَصَب — nerve
عَصَبَة — neuron
عُصْعُص — coccyx
عَصِيرٌ خَلَوِيّ — cell sap
عَضُد — humerus
عَضَلَة — muscle
العَضَلَةُ ذَاتُ الرَّأْسَيْن — biceps
عُضْو — organ
عُضْوٌ أَثَرِيّ — vestigial organ
عُضْو الإِنْتَاج — armature
عُضْوُ تَبْدِيل ، عُضْوُ تَوْحِيد — commutator
عُضْوٌ لاَ وَظِيفِيّ — vestigial organ
عُضْوِيّ — organic
العَطَالَة — inertia
عَظْم — bone
عَظْمُ الصَّدْر — breastbone
عَظْمُ العَانَة — pubis

عَظْمُ العَضُد	humerus
عَظْمُ الفَخِذ	femur
العَظْمُ المِطْرَقِيّ	hammer
العَفَج	duodenum
عَفَن	mould
عَفوِيّاً	spontaneously
عَقّار	drug
عَقّار مُسَكِّن	sedative
عُقال	cramp
عُقْدَة عَصَبِيَّة	ganglion
عَكِر	turbid
عَكُوس	reversible
العَلاة	anvil
عَلَفٌ سَلْوِيّ ، عَلَفٌ مَطْمُور	silage
عِلْمُ البِيئَة	ecology
عِلْمُ التَّشْرِيح	anatomy
عِلْمُ الأَجِنَّة	embryology
عِلْمُ الأَحْياء	biology
عِلْمُ الحَيَوان	zoology
عِلْمُ الصَّوْت	acoustics
عِلْمُ النَّبات	botany
عِلْمُ الوِراثَة	genetics
عِلْمُ وَظائِف الأَعْضاء	physiology
عُلَيْبَة	capsule
عَمَى الأَلْوان ، العَمَى اللَّوْنِي	colour blindness
عَمَلِيَّة	process
عَمُود ، خَلِيَّة (كَهربائيَّة)	cell
عَمُودٌ فَقَرِيّ	backbone
عَمِيرَة	colony
عُنْصُر	element
عُنْصُرٌ مُكَوِّن	component
عُنُق	stalk
عَنَمَة	tendril
عَوالِق	plankton
عَيْن	eye
عَيْنِيَّة	eyepiece

غ

غائِط	faeces
غاز	gas
غازُ الأُوزون	ozone
غازُ الاسْتِصْباح	coal gas
غازُ الأَسِيتيلين (إيثاين)	acetylene
غازُ البيُوتان	butane
الغازُ الطَّبِيعِيّ	natural gas
غازُ الفَحْم	coal gas
غازُ الكْلُور	chlorine
غازُ النَّشادِر	ammonia
غازُ النِّيُون	neon
غازُ الهِلْيُوم	helium
غازُ الهِيدْرُوجِين	hydrogen
غازُولِين	(gas)oline; petrol
غازِيّ	gaseous
غُبارُ الطَّلْع	pollen
غُثاء	scum
غُدَّة	gland
الغُدَّة الصَّعْتَرِيَّة	thymus
غُدَّة صَمّاء (لا قَنَوِيَّة)	ductless gland
غُدَّة عَرَقِيَّة	sweat gland
غُدَّةُ الكُظْر	adrenal body
الغُدَّة النُّخامِيَّة	pituitary gland
الغُدَّة النَّكَفِيَّة	parotid gland

غرافيت	graphite
غرافيت تِجاريّ	black lead
غرام	gram
غَرَوانيّ	colloid
غَرَوانيّ هُلاميّ القَوام	gel
غَريزة	instinct
غِرْيَن	silt
غَزير	copious; abundant
غِشاء	membrane
غِشاءُ الجَفْنِ الباطِنُ	conjunctiva
غِشاءٌ مُنْفِذٌ أو نَفيذ	permeable membrane
غُصَيْن	twig
غُصَيْنٌ عَصَبيّ	dendron
غُضْروف	cartilage; gristle
غِلافُ البِذْرة (أو الثَّمَرة)	pericarp
غَلْصَم	gill
غَلْصَمة	epiglottis
غلفانومتر	galvanometer
غَلْفَن	galvanize
غلوكوز	glucose; grape sugar
غَلَيان	boiling
غيرُ ثابِت	unstable
غيرُ ذَوّاب	insoluble
غيرُ شَفّاف	opaque
غيرُ عُضْويّ	inorganic
غيرُ فَعّال	inert
غيرُ مُتَبَلْوِر	amorphous
غيرُ مُسْتَقِرّ	unstable
غيرُ مُنْفِذ	impervious
غيرُ مُنْفِذ للضَّوء	opaque
غَيْمة	cloud

ف

فِئةُ الدَّم	blood group
فاصِمة انصِهاريّة	fuse
فِبْر ، لِيفة	fibre
فُتْحة	aperture
فَتْرة	period
فَتْرةُ الحَضانة	incubation period
فَتيلة	filament
فحم الانتراسيت	anthracite
فَحْم (حَجَريّ)	coal
الفحم الحيواني	animal charcoal
الفَحْمُ العَظْميّ	boneblack
فَحْمُ الكوك	coke
فَخّاريّات	earthenware
فَخِذ	femur
فَرّازة	centrifuge
فَراغ	vacuum
الفَرْج	vulva
فِرْجار الثُّخَن	callipers
فَرْخُ الضِّفْدَع	tadpole
فَرْضٌ ، فَرَضِيّة	hypothesis
فَرْطُ التَّبْريد	supercooling
فُرْن	furnace
فُرْنُ الصَّهْر ، الفُرْنُ العالي	blast furnace
فَرْو	fur
فُسْفات الكالْسيوم	calcium phosphate
الفُسْفور	phosphorus
فَسيلة	cutting
الفِسيولوجيّة	physiology

فَصَلَ بالتَّقطِير	distil
فُضَالَـة	residue
الفِضَّـة	silver
فَضَلات	waste products
فَضْلَـة	residue
فُطْر	fungus
فُطْر صَغِير	mould
فَطَمَ	wean
فِطْنَة ، ذكاء	intelligence
فَعَّـال	reactive
فَعَّالِيَّة ، كفايَة	efficiency
فَقَـارَة	vertebra
فَقْد اللَّمْعَة	tarnish
فَقْرُ الدَّم	anaemia
فِقْرَة	vertebra
فَقْرَة العنق الثَّانِية	axis
فَقْرَةُ العُنُقِ الأُولَى	atlas
فَـكّ	jaw
فِلِزّ	metal
فِلِزّاتٌ قلوِيَّة	alkali metals
فَلْس	scale
فُلْـط	volt
فُلْطمِتر	voltmeter
فُلْطِيَّـة	voltage
فِلْقَـة	segment
فِلْقَة (البِزْرَة)	cotyledon
فَلَـك	orbit
فَلْوَرِيَّـة	fluorescence
فِلِّين	cork
فَهْقَـة	atlas
فَوَّار	effervescent
الفُوسفُور	phosphorus

فَوقَ تُربِيّ ، فوق سَطْحِي	epigeal
الفُولاذ	steel
فُولاذٌ لا يَصْدَأ	stainless steel
فُولط ، فولت	volt
الفيتامينات	vitamins
فَيرُوس ، حُمَة	virus
فَيْلَجَـة	cocoon
فَيْلَسُوف	philosopher

ق

قابِلٌ للانْشِطَار	fissile
قابِل للانْعِكَاس	reversible
قابِل للانْفِجار	explosive
قابِل للذَّوَبَان	soluble
قابِل للطَّرْق	malleable
قابِلِيَّة الاستِثَارَة	irritability
قَـار	pitch; tar
قارُ الفحم الحَجَرِيّ	coal tar
قـارِبٌ	boat
قارِتٌ ، عاشِبٌ لاحِم	omnivorous
قارِضٌ ، قاضِم	rodent
قَازِب ، برمائي	amphibious
قاطِعَـة	incisor
قَـاعِدَة	base
قَـاعِدِيّ	basic
قاعِدِيَّـة	basicity
ألقَـالِي	alkali
قابِطة شَبَك	bosshead
قَبْلِي ، امامي	anterior
قِحْف	cranium

قُدرة	power
قُدرَةٌ حِصَانِيَّة	horsepower
القُدرَة الكَهربائِيَّة	electric power
القُدرة النوَوِيَّة	nuclear power
قَدَمَة	callipers
قَذف	egestion; ejection
قُرارَة	deposit; sediment
قُرصُ النَّورة	receptacle
قُرَمَة	corm
قَرنُ استِشعار	antenna
قَرنُ (البَقل)	legume
القرنِيَّة ، قرنِيَّة العَين	cornea
قَزحِيَّة (العَين)	iris
قِشر	bark; cortex
قِشرة ، حَرشفة	scale
قِشرة كِلسِيَّة	scale; fur
قَصّ	breastbone; sternum
القَصَبَة الصُغرى	fibula
قصبةُ نَفخ	blowpipe
القَصَبَة الهوائِيَّة	trachea; windpipe
القصدير	tin
قَصر	bleaching
قِصَرُ البَصَر	myopia; short sight
قَصِفٌ ، قصيم	brittle
القُصورُ الذَّاتي	inertia
قَصِيّ	distal
قَضيب (الذَّكَر)	penis
قُطارة	distillate
قُطب	electrode
قُطب (المِرآة) ، قُطب (المغنطيس)	pole
قَطَّرَ	distil
قَطِران	tar
قَطِران الفَحم	coal tar
قطعَة دائرية	segment
قُلْب	cambium
قَلْب	heart
قِلف	bark
قَلَم (الريشة)	quill
قَلم (الزهرة)	style
قِلْي	alkali
قَمَّام	scavenger
قِمْع	funnel
قِمعُ القَطر ، قمع قَطَّار	dropping funnel
قمين ذريّ	atomic pile
قُنابَة	bract
قَنَاة	canal
قَناةُ الصَّفْراء	bile duct
قَنَاةُ الهَضم	alimentary canal; gut
القَنْد	sugar
قوازِب	amphibia
قُوَّة	force
قُوَّةُ الاستِمرَار	inertia
قُوَّةُ التَّكافُؤ	valency
قُوَّةٌ دافِعَةٌ كَهربائِيَّة	electromotive force
قُوَّةُ الطَّرْدِ المَرْكَزِيّ	centrifugal force
قُوَّة (العَدَسَة)	power
قُوَّة نابِذَة	centrifugal force
قَوقَعة (الأُذُن)	cochlea
قُولُون	colon
قَيح	pus
قِير	pitch; tar
قِيمَةُ الذُّرْوَة ، القيمة الذُروِيَّة	peak value

ك

كَائِنٌ حَيّ	organism
كائنٌ مُمْرِض	pathogen
كـاثُود	cathode
كـأس	beaker
كأسُ الزَّهْرة	calyx
كاسياتُ البزر	Angiospermae
كأسيَّة	sepal
كـاشِف	indicator; reagent
كـافُور	camphor
الكالسيوم	calcium
كالُوري	calorie
كالُوريمتر	calorimeter
كاميرا	camera
كـاوٍ	caustic
كَبِـد	liver
كَبِـديّ	hepatic
الكِبريت	sulphur
كِبريتُ العَمُود	brimstone
كِبريتات الكالسيُوم	calcium sulphate
كِبريتات الكالسيوم المائيَّة	gypsum
كِبريتات النُّحاس	copper sulphate
كُتلَـة	mass
كُتلَة مَعدِنيَّة مَصبوبَة	ingot
كَتيم	impervious
كَثافَـة	density
الكَثافَة النِّسبيّة	relative density
كَثَّف	condense
كُحول أثيلي	ethanol

كُحُولٌ صِرْف	absolute alcohol
كَـدَّر	tarnish
كَـدِر	turbid
كَرْبَلَة ، خِباء	carpel
كَربُون	carbon
كَربُونات	carbonates
كَربونٌ مُنَشَّط	activated carbon
كَربُوهِيدرات	carbohydrates
كَرَّر	refine
كُرسِيّ الزهرة	receptacle
كروموسُوم	chromosome
كريات الدمِ البَيضاءُ	white blood cells
كريات الدم الحمراء	red blood cells
كُرَيَّـة	corpuscle
كُرَيَّة (دمٍ) بَيْضاءُ ، كُرَيْضَة	leucocyte
كُرَيَّة (دمٍ) حَمراءُ	erythrocyte
الكُزاز	tetanus
الكُساح ، كُساح الأطفال	rickets
كُسوف (الشمس)	eclipse of the sun
كَشَف	detect
الكُظر	adrenal body
كُظْرين	adrenalin
كَظيمـة	thermos flask
كَعبٌ بَصَليّ	corm
كِفايـة	efficiency
كَـلال	fatigué
كَلبيّ	canine
كِلْس	lime
الكَلْسيُوم	calcium
كُلْوَة	kidney
كلُور	chlorine
كلُورور ، كلوريد	chloride

كلوروفيل	chlorophyll
كُلْيَة	kidney
كِمّ (الزَّهرة)	perianth
كَمبيوم	cambium
كَمِّيَّة التحرُّك	momentum
كَمِّيَّة ثابِتَة	constant quantity
كَمِّيَّة الحرارة	heat quantity
كَمِّيَّة مُوَجَّهة	vector quantity
الكهربائيّة الساكنة	static electricity
كَهْرَمان	amber
كُهَيْرِب	electron
كوارتز ، مرو	quartz
كُوب	beaker
كُوَّة	aperture; fenestra
كُوزٌ صنوبريّ	cone
كُوك	coke
كُوكايين	cocaine
الكيروسين	paraffin oil
كِيسٌ هَوائِيّ	air sac
الكِيمياءُ القَديمة	alchemy
كُيَيْس غِشائِيّ ، كُيَيْس مَثانِيّ	cyst

ل

لاامتزاجيّ	immiscible
لابِلَّوْري	amorphous
لاتَزاوُجِيّ ، لاجِنسي	asexual
لاحِم	carnivore
لاخَلُوط	immiscible
لاذِع	pungent
لامائِليّ	aneroid
لاشَكليّ	amorphous
لاعُضويّ	inorganic
لافَقاريّ ، لافقري	invertebrate
لامائيّ	anhydrous
لَبَن	milk
لَبُون	mammal
لِتْر	litre
لِحاء	phloem
لِحاءٌ داخليّ	bast
لِحاء فلّينيّ	cork
لِحاء قشري	cortex
لِحاء قِلْفي	bark
لِحام	solder; welding
ألّدائن	plastics
لدائني لَدْن	plastic
لَزِج	viscous
لُزوب ، امتزاز	adsorption
لِسان	tongue
لِسانُ المِزمار	epiglottis
لُعاب	saliva
لَقاح (تطعيم)	vaccine
لَقاح (الزهرة)	pollen
لَمْس	touch
لِمْف ، لِنْف	lymph
لَهَب	flame
لَهُوب	flammable; inflammable
لَوزتا الحَلْق	tonsils
لَون	colour
لَونٌ صِبغيّ	pigment
لِيفة	fibre
لُيَيْفَة	filament

م

مـاء	water
ألماءُ الثَّقيل	heavy water
ماء الصودا	soda water
مـائع	fluid
مائع ، متميّع	deliquescent
ماءٌ عَسِر	hard water
ماءٌ غازيّ	soda water
ماءٌ مُقطَّر	distilled water
مـائيّ	aquatic; aqueous
ماءٌ يَسِر	soft water
مِئبَر	anther
مادّة استشفافيّة ، مادة تتبُّع	tracer
مادّةُ تزليق	lubricant
مادّة حفّازَة	catalyst
مادّة عازِلَة	insulator
مادة غروانيّة	colloid
مادّة متفجّرة	explosive
مادّة مُذابة	solute
مادّة مُذيبَة	solvent
مادّةٌ مُؤكْسِدَة	oxidant
مـازوت	fuel oil
مـاس	diamond
ماصّة (مُدَرَّجة)	pipette
ماصّ الرُّطوبة	hygroscopic
مِنْفـاق	periscope
مانِعٌ لِلعُفونة	antiseptic
مُبَرِّد	coolant
مُبَـدِّل	commutator
مُبيدُ آلجَراثيم	disinfectant
مُبيدٌ حَشَريّ	insecticide
مَبيض	ovary
مُبَيِّن ، دليل	indicator
مُتابِع ، مُرَحِّل	relay
مُتَبَلِّر ، مُتبلور	crystalline
مُتَجَانِس	homogeneous
مُتَّجِـه	vector
مُتَّحِدُ آلمَركز	concentric
مُتَحَرِّض	armature
مُتَحَرِّك	mobile
مِتْر	metre
مُتَسَيِّل	deliquescent
مُتَطاير	volatile
مُتعـادِل	neutral
مُتَعَضٍّ	organism
مُتَعَكِّر	turbid
مُتَفاعِـل	reactive
مُتَفَجِّر	explosive
مُتَفَرِّد	discrete
مُتَقَبِّـل	receptor
مُتماكِنات	isotopes
مُتَمركِز	concentric
مُتَمَوِّه ، مُتَمَيِّه	hydrated
مُتَمَيِّز	discrete
مُتَمَيِّع	deliquescent
مُتناسِب	proportional
مُتَناسِبٌ عَكسِيّاً	inversely proportional
مُتَنَحٍّ	recessive
مُتَنَقِّـل	mobile
مُتَوازِي أَضلاع	parallelogram
مُتَوَسِّـط	median

مَثَـانَة	bladder; urinary bladder
مَثَانَةٌ هَوائِيَّة	air bladder
مُثَبِّتَةُ درجة الحرارة	thermostat
مَثْعَب	siphon
مُثِير	stimulus
مَجـال	field
مَجال كهربائي	electric field
مَجالٌ مِغنطيسي	magnetic field
مُجْتَرّ	ruminant
مُجَفِّف	drying agent
مُجَفِّفَـة	desiccator
مَجْلَـة	ampulla
مَجموعـة	group; assemblage
مِجْهـار	loudspeaker; microphone
مِجْهَر	microscope
مَجْهُود	effort
مُحّ	yolk
مُحَايِـد	neutral
مَحجِرَ (العين)	orbit
مُحَـدَّب	convex
مُحَدَّب ٱلوَجهين	biconvex
مِحرار	thermometer
مِحْرق	focus
مُحَرِّكٌ كهربائيّ	electric motor
مُحَصِّلَـة	resultant
مِحقَنَـة	syringe
مَحلُول	solution
مَحلولٌ عياريّ	standard solution
(مَحلولٌ) قِلويّ	alkaline
محلولٌ كُحوليّ	tincture
مَحلول كهربائي	electrolyte
مَحلولٌ مُبَرِّد	coolant

مَحلولٌ مِلحيّ	brine
مِحوَر	axis
مِحورُ العَصَبة	axon
مُحول	biennial
مُحَوِّل	transformer
مُحيط ، بيئة	environment
مُحيطُ ٱلدّائِرَة	circumference
مُخّ	cerebrum
مُخـاط	mucus
مِخبار مُدَرَّج	graduated cylinder
مُخَـدِّر	anaesthetic
مَخروط	cone
مُخْصِب	fertilizer
مُخَطَّطٌ بيانيّ	graph
مُخَفِّف	diluent
مُخَفَّف	dilute
مُخْـل	lever
مُخَلَّفات الاحتِراق	clinker
مَخلوط	mixture
مُخَيخ	cerebellum
مَـدار	orbit
مَدُّ البَصرِ	hypermetropia; long sight
مُدَّخِرة كهربائيَّة	accumulator
مِدَقَّـة	pestle
مِدَقَّة (الزهرة)	pistil
مُـذاب	solute
مُذيب	solvent
مِرآة	mirror
مَرارة	gall bladder
مِرَّة	bile
مُرتَـكَز	fulcrum
مَرجـان	coral

مُرَحِّل ، مُرَحِّلَة	relay
مُرْدٍ	antibiotic
مَردود ، كِفاية	efficiency
مِرذاذٌ بالغاز المَضغوط	aerosol
مُرَسِّخ (الصِّبغة)	mordant
مُرَشِّح	filter
مُرَشِّحُ أَلوان	colour filter
مَرَض	disease
مِرطاب	hygrometer
مَرعى	pasture
مِرفاعٌ لَوْلَبِيّ	screw jack
مِرقَب	telescope
مُرَكَّب	compound
مُرَكَّب ، مُعَقَّد	complex
مُرَكَّبٌ إسهاميّ التَّرابُط	covalent compound
مُرَكِّبَة	component
مُرَكَّبٌ كيماويّ	chemical compound
مُرَكَّز	concentrated
مَرْكَزُ الثِّقَل	centre of gravity
مُرَكِّم ، مِرْكَم	accumulator
مَرْمَر ، رُخام	marble
المَرْو	quartz
مِرواز	barometer
مُرونَة	elasticity
المَريء	oesophagus
مُزدَوِجَة	couple
مُزدَوِجة حراريّة	thermocouple
مُزَلِّق	lubricant
مِزمار (الحَنجَرة)	glottis
مَزيج	mixture; blend
مَزيجٌ مُعلَّق	suspension
مُزيلٌ للأوساخ	detergent
مُزيلُ الرّائحة	deodorant
مِساحَة	area
مَسارٌ مَداريّ	orbit
مَسارُ المَقذوف	trajectory
مُساعِدُ صَهر	flux
مَسامِيّ	porous
مُستحاثَة ، مُستحجرة ، أُحفورة	fossil
مُستَحلَب	emulsion
مُستَرطِب	hygroscopic
مُستَعلَق	suspension
مُستَعمَرة	colony
مُستَقبِل	receiver
المستقيم	rectum
مستقيم مُتوسِّط	median
مُستَنبَت	culture
مُستوٍ	plane
مستوى بُؤرِيّ	focal plane
مَسحوقُ البارود	gunpowder
مسحوقُ الخَبيز	baking powder
مَسْحُوقُ القَصْر	bleaching powder
مِسْعَر	calorimeter
مُسَكِّن	sedative
مُسهِل	laxative
مِسيَل	hydrometer
مُشِعّ	radioactive
المَشيمَة	placenta
مَصّ	absorption
مَصّاصَة	aspirator
مِصباحٌ قوسيّ	arc light
مُصدِر	efferent
مَصْدَر	origin
مُصدِرُ الفَقاقيع	effervescent

مِصراع ، صِمام	valve
مُصطنع	synthetic
مَصْعَد	anode
مَصْل	serum
مَصْلُ الدّم	plasma
مِصْهَر	fuse
مَصِير ، مصران	intestine
مُضادٌّ حَيَوِيّ	antibiotic
مِضَخَّة	pump
مِضَخّة دافِعة ، مضخة دَفْقٍ قَسْرِيّ	force pump
مِضَخّة رافِعة	lift pump
مُضخِّم	amplifier
مَضْغ	mastication
مِطرقة	hammer
مُطفِئة حَرِيق ، مِطفأة حريق	fire extinguisher
مِطفَأةُ حَرِيقٍ رغويّة	foam fire extinguisher
مُطَهِّر	antiseptic; disinfectant
مُطَهَّر	aseptic
مِعًى	intestine
المِعَى المُستقيم	rectum
مُعادَلة (جَبريّة او كِيماوِيّة)	equation
مُعادَلَة (الحامض او القلي)	neutralization
مُعامِلُ الإنكِسار	refractive index
المُعايَرة بالتحليل الحجمي	titration
مُعبِل	deciduous
مَعِدَة	stomach
مَعْدِن	mineral
مَعْدِن فِلِزّي	metal
مَعِدِيّ	gastric
مَعْص	cramp
مِعْصَم	wrist
المِعْقَد	pancreas

مُعقَّدُ التَّركِيب	complex
مُعَقَّم	aseptic
مِعلاق	tendril
مُعَمِّر	perennial
مُعوَجَّة	retort
مُعيقُ التَّجَمُّد	antifreeze
مُعَيَّنِيّ	rhombic
مِغْبَر (الزَّهر)	nectar
مَغْرِز	socket
مِغْزَل	spindle
مَغطَس رمليّ	sand bath
مَغْطَسٌ مائيّ	water bath
المَغْنِيسوم	magnesium
مِغنطيس كهربائيّ	electromagnet
مغنطيسيّة الأرض	earth's magnetism
مُفاعِل (كيماويّ)	reagent
مُفاعِل (نوويّ)	reactor
مُفاعِلٌ ذَرِّيّ	atomic pile
مُفتلِحٌ	arable
مُفرِّعُ التَّيَّار	shunt
مُفْرَز	secretion
مَفْصِل	joint
مُقاوَمَة	resistance
مُقاوِمُ التجَمُّد	antifreeze
مُقتَفٍ	tracer
مِقراب	telescope
مِقرابٌ فَلَكيّ	astronomical telescope
مِقْطَر	still
مُقَعَّر	concave
مُقعر الوَجْهَين	biconcave
مُقَوِّم ، مكوِّن	constituent
مقياسُ الارتِفاع	altimeter

مِقياسُ الأمبير	ammeter
مقياسُ دَرَجَةِ الحَرَارَةِ	thermometer
مقياس الرُّطوبة النسبيَّة	hygrometer
مِقياسُ الضغط الجوّيّ	barometer
مقياسُ الفلطيَّة	voltmeter
مُكَبِّرُ الصَّوت	loudspeaker
مِكْبَس هَيدرُولي، مكبس مائيّ	hydraulic press
مِكْثاف السوائل	hydrometer
مُكَثِّف (كهربائي)	condenser; capacitor
مُكَثِّفَة (بصريَّة)	condenser
مِكْرُوب	germ
مِكشاف كهربائي	electroscope
مُكَعَّب	cubic
مَكِنَــة	machine
مُكَوِّن	component
مَلاريــا	malaria
مِــلاط	cement; mortar
مُلتحمة	conjunctiva
مُلتهِب	flammable
مِلْح	salt
مِلْحٌ حامِضِيٌّ	acid salt
مِلْحُ الطَّعام	table salt
مِلحٌ قاعِديٌّ	basic salt
مُلْغَم	amalgam
مِلَفٌّ خانِق	choke
مِلَفٌّ لولَبِيٌّ	solenoid
مِلْقَط	forceps; tongs
مَلِكَة	queen
مِلْوَق	spatula
مِليلِتر	millilitre
مُلَيِّن	laxative
مُمارِسُ الكيمياءِ القديمة	alchemist
مَمَــال	gradient
مُمرِض	pathogen
مَمَص	siphon
مُمَيًّا ، مُمَيَّه	hydrated
مُمَيِّز	characteristic
مَناعَــة	immunity
مُناوبة المَحاصيل	rotation of crops
مُنْبِت	habitat
مُنْبَسِط	plane
مُنَبِّــه	stimulus
مُنْتَجٌ ثانَوِيٌّ	by-product
مُنْتَجٌ فُضالِيٌّ	waste product
مُنْحَسِر	recessive
مُنْحَلٌّ كهربائي	electrolyte
مَنسوجات	textiles
مَنْشَأ	origin
مَنْشور	prism
مِنْطَقَــة	zone
مِنْظارٌ ثُنائِيُّ العَيْنِيَّة	binoculars
مُنَظِّف	detergent
مُنَوِّب	alternator
ألمَنِيّ	semen
مَهْبِــط	cathode
مَهْبِــل	vagina
مُهَدِّىء (النيوترونات)	moderator
المواد اللدائنية	plastics
مُوتور كهربائي	electric motor
مَوْجَــة	wave
مُوَرِّثــة	gene
مُوَرِّد	afferent
مَوْشور	prism
مُوَصِّــل	oonductor

مَوْطِن	habitat
مُؤَكسِد	oxidant
مُوَلَّد ، هَجِين	hybrid
مُوَلِّد	generator
مُوَلِّد التَّيار المُتَناوِب	alternator
مُوَلِّدٌ كَهربائيّ	dynamo; generator
مُوَلِّد المُضَاد	antigen
مِيزَان	balance
ميزان زُنبركيّ	spring balance
مِيزان قَبَّانيّ	steelyard
مِيزَة	property; characteristic
مِيْسَم	stigma
منفاق	periscope
ميكروسكوب	microscope
مِيكروفُون	microphone
المَيْلُ (المغنطيسي)	dip
مُيَّه ، مُمَيَّه	hydrated

ن

نابٌ	canine
نابِذَة	centrifuge
نابِيّ	canine
نافِذة	fenestra
ناقِل	conductor
ناقِلُ جراثيم	vector
ناقِلٌ من الطرف الى ٱلمركز	afferent
ناقِلٌ مِن المَرْكَزِ الى الأطراف	efferent
نامٍ فوقَ سطحِ الأرض	epigeal
نباتٌ أحاديّ الفلقة	monocotyledon
نَبَاتٌ ثُنائي ٱلحَوْل ، نبات مُحوِل	biennial
النباتات الحَوليّة	annuals
نباتٌ دائمُ الخُضْرَة	evergreen
نبات مائيّ	hydrophyte
نباتٌ من ذوات الفِلْقَتَيْن	dicotyledon
نَبض ، نَبضة	pulse
نِتَاجٌ جَانِبيّ	by-product
ألنَّتْح	transpiration
النِّتروجين	nitrogen
نُحَاس	copper
نُحاسٌ أصفَر	brass
نُخاعٌ شَوكيّ	spinal cord
نُخاعُ العَظْم	marrow
نَدَب ، نَدبة	scar
نَزْعُ الماء	dehydration
النَّزْلة الوافِدة	influenza
نِسبيّ	proportional
نُسْغ	sap
نَسَق	lattice
نَسِيج	tissue
نسيجُ الخشَب	xylem
نسيجٌ شَبكيّ	gauze
ألنَّشا	starch
نَشر ، انتشَر	diffuse
نَشر ، انتِشَار	diffusion
نِصْفُ شَفَّاف	translucent
نَصْلُ الرِّيشة	vane
نَصَّل (اللّون)	decolorize
نَصْلُ (الوَرَقة)	lamina
نِطاق ، حِزام	girdle
نِطاق ، مِنطَقة	zone
نُطْفَة	sperm
نَظَائِر	isotopes

نَظَرِيَّة	theory
نظريةُ النُّشوء والإرتقاء	evolution
نَغْل	hybrid
نُفايَةُ الحَدائِد	scrap metal
نَفِضيّ ، مُعبل ، سَليب	deciduous
النِّفط ، الزَّيْت	petroleum; oil
نَقَّى	refine
نُقطةَ إرتكاز	fulcrum
نُقطةُ الأنصِهار	melting point
نُقطةُ التَّجَمُّد	freezing point
نُقطةُ الغَلَيان	boiling point
نُقطةُ النَّدى	dew point
نَقْل	conduction
نَقْلُ الدَّم	transfusion
نِقْي	marrow
نَماء ، نُمُوّ	growth
نواة (الخليّة او الذَّرَّة)	nucleus
نَوَّاس	pendulum
نُور	light
نَوْرَة	flower
نَوَسان	oscillation
نَوع	species
نَوعِيّ	specific
النِّيكل	nickel
النِّيُون	neon

هـ

هاتِف	telephone
هاوِن	mortar
هَباءٌ جَوِّيّ	aerosol
هُجوع	dormancy
هَجين	hybrid
هُدْب	cilia
هَدْرَجة	hydrogenation
هُرْب	peritoneum
هُرْمون	hormone
هَضْم	digestion
هِلاَليَّة	meniscus
الهِليُوم	helium
الهوابِطُ والصَّواعِدُ	stalactites and stalagmites
هَيْجرومِتْر ، مِرطاب	hygrometer
هَيدرُوجين	hydrogen
الهيدرُوجين الثَّقيل	deuterium
هَيْدروكَربونات	hydrocarbons
هَيدرُوكسيد	hydroxide
هَيدرُومِتْر	hydrometer
هيكلٌ عَظْمِيّ	skeleton
الهَيُولى	protoplasm
هيموغلوبين ، يحمور	haemoglobin

و

وارِد	afferent
وَاط	watt
وافِر	copious
وَتَر	tendon
وَتَرٌ صَوتِيّ	vocal cord
وَتَرُ العُرقُوب	Achilles tendon
وَتين	aorta
وَجْه	face
وُجَيْه	facet

وَحدةُ تبريد ، بَرّاد	refrigerator
وَحْدَةُ الضَّغْطِ الجَوِّي	atmosphere
وَحْدَة (قِياس)	unit
وَحدةُ الكُتلَة الذرِّية	atomic mass unit
وِراثـة	heredity
وَرَق	paper
وَرقُ ترشيح	filter paper
وَرَقَةٌ تُوَيْجيَّة	petal
وَرَقَةُ نَبات	leaf
وَرنيش	varnish
وُرود (الأشعَّة)	incidence
وَريـد	vein
ألوريدُ الأَجوَف	vena cava
وُرَيقَـة	leaflet
وَزْن	weight
الوزنُ النَّوعيّ	specific gravity
وَسَط ، بيئة	environment
وَشَـلَ	percolate
وَشيعَـة	spindle
وَصْلَـة	bond
وَضْع ، حَالة	state
وَظيفَـة	function
وِعَـاء	vessel
وِعاءُ استِقْبال	receiver
وِعاءُ تَجْفيف	desiccator
وِعاءٌ مَسَامِيّ	porous pot
وِعَـائِيّ	vascular
وِعائِيَّاتُ البُزور	Angiospermae
وَعْي	consciousness
وَقْب ، وَقْبَة	socket
وَقود	fuel
وَلُود	viviparous
وَهَن ، كَلال	fatigue

ي

يَخْمُور	haemoglobin
يَخْضُور	chlorophyll
يَدُ الهَاوَن	pestle
يَرَقانَـة	larva
يَرَقَانَةُ الشَّريطية	bladderworm
يَرَقَانَةُ العُثّ والفراش	caterpillar
يَرَقَـة	larva
يَرَقَةٌ ذُبابِيَّة	maggot
يَعْسُوب	drone
أليُود	iodine

ABBREVIATIONS. إخْتِصَارَاتٌ

a. = adjective.	صفة	*ppr. = present participle.*	اسم فاعل
ad. = adverb.	حال او ظرف	*p. pron. = personal pronoun.*	ضمير
con. = conjunction.	حرف عطف	*int. = interrogation.*	اسم استفهام
n. = noun.	اسم	*rel. = relative.*	اسم موصول
pl. = plural.	جمع	*dem. = demonstrative.*	اسم إشارة
pp. = past participle.	اسم مفعول	*pp. = preposition.*	حرف جر

ENGLISH-ARABIC DICTIONARY

قاموس انكليزي وعربي

A

A *or* **an.** حَرْفُ نَكِرَة

Abaft *ad.* عِنْدَ مُؤَخَّرِ ٱلْمَرْكَبِ

Abandon *v. t.* تَرَكَ . هَجَرَ

Abase *v. t.* أَذَلَّ . وَضَعَ . حَطَّ

Abasement *n.* ذِلٌّ . ضِعَةٌ

Abash *v. t.* خَجَّلَ . أَخْجَلَ

Abate *v. t.* or *i.* نَقَّصَ . نَقَصَ

Abatement *n.* تَقْلِيلٌ . تَخْفِيضٌ

Abbess *n.* رَئِيسَةُ دَيْرٍ

Abbey *n.* دَيْرٌ

Abbot *n.* رَئِيسُ دَيْرٍ

Abbreviate *v. t.* قَصَّرَ . إِخْتَصَرَ

Abbreviation *n.* تَقْصِيرٌ . إِخْتِصَارٌ

Abdicate *v. t.* or *i.* خَلَعَ نَفْسَهُ مِن

Abdication *n.* تَنَازُلٌ عَنْ

Abdomen *n.* بَطْنٌ

Abdominal *a.* بَطْنِيٌّ

Abduct *v. t.* خَطَفَ . إِخْتَلَسَ

Abduction *n.* خَطْفٌ . إِخْتِلَاسٌ

Abet *v. t.* حَرَّضَ . عَاوَنَ . عَاضَدَ

Abhor *v. t.* مَقَتَ . كَرِهَ

Abhorrence *n.* مَقْتٌ . كَرَاهَةٌ

Abide *v. i.* or *t.* أَقَامَ بِ . إِنْتَظَرَ

Abiding *a.* ثَابِتٌ . مُسْتَمِرٌ

Ability *n.* قُدْرَةٌ . طَاقَةٌ . إِسْتِطَاعَةٌ

Abject *a.* ذَلِيلٌ . دَنِيٌّ . حَقِيرٌ

Abjure *v. t.* رَفَضَ . إِرْتَدَّ عَنْ

Able *a.* قَادِرٌ . مُسْتَطِيعٌ

Able-bodied *a.* صَحِيحُ ٱلْجِسْمِ

Ablution *n.* غَسْلٌ . وُضُوءٌ

Ably *ad.* بِقُدْرَةٍ . بِمَهَارَةٍ

Abnegation *n.* إِنْكَارُ ٱلنَّفْسِ

Abnormal *a.* غَيْرُ قِيَاسِيٍّ . شَاذٌّ

Aboard *ad.* فِي ٱلسَّفِينَةِ

Abode *n.* مُقَامٌ . مَنْزِلٌ . مَسْكِنٌ

Abolish *v. t.* نَسَخَ . ـــَ أَلْغَى . أَبْطَلَ

Abolition *n.* نَسْخٌ . إِلْغَاءٌ

Abominable *a.* كَرِيهٌ . قَبِيحٌ

Abominate *v. t.* كَرِهَ ـــَ إِسْتَقْبَحَ

Abomination *n.* قَبِيحَةٌ . رِجْسٌ

Aborigines *n. pl.* (سُكَّانٌ) أَصْلِيُّونَ

Abortion *n.* سِقْطٌ . إِسْقَاطُ ٱلْجَنِينِ

Abortive *a.* مُخَيِّبٌ . غَيْرُ مُنْتِجٍ

Abound *v. i.* كَثُرَ . ـــُ وَفَرَ يَفِرُ

About *pr.* حَوْلَ نَحْوَ

Above *pr.* فَوْقَ . أَكْثَرُ مِنْ

Abrasion *n.* كَشْطٌ . إِحْتِكَاكٌ

Abridge *v. t.* قَصَّرَ . أَوْجَزَ . إِخْتَصَرَ

Abridgement *n.* إِيجَازٌ . إِخْتِصَارٌ

Abroad *ad.* خَارِجًا . فِي ٱلْخَارِجِ

Abrogate *v. t.* أَلْغَى . أَبْطَلَ . نَسَخَ

Abrupt *a.* فُجَائِيٌّ . مَقْطُوعٌ

Abruptness *n.* مُفَاجَأَةٌ . إِنْقِطَاعٌ

Abcess *n.* خُرَاجٌ . خُرَّاجَةٌ

Abscond *v. i.* تَوَارَى . إِخْتَفَى . إِنْسَلَّ

Absence *n.* غَيْبَةٌ . غِيَابٌ

Absent *a.* **Absentee** *n.* غَائِبٌ

Absolute *a.* غَيْرُ مُقَيَّدٍ . مُطْلَقٌ

Absolutely *ad.* مُطْلَقًا . قَطْعًا

Absolution *n.* حَلٌّ . غُفْرَانٌ

Absolve *v. t.* حَلَّ ـُ . غَفَرَ ـِ

Absorb *v. t.* إِمْتَصَّ . إِسْتَغْرَقَ

Absorption *n.* إِمْتِصَاصٌ

Abstain *v. i.* إِمْتَنَعَ عَنْ

Abstenious *a.* قَلِيلُ ٱلْأَكْلِ . عَفِيفٌ

Abstinence *n.* إِمْتِنَاعٌ . عِفَّةٌ

Abstinent *a.* زَاهِدٌ عَفِيفٌ

Abstract *v. t.* جَرَّدَ . إِخْتَلَسَ

Abstract *a.* مُجَرَّدٌ . تَجْرِيدِيٌّ

Abstraction *n.* تَجْرِيدٌ . (غَيْبَةٌ)

Abstractly *ad.* مُجَرَّدًا

Abstruse *a.* عَوِيصٌ مُشْكِلٌ

Absurd *a.* بَاطِلٌ . مُخَالِفُ ٱلْعَقْلِ

Absurdity *n.* بُطْلٌ . بُطْلَانٌ

Abundance *n.* كَثْرَةٌ . وَفْرٌ

Abundant *a.* كَثِيرٌ . وَافِرٌ

Abuse *v. t.* شَتَمَ ـ أَسَاءَ ٱسْتِعْمَالَهُ

Abuse *n.* شَتِيمَةٌ . سُوءُ ٱلاسْتِعْمَالِ

Abusive *a.* شَاتِمٌ مُهِينٌ

Abyss *n.* هَاوِيَةٌ . وَهْدَةٌ

Acacia *n.* شَجَرُ ٱلسَّنْطِ

Academy *n.* مَدْرَسَةُ ٱلْعُلُومِ أَوْ مَجْمَعُهَا

Accede *v. t.* قَبِلَ . رَضِيَ بِهِ ـ

Accelerate *v. t.* اسْرَعَ . عَجَّلَ

Accent *n.* شَدَّةٌ فِي ٱللَّفْظِ . نَبْرَةٌ

Accentuate *v. t.* شَدَّدَ . أَظْهَرَ أَهَمِّيَّتَهُ

Accept *v. t.* قَبِلَ ـ رَضِيَ

Acceptable *a.* مَقْبُولٌ . مَرْضِيٌّ

Acceptance *n.* قُبُول

Acceptation *n.* قُبُولٌ . مَعْنًى

Accepted *a.* مَقْبُولٌ

Access *n.* دُخُولٌ . وُصُولٌ

Accessible *a.* سَهْلُ ٱلْوُصُولِ إِلَيْهِ

Accession *n.* زِيَادَةٌ . وُصُولٌ / جُلُوسٌ (ملك)

Accident *n.* عَرَضٌ . آفَةٌ

Accidental *a.* عَرَضِيٌّ . إِتِّفَاقِيٌّ

Acclamation *n.* تَصْفِيقٌ . إِسْتِحْسَانٌ

Acclimate / Acclimatize *v. t.* عَوَّدَ عَلَى ٱلْمَنَاخِ

Acclimation *n.* تَعَوُّدُ ٱلْمَنَاخِ

Acclivity *n.* مَطْلَعٌ . مَصْعَدٌ

Accommodate *v. t.* أَمَدَّ . وَفَّقَ

Accommodating *a.* مُوَفِّقٌ. مُلاطِفٌ
Accommodation *n.* مُوَافَقَةٌ
Accompaniment *n.* مُرَافَقَةٌ
Accompany *v. t.* رَافَقَ
Accomplice *n.* شَرِيكٌ فِي ذَنْبٍ
Accomplish *v. t.* أَكْمَلَ . أَنْجَزَ
Accomplishment *n.* إِنْجَازٌ . إِتْمَامٌ
Accord *n.* إِتِّفَاقٌ . إِتِّحَادٌ
Accordance *n.* إِتِّفَاقٌ
According to. عَلَى مُوجِبِ . بِحَسَبِ
Accordingly *ad.* لِذَلِكَ
Accost *v. t.* خَاطَبَ كَلَّمَهُ أَوَّلاً
Account *v. t.* حَسَبَ ـُ . عَدَّ
Account *n.* حِسَابٌ . قِصَّةٌ . خَبَرٌ
Accountability *n.* مَسْؤُولِيَّةٌ
Accountable *a.* مَسْؤُولٌ
Accountant *n.* كَاتِبُ ٱلْحِسَابَاتِ
Accrue *v. i.* زَادَ . نَشَأَ ـَ أُضِيفَ

Accumulate *v. t.* or *i.* جَمَعَ ـَ . إِزْدَادَ
Accumulation *n.* إِزْدِيَادٌ . تَجَمُّعٌ
Accumulative *a.* جَامِعٌ . مُزْدَادٌ
Accuracy *n.* ضَبْطٌ . إِتْقَانٌ
Accurate *a.* مَضْبُوطٌ . مُتْقَنٌ
Accurately *ad.* بِضَبْطٍ . بِإِتْقَانٍ
Accursed *a.* مَلْعُونٌ
Accusation *n.* إِشْتِكَاءٌ . شِكَايَةٌ
Accuse *v. t.* شَكَا . إِتَّهَمَ . سَعَى بِهِ
Accuser *n.* شَاكٍ . مُتَّهِمٌ
Accustom *v. t.* عَوَّدَ
Acerbity *n.* حَرَافَةٌ . فَظَاظَةٌ
Ache *n.* وَجَعٌ . أَلَمٌ
Ache *v. i.* تَوَجَّعَ . تَأَلَّمَ
Achieve *v. t.* عَمِلَ . تَمَّمَ . فَازَ
Achievement *n.* عَمَلٌ . إِنْجَازُ أَمْرٍ
Acid *n.* حَامِضٌ
Acidity *n.* حُمُوضَةٌ

Acknowledge *v. t.* إعترف . أقرَّ
Acme *n.* رأسٌ . قمَّةٌ
Acknowledgement *n.* إعترافٌ
Acorn *n.* بلُّوطٌ
Acoustics *n.* عِلمُ ٱلسمعيَّاتِ
Acquaint *v. t.* أعلمَ . عرَّفَ
Acquaintance *n.* معرفةٌ. أحدُ المعارفِ
Acquiesce *v. t.* قبلَ . رضيَ ب
Acquire *v. t.* حصلَ . إقتنى
Acquisition *n.* تحصيلٌ . قنيةٌ
Acquit *v. t.* برّأ . أطلقَ
Acquittal *n.* تبرئةٌ . إطلاقٌ
Acre *n.* فدَّانٌ (إنكليزيٌّ)
Acreage *n.* عددُ ٱلفدادينِ في ارضٍ
Acrid *a.* قارصٌ . حرّيفٌ
Acrimony *n.* حرافةٌ . حدَّةٌ
Across *pr.* عرضًا . عبْرَ
Act *n.* فِعلٌ . عملٌ
Act *v. t.* or *i.* فعلَ . عملَ ـ . تصرَّفَ
Action *n.* فِعلٌ . معركةٌ . دعوى
Active *a.* فعَّالٌ ـ نشيطٌ
Actively *ad.* بنشاطٍ . بهمَّةٍ
Activity *n.* نشاطٌ . همَّةٌ
Actor *n.* فاعلٌ . مشخِّصٌ في ملعبٍ
Actual *a.* فعليٌّ . حقيقيٌّ
Actually *ad.* فعلاً . حقًّا
Actuate *v. t.* حملهُ على . ساقَ إلى
Acumen *n.* ذكاءٌ . حذاقةٌ
Acuminate *a.* محدَّدُ ٱلرَّأسِ. مسنَّنٌ
Acute *a.* حادٌّ . ذكيٌّ . حاذقٌ
Acuteness *n.* حدَّةٌ . حذاقةٌ
Adage *n.* مثلٌ
Adamant *n.* حجرٌ صلبٌ . ماسٌ
Adapt *v. t.* ناسبَ . وافقَ
Adapted *a.* جديرٌ بهِ . مناسبٌ
Adaptable *a.* قابلُ ٱلمناسبةِ

Adaptation *n.* مناسبة . موافقة

Add *v. t.* جمع ـ أضاف إلى

Adder *n.* أفعى ج أفاع

Addict *v. t.* اولع ب . عكف على

Addicted *pp.* مولع . منعكف

Addition *n.* جمع . إضافة

Additional *a.* مضاف . زائد

Addle *v. t. & a.* أفسد . قذر

Address *v. t.* خاطب . عنون

Address *n.* خطاب . عنوان . حذاقة

Adduce *v. t.* أورد . جاء ب

Adept *n.* ماهر . لبيب

Adequate *a.* كاف . مساو

Adhere *v. t.* لصق . لزق ـ

Adherence *n.* لصق . لزوق

Adherent *a. n.* حليف . ملتصق ب

Adhesion *n.* لصق . إلتصاق

Adhesive *a.* لزج . دابق

Adieu *ad.* أستودعكم الله

Adjacent *a.* مجاور . متاخم

Adjective *n.* نعت . صفة

Adjoin *v. t.* or *i.* اتصل ب . جاور

Adjoining *a.* متصل ب

Adjourn *v. t.* أجل . اخر

Adjournment *n.* تأجيل . تأخير

Adjudicate *v. t.* قضى ـ حكم

Adjunct *n.* or *a.* مضاف . ملحق

Adjure *v. t.* إستحلف

Adjust *v. t.* ناسب . ضبط

Adjustment *n.* ضبط . تعديل

Adjutant *n.* معاون عسكري

Administer *v. t.* أدار . أجرى

Administration *n.* إدارة . إجراء

Administrator *n.* مدير . وكيل

Admirable *a.* عجيب . باهر

Admiral *n.* أمير البحر

Admiralty *n.* إِمَارَةُ ٱلْبَحْرِيَّةِ

Admiration *n.* تَعَجُّبٌ . اِسْتِحْسَانٌ

Admire *v. t.* تَعَجَّبَ مِنْ . اِسْتَحْسَنَ

Admissible *a.* مُسَلَّمٌ بِهِ . جَائِزٌ

Admission *n.* تَسْلِيمٌ بِ . دُخُولٌ

Admit *v. t.* سَلَّمَ بِهِ . أَدْخَلَ

Admittance *n.* دُخُولٌ . تَسْلِيمٌ

Admix *v. t.* مَزَجَ ـُ . خَلَطَ ـِ

Admixture *n.* مَزِيجٌ

Admonish *v. t.* نَبَّهَ . أَنْذَرَ

Admonition *n.* إِنْذَارٌ . نَصِيحَةٌ

Admonitive *a.* / Admonitory *a.* مُنْذِرٌ

Ado *n.* تَعَبٌ . ضَجِيجٌ

Adolescence *n.* شُبُوبِيَّةٌ . مُرَاهَقَةٌ

Adopt *v. t.* تَبَنَّى . اِتَّخَذَ

Adoption *n.* تَبَنٍّ . اِتِّخَاذٌ

Adorable *a.* مُسْتَحِقٌّ ٱلْعِبَادَةِ

Adoration *n.* عِبَادَةٌ . مَحَبَّةٌ فَائِقَةٌ

Adore *v. t.* عَبَدَ ـُ أَحَبَّ

Adorn *v. t.* زَيَّنَ . زَخْرَفَ

Adornment *n.* تَزْيِينٌ . زِينَةٌ

Adrift *a.* or *ad.* عَائِمٌ . سَائِبٌ

Adroit *a.* مَاهِرٌ . أَرِيبٌ . حَاذِقٌ

Adroitness *n.* مَهَارَةٌ . حَذَاقَةٌ

Adulation *n.* تَمَلُّقٌ . إِطْرَاءٌ

Adulatory *a.* مُتَمَلِّقٌ . مُطْرٍ

Adult *n.* بَالِغُ ٱلسِّنِّ

Adulterate *v. t.* أَفْسَدَ . غَشَّ

Adulterer *n.* / Adulterous *a.* زَانٍ

Adultery *n.* زِنًى

Advance *v. i.* or *t.* تَقَدَّمَ . قَدَّمَ . رَقَّى

Advance *n.* تَقَدُّمٌ . تَرَقٍّ

Advance guard *n.* طَلِيعَةُ ٱلْجَيْشِ

Advanced *a.* مُقَدَّمٌ . مُرَقًّى . مُتَقَدِّمٌ

Advancement *n.* تَقْدِيمٌ . تَرْقِيَةٌ

Advantage *n.* فَائِدَةٌ . مَصْلَحَةٌ

Advantageous *a.* مُفِيدٌ . نَافِعٌ

Advent *n.* مَجِيءٌ . ظُهُورٌ

Adventitious *a.* عَرَضِيٌّ

Adventure *n.* حَادِثَةٌ غَرِيبَةٌ
مَشْرُوعٌ

Adventurous / Adventuresome } *a.* مُخَاطِرٌ بِنَفْسِهِ

Adverb *n.* ظَرْفٌ أَو حَالٌ

Adverbial *a.* ظَرْفِيٌّ أَو حَالِيٌّ

Adversary *n.* خَصْمٌ . مُقَاوِمٌ

Adverse *a.* مُضَادٌّ . مُعَاكِسٌ

Adversity *n.* مُصِيبَةٌ . بَلِيَّةٌ

Advert *v. i.* إِلْتَفَتَ إِلَى . أَشَارَ

Advertise *v. t.* أَعْلَنَ . اخْبَرَ

Advertisement *n.* إِعْلَانٌ . إِخْبَارٌ

Advice *n.* نَصِيحَةٌ . مَشُورَةٌ

Advisable *a.* مُوَافِقٌ . مُسْتَحْسَنٌ

Advise *v. t.* نَصَحَ . أَخْبَرَ

Advisory *n.* شُورِيٌّ

Advocacy *a.* مُحَامَاةٌ . شَفَاعَةٌ

Advocate *n.* مُحَامٍ (أَفُوكَاتُو)

Advocated *v. t.* حَامَى عَنْ . عَضَدَ

Advocation *n.* مُحَامَاةٌ . إِحْتِجَاجٌ

Adz or Adge *n.* قَدُومٌ

Aerial *a.* هَوَائِيٌّ . عَالٍ

Aerolite *n.* حَجَرٌ جَوِّيٌّ . نَيْزَكٌ

Aeronaut *n.* مُسَافِرٌ فِي ٱلْهَوَاءِ

Aesthetics *n. pl.* عِلْمُ ٱلْجَمَالِ

Afar *ad.* عَلَى بُعْدٍ

Affability *n.* انسٌ وَبَشَاشَةٌ

Affable *a.* انيسٌ . لَيِّنُ ٱلْجَانِبِ

Affably *ad.* بِبَشَاشَةٍ . بِلُطْفٍ

Affair *n.* أَمْرٌ . شَأْنٌ . قَضِيَّةٌ

Affect *v. t.* أَثَّرَ فِي . هَيَّجَ . تَصَنَّعَ

Affectation *n.* تَصَنُّعٌ

Affected *a.* مُتَأَثِّرٌ . مُصَابٌ . مُتَصَنِّعٌ

Affecting *a.* مُؤَثِّرٌ

Affection *n.* مَحَبَّةٌ . مَوَدَّةٌ

Affectionate *a.* مُحِبٌّ . وَدُودٌ

Affective *a.* مُهَيِّجُ الْعَوَاطِفِ

Affiance *v. t.* خَطَبَ ـُ (ٱلْمَرْأَةَ)

Affidavit *n.* إِقْرَارٌ بِالْيَمِينِ

Affiliate *v. t.* تَبَنَّى . أَشْرَكَ

Affiliation *n.* تَبَنٍّ . إِشْرَاكٌ

Affinity *n.* قَرَابَةٌ . مُجَانَسَةٌ

Affirm *v. t.* حَقَّقَ . أَكَّدَ

Affirmable *a.* مُمْكِنٌ تَأْكِيدُهُ

Affirmation *n.* تَأْكِيدٌ . إِيجَابٌ

Affirmative *a.* or *n.* إِيجَابِيٌّ . مُوجَبٌ

Affirmatory *a.* مُثْبِتٌ

Affix *v. t.* أَلْصَقَ بِ . وَصَلَ

Affix *n.* مُضَافٌ

Afflict *v. t.* كَدَّرَ . ضَايَقَ

Afflicting / Afflictive مُكَدِّرٌ . مُغِمٌّ

Affliction *n.* ضِيقَةٌ . بَلِيَّةٌ

Affluence *n.* غِنًى . وَفْرَةٌ

Affluent *a.* غَنِيٌّ . وَافِرٌ

Afford *v. t.* أَنْتَجَ . قَدَّمَ . قَدَرَ عَلَى

Affray *n.* مُشَاجَرَةٌ . شَغَبٌ

Affright *v. t.* أَفْزَعَ . خَوَّفَ

Affront *v. t.* أَهَانَ . عَيَّرَ

Affront *n.* إِهَانَةٌ . تَعْيِيرٌ

Affusion *n.* سَكْبٌ . رَشٌّ

Afloat *ad.* عَائِمٌ

Afoot *ad.* مَاشٍ . جَارٍ

Aforesaid *a.* الْمَارُّ ذِكْرُهُ

Afraid *a.* خَائِفٌ . مُرْتَعِبٌ

Afresh *ad.* حَدِيثًا . أَيْضًا

Aft *a.* or *ad.* عِنْدَ الْمُؤَخَّرِ

After *ad.* or *pr.* بَعْدُ . خَلْفُ . بِحَسَبِ

Afternoon *n.* بَعْدَ الظُّهْرِ

After-thought *n.* تَأَمُّلٌ . مُعَادٌ

Afterwards *ad.* بَعْدَ ذَلِكَ

Again *ad.* أَيْضًا . مَرَّةً أُخْرَى

Against *pr.*	ضدّ . تجاه
Age *n.*	عمرٌ . عصرٌ
Aged *a.*	طاعنٌ في السنّ
Agency *n.*	فاعليّة . وكالة
Agent *n.*	فاعلٌ . وكيلٌ
Agglomerate *v. t.*	كتّل
Agglomeration *n.*	تكتيلٌ . تراكم
Agglutinate *v. t.*	غرّى . ألصق
Agglutination *n.*	تغرية . إلزاقٌ
Aggrandize *v. t.*	عظّم . كبّر
Aggrandizement *n.*	تعظيمٌ
Aggravate *v. t.*	زاد . بالغ في
Aggravation *n.*	زيادة . تثقيلٌ
Aggregate *v. t.*	جمع ـَ . بلغ ـُ
Aggregate *n.* or *a.*	الكلّ . مجموعٌ
Aggregation *n.*	جمعٌ
Aggress *v. t.*	تعدّى على
Aggression *n.*	تعدٍّ
Aggressive *a.*	متعدٍّ
Aggressor *n.*	
Aggrieve *v. t.*	أحزن . كدّر
Aghast *ad.*	منذهلٌ . مرعوبٌ
Agile *a.*	حركٌ . خفيفٌ
Agility *n.*	خفّة . سرعة
Agitate *v. t.*	حرّك . هيّج . أقلق
Agitation *n.*	تحريكٌ . إنزعاجٌ
Agitator *n.*	مهيّجٌ . محرّكٌ
Ago *ad.*	سابقا . من مدّة
Agonize *v. i.*	تعذّب
Agony *n.*	ألمٌ شديدٌ . نزعٌ
Agrarian *a.*	مختصٌّ بالحقول
Agrarian *n.*	من يطلب قسمة الأراضي بالتساوي
Agree *v. i.*	إتفق على . سلّم بِ
Agreable *a.*	مرضٍ . سارٌّ
Agreement *n.*	إتفاقٌ . عهدٌ
Agricultural *a.*	زراعيٌّ . فلاحيٌّ

Agriculture *n.* اَلْفِلَاحَةُ . اَلزِّرَاعَةُ

Agriculturist *n.* فَلَّاحٌ . زَارِعٌ

Aground *ad.* عَلَى ٱلْأَرْضِ (مَرْكَبٌ)

Ague *n.* بُرَدَاءُ . بَرْدِيَّةٌ

Ah ! / Aha ! *ex.* آه . آهاً

Ahead *ad.* امَامَ . إِلَى قُدَّامٍ

Aid *v. t.* سَاعَدَ . أَعَانَ

Aid *n.* مُسَاعَدَةٌ . عَوْنٌ . مَدَدٌ

Ail *v. i.* إِعْتَلَّ . تَشَكَّى مِنْ مَرَضٍ

Ail *n.* / Ailment *n.* عِلَّةٌ . مَرَضٌ

Aim *v. t.* or *i.* قَصَدَ . إِعْتَرَضَ . صَوَّبَ

Aim *n.* قَصْدٌ . غَرَضٌ

Aimless *a.* بِلَا قَصْدٍ أَوْ غَرَضٍ

Air *n.* هَوَاءٌ . نَغْمَةٌ . هَيْئَةٌ

Air *v. t.* عَرَّضَ لِلْهَوَاءِ . هَوَّى

Airing *n.* تَنَزُّهٌ

Airless *a.* بِلَا هَوَاءٍ

Airy *a.* مَكْشُوفٌ لِلْهَوَاءِ . مَرِحٌ

Akin *a.* ذُو قَرَابَةٍ . نَسِيبٌ

Alacrity *n.* إِسْتِعْدَادٌ لِلْعَمَلِ . نَشَاطٌ

Alarm *v. t.* خَوَّفَ . أَرْعَبَ

Alarm *n.* إِنْذَارٌ بِٱلْخَطَرِ . خَوْفٌ

Alarm-clock *n.* سَاعَةٌ مُنَبِّهَةٌ

Alarming *a.* مُخِيفٌ . مُفْزِعٌ

Alas ! *ex.* وَا أَسَفَاهُ

Albeit *ad.* مَعَ أَنَّ وَلَوْ أَنَّ

Albumen *n.* زُلَالٌ

Alchemy *n.* اَلْكِيمْيَاءُ ٱلْقَدِيمَةُ

Alcohol *n.* (اَلْكُحُولُ)

Alcoholic *a.* (كُحُولِيٌّ)

Alderman *n.* شَيْخُ بَلَدٍ

Ale *n.* جِعَةٌ

Alert *a.* مُنْتَبِهٌ . مُتَيَقِّظٌ . خَفِيفٌ

Alertness *n.* خِفَّةٌ . يَقَظَةٌ . نَشَاطٌ

Algebra *n.* عِلْمُ ٱلْجَبْرِ

Algebraist *n.* مَاهِرٌ فِي عِلْمِ ٱلْجَبْرِ

Algerine *a.*. جَزَائِرِيٌّ
Alien *a.* or *ad.* أَجْنَبِيٌّ
Alienate *v. t.* نَقَلَ . أَبْعَدَ
Alienation *n.* بَيْعٌ . نَقْلٌ . هِجْرَانٌ
Alight *v. i.* تَرَجَّلَ . وَقَعَ عَلَى
Alignment *n.* تَرْتِيبٌ عَلَى خَطٍّ
Alike *a.* شَبِيهٌ . نَظِيرٌ
Aliment *n.* غِذَاءٌ ج أَغْذِيَةٌ
Alimental, alimentary *a.* مُغَذٍّ
Alive *a.* حَيٌّ
Alkali *n.* أَلْقِلْيُ . الْقِلَى
Alkaline *n.* قَلَوِيٌّ
Alkoran *n.* الْقُرْآنُ
All *a.* or *n.* كُلٌّ . الْكُلُّ
Allay *v. t.* أَخْمَدَ . خَفَّفَ . خفض
Allegation *n.* تَأْكِيدٌ . حجةٌ . إِدِّعَاءٌ
Allege *v. t.* صَرَّحَ . إِدَّعَى
Allegiance *n.* طَاعَةٌ . امَانَة

Allegory *n.* مَجَازٌ . رَمْزٌ
Alleviate *v. t.* خَفَّفَ . لَطَّفَ
Alleviation *n.* تَسْكِينٌ . تَلْطِيفٌ
Alley *n.* زُقَاقٌ ج أَزِقَّةٌ
Alliance *n.* معاهَدَةٌ . مُحَالَفَةٌ . مُصَاهَرَةٌ
Allied *pp.* متعاهِدٌ . منْتَسِبٌ . مُصَاهِرٌ
Alligator *n.* ضَرْبٌ مِنَ التِّمْسَاحِ
Allot *v. t.* خَصَّصَ . اعْطَى نَصِيبًا
Allotment *n.* نَصِيبٌ . تقسِيمٌ
Allow *v. t.* سَمَحَ . أَذِنَ . أَجاز
Allowable *a.* جَائِزٌ . مُبَاحٌ
Allowance *n.* إِذْنٌ . رَاتِبٌ
Alloy *v. t.* or *n.* مَزِيجُ الْجَيِّدِ مَعَ الرَّدِي
Allude *v. t.* اشَارَ أَوْ لَمَّحَ إِلَى
Allure *v. t.* إِسْتَمَالَ . إِجْتَذَبَ . اغوَى
Allurement *n.* جذبٌ . إِسْتِمَالَةٌ . إِغْوَاءٌ
Alluring *a.* مستَمِيلٌ . مغْوٍ

Allusion *n.* إشارة . تلميح

Alluvium *n.* غَرْبَل . رُسُوبُ آلْمَاء

Ally *n.* or *v. t.* مُحالِف . مُعاهِد . حالف

Almanac *n.* رُزْنامة . تقويم آلسنة

Almighty *a.* or *n.* قادِر على كلّ شيء

Almond *n.* لوز

Almoner *n.* وكيل او موزع صدقات

Almost *ad.* تقريبا

Alms *n.* صدقة . إحسان

Aloft *ad.* في آلعالي . فوق

Alone *a.* على انفراد . وحدة

Along *ad.* or *pr.* إلى قدام . بجانب

Aloof *ad.* بمعزل عن . على بعد

Aloud *ad.* بصوت واضح او عال

Alphabet *n.* حروف آلهجاء

Alphabetic *a.* نسبة لحروف آلهجاء

Alpine *a.* مختص بجبل عال

Already *ad.*

Also *ad.* ايضا . كذلك

Altar *n.* مذبح

Alter *v. t.* غيّر . بدّل . حوّل

Alterable *a.* قابل آلتغيير

Alteration *n.* تغيير . تحويل

Altercation *n.* مخاصمة . مشاجرة

Alternate *a.* متبادل . متعاقب

Alternate *v. i.* بادل . ناوب

Alternation *n.* تبادل . تناوب

Alternative *n.* احد امرين

Although *con.* مع ان . ولو ان

Altitude *n.* علو . إرتفاع

Altogether *ad.* جملة . آلكل معاً

Alum *n.* شب ابيض

Always *ad.* دائما . على آلدوام

Amalgamate *v. t.* خلط معدنا بالزئبق مزج

Amalgamation *n.* مزج المعادن بالزئبق

Amanuensis *n.* كَاتِبُ مَا يُمْلَى عَلَيْهِ
Amass *v. t.* جَمَّعَ . كَوَّمَ
Amateur *n.* مُغْرَمٌ بِالفُنُونِ هاوٍ
Amatory *a.* حُبِّيٌّ . عِشْقِيٌّ
Amaze *v.t.* أَدْهَشَ . أَذْهَلَ
Amazement *n.* دَهْشَةٌ . إِنْذِهَالٌ
Amazing *a.* مُدْهِشٌ . عَجِيبٌ
Amazon *n.* إِمْرَأَةٌ حَرْبِيَّةٌ . سَلِيطَةٌ
Ambassador *n.* سَفِيرٌ ج سُفَرَاءُ
Amber *n.* كَهْرَبَاءُ
Ambergris *n.* عَنْبَرٌ
Ambiguity *n.* إِلْتِبَاسٌ . إِبْهَامٌ
Ambiguous *a.* مُلْتَبِسٌ . مُبْهَمٌ
Ambition *n.* طَلَبُ الرِّفْعَةِ . حُبُّ الرِّآسَةِ
Ambitious *a.* طَالِبُ الرِّفْعَةِ . مُحِبُّ الرِّآسَةِ
Amble *v. i.* خَبَّ ـُ . رَهَا ـُ

Ambler *n.* خَابٌّ . رَهْوَانٌ
Ambrosia *n.* عَنْبَرِيَّةٌ . طَعَامُ الآلِهَةِ
Ambulance *n.* مَحْمَلُ الْمَرْضَى
Ambuscade *n.* مَكْمَنٌ
Ambush *n.* كَمِينٌ
Ameliorate *v. t.* حَسَّنَ . أَصْلَحَ
Amelioration *n.* تَحْسِينٌ
Amenable *a.* مَسْئُولٌ . مُطَالَبٌ
Amend *v. t.* أَصْلَحَ . عَدَّلَ . حَسَّنَ
Amendment *n.* إِصْلَاحٌ . تَحْسِينٌ
Amends *n.* تَعْوِيضٌ
Amenity *n.* لُطْفٌ . أُنْسٌ
Amerce *v. t.* غَرَّمَ
Amethyst *n.* جَمَشْتٌ . بَنَفْشٌ
Amiable *a.* أَنِيسٌ . مَحْبُوبٌ
Amiably *ad.* بِلُطْفٍ . بِرِقَّةٍ . بِوُدٍّ
Amiable *a.* سِلْمِيٌّ . وِدَادِيٌّ
Amid *pr.* بَيْنَ . فِيمَا بَيْنَ

Amiss *a.* or *ad.* غَيْرُ مُوَافِقٍ . بِخَطَاءٍ

Amity *n.* مَحَبَّةٌ . صُحْبَةٌ

Ammonia *n.* نُشَادِرٌ

Ammunition *n.* مُؤُونَةُ ٱلْحَرْبِ

Amnesty *n.* أَمَانٌ . عَفْوٌ

Among / **Amongst** } *pr.* بَيْنَ . فِيمَا بَيْنَ

Amorous *a.* عَاشِقٌ . غَرَامِيٌّ

Amount *v. i.* or *n.* بَلَغَ . مَبْلَغٌ

Amphibious *a.* (حَيَوَانٌ) مَائِيٌّ بَرِّيٌّ

Amphitheatre *n.* مَلْعَبٌ مُدَوَّرُ ٱلْبِنَاءِ

Ample *a.* فَسِيحٌ . وَاسِعٌ . كَافٍ

Amplification *n.* تَوْسِيعٌ . إِسْهَابٌ

Amplify *v. t.* وَسَّعَ . أَسْهَبَ

Amplitude *n.* إِتِّسَاعٌ . كِبَرٌ

Amply *ad.* كِفَايَةً . بِسِعَةٍ

Amputate *v. t.* بَتَرَ . قَطَعَ

Amputation *n.* بَتْرٌ . قَطْعٌ

Amulet *n.* عَوْذَةٌ . تَمِيمَةٌ

Amuse *v. t.* سَلَّى . أَلْهَى

Amusement *n.* تَسْلِيَةٌ

Amusing *a.* مُسَلٍّ . مُضْحِكٌ

Anachronism *n.* خَطَأٌ تَارِيخِيٌّ

Anæsthetic *n.* مُخَدِّرٌ

Analogous *a.* مُمَاثِلٌ . تَمْثِيلِيٌّ

Analogy *n.* تَمْثِيلٌ . مُمَاثَلَةٌ

Analysis *n.* تَحْلِيلٌ . تَفْصِيلٌ

Analytic *a.* تَحْلِيلِيٌّ . مُفَصَّلٌ

Analyze *v. t.* حَلَّلَ . فَصَّلَ

Anarchic *a.* بِلَا حُكُومَةٍ أَوْ تَرْتِيبٍ

Anarchy *n.* عَدَمُ ٱلْحُكْمِ . فَوْضَى

Anathema *n.* حَرْمٌ

Anathematize *v. t.* حَرَمَ

Anatomical *a.* تَشْرِيحِيٌّ

Anatomist *n.* عَالِمٌ فِي ٱلتَّشْرِيحِ

Anatomy *n.* عِلْمُ ٱلتَّشْرِيحِ

Ancestor *n.* سَلَفٌ . جَدٌّ

Ancestral *a.* مُختَصٌّ بالأجدادِ

Ancestry *n.* سلسِلَةُ ٱلأَجْدَادِ نَسَبٌ

Anchor *n.* مِرْساةٌ ج مَرَاسٍ

Anchorage *n.* مَرْسًى . مَوْقِفٌ

Anchorite *n.* نَاسِكٌ . زَاهِدٌ

Ancient *a.* قَدِيمٌ

Ancients *n. pl.* القُدَمَاء

And *con.* وَاوُ ٱلعطف

Anecdote *n.* حِكَايَةٌ . قِصَّةٌ

Anemone *n.* شَقِيقَةٌ . (نَبَاتٌ)

Anew *ad.* جَدِيدًا . أَيْضًا

Angel *n.* مَلَاكٌ

Angelic *a.* مَلَكِيٌّ

Anger *n.* غَضَبٌ . غَيظٌ

Angle *n.* زَاوِيَةٌ ج زَوَايَا

Angle *v.i.* صَادَ (ٱلسَّمَكَ) بِالصِّنَّارَةِ

Angler *n.* صَيَّادٌ بِٱلصِّنَّارَةِ

Anglican *a.* تَابِعُ ٱلكَنِيسَة ٱلإِنْكِلِيزِيَّةِ

Anglicism *n.* لَهْجَةٌ إِنْكِلِيزِيَّةٌ

Anglicize *v. t.* حَوَّلَ إِلَى ٱلانكليزِي

Angling *n.* صَيْدٌ بِٱلصِّنَّارَةِ

Angrily *ad.* بِغَيظٍ . بِغَضَبٍ

Angry *a.* غَضْبَانُ . مُغْتَاظٌ

Anguish *v.* عَذَابٌ . أَلَمٌ شَدِيدٌ

Angular *a.* ذُو زَوَايَا

Animadversion *v.* مَلَامَةٌ . تَنْكِيتٌ

Animadvert *v. i.* إِلْتَفَتَ إِلَى . نَكَّتَ

Animal *n.* حَيَوَانٌ

Animalcule *n.* حُوَيْوِينَةٌ

Animate *v. t.* أَحْيَا . أَنعَشَ . نَشَّطَ

Animating *a.* مُحْيِي . مُنَشِّطٌ

Animation *n.* نَشَاطٌ . حَيَاةٌ . رُوحٌ

Animosity *n.* بُغْضٌ . حِقْدٌ

Ankle *n.* رُسْغُ ٱلقَدَمِ

Anklet *n.* خَلْخَالٌ

Annalist *n.* مُؤَرِّخٌ

Annals *n.* أخبارٌ سنويةٌ متتابعةٌ

Annex *v. t.* أوْصلَ اضافَ

Annexation *n.* إيصالٌ . إضافةٌ

Annihilate *v. t.* أعدمَ . أبادَ

Annihilation *n.* إعدامٌ . إبادةٌ

Anniversary *n.* or *a.* عيدٌ سنويٌّ

Annotate *v. t.* شرحَ . حشّى

Annotation *n.* شرحٌ . حاشيةٌ

Annotator *n.* شارحٌ . مُحشٍّ

Announce *v. t.* أعلنَ . أخبرَ . أنبأَ

Announcement *n.* إعلانٌ إنباءٌ

Annoy *v. t.* كدّرَ . أزعجَ

Annoyance *n.* إزعاجٌ . أمرٌ مُكدّرٌ

Annual *a.* or *n.* سنويٌّ . نباتٌ سنويٌّ

Annually *ad.* سنويًّا

Annuity *n.* معاشٌ سنويٌّ

Annul *v. t.* ألغى . أبطلَ

Annular *a.* حلقيٌّ . مُستديرٌ

Annulment *n.* إلغاءٌ إبطالٌ

Annulet *v. t.* زردةٌ . حلقةٌ

Annunciate *v. t.* أعلنَ . أتى بأخبارٍ

Annunciation *n.* إعلانٌ . خبرٌ . بشارةٌ

Anoint *v. t.* مسحَ

Anointing *n.* مسحٌ

Anomalous *a.* غيرُ قياسيٍّ . شاذٌّ

Anomaly *n.* شذوذٌ . عدمُ نظامٍ

Anon *ad.* عن قريبٍ . حالاً

Anonymous *a.* بلا اسمٍ

Another *a.* آخرُ غيرُ

Answer *n.* or *v. t.* جوابٌ . اجابَ

Answerable *a.* مسئولٌ . موافقٌ

Ant *n.* نملةٌ

Antagonism *n.* مضادّةٌ . مقاومةٌ

Antagonist *n.* مقاومٌ . خصمٌ

Antagonistic *a.* مضادٌّ . مقاومٌ

Antagonize *v. t.* ضادَّ . قاومَ

Antractic a. مختصٌّ بالقطبِ ٱلجنوبيِّ
Antecedence n. أسبقيّة . سبق
Antecedent a. سابقٌ
Antechamber n. غرفة مقدَّمة
Antedata v. t. أرَّخ قبلُ (التاريخ الحقيقيّ)
Antediluvian a. or n. قبلَ ٱلطّوفانِ
Antelope n. رئمٌ ج آرام
Antepenult a. مقطعُ ٱلكلمةِ قبلَ ٱلأخيرِ
Anterior a. سالفٌ . متقدِّمٌ
Anthem n. نشيدٌ
Anteroom n. غرفةٌ . قدّام غرفةٍ
Anther n. طرفُ سداةِ النباتِ
Anthracite n. فحمٌ حجريٌّ صلبٌ
Anthropology n. علمٌ يبحثُ عنِ ٱلإنسانِ
Antichrist n. ضدّ ٱلمسيحِ

Anticipate v. t. سبقَ ـ رأى من قبلُ
Anticipation n. سبقٌ . حسٌّ . سابقٌ
Antidote n. ترياق
Antimony n. إثمدٌ . انتيمن
Antipathy n. نفورٌ . كراهةٌ
Antipodes n. السّاكنون أقطارَ ٱلأرضِ ٱلمتقابلةِ
Antiquarian a. مختصٌّ بالزمانِ ٱلقديمِ
Antiquarian n. }
Antiquary n. } عالمٌ بالآثارِ ٱلقديمةِ
Antiquated a. or pp. قديمٌ . عتيقٌ
Antique a. or n. أثرٌ قديمٌ . قديمٌ
Antiquity n. ٱلزمانُ ٱلقديمُ . أثرٌ قديمٌ
Antiseptic a. or n. مضادٌّ ٱلفسادِ وٱلعفونةِ
Antithesis n. تباينٌ في ٱلكلامِ
Antitype n. ٱلمرموزُ إليهِ

Antler *n.* قرن الوعل

Anus *n.* إست

Anvil *n.* سندان . زبرة

Anxiety *n.* هم . قلق

Anxious *a.* مهتم . مشغول البال

Any *a.* احد . ايا كان

Apace *ad.* سريعاً

Apart *ad.* على جانب . على حدة

Apartment *n.* غرفة . مخدع

Apathetic *a.* غير حاس أو مبال

Apathy *n.* عدم الاكتراث أو المبالاة

Ape *n.* or *v. t.* قرد . قلد

Aperient *a.* مسهل . خفيف . ملين

Aperture *n.* نافذة . ثقب

Apex *n.* قمة . رأس

Apiary *n.* منحلة

Apiece *ad.* نصيب كل . لكل واحد

Apish *a.* قردي . نظير القرد

Apocalypse *n.* الرؤيا . سفر الرؤيا

Apocrypha *n.* الكتب غير القانونية

Apocryphal *a.* غير ثابت . باطل

Apologetic *a.* إعتذاري . إحتجاجي

Apologist *n.* محتج . محام

Apologize *v. i.* إعتذر . دافع عن

Apology *n.* اعتذار . محاماة

Apoplexy *n.* داء السكتة

Apostasy *n.* إرتداد . جحود الدين

Apostate *n.* مرتد . جاحد

Apostatize *v. t.* إرتد . جحد الايمان

Apostle *n.* رسول ج رسل

Apostleship *n.* رسولية . رسالة

Apostolic *a.* رسولي

Apostrophe *n.* حذف حرف وعلامته

Apothecary *n.* اجزائي (صيدلاني)

Appall *v. t.* أرعب . راع

Appalling *a.* مُرْعِبٌ . رَائِعٌ

Apparatus *n.* ادَوَاتٌ

Apparel *n.* لِبَاسٌ . كِسَاءٌ

Apparent *a.* ظَاهِرٌ . وَاضِحٌ

Apparently *ad.* بِحَسَبِ الظاهِرِ

Apparition *n.* ظُهُورٌ . طَيْفٌ

Appeal *v. t.* رَفَعَ الدَّعْوَى

Appeal *n.* إِسْتِئْنَافٌ .رَفْعُ الدَّعْوى

Appear *v. t.* ظَهَرَ ـَ . بانَ ـَ

Appearance *n.* ظُهُورٌ

Appease *v. t.* سَكَّنَ (غَيْظَهُ) . هَدَّأَ

Appellant *n.* رَافِعُ الدَّعْوَى

Appellation *n.* لَقَبٌ . تسْمِيَةٌ

Appellative *a.* or *n.* عَامٌّ .إِسْمٌ عَامٌّ

Append *v. t.* عَلَقَ اوْ الْحَقَ بِ

Appendage *n.* مُلْحَقٌ . ذَيْلٌ

Appendix *n.* مُلْحَقٌ .ذَيْلُ كِتاب

Appertain *v. i.* إِخْتَصَّ ب

Appetite *n.* (قَابِلِيَّةٌ) شَهْوَةُ الْأَكْلِ

Appetizing *a.* مُهَيِّجٌ لِشَهْوَةِ الْأَكْلِ

Applaud *v. t.* مَدَحَ . صَفَقَ مَدْحاً

Applause *n.* مَدْحٌ . تَصْفِيقٌ آسْتِحسانٍ

Apple *n.* تُفَاحَةٌ

Appliance *n.* وضْعٌ. تَخْصِيصٌ. وَاسِطَةٌ

Applicable *a.* مُطَابِقٌ . مُوَافِقٌ

Applicant *n.* طَالِبٌ ج طَلَبَةٌ

Application *n.* مُوَاظَبَةٌ. طَلَبٌ. وَضْعٌ

Apply *v. t.* or *i.* أَطْلَقَ عَلَى . إِسْتَعْمَلَ لِ

Apply to-for *v. t.* طَلَبَ مِنْ

Appoint *v. t.* عَيَّنَ. اقَامَ عَلَى

Appointee *n.* مُعَيَّنٌ لِوَظِيفَةٍ

Appointment *n.* تَعْيِينٌ . رَاتِبٌ

Apportion *v. t.* قَسَّمَ . أَحَصَّ

Apportionment *n.* تَقْسِيمٌ .إِخْصَاصٌ

Apposite *a.* مُوَافِقٌ . لائِقٌ

Apposition *n.* بَدَلٌ (فِي النَّحْوِ)

Appraisal, **Appraisment** *n.* تَثْمِينٌ. (تَقْدِيرٌ)

Appraise *v. t.* ثَمَّنَ (قَدَّرَ)

Appreciable *a.* قَابِلُ ٱلتَّثْمِينِ وَٱلتَّقْدِيرِ

Appreciate *v. t.* ثَمَّنَ. إِعْتَبَرَ

Appreciation *n.* تَثْمِينٌ. إِعْتِبَار

Apprehend *v. t.* فَهِمَ. أَدْرَكَ. قَبَضَ

Apprehension *n.* إِدْرَاكٌ. خَوْفٌ

Apprehensive *a.* مُدْرِكٌ. خَائِفٌ

Apprentice *n.* تِلْمِيذُ صِنَاعة

Apprise *v. t.* أَخْبَرَ. اعْلَمَ

Approach *v. t.* دَنَا ـُ. قَرُبَ ـُ. مِنْ

Approachable *a.* سَهْلُ ٱلإِقْتِرَابِ إِلَيْهِ

Approbation *n.* إِسْتِحْسَانٌ. رِضًى

Appropriate *v. t.* خَصَّصَ. أَفْرَزَ

Appropriate *n.* مُنَاسِبٌ. لَائِقٌ

Appropriate *a.* تَخْصِيصٌ

Approval *n.* إِسْتِحْسَانٌ. قَبُولٌ

Approve *v. t.* إِسْتَحْسَنَ. رَضِيَ بِهِ

Approximate *v. t.* or *a.* إِقْتَرَبَ إِلَى. تَقْرِيبِيٌّ

Approximately *ad.* تَقْرِيباً

Approximation *n.* تَقْرِيبٌ. إِقْتِرَابٌ

Appurtenance *n.* مُلْحَقٌ. مُخْتَصٌّ

Apricot *n.* مِشْمِشَةٌ

April *n.* نِيسَانٌ

Apron *n.* (مَرْيُولٌ) وَزْرَةٌ

Apt *a.* مُسْتَعِدٌّ. خَلِيقٌ ب

Aptitudes, **Aptness** *n.* مَيْلٌ طَبِيعِيٌّ. اهْلِيَّةٌ

Aptly *ad.* كَمَا يَجِبُ. بِلِيَاقَةٍ

Aquarium *n.* حَوْضُ السَّمَكِ • النَّبَاتَاتِ

Aquatic *a.* عَائِش ي ٱلْمَاءِ

Aqueduct *n.* قَنَاةُ مَاءٍ

Aqueous *a.* مَائِيٌّ

Arabian *a.* عَرَبِيٌّ

Arabic *n.* أَلْعَرَبِيَّةُ

Arable *a.* صَالِحٌ لِلْحَرْثِ او ٱلزَّرْعِ

Arbiter, **Arbitrator** *n.* فَيْصَلٌ. حَكَمٌ

Arbitrary *n.* غيرُ مقيَّد . مُستَبِدٌّ

Arbitrate *v. t.* or *i.* توسَّطَ بِحُكْمٍ بَيْنَ

Arbitration *n.* حُكْمُ ٱلْفَيَاصِلِ

Arbour *n.* عَرِيشٌ ج عَرَائِشُ

Arboreous *a.* شَجَرِيٌّ

Arc *d.* قَوْسٌ ج قِسِيٌّ

Arcade *n.* رِوَاقٌ ج أَرْوِقَةٌ

Arch *n.* or *v. t.* قَنْطَرَةٌ . قَنْطَرَ

Archæology *n.* عِلمُ ٱلآثَارِ ٱلْقَدِيمَةِ

Archaic *a.* قَدِيمٌ

Archangel *n.* رَئِيسُ مَلَائِكَةٍ

Archbishop *n.* رَئِيسُ أَسَاقِفَةٍ

Archbishopric *n.* مقامُ رَئِيسِ ٱلأَسَاقِفَةِ

Archduchess *n.* أَمِيرَةٌ فِي دَوْلَةِ ٱلنَّمْسَا

Archduke *n.* امِيرٌ فِي دَوْلَةِ ٱلنَّمْسَا

Arched *a.* مُقَوَّسٌ . مقبوٌّ

Archer *n.* رَامِي ٱلسِّهَامِ . رَامٍ

Archery *n.* صِنَاعَةُ ٱلرَّمْيِ بِٱلْقَوْسِ

Archetype *n.* أُنْمُوذَجٌ أَصْلِيٌّ

Archipelago *n.* مجموعُ جَزَائِرَ . أَرْخَبِيلٌ

Architect *n.* مُهَنْدِسٌ بنَّاءٌ

Architectural *a.* مُتَعَلِّقٌ بِعِلْمِ ٱلْبِنَاءِ

Architecture *n.* عِلْمُ ٱلْبِنَاءِ وَهَنْدَسَتُهُ

Archives *n. pl.* سِجِلَّاتٌ وَخَزَائِنُهَا

Archway *n.* مَمْشًى تَحْتَ قَنَاطِرَ

Arctic *a.* مُخْتَصٌّ بِٱلْقُطْبِ ٱلشَّمَالِيِّ

Ardent *a.* حَارٌّ . غَيُورٌ

Ardour *n.* حَرَارَةٌ . حَمِيَّةٌ . حَمَاسَةٌ

Arquous *a.* صَعْبٌ . شَاقٌّ

Area *n.* سَاحَةُ أَرْضٍ . إِتِّسَاعُهَا

Arena *n.* مَيْدَانٌ ج مَيَادِينُ

Arenaceous *a.* رَمْلِيٌّ

Argillaceous *a.* صَلْصَالِيٌّ

Argue *v. i.* or *t.* نَاظَرَ . إِحْتَجَّ . جَادَلَ

Argument *n.* دَلِيلٌ . حُجَّةٌ

Argumentation *n.* إِقَامَةُ ٱلدَّلِيلِ

Argumentation *n.* إِحتِجاجيٌّ

Arid *a.* قاحِلٌ . جافٌّ

Aridity *n.* قُحُولَةٌ . يُبُوسَةٌ

Aries *n.* بُرْجُ ٱلْحَمَلِ

Aright *ad.* مُسْتَقِيمًا

Arise *v. i.* قامَ ـُ . طَلَعَ . ظَهَرَ ـَ

Aristocracy *n.* الأَشْرافُ . حُكُومَتُهُمْ

Aristocrat *n.* أَحَدُ ٱلأَشْرافِ

Aristocratic *a.* مُخْتَصٌّ بِٱلاشْرافِ

Arithmetic *n.* عِلْمُ الحِسابِ

Arithmetical *a.* حِسابِيٌّ

Arithmetician *n.* عالِمٌ بِٱلْحِسابِ

Ark *n.* فُلْكٌ . تابُوت

Arm *n.* ذِراعٌ . ساعِدٌ . فَرْعٌ مِنَ ٱلْعَسْكَرِ

Arm *v. t.* سَلَّحَ

Armada *n.* مَجْمُوعُ بَوارِجَ . اسْطُولٌ

Armament *n.* جِهازٌ لِلْحَرْبِ

Arm-chair *n.* كُرْسِيٌّ ذُو يَدَيْنِ

Armful *n.* مِلْءُ قَبضَةِ الذِراعِ

Armhole *n.* ثَقْبُ ثَوب لِلذِراعِ

Armistice *n.* هُدْنَة

Armlet *n.* سِوارٌ

Armour *n.* عُدَّةُ حَرْب . سِلاحٌ

Armoured *a.* مُصَفَّحٌ بِٱلْحَدِيدِ
مُلَبَّسٌ بِصَفائِحِ حَدِيدٍ

Armourer *n.* صانِعُ أَسْلِحةٍ أَوْ بائِعُها

Armoury *n.* مَخْزَنُ اسلِحةٍ

Armpit *n.* إِبْطٌ ج آباطٌ

Arms *n. pl.* عُدَّةُ حَرْب . اسْلِحة

Army *n.* جَيْشٌ ج جُيُوشٌ

Aroma *n.* رائِحةٌ عِطْرِيَّةٌ

Aromatic *a.* عِطْرٌ . طيِّبٌ

Around *pr.* or *ad.* حَوْلَ

Arouse *v. t.* أَيقَظَ . نبهَ . حَرَّضَ

Arraign *v. t.* دَعِيَ لِلمُحاكَمَةِ

Arraignment *n.* مُحاكَمَةٌ

Arrrange *v. t.* رَتَّبَ . دَبَّرَ

Arrangement *n.* تَرْتِيبٌ . تَدْبِيرٌ

Arrant *a.* شَهِيرٌ بِٱلشَّرِّ

Array *n.* مَصَافٌّ . لِبَاسٌ

Array *v. t.* صَفَّ . لَبَّسَ . زَيَّنَ

Arrears *n. pl.* بَقَايَا دَيْنٍ مُسْتَحِقٍّ

Arrest *v. t.* أَلْقَى ٱلْقَبْضَ عَلَى . وَقَّفَ

Arrest *n.* إِلْقَاءُ ٱلْقَبْضِ . تَوْقِيفٌ

Arrival *n.* مَجِيءٌ . وُصُولٌ

Arrive *v. i.* أَتَى . وَصَلَ . بَلَغَ

Arrogance *n.* غَطْرَسَةٌ . تَكَبُّرٌ

Arrogant *a.* مُتَجَبِّرٌ . مُتَكَبِّرٌ

Arrogate *v. t.* إِدَّعَى . نَسَبَ لِنَفْسِهِ

Arrow *n.* سَهْمٌ ج سِهَامٌ

Arsenal *n.* مَخْزَنُ مُؤْنَةٍ حَرْبِيَّةٍ

Arsénic *n.* زِرْنِيخٌ . سَمُّ ٱلْفَارِ

Arson *n.* حَرْقُ بَيْتٍ عَنْ ضَغِينَةٍ

Art *n.* فَنٌّ . صِنَاعَةٌ . مَكْرٌ

Arterial *a.* شِرْيَانِيٌّ

Artery *n.* شِرْيَانٌ ج شَرَايِينُ

Artful *a.* مَكَّارٌ . مَاهِرٌ

Artichoke *n.* (أَرْضِي شَوْكِي) خُرْشُوفٌ

Article *n.* بَنْدٌ . مَادَّةٌ . آل ٱلتَّعْرِيفِ

Articulate *a.* ذو مَفَاصِلَ أَوْ مَقَاطِعَ

Articulate *v. t.* لَفَظَ وَاضِحًا

Articulation *n.* لَفْظٌ . مَفْصِلٌ . إِتِّصَالٌ

Artifice *n.* حِيلَةٌ تَدْبِيرٌ

Artificer *n.* صَاحِبُ حِرْفَةٍ . مُخْتَرِعٌ

Artificial *a.* مُصْنَعٌ . غَيْرُ حَقِيقِيٍّ

Artillery *n.* مَدَافِعُ (طُوبْجِيَّةٌ)

Artisan *n.* صَاحِبُ صِنَاعَةٍ

Artist *n.* إِسْتَاذُ صِنَاعَةٍ . مُصَوِّرٌ

Artistic *a.* مُطَابِقٌ لِلْصِنَاعَةِ . نَفِيسٌ

Artless *a.* سَاذِجٌ سَلِيمُ ٱلنِّيَّةِ

As *ad.* كَمَا . مِثْلُ . لَمَّا . بَيْنَمَا

Ascend *v. t.* or *i.* صَعِدَ . طَلَعَ ـَ

Ascendant *a.* or *n.* فَائِقٌ . سَطْوَةٌ

Ascendency *n.* سَطْوَةٌ . سُلْطَةٌ

Ascension *n.* صُعُودٌ

Ascent *n.* طُلُوعٌ . مَرْقًى . إِرْتِقَاءٌ

Ascertain *v. t.* كَشَفَ ـَ حَقَّقَ

Ascetic *n.* نَاسِكٌ . زَاهِدٌ

Asceticism *n.* تَنَسُّكٌ . زُهْدٌ

Ascribe *v. t.* نَسَبَ ـِ إِلَى

Ascription *n.* نَسْبَةٌ . تَخْصِيصٌ

Ash *n.* دَرْدَارٌ (شَجَرَة)

Ashamed *a.* خَجْلَانُ . مُسْتَحٍ

Ashen *a.* دَرْدَارِيٌّ . رَمَادِيٌّ

Ashes *n. pl.* رَمَادٌ

Ashore *ad.* عَلَى ٱلْبَرِّ اوْ إِلَيهِ

Ashy *a.* رَمَادِيٌّ . مُصْفَرٌّ

Asiatic *a.* نِسبَةٌ لآسيَا

Aside *ad.* عَلَى جَانِبٍ . عَلَى إِنفِرَادٍ

Asinine *a.* حِمَارِيٌّ . بَلِيدٌ

Ask *v. t.* طَلَبَ ـُ سَأَلَ

Asleep *a.* نَائِمٌ . رَاقِدٌ

Asp *n.* صِلٌّ . افْعَى

Asparagus *n.* هَلْيُونٌ

Aspect *n.* مَنْظَرٌ . هَيْئَةٌ

Asperity *n.* خُشُونَة . غِلَاظَةٌ

Asperse *v. t.* قذف ـِ طَعَنَ في

Aspersion *n.* قَذْفٌ . طَعْنٌ . رَشٌّ

Asphyxia *n.* إِخْتِنَاقٌ

Aspirant *n.* طَالِبٌ . تَوَّاقٌ

Aspirate *n.* صَوْتٌ كَالْهَاءِ

Aspiration *n.* شَوْقٌ . مَطْلَبٌ . تَلَهُّفٌ

Aspire *v. i.* طَلَبَ بِشَوْقٍ . تَاقَ إِلَى

Ass *n.* حِمَارٌ ج حَمِيرٌ

Assail *v. t.* هَجَمَ عَلَى . إِقْتَحَمَ

Assailant *n.* مُهَاجِمٌ . مُقْتَحِمٌ

Assassin *n.* قاتلٌ سِرًّا

Assassinate *v. t.* قتلَ سِرًّا

Assassination *n.* قتلٌ سِرًّا

Assault *v. t.* or *n.* هَاجَمَ مُهَاجَمَةٌ

Assay *v. t.* or *i.* or *n.* جرَّبَ إِمتِحَان

Assayer *n.* مُمتحِنُ ٱلمَعَادِنِ

Assemblage *n.* إِجتِمَاعٌ . مَحفَلٌ

Assemble *v. i.* or *t.* جَمَعَ . إِجتَمَعَ

Assembly *n.* مَجمَعٌ . مَجلِسٌ

Assent *v. i.* or *n.* سَلَّمَ . تسلِيمٌ

Assert *v. t* زَعَمَ . إِدَّعى . تَاكَّدَ

Assertion *n.* زَعمٌ . إِدِّعَاءٌ . تَأكِيدٌ

Assess *v. t.* قَدَّرَ . ثَمَّنَ

Assessment *n.* تثمِينٌ

Assessor *n.* مُثَمِّنٌ . مَن يَضَعُ الوَسمَ

Assets *n. pl.* مَوجُودَاتٌ

Asseverate *v. t.* اكَّدَ صَرَّحَ

Assiduity *n.* مُوَاظَبَةٌ . مُثابَرَةٌ

Assiduous *a.* مُوَاظِبٌ . مُثابِرٌ

Assign *v. t.* خَصَّصَ . أفرَزَ

Assignation *n.* تعيِينٌ . ميعَادُ لِقَاءٍ

Assignee *n.* مَن يُسلَّمُ لَهُ شيءٌ

Assignment *n.* تعيِينٌ . تحوِيلٌ . إِحالَةُ امُورِ مفلِسٍ إِلى وُكَلاءَ

Assimilate *v. t.* مَثَّلَ . شَبَّهَ . أَدغَمَ

Assist *v. t.* أَعَانَ . سَاعَدَ . اغَاثَ

Assistance *n.* مُسَاعَدَةٌ . عَونٌ

Assistant *n.* مُسَاعِدٌ . مُعِينٌ

Assizes *n.* محكَمَةٌ . مَجلِسُ ٱلحقُوقِ

Associate *v. t.* or *i.* اشرَكَ . إِشتَرَكَ

Associate *n.* or *a.* شَرِيكٌ . رَفِيقٌ

Association *n.* مشارَكَةٌ . جَمعِيَّةٌ

Assort *v. t.* رَتَّبَ . جَنَّسَ

Assorted *a.* متنوِّعٌ . مُشَكَّلٌ

Assortment ترتِيبٌ . بَضَائِعُ متنوِّعَةٌ

Assuage *v. t.* خَفَّفَ . اخمَدَ

Assume *v. t.* ادَّعى . إتَّخذ

Assuming *a.* مُدَّعٍ . مُتكبّرٌ . مُعْجبٌ

Assumption *n.* إدّعاء . إتّخاذٌ

Assurance *n.* تأكيدٌ . يقينٌ

Assure *v. t.* أكَّد . حقق

Asteroid *n.* سيَّارٌ صغيرٌ

Astern *ad.* على مُؤخَّرِ السَّفينةِ أوْ خَلْفَها

Asthma *n.* داءُ آلرَّبْوِ

Asmatic *a.* مُصابٌ بداءِ آلرَّبْوِ

Astonish *v. t.* أذهش . حيَّر

Astonishing *a.* مُدْهِشٌ . مُحيّرٌ

Astonishment *n.* دَهشةٌ . تعجُّبٌ

Astound *v. t.* أذْهش حيَّر

Astray *ad.* تائهاً . شارِداً

Astrine *ad.* مفرْشحاً

Astringent *a.* or *n.* قابِضٌ ج قوابِضُ

Astrologer *n,* مُنجِّمٌ

Astrology *n.* عِلْمُ آلتنجيمِ

Astronomer *n.* عالِمٌ بِعِلْمِ آلْهيئةِ

Astronomy *n.* عِلْمُ آلْهيئةِ

Astute *a.* ذكِيٌّ . حاذِقٌ

Astuteness *n.* دَهاءٌ فِراسةٌ

Asunder *ad.* مفصُولاً عنْ

Asylum *n.* مَلْجأٌ . بيمارِستانٌ

At *pr.* عِندَ . في

Atheism *n.* إنكارُ وُجُودِ آللهِ

Atheist *n.* مُنكِرُ وُجُودِ آللهِ . مُلْحِدٌ

Athirst *a.* عطشان . ظمآن

Athlete *n.* مُصارِعٌ . مُتقِنُ آلرِّياضةِ

Athletic *a.* قويُّ آلْجِسْمِ . ضليعٌ

Athwart *ad.* عرْضاً

Atlas *n.* (أطلسٌ . مجْمُوعُ خارِطاتٍ)

Atmosphere *n.* هواءٌ . جوٌّ

Atmospheric *a.* هوائيٌّ . جوّيٌّ

Atom *n.* ذرَّةٌ . جوْهرُ آلْفرْدِ

Atomic *a.* مختصٌّ بجوْهرِ آلْفرْدِ

Atone v. t. or i. كفّر عن

Atonement n. كفّارة

Atrocious a. فظيع . فاحش

Atrocity n. كبيرة . فظاعة

Attach v. t. وصل ـِ . علّق

Attachment n. ضبط . حجز (الاموال) . ودّ

Attack v. t. or n. هاجم . مهاجمة

Attain v. t. حصّل . بلغ ـُ

Attainment n. تحصيل . بلوغ

Attaint v. t. أفسد . أثبت خيانته

Attempt v. t. or n. جرّب . حاول تجربة

Attend v. t. or i. رافق . إعتنى . حضر

Attendance n. حضور . ملازمة

Attendant n. تابع . خادم . إصغاء

Attention n. إنتباه . معروف

Attentive a. مصغ . ملازم

Attenuate v. t. رقّق . خفّف

Attenuation n. ترقيق . تخفيف

Attest v. t. شهد . اثبت . أكّد

Attestation n. شهادة . إثبات

Attire v. t. or n. ألبس . لباس

Attitude n. حالة . هيئة

Attorney n. وكيل دعاو

Attract a. t. جذب ـِ إستمال

Attraction n. جذب . جاذبية

Attracting / Attractive a. جاذب . مستميل . سارّ

Attractiveness n. صفة الجذب جاذبية . حسن

Attribute v. t. or n. نسب إلى . صفة

Attribution n. نسبة . وصف

Attrition n. فرك . سحق

Attuned pp. موفّق . مدوزن

Auction n. مزاد . حراج

Auctioneer n. دلّال

Audacious *a.* جَسُورٌ . وَقِحٌ
Audacity *n.* جَسَارَةٌ . وَقَاحَةٌ
Audible *a.* مَسْمُوعٌ
Audience *n.* اَلسَّامِعُونَ اَلْحَاضِرُونَ
Audit *v. t.* فَحَصَ حِسَابًا وَضَبَطَهُ
Auditor *n.* فَاحِصُ حِسَابٍ . سَامِعٌ
Auditory *a.* سَمْعِيٌّ
Auger *n.* مِثْقَبٌ
Aught *n.* شَيْءٌ مَا
Augment *v. t.* or *i.* زَادَ . إِزْدَادَ
Augment / **Augmentation** *n.* زِيَادَة
Augury *n.* فَأْلٌ . تَطَيُّرٌ
August *a.* عَظِيمٌ . سَامِي ٱلشَّأْنِ
August *n.* شَهْرُ آبٍ
Aunt *n.* عَمَّةٌ أَوْ خَالَةٌ
Auricle *n.* صِيوَانَةُ ٱلاُذُنِ أُذَيْنَةُ ٱلْقَلْبِ
Auriferous *a.* ذُو ذَهَبٍ

Aurora *n.* شَفَقٌ
Auspicious *a.* ذُو حَظٍّ . سَعِيدٌ
Austere *a.* عَابِسٌ . صَارِمٌ
Austerity *n.* صَرَامَةٌ . عُبُوسٌ
Authentic *a.* حَقِيقِيٌّ
Authenticate *v. t.* حَقَّقَ . أَثْبَتَ
Authenticity *n.* حَقِيقَةٌ . حَقَّانِيَّةٌ
Author *n.* مُؤَلِّفٌ . مُصَنِّفٌ . مُسَبِّبٌ
Authoritative *a.* جَازِمٌ . ذُو سُلْطَةٍ
Authority *n.* سُلْطَةٌ . حَقُّ ٱلتَّسَلُّطِ
Authorization *n.* تَفْوِيضٌ . إِجَازَةٌ
Authorize *v. t.* فَوَّضَ . أَجَازَ . رَخَّصَ
Authorship *n.* صِنَاعَةُ ٱلتَّأْلِيفِ
Autobiography *n.* تَرْجَمَةُ ٱلْإِنْسَانِ لِحَيَاتِهِ
Autocracy *n.* سُلْطَةٌ مُطْلَقَةٌ
Autocrat *n.* حَاكِمٌ مُطْلَقٌ
Autograph *n.* خَطُّ ٱلْمُؤَلِّفِ . إِمْضَاءٌ

Automatic *a.* مُتحَرِّكٌ مِنْ ذَاتِهِ

Autonomy *n.* حُكْمٌ ذاتِيٌّ إِسْتِقْلَالِيٌّ

Autopsy *n.* تَشْرِيحُ جُثَّةٍ

Autumn *n.* أَلْخَرِيفُ

Autumnal *a.* خَرِيفِيٌّ

Auxiliary *a.* or *n.* مُسَاعِدٌ

Avail *v. i.* or *t.* or *n.* نَفَعَ. أَفَادَ. نفعٌ

Available *a.* مَوْجُودٌ. مُفِيدٌ

Avails *n. pl.* اَلْحَاصِلُ مِنْ بَيْعٍ

Avalanche *n.* هَيَارُ ٱلثَّلْجِ مِنْ جَبَلٍ

Avarice *n.* بُخْلٌ. شُحٌّ

Avaricious *a.* بَخِيلٌ. شَحِيحٌ

Avenge *v. t.* إِنْتَقَمَ مِنْ. عَاقَبَ

Avenger *n.* مُنْتَقِمٌ

Avenue *n.* شَارِعٌ عَرِيضٌ. مَدْخَلٌ

Aver *v. t.* اكَّدَ. جَزَمَ

Average *n.* or *v. t.* مُعَدَّلٌ. عَدَّلَ

Averse *a.* كَارِهٌ. مُنَافٍ. غَيْرُ رَاضٍ

Aversion *n.* نفورٌ. كَرَاهَةٌ

Avert *v. t.* حَوَّلَ عَنْ. مَنَعَ

Aviary *n.* قَفَصٌ. بَيْتُ ٱلطُّيُورِ

Avidity *n.* شَرَهٌ. حِرْصٌ

Avocation *n.* حِرْفَةٌ. مَشْغَلَةٌ

Avoid *v. t.* جَانَبَ. تَحَوَّلَ عَنْ

Avoirdupois *n.* عِيَارٌ فِيهِ ٱللِّيبْرَا ١٦ أُوقِيَّةً إِنْكِلِيزِيَّةً

Avouch *v. t.* اكَّدَ. صَرَّحَ بِ

Avow *v. t.* صَرَّحَ. أَقَرَّ بِ

Avowal *n.* إِقْرَارٌ. إِشْهَارٌ

Await *v. t.* إِنْتَظَرَ. تَوَقَّعَ

Awake / **Awaken** *v. t.* or *i.* ايقظَ. إِسْتَيْقَظَ

Awake *a.* يَقْظَانُ

Award *v. t.* or *n.* حَكَمَ. قَضَى. حُكْمٌ

Aware *a.* عَارِفٌ. مُنْتَبِهٌ

Away *ad.* عَلى بُعْدٍ . غائِباً

Awe *n.* or *v. t.* رَوْعَةٌ . خشية . ارْعب

Awe-struck *a.* مُرْتَعِدٌ . رَاهِبٌ

Awful *a.* مُخِيفٌ . هَائِلٌ

Awhile *ad.* إِلى حِينٍ . مُدَّةً

Awkward *a.* أَخْرَقُ . مُتَلَبِّكٌ

Awkwardness *n.* خَرَقٌ . تَلَبُّكٌ

Awl *n.* مِخْرَزٌ ج مَخارِزُ

Awning *n.* مَظَلَّةٌ ج مَظالُّ

Awry *a.* or *ad.* مُنْحَرِفٌ مُعَوَّجٌ بِانْحِرَافٍ

Ax *or* **Axe** *n.* فَأْسٌ ج فُؤُوسٌ

Axillary *a.* اِبْطِيٌّ

Axiom *n.* مَبْدَأٌ . اوَّلِيَّةٌ

Axiomatic *a.* مَبْدَئِيٌّ . اوَّلِيٌّ

Axail *a.* مِحْوَرِيٌّ

Axis *n.* مِحْوَرٌ

Axle *n.* مِحْوَرُ دُولابٍ . قُطْبٌ

Ay *or* **Aye** *adv.* بَلَى . نَعَمْ . دَائِماً

Azure *a.* or *n.* اسمانجوني

B

Babble *v. i.* or *n.* بَقَّ ـ هَذَرَ ـ هَذْرٌ

Babbler *n.* بِقْبَاقٌ . مِهْذارٌ

Babe *or* / **Baby** } *n.* طِفْلٌ ج اطْفَالٌ

Baboon *n.* نَوْعٌ مِن القُرُودِ

Babyish *a.* سَرِيعُ التَّكَدُّرِ كَالطِّفْلِ

Bachelor *n.* عَزَبٌ ج عُزَّابٌ

Bachelorship *n.* عُزُوبَةٌ

Back *n.* or *ad.* ظَهْرٌ ج ظُهُورٌ
إِلَى ٱلْوَرَاءِ

Back and forth *ad.* إِقْبَالًا وَإِدْبَارًا

To go back رَجَعَ ـِ

Backbite *v. t.* غَابَ . إِغْتَابَ

Backbiting *n.* غِيبَةٌ . إِغْتِيَابٌ

Backbone *n.* اَلسِّلْسِلَةُ ٱلْفَقْرِيَّةُ

Backing *n.* عَوْنٌ . سَنَدٌ . بِطَانَةٌ

Backside *n.* ظَهْرٌ . قَفَاءٌ

Backslide *v. i.* مَالَ عَنْ . إِرْتَدَّ

Backward *ad.* or *a.* إِلَى ٱلْخَلْفِ . مُتَأَخِّرٌ

Bacon *n.* لَحْمُ خِنْزِيرٍ مُجَفَّفٌ

Bad *a.* شِرِّيرٌ . رَدِيٌّ . مُضِرٌّ

Bade *v. t.* أَمَرَ (مَاضِي bid)

Badge *n.* عَلَامَةٌ (نِيشَانٌ)

Baffle *v. t.* خَيَّبَ . غَلَبَ بِحِيلَةٍ

Bag *n.* كِيسٌ ج أَكْيَاسٌ

Bag *v. t.* وَضَعَ فِي كِيسٍ

Baggage *n.* أَمْتِعَةُ ٱلسَّفَرِ

Bagging *n.* خَيْشٌ لِلْأَكْيَاسِ

Bail *n.* or *v. t.* كَفِيلٌ كَفَالَةٌ
أَطْلَقَ بِكَفَالَةٍ

Bait *n.* or *v. t.* طُعْمٌ لِلسَّمَكِ . طَعَّمَ

Bake *v. t.* طَبَخَ بِفُرْنٍ . خَبَزَ

Baker *n.* فَرَّانٌ . خَبَّازٌ

Bakery *n.* مَخْبَزٌ . دُكَّانُ ٱلْخُبْزِ

Balance *n.* or *v. t.* مِيزَانٌ . وَازَنَ

Balcony *n.* شُرْفَةٌ . كُشْكٌ

Bald *a.* أَقْرَعُ

Baldness *n.* قَرَعٌ

Bale *n.* (طَرْدٌ) حُزْمَةٌ ج حُزَمٌ

Baleful *a.* مُضِرٌّ . مُحْزِنٌ . مُكَدِّرٌ

Balk *v. t.* خَيَّبَ أَعَاقَ

Ball *n.* كُرَةٌ . رَصَاصَةٌ (طَابَةٌ)

Ballad *n.* أُغْنِيَّةٌ . أَغَانٍ

Ballast *n.* or *v. t.* صَابُورَةٌ . صَبَّرَ

Balloon *n.* مَرْكَبَةٌ هَوَائِيَّةٌ (بالُون)

Ballot *n.* or *v. t.* وَرَقَةُ انتِخاب. إِنْتَخَبَ بِهَا

Balm *n.* رَيحان. مَرْهَمٌ عِطرٌ

Balmy *a. n.* عِطرٌ. لطِيفٌ. لَذِيذٌ

Balsam *n.* بَلْسَمٌ

Balustrade *n.* دَرَابزُون

Bamboo *n.* خَيزُرَان

Ban *n.* نَهْيٌ عامٌ. لَعْن (حِرْمٌ)

Banana *n.* مَوْزٌ

Band *n.* or *v. t.* رِباطٌ. فِرْقَة. إِرْتَبَطَ

Bandage *n.* or *v. t.* عِصَابَةٌ. ضِمَادَةٌ
لَفَّ ـُ. ضَمَدَ

Bandbox *n.* عُلبَةٌ لِلبَرَانِيطِ

Bandit *n.* قَاطِعُ الطَّرِيقِ

Bane *n.* سَمٌّ. أَذِيَّةٌ. شَرٌّ

Baneful *a.* سَامٌّ. مُضِرٌّ. مُهلِكٌ

Bang *v. t.* or *n.* ضَرَبَ ـِ. صَوْت بِشِدَّة. ضَرْبَةٌ

Banish *v. t.* نَفَى ـ طَرَدَ ـُ

Banishment *n.* نَفْيٌ

Bank *n.* شَطٌّ. سَدٌّ. مَقْعَدٌ. بَنْكٌ

Bank-bill / Bank-note *n.* إِيرَاد بَنْكٍ. بنكنوت

Banker *n.* صَاحِبُ بَنْكٍ
صَرَّافٌ ج صَيَارِفَةٌ

Banking *n.* (صِرَافَة)

Bankrupt *a.* or *n.* مُفلِسٌ

Bankruptcy *n.* إِفلاسٌ

Bank-stock *n.* أَسْهُمُ بَنْكٍ

Banner *n.* رَايَةٌ. بَيْرَقٌ

Banquet *n.* وَلِيمَةٌ. مأْدُبَة

Banter *v. i.* or *n.* مزح ـَ. سخِرَ ـَ مَزْحٌ

Baptism *n.* مَعْمُودِيَّةٌ

Baptist *n.* مُعْتَقِدٌ بالتَّغطِيس
فِي الْمَعْمُودِيَّةِ

Baptize *v. t.* عَمَّدَ

Bar *n.* or *v. t.* قَضِيبٌ. سَدٌّ. (دِقْرٌ)

Barb *n.* سِنَان . شَوْكَةٌ

Barbarian *n.* بَرْبَرِيٌّ . مُتَوَحِّشٌ

Barbaric / Barbarous *a.* بربري . فظيع

Barbarism *n.* بَرْبَرِيَّةٌ . تَوَحُّشٌ

Barbarity *n.* فَظَاظَةٌ . قَسَاوَةٌ

Barbed *n.* ذُو سِنَانٍ اوْ شَوْكٍ

Barber *n.* حَلَّاقٌ

Bard *n.* شَاعِرٌ . مُغَنٍّ . مُنْشِدٌ

Bare *a.* or *v. t.* عَارٍ . مُجَرَّدٌ . عَرَّى

Barefaced *a.* وَقِحٌ بِدُونِ حَيَاءٍ

Barefoot *a.* حَافٍ

Bareheaded *a.* مَكْشُوفُ ٱلرَّأْسِ

Barely *ad.* بِٱلْجَهْدِ . فَقَطْ

Bareness *n.* عُرِيَّةٌ

Bargain *n.* or *v. i.* مُسَاوَمَةٌ . سَاوَمَ

Barge *n.* جَرْمٌ . سَفِينَةٌ لِلشَّحْنِ

Bark *n* or *v. t.* or *i.* قِشْرٌ . قَشَّرَ . قَلَّفَ . نَبَحَ

Bark / Barque *n.* سَفِينَةٌ بِثَلَاثَةِ صَوَارٍ

Barking *n.* نَبِيحٌ . عُوَاءٌ

Barley *n.* شَعِيرٌ

Barn *n.* هُرْيٌ . بِنَاءٌ لِلْمَوَاشِي

Barometer *n.* مِيزَانٌ لِلْهَوَاءِ

Baron *n.* (بَارُونٌ)

Baronage *n.* رُتْبَةٌ مِنَ ٱلْأَشْرَافِ

Baronet *n.* رُتْبَةٌ دُونَ ٱلْبَارُونِ

Barrack *n.* قِشْلَاقٌ . ثُكْنَةٌ

Barrel *n.* بِرْمِيلٌ

Barren *a.* عَاقِرٌ . عَقِيمٌ . مَحْلٌ

Barrenness *n.* عُقْرٌ . مَحْلٌ

Barricade *n.* or *v. t.* سَدٌّ . حَاجِزٌ . سَدَّ

Barrier *n.* سَدٌّ . حَاجِزٌ . حَدٌّ . مَانِعٌ

Barrister *n.* وَكِيلُ دَعَاوٍ

Barter *n.* or *v.t.* مُبَادَلَةٌ . بَادَلَ ٱلْبَضَائِعَ

Basalt *n.* حَجَرٌ نَارِيٌّ أَسْوَدُ

Base *n.* or *a.* قَاعِدَةٌ . دَنِيءٌ . خَسِيسٌ

Baseless *a.* بِلَا أَسَاسٍ . بَاطِلٌ

Basement *n.* طَبَقَةُ ٱلْبَيْتِ ٱلسُّفْلَى

Baseness *n.* دَنَاءَة . لُؤْمٌ

Bashful *a.* مُسْتَحٍ . خَجِلٌ

Bashfulness *n.* حِشْمَةٌ . حَيَاءٌ

Basin *n.* طَسْت . حَوْضٌ

Basilisk *n.* حَيَّةٌ خُرَافِيَّةٌ اوْ تِنِّين

Basis *n.* أَسَاسٌ . أَصْلٌ

Bask *v. i.* تَشَمَّسَ

Basket *n.* سَلَّةٌ ج سِلَالٌ . قُفَّةٌ ج قُفَفٌ

Bastard *n.* نَغْلٌ إِبْنُ زِنا

Baste *v. t.* شَلَّ ـُ شَرَّجَ

Bastinade / **Bastinado** *v. t.* or *n.* ضَرَبَ بِعَصاً خَاصَّةً عَلَى أَسْفَلِ ٱلْقَدَمَيْن . ضَرْبٌ بِهِ

Bastion *n.* بُرْجٌ اوِ ٱلْبَارِزُ مِنْهُ

Bat *n.* وَطْوَاطٌ . خُفَّاشٌ

Batch *n.* كَمِّيَّةٌ مِقْدَارٌ

Bated *a.* خَفِيٌّ (صَوْت)

Bath *n.* حَمَّامٌ

Bathe *v.t.* or *i.* حَمَّمَ . غَسَلَ . إِسْتَحَمَّ

Bathing *n.* إِسْتِحْمَامٌ . إِغْتِسَالٌ

Battalion *n.* تَابُورٌ ج تَوَابِيرُ . اورْطَة

Batter *v. t.* هَدَمَ ـِ . هَدَّ

Battering-ram *n.* مَنْجَنِيقٌ

Battery *n.* مَجْمُوعُ مَدَافِعَ . بَطَّارِيَّةٌ

Battle *n.* قِتَالٌ . مَعْرَكَةٌ . حَرْبٌ

Battle-axe *n.* بَلْطَةٌ

Battlement *n.* شُرْفَة ج شُرَفٌ

Bauble *n.* لُعْبَةٌ . شَيْءٌ زَهِيدٌ

Bawl *v. i.* صَرَخَ ـُ . صَيَّحَ

Bay *a.* أَحْمَرُ ٱللَّوْنِ

Bay *n.* خَلِيجٌ . شَجَرُ ٱلْغَارِ

Bayonet *n.* حَرْبَةٌ

Bazaar *n.* سُوقٌ ج أَسْوَاقٌ

Be *v. i.* (was, been) كَانَ يَكُونُ

Beach *n.* شَطٌّ (رَمْلِيٌّ) شَاطِئٌ

Beacon *n.*	مَنَارَةٌ ج مَنَائِرُ
Bead *n.*	خَرَزَةٌ ج خَرَزٌ
Beak *n.*	مِنقادٌ . مِنقارٌ
Beaker *n.*	كَأسٌ قَدَحٌ
Beam *v. t.*	اشْرَقَ لاَحَ
Beam *n.*	جِسْرٌ خَشَبٌ . شُعَاعٌ
Bean *n.*	حَبَّةٌ مِنَ آللُّوبْيَا اوْ آلْفُولِ
Bear *n.*	دَبٌّ ج اَدْبَابٌ . شَرِسٌ
Bear *v. t. or i.*	حَمَلَ ـِ وَآحْتَمَلَ . اثْمَرَ
Bearable *a.*	مَا يُحْتَمَلُ اوْ يُطَاقُ
Beard *n.*	لِحْيَةٌ ج لِحًى
Bearded *a.*	ذُو لِحْيَةٍ أَوْ شَوْكٍ
Beardless *a.*	بِلاَ لِحْيَةٍ . امْرَدُ
Bearer *n.*	حَامِلٌ . نَاقِلٌ
Beast *n.*	بَهِيمَةٌ ج بَهَائِمُ . وَحْشٌ
Beat *v. t.*	ضَرَبَ ـِ غَلَبَ ـُ
Beating *n.*	ضَرْبٌ بَالِغٌ
Beatitude *n.*	غِبْطَةٌ . طُوْبَى
Beau *n.*	لَبِقٌ . بَشُوشٌ لِلنِّسَاءِ
Beau-ideal *n.*	خَيَالٌ . غَايَةُ آلْجَمَالِ
Beauteous *a.*	حَسَنٌ . جَمِيلٌ
Beautiful *a.*	حَسَنٌ . جَمِيلٌ
Beautify *v. t*	حَسَّنَ . زَخْرَفَ
Beauty *n.*	حُسْنٌ . جَمَالٌ
Beaver *n.*	كَلْبُ آلْمَاءِ
Becalm *v. t.*	هَدَّأَ . سَكَّنَ
Because *con.*	لِأَنَّ . بِسَبَبِ ان
Beckon *v. t.*	أَوْمَأَ . أَشَارَ
Become *v. i. or t.*	صَارَ ـِ . لاَقَ
Becoming *a.*	لاَئِقٌ . مُوَافِقٌ
Bed *n.*	فِرَاشٌ . مَجْرَى (نَهْرٍ)
Bedaub *v. t.*	طَلَى . دَهَنَ ـُ
Bedding *n.*	فِرَاشٌ وَمَفْرُوشَاتُهُ
Bedeck *v. t.*	زَيَّنَ . زَخْرَفَ
Bedew *v. t.*	نَدَّى
Bedim *v. t.*	اظْلَمَ

Bedlam *n.* بِيمَارِسْتَانٌ
Bed-quilt *n.* لِحَافٌ ج لُحُفٌ
Bedridden *n.* مُلازِمُ ٱلفِرَاشِ
Bedroom *n.* غُرْفَةُ ٱلنَّوْمِ
Bedstead *n.* تَخْتٌ . سَرِيرٌ
Bee *n.* نَحْلَةٌ
Beef *n.* لَحْمُ بَقَرٍ
Beefsteak *n.* شَرِيحَةُ بَقَرٍ لِلشَّيِّ
Bee-hive *n.* خَلِيَّةٌ . كُوَارَةٌ
Beer *n.* جِعَةٌ (بِيرَا)
Beeswax *n.* شَمْعٌ عَسَلِيٌّ
Beet *n.* (شَمَنْدُورٌ) . (بَنْجَرٌ)
Beetle *n.* خُنْفُسَاءُ
Beeves (*pl.* of ***beef.***) بَقَرٌ
Befall *v. t.* اصَابَ . إِعْتَرَى
Befit *v. t.* نَاسَبَ . لاَقَ بِـ
Befool *v. t.* إِفْتَتَنَ . خَدَعَ
Before *ad.* or *pr.* قَبْلُ . قُدَّامُ . امَامُ
Beforehand *ad.* قَبْلاً . مِنْ قَبْلُ
Befoul *v. t.* وَسَّخَ . دَنَّسَ . لَوَّثَ
Befriend *v. t.* وَالَى . اعَانَ
Beg *v. t.* or *i.* إِلْتَمَسَ . تَسَوَّلَ
Beget *v. t.* وَلَدَ يَلِدُ . أَنْتَجَ
Beggar *n.* or *v. t.* شَحَّاذٌ . افْقَرَ
Beggarly *a.* حَقِيرٌ . دَنِيءٌ
Beggary *n.* فَقْرٌ . مَسْكَنَةٌ
Begging *n.* تَسَوَّلَ . شِحَاذَةٌ
Begin *v. t.* بَدَأَ ـَ . إِبْتَدَأَ بِـ
Beginning *n.* بَدْءٌ . بَدَاءَةٌ
Begird *v. t.* زَنَّرَ . نَطَّقَ . طَوَّقَ
Begrudge *v. t.* حَسَدَ ـُ عَلَى
Beguile *v. t.* غَرَّ ـُ . خَدَعَ
Begun(*pp.* of ***Begin***) مَبْدُوءٌ
Behalf *n.* مَنْفَعَةٌ . لِأَجْلِ . بِالنِّيَابَةِ عَنْ
Behave *v. i.* تَصَرَّفَ . أَحْسَنَ سُلُوكَهُ
Behaviour *n.* تَصَرُّفٌ . سِيرَةٌ

Behead *v. t.* قَطَعَ رَأْسَهُ

Beheld *v. t.* (*Behold.* رَأَى (مَاضِي

Behind *pr.* or *ad.* وَرَآءَ . خَلْفُ

Behindhand *ad.* مُتَأَخِّراً

Behold *v.t.* or *ad.* رَأَى ـ هُوَ ذَا

Beholden *a.* (to) شَاكِرٌ لِ

Beholder *n.* مُشَاهِدٌ . مُعَايِنٌ

Behoove *v. t.* لَزِمَ ـَ . وَجَبَ ـِ

Being *n.* كَوْنٌ . وُجُودٌ . كَائِنٌ

Belabour *v. t.* ضَرَبَ ـِ كَثِيرًا

Belate *v. t.* أَخَّرَ . أَبْطَأَ

Belch *v. t.* قَذَفَ ـِ تَجَشَّأَ

Beleaguer *v. t.* حَاصَرَ . أَحَاطَ بِ

Belfry *n.* قُبَّةُ ٱلْجَرَسِ

Belie *v. t.* كَذَّبَ

Belief *n.* تَصْدِيقٌ . إِعْتِقَادٌ

Believe *v. t.* صَدَّقَ . إِعْتَقَدَ . آمَنَ

Believer *n.* مُصَدِّقٌ . مُؤْمِنٌ

Bell *n.* جَرَسٌ ج أَجْرَاسٌ

Belle *n.* إِمْرَأَةٌ حَسَنَةٌ . حَسْنَاء

Belles-lettres *n.* آدَابُ ٱللُّغَةِ

Belligerent *a.* مُحَارِبٌ

Bellow *v. i.* or *n.* جَأَرَ . صَرَخَ . جُأَرٌ

Bellows *n.* مِنْفَخٌ . مِنْفَاخٌ

Belly *n.* بَطْنٌ . جَوْفٌ

Belly-band *n.* حِزَامُ ٱلْفَرَسِ

Belong *v. i.* إِخْتَصَّ بِ

Belonging *a.* مُخْتَصٌّ . ذَيْلٌ

Beloved *a.* مَحْبُوبٌ . حَبِيبٌ

Below *pr.* or *ad.* تَحْتَ . دُونَ

Belt *n.* زُنَّارٌ . حِزَامٌ . مِنْطَقَةٌ

Bemoan *v. t.* نَدَبَ ـُ . نَاحَ ـُ

Bench *n.* مَقْعَدٌ . دَكَّةُ ٱلْقُضَاةِ

Bend *v. t.* or *i.* حَنَا . ثَنَى . تَلَوَّى

Bend *n.* حَنْوٌ . ثَنْيٌ . عَطْفٌ

Beneath *pr.* or *ad.* تَحْتَ . أَسْفَلَ

Benediction *n.* بَرَكَةٌ إِنْعَامٌ
Benefaction *n.* إِحْسَانٌ . خَيْرٌ
Benefactor *n.* مُحْسِنٌ . عَامِلُ خَيْرٍ
Beneficence *n.* إِحْسَانٌ عَمَلُ آلْخَيْرِ
Beneficent *a.* مُحْسِنٌ . جَوَّاد
Beneficial *a.* مُفِيدٌ . نَافِعٌ
Beneficiary *n,* أَلْمُحْسَنُ إِلَيْهِ
Benefit *n.* نَفْعٌ فَائِدَةٌ
Benevolence *n.* إِحْسَانٌ جُودٌ
Benevolent *n.* مُحْسِنٌ . مُحِبُّ آلْخَيْرِ
Benighted *a.* ذَاهِبٌ فِي الظَّلَامِ
Benign *a.* حَلِيمٌ . لَطِيفٌ
Benignity *n.* حِلْمٌ . لُطْفٌ
Bent *a.* or *n.* مَعْطُوفٌ . مَيْلٌ
Benumb *v. t.* خَدَّرَ
Bequeath *v. t.* وَصَّى بِ
Bequest *n.* وَصِيَّةٌ . آلْمُوصَّى بِهِ
Berate *v. t.* عَنَّفَ . وَبَّخَ
Bereave *v. t.* اثْكَلَ . أَفْقَدَ
Bereavement *n.* فُقْدَانُ الْحَبِيبِ
Bereft *(pp. of Bereave).* فَاقِدٌ
Berry *n.* تُوتَةٌ . حَبَّةُ تُوتٍ
Berth *n.* سَرِيرٌ فِي سَفِينَةٍ . مَنْصَبٌ
Beseech *v. t.* تَوَسَّلَ تَضَرَّعَ إِلَى
Beseem *v. t.* لَاقَ . وَافَقَ
Beseemly *a.* لَائِقٌ . مُوَافِقٌ
Beset *v. t.* أَحَاطَ . لَازَم
Besetting *a.* مُحِيطٌ . مُلَازِمٌ
Beside *pr.* بِجَانِبِ عِنْدَ
Besides *ad.* فَضْلاً عَنْ . عَدَا . غَيْرَ
Besiege *v. t.* حَاصَرَ
Besmear *v. t.* طَلَى . لَوَّثَ
Besotted *a.* سَكِيرٌ . أَبْلَهُ
Besought *(pret of Beseech).* تَوَسَّلَ
Bespangle *v. t.* زَيَّنَ . رَصَّعَ
Bespatter *v. t.* لَطَخَ

Besprinkle *v. t.* رَشَّ

Best *a.* أَلْأَحْسَنُ. الأَفْضَلُ

Bestial *a.* بَهِيمِيٌّ . قَذِرٌ

Bestir *v. t.* حرَّكَ

Bestow *v. t.* اعطَى وَهبَ يَهِبُ

Bestowal / **Bestowment** *n.* إِعطَآءٌ . مَنْحٌ

Bestride *v. t.* فَرْشَحَ رَكِبَ

Bet *n.* or *v. t.* or *i.* مُرَاهَنَةٌ . رَاهَنَ

Betake *v. t.* لَجَأَ إِلَى . عكَفَ

Bethink *v. t.* فَطِنَ ـُ . تأمَّلَ

Betide *v. t.* or *i.* حَدَثَ ـُ . صارَ ـِ

Betimes *ad.* فِي وَقتٍ مُنَاسِبٍ . بَاكِراً

Betoken *v. t.* أَشارَ . دلَّ ـِ

Betray *v. t.* سَلَّمَ . خَانَ

Betrayal *n.* تَسلِيمٌ. خِيَانَةٌ

Betroth *v. t.* خَطَبَ ـُ (إِمْرَأَةً)

Betrothal *n.* خُطْبَةٌ

Better *a.* احْسَنُ . افضَلُ . خَيْرٌ

Bettor *n.* مُرَاهِنٌ

Between / **Betwixt** *pr.* بَيْنَ . مَا بَيْنَ

Beverage *n.* شرَابٌ . مَشْرُوبٌ

Bevy *n.* سِرْبٌ . جَمَاعَةٌ

Bewail *v. t.* نَاحَ . نَدَبَ ـُ

Beware *v. t.* حَذِرَ ـ . تَحَرَّزَ مِنْ

Bewilder *v. t.* حَيَّرَ

Bewitch *v. t.* إِفْتَتَنَ . سَحَرَ

Beyond *ad.* or *pr.* عَبْرَ . بَعدَ

Bias *n.* or *v. t.* مَيلٌ. إِنحِرَافٌ. امَالَ

Bib *n.* صُدْرِيَّةُ الطِّفلِ

Bibber *n.* شِرِّيبٌ

Bible *n.* الكِتَابُ المُقَدَّسُ

Biblical *a.* مُختَصٌّ بِالكِتَابِ المُقَدَّسِ

Bibliography *n.* تارِيخُ الكُتُبِ أَوْ وَصفُهَا

Bicephaleus *a.* ذو رَأْسَينِ

Bid *v. t.* or *n.* امَرَ ـُ . زَايَدَ . دَفعٌ

Bidden *(pp. Bid)* مَأْمُورٌ

Bidding *n.* أمْرٌ . دَعْوَةٌ

Bid *v. t.* or *i.* إِنتظر. أَقَامَ. سَكَنَ

Biennial *a.* حَادِث مَرَّةً كُلَّ سنتَيْنِ

Bier *n.* نَعْشٌ ج نُعُوشٌ

Bifold *a.* مُزْدَوِجٌ . ذُو ثَنْيَتَيْنِ

Big *a.* كَبِيرٌ. ضَخْمٌ

Bigamy *n.* أَلتَّزَوُّجُ بِامْرَأَتَيْنِ مَعاً

Bight *n.* خَلِيجٌ صَغِيرٌ

Bigness *n.* كُبْرٌ. ضَخَامَة

Bigot *n.* / **Bigoted** *a.* } مُتَعَصِّبٌ بالدِّينِ

Bigotry *n.* تَعَصُّبٌ بِالدِّينِ

Bile *n.* صَفْرَاءُ . مِرَّةٌ

Bilingual *n.* ذُو لُغَتَيْنِ

Bilious *a.* صَفْرَاوِيٌّ

Bill *n.* مِنْقَارٌ . قَائِمَةُ حِسَابٍ

Bill of exchange *n.* سُفْتَجَة

Billet *n.* رُقْعَةٌ. كُتَيْبَةٌ

Bil-lion *n.* أَلْفُ مَلْيُون أو أَلْفُ أَلْفِ أَلْفٍ

Billow *n.* مَوْجَةٌ ج مَوْجَاتٌ

Billowy *a.* مُتَمَوِّجٌ

Bimonthly *a.* ما يظْهَرُ كُلَّ شَهْرَيْنِ

Bin *n.* صُنْدُوقٌ لِلْمُؤْنَةِ

Binary *a.* مُزْدَوِجٌ . ثُنَائِيٌّ

Bind *v. t.* رَبَطَ ـُ . أَوْثَقَ . جَلَّدَ

Binder *n.* مُجَلِّدُ كُتُبٍ

Bindery *n.* مَحَلُّ ٱلتَّجْلِيدِ

Binding *n.* رَبْطٌ . تَجْلِيد

Biographer *n.* كَاتِبُ تَرْجَمَةِ إِنْسَانٍ

Biography *n.* تَرْجَمَةُ إِنْسَانٍ

Biology *n.* عِلْمُ ٱلْحَيَاةِ

Biped *n.* ذُو رِجْلَيْنِ او سَاقَيْنِ

Birch *n.* بَتُولاَ (شَجَرٌ) قَضِيبٌ

Bird *n.* طَائِرٌ . عُصْفُورٌ

Bird-lime *n.* دَابُوقٌ (دِبْقٌ)

Birth *n.* وِلاَدَة . مَوْلِدٌ

Birthday *n.* مِيلَادٌ . مَوْلِدٌ

Birthplace *n.* مَسْقَطُ ٱلرَّأْسِ . مَوْلِدٌ

Birthright *n.* بَكُورِيَّة

Biscuit *n.* (بَقْسَماط)

Bisect *v. t.* نَصَّفَ . شَطَرَ ـُ

Bisection *n.* شَطْرٌ . تَنْصِيفٌ

Bishop *n.* أُسْقُفٌ ج اساقِفة

Bishopric *n.* أَبْرَشِيَّةٌ اسقُفٍ

Bisextile *n.* سَنَةٌ كَبِيسَة

Bison *n.* جَامُوسٌ أَمْرِيكَانِيٌّ

Bit *n.* شَكِيمَة . قِطْعَةٌ صَغِيرَة

Bitch *n.* كَلْبَةٌ

Bite *v. t.* or *n.* عَضَّ ـُ . عَضَّةٌ

Bitter *a.* مُرٌّ . شَدِيدٌ . مُحْزِن

Bitterness *n.* مَرَارَةٌ . بُغْضَةٌ . حزْن

Bitumeen *n.* حُمَرٌ وَحُمَّرٌ

Bituminous *a.* حُمَرِيٌّ

Bivalve *n.* or *a.* صَدَفٌ . صدَفِيٌّ

المَبِيتُ فِي ٱلْعَرَاءِ بَاتَ بدُونِ خِيَمٍ

Bivouac *n.* or *v. t.*

Blab *v. t.* or *i.* أَفْشَى ٱلسِّرَّ . هَذِرَ

Blackguard *n.* ثَالِبٌ . وَبَشٌ

Block *a.* or *n.* أَسْوَدُ . زِنْجِيٌّ

Blackberry *n.* تُوتٌ اسْوَدُ

Blackboard *n.* لَوْحٌ أَسْوَدُ

Blacken *v. t.* سَوَّدَ

Blacksmith *n.* حَدَّادٌ

Bladder *n.* مَثَانَة

Blade *n.* نَصْلٌ . وَرَقَةُ عِشْبٍ

Blamable } *n.* مُسْتَحِق ٱللَّوْمِ
Blameworthy }

Blame *n.* or *v.t.* لَوْمٌ . لَامَ ـُ . عَاتَبَ

Blameless *a.* بلَا لَوْمٍ . بَرِيءٌ

Blanch *v. t.* بَيَّضَ . قَصَّرَ

Bland *a.* لطِيفٌ . أَنِيسٌ

Blandish *v. t.* لَاطَفَ . ملقَ ـُ

Blandishment *n.* مُلَاطَفَةٌ . ملَقٌ

Blandness *n.* لطْفٌ . مُؤَانسة

Blank *a.* or *n.* خَالٍ . وَرَقَةٌ بَيْضَآءُ

Blanket *n.* حِرَامٌ . دِثَارٌ

Blaspheme *v. t.* جَدَّفَ

Blasphemous *a.* تَجْدِيفِيٌّ . مُجَدِّفٌ

Blasphemy *n.* تَجْدِيفٌ

Blast *v. t.* لَفَحَ ـَ . فَجَّرَ (بِلُغْمٍ)

Blast *n.* هَبَّةُ رِيحٍ . لَفْحٌ . (لُغْمٌ)

Blaze *v. i.* or *n.* إِلْتَهَبَ . أَذَاعَ . لَهِيبٌ

Bleach *v. t.* بَيَّضَ . قَصَرَ ـِ

Bleaching *n.* تَبْيِيضٌ . قِصَارَةٌ

Bleak *a.* بَارِدٌ . مُعَرَّضٌ لِلرِّيحِ ٱلْبَارِدَةِ

Blear *v t.* سَدَّبَ ٱلْعَمَشَ

Blear-eyed *a.* اعْمَشُ

Bleat *v. i.* or *n.* ثَغَا يَثْغُو . ثُغَآءٌ

Bleed *v. i.* or *i.* فَصَدَ ـِ . نَزَفَ

Bleeding *n.* فِصَادٌ . نَزْفٌ

Blemish *v. t.* or *n.* أَعَابَ . عَيْبٌ

Blend *v. t.* or *i.* مَزَجَ ـُ . إِمْتَزَجَ

Bless *v. t.* بَارَكَ . حَمَدَ ـَ

Blessed *a.* مُبَارَكٌ . مَغْبُوطٌ . سَعِيدٌ

Blessedness *n.* غِبْطَةٌ . سَعَادَةٌ

Blessing *n.* بَرَكَةٌ . نِعْمَةٌ

Blight *v. t.* or *n.* لَفَحَ ـَ لُفُوحٌ . آفَةٌ

Blind *a.* or *n.* أَعْمَى . ضَرِيرٌ . غَبِيٌّ

Blind *v. t.* أَعْمَى . عَمَّى

Blindfold *v. t.* غَطَّى ٱلْعَيْنَيْنِ

Blindness *n.* عَمًى . غَبَاوَةٌ

Blindly *ad.* بِدُونِ فِكْرٍ . بِغَبَاوَةٍ

Blink *v. i.* غَمَزَ ـِ . جَهَرَ ـَ

Bliss / **Blissfulness** } *n.* سَعَادَةٌ . غِبْطَةٌ

Blissful *a.* سَعِيدٌ . مَغْبُوطٌ

Blister *n.* or *v. t.* نَفْطَةٌ . حَرَّاقَةٌ . نَقَّطَ

Blithe / **Blithsome** } *a.* فَرِحٌ . مُبْتَهِجٌ . مَسْرُورٌ

Bloat *v. t.* or *i.* وَرَّمَ . نَفَخَ . إِنْتَفَخَ

Block *n.* or *v. t.* قِطْعَةُ خَشَبٍ . سَدَّ

Blockade *v. t.* or *n.* حَاصَرَ . احَاطَ . حِصَارٌ

Blockhead n.	بَلِيدٌ . أَبْلَهُ
Block-house n.	بُرْجٌ مِنْ أَخْشَابٍ ضَخْمَةٍ
Blood n.	دَمٌ
Blood-hound n.	كَلْبُ صَيْدٍ كَبِيرٌ
Bloodless a.	بِلَا دَمٍ
Bloodshed n.	سَفْكُ ٱلدَّمِ . قَتْلٌ
Blood-thirsty a.	سَفَّاكُ ٱلدَّمِ
Blood-vessel n.	وِعَاءٌ دَمَوِيٌّ . عِرْقٌ
Bloody n.	دَمَوِيٌّ . مُلَطَّخٌ بِالدَّمِ
Bloom n. or v. i.	زَهْرَةٌ . جَمَالٌ . أَزْهَرَ
Blooming a.	مُزْهِرٌ . نَضِيرٌ . جَمِيلٌ
Blossom n. or v. i.	زَهْرَةٌ . أَزْهَرَ
Blot n. or v. t.	لَطْخَةٌ . عَارٌ . لَطَخَ . مَحَا ـُ
Blotch n.	لَمْعَةٌ . بَثْرَةٌ
Blotting-paper n.	وَرَقٌ نَشَّاشٌ
Blow n. or v. t. or i.	ضَرْبَةٌ . هَبَّ ـُ
Blower n.	نَافِخٌ . مِنْفَخٌ
Blubber n.	شَحْمُ ٱلحُوتِ
Blue a.	أَزْرَقُ
Blueness n.	زُرْقَةٌ
Bluff n. or a.	جُرْفٌ شَاهِقٌ . فَظٌّ
Bluish a.	ضَارِبٌ إِلَى ٱلزُّرْقَةِ
Blunder n. or v. i.	خَطَأٌ . غَلِطَ ـَ
Blundering a.	كَثِيرُ ٱلْخَطَإِ
Blunt a. or v. t.	كَلِيلٌ . شَرِسٌ . فَلَّ حَدَّ ٱلسِّكِّينِ
Bluntness n.	كَلَالٌ . خُشُونَةٌ
Blur n. or v. t.	لَطْخَةٌ . لَاثَ ـُ
Blurred pp.	غَيْرُ وَاضِحٍ
Blush v.i. or n.	خَجِلَ ـَ . إِحْمِرَارٌ
Bluster v. t. or n.	هَاجَ . تَصَلَّفَ . تَصَلُّفٌ
Boa n.	ضَرْبٌ مِنَ ٱلْحَيَّاتِ ٱلضَّخْمَةِ
Boar n.	خِنْزِيرٌ
Board n.	لَوْحُ خَشَبٍ . قُوتٌ . مَجْلِسٌ
Board v. t. or i.	غَطَّى بِالْوَاحٍ . صَعَدَ إِلَى مَرْكَبٍ . أَكَلَ قَاتَ ـُ
Boarder n.	نَزِيلٌ بِالأُجْرَةِ

Boarding *n.* تَسْمِيرُ الْوَاح . طعامٌ
Boast *v. i.* or *n.* إِفتخرَ . إِفْتِخَارٌ
Boastful *a.* مفْتخِرٌ . مُتَعَظِّمٌ
Boasting *n.* إِفْتِخَارٌ . تعظمٌ
Boat *n.* قَارِبٌ . زَوْرَقٌ . سفِينَةٌ
Boating *n.* أَلتَّنَزُّهُ بِالْقَارِب
Boatman *n.* بَحْرِيٌّ
Boatswain *n.* مُدِيرُ قَارِبِ
Bob *v. i.* إِهْتَزَّ . إِرْتَجَّ
Bode *v. t.* or *i.* انْبَا بِهِ . شَوَّمَ
Bodiless *a.* بِلَا جِسْمٍ اوْجسدٍ
Bodily *a.* or *ad.* جَسَدِيٌّ . كُلِّيًّا
Body *n.* جِسْمٌ . جَسَدٌ . بَدَنٌ
Bog *n.* مُسْتَنْقَعٌ
Boggy *a.* مُسْتَنْقَعِيٌّ
Bogus *a.* مُزَوَّرٌ . كاذِبٌ
Boil *n.* or *v. i.* or *v. t.* دُمَّلٌ . غَلَى ـ . سَلَقَ ـ
Boiler *n.* مرْجَلٌ (دَسْتٌ)
Boisterous *a.* هائِجٌ . صَيَّاح
Bold *a.* جَسُورٌ . شُجَاعٌ
Boldness *n.* جسارَةٌ شَجَاعة
Bolster *n.* or *v. t.* وِسَادَةٌ . سندَ
Bolt *n.* or *v. t.* مِزْلَاجٌ (دُقرَة . دَقر)
Bomb *n.* قُنبُلَة (قنبرَةٌ)
Bombard *v. t.* رَمَى بِالْقَنَابِلِ
Bombardment *n.* اطْلَاقُ الْقَنَابِلِ
Bombast *n.* التفخر فِي الْكَلَامِ
Bond *n.* قيد . رِبَاط . عهد
Bondage *n.* عبُودِيه
Bondman / **Bondservant** *n.* عبْدٌ . رَقِيقٌ
Bondsman *n.* كافِلٌ . ضامِنٌ
Bone *n.* عظمٌ ج عِظَام
Bone-setter *n.* مُجبِّرُ الْعِظَام
Bonfire *n.* نارٌ تُشْعَلُ لِلْفرح
Bonnet *n.* قُبَّعَةٌ . بُرْنَيْطَةٌ
Bonny *a.* جمِيلٌ . بَدِيعٌ . فرِحٌ

Bonus *n.* نافِلَةٌ . جزءٌ فَوْقَ ٱلْمَفرُوض

Bony *a.* كَثِيرُ ٱلْعِظَامِ . ضَلِيعٌ

Boody *n.* أَبْلَهُ . غَبِيٌّ

Book *n.* كِتَابٌ . سِفْرٌ

Book-binder *n.* مُجَلِّد كُتُبٍ

Book-case *n.* خِزَانَةُ كُتُبٍ

Book-keeping *n.* مَسْكُ ٱلدَّفَاتِرِ

Book-store *n.* مَخْزَنُ كُتُبٍ

Book-worm *n.* مغرَمٌ بِٱلْكُتُبِ

Boom *v. i.* or *n.* عَجَّ . هَدَرَ . زَئِيرٌ

Booming *n.* منقضٌّ بِشِدَّةٍ . عَاجٌّ

Boon *n.* or *a.* هِبَةٌ . بَشُوشٌ

Boor *n.*
Boorish *a.* } غَلِيظٌ . جافٍ . غَيرُ مُهَذَّبٍ

Boot *n.* or *r. t.* حِذاءٌ (جَزْمَةٌ) . نَفَعَ ـُ

Booth *n.* خَيْمَةٌ . مَظَلَّةٌ

Bootless *n.* غَيْرُ نَافِعٍ . عَبَثٌ

Booty *n.* غنِيمَةَ

Borax *n.* بَوْرَقٌ

Border *n.* حافَةٌ . حَدٌّ . تَخْمٌ

Bore *v. t.* قَدَحَ ـَ . أَتْعَبَ . اضجَرَ

Bore *n.* (قَدْحٌ) ثَقْبٌ . مُضْجِرٌ

Boreal *n.* شِمَالِيٌّ

Born *p.p.* of *bear.* مَوْلُودٌ

Borne *p.p.* of *bear.* مَحْمُولٌ

Borrow *v. t.* إِسْتَعَارَ . إِسْتَقْرَضَ

Bosom *n.* حُضْنٌ . صَدْرٌ

Botanist *a.* عَالِمٌ بِالنَّبَاتِ

Botanize *v. t.* جَمَعَ ٱلنَّبَاتَ

Botany *n.* عِلْمُ ٱلنَّبَاتِ

Botch *n.* or *v. t.* رَقْعٌ رَدِيٌّ . رَقَعَ رَدِيئاً

Both *a.* كِلَا وَكِلْتَا

Bother *n.* or *v. t.* إِنْزِعَاجٌ . ازعَجَ

Bottle *n.* زُجَاجَةٌ . قَارُورَةٌ

Bots *n. pl.* دُودُ إِمعَاءِ ٱلْخَيْلِ

Bottom *n.* قَعْرٌ . قَاعٌ . اسفَل

Bottomless *a.* بِلَا قَعْرٍ

Bough *n.* غُصْنٌ

Bought *p.p.* of *buy.* مُبْتَاعٌ

Bounce *v. i.* or *n.* وَثَبَ . وَثْبَةٌ

Bound *p.p.* of *bind.* مُقَيَّدٌ . مُلْتَزِمٌ

Bound *v. t.* or *i.* حَدَّدَ . قَفَزَ

Bound / **Boundary** } *n.* حَدٌّ . تَخْمٌ

Bounteous / **Bountiful** } *a.* كَرِيمٌ . جَوَّادٌ

Bounty *n.* كَرَمٌ . سَخَاءٌ

Bouquet *n.* بَاقَةُ زُهُورٍ

Bout *n.* دَوْرٌ

Bovine *a.* بَقَرِيٌّ

Bow *v. t.* or *i.* حَنَا ـُ إِنْحَنَى

Bow *n.* إِنْحِنَاءٌ . قَوْسٌ

Bowlder *n.* صَخْرَةٌ كَبِيرَةٌ كُرَوِيَة

Bowman *n.* رَامٍ بِالْقَوْسِ

Bowels *n. pl.* امْعَاءٌ . احْشَاءٌ

Bower *n.* مَظَلَّةٌ . عَرِيشٌ

Bowl *n.* كَاسٌ . طَاسٌ

Bowsprit *n.* خَشَبَةُ مُقَدَّمِ ٱلسَّفِينَةِ

Bowstring *n.* وَتَرُ ٱلْقَوْسِ

Box *n.* or *v. t.* صُنْدُوقٌ . لَكَمَ

Boxer *n.* مُقَاتِلٌ بِقَبْضَةِ ٱلْيَدِ

Boy *n.* صَبِيٌّ . غُلَامٌ

Boyhood *n.* صَبْوَةٌ

Boyish *a.* وَلَدِيٌّ . طَفِيفٌ

Brace *n.* or *v. t.* مَشَدٌّ . شَدَّ ـُ

Bracelet *n.* سُوَارٌ ج اسَاوِرُ

Bracket *n.* رَفٌّ صَغِيرٌ بَارِزٌ مِنَ ٱلْحَائِطِ

Brackets *n. pl.* هِلَالَانِ كَذَا ( )

Brackish *a.* مَالِحٌ . مَائِلٌ لِلْمُلُوحَةِ

Brad *n.* مِسْمَارٌ صَغِيرٌ بِلَا رَأْسٍ

Brag *v. i.* تَصَلَّفَ . فَاخَرَ

Braggadocio / **Braggart** } *n.* مُتَصَلِّفٌ . نَفَّاخٌ

Braid *v. t.* or *n.* ضَفَرَ ـِ . ضَفِيرَةٌ

Brain *n.* دِمَاغٌ ج ادْمِغَةٌ

Brake *n.* آلَةٌ لِتَوْقِيفِ دُولَابٍ . (فَرْمَلَة)

Bramble *n.*	عَوْسَجٌ . عُلَّيْقٌ
Bran *n.*	نُخَالَةٌ
Branch *n.* or *v. i.*	غُصْنٌ . تَفَرَّعَ
Brand *v. t.*	وَسَمَ ـِ . عَابَ ـ
Brand *n.*	وَسْمٌ أَوْسِمَةٌ . عَيْبٌ
Brandish *v. t.*	هَزَّ . حَرَّكَ
Brandy *n.*	كُونْيَاكُ
Brasier *n.*	كَانُونٌ . نَحَّاسٌ
Brass *n.*	نُحَاسٌ أَصْفَرُ
Brassy *n.*	نُحَاسِيٌّ
Bravado *n.*	تَصَلُّفٌ . تَعَظُّمٌ
Brave *a.* or *n.*	شُجَاعٌ . بَاسِلٌ
Brave *v. t.*	إِقْتَحَمَ . بَارَزَ
Bravery *n.*	شَجَاعَةٌ . بَسَالَةٌ
Bravo *n.* or *int.*	جَسُورٌ . أَحْسَنْتَ
Brawl *n.* or *v. i.*	مُشَاجَرَةٌ . تَشَاجَرَ
Brawny *a.*	قَوِيٌّ . ضَلِيعٌ
Bray *v. t.* or *i.*	سَحَقَ ـ . شَهَقَ ـُ
Bray / **Braying** } *n.*	شَهِيقٌ . نَهِيقٌ
Brazen *a.*	نُحَاسِيٌّ
Brazen / **Brazen-faced** } *a.*	جَسُورٌ . وَقِحٌ
Breach *n.*	خَرْقٌ . نَكْثٌ
Bread *n.*	خُبْزٌ . عَيْشٌ
Breadstuff *n.*	دَقِيقٌ . حُبُوبٌ
Breadth *n.*	عَرْضٌ
Break *v. t.* or *i.*	كَسَرَ ـِ . إِنْكَسَرَ
Break *n.*	كَسْرٌ . فَتْحَةٌ
Breakage *n.*	كَسْرٌ
Breaker *n.*	كَاسِرٌ . صَخْرَةٌ بَحْرِيَّةٌ
Breakfast *n.* or *v. i.*	فُطُورٌ . فَطَرَ ـُ (تَرَوَّقَ)
Breakwater *n.*	سَدٌّ لِمَنْعِ الأَمْوَاجِ
Breast *n.* or *v. t.*	صَدْرٌ . صَادَرَ
Breastplate *n.*	دِرْعٌ ج دُرُوعٌ
Breastwork *n.*	مَتْرَاسٌ
Breath *n.*	نَفَسٌ . نَسْمَةٌ
Breathe *v. i.*	تَنَفَّسَ

Breathing *n.* تَنَفُّسٌ

Breathless *n.* مَقْطُوعُ ٱلنَّفَسِ

Breeches *n. pl.* سَرَاوِيلُ. (سِرْوَالٌ)

Breed *v. t.* or *i.* وَلَّدَ. رَبَّى. وَلَدَ

Breed *n.* ذُرِّيَّةٌ. نَسْلٌ. جِنْسٌ

Breeding *n.* تَوْلِيدٌ. تَرْبِيَةٌ. سَجَايَا

Breeze *n.* نَسِيمٌ

Brethren *n. pl.* of *brother.* إِخْوَةٌ

Brevity *n.* إِخْتِصَارٌ. إِيجَازٌ

Brew *v. t.* خَمَّرَ (جِعَةً (بِيرَا)

Brewery *n.* مَصْنَعُ ٱلْجِعَةِ

Bribe *n.* or *v. t.* بَرْطِيلٌ. بَرْطَلَ

Bribery *n.* بَرْطَلَةٌ. رَشْوَةٌ

Brick *n.* آجُرٌّ. قِرْمِيدٌ

Brick-bat *n.* قِطْعَةُ قِرْمِيدٍ

Brick-kiln *n.* أَتُونُ ٱلْآجُرِّ

Bridal *a.* or *n.* عُرْسِيٌّ. عُرْسٌ

Bride *n.* عَرُوسٌ

Bridegroom *n.* عَرِيسٌ

Bridemaid / Bride's maid } *n.* شَبِينَةُ ٱلْعَرُوسِ

Bridge *n.* or *v. t.* جِسْرٌ. قَنْطَرَةٌ. نَصَبَ جِسْرًا

Bridle *n.* or *v. t.* لِجَامٌ. أَلْجَمَ

Brief *a.* or *n.* قَصِيرٌ. عَرْضُحَالٌ. مُخْتَصَرٌ

Brier *n.* عُلَيْقٌ. عَوْسَجٌ

Brig *n.* سَفِينَةٌ ذَاتُ صَارِيَيْنِ

Brigade *n.* لِوَاءٌ مِنَ ٱلْجُنْدِ

Brigadier *n.* قَائِدٌ فَوْقَ امِيرِ الآيِ. لِوَاءٌ

Brigand *n.* لِصٌّ. قَاطِعُ طُرُقٍ

Brigandage *n.* قَطْعُ ٱلطُّرُقِ

Bright *a.* لَامِعٌ. بَرَّاقٌ. ذَكِيٌّ

Brighten *v. t.* or *i.* أَنَارَ. لَمَعَ

Brightness *n.* لَمَعَانٌ. رَوْنَقٌ

Bright's disease *n.* مَرَضٌ فِي ٱلْكُلْيَتَيْنِ

Brilliancy *n.* رَوْنَقٌ. بَهَاءٌ

Brilliant *a.* بَهِيٌّ. لَامِعٌ

Brim *n.* شَفَةٌ. حَرْفٌ. حَافَّةٌ

Brimful / Brimming } *a.* مَمْلُوءٌ إِلَى شَفَتِهِ

Brimstone *n.* كِبْرِيتٌ

Brine *n.* مَاءٌ كَثِيرُ ٱلْمُلوحة

Bring *v. t.* أَتَى بِهِ . احضر

Brink *n.* حَافَةٌ

Brisk *a.* نَشِيطٌ . سَرِيعٌ . خَفِيفٌ

Briskness *n.* نَشَاطٌ . خِفَّةٌ

Bristle *n.* or *v. i.* هُلْبَةٌ . تَنَفَّشَ

Bristly *a.* اهْلَبُ او هُلْبِيٌّ

Brittle *a.* قَصِمٌ . قَصِفٌ

Brittleness *n.* سُرْعَةُ ٱلإِنْكِسارِ

Broad *a.* عَرِيضٌ . مُتَسِعٌ

Broadcloth *n.* جُوخٌ

Broaden *v. t.* or *i.* أَوْسَعَ . عَرَّضَ . إِتَّسَعَ

Broadside *n.* إِطْلاقُ مَدَافِعِ جَانِبِ ٱلْبَارِجَةِ

Brocade *n.* دِيبَاجٌ . سُنْدُسٌ

Brochure *n.* كُرَّاسَةٌ

Brouge *n.* لَفْظٌ فَاسِدٌ

Broil *v.t.* or *n.* شَوَى . إِنْشَوَى . خِصَامٌ

Broken *pp.* (break مَكْسُورٌ (مِنْ

Broker *n.* سِمْسَارٌ ج سَمَاسِرَةٌ

Brokerage *n.* سَمْسَرَةٌ

Bronchitis *n.* إِلْتِهَابُ شُعَبِ ٱلرِّئَةِ

Bronze *n.* خَلِيطٌ مِنْ نُحَاسٍ وَقَصْدِيرٍ

Brooch *n.* دَبُّوسٌ لِلصَّدْرِ

Brood *n.* فَرْخٌ ج فِرَاخٌ . نَسْلٌ

Brood *v. t.* حَضَنَ ٱلْفِرَاخِ

Brood *v. i.* ثَابَرَ عَلَى ٱلْهَمِّ

Brook *n.* or *v. t.* سَاقِيَةٌ . إِحْتَمَلَ

Brooklet *n.* سَاقِيَةٌ صَغِيرَةٌ

Broom *n.* مِكْنَسَةٌ ج مَكَانِسُ

Broomstick *n.* قَضِيبُ مِكْنَسَةٍ

Broth *n.* مَرَقٌ

Brothel *n.* بَيْتُ ٱلْعَوَاهِرِ

Brother *n.* أَخٌ . إِخْوَةٌ

Brotherhood *n.* اخُوَّةٌ ج إِخَاءٌ

Brought *pp.* of *bring.* مُحْضَرٌ . مُؤْتًى بِهِ

Brow *n.* جَبْهَةٌ . جَبِينٌ . حَافَةٌ

Brown *a.* or *v. t.* أَسْمَرُ . جَعَلَهُ اسْمَرَ

Brownish *a.* مَائِلٌ إِلَى ٱلسُّمْرَةِ

Browse *v. t.* or *i.* رعى . إِرْتَعَى

Bruin *n.* لَقَبٌ لِلدُّبِّ

Bruise *v. t.* رَضَّ ـُ رَضْرَضَ

Brunt *n.* شِدَّةٌ . صَدْمَةٌ

Brush *n.* فُرْشَةٌ . اغصانٌ مقطوعة

Brush *v. i.* or *t.* مَسَحَ (بِالفُرْشَةِ)

Brusque *a.* خَشِنُ ٱلْمُعَامَلَةِ . عنيفٌ

Brutal / Brutish } *a.* وحشِيٌّ . فظٌّ

Brutality *n.* وحشِيَّةٌ . فَظَاظَة

Brutalize *v. t.* وَحَّشَ

Brute *n.* وَحْشٌ . جِلفٌ . قاس

Bubble *n.* فُقَّاعةٌ . مشْرُوعٌ بَاطِلٌ

Buck *n.* ذَكَرُ ٱلْغَنَمِ وَٱلْوَعْلِ

Bucket *n.* دَلْوٌ . سَطل

Buckle *n.* or *v.t.* إِبْزِيمٌ . شَدَّ (بِهِ)

Buckler *n.* تُرْسٌ ج اتْرَاسٌ

Bud *n.* or *v. i.* بُرْعُمٌ . أَخْرَجَ البَرَاعِمَ

Budge *v. i.* تحرَّكَ . إِنْطَلَقَ

Budget *n.* قَائِمةٌ مَالِيَةٌ . مِيزانيَّة

Buffalo *n.* جامُوسٌ ج جَوَامِيسُ

Buffet *v. t.* لكمَ ـُ . لطَمَ ـِ . قَاوَمَ

Buffoon *n.* مازِحٌ . مَاجِنٌ

Bug *n.* بقَّة . فسفسٌ ج فسافِس

Bugbear *n.* هائلٌ . وَهمِيٌّ

Bugle *n.* نَفِير

Build *v. t.* بنى ـِ عمَّرَ

Building *n.* بَناءٌ . عمَارٌ

Built *pp.* of *build.* مبنِيٌّ

Bulb *n.* بَصلَةُ نباتٍ

Bulbous *a.* ذُو بصلٍ

Bulge *v. i.* تَقَبَّبَ . بَرَزَ

Bulk *n.* حجم . مِقْدَارٌ

Bulky *n.* جسِيمٌ . ضخمٌ . كبيرٌ

Bull *n.* ثورٌ ج ثيرَان

Bull-dog *n.* كَلْبٌ كَبِيرٌ ضَارٌّ

Bullet *n.* كُلَّةُ بُنْدُقِيَّةٍ . رَصَاصَةٌ

Bulletin *n.* تَقْرِيرٌ رَسْمِيٌّ

Bull-frog *n.* ضِفْدَعٌ كَبِيرٌ

Bullion *n.* سَبَائِكُ ذَهَبٍ أَوْ فِضَةٍ

Bullock *n.* ثَوْرٌ صَغِيرٌ اَوْ خَصِيٌّ

Bully *n.* مُتَوَعِّدٌ . مُتَصَلِّفٌ

Bullrush *n.* حَلْفَاةٌ . بَرْدِيٌّ

Bulwark *n.* حِصْنٌ . مِتْرَاس

Bumble-bee *n.* نَحْلَةٌ كَبِيرَةٌ

Bump *n.* صَدْمَةٌ . لَطْمَةٌ . وَرَمٌ .

Bump *v. t.* or *i.* صَدَمَ بِصَوْتٍ قَوِيٍّ

Bumper *n.* كَأْسٌ مَمْلُوءَةٌ

Bun *n.* نَوْعٌ مِنَ ٱلْكَعْكِ

Bunch *n.* or *v. t.* عُنْقُودٌ . عِذْقٌ . جَمَعَ

Bundle *n.* رَبْطَةٌ . رِزْمَةٌ . حُزْمَة

Bung *n.* سِدَادُ بَرْمِيلٍ

Bungle *v. i.* خَبَّصَ

Bunion *n.* ثُؤْلُولٌ فِي ٱلرِّجْلِ

Bunting *n.* نَسِيجُ صُوفٍ لِلرَّايَاتِ

Buoy *n.* عَوَّامَةٌ لِدَلَالَةِ ٱلْمَرَاكِبِ

Buoyant *n.* عَائِمٌ . خَفِيف . مَسْرُورٌ

Bur or burr *n.* غُلَافُ نَبَاتٍ ذُو شَوْكٍ

Burden *n.* or *v. t.* حِمْلٌ . ضَايَق

Burdensome *a.* ثَقِيلٌ مُتْعِبٌ

Bureau *n.* خِزَانَةٌ . مَكْتَبٌ

Burglar *n.* سَارِقُ بَيْتٍ بِٱللَّيْلِ

Burglary *n.* سِرْقَةُ بَيْتٍ بِٱللَّيْلِ

Burial *n.* دَفْنٌ . جِنَازَةٌ

Burlesque *a* or *n.* مُضْحِكٌ . أُضْحُوكَةٌ

Burly *a.* جَسِيمٌ . ضَخْمٌ

Burn *v. t.* or *n.* حَرَقَ ـِ . إِحْتَرَقَ . كَيٌّ

Burnish *v. t.* صَقَلَ ـُ

Burrow *n.* or *v. i.* وِجَارٌ . إِحْتَفَرَ

Burst *v. t.* or *i.* فَجَرَ . إِنْفَجَرَ . إِنْفَلَق

Bury *v. t.* دَفَنَ ـِ . قَبَرَ ـِ

Bush *n.*	شُجَيْرَةٌ . دَغَلٌ
Bushel *n.*	مِكْيَالٌ انكليزيٌّ
Bushy *a.*	كَثٌّ
Busily *ad.*	بِجِدٍّ أَوْ بِاجْتِهَادٍ
Business *n.*	شُغْلٌ . مَصْلَحَةٌ . حِرْفَةٌ
Bust *n.*	تِمْثَالُ ٱلرَّاسِ إِلَى ٱلصَّدْرِ
Bustle *n.* or *v. i.*	جَلَبَةٌ . عَجَلَةٌ . — ضَجَّ
Busy *a.*	مَشْغُولٌ . مُهْتَمٌّ
Busybody *n.*	فُضُولِيٌّ
But *conj.* or *pr.*	لَكِنَّ . غَيْرَ ان . إِلاَّ
Butcher *n.*	لَحَّامٌ . قَصَّابٌ . جَزَّارٌ
Butchery *n.*	ذَبْحٌ . قَتْلٌ عَظِيمٌ
Butler *n.*	سَاقِي ٱلْخَمْرِ
Butt *n.*	هَدَفٌ . بَرْمِيلٌ كَبِيرٌ
Butter *n.*	زُبْدَةٌ . سَمْنٌ
Buttery *n.*	بَيْتُ ٱلْمُونَةِ
Butterfly *n.*	فَرَاشَةٌ ج فَرَاشٌ
Buttock *n.*	عَجُزٌ ج أَعْجَازٌ
Button *n.*	زِرٌّ ج ازْرَارٌ
Buttonhole *n.*	عُرْوَةٌ لِلزِّرِّ
Buttress *n.*	دِعَامَةٌ
Buxom *a.*	جَسِيمٌ . طَرِبٌ
Buy *v. t.*	إِبْتَاعَ . إِشْتَرَى
Buzz *v. i.* or *n.*	دَوَى . دَوِيٌّ
Buzzard *n.*	ضَرْبٌ مِنَ ٱلْبَازِ
By *pr.*	عِنْدَ . قُرْبَ . بِ
By-and-by *ad.*	بَعْدَ حِينٍ
By-path / **By-way** *n.*	مَسْلَكٌ صَغِيرٌ
By-word *n.*	عِبْرَةٌ . مَثَل

C

Cab *n.*	نوعٌ مِنَ ٱلْمَرْكَبَاتِ
Cabal *n.*	عُصْبةٌ سِرِّيَّةٌ
Cabbage *n.*	كُرُنبٌ . مَلْفوفٌ
Cabin *n.*	كُوخٌ . حُجْرَةٌ في سفِينَةٍ
Cabinet *n.*	خِزَانَةٌ . وِزَارةٌ
Cabinet-maker *n.*	نَجَّارٌ
Cable *n.*	جُمَلٌ (حبلُ المِرْساة أَوْ سلسِلتها) . حبلٌ غليظٌ
Cackle *v. i.* or *n.*	قاقَ ـُ . قوْق
Cadaverous *a.*	شَبِيهٌ بالجثةِ . مصفَرٌّ
Cadence *n.*	هُبُوط ٱلصَّوت . لَحْنٌ
Cadet *n.*	تِلْمِيذ مَدْرَسَةٍ حربِيَّةٍ
Café *n.*	قَهْوَةٌ
Cage *n.*	قفَصٌ
Cajole *v. t.*	دَاهَنَ . تَمَلَّقَ
Cake *n.*	قُرصٌ . كَعْكَةٌ
Calamitous *a.*	مُسِيءٌ . نَكَبِيٌّ
Calamity *n.*	مُصِيبَةٌ . بَلِيَّةٌ
Calcareous *a.*	كِلْسِيٌّ
Calcedony *n.*	عقيقٌ أَبْيَضُ
Calcine *v. t.*	كَلَّسَ بِالنَّارِ
Calculate *v. t.*	حسَبَ ـُ . احصى
Caldron *n.*	قِدْرٌ . خلقِيْنٌ
Calendar *n.*	تَقْوِيمُ ٱلسَّنَةِ (رُزْنامةٌ)
Calf (*pl.* calves) *n.*	عِجْلٌ ج عُجُولٌ
Calf of the leg *n.*	بطْنُ السَّاقِ
Calibre *n.*	قُطْرٌ . إِتِّسَاعٌ . عيارٌ
Calico *n.*	شيتٌ . خامٌ
Call *v. t.* or *i.*	دعَا . سمَّى . نادَى

Call *n.* دَعْوَةٌ . طَلَبٌ . مناداة

Calling *n.* حِرْفَةٌ . مَصْلَحَةٌ . مُنَادَاةٌ

Callous *a.* مُتَصَلِّبٌ. مُكَنَّبٌ

Calm *a.* or *v. t.* هَادِئٌ . هَدَّأَ . اسْكَنَ

Calm / Calmness *n.* هُدُوءٌ. سُكُونٌ

Caloric *n.* أَلْحَرَارَةُ

Calorific *n.* مُوَلِّدٌ لِلْحَرَارَةِ

Calumniate *v. t.* وَشَى بِ . نَمَّ ـُ ـِ

Calumny *n.* نَمِيمَةٌ . إِفْتِرَاءٌ

Calve *v. t.* وَلَدَتْ (أَلْبَقَرَةُ)

Calyx *n.* كَأْسُ ٱلزَّهْرَةِ

Came (Come ماضي) *v. i.* جَاءَ . أَتَى

Camel *n.* جَمَلٌ . بَعِيرٌ . نَاقَةٌ

Camelopard *n.* زَرَافَةٌ

Cameo *n.* حَجَرٌ كَرِيمٌ نَافِرُ ٱلنَّقْشِ

Camera *n.* آلَةٌ لِلتَّصْوِيرِ ٱلشَّمْسِيِ

Camomile / Chamomile *n.* بَابُونَجٌ

Camp *n.* محلَّة . مُعَسْكَرٌ

Campaign *n.* غَزْوَةٌ . حَرْبٌ

Camphor *n.* كَافُورٌ

Can *v. i.* or *n.* قَدَرَ ـُ . كُوزٌ

Canal *n.* قَنَاةٌ . تُرْعَةٌ

Canary *n.* عُصْفُورٌ مُغَرِّدٌ

Cancel *v. t.* مَحَا . أَلْغَى . أَبْطَلَ

Cancellation *n.* مَحْوٌ

Cancer *n.* سَرَطَانٌ

Cancerous *a.* سَرَطَانِيٌّ

Candid *a.* مُخْلِصٌ . سَلِيمُ ٱلنِّيَّةِ

Candidate *n.* طَالِبُ ٱلْإِنتخاب

Candidly *ad.* بِإِخْلَاصٍ . مُخْلِصًا

Candy *n.* قَنْدٌ . نَوْعٌ من الحَلْوَى

Candle *n.* شَمْعَة . قِنْدِيلٌ

Candlestick *n.* شَمْعَدَانٌ . مَنَارَةٌ

Candour *n.* إِخْلَاصٌ . سلامة ٱلنِّيَّة

Cane *n.* قَصَبَةٌ . عَصًا

Canine *a.* كَلْبِيّ

Canine-tooth *n.* نَابٌ

Canker *n.* or *v i.* قَرْحٌ اكَّالٌ .فسَدَ — ـُ
Canker-worm *n.* دُودُ النَّبَاتَات
Cannibal *n.* آكل لحُوم البَشَر
Cannibalism *n.* أَكْلُ لحُومِ ٱلْبَشَر
Cannon *n.* مَدْفَعٌ ج مَدَافِعُ
Cannonade *n.* ضَربٌ بِالْمَدَافِع
Cannoneer / Cannonier *n.* أَلرَّامي بِالْمَدَافِع
Canoe *n.* قَارِبٌ هِنْدِيٌّ
Canon *n.* قانونٌ
Canonical *a.* قَانُونِيٌّ
Canonize *v. t.* صَرَّحَ بِقِدَاسةِ مَيْت
Canopy *n.* مِظَلَّةٌ
Cant *n.* or *v. i.* تظاهرٌ بكَلَامِ ٱلتقوى.تظاهَرَ
Canter *v. i.* or *n.* خَبَّ .خَبَبٌ
Canto *n.* قصيدَةٌ
Canton *n.* مُقَاطَعَةٌ . إِقليمٌ
Cantonment *n.* مَحلَّة
Canvas *n.* جنفيصٌ .خَيْشٌ
Canvass *v. t.* بحَثَ عَنْ — طَلَبَ
Cap *n.* or *v. t.* (طَرْبوشٌ) . غطَّى
Capability *n.* مقدَرَةٌ . طَاقَةٌ
Capable *a.* قادِرٌ. اهلٌ
Capacious *a.* متسعٌ فسيحٌ
Capacity *n.* سعة . قُدْرَة
Cap-a-pie *ad.* مِنَ ٱلرَّأْسِ إِلَى ٱلقدَم
Cape *n.* رَاسُ (أَرْض) .بُرْنُسٌ
Capillary *a.* or *n.* شَعْرِيٌّ
Capital *n.* or *a.* رَاسُ مَالٍ . قصبَة مَملكَةٍ . رَئيسِيٌّ . نَفيسٌ
Capitalist *n.* ذُو مَال مُثْرٍ
Capitol *n.* سَرَايُ ٱلحُكومة ٱلأميركيَّةِ
Capitulate *v. i.* سلَّمَ تحتَ شُرُوطٍ
Caprice *n.* تَقَلُّبُ ٱلخَاطِرِ
Capricious *a.* مُتقلِّبٌ
Capsize *v. t.* or *i.* قلَبَ . إِنقَلَب
Captain *n.* قبْطَان . يُوزبَاشِي

Capricorn *n.* بُرْجُ الْجَدْي

Captious *a.* كَثِيرُ الانتِقاد

Captivate *v. t.* أَسَرَ — ِ ُ إِفتَتَن

Captive *n.* or *a.* أَسِيرٌ . مسْبِيٌّ

Captivity *n.* أَسْرٌ . سَبِيٌّ

Captor *n.* آسِرٌ . سالبٌ

Capture *n.* or *v. t.* قَبْضٌ. قبَض عَلى

Car *n.* عَجلَة. مَرْكَبة

Carat *n.* قيراط (في وزن ٱلذهبِ)

Caravan *n.* قَافِلَةٌ ج قوَافِلُ

Caraway *n.* كَرَوْيَاء (كَرَاويا)

Carbine *n.* (قَرَابِينَة) بُنْدُقيةٌ قَصِيرَةٌ

Carbon *n.* فحْمٌ (كَرْبُونٌ)

Carbonaceous *a.* فَحْمِيٌّ

Carbonize *v. t.* صَيَّرَهُ فحْماً

Carbuncle *n.* دُمَّلٌ كبيرٌ

Carcass *n.* جُثَّةٌ جيفَة

Card *n.* وَرَقةُ زِيارَةٍ . مُشْطٌ للصُّوف

Card *v. t.* مَشَّط . حلَج

Cardiac *a.* مُختَصٌّ بِالقَلْب

Cardinal *n.* or *a.* كردِنالٌ . أوَّليٌّ

Care *n.* or *v. i.* إعتِناء . همٌّ . إعْتَنَى

Careen *v.i.* or *t.* مَالَتْ السَّفِينَةُ . أمالها

Career *n.* مَجْرًى . مَسِيرٌ

Careful *a.* حذِرٌ . كثِيرُ الاعتِنَاء

Carefulness *n.* إعْتِنَاء . مُبالاَة

Careless *a.* غيرُ مُبالٍ . غافِلٌ

Carelessness *n.* إهمَالٌ . غَفْلَةٌ

Caress *v. t* or *n.* لاطَف. دَلَّل. مُلاطفةٌ

Cargo *n.* شَحْنٌ . وَسْقُ سَفِينَةٍ

Caricature *n.* صُورَةٌ هزْلِيَّةٌ

Carious *a.* نَخِرٌ

Carmine *n.* لونٌ دُودِيٌّ

Carnage *n.* مَلْحَمَةٌ . مَقْتَلَةٌ عظيمَةٌ

Carnal *a.* جسدَانِيٌّ . شَهْوَانِيٌّ

Carnally *ad.* بشَهْوَةٍ جَسَدِيَّةٍ

Carnival *n.* مَرْفَعٌ ج مَرَافِعُ

Carnivorous *a.* آكِلُ لُحُومٍ . ضارٍ

Carob *n.* خَرُّوبٌ

Carol *n.* or *v. i.* اغْنِيَّةٌ . غَنَّى

Carousal *n.* وَلِيمَةٌ لِلشُّرْبِ وَالْفَرَحِ

Carouse *v. i.* شَرِبَ وَفَرِحَ . قصف

Carp *v. i.* لامَ ـُ . عذلَ ـُ

Carpenter *n.* نَجَّارٌ

Carpet *n.* سُجَّادَةٌ . بِسَاطٌ

Carriage *n.* مَرْكَبَةٌ . (عَرَبِيَّةٌ)

Carrion *n.* جيفَةٌ لَحْمٌ نَتِنٌ

Carrot *n.* جَزَرَةٌ ج جَزَرٌ

Carry *v. t.* حَمَلَ ـِ نَقَلَ ـُ

Cart *n.* عَجَلَةُ النَّقْلِ

Cartage *n.* نَقْلٌ . اجْرَةُ النقلِ

Carter *n.* سَائِقُ عَجَلَةِ النَّقْلِ

Cartilage *n.* غُضْرُوفٌ ج غَضَارِيفُ

Cartilaginous *a.* غُضْرُوفِيٌّ

Cartridge *n.* (فَشَكَةٌ ج فَشَكٌ)

Carve *v. t.* نَقَشَ ـُ قَطَعَ (لَحْماً)

Cascade *n.* شَلَّالٌ

Case *n.* صُنْدُوقٌ . حَالٌ . قَضِيَّةٌ

Casement *n.* صُنْدُوقُ شُبَّاكٍ

Cash *n.* or *v. t.* نُقُودٌ . قَبَضَ ـِ نَقْدًا

Cash-book *n.* دَفْتَرُ النقود

Cashier *n.* or *v. t.* أَمِينُ الصُّنْدُوقِ . عَزَلَ

Cashmere *n.* كَشْمِيرٌ

Casing *n.* غِطَاءٌ . بِرْوَازٌ

Cask *n.* بَرْمِيلٌ

Casket *n.* عِلْبَةٌ لِلْحُلِيِّ أَوْ اكلِّ شَيْءٍ ثَمِينٍ

Casque *n.* خُوذَةٌ ج خُوَذٌ

Cast *v. t.* رَمَى . صَبَّ . سَبَكَ

Cast *n.* رَمْيَةٌ . هَيْئَةٌ . سَبِيكَةٌ

Castaway *n.* مَرْفُوضٌ . مَرْذُولٌ

Caste *n.* طَائِفَةٌ . فِئَةٌ

Castigate *v. t.* أدب. ضَرَبَ بِالسَّوْطِ

Casting *n.* رَمْيٌ . سبيكة

Cast-iron *n.* حَدِيدٌ صَبٍّ

Castor-oil *n.* زَيتُ خَرْوَع

Castle *n.* حصنٌ . قَلْعَةٌ . صَرْحٌ

Castrate *v. t.* خَصَى —

Casual *a.* عرَضِيٌّ . إِتِفَاقِيٌّ

Casually *ad.* عرَضاً . إِتِّفاقاً

Casualty *n.* حَادِثَةٌ عَرَضِيَّةٌ

Cat *n.* قِطٌّ . هِر

Catacomb *n.* مَغَارَةٌ لِلدَّفْن تَحْتَ ٱلأرْضِ

Catalogue *n.* قَائِمَةٌ . جَدْوَلٌ

Cataract *n.* شَلَّالٌ . مَآءٌ أَزْرَقُ فِي ٱلعَيْنَيْنِ

Catarrh *n.* زُكَامٌ

Catastrophe *n.* مُصِيبَةٌ . نَكْبَةٌ

Catch *v. t.* أَدْرَكَ . قَبَضَ . تَنَاوَلَ

Catching *a.* مُعْدٍ

Catechetical *a.* بِالسُّؤَالِ وَٱلجْوَابِ

Catechise *v. t.* عَلَّمَ بِالسُّؤَالِ

Catechism *n.* اصُولُ ٱلإِيمَانِ

Categorical *a.* صَرِيحٌ . قَاطِعٌ

Category *n.* صَفٌّ . طَبَقَةٌ

Cater *v. t.* رَوَّدَ . قَدَّمَ طَعَاماً

Caterpillar *n.* دُودَةٌ . فَرَاشَةٌ

Catgut *n.* وَتَرٌ مِن مَعًى

Cathartic *n.* or *a.* مُسْهِلٌ

Cathedral *n.* كَنِيسَةُ اسْقُفٍ

Catholic *a.* جَامِعٌ . كَاثُولِيكِيٌّ

Catholocism *n.* النِّظَامُ ٱلكَاثُولِيكِيُّ

Cattle *n. pl.* ماشِيَةٌ ج مَوَاشٍ

Caudal *a.* ذَنَبِيٌّ

Caught *pp.* of *catch.* مَقْبُوضٌ

Caul *n.* ثَرْبٌ

Cauliflower *n.* قَرْنَبِيط أو قنبيط

Causal *a.* سَبَبِيٌّ

Causalty *n.* سَبَبِيَّةٌ

Causation *n.* تَسْبِيبٌ

Causative *a.* مُسَبِّبٌ	**Celebrated** *a.* مشهُورٌ
Cause *n.* سَبَبٌ . عِلةٌ	**Celebrity** *n.* شُهْرَةٌ . صِيتٌ
Caustic *a.* or *n.* حَارِقٌ . كَاوٍ	**Celerity** *n.* سُرْعة . عَجَلَةٌ
Cauterize *v. t.* كَوَى ـِ . وَسَمَ ـِ	**Celery** *n.* كرَفسٌ
Cautery *n.* كَيٌّ	**Celestial** *a.* سَمَاوِيٌّ
Caution *n.* or *v. t.* حذرٌ . حذَّرَ	**Celibacy** *n.* عزُوبة . عزبة
Cautious *a.* حَذِرٌ . مُحترِسٌ	**Cell** *n.* صومَعَة . خَلِيَّةٌ . حُوَيصلَةٌ
Cavalcade *n.* موْكِبُ فُرْسانٍ	**Cellar** *n.* قبْوٌ. بَيتٌ تَحْتَانِيٌّ
Cavalier *n.* فارسٌ . خيَّالٌ	**Cellular** *n.* حُوَيصلِيٌّ . ذُو تَجَاوِيفٌ
Cavalry *n.* فُرْسَانٌ . خَيَّالة	**Cement** *n.* or *v. t.* مِلاط. ملَّطَ
Cave / **Cavern** } *n.* مَغَارَةٌ ج مغائِرُ	**Cemetry** مَقْبَرَة
Cavil *v. i.* or *n.* ماحك. مُمَاحَكة	**Censer** *n.* مبخَرَةٌ . مِجمَرَةٌ
Cavity *n.* وَقْبَةٌ . تجْوِيفٌ	**Censor** *n.* مُرَاقِبٌ . مُؤَدِّبٌ . منتَقِدٌ
Cease *v. i.* كفَّ عَنْ . إِنْقَطَعَ	**Censorious** *a.* قاسٍ . كَثِيرُ ٱلْمَلامَةَ
Cedar *n.* ارْز	**Censurable** *a.* قَابِلُ ٱلْمَلامَةِ
Cede *v. t.* تركَ ـُ : تخَلَّى عَن	**Censure** *v. t.* or *n.* لَامَ. مَلامَةٌ
Ceil *v. t.* سَقَفَ ـُ طَيَّنَ . بطَّن	**Census** *n.* تعدَادُ ٱلنُّفُوسِ
Ceiling *n.* سَقْفٌ (طوَان)	**Cent** *n.* جُزْءٌ مِنَ ٱلْمِئة منَ ٱلرِّيَال
Celebrate *v. t.* عظمَ . إِحتَفَل	**Centaur** *n.* فرَس خُرَافِيٌّ لَهُ رَاسُ إِنسان

Centennial *a.* مَرَّةً كُلَّ مِئَةِ سَنَةٍ

Centenarian *n.* ذُو مِئَةِ سَنَةٍ

Centigrade *a.* قِيَاسُ مِئَةِ دَرَجَةٍ

Centipede *n.* ذُو مِئَةِ رِجْلٍ . أُمُّ أَرْبَعٍ وَأَرْبَعِينَ

Central *a.* مَرْكَزِيٌّ

Centrality *n.* مَرْكَزِيَّةٌ

Centre *n.* مَرْكَزٌ . وَسْط

Centrifugal *a.* مَائِلٌ عَنِ ٱلْمَرْكَزِ

Centripetal *n.* مَائِلٌ إِلَى ٱلْمَرْكَزِ

Centurion *n.* قَائِدُ مِئَةٍ

Century *n.* مِئَةُ سَنَةٍ . قَرْن

Cereals *n. pl.* حُبُوبٌ تُؤْكَلُ

Cerebrum *n* الدِّمَاغُ

Cerebral *a.* دِمَاغِيٌّ

Ceremonial *a.* إِحْتِفَالِيٌّ . طَقْسِي

Ceremonial, Ceremony } *n.* إِحْتِفَالٌ . طَقْسٌ

Certain *a.* أَكِيدٌ . مُحَقَّقٌ

Certainly *n.* مُحَقَّقًا

Certainty *n.* يَقِينٌ . قَطْع

Certificate *n.* شَهَادَةٌ . وَثِيقَة

Certify *v. t.* حَقَّقَ . شَهِدَ بِ

Certitude *n.* يَقِينٌ . عَدَمُ ٱلشَّكِّ

Cerulean *a.* سَمَاوِيُّ ٱللَّوْنِ

Cessation *n.* إِنْقِطَاعٌ . تَوَقُّف

Cession *n.* تَسْلِيمٌ . تَخْلِيَة

Cess-pool *n.* مَحَلُّ ٱلْأَقْذَارِ . بَالُوعَةٌ

Chafe *v.i.or t.* دَعَكَ ـَ . ضَجِرَ ـَ

Chaff *n.* or *e. i.* عُصَافَةٌ . مَازَح

Chaffer *v. i.* سَاوَمَ

Chagrin *n.* or *v.t.* } خَجَلٌ . ضَجَر . أَزْعَجَ

Chain *n.* or *v. i.* سِلْسِلَةٌ . رَبَطَ بِهَا

Chair *n.* كُرْسِيٌّ ج كَرَاسِي

Chairman *n.* صَاحِبُ ٱلْكُرْسِيِّ

Chaise *n.* مَرْكَبَةٌ بِعَجَلَتَيْنِ

Chalcedony *n.* عَقِيق أَبْيَض

Chalice *n.* كأسُ ٱلْعَشَاءِ ٱلرَّبَّانِي

Chalk *n.* طَبَاشِيرُ

Challenge *v. t.* or *n.* إِسْتَدْعَى لِلْمُبَارَزَةِ . تَحَدٍّ

Chamber *n.* غُرْفَةٌ . حُجْرَةٌ

Chamberlain *n.* حَاجِب

Chameleon *n.* حِرْبَاءَة

Champ *v.t.*or *i.* صَكَّمَ عَلَى . عَضَّ

Champagne *n.* شَمْبَانِيَا

Champion *n.* مُبَارِزٌ . مُحَامٍ . بَطَلٌ

Chance *n.* صُدْفَةٌ . عَرَضٌ . إِتِّفَاقٌ

Chance *v. i.* إِتَّفَقَ . حَدَثَ

Chancellor *n.* وَزِيرٌ . رَئِيسُ قُضَاةٍ

Chandler *n.* بَائِعُ شَمْعٍ

Change *n.* or *v. t.* تَغْيِيرٌ . غَيَّرَ

Changeable *a.* قَابِلُ ٱلتَّغْيِيرِ . مُتَقَلِّبٌ

Channel *n.* مَجْرَى . مَضِيقٌ . تَلْم

Channelled *a.* مُتَلَّمٌ

Chant *v. t.* or *i.* or *n.* أَنْشَدَ . غَنَى . نَشِيد

Chaos *n.* هَيُولِيٌّ . عَدَمُ ٱنْتِظَام

Chaotic *a.* غَيْرُ مُنتظم . مُشَوَّشٌ

Chapel *n.* مَعْبَدٌ . كَنِيسَةٌ

Chaplain *n.* قِسِّيسٌ فِي ٱلْجَيْش

Chaplet *n.* إِكْلِيلُ زَهْرٍ او أَوْرَاقٍ

Chapter *n.* بَابٌ . فَصْلٌ

Char *v. t.* صَبَّرَ فَحْمًا . حَرَق

Character *n.* سَجِيَّةٌ . خُلْق . صِفَة

Characteristic *a.*or *n* خَاصٌّ . مَزِيَّةٌ

Characterize *v. t.* وَصَفَ . مَيَّزَ

Charcoal *n.* فَحْمٌ (مِنْ حَطَب)

Charge *v. t.* or *n.* هَاجَمَ . شَكَا . أَوْصَى . دَكٌّ . مُهَاجَمَةٌ . شَكْوَى

Charge *n.* قَيْدٌ فِي حِسَابٍ

Charger *n.* صِحْفَةٌ . جَوَادٌ

Chariot *n.* مَرْكَبَةٌ

Charitable *a.* مُحْسِنٌ . مُتَصَدِّق

Charity *n.* صَدَاقَةٌ . إِحْسَان

Charlatan *n.* دَجَّالٌ

Charm *n.* طَلْسَمٌ . حُسْنٌ . لُطْفٌ

Charm *v.t.* سَحَرَ ـَ . فَتَنَ ـِ . ابْهَجَ

Charming *a.* سَارٌّ جِدًّا . مُبْهِجٌ

Chart *n.* خَرِيطَةٌ

Charter *n.* or *v. t.* صَكٌّ . إِمْتِيَازٌ . إِسْتَأْجَرَ

Chary *a.* حَذِرٌ . مُتَيَقِّظٌ

Chase *v. t.* طَارَدَ . إِصْطَادَ

Chase *n.* مُطَارَدَةٌ . صَيْدٌ

Chasm *n.* شَقٌّ عَمِيقٌ فِي الْأَرْضِ

Chaste *a.* عَفِيفٌ

Chasten *v. t.* أَدَّبَ

Chastise *v. t.* قَاصَّ . ادَّبَ

Chastisement *n.* قِصَاصٌ . تَأْدِيبٌ

Chastity *n.* عِفَّةٌ

Chat *v. i.* حَادَثَ . كَالَمَ

Chatter *v. i.* هَذَرَ . بَقَّ ـُ

Chatterer *n.* بَقْبَاقٌ

Cheap *a.* رَخِيصٌ

Cheapen *v. t.* رَخَّصَ

Cheapness رُخْصٌ

Cheat *v. t.* غَشَّ ـُ . غَبَنَ ـِ

Cheat *n.* مُحْتَالٌ . خِدَاعٌ

Check *v. t.* رَدَعَ . اوْقَفَ . عَاقَ

Check *n.* رَدْعٌ . تَوْقِيفٌ . تَحْوِيلٌ

Checker *v. t.* نَوَّعَ

Checkers *n. pl.* لِعْبُ الدَّامَا

Cheek *n.* خَدٌّ . خُدُودٌ . وَجْنَةٌ

Cheer *v. t.* or *n.* فَرَّجَ . شَرَحَ . إِنْشِرَاحٌ

Cheerful / **Cheery** } *n.* مَسْرُورٌ . بَشَّاشٌ

Cheese *n.* جُبْنٌ

Chemical *a.* كِيمِيٌّ اوْ كِيمَاوِيٌّ

Chemicals *n. pl.* مَوَادٌّ كِيمِيَّةٌ

Chemise *n.* قَمِيصُ امْرَأَةٍ

Chemist *n.* عَالِمٌ بِالْكِيمِيَا

Chemistry *n.* أَلْكِيمِيَا

Cheque *n.*	تحويلٌ (ماليٌّ)
Cherish *v. t.*	ربّى. أعزّ. لاطف
Cherry *n.* or *a.*	كرز. كرزيُّ اللون
Cherub *n.*	كروبٌ أو كروبيم
Chess *n.*	شطرنجٌ
Chest *n.*	صندوق. صدرٌ
Chestnut *n.*	كستنا. أبو فروة
Chevalier *n.*	فارسٌ (شفليرٌ)
Chew *v. t.*	مضغ ـَ
Chick / **Chicken** *n.*	فرخ ج فروخ وفراخ
Chicken-pox *n.*	جدريُّ الماء
Chick-peas *n. pl.*	حمّصٌ
Chide *v. t.*	عاتب. زجر ـُ
Chief *a.*	رئيسيٌّ. أوّليٌّ. اهمُّ
Chief / **Chieftain** *n.*	رئيسٌ. قائدٌ
Chiefly *ad.*	خصوصاً. بالأخصّ
Child *pl.* **Children** *n.*	ولدٌ ج اولادٌ
Childhood *n.*	زمان الصبا. صبوة
Childish *a.*	ولديٌّ. باطلٌ
Chill *a.* or *n.*	باردٌ. قشعريرة
Chilly *v. t.*	برّد
Chilly *a.*	باردٌ
Chime *n.*	ألحان اجراسٍ موقّعةٍ
Chimera *n.*	تصوّرٌ وهميٌّ
Chimerical *a.*	وهميٌّ. باطلٌ
Chimney *n.*	مدخنةٌ. داخنةٌ
Chin *n.*	ذقنٌ ج ذقونٌ
China *n.*	خزفٌ صينيٌّ. بلادُ الصين
Chinese *a.*	صينيٌّ
Chine *n.*	فقارةٌ
Chink *n.*	شقٌّ ضيّقٌ
Chink *v. i.* or *t.*	إنشقّ. طنّ. أطنّ
Chintz *n.*	شيتٌ مختلفُ الألوان
Chip *n.*	قطعةُ خشبٍ صغيرةٌ
Chirography *n.*	خطّ. صناعة الكتابة
Chirp *v. i.*	غرّد. صوّت

Chisel n. or v. t. إِزْمِيلٌ ج ازاميل. نَحَتَ بِهِ
Chivalrous a. شَرِيفٌ . ذُو شَهَامَةٍ
Chivalry n. فُرُوسِيَّةٌ . بَسَالَةٌ
Chloroform n. بَنْجٌ (كلورُفورم)
Chocolate n. (شُوكلاتا)
Choice n. or a. إِخْتِيَارٌ . نفيسٌ. فاخِرٌ
Choir n. زُمْرَةُ مُرَنِّمِين
Choke v. t. or i. خَنَقَ.سَدَّ.إِخْتَنَقَ
Choler n. صَفْرَاءُ . غَضَبٌ
Cholera n. أَلْهَوَاءُ ٱلأَصْفَرُ
Choleric a. سَرِيعُ ٱلْغَضَبِ. غضوبٌ
Choose v. i. إِخْتَارَ . إِنْتَخَبَ
Chop v. t. or n. قَطَعَ . قطعَةُ لَحْمٍ
Chord n. وَتْرٌ وَوَتَرٌ ج أَوْتَارٌ
Chorister n. مغَنٍّ . مُرَنِّمٌ
Chorus n. قَرَارٌ فِي ٱلتَّرْنِيمِ . زُمْرَةُ مُرَنِّمِينَ
Christ n. اَلْمَسِيحُ

Christen v. t. عَمَّدَ . سَمَّى
Christendom n. أَلْعَالَمُ ٱلْمَسِيحِي
Christening n. مَعْمُودِيَّةٌ مَعَ تَسْمِيَةٍ
Christian a. or n. مَسِيحِيٌّ
Christianity n. أَلدِّيَانَةُ ٱلْمَسِيحِيَّةُ
Christianize v. t. نَصَّرَ
Christmas n. عِيدُ ٱلْمِيلَادِ
Chromatic a. مُخْتَصٌّ بِالأَلْوَانِ
Chronic n. مُزْمِنٌ
Chronicle n. سِفْرُ ٱلأَخْبَار. تَأْرِيخٌ
Chronological a. تَارِيخِيٌّ
Chronologer / Chronologist n. عَالِمٌ بالتَّارِيخِ
Chronology n. حِسَابُ ٱلتَّوَارِيخِ
Chronometer n. سَاعَةٌ تَضْبُطُ نَفْسَهَا
Chrysalis n. شَرْنَقَةٌ ج شَرَانِق
Chubby a. ضَخْمُ ٱلْجِسْمِ وَقَصِيرُهُ
Chuckle v. i. ضَحِكَ سِرًّا
Chum n. زَمِيلٌ . رَفِيق

Church *n.* كنيسة	**Circulate** *v. i.* or *t.* دَارَ . نَشَرَ ـُ
Churchyard *n.* مَقْبَرَة	**Circulation** *n.* دَوَرَانٌ . نَشْرٌ
Churl *n.* خَشِنٌ . فَظٌّ	**Circulatory** *a.* دَائِرٌ
Churn *v. t.* or *n.* مَخَضَ ـُ مِمْخَضٌ	**Circumambulate** *v. t.* طَافَ ـُ حَوْلَ
Cicatrice / **Cicatrix** *n.* نَدْبَة	**Circumcise** *v. t.* خَتَنَ ـُ . طَهَّرَ
Cider *n.* عَصِيرُ ٱلتُّفَّاحِ	**Circumcision** *n.* خِتَان
Cigar *n.* سِيكَارَةٌ	**Circumference** *n.* مُحِيط
Ciliary *a.* هُدْبِيٌّ . شَعْرِيٌّ	**Circumflex** *n.* (ˆ) عَلَامَةُ مَدِّ حَرْف
Cimeter / **Cimerer** *n.* سَيْفٌ مُقَوَّسٌ	**Circumjacent** *a.* مُحِيطٌ (بِهِ)
Cincture *n.* زُنَّارٌ . مِنْطَقَةٌ	**Circumlocution** *n.* إِسْهَابٌ
Cinders *n. pl.* بَقَايَا ٱلْوَقِيدِ ٱلْمَحْرُوقِ	**Circumnavigate** *v. t.* طَافَ بَحْراً
Cinnamon *n.* قِرْفَةٌ	**Circumnavigation** *n.* اَلطَّوَافُ بَحْراً
Cipher *n.* صِفْرٌ	**Circumscribe** *v. t.* أَحَاطَ بِهِ . حَصَرَ ـُ ـِ
Ciphering *v.* حِسَابُ ٱلْأَرْقَامِ	**Circumscription** *n.* إِحَاطَةٌ . حَصْرٌ
Circle *n.* or *v. i.* دَائِرَةٌ . دَارَ ـُ	**Circumspect** *a.* حَذِرٌ . مُحْتَرِسٌ
Circuit *n.* دَوَرَانٌ . إِقْلِيمٌ	**Circumspection** *n.* حَذَرٌ . إِحْتِرَاسٌ
Circuitous *a.* دَوْرِيٌّ . غَيْرُ مُسْتَقِيمٍ	**Circumspectly** *ad.* بِحَذَرٍ . إِحْتِرَاساً
Circular *a.* مُدَوَّرٌ . نَشْرَةٌ	**Circumstance** *n.* حَالَةٌ . ظَرْفٌ

Circumstantial *a.* مفصَّلٌ. عَرَضِيٌّ

Circumvent *v. t.* غلَبَهُ بِاْلحِيلَةِ

Circus *n.* ملْعَبٌ مُسْتَدِيرٌ لِلْخَيْلِ

Cistern *n.* صِهْرِيجٌ . حَوْضٌ

Citadel *n.* بُرْجٌ. قَلْعَةٌ

Citation *n.* إِقتِبَاس . إِستِدْعَآءٌ

Cite *v. t.* إِقتَبَسَ. إِستَشْهَدَ. إِستَدْعَى

Citizen *n.* مَدَنِيٌّ تابِعٌ لِدَولةِ

Citizenship *n.* حقوقُ اْلمَدَنِيَّةِ

Citron *n.* لَيمُونٌ حَامِضٌ . اتْرُجٌّ

Citric *n.* لَيمُونِيٌّ . اتْرُجِيٌّ

City *n.* مَدِينَةٌ . بَلْدَةٌ

Civil *a.* مَدَنِيٌّ . سِياسِيٌّ . انِيسٌ

Civilian *n.* مَدَنِيٌّ. عَالِمٌ بِالشَّرِيعة اْلمَدَنِيةِ

Civilry *n.* انسٌ . لطفٌ

Civilization *n.* تمَدُّنٌ . تهذِيب

Civilize *v. t.* مدن . هَذَّبَ

Clack *v. i.* or *n.* طقطق . قَعْقَعَ . طقْطَقَةَ

Clad *pp.* of clothe لابسٌ. مَكْسُوٌّ

Claim *v. t.* or *n.* إِدَّعَى بِهِ. إِدِّعَآءٌ

Claimant *n.* طالبٌ . مُدَّعٍ

Clam *n.* بَطْلِينُوس

Clamber *v. i.* تسَلَّق

Clammy *a.* دَبِقٌ . لزِجٌ

Clamour *n.* صِيَاحٌ. ضجَّةٌ

Clamorous *a.* صَيَاح . صَخاب

Clamp *v. t.* or *n.* شَدَّ بكلاب. كُلَّابٌ

Clan *n.* عَشِيرَةٌ . قَبِيلَةٌ

Clandestine *a.* خفِيٌّ . مستورٌ

Clang *v. t.* or *n.* طَنَّ . رَنَّ

Clangour *n.* طنِينٌ

Clank *n.* or *v.* t. قَعْقَعَةٌ . قعقع

Clap *v. t.* or *n.* صَفَّقَ . تصفِيقٌ

Claper *n.* مِدَقُّ اْلجرَسِ او اْلبَاب

Claret *n.* نوعُ خمْرٍ فرنسَاويةِ

Clarify *v. t.* صَفَّى . رَوَّقَ

Clarion *n.* بُوقٌ ج أَبْوَاقٌ

Clash *v. i.* or *t.* إِصْطَدَمَ . ضَادَّ

Clashing *n.* or *a.* تَصَادُمٌ . تَعَارُضٌ

Clasp *n.* or *v. t.* إِبْزِيمٌ . عَانَقَ . قَبَضَ

Class *n.* صَفٌّ . فَصِيلَةٌ . رُتْبَةٌ

Classic *a.* or *n.* مُؤَلِّفٌ شَهِيرٌ

Classification *n.* صَفٌّ . تَرْتِيبٌ

Classify *v. t.* صَفَّ . رَتَّبَ

Clatter *n.* or *v. i.* طَقْطَقَ . طَقْطَقَةٌ

Clause *n.* جُزْءُ جُمْلَةٍ . عِبَارَةٌ

Clavicle *n.* تَرْقُوَةٌ ج تَرَاقٍ

Claw *n.* or *v. t.* مِخْلَبٌ . خَلَبَ ـِ

Clay *n.* طِينٌ . صَلْصَالٌ

Clayey *a.* طِينِيٌّ . صَلْصَالِيٌّ

Clean *a.* or *ad.* نَظِيفٌ . نَقِيٌّ . تَمَاماً

Clean *v. t.* نَظَّفَ . نَقَّى

Cleanliness *n.* نَظَافَةٌ . نَقَاوَةٌ

Cleanse *v. t.* طَهَّرَ . نَقَّى

Clear *a.* صَافٍ . رَائِقٌ

Clear *v. t.* or *i.* صفى . بَرَّأَ . إِنْجَلَى

Clearance *n.* تَصْفِيَةٌ . إِجَازَةٌ

Clearly *ad.* وَاضِحًا . جَلِيًّا

Clearness *n.* وُضُوحٌ . بَيَانٌ . بَهَاءٌ

Cleavage *n.* شَقٌّ . شَقٌّ إِلَى طَبَقَاتٍ

Cleave *v. t.* or *i.* شَقَّ ـُ . إِلْتَصَقَ

Cleft *n.* or *pp.* شَقٌّ . مَشْقُوقٌ

Clemency *n.* رَأْفَةٌ . حِلْمٌ

Clement *a.* رَؤُوفٌ . حَلِيمٌ

Clergy *n.* إِكْلِيرُوسٌ

Clergyman *n.* قَسٌّ أَوْ قِسِّيسٌ

Clerical *a.* إِكْلِيرِيٌّ

Clerk *n.* كَاتِبٌ ج كُتَّابٌ

Clerkship *n.* مَقَامُ ٱلْكَاتِبِ

Clever *a.* ذَكِيٌّ . حَاذِقٌ . أَرِيبٌ

Cleverness *n.* ذَكَاءٌ . حَذَاقَةٌ

Clew *n.* دَلِيلٌ . إِشَارَةٌ

Click *v. i.* or *a.* تَكْتَكَ . تَكْتَكَةٌ

Client *n.* زَبُونُ ٱلْمُحَامِي . تَابِعٌ

Cliff *n.* صَخْرَةٌ شَاهِقَةٌ

Climate, Clime *n.* مَنَاخٌ . إِقْلِيمٌ

Climatic *a.* إِقْلِيمِيٌّ

Climax *n.* نِهَايَةٌ . تَدَرُّجٌ

Climb *v. t.* or *i.* تَسَلَّقَ . صَعِدَ ـَ

Clinch *v. t.* ضَبَطَ ـِ . شَدَّ ـُ . أَثْبَتَ

Clincher *n.* كُلَّابٌ . بُرْهَانٌ قَاطِعٌ

Cling *v. i.* إِلْتَصَقَ بِ . تعلق عَلَى

Clinic, Clinical *n.* (كلينيك) . سَرِيرِيٌّ

Clink *v. i.* or *t.* طَنَّ ـِ . رَنَّ ـِ

Clip *v. t.* قَرَمَ ـُ . قصَّر . قَلَّمَ

Clipper *n.* سَفِينَةٌ سَرِيعَةُ ٱلسَّيْرِ

Clique *n.* عُصْبَةٌ

Cloak *n.* or *v.t.* رِدَاءٌ . سَتَرَ ـِ

Clock *n.* سَاعَةٌ كَبِيرَةٌ

Clock-maker *n.* سَاعَاتِيٌّ

Clockwork *n.* آلَاتُ سَاعَةٍ

Clod *n.* or *v. i.* مَدَرٌ . تَكَتَّلَ

Clog *v. t.* or *n.* عَاقَ . ثَقَّلَ . عَائِقٌ

Cloister *n.* دَيْرٌ

Close *v. t.* or *n.* غَلَقَ . أَنْجَزَ . خِتَامٌ

Close *a.* ضَيِّقٌ . مَحْصُورٌ . قَرِيبٌ

Closely *ad.* مُلَاصِقًا . عَنْ قُرْبٍ

Closet *n.* مُخْدَعٌ . حُجْرَةٌ صَغِيرَةٌ

Closing *n.* or *a.* نِهَايَةٌ . خِتَامٌ . آخِرٌ

Closure *n.* إِنْجَازٌ . خَتْمٌ . حَوْشٌ

Clot *n.* or *v. i.* خِثْرَةٌ . خَثَرَ ـَ

Cloth *n.* نَسِيجٌ . قُمَاشٌ . جُوخٌ

Clothe *v. t.* كَسَا ـُ . أَلْبَسَ

Clothes, Clothing *n.* لِبَاسٌ . ثِيَابٌ . كِسْوَةٌ

Clothes-line *n.* حَبْلُ ٱلْغَسِيلِ

Clothier *n.* صَانِعُ ثِيَابٍ وَبَائِعُهَا

Cloud *n.* غَيْمٌ . سَحَابٌ

Cloud *v. t.* or *i.* اظلَمَ . سَوَّدَ . تغَيَّمَ

Cloudiness *n.* تغَيُّمٌ

Cloudy *a.* مُغَيِّمٌ . مُظْلِمٌ

Cloves *n. pl.* كَبْشُ القرَنفل

Cloven *pp.* of cleave. مَشْقُوق

Cloven-footed *a.* مَشقوق الظِّلْفِ

Clover *n.* نَفَلَةٌ . بَرْسِيمٌ

Clown *n* فَظٌّ . مُهَرِّجٌ

Clay *v. t.* مَلاَ . أَشْبَعَ

Club *n.* عصاً . نَبُّوتٌ . مُنتَدًى

Club-footed أَخْنَفُ

Clue *see* clew دَلِيلٌ . إِشارَة

Clump *n.* دَغَلٌ (مِنْ شَجَرٍ)

Clumsy *a.* أَخْرَقُ

Clung *pp.* of cling. تَعَلَّقَ عَلَى وَبِ

Cluster *n.* or *v. i.* عنقودٌ . تجَمَّعَ

Clutch *v. t.* or *n.* قبَضَ بِ . قبْضٌ

Coach *n.* عَجَلَةٌ . عَرَبَةٌ . مَرْكَبة

Coachman *n.* سَائِقُ مَرْكَبَة

Coadjutor *n.* مُعَاوِنٌ . مُسَاعِدٌ

Coagulate *v. t.* or *i.* خثَرَ . خَثُرَ

Coagulation *n.* رَوْبٌ . تجَمُّدٌ . خثْرٌ

Coal *n.* فَحْمٌ . فحمٌ حَجَرِيٌّ

Coal *v.* إتحدَ . إِتَّصَلَ

Coaling *n.* تقدِيمُ فحمٍ

Coalition *n.* إِعتِصابٌ . إتحاد

Coal-mine *n.* معدِنُ فَحْمٍ حَجَرِي

Coarse *a.* خَشِنٌ . ثَخِين . غَلِيظ

Coarseness *n.* خُشُونَةٌ . فَظَاظَةٌ

Coast *n.* شَاطِئُ الْبَحْرِ

Coaster *n.* مُسَافِرٌ قُرْبَ الشَّاطِئِ

Coat *n.* رِدَاءٌ . جُبَّةٌ

Coating *n* تغْطِيَةٌ . غطَاءٌ

Coax *v. t.* تملَّقَ

Cobble *v. t* رَقَعَ (أحذِيَةً)

Cobble-stone *n.* حَصَاةٌ مُسْتَدِيرَة

Cobbler *n.* مُرَقِّعُ احذِيَةٍ

Cobweb *n.* نسيجُ ٱلعنكبوت

Cock *n.* دِيكٌ . حَنَفِيَّةٌ

Cockade *n.* عُقْدَةُ شَرِيطٍ لِلرَّأسِ

Cockatrice *n.* افعُوَان

Cockle *n.* نَوْعٌ مِنَ ٱلصَّدَفِ

Cockroach *n.* صُرْصُورٌ

Cockscomb *n.* عُرْفُ ٱلدِّيكِ

Cockswain *n.* رَئِيسُ قَارب

Cocoanut *n.* جَوْزُهِندٍ . نَارجِيلٌ

Cocoon *n.* شَرَنقَةٌ

Cod
Codfish } *n.* نَوْعٌ مِنَ ٱلسَمَك

Coddle *v. t.* دَلَّلَ

Code *n.* دُسْتُورُ شَرَائِعَ . مَجلَّةٌ

Codicil *n.* ذَيْلُ وَصِيَّةٍ

Codify *v. t.* جَمَعَ . لَخَّصَ ٱلشرائِعَ

Co-efficient *n.* or *a.* مُعَيِن. مُسَاعِدٌ

Co-equal *a.* كُفُوءٌ . مَثِيلٌ . عَدِيلٌ

Coerce *v. t.* غَصَبَ . أَجبَرَ

Coercion *n.* غَصْبٌ . إِجبَارٌ

Coercive *a.* غَاصِبٌ . مُجبِرٌ

Coeval *a.* or *n.* مُعَاصِرٌ . متَسَاوٍ

Co-existent *a.* مَوْجُودٌ فِي زَمانٍ وَاحِدٍ

Co-existence *n.* أَلتعَادُلُ فِي ٱلوُجُودِ

Co-extensive *a.* مُعَادِلٌ فِي الامتِدَاد

Coffee *n.* بُنٌّ . قَهْوَةٌ

Coffer *n.* صُنْدُوقٌ لِلْمَالِ

Coffin *n.* تَابُوتٌ نَعْشٌ

Cog *n.* سِنُّ دُولَابٍ

Cogency *n.* قُوَّةٌ . شِدَّةٌ

Cogent *a.* قَوِيٌّ . مُقْنِعٌ

Cogitate *v. i.* تَأَمَّلَ . فَكَّرَ

Cogitation *n.* تَأَمُّلٌ . تَفْكِيرٌ

Cognate *n.* نَسِيبٌ . مُجانِسٌ

Cognition *n.* عِلْمٌ . إِدْرَاكٌ

Cognizable *a.* قَابِلُ ٱلمَعْرِفَةِ

Cognomen *n.* إِسْمُ ٱلعَائِلَةِ

Cogwheel *n.* دُوْلاَبٌ ذُوْ اسْنَانٍ

Colhabit *v. i.* سَاكَنَ

Co-heir *n.* قَسِيمُ ٱلمِيرَاثِ

Cohere *v. i.* إِلْتَصَقَ . إِتَّحَدَ

Coherence / **Cohesion** } *n.* إِلْتِصَاقٌ . إِلْتِحَامٌ

Coherent *a.* مُلْتَصِقٌ . مُنْتَظِمٌ

Cohesive *a.* لَزِجٌ مُلْتَصِقٌ

Cohort *n.* كَتِيبَةٌ

Coil *v. t.* or *n.* لَفَّ . طَوَى ـ لَفَّةٌ

Coin *n.* or *v. t.* قِطْعَةُ نُقُوْدٍ . سَكَّ ـُ

Coinage *n.* سَكُّ ٱلنُّقُوْدِ . أَلْمَسْكُوكَات

Coincide *v. i.* إِتَّفَقَ

Coincidence *n.* إِتِّفَاقٌ . مُطَابَقَةٌ

Coincident *n.* مُتَّفِقٌ . مُطَابِقٌ

Coke *n.* نَوْعُ فَحْمٍ حَجَرِيٍّ

Cold *a.* or *n.* بَارِدٌ . بَرْدٌ . زُكَامٌ

Coldly *ad.* بَارِداً . بِعَدَمِ اكْتِرَاثٍ

Coldness *n.* بُرُوْدَةٌ . بَرْدٌ

Colic *n.* مَغْصٌ . (قُولَنْجٌ)

Collaborator *n.* شَرِيكٌ فِي عَمَلٍ

Collapse *v. i.* or *n.* هَبَطَ ـُ . تَهَوُّرٌ

Collar *n.* or *v.t.* طوق . قبة . طَوَّقَ

Collate *v. i.* قَابَلَ . جَمَعَ . رَتَّبَ

Collateral *a.* مُجَانِبٌ مُرَافِقٌ

Collation *n.* مُقَابَلَةٌ . لُمْجَةٌ

Colleague *n.* شَرِيكٌ . رَصِيفٌ

Collect *v. t.* or *i.* جَمَعَ . إِجْتَمَعَ

Collected *pp.* or *a.* مَجْمُوْعٌ . رَزِينٌ

Collection *n.* جَمْعٌ . مَجْمُوْعٌ

Collectively *ad.* جُمْلَةً . بِالإِجْمَالِ

Collector *n.* جَامِعٌ . جَابٍ

College *n.* مَدْرَسَةٌ عَالِيَةٌ أَوْ كُلِّيَّةٌ

Collegiate *a.* مُخْتَصٌّ بِمَدْرَسَةٍ كُلِّيَّةٍ

Collide *v. i.* تَصَادَمَ

Collier *n.* فَحَّامٌ . سَفِينَةٌ لِحَمْلِ ٱلفَحْمِ

Colliery *n.* مَعْدِنُ ٱلْفَحْمِ

Collision *n.* تَصَادُمٌ

Collocate *v. t.* رَتَّبَ . نَظَّمَ

Colloquial *n.* عَامِيٌّ . تَحَاوُرِيٌّ

Colloquy *n.* مُحَاوَرَة

Collude *v. i.* تَآمَرَ

Collusion *n.* مُؤَامَرَةٌ لِلْخِدَاعِ

Collusive *a.* خِدَاعِيٌّ

Colon *n.* عَلَامَةُ وَقْفٍ (:)

Colonel *n.* أَمِيرُ آلَايٍ

Colonial *a.* مُخْتَصٌّ بِمُسْتَعْمَرَةٍ

Colonist *n.* مُسْتَعْمِرٌ . مُهَاجِرٌ

Colonization *n.* إِنْشَاءُ مُسْتَعْمَرَاتٍ

Colonize *v. t.* أَنْشَأَ مُسْتَعْمَرَةً

Colonade *n.* صَفٌّ أَعْمِدَة

Colony *n.* مُسْتَعْمَرَةٌ . مُهَاجِرُونَ

Colossal *a.* جَسِيمُ ٱلْقَدِّ

Colossus *n.* تِمْثَالٌ عَظِيمُ ٱلْقَدِّ

Colour *n.* or *v. t.* or *i.* لَوْنٌ . لَوَّنَ . إِحْمَرَّ

Colouring *n.* تَلْوِينٌ . تَلَوُّنٌ . صَبْغٌ

Colours *n. pl.* رَايَةٌ . عَلَمٌ

Colporteur *n.* بَيَّاعٌ يَدُورُ بِكُتُبٍ

Colt *n.* فِلْوٌ . مُهْرٌ

Column *n.* عَمُودٌ ج أَعْمِدَةٌ

Columnar *a.* عَمُودِيٌّ

Comb *n.* مُشْطٌ ج أَمْشَاطٌ

Combat *n.* or *v. t* قِتَالٌ . قَاتَلَ

Combatant *n.* مُقَاتِلٌ

Combative *a.* مَائِلٌ إِلَى ٱلْقِتَالِ . خَصُومٌ

Combination *n.* إِتِّحَادٌ . إِتِّفَاقٌ

Combine *v. i.* or *t.* إِجْتَمَعَ . جَمَعَ

Combustible *a.* قَابِلُ ٱلْإِشْتِعَالِ

Combustion *n.* إِشْتِعَالٌ . إِحْتِرَاقٌ

Come *v. i.* (came, come) جَاءَ . اتى

Comedian *n.* كَاتِبُ رِوَايَاتٍ هَزْلِيَّةٍ . مُشَخِّصُهَا

Comedy *n.* رِوَايَةٌ هَزْلِيَّةٌ

Comely *a.* حَسَنُ ٱلصُّورَةِ

Comet *n.* نَجْمٌ ذُو ذَنَبٍ

Comfort *n.* or *v. t.* تعزِيَةٌ . عَزَّى

Comfortable *a.* مُرِيحٌ . مُسْتَرِيحٌ

Comforter *n.* مُعزٍّ . أَلرُّوحُ ٱلقُدُسُ

Comic } *a.* مُضْحِكٌ . هَزْلِيٌّ
Comical }

Coming *a.* or *n.* آتٍ إِتْيَانٌ . مَجِيٌّ

Comma *n.* (,) عَلامَةُ وَقْفٍ قَصيرٍ

Command *v. t.* or *n.* أمَرَ . أَمْرٌ

Commandant } *n.* أَمِيرٌ . قَائِدٌ
Commander }

Commanding *ppr.* آمِرٌ . مُشْرِفٌ عَلَى

Commandment *n.* أمْرٌ . وَصِيَّةٌ

Commemorable *a.* مُسْتَحِقٌّ ٱلذِّكْرِ

Commemorate *v. t.* إِحتَفَلَ . عَيَّدَ

Commemorative *a.* تَذْكَارِيٌّ

Commence *v. t.* or *i.* بَدَا . إِبْتَدَأَ

Commencement *n.* بدَاء

Commend *v. t.* مَدَحَ . إِستَوْدَعَ

Commendable *a.* مُسْتَحِقٌّ ٱلْمَدْحِ

Commendation *n.* مَدْحٌ . تَوْصِيَةٌ

Commensurable } *a.* مُتَسَاوٍ
Commensurate }

Comment *v. i.* or *n.* شَرَحَ . تَفْسِيرٌ

Commentary *n.* تَفْسِيرٌ . شَرْحٌ

Commentator *n.* مُفَسِّرٌ . شَارِحٌ

Commerce *n.* تِجَارَةٌ . مَتْجَرٌ

Commercial *a.* تِجَارِيٌّ . مَتْجَرِيٌّ

Commingle *v. t.* or *i.* مَزَجَ . إِمتَزَجَ

Commiserate *v. t.* أَشفَقَ عَلَى

Commiseration *n.* شَفَقَةٌ

Commissary *n.* } مُفَوَّضٌ . مَأْمُورُ ٱلْمَأْكُولَاتِ فِي جَيْشٍ

Commission *n.* وَكَالَةٌ . لَجْنَةٌ

Commission *v. t.* فَوَّضَ إِلَى

Commissioner *n.* وَكِيلٌ مُفَوَّضٌ

Commit *v. t.* سَلَّمَ . إِرتَكَبَ

Commitment *n.* إِيدَاعٌ . سِجْنٌ

Committal *n.* تَسْلِيمٌ . إِرْتِكَابٌ

Committee *n.* لجنةٌ . وُكلاءُ

Commodious *a.* مُرِيحٌ . رَحْبٌ

Commodity *n.* سِلعةٌ . بِضاعةٌ

Commodor *n.* رَئِيسُ أُسطُولٍ

Common *a.* عامٌّ . إِعتِيادِيٌّ

Commoner *n.* احَدُ ٱلْعَامَّةِ

Commonly *a.* غَالبًا . إِعتِيَادِيًّا

Common-wealth *n.* حُكُومَةٌ جَمْهُورِيَّةٌ

Commotion *n.* ضَجَّةٌ . إِضطِرَابٌ

Commune *v. i.* إِشْتَرَكَ . كالَمَ

Communicant *n.* مُشْتَرِكٌ

Communicate *v. t.* ابْلَغَ . أَخبَرَ

Communication *n.* تَبلِيغٌ . مُرَاسَلَةٌ

Communicative *a.* مُبَلِّغٌ

Communion *n.* مُخَالَطَةٌ . إِشْتِرَاكٌ

Community *n.* جَمَاعَةٌ . إِشْتِرَاكٌ

Commutable *a.* قَابِلُ ٱلاستِبْدَالِ

Commutation *n.* تبادُلٌ . إِستِبْدَالٌ

Commute *v. t.* إِستَبدَلَ . غيَّرَ

Compact *a.* or *n.* مُتَلَبِّدٌ . مُعَاهَدَةٌ

Compactness *n.* تلبُّدٌ . مَتَانَةٌ

Companion *n.* رَفِيقٌ . عَشِيرٌ

Companionable *a.* أَنِيسٌ

Companionship *n.* مُعَاشَرَةٌ . صُحْبَةٌ

Company *n.* جَمَاعَةٌ . شِرْكَةٌ

Comparable *a.* قابِلُ ٱلْمُقَابَلَةِ

Comparative *a.* or *n.* نِسبِيٌّ . أَفْعَلُ التَّفضِيلِ

Compare *v. t.* or *i.* قَابَلَ . شَابَهَ

Comparison *n.* مُقَابَلَةٌ . مُشَابَهَة

Compartment *n.* قِسْمٌ . بَيْتٌ

Compass *v.t.* أَحَاطَ بِ . أَنْجَزَ . نَالَ

Campass *n.* مُحِيطٌ . حُكّ

Compasses *n. pl.* بِرْكَارٌ أو بيكارٌ

Compassion شفقة . رَأفة

Compassionate *a.* شَفُوقٌ . رَؤُوفٌ

Compatibility *n.* مُوَافَقَةٌ . مُلاءَمة

Compatible *a.* مُوَافِقٌ . مُلاَئِم

Compeer *n.* قَرِينٌ . شَرِيك

Compel *v.* أَجبَرَ . أَلْزَمَ . غَصَبَ

Compend / **Compendium** *n.* مُخْتَصَرٌ

Compensate *v. t.* عَوَّضَ . كَافَأَ

Compensation *n.* مُكافَاةٌ . تَعوِيضٌ

Compete *v. i.* سَابَقَ . بَارَى . نَاظَرَ

Competence / **Competency** *n.* كِفَايَةٌ . جدَارة

Competent *a.* جَدِيرٌ . قَادِرٌ عَلَى

Competition *n.* مُسَابَقَةٌ . مُبَارَاة

Competitor *n.* مُسَابِقٌ . مُبَارٍ

Competitive *a.* سِبَاقِيٌّ

Compilation *n.* مَجْمُوعة . تَأْلِيف

Compile *v. t.* جَمَعَ . أَلَّفَ

Complacence *n.* سُرُورٌ بِـ . رِضًى بِـ

Complacent *a.* رَاضٍ بِـ . مَسْرُورٌ بِـ

Complain *v. i.* شَكَا . تَظَلَّمَ مِنْ

Complainant / **Complainer** *n.* مشْتَكٍ

Complaint *n.* شَكَايَةٌ . عِلَّةٌ

Complaisance *n.* مُلاطَفَةٌ . مُرَاعَاةٌ

Complaisant *a.* مُلاطِفٌ . مُرَاعِي الْخَاطِرِ

Complement *n.* تَتِمَّةٌ . تَكْمِلَةٌ

Complemental *a.* مُتَمِّمٌ . تَكْمِيلِيٌّ

Complete *v. t.* or *a.* تَمَّمَ . أَكْمَلَ . كَامِلٌ

Completely *ad.* تَمَاماً

Completement / **Completion** *n.* إِتمَامٌ . تَكْمِيلٌ

Complex *a.* مُرَكَّبٌ . مُشْتَبَكٌ

Complexion *n.* لَوْنُ الْوَجْهِ

Complexity *n.* إِشْتِبَاكٌ . تَعَقُّدٌ

Compliance *n.* إِذْعَانٌ . إِجَابَةٌ

Compliant *a.* مُذْعِنٌ . مُنْقَادٌ

Complicate *v.t.* or *a.* عَرْقَلَ . مُعَقَّدٌ

Complicated *a.* مُعَرْقَلٌ . مُعَقَّدٌ

Complication *n.* عَرْقَلَةٌ . تَشْوِيشٌ

Complicity *n.* إِشْتِرَاكٌ فِي ذَنْبٍ

Compliment *n.* قَولُ مَدْحٍ . تَحِيَّةٌ

Complimentary *a.* مَادِحٌ

Comply *v. i.* أَذْعَنَ . أَجَابَ . إِنْقَادَ

Component *a.* or *n.* تَرْكِيبِيٌّ . جُزْءٌ

Comport *v. i.* وَافَقَ . لَاءَمَ

Compose *v. t.* رَكَّبَ . أَلَّفَ . هَدَّأَ

Composed *a.* مُرَكَّبٌ . مُؤَلَّفٌ رَزِينٌ

Composer *n.* مُؤَلِّفٌ . جَامِعٌ

Composite *a.* مُرَكَّبٌ مِنْ أَجْزَاءٍ

Composition *n.* تَرْكِيبٌ . تَأْلِيفٌ

Compositor *n.* صَفَّافُ أَحْرُفٍ لِلطَّبْعِ

Compost *n.* سَمَادٌ

Composure *n.* رَزَانَةٌ . هُدُوءٌ

Compound *a.* or *n.* مُرَكَّبٌ . مَزِيجٌ

Compound *v. t.* رَكَّبَ . مَزَجَ ـُ

Component *a.* or *n.* مُرَكَّبٌ . جُزْءٌ جَوْهَرِيٌّ

Comprehend *v. t.* أَدْرَكَ . فَهِمَ ـَ

Comprehensible *a.* مُمْكِنٌ إِدْرَاكُهُ

Comprehension *n.* إِدْرَاكٌ . شُمُولٌ

Comprehensive *a.* شَامِلٌ . جَامِعٌ

Compress *v. t.* كَبَسَ ـِ ضَغَطَ ـَ

Compression *n.* كَبْسٌ

Comprise *v. t.* تَضَمَّنَ . إِشْتَمَلَ عَلَى

Compromise *v.t.* or *n.* اِتَّفَقَ . إِتِّفَاقٌ

Compulsion *n.* غَصْبٌ . إِكْرَاهٌ

Compulsive / Compulsory *a.* غَاصِبٌ . مُجْبِرٌ

Compunction *n.* تَوْبِيخُ الضَّمِيرِ

Computable *a.* قَابِلُ الإِحْصَاءِ

Compute *v. t.* أَحْصَى . حَسَبَ ـُ

Comrade *n.* رَفِيقٌ . صَاحِبٌ

Con *v. t.* تَأَمَّلَ . دَرَسَ ـُ

Concatenation *n.* تَسَلْسُلٌ . سِلْسِلَةٌ

Concave *a.* مُقَعَّرٌ . مُجَوَّفٌ

Concavity *n.* تَجْوِيفٌ . قَعْرَةٌ

Conceal *v. t.* اخفى . سَتَرَ ـِ . كتم ـُ

Concealment *n.* إِخفَاء . كِتمَان

Concede *v. t.* منح — سلّم بهِ

Conceit *n.* تخيّل . رأي . عُجْب

Conceited *a.* مُعجَب بنفسهِ

Conceivable *a.* مُمكن تصوُّره

Conceive *v. t.* تصوّر في الذهن

Concentrate *v. t.* جمع في مركزٍ

Concentration *n.* جمع . تجمّع

Concentric *a.* ذو مركزٍ واحدٍ

Conception *n.* تصوُّر . فكر . حَبَل

Concern *v. t.* or *n.* همّ ـُ . همّ . قضية

Concerning *pr.* بخصُوص . من جهة

Concert *v. t.* or *i.* دبّر . إتّفق

Concert *n.* إتّفاق . محفل موسيقيّ

Concession *n.* تسليم.هبة. رُخصة

Conciliate *v. t.* سالم . وفّق بين

Conciliation *n.* مُسالمة

Conciliatory *a.* مُستعطف . مُسالم

Concise *a.* مختصر . وجيز

Conciseness *n.* إختصار . إيجاز

Conclave *n.* مجمع سرّي

Conclude *v. t.* or *i.* انهى . إستنتج

Concluding *a.* خاتم . أخير

Conclusion *n.* خاتمة . نتيجة

Conclusive *a.* قاطع . جازم

Concoct *v.* دبّر . ركّب طبيخاً

Concoction *n.* هضم . تدبير

Concomitant *a.* مرافق . مُلازم

Concord *n.* إتّفاق . وفاق

Concordance *n.* فهرس

Concordat *n.* صكّ . إتّفاق

Concourse *n.* إجتماع

Concrete *a.* or *n.* مُتجمّد . مُركّب

Concretion *n.* كُتلة مُتجمّدة

Concubine *n.* سرّيّة ج سراريّ

Concupiscence *n.* شَهْوَة . هَوًى

Concur *v. i.* إِتَّفَقَ

Concurrence *n.* إِتِّفاقٌ

Concurrent *a.* مُرَافِقٌ . مجَارٍ

Concussion *n.* هَزٌّ . صَدْمَةٌ

Condemn *v. t.* حكَمَ على . دَانَ ـِ

Condemnation *n.* حُكْمٌ . دَيْنُونَةٌ

Condemnatory *a.* دائِنٌ . حاكِمٌ بِدَيْنُونَةٍ

Condensation *n.* تكْثِيفٌ

Condense *v. t.* كَثفَ . اوْجَزَ . قَطَّرَ

Condescend *v. i.* تنازَلَ . تَساهَلَ

Condescension *n.* تَنَازُلٌ

Condign *a.* مُسْتَحِقٌّ . مُوَافِق

Condiment *n.* تابلٌ ج توَابل

Condition *n.* or *v. t.* حالَةٌ . شَرْط . إِشترَطَ

Conditional *a.* شرْطِيٌّ

Conditioned *a.* مشرُوطٌ اوْ مُشْترَط

Condole *v. i.* or *t.* حزِنَ معَ غَيْرِهِ

Condolence *n.* الأَسَفُ معَ الغَيْرِ

Condone *v. t.* غفرَ ـِ . سَامَحَ

Condor *n.* حَدَأَة أميركِيَّة كَبِيرَة

Conduce *v. i.* أفضى أوْ آلَ إِلى

Couducible / Conducive *a.* مُفْضٍ أوْ آيِلٌ إِلى

Conduct *v. t.* قادَ . أدارَ

Conduct *n.* تصَرُّفٌ . قِيادَة

Conductor *n.* قائِدٌ . مُوْصِلٌ كَهْرَبائِيٌّ

Conduit *n.* قَنَاةٌ ج قُنِيٌّ وَقَنَوَات

Cone *n.* مَخْرُوطٌ

Confection / Confectionery *n.* حَلْوَى أوْحَلْوَاء

Confectioner *n.* حَلْوانِيٌّ

Confederacy *n.* عُصْبَة . مُعَاهدة

Confederate *v. i.* or *a.* إِعْتَصَبَ . متعَاهِد

Confederation *n.* تعاهُدٌ . تحَالفٌ

Confer *v.i.* or *t.* تشَاوَرَ . مَنَح ـَ

Conference *n.* مشاوَرَة . مُؤْتَمَر

Confess *v. t.* أقَرَّ . إعْتَرَفَ

Confessedly *ad.* بإِقْرَار ٱلعُمُوم

Confession *n.* إعتِرَافٌ . إقْرَارٌ

Confessional *n.* كرْسِيُّ ٱلاعتِرَاف

Confessor *n.* معَرِّفٌ . مُعْتَرِفٌ

Confidant *n.* صفِيٌّ . خلٌّ امِيْنٌ

Confide *v. i.* or *t.* امِنَ ـَ أَرْكَنَ إلَى

Confidence *n.* ثقَة . إِذْ كَان

Confident *a.* مُتأكِّدٌ . واثِق

Confidential *a.* سِرِّيٌّ . امِيْن

Configuration *n.* صُوْرَة . هَيْئَة

Confine *v. t.* حَجَزَ ـُ . حصَرَ ـِ ـُ

Confinement *n.* حَصرٌ . حَبْسٌ

Confirm *v. t.* اثْبَتَ . شَدَّدَ

Confirmation *n.* إِثبَاتٌ . تَأْيِيْد

Confirmative / Confirmatory *a.* مُثبّت . مُؤَيِّد

Confiscate *v. t.* ضَبَطَ مُلْكاً (الحكومة)

Confiscation *n.* ضَبْطُ ٱلملك

Conflagration *n.* إِحْتِرَاقٌ . حَرِيق

Conflict *n.* or *v.t.* قِتَالٌ . خِصَامٌ . نَازِع

Conflicting *a.* مُتَنَاقِضٌ . مُتَخَالِفٌ

Confluent *a.* جَارٍ مَعَ غَيْرِه

Conform *v. t.* or *i.* شَاكَلَ . إِمْتَثَلَ

Conformable *a.* مُطَابِقٌ . مُوَافِقٌ

Conformation *n.* تَرْكِيبٌ . جِبْلَة

Conformity *n.* مُوَافَقَة . مُطَابَقَة

Confound *v. t.* خلَطَ . حَيَّرَ

Confounded *a.* مُخْتَلِطٌ . مُتَحَيِّرٌ

Confront *v. t.* وَاجَهَ . قَابَلَ

Confuse *v. t.* خلَطَ ـِ . بَلْبَلَ . أَخْجَلَ

Confusion *n.* بِلْبَالٌ . تَشْوِيْشٌ

Confutation *n.* دَحْضٌ . إِبطَالٌ

Confute *v. t.* ادْحَض . أَبْطَلَ

Congeal *v. t.* or *t.* جَمَّدَ . جَمُدَ ـُ

Congelation *n.* جَمْدٌ أَوْ جُمُوْد

Congenial *n.* مِنْ خُلُقٍ وَاحِدٍ . مُوَافِق

Congeniality *n.* مُوافَقَةُ ٱلْخُلق

Congenital *a.* خلقيٌّ . مِنَ الخِلْقَـةِ

Congested *a.* مُحْتَقِنٌ

Congestion *n.* إِحتِقَانٌ

Conglomerate v. t. or a. كـتل . مُكتَّلٌ

Conglomeration *n.* تَكَتُّلٌ

Congratulate *v. t.* هَنَّأ

Congratulation *n.* تَهْنِئَة

Congratulatory *a.* مُهَنِّي

Congregate v. t. or i. حَشَدَـُ . إِحْتَشَدَ

Congregation *n.* جَمَاعَة. مَحْفَلٌ

Congregational *a.* جُمْهُورِيٌّ (فِي الدِّينِ)

Congress *n.* مُؤْتَمَرٌ . مَجْمَعٌ

Congruity *n.* مُنَاسَبَة . مُطابَقَة

Congruous *a.* مُنَاسِبٌ . مُوَافِقٌ

Conical *a.* مَخْرُوطِيُّ ٱلشَّكْلِ

Conicsections *n.* عِلْمُ قَطْعِ ٱلمخْرُوطِ

Coniferous *a.* ذو ثمر كالصَّنَوْبَرِ

Conjectural *a.* حَدْسِيٌّ . تخمينيٌّ

Conjecture *n.* حَدْسٌ . تَخْمين

Conjoin *v. t.* وَصَلَ ـِ . قَرَنَ ـِ

Conjointly *ad.* معاً

Conjugal *a.* زَوَاجِيٌّ . بَعْلِيٌّ

Conjugate *v. t.* صَرَّفَ (ٱلفِعْلَ)

Conjugation *n.* تصْرِيفُ ٱلفِعلِ

Conjunction *n.* وَصْلٌ . حَرْفُ عطف

Conjunctive *a.* عَاطِفٌ. مُوْصِلٌ

Conjuncture *n.* إِتِّحَادٌ . وَقْتٌ مُهِمٌّ

Conjure *v. t.* or *i.* رَقَى ـِ . إِسْتَحْلَفَ

Conjurer *n.* رَاقٍ . مُشَعْوِذٌ

Connect *v. t.* وصلَ ـِ . قَرَنَ ـِ

Connection / Connexion *n.* وَصْلٌ . إِتِّصَالٌ

Connective *n.* or *a.* مُوْصِلٌ . رَابِط

Connivance *n.* إِغْضَاءٌ عَنْ زَلَّةٍ

Connive *v. t.* تغاضى عن

Connubial *a.* زيجيٌّ أوْ زَوْجِيٌّ

Conoid / Conoidal *a.* شَبِيهٌ بِالْمَخْرُوط

Conquer *v. t.* غَلَبَ ـِ . ظَفِرَ بِ ـَ

Conqueror *n.* غَالِبٌ . ظَافِرٌ . فَاتِح

Conquest *n.* غَلَبَةٌ . ظَفَرٌ . فَتْحٌ . فتوح

Consanguinity *n.* قَرَابَة . نَسَبٌ

Conscience *n.* اَلضَّمِيرُ . ذِمَّة

Conscientious *a.* صَاحِبُ ذِمَةٍ . أَمين

Conscientiousness *n.* ذِمَّة . امانة

Conscious *a.* عَارِفٌ . يقظان

Consciously *ad.* عَنْ عِلْمٍ . عَمْداً

Consciousness *n.* إِدْرَاك . يقظة

Conscript *a.* جُنْدِيٌّ مَاخُوذ بالقُرْعَةِ

Conscription *n.* قُرْعَةُ الْعَسْكَرِ / إِكْتِتَابٌ

Consecrate *v. t.* قَدَّسَ . كَرَّسَ

Consecration *n.* تَقْدِيسٌ . تَكْرِيسٌ

Consecutive *a.* مُتَتَابِعٌ . مُتَوَالٍ

Consent *n.* or *v. i.* رِضى . رَضِيَ ب

Consentient *a.* مُتفق اَلرَّأْي

Consequence *n.* نَتِيجَةٌ . اهَمِّيَة

Consequent *a.* or *n.* تَابِعٌ . تَالٍ

Consequential *a.* نَاتِجٌ . مُهِمٌّ . مُعْجَبٌ

Consequently *ad.* مِن ثَمَّ . إِذاً

Conservation *n.* حِفْظٌ . وِقَايَةٌ

Conservatism *n.* اَلْمُحَافَظَةُ عَلَى / اَلنِّظَامُ اَلْحَالِيِّ

Conservative *a.* or *n.* مُحَافِظٌ

Conservatory *a.* or *n.* حَافِظ . كِنٌّ لِلنبَاتِ

Conserve *v. t.* حَفِظَ ـَ . صَانَ ـُ

Consider *v. t.* or *i.* إِعْتَبَرَ . تَبَصَّرَ

Considerable *a.* مُسْتَحِقٌّ الاِعْتِبَارِ . وَافِرٌ

Considerate *a.* مُتَبَصِّرٌ . حَازِمٌ

Consideration *n.* تَفَكُّرٌ . إِعْتِبَارٌ

Considering *ppr.* نظراً إِلَى . مُتَأَمِّلٌ

Consign *v. t.* سَلَّمَ إِلَى . اوْدَعَ

Consignee *n.* اَلْمُتَسَلِّمُ . اَلْمُرْسَلُ إِلَيْهِ

Consignment *n.*	تسليمٌ . إرسالية
Consist *v. i.*	تكوّن (مِنْ)
Consistence / **Consistency** *n.*	قوامٌ . موافقة
Consistent *a.*	جامدٌ . موافق
Consistently *ad.*	مطابقةً ل
Consolable *a.*	قابلُ التعزية
Consolation *n.*	تعزيةٌ . سلوى
Consolatory *a.*	معزٍّ . مسلٍّ
Console *v. t.*	عزى . سلى
Consolidate *v. t.* or *i.*	ثبّتَ . مكّن . تجمد
Consolidation *n.*	تثبيتٌ . تجمّدٌ
Consonant *a.* or *n.*	موافقٌ . الحرف الصحيحُ
Consort *n.*	زوجٌ او زوجةٌ . قرينٌ
Consort *v. i.*	تشاركَ . ترافق
Conspicuous *a.*	بيّنٌ . جليٌّ . ظاهرٌ
Conspiracy *n.*	فتنة . مؤامرة
Conspirator *n.*	متآمرٌ
Conspire *v. i.*	فتنَ ـ . تآمر
Constable *n.*	مأمورٌ لحفظِ السلام
Constant *a.*	ثابتٌ . دائمٌ . امينٌ
Constancy *n.*	ثباتٌ . عزمٌ . امانةٌ
Constantly *ad.*	على الدوام
Constellation *n.*	جماعةُ نجومٍ . برجٌ
Consternation *n.*	دهشةٌ . رعبٌ
Constipate *v. t.*	قبّضَ الامعاء
Constipation *n.*	قبضُ الامعاء
Constituency *n.*	جماعةُ المنتخبين
Constituent *a.* or *n.*	مكوّن . موكِّلٌ . جوهريٌّ
Constitute *v. t.*	قامَ . نصبَ . ركّب
Constitution *n.*	بُنيةٌ . نظامٌ
Constitutional *a.*	نظاميٌّ . مزاجيٌّ
Constitutive *a.*	مقيمٌ . مكوِّن
Constrain *v. t.*	اجبرَ . الزمَ
Constraint *n.*	إلزامٌ . حصر
Constrict *v. t.*	شدّ ـُ . ضغط ـ

Constriction *n.* شدٌّ. ضغطٌ. إنقباضٌ

Constringent *a.* قَابِضٌ . مُقلّصٌ

Construct *v. t.* بنى ـ انشأ . دبّر

Construction *n.* بنَاءٌ . تركِيبٌ

Constructor *n.* بَان . بنَّاءٌ

Constructive *a.* بَانٍ . إستِدْلاليٌّ

Construe *v. i.* فسّرَ معْنىً . أعْرَبَ

Consul *n.* قنْصُلٌ ج قنَاصِلُ

Consular *a.* قُنْصليٌّ

Consulship *n.* مقَامُ القُنْصلِ

Consulate *n.* مكْتبُ القُنْصلِ

Consult *v. t.* or *i.* شاوَرَ . تشَاوَرَ

Consultation *n.* مُشَاوَرَةٌ . مفَاوَضَةٌ

Consume *v. t.* or *i.* أتْلفَ . ابَاد . فنِيَ ـ

Consumer *n.* آكِلٌ . مُسْتعْمِلٌ. نَافِذٌ

Consummate *a.* تَامٌّ . مُكمَّلٌ

Consummate *v. t.* كمَّلَ . تمَّمَ

Consummation *n.* إتمَامٌ . إنجَازٌ

Consumption *n.* إتْلافٌ . دَاءُ السُّلِّ

Consumptive *a.* مُصَابٌ بالسُّلِّ

Contact *n.* مُمَاسَّةٌ . مُلامَسَة

Contagion *n.* عَدْوَى مِنَ المُمَاسةِ

Contagious *a.* مُعْدٍ بمُمَاسةٍ

Contain *v. t.* وَسِعَ ـ . إحتوَى

Contaminate *v. t.* أفْسَدَ . دَنَّسَ

Contamination *n.* إفسَاد . تنْجيسٌ

Contemn *v. t.* أهَانَ . كرِهَ ـ

Contemplate *v. t.* or *i.* تامّلَ . قَصَدَ ـ

Contemplation *n.* تأمُّلٌ

Contemplative *a.* مُتفَكِّر

Contemporaneous *a.* مُعَاصِرٌ

Contempt *n.* إهَانَةٌ . إحْتِقَارٌ

Contemptible *a.* مُحْتقَرٌ . دَنِيءٌ

Contemptuous *a.* مُحْتقِرٌ . مُهِينٌ

Contend *v. t.* نَازَعَ . حَاجَّ . قَاوَمَ

Content *v. t.* أرْضَى . أقْنَعَ

Content *n.* المضمون . فحوى

Content / Contented } *n.* راض . مكتف . قانع

Contention *n.* منازعة . مشاجرة

Contentious *a.* مشاجر . خصوم

Contentment *n.* قناعة . رضى

Contest *n.* مجاهدة . مقاومة

Contest *v. t.* نازع . قاوم . ناظر

Contstant *n.* مقاوم . مناظر

Conterminous *a.* متاخم . مجاور

Context *n.* قرينة . سياق الكلام

Contiguity *n.* مماسة . قرب

Contiguous *a.* مماس . متصل ب

Continence / Continency } *n.* عفة . إمساك

Continent *a.* or *n.* عفيف . قارة

Continental *a.* مختص بقارة

Contingence / Contingency } *n.* حادثة عرضية

Contingent *a.* or *n.* عرضي . مشروط . عارض

Contingently *ad.* عرضاً . اتفاقاً

Continual *a.* دائم . مستمر

Continuance *n.* دوام . بقاء

Continuation *n.* تتابع . توال

Continue *v. i.* or *t.* دام ـُ . داوم

Continuity *a.* مواصلة . إتصال

Continuous *a.* متصل . دائم

Contortion *n.* إعوجاج . تفتل

Contort *v. t.* فتل ـِ . لوى ـ

Contour *a.* صورة حدود الشيء

Contraband *a.* ممنوع شرعاً

Contract *n.* عقد . شرط . إتفاق

Contract *v. t.* or *i.* } قلص . شارط . تقبض

Contracted *a.* متقلص . منقبض . ضيق

Contractible *a.* قابل التقلص

Contraction *n.* تقلص . إنقباض

Contractor *n.* مشارط . معاقد . مقاول

Contradict *v. t.* ناقض . ضاد . نافى

Contradiction *n.* مناقضة . تناقض

Contradictory *a.* مُتناقِضٌ
Contrariety *n.* مُعاكسة . مغايرة
Contraries *n. pl.* اضْدادٌ
Contrary *n.* مُضادٌّ . ضِدٌّ . مُخالِفٌ
Contrast *n.* or *v. t.* or *i.* تبَايَن . قابَلَ . ميَّزَ بَين
Contravene *v. t.* خالَفَ . عارَضَ
Contravention *n.* مُخالَفَةٌ . مُعارَضة
Contribute *v. t.* وَهَبَ . أعْطَى
Contribution *n.* هِبَةٌ . إعْطاءٌ
Contributive *a.* آئِلٌ إلى . مفيدٌ
Contributor *n.* مُعْطٍ
Contrite *a.* مُنكَسِرُ القَلْبِ . مُتَخَشِّعٌ
Contrition *n.* إنكِسارُ القَلْبِ . تَخَشُّعٌ
Contrivance *n.* حِيلَة . تدْبيرٌ
Contrive *v. t.* دَبَّرَ . إبْتَدَعَ
Control *n.* or *v. t.* سُلْطَة . ادارَ . سادَ
Controllable *a.* مُمكِنٌ إدارَتُهُ
Controller *n.* مُدِيرٌ . مُراقِبٌ

Controversial *a.* جَدَلِيٌّ
Controversy *n.* جِدالٌ . مُناظَرَة
Controvert *v. t.* خاصَمَ . جادَلَ
Controvertible *n.* مُمكِنٌ مقاوَمَتهُ
Contumacious *a.* عَنيدٌ . مارِدٌ
Contumacy *n.* عِنادٌ
Contumelious *a.* مُهِين . عاتٍ . شاتِمٌ
Contumely *n.* شَتيمَةٌ . إهانَة
Contusion *n.* رَضٌّ . رَضَّة
Conundrum *n.* ضَرْبٌ مِنَ اللُّغْزِ
Convalescense *n.* نَقَهٌ . تعافٍ
Convalescent *a.* ناقِهٌ . مُتَعافٍ
Convene *v. t.* or *i.* جَمَعَ . إلْتَأَمَ
Convenience *n.* مُوافَقة . راحة
Convenient *a.* مُوافِق . ملائِمٌ . مُرِيح
Conveniently *ad.* بِسُهُولَةٍ . بِراحةٍ
Convent *n.* دَيْرٌ ج أدْيِرَة
Conventicle *n.* إجْتِماعٌ دِينيٌّ

Convention *n.* مَجْمَعٌ. مُؤْتَمَرٌ. مُعَاهَدَة

Conventional *a.* إِصْطِلاحِيٌّ. إِعْتِيَادِيٌّ

Converge *v. i.* إِتَّجَهَ إِلَى مَرْكَزٍ

Convergence *n.* إِتِّجَاهٌ إِلَى مَرْكَزٍ

Convergent / Converging } *a.* مُتَقَارِبٌ. مُتَجِهٌ إِلَى مَرْكَزٍ

Conversant *a.* عَارِفٌ. خَبِيرٌ

Conversation *n.* مُفَاوَضَةٌ. حَدِيث

Conversational *a.* مُخْتَصٌّ بِٱلْحَدِيثِ

Converse *v. i.* تَفَاوَضَ. تَحَادَثَ

Converse *n.* or *a.* عَكْسٌ. مَعْكُوسٌ

Conversly *ad.* بِٱلْعَكْسِ

Conversion *n.* تَحْوِيلٌ. تَوْبَة

Convert *v. t.* حَوَّلَ. بَدَّلَ. هَدَى

Convert *n.* مُهْتَدٍ إِلَى دِينٍ

Convertible *a.* قَابِلُ ٱلتَّبْدِيل

Convex *a.* مُحَدَّبٌ

Convexity *n.* تَحَدُّبٌ

Convey *v. t.* نَقَلَ. حَمَلَ ـِ

Conveyance *n.* نَقْلٌ. مَرْكَبَة

Convict *v.* t. or *n.* } أَثْبَتَ ذَنْبَهُ. مُذْنِبٌ

Conviction *n.* إِثْبَاتُ ٱلذَّنْبِ. يَقِين

Convince *v. t.* اقْنَعَ

Convivial *a.* مُنْبَهِجٌ. قَصُوفِيٌّ

Conviviality *n.* إِنْشِرَاحٌ. قَصُوفٌ

Convocation *n.* جَمْعٌ. مَجْمَعٌ

Convoke *v. t.* إِسْتَدْعَى. جَمَعَ ـَ

Convolute / Convoluted } *a.* مُلْتَفٌّ

Convolution *n.* لَفٌّ. إِلْتِفَافٌ

Convoy *v. t.* or *n.* خَفَرَ ـِ. خَفَرٌ

Convulse *v. t.* شَنَّجَ. رَجَّ ـُ

Convulsive *a.* مُشَنِّجٌ

Cony *n.* وَبْرٌ ج وُبُورٌ

Coo *v. i.* هَدَرَ. سَجَعَ ـَ

Cook *v. t.* or *n.* } طَبَخَ ـَ. طَبَّاخٌ (عَشِّيٌّ)

Cookery *n.* صِنَاعَةُ ٱلطَّبْخ

Cool *a.* بَارِدٌ . مُعْتَدِلُ ٱلْبرُودَةِ

Cool *v. t.* or *i.* بَرَّدَ . هَدَّأَ . بَرَدَ ـُ

Cooler *n.* بَرَّادَةٌ . مُبَرِّدٌ

Coolly *ad.* بِهُدُوءٍ . بِضَبْطِ ٱلنفسِ

Coolness *n.* بُرُودَةٌ . رِبَاطَةُ جَأْشٍ

Coop *n.* or *v. t.* قَفَصٌ . حَبَسَ في قَفَصٍ

Cooper *n.* صَانِعُ بَرَامِيلَ

Co-operate *v. i.* تعَاوَنَ . تَشَارَكَ

Co-operative *a.* مُشْتَرِكٌ في عَمَلٍ

Co-ordinate *a.* مُتَسَاوِي ٱلرُّتْبَةِ

Co-partner *n.* شَرِيكٌ ج شُرَكَاءُ

Co-partnership *n.* شِرْكَة

Cope *v.i.* بَارَى . سَابَقَ . نَاظَرَ

Copious *a.* وَافِرٌ . غَزِيرٌ

Copper *n.* نُحَاسٌ احْمَرُ

Copperas *n.* زَاجٌ

Copper-smith *n.* نَحَّاسٌ

Copse *n.* غَابَةُ اشْجَارٍ صغيرَةٍ . دَغَلٌ

Copt *n.*, Coptic *a.* قُبْطِيٌّ

Copula *n.* رَابِط . صلة

Copulate *v. t.* or *i.* جَامَعَ

Coping *n.* إِفْرِيز . سَقِيفَةُ حائطٍ

Copy *n.* or *v. t.* نُسْخَةٌ . نَسَخَ ـَ

Copyer, Copyist *n.* نَاسِخ

Copyright *n.* حقُّ طبْعِ كِتَاب

Coquet *v. i.* غَنِجَ ـَ

Coquetry *n.* غُنْجٌ ـ غُنَاجٌ

Coquette *n.* غَنِيجَةٌ . (غنوجة)

Coquettish *a.* غَانِجٌ . غَنِجٌ

Coral *n.* or *a.* مَرْجَانٌ . مَرْجَانِيٌّ

Cord *n.* or *v. t.* مَرَسٌ . شدَّ بِمَرَسٍ

Cordage *n.* حِبَالُ ٱلسَّفِينَةِ

Cordate *a.* قَلْبِيُّ ٱلشَّكْلِ

Cordial *v.* or *n.* قَلْبِيٌّ . مُخْلِصٌ . شرَابٌ مُنْعِشٌ

Cordiality *n.* وُدٌّ . إِخْلَاصٌ

Cordon *n.* نطاقٌ مِنَ الْجُنْد

Core *n.* قَلْبٌ . لُبٌّ

Coriander *n.* كزبرةٌ

Cork *n.* or *v. t.* { (فَلِّينٌ) .سدَّادةٌ. سَدَّ بِهَا

Corky *a.* (فَلِّينِيٌّ)

Cork-screw *n.* بِيرَمٌ . (بَرِّيمَةٌ)

Corn *n.* حبٌّ . ذُرَةٌ . مِسْمَارٌ

Cornea *n.* قَرْنِيةُ الْعَيْنِ

Cornelian *n.* عقيقٌ

Corner *n.* زَاوِيَةٌ . قُرْنَةٌ

Corner-stone *n.* حجَرُ الزَّاوِيَةِ

Cornet *n.* صُورٌ . نَفِيرٌ

Cornice *n.* إِفْرِيزٌ . طُنُفٌ

Corolla *n.* تُوَيْجُ زَهْرَةٍ

Corollary *n.* تابعة . نتيجة

Coronation *n.* تَتْوِيجٌ

Coroner *n.* { مَأْمُورٌ يفحصُ سَبَبَ مَوْتٍ فُجَائِيٍّ

Coronet *n.* تاجُ الأشرافِ . إِكْلِيل

Corporal *a.* or *n.* { جَسَدِيٌّ . (أُونْبَاشِي)

Corporation *n.* شرْكةٌ

Corporeal *a.* ذو جَسَدٍ . جسدَانِيٌّ

Corps *n.* فَيْلَقُ عسْكَرٍ . جَمَاعَةٌ

Corpse *n.* جُثَّةُ الْمَيْتِ

Corpulence / Corpulency } *n.* سَمَانَةٌ . جسَامَةٌ

Corpulent *a.* سمينٌ . جَسِيمٌ

Corpuscle *n.* ذَرَّةٌ . جُسَيْمٌ

Correct *v. t.* اصلَحَ . نقَّحَ . ادَّب

Correct *a.* صَحِيحٌ . مَضْبُوط

Correction *n.* إِصْلَاحٌ . تَنْقِيحٌ تَأْدِيبٌ

Corrective *a.* مُصْلِحٌ . تَأْدِيبِيٌّ

Correctly *ad.* بِضَبْطٍ . تماماً

Correctness *n.* ضَبْط . مُطابقَةٌ لِلْحقِّ

Correlate *v.t.* or *i.* ناسَبَ . تَنَاسَبَ

Correlation *n.* نسبَةٌ . مُناسبة

Correlation *n.* نسبَةٌ مُتبادلة

Correlative *a.* or *n.* { نِسبي مُتَبَادَلٌ . ذُو نِسبَةٍ مُتبادَلةٍ

Correspond *v. i.* طابَقَ . رَاسَلَ

Correspondence *n.* مُرَاسلَةٌ . مناسبَة

Correspondent *n.* or *a.* مُرَاسِلٌ . مُنَاسِبٌ

Corridor *n.* رِوَاق . أَزْوِقة

Corroborate *v. t.* شَدَّدَ . اثبَتَ . أَيَّدَ

Corroboration *n.* إِثْبَاتٌ . تأْيِيدٌ

Corrode *v. i.* or *t.* صَدِيءَ . قرضَ ـِ

Corrodent / Corrosive } *a.* آكِلٌ . قارِضٌ

Corrosion *n.* صَدَأٌ . قَرْضٌ

Corrugation *n.* تجعُّدٌ

Corrupt *v. t.* or *a.* { افسَدَ . نجَّس . فاسِدٌ

Corruptible *a.* فاسِدٌ . فَانٍ

Corruption *n.* فسَادٌ . نجاسة

Corruptive *a.* مُفسِدٌ . مُنَجِّسٌ

Corruptness *n.* فسَادٌ

Corsair *n.* قُرصَانُ البَحْرِ

Corselet *n.* زَرْدِيَّةٌ . دِرْعٌ

Corset *n.* مَشَدٌّ لِلنِّسَاءِ

Cortege *n.* مَوْكِبٌ

Coruscate *v. i.* بَرَقَ . لَمَعَ ـَ

Corvée *n.* سُخْرَةٌ

Corvette *n.* بَارِجَة صَغِيرَةٌ

Cosmetic *a.* or *n.* } مُحَسِّنٌ لِلَوْنِ الوَجْهِ

Cosmogony *n.* عِلمُ تكوينِ الكَوْنِ

Cosmography *n.* عِلمُ وَصفِ الكَوْنِ

Cosmology *n.* عِلمٌ يَبحَثُ عَنِ الكَوْنِ

Cosmopolitan *n.* رَجُلٌ وَطنُهُ العَالَمُ

Cost *n.* or *v. t.* or *i.* قِيمَةٌ . سِعْرٌ . كلَّفَ

Costal *a.* ضِلْعِيٌّ

Costive *a.* قابِضُ الامعَاءِ

Costiveness *n.* قَبْضُ الامعَاءِ

Costliness *n.* غَلاَءٌ

Costly *a.* غالٍ

Costume *n.* زِيٌّ ج أَزْيَاءٌ

Cot *n.* كُوخ . فِرَاشٌ صَغِيرٌ

Cote *n.* حَظِيرَةٌ . صِيرَةٌ

Coterie *n.* جَمَاعَةُ اصْحَابٍ

Cotemporaneous *a.* / Cotemporary *n.* مُعَاصِرٌ

Cottage *n.* كُوخ . بَيْتٌ صَغِيرٌ

Cottager *n.* سَاكِنُ كُوخٍ

Cotton *n.* or *a.* قُطْنٌ . قُطْنِيٌّ

Cotton-gin *n.* مَحْلَجُ ٱلْقُطْنِ

Cotyledon *n.* فِلْقَةُ بِزْرَةٍ

Couch *v. i.* or *t.* اِضْطَجَعَ . كَمَنَ أَضْجَعَ

Couch *n.* فِرَاشٌ

Cough *v. i.* or *n.* سَعَلَ ـُ سُعَالٌ

Council *n.* مَجْلِسُ ٱلشُّورَى

Councillor *n.* عَضْوُ مَجْلِسٍ . مُشِيرٌ

Counsel *n.* or *v. t.* نَصِيحَةٌ . نَصَحَ

Counsellor *n.* نَاصِحٌ . مُشِيرٌ . فَقِيهٌ

Count *v. t.* or *n.* عَدَّ . احْصَى . اَمِيرٌ

Countenance *n.* مُحَيًّا . طَلْعَةٌ

Countenance *v. t.* عَضَدَ ـَ

Counter *n.* or *ad.* مَائِدَةُ مَخْزَنٍ . ضِدَّ

Counteract *v. t.* ضَادَّ . خَيَّبَ

Counteraction *n.* مُضَادَّة . إِبْطَالٌ

Counterbalance *n.* or *v. t.* مُوَازَنَة . وَازَنَ . عَادَلَ

Counterfeit *a.* or *n.* or *v. t.* مُزَوَّرٌ . زَوَّرَ

Countermand *n.* or *v. t.* أَمْرٌ يُبْطِلُ امْراً . أَلْغَى

Countermarch *v. i.* or *n.* قَهْقَرَ . قَهْقَرَى

Counterpane *n.* لِحَافُ فِرَاشٍ

Counterpart *n.* قِسْمٌ مقَابِلَ قِسْمٍ

Counterplot *n.* حِيلَةٌ ضِدَّ حِيلَةٍ

Counterpoise *n.* or *v. t.* ثِقْلٌ . مُوَازِنٌ . وَازَنَ

Countersign *n.* كَلِمَةُ سِرِّ ٱللَّيْلِ

Countersign *v. t.* امْضَى إِثْبَاتاً لِلإِمْضَاءِ

Countess *n.* امِيرَةٌ

Counting-house *n.* مَكْتَبُ ٱلتَّاجِرِ

Countless *a.* مَا لا يُحصَى

Country *n.* بِلَاد . بَرِّيَّة

Countryman *n.* إِبْنُ بِلَادٍ . فلاحٌ

County *n.* لِوَاءٌ مِن بِلَادٍ

Couple *n.* or *v. t.* زَوْجٌ . إِثْنَانِ . وَصَلَ

Couplet *n.* بَيْتَا شِعْرٍ

Coupling *n.* رَابِطٌ . مُوْصِلٌ . وَصلٌ

Courage *n.* شَجَاعَة . بسَالَة

Courageous *a.* شُجَاعٌ . بَاسِلٌ

Courier *n.* رَسُوْلٌ . بَرِيْدٌ

Course *n.* سَيْرٌ . طَرِيقٌ . ناحية

Courser *n.* فَرَسٌ سَرِيعٌ

Court *n.* or *v. t.* دَارٌ . مَحكمة . تَملق

Courteous *a.* انِيْسٌ . ادِيْبٌ

Courtesan *n.* زَانِيَةٌ . فاجِرَةٌ

Courtesy *n.* انسٌ . ادَبٌ . إِنسَانِيةٌ

Courtier *n.* مُلازِمُ بلَاطِ آلمَلِك

Courtliness *n.* ادَبٌ . لُطفٌ مَعَ شَرَفٍ

Courtly *a.* ادِيبٌ . شرِيفٌ

Court-martial *n.* محكمَة عسكَرِيَّة

Court-plaster *n.* لَزُوقٌ من حَرِيْرٍ

Courtship *n.* تَملُّقٌ

Courtyard *n.* حوشٌ . دَارٌ

Cousin *n.* إِبْنُ عَمٍّ اوْ عَمَّةٍ او خَالٍ اوْ خالَةٍ او إِبْنَتهُمْ

Cove *n.* خلِيجٌ صَغِيرٌ . خوْرٌ

Covenant *n.* or *v. t.* عهْدٌ . عَاهَدَ

Cover *v. t.* or *n.* ستَرَ . غطَّى . غِطَاءٌ

Covering *n.* غِطَاءٌ . سِتْرٌ

Coverlet *n.* لحَافٌ . دِثَارٌ

Covert *n.* or *a.* مَأوًى . مَستُوْرٌ . سرِّيٌّ

Covertly *ad.* سرًّا . خُفيَةً

Covet *v. t.* إِشتهَى . طمِعَ فِي-

Covetous *a.* مُشتهٍ . طَمَّاعٌ

Covetousness *n.* شهْوَةٌ . طمَعٌ

Covey *n.* سِربٌ مِنْ (طيُوْرٍ)

Cow *n.* بقَرَةٌ

Coward *n.* جَبَانٌ ج جُبَنَاء

Cowardice *n.* جَبَانَة . جُبْن

Cowardly *a.* or *ad.* جَبَانٌ . بِجَبَانَةٍ

Cower *v. i.* خَرَّ أَوْ تَرَدَّدَ مِنَ ٱلْخَوْفِ

Cowherd *n.* رَاعِي بَقَرٍ

Cowhide *n.* جِلْدُ بَقَرٍ أَوْ سَوْطٌ مِنْهُ

Cowl *n.* قَلَنْسُوَةٌ ج قَلَانِسُ

Coxcomb *n.* مُعْجَبٌ . مُتَحَذْلِقٌ . بَلْتَعَانِيٌّ

Cowpox *n.* جُدَرِيُّ ٱلْبَقَرِ

Coy *a.* مُتَصَاوِنٌ . مُعْتَزِلٌ عَنْ ٱلْمُعَاشَرَةِ

Cozen *v. t.* خَدَعَ ـَ . غَشَّ

Cozy *a.* مُسْتَرِيحٌ

Crab *n.* سَرَطَانٌ

Crabbed *a.* خَشِنُ ٱلْجَانِبِ . فَظٌّ

Crack *n.* or *v. t.* or *i.* شَقٌّ . شَقَّ . تَشَقَّقَ (طَقَّ)

Cracker *n.* كَعْكٌ يَابِسٌ . بَقْسُمَاط

Crackle *v. i.* (قَرْقَعَ . طَقْطَقَ)

Cradle *n.* or *v. t.* سَرِيرٌ . وَضَعَ فِي سَرِيرٍ

Craft *n.* حِرْفَة سَفِينَةٌ صَغِيرَة

Craft / **Craftiness** *n.* دَهَاءٌ . مَكْرٌ

Craftsman *n.* صَانِعٌ . مُحْتَرِفٌ

Crafty *a.* دَاهٍ . مُحْتَالٌ

Crag *n.* صَخْرٌ شَاهِقٌ . غَلِيظ

Cragged / **Craggy** *a.* صَخْرِيٌّ . غَلِيظ

Cram *v. t.* or *i.* حَشَا ـُ أَفْعَمَ

Cramp *n.* or *v. t.* كُزَازٌ . كُلَّابٌ . ضَيَّقَ عَلَى . اعَاقَ

Crane *n.* كُرْكِيٌّ . آلَة لِرَفْعِ ٱلْأَثْقَالِ

Cranial *a.* قِحْفِيٌّ

Cranium *n.* جُمْجُمَة . قِحْفٌ

Crank *n.* يَدُ دُولَابٍ أَوْ آلَةُ ٱلتَّدْوِيرِ

Crape *n.* (كُرَيْشَة) . نَسِيجٌ

Crash *v.i.* or *n.* صَوَّتَ صَوْتُ كَسْرٍ

Crass *a.* خَشِنٌ . غَلِيظ

Crate *n.* قَفَصٌ لِنَقْلِ صُحُونٍ فخارِيةٍ

Crater *n.* فُوهُ بُرْكَان

Craunch *v. t.* مَضَغَ . سَحَقَ بِالأسْنان

Cravat *n.* رَبْطَة رَقَبَة

Crave *v. t.* طَلَبَ . إشْتَهَى إشْتَاق

Craven *a.* or *n.* جَبَانٌ . نَذْلٌ

Craving *n.* تلهُّفٌ . إشْتِهَاء

Crawl *v. i.* دَبَّ ـِ . زَحفَ ـَ

Crayon *n.* or *v. t.* قَلَمُ رَصَاصٍ . رَسَمَ به

Craze *v. t.* جَنَّنَ

Craziness *n.* جُنُونٌ . إخْتِلالُ ٱلْعَقْلِ

Crazy *a.* مَجْنُونٌ . مُخْتَلُّ ٱلْعَقْلِ

Creak *v. i.* صَرَفَ ـِ صريفًا

Cream *n.* زُبْدَة اللَّبَن . قِشدَة

Crease *v. t.* or *n.* غضَّنَ . غَضْنٌ

Create *v. t.* خَلَقَ ـُ . بَرَأَ ـَ ابدَعَ

Creation *n.* خَلْقٌ خليقَةٌ . بَرِيَّة

Creative *a.* خَالِقٌ . مُبْدِعٌ

Creator *n.* خَالِق . ألْبَارِئ

Creature *n.* خَلِيقَة . مخلوقٌ . برِية

Credence *n.* ثِقَةٌ . تَصْدِيقٌ

Credentials *pl.* شَهَادَاتٌ رَسْمِيَّة

Credibility *n.* إستِحْقَاقُ ٱلتصْدِيقِ

Credible *a.* مُسْتَحَقُّ ٱلتَّصْدِيقِ

Credit *n.* or *v. t.* ثِقَة . امَّن

Creditable *a.* مَوْثُوق بِهِ . مُعتَبَرٌ

Creditor *n.* دَائِنٌ . صَاحِبُ دَيْنٍ

Credulity *n.* سُهُولَةُ ٱلتَّصْدِيق

Credulous *a.* سَهْلُ ٱلتَّصْدِيقِ

Creed *n.* مذهَبٌ . قَانُون الإيمَانِ

Creek *n.* جُون . نَهْرٌ صَغِيرٌ

Creep *v. i.* دبَّ ـِ . زَحَفَ ـَ

Creeper *n.* نبْتٌ مُتعَرِّشٌ اوْ مُتَسلِّق

Cremation *n.* حَرْق . حَرْقُ ٱلْجُثَّة

Crescent *n.* هِلالٌ

Cress *n.* رَشَاد . قُرَّةُ ٱلْعَيْنِ

Crest *n.* قُنبُرَة . قِمَّة

Crest-fallen *a.* مُنحَط . ذليلٌ

Cretacious *a.* طَبَاشِيْرِيٌّ

Crevice *n.* شَقٌّ ج شُقُوقٌ

Crew *n.* مَلَّاحُو ٱلسَّفِيْنَةِ . جَمَاعَةٌ

Crib *n.* مِذْوَدٌ . مَهْدٌ

Cricket *n.* صُرْصُرٌ

Crier *n.* مُنَادٍ . مُؤَذِّنٌ

Crime *n.* جَرِيمَةٌ . جِنَايَةٌ . جُنَاحٌ

Criminal *n.* or *a.* مُذْنِبٌ . جِنَائِيٌّ

Criminality *n.* جِنَائِيَّةٌ . ذَنْبِيَّةٌ

Criminate *v. t.* إِسْتَذْنَبَ . جَنَّحَ

Crimination *n.* إِسْتِذْنَابٌ . تَجْنِيْحٌ

Crimp *v. t.* or *a.* جَعَّدَ . قَصِمٌ

Crimson *n.* or *a.* قِرْمِزٌ . قِرْمِزِيٌّ

Cringe *v. i.* تَذَلَّلَ لِ

Cringer / Cringeling } *n.* مُتَذَلِّلٌ

Cripple *n.* or *v. t.* كَسِيْحٌ . صَيَّرَ كَسِيْحاً

Crisis *n.* بُحْرَانٌ . نُقْطَةُ ٱلْخَطَرِ وَٱلتَّغَيُّرِ . أَزْمَةٌ

Crisp *a.* قَصِمٌ . مُجَعَّدٌ

Criterion *n.* دَلِيْلٌ . مِقْيَاسٌ

Critic *n.* مُنْتَقِدٌ . مُنَكِّتٌ

Critical *a.* إِنْتِقَادِيٌّ . مُدَقِّقٌ . مُخْطِرٌ

Criticise *v. t.* إِنْتَقَدَ . نَكَّتَ

Criticism / Critique } *n.* إِنْتِقَادٌ . تَنْكِيْتٌ

Croak *v. i.* or *n.* نَعَقَ ـَ . نَعِيْقٌ

Croaker *n.* نَاعِقٌ . مُتَذَمِّرٌ

Crockery *n.* خَزَفٌ . فَخَّارٌ

Crocodile *n.* تِمْسَاحٌ

Crocus *n.* زَعْفَرَان

Crony *n.* خِلٌّ . نَدِيْمٌ

Crook *v. t.* or *n.* عَقَفَ ـِ . عَصَا ٱلرَّاعِي

Crooked *a.* أَعْقَفُ . مُلْتَوٍ

Crookedness *n.* إِعْوِجَاجٌ . إِنْعِقَافٌ

Crop *n.* غَلَّةٌ . حَوْصَلَةٌ

Crosier *n.* عُكَّازُ ٱلْأُسْقُفِ

Cross *n.* or *a.* صَلِيْبٌ . نَكِدٌ

Cross *v. t.* or *i.* عَبَرَ ـُ عارَضَ
Cross-bow *n.* قَوْسُ ٱلسِّهَامِ
Cross-eyed *a.* أَحْوَلُ
Crossing *n.* معبَرٌ . عُبُورٌ
Crossgrained *a.* شَابِكٌ . نَكِدٌ
Crosslegged *a.* مُتَرَبِّعٌ
Cross-purpose *n.* قَصْدٌ مُتَضَادٌّ
Cross-question *v. t.* إِسْتَنطَقَ . حقق
Cross-road *n.* مُصَلَّبُ ٱلطُّرُقِ
Crosswise *ad.* عَرْضاً
Crotch *n.* مَفْرَقُ أَغْصانٍ
Crotchet *n.* وَهْمٌ . تَصَوُّرٌ بَاطِلٌ
Crouch *v. i.* رَبَضَ . جَثَا ـُ
Croup *n.* دَآءُ ٱلذَّبْحَةِ
Crow *n.* or *v. i.* غُرَابٌ . صَاحَ (ٱلدِّيكُ)
Crow-bar *n.* مُخْلٌ ج أَمْخَالٌ
Crowd *n.* or *v. t.* زَحْمَةٌ . زَاحَمَ
Crown *n.* or *v. t.* تَاجٌ . تَوَّجَ

Crown-prince *n.* وَلِيُّ ٱلْعَهْدِ
Crucial *a.* صَلِيبِيٌّ . شَدِيدٌ . حَتْمِيٌّ
Crucible *n.* بُوتَقَةٌ
Crucifix *n.* صَلِيبٌ عَلَيْهِ صُورَةُ ٱلْمَسِيحِ
Crucifixion *n.* صَلْبٌ
Cruciform *a.* صَلِيبِيُّ ٱلشَّكْلِ
Crucify *v. t.* صَلَبَ ـِ
Crude *a.* نِيٌّ . غَيْرُ مُتْقَنٍ
Crudity / Crudeness *n.* عَدَمُ إِتْقَانٍ . فَجَاجَةٌ
Cruel *a.* قَاسٍ . صَارِمٌ
Cruelty *n.* قَسَاوَةٌ . صَرَامَةٌ
Cruet *n.* قَارُورَةٌ
Cruise *n.* or *v. i.* طَافَ ـُ . طَوَافٌ بَحْراً
Cruiser *n.* بَارِجَةٌ طَوَّافَةٌ أَوْ سَرِيعَةٌ
Crum / Crumb *n.* كِسْرَةٌ صَغِيرَةٌ
Crumble *v. t.* or *i.* فَتَّتَ . تَفَتَّتَ
Crumple *v. t.* or *i.* غَضَّنَ تَغَضَّنَ
Crupper *n.* (قُوشٌ) . (اصَالٌ)

Crusade *n.* حَرْبُ ٱلصَّلِيبِيَّةِ . جِهَادٌ

Crusader *n.* مُحَارِبٌ صَلِيبِيٌّ

Crush *v. t.* سَحَقَ . حطَّمَ . اذَلَّ

Crust *n.* or *v. t.* قُشْرٌ . لَبَّسَ بِقِشْرٍ

Crustacious *a.* ذُوْ قِشْرٍ أَوْصَدَفَةٍ

Crusty *a.* فظٌّ . شَرِسٌ . قِشرِيٌّ

Crutch *n.* عُكَّازٌ

Cry *v. i.* or *n.* صَرَخَ ـُ . بَكى ـِ . صُرَاخ

Crying *a.* صَارِخٌ . مَشْهُوْرٌ . عَظِيمٌ

Crypt *n.* مُخْدَعٌ تَحْتَ ٱلأَرْض

Crystal *n.* بَلُّوْرٌ وَبِلَّوْرٌ

Crystalline *a.* بَلُّوْرِيٌّ . شَفَّافٌ

Crystallize *v. i.* or *t.* تَبَلْوَرَ . بِلْوَرَ

Cub *n.* جَرْوٌ . شِبْلٌ

Cube *n.* or *v. t.* كَعْبٌ . مُكَعَّبٌ . كَعَّبَ

Cubic / Cubiform } *a.* مُكَعَّبُ ٱلشَّكْلِ

Cubit *n.* ذِرَاعٌ ج أَذْرُع

Cucumber *n.* خِيَارٌ . قُثَّاء

Cud *n.* جِرَّةٌ

Cuddle *v. i.* or *t.* إِستَكَنَّ عِنْدَ . حضَنَ

Cudgel *n.* نبُّوْتٌ . هرَاوَةٌ

Cue *n.* ذيْلٌ . إِشَارَة . تَلْمِيحٌ

Cuff *n.* or *v. t.* كُمُّ ٱلقَمِيصِ . لَطَمَ ـِ

Cuirass *n.* دِرْعٌ ج اَدْرَاعٌ وَدُرُوْعٌ

Cuirassier *n.* لَابِسُ دِرْعٍ . مُدَرَّعٌ

Culinary *a.* طَبْخِيٌّ

Cull *v. t.* نخَبَ ـُ . إِنْتَخَبَ

Cullender *n.* مِصفَاةٌ

Culminate *v. i.* بَلَغَ اعْلَاهُ

Culmination *n.* غَايَةُ ٱلبُلُوغِ

Culpable *a.* مَلُوْمٌ . مُخْطِيٌّ

Culpability *n.* ذَنْبٌ . إِسْتِحْقَاقُ ٱللَّوْمِ

Culprit *n.* مُذْنِبٌ

Cultivable *a.* قَابِلُ ٱلحِرَاثَةِ

Cultivate *v. t.* حَرَثَ ـُ . هَذَّبَ

Cultivation / Culture } *n.* حِرَاثَةٌ . تَهْذِيبٌ

Cumber *v. t.* ثَقَّلَ . أَعَاقَ . لَبَّكَ

Cumbersome / **Cumbrous** *a.* ثَقِيلٌ . مُلَبِّكٌ

Cumulate *v. t.* رَكَمَ ـُ كَوَّمَ

Cumulative *a.* مُتَجَمِّعٌ . مُتَزَايِدٌ

Cuneiform / **Cuniform** *a.* إِسْفِينِيُّ ٱلشَّكْلِ

Cunning *a.* or *n.* دَاهٍ . دَاهِيَة . دَهَاءٌ

Cup *n.* or *v. t.* كَاسٌ . فِنْجَان . حَجَمَ ـُ

Cupbearer *n.* سَاقٍ . سَاقِي مَلِكٍ

Cupboard *n.* (خِزَانَةٌ) (دُوْلَابٌ)

Cupidity *n.* طَمَعٌ . جَشَعٌ

Cupola *n.* قُبَّةٌ

Cur *n.* كَلْبٌ . شَاكِسٌ . فَظٌّ

Curable *a.* قَابِلُ ٱلشِّفَاءِ

Curacy *n.* مَقَامُ قَسِّيسٍ أَوْ خُورِيّ

Curate *n.* قَسِّيسٌ . خُورِيٌّ

Curative *a.* شَافٍ

Curator *n.* وَكِيلٌ . حَافِظ

Curb *n.* or *v. t.* شَكِيمَة . صَدٌّ . كَبَحَ ـَ

Curd *n.* رَوْبٌ . خَثْرَة . لَبَنٌ رَائِبٌ

Curdle *v. i.* or *t.* خَثَرَ . خَثَّرَ

Cure *v. t.* or *n.* شَفَى . شِفَاءٌ

Curiosity *n.* إِسْتِطْلَاعٌ . نَادِرَة

Curious *a.* مُسْتَطْلِعٌ . نَادِرٌ

Curl *n.* or *v. t.* or *i.* جُعْدَة . جَعَّدَ . تَجَعَّدَ

Curly *a.* مُتَجَعِّدٌ . جُعْدِيٌّ

Currants *n. pl.* عِنَبُ ٱلثَّعْلَبِ . كِشْمِشٌ

Currency *n.* مُعَامَلَة . نُقُوْدٌ . جَرَيَانٌ

Current *a.* or *n.* جَارٍ . مَجْرًى

Currier *n.* مُصْلِحُ جُلُوْدٍ مَدْبُوغَةٍ

Curry *v. t.* اصْلَحَ (جُلُوداً) حَسَّ (فَرَساً)

Curse *v. t.* or *n.* لَعَنَ . لَعْنَة

Cursed *a.* مَلْعُونٌ . مَكْرُوهٌ

Cursorily *ad.* بِسُرْعَةٍ . بِلَا دِقَّةٍ

Cursory *a.* سَرِيعٌ . غَيْرُ مُدَقِّق

Curt *a.* قَصِيرٌ . فَظٌّ

Curtail *v. t.* قَصَّرَ . اوْجَزَ

Curtain *n.* or *v. t.* سِتارٌ نصبَ سِتاراً

Curvature / **Curve** *n.* إِنْحِنَاءٌ . قَوْسٌ

Curve *v. t.* or *i.* قوَّسَ . إِنْحَنَى

Cushion *n.* وِسادَة . مخدَّة

Custodian *n.* وَكِيلٌ . مُحَافِظ

Custody *n.* وِكَالَة . مُحافظة . حبسٌ

Custom *n.* عَادَة . دأْبٌ

Customary *a.* إِعتِيَادِيٌّ . مَأْلُوفٌ

Cutomer *n.* زُبُون ج زُبَنَاءُ

Custom-house *n.* (جُمْرُكٌ) دِيوَان الرُّسُومَاتِ

Customs *n.* رُسُومَاتٌ . (جمَارِك)

Cut *v. t.* or *n.* قطعَ . قطْعٌ

Cutaneous *a.* جلْديٌّ

Cuticle *n.* بَشرَةُ الجِلْدِ

Cutlass *n.* سَيْفٌ عَرِيضٌ قصِيرٌ

Cutlery *n.* ادوَاتُ القَطْعِ كالسَّكَاكِينِ

Cutlet *n.* قِطعة لَحمٍ لِلشَّيِّ (كستلاتا)

Cutter *n.* سَفِينَة صَغِيرة

Cutting *a.* or *n.* قاطِعٌ . مُؤْلِمٌ . قطعَة

Cwt *n.* عَلامَةُ مئةِ لِيبْرَا انكليزِيَةٍ

Cyclamen *n.* بَخُورُ مَرْيَمَ (نبات)

Cycle *n.* دَائِرَة . دَوْرٌ

Cyclone *n.* زَوْبَعَةٌ عظِيمة

Cyclopean *a.* كَبِيرٌ جِدًّا

Cyclopedia *n.* دَائِرَةُ المَعَارِفِ

Cylinder *n.* اسْطُوَانَةٌ ج اسَاطِينُ

Cylindrical *a.* اسْطُوَانِيٌّ

Cymbal *n.* صَنْجٌ ج صُنوجٌ

Cynic *n.* / **Cynical** *a.* شَرِسٌ . فَظٌّ

Cypress *n.* سَرْوٌ . سَرْوَة

Cyprian / **Cypriote** *a.* or *n.* قبْرُسِيٌّ

Cyst *n.* كِيسٌ غِشائِيٌّ

Czar *n.* قَيْصَرُ رُوسِيَّا

Czarina *n.* إِمْرَاةُ القَيصرِ

Czarowitz *n.* وَلِيُّ عهْدِ رُوسِيَّا

D

Dab *v. t.* مَلَثَ ـُ . لطخَ ـَ

Dabble *v. i.* لَعِبَ فِي وبٍ . لَطخَ

Dad / **Daddy** } *n.* أَبٌ (بِلُغَةِ ٱلْاوْلَادِ)

Daft *a.* بَلِيدٌ . مَجنُونٌ

Dagger *n.* خَنْجَرٌ ج خَنَاجِرُ

Dahlia *n.* دَالِيَا (نَبَاتٌ)

Daily *a.* or *ad.* يَوْمِيٌّ . يَوْمِيًّا

Daintly *ad.* بِتَأَنُّقٍ

Daisy *n.* أُقحُوَانٌ

Dainty *a.* نَفِيسٌ . أَنِيقٌ

Dairy *n.* مَلْبَنٌ . مَجْبَنَةٌ

Dale *n.* وَادٍ ج اوْدِيَةٌ

Dalliance *n.* مُدَاعَبَةٌ . مُلَاعَبَةٌ

Dally *v. i.* دَاعَبَ . غَازَلَ . لَاعَبَ

Dam *v. t.* سدَّ ـُ . حَجَرَ

Dam *n.* سَدٌّ . امُّ بَهِيمَةٍ

Damage *n.* or *v. t.* ضَرَرٌ . أَضرَّ

Damask *n.* نَسِيجٌ نَفِيسٌ مُنَقَّشٌ

Dame *n.* سَيِّدَةٌ

Damn *v. t.* دَانَ ـِ . لعنَ ـَ

Damnable *a.* مَلْعُونٌ . مَكْرُوهٌ

Damnation *n.* دَيْنُونَةٌ . هَلَاكٌ

Damp *a.* or *n.* رَطِبٌ . رُطُوبَةٌ

Dampen *v. t.* رَطَّبَ . بَلَّ ـُ

Damper *n.* صِمَامُ مَدْخَنَةٍ

Dampness *n.* رُطُوبَةٌ

Damsel *n.* فَتَاةٌ . بِنْتٌ

Dance *v. i.* or *n.* رَقَصَ ـُ . رَقصٌ

Dandelion *n.* نَابُ الْاسدِ (نَبَاتٌ)

Daddle *v. t.* رَقَّصَ (طِفلاً) . دَلَّلَ

Dandruff *n.* هِبْرِيَةُ الرَّأْسِ . أَقِشْرَةُ

Dandy *n.* أَنِيقٌ . مُتَأَنِّقٌ

Danger *n.* خَطَرٌ

Dangerous *a.* خَطِرٌ . مُخْطِرٌ

Dangle *v. i.* تَدَلَّى

Dank *a.* مُبْتَلٌّ . رَطْبٌ

Dapple / **Dappled** *a.* أَرْقَطُ

Dard *v. i.* or *t.* تَجَاسَرَ . إِقْتَحَمَ

Daring *a.* مِتَجَاسِرٌ . جَسُورٌ

Dark *a.* or *n.* مُظْلِمٌ . أَغْبَشُ . ظَلَامٌ

Darken *v. t.* or *i.* أَظْلَمَ . عَتَّمَ

Darkly *ad.* مُظْلِماً

Darkness *n.* ظَلَامٌ . قِتَامٌ

Darling *a.* or *n.* عَزِيزٌ . حَبِيبٌ

Darn *v. t.* رَتَقَ ـُـ . رفا ـَـ

Darnel *n.* زَوَانٌ

Dart *n.* or *v. t.* or *i.* سَهْمٌ . رَمَى . إِنْقَضَّ

Dash *v. t.* صَدَمَ ـِـ . إِقْتَحَمَ . كَسَّرَ

Dash *n.* علامةُ فَصْلٍ كَذَا (—)

Dastard *n.* خسِيسٌ . لَئِيمٌ

Dastardly *a.* جَبَانٌ . لَئِيمٌ

Data *n. pl.* مَوَادٌّ . مَوْضُوعٌ

Date *n.* or *v. t.* تَارِيخٌ . تَمْرَةٌ . أَرَّخَ

Daub *v. t.* طَيَّنَ . دَهَنَ

Daughter *n.* بِنْتٌ أَوْ ابْنَةٌ

Daughter-in-law *n.* كَنَّةٌ

Daunt *v. t.* افْزَعَ . ارْهَبَ

Dauntless *a.* جَسُورٌ . جَرِيٌّ

Dauphin *n.* وَلِيُّ عَهْدِ فَرَنْسَا

Dawn *n.* or *v. i.* فَجْرٌ . أَفْجَرَ

Day *n.* يَوْمٌ . نَهَارٌ

Day-break / **Day-spring** *n.* فَجْرٌ . فَلَقٌ

Daylight *n.* ضَوْءُ النَّهَارِ

Daze / **Dazzel** *v. t.* جَهَرَ ـَـ . أَسْدَرَ

Deacon *n.* شَمَّاسٌ ج شَمَامِسَةٌ

Dead *a.* or *n.* مَيْتٌ ج أَمْوَاتٌ

Deaden *v. t.* أَضْعَفَ . أَخْمَدَ

Dead-letter *n.* مُهْمَلٌ

Deadlock *n.* وَرْطَةٌ . مُعْضِلَةٌ

Deadly *a.* مُهْلِكٌ . مُمِيتٌ

Deaf *a.* اصَمُّ . اطرَشُ

Deafen *v. t.* أَصَمَّ

Deaf-mute *n.* أَطرَشُ . اخرَسُ

Deafness *n.* صمَمٌ . طرَشٌ

Deal *v. t.* or *i.* وَزَّعَ . تَاجَرَ . عَامل

Dealer *n.* تَاجِرٌ . بَيَاعٌ

Dean *n.* ثَانِي ٱلْاسقُفِ . رَئِيسُ عُمْدَةِ مَدرَسَةٍ أَوْ كَاتِبُهَا

Dear *a.* عزِيزٌ . غَال

Dearth *n.* مجَاعَةٌ . قَحْطٌ

Death *n.* مَوْتٌ

Deathless *a.* خَالِدٌ

Debar *v. t.* مَنَعَ ـ . صدَّ عَنْ

Debase *v. t.* أَذلَّ . افْسَدَ

Debasement *n.* إِذْلَالٌ . دَنَاءَةٌ

Debasing *a.* مُفْسِدٌ . مذِلٌّ

Debate *v.t.* or *n.* نَاظَرَ بَاحَثَ . مُنَاقَشَةٌ

Debauch *n.* or *v. t.* خلَاعَة . أَفْسَدَ

Debauchery *n.* خلَاعَةٌ . فسْقٌ

Debilitate *v. t.* أَضْعَفَ . اوْهَنَ

Debility *n.* ضَعفٌ . وَهْنٌ . وَنَاءٌ

Debt *n.* دَيْنٌ ج دُيُونٌ

Debtor *n.* مَدْيُون

Decade *n.* مُدَّةُ عَشْرِ سِنِينَ

Decadence *n.* إِنحِطَاطٌ

Decalogue *n.* أَلْوَصَايَا ٱلْعَشْرُ

Decamp *v. i.* بَرِحَ ٱلْمَحَلَةَ . إِنسَلَّ

Decanter *n.* قَنِّينَة

Decapitate *v. t.* قَطعَ ٱلرَّأْسَ

Decay *v. i.* or *n.* إِنحَطَّ . فَنِيَ ـ فَنَاءٌ

Decease *v. i.* or *n.* مَاتَ . مَوْتٌ . وَفَاة

Deceased *a.* مَيتٌ . مَرْحُومٌ

Deceit *n.* غِش . مَكرٌ . خَدِيعَة

Deceitful *a.* غَاشٌّ . خَدَّاعٌ

Deceive *v. t.* غَشَّ ـُ . خَدَعَ . خَادع

December *n.* شَهْرُ كَانُون الأوَّل

Decency *n.* لِيَاقة . حِشْمَة

Decennial *a.* حَادِثٌ كُلَّ عَشْرِ سنِين مَرَّةً

Decent *a.* لاَئقٌ . مُوَافِقٌ

Deception *n.* خَدِيعَة . غرُورٌ . غش

Deceptive *a.* غرَّارٌ . غَاشٌّ

Decide *v. t.* عَزَمَ ـِ . حتمَ ـ . أنهى

Decided *a.* مَحتُومٌ . عَزُومٌ . وَاضِحٌ

Decimal *a.* عَشْرِيٌّ

Decimate *v. t.* قَتلَ عُشْراً

Decipher *v. t.* فَسَّرَ . حلَّ

Decision *n.* حَتْمٌ . حُكمٌ . فَتوى

Decisive *a.* قاطِع . جازمٌ . حَتمِيٌّ

Deck *v.t.* or *n.* زيَّنَ . ظَهْرُ السفِينَة

Declaim *v. i.* خَطَبَ ـُ . اكْثَرَ الكَلام

Declamation *n.* خطَابٌ . خُطْبَة

Declamatory *a.* خِطابِيٌّ كَثِيرُ الكَلام

Declaration *n.* قرارٌ . تصْرِيحٌ

Declare *v. t.* اقرَّ . صَرَّحَ بِ . شهرَ

Declension *n.* تصْرِيفُ الأسْمَاءِ إنحرَافٌ

Declination *n.* إنحرَافٌ . رَفْضٌ

Decline *v. t.* or *i.* صرَفَ . إنحَرَفَ . إنحط

Declivity *n.* احْدُورٌ . متَحدِّرٌ

Decoct *v. t.* غلَى ـ

Decoction *n.* مغلِيٌّ

Decompose *v.t.* or *i.* حلَّ . فَسدَ ـُ

Decomposition *n.* إنحِلاَلٌ . فَسَادٌ

Decorate *v. t.* زيَّنَ . زَخْرَفَ

Decoration *n.* زِينَةٌ . نِيشَانٌ

Decorative *a.* مُزَيَّنٌ. مُزَخْرَفٌ

Decorous *a.* اَدِيبٌ. لائِقٌ

Decorum *n.* أَدَبٌ. لِيَاقَةُ التَّصَرُّفِ

Decoy *v. t* or *n.* أَغْوَى. حِيلَةٌ

Decrease *v. t.* or *i.* or *n.* قَلَّلَ. نَقَصَ ـُ نَقْصٌ

Decree *v. t.* or *n.* أَصْدَرَ أَمْرًا. أَمْرٌ

Decreed *a.* or *pp.* مَحْتُومٌ. مُقَدَّرٌ

Decrepitude *n.* هَرَمٌ. عَجْزٌ

Dedicate *v. t.* قَدَّسَ. كَرَّسَ (دَشَّنَ)

Dedication *n.* تَقْدِيسٌ. تَكْرِيسٌ

Deduce *v. t.* إِسْتَدَلَّ. إِسْتَنْتَجَ

Deducible *a.* مُمْكِنٌ إِسْتِنْتَاجُهُ

Deduct *v. t.* طَرَحَ ـَ أَسْقَطَ

Deduction *n.* إِسْقَاطٌ. إِسْتِنْتَاجٌ

Deed *n.* عَمَلٌ. فِعْلٌ

Deem *v. t.* or *i.* ظَنَّ ـُ إِرْتَأَى

Deep *a.* or *n.* عَمِيقٌ. اَلْبَحْرُ

Deepen *v. t.* or *i.* عَمَّقَ. زَادَ عُمْقًا

Deer *n.* اِبِّلٌ إِبِلٌ ج ايَائِلُ

Deface *v. t.* شَوَّهَ. مَحَا ـُ

Defacement *n.* تَشْوِيهٌ

Defalcation *n.* إِخْتِلَاسٌ

Defamation *n.* هَتْكَةٌ. وِشَايَةٌ

Defame *v. t.* وَشَى يَشِي بِهِ. هَتَكَ

Default *v. t.* or *n.* إِخْتَلَسَ مالاً قَصَّرَ عَنْ

Default *n.* إِخْتِلَاسٌ. ذَنْبٌ. تَقْصِيرٌ

Defeat *v. t.* or *n.* غَلَبَ ـِ هَزَمَ ـ هَزِيمَةٌ

Defect *n.* نَقْصٌ. خَلَلٌ. عَيْبٌ

Defection *n.* تَرْكٌ. خِيَانَةٌ

Defective *a.* نَاقِصٌ. كَثِيرُ الخَلَلِ

Defence / Defense *n.* حِمَايَةٌ. مُدَافَعَةٌ

Defenceless *a.* خَالٍ مِنَ الحِمَايَةِ

Defend *v. t.* حَمَى. دَفَعَ عَنْ

Defendant *n.* مُدَافِعٌ مُدَّعًى عَلَيْهِ

Defender *n.* مُحَامٍ. مُدَافِعٌ

Defensive *a.* دِفَاعِيٌّ

Defer *v. t.* أَمْهَلَ . أَخَّرَ . أَجَّلَ

Deference *n.* إِحْتِرَامٌ . إِعْتِبَارٌ

Deferential *a.* إِحْتِرَامِيٌّ

Defiance *n.* تَحَدٍّ . تَعْيِيرٌ

Deficiency *n.* نَقْصٌ . قُصُورٌ

Deficient *a.* نَاقِصٌ . قَاصِرٌ

Deficit *n.* نَقْصٌ فِي ٱلْمَالِ

Defile *v. t.* or *i.* دَنَّسَ . مَشَى صَفًّا

Defile *n.* مَضِيقٌ

Defilement *n.* نَجَاسَةٌ . تَدْنِيسٌ

Definable *a.* قَابِلُ ٱلتَّحْدِيدِ

Define *v. t.* حَدَّدَ . عَرَّفَ . بَيَّنَ

Definite *a.* مَحْدُودٌ . وَاضِحٌ

Definition *n.* حَدٌّ . تَعْرِيفٌ

Definitive *a.* مُحَدِّدٌ . قَاطِعٌ . جَازِمٌ

Deflect *v. t.* or *i.* حَرَّفَ . إِنْحَرَفَ

Deflection *n.* تَحْرِيفٌ . إِنْحِرَافٌ

Deform *v. t.* شَوَّهَ . بَشَّعَ

Deformed *a.* مُشَوَّهٌ . مَعْيُوبُ ٱلْخِلْقَةِ

Deformity *n.* عَيْبُ ٱلْخِلْقَةِ

Defraud *v. t.* غَبَنَ ـ . خَدَعَ ـ

Defry *v. t.* قَامَ بِٱلنَّفَقَةِ

Defunct *a.* مُتَوَفًّى . مَيْتٌ

Defy *v. t.* تَحَدَّى . بَارَزَ . عَيَّرَ

Degenerate *a.* or *v. i* مُنْحَطٌّ . إِنْحَطَّ . فَسَدَ

Degeneracy / **Degeneration** } *n.* فَسَادٌ . إِنْحِطَاطٌ

Degradation *n.* ذُلٌّ . هَوَانٌ

Degrade *v. t.* اذَلَّ . حَطَّ الشَّانَ ـُ

Degraded *a.* مُذَلٌّ . مُحْتَقَرٌ

Degrading *a.* مُذِلٌّ . شَائِنٌ

Degree *n.* رُتْبَةٌ . دَرَجَةٌ

Deify *v. t.* أَلَّهَ

Deign *v. i.* تَنَازَلَ . تَكَرَّمَ

Deism *n.* إِعْتِقَادٌ بِٱللهِ دُونَ ٱلْوَحْيِ

Deist *n.* مُعْتَقِدٌ بِٱللهِ دُونَ ٱلْوَحْيِ

Deity *n.* الوهيَّةٌ . إِلٰهٌ

Deject *v. t.* اغَمَّ . بَرَّدَ هِمَّتَهُ

Dejected *a.* كَئِيبٌ . مَغْمُومٌ

Dejection *n.* غَمٌّ . كَآبَةٌ

Delay *v.t.* or *n.* أَخَّرَ . أَعَاقَ . تَاخُرٌ

Delectable *a.* مُبْهِجٌ . سَارٌّ جِدًّا

Delegate *v. t.* or *n.* فَوَّضَ . نَائِبٌ . رَسُولٌ

Delegation *n.* تَفْوِيضٌ . جَمَاعَةُ نُوَّابٍ

Deleterious *a.* ضَارٌّ . مُؤْذٍ . مُهْلِكٌ

Deliberate *v. i.* or *t.* تَأَمَّلَ . تَبَصَّرَ

Deliberate *a.* مُتَمَهِّلٌ . مَقْصُودٌ . مُتَأَمِّلٌ

Deliberately *ad.* مُتَمَهِّلاً . عَمْداً

Deliberation *n.* تَأَمُّلٌ . تَبَصُّرٌ . تَمَهُّلٌ

Delicacy *n.* رِقَّةٌ . حِشْمَةٌ . لَذَّةٌ

Delicate *a.* بَضٌّ . لَطِيفٌ . لَذِيذٌ

Delicious *a.* شَهِيٌّ . لَذِيذٌ

Delight *n.* or *v. i.* بَهْجَةٌ . إِبْتَهَجَ

Delighted *a.* مُبْتَهِجٌ . مَسْرُورٌ جِدًّا

Delightful *a.* مُبْهِجٌ . سَارٌّ

Delineate *v. t.* رَسَمَ ـُ صَوَّرَ . وَصَفَ ـِ

Delineation *n.* رَسْمٌ . وَصْفٌ

Delinquency *n.* قُصُورٌ . خَطَاءٌ

Delinquent *a.* مُقَصِّرٌ . مُذْنِبٌ

Delirious *a.* هَاذٍ

Delirium *n.* هَذَيَانٌ (بُحْرَانٌ)

Deliver *v. t.* نَجَّى . اطْلَقَ . سَلَّمَ

Deliverance *n.* نَجَاةٌ . إِطْلَاقٌ . تَخْلِيصٌ

Delivery *n.* نَجَاةٌ . تَسْلِيمٌ . وِلَادَةٌ

Dell *n.* وَادٍ صَغِيرٌ

Delta *n.* قِطْعَةُ أَرْضٍ مُثَلَّثَةٌ

Delude *v. t.* خَدَعَ ـَ أَغْوَى . اضَلَّ

Deluge *n.* or *v. t.* طُوفَانٌ . غَمَرَ ـَ

Delusion *n.* وَهْمٌ . ضَلَالٌ . غُرُورٌ

Delusive *a.* خَادِعٌ . مُضِلٌّ

Demagogue *n.* زَعِيمُ ٱلْعَوَامِّ . مُهَيِّجُهُمْ

Demand *v.t.* or *n.* طَلَبَ ـُ . طَلَبٌ

Demarcation, Demarkation *n.* تَخْطِيطُ ٱلْحُدُودِ

Demean *v. t.* سَلَكَ ـُ. تَصَرَّفَ. دَنَّا
Demeanor *n.* سُلُوْكٌ. تَصَرُّفٌ
Demented *a.* مُخْتَلُّ ٱلعَقْلِ
Demerit *n.* نَقْصٌ ادبِيٌّ. قُصُوْر
Demigod *n.* نِصفُ إِلهٍ. بَطَلٌ
Demise *n.* وَفَاةٌ. مَوْتٌ
Democracy *n.* حُكْمٌ جُمْهُوْرِيٌّ
Democrat *n.* أحَدُ حِزْبِ ٱلجُمْهُورِيّينَ
Democratic / **Democratical** *a.* جُمْهُوْرِيٌّ
Demolish *v. t.* هَدَمَ ـِ. هدَّ ـُ
Demolition *n.* هَدْمٌ. هدٌّ
Demon *n.* جِنِّيٌّ. رُوْحٌ نجِسٌ
Demoniac *n.* مَن بِهِ رُوْحٌ نجِسٌ. مَجْنُوْنٌ
Demonstrate *v. t.* بَرْهَنَ. أثْبت
Demonstration *n.* إِثْبَاتٌ. دَلاَلَةٌ
Demonstrative *a.* دَالٌّ مُظهِرٌ عَوَاطِفِهِ
Demoralization *n.* فَسَادُ ٱلآدَابِ
Demoralize *v. t.* افسَدَ ٱلآدَابَ اوِ ٱلنخْوَةَ
Demur *v. i.* تَرَدَّدَ فِيْ. تَأخرَ
Den *n.* عرِينٌ. عِرِّيسٌ
Denial *n.* إِنكَارٌ. رَفضٌ
Denizen *n.* سَاكِنٌ
Denominate *v. t.* لَقَّبَ. سَمَّى
Denomination *n.* تسمِيَةٌ. طَائِفَةٌ
Denominator *n.* مَخْرَجُ ٱلكُسُوْرِ
Denote *v. t.* أشَارَ إِلَى. دَلَّ على
Denounce *v. t.* شَهَّرَ. إِشتَكى على
Dense *a.* كَثِيفٌ. مُلْتَفٌّ. مُتَلَبِّدٌ
Density *n.* كَثَافَة
Dent *n.* or *v. t.* نقيْرَةٌ. نقرَ قَلِيلاً
Dental *a.* سِنِّيٌّ او ضِرْسِيٌّ
Dentate *n.* ذُوْ اسنَانٍ
Dentiform *a.* شَبِيهٌ بالسِّنِّ
Dentist *n.* طَبِيبُ ٱلأَسْنَانِ
Dentistry *n.* طِبُّ ٱلاسنَانِ

Dentition *n.* زَمَنُ ٱلتَّسنينِ . بُرُوزُ ٱلأَسْنَانِ

Denude *v. t.* عرَّى . جرَّدَ

Denunciation *n.* تَعْذِيلٌ . تَهْدِيدٌ

Deny *v. t.* أَنْكَرَ . رَفَضَ طَلَبًا

Deodorize *v. t.* أَزَالَ ٱلرَّائِحَةَ

Depart *v. i.* ذَهَبَ ـَ رَحَلَ

Department *n.* دائِرَةُ اعمَالٍ . قِسْمٌ

Departure *n.* ذهَابٌ . رَحِيلٌ

Depend *v. i.* إِسْتَنَدَ إِلَى . وَثِقَ ب . تَدَلَّى

Dependence *n.* إِتِّكَالٌ . إِسْتِنَادٌ . تَعَلُّقٌ

Dependent *a.* مُستَنِدٌ . تَابِعٌ او خاضِعٌ لِ

Depict *v. t.* صَوَّرَ . وَصَفَ ـِ

Deplorable *a.* مُحْزِنٌ . مَا يُرْثَى لَهُ

Deplore *v. t.* اسِفَ ـَ عَلَى . حَزِنَ على

Depopulate *v. t.* قرَضَ ٱلسُّكَّانَ

Depopulation *n.* إِنقِرَاضُ ٱلسُّكَّانِ

Deport *v. t.* تَصَرَّفَ . نَقَلَ . نَفَى

Deportation *n.* إِجلاءُ ٱلسُّكَّانِ

Deportment *n.* تَصَرُّفٌ . سُلُوكٌ

Depose *v. t.* or *i.* عزَلَ ـِ شَهِدَ ـَ

Deposit *v. t.* or *n.* أَوْدَعَ . وَضَعَ ـَ وَدِيعَةٌ

Deposition *n.* عَزْلٌ . شَهَادَةٌ

Depository *n.* مَخْزَنٌ . مُسْتَوْدَعٌ

Depot *n.* مَخْزَنٌ . مَحطَّةٌ

Deprave *v. t.* أَفْسَدَ

Depraved *a.* فَاسِدٌ . شِرِّيرٌ

Depravity *n.* فَسَادٌ . شَرٌّ

Deprecate *v. t.* توَسَّلَ . أَسِفَ عَلَى

Depreciate *v. t.* or *i.* وَكَّسَ . وَكَسَ

Deprecia-tion *n.* إِسْتِخْفَافٌ . هُبُوط ٱلقِيمَةِ

Depredation *n.* سَلْبٌ . نَهْبٌ

Depress *v. t.* خَفَّضَ . أَذَلَّ . أَغَمَّ

Depressing *a.* مُكَدِّرٌ . مُغِمٌّ

Depression n. تَخَفُّضٌ . كَآبَةٌ . كَسادٌ

Deprivation n. نَزْعٌ . فُقْدانٌ . حِرمانٌ

Deprive v. t. أَخَذَ مِنْ . نَزَعَ ـِ

Depth n. عُمْقٌ

Deputation n. تَوْكِيلٌ . وَفْدٌ

Depute v. t. وَكَّلَ . أَوْفَدَ

Deputy n. نائِبٌ . وَكِيلٌ . وَافِدٌ

Derange v. t. قَلَبَ ـِ . شَوَّشَ

Deranged a. مَقلوبٌ . مُشَوَّشٌ . مُختَلٌّ

Derangement n. تَشْوِيشٌ . إِختِلالٌ

Deride v. t. إِزْدَرَى بِ . هَزأَ بِ ـَ

Derisive / Derisory a. إِستِهزائِيٌّ . إِزدرائِيٌّ

Derision n. إِزدِراءٌ . هُزْءٌ

Derivation n. إِشْتِقاقٌ

Derivative a. or n. مُشْتَقٌّ

Derive v. t. إِشْتَقَّ . إِستَخْرَجَ مِنْ

Derogate v. t. or i. نَقَصَ . إِستَخَفَّ بِ

Derogative / Derogatory a. مُستَخِفٌّ . مُستَحقِرٌ

Dervish n. دَرْوِيشٌ

Descend v. i. نَزَلَ ـِ . إِنْحَدَرَ

Descendant n. سَلِيلٌ . أَحَدُ الذُّرِّيَّةِ

Descent n. نُزُولٌ . أُحْدُورٌ

Describe v. t. وَصَفَ ـِ . أَوْضَحَ

Description n. وَصْفٌ

Descriptive a. وَصْفِيٌّ . وَاصِفٌ

Descry v. t. رَأَى . أَوْ مِنْ بَعِيدٍ

Desecrate v. t. نَجَّسَ . دَنَّسَ

Desert v. t. or i. تَرَكَ ـُ . هَجَرَ ـُ

Desert n. قَفْرٌ . صَحْرَاءُ . إِستِحقاقٌ

Deserter n. هارِبٌ . آبِقٌ

Deserve v. t. إِستَحَقَّ . إِستَوْجَبَ

Desiccate v. t. نَشَّفَ . جَفَّفَ

Desideratum n. مَطْلوبٌ . بُغْيَةٌ

قَصَدَ ـُ . نَوَى ـِ . قَصْدٌ

Design v. t. or n. رَسَمَ ـُ . رَسْمٌ

Designate v. t. أَشَارَ إِلَى . عَيَّنَ . دَلَّ

Designation *n.* تَعيِينٌ . دَلالَة

Designedly *ad.* قَصْدًا . عَمْدًا

Designer *n.* مُسْتَنْبِطٌ. رَاسِمٌ. مُصَوِّرٌ

Designing *a.* رَاسِمٌ . مُحْتَالٌ . دَاهٍ

Desirable *a.* مَرْغُوبٌ . مُبْتَغًى

Desire *n.* or *v. t.* رِغْبَة.بُغْيَة.إِبْتَغَى

Desirous *a.* رَاغِبٌ . مُبْتَغٍ

Desist *v. i.* كَفَّ عَنْ ـُ . عَدَلَ عَنْ

Desistance *n.* تَرْكٌ . كَفٌّ عَنْ

Desk *n.* مائِدَةٌ لِلْكِتَابَةِ

Desolate *v. t.* or *a.* دَمَّرَ . خَرَّبَ . مُقْفِرٌ

Desolation *n.* دَمَارٌ.وَحْشَةٌ . خَرَابٌ

Despair *v. i.* or *n.* يَئِسَ ـَ . يَأْسٌ. قُنُوطٌ

Despairing *a.* يَائِسٌ . بِلاَ رَجَاءٍ

Despatch *see* Dispatch.

Desperado *n.* / **Desperate** *a.* } يَائِسٌ. فَاتِكٌ . هَائِجٌ

Desperation *n.* يَأْسٌ . قُنُوطٌ

Despicable *a.* خَسِيسٌ.مُحْتَقَرٌ. مُهَانٌ

Despise *v. t.* إِحْتَقَرَ . اهَانَ

Despite *n.* ضَغِينَةٌ . حِقْدٌ

Despite of. رَغْمًا عَنْ

Despoil *v. t.* نَهَبَ . سَلَبَ

Despond *v. i.* يَئِسَ ـَ . قَنِطَ

Despondency *n.* يَأْسٌ . قُنُوطٌ

Despondent / **Desponding** } *a.* خَائِبُ الأَمَلِ. قَانِطٌ

Despot *n.* / **Despotic** *a.* } حَاكِمٌ مُطْلَقٌ.ظَالِمٌ

Despotism *n.* سُلْطَةٌ مُطْلَقَةٌ . ظُلْمٌ

Dessert *n.* فَاكِهَةٌ أَوْحَلْوَى بَعْدَ الطَّعَامِ

Destination *a.* مَكَانٌ مَقْصُودٌ

Destinate / **Destine** } *v. t.* قَدَّرَ. عَيَّنَ. خَصَّصَ

Destiny *n.* قَدَرٌ . قِسْمَةٌ . نَصِيبٌ

Destitute *a.* مُحْتَاجٌ. خَالٍ مِنْ . فَقِيرٌ

Destitution *n.* فَاقَةٌ . عَوَزٌ

Destroy *v. t.* اهْلَكَ . أَبَادَ . ازَالَ

Destruction *n.* إِبَادَةٌ. هَلاَكٌ

Destructive *a.* مُهْلِكٌ . مُمِيتٌ

Desultory *a.* غَيْرُ مُنْتَظِمٍ . مُنْقَطِعٌ

Detach *v. t.* فصل ـ . فكّ ـ

Detachment *n.* سريّة من الجند

Detail *n.* or *v. t.* تفصيل . اسهاب . اسهب

Detain *v. t.* حجز ـ . صدّ ـ . منع ـ

Detect *v. t.* كشف ـ . وجد ـ

Detection *n.* كشف . إظهار

Detention *n.* حجز . توقيف . تأخير

Deter *v.t.* أعاق . صدّ . منع ـ

Deteriorate *v.i.* إنحطّ . فسد ـ

Deterioration *n.* إنحطاط . فساد

Determinable *a.* قابل التحديد أو التعريف

Determinate *a.* محدود . جازم

Determination *n.* تحديد . عزم . حكم

Determine *v. t.* حكم في . عزم على . حقّق

Determined *a.* عزوم . محكوم به

Detest *v. t.* كره ـ . مقت ـ

Detestable *a.* مكروه . ممقوت

Detestation *n.* كره . مقت

Dethrone *v. t.* خلع عن الملك

Dethronement *n.* خلع

Detonation *n.* صوت انفجار

Detour *n.* دورة

Detract *v. t.* قلّل . ذمّ ـ

Detraction *n.* ذمّ . نميمة

Detriment *n.* ضرر . خسارة

Detrimental *a.* مضرّ

Deuteronomy *n.* سفر التثنية

Devastate *v. t.* خرّب . دمّر

Devastation *n.* تخريب . دمار

Develop *v.i.* or *t.* نشأ ـ . إنتشر ـ . نشر

Development *n.* نشوء . نشر

Deviate *v. i.* حاد ـ . مال ـ

Deviation *n.* إنحراف . حيدان

Device *n.* حيلة . تدبير . علامة

Devil *n.* شَيْطَانٌ

Devilish *a.* شَيْطَانِيٌّ . خَبِيثٌ

Deviltry *n.* شَيْطَنَةٌ . تَصَرُّفٌ شَيْطَانِيٌّ

Devious *a.* زَائِغٌ . مُنْحَرِفٌ مُعْوَجٌّ

Devise *v. t.* دَبَّرَ . إِخْتَرَعَ . وَصَّى بَعْدَ ٱلْمَوْتِ

Devoid *a.* خَالٍ . مُجَرَّدٌ . فَارِغٌ

Devolve *v. t.* or *i.* كَلَّفَ . سَلَّمَ . إِنْتَقَلَ

Devote *v. t.* أَفْرَزَ . خَصَّصَ

Devoted *a.* مُفْرَزٌ

Devotedness *n.* غَيْرَةٌ . وُلُوعٌ

Devotee *n.* زَاهِدٌ . مُتَعَبِّدٌ

Devotion *n.* غَيْرَةٌ . عِبَادَةٌ

Devour *v. t.* إِبْتَلَعَ . إِفْتَرَسَ

Devout *a.* دَيِّنٌ . تَقِيٌّ

Dew *n.* نَدًى . طَلٌّ

Dexterity *n.* خِفَّةٌ . مَهَارَةٌ

Dexterous *a.* خَفِيفٌ . مَاهِرٌ

Diabolic / Diabolical *a.* شَيْطَانِيٌّ خَبِيثٌ

Diadem *n.* تَاجٌ . عِصَابَةٌ

Diagnosis *n.* تَشْخِيصٌ

Diagonal *n.* خَطٌّ بَيْنَ زَاوِيَتَيْنِ مُتَقَابِلَتَيْنِ

Diagram *n.* رَسْمٌ . شَكْلٌ هَنْدَسِيٌّ

Dial *n.* مِينَا سَاعَةٍ . شَمْسِيَّةٌ

Dialect *n.* لُغَةٌ . لَهْجَةٌ

Dialectic / Dialectical *a.* نُطْقِيٌّ . لَهْجِيٌّ

Dialogue *n.* مُحَاوَرَةٌ . مُكَالَمَةٌ

Diameter *n.* قُطْرُ دَائِرَةٍ

Diametrical *a.* قُطْرِيٌّ أَبْعَدُ مَا يُمْكِنُ

Diamond *n.* مَاسٌ

Diaphragm *n.* حِجَابٌ . اَلْحِجَابُ ٱلْحَاجِزُ (فِي ٱلطِّبِّ)

Diarrhœa *n.* إِسْهَالٌ

Diary *n.* يَوْمِيَّةٌ

Dice *n. pl.* of *Die* زَهْرُ ٱلنَّرْدِ

Dicephalous *a.* ذُو رَأْسَيْنِ

Dictate *v.* or *n.* أَمْلَى عَلَى . أَمَرَ ـُ . أَمْرٌ

Dictation *n.* إِمْلَاءٌ . أَمْرٌ

Dictator *n.* مُطْلَقُ ٱلسُّلْطَةِ

Dictatorial *a.* مُسْتَبِدٌّ

Diction *n.* أُسْلُوبُ ٱلْكَلَامِ

Dictionary *n.* قَامُوسٌ ج قَوَامِيسُ

Dictum *n.* قَوْلٌ جَازِمٌ

Didactic / **Didactical** *a.* تَعْلِيمِيٌّ . مُوَافِقٌ لِلتَّعْلِيمِ

Die *v. i.* مَاتَ ـُ . تُوُفِّيَ

Diet *n.* or *v. i.* طَعَامٌ . إِحْتَمَى بِالطَّعَامِ

Differ *v. i.* إِخْتَلَفَ . تَبَايَنَ

Difference *n.* إِخْتِلَافٌ . فَرْقٌ

Different *a.* مُخْتَلِفٌ

Difficult *a.* صَعْبٌ . عَسِرٌ . شَاقٌّ

Difficulty *n.* صُعُوبَةٌ . عَاقَةٌ . إِرْتِبَاكٌ

Diffident *a.* غَيْرُ وَاثِقٍ بِنَفْسِهِ

Diffuse *v. t.* or *a.* نَشَرَ ـُ . مُنْتَشِرٌ . مُسْهِبٌ

Diffusion *n.* نَشْرٌ . إِمْتِدَادٌ

Diffusive *a.* مُمْتَدٌّ . مُنْتَشِرٌ . مُسْهِبٌ

Dig *v. t.* or *i.* (dug) حَفَرَ ـِ . نَقَبَ ـُ

Digest *v. t.* or *n.* هَضَمَ ـِ . مَجْمُوعُ شَرَائِعَ

Digestible *a.* سَهْلُ ٱلْهَضْمِ

Digestion *n.* هَضْمٌ

Digestive *a.* هَاضِمٌ

Dignified *a.* ذُو وَقَارٍ

Dignify *v.t.* كَرَّمَ . شَرَّفَ . وَقَّرَ

Dignitary *n.* صَاحِبُ رُتْبَةٍ عَالِيَةٍ

Dignity *n.* وَقَارٌ . كَرَامَةٌ . جَاهٌ

Digress *v. i.* حَادَ ـِ . إِسْتَطْرَدَ

Digression *n.* حَيَدَانٌ . إِسْتِطْرَادٌ

Digressive *a.* مُسْتَطْرِدٌ . مُعْتَسِفٌ

Dike *n.* سَدٌّ . خَنْدَقٌ

Dilapidated *a.* خَرِبٌ . مُتَسَاقِطٌ

Dilate *v. t.* or *i.* وَسَّعَ . مَدَّ ـُ . إِتَّسَعَ

Dilatory *a.* بَطِيءٌ . مُتَكَاسِلٌ . مُتَرَاخٍ

Dilemma *n.* مُشْكِلٌ . وَرْطَةٌ

Diligence *n.* جَدٌّ . مثَابَرَةٌ . مُوَاظَبَة

Diligent *a.* مُجْتَهِدٌ . مثَابِرٌ

Dilute *v. t.* خَفَّفَ سَائلاً . أضَافَ مَاءً

Dilution *n.* تَخْفِيفٌ

Dim *a.* or *v. t.* مُظْلِمٌ . مُكَدِّرٌ . كَدَّرَ

Dimension *n.* قِيَاسٌ . إمْتِدَادٌ . قَدْرٌ

Diminish *v. t.* or *i.* قَلَّلَ . نَقَصَ . قَلَّ . نَقَصَ

Diminution *n.* تَقْلِيلٌ . نَقْصٌ

Diminutive *n.* or *a.* إِسْمُ التَّصْغِيرِ . صَغِيرٌ جِدًّا

Dimly *ad.* مُكَدَّرًا

Dimple *n.* نُونَة . (غَمَّازَة)

Dimpled *a.* ذُو نُونَاتٍ

Din *n.* or *v. t.* صَخَبٌ . قَعْقَعة . قَعْقَعَ

Dine *v. i.* تَغَدَّى . تَعَشَّى

Dinginess *n.* غُبْسَة

Dingy *a.* مُكْمَدُّ اللَّوْنِ

Dinner *n.* غدَاءٌ . فُطُورٌ

Diocese *n.* ابرَشِيَّة

Dip *v. t.* or *n.* غَمَسَ ـ حُدُورٌ

Diphthong *n.* إجْتِمَاعُ حَرْفَيْ عِلَّةٍ بِصَوْتٍ وَاحِدٍ

Diploma *n.* شَهَادَةٌ مَدْرَسِيَّةٌ

Diplomacy *n.* سِيَاسَةُ الدُّوَلِ

Diplomatic *a.* مختَصٌّ بِالسِّيَاسَةِ

Diplomatist *n.* خَبِيرٌ بِالسِّيَاسَةِ الدَّوْلِيةِ

Dipper *n.* غَاطِسٌ . مِغْرَفَة

Dire *a.* هَائِلٌ . مُرْعِبٌ

Direct *v. t.* or *a.* أرْشَدَ . أدَارَ . أمَرَ ـُ . مُسْتَقِيمٌ

Direction *n.* جِهَةٌ . إرْشَادٌ . أمْرٌ

Directly *ad.* رَأساً . بِإسْتِقَامَةٍ . حَالاً

Directness *n.* إسْتِقَامَةٌ . خلُوصٌ

Director *n.* مُدِيرٌ . مُدَبِّرٌ . نَاظِرٌ

Directory *n.* جَمَاعَةُ مُدِيرِينَ كِتَابُ مُرْشِدٌ . دَلِيلٌ

Direful *a.* هَائِلٌ . رَائِعٌ

Dirge *n.* تَرْنِيمَةُ جَنَازَةٍ

Dirk *n.* خَنْجَرٌ ج خَنَاجِرُ

Dirt *n.* وَسَخٌ . قَذَرٌ

Dirtly *a.* وَسِخٌ . قَذِرٌ

Disability *n.* عَجزٌ . عَدَمُ اقتِدَار

Dısable *v. t.* اعجَزَ . أَوْهَنَ

Disabuse *v. t.* بَيَّنَ غلطَهُ . أصلَحَ فِكرَهُ

Disadvantage *n.* خِسارَةٌ . عاقةٌ

Disadvantageous *a.* غَيرُ نافعٍ

Disaffected *a.* فَاتِرُ المَحَبَّةِ . سَاخِطٌ

Disagree *v. i.* تخَالَفَ

Disagreeable *a.* غَيرُ مُرْضٍ . غيرُ مقبُولٍ

Disagreement *n.* إختِلافٌ . إنشِقَاقٌ

Disallow *v. t.* أَنكَرَ عَلَى . رَفَضَ

Disappear *v. i.* غابَ ـِ . تَوارَى

Disappearance *n.* مُوارَاة . إختِفاءٌ

Disappoint *v. t.* خيَّبَ . خَذَلَ ـُ

Disappointment *n.* خيبَة . خِذلانٌ

Disapprobation / **Disapproval** *n.* إنكارٌ عَلَى . عدَمُ رضًى

Disapprove *v. t.* أنكَرَ عَلَى . عابَ

Disarm *v. t.* جرَّدَ مِنَ السِّلاحِ . نَزَعَ القُوَّةَ

Disarrange *v. t.* أخلَّ بالتَّرتِيبِ . قلَبَ ـِ

Disaster *n.* مُصيبة . نازِلَة . نَكبَةٌ

Disastrous *a.* مشؤُومٌ . جالِبُ مُصيبةٍ

Disavow *v. t.* أنكَرَ . رَفَضَ ـِ

Disavowal *n.* إنكارٌ . رَفضٌ

Disband *v. t.* فضَّ . فرَّق

Disbelief *n.* عدمُ تصدِيقٍ

Disbelieve *v. t.* أنكرَ . كفَرَ

Disburden *v. t.* نزَعَ حِملَهُ

Disburse *v. t.* انفق . صرَفَ

Disbursement *n.* إنفَاقٌ . صَرفٌ

Disc *n. see* **Disk.**

Discard *v. t.* رفضَ ـِ . أبعدَ . طَرَحَ ـَ

Discern *v. t.* رَأى ـَ . مَيَّزَ

Discernible *a.* مُمْكِنٌ مشاهَدَته

Discerning *a.* مُمَيِّزٌ . بصيرٌ

Discernment *n.* تَمْيِيز. إدْرَاك. فطنة

Discharge *v. t.* **or** *n.* أَطلقَ.طَرَدَ.صَرَفَ أَجْرَى. تخْلِيَة

Disciple *n.* تِلْمِيذٌ ج تلاميذ وتَلامِذَة

Disciplinary *a.* تَأْدِيبِيٌّ

Disicpline. *v. t.* **or** *n.* أَدَّبَ .هذَّبَ . تَأْدِيبٌ

Disclaim *v. t.* انـكرَ . رَفَضَ ـُ

Disclose *v. t.* أَظْهَرَ . بَيَّنَ . أَعْلَنَ

Disclosure *n.* إِظْهَارٌ. إِعْلَانٌ. إِباحة

Discolour *v. t.* غَيَّرَ لوْنَهُ . لَطَّخَ

Discomfit *v. t.* هَزَمَ ـِ . كَسَرَ ـِ

Discomfiture *n.* هَزِيمَةٌ . خيبَة

Discomfort *n.* كَدَرٌ . عَدَمُ رَاحَةٍ

Discommode *v. t.* أَقْلَقَ . ثَقُلَ عَلى

Discompose *v. t.* شَوَّشَ . بَلْبَلَ

Disconcert *v. t.* اقْلَقَ . حَيَّرَ

Disconnect *v. t.* فصلَ ـِ . قَطَعَ ـَ

Disconsolate *a.* كَئِيبٌ . حَزِينٌ

Discontented *a.* غيْرُ رَاضٍ. ضَجِرَ

Discontent / **Discontentment** } *n.* عدَمُ رِضًى ضَجَرٌ

Discontinue *v. t.* **or** *i.* ابْطَلَ . إِنْقَطَعَ

Discontinuous *a.* مُنْقَطِعٌ

Discord *n.* خِصَامٌ . عَدَمُ إِتِّفاقٍ

Discordant *a.* غيْرُ متفق . مغايِرٌ

Discount *v. t.* **or** *n.* حَطَّ الثمَنَ. إِسْقَاطٌ (خَصْمٌ)

Discountenance *v. t.* عارَضَ.قاوَمَ

Discourage *v. t.* بَرَّدَ هِمتَهُ

Discouragement *n.* فشَلٌ . ضَعْفُ الْعَزْمِ

Discouraging *a.* مُضْعِفُ الْعَزْمِ وَالرَّجَاءِ

Discourse *n.* **or** *v.i.* خِطَابٌ . خَاطَبَ

Discourtesy *n.* سُوءُ الادَب . فَظَاظَةٌ

Discover *v. t.* كَشَفَ ـِ وَجَدَ ـِ اِكْتَشَفَ

Discovery *n.* اِكْتِشَافٌ . إِخْتِرَاعٌ

Discredit *v. t.* or *n.* لَمْ يُصَدِّقْ . شَيْنٌ

Discreditable *a.* شَائِنٌ . مُخِلٌّ بِالشَّرَفِ

Discreet *a.* عَاقِلٌ . حَازِمٌ

Discreetness / **Discretion** *n.* تَعَقُّلٌ . بَصِيرَةٌ . تَمْيِيزٌ

Discretionary *a.* مَتْرُوكٌ لِحُكْمِهِ

Discrepance / **Discrepancy** *n.* إِخْتِلَافٌ . مُغَايَرَةٌ

Discriminate *v. t.* مَيَّزَ بَيْنَ

Discuss *v. t.* بَحَثَ ـَ فِي اوْ بَاحَثَ

Discussion *n.* مُبَاحَثَةٌ

Disdain *v. t.* or *n.* إِزْدَرَى بِ . إِحْتِقَارٌ

Disdainful *a.* مُسْتَحْقِرٌ . مُتَعَجْرِفٌ

Disease *n.* مَرَضٌ . دَاءٌ . عِلَّةٌ

Diseased *a.* مَرِيضٌ . سَقِيمٌ

Disembark *v. t.* or *i.* نَزَّلَ أَوْ نَزَلَ مِنْ سَفِينَةٍ

Disembarrass *v. t.* أَزَالَ ٱرْتِبَاكًا

Disenchant *v. t.* حَرَّرَ مِنْ سِحْرٍ اوْ رُقْيَةٍ

Disencumber *v. t.* حَرَّرَ مِنْ أَثْقَالٍ

Disengage *v. t.* فَكَّ مِنْ عَهْدٍ . أَطْلَقَ

Disentangle *v. t.* فَكَّ ـُ . حَلَّ ـُ

Disfavour *n.* عَدَمُ قُبُولٍ . نُفُورٌ

Disfiguration *n.* تَشْوِيهٌ

Disfigure *v. t.* شَوَّهَ . أَخَلَّ بِالْهَيْئَةِ

Disfranchise *v. t.* نَزَعَ ٱلْحُقُوقَ ٱلسِّيَاسِيَّةَ

Disgorge *v. t.* اخْرَجَ . قَذَفَ . إِسْتَفْرَغَ

Disgrace *v. t.* or *n.* فَضَحَ ـَ . شَانَ . عَيَّبَ . عَارٌ

Disgraceful *a.* شَائِنٌ . مُعِيبٌ

Disguise *v.t.* or *n.* سَتَّرَ . اخْفَى . تَسَتُّرٌ . تَنَكُّرٌ

Disgust *n.* or *v. t.* كُرْهٌ . قَزَّزَ

Disgusting *a.* مُقَزِّزٌ . كَرِيهٌ

Dish *n.* صَحْنٌ . قَصْعَةٌ . طَبَقٌ

Dishearten *v. t.* أَضْعَفَ ٱلْعَزْمَ اوِ ٱلْهِمَّةَ

Dishonest *a.* غَيْرُ أَمِينٍ . غَابِنٌ

Dishonesty *n.* غَبْنٌ . عدمُ أمَانَةٍ

Dishonour *n.* or *v. t.* هَوَانٌ.عَارٌ . أهَانَ

Dishonorable *a.* شَائِنٌ . مُعِيبٌ

Disinclination *n.* مَيْلٌ عَنْ . نُفُورٌ

Disincline *v. t.* أمَالَ عَنْ . نَفَّرَ

Disinfect *v.t.* طَهَّرَ مِنْ أسبَابِ ٱلْعَدوى

Disingenuous *a.* غَيْرُ مُخلِصٍ

Disinherit *v. t.* حَرَمَ مِنَ ٱلْإِرْثِ

Disintegrate *v.t.* حَلَّ . فَرَّقَ أجزَاءَهُ

Disinterested *a.* صَافِي ٱلنِّيَّةِ

Disjoin *v.t.* فَصَلَ ـِ

Disjoint *v. t.* خَلَعَ ـَ

Disk or Disc *n.* قُرْصٌ ج اقْرَاصٌ

Dislike *v. t.* or *n.* كَرِهَ ـَ . سَئِمَ ـَ

Dislocate *v. t.* خَلَعَ ـَ ازَاحَ

Dislocation *n.* خَلْعٌ . إِزاحَةٌ

Dislodge *v. t.* أخْرَجَ مِنْ مَكَانِهِ

Disloyal *a.* خَائِنٌ . غَيْرُ امِين

Disloyalty *n.* خِيانَةٌ عَدَمُ امانةٍ

Dismal *a.* مُظْلِمٌ . مُغِمٌّ

Dismantle *v. t.* عَرَّى . نَزَعَ أدَوَاتِ ٱلتَّحصِينِ

Dismast *v. t.* نَزَعَ سَوَارِيَ سَفِينَةٍ

Dismay *n.* or *v. t.* رَوْعٌ . رَوَّعَ

Dismember *v. t.* فصلَ ـِ ٱلاجزَاءَ

Dismiss *v. t.* صَرَفَ ـِ . طَرَدَ ـُ

Dismissal / **Dismission** } *n.* فَصْلٌ . عَزْلٌ

Dismount *v. i.* or *t.* نزَلَ عَنْ دَابَّةٍ. نَزَّلَ

Disobedience *n.* عدمُ طَاعَةٍ . عِصْيَانٌ

Disobey *v.t.* عَصَى ـِ . خَالَفَ أمْرًا

Disoblige *v. t.* خَالَفَ خَاطِرَهُ اوْ كَدَّرَهُ

Disorder *n.* or *v. t.* تَشْوِيشٌ . شَوَّشَ

Disorderly *a.* مُشَوَّشٌ . غَيْرُ مُنْتَظِمٍ

Disorganize *v. t.* أخَلَّ بِنِظَامٍ او تَرْتِيبٍ

Disown *v. t.* رفضَ ـُ . أنْكَرَ

Disparage *v. t.* عَيَّبَ . إِحْتَقَرَ

Dispassionate رَزِينٌ. هادئُ ٱلطَّبْعِ

Dispatch *v.t.* ارْسَلَ. أَنْجَزَ

Dispatch *n.* سِرْعَةٌ. رِسَالَةٌ

Dispel *v. t.* بَدَّدَ. ازَالَ

Dispensary *n.* صَيْدَلِيَّةٌ. مَجَّانِيَّةٌ

Dispensation *n.* نِظَامٌ. تَحْلِيلٌ. إِجَازَةٌ

Dispense *v.t.* اعفَى مِنْ. وزَّعَ. اجْرَى

Disperse *v. t.* بَدَّدَ. شَتَّتَ

Dispersion *n.* تَشْتِيتٌ. تَشَتُّتٌ

Dispirited *a.* فَشِلٌ. مُنْكَسِرُ ٱلعَزْمِ

Displace *v. t.* أَزَاحَ مِنْ مَكَانِهِ

Displacement *n.* إِزَاحةٌ مِنْ مَكَانِهِ

Display *v.t.* or *n.* اظْهَرَ. مَنْظَرٌ بَاطِلٌ

Displease *v. t.* كَدَّرَ. غَمَّ ـُ. احْزَنَ

Displeasure *n.* كَدَرٌ. غَمٌّ. (زَعَلٌ)

Disposal *n.* تَصَرُّفٌ. تَرْتِيبٌ. تَدْبِيرٌ

Dispose *v. t.* رَتَّبَ. تَصَرَّفَ في. امَالَ

Disposition *n.* تَرْتِيبٌ. خُلْقٌ. مَيْلٌ

Dispossess *v. t.* حَرَمَهُ مُلْكَهُ. سَلَبَ ـُ

Disproportion *n.* عَدَمُ تَنَاسُبٍ اوْ تَعَادُلٍ

Disproof *n.* إِدْحَاضٌ. رَدٌّ

Disprove *v. t.* أَدْحَضَ. رَدَّ

Disputable *a.* قَابِلُ ٱلرَّدِّ. فِيهِ خِلَافٌ

Disputant *n.* مُنَاظِرٌ. مُجَادِلٌ

Disputation *n.* مُجَادَلَةٌ. مُنَاظَرَةٌ

Dispute *v. t.* or *i.* جَادَلَ. نَازَعَ

Disqualify *v.t.* ازَالَ اهْلِيَّتَهُ. اعْجَزَ

Disquiet *v. t.* أَزْعَجَ. أَخَلَّ بِٱلرَّاحَةِ

Disregard *v. t.* or *n.* إِسْتَخَفَّ بِهِ. إِهْمَالٌ

Disrelish *n.* or *v. t.* كُرْهٌ. تَقَزَّزَ

Disreputable *a.* شَائِنٌ. مُضِرٌّ بالصِّيتِ

Disrepute *n.* صِيتٌ رَدِيٌّ اوْ مُعِيبٌ

Disrespect *n.* جَفَاءٌ. عَدَمُ ٱحْتِرَامٍ

Disrespectful *a.* جَافٍ. مُهِينٌ

Disrobe *v. t.* خَلَعَ ـَ ٱلثِّيَابَ

Dissatisfaction *n.* عَدَمُ ٱلرِّضى
Dissatisfactory *a.* غَيْرُ رَاضٍ
Dissatisfied *a.* غَيْرُ رَاضٍ أَوْ مُكْتَفٍ
Dissatisfy *v. t.* أَضْجَرَ . لَمْ يُرْضِ
Dissect *v. t.* شَرَّحَ
Dissemble *v. t.* or *i.* تَظَاهَرَ . تَسَتَّرَ . رَاءَى
Disseminate *v. t.* بَثَّ ـُ . نَثَرَ ـُ
Dissension *n.* إِنْشِقَاقٌ . نِزَاعٌ
Dissent *v. i.* or *n.* خَالَفَ الرَّأْيَ . خِلَافٌ
Dissenter *n.* مُخَالِفٌ خَاصَّةً فِي الدِّينِ
Dissertation *n.* خِطَابٌ . مَقَالَةٌ
Dissever *v. t.* فَصَلَ ـِ . قَطَعَ ـَ
Dissimilar *a.* مُخْتَلِفٌ . غَيْرُ مُشَابِهٍ
Dissimilarity } *n.* إِخْتِلَافٌ
Dissimiltude
Dissimulation *n.* تَظَاهُرٌ . رِيَاءٌ
Dissipate *v. t.* بَذَّرَ . أَسْرَفَ . شَتَّتَ
Dissipated *a.* مُتَشَتِّتٌ . خَلِيعٌ
Dissipation *n.* خَلَاعَةٌ . لَهْوٌ . إِسْرَافٌ

Dissoluble *a.* قَابِلُ ٱلذَّوَبَانِ
Dissolute *a.* خَلِيعٌ . فَاجِرٌ
Dissolution *n.* إِنْحِلَالٌ . فَنَاءٌ . مَوْتٌ
Dissolve *v. t.* or *i.* ذَوَّبَ . حَلَّ ـُ . ذَابَ ـُ
Dissolvent *n.* مُحَلِّلٌ . مُذِيبٌ
Dissuade *v. t.* ثَنَى عَنْ
Dissuasion *n.* إِقْنَاعٌ بِالْعُدُولِ عَنْ
Dissuasive *a.* مُمِيلٌ عَنْ . ثَانٍ عَنْ
Dissyllable *n.* لَفْظَةٌ ذَاتُ مَقْطَعَيْنِ
Distaff *n.* عِرْنَاسٌ ج عَرَانِيسُ
Distance *n.* or *v. t.* بُعْدٌ . مَسَافَةٌ . سَبَقَ ـِ
Distant *a.* بَعِيدٌ
Distaste *n.* عَيْفٌ . كَرَاهَةٌ
Distasteful *a.* كَرِيهٌ . غَيْرُ لَذِيذٍ
Distemper *n.* مَرَضٌ . سُوءُ الْخُلُقِ
Distend *v.t.* or *i.* وَسَّعَ . مَدَّدَ . إِنْتَفَخَ
Distill *v. t.* or *i.* قَطَّرَ . تَقَطَّرَ
Distillery *n.* مَعْمَلُ المسكرات

Distinct *a.* وَاضِحٌ . بَيِّنٌ . مُمْتَازٌ

Distinction *n.* تَمْيِيزٌ . سُمُوٌّ . رِفْعَةٌ

Distinctive *a.* مُمَيِّزٌ . فَاصِلٌ

Distinctly *ad.* وَاضِحاً . بَيِّناً

Distinctness *n.* وُضُوحٌ . صَرَاحة

Distinguish *v. t.* مَيَّزَ . فَصَلَ بَيْنَ

Distinguished *a.* مُمْتَازٌ . شَهِيرٌ

Distort *v. t.* لَوَى . عَوَّجَ . حَرَّفَ

Distract *v. t.* شَوَّشَ . حَيَّرَ . أَلْهَى

Distraction *n.* تَشْوِيشٌ . لَهْوٌ

Distress *n.* or *v.t.* ضِيقٌ . أَلَمٌ شَدِيدٌ . ضَايَقَ

Distressing / **Distressful** *a.* مُؤْلِمٌ . شَاقٌّ . مُكَدِّرٌ

Distribute *v. t.* وَزَّعَ . قَسَّمَ

Distribution *n.* تَوْزِيعٌ . تَقْسِيمٌ

District *n.* اقْلِيمٌ . كُورَةٌ . مَرْكَزٌ

Distrust *n.* or *v. t.* عَدَمُ ثِقَةٍ . إِرْتَابَ

Distrustful *a.* غَيْرُ وَاثِقٍ . مُرْتَابٌ

Disturb *v. t.* أَقْلَقَ . شَوَّشَ . ازْعَجَ

Disturbance *n.* تَشْوِيشٌ . إِضْطِرَابٌ

Disunion *n.* إِنْشِقَاقٌ . إِنْفِصَالٌ

Disunite *v. t.* فَصَلَ ـِ . فَرَّقَ

Disuse *v. t.* or *n.* أَهْمَلَ . إِهْمَالٌ

Ditch *n.* خَنْدَقٌ . حُفْرَةٌ

Ditto *n.* مِثْلُهُ . ذَاتُ ٱلشَّيْءِ

Diurnal *a.* يَوْمِيٌّ . نَهَارِيٌّ

Divan *n.* دِيْوَانٌ . مَقْعَدٌ

Dive *v. i.* or *n.* غَطَسَ ـِ . غَاصَ ـُ غَطْسَةٌ

Diverge *v. i.* إِفْتَرَقَ . إِنْحَرَفَ

Divergence *n.* تَشَعُّبٌ . إِفْتِرَاقٌ

Divergent / **Diverging** *a.* مُفْتَرِقٌ . مُنْفَصِلٌ

Divers / **Diverse** *a.* مُخْتَلِفٌ . مُتَنَوِّعٌ

Diversify *v. t.* نَوَّعَ . جَعَلَهُ أَشْكَالاً

Diversion *n.* تَحْوِيلٌ . لَهْوٌ . تَسْلِيَةٌ

Diversity *n.* تَنَوُّعٌ . تَعَدُّدُ ٱلاشْكَال

Divert *v. t.* أَلْهَى عَنْ . سَلَّى

Diverting *a.* مُلْهٍ . مُسَلٍّ . مُحَوِّلٌ

Divest *v. t.* عَرَّى . نَزَعَ ـَ

Divide *v. t.* قَسَمَ ـِ . جَزَّأَ . فَصَلَ ـِ

Dividend *n.* حِصَّةٌ . اَلْعَدَدُ الْمَقْسُومُ

Divider *n.* قَاسِمٌ . قَسَّامٌ

Divine *a.* or *v. t.* إِلَهِيٌّ . تَكَهَّنَ

Divinity *n.* أُلُوهِيَّةٌ . لَاهُوتٌ

Divisible *a.* قَابِلُ الْقِسْمَةِ

Division *n.* قِسْمَةٌ . تَقْسِيمٌ . فِرْقَة

Divisor *n.* مَقْسُومٌ عَلَيْهِ

Divorce *v. t.* or *n.* طَلَّقَ . طَلَاقٌ

Divulge *v. t.* اذاعَ . بَاحَ ب

Dizziness *n.* دُوَارٌ . رَنَحٌ

Dizzy *a.* مُصَابٌ بِالدُّوَار . مُتَرَنِّحٌ

Do *v. t.* (did, done). عَمِلَ ـَ فَعَلَ ـَ

Docile *a.* سَهْلُ التَّعْلِيمِ . مُطِيعٌ

Docility *n.* إِنْقِيَادٌ

Dock *n.* or *v.t.* مَرْبَطُ السُّفُنِ . قَصَّرَ

Dockyard *n.* تَرْسَخَانَةٌ

Doctor *n.* طَبِيبٌ (دَكْتُورٌ)

Doctorate *n.* رِتْبَةُ الدَّكْتُورِ

Doctrine *n.* تَعْلِيمٌ دِينِيٌّ . عَقِيدَةٌ

Document *n.* رَقِيمٌ . صَكٌّ

Doged *v. t.* or *i.* جَانَبَ . تَنَحَّى عَنْ

Doe *n.* ظَبْيَةٌ . انثى الإِيَّلِ او الوَعْلِ

Doff *v. t.* نَزَعَ ـَ كُسْوَةً

Dog *n.* كَلْبٌ ج كِلَابٌ

Dog-days *n. pl.* ايامُ الشِّعْرَى

Dogged *a.* عَنِيدٌ . عَازِمٌ . فَظ

Dogma *n.* عَقِيدَةٌ . مَذْهَبٌ

Dogmatic / **Dogmatical** } *a.* جَازِمُ الرَّأْيِ . تَجَبُّرٌ

Dogmatism *n.* جَزْمُ الرَّأْيِ . تَجَبُّرٌ

Dogmatize *v. t.* جَزَمَ فِي الرَّأْيِ

Dog-star *n.* الشِّعْرَى (نَجْمَةٌ)

Dole *n.* or *v. t.* نَصِيبٌ . هِبَةٌ حَقِيرَةٌ . اعطى صَدَقَةً زَهِيدَةً

Doleful *a.* مُغِمٌّ . مُحْزِنٌ

Doll *n.* الْعُوْبَة . لُعْبَةٌ

Dollar *n.* رِيَالٌ ج رِيَالاَتٌ

Dolorous *a.* مُؤْلِمٌ . مُحْزِنٌ

Dolphin *n.* دُلْفِينٌ ج دَلاَفِينُ

Dolt *n.* بَلِيدٌ . أَبْلَهُ

Domain *n.* مُلْكٌ . رِزقٌ . مَمْلَكَةٌ

Dome *n.* قُبَّةٌ

Domestic *a.* بَيْتِيٌّ . عَائِلِيٌّ . دَاجِنٌ

Domesticate *v. t.* دَجَّنَ . انَّسَ

Domicile *n.* or *v. t.* مَسْكَنٌ . مَقَامٌ . اسْكَنَ

Dominant *a.* مُتَسَلِّطٌ . سَائِدٌ . شَائِعٌ

Domination *n.* تَسَلُّطٌ . سِيَادَةٌ

Domineer *v. i.* تسَلَّطَ . بِغَطْرَسةٍ وَتَعَجْرُفٍ

Dominion *n.* مَمْلَكَةٌ . تَسَلُّطٌ

Don *v. t.* لَبِسَ ـَ

Donate *v. t.* مَنَحَ ـَ وَهَبَ . يَهِبُ

Donation *n.* هِبَةٌ . هَدِيَّةٌ

Donkey *n.* حِمَارٌ ج حَمِيرٌ

Donor *n.* وَاهِبٌ . مُعْطٍ

Doom *n.* قَضَاءٌ . نَصِيبٌ . هَلاَكٌ

Doomsday *n.* يَوْمُ ٱلدَّيْنُونَةِ

Door *n.* بَابٌ . مَدْخَلٌ

Dormant *n.* نَائِمٌ . غَيْرُ عَامِلٍ

Dormitory *n.* غُرْفَةُ ٱلنَّوْمِ . مَنَامٌ

Dorsal *a.* ظَهْرِيٌّ

Dose *n.* or *v. t.* جَرْعَةٌ . سقى جُرْعةً

Dot *n.* or *v. t.* نُقْطَة . نَقَطَ

Dotage *n.* خَرَفٌ . ضَعْفُ الْعَقْلِ كِبَرًا

Dotard *n.* خَرِفٌ

Dote *v. i.* خَرِفَ ـَ وَلِعَ

Double *a.* or *v. t.* مزْدَوِجٌ . ضَاعَفَ

Double-dealing *n.* خِدَاعٌ . مخَاتَلَةٌ

Doubt *n.* or *v. t.* شَكٌّ . رَيْبٌ . شَكَّ ـُ

Doubtful *a.* مَشْكُوكٌ فِيهِ . مُرْتَابٌ

Doubtless *ad.* بلاَ شَكٍّ أَوْ رَيْبٍ

Dough *n.* عَجِينٌ

Dove *n.* حَمَامَةٌ ج حَمَامٌ

Dove-cote *n.* بُرْجُ حَمَامٍ

Dower / **Dowry** *n.* صَدَاقٌ . مَهْرٌ

Down *pr.* or *n.* إِلَى تَحْتٍ . زَغَبٌ

Downfall *n.* هُبُوطٌ . خَرَابٌ

Downcast / **Downhearted** *a.* مَكْسُورُ ٱلْخَاطِرِ مَغْمُومٌ

Downright *a.* واضحٌ . صَافٍ . مُسْتَقِيمٌ

Downward / **Downwards** *ad.* إِلَى تَحْت او اسفَل

Doxology *n.* تَسْبِحَةٌ

Doze *v. i.* نَعَسَ ـَ نَامَ خَفِيفاً

Dozy *a.* نَاعِسٌ . نَعْسَانٌ

Dozen *n.* إِثْنَا عَشَرَ (دَزِّينَة)

Drachm *n.* دِرْهَمٌ

Draft *n.* سَحْبٌ . سفتجة . حوالة

Drag *v. t.* or *i.* سَحَبَ ـَ جَرَّ ـَ تَأَخَّرَ

Dragoman *n.* تُرْجُمَانٌ

Dragon *n.* تِنِّينٌ

Dragoon *n.* جُنْدِيٌّ مِنَ ٱلْفُرسانِ

Drain *n.* or *v. t.* قَنَاةٌ . فَرَّغَ بِقَنَاةٍ

Drainage *n.* صَرْفٌ . قَنَوَاتُ مَاءٍ

Drake *n.* ذَكَرُ ٱلْبَطِّ

Dram *n.* دِرْهَمٌ . جُرْعَةٌ مُسْكِرَةٌ

Drama *n.* رِوَايَةٌ تَشْخِيصِيَّةٌ

Dramatic *a.* مُخْتَصٌّ بِرِوَايَةٍ تَشْخِيصِيَّةٍ

Dramatist *n.* مُؤَلِّفُ رِوَايَاتٍ

Dramatize *v. t.* كَتَبَ رِوَايَاتٍ تَشْخِيصِيَّةً

Drape *v. t.* غَطَّى بِسُتْرٍ او سُجُوفٍ

Draper *n.* تَاجِرٌ بِالنسجِ ٱلصُّوفِيَّةِ

Drapery *n.* أَصْوَافٌ سُجُوفٌ

Draught *n.* مَجْرَى هَوَاءٍ . جَرْعة

Draughts *n.* لَعْبُ ٱلدَّامَا

Draughtsman *n.* رَسَّام

Draw *v. t.* سَحَبَ ـَ جَرَّ ـُ جذب

Drawback *n.* عَاقَة . مَانِعٌ

Drawer *n.* سَاحِبٌ . (جَرَّارٌ) . (دُرْجٌ)

Drawers *n. pl.* سِرْوَالٌ تَحْتِيٌّ

Drawing *n.* رَسْمٌ . تَخْطِيطٌ . سَحْبٌ

Drawing-room *n.* غُرْفَةُ إِسْتِقْبَالٍ

Drawl *v. i.* or *n.* اطَالَ ٱلصَّوْتَ فِي ٱلنُّطْقِ

Dray *n.* مَرْكَبَةٌ لِنَقْلِ ٱلْبَضَائِعِ

Dread *n.* or *v. t.* خَوْفٌ . هَوْلٌ . خَافَ

Dreaded / **Dreadful** *a.* هَائِلٌ . مُخِيفٌ

Dream *n.* or *v. i.* حُلْمٌ . حَلَمَ ـُ

Dreamless *a.* خَالٍ مِنَ ٱلأَحْلَامِ

Dreamy *a.* كَثِيرُ الاحْلَامِ

Dreariness *n.* وَحْشَةٌ . كَآبَة

Dreary *a.* مُغِمٌّ . مُسْتَوْحِشٌ

Dredge *v. t.* or *n.* جَرَفَ ـُ . مِجْرَفَةٌ بَحْرِيَّةٌ

Dregs *n. pl.* ثُفْلٌ . دُرْدِيٌّ

Drench *v. t.* بَلَّلَ

Dress *n.* or *v. t.* لِبَاسٌ . البَسَ . كسا

Dressmaker *n.* خَيَّاطَةٌ

Dribble *v. i.* قَطَرَ ـُ

Driblet *n.* كَمِّيَّةٌ قَلِيلَةٌ . جُزْءٌ صَغِيرٌ

Drift *v. i.* or *n.* تَكَوَّمَ إِنْسَاقَ . كَوْمَةُ ثَلْجٍ

Drill *n.* تَمْرِينُ ٱلْجُنُودِ . مِثْقَبٌ

Drill *v. t.* ثَقَبَ . مَرَّنَ ٱلْجُنُودَ

Drink (drank, drunk) *v. t.* شَرِبَ ـَ

Drip *v. i.* قَطَرَ ـُ

Drive *v. t.* or *i.* سَاقَ ـُ . حَرَّضَ . أَلْزَمَ

Drizzle *v. i.* or *n.* أَرَذَّ . نَضَّ . رَذَاذٌ

Droll *a.* مُضْحِكٌ

Drollery *n.* مَزْحٌ . دُعَابَةٌ

Dromedary *n.* بَعِيرٌ مُسْرِعٌ . هَجِينٌ

Drone *n.* ذَكَرُ ٱلنَّحْلِ . كَسْلَانٌ

Droop *v. i.* ذَبُلَ ـُ . ضَنِيَ ـَ

Drop *n.* or *v. t.* قَطْرَةٌ . قَطَرَ . أَسْقَطَ

Dropsy *n.* إِسْتِسْقَاءٌ

Dropsical *a.* مُسْتَسْقٍ

Dross *n.* رَغْوَةُ مَعْدَنٍ (زَغَلٌ)

Drought *n.* قَيْظٌ . قَحْطٌ

Drove *n.* قَطِيعٌ ج قُطْعَانٌ

Drown *v. t.* or *i.* غَرَّقَ . غَرِقَ ـَ

Drowsiness *n.* نعاسٌ

Drowsy *a.* نَعْسَانُ

Drudge *n.* or *v. i.* كَثِيرُ ٱلْكَدِّ . كَدَّ . جَدَّ

Drudgery *n.* عَنَآءٌ . شُغْلٌ مُمِلٌّ

Drug *n.* or *v. t.* عَقَارٌ . عَالَجَ بِٱلْعَقَاقِيرِ

Drugget *n.* لِبْدٌ ج لُبُودٌ

Druggist *n.* صَيْدَلَانِيٌّ . اجزَائِيٌّ

Drum *n.* or *v. i.* طَبْلٌ . طَبَّلَ

Drummer *n.* طَبَّال

Drunk / Drunken *a.* سَكْرَانُ ج سكَارَى

Drunkard *n.* سِكِّيرٌ

Drunkenness *n.* سُكْرٌ

Dry *a.* or *v. t.* يَابِسٌ . يَبَّسَ

Dry-goods *n. pl.* مَنْسُوجَاتٌ

Dryly *ad.* بِتَهَكُّمٍ

Dryness *n.* يُبُوسَةٌ

Dual *a.* مُثَنًّى

Dub *v. t.* سَمَّى . لَقَّبَ

Dubious *a.* مَشْكُوكٌ فِيهِ . مُشْتَبَهٌ

Ducal *a.* أَمِيرِيٌّ . دُوقِيٌّ

Ducat *n.* دِينَارٌ اورُبِيٌّ

Duchess *n.* أَمِيرَةٌ . إِمْرَأَةُ دُوقٍ

Duchy / Dukedom *n.* إِيَالَةُ دُوقٍ

Duck *n.* or *v. t.* بَطٌّ . غطَسَ

Duckling *n.* فَرْخُ ٱلْبَطِّ

Duct *n.* انْبُوبَةٌ . قَنَاةٌ

Ductile *a.* مُتَمَغِّطٌ . مَرِنٌ

Ductility *n.* لِينَة . إِمْتِغَاطِيَّةٌ

Due *n.* or *a.* حَقٌّ . مُسْتَحَقٌّ . مَطْلُوبٌ

Duel *n.* مُبَارَزَةُ ٱثْنَيْنِ

Duelist / Dueller *n.* مُبَارِزٌ

Dug *pp.* or *n.* مَحْفُورٌ . ضَرْعٌ ج ضُرُوعٌ

Duke *n.* اميرٌ (دُوقٌ)

Dull *a.* or *v. t.* كَالٌّ . بَلِيدٌ . اكلَ

Dullness *n.* كَلاَلَةٌ . بَلاَدَةٌ . بَلاَهة

Duly *ad.* كَمَا يَجِبُ . فِي حِينِهِ

Dumb *a.* أَخْرَسُ . أَبْكَمُ

Dumbness *n.* خَرَسٌ . بَكَمٌ

Dumpish *a.* كَئِيبٌ . مَغْمُومٌ . بَلِيدٌ

Dun *a.* or *v. t.* كُمَيْتُ ٱللَّوْنِ . طَلَبَ بِلَجَاجَةٍ

Dunce *n.* غَبِيٌّ . أَبْلَهُ

Dung *n.* or *v. t.* زِبْلٌ . سَمَادٌ . دمالٌ . سَمَّدَ

Dungeon *n.* حَبْسٌ . غَائِرٌ

Duodecimal *a.* or *n.* إِثْنَاعَشَرِيٌّ . جُزْءٌ مِنْ ١٢

Duodenum *n.* أَلْمَعَى ٱلاِثْنَا عَشَرِيٌّ

Dupe *n.* or *v. t.* غَرِيرٌ . غَرَّ ـُ

Duplicate *n.* or *v. t.* نُسْخَةٌ ثَانِيَةٌ . ثَنَّى

Duplicity *n.* مُخَادَعَةٌ . مُخَاتَلَةٌ

Durability / Durableness } *n.* صِفَةُ ٱلْبَقَاءِ

Durable *a.* مُسْتَمِرٌّ . بَاقٍ

Duration *n.* بَقَاءٌ . دَوَامٌ . مُدَّةٌ

During *pr.* اثْنَاءَ . مُدَّةَ . خِلاَلَ

Dusk *n.* غَسَقٌ . غَبَشٌ

Dusky *a.* غَاسِقٌ . مَائِلٌ إِلَى ٱلسَّوَادِ

Dust *n.* or *v. t.* غُبَارٌ . مَسَحَ مِنَ ٱلْغُبَارِ

Duster *n.* مَاسِحُ ٱلْغُبَارِ . مِمْسَحَةٌ

Dustpan *n.* مَجْرُودُ ٱلْغُبَارِ

Dusty *a.* مُغَبَّرٌ . مُتَعَفِّرٌ

Duteous / Dutiful } *a.* مُتَمِّمٌ وَاجِبَاتِهِ . مُطِيعٌ

Duty *n.* فَرْضٌ . وَاجِبٌ . رَسْمٌ جُمْرُكٍ

Dwarf *n.* or *a.* / Dwarfish *a.* } قَزَمٌ . قَصِيرُ ٱلْقَدِّ

Dwarf *v. t.* صَيَّرَهُ قَزَماً . مَنَعَ نُمُوَّهُ

Dwell *v. i.* سَكَنَ ـُ . قَطَنَ ـُ

Dwelling *n.* مَسْكَنٌ . بَيْتٌ

Dwindle *v. i.* صَغُرَ . إِنْحَطَّ . قَلَّ

Dye *v. t.* or *n.* صَبَغَ ـُ . صِبْغَةٌ . صِبَاغٌ

Dyeing *n.* صَبْغٌ صِبَاغَةٌ

Dyer *n.* صَبَّاغٌ

Dying *pp.* of *die.* مَائِتٌ . فَانٍ

Dynasty *n.* دَوْلَةٌ مُلُوكٍ

Dysentery *n.* سَحْجٌ . دُوسَنْطَارْيَا

Dyspepsia *n.* سُوءُ ٱلْهَضْمِ . تُخْمَةٌ

Dyspeptic *a.* or *n.* مُتَعَلِّقٌ بِالتُّخْمَةِ . مُصَابٌ بِهَا

E

Each *a.* كُلٌّ . كُلُّ وَاحِدٍ

Eager *a.* رَاغِبٌ . تَائِقٌ . مُلْهِفٌ لِ

Eagerness *n.* رَغْبَةٌ . شَوْقٌ

Eagle *n.* نَسْرٌ ج نُسُورٌ

Eaglet *n.* فَرْخُ نَسْرٍ

Ear *n.* أُذُنٌ ج آذَانٌ

Ear of corn *n.* سُنْبُلَةٌ

Earl *n.* رُتْبَةٌ بَيْنَ امْرَاءِ الانكليزِ

Early *a.* or *ad.* مُبَكِّرٌ . بَاكِراً

Earn *v. t.* إِسْتَحَقَّ اجْرَةً . كَسَبَ ـِ

Earnest *a.* or *n.* جَادٌّ . عَرْبُونٌ

Earnestness *n.* غَيْرَةٌ . جِدٌّ . إِهْتِمَامٌ

Earnings *n.* أَجْرٌ . كَسْبٌ

Ear-ring *n.* قُرْطٌ ج أَقْرَاطٌ

Earth *n.* الأَرْضُ . تُرَابٌ

Earthen *a.* تُرَابِيٌّ . مِنْ طِينٍ

Earthen-ware *n.* أَوَانٍ خَزَفِيَّةٌ

Earthquake *n.* زَلْزَلَةٌ ج زَلَازِلُ

Ease *n.* or *v. t.* رَاحَةٌ سُهُولَةٌ . ارَاحَ

Easiness *n.* سُهُولَةٌ . رَاحَةٌ

East *n.* الشَّرْقُ . ٱلْمَشْرِقُ

Easter *n.* عِيدُ ٱلْفِصْحِ

Easterly / Eastern } *a.* شَرْقِيٌّ

Eastward *ad.* نَحْوَ ٱلشَّرْقِ . شَرْقاً

Easy *a.* سَهْلٌ . هَيِّنٌ

Eat *v.t.* or *i.* أَكَلَ ـُ

Eatable *n.*or *a.* مَأْكُولٌ . مَا يُؤْكَلُ

Eaves *n. pl.* أَطْنَافُ ٱلسَّقْفِ

Ebb *v. i.* or *n.* جَزْرٌ . جَزَرَ ـِ

Ebony *n.* أَبَنُوسٌ

Ebullition *n.* غَلَيَانٌ . فَوَرَانٌ

Eccentric *n.* or *a.* مُنْحَرِفٌ . غَرِيبٌ

Ecclesiastic *n.* / Ecclesiastical *a.* } أَكْلِيرِكِيٌّ كَنَائِسِيٌّ

Eaves *n.* or *v. i.* or *t.* صَدًى . أَصْدَى

Eclipse *n.* كُسُوفٌ . خُسُوفٌ

Ecliptic *n.* مَدَارُ ٱلشَّمْسِ

Economic / Economical } *a.* إِقْتِصَادِيٌّ

Economize *v. t.* or *i.* إِقْتَصَدَ

Economy *n.* إِقْتِصَادٌ

Ecstasy *n.* شَغَفٌ . ذُهُولٌ

Ecstatic *n.* شَغَفِيٌّ . مُفْتَتِنٌ

Eddy *n.* دَرْدُورٌ

Eden *n.* عَدْنٌ

Edge *n.* حَدٌّ . حَافَةٌ

Edgewise *ad.* جَانِبِيًّا

Edible *see* eatable.

Edict *n.* أَمْرٌ سُلْطَانِيٌّ . فَرَمَانٌ

Edifice *n.* بِنَاءٌ . عِمَارَةٌ

Edify *v. t.* بَنَى . أَفَادَ . هَذَّبَ

Edit *v.t.* هَذَّبَ لِلطَّبْعِ . نَقَّحَ

Edition *n.* طَبْعٌ . طَبْعَةٌ

Editor *n.* مُهَذِّبٌ . رَئِيسُ تَحْرِيرِ جَرِيدَةٍ

Educate *v. t.* عَلَّمَ . رَبَّى . دَرَّبَ

Education *n.* تَعْلِيمٌ . تَرْبِيَةٌ . تَهْذِيبٌ

Educe *v. t.* إِسْتَخْرَجَ . اِنْتَجَ

Eel *n.* سَمَكٌ كَالْحَيَّةِ . حَنْكَلِيسٌ

Efface *v. t.* مَحَا ـُ . طَلَسَ ـِ

Effect *n.* or *v. t.* نَتِيجَةٌ . تَأْثِيرٌ . سَبَّبَ

Effective / Effectual } *a.* فَعَّالٌ . مُنْتِجٌ . عَامِلٌ

Effects *n. pl.* أَمْتِعَة . أَثَاثٌ

Effeminacy *n.* خُنَاثَة . تَخَنُّثٌ

Effeminate *a.* or *v. t.* خَنِث . خَنَّثَ

Effervesce *v. t.* فَارَ . ازْبَدَ

Effervescence *n.* فَوَرَانٌ

Effervescent *a.* فَوَّارٌ . مُزْبِدٌ

Effete *a.* غَيْرُ مُنْتِجٍ . مَنْهُوك

Efficacious *a.* فَعَّالٌ . عَامِلٌ

Efficacy / **Efficiency** } *n.* قُوَّة فَعَّالة . فَاعِلِيَّة

Efficient *a.* فَعَّالٌ . مُنْتِجٌ

Effigy *n.* تِمْثَالٌ . صُورَة

Efflorescence *n.* إِزْهَارٌ

Effort *n.* إِجْتِهَادٌ . سَعْيٌ

Effrontery *n.* وَقَاحَة . عَجْرَفَة

Effulgence *n.* بَهَاءٌ . رَوْنَقٌ

Effulgent *a.* بَهِيٌّ . لَامِعٌ

Effusion *n.* سَفْكٌ . إِهْرَاقٌ

Egg *n.* بَيْضَة ج بُيُوضٌ وَبَيْضَات

Egg-plant *n.* بَاذِنْجَانٌ

Egoism / **Egotism** } *n.* عُجْبٌ . تَعْظِيمُ ٱلذَّات

Egotist *n.* / **Egotistic** *a.* } مُعْجَبٌ بِنَفْسِهِ

Egregious *a.* فَائِق (فِي ٱلسُّوءِ)

Egress *n.* خُرُوجٌ . مَخْرَجٌ

Egyptian *a.* مِصْرِيٌّ

Eight *n.* ثَمَانِيَة . ثَمَانٍ

Eighth *a.* أَلثَّامِن

Eighteen *n.* ثَمَانِيَةَ عَشَرَ وَثَمَانِي عَشْرَةَ

Eighty *n.* ثَمَانُونَ

Either *a.* or *pron.* إِمَّا . كُلٌّ مِنِ ٱثْنَيْنِ

Ejaculate *v. t.* نَطَقَ بِصُرَاخٍ أو دُعَاء

Eject *v. t.* قَذَفَ . أَخْرَجَ . طَرَدَ ـُ

Ejection *n.* قَذْفٌ . إِخْرَاجٌ

Elaborate *v. t.* or *a.* تَمَّمَ . أَتْقَنَ . مُتْقَنٌ

Elapse *v. i.* مَضَى ـِ . إِنْقَضَى

Elastic *a.* مَرِنٌ . لَدْن

Elasticity *n.* مُرُونَة . لُدُونَة

Elated *pp.* مُفْتَخِرٌ . مُبْتَهِجٌ

Elation *n.* تشامخ . إِبْتِهَاجٌ

Elbow *n.* or *v. t.* مِرْفَقٌ دَفَعَ بِهِ

Elder *a.* or *n.* اكْبَرُ عُمْراً . شَيْخٌ

Elder *n.* (plant). بَلَسَانٌ

Elderly *a.* مُتَقَدِّمٌ فِي ٱلسِّنِّ

Eldest *a.* الأَكْبَرُ فِي ٱلْعُمْرِ

Elect *v. t.* or *a.* or *n.* إِنْتَخَبَ . مُخْتَارٌ

Election *n.* إِنْتِخَابٌ

Electric / Electrical } *a.* كَهْرَبَائِيٌّ

Electricity *n.* كَهْرَبَائِيَّةٌ

Electrify *v. t.* كَهْرَبَ

Elegance *n.* ظَرَافَةٌ . لَبَاقَةٌ

Elegant *a.* ظَرِيفٌ . كَيِّسٌ . مَلِيحٌ

Elegy *n.* مَرْثَاةٌ ج مَرَاثٍ

Element *n.* عُنْصُرٌ . مَبْدَأٌ

Elemental / Elementary } *a.* عُنْصَرِيٌّ . اوَّلِيٌّ

Elephant *n.* فِيلٌ ج افيال

Elevate *v. t.* رَفَعَ . رَقَى . على

Elevation *n.* رَفْعٌ . إِرْتِفَاعٌ

Elevator *n.* رَافِعٌ . مُعَلٍّ

Eleven *n.* احَدَ عَشَرَ

Eleventh *a.* ٱلْحَادِي عَشَرَ

Elicit *v. t.* إِسْتَخْرَجَ . إِسْتَبَانَ

Elide *v. t.* حَذَفَ

Eligible *a.* جَدِيرٌ بِالاِنْتِخَابِ

Eliminate *v. t.* اخْرَجَ . حَذَفَ

Elimination *n.* إِخْرَاجٌ

Elision *n.* حَذْفٌ

Elk *n.* نَوْعٌ مِنَ ٱلإِيَّلِ

Ellipse *n.* إِهْلِيلَجٌ

Elliptical *a.* إِهْلِيلَجِيُّ ٱلشَّكْلِ

Elm *n.* دَرْدَارٌ (نَوْعٌ مِنَ ٱلشجرِ)

Elocution *n.* نُطْقٌ . فَصَاحَةٌ

Elocutionist *n.* إِسْتَاذُ ٱلْخِطَابَةِ

Elongate *v. t.* أَطَالَ طَوَّلَ

Elope *v. i.* هَرَبَ سِرًّا

Eloquence *n.* فَصَاحَةٌ. بَلاغَةٌ

Eloquent *a.* فَصِيحٌ. بَلِيغٌ

Else *pron.* or *a.* غَيْرُ. وَإِلا

Elsewhere *ad.* بِغَيْرِ مَكَانٍ

Elucidate *v. t.* اوْضَحَ. شَرَحَ ـَ

Elude *v. t.* تَمَلَّصَ مِنْ. تَجَنَّبَ

Emaciate *v. i.* or *t.* هُزِلَ ـُ

Emaciation *n.* هُزَالٌ

Emancipate *v. t.* حَرَّرَ. اعْتَقَ

Emancipation *n.* تَحْرِيرٌ

Emanate *v. i.* نَشَأَ ـَ. صَدَرَ ـُ

Emasculate *v. t.* اضْعَفَ. خَصَى

Embalm *v. t.* حَنَطَ

Embankment *n.* سَدٌّ. حَاجِزٌ

Embargo *n.* حَجْزُ ٱلسُّفُنِ عَنِ ٱلسفرِ

Embark *v. t.* رَكِبَ سَفِينَةً. بَاشَرَ

Embarkation *n.* نُزُولٌ فِي سَفِينَةٍ

Embarrass *v. t.* لَبَّكَ. رَبَكَ ـُ

Embarrassment *n.* إِرْتِبَاكٌ. لَبْكَةٌ

Embassy *n.* سَفَارَةٌ

Embellish *v. t.* زَيَّنَ. زَخْرَفَ

Embellishment *n.* زِينَةٌ. زَخْرَفَةٌ

Embezzle *v.* إِخْتَلَسَ

Embezzlement *n.* إِخْتِلَاسٌ

Emblem *n.* رَمْزٌ. كِنَايَةٌ

Emblematic / **Emblematical** } *a.* رَمْزِيٌّ

Embody *v. t.* جَسَّمَ. ضَمَّنَ

Embolden *v. t.* شَجَّعَ. جَرَّأَ

Embrace *v. t.* or *n.* عَانَقَ. تَضَمَّنَ. مُعَانَقَةٌ

Embroider *v. t.* طَرَّزَ

Embroidery *n.* تَطْرِيزٌ

Embroil *v. t.* شَوَّشَ. هَيَّجَ. افْتَنَ

Embryo *n.* جَنِينٌ ج اجِنَّةٌ. جُرْثُومَةٌ

Embryology *n.* عِلْمٌ يَبْحَثُ عَنِ ٱلاجِنَّةِ

Emerald *n.* زُمُرُّدٌ

Emerge *v. i.* خَرَجَ ـُ . ظَهَرَ ـَ

Emergency *n.* حَادِثَةٌ غَيْرُ مُنْتَظَرَةٍ ضَرُورَة

Emetic *a.* or *n.* مُقيّء

Emigrant *n.* مُهَاجِرٌ

Emigrate *v. i.* هَاجَرَ اَلْوَطَنَ

Emigration *n.* مُهَاجَرَةٌ

Eminence *n.* إِرْتِفَاعٌ . سُمُوٌّ

Eminent *a.* سَامٍ . شَهِيْرٌ

Emissary *n.* رَسُوْلٌ . جَاسُوْسٌ

Emission *n.* إِصْدَارٌ . نَشْرٌ

Emit *v. t.* اَصْدَرَ . نَشَرَ ـ

Emollient *a.* مُلَيِّنٌ

Emotion *n.* انْفِعَالٌ نَفْسَانِيٌّ

Emotional *a.* انْفِعَالِيٌّ . سَرِيْعُ الاِنْفِعَالِ

Empale *v. t.* خَوْزَقَ

Emperor *v. t.* سُلْطَانٌ (امْبَرَاطُورٌ)

Emphasis *n.* تَأْكِيْدٌ . تَشْدِيْدُ الصَّوْتِ

Emphasize *v. t.* أَكَّدَ . شَدَّدَ . اللَّفْظَ

Emphatic *a.* مُؤَكَّدٌ . مُشَدَّدٌ

Empire *n.* مَمْلَكَةٌ . سَلْطَنَة

Employ *v. t.* إِسْتَخْدَمَ . شَغَّلَ

Employé *n.* مُسْتَخْدَمٌ . اجِيْرٌ

Employer *n.* مُسْتَخْدِمٌ . مُشَغِّلٌ

Employment *n.* شُغْلٌ . مَصْلَحَة

Empower *v. t.* قَدَّرَ . مَكَّنَ . فَوَّض

Empress *n.* سُلْطَانَة (أَمبَرَاطُورَة)

Emptiness *n.* فَرَاغ . خُلُوٌّ

Empty *a.* خَالٍ . فَارِغٌ . بَاطِلٌ

Empty *v. t.* افْرَغَ

Emulate *v. t.* نَافَسَ . بَارَى

Enable *v. t.* قَدَّرَ . مَكَّنَ

Enact *v. t.* سَنَّ . رَسَمَ ـُ

Enactment *n.* سُنَّةٌ . شَرِيْعَة

Enamel *n.* or *v. t.* مِيْنَاءٌ . غَشَّى بِالْمِيْنَاء

Enamour *v. t.* عَشِقَ . افْتَتَنَ

Encamp *v. t.* or *i.* نَزَلَ ـِ . عَسْكَرَ

Encampment *n.* مَحَلَة . معسكَرٌ

Enchain *v. t.* غَلَّ . سَلْسَلَ . أَوْثَقَ

Enchant *v. t.* سَحَرَ ـَ . فَتَنَ ـِ . رَقَى

Enchantment *n.* سِحْرٌ . رُقْيَةٌ

Encircle *v. t.* أَحَاطَ . أَحْدَقَ بِ

Enclosure *n.* حَوْشٌ . سِيَاجٌ

Encompass *v. t.* احَاطَ . أَحْدَقَ بِ

Encounter *n.* مُصَادَفَةٌ . معرَكَةٌ .
or *v. t.* صَادَفَ . بَارَزَ

Encourage *v. t.* شَجَّعَ ؛ حَرَّضَ عَلَى

Encouragement *n.* تَشْجِيعٌ

Encouraging *a.* مُشَجِّعٌ . مُقَوِّي ٱلْأَمَلِ

Encroach *v. t.* تعدى عَلَى

Encroachment *n.* تَعَدٍّ عَلَى

Encumber *v. t.* ثَقَّلَ . أَعَاقَ . عَرْقَلَ

Encumbrance *n.* ثِقْلٌ . إِعَاقَةٌ

Encyclopedia *n.* دَائِرَةُ ٱلْمَعَارِفِ

End *n.* or *v. t.* نِهَايَةٌ . غَايَة . أَنهى

Endanger *v. t.* أَوقعَ فِي ٱلْخَطَرِ

Endear *v. t.* حَبَّبَ . صَيَّرَ عَزِيزاً

Endeavour *v. t.* or *n.* إِجْتَهَدَ . سَعَى ـَ

Ending *n.* إِنْتِهَاءٌ . خِتَامٌ

Endless *a.* غَيْرُ مُتَنَاهٍ . بِلاَ نِهَايَةٍ

Endow *v. t.* وَقَفَ لَهُ رِزْقًا . امْهَرَ

Endowment *n.* وَقْفٌ . مَهْرٌ

Endurable *a.* مُمْكِنٌ إِحْتِمَالُهُ . محتَمِلٌ

Endurance *n.* إِحْتِمَالٌ . بَقَاءٌ

Endure *v. t.* or *i.* بَقِيَ ـَ . إِحْتَمَلَ

Enemy *n.* عَدُوٌّ ج أَعْدَاءٌ

Energetic / **Energetical** } *a.* نَشِيطٌ . هُمَامٌ

Energize *v. t.* قَوَّى . شَدَّدَ

Energy *n.* هِمَّةٌ . جِدٌّ . نَشَاطٌ

Enervate / **Enfeeble** } *v. t.* اضْعَفَ . أَوْهَنَ

Enforce *v. t.* أَجْرَى . أَنْفَذَ

Enforcement *n.* إِجْرَاءٌ . إِنْفَاذٌ

Enfranchise *v. t.* مَنَحَ حُقُوقَ ٱلْامَّةِ

Engage *v. t.* عَاهَدَ . إِسْتَخْدَمَ . بَارَزَ

Engaged *a.* مَشْغُولٌ . مُقَيَّدٌ . مَخْطُوبٌ

Engagement *n.* وَعْدٌ . خِطْبَةٌ قِتَالٌ

Engaging *a.* فَاتِنٌ . مُسْتَمِيلُ ٱلْعَوَاطِفِ

Engender *v. t.* وَلَّدَ . أَوْجَدَ . سَبَّبَ

Engine *n.* آلَة بُخَارِيَّة

Engineer *n.* مُهَنْدِسٌ

English *a.* or *n.* إِنْكِلِيزِيٌّ . ٱلْإِنْكِلِيزُ

Engrave *v. t.* حَفَرَ ـِ . نَقَشَ ـُ

Engraver *n.* حَفَّارٌ . نَقَّاشٌ

Engraving *n.* نَقْشٌ . صُورَةٌ مَحْفُورَةٌ

Engross *v. t.* شَغَلَ . نَسَخَ بِخَطٍّ وَاضِحٍ

Engulf *v. t.* إِبْتَلَعَ

Enhance *v. t.* رَقَّى . عَظَّمَ

Enigma *n.* لُغْزٌ . احْجِيَةٌ

Enigmatic, Enigmatical *a.* لُغْزِيٌّ . غَامِضٌ

Enjoin *v. t.* أَمَرَ ـُ

Enjoy *v. t.* إِلْتَذَّ . تَمَتَّعَ بِ

Enjoyable *a.* لَذِيذٌ . مُفْرِحٌ

Enjoyment *n.* لَذَّةٌ . حظ . تَمَتُّعٌ

Enlarge *v. t.* or *i.* وَسَّعَ . إِتَّسَعَ

Enlargement *n.* تَوْسِيعٌ . تَوَسُّعٌ

Enlighten *v. t.* عَلَّمَ . أَنَارَ

Enlist *v. t.* or *i.* ضَمَّ . دَوَّنَ ٱسْماً

Enlistment *n.* تَقْيِيدٌ . تَدْوِينٌ

Enliven *v. i.* انعش . أَبْهَجَ

Enmity *n.* عَدَاوَةٌ

Ennoble *v. t.* شَرَّفَ . رَقَّى

Enormity *n.* جَسَامَةٌ . فَظَاعَة

Enormous *a.* عَظِيمٌ جِدًّا . مُفْرِطٌ

Enough *n.* or *ad.* كاف

Enrage *v. t.* أَغَاظَ . أَغْضَبَ

Enrich *v. t.* اغنى . أَخْصَبَ

Enrol *v. t.* سجَّلَ . دَوَّنَ

Ensign *n.* عَلَمٌ . ضَابِطٌ

Enslave *v. t.* إستعبد . إسترق

Ensnare *v. t.* أخذ بحيلة . شبك

Ensue *v. i.* تلا ـ تبع ـ

Entail *v. t.* أوقف . جر

Entangle *v. t.* عرقل . شبك ـ

Enter *v. t.* **or** *i.* أدخل أو دخل ـ

Enterprise *n.* مسعى . مشروع

Eeterprising *a.* ذو إقدام . همام

Entertain *v. t.* ضاف . سلى

Entertaining *a.* مسل . سار

Entertainment *a.* تسلية . ضيافة

Enthrone *v. t.* أجلس على العرش

Enthusiasm *n.* حماسة . نشاط

Enhusiast *n.* / **Enthusiastic** *a.* } حمس . نشيط

Entice *v. t.* أغوى . راود . تملق

Entire *a.* كامل . كل . صحيح

Entirely *ad.* تماماً . بكليته

Entitle *v. t.* لقب . أعطى حقاً في

Entomb *v. t.* قبر ـ . دفن ـ

Entrails *n. pl.* أحشاء . أمعاء

Entrance *n.* مدخل . دخول

Entrance *v. t.* سحر ـ . أبهج

Entrap *v. t.* شبك ـ . أخذ بحيلة

Entreat *v. t.* توسل . تضرع

Entreaty *n.* توسل . إلتماس

Entry *n.* دخول . مدخل . تقييد

Entwine *v. t.* فتل ـ . حبك ـ

Enumerate *v. t.* عد ـ . أحصى

Enunciate *v. t.* أعلن . نطق ـ

Envelop *v. t.* غلف . لف ـ

Envelope *n.* غلاف . ظرف

Envenom *v. t.* صم ـ . أحقد

Enviable *a.* مهيج الحسد . مشتهى

Envious *a.* حاسد . حسود

Environ *v. t.* أحاط . أحدق به

Environment *n.* إحاطة

Environs *n. pl.* سَوَادٌ . ضَوَاحٍ

Envoy *n.* رَسُولٌ . مُعْتَمَدٌ . سَفِيرٌ

Envy *n.* or *v. t.* حَسَدٌ . حَسَدَ ـ

Ephemeral *a.* فَانٍ . قَلِيلُ ٱلْبَقَاءِ

Epic *a.* or *n.* قِصَّةٌ شِعْرِيَّةٌ

Epicure *n.* / Epicurean *a.* } مُتَنَعِّمٌ . شَهْوَانِيٌّ

Epidemic *n.* or *a.* وَبَأٌ . وَبَائِيٌّ

Epidermis *n.* بَشَرَةٌ

Epiglottis *n.* لِسَانُ ٱلْمِزْمَارِ

Epigram *n.* شِعْرٌ . قَصِيرٌ . فَكِهٌ

Epilepsy *n.* دَآءُ ٱلصَّرْعِ

Epileptic *a.* صَرِيعٌ . مُصَابٌ بِٱلصَّرْعِ

Episcopal *a.* / Episcopalian *n.* } أُسْقُفِيٌّ

Episode *n.* حَادِثَةٌ . إِسْتِطْرَادِيَّةٌ

Epistle *n.* رِسَالَةٌ

Epitaph *n.* كِتَابَةٌ عَلَى قَبْرٍ

Epithet *n.* صِفَةٌ . لَقَبٌ

Epitome *n.* مُخْتَصَرٌ . خُلَاصَةٌ

Epitomize *v. t.* لَخَّصَ . أَوْجَزَ . إِخْتَصَرَ

Epoch *n.* عَصْرٌ . زَمَنٌ

Equable *a.* مُتَسَاوٍ

Equal *a.* or *n.* or *v. t.* مُسَاوٍ . قَرِينٌ . سَاوَى

Equality *n.* مُسَاوَاةٌ . مُعَادَلَةٌ

Equalize *v. t.* سَاوَى . عَدَّلَ

Equanimity *n.* هُدُوءُ ٱلْعَقْلِ

Equation *n.* تَسْوِيَةٌ . مُعَادَلَةٌ جَبْرِيَّةٌ

Equator *n.* خَطُّ ٱلْإِسْتِوَآءِ

Equatorial *a.* مَنْسُوبٌ لِخَطِّ ٱلْإِسْتِوَآءِ

Equestrian *a.* or *n.* مُتَعَلِّقٌ بِرُكُوبِ ٱلْخَيْلِ . خَيَّالٌ . فَارِسٌ

Equiangular *a.* مُتَسَاوِي ٱلزَّوَايَا

Equidistant *a.* مُتَسَاوِي ٱلْبُعْدِ

Equilateral *a.* مُتَسَاوِي ٱلْأَضْلَاعِ

Equilibrium *n.* تَوَازُنٌ

Equinoctial *a.* إِعْتِدَالِيٌّ

Equinox *n.* إِعْتِدَالُ ٱللَّيْلِ وَٱلنَّهَارِ

Equip *v.t.* جوز . أهب

Epuipage *n.* مهمات . اتباع

Equipment *n.* تجهيز . جهاز

Equitable *a.* عادل . منصف

Equity *n.* عدل . إنصاف

Equivalent *n.* مساوٍ . معادل

Equivocal *a.* ذو معنيين . مشتبه

Equivocate *v. t.* لبس في الكلام

Era *n.* عصر . مدة

Eradicate *v. t.* إستأصل

Erase *v. t.* محا ـُ . سحق ـَ

Erasure *n.* محو

Ere *ad.* قبل أن . قبل

Erect *a.* or *v. t.* منتصب . نصب ـُ . اقام

Erection *n.* إقامة . نصب

Erelong *ad.* بعد قليل

Erosion *n.* قضم . قرض

Erosive *a.* آكل . قاضم

Err *v. i.* غلط ـَ . ضل ـِ . خطئ

Errand *n.* عرض

Erratic *a.* ضال . زائغ . غير مضبوط

Erratum *n.* / Errata *pl. n.* غلط . خطأ

Erroneous *a.* مغلوط

Error *n.* غلط . خطأ

Erudition *n.* علم غزير

Eruption *n.* إنفجار . بثر

Erysipelas *n.* مرض الحمرة

Escape *n.* or *v. i.* نجاة . نجا ـُ

Eschew *v. t.* رفض ـِ . تنحى عن

Escort *v. t.* or *n.* خفر ـِ ـُ . خفر

Esophagus *n.* المريء

Especial *a.* خاص . خصوصي

Especially *ad.* خاصة

Espouse *v. t.* خطب ـُ (إمرأة)

Espy *v. t.* إستطلع . إستكشف

Esquire *n.* سيد

Essay *v. t.*	جَرَّبَ
Essay *n.*	تجربة . مَقَالَةٌ
Essence *n.*	مَاهِيَّةٌ . عِطْرٌ
Essential *a.*	جَوْهَرِيٌّ . ضَرُورِيٌّ
Essentially *ad.*	حَقِيقَةً
Establish *v. t.*	اقَامَ . ثَبَّتَ
Establishment *n.*	إِقَامَةٌ . بِنَاءٌ
Estate *n.*	حَالٌ . مُلْكٌ
Real-estate *n.*	أَلْأَمْلَاكُ غَيْرُ ٱلْمَنْقُولَةِ
Esteem *n.* or *v. t.*	إِعْتِبَارٌ . إِعْتَبَرَ
Estimable *a.*	مُسْتَحِقُّ ٱلْمَدْحِ
Estimate *v. t.*	حَسَبَ . ثَمَّنَ
Estimation *n.*	تَثْمِينٌ . إِعْتِبَارٌ
Estrange *v. t.*	نَفَّرَ
Estuary *n.*	مَصَبُّ نَهرٍ
Eternal *a.*	سَرْمَدِيٌّ . أَبَدِيٌّ
Eternity *n.*	أَلْأَبَدُ . أَلْأَزَلُ
Ether *n.*	إِثِيرٌ
Ethical *a.*	ادَبِيٌّ
Ethics *n. pl.*	عِلْمُ ٱلْآدَابِ
Ethnology *n.*	أَلْبَحْثُ عَنْ أَجْنَاسِ ٱلْبَشَرِ
Etiquette *n.*	آدَابُ ٱلْإِكْرَامِ
Etymology *n.*	إِشْتِقَاقُ ٱلْكَلَامِ
Eulogy *n.*	تَقْرِيظٌ . تَأْبِينٌ
Eunuch *n.*	خَصِيٌّ
European *n.*	اوْرُبِيٌّ
Evacuate *v. t.*	أَخْلَى . تَرَكَ
Evacuation *n.*	إِخْلَاءٌ . تَرْكٌ
Evade *v. t.*	إِجْتَنَبَ . مَلِصَ مِنْ
Evanescent *a.*	فَانٍ . زَائِلٌ
Evangelical *a.*	إِنْجِيلِيٌّ
Evangelist *n.*	مُبَشِّرٌ إِنْجِيلِيٌّ
Evaporate *v. i.*	تَحَوَّلَ بُخَاراً
Evasion *n.*	إِجْتِنَابٌ . مُوَارَبَةٌ
Evasive *a.*	مُجْتَنِبٌ . مُحَاوِلٌ . مُوَارِبٌ
Eve, Evening *n.*	مَسَاءٌ . عَشِيَّةٌ

Even *a.* سَهْلٌ . مُسْتَوٍ
Even *ad.* حَتَّى . كَذٰلِكَ . ايضاً
Event *n.* حَادِثَةٌ . نَتِيجَةٌ
Eventful *a.* كَثِيرُ ٱلْحَوَادِثِ
Eventually *a.* فِي ٱلنِّهَايَةِ . أَخِيراً
Ever *ad.* دَائِماً . كُلَّ حِينٍ
Evergreen *n.* نَبَات دَائِمُ ٱلْإِخْضِرَارِ
Everlasting *a.* أَبَدِيٌّ . بَاقٍ
Evermore *ad.* دَائِماً . أَبَداً
Every *a.* كُلّ
Everywhere *ad.* فِي كُلِّ مَكَانٍ
Evict *v. t.* أَخْرَجَ . طَرَدَ ـُ
Evidence *n.* بُرْهَانٌ . دَلِيلٌ . شَهَادَةٌ
Evident *a.* وَاضِحٌ . ظَاهِرٌ . جَلِيٌّ
Evil *n.* or *a.* شَرٌّ . شِرِّيرٌ
Evince *v. t.* اظْهَرَ . بَيَّنَ
Evoke *v. t.* إِسْتَدْعَى
Evolution *n.* نَشْرٌ . نُشُوءٌ
Evolve *v. t.* نَشَرَ ـُ اخْرَجَ
Ewe *n.* شَاةٌ . نَعْجَةٌ
Exact *a.* or *v. t.* مَضْبُوطٌ . أَلْزَمَ
Exaction *n.* بَلْصٌ . ظُلْمٌ فِي ٱلْأَخْذِ
Exactly *ad.* تَمَاماً . بِضَبْطٍ
Exactness *n.* ضَبْطٌ . إِتْقَانٌ
Exaggerate *v. t.* بَالَغَ . غَالَى فِي
Exaggeration *n.* مُبَالَغَةٌ . مُغَالَاةٌ
Exalt *v. t.* رَقَّى . عَظَّمَ . فَخَّمَ
Exaltation *n.* تَرْقِيَةٌ . سُمُوٌّ . رِفْعَةٌ
Exalted *a.* مُرْتَفِعٌ . سَامٍ
Examination *n.* فَحْصٌ . إِمْتِحَانٌ
Examine *v. t.* فَحَصَ . إِمْتَحَنَ
Example *n.* مِثَالٌ . نَمُوذَجٌ . قِدوَة
Exasperate *v. i.* أَغَاظَ . أَسْخَطَ
Exasperation *n.* إِغَاظَةٌ . حَنَقٌ
Excavate *v. t.* حَفَرَ ـِ . نَبَشَ ـُ
Excavation *n.* حَفْرٌ . حُفْرَةٌ

Exceed *v.t.* or *i.* زَادَ ـِ . فَاقَ ـُ . جَاوَزَ

Exceeding *a.* فَائِقٌ . عَظِيمٌ جِدًّا

Exceedingly *ad.* جِدًّا . لِلْغَايَةِ

Excel *v. t.* or *i.* فَاقَ ـُ . سَبَقَ ـُ

Excellence / Excellency *n.* فَضْلٌ . جُوْدَةٌ . سُمُوٌّ

Excellent *a.* فَاضِلٌ . فَاخِرٌ . نَفِيسٌ

Except *v. t.* إِسْتَثْنَى مِنْ

Except / Excepting *pr.* إِلاَّ . غَيْرُ . مَا عَدَا

Exception *n.* إِسْتِثْنَاءٌ . شُذُوذٌ

Exceptional *a.* شَاذٌّ . إِسْتِثْنَائِيٌّ

Excess *n.* زِيَادَةٌ . مُجَاوَزَةُ ٱلْحَدِّ

Excessive *a.* زَائِدٌ جِدًّا . مُفْرِطٌ

Exchange *v. t.* or *n.* بَادَلَ . مُبَادَلَةٌ

Excision *n.* قَطْعٌ . بَتْرٌ

Excitable *a.* سَرِيعُ ٱلْهَيَجَانِ

Excite *v. t.* هَيَّجَ . أَثَارَ . حَرَّكَ

Excited *a.* مُتَهَيِّجٌ . ثَائِرٌ

Exciting *a.* مُهَيِّجٌ . مُحَرِّكٌ

Excitement *n.* هَيَجَانٌ . ثَوَرَانٌ

Exclaim *v. i.* صَاحَ ـِ . صَرَخَ ـُ

Exclamation *n.* صُرَاخٌ . صَيْحَةٌ

Exclude *v.t.* أَخْرَجَ . إِسْتَثْنَى

Exclusion *n.* إِخْرَاجٌ . نَفْيٌ . مَنْعٌ

Exclusive *a.* نَافٍ . مَانِعٌ . خَاصٌّ

Excommunicate *v. t.* حَرَمَ ـِ

Excommunication *n.* حِرْمٌ

Excrement *n.* بَرَازٌ . رَوْثٌ

Excrescence *n.* نُتُوءٌ غَيْرُ طَبِيعِيٍّ

Excretion *n.* إِفْرَازُ ٱلْفُضُولِ

Excruciating *a.* أَلِيمٌ جِدًّا . مُعَذِّبٌ

Exculpate *v. t.* بَرَّأَ . زَكَّى

Excursion *n.* سَفْرَةٌ قَصِيرَةٌ

Excusable *a.* مَعْذُورٌ

Excuse *v. t.* عَذَرَ ـِ . سَامَحَ

Excuse *n.* عُذْرٌ

Execrate *v. t.* لَعَنَ ـَ . كَرِهَ ـَ

Execute *v. t.* انجز . أعدم (الحياة)

Executioner *n.* معدم الحياة . جلاد

Executive *a.* or *n.* مجر . منفذ . رئيس

Executor *a.* وكيل تركة . وصي

Exemplary *a.* مستحق الاقتداء به

Exemplify *v. t.* مثل . نسخ ـ

Exempt *v. t.* أعفى من

Exemption *n.* إعفاء . تحرير من

Exercise *n.* ممارسة . رياضة

Exert *v. t.* بذل الجهد ـ . سعى ـ

Exertion *n.* إجتهاد . سعي . جد

Exhale *v. i.* or *t.* زفر ـ

Exhaust *v. t.* فرغ . أفنى

Exhaustion *n.* نفاد . كلال

Exhaustive *a.* مدقق البحث . كامل

Exhibit *v. t.* أظهر . عرض ـ

Exhibiton *n.* إظهار . معرض

Exhilarate *v. t.* ابهج . أنعش

Exhort *v.* وعظ . انذر . حث ـ

Exhortation *n.* وعظ . إنذار

Exhume *v. t.* نبش ـ المدفون

Exigence / **Exigency** *n.* إحتياج . إضطرار

Exile *n.* or *v. t.* منفى . نفى ـ

Exist *v. i.* كان ـ . وجد

Existence *n.* وجود

Existent *a.* / **Existing** *ppr.* or *a.* موجود . كائن

Exodus *n.* خروج . سفر الخروج

Exonerate *v. t.* برأ

Exorbitant *a.* مفرط . باهظ

Exotic *a.* or *n.* أجنبي . (نبات)

Expand *v. t.* or *i.* مد ـ . إمتد

Expanse *n.* إنبساط . فسحة

Expantiate *v. i.* اطنب . توسع في

Expatriate *v. t.* أجلى عن الوطن

Expect *v. t.* إنتظر . توقع

Expectancy / **Expectation** *n.* إنتظار . توقع

Expectorate *v. t.* بَصَقَ ـُ . نَفَثَ ـُ

Expectoration *n.* بصق . نفث

Expedience / Expediency *n.* مُوَافَقَةٌ . مناسبَةٌ

Expedient *a.* مُوَافِق . نافع

Expedient *n.* وَسِيلَة . واسطَةٌ

Expedite *v. t.* عجل . بعث ـَ

Expedition *n.* سرعة . إرساليَّة

Expel *v. t.* طرد ـُ . أخرج

Expend *v. t.* صرف ـ . أنفق

Expenditure *n.* صرف . نفقة

Expense *n.* نفقة . مصروف

Expensive *a.* غَال . (مكلِف)

Experience *n.* or *v. t.* إختبارٌ . إختبر

Experienced *a.* خبيرٌ . مختبر

Experiment *n.* إمتحان . تجربة

Expert *n.* ماهر . بارع . خبير

Expiate *v. t.* كفّر عن

Expiration *n.* إنقضاء . نهاية

Expire *v. i.* مات . إنقضى . زفر ـِ

Explain *v. t.* فسّر . أوضح

Explanation *n.* تفسير . إيضاح

Explanatory *a.* مفسر . تفسيري

Explicit *a.* صَريح . واضح

Explode *v. i.* إنفجر

Exploration *n.* إكتشاف . رود

Explore *v. t.* راد ـُ . إكتشف

Explosion *n.* إنفجار

Explosive *a.* or *n.* مسبّبُ الإنفجار

Export *v. t.* أصدر بضائع

Exports *n. pl.* بضائع صادرة

Expose *v. t.* كشف ـِ . عرض ـ

Exposition *n.* عرض . تفسير

Expostulate *v. i.* نصح ـ عاقب

Exposure *n.* كشف . عرض

Expound *v. t.* فسّر . شرح ـ

Express *a.* or *n.* صَرِيح . خاص

Express *n.* رَسُولٌ خاصٌّ . مَرْكَبَةٌ خاصَّة

Express *v. t.* عَصَرَ ـِ أَظْهَرَ

Expressed *a.* مقولٌ . منطوق بِهِ

Expression *n.* عبارَةٌ . أُسلوبُ النُّطْقِ

Expressive *a.* بَلِيغٌ . مفيدُ المعنى

Expressly *ad.* خاصَّةً . صَرِيحاً

Expulsion *n.* طَرْدٌ . إِخْرَاجٌ

Expunge *v. t.* مَحَا ـُ أَزَال

Expurgate *v. t.* طَهَّرَ . نَقَّحَ

Exquisite *a.* نَفِيسٌ . فَاخِرٌ

Extant *a.* بَاقٍ فِي الْوُجُود

Extemporaneous / **Extemporary** } *a.* مُرْتَجَلٌ

Extempore *ad.* إِرْتِجَالاً

Extemporize *v. t.* إِبتَدَهَ . إِرْتَجَل

Extend *v. t.* or *i.* مَدَّ . إِمْتَدَّ

Extension *n.* مَد . إِمْتِدَادٌ . إِتِّسَاعٌ

Extensive *a.* مُمْتَدٌّ . مُتَّسِعٌ

Extent *n.* إِمْتِدَادٌ . سِعَةٌ

Extenuate *v. t.* خَفَّفَ . خَفَّضَ

Exterior *a.* or *n.* خَارِجِيٌّ . الْخَارِجُ

Exterminate *v. t.* إِستَأْصَلَ . أَبَادَ

External *a.* خَارِجِيٌّ . عَرَضِيٌّ

Extinct *a.* مُنقَرِضٌ . مَعْدُومٌ

Extinction *n.* إِنْقِرَاضٌ

Extinguish *v. t.* أَطْفَأَ . أَزَالَ

Extirpate *v. t.* إِستَأْصَلَ . أَبَادَ

Extol *v. t.* مَجَّدَ . فَخَّمَ

Extort *v. t.* بَلَصَ

Extortion *n.* بَلْصٌ

Extortionate *a.* / **Extortioner** *n.* } بَلَّاصٌ

Extra *n.* or. *a.* زِيَادَةٌ . زَائِد

Extract *n.* جملةٌ مقتبسةٌ . خُلاصَةٌ

Extract *v. t.* إِستَخْرَجَ . إِقْتَبَسَ

Extraction *n.* إِستَخْرَجَ . نَسَبٌ

Extraordinary *a.* فوقَ العَادَةِ . غَرِيبٌ

Extravagance *n.* إِسْرَافٌ . إِفْرَاطٌ
Extravagant *a.* مُسْرِفٌ . مُفْرِطٌ . مُبَالِغٌ
Extreme *a.* اقْصَى . اشَدّ
Extremely *ad.* لِلْغَايَةِ . جِدًّا
Extreme / Extremity *n.* طَرَفٌ . حَاجَةٌ شَدِيدَةٌ
Extricate *v. t.* نَشَلَ ـَ . أَنْقَذَ . فَكّ
Exuberance *n.* وَفْرَةٌ . غَزَارَةٌ . خِصْبٌ
Exude *v. t.* or *i.* رَشَحَ . أَفْرَزَ
Exult *v. i.* إِبْتَهَجَ . تَهَلَّلَ

Eye *n.* or *v. t.* عَيْنٌ ج أَعْيُن . رَاقَبَ
Eyeball *n.* مُقْلَة . مُقَلٌ
Eye-brow *n.* حَاجِبٌ ج حَوَاجِبُ
Eye-glass *n.* مَنْظَرٌ
Eye-lashes *n. pl.* هُدْبٌ ج أَهْدَابٌ
Eyelid *n.* جَفْنٌ ج أَجْفَانٌ
Eye-sight *n.* بَصَرٌ . عِيَان
Eye-tooth *n.* Tusk. نَابٌ ج أَنْيَابٌ

F

Fable *n.* خُرَافَةٌ . خُزَعْبَلَةٌ
Fabric *n.* بِنْيَةٌ . نَسِيجٌ
Fabricate *v. t.* صَنَعَ . إِخْتَلَقَ
Fabulous *a.* خُرَافِيٌّ . خُزَعْبَلِيٌّ

Face *n.* or *v. t.* وَجْهٌ . سَطْحٌ . وَاجَهَ
Facetious *a.* مَازِحٌ . هَازِلٌ
Facilitate *v. t.* سَهَّلَ . يَسَّرَ
Facility *n.* سُهُولَةٌ . يُسْرٌ

Fac-simile *n.* نُسْخَة طِبق ٱلْأَصْلِ
Fact *n.* حَقِيقَة . أَمْرٌ . وَاقِعٌ
Faction *n.* عُصْبَة . حِزْبٌ
Factious *a.* تَحَزُّبِي . مُتَحَزِّبٌ
Factitious *a.* مُصْطَنَعٌ
Factor *n.* عَامِلٌ . أَصْلُ الْحَاصِلِ . ضِلعٌ
Factory *n.* مَعْمَلٌ
Faculty *n.* قُوَّةٌ . طَاقَة . (عُمْدَةٌ)
Fade *v. i.* ذَبُلَ ـُ . جَرِدَ ـَ . بَاخَ ـُ
Fagot *n.* حُزْمَةُ قُضْبَانٍ
Fail *v. t.* or *i.* خَابَ ـِ اَفْلَسَ
Failure *n.* خَيْبَةٌ . إِفْلَاسٌ
Fain *a.* or *ad.* مَسْرُورٌ . بِرِضَى
Faint *a.* or *v. i.* مُعْيٍ . أَعْيَى . غُشِيَ عَلَيْهِ
Faint-hearted *a.* جَبَانٌ . خَائِفٌ
Faintly *ad.* بِضُعْفٍ . قَلِيلاً
Faintness *n.* إِعْيَاءٌ . إِغْمَاءٌ
Fair *a.* or *n.* حَسَنٌ . صَافٍ . سُوقٌ
Fairly *ad.* بِإِسْتِقَامَةٍ . بِعَدْلٍ
Fairness *n.* عَدَالَةٌ . حُسْنٌ . بَيَاضٌ
Fairy *n.* or *a.* جِنِّيَة . جِنِّيٌّ
Faith *n.* إِيمَانٌ . إِعْتِقَاد . مَذْهَبٌ
Faithful *a.* أَمِين . صَادِقٌ
Faithfulness *n.* أَمَانَةٌ
Faithless *a.* غَيْرُ مُؤْمِنٍ . خَائِنٌ
Falcon *n.* بَازٌ . صَقْرٌ
Falconer *n.* مُرَبِّي او مُطَبِّعُ ٱلْبُزَاةِ
Fall *v. i.* or *n.* سَقَطَ ـُ وَقَعَ ـَ . سُقُوطٌ
Fallacious *a.* خَادِعٌ . سَفْسَطِيٌّ
Fallacy *n.* خَطَأٌ . إِسْتِدْلَالٌ . فَاسِدٌ
Fallible *a.* قَابِلُ ٱلْخَطَا اوْ ٱلزَّلَلِ
Fallow *a.* or *n.* أَرْضٌ غَيْرُ مَزْرُوعَةٍ
False *a.* كَاذِبٌ . مُزَوَّرٌ . بَاطِلٌ
Falsehood *n.* كِذْبٌ . زُورٌ
Falsify *v. t.* or *i.* زَوَّرَ . كَذَّبَ
Falter *v. i.* تَرَدَّدَ . قَصَّرَ . لَعْثَمَ

Fame *n.* صِيتٌ عَظِيمٌ . شُهْرَةٌ

Famed *a.* مَشْهُورٌ . شَهِيرٌ

Familiar *a.* or *n.* مَأْلُوفٌ . مَعْرُوفٌ

Familiarity *n.* أُلْفَةٌ . صَدَاقَةٌ . مَعْرِفَةٌ

Familiarize *v. t.* أَلَّفَ . عَوَّدَ . سَهَّلَ

Family *n.* عَائِلَةٌ . آلٌ . نَسَبٌ

Famine *n.* مَجَاعَةٌ . قَحْطٌ . غَلَاءٌ

Famish *v. i.* or *t.* مَاتَ جُوعاً . جَوَّعَ

Famous *a.* شَهِيرٌ . كَثِيرُ ٱلذِّكْرِ

Fan *n.* or *v. t.* مَرْوَحَةٌ . هَوَّى . رَوَّحَ

Fanatic *n.* / **Fanatical** *a.* مُتَعَصِّبٌ فِي ٱلدِّينِ

Fancied *a.* مَوْهُومٌ . مُتَصَوَّرٌ

Fanciful *a.* وَهْمِيٌّ . تَصَوُّرِيٌّ

Fancy *n.* or *v. t.* or *i.* وَهْمٌ . تَصَوُّرٌ . تَصَوَّرَ

Fang *n.* نَابٌ . مِخْلَبٌ

Fantasm *n.* وَهْمٌ . خَيَالٌ

Fantastic / **Fantastical** *a.* وَهْمِيٌّ . خَيَالِيٌّ

Fantasy *n.* وَهْمٌ . تَصَوُّرٌ . بَاطِلٌ

Far *a.* or *ad.* بَعِيد . بَعِيداً

Farce *n.* رِوَايَةٌ سُخْرِيَّةٌ . بُطْلٌ

Farewell *n.* اَلْوِدَاعُ

Farm *n.* or *v. t.* مَزْرَعَةٌ . فَلَجَ ـَ . اقْطَعَ

Farmer *n.* فَلَّاحٌ . مُلْتَزِمٌ

Farming *n.* فِلَاحَةٌ

Farrier *n.* بَيْطَارٌ ج بَيَاطِرَة

Farther *a.* أَبْعَدُ . أَيْضاً

Farthing *n.* فَلْسٌ ج فُلُوسٌ

Fascinate *v. t.* فَتَنَ ـِ . خَلَبَ ـُ

Fascination *n.* إِفْتِتَانٌ

Fashion *n.* or *v. t.* زِيٌّ . عَادَةٌ . جَبَلَ ـُ

Fashionable *a.* بِحَسَبِ ٱلزِّيِّ اوٱلْعَادَةِ

Fast *a.* سَرِيعٌ . ثَابِتٌ . مَاكِنٌ

Fast *n.* or *v. i.* صَوْمٌ . صَامَ ـُ

Fasten *v. t.* مَكَّنَ . ثَبَّتَ . شَدَّ ـُ

Fastidious *a.* صَعْبُ ٱلْإِرْضَاءِ

Fat *n.* or *a.* دُهْنٌ . سَمِين

Fatal *a.* مُمِيتٌ . مُهْلِكٌ

Fatalism *n.* آلاِعتِقَادُ بِالقَدَرِ

Fatalist *n.* مُعْتَقِدٌ بِالقَدَرِ

Fatally *ad.* مُمِيتاً

Fatality / **Fate** } *n.* قَدَرٌ . قَضَآءٌ

Fated *a.* مُقَدَّرٌ . مَقْضِيٌّ بِهِ

Fates *n. pl.* تَقَادِيرُ

Father *n.* أَبٌ ج آبَآءٌ . وَالِدٌ

Father-in-law *n.* حَمٌ أَوْ حَمُو

Fatherland *n.* وَطَنٌ ج أَوْطَانٌ

Fatherless *a.* بلاَ أَبٍ . يَتِيمٌ

Fatherly *a.* أَبَوِيٌّ

Fathom *n.* or *v. t.* قَامَةٌ . سَبَرَ ـُ

Fathomless *a.* عَمِيقٌ لاَ يُسْبَرُ غَوْرُهُ

Fatigue *n.* or *v. t.* وَنَى . تَعَبٌ . أَتْعَبَ

Fatling *n.* مُسَمَّنٌ . مَعْلُوفٌ

Fatness *n.* سَمَانَةٌ . دَسَمٌ

Fatten *v. t.* سَمَّنَ . دَسَّمَ

Fatty *a.* دَسِمٌ . دَهِنٌ

Faucet *n.* انبُوبَةٌ . حَنَفِيَّةٌ

Fault *n.* عَيْبٌ . ذَنْبٌ . غَلَطٌ

Faultless *a.* بلاَ عَيْبٍ . كَامِلٌ

Faulty *a.* عَائِبٌ . مَغْلُوطٌ . نَاقِصٌ

Favour *v. t.* أَحْسَنَ إِلَى . اعَانَ

Favour *n.* مَعْرُوفٌ . نِعْمَةٌ . رِضًى

Favourable *a.* مُوَافِقٌ . لَطِيفٌ

Favourite *n.* or *a.* خَلِيلٌ . عزِيزٌ . حَبِيبٌ

Favouritism *n.* مُحَابَاةٌ

Fawn *v. t.* تَذَلَّلَ لَهُ . دَاهَنَ

Fawn *n.* or *a.* وَلَدُ آلاِيلِ . مِنْ لَوْنِهِ

Fealty *n.* أَمَانَةٌ . طَاعَةٌ

Fear *n.* or *v. t.* خَوْفٌ . خَافَ ـَ

Fearful *a.* خَائِفٌ . مُخِيفٌ . رَائِعٌ

Fearfulness *n.* خَوْفٌ . حَالَتُهُ

Fearless *a.* بِلاَ خَوْفٍ . جَسُورٌ

Feasible *n.* مُمْكِنٌ فِعْلُهُ

Feast *n.* or *v. t.* or *i.* عِيدٌ . وَلِيمَةٌ . أَوْلَمَ

Feat *n.* عَمَلٌ . عَجِيبٌ

Feather *n.* رِيشَةٌ ج رِيشٌ

Feature *n.* هَيْئَةٌ . طَلْعَةٌ . صِفَةٌ

February *n.* شَهْرُ شُبَاطٍ (فبراير)

Fecund *a.* مُخْصِبٌ . مُثْمِرٌ (لِلْحَيَوَانِ)

Fee *n.* or *v. t.* أُجْرَةٌ . هِبَةٌ . آجَرَ

Feeble *a.* ضَعِيفٌ . عَاجِزٌ

Feebleness *n.* ضَعْفٌ . وَهْنٌ

Feed *a.* or *v. t.* عَلَفٌ . أَطْعَمَ

Feel *v. t.* or *i.* لَمَسَ ـِ . حَسَّ ـُ

Feeling *n.* حِسٌّ . شُعُورٌ . إِنْفِعَالٌ

Feign *v. t.* تَظَاهَرَ . تَرَآءَى

Feint *n.* حِيلَةٌ . تَظَاهُرٌ

Felicitate *v. t.* هَنَّأَ

Felicity *n.* سَعَادَةٌ . غِبْطَةٌ

Fell *v. t.* رَمَى . أَلْقَى

Fellow *n.* رَفِيقٌ . قَرِينٌ

Fellowship *n.* أُلْفَةٌ . صُحْبَةٌ . شِرْكَةٌ

Felon
Felonious *a.* } مُجْرِمٌ بِذَنْبٍ عَظِيمٍ

Felony *n.* جَرِيمَةٌ عَظِيمَةٌ . جِنَايَة

Felt *n.* لِبْدٌ ج لُبُودٌ . وَأَلْبَادٌ

Female *n.* or *a.* أُنْثَى ج إِنَاثٌ

Feminine *a.* مُؤَنَّثٌ . أُنْثَوِيٌّ

Fen *n.* مُسْتَنْقَعٌ

Fence *n.* or *v. t.* سِيَاجٌ . سَيَّجَ

Ferment
Fermentation } *a.* إِخْتِمَارٌ . هَيَجَانٌ

Ferment *v. i.* or *t.* خَمَرَ ـُ . إِخْتَمَرَ

Fern *n.* خَنْشَارٌ (نَبَاتٌ)

Ferocious *a.* ضَارٍ . مُفْتَرِسٌ

Ferocity *n.* تَوَحُّشٌ . قَسَاوَةٌ

Ferry *n.* or *v. t.* مَعْبَرٌ . عَبَّرَ

Fertile *a.* مُخْصِبٌ . مُثْمِرٌ

Fertility *n.* خِصْبٌ

Fertilize *v. t.* خَصَّبَ . لَقَّحَ

Fervency *n.* حَرَارَةٌ . حَمَاسَةٌ

Fervent / **Fervid** *a.*	حَارٌّ . غَيُورٌ . حَادٌّ
Fervour *n.*	حَرَارَةٌ . حَمَاسَةٌ . حَمِيَّةٌ
Festal *a.*	مُفْرِحٌ . عِيدِيٌّ
Fester *v. i.* or *n.*	تَقَيَّحَ . قَيْحٌ
Festival *n.*	عِيدٌ . فَرَحٌ
Festivity *n.*	فَرَحٌ . بَسْطٌ . عِيدٌ
Fetch *v. t.*	جَاءَ بِهِ . أَحْضَرَ
Fetid *a.*	مُنْتِنٌ . مُخِمٌ
Fetter *n.* or *v. t.*	قَيْدٌ . قَيَّدَ
Fetus *n.*	جَنِينٌ ج أَجِنَّة
Feud *n.*	نِزَاعٌ . شِقَاقٌ
Fever *n.*	حُمَّى
Feverish *a.*	مَحْمُومٌ
Few *a.*	قَلِيلٌ . يَسِيرٌ
Fib *n.* or *v. i.*	كِذْبَةٌ . كَذَبَ
Fibre / **Fibril** *n.*	لِيفَةٌ . لِيفٌ . لُوَيْفَة
Fickle *a.*	مُتَقَلِّبٌ . مُتَرَدِّدٌ
Fickleness *n.*	تَقَلُّبٌ . طَيْشٌ
Fiction *n.*	خُرَافَةٌ . كِذْبٌ
Fictitious *a.*	كَاذِبٌ . وَهْمِيٌّ
Fiddle *n.*	كَمَنْجَة
Fidelity *n.*	أَمَانَةٌ . صِدْقٌ
Fidget *v. t.*	قَلِقَ . ضَجِرَ
Fidgety *a.*	قَلِقٌ . مُضْطَرِبٌ . ضَجِرٌ
Field *n.*	حَقْلٌ . سَاحَة
Field-piece *n.*	مَدْفَعٌ صَغِيرٌ
Fiend *n.*	عَدُوٌّ . خَبِيثٌ . شَيْطَان
Fierce *a.*	عَنِيفٌ . حَادٌّ . شَرِسٌ
Fiery *a.*	نَارِيٌّ . حَادُّ ٱلطَّبْعِ
Fife *n.*	مِزْمَارٌ
Fifteen *a.*	خَمْسَةَ عَشَرَ . خَمْسَ عَشْرَةَ
Fifteenth *a.*	أَلْخَامِسَ عَشَرَ
Fifth *a.* or *n.*	خَامِسٌ . خُمْسٌ
Fiftieth / **Fifty** *a.*	أَلْخَمْسُونَ . خَمْسُونَ
Fig *n.*	تِينَةٌ
Fight *n.* or *v. t.*	قِتَالٌ . قَاتَلَ

Figurative *a.* مَجَازِيٌّ . إِسْتِعَارِيٌّ

Figure *n.* or *v.t.* or *i.* صُورَةٌ . صَوَّرَ . حَسَبَ . ظَهَرَ

Filbert *n.* بُنْدُقَةٌ

Filch *v. t.* سَرَقَ ـِ . أَسَلَّ

File *n.* or *v. t.* مِبْرَدٌ . صَفٌّ . بَرَدَ ـُ

Filial *a.* بَنَوِيٌّ . وَلَدِيٌّ

Fill *v. t.* مَلأَ . أَفْعَمَ

Filly *n.* فُلُوٌّ . مُهْرَةٌ

Film *n.* غُشَاوَةٌ

Filter *n.* or *v. t.* مِصْفَاةٌ . صَفَّى

Filth / **Filthness** } *n.* وَسَخٌ . قَذَرٌ

Filthy *a.* وَسِخٌ . قَذِرٌ

Filtrate *v. t.* صَفَّى

Fin *n.* زِعْنِفَةُ (ٱلسَّمَكِ)

Final *a.* نِهَائِيٌّ . أَخِيرٌ

Finally *ad.* أَخِيرًا

Finance *n.* مَالِيَّةٌ

Financial *a.* مَالِيٌّ

Financier *n.* مَاهِرٌ بِٱلْأُمُورِ ٱلْمَالِيَّةِ

Find *v. t.* (*pp.* Found) وَجَدَ ـِ

Fine *a.* دَقِيقٌ . نَاعِمٌ

Fine *n.* or *v. t.* غَرَامَةٌ . غَرَّمَ

Fineness *n.* دِقَّةٌ . رِقَّةٌ

Finery *n.* زِينَةٌ . حِلْيَةٌ

Finesse *n.* دَهَاءٌ . حِيلَةٌ

Finger *n.* or *v.t.* إِصْبَعٌ . مَسَّ . جَسَّ ـُ

Finish *v. t.* أَنْهَى . أَنْجَزَ . أَكْمَلَ

Finite *a.* مَحْدُودٌ . مُتَنَاهٍ

Fir *n.* شَرْبِينٌ . (شَجَرٌ)

Fire *n.* نَارٌ . حَرَارَةُ ٱلْخُلْقِ

Fire *v. t.* أَوْقَدَ . أَطْلَقَ (ٱلْأَسْلِحَةَ)

Fire-arms *n. pl.* أَسْلِحَةٌ . نَارِيَّةٌ

Fire-engine *n.* آلَةٌ لِإِطْفَاءِ ٱلنَّارِ

Firefly *n.* حُبَاحِبُ

Fire-place *n.* مَوْقِدٌ

Fireside *n.* مَوْقِدُ ٱلْعَائِلَةِ . أَلْبَيْتُ

Fireworks *n. pl.* أَلْعَابٌ . نارِيَةٌ

Firm *a.* or *n.* ثابتٌ. رَاسِخ شِرْكَةٌ (تجار)

Firmament *n.* جَلَدٌ . جوٌ

Firman *n.* فرَمان

Firmly *ad.* بِثَبَاتٌ . بِعزمٍ

Firmness *n.* ثَبات . عزْمٌ . مَتَانَةٌ

First *a.* or *ad.* ألاوَّل. أَوَّلاً. إِبتِدَاءً

First-born *n.* بِكْرٌ ج ابكارٌ

First-rate *a.* عال . فَائِقٌ

Fiscal *a.* مُختصٌّ بِالْمَالِيَّةِ

Fish *n.* or *v. t.* or *i.* سَمَكٌ. صادَ ـِ

Fisherman *n.* صَيَّادُ سَمَكٍ

Fishery *a.* صيدُ السَّمَكِ او مَحلهُ

Fish-hook *n.* صِنَارَةُ الصَّيدِ

Fishing *n.* صَيْدُ السمَكِ

Fissure *n.* شِقٌّ . فَلْقٌ

Fist *n.* قَبْضَةُ اليَدِ

Fit *n.* نَوْبةٌ. صَرْعٌ . دَوْرٌ

Fit *a.* or *v. t.* مُنَاسِبٌ. نَاسَبَ

Fitful *a.* مُتَغَيِّرٌ . غيرُ مضبُوطٍ

Fitness *n.* لِيَاقَة . مُنَاسَبَةٌ

Five *n.* or *a.* خَمْسَةٌ

Fivefold *a.* or *ad.* خَمْسَةُ أَضْعَافٍ

Fix *v. t.* or *i.* ثَبَّتَ . مَكَّنَ . أَرْسَخَ ـَ

Fizz *v. i.* }
Fizzle *v. i.* } صفرَ ـِ (نارٌ)

Flabby }
Flaccid } *a.* رَخْوٌ . مُرْتَخٍ

Flag *n.* حلفَاءُ . رَايَةٌ . بَلاَطَةٌ

Flag *v. t.* ضعفَ ـُ. إِستَرْخَى

Flagitious *a.* خَبِيث .فَاجِرٌ

Flagon *n.* إِبْرِيقٌ لِلْمُسْكِرَاتِ

Flagrant *a.* مُفْرِط . قَبِيحٌ

Flag-ship *n.* بَارِجَةُ أَمِيرِ البَحْرِ

Flag-staff *n.* سَارِيَةُ الرَّايَةِ

Flag-stone *n.* بَلاَطَةٌ

Flake *n.* صُفَيحَةٌ رَقِيقَةٌ

Flame *n.* or *v. i.* لَهِيبٌ . إِلْتَهَبَ

Flaming *a.* مُلْتَهِبٌ . بَرَّاقٌ . مُحْتَدٌّ

Flank *n.* or *v.* خَاصِرَةٌ أَتَى ٱلْجَانِبَ

Flannel *n.* نَسِيجٌ صُوفِيٌّ (فَلاَنِلاَّ)

Flap *n.* or *v. t.* or *i.* ذَيْلٌ (ثَوْبٍ) خَفَقَ ـِ

Flare *v. i.* خَفَقَ (ٱللَّهِيبُ) تَأَلَّقَ

Flash *n.* or *v. i.* وَمِيضٌ . أَوْمَضَ . بَرَقَ ـُ

Flask *n.* قَنِّينَةٌ . قَارُورَةٌ

Flat *a.* or *n.* مُسَطَّحٌ . طَبَقَةٌ . سَهْلٌ

Flatten *v. t.* or *i.* سَطَّحَ . تَسَطَّحَ

Flatter *v. t.* مَلَقَ ـَ . دَاهَنَ

Flatterer / **Flattering** } مُتَمَلِّقٌ . مُدَاهِنٌ

Flattery *n.* مَلَقٌ . مُدَاهَنَةٌ

Flavour *n.* or *v. t.* طَعْمٌ . رَائِحَةٌ . تَبَّلَ

Flaw *n.* عَيْبٌ . خَلَلٌ . شَقٌّ

Flax *n.* كَتَّانٌ (نَبَاتٌ) قِنَّبٌ

Flay *v. t.* سَلَخَ ـُ . كَشَطَ ـِ

Flea *n.* بُرْغُوثٌ ج . بَرَاغِيثُ

Flee(Fled) *v. i.* هَرَبَ ـُ . فَرَّ ـِ

Fleece *n.* or *v. t.* جَزَّةٌ . جَزَّ . سَلَبَ

Fleet *a.* or *n.* سَرِيعٌ . اسْطُولٌ

Fleeting *a.* وَقْتِيٌّ . فَانٍ

Flesh *n.* لَحْمٌ . جَسَدٌ . ٱلْبَشَرُ

Fleshly *a.* حَيَوَانِيٌّ . شَهْوَانِيٌّ

Fleshy *a.* سَمِينٌ . لَحْمِيٌّ

Flew *pret. of fly* طَارَ

Flexibility *n.* لِينٌ . مُرُونَةٌ

Flexible *a.* لَيِّنٌ . مَرِنٌ . مُنْقَادٌ

Flicker *v. i.* خَفَقَ ـِ لَأْلَأَ

Flight *n.* طَيَرَانٌ . هَرَبٌ . فِرَارٌ

Flighty *a.* طَائِشٌ . مُتَخَيِّلٌ

Flimsy *a.* سَخِيفٌ . ضَعِيفٌ . بَاطِلٌ

Fling *v. t.* or *n.* رَمَى ـِ . طَرَحَ ـَ . رَمْيٌ

Flint *n.* صَوَّانٌ

Flippant *a.* خَفِيفُ ٱلْكَلَامِ . بِقْبَاقٌ

Flirt *v. t., i.* or *n.* غَازَلَ . غَنِجَ . غُنْجَةٌ

Flirtation *n.* غُنْجٌ . مُغَازَلَةٌ

Flit *v. i.* / **Flitter** *v. i.* هفت ـِ . حام ـُ
Float *v. t.* or *i.* عام ـَ . سبّح
Flock *n.* or *v.i.* قطيع . سِرب تجمّع
Flog *v. t.* جلد ـِ . ساط ـُ
Flogging *n.* جلد . سوط
Flop *v. t.* صفق . تقلّب
Flood *n.* or *v. t.* طوفان . غمر ـُ
Floor *n.* or *v. t.* أرض البيت . طبقة . بلّط
Flora *n.* نبات إقليم . شرحه
Floral *a.* زهري
Florid *a.* أحمر . زاهر . مزوّق
Florist *n.* مربي الزهور
Flotilla *n.* أسطول صغير
Flounce / **Flounder** *v. i.* تمرّغ . تقلّب
Flour *n.* طحين . دقيق
Flourish *v.t.* or *i.* هزّ ـِ . أزهر . أفلح
Flow *v. i.* جرى ـِ سال ـِ . نبع ـِ
Flower *n.* زهرة . زبدة
Flowery *a.* زهريّ . أزهر . زاهر
Flown *see* **Fly.** طار . طيّر
Fluctuatte *v.i.* تقلّب . تردّد
Fluency *n.* طلاقة اللسان
Fluent *a.* ذلق . طلق اللسان
Fluid *n.* سائل . مائع
Fluidity *n.* سيلان . ميْع
Flush *n.* or *v. i.* إحمرار . إحمرّ
Flute *n.* ناي
Flutter *v. i.* or *n.* خفق ـِ . خفقان
Fly *v. i.* or *t.* طار . طيّر
Fly *n.* ذبابة ج ذِبّان وذُباب
Fly-leaf *n.* ورقة بيضاء في كتاب
Foal *n.* or *v. i.* فلو . ولدت (فرس)
Foam *n.* or *v. i.* رغوة . زبد . أزبد
Foamy / **Foaming** *a.* مزبد
Focus *n.* نقطة الإحتراق
Fodder *n.* or *v. t.* علف . علف ـِ

Foe *n.* عَدُوٌّ . خَصْمٌ

Fog *n.* ضَبَابٌ

Foil *v. t.* or *n.* خَيَّبَ . صَفِيحَة . رَقِيقَة

Fold *n.* ضِعْفٌ . ثِنْيٌ . حَظِيرَةٌ

Fold *v. t.* ثَنَى ـِ . زَرَبَ ـُ

Foliage *n.* أَوْرَاقُ ٱلنَّبَاتِ

Folk *n.* أَهْلٌ . قَوْمٌ . انَاسٌ

Follow *v. t.* or *i.* تَبِعَ ـَ . نَتَجَ مِنْ

Follower *n.* تَابِعٌ . تِلْمِيذٌ

Following *n.* قَوْمٌ . اتْبَاعٌ

Folly *n.* جَهَالَةٌ . حَمَاقَة . سَفَهٌ

Foment *v. t.* اثَارَ . هَيَّجَ

Fond *a.* مُوْلَعٌ . مُحِبٌّ

Fondle *v. t.* دَلَّلَ . لَاطَفَ

Fondness *n.* غَرَامٌ . وَدَادٌ

Font *n.* طَقْمُ احْرُف . نَبْعٌ

Food *n.* طَعَام . قُوْتٌ

Fool *n.* / **Foolish** *a.* } جَاهِلٌ . غَبِيٌّ . سَفِيهٌ

Foolishness *n.* جَهْلٌ . حَمَاقَةٌ

Foolhardy *a* مُتَهَوِّرٌ . مُخَاطِرٌ بِنَفْسِهِ جَهْلاً

Foot *n.* قَدَمٌ رِجْلٌ . وَزْنُ شِعْرٍ

Footman *n.* خَادِمٌ . تَابِعٌ

Foot-path *n.* مَمْشًى . مَسْلَكٌ (لِلرَّاجِلِ)

Footstep *n.* خَطْوَةٌ . أَثَرُ ٱلْقَدَمِ

Footstool *n.* كُرْسِيٌّ لِلرِّجْلَيْنِ

For *pr.* or *conj.* لِأَجْلِ . لِ . لِأَنْ

Forage *n.* عَلَفٌ . عُلُوفَةٌ

Forasmuch *conj.* حَيْثُ . بِمَا أَنْ

Foray *n.* غَزْوَةٌ . غَارَةٌ

Forbear *v. t.* or *i.* إِمْتَنَعَ . كَفَّ ـُ

Forbearance *n.* إِحْتِمَالٌ . إِمْتِنَاعٌ

Forbid *v. t.* نَهَى ـَ . مَنَعَ ـَ

Force *n.* or *v. t.* قُوَّةٌ . فَاعِلِيَّةٌ . أَلْزَمَ

Forceps *n. pl.* مِلْقَط . جِرَاحِيٌّ

Forcible *a.* قَوِيٌّ . فَعَّالٌ

Ford *n.* or *v. t.* مَخَاضَةٌ . خَاضَ ـَ

Fore-arm *n.* سَاعِدٌ

Forebode *v.t.* تَشَاءَمَ . أَنْبَأَ بِشَرٍّ

Forecast *n.* or *v.t.* تَدْبِيرٌ سَابِقٌ . دَبَّرَ

Forecastle *n.* أَعْلَى مُقَدَّمِ ٱلسَّفِينَةِ

Forefather *n.* جَدٌّ . سَلَفٌ

Forefinger *n.* سَبَّابَةٌ

Forefoot *n.* قَائِمَةٌ . مُقَدَّمَةٌ لِلْبَهِيمَةِ

Forego *v. t.* تَنَازَلَ عَنْ . تَرَكَ ـُ

Foregoing *a.* مُتَقَدِّمٌ . سَالِفٌ

Foregone *a.* مَعْزُومٌ عَلَيْهِ . مَحْتُومٌ

Forehead *n.* جَبْهَةٌ

Foreign / **Foreigner** *n.* أَجْنَبِيٌّ . غَرِيبٌ

Forejudge *v. t.* سَبَقَ فَقَضَى

Foreknow *v. t.* سَبَقَ فَعَرَفَ

Foreknowledge *n.* عِلْمٌ سَابِقٌ

Forelock *n.* نَاصِيَةٌ ج نَوَاصٍ

Foreman *n.* نَاظِرٌ . رَئِيسُ شُغْلٍ

Foremast *n.* سَارِيَةُ ٱلْمُقَدَّمِ

Foremost *a.* الاوَّلُ . أَلْمُتَقَدِّمُ

Forenoon *n.* مَاقَبْلَ ٱلظُّهْرِ

Foreordain *v. t.* سَبَقَ فَعَيَّنَ

Foresee *v. t.* سَبَقَ فَنَظَرَ أَو عَرَفَ

Foresight *v.* سَبْقُ ٱلنَّظَرِ . عِنَايَة

Forest *n.* غَابَةٌ . عَرِينٌ

Forestall *n. n.* سَبَقَ إِلَى

Foretell *v. t.* سَبَقَ فَاخْبَرَ . أَنْبَأَ

Forethought *n.* فِكْرٌ سَابِقٌ . تَبَصُّرٌ

Forever *ad.* إِلَى ٱلْابَدِ

Forewarn *v.t.* سَبَقَ فَحَذَّرَ . انْذَرَ

Forfeit *v.t.* or *n.* غَرَّمَ فِي جِنَايَةٍ . غَرَامَة

Forge *n.* or *v. t.* كُورٌ . زَوَّرَ

Forger *n.* حَدَّادٌ . مُزَوِّرٌ

Forgery *n.* تَزْوِيرٌ . زَيْفٌ

Forget *v. t.* (Forgot) نَسِيَ ـَ

Forgetful *a.* نَاسٍ . غَافِلٌ

Forgetfulness *n.* نِسْيَانٌ . غَفَلٌ

Forgive *v. t.* غَفَرَ لَهُ

Forgiveness *n.* غُفْرَانٌ . مَغْفِرَةٌ

Fork *n.* or *v. t.* شَوْكَةٌ . تَشَعَّبَ

Forked *a.* مُتَشَعِّبٌ . مُتَفَرِّعٌ

Forlorn *a.* مُهْمَلٌ . بَائِسٌ

Form *n.* رَسْمٌ . شَكْلٌ . هَيْئَةٌ

Form *v. t.* كَوَّنَ . صَوَّرَ . عَمِلَ

Formal *a.* رَسْمِيٌّ . خَارِجِيٌّ

Formality *n.* عَادَةٌ رَسْمِيَّةٌ . تَكْلِيفٌ

Formally *ad.* رَسْماً . بِالظَّاهِرِ فَقَط

Formation *n.* تَكْوِينٌ . تَرْكِيبٌ

Former *a.* سَابِقٌ . اوَّلُ اثْنَيْنِ

Formerly *ad.* سَابِقاً . قَبْلاً

Formidable *a.* عَظِيمٌ . مُخِيفٌ

Formulate *v. t.* صَرَّحَ بِهِ رَسْمِيّاً

Formication *n.* زِنَى . عِهَارَةٌ

Forsake *v. t.* تَرَكَ . هَجَرَ

Forsaken *a.* مَتْرُوكٌ

Fort *n.* حِصْنٌ . قَلْعَةٌ

Forth *ad.* خَارِجاً . فَصَاعِداً

Forthcoming *a.* آتٍ . قَرِيبُ الْحُضُورِ

Forthwith *ad.* حَالاً . عَلَى الْفَوْرِ

Fortieth *a.* الْأَرْبَعُونَ

Fortification *n.* حِصْنٌ . تَحْصِينٌ

Fortify *v. t.* حَصَّنَ . قَوَّى

Fortitude *n.* تَجَلُّدٌ . عَزْمٌ . ثَبَاتٌ

Fortnight *n.* اسْبُوعَانِ

Fortress *n.* حِصْنٌ . قَلْعَةٌ

Fortuitous *a.* عَرَضِيٌّ . إِتِّفَاقِيٌّ

Fortunate *a.* سَعِيدٌ . حَظِيظٌ

Fortune *n.* حَظٌّ . نَصِيبٌ

Forty *a.* أَرْبَعُونَ

Forward *a.* or *ad.* مُقَدَّمٌ . إِلَى قُدَّامٍ

Forward *v. t.* أَرْسَلَ . عَجَّلَ

Fossil *n.* or *a.* مُتَحَجِّرٌ

Foster *v. t.* رَبَّى . عَالَ . اعَانَ

Foul *a.* قَذِرٌ . نَجِسٌ . قَبِيحٌ

Foul *v. t.* وَسَّخَ . نَجَّسَ . لَوَّثَ

Found *v. t.* اسَّسَ . انشأَ . سَبَكَ

Foundation *n.* اساسٌ . اصلٌ

Founder *n.* مُؤَسِّسٌ . سَبَّاك

Foundling *n.* وَلَد . لَقِيطٌ

Foundry / **Foundery** *n.* مَعْمَلُ ٱلسَّبْكِ

Fount / **Fountain** *n.* نَبْعٌ . يَنْبُوعٌ

Four *a.* ارْبَعَة او ارْبَعُ

Fourfold *a.* ارْبَعَةُ اضعَافٍ

Fourfooted *a.* ذَوَاتُ ٱلْارْبع

Fourscore *a.* ثمَانُونَ

Fourteen *a.* ارْبَعَةَ عشَرَ . ارْبَعَ عَشَرة

Fourteenth *a.* الرَّابعُ عشَرَ

Fowl *n.* طَيْرٌ . دُجَاجة

Fowler *n.* صَيَّادٌ

Fowling-piece *n.* بَارُودَة . بُنْدُقِيَّة

Fox *n.* ثَعْلَبٌ . مَكَّار

Fraction *n.* كَسْرٌ . جُزْءٌ

Fracture *n.* or *v. t.* كَسْرٌ . كَسَرَ

Fragile *a.* قَصِمٌ . سَهْلُ ٱلْانْكِسَارِ

Fragment *n.* قِطْعَةٌ كِسْرَةٌ

Fragmentary *a.* مُؤَلَّفٌ مِنْ كِسَرٍ

Fragrance *n.* رَائِحَة . ذَكِيَّةٌ

Fragrant *a.* عَطِرٌ . ذَكِيُّ ٱلرَّائِحَةِ

Frail *a.* نَحِيفٌ . ضَعِيفٌ . وَاهٍ

Frailty *n.* ضَعْفٌ . وَهْنٌ . عَجْزٌ

Frame *n.* بِنْيَةٌ . قَالِبٌ . بِرْوَازٌ

Franchise *n.* إِمْتِيَازٌ سِيَاسِيٌّ

Frank *a.* or *n.* مُخْلِصٌ . سَلِيمُ ٱلنِّيَّةِ . إِفْرَنْجِيٌّ

Frankincense *n.* بَخُورٌ . لُبَانٌ

Frankness *n.* إِخْلَاصٌ . صَفْوُ ٱلنِّيَّةِ

Frantic *a.* مَجْنُونٌ . هَائِجٌ غَيْظًا

Fraternal *a.* أَخَوِيٌّ

Fraternity *n.* إِخَاءٌ وَإِخَاوَة . شِرْكَةٌ

Fraternize *v. t.* آخَى . تَآخَى

Fratricide *n.* قَاتِلُ ٱلْأَخِ . قتل ٱلأخِ

Fraud *n.* خِدَاعٌ . غُبْنٌ . مَكْرٌ

Freak *n.* غَرَابَةُ خلقٍ أو فِعلٍ

Freckle *n.* or *v. t.* كَلَفٌ . كَلِفَ ـ كَلَفَ ـ

Freckled
Freckly } *a.* أَكْلَفُ

Free *v. t.* حَرَّرَ . أَعتَقَ

Free *a.* حُرٌّ . بَرِيءٌ . مَجَّانِيٌّ

Freedom *n.* حُرِّيَّةٌ . بَرَاءَةٌ . خُلُوصٌ

Freely *ad.* مجَّانًا . طَوْعًا . بِسَخَاءٍ

Freeman *n.* حُرٌّ

Freemason *n.* فَرْمَاسُون

Freeness *n.* حُرِّيَّةٌ . سَخَاءٌ

Free-thinker *n.* مُنْكِرُ ٱلْوَحْيِ

Freewill *n.* إِرَادَةٌ حُرَّةٌ

Freeze *v. t.* or *i.* قَرَّسَ . قَرِسَ ـ

Freight *n.* شَحْنٌ . اجْرَتُهُ

French *n.* or *a.* فَرَنسَاوِيٌّ

Frenzy *n.* جُنُونٌ . غَيظٌ

Frequent *a.* كَثِيرُ ٱلْوُقُوعِ . مُتَوَاتِرٌ

Frequent *v. t.* تَرَدَّدَ إِلى . لَازَمَ

Frequently *ad.* تكرَارًا . كَثِيرًا مَا

Fresco *n.* or *v. t.* تَصْوِيرٌ على جَصٍّ

Fresh *a.* جَدِيدٌ . رَطْبٌ

Freshen *v.t.* or *i.* حَلَّى . رَطَّبَ . أَنْعَشَ . إِشتَدَّ

Freshet *n.* سَيلٌ . طُغْيَانٌ

Freshman *n.* مُبتَدِئٌ (في مَدْرَسَةٍ)

Freshness *n.* نَضَارَةٌ . عُذُوبَةٌ

Fret *v.t.* or *i.* كَدَّرَ . تَكَدَّرَ . ضَجِرَ

Fretful *a.* نَكِدٌ . شَاكٍ

Fretfulness *n.* نَكَدٌ . ضَجَرٌ

Friar *n.* رَاهِبٌ ج رُهْبَانٌ

Friction *n.* فَرْكٌ . حَكٌّ . دَلْكٌ

Friday *n.* يوم ٱلْجُمْعَةِ

Friend *n.* صَاحِبٌ . صَدِيقٌ . خِلٌّ

Friendless *a.* بِلَا صَدِيقٍ . مُهْمَلٌ

Friendly *a.* وَدُودٌ . مُسَالِمٌ

Friendship *n.* صَدَاقَةٌ . الفَةٌ

Frigate *n.* بَارِجَةٌ حَرْبِيَّةٌ

Fright *n.* خَوف . فَزَعٌ . رُعْبٌ

Frighten *v. t.* خَوَّفَ . افزعَ

Frightful *a.* مُرْعِبٌ . مُخِيف . هَائِلٌ

Frigid *a.* بَارِدٌ . قَارِسٌ

Frill
Fringe } *n.* هُدْبٌ . حَاشِيَةٌ

Frisk *v. t.* قَفَزَ فَرَحاً . مَرِحَ ـ

Frisk
Erisky } *a.* مَرِحٌ . خَفِيف

Frivolity *n.* طَيْشٌ . بطْلٌ

Frivolous *a.* عَبَثٌ . بَاطِلٌ

Frock *n.* قُفْطَانٌ . (فسطَانٌ)

Frog *n.* ضَفْدَعٌ ج ضَفَادِعُ

Frolic *n.* or *v. i.* لِعْبٌ . مَرِحَ ـ

From *pr.* مِنْ . عَنْ . من عِند

Front *n.* مُقَدَّمٌ . صَدْرٌ

Frontier *n.* حَدٌّ . تخْمٌ

Frost *n.* صَقِيعٌ . جَلِيدٌ

Froth *n.* رَغْوَةٌ . زَبَدٌ

Froward *a.* مُتَمَرِّدٌ . عَاتٍ

Frown *n.* or *v. t.* عُبُوسَةٌ . عَبَسَ ـِ

Froze *see* Freeze. فَرَّسَ

Fructify *v. t.* جَعَلَهُ مثمِراً . لَقَّحَ

Frugal *a.* مقْتَصِدٌ

Frugality *n.* إِقتِصَادٌ

Fruit *n.* ثَمَرٌ . فَاكِهَةٌ . حَاصِلٌ

Fruitful *a.* مثْمِرٌ . مُخْصِبٌ . مُنتِجٌ

Fruitlessly *ad.* عَبَثاً . بَاطِلاً

Frustrate *v. t.* خَيَّبَ . أَبطَلَ

Fry *v. t.* or *i.* قَلَى ـ . إِنْقَلَى

Frying-pan *n.* مِقْلاةٌ

Fuel *n.* وَقِيدٌ . وُقُود

Fugitive *n.* or *a.* هَارِبٌ . زَائِلٌ

Fulcrum *n.* مُسْنَدٌ . دَارِكٌ

Fulfil *v. t.* اكْمَلَ . اتَمَّ

Fulfilment *n.* إِتمَامٌ . وَفَاءٌ

Full *a.* or *v.t.* مَلآنٌ. وَافِرٌ. تَامٌّ. قَصَرَ

Fuller *n.* قَصَّارٌ

Fully *ad.* تَمَاماً

Fume *n.* or *v. i.* بُخَارٌ. إِغْتَاظَ. دَخَّنَ

Fumigate *v. t.* بَخَّرَ. دَخَّنَ

Fumigation *n.* تَبْخِيرٌ. تَدْخِينٌ

Fun *n.* مُزَاحٌ. هَزْلٌ

Function *n.* وَظِيفَةٌ. شُغْلٌ

Fund *n.* مَالٌ. رَأْسُ مَالٍ

Fundamental *a.* أَسَاسِيٌّ. جَوْهَرِيٌّ

Funeral *n.* جِنَازَةٌ

Fungus *n.* فُطْرٌ (نَبَاتٌ)

Funnel *n.* قِمْعٌ. مِدْخَنَةٌ

Funny *a.* مُضْحِكٌ

Fur *n.* فَرْوٌ. بَيَاضُ ٱللِّسَانِ

Furious *a.* هَائِجٌ غَضَباً. مُزْبِدٌ

Furl *v. t.* طَوَى ـِ. لَفَّ ـُ

Furlong *n.* فَرْسَخٌ ج فَرَاسِخ

Furlough *n.* رُخْصَةٌ لِلْغِيَابِ (إِجَازَةٌ)

Furnace *n.* كُورٌ. أَتُونٌ

Furnish *v. t.* جَهَّزَ. أَهَّبَ

Furniture *n.* أَثَاثٌ. أَمْتِعَةٌ

Furrier *n.* فَرَّاءٌ. تَاجِرُ ٱلْفَرْوِ

Furrow *n.* or *v. t.* ثَلْمٌ. خَدَّةٌ. خَدَّ ـُ

Further *a.* or *ad.* أَبْعَدُ. ثُمَّ. أَيْضاً

Further *v. t.* سَاعَدَ. أَيَّدَ

Furthermore *ad.* ثُمَّ. أَيْضاً

Furthermost / **Furthest** } *a.* الْأَبْعَدُ. ٱلْأَقْصَى

Furtive *a.* سِرِّيٌّ. خَفِيٌّ

Fury *n.* غَيْظٌ مُزْبِدٌ. جُنُونٌ

Fuse *v. t.* or *i.* أَذَابَ. ذَابَ ـُ

Fuse *n.* فَتِيلَةُ ٱللُّغْمِ

Fuss *n.* ضَجِيجٌ. شَغَبٌ

Futile *a.* بَاطِلٌ. عَبَثٌ

Futility *n.* عَبَثٌ. عَدَمُ ٱلْفَائِدَةِ

Future *n.* or *a.* مُسْتَقْبَلٌ. آتٍ

Futurity *n.* الزَّمَانُ ٱلْمُقْبِلُ

G

Gabble *v. i.* or *n.* ثَرْثَرَ . ثَرْثَرَة

Gable *n.* (جَمْلُون)

Gag *v. t.* or *n.* سَدَّ الفم

Gage *n.* or *v. t.* رَهْنٌ . عِيار . عايَرَ

Gaily / Gayly *ad.* سُرُوراً . بَهْجَةً

Gain *n.* or *v. t.* or *i.* كَسْبٌ . رَبِحَ

Gainful *a.* مُكْسِبٌ . مُرْبِحٌ

Gainings *n. pl.* أرْبَاح

Gainsay *v. t.* نَاقَضَ . قاوَمَ

Gait *n.* المَشْيُ أو نوعُه

Gaiter *n.* جُرْمُوق

Galaxy *n.* المَجَرَّةُ . مَوْكِبٌ

Gale *n.* رِيحٌ شَدِيدَةٌ . عَاصِفَةٌ

Gall *n.* صفْرَاء . مَرَارَةٌ . عَفْصٌ

Gallant *a.* شُجَاع . لَطِيف . عاشِق

Gallantry *n.* بسالة . شهامة

Gallery *n.* رِواق . دِهلِيز

Galley *n.* نوع مِن السفن

Gallic *a.* غاليّ . فرنساويّ

Gallon *n.* مِكيالٌ للسائلاتِ

Gallop *n.* or *v. i.* رَكْضُ (الفَرَسِ)

Gallows *n. pl.* مِشنقة

Galvanic *a.* كهربائيّ . كلفانيّ

Galvanize *v.t.* كهربَ . لبَّسَ بالمعدنِ

Gamble *v. t.* or *i.* قامَرَ

Gambler *n.* مُقامِر

Gambling *n.* مُقامَرة

Gambol *n.* or *v. i.* قَمَصَ . قَمْص

Game *n.* لِعبَة . قَنَص . صَيداً

Gamester *n.* لاَعِبٌ . مقَامِر

Gander *n.* ذَكَرُ الوَزّ

Gang *n.* زُمْرَةٌ . جماَعَة

Gangrene *n.* or *v. i.* غَنغَرِين تَغنْغَرَ

Gangway *n.* مَعْبَرٌ . مَمَرٌّ

Gaol *n.* سجن . حَبْس

Gap *n.* شَقٌّ . فَتحَة

Gape *v. t.* فَغَرَ ـِ

Garb *n.* لبَاَسٌ . هيئَة

Garden *n.* بستَانٌ . جنَيْنَة

Gardener *n.* بستاَنيٌّ

Gargle *v. t.* or *n.* غَرْغَر . غرْغَرة

Garland *n.* إِكْلِيلُ زَهرٍ

Garlic *n.* ثُومٌ

Garment *n.* ثَوْبٌ . كسَاء

Garner *n.* or *v. t.* شُوْنَة . خَزَنَ ـِ

Garnish *v. t.* زَيَنَ . زَخْرَف

Garrison *a.* or *v. t.* حَرَسُ حصْنٍ . جَهَّزَ بِحَرَس

Garrulity *n.* ثَرثَرَة . بقَاق

Garrulous *a.* ثَرثَار . بِقْبَاق

Garter *n.* رُبَاط ٱلساق . (وِسَامٌ إِنْكِلِيزيٌّ)

Gas *n.* غَاز

Gaseous *a.* غَازيٌّ

Gash *n.* جُرْحٌ

Gas-light *n.* نورُ غاز

Gasometer *n.* مِقيَاسُ غاز . مخزنه

Gasp *v. i.* or *n.* إِلتهث . لَهثَة

Gastric *a.* معِدِيٌّ

Gate *n.* بَابٌ . مدخَلٌ

Gateway *n.* مدْخَل في حائِط

Gather *v. t.* or *i.* جَمَعَ . إِجتمع

Gaudy *a.* مزخرَف بلاَ ذَوقٍ

Gauge *v. t.* or *n.* قَاس . مِقيَاسٌ

Gaunt *a.* هزِيل . ضامِر . اعجَفُ

Gauntlet *n.* كفٌّ مِن حَدِيدٍ

Gawky *a.* or *n.* غَشِيم . غَلِيظ ٱلتَّصرُّفِ
Gauze *n.* نَسِيج رَقِيق
Gay *a.* مُبتهِج . مَرِح . فَاخِر
Gayety *n.* بهجة . بسط . سُرُور
Gaze *n.* or *v.t.* نظرة ثابتة . تفرَّس
Gazelle *n.* غزَال ج غِزلان
Gazette *n.* جرِيدة ج جرَائِد
Gazetteer *n.* كتَابُ وَصفِ ٱلبُلدَانِ
Gear *n.* عُدَّة . جِهَاز . أدوَات
Gear *v. t.* لَبَّسَ بِعُدَّةٍ
Gelatine *n.* هُلَام
Gelding *n.* حِصَان مَخْصِيّ
Gem *n.* جوْهَرَة . فَصّ
Gender *n.* جِنْس، ج أَجنَاس
Genealogical *a.* نَسَبِيّ
Genealogy *n.* سِلْسِلَةُ ٱلنَسَب
General *a.* or *n.* عَامّ . شَائِع . قَائِد
Generality *n.* عُمُومِيَّة . اغلَبِية
Generalize *v. t.* عَمَّمَ
Generally *ad.* غَالِباً . عُمُوماً
Generate *v. t.* وَلَدَ . سَبَّبَ . أحدث
Generation *n.* جِيل . تَنَاسُل
Generative *a.* مُوَلِّد . مُنتِج
Generic / **Generical** } *a.* جِنسِيّ . شَامِل
Generosity *n.* سخَاء . كَرَم
Generous *a.* كرِيم . سَخِيّ
Genesis *n.* تَولِيد . سِفرُ ٱلتكوِين
Genial *a.* مُبهِج . بشُوش
Genii *n. pl.* جَانّ
Genitive *n.* ٱلمُضَافُ إِلَيهِ
Genius *n.* حذق . قَرِيحَة . صَاحِبُهَا
Genteel *a.* مُهَذَّب . لطِيف
Gentile *n.* or *a.* اممي . وَثَنِيّ
Gentility *n.* رِقَّة . تهذِيب . ادَب
Gentle *a.* لطِيف . دَمِث . انيس
Gentleman *n.* مُهَذَّب . (خواجا) سَيِّد

Gentleness *n.* رقة . دَمَاثَةٌ . لطفٌ

Gently *ad.* بلطافة . برقة

Gentry *n.* أَلخاصة . النجبآء . ألاعيان

Genuine *a.* حَقِيقِيٌّ . صَحِيح . خالص

Genuineness *n.* حقيقة . حقيقية

Genus (*pl.* Genera) *n.* جنس . نوع

Geographic / **Geographical** *a.* جغرافيٌّ

Geography *n.* جغرافيا . رَسمُ الارض

Geologic / **Geological** *a.* جيولوجيٌّ

Geologist *n.* عالم بالجيولوجيا

Geology *n.* علمُ طبقات الأرض

Geometric / **Geometrical** *a.* هندسيٌّ

Geometrician *n.* ماهر بعلم الهندسة

Geometry *n.* علمُ الهندسة

Germ *n.* جُرثُومة . اصل

German / **Germanic** *a.* ألمانيٌّ . جرمانيٌّ

Germinate *v. i.* نبت ـُ . افرخ

Gestation *n.* حَملٌ . مُدة الحمل

Gesticulate *v. i.* اومأ في الخطاب

Gesticulation / **Gesture** *n.* إيماء . حركة جسدية

Get (Got) *v. t.* حصل . إقتنى

Ghastliness *n.* إصفرار الوجه

Ghastly *a.* فظيع المنظر

Ghost *n.* رُوح . طيفٌ . خيالٌ

Ghostly *a.* خياليٌّ . رُوحانيٌّ

Ghoul *n.* غولٌ ج غيلانٌ

Giant *n.* or *a.* جبار . عظيمٌ جدًّا

Gibberish *n.* تمتمة

Gibbet *n.* or *v. t.* مشنقة . شنق

Gibe *v. i.* or *n.* إزدرى . هزأ . هزء

Gibralter *n.* جبل طارق

Giddiness *n.* دُوارٌ . طيش

Giddy *a.* مُصاب بالدوار . طائشٌ

Gift *n.* عطية . هبة

Gifted *a.* حاذق . ذو مواهب

Gig *n.* مَرْكَبَةٌ ذَاتُ دُولاَبَيْنِ

Gigantic *a.* كَبِيرٌ جداً . ضَخْمٌ

Gild *v. t.* مَوَّهَ . ذَهَّبَ

Gilt *n.* مِكْيَالٌ صَغِيرٌ لِلسَّوَائِلِ

Gilt *a.* مُذَهَّبٌ . مُمَوَّه

Gimlet *n.* بَيْرَمٌ صَغِيرٌ . بَرِّيمَةٌ

Gin *n.* نَوْعٌ مِنَ ٱلْعَرَقِ . فَخٌّ

Ginger *n.* زَنْجَبِيلٌ

Gipsy / Gypsy *n.* نُورِي . غَجَرِي

Giraffe *n.* زَرَافَةٌ

Gird *v. t.* نَطَّقَ . زَنَّرَ ـَ . رَبَطَ ـِ

Girder *n.* جِسْرٌ كَبِيرٌ

Girdle *n.* مِنْطَقَةٌ . زُنَّارٌ . حِزَامٌ

Girl *n.* صَبِيَّةٌ . إِبْنَةٌ . فَتَاةٌ

Girth *n.* حِزَامٌ

Gist *n.* خُلَاصَةٌ . زُبْدَةٌ . جل

Give *v. t.* أَعْطَى . وَهَبَ ـَ

Giving *n.* إِعْطَاءٌ . إِهْدَاءٌ

Gizzard *n.* قَانِصَةٌ ج قَوَانِصُ

Glacier *n.* جُرْفُ جَلِيدٍ

Glad *a.* مَسْرُورٌ . فَرْحَانٌ . مَبْسُوطٌ

Gladden *v. t.* فَرَّحَ . أَسَرَّ . ابْهَجَ

Glade *n.* مَعْبَرٌ او فسحةٌ فِي غَابَةٍ

Gladiator *n.* مُصَارِعٌ

Gladness *n.* سُرُورٌ . فَرَحٌ . بسط

Glance *n.* or *v. i.* لَمْحَةٌ . لَمَحَ ـَ . إِنْعَكَسَ

Gland *n.* غُدَّةٌ ج غدد

Glandular / Glandulous *a.* غُدِي ذُو غُدَدٍ

Glare *n.* or *v.i.* لَمَعَانٌ . مُبْهِرٌ . تَوَهَّجَ

Glaring *a.* لَامِعٌ . مُبْهِرٌ . فَاحِشٌ

Glass *n.* زُجَاجٌ . مِرْآةٌ . نَظَّارَةٌ

Glassy *a.* زُجَاجِيٌّ

Glaze *v. t.* جَهَّزَ بِزُجَاجٍ

Gleam *n.* or *v. i.* وَمِيضٌ . بَرْقٌ . وَمَضَ ـِ

Glean *v. t.* إِلْتَقَطَ . جَمَعَ ٱلْفَضَلَاتِ

Glee *n.* سُرُورٌ . إِبْتِهَاجٌ

Gleeful *a.* مَسْرُورٌ. فَرِحٌ . مُبْتَهِجٌ

Glen *n.* وَادٍ ضَيِّقٌ مُنْفَرِدٌ

Glibness *n.* نُعُومَةٌ. طَلَاقَةُ اللِّسانِ

Glide *v. i.* تَزَلَّقَ تزَلجَ

Glimmer *v. i.* تَلَأْلَأَ . خَفِيفاً

Glimmering *n.* تَلَأْلُؤٌ

Glimpse *n.* لمحةٌ. نَظْرَةٌ قَصِيرَةٌ

Glisten / Glitter } *v. i.* or *n.* تَلَأْلَأَ .لمعَان

Gloat *v. i.* تَفَرَّسَ بِعَيْنِ الشَّرِّ

Globe *n.* كُرَةُ .الأَرْضِ

Globular / Globulous } *a.* كُرَوِيٌّ

Globule *a.* كُرَيَّةٌ

Glomerate *v. t.* كَتَّلَ

Gloom *n.* قتامٌ . غَمٌّ

Gloomy *a.* مُغِمٌّ . مُكَدِّرٌ

Glorify *v. t.* مَجَّدَ. عَظَّمَ . اجَلَّ

Glorious *a.* مجيدٌ .جَليلٌ

Glory *n.* مجدٌ. جلالَةٌ . شهرَةٌ

Gloss / Glossiness } *n.* لمَعَانٌ. تأْوِيل

Glossary *n.* فِهْرِسُ كَلِماتٍ مَشْرُوحَةٍ

Glossy *a.* مَصْقُولٌ. لاَمِعٌ

Glottis *n.* مِزْمارُ الْحَنْجَرَة

Glove *n.* كَفٌّ ج كُفُوف

Glow *n.* or *v.i.* تَوَهجٌ. تَوَقَّدَ. إِحْتَدَمَ

Glowing *a.* مُتَوَهِجٌ. مُتَأَجِّجٌ. لاَمِعٌ

Glow-worm *n.* يَرَاعَة (حَشَرَةٌ)

Glue *n.* or *v. t.* غِرَاءٌ. غَرَّى

Glum *a.* مَغْمُومٌ. عَبُوسٌ

Glut *v. t.* أَشْبَعَ

Glutinous *a.* دَبِقٌ. لَزِجٌ

Glutton *n.* / Gluttonous *a.* } أَكُولٌ. نَهِمٌ. شَرِهٌ

Gluttony *n.* شَرَهٌ . نَهَمٌ

Gnarled / Gnarly } *a.* معقدٌ. ملْتَفٌّ

Gnash *v. t.* صَرَّ اسْنَانَهُ

Gnat *n.* بَعُوضَةٌ. نَامُوسَةٌ

Gnaw *v. t.* قَرَضَ ـِ . قَضَمَ ـِ

Go (went, gone) v. i. ذَهَبَ ـَ . مضَى ـ

Goad n. or v. t. منْخَس . نخَس ـ

Goal n. أَمد . غاية . غَرَض

Goat n. ماعِز . عَنْز . تَيْس

Goat-herd n. مَعاز

Gobble v. t. or i. إِزْدَرَدَ . لَهِم

Go-between n. وَسيط

Goblet n. قَدَح . كَأْس

Goblin n. جِنّي . عَفْرِيت

God n. إِلَه ج آلِهَة . الله

Goddess n. إِلاَهة

Godfather n. عَرَّاب

Godless a. كافِر . شِرِّير . فاجِر

Godliness n. تَقوَى

Godly a. تَقِيّ . صالِح

Godson n. فَلْيُون

Gold n. ذَهَب

Golddust n. دَقِيقُ الذَّهَبِ . تِبْر

Golden a. ذَهَبِي

Goldfinch n. حَسُّون . (طَائِر)

Goldsmith n. صائِغ ج صاغة

Gondola n. زَوْرَق . قارِب

Gong n. نَاقُوس

Good a. صالِح . جيد . طَيِّب

Good n. خير . نفْع . فَائِدَة

Good-by / Good-bye } n. or int. تَوْدِيع . بِأمانِ اللّٰهِ

Good-humour n. بَشَاشَة

Goodly a. جَمِيل . حسن

Good-natured a. حَسَنُ الأَخْلاَق

Goodness n. صلاَح . جُوْدَة . فَضِيلَة

Goods n. pl. بضائِع . سِلَع . أَملاَك

Good-will n. إِحسان . مَسَرَّة . معرُوف

Goose n. (pl. geese) وَزَّة . غَبِي

Gore v. or v.t. دَم . نطَح ـَ . طعَن ـ

Gorge v. t. إِلْتَهَم

Gorgeous *a.* فَاخِرٌ . زَاهٍ . بَهِيٌّ
Gorilla *n.* اكبرُ القُرُودِ . جُورِلاَّ
Gory *a.* دَمَوِيٌّ . مُضَرَّجٌ بِالدَّمِ
Gosling *n.* فَرْخُ الوَزِّ
Gospel *n.* إِنْجِيلٌ . بِشَارَة
Gossip *n.* or *v. i.* فُضُولِيٌّ . مِهذَارٌ . هَذَرَ ـ
Gouge *n.* or *v. t.* إِزمِيلٌ . نقرَ ـ
Gourd *n.* قَرْعٌ . (نَبَاتٌ)
Gout *n.* نقرسٌ . دَاءُ المُلُوكِ
Gouty *a.* مُصَابٌ بِالنِّقرِسِ
Govern *v. t.* مَلَكَ . سَادَ . حكمَ
Governess *n.* مُعَلِّمَةُ عائلة
Government *n.* حُكُومَة . سِيَاسَة
Governor *n.* حَاكِمٌ . وَالٍ . مدِيرٌ
Governorship *n.* منصبُ الحَاكِمِ . ولاَيَة
Gown *n.* قفطَانٌ . جُبةُ العُلَمَاءِ
Grab *v.t.* or *n.* مسكَ . خطفَ . خطفٌ
Grace *n.* نعمَة . عفو . حسن

Grace *v. t.* زَيَّنَ . ظَرَّفَ . اكرَمَ
Graceful *a.* رَقِيقٌ . لَطِيفٌ . مُهَذَّبٌ
Graceless *a.* شِرِّيرٌ . خَبِيثٌ
Gracious *a.* منعِمٌ . جوَّادٌ . رَحِيمٌ
Graciously *ad.* بلطَافةٍ . تكَرُّماً
Gradation *n.* تَدْرِيجٌ . تَدَرُّجٌ
Grade *n.* دَرَجة . رِتبة
Gradual *a.* تَدرِيجِيٌّ
Graduate *v. i.* نَالَ رِتْبَةً عِلمِيَّةً
Graduation *n.* نَيل رِتبَةٍ . تَدْرِيجٌ
Graft *n.* or *v.t.* تَطْعِيمُ الغُصْنِ . طَعَّمَ
Grain *n.* حَبَّة . حُبُوبٌ . حِنطَةٌ
Gram *n.* وَزْنُ الجرَامِ
Grammar *n.* عِلْمُ الصَّرْفِ وَالنحوِ
Grammarian *n.* نَاحٍ ج نُحَاةٌ
Grammatical *a.* حسَبَ النَّحْوِ
Granary *n.* مَخزَنُ الحُبُوبِ . هرْيٌ
Grand *a.* عَظِيمٌ . فاخِرٌ . جَلِيلٌ

Grand-child *n.* حَفِيدٌ . حَفِيدَةٌ

Granted *pp.* مُسَلَّمٌ بِهِ . لِنَفْرِضَ

Grandee *n.* احَدَ ٱلشُّرَفَاءِ او ٱلْاعْيَانِ

Grandeur *n.* عَظَمَةٌ . سُمُوٌّ . فَخَامَةٌ

Grandfather / **Grandsire** *n.* جَدٌّ ج جُدُودٌ

Grandma / **Grandmother** *n.* جَدَّةٌ

Grandson *n.* حَفِيدٌ

Granite *n.* نَوْعٌ مِنَ ٱلْحَجَرِ ٱلصُّلْبِ

Grant *n.* or *v.t.* هِبَةٌ وَهَبَ ـِ . أَجَابَ

Granular / **Granulate** *a.* حَبِّيٌّ . مُحَبَّبٌ

Granulate *v. t.* or *i.* حَبَّبَ . تَحَبَّبَ

Granule *n.* حُبَيْبَةٌ . دَقِيقَةٌ

Grape *n.* حَبَّةُ عِنَبٍ

Grape-shot *n.* دَكَّة رَصَاصَاتٍ

Grape-vine *n.* دَالِيَةٌ . كَرْمَةٌ

Graphic / **Graphical** *a.* خَطِّيٌّ . بَلِيغُ ٱلْوَصْفِ

Grapple *v. t.* or *n.* قَبَضَ . صَارَعَ . قَبْضٌ

Grasp *v.t.* or *n.* قَبَضَ . مَسَكَ . قَبْضٌ

Grasping *a.* طَمَّاعٌ

Grass *n.* حَشِيشٌ . كَلَأٌ . عُشْبٌ

Grasshopper *n.* جُنْدُب

Grassy *a.* عَشِبٌ . مُعْشِبٌ

Grate *v. t.* or *i.* حَكَّ . كَدَّرَ . صَرَفَ

Grate *n.* كَانُونٌ . وُجَاق

Grateful *a.* شَكُورٌ . مُرْضٍ

Gratefulness *n.* إِمْتِنَانٌ . شُكْرٌ

Gratification *n.* إِرْضَاءٌ . جَبْرُ ٱلْخَاطِرِ

Gratify *v. t.* أَرْضَى . طَيَّبَ ٱلْخَاطِرَ

Grating *n.* شَعْرِيَّةٌ

Gratis *ad.* مَجَّانًا

Gratitude *n.* شُكْرٌ

Gratuitous *a.* مَجَّانِيٌّ . بِلَا دَاعٍ

Gratuity *n.* عَطِيَّةٌ . هَدِيَّةٌ

Grave *n.* or *a.* قَبْرٌ . مُهِمٌّ . رَصِينٌ

Gravel *n.* or *v. t.* حَصًى او دَقِيقُهَا . فَرَشَ بِهِ

Graven *a.* مَنْحُوتٌ . مَنْقُوشٌ

Graver *n.* نَقَّاش . حَفَّار

Gravestone *n.* رُجْمَة ج رُجَم

Graveyard *n.* مَقْبَرَة

Gravitate *v. i.* مَالَ إِلَى . إِنْجَذَبَ

Gravity *n.* رَزَانَة . عَظَمَة أَلْجَاذِبِيَّة

Gravy *n.* مَرَق

Gray *a.* أَشْيَب . أَشْهَب

Grayish *a.* ضَارِب إِلَى ٱلشَّيْب

Grayness *n.* شَيْب . شُبْهَة

Graze *v. t.* or *i.* رَعَى ـَ . مَسّ ـَ

Grazing *n.* مَرْعًى

Grease *n.* or *v. t.* دُهْن . دَهَنَ ـُ

Greasiness *n.* دُهْنِيَّة

Greasy *a.* دَهِن

Great *a.* عَظِيم . كَبِير . سَامٍ

Greatly *ad.* كَثِير جِدًّا

Greatness *n.* عَظَمَة . سُمُوّ . كِبْر

Greaves *n. pl.* جُرْمُوق . دِرْع لِلْأَرْجُل

Grecian *a.* يُونَانِيّ . رُومِيّ

Greedily *ad.* شَرِهًا . نَهْمًا . تَائِقًا

Greediness *n.* شَرَه . شَهْوَة . طَمَع

Greedy *a.* شَرِه . أَكُول . طَامِع

Greek *a.* or *n.* يُونَانِيّ

Green *a.* أَخْضَر . فَجّ . عَدِيم ٱلْخِبْرَة

Greenhouse *n.* كِنَان لِتَرْبِيَةِ ٱلنَّبَات

Greens *n. pl.* خُضَر . بُقُول

Greet *v. t.* حَيَّا . سَلَّمَ عَلَى

Greeting *n.* تَحِيَّة . سَلَام

Greyhound *n.* كَلْب سَلُوقِيّ

Griddle / Gridion } *n.* (مِصْبَع) . سَفُّود . مِقْلَاة

Grief *n.* حُزْن . كَآبَة

Gregarious *a.* (حيوان) عَائِش سِرْبًا

Grievance *n.* شَكْوَى . ضِيق . اذِيَّة

Grieve *v. i.* or *t.* حَزِنَ ـَ . أَحْزَنَ

Grievous *a.* مُحْزِن . شَاقّ . شَدِيد

Grill *v. t.* شَوَى ـ

Grim *a.*	عَبُوس.هَائِل.شَرِس
Grimace *n.*	إِعوِجَاجُ ٱلْوَجْهِ لِقَصدٍ
Grime *v. t.* or *n.*	قَذَرَ.لَوَّث.وَسَخ
Grin *n.* or *v. t.*	كَشْرَة. كَشَرَ ـِ
Grind *v. t.*	سَنَّنَ.طَحَنَ ـَ. جَرَشَ ـِ
Grind *v.t.* (the teeth)	قَرَعَ اسْنَانَهُ
Grinder *n.*	سَنَّان. مِطْحَنَة. ضِرْس
Grindstone *n.*	جلْخ . مِسَنّ
Grip / Gripe *n.* or *v. t.*	قَبْض.قَبَضَ ـَ. مَغْص
Grist *n.*	طَحْنَة
Gristel *n.*	غضرُوف ج غضَارِيف
Gristmill *n.*	طَاحون ج طوَاحِين
Grit *n.*	رَمل . جَرِيشُ ٱلطَّحِين
Grizzled / Grizzly *a.*	اَشْيَبُ . أَزْبَد
Groan *v. t.* or *n.*	اَن . تَأَوَّهَ. انِين
Groaning *n.*	انِين . تَأَوُّه
Grocer *n.*	بَدَّال (بقَّال) . عطَّار
Grocery *n.*	دُكان آلمأ كُولَاتِ
Grog *n.*	شَرَاب مُسَكِّر
Groin *n.*	ارْبِيَة
Groom *n.* or *v. t.*	سَائِس . سَاسَ ـُ (آلخَيل)
Groove *n.*	خُدَّة . خط محفُور . ثِلم
Grope *v. i.*	تَلَمَّسَ .تَجَسَّسَ
Gross *a.*	غَلِيظ . ضَخم . فَظّ .
Gross *n.*	جُمْلَة. ١٢ دستَة (دَزِّينَة)
Grossness *n.*	غَلَاظَة. خُشُونَة
Grotto *n.*	كَهْف ج كُهُوف
Grotesque *a.*	غَرِيب . مضْحِك
Ground *n.*	ارْض . اسَاس . دَلِيل
Ground *v. t.* or *i.*	اسَّسَ . شَطَّطَتْ (سفِينَة)
Groundless *a.*	بَاطِل . لَا اصْلَ له
Groundwork *n.*	اسَاس . أَصل
Group *n.* or *v. t.*	جَمَاعَة . زُمْرَة . جَمَّعَ
Grove *n.*	غَابَة . حَرَجَة
Grovel *v. t.*	تَذَلَّلَ . دَبَّ ـِ
Grow *v. t.* or *i.*	ربى . نَمَا . زَادَ ـِ

Growl *v. t.* or *i.* هَمْهَمَ . تقمقم

Growth *n.* نُمُوٌّ . زِيَادَةٌ . تَقَدُّم

Grub *n.* شحمةُ ٱلْأَرْض
دودة ٱلخنفساء

Grudge *n.* or *v. t.* ضغينةٌ . حَسَدَ ـُ

Gruel *n.* ثَرِيدٌ لِلْمَرِيض

Gruff *a.* عبُوس . شَرِسٌ

Grumble *v. i.* تذمَّرَ . أتقمقم

Grunt *v. i.* or *n.* قبعَ ـَ . قبيعة

Guarantee *v. t.* or *n.* كفَلَ ـِ . كفَالَة . كَفِيلٌ

Guard *n.* or *v. t.* حِرَاسَةٌ . حرَّاسٌ حَرَسَ ـُ

Guardian *n.* حَارِسٌ . وَصِيٌّ . وَلِيٌّ

Guardianship *n.* وِصَايَة . حِرَاسَةٌ

Guess *v. t.* or *n.* خمَّنَ . تخمينٌ

Guest *n.* ضَيف ج ضُيُوف

Guidance *n.* إِرْشَاد . هِدَايَة . دِلَالَة

Guide *v. t.* ارشد . دَلَّ ـُ . هدَى ـِ

Guide *n.* مرشِدٌ . دَلِيلٌ

Guile *n.* مكرٌ . خدَاعٌ . غِشٌّ

Guileless *a.* مُخلِصٌ . بَرِيءٌ

Guillotine *n.* آلَةٌ لِلإِعْدَام بِقَطْع ٱلرَّأْس

Guilt, Guiltiness *n.* ذَنْبٌ

Guiltless *a.* بريءٌ لا ذَنْبَ فِيهِ

Guilty *a.* مُذْنِبٌ . مستحِقٌّ ٱلْقِصَاص

Guinea *n.* ٢١ شِلِنًا . جنيهٌ

Guise *n.* اسلُوبٌ . هيئَةٌ . زِيٌّ

Guitar *n.* قِيثَارٌ . ج قيَاثِير

Gulf *n.* خَلِيجٌ . جُوْن

Gull *v. t.* or *n.* خدَعَ . طَائِرٌ بحرِيٌّ

Gullet *n.* أَلْمَرِيءُ . أَلْبُلْعُوْمُ

Gully *n.* مَجْرًى عَمِيقٌ ضيقٌ

Gulp *v. t.* or *n.* لهمَ . جرَعَ . جرْعة

Gum *n.* لِثَةٌ . صَمْغٌ

Gun *n.* بُارُودَةٌ . بنْدُقية . مَدْفع

Gunner *n.* طوبجيٌّ

Gunpowder *n.* بارُودٌ

Gunsmith *n.* صانعُ ٱلأسلحةِ

Gurgle *v. i.* تغرغر

Gush *v. i.* دفق ـ

Gust *n.* نفخة ريحٍ قويّة

Gust *n.* مِعى ج أمعاء

Gutter *n.* قناة . بالوعة

Guttural *a.* or *n.* حلقيّ . حرفُ ٱلحلق

Guy *n.* حبلٌ للإسنادِ

Gymnasium *n.* مدرسةُ ٱلرّياضةِ

Gymnastic *a.* رياضيّ . جسديّ

H

Ha ! *ex.* عجبًا . ها

Habiliment *n.* ثوبٌ

Habit *n.* عادة . دأبٌ . ثوبٌ

Habitable *a.* قابلُ ٱلسُّكنى

Habitation *n.* مسكنٌ

Habitual *a.* عاديّ . إعتياديّ

Habituate *v.t.* عوّد . ألَّف

Habitude *n.* عادةٌ

Hack *v. t.* or *n.* قطع . فرّض . كديشٌ

Hackneyed *a.* كثيرُ ٱلإستعمالِ

Hackney-coach *n.* مركبةٌ للكراء

Haddock *n.* نوعٌ من ٱلسَّمك

Haft *n.* مقبضٌ ومِقبضٌ . نِصابٌ

Hag *n.* عجوزٌ . قبيحةٌ

Haggard *a.* خاسِفُ ٱلوجهِ

Haggle *v. t.* or *i.* دقّق في ٱلمساومة . قطّع

Hail *n.* or *v. t.* بَرَد . نادى . حيا

Hailstones *n. pl.* بَرَد

Hair *n.* شَعْر . شَعْرَة

Hairless *a.* أَجْرَدُ

Hairy *a.* أَشْعَر

Hale *a.* مُتَعافٍ . صَحِيحُ الْجِسْمِ

Half *n.* (*pl.* **Halves**) نِصْف

Hall *n.* دِهْلِيز . قَاعَة . مُنْتَدًى

Halloo *n.* or *v. i.* صَيْحَة . صاحَ ـِ

Hallow *v. t.* قَدَّس

Hallucination *n.* وَهْم . تَوَهُّم

Halo *n.* هَالَة . دائِرَة مُنِيرَة

Halt *n.* or *a.* وُقُوف . أَعْرَجُ

Halt *v. t.*, or *i.* وَقَّفَ. وَقَفَ ـِ . عَرَجَ ـُ

Halter *n.* or *v.t.* رَسَن. شِنَاق. رَسَنَ

Halve *v. t.* نَصَفَ ـُ . شَطَرَ ـُ

Ham *n.* فَخْذُ خِنْزِيرٍ مُمَلَّح

Hamlet *n.* مَزْرَعَة

Hammer *n.* مِطْرَقَة . شَاكُوش

Hammer *v. t.* طَرَقَ ـُ . دَقَّ ـُ

Hammock *n.* سَرِيرٌ مُعَلَّق

Hamper *n.* or *v. t.* قُفَّة . عاقَ . قَيَّدَ

Hamstring *n.* or *v. t.* عُرْقُوب . عَرْقَبَ

Hand *n.* or *v.t.* يَدٌ . كَفٌّ . نَاوَلَ

Handbook *n.* كِتَابٌ مُخْتَصَرٌ لِلدِّلاَلَة

Handcraft / **Handicraft** } *n.* حِرْفَة . صَنْعَةُ الْيَدِ

Handcuff *n.* غُلٌّ . قَيْدُ الْيَدِ

Handful *n.* قَبْضَة . شِرْذِمَة

Handily *ad.* بِمَهَارَةٍ . بِسُهُولَةٍ

Handiwork *n.* شُغْلُ الْيَدِ

Handkerchief *n.* (مَحْرَمَة) . مِنْدِيل

Handle *n.* or *v. t.* مِقْبَض . مَسَّ ـَ

Handmaid *n.* جَارِيَة . أَمَة

Hand-mill *n.* جَارُوش ج جَوَارِيش

Handsome *a.* جَمِيل . حَسَن

Handy *a.* مَاهِر . قَرِيب

Hang *v. t.* or *i.* عَلَّقَ . شَنَقَ . تَعَلَّقَ

Hangings *n. pl.* سَتَائِرُ . مُعَلَّقَات

Hangman *n.* جَلَّادٌ

Hanker *v. i.* تَاقَ ـُ إِلَى

Hap-hazard *n.* عَرَضٌ . صُدْفَةٌ

Hapless *a.* نحس . مَنْكُودُ ٱلْحَظِّ

Happen *v. i.* حَدَثَ ـُ صَارَ ـِ

Happiness *n.* سَعَادَةٌ . غِبْطَةٌ

Happy *a.* سَعِيدٌ . مَغْبُوطٌ . فَرِحٌ

Harangue *n.* or *v. t.* خِطَابٌ . خَاطَبَ

Harass *v. t.* أَزْعَجَ . أَضْجَرَ . أَتْعَبَ

Harassing *a.* مُزْعِجٌ . مُتْعِبٌ

Harbinger *n.* سَابِقٌ . مُبَشِّرٌ

Harbour *n.* or *v. t.* مِينَاءٌ . مَرْفَأٌ . آوَى

Hard *a.* قَاسٍ . صُلْبٌ . صَعْبٌ

Harden *v. t.* or *i.* صَلَّبَ . قَسَّى . تَصَلَّبَ

Hard-hearted *a.* قَاسِي ٱلْقَلْبِ

Hardihood *n.* جَرَاءَة . إِقْدَامٌ

Hardly *ad.* بِصُعُوبَةٍ . بِالْجهد

Hardness *n.* صَلَابَة . قَسَاوَة

Hardship *n.* مَشَقَّةٌ . صُعُوبَةٌ

Hardware *n.* بَضَائِعُ مَعْدِنِيَّةٌ

Hardy *a.* شَدِيدٌ . بَاسِلٌ . ضَلِيعٌ

Hare *n.* أَرْنَبٌ

Hare-brained *a.* طَائِشٌ

Harelip *n.* شَفَةٌ شَرْمَاءُ

Harem *n.* حَرِيمٌ

Hark *v. i.* أَصْغَى إِلَى

Harlot *n.* زَانِيَةٌ . عَاهِرَةٌ

Harm *n.* or *v. t.* أَذِيَة . ضَرَرٌ . آذَى

Harmful *a.* مُؤْذٍ . مُضِرٌّ

Harmless *a.* غيرُ مُضِرٍّ . سَلِيمٌ

Harmonious *a.* مُتَوَافِقٌ . مُتَنَاسِبٌ

Harmonize *v. t.* وَفَّقَ . سَاوَى

Harmony *n.* إِتِّفَاقٌ . مُوَازَنَةٌ

Harness *n.* عُدَّةُ ٱلْفَرَسِ او ٱلْعَسْكَرِيِّ

Harness *v. t.* أَلْبَسَهُ ٱلْعُدَّةَ . كَدَنَ ـُ

Harp *n.* or *v. i.* عُودٌ . ضَرَبَ عَلَيْهِ

Harper *n.* ضارِبٌ بالْعُودِ

Harpoon *n.* خُطَّافُ ٱلصَّيْد

Harrow *n.* or *v. t.* مسلفة . كدر . سلف

Harry *v. t.* نَهَبَ . سَلَبَ . ازعج

Harsh *a.* صَارِمٌ . فَظ . خَشِن

Harshness *n.* جَفَاءٌ . خشونة

Hart *n.* إِيِلٌ . وَعِلٌ ج وُعُول

Harvest *n.* or *v. t.* حِصَادٌ . حَصَدَ ـُ

Hash *n.* or *v. t.* (لَحْم مفرُوم) . قطع

Haste / Hasten *v. i.* or *t.* أَسْرَعَ . عَجَّلَ

Haste *n.* عَجَلَةٌ . مُبَادَرة

Hasty *a.* عَجُولٌ . مُسْرِعٌ . حَادٌّ

Hat *n.* بُرْنَيطَةٌ . قَلَنسُوَة

Hatch *v.t.* or *i.* فَقَسَ ـِ . إِنفقس

Hatchet *n.* فَأْسٌ

Hatchway *n.* مَدْخَل في ٱلسفينة

Hate *n.* or *v. t.* بُغْضٌ . أَبغض . مقت

Hateful *a.* مَمْقُوتٌ . مَكْرُوه

Hatred *n.* بُغضٌ . مقتٌ

Hatter *n.* صَانِعُ ٱلْبَرَانِيطِ او بَائِعها

Haughty *a.* مُتَكَبِّرٌ . متعجرف

Haul *v. t.* جَذَبَ . سَحَبَ

Haunch *n.* وَرْكٌ

Haunt *n.* or *v. t.* مَزَارٌ . تَرَدَّدَ إِلَى

Haunted *a.* مَأْوَى ٱلْجَانّ أَو ٱلطيف

Have *v. t.* مَلَكَ ـِ . لَهُ

Haven *n.* مِينَاءٌ . مرسى

Havoc *n.* خَرَاب . مَقتلة

Hawk *n.* بَازٍ ج بُوَاز . صقر ج صُقُور

Hawser *n.* حَبْلٌ ضَخم

Hawthorn *n.* زعرور (نَبَاتٌ)

Hay *n.* قَشٌّ . تِبْنٌ . كَلأٌ

Hazard *n.* or *v.t.* خَطَرٌ . خَاطَرَ بِ

Hazardous *a.* مُخطِرٌ . خطِرٌ

Haze *n.* ضَبَابَةٌ . إِغْبِرَارٌ

Hazel *n.* or *a.* شَجَرُ ٱلْبندق . بندقيٌّ

Haziness *n.* إِغبرار

Hazy *a.* ضَبَابِيٌّ . مُغْبَرٌّ

He *pron.* هُوَ

Head *n.* or *v. t.* رَأْسٌ . قَادَ . تَرَأَّسَ

Headache *n.* وَجَعُ ٱلرَّأْسِ . صُدَاعٌ

Head-dress *n.* كِسَاءُ ٱلرَّأْسِ

Heading *n.* أَوَّلُ ٱلشَّيْءِ . عُنْوَانٌ

Headland *n.* رَأْسٌ (فِي ٱلْبَحْرِ)

Headlong *a.* or *ad.* ٱلرَّأْسُ إِلَى أَسْفَلِ

Head-quarters *n.* مَرْكَزُ ٱلْقَائِدِ أَوِ ٱلْحُكُومَةِ

Headship *n.* رِئَاسَةٌ

Headstrong *a.* عَنِيدٌ . صَلْبُ ٱلرَّأْسِ

Heal *v.t.* or *i.* شَفَى ـِ . تَعَافَى . إِنْدَمَلَ

Health *n.* صِحَّةٌ . عَافِيَةٌ

Healthful *a.* مُتَعَافٍ . مُفِيدٌ لِلصِّحَّةِ

Healthfulness, Healthiness *n.* صِحَّةٌ . عَافِيَةٌ

Healthy *a.* صَحِيحٌ . نَافِعٌ لِلصِّحَّةِ

Heap *n.* or *v. t.* كَوْمَةٌ . عُرْمَةٌ . كَوَّمَ

Hear *v. t.* سَمِعَ ـَ . اصْغَى . أَطَاعَ

Hearing *n.* سَمْعٌ . مَسْمَعٌ

Hearken *v. t.* أَصْغَى . إِسْتَمَعَ

Hearsay *n.* قَوْلٌ . قَالٌ وَقِيلٌ

Hearse *n.* مَرْكَبَةٌ لِحَمْلِ ٱلْمَوْتَى

Heart *n.* قَلْبٌ . لُبٌّ

Heart-felt *a.* قَلْبِيٌّ . مُخْلِصٌ

Hearth *n.* مَوْقَدَةٌ

Heartily *a.* قَلْبِيًا . بِنَشَاطٍ

Heartiness *n.* خُلُوصٌ . هِمَّةٌ

Heartless *a.* قَاسٍ . بِلَا رَأْفَةٍ

Hearty *a.* قَلْبِيٌّ . مُخْلِصٌ . مُتَعَافٍ

Heat *n.* or *v. t.* حَرَارَةٌ . سَخَّنَ

Heathen *n.*, Heathenish *a.* وَثَنِيٌّ

Heathenism *n.* الدِّيَانَةُ ٱلْوَثَنِيَّةُ

Heave *v. t.* رَفَعَ ـَ رَمَى ـِ

Heaven *n.* ٱلسَّمَاءُ

Heavenly *a.* سَمَاوِيٌّ

Heaviness *n.*	ثِقل . غمّ
Heavy *a.*	ثَقِيلٌ . شَدِيد . بطِيء
Hebraic *a.* / **Hebrew** *n.*	عِبْرَانِيٌّ
Hedge *n.* or *v. t.*	سِياجٌ . سَيَّجَ
Hedgehog *n.*	قنفذ ج قنافذ
Heed *v. t.*	بالى . أصغى إِلى
Heed *n.*	إِكْتِرَاثٌ . إِعتناء
Heedful *a.*	مُبالٍ . منتبِهٌ
Heedless *a.*	غافلٌ . غيرُ مُبالٍ
Heedlessness *n.*	عدمُ ٱلْمُبَالاَة
Heel *n.*	عَقِبٌ ج اعقابٌ
Hegira *n.*	هِجْرَةٌ
Heifer *n.*	عِجْلَةٌ
Height *n.*	عُلُوٌّ
Heighten *v. t.*	علّى . زادَ
Heinous *a.*	فظيعٌ
Heir *n.*	وَارِثٌ ج وَرَثَةٌ
Heir-apparent *n.*	وَلِيُّ عهد
Hell *n.*	جهنّم . جحيم
Hellenic *a.*	يونانيٌّ
Helm *n.*	دفة . قِيادَةٌ
Helmet *n.*	خُوذَةٌ ج خُوذٌ
Helmsman *n.*	مدِيرُ ٱلدفَّة
Help *v. t.* or *n.*	ساعدَ . مُساعدةٌ
Helpful *a.*	مُساعِدٌ . مُعاون
Helpless *a.*	عاجزٌ . لا مُعِينَ له
Helpmate *n.*	مُعِين . رَفيق
Hem *n.* or *v.t.*	كفة . حاشِيَةٌ . كَفَّ
Hemisphere *n.*	نِصفُ كُرَةٍ
Hemlock *n.*	شوْكرانٌ
Hemorrhage *n.*	نزْفُ ٱلدَّمِ
Hemp *n.*	قِنَّبٌ
Hen *n.*	دُجاجَةٌ
Henbane *n.*	بَنجٌ (نبَاتٌ)
Hence *ad.*	من هنا . لهذَا . إِذاً
Henceforth / **Henceforward** *ad.*	منَ ٱلآنِ فصاعداً

Hencoop *n.*	قَفَص . قنّ
Heptagon *n.*	مُسَبَّع
Her *pro.*	لَهَا . هَا (ضمير)
Herald *n.* or *v. t.*	مُنادٍ. مخبّر . اخبَرَ
Herb *n.*	عُشْب . بقْل . نَبْت
Herbaceous *a.*	عُشْبِيّ
Herbage *n.*	كَلأ . خضْرَة
Herbarium *n.*	مَنْبَت
Harbivorous *a.*	آكِلُ ٱلنَّبَاتِ
Herculean *a.*	عَظِيم جِدًّا . صَعْب
Herd *n.* or *v. i.*	قَطِيع . إِجْتَمَعَ
Herdsman *n.*	رَاعٍ ج رُعاة
Here *ad.*	هُنَا . هَا هُنَا
Hereabouts *ad*	فِي هذِهِ ٱلنَّوَاحِي
Hereafter *ad.*	فِيمَا بعدُ . بَعْدَ هٰذَا
Hereby *ad.*	بِهٰذَا . مِنْ هٰذَا
Hereditary *a.*	إِرْثِيّ . مَوْرُوث
Herein *ad.*	فِي هٰذَا . مِنْ هٰذَا . لِهٰذَا
Heresy *n.*	(هَرْطَقَة) بِدْعَة
Heretic *n.* / Heretical *a.*	(هَرْطُوقِيّ) . خَارِجِيّ
Heretofore *ad.*	فِيمَا مَضَى . سَابِقًا
Hereupon *ad.*	عِنْدَ ذَلِكَ . مِنْ ثَمَّ
Herewith *ad.*	بِهٰذَا . مِنْ هٰذَا
Heritage *n.*	مِيرَاث
Hermetically *ad.*	بِضَبْطٍ (مَسْدُود)
Hermit *n.*	نَاسِك . زَاهِد
Hermitage *n.*	مَنْسَك
Hernia *n.*	فِتْق
Hero *n.* (*pl.* Heroes).	صِنْدِيد . بَطَل
Heroic *a.*	صِنْدِيدِيّ . مَجِيد
Heroine *n.*	صِنْدِيدَة . بَطَلَة
Heroism *n.*	بَسَالَة . إِقْدَام
Herring *n.*	نَوْع مِنَ السَّمَكِ
Herself *pro.*	نَفْسُهَا . ذَاتُهَا
Hesitancy / Hesitation *n.*	تَرَدُّد . إِرْتِيَاب
Hesitate *v. i.*	تَرَدَّدَ . إِرْتَابَ
Heterogeneous *a.*	مُخْتَلِفُ ٱلْجِنْسِ
Hew *v. t.*	نَحَتَ ـ . قَطَعَ

Hexagon *n.*	مُسَدَّسٌ
Hexangular *a.*	مُسَدَّسُ ٱلزَّوَايَا
Hibernal *a.*	شَتَوِيٌّ
Hibernate *v. i*	شَتَّى (لِلْبَهَائِمِ)
Hibernian *n.*	إِرْلَانْدِيٌّ
Hiccough *n.* or *v. i.*	فُوَاق . فَاقَ ــَ
Hidden *a.*	مُخْفِيٌّ . مَسْتُور
Hide *v. t.* or *i.*	أَخْفَى . إِخْتَفَى
Hideous *a.*	قَبِيحٌ . كَرِيهُ ٱلْمَنْظَرِ
Hierarchy *n.*	رِئَاسَة دِينِيَّة
Hieroglyphics *n. pl.*	خَط بِصُوَر
High *a.*	عَالٍ . سَامٍ
Highland *n.*	نَجْد . ارض جَبَلِيَّة
Highly *ad.*	كَثِيراً . جِدّاً
Highness *n.*	سُمُوٌّ . رِفْعَة
High-priest *n.*	رَئِيسُ ٱلْكَهَنَةِ
Hight *see* **Height** *n.*	عُلُوٌّ
High-water *n.*	أَعْلَى ٱلْمَدّ
Highway *n.*	سِكَّة سُلْطَانِيَّة
Highwayman *n.*	قَاطِعُ ٱلطُّرُقِ
Hilarity *n.*	طَرَب فَرَحٌ
Hill *n.*	تَلٌّ . أَكَمَةٌ
Hillock *n.*	قَلِيل . كَثِيب
Hilly *a.*	كَثِيرُ ٱلتِّلَالِ
Hilt *n.*	مِقْبَضٌ . نِصَابٌ
Himself *pro.*	نَفْسُهُ . ذَاتُهُ
Hind *a.* or *n.*	مُؤَخَّرُ ٱلشَّيْءِ . إِيَّلَةٌ
Hinder *v. t.*	عَاقَ . صَدَّ ــُ مَنَعَ ــَ
Hinderance / **Hindrance** *n.*	عَائِقٌ . مَانِعٌ
Hindermost / **Hindmost** *a.*	أَلاخِيرُ
Hindoo *n.*	هِنْدِيٌّ
Hinge *n.* or *v. i.*	مَفْصَلَة . دَار عَلَى
Hint *v. t.* or *i.* or *n.*	اومأَ . لَمَّحَ . إِيمَاء . تَلْمِيح
Hip *n.*	وِرْكٌ
Hippodrome *n.*	مِيدَانٌ لِلْخَيْلِ
Hippopotamus *n.*	فَرَسُ ٱلْمَاءِ
Hire *n.* or *v. t.*	اجرٌ . كِرَاء . إِسْتَأْجَرَ
Hireling *n.* or *a.*	اجِيرٌ

His *pro.*	لهُ
Hiss *v. t.* or *i.* or *n.*	صفرَ ـِ . فحَّ ـُ . فَحيحٌ
Historian *n.*	مُؤَرّخ
Historical *a.*	تاريخيٌّ
History *n.*	تأريخٌ
Hit *v. t.* or *n.*	اصابَ . إصابة
Hitch *v. t.* or *n.*	علقَ . رَبَطَ . عرْقَلَة
Hither *ad.*	إِلَى هُنَا
Hitherto *ad.*	إِلَى الآنَ
Hive *n.*	قَفِيرٌ
Hoar / Hoary *a.*	أَشيبُ . أبيَضُ
Hoard *v. t.* or *n.*	ذَخَرَ ـَ . ذَخيرَة
Hoarfrost *n.*	مَلاَّحٌ . صَقِيعٌ
Hoariness *n.*	شيب
Hoarse *a.*	ابَحٌّ . مَبْحُوحٌ
Hoarseness *n.*	بُحَّةٌ
Hoax *n.* or *v. t.*	غشٌّ . أُلعُوبَة . غَشَّ . مَكَرَ
Hobble *v. i.* or *t.*	عرِج . شَكَّلَ
Hobby / Hobbyhorse *n.*	ما يُولَعُ بِهِ
Hobgoblin *n.*	غُولٌ
Hock *n.* or *v. t.*	عرُقوبٌ . عَرْقَبَ
Hod *n.*	نَقِيرٌ ج نُقْرَان
Hoe *n.* or *v. t.*	مِجْرَفَة . مِعزَقَة . عَزَقَ ـِ
Hog *n.*	خنْزِير ج خنَازِير
Hogshead *n.*	بَرْمِيل كبير
Hog-sty *n.*	زَرِيبَةُ الخَنَازِيرِ
Hoist *v. t.*	رَفَعَ ـَ
Hold *n.*	ضَبْطٌ . دَاخِلُ سفِينَةٍ
Holde *v. t.*	ضَبطَ . حَجَزَ ـُ . وَسِعَ ـَ
Hole *n.*	ثَقْبٌ . خَرْق . وَجَار
Holiday *n.*	يَوْمُ بطالَةٍ
Holiness *n.*	قَدَاسَة
Hollow *a.*	فَارِغٌ . مُجَوَّفٌ . بَاطِلٌ
Hollow *v. t.*	جوَّفَ
Hollow *n.*	إِنخِفَاضٌ . غَوْطٌ . جوف
Hollow-hearted *a.*	خَائِنٌ . مُرَآءٍ
Hollyhock *n.*	اخْطِيٌّ

Holy *a.*	مقدّس . قدّوس	Honorary *a.*	إكرامي
Homage *n.*	إكرام . عبادة . إحترام	Hood *n.*	قلنسوة . قبّعة
Home *n.*	بيت . وطن	Hoodwink *v. t.*	خدع . ختل ـِ
Homely *a.*	عديم الحسن . بيتيّ	Hoof *n.*	حافر . ظلف ج ظلوف
Homeopathy *n.*	العلاج بالمثل	Hook *n.*	شصّ . كلاب . خطّاف
Homesick *a.*	مشتاق للوطن او للبيت	Hoop *n.* or *v.t.*	إطار . طوق . شدّ بإطار
Homestead *n.*	دار عائلة	Hooping-cough *n.*	مرض الشهقة
Homeward *ad.*	نحو البيت او الوطن	Hoot *n. v. i.*	صيحة . نعق . نعق ـَ
Homicide *n.*	قاتل . قتل	Hop *v. i.*	قفز على رجل واحدة
Homogeneous *a.*	متجانس	Hop *n.*	قفزة . حشيشة الدينار
Hone *n.* or *v. t.*	مسنّ رفيع . سنّ ـُ	Hope *n.* or *v. i.*	رجاء . رجا ـُ
Honest *a.*	مستقيم . أمين . مخلص	Hopeful *a.*	كثير الرجاء . مرجوّ
Honesty *n.*	أمانة . إستقامة	Hopeless *a.*	بلا رجاء . بائس
Honey *n.*	عسل	Horde *n.*	قوم . قبيلة
Honeycomb *n.*	شهد العسل	Horizon *n.*	افق
Honeymoon *n.*	شهر الزواج	Horizontal *a.*	افقيّ
Honour *n.* or *v.t.*	إكرام . أكرم	Horn *n.*	قرن . بوق . ناقور
Honorable *a.*	مكرم . شريف	Horned *a.*	ذو قرون

Hornet *n.*	زُنْبُورٌ
Horrible *a.*	هَائِلٌ . فَظِيعٌ
Horrid *a.*	فَظِيعٌ . قَبِيحٌ
Horrify *v. t.*	أَرْعَبَ . أَفْظَعَ
Horror *n.*	هَوْلٌ . رُعْبٌ
Horse *n.*	فَرَسٌ . حِصَانٌ ج احْصِنَةٌ
Horseback *n.*	ظَهْرُ ٱلْفَرَسِ
Horseman *n.*	خَيَّالٌ . فَارِسٌ
Horsemanship *n.*	فَنُّ رُكُوبِ ٱلْخَيْلِ
Horseshoe *n.*	نَعْلُ ٱلْفَرَسِ
Horsewhip *n.*	سَوْطٌ . كُرْبَاجٌ
Hospitable *a.*	مِضْيَافٌ . كَرِيمٌ
Hospital *n.*	مُسْتَشْفًى
Hospitality *n.*	تَضْيِيفٌ . ضِيَافَةٌ
Host / **Hostess** *n.*	مُضِيفٌ مُضَيِّفٌ . مُضِيفَةٌ
Hostage *n.*	رَهْنٌ . رَهِينٌ
Hostile *a.*	عِدَائِيٌّ . مُضَادٌّ
Hostility *n.*	عَدَاوَةٌ . خِصَامٌ
Hostler *n.*	سَائِسُ ٱلْخَيْلِ
Hot *a.*	حَارٌّ . سُخْنٌ . حَامٍ
Hotel *n.*	فُنْدُقٌ . لوكَنْدَة
Hotly *ad.*	بِحَمِيةٍ . بِشِدَّةٍ
Hound *n.*	كَلْبُ ٱلصَّيْدِ
Hour *n.*	سَاعَةٌ . زَمَان
Hour-glass *n.*	سَاعَةٌ . رَمْلِيَّةٌ
Hourly *a.* or *ad.*	كُلَّ سَاعَةٍ
House *n.*	بَيْتٌ . دَوْلَةٌ . شِرْكَة
House-breaker *n.*	لِصٌّ ج لُصُوص
Household *n.*	أَهْلُ ٱلْبَيْتِ
Housekeeper *n.*	مُدَبِّرُ ٱلْمَنْزِلِ .
Houseless *a.*	بِلَا مَسْكَنٍ
Hovel *n.*	كُوخٌ . خُصٌّ
Hover *v. i.*	حَامَ ـُ . تَرَدَّدَ بِقُرْبٍ
How *ad.*	كَيْفَ
However *ad.*	كَيْفَمَا . إِلَّا أَنَّ
Howl *v. i.* or *n.*	عَوَى ـِ . عُوَاءٌ

Hub *n.* بَطِّيخَة ٱلدُّولَاب

Hubbub *n.* ضَوْضَاء . ضَجِيج

Huddle *v. t.* أَسْرَعَ . خَلَطَ ـِ إِزْدَحَمَ

Hue *n.* لَوْن

Hug *v. t.* or *n.* عَانَقَ . عِنَاق

Huge *a.* كَبِير جِدًّا . جَسِيم

Hull *n.* قِشْرُ ٱلْجَوْزَةِ . بَدَنُ ٱلسَّفِينَةِ

Hull *v. t.* قَشَّرَ

Hum *v. i.* or *n.* دَنْدَنَ . دَنْدَنَة . دَوِيّ

Human *a.* بَشَرِيّ . إِنْسَانِيّ

Humane *a.* ذُو إِنْسَانِيَّةٍ . لَطِيف

Humanity *n.* إِنْسَانِيَّة . لُطْف

Humble *a.* وَدِيع . مُتَوَاضِع

Humble *v. t.* ذَلَّلَ . وَضَعَ ـَ . حَطَّ ـُ

Humbug *n.* or *v. t.* شَعْبَذَة . غِشّ ـُ

Humid *a.* رَطْب . مُنَدًّى

Humidity *n.* رُطُوبَة . نَدًى

Humiliate *v. t.* ذَلَّلَ . حَطَّ شَأْنَهُ

Humiliation *n.* ذُلّ . إِنْحِطَاط

Humility *n.* تَوَاضُع . خُشُوع

Humour *v. t.* لَاطَفَ . دَارَى

Humour *n.* طَبْع . سَجِيَّة . فُكَاهَة

Humorist *n.* / **Humorous** *a.* } مَازِح . مُضْحِك

Hump *n.* حَدَبَة . سَنَام

Humpback / **Hunchback** } *n.* أَحْدَب . حَدْبَاء

Hundred *n.* مِئَة وَمِائَة

Hundredth *a.* أَلْمِئَة

Hunger *n.* or *v. i.* جُوع . جَاعَ

Hungry *a.* جَائِع . جَوْعَان

Hunt *v. t.* or *n.* إِصْطَادَ . صَيْد . قَنَص

Hunter / **Huntsman** *n.* } قَانِص . صَيَّاد

Hurl *v. t.* or *n.* أَلْقَى . رَمَى ـِ رَمْيَة

Hurrah! *ex.* هُتَافُ ٱلْفَرَحِ

Hurricane *n.* زَوْبَعَة

Hurry *v. t.* or *i.* عَجَّلَ . إِسْتَعْجَلَ

Hurt *n.* or *v. t.* ضَرَر . أَضَرَّ . آذَى

Hurtful *a.*	مُؤْذٍ . مضِر
Husband *n.* or *v. t.*	زَوْج . بَعْل . إقتصد
Husbandman *n.*	فلاحٌ . كرَّامٌ
Husbandry *n.*	فلاحةٌ
Hush *v. t.* or *i.*	اسْكت . سَكت ـُ
Husk *n.* or *v. t.*	قِشْرةٌ . قشر
Husky *a.*	أَبَحُّ
Hustle *v. t.*	زَحَمَ ـَ . دفع ـَ عجَّل
Hut *n.*	كُوخٌ
Huzza *n.*	هِتَافُ ٱلاِسْتِحْسَانِ
Hybrid *n.*	مَوْلُودٌ مِنْ نَوْعَيْنِ
Hydraulics *n. sing.*	عِلْمُ ٱلسَّوَائِلِ
Hydrogen *n.*	هِدْرُوجِينٌ
Hydrophobia *n.*	دَاءُ ٱلْكَلَبِ
Hygiene / **Hygienics** } *n.*	عِلْمُ حِفْظِ ٱلصِّحَّةِ
Hyena *n.*	ضَبُع ج ضِبَاعٌ
Hymn *n.*	تَرْنِيمَةٌ
Hymnal *n.*	كِتَابُ تَرْنِيمَاتٍ
Hyperbola *n.*	قَوْسُ قَطْعِ ٱلْمَخْرُوطِ
Hyperbole *n.*	مبالغة
Hyphen *n.*	علامةُ وصلٍ (ـ)
Hypochondria *n.*	سَوْدَاء
Hypocrisy *n.*	رِيَاء . نفاقٌ
Hypocrite *n.*	مُرَاءٍ . مُنَافِقٌ
Hypothenuse *n.*	وَتَرُ زَاوِيَةٍ قَائِمَةٍ
Hypothssis *n.*	حَدَس . فَرْضٌ
Hyssop *n.*	زُوفَا
Hysterical *a.*	(هِسْتِيرِي)
Hysteria / **Hysterics** } *n.*	(هِسْتِيرِيَا)

I

I *pro.* انا

Ice *n.* جَلِيدٌ

Iceberg *n.* جَبَلُ جَلِيدٍ عَائِمٌ

Ice-cream *n.* (بُوزٌ جِلاته . دَنْدُرْمَه)

Icicle *n.* جَلِيدٌ مَخْرُوطِيُّ ٱلشَّكْلِ

Icy *a.* جَلِيدِيٌّ . قَارِسٌ

Idea *n.* صُورَةٌ عَقْلِيَّةٌ . فِكْرٌ

Ideal *a.* تَصَوُّرِيٌّ . كَامِلٌ

Idealize *v. t.* تَصَوَّرَ

Identic / Identical } *a.* عَيْنُهُ . ذَاتُهُ

Identify *v. t.* حَقَّقَ أَنَّهُ هُوَ

Idiocy *n.* بَلَاهَةٌ . عَتَهٌ

Idiom *n.* إِصْطِلَاحٌ

Idiomatic / Idiomatical } *a.* إِصْطِلَاحِيٌّ

Idio *n.* / Idiotic *a.* } أَبْلَهُ . مَعْتُوهٌ

Idle *a.* / Idler *n.* } بَطَّال . كَسْلَانٌ

Idleness *n.* كَسَلٌ . بطَالَةٌ

Idol *n.* صَنَمٌ . وَثَنٌ

Idolater *n.* وَثَنِيٌّ . عَابِدُ اصْنَامٍ

Idolatrous *a.* مُخْتَصٌّ بِعِبَادَةِ ٱلأَوْثَانِ

Idolize *v. t.* أَفْرَطَ فِي ٱلْحُبِّ . وَلِعَ بِ

Idolatry *n.* عِبَادَةُ ٱلْأَوْثَانِ

If *conj.* لَوْ . إِنْ . إِذَا

Igneous *a.* نَارِيٌّ

Ignite *v. t.* أَوْقَدَ . أَشْعَلَ

Ignoble *a.* دَنِيءٌ . خَسِيسٌ

Ignominious *a.* مُوجِبُ ٱلْعَارِ . مُخْزٍ

Ignominy *n.* عَارٌ . فَضِيحَةٌ . إِبَةٌ

Ignoramus *n.* / Ignorant *a.* } جَاهِلٌ . غَبِيٌّ

Ignorance *n.* جَهَالَة . غَبَاوَة

Ignore *v. t.* تَجَاهَلَ . أَهمَلَ

Ill *a.* or *a.* مَرِيضٌ . سُوءٌ

Ill-bred *a.* غَيْرُ مُهَذَّبٍ . فَظ

Illegal *a.* غَيْرُ شَرْعِيٍّ

Illegible *a.* مُمْتَنِعٌ قِرَاءَتُهُ

Illegitimate *a.* غَيْرُ شَرْعِيٍّ . نَغْل

Ill-fated *a.* نَحِس . مَشْؤُومٌ

Ill-favoured *a.* اشْوَهُ . سَيِّءُ ٱلْمَنْظَرِ

Illiberal *a.* بَخِيلٌ . خَسِيس

Illicit *a.* مُحَرَّمٌ . مَمْنُوع

Illimitable *a.* غَيْرُ مَحْدُودٍ

Illiterate *a.* أُمِّيٌّ

Ill-nature *n.* سُوءُ ٱلطَّبْعِ

Illness *n.* مَرَضٌ . عِلَّة

Illogical *a.* غَيْرُ مَنْطِقِيٍّ

Ill-omened *a.* مَشْؤُوم

Ill-starred *a.* مَشْؤُومٌ

Ill-timed *a.* فِي غَيْرِ وَقْتِهِ

Illumine / Illuminate } *v. t.* أَنَارَ . اضَاءَ

Illumination *n.* إِنَارَةٌ

Illusion *n.* وَهْمٌ

Illusive / Illusory } *a.* غَرَّارٌ . غَيْرُ حَقِيقِيٍّ

Illustrate *v. t.* بَيَّنَ . شَرَحَ

Illustration *n.* إِيضَاحٌ . تَصْوِيرٌ

Illustrious *a.* شَهِيرٌ . جَلِيل

Ill-will *n.* ضَغِينَة . سُوءُ نِيَّةٍ

Image *n.* تِمْثَالٌ . صُورَةٌ

Imagery *n.* اَلتَّصَوُّرُ فِي ٱلْكَلَامِ

Imaginable *a.* قَابِلُ ٱلتَّصَوُّرِ

Imaginary *a.* تَصَوُّرِيٌّ . وَهْمِيٌّ

Imagination *n.* اَلتَّصَوُّرُ . اَلْمُخَيِّلَةُ

Imaginative *a.* كَثِيرُ ٱلتَّصَوُّرِ

Imagine *v. t.* تَصَوَّرَ . تَخَيَّلَ

Imbecile *a.* سَخِيف . عَاجِز

Imbecility *n.*	سخافة . عجز
Imbedded *pp.*	مغروز . مدفون
Imbibe *v. t.*	شرب ــ . تشرب
Imbrue *v. t.*	بلل . نقع . لطخ
Imbue *v. t.*	صبغ ــ . أثر
Imitate *v. t.*	تمثل به . حاكى
Imitation *n.*	إقتداء . تزوير
Immaculate *a.*	بلا دنس . نقي
Immalleable *a.*	لا يمطل بالطرق
Immaterial *a.*	غير مادي . غير مهم
Immature *a.*	فج . غير بالغ
Immeasurable / Immensurable *a.*	لا يقاس
Immediate *a.*	غير متأخر . قريب
Immediately *ad.*	حالاً . على الفور
Immemorial *a.*	قديم جداً
Immense *a.*	عظيم جداً
Immensity *n.*	كبر لا يقاس
Immerse *v. t.*	غطس ب . غمس ب

Immersion *n.*	غطس . غمس
Immigrant *a.*	مهاجر إلى
Immigrate *v. i.*	هاجر إلى
Imminent *a.*	قريب . موشك
Immoderate *a.*	مفرط . متجاوز الحد
Immodest *a.*	عديم الحشمة او الحياء
Immolate *v. t.*	ذبح ــ
Immoral *a.*	فاسد . فاجر
Immorality *n.*	فساد الآداب
Immortal *a.*	خالد
Immortality *n.*	خلود
Immortalize *v. t.*	خلد
Immovable *a.* in *pl. n.*	ثابت . راسخ . عقار
Immunity *n.*	براءة . إمتياز
Immure *v. t.*	حبس ــ
Immutability *n.*	عدم التغير
Immutable *a.*	عديم التغير
Imp *n.*	عفريت صغير

Impact *n.* صَدمٌ . دَفعٌ

Impair *v. t.* أفسَدَ . أخلَّ بهِ . أضرَّ

Impale *v. t.* خَوزَقَ

Impalpable *a.* مَا لاَ يُدرَكُ باللمسِ

Impart *v. t.* مَنَحَ . ـــ . أخبَرَ بهِ

Impartial *a.* عَدِيمُ المُحابَاةِ . عَادِل

Impartiality *n.* عَدَمُ المحابَاةِ

Impassable *a.* مَا لاَ يُعبَرُ

Impassioned *a.* ثَائِرٌ . مُهيَّجٌ . متهيّج

Impatience *n.* عدَمُ الصبرِ

Impatient *a.* عَدِيمُ الصَّبرِ . جَزِعٌ

Impeach *v. t.* أقَامَ دَعوَى عَلَيهِ

Impede *v. t.* عَاقَ

Impediment *n.* عَائِقٌ

Impel *v. t.* دَفَعَ ـــ حَرَّضَ

Impending *a.* مُوشِكٌ . مُتوَعِّد

Impenetrable *a.* غَيرُ قَابِلِ الإختِرَاق

Impenitence *n.* عَدَمُ التَّوبَةِ

Impenitent *a.* عَدِيمُ التَّوبَةِ

Imperative *a.* or *n.* ضَرُورِيٌّ . أمْرٌ

Imperceivable / **Imperceptible** *a.* لاَ يُشعَرُ بهِ

Imperfect *a.* نَاقِصٌ . غَيرُ كَامِلٍ

Imperfection *n.* نَقصٌ

Imperial *a.* سُلطَانِيٌّ

Imperil *v. t.* اوقَعَ في خطَرٍ

Imperious *a.* مُتَجَبِّرٌ . ضَرُورِيٌّ

Imperishable *a.* عَدِيمُ الزَّوَالِ

Impermeable *a.* مَا لاَ يَتَخَلَّلُهُ سَائِلٌ

Impersonal *a.* غَيرُ شَخصِيٍّ

Impersonate *v. t.* شَخَّصَ

Impertinence *n.* وَقَاحَة

Impertinent *a.* وَقِحٌ . فُضُولِيٌّ

Imperturbable *a.* رَكِينٌ لاَ يُقلَقُ

Impervious *a.* مَا لاَ يُخرَقُ أو يُتخَلَّلُ

Impetuosity *n.* إقتِحَامٌ . حِدَّة

Impetuous *a.* مُقتَحِمٌ . مُحتَدّ

Impetus *n.* قُوَّةٌ دَافِعَةٌ

Impiety *n.* عَدَمُ ٱلتَّقوَى

Impious *a.* شِرِّيرٌ . أَثِيمٌ

Implacable *a.* حَنِقٌ لَا يُرْضَى

Implant *v. t.* غَرَسَ فِي . أَدْخَلَ

Implement *n.* آلَةٌ . أَدَاةٌ

Implicate *v. t.* أَوْقَعَ فِي . عَرَّضَ

Implication *n.* تَضَمُّنُ مَعْنًى

Implicit *a.* مُتَضَمَّنٌ . مَوْثُوقٌ بِهِ

Implicitly *ad.* بِثِقَةٍ تَامَّةٍ . مَعْنَوِيًّا

Implore *v. t.* تَوَسَّلَ . إِسْتَغَاثَ

Imply *v. t.* تَضَمَّنَ . دَلَّ عَلَى

Impolite *a.* قَلِيلُ ٱلأَدَبِ . فَظٌّ

Impoliteness *n.* قِلَّةُ ٱلادَبِ

Impolitic *a.* بِغَيْرِ حِكْمَةٍ . غَيْرُ مُنَاسِبٍ

Imponderable *a.* عَدِيمُ ٱلثِّقَلِ

Import *v. t.* جَلَبَ ـِ . ادْخَلَ إِلَى

Import *n.* وَارِدٌ . مَعْنًى . اهَمِيَّةٌ

Importance *n.* أَهَمِيَّةٌ . عَظَمَةٌ

Important *a.* مُهِمٌ . خَطِيرٌ

Importation *n.* جَلْبٌ مِنْ خَارِجٍ

Importunate *a.* لَجُوجٌ . مُلِحٌّ

Importune *v. t.* لَجَّ ـِ . أَلَحَّ عَلَى

Importunity *n.* لَجَاجَةٌ . إِلحَاحٌ

Impose *v. t.* وَضَعَ ـَ عَلَى . غَشَّ ـُ

Imposing *a.* عَظِيمٌ . مُؤَثِّرٌ

Imposition *n.* تَكْلِيفٌ . مَكْرٌ

Impossibility *n.* عَدَمُ ٱلإِمْكَانِ

Impossible *a.* غَيْرُ مُمْكِنٍ . مُسْتَحِيلٌ

Impost *n.* ضَرِيبَةٌ . مَكْسٌ

Impostor *n.* خَدَّاعٌ . دَجَّالٌ

Imposture *n.* خُدْعَةٌ

Impotence *n.* عَجْزٌ . وَهنٌ

Impotent *a.* عَاجِزٌ . وَاهِنٌ

Impoverish *v. t.* أَفْقَرَ . أَعْوَزَ

Impracticable *a.* مُمْتَنِعٌ عَمَلُهُ

Imprecate *v. t.* دعا على

Impregnable *a.* منيع

Impregnate *v. t.* لقح . أشرب

Impregnation *n.* تلقيح . إشراب

Impress *v. t.* أثر . سخر . ختم

Impress *n.* رسم . أثر . صورة

Imprsesion *n.* ظن . علامة . طبعة

Impressive *a.* مؤثر

Imprint *v. t.* or *n.* طبع ـ . وسم ـ . وسم

Imprison *v. t.* حبس ـ . سجن ـ

Imprisonment *n.* حبس . سجن

Improbable *a.* غير محتمل

Improper *a.* غير لائق

Impropriety *n.* عدم لياقة

Improve *v. t.* or *i.* حسن . تقدم

Improvement *n.* تحسن . تقدم

Improvident *a.* عديم العناية . متغفل

Improvise *v. i.* إرتجل . إبتده

Imprudence *n.* قلة الحزم أو البصيرة

Imprudent *a.* غير بصير أو حازم

Impudence *n.* وقاحة . سفه

Impudent *a.* وقح . سفيه

Impugn *v. t.* ناقض . عارض

Impulse / Impulsion *n.* قوة دافعة

Impulsive *a.* مندفع . دافع

Impunity *n.* عدم عقاب . أمن

Impure *a.* فاسد . نجس

Impurity *n.* فساد . قذر

Imputation *n.* إتهام . ذم

Impute *v. t.* نسب إلى . حسب له

In *pr.* في . ب . داخل

Inability *n.* عجز . عدم قدرة

Inaccessible *a.* منيع

Inaccuracy *n.* عدم ضبط أو صحة

Inaccurate *a.* غير مضبوط أو صحيح

Inaction / Inactivity *n.* عدم حركة . بطالة

Inactive *a.* سَاكِنٌ . مُتَكَاسِلٌ
Inadequate *a.* غَيْرُ كَافٍ . نَاقِصٌ
Inadmissible *a.* مُمْتَنَعٌ قَبُولُهُ
Inadvertence / Inadvertency *n.* غَفْلَةٌ . سَهْوٌ
Inalienable *a.* لاَ يُبَاعُ وَلاَ يُوهَبُ
Inane *a.* فَارِغٌ . غَيْرُ مُفِيدٍ . خَاوٍ
Inanimate *a.* عَدِيمُ ٱلْحَيَاةِ
Inapplicable *a.* غَيْرُ مطَابِقٍ
Inappreciable *a.* مَالاَ يُحْسَبُ . زَهِيدٌ
Inappropriate *a.* غَيْرُمنَاسِبٍ
Inapt *a.* غَيْرُ جَدِيرٍ . غَيْرُ مُنَاسِب
Inaptitude *a.* عَدَمُ جَدَارَةٍ أَوْ مُنَاسَبَةٍ
Inarticulate *a.* غَيْرُ مَلْفُوظٍ
Inasmuch *ad.* بِمَا انَّ
Inattention *n.* عَدَمُ مُبَالاَةٍ . غَفْلَةٌ
Inattentive *a.* غَيْرُ مُبَالٍ . مُتَغَافِلٌ
Inaudible *a.* غَيْرُ مَسْمُوعٍ
Inaugural *a.* إِفْتِتَاحِيٌّ . إِحتِفَالِيٌّ

Inaugurate *v. t.* إِفْتَتَحَ . رَسَمَ . قَلَّدَ
Inauguration *n.* إِفْتِتَاحٌ . تَقْلِيدٌ
Inauspicious *a.* مَشْؤُومٌ
Inborn / Inbred *a.* غرِيزِيٌّ . طَبِيعِيٌّ
Incalculable *a.* مَالاَ يُحْصَى
Incandescent *a.* وَهَّاجٌ
Incantation *a.* رُقْيَةٌ
Incapability *n.* عَجز . قُصُورٌ
Incapable *a.* عَاجِزٌ . غَيْرُ قَادِرٍ
Incapacitate *v. t.* اعْجَزَ
Incapacity *n.* عَجز
Incarcerate *v. t.* حبس
Incarceration *n.* حَبْس
Incarnate *a.* مُتَجَسِّدٌ
Incarnation *n.* تجَسُّد
Incase *v. t.* وَضَعَ فِي صُنْدُوق
Incautious *a.* غَافِلٌ . غَيْرُ مُتَحَذِّرٍ
Incendiary *a.* or *n.* حَارِقُ بُيُوتٍ عَمْدًا
Incense *n.* / Incense *v. t.* بَخُورٌ . بَخَّرَ . اغَاظَ

Incentive *n.*	باعِث . حَثّ
Inception *n.*	بداءة . شرُوعٌ
Incertitude *n.*	عدمُ يقينٍ . شك
Incessant *a.*	غيرُ منقطِعٍ
Incest *n.*	ألزِّنا بين اقرِباء
Inch *n.*	عقدة
Incidence *n.*	وُقوعٌ . حدُوث
Incident *n.*	وَاقِعٌ . حادِثة
Incidental *a.*	عَرَضي . إتفاقيٌّ
Incipient *a.*	إبتداِئيٌّ
Incision *n.*	شقٌّ . تشريط
Incisive *a.*	قاطِعٌ . صارِمٌ . حادٌّ
Incisor *n.*	قاطِعٌ . ثنِية . (سِن)
Incite *v. t.*	حمَل على. أغوى. هيَّج
Incivility *n.*	غلاظةٌ . عدمُ انسٍ
Inclement *a.*	صارمٌ . قارسٌ
Inclinable *a.*	مائِلٌ إلى
Inclination *n.*	ميلٌ

Incline *v. t.* or *i.*	أمالَ . مالَ ـِ
Inclose *v. t.*	أحاطَ . سيَّج . ضمَّنَ
Inclosure *n.*	حائِط . حظِيرة . ضِمنٌ
Include *v. t.*	حوى ـِ . شمِلَ ـَ
Including *pp.* / Inclusive *a.*	شامِلٌ . حاوٍ
Incognito *n.* or *ad.*	تنكُّرٌ
Incoherence *n.*	عدمُ ارتباطٍ . هذيٌ
Incoherent *a.*	هذاء . بلا مطابقةٍ
Incombustible *a.*	مالا يُحرق
Income *n.*	إيرادٌ . دخلٌ
Incommode *v. t.*	ثقل على . اتعبَ
Incommodious *a.*	متعِبٌ
Incommunicative *a.*	كتوم
Incomparable *a.*	فريد
Incompatible *a.*	مغايِرٌ . متنافٍ
Incompetence *n.*	قصورٌ . عجزٌ
Incompetent *a.*	قاصِرٌ . عاجزٌ
Incomplete *a.*	ناقِصٌ

Incompleteness *n.* نَقْصٌ

Incomprehensible *a.* مُمْتَنِعٌ إِدْرَاكُهُ

Inconceivable *a.* مَالَا يُتَصَوَّرُ

Inconclusive *a.* غَيْرُ مُقْنِعٍ

Incongruent / **Incongruous** *a.* غَيْرُ مُتَنَاسِبٍ

Incongruity *n.* عَدَمُ تَنَاسُبٍ

Inconsiderable *a.* زَهِيدٌ

Inconsiderate *a.* غَيْرُ مُبَالٍ

Inconsistency *n.* تَنَاقُضٌ

Inconsistent *a.* مُخَالِفٌ . مُنَاقِضٌ

Inconsolable *a.* لَا يَتَعَزَّى

Inconspiciuous *a.* غَيْرُ بَيِّنٍ أَوْ وَاضِحٍ

Inconstancy *n.* تَقَلُّبٌ

Inconstant *a.* مُتَقَلِّبٌ . مُتَغَيِّرٌ

Incontestable *a.* مَالَا يُنْكَرُ

Incontinence / **Incontinency** *n.* عَدَمُ ٱلْعِفَةِ وَٱلضَّبْطِ

Incontinent *a.* غَيْرُ عَفِيفٍ . فَاسِقٌ

Incontrovertible *a.* مَالَا يُرَدُّ

Inconvenience *n.* عَائِقٌ

Inconvenient *a.* غَيْرُ مُوَافِقٍ

Incorporate *v. t.* ضَمَّ إِلَى . أَدْخَلَ
أَقَامَ شَرْعًا

Incorporeal *a.* غَيْرُ مَادِّيٍّ . بِلَا جِسْمٍ

Incorrect *a.* غَيْرُ مُصِيبٍ . خَطَأٌ

Incorrectness *n.* خَطَأٌ . عَدَمُ ضَبْطٍ

Incorrigible *a.* مَا لَا يُصْلَحُ

Incorrupt *a.* غَيْرُ فَاسِدٍ . طَاهِرٌ

Incorruptible *a.* عَدِيمُ ٱلْفَسَادِ

Increase *v. t.* or *i.* زَادَ — ِ نَمَا — ُ

Increment / **Increase** *n.* زِيَادَةٌ . نُمُوٌّ

Incredible *a.* مُمْتَنِعٌ تَصْدِيقُهُ

Incredulity *n.* عَدَمُ تَصْدِيقٍ

Incredulous *a.* غَيْرُ مُصَدِّقٍ

Incriminate *v. t.* إِسْتَذْنَبَ . إِتَّهَمَ

Incrust *v. t.* لَبَّسَ بِقِشْرَةٍ

Incubation *n.* حَضَانَةٌ . رَخْمٌ

Incubus *a.* كَابُوسٌ ج كَوَابِيسُ

Inculcate *v. t.* اوصى . ألحّ . علّم

Incumbent *a.* or *n.* واجب على . متوظف

Incumbrance *n.* عائق . ثقل

Incur *v.t.* تعرّض له . جلب على نفسه

Incurable *a.* عديم الشفاء

Incursion *n.* غزوة . غارة

Indebted *n.* مديون

Indecency *n.* رذيلة . قباحة

Indecent *a.* رذيل . قبيح

Indecipherable *a.* مالا يقرأ أو يحل

Indecision *n.* تردد . عدم ثبات

Indecisive *a.* غير حازم

Indeclinable *a.* غير متصرف . مبني

Indecorous *a.* مخالف الادب

Indecorum *n.* مخالفة الادب

Indeed *ad.* حقاً . صحيح

Indefatigable *a.* جادّ لا يكل

Indefensible *a.* مالا يحامى عنه

Indefinite *a.* غير محدود . مبهم

Indefiniteness *n.* عدم تحديد

Indelible *a.* ثابت لا يمحى

Indelicacy *n.* قلة الادب

Indelicate *a.* قليل الادب

Indemnification, **Indemnity** *n.* تعويض غرامة

Indemnify *v. t.* عوّض عن

Indent *v. t.* فرض — . قيد لخدمة

Indentation *n.* فرض . أثر

Independence, **Independency** *n.* استقلال

Independent *a.* مستقل

Indescribable *a.* مالا يوصف

Indestructible *a.* مالا يفنى

Indeterminable *a.* مالا يحدد

Indeterminate *a.* غير محدد

Index *n.* دليل . فهرس . سبابة

Indian *n.* هندي

Indiaman *n.* سفينة تسافر الى الهند

India-rubber n. (لستك) . (مُغيطٌ)

Indicate v. t. اشارَ إِلَى . دَلَّ

Indication n. إِشارَةٌ . دَلَالَةٌ

Indicative a. / Indicator n. مُشيرٌ . دَالٌّ

Indict v. t. أَقامَ دَعْوَى عَلَيهِ

Indictment n. إِقامةُ الدَّعْوَى

Indifference n. عدمُ اكتِرَاثٍ

Indifferent a. غَيْرُ مُكْتَرِثٍ . سوَآء

Indigence n. فَقْرٌ . فَاقَةٌ

Indigenous a. وَطَنِي . بَلَدِيٌّ

Indigent a. فَقيرٌ . مُعْوِزٌ

Indigestible a. مَالَا يُهْضَمُ

Indigestion n. تُخَمَةٌ . سُوءُ هضمٍ

Indignant a. مُغْتَاظٌ

Indignation n. غَيْظٌ . غَضَبٌ .

Indignity n. إِهَانَةٌ . إِحتِقَارٌ

Indigo n. نِيلٌ (الصباغ المعروف)

Indirect a. غَيْرُ مُستَقِيمٍ . مُنْحَرِفٌ

Indirectness n. إِنحِرَافٌ

Indiscernible a. مَالَا يُرَى أَوْ يُمَيَّزُ

Indiscoverable a. مَالَا يُكْشَفُ

Indiscreet a. غَيْرُ حَازِمٍ او بَصِيرٍ

Indiscretion n. حَمَاقَةٌ . رُعُونَةٌ

Indiscriminate a. غَيْرُ مُمَيِّزٍ . بِلَا فَرْقٍ

Indiscrimination n. عَدَمُ تَمييزٍ

Indispensable a. ضَرُورِيٌّ

Indisposed a. مُنْحَرِفُ الصِّحَّةِ نَافِرٌ مِنْ

Indisposition n. إِنْحِرَافُ الصِّحَّةِ

Indisputable a. مَالَا يُنْكَرُ . مُسَلَّمٌ

Indissoluble / Indissolvable a. مَالَا يَنْحَلُّ

Indistinct n. غَيْرُ وَاضِحٍ . مُبْهَمٌ

Indistinctness n. عدمُ وُضُوحٍ

Indistinguishable a. مَالَا يُمَيَّزُ

Indite v. t. أَلَّفَ . كَتَبَ . أملَى ب

Individual n. شَخْصٌ . فَرْدٌ

Individualism / Individuality n. ذَاتِيَّةٌ . فَرْدِيَّةٌ

Individualize *v. t.* مَيّزَ على حدَة

Individually *ad.* إفراداً . شخصياً

Indivisible *n.* مَالاَ ينقَسِم

Indocile *a.* غيرُ طَائِعٍ . عَاص

Indolence *n.* كسَلٌ . توَانٍ

Indolent *a.* كَسْلاَنُ

Indomitable *a.* مالاَ يقْهَرُ اويُذَلَّل

Indorse *v. t.* صَادَق علي

Indorsement *n.* مُصَادقَةٌ على

Indubitable *a.* لاَ رَيب فيهِ

Induce *v. t.* اغرَى . امَال . رَغب

Inducement *n.* دَاعٍ . مُوجِبٌ

Induction *n.* إدْخَال . إستِدلاَل

Inductive *a.* إستْدلاَلِيٌّ

Indue *v. t.* منَح — . البَس . قلدَ

Indulge *v. t.* or *i.* ارْضى . اولِعَب

Indulgence *n.* تَلذُّذٌ . عفو

Indulgent *a.* مدَلِّلٌ . مُسَامِحٌ

Industrial *a.* صِنَاعِيٌّ

Industrious *a.* جَادٌّ . مثَابِرٌ

Industry *n.* جِدٌّ . مثَابرَةٌ . صِنَاعةٌ

Inebriate *v. t.* or *n.* أَسْكَرَ . سِكّيرٌ

Inebriation, Inebriety *n.* سُكْرٌ

Inedited *a.* غيرُ مطبُوعٍ

Indeffable *a.* مالاَ يعبَرُ عَنهُ

Ineffaceable *a.* مالاَ يُمحَى

Ineffective, Ineffectual, Inefficacious *a.* غيرُ فعالٍ . عبَثٌ

Inefficacy, Inefficiency *n.* عدَمُ فاعِليَةٍ

Inefficient *a.* غيرُ فعَّالٍ . عَاجِز

Inelegant *a.* غيرُ ظريفٍ

Inelegant *a.* لاَ يجُوزُ إنتِخَابهُ

Inequality *n.* عدَمُ مُسَاوَاةٍ

Inert *a.* غيرُ مُتحَرِّكٍ . بَلِيدٌ

Inestimable *a.* فَائِقُ ٱلتثمِين

Inevitable *a.* مَالاَ مفَرَّ مِنه

Inexact *a.* غيرُ مضبُوطٍ
Inexactness *n.* عدمُ ضبطٍ . غلطٌ
Inexcusable *a.* بلا عذرٍ
Inexhaustible *a.* مالا يفرغ
Inexorable *a.* غيرُ متغيرٍ. ثابتُ العزمِ
Inexpedience / Inexpediency عدمُ مناسبةٍ
Inexpedient *a.* غيرُ مناسبٍ
Inexpensive *a.* رخيصٌ
Inexperience *n.* عدمُ الإختبارِ
Inexpiable *a.* مالا يُعفى أو يُكفرُ عنهُ
Inexplicable *a.* مالا تفسيرَ لهُ
Inexpressible *a.* مالا يُعبرُ عنهُ
Inexpressive *a.* غيرُ معبرٍ عن
Inextinguishable *a.* مالا ينطفئُ
Inextricable *a.* مالا يُحلُّ . مُعقدٌ
Infallibility *n.* عِصمةٌ
Infallible *a.* معصُومٌ
Infamous *n.* كريهُ الصيتِ

Infamy *n.* فضيحةٌ .عارٌ. قبيحةٌ
Infancy *n.* طفُوليةٌ
Infant *n.* طفلٌ . رضيعٌ
Infanticide *n.* قتلُ الأطفالِ
Infantile / Infantine *a.* طِفليٌ
Infantry *n.* جنودٌ مشاةٌ
Infatuate *v. t.* فتنَ . شغفَ حُباً
Infatuation *n.* إفتتانٌ. كلفٌ. وُلوعٌ
Infect *v. t.* اعدى. افسدَ
Infection *n.* عدوى. إفسادٌ
Infectious *a.* معدٍ. مفسدٌ
Infelicitous *a.* نحسٌ . في غيرِ محلهِ
Infelicity *n.* نحسٌ . بليةٌ
Infer *v. t.* إستنتجَ. إستدلَ
Inferable / Inferential *a.* ناتجٌ عن. مُستدلٌ
Inference *n.* نتيجة . إستدلالٌ
Inferior *a.* دني٤. دُونٌ
Inferiority *n.* دُونيةٌ . اسفليةٌ

Infernal *a.* جهنمي . جحيمي

Infertility *n.* عدم خصب

Infest *v. t.* كدّر . أكثر في

Infidel *n.* كافر ج كفّار وكفرة

Infidelity *n.* كفر . خيانة

Infinite *a.* غير محدود

Infinitely *ad.* بلا نهاية . جدًّا

Infiniteness } *n.* عدم حدّ أو نهاية
Infinity

Infinitesimal *a.* دقيق جدًّا

Infinitive *a.* صيغة المصدر

Infirm *a.* عاجز . ضعيف

Infirmary *n.* مستشفى

Infirmity *n.* ضعف . عجز

Inflame *v. t.* اضرم . هيّج

Inflammable *a.* قابل الالتهاب

Inflammation *n.* التهاب

Inflammatory *a.* ملهب . مهيّج

Inflate *v. t.* نفخ — . ملأهواء

Inflect *v. t.* حنى — . صرّف

Inflection } *n.* حناية . تصريف
Inflexion

Inflexibility *n.* صلابة . إصرار

Inflexible *a.* لا ينحني . مصرّ

Inflict *v. t.* أبلى به . حمّل به

Infliction *n.* بلية . عقاب

Influence *n.* تأثير . نفوذ . قوّة

Influence *v. t.* أثّر في . أمال

Influential *a.* ذو سطوة او نفوذ

Influenza *n.* زكام وافدي

Influx *n.* ورود بوفرة

Infold *v. t.* لفّ — . عانق

Inform *v. t.* أخبر . أعلم

Informal *a.* غير رسمي

Informality *n.* مخالفة الرسوم

Information *n.* خبر . إنباء

Infraction } *n.* نكث . تعدّ
Infringement

Infrequent *a.* نادر

Infringe v. t.	خَالَفَ . تعَدَّى علَى
Infuriate v. t.	أغَاظَ .هيَّجَ غَضَباً
Infuse v. t.	ادْخَلَ . نَقَعَ
Infusion n.	إِدْخَال . تَقِيعٌ
Ingathering n.	حصَاد . جَمْعٌ
Ingenious a.	حَاذِقٌ . لَبِيبٌ
Ingenuity n.	حذَاقَةٌ . مهَارَةٌ
Ingenuous a.	صَفِيٌّ . مُخْلِصٌ . نَبِيل
Inglorious a.	عَدِيمُ آلمجد . مُخْزٍ
Ingot n.	سَبِيكَةٌ ج سبائك
Ingratiate v. t.	إِستَعطفَ
Ingratitude n.	كُنُودٌ. عَدَمُ الشُّكرِ.
Ingredient a.	عُنْصُرٌ مَزِيج
Ingress n.	دُخُول . مَدْخَل
Ingulf v. t.	إِبْتَلَعَ
Inhabit v. t. or i.	سَكَنَ ـُ . قطنَ ـُ
Inhabitable a.	قَابِلُ السَّكن
Inhabitant n.	سَاكِن . قَاطِن
Inhale v. t.	إِستَنشَقَ
Inhere v. i.	إِخْتَصَّ بِهِ. طُبِعَ عَلَيْهِ
Inherent a.	مُلاَزِمٌ . حَال فِي
Inherit v. t.	وَارِثَ ـُ
Inheritance n.	مِيرَاثٌ ج مَوَارِيث
Inheritor n.	وَارِثٌ ج ورَثَةٌ
Inhibit v. t.	نَهَى ـَ .مَنَعَ ـَ عَارَضَ
Inhospitable a.	غَيْرُ مِضْيَافٍ
Inhospitality n.	عَدَمُ إِكْرَامِ الضَّيفِ
Inhuman a.	عَدِيمُ الإِنْسَانِيَّةِ
Inhumanity n.	عَدَمُ الإِنْسَانِيَّة
Inimical a.	عُدْوَانِيٌّ . مُقَاوِمٌ
Inimitable a.	لاَ يُحَاكَى .لاَ مَثِيلَ لَهُ
Iniquitous a.	اثِيمٌ . شِرِّيرٌ جِدًا
Iniquity n.	إِثْمٌ . شَرٌّ
Initial a. or n.	إِبتِدَائِيٌّ . اوَّلُ آسْمٍ
Initiate v. t.	أَدخَلَ فِي. بَدَأَ . عَلَّمَ
Initiative, Initiatory a.	إِبتِدَائِي . إِنْشَائِيٌّ

Inject *v. t.*	حَقَنَ ـِ . أَدخَلَ فِي
Injection *n.*	حُقْنَةٌ
Injudicious *a.*	غيرُ مُوَافِقٍ او بَصِيرٍ
Injunction *n.*	أَمْرٌ . حُكْمٌ
Injure *v. t.*	أَضَرَّ . آذَى
Injurious *a.*	مُضِرٌّ . مُؤْذٍ
Injury *n.*	ضَرَرٌ . أَذِيَّةٌ
Injustice *n.*	ظُلْمٌ . جَوْرٌ . بَغْيٌ
Ink *n.*	حِبْرٌ . مِدَادٌ
Inkhorn / **Inkstand** } *n.*	دَوَاةٌ . مِحْبَرَةٌ
Inkling *n.*	تَلْمِيحٌ . إِشَارَةٌ
Inland *n.*	دَاخِلُ ٱلْبَرِّ
Inlay *v. t.* (*pp.* **inlaid**)	رَصَّعَ
Inlet *n.*	مَدْخَلٌ . خَلِيجٌ . جُونٌ
Inmate *n.*	سَاكِنٌ مَعَ غَيْرِهِ
Inmost / **Innermost** } *a.*	الاكثَرُ دَاخِلِيَّةً
Inn *n.*	فُنْدُقٌ . خَانٌ
Innate *a.*	غَرِيزِيٌّ . بَدِيهِيٌّ
Inner *a.*	دَاخِلِيٌّ
Inkeeper *n.*	صَاحِبُ ٱلْفُنْدُقِ . خَانَاتِيٌّ
Innocence *n.*	بَرَاءَةٌ . طَهَارَةٌ
Innocent *a.*	بَرِيءٌ . سَلِيمُ ٱلْقَلْبِ
Innocuous *a.*	غيرُ مُضِرٍّ . سَلِيمٌ
Innovation *n.*	بِدْعَةٌ . إِحْدَاثٌ
Innovator *n.*	مُبْدِعٌ . مُحْدِثٌ
Innoxious *a.*	غيرُ مُضِرٍّ . سَلِيمٌ
Innuendo *n.*	تَلْمِيحٌ خَفِيٌّ . دَسِيسَةٌ
Innumerable *a.*	فَائِقُ ٱلإِحْصَاءِ
Innutricious / **Innutritive** } *a.*	غيرُ مُغَذٍّ
Inoculate *v. t.*	طَعَّمَ . لَقَّحَ
Inoculation *n.*	تَطْعِيمٌ . تَلْقِيحٌ
Inodorous *a.*	عَدِيمُ ٱلرَّائِحَةِ
Inoffensive *a.*	غيرُ مُسِيءٍ . بَسِيطٌ
Inoperative *a.*	غيرُ عَامِلٍ
Inopportune *a.*	فِي غَيْرِ أَوَانِهِ

Inordinate *a.*	مُفْرِطٌ . زَائِدٌ
Inorganic *a.*	غيرُ آلِيٍّ . غيرُ عضويٍّ
Inquest *n.*	فَحْصٌ . تَفْتِيشٌ
Inquire *v. t.*	إِسْتَخْبَرَ . سَأَلَ
Inquirer *n.*	مُسْتَخْبِرٌ . طَالِبٌ
Inquiry *n.*	سُؤَالٌ . فَحْصٌ . بَحْثٌ
Inquisition *n.*	تَفْتِيشٌ . دِيوَانُهُ
Inquisitive *a.*	كَثِيرُ ٱلسُّؤَالِ
Inquisitor *n.*	مُفَتِّشٌ . فَاحِصٌ
Inroad *n.*	غَزْوَةٌ . هَجْمَةٌ
Insalubrious *a.*	وَخِيمٌ . وَبِيلٌ
Insalubrity *n.*	وَبَالٌ . وَخَامَةٌ
Insane *a.*	مَجْنُونٌ . مُخْتَلُّ ٱلعَقْلِ
Insanity *n.*	جُنُونٌ . إِخْتِلَالُ ٱلعَقْلِ
Insatiable / **Insatiate** } *a.*	لَا يَشْبَعُ
Inscribe *v. t.*	كَتَبَ . حَفَرَ
Inscription *n.*	كِتَابَةٌ
Inscrutable *a.*	مَا لَا يُكْشَفُ لَا يُفْهَمُ
Insect *n.*	دُوَيبَّةٌ . حَشَرَةٌ
Insectivorous *a.*	آكِلُ ٱلْحَشَرَاتِ
Insecure *a.*	غَيْرُ مُطْمَئِنٍّ . خَطِرٌ
Insecurity *n.*	عَدَمُ ٱلأَمْنِ
Insensate *a.*	عَدِيمُ ٱلحِسِّ . بَلِيدٌ
Insensibility *n.*	عَدَمُ ٱلْحِسِّ
Insensible *a.*	عَدِيمُ ٱلْحِسِّ
Inseparable *a.*	مَا لَا يُفْصَلُ أَوْ يَنْفَكُ
Insert *v. t.*	أَدْخَلَ . أَدْرَجَ
Insertion *n.*	إِدْخَالٌ . إِدْرَاجٌ
Inside *ad.* or *a.* or *n.*	دَاخِلاً . دَاخِلٌ
Insidious *a.*	غَدَّارٌ . مُخَاتِلٌ
Insight *n.*	بَصِيرَةٌ . فِطْنَةٌ
Insignia *n.*	عَلَامَاتٌ
Insignificant *a.*	زَهِيدٌ . طَفِيفٌ
Insincere *a.*	غَيْرُ مُخْلِصٍ
Insincerity *n.*	عَدَمُ إِخْلَاصٍ
Insinuate *v. t.*	لَمَّحَ . دَسَّ

Insinuation *n.* تلميح . دَسِيسة
Insipid *a.* تفه . بارد . ناشف
Insipidity *n.* تفاهة . بلادة
Insist *v. i.* أصرّ . ألحّ
Insistence *n.* إِصرار . إلحاح
Insolence *n.* وقاحة . عتوّ
Insolent *n.* وقح . عاتٍ
Insolubility *n.* عدم الذوبان
Insoluble *a.* ما لا يذوب . لا يحل
Insolvable *a.* ما لا يحل . لا يفسّر
Insolvency *n.* إفلاس
Insolvent *a.* مفلس
Insomuch *ad.* حتى أن
Inspect *v. t.* فحص ـ فتّش
Inspection *n.* فحص . تفتيش
Inspector *n.* ناظر . مفتّش
Inspiration *n.* شهيق . وحي
Inspire *v. t.* شهق ـ ألهم
Inspiring *a.* مشجع . مفرّح . منشّط
Instability *n.* عدم ثباتٍ . تقلّب
Instable *a.* غير ثابتٍ . متغيّر
Install *v. t.* قلّد منصباً . أقام
Installment *n.* قسط . تقليد
Instance *n.* مثال . حادثة
Instant *a.* or *n.* حالي . مهم . لحظة
Instantaneous *a.* حالي . فجائي
Instantly *ad.* حالاً . على الفور
Instead *ad.* عوضاً عن
Instep *n.* ظهر القدم
Instigate *v. t.* حمل على . أغرى
Instigation *n.* إغراء . تهييج
Instigator *n.* مغرٍ . مهيج
Instill *v. t.* ادخل . تدريجاً . لقّن
Instinct *n.* سليقة . فطرة . غريزه
Instinctive *a.* غريزي
Institute *v. t.* اقام . انشا

Institution *n.* إقامة . منصب . دار للتعليم وما أشبه

Instruct *v. t.* علم . أوصى

Instruction *n.* تعليم . أمر

Instructive *a.* مفيد . مثقف

Instructor *n.* معلم . مدرس

Instrument *n.* آلة . واسطة

Instrumental *a.* آلي . مفض إلى

Instrumentality *n.* واسطة

Insubordination *n.* عصيان

Insufferable *a.* مالا يطاق

Insufficiency *n.* نقص

Insufficient *a.* غير كاف . ناقص

Insular *a.* مختص بجزيرة . محاط بماء

Insulate *v. t.* أفرد . قطع عن

Insulator *n.* قاطع مجرى الكهربائية

Insult *n.* or *v. t.* إهانة . أهان

Insulting *a.* مهين . شاتم

Insuperable *a.* مالا يغلب

Insupportable *a.* مالا يحتمل

Insurance *n.* تأمين . ضمان

Insure *v. t.* أمن . ضمن

Insurgent *a.* ثائر . مارد . عاص

Insurmountable *a.* مالا يقوى عليه

Insurrection *n.* ثورة . فتنة

Insusceptible *a.* غير متأثر

Intangible *a.* مالا يحس به

Intact *a.* كامل . سالم . غير ممسوس

Integer *n.* عدد صحيح او تام

Integral *n.* or *a.* صحيح . كامل

Integrate *v. t.* تمم . شمل . جدد

Integrity *n.* إستقامة . كمال

Intellect *n.* عقل . ذهن

Intellectual *a.* عقلي . ذكي

Intelligence *n.* فهم . ذكاء

Intelligent *a.* ذكي . عاقل

Intelligible *a.*	مَفْهُومٌ . معقُول
Intemperance *n.*	افْرَاطٌ . سُكْر
Intemperate *a.*	مُفْرِط . سِكّيرٌ
Intend *v. t.* or *i.*	قصَدَ ـ . نوَى ـ
Intense *a.*	شَدِيدٌ جدًّا
Intensely *ad.*	جِدًّا . بِشِدةٍ
Intensify *v. t.*	شَدَّدَ . قوَّى
Intensive *a.*	مشَدِّدٌ . مقوٌّ
Intent *n.* or *a.*	قَصْدٌ . مُنْصَبٌّ على
Intention *n.*	قَصْدٌ . نِيَّةٌ
Intentional *a.*	مَقْصود . عَمْدِيٌّ
Intentionally *ad.*	عَمْدًا
Inter *v. t.*	دَفَنَ ـ . قَبَرَ ـ
Intercede *v. i.*	شَفَعَ . تَوَسَّطَ
Intercept *v. t.*	عَارَضَ . وَقَّفَ
Interception *n.*	مُعَارَضَةٌ . تَوْقِيفٌ
Intercession *n.*	شَفَاعَةٌ
Intercessor *n.*	شَفِيعٌ . وَسِيطٌ
Interchange *v.t.* or *n.*	بَادَلَ . تبَادُلٌ
Intercourse *n.*	مُبَاشَرَةٌ . مُخَالَطَةٌ
Interdict *v.t.* or *n.*	مَنَعَ . نهيٌ
Interest *n.*	فَائِدَةٌ . رَغْبَةٌ . نَفْعٌ
Interest *v. t.*	إِستَعْمَالَ . رَغبَ
Interested *a.*	مَائِلٌ . مُهْتَمٌّ
Interesting *a.*	مُلِذٌّ . مُفِيدٌ
Interfere *v. i.*	تَدَاخَلَ في . عَارَضَ
Interference *n.*	مُدَاخَلَةٌ . مُعَارَضَةٌ
Interim *n.*	اثْنَاء . خِلَالَ
Interior *a.* or *n.*	دَاخِلِيٌّ . أَلدَّاخِلُ
Interjection *n.*	حَرْفُ نِدَاء
Interlace *v. t.*	شَبَكَ ـ
Interleave *v. t.*	أَدْخَلَ أَوْرَاقًا بَيْنَ غَيْرِهَا
Interline *v. t.*	خَطَّ بَيْنَ خطُوطٍ
Interloper *n.*	فُضُولِيٌّ . طُفَيْلِيٌّ
Intermarriage *n.*	تزَاوُجٌ
Intermeddle *v. i.*	تَدَاخَلَ

Intermediate *a.* مُتَوَسِّط

Intermediation *n.* وَسَاطَةٌ . تَوَسُّط

Interment *n.* دَفْنٌ . جِنَازَةٌ

Interminable *a.* لاَنِهَايَةَ لَهُ

Intermingle *v.t.* or *i.* خَالَطَ . تخَالَط

Intermission *n.* فَتْرَةٌ . تَوَقُّفٌ

Intermit *v. t.* or *i.* وَقَّفَ . تَوَقَّفَ

Intermittent *a.* مُتَقَطِّعٌ . مُتَنَاوِبٌ

Intermix *v. t.* or *i.* مازَجَ . تَخَالَطَ

Internal *a.* دَاخِلِيٌّ . بَاطِنِيٌّ

International *a.* مُشْتَرِكٌ بَيْنَ اَلامَمِ

Internecine *a.* مُتَبَادِلُ الْقَتْلِ . مُهْلِكٌ

Interpalate *v. t.* أَفْسَدَ كِتَاباً اوْ ادْخَلَ فِيهِ

Interpose *v. i.* ادخَلَ أَوْ دَخَلَ بَيْنَ

Interposition *n.* مُدَاخَلَةٌ . تَوَسُّطٌ

Interpret *v. t.* تَرْجَمَ . فَسَّرَ

Interpretation *n.* تَرْجَمَةٌ . تَفْسِيرٌ

Interpreter *n.* مُتَرْجِمٌ . مُفَسِّرٌ

Interregnum *n.* فَتْرَةٌ فِي اَلسَّلْطَنَةِ

Interrogate *v.t.* سَأَلَ ـَ . (إِسْتَنْطَقَ)

Interrogation *n.* سُؤَالٌ . (إِسْتِنْطَاقٌ)

Interrogative *a.* إِسْتِفْهَامِي

Interrupt *v. t.* قَطَعَ ـَ . تَعَرَّضَ لِ

Interruption *n.* قَطْعٌ . إِنْقِطَاعٌ . مَانِعٌ

Intersect *v. t.* قَاطَعَ . تَقَاطَعَ

Intersection *n.* تَقَاطُعٌ

Intersperse *v. t.* بذرَ بَيْنَ

Interstice *n.* فسحَةٌ ضَيِّقَةٌ

Intertwine / **Intertwist** *v.t.* شَبَكَ ـِ . حَبَكَ ـُ

Interval *n.* خِلاَلُ . فَتْرَةٌ

Intervene *v. i.* تَخَلَّلَ . تَوَسَّطَ

Intervention *n.* مُدَاخَلَةٌ . تَوَسُّطٌ

Interview *n.* مُقَابَلَةٌ . مُحَادَثَةٌ

Interweave *v. t.* حَاكَ . نَسَجَ مَعاً

Intestate *a.* بِدُونِ وَصِيَّةٍ

Intestine *a.* دَاخِلِي . وَطَنِيٌّ

Intestines *n. pl.* أمعاء

Inthrall *v. t.* إستعبد

Intimacy *n.* مودة . خاصة

Intimate *v. t.* اشار . لمح

Intimate *a.* or *n.* خاص . خليل

Intimation *n.* تلميح . إعلان

Intimidate *v. t.* أخاف . هدد

Intimidation *n.* تهديد

Into *prep.* في . إلى داخل

Intolerable *a.* مالا يطاق

Intolerance *n.* تعصب

Intolerant *a.* متعصب

Intone *v. t.* نغم . لحن في القراءة

Intoxicate *v. t.* أسكر

Intoxication *n.* سكر

Intractable *a.* مالا يذلل . عنيد

Intransitive *a.* لازم (فعل)

Intrench *v. t.* خندق . حصن

Intrenchment *n.* تحصين . متراس

Intrepid *a.* جسور . شجاع

Intrepidity *n.* جسارة . جراءة

Intricacy *n.* تعقيد

Intricate *a.* معقد . مشكل

Intrigue *n.* or *v. i.* دسيسة . إحتال

Intriguer *n.* محتال . صاحب دسائس

Intrinsic *a.* حقيقي . جوهري

Introduce *v. t.* دخل . عرف . أنشأ

Introduction *n.* إدخال مقدمة

Introductory *a.* إفتتاحي . ديباجي

Introspection *n.* نظر إلى داخل

Intrude *v. i.* تطفل . تعدى

Intrusion *n.* تطفل

Intrusive *a.* متطفل

Intrust *v. t.* امن . أودع

Intuition *n.* بداهة . فطرة

Intuitive *a.* بديهي

Inundate *v. t.* غَمَرَ ـُ . اغرق

Inundation *n.* طُفُوحٌ . فَيَضَانٌ

Inure *v. t.* عَوَّدَ

Inutility *n.* عَدَم فَائِدَةٍ

Invade *v. t.* هَجَمَ عَلَى . إِفْتَتَحَ

Invader *n.* مُهَاجِمٌ . فَاتِحٌ . غَازٍ

Invalid *a.* or *n.* مَرِيضٌ . بَاطِلٌ

Invalidate *v. t.* أَبْطَلَ . أَوْهَنَ

Invalidity *n.* بُطْلَانٌ . فَسَادٌ

Invaluable *a.* فَائِقُ ٱلثَّمَنِ . سَامٍ

Invariable *a.* غَيْرُ مُتَغَيِّرٍ . ثَابِتٌ

Invasion *n.* مُهَاجَمَةٌ . فُتُوحٌ . غَزْوٌ

Invective *n.* شَتِيمَةٌ . سَبٌّ

Inveigh *v. t.* طَعَنَ ـَ . سَعَى بِهِ

Inveigle *v. t.* اغوى . أَضَلَّ . وَرَّطَ

Invent *v. t.* إِخْتَرَعَ . إِخْتَلَقَ

Invention *n.* إِخْتِرَاعٌ . إِخْتِلَاقٌ

Inventive *a.* }
Inventor *n.* } مُخْتَرِعٌ . مُبْدِعٌ

Inventory *n.* قَائِمَةٌ . تَقْيِيدٌ

Inversion *n.* عَكْسٌ . قَلْبٌ

Invert *v. t.* عَكَسَ ـِ . قَلَبَ ـِ

Invertebrate *a.* عَدِيمُ ٱلْفَقَرَاتِ

Inverse *a.* مُنْعَكِسٌ . مَقْلُوبٌ

Inverted *a.* مَقْلُوبٌ . مَعْكُوسٌ

Invest *v. t.* قَلَّدَ . وَقَفَ لِلْفَائِدَةِ

Investigate *v. t.* فَحَصَ . إِسْتَقْصَى

Investigation *n.* فَحْصٌ . إِسْتِقْصَاءٌ

Investiture *n.* تَقْلِيدٌ . إِقَامَةٌ

Investment *n.* إِلْبَاسٌ . وَضْعُ مَالٍ

Inveterate *a.* مُتَأَصِّلٌ . مُتَعَوِّدٌ

Invidious *a.* مُهَيِّجُ ٱلْحَسَدِ أَوِ ٱلْبُغْضِ

Invigorate *v. t.* قَوَّى . شَدَّدَ . نَشَّطَ

Invincible *a.* مَنِيعٌ . لَا يُغْلَبُ

Inviolable *a.* مُحَرَّمٌ . مَا لَا يُنْقَضُ

Inviolate *a.* مَصُونٌ . مَحْفُوظٌ

Invisible *a.* غَيْرُ مَنْظُورٍ

Invitation *n.* دَعْوَةٌ . إِسْتِدْعَآءٌ

Invite *v. t.* دَعَا . إِسْتَدْعَى

Invocation *n.* دُعَآءٌ . صَلَاةٌ

Invoice *n.* قَائِمَةُ بَضَائِعَ

Invoke *v. t.* دَعَا . إِسْتَغَاثَ

Involuntary *a.* غَيْرُ إِخْتِيَارِيٍّ

Involution *n.* تَرْقِيَةُ ٱلْعَدَدِ (في الحساب)

Involve *v. t.* لَفَّ . تَضَمَّنَ . عَرْقَلَ

Invulnerable *a.* مَصُونٌ . مَا لَا يُجْرَحُ

Inward *a.* دَاخِلِيٌّ . بَاطِنِيٌّ

Inwrought *a.* مُرَصَّعٌ . مُوَشًّى

Iodine *n.* يُودٌ (دوا)

Irascible *a.* نَزِقٌ . سَرِيعُ ٱلْغَضَبِ

Ire *n.* غَضَبٌ . غَيْظٌ

Iridiscent *a.* مُلَوَّنٌ كَقَوْسِ قُزَحَ

Iris *n.* قَوْسُ قُزَحَ . قُزَحِيَةُ ٱلْعَيْنِ

Irksome *a.* مُمِلٌ . مُضْجِرٌ . مُتْعِبٌ

Iron *n.* or *a.* حَدِيد . حَدِيدِي

Ironical *a.* تَهَكُّمِيٌّ . إِسْتِهْزَائِيٌّ

Irony *n.* تَهَكُّمٌ . إِسْتِهْزَآءٌ

Irradiate *v. t.* أَضَاءَ . أَشَعَّ . انَارَ

Irrational *a.* غَيْرُ مَعْقُولٍ

Irreclaimable *a.* مَالَا يُسْتَرَدُّ

Irreconcilable *a.* مَالَا يُصَالَحُ

Irrecoverable *a.* مَالَا يُرَدُّ . مَالَا يُعَادُ

Irredeemable *a.* مَالَا يُفْدَى اوْ يُفَكُّ

Irrefutable *a.* مَالَا يُدْحَضُ

Irregular *a.* غَيْرُ قِيَاسِيٍّ . شَاذٌّ

Irregularity *n.* عَدَمُ ٱنْتِظَامٍ . شُذُوذٌ

Irrelevant *a.* غَيْرُ مُطَابِقٍ

Irreligion *n.* كُفْرٌ . زَنْدَقَةٌ

Irreligious *a.* قَلِيلُ ٱلدِّينِ

Irremediable *a.* مَالَا يُشْفَى اوْ يُصْلَحُ

Irremovable *a.* مَالَا يُنْقَلُ اوْ يُنْزَعُ

Irreparable *a.* مَالَا يُعَوَّضُ

Irrepressible *a.* مَالَا يُرْدَعُ اوْ يُضْبَطُ

Irreproachable *a.* مَالاَ يُلاَمُ

Irresistible *a.* مَالاَ يُقَاوَمُ اوْ يُدْفَعُ

Irresolute *a.* مُتَرَدِّدٌ . مُتَقَلْقِل

Irresoluteness / **Irresolution** *n.* تَرَدُّدٌ . تَقَلُّبٌ

Irrespective *a.* بِلاَ ٱلْتِفَاتٍ إِلَى

Irresponsible *a.* غيرُ مسؤُولٍ

Irretrievable *a.* مَالاَ يُعَوَّضُ

Irreverence *n.* عَدَمُ ٱحْتِرَامٍ

Irrevocable *a.* مَالاَ يُلْغَى اوْ يُرَد

Irrigate *v. t.* سَقَى ـِ أَرْوَى

Irrigation *n.* سَقْيٌ . رَيٌّ

Irritabiliy *n.* سُرْعَةُ ٱلتَّهَيُّجِ

Irritable *a.* نَكِدٌ . نَزِق

Irritant *a.* or *n.* مُهَيِّجٌ

Irritate *v. t.* هَيَّجَ . أَثَارَ . أَغَاظَ

Irritation *n.* تَهْيِيجٌ . إِلْتِهَابٌ

Irruption *n.* هُجُومٌ . غَارَةٌ . إِنْفِجَارٌ

Is (see *to be*) كَائِنٌ . يَكُونُ

Islam / **Islamism** *n.* اَلْإِسْلاَمُ

Island / **Isle** *n.* جَزِيرَةٌ ج جَزَائِر

Islet *n.* جَزِيرَةٌ صَغِيرَةٌ

Isolate *v. t.* أَفْرَدَ

Isosceles *n.* مُتَسَاوِي ٱلضِّلْعَيْنِ

Israelite *n.* إِسْرَائِيلِيٌّ

Issue *v. t.* or *i.* أَصْدَرَ . صَدَرَ ـُ

Issue *n.* نَتِيجَةٌ . نَسْلٌ . صُدُورٌ

Isthmus *n.* بَرْزَخٌ

It *pro.* هُوَ . هِيَ

Italian *n.* or *a.* إِيطَالِيٌّ

Italics *n. pl.* حُرُوفُ ٱلطَّبْعِ ٱلْمَائِلَةُ

Itch *n.* or *v. t.* جَرَبٌ . حِكَّةٌ . حَكَّ

Item *n.* أَيْضًا . نُبْذَةٌ

Iterate *v. t.* كَرَّرَ

Itinerant *a.* دَائِرٌ . جَائِلٌ

Itinerate *v. i.* دَارَ . جَالَ ـُ

Itinerary *n.* سياحة أو كتابها

Itself *pro.* ذاته. نفسه

Ivory *n.* or *a.* عاج. عاجي

Ivy *n.* لبلاب أو عاشق الشجر (نبات)

J

Jabber *v. i.* بقَّ ـُ. تمتم

Jack *n.* آلة لقلع الأحذية او لرفع الأثقال

Jackal *n.* إبن آوى ج بنات آوى

Jackass *n.* حمار ج حمير

Jackdaw *n.* نوع من الزاغ

Jacket *n.* جبة قصيرة

Jack-knife *n.* سكين الجيب

Jade *n.* كديش. جارية

Jaded *a.* معيٍ. تعب

Jagged *a.* محزوز. مشقوق

Jail *n.* حبس. سجن

Jailer *n.* سجان

Jam *n.* or *v. t.* مربى. زحمة. زحم ـَ

Janitor *n.* حاجب. بواب

Janizary *n.* إنكشاري. يسقجي

January *n.* كانون الثاني. يناير

Jar *v. t.* or *i.* هزَّ ـُ. إهتز

Jar *n.* جرة. حزة. خصام

Jargon *n.* رطانة

Jasmine / Jessamine *n.* ياسمين. فل

Jasper *n.* يشب

Jaundice *n.* يرقان

Jaunty *n.* مرح. خفيف

Javelin *n.*	مِزْرَاقٌ ج مَزَارِيقُ
Jaw *n.*	فَكٌّ ج فُكُوكٌ
Jealous *a.*	غَيُورٌ . مِغْيَارٌ
Jealousy *n.*	غَيْرَةٌ
Jeer *v. i.* or *n.*	هَزَأَ ـَ . هَزْءٌ
Jelly *n.*	هُلَامٌ
Jeopard / **Jeopardize** } *v. t.*	أَلْقَى فِي خَطَرٍ
Jeopardy *n.*	خَطَرٌ
Jerboa *n.*	يَرْبُوعٌ ج يَرَابِيعُ (حَيَوَان)
Jerk *v. t.*	رَمَى . شَدَّ بَغْتَةً
Jest *v. i.* or *n.*	مَزَحَ ـَ مَزْحٌ
Jester *n.*	مَازِحٌ . مَاجِنٌ
Jesting *n.*	مَزْحٌ
Jesuit *n.* / **Jesuitical** *a.* }	يَسُوعِيٌّ
Jesuitism *n.*	مَبَادِئُ يَسُوعِيَّةٌ
Jet *n.*	غَايَةُ ٱلسَّوَادِ . فَوَّارَةٌ
Jetty *n.*	لِسَانٌ صِنَاعِيٌّ فِي ٱلْبَحْرِ
Jew *n.* / **Jewish** *a.* }	يَهُودِيٌّ
Jewel *n.*	جَوْهَرَةٌ . دُرَّةٌ
Jeweller *n.*	صَائِغٌ . جَوْهَرِيٌّ
Jewelry *n.*	مَصَاغٌ . حُلِيٌّ
Jib *n.*	شِرَاعُ مُقَدَّمِ ٱلسَّفِينَةِ
Jibe *v. i.* or *n.*	هَزَأَ ـَ . هَزْءٌ
Jilt *v. t.*	رَفَضَتْ عَاشِقَهَا
Jingle *v. t.*	طَنَّ ـِ . رَنَّ ـِ
Job *n.* (أَيُّوبُ ٱلنَّبِيُّ)	شَغْلَةٌ . مُقَاوَلَةٌ .
Jockey *n.*	تَاجِرٌ بِٱلْخَيْلِ . مُكَارٍ
Jocose / **Jocular** } *a.*	مَازِحٌ . دَاعِبٌ
Jog / **Joggle** } *v. t.*	هَزَّ ـِ . وَكَزَ يَكِزُ
Jog on *v. t.* or *i.*	مَشَى عَلَى مَهْلٍ
Join *v. t.* or *i.*	وَصَلَ ـِ . إِتَّصَلَ
Joiner *n.*	نَجَّارٌ
Joint *n.* or *a.*	مَفْصِلٌ . عُقْدَةٌ . مُشْتَرِكٌ
Jointed *a.*	ذُو مَفَاصِلَ او عُقَدٍ
Jointly *ad.*	مَعاً . بِٱشْتِرَاكٍ
Joist *n.*	جِسْرٌ . خَشَبَةٌ مُعْتَرِضَةٌ

Joke *n.* or *v. t.* مَزْحٌ. هزْل. هزَلَ ـِ. مَزَحَ

Jolly *a.* مَرِح. فَرِح. بَهِيْجٌ

Jolt *v. t.* or *i.* رَجَّ ـُ. (خَضَّ ـُ) إِرْتَجَّ

Jostle *v. t.* صَدَمَ. رَجَّ ـُ

Jot *n.* or *v. t.* جُزْءٌ دَقِيقٌ. دَوَّنَ

Journal *n.* (يَوْمِيَّةٌ. جَرِيدَة)

Journalism *n.* كِتابةُ جَرِيدَةٍ. تَحْرِيرٌ

Journalist *n.* كَاتِبُ جَرِيدَةٍ. مُحَرِّرٌ

Journey *n.* or *v. i.* سَفَرٌ. سَافَرَ

Jovial *a.* مَرِحٌ. فَرِحٌ

Jowl *n.* خَدٌّ. فَكٌ

Joy *n.* فَرَحٌ. سُرُورٌ. بَهْجَة

Joyful / **Joyous** } *a.* فَرِحٌ. مُبْتَهِج مَسْرُورٌ

Joyless *a.* عَدِيمُ ٱلْفَرَحِ. كَئِيبٌ

Jubilant *a.* كَثِيرُ ٱلابْتِهَاجِ. مُتَهَلِّلٌ

Jubilee *n.* يُوبِيلٌ

Judaism *n.* دِيَانَةُ ٱلْيَهُودِ

Judge *n.* قَاضٍ. دَيَّانٌ

Judge *v. t.* قَضَى ـِ. حَكَمَ ـُ

Judgment *n.* قَضَاءٌ. حُكْمٌ. تَمْيِيزٌ

Judicatory *a.* مُخْتَصٌّ بِمَحْكَمَةٍ. حُكْمِيٌّ

Judicial *a.* قَضَائِيٌّ. قِصَاصِيٌّ

Judiciary *a.* or *n.* قَضَائِيٌّ. دَائِرَةُ ٱلْقُضَاة

Judicious *a.* حَكِيمٌ. حَازِمٌ

Jug *n.* إِبْرِيقٌ. كُوزٌ

Juggle *v. i.* شَعْوَذَ. غَبَنَ ـِ

Juggler *n.* مُشَعْوِذٌ. مَكَّارٌ

Jugglery / **Juggling** } *n.* شَعْوَذَةٌ

Jugular *a.* or *n.* عُنُقِيٌّ. حَبْلُ ٱلْوَرِيدِ

Juice *n.* عَصِيرٌ. عُصَارَةٌ

Juicy *n.* غَضٌّ. ذُو عُصَارَةٍ

July *n.* تَمُّوزُ. يُولْيُو

Jumble *v. t.* or *n.* خَلَطَ. خِلْطٌ

Jump *v. i.* or *n.* قَفَزَ. قَفْزَةٌ

Junction *n.* وَصْلٌ. مُلْتَقًى

Juncture *n.* آن . وَقتٌ مُهِمٌّ

June *n.* حَزِيرَانُ . يُونِيُو

Jungle *n.* غَابَةٌ . اجَمٌ

Junior *n.* اصغرُ عُمْراً

Juniper *n.* عَرْعَرٌ (نَبَاتٌ)

Junk *n.* سَفِينَةٌ صِينِيَّةٌ . مَوَاد عتِيقَةٌ

Juno *n.* الإِلَاهَةُ رُومَانِيَّةٌ . إِحدَى ٱلسَّيَّارَاتِ ٱلصَّغِيرَةِ

Jupiter *n.* الْمُشْتَرِي (سَيَّارٌ)

Jurisdiction *n.* حُكْمٌ أَوْ دَائِرَتُهُ

Jurisprudence *n.* علمُ ٱلْفِقْهِ

Juror / **Juryman** *n.* عضوُ محكمَةِ ٱلتَّحقِيقِ

Jury *n.* محكمَةٌ تحقِيقِيَّةٌ

Just *a.* or *ad.* عَادِلٌ . بَارٌّ . تَمَامًا

Justice *n.* عَدْلٌ . إِستِقَامَةٌ . قَاضٍ

Justifiable *a.* يتبرَّرُ . جَائِزٌ

Justification *n.* تبرِيرٌ . تبرِئَةٌ

Justify *v. t.* بَرَّرَ . بَرَّأَ

Justly *ad.* بِعَدْلٍ . بِٱستِحقَاقٍ

Jut *v. i.* بَرَزَ ـ نَتَأَ ـ

Juvenile *a.* or *n.* وَلَدِيٌّ . وَلَدٌ

Juxtaposition *n.* مُقَارَبَةٌ

K

Keel *n.* قاعِدَةُ ٱلسفِينَةِ

Keen *a.* حَادٌّ . ذَكِيٌّ

Keep *v. t.* حفظَ ـ . ضَبطَ ـ

Keeper *n.* حَافِظٌ . حَارِسٌ

Keepsake *n.* شيءٌ للتذْكَارِ

Keg *n.* بَرْمِيلٌ صَغِيرٌ

Ken *v. t.* or *n.* عَلِمَ ـَ . عِلْمٌ

Kennel *n.* زَرِيبَةُ ٱلْكِلاَبِ

Kerchief *n.* مِنْدِيلٌ

Kernel *n.* حَبَّةٌ . نَوَاةٌ . لُبٌّ

Kerosene *n.* زَيْتٌ مَعْدَنِيٌّ

Kettle *n.* قِدْرٌ . غَلاَّيَةٌ

Key *n.* مِفْتَاحٌ . تَفْسِيرٌ

Key-stone *n.* أَعْلَى حَجَرِ ٱلْقَنْطَرَةِ

Kick *v. t.* or *i.* or *n.* لَبَطَ ـُ . رَفَسَ ـِ

Kid *n.* جَدْيٌ ج جِدَاءٌ

Kidnap *v. t.* إِخْتَلَسَ بَشَرًا

Kidney *n.* كُلْيَةٌ ج كُلًى

Kill *v. t.* قَتَلَ ـُ . اخْمَدَ

Kiln *n.* أَتُّونٌ

Kilo / **Kilogramme** } *n.* أَلْفُ جِرَامٍ

Kilometre *n.* أَلْفُ مِتْرٍ

Kin *n.* اقَارِبُ . أَنْسِبَاءُ

Kind *a.* or *n.* لَطِيفٌ . مُحْسِنٌ . نَوْعٌ

Kindle *v. t.* اضْرَمَ . اشْعَلَ

Kindliness *n.* لُطْفٌ . مَعْرُوفٌ

Kindly *ad.* or *a.* بِلُطْفٍ . لَطِيفٌ

Kindness *n.* لُطْفٌ . مَعْرُوفٌ

Kindred *n.* اقَارِبُ . أَنْسِبَاءُ

Kine *n. pl.* بَقَرٌ

King *n.* مَلِكٌ ج مُلُوكٌ

Kingdom *n.* مَمْلَكَةٌ

Kink *v. i.* or *n.* إِلْتَوَى . لَيَّةٌ

Kinsman *n.* نَسِيبٌ . قَرِيبٌ

Kiss *n.* or *v. t.* قُبْلَةٌ . قَبَّلَ

Kitchen *n.* مَطْبَخٌ

Kite *n.* حِدَأَةٌ . طَيَّارَةٌ

Kitten *n.* جِرْوُ ٱلْقِطِّ . قُطَيْطَةٌ

Knack *n.* خِفَّةٌ . بَرَاعَةٌ . مَلَكَةٌ

Knapsack *n.* مِزْوَدُ ٱلْجُنْدِيِّ

Knarled *a.* مُعقّد

Knave *n.* / Knavish *a.* } خبيث . مكّار

Knavery / Knavishness } *n.* خباثة . مكر

Knead *v. t.* عجن ـُ ـِ

Knee *n.* رُكبة ج رُكَب

Kneel *v. i.* ركع ـَ . جثا ـُ

Knee-pan *n.* رضفة الرُّكبة

Knell *n.* دقّ الجرس لميْت

Knife *n.* سكّين

Knight *n.* فارس . لقب شرف

Knighthood *n.* فروسيّة رتبة شرف

Knit *v. t.* or *i.* حبك ـُ . إحتبك

Knob *n.* عجرة

Knock *v. t.* or *n.* قرع ـَ . ضربة

Knocker *n.* مقرعه . مطرقه

Knoll *n.* تلّة . رابية صغيرة

Knot *n.* or *v. t.* عقدة . عقّد

Knotted / Knotty } *a.* مُعقّد . كثير العقد

Know *v. t.* علم ـَ . عرف ـِ

Knowable *a.* ما يُعلم أو يُعرف

Knowingly *ad.* عمدًا

Knowledge *n.* علم . معرفة

Knuckle *n.* مفصل الإصبع

Koran *n.* القرآن

L

Label *n.* or *v. t.* وُرَيقة لعنوان . عنون

Laboratory *n.* معمل لفنّ

Laborious *a.* شاقّ . كدود

Labour *n.* or *v. i.* كدّ . إشتغل

Labourer *n.* فاعلٌ . شغّالٌ

Labyrinth *n.* أمرٌ معقّدٌ . ألغازٌ

Lace *n.* or *v. t.* (تخريم). شدّ بخيطٍ

Lacerate *v. t.* شرّط . مزّق

Laceration *a.* تشريطٌ . تمزيقٌ

Lachrymal *a.* دمعيٌّ

Lack *n.* or *v. t.* or *i.* عوزٌ . عازَ . أعوزَ

Laconic / **Laconical** *a.* ما قلّ ودلّ (من الكلام)

Lacteal / **Lactic** *a.* لبنيّ

Lad *n.* صبيٌّ . ولدٌ . فتىً

Ladder *n.* سُلّمٌ ج سلالمُ

Lade *v. t.* حمَلَ . شحنَ ـَ

Lading *n.* حمْلٌ . شحنٌ

Ladle *n.* مغرفةٌ

Lady *n.* سيّدةٌ . خاتونٌ

Ladyship *n.* مقامُ السيّدة

Lag *v. i.* تأخّر . أبطأ

Laggard *n.* متأخّرٌ . متكاسلٌ

Lagoon *n.* بحيرةٌ قليلةُ الماء

Laid, lain, *see* **Lay.** موضوعٌ

Lair *n.* عرينٌ . وجارٌ ج أوجرة

Laity *n.* العوامُّ . غيرُ الإكليرس

Lake *n.* بُحيرةٌ

Lamb *n.* خروفٌ . حمَل

Lambkin *n.* خروفٌ صغيرٌ

Lame *a.* or *v. t.* أعرجُ . عرّج

Lameness *n.* عرجٌ

Lament *n.* or *v. t.* ناحَ ـُ . رثى ـِ

Lamentable *a.* محزنٌ . ما يُرثى له

Lamentation *n.* نوحٌ . مرثاةٌ

Lamp *n.* مصباحٌ . سراجٌ . قنديلٌ

Lampoon *v. t.* or *n.* هجا . هجوٌ

Lance *n.* or *v. t.* رُمحٌ . رمَحَ . طعنَ ـَ

Lanceolate *a.* رمحيُّ الشكلِ

Lancet *n.* مشرطٌ . مِبضعٌ

Land *n.* ارضٌ . برٌّ . بلادٌ

Land *v. t.* or *i.* انزَلَ او نزَلَ من سفينة
Landlocked *a.* مُحاط بالبَرِّ
Landlord *n.* ربُّ ارضٍ او منزِلٍ
Landmark *n.* علامة حدٍ. تخمٌ
Landscape *n.* منظرٌ من الارضِ
Lane *n.* زُقاقٌ. مضيقٌ
Language *n.* لُغة. كلامٌ. لِسانٌ
Languid *a.* متوانٍ. متراخٍ
Languish *v. i.* خارَ. إنضنى. إرتخى
Languor *n.* رخاوةٌ. ضعفٌ
Lank *a.* رخوٌ. نحيفٌ
Lantern *n.* (فنارٌ. فانوسٌ)
Lap *n.* ذيلٌ. حضنٌ. حجرٌ
Lap *v. t.* or *i.* ولغ. طوى. إنثنى
Lapse *v. i.* مضى وقتُه. سقطَ
Larceny *n.* سرقةٌ
Lard *n.* دهنُ الخنزيرِ
Larder *n.* بيتُ المؤونه

Large *a.* كبيرٌ. فسيحٌ
Largely *ad.* وفرة. كثيراً
Lark *n.* قُبَّرأو قُنبرة (طائرٌ)
Larynx *n.* حنجرةٌ ج حناجرُ
Lascivious *a.* شهوانيٌّ. فاسقٌ
Lash *n.* or *v.t.* سوطٌ. ساط. شدَّ
Lass *n.* فتاةٌ. صبيةٌ
Lassitude *n.* إسترخاءٌ. عياءٌ
Last *n.* or *a.* قالبُ الحذاء الأخيرُ
Last *v. i.* بقي. دام. إستمرَّ
Lastly *ad.* أخيراً
Latch *n.* or *v. t.* سقاطةٌ. اوصدَ (الباب)
Latchet *n.* شِراكٌ. سيرٌ
Late *a.* متأخرٌ
Lately *ad.* حديثاً
Lateness *n.* تأخرٌ. فواتُ الوقت
Latent *a.* مُستترٌ. كامنٌ
Lateral *a.* جنبيٌّ. جانبيٌّ

Lather *n.* مَخرَطَةٌ
Lather *n.* رَغْوَةُ ٱلصابُون
Latin *a.* or *n.* لاتِينيٌّ. أَللغةُ ٱللاتينِيَّةُ
Latitude *n.* عَرْضٌ
Latter *a.* أَلاخِيرُ. أَلثَّاني
Latterly *ad.* حَدِيثًا
Lattice *n.* شُبَّاكٌ
Laud *v. t.* مَدَحَ. حَمَدَ
Laudable *a.* مَمدوحٌ. جَدِيرٌ بِالْمَدْحِ
Laudanum *a.* صِبغَةُ أَفيُونٍ
Laudatory *a.* مَدْحِيٌّ. مَادِحٌ
Laugh *n.* or *v. i.* ضِحْكَةٌ. ضَحِكَ
Laughable *a.* مُضحِكٌ
Laughing / Laughter *n.* ضَحِكٌ
Laughing-stock *n.* اُضحُوكَةٌ
Launch *v. t.* أَنزَلَ فِي ٱلْمَاءِ
Laundress *n.* غَسَّالَةٌ
Laundry *n.* مَغسَلٌ

Laurel *n.* غَارٌ (شَجَرٌ)
Lava *n.* مَوَادُ تُقْذَفُ مِنْ جَبَلِ ٱلنَّار
Lavatory *n.* مَرْحَضَةٌ. مَغْسَلَةٌ. حَمَّامٌ
Lave *v. t.* غَسَلَ
Laver *n.* مِرْحَضَةٌ. جُرْنٌ لِلغسلِ
Lavish *a.* or *v. t.* مُسْرِفٌ. أَسرَفَ. بَذَّرَ
Law *n.* شَرِيعَةٌ. نَامُوسٌ. سُنَّةٌ
Lawful *a.* شَرْعِيٌّ. جَائِزٌ. مُبَاحٌ
Lawfulness *n.* جَوَازٌ
Lawless *a.* مُخَالِفُ ٱلشَّرِيعةِ. عَاصٍ
Lawn *n.* سَهْلَةٌ خَضْرَاءُ. (شَاشٌ)
Lawsuit *n.* دَعْوَى ج دَعَاوٍ
Lawyer *n.* فَقِيهٌ. مُحَامٍ (أَفُوكَاتُو)
Lax *a.* مُتَرَاخٍ. مُتَسَاهِلٌ
Laxative *a.* مُسَهِّلٌ
Laxity *n.* تَرَاخٍ. فَسَادٌ
Lay *n.* or *a.* نَشِيدٌ. عَامِيٌّ
Lay *v. t.* وَضَعَ. نَظَمَ. بَسَطَ

Layer *n.* طَبَقَةٌ

Laziness *n.* كَسَل . توانٍ

Lazy *a.* كَسْلَانٌ

Lead *n.* رَصَاصٌ

Lead *v. t.* قَادَ ـُ . هدى ـ

Leader *n.* قَائِدٌ . مرشد

Leadership *n.* قِيَادةٌ . رِيَاسَة

Leaf *n.* وَرَقَةٌ . مِصْرَاعٌ

Leaflet *n.* وُرَيْقَةٌ

Leafy *a.* مُورِقٌ . ذو ورق

League *n.* مُحَالَفَةٌ . عصْبَةٌ . فَرْسَخٌ

Leak *n.* or *v. i.* فُجْرَةٌ . وكَفَ ـ

Leakage *n.* وكْفٌ . تَلَفٌ منه

Leaky *a.* واكِفٌ . غيرُ مضبوطٍ

Lean *a.* or *v. i.* نَحِيفٌ . هزيل . مَالَ ـ

Leanness *n.* هزَالٌ . نَحَافة

Leap *n.* or *v. t.* قَفْزَةٌ . قَفَزَ ـ . وثَبَ

Leap-year *n.* سنة كَبيسةٌ

Learn *v. t.* تَعَلَّمَ . عَلِمَ ـ

Learned *a.* عَالِمٌ . مَاهِرٌ

Learner *n.* متعلِّم . تلميذ

Learning *n.* عِلْمٌ . معرِفَة

Lease *n.* or *v. t.* إِيجَارٌ . آجر

Least *a.* الأَصغرُ . الأَقَلّ . الأدنى

Leather *n.* جلْدٌ مدبُوغ

Leathern / **Leathery** } *a.* مِن جِلْدٍ . جلدي

Leave *n.* or *v. t.* إِذْنٌ . تركَ ـ

Leaven *n.* or *v. t.* خَمِيرة . خَمَّرَ ـ

Lecture *n.* خِطَابٌ

Lecturer *n.* خطيبٌ . مُدرِّسٌ

Led *pp.* of **Lead.** مقُودٌ

Ledge *n.* طَبَقَة . صخور بَارِزَة

Ledger *n.* دفترٌ مُختصرِ الحسابات

Leech *n.* عَلَقَة

Lee *n.* or *a.* الجانبُ المَخفور مِن الرِّيحِ

Leeward *a.* or *ad.* مع الرِّيحِ

Leeway *n.* حَرَكَةٌ جَنْبِيَّةٌ مَعَ الرِّيحِ

Left *a.* or *n.* يَسَارٌ . شِمَالٌ

Left-handed *a.* أَعْسَرُ

Leg *n.* رِجْل . سَاقٌ . قَائِمَة

Legacy *n.* وَصِيَّةٌ . وَقْفٌ

Legal *a.* شَرْعِيٌّ . قَانُونِيٌّ . جَائِزٌ

Legality *n.* شَرْعِيَّةٌ . جَوَازٌ

Legalize *v. t.* جعله شُرْعِيًّا

Legate *n.* نَائِبٌ . قَاصِدٌ

Legatee *n.* أَلْمُوصَى لَهُ . وَارِثٌ

Legation *n.* سِفَارَةٌ

Legend *n.* خُرَافَةٌ . عِنْوَانٌ

Legendary *a.* خُرَافِيٌّ

Legerdemain *n.* شَعْوَذَةٌ . شَعْبَذَةٌ

Legging *n.* جَوْرَبٌ لِلرِّجْلِ

Legible *a.* مَا يُقْرَأُ . وَاضِحٌ

Legion *n.* كَتِيبَةٌ . جَوْقٌ

Legislate *v. i.* سَنَّ شَرَائِعَ

Legislation *n.* سَنُّ الشَّرَائِعِ

Legislative *a.* مُخْتَصٌّ بِسَنِّ الشَّرَائِعِ

Legislator *n.* مُشْتَرِعٌ

Legislature *n.* مَجْلِسُ الْمُشْتَرِعِينَ

Legitimacy *n.* شَرْعِيَّةٌ

Legitimate *a.* شَرْعِيٌّ . نِظَامِيٌّ

Leisure *n.* عُطْلَةٌ . فَرَاغٌ

Leisurely *ad.* بَطِيئًا . رُوَيْدًا

Lemon *n.* لَيْمُونٌ

Lemonade *n.* شَرَابُ اللَّيْمُونِ

Lend *v. t.* أَقْرَضَ . أَعَارَ

Length *n.* طُول

Lengthen *v.t.* or *i.* أَطَالَ . طَالَ

Lengthwise *ad.* طُولاً

Lengthy *a.* طَوِيلٌ

Lenient *a.* لَطِيفٌ . حَلِيم

Lenity *n.* لُطْفٌ . مُسَاهَلَةٌ

Lens *n.* بَلُّورَةٌ مُحَدَّبَةٌ اوْ مقعرة

Lent *n.* or *pp.*	اَلصَّوْمُ الكَبِيرُ . مُقْرَضٌ
Lentil *n.*	عَدَسَةٌ
Leopard *n.*	نِمْرٌ . نَمِرٌ
Leper *n.* / **Leprous** *a.* } *a.*	مَجْذُومٌ
Leprosy *n.*	جُذَامٌ
Less *a.*	أَقَلُّ
Lesion *n.*	أَذِيَّةٌ . ضَرَرٌ . هَتْكٌ
Lessen *v. i.* or *t.*	قَلَّ ـِ . نَقَصَ ـُ . قَلَّلَ
Lesson *n.*	مَقَالَةٌ . تَعْلِيمٌ . عِبْرَةٌ
Lest *conj.*	لِئَلَّا
Let *v. t.*	سَمَحَ ـَ . رَخَّصَ . آجَرَ
Lethargy *n.*	سُبَاتٌ . تَغَافُلٌ
Letter *n.*	حَرْفٌ . كِتَابٌ . تَحْرِيرٌ
Letters *pl.*	آدَابٌ . تَهْذِيبٌ
Lettuce *n.*	خَسٌّ
Levant *n.*	شَرْقِيُّ بَحْرِ الرُّومِ
Level *a.* or *v.t.*	مُسْتَوٍ . سَهْلٌ . سَوَّى
Level *n.*	سَطْحٌ مُسْتَوٍ مِيزَانٌ (مَنْسُوبٌ)

Levelling *n.*	تَسْوِيَةٌ . تَسْطِيحٌ
Lever *n.*	مُخْلٌ . عَتَلَةٌ
Levity *n.*	خِفَّةٌ . طَيْشٌ
Levy *v. t.*	ضَرَبَ عَلَى . جَبَى ـِ
Lewd *a.*	شَهْوَانِيٌّ . مُفْسِدٌ . فَاسِقٌ
Lewdness *n.*	فِسْقٌ . فُجُورٌ
Lexicographer *n.*	مُؤَلِّفُ قَامُوسٍ
Lexicon *n.*	قَامُوسٌ
Liable *a.*	مُعَرَّضٌ لِ . مَسْؤُولٌ
Liability *n.*	تَعَرُّضٌ لِ . مَسْؤُولِيَةٌ
Liar *n.*	كَذَّابٌ
Libel *n.*	هَجْرٌ . طَعْنٌ (قَذْفٌ)
Libeler *n.*	هَاجٍ . طَعَّانٌ (قَاذِفٌ)
Libelous *a.*	هَجَائِي . طَاعِنٌ
Liberal *a.*	سَخِيٌّ . كَرِيمٌ
Liberality *n.*	سَخَاءٌ . كَرَمٌ
Liberalize *v. t.*	حَرَّرَ مِنَ التَّعَصُّبِ
Liberate *v. t.*	حَرَّرَ . أَعْتَقَ . أَطْلَقَ

Liberation *n.*	تحرير . إطلاق
Liberator *n.*	محرر . معتق
Libertine *n.*	خليع . فاسق . فاجر
Liberty *n.*	حرية . إستقلال
Librarian *n.*	مدير مكتبة
Library *n.*	مكتبة
Lice *n. pl.*	قمل
License *n.*	إجازة . غلو . خلاعة
Licensed *a.* / Licentiate *n.*	ذو امتياز او رخصة
Licentious *a.*	شهواني . خليع
Licentiousness *n.*	خلاعة . دعارة
Lick *v. t.*	لحس ـ . لعق ـ
Licorice / Liquorice } *n.*	سوس (نبات)
Lid *n.*	غطاء ج اغطية
Lie *n.*	كذب
Lie *v. i.*	كذب . إضطجع . إتجه . مكث
Lieutenant *n.*	نائب . (ملازم)
Life *n.*	حياة . عمر . نشاط
Life-boat *n.*	قارب لا يغرق
Lifelike *a.*	مثله . طبق الاصل
Lifelong *a.*	ما يدوم مدى الحياة
Lift *v. t.* or *n.*	رفع ـ . علّى . رفع
Ligament *n.*	رباط . عصب
Ligature *n.*	عصابة
Light *n.* or *a.*	نور . ضوء . خفيف
Light / Lighten } *v. t.*	أنار . أضاء
Lighten *v. i.* or *t.*	برق ـ . خفف
Lighter *n.*	جرم . ماعون
Light-headed *a*	طائش . فرفار
Light-house *n.*	منارة
Lightly *ad.*	بخفة
Lightness *n.*	خفة . فرفرة
Lightning *n.*	برق
Lightsome *a.*	نير . فرح . مفرح
Like *ad.*	على مثال
Like *a.* or *n.*	مثل . شبيه . نظير

Like *v. t.* احبّ . إستحسن

Likely *a.* or *ad.* مُحتمَلٌ . مُمكِنٌ

Liken *v. t.* شبَّهَ . مثَّلَ

Likeness *n.* شِبْهٌ . صُورةٌ

Likewise *ad.* ايضاً . كذلك

Liking *n.* إستحسانٌ . ميلٌ إلى

Lily *n.* زَنبقٌ . سُوسن

Limb *n.* غُصنٌ . عضوٌ

Line *n.* كِلسٌ . (جيرٌ)

Lime-kiln *n.* أَتُّون كِلسٍ

Lime-stone *n.* حجرُ الكِلسِ

Limit *n.* or *v. t.* حدٌّ . تخمٌ . حدَّدَ

Limitable *a.* قابلُ التحديدِ

Limitation *n.* تحديدٌ . حصرٌ

Limitless *a.* لاحدَّ . غيرُ محدودٍ

Limp *v. i.* or *a.* عرَجَ . رَخوٌ

Limpid *a.* صافٍ . رائقٌ

Line *n.* خطٌّ . سطرٌ . صفٌّ . مرسٌ

Line *v. t.* بطَّنَ . خطَّطَ . سطَّرَ

Lineage *n.* نسبٌ . ذُرِّيّةٌ

Lineal *a.* نسبيٌّ

Lineament *n.* رسمٌ . هيئةٌ

Linear *a.* خطّي . مُستقيمٌ

Linen *n.* كتّانٌ . ثيابٌ من كتّانٍ

Linger *v. i.* ابطأ . تردّد

Lingering *a.* إبطاءٌ . تأخرٌ

Lingual *a.* لسانيٌّ

Linguist *n.* عالِمٌ باللُّغاتِ

Linguistic / Linguistical } *a.* مختصٌّ بعلمِ اللُّغاتِ

Lining *n.* بِطانةٌ . تبطِينٌ

Liniment *n.* مرهمٌ . دِهنٌ

Link *n.* or *v. t.* حلقةٌ . زردةٌ . سلسلَ

Linseed *n.* بزرُ كتّانٍ

Lint *n.* كتيتٌ . مشاقةٌ

Lintel *n.* عتبةٌ ج . عتبٌ

Lion *n.* أسدٌ ج اسُودٌ

Lioness *n.* لَبْوَةٌ

Lip *n.* شِفَةٌ

Liquify *v. t.* ذَوَّبَ . اماع

Liquid *n.* مائِعٌ . سائِلٌ

Liquidate *v. t.* صَفَّى ٱلحساب . اوْفَى ـِ

Liquidation *n.* تصْفِيَةُ ٱلحسَابِ إِيفَاءٌ

Liquor *n.* سَائِلٌ . شَرابٌ . مُسْكِرٌ

Liquorice *n.* نَبَاتُ ٱلسُّوسِ اورُبُّهُ

Lisp *v. i.* or *n.* لَثِغَ ـَ . لُثْغَةٌ

List *n.* قَائِمَةٌ . جَدْولٌ . مَيْلٌ

Listen *v. i.* اصغَى إِلَى . إِستَمَعَ

Listless *a* غَافِلٌ . غيْرُ مُبَالٍ

Literal *a.* حرْفِيٌّ

Literary *a.* آدَابِيٌّ . علْمِيٌّ

Literature *n.* آدَابُ ٱللُّغَةِ . كُتُبٌ

Lithe / **Lithesome** } *a.* مَرِنٌ . لَيِّنٌ

Lithograph *v. t.* or *n.* طَبَعَ على حجرٍ

Lithographer *n.* طَابِعٌ على حجر

Lithography *n.* صِناعَةُ ٱلطَّبْعِ ٱلحَجَرِيّ

Litigant *n.* خصِيمٌ . مُدَّعٍ

Litigate *v. i.* خَاصَمَ . اقام دَعْوَى

Litigation *n.* مخاصَمَةٌ . إِجرَاءُ ٱلدَّعاوي

Litter *n.* مَحْمَلٌ . نُثَارَةٌ . أَجْرِيَةٌ

Little *a.* or *ad.* صَغيرٌ . قَليلٌ . قَلِيلاً

Liturgy *n.* خِدْمَةُ ٱلعِبَادةِ

Live *v. i.* عَاشَ ـِ . أَقَامَ بِ . تصرَّف

Live *a.* حَيٌّ . نَشِيطٌ

Livelihood *n.* مَعَاشٌ . مَعيشة

Liveliness *n.* خِفَّةٌ . نَشَاط

Lively *a.* خَفِيفٌ . نَشِيط . بَشَّاشٌ

Liver *n.* كَبِدٌ ج اكْبَادٌ

Livery *n.* زِيٌّ رَسْمِيٌّ لِلْخَدم

Live-stock *n.* خيلٌ . مَواشٍ

Livid *a.* ازرَقُ مُسْوَدٌّ

Living *a.* or *n.* حَيٌّ . مَعِيشَةٌ

Lizard *n.* حرْذَوْن . ضَب

Lo ! *ex.*	هوَذَا . إِذَا بِ . هَا
Load *n.* or *v. t.*	حِمْلٌ . حَمَلَ . شَحَنَ ـ
Loadstone *n.*	حَجَرُ مَغْنَطِيس
Loaf *n.*	رَغِيفٌ . قَالِبُ (سُكر)
Loafer *n.*	بَطَّال . كَسْلَان
Loam *n.*	تُربَةٌ مُخْصِبَة
Loan *v.* or *n.*	اقْرَضَ . اعَارَ . قَرْضٌ
Loath *a.*	غَيرُ رَاضٍ . نَافِرٌ
Loathe *v. t.*	كَرِهَ ـ . سَئِمَ
Loathsome *a.*	مَكْرُوهٌ
Loathsomeness *n.*	كَرَاهة
Lobe *n.*	فَصٌّ ج فُصُوصٌ
Lobster *n.*	سَرطَانٌ بَحْرِيٌّ
Local *a.*	مَحَلِّيٌّ
Locality *n.*	مَحَلٌّ . موقِعٌ
Locate *v. t.*	وَضَعَ ـ . انْزَلَ
Location *n.*	وَضْعٌ . مَوْضِعٌ
Lock *n.* or *v. t.*	قُفْلٌ . اقفَلَ
Locket *n.*	حَمِيلَةٌ
Locksmith *n.*	قَفَّالٌ . (قَرَدَحجي)
Locomotion *n.*	سَيْرٌ . إِنْتِقَالٌ
Locomotive *n.*	آلَةُ ٱلْبُخَارِ لِلسَّيْرِ
Locust *n.*	جَرَادَةٌ
Lodge *n.* or *v. i.*	مَأْوَى . آوَى . بَاتَ ـ
Lodger *n.*	نَزِيلٌ . بَائِتٌ
Lodging *n.*	مَبِيتٌ . مَنزِلٌ
Loftiness *n.*	عُلُو . تَشَامُخٌ
Lofty *a.*	عَالٍ . رَفِيعٌ . مُتَشَامِخٌ
Log *n.*	خَشَبَةٌ ضَخْمَة
Logarithms *n. pl.*	عِلْمُ ٱلْأَنْسَابِ
Log-book *n.*	كِتَابُ سَيْرِ سَفِينَةٍ
Logic *n.*	عِلْمُ ٱلْمَنْطِقِ
Logical *a.*	مَنطِقِيٌّ . قِيَاسِيٌّ
Logician *n.*	عَالِمٌ بِٱلْمَنْطِقِ
Loin *n.*	صُلْبٌ ج اصْلَابٌ
Loiter *v. t.*	تَاخَّرَ . أَبطَأَ

Lone *a.* مُنْفَرِدٌ . مُتَوَحِّدٌ

Loneliness *n.* وَحْدَةٌ

Lonely / **Lonesome** *a.* مُسْتَوْحِشٌ

Long *a.* or *v. i.* طَوِيلٌ . تَاقَ . إِشْتَاقَ

Longevity *n.* طُولُ ٱلْعُمْرِ

Longing *n.* إِشْتِيَاقٌ . شَوْقٌ

Longitude *n.* طُولٌ

Long-suffering *n.* or *a.* طُولُ ٱلْأَنَاةِ . طَوِيلُهَا

Look *v. i.* نَظَرَ ـُ . فَتَّشَ . ظَهَرَ ـَ

Looking-glass *n.* مِرْآةٌ

Loom *n.* or *v. i.* نَوْلٌ . ظَهَرَ ـَ

Loop *n.* عُرْوَةٌ

Loop-hole *n.* فَرَاغُ ٱلْعُرْوَةِ . مَهْرَبٌ

Loose / **Loosen** *v.t.* حَلَّ ـُ . فَكَّ ـُ . أَطْلَقَ

Loose *n.* مَحْلُولٌ . رَخْوٌ . مُسْتَرْسِلٌ

Looseness *n.* رَخَاوَةٌ . إِنْحِلَالٌ

Lop *v. t.* قَضَبَ ـَ . إِسْتَمَالَ

Loquacious *a.* كَثِيرُ ٱلْكَلَامِ

Lord *n.* رَبٌّ . سَيِّدٌ . شَرِيفٌ

Lordly *a.* شَرِيفٌ . مُتَعَظِّمٌ . سَامٍ

Lordship *n.* رَبُوبِيَّةٌ . سِيَادَةٌ

Lose *v. t.* ضَيَّعَ . خَسِرَ ـَ . فَقَدَ ـِ

Loss *n.* خِسَارَةٌ . فَقْدٌ . تَلَفٌ

Lot *n.* نَصِيبٌ . حِصَّةٌ . قُرْعَةٌ

Lotion *n.* غَسْلٌ . غِسْلَةٌ

Lottery *n.* قُرْعَةٌ . قِمَارٌ

Lotus *n.* جَنْدَقُوقٌ

Loud *a.* عَالٍ . مُجْهِرٌ . جَهُورٌ

Loudness *n.* عُلُوٌّ (ٱلصَّوْتِ) . جَهَارَةٌ

Lounge *v. i.* تَقَاعَدَ . تَكَاسَلَ

Louse *n.* (*pl.* Lice). قَمْلَةٌ ج قَمْلٌ

Lovable / **Lovely** *a.* مَحْبُوبٌ . جَدِيرٌ بِٱلْمَحَبَّةِ

Love *n.* or *v. t.* مَحَبَّةٌ . أَحَبَّ

Loveliness *n.* حُسْنٌ . جَمَالٌ

Lover *n.* / **Loving** *a.* مُحِبٌّ . عَاشِقٌ

Low *a.* مُنْخَفِضٌ . دَنِيٌّ . رَخِيصٌ

Lower *v. t.* خَفَّضَ . أنْزَلَ
Lowering *a.* مُظْلِمٌ . عَابِسٌ
Lowland *n.* أَرْضٌ مُنْخَفِضَة
Lowliness *n.* مَسْكَنَةٌ . ضعة
Lowly *a.* مُتَوَاضِعٌ . وَدِيعٌ
Low-spirited *a.* كَئِيبٌ
Loyal *a.* أَمِين . مُخْلِص ٱلطَّاعة
Loyalty *n.* أَمَانَةٌ . طَاعَة
Lubricate *v. t.* دهَّنَ. زَيَّت . ملَّس
Lucid *a.* وَاضِحٌ . صَاف
Lucidness / **Lucidity** *n.* وُضُوحٌ . صفَآءٌ
Luck *n.* حَظٌّ . نَصِيبٌ
Luckily *ad.* بِحُسْنِ ٱلْحَظِّ . بِسعْدٍ
Luckless *a.* مَنْكُودُ ٱلْحَظِّ
Lucky *a.* حَظِيظ . سعِيدٌ
Lucrative *a.* مُكْسِبٌ . مفِيد
Lucre *n.* رِبْحٌ . مَكْسَبٌ
Ludicrous *a.* مُضْحِك

Luggage *n.* أَمْتِعة
Lukewarm *a.* فَاتِرٌ
Lull *v.t.* or *i.* or *n.* هدَّأ . هَدَا . هدوٌّ
Lumbre *n.* سَقطُ ٱلمَتَاع . اخْشَاب
Luminary *n.* جِرْمٌ مُضِيٌّ
Luminous *a.* مُضِيٌّ نَيِّرٌ
Lump *n.* كُتْلَةٌ . جُمْلة
Lunacy *n.* جُنُونٌ
Lunar / **Lunary** *a.* قَمَرِيٌّ
Lunatic *n.* or *a.* مَجْنُونٌ . جُنُونِيٌّ
Lunatic-asylum *n.* بِيمَارِسْتَانٌ
Lunch *n* or *v. i.* غَدَآءٌ . تغَدَّى
Lung *n.* رِئَةٌ
Lurch *v. i.* or *n.* إِنْدَفَعَ جَانِبًا
Lure *v. t.* اغْوَى . غرَّ ـُ
Lurid *a.* مُصْفَرٌّ . مغِمٌّ . مُكَدَّرٍ
Lurk *v. i.* كمنَ ـُ . إِخْتَبَأَ
Luscious *a.* حلْوٌ . لَذِيذٌ

Lust *n.* or *v. i.*	شَهْوَةٌ . إشْتَهى
Lustful *a.*	شَهْوَانِيٌّ
Lustily *a.*	بِبَأْسٍ بِشِدَةٍ
Lustre *n.*	بَهَاءٌ . رَوْنَقٌ . شهرةٌ
Lustrous *a.*	لاَمِعٌ . بهِيٌّ
Lusty *a.*	ضَلِيعٌ . نَشِيطٌ
Lute *n.*	عُودٌ
Luxuriance *n.*	رَتْعٌ .خصبٌ . تَرَفٌ
Luxuriant *a.*	خصبٌ . تَارِفٌ
Luxuriate *v. i.*	رُتِعَ . تنعم
Luxurious *a.*	متنعمٌ . مُتْرَفهٌ
Luxury *n.*	تَرَفٌ . تنعُّمٌ . رفاهة
Lyceum *n.*	جمْعِيةٌ عِلْمِيَّةٌ
Lying *n.* or *a.*	كِذْبٌ . كَاذِبٌ
Lynch *v. t.*	قاصَّ او قتَلَ بِلاَ حُكمٍ شرعِيٍّ
Lynx *n.*	نَوْعٌ من الفَهْدِ
Lyre *n.*	قِيثَارٌ
Lyric, **Lyrical** *a.*	غنائِيٌّ . قِيثَارِيٌّ

M

Macadamize *v. t.*	رَصَفَ بالحَصى
Mace *n.*	عصاً . صَوْلجَانٌ
Macerate *v. t.*	نَقَعَ . انْحَفَ
Machination *n.*	مؤامرةٌ . مَكرٌ
Machine *n.*	آلَةٌ
Machinery *n.*	آلاتٌ او اجزَاؤُهَا
Machinist *n.*	صَانِعُ الآلاتِ
Mackerel *n.*	سمكٌ بحرِيٌّ منقطٌ

Mackintosh *n.* مُشَمَّعٌ

Mad *a.* مَجْنُونٌ . أحمق

Madam *n.* سَيِّدَة

Madden *v. t.* أغضَبَ . جَنَّنَ

Madhouse *n.* بِيمَارِسْتَان

Madly *ad.* بِجُنُونٍ . بِحَمَاقَةٍ

Madman *n.* مَجْنُونٌ

Madness *n.* جُنُونٌ . حَمَاقَةٌ

Magazine *n.* مَخْزَن (جريدة)

Maggot *n.* دُودَةٌ

Magic *n.* سِحْرٌ . رُقْيَةٌ

Magic, Magical *a.* سِحْرِيٌّ

Magician *n.* سَاحِرٌ . رَاقٍ

Magisterial *a.* سُلْطَانِيٌّ . مُتَجَبِّرٌ

Magistracy *n.* مَأْمُورِيَّةُ حَاكِمٍ

Magistrate *n.* حَاكِم . مَأْمُور

Magnanimity *n.* شَرَفُ ٱلنَّفْس

Magnanimous *a.* شَرِيفُ ٱلنفسِ

Magnate *n.* عَظِيم . كَبِيرٌ . وَجِيهٌ

Magnet *n.* مَغْنَطِيسٌ

Magnetic, Magnetical *a.* مَغْنَطِيسِيٌّ

Magnetism *n.* مَغْنَطِيسِيَّةٌ

Magnetize *v. t.* مَغْنَطَ

Magnificence *n.* جَلَالٌ . بَهَاءٌ

Magnificent *a.* بَهِيٌّ . فَاخِرٌ . جَلِيلٌ

Magnify *v. t.* كَبَّرَ . عَظَّمَ . بَجَّلَ

Magnitude *n.* كِبَرٌ . قَدْرٌ . أَهَمِّيَةٌ

Magpie *n.* نَوْعٌ مِنَ ٱلْعَقْعَقِ (طَائِر)

Maid, Maiden *n.* فَتَاة . عذرَاءُ . جَارِيَة

Maiden-hair *n.* كُزْبَرَةُ ٱلْبِئْرِ (نبات)

Mail *n.* بَرِيدٌ . دِرْعٌ

Mail *v. t.* أَرْسَلَ بِٱلْبَرِيد . دَرَّعَ

Maim *v. t.* جَدَعَ . بَتَرَ

Main *a.* or *n.* رَئِيسِيٌّ . اهَمُّ . قُوَّة

Mainland *n.* اليَابسةُ . (غيرُ جزيرةٍ)

Mainly *ad.* غَالِبًا . في ٱلأكثرِ

Mainmast *n.* الصَّارِي ٱلاكْبَر

Mainsail *n.* الشِّرَاعُ الأَكْبَرُ

Maintain *v. t.* حَفِظَ . قَامَ بِ . أَكَّدَ

Maintenance *n.* إِعَالَةٌ . حِفْظٌ . قِيَامٌ

Maize *n.* ذُرَةٌ صَفْرَاءُ

Majestic *a.* جَلِيلٌ . رَفِيعٌ . عَظِيمٌ

Majesty *n.* جَلَالَةٌ . عَظَمَةٌ

Major *a.* or *n.* أَكْبَرُ . كُبْرَى . (بِكْبَاشِي)

Major-general *n.* قَائِدُ لِوَاءٍ

Majority *n.* أَلْاكْثَرِيَّةُ . سِنُّ ٱلْبُلُوغِ

Make *v. t.* عَمِلَ ـَ . صَنَعَ ـَ . اوْجَبَ

Maker *n.* عَامِلٌ . صَانِعٌ . خَالِقٌ

Maladministration *n.* سُوءُ إِدَارَةٍ

Malady *n.* مَرَضٌ . عِلَّةٌ . دَاءٌ

Malaria *n.* فَسَادُ ٱلْهَوَاءِ . مَلَارِيَا

Malcontent *a.* غَيْرُ رَاضٍ

Male *n.* ذَكَرٌ ج ذُكُورٌ

Malediction *n.* لَعْنَةٌ . شَتِيمَةٌ

Malefactor *n.* مُذْنِبٌ . مُجْرِمٌ

Malevolent *a.* سَيِّءُ ٱلنِّيَّةِ . ضَاغِنٌ

Malformation *n.* سُوءُ ٱلْخِلْقَةِ . تَشَوُّهٌ

Malice *n.* ضَغِينَةٌ . حِقْدٌ

Malicious *a.* ضَاغِنٌ . حَقُودٌ

Malign *v. t.* هَتَكَ . نَمَّ ـُ . إِفْتَرَى

Malignancy / **Malignity** *n.* ضَغِينَةٌ . خَبَاثَةٌ

Malignant *a.* ضَاغِنٌ . حَقُودٌ . خَبِيثٌ

Malleable *a.* قَابِلُ ٱلْمَطْلِ بِٱلتَّطْرِيقِ

Mallet *n.* مِطْرَقَةٌ

Malpractice *n.* سُوءُ ٱلْعَمَلِ

Maltreat *v. t.* عَامَلَ بِٱلسُّوءِ

Maltreatment *n.* مُعَامَلَةٌ . سَيِّئَةٌ

Mameluke *n.* مَمْلُوكٌ ج مَمَالِيكُ

Mamma *n.* أُمٌّ

Mammali *n.* / **Mammalia** *n. pl.* ذَوَاتُ ٱلثُّدِيِّ

Man *n.* (*pl.* Men) الإِنْسَانُ . رَجُلٌ

Manacle *v.t.* or *n.* غَلَّ ـُ . غُلٌّ ج اغْلَالٌ

Manage *v. t.* ادار . ساس ـُ . دَبَّرَ

Manageable *a.* سهلُ ٱلتَّدْبِيرِ وٱلضبْطِ

Management *n.* تَدْبِيرٌ . إِدارةٌ

Manager *n.* مُدِيرٌ . مدبّرٌ

Mandate *n.* أَمْرٌ رَسْمِيٌّ

Mandrake *n.* لُفَّاحٌ (نَبَاتٌ)

Mane *n.* عُرْفُ ٱلفَرَسِ

Maneuvre / Manœuvre *n.* حَرَكاتُ ٱلعَسْكرِ حِيلَةٌ

Manful *a.* رُجُلِيٌّ . شَهْمٌ

Mange *n.* جَرَبُ ٱلحَيَوانَاتِ

Manger *n.* مِذْوَدٌ . مَعْلِفٌ

Mangle *v. t.* مَزَّقَ . قَرَّضَ

Mangy *a.* أَجْرَبُ

Manhood *n.* رُجُولَةٌ . مُرُوءةٌ

Mania *n.* جُنُونٌ . وَلَعٌ . (هوسٌ)

Maniac *n.* / Maniacal *a.* مَجْنُونٌ

Manifest *a.* or *v. t.* ظَاهِرٌ . بَيِّنٌ . أَظْهَرَ

Manifestation *n.* إِظْهَارٌ . بَيَانٌ

Manifesto *n.* إِعْلانٌ . مَنْشُورٌ

Manifold *a.* مُتَنَوِّعٌ . شَتَّى

Mankind *n.* نَوْعُ ٱلإِنْسَان . ٱلْبَشَرُ

Manfully *ad.* بِمُرُوءَةٍ . بِشَهامَةٍ . بِشَجاعَةٍ

Manliness *n.* رجولِيَّةٌ . شَهَامَةٌ

Manly *a.* شَهْمٌ . ذُو مروءةٍ

Manna *n.* مَنٌّ

Manner *n.* كَيفيةٌ . اسلوبٌ . دَأْبٌ

Manners *n. pl.* آدابٌ

Man-of-war *n.* بَارِجَةٌ حَرْبِيَّةٌ

Manœuvre *see* Maneuvre.

Manor *n.* عِقَارٌ . إِقْطَاعَةٌ

Mansion *n.* دارٌ . قَصْرٌ

Manslaughter *n.* أَقَتْلُ خطأً

Mantel *n.* رفٌّ فوقَ ٱلْمَوْقِدِ

Mantle *n.* رِدَآءٌ . جبةٌ

Manual *a.* or *n.* شُغْلُ ٱليَدِ . كِتَابٌ مُخْتَصرٌ

Manufactory *n.* مَعْمَلٌ

Manufacture *n.* or *v. t.*	عَمَلٌ . إِصْطِنَاعٌ
Manufacturer *n.*	صَانِعٌ . صَاحِبُ مَعْمَلٍ
Manure *n.*	زِبْلٌ . سَمَادٌ . سِرْقِينٌ
Manuscript *n.*	كِتَابُ خَطٍّ
Many *a.*	كَثِيرٌ . عَدِيدٌ
Map *n.*	(خَارِطَةٌ) . رَسْمُ بِلَادٍ
Mar *v. t.*	أَضَرَّ . أَفْسَدَ . شَوَّهَ
Marauder *n.* / **Marauding** *a.*	نَهَّابٌ . مُغِيرٌ لِلسَّلْبِ
Marble *n.*	رُخَامٌ . مَرْمَرٌ
March *n.* or *v. i.*	اذَارُ . مَسِيرٌ . سَارَ ـِ
Mare *n.*	أُنثَى ٱلْفَرَسِ
Margin *n.*	حَاشِيَةٌ . حَرْفٌ . شَفِيرٌ
Marine *a.* / **Mariner** *n.*	بَحْرِيٌّ
Marital *a.*	زَوْجِيٌّ
Maritime *a.*	بَحْرِيٌّ . مُجَاوِرُ ٱلْبَحْرِ
Mark *n.*	عَلَامَةٌ . أَثَرٌ . هَدَفٌ
Mark *v. t.*	عَلَّمَ عَلَى . لَاحَظَ
Market *n.*	سُوقٌ ج أَسْوَاقٌ
Marketable *a.*	رَائِجٌ
Marksman *n.*	رَامٍ . مَاهِرٌ بِٱلرَّمْيِ
Marmalade *n.*	نَوْعٌ مِنَ ٱلْمُرَبَّى
Marriage *n.*	عُرْسٌ . زَوَاجٌ
Marriageable *a.*	خَلِيقٌ بِٱلزَّوَاجِ
Marrow *n.*	مُخٌّ . لُبٌّ
Marry *v. t.* or *i.*	زَوَّجَ . تَزَوَّجَ
Mars *n.*	أَلْمَرِّيخُ (سَيَّارٌ) . إِلٰهُ ٱلْحَرْبِ
Marsh *n.*	مُسْتَنْقَعٌ . سَبْخَةٌ
Marshal *n.* or *v. t.*	اكْبَرُ ٱلْقُوَّادِ . صَفَّ
Marshy *a.*	مُسْتَنْقَعِيٌّ . سَبِخٌ
Martial *a.*	حَرْبِيٌّ . عَسْكَرِيٌّ
Martyr *n.*	شَهِيدٌ ج شُهَدَاءُ
Martyrdom *n.*	إِسْتِشْهَادٌ
Marvel *v. i.* or *n.*	تَعَجَّبَ . عَجِيبَةٌ
Marvelous *a.*	عَجِيبٌ . غَرِيبٌ
Masculine *a.*	مُذَكَّرٌ
Mash *v. t.*	دَقَّ ـُ . خَبَصَ ـِ

Mask *n.* or *v. t.* وَجْهٌ عَارِيَةٌ . نَكَّرَ . سَتَرَ

Mason *n.* بَنَّاءٌ . مِعْمَارٌ

Masonic *a.* مَاسُونِيٌّ

Masonry *n.* صِنَاعَةُ ٱلْبِنَاءِ . مَاسُونِيَّةٌ

Masquerade *v. i.* or *n.* تَنَكَّرَ . تَنَكُّرٌ لِلسُّخْرِيَةِ

Mass *n.* كَوْمٌ . مِقْدَارٌ . قُدَّاسٌ

Massacre *n.* or *v. t.* ذَبْحٌ . مَقْتَلَةٌ . قَتَلَ ـُ

Massive *a.* جَسِيمٌ . غَلِيظٌ

Mast *n.* صَارٍ . دَقَلٌ

Master *n.* or *v. t.* سَيِّدٌ . مُعَلِّمٌ . رَئِيسٌ . غَلَبَ

Master-piece *n.* شُغْلٌ سَامٍ فِي بَابِهِ

Mastery *n.* ظَفَرٌ . تَسَلُّطٌ

Mastic *n.* عِلْكٌ . (مَصْطِكَى)

Masticate *v. t.* مَضَغَ ـَ . عَلَكَ ـُ

Mastication *n.* مَضْغٌ . عَلْكٌ

Mastiff *n.* كَلْبٌ . كَبِيرٌ . قَوِيٌّ

Mat *n.* or *v. i.* حَصِيرَةٌ . تَلَبَّدَ

Match *n.* عُودٌ كِبْرِيتِيٌّ . قَرِينٌ . سِبَاقٌ

Match *v. t.* وَفَّقَ . أَزْوَجَ

Matchless *a.* لاَ نَظِيرَ لَهُ

Mate *n.* رَفِيقٌ . قَرِينٌ . ثَانِي قُبْطَانٍ

Material *n.* or *a.* مَادَّةٌ . مَادِيٌّ

Materialism *n.* مَذْهَبُ ٱلْمَادِّيِّينَ

Materialist *n.* دَهْرِيٌّ

Materially *ad.* مَادِيًّا

Maternal *a.* أُمِّيٌّ

Maternity *n.* أُمِيَّةٌ . وَظِيفَةُ ٱلْأُمِّ

Mathematical *a.* رِيَاضِيٌّ

Mathematician *n.* عَالِمٌ بِٱلرِّيَاضِيَّاتِ

Mathematics *n. pl.* أَلْعُلُومُ ٱلرِّيَاضِيَّةُ

Matricide *n.* قَتْلُ ٱلْأُمِّ

Matriculate *v. t.* تَسَجَّلَ فِي مَدْرَسَةٍ عَالِيَةٍ

Matrimonial *a.* مُتَعَلِّقٌ بِٱلزِّيجَةِ

Matrimony *n.* أَلزِّيجَةُ

Matron *n.* شَيْخَةٌ . رَئِيسَةٌ . قَهْرَمَانَةٌ

Matted *a.* مُتَلَبِّدٌ

Matter *v. i.* هَمَّ . اغث

Matter *n.* مَادَّةٌ . هيُولَى . أمرٌ

Mattock *n.* مِعْوَلٌ ج معَاوِلُ

Mattress *n.* فِرَاشٌ

Mature *a.* or *v. i.* ناضِجٌ . بَالِغٌ . نَضَجَ

Matureness / **Maturity** } *n.* نَضْجٌ . بُلُوغٌ

Maul *v. t.* ضرَبَ شَدِيداً بعصا . جرَحَ

Mausoleum *n.* مقَامٌ . مزخرَفٌ لِمَيْتٍ

Maxim *n.* قَاعِدَةٌ . حِكْمَةٌ ج حِكَمٌ

Maximum *n.* غَايَةٌ . اعلَى دَرَجَةٍ

May *n.* or *v. i.* أَيَّارُ . (مايو) . أمْكَنَ

Mayor *n.* حَاكِمُ مَدِينَةٍ . رئِيسُ بلَدِيَةٍ

Maze *n.* إرْتِبَاكٌ . ورْطَةٌ

Mazy *a.* مُرْتَبِكٌ . مبهم

Me *pron.* ضَمِيرُ المُتَكَلِّمِ . بي . ي

Meadow *n.* مَرْجٌ . رَوْضَةٌ

Meagre *a.* هَزِيل . زَهِيدٌ . سَخِيفٌ

Meal *n.* طَحِينٌ . أَكْلَةٌ وَاحِدَةٌ

Mealy *a.* ناعِمٌ كَالطَّحِينِ

Mean *a.* حقِيرٌ . دَنِيٌّ . وَسَطٌ

Mean *v. t.* عنَى ـِ . قَصَدَ ـِ . نَوَى ـ

Meander *v. t.* إنْعَرَجَ . جرَى عِوَجاً

Meaning *n.* معنًى . مُرَاد . مَرَامٌ

Meanly *ad.* بِدَنَاءَةٍ . خِسَّةً

Meanness *n.* خسيسةٌ . دَنَاءَةٌ

Means *n. pl.* وَاسِطَةٌ . ثروَةٌ

Meantime / **Meanwhile** } *ad.* في اثْنَاءِ ذَلِكَ

Measles *n. pl.* حَصْبَةٌ (مَرَضٌ)

Measurable *a.* قَابِلُ القِيَاسِ أو الكَيْلِ

Measure *v. t.* قَاسَ . كَالَ ـِ . مَسَحَ ـَ

Measure *n.* قِيَاسٌ . كَيْلٌ . وَسِيلَةٌ

Measurement *n.* قِيَاسٌ . مِسَاحَة

Meat *n.* لَحْمٌ . طَعَامٌ

Mechanic *n.* فَاعِلٌ يَعْمَلُ بالآلاتِ

Mechanical *a.* آلِيٌّ . صِنَاعِيٌّ

Mechanics *n. pl.* عِلْمُ الحِيَلِ

Mechanism *n.*	تَرْكِيبُ آلاَتٍ
Medal *n.*	نِيشَانٌ . سِكَّةٌ تَذْكَارِيَّةٌ
Medallion *n.*	سِكَّةٌ كَبِيرَةٌ . وِسَامٌ
Meddle *v. i.*	تَطَفَّلَ . تَحَرَّشَ
Meddler *n.* / Meddlesome *a.*	مُتَحَرِّشٌ . مُتَطَفِّلٌ
Mediaeval *a.*	مِنَ الْقُرُونِ الْمُتَوَسِّطَةِ
Mediate *v. t.*	تَوَسَّطَ . تَشَفَّعَ فِي
Mediation *n.*	شَفَاعَةٌ . تَوَسُّطٌ
Mediator *a.*	وَسِيطٌ . شَفِيعٌ
Medical *a.*	طِبِّيٌّ
Medicate *v. t.*	خَلَطَ بِعَقَاقِيرَ . عَالَجَ
Medicinal *a.*	عِلاَجِيٌّ . دَوَائِيٌّ
Medicine *n.*	دَوَاءٌ . عِلاَجٌ
Mediocre *a.*	وَسَطٌ أَوْ أَقَلُّ مِنْهُ
Mediocrity *n.*	إِعْتِدَالٌ . قِلَّةٌ
Meditate *v. t.* or *i.*	تَأَمَّلَ . تَفَكَّرَ . نَوَى
Meditation *n.*	تَأَمُّلٌ . تَفَكُّرٌ
Mediterranean *n.*	اَلْبَحْرُ الْمُتَوَسِّطُ

Medium *n.*	وَاسِطَةٌ . وَسَطٌ . وَسِيطٌ
Medley *n.*	خَلِيطٌ . عَدَمُ نِظَامٍ
Meek *a.*	وَدِيعٌ . حَلِيمٌ . لَطِيفٌ . طَائِعٌ
Meekness *n.*	وَدَاعَةٌ . حِلْمٌ
Meet *v. t.* or *i.*	لَقِيَ . إِلْتَقَى . إِجْتَمَعَ
Meet *a.*	لاَئِقٌ . مُوَافِقٌ
Meeting *n.*	إِجْتِمَاعٌ . مَجْمَعٌ . لِقَاءٌ
Melancholy *n.*	غَمٌّ . سَوْدَاءُ
Meliorate *v.t.*	حَسَّنَ . أَصْلَحَ
Melioration *n.*	تَحْسِينٌ
Mellow *a.*	نَاضِجٌ . لَيِّنٌ . رَخْوٌ
Mellow *v. t.* or *i.*	نَضِجَ . نَضَّجَ
Melodious *a.*	مُطْرِبٌ . رَخِيمٌ
Melody *n.*	حُسْنُ الأَلْحَانِ . إِيقَاعُهَا
Melon *n.*	جَبَسٌ . بَطِّيخٌ
Melt *v. t.* or *i.*	أَذَابَ . ذَابَ
Member *n.*	عُضْوٌ . جُزْءٌ
Membership *n.*	عَضْوِيَّةٌ

Membrane *n.* غِشَاءٌ . نَسِيجٌ

Membranaceous / **Membranous** *a.* غِشَائِيٌّ

Memento *a.* تَذْكِرَةٌ

Memoir *n.* تَرْجَمَةٌ . تَقْرِيرٌ

Memorable *a.* مُسْتَحِقُّ ٱلذِّكْرِ

Memorialize *v. t.* قدم عَرْضَ حَالٍ إِلَى

Memorandum *n.* تَذْكِرَةٌ . مُفَكِّرَةٌ

Memorial *n.* or *a.* تَذْكِرَةٌ . تَقْرِيرٌ لِلتَّذْكَارِ

Memorize *v. t.* حَفِظَ . غَيَّبَ

Memory *n.* ذِكْرٌ . الذَّاكِرَةُ . الحَافِظَةُ

Menace *v. t.* or *n.* هَدَّدَ . تَوَعَّدَ . وَعِيدٌ

Menagerie *n.* مَعْرِضُ ٱلْحَيَوَانَاتِ

Mend *v. t.* or *i.* أَصْلَحَ . رَقَّعَ . تحسن

Mendacious *a.* كَاذِبٌ

Mendacity *n.* كِذْبٌ

Mendicancy / **Mendicity** *n.* تَسَوُّلٌ . شِحَاذَة

Mendicant *n.* شَحَّاذ . متسوّل

Menial *a.* or *n.* دَنِيٌّ . ذَلِيلٌ . اجِيرٌ

Menses *n. pl.* / **Menstruation** *n.* حَيْضٌ ، طَمْثٌ

Menstrual *a.* حَيضِيٌّ . شَهْرِيٌّ

Menstruate *v. i.* حَاضَتْ . طَمِثَتْ

Mensuration *n.* قِيَاسٌ . مِسَاحَةٌ

Mental *a.* عَقْلِيٌّ . ذِهْنِيٌّ

Mention *n.* or *v. t.* ذِكْرٌ . ذَكَرَ

Mercantile *a.* تِجَارِيٌّ

Mercenary *a.* or *n.* مُسْتَأْجَرٌ . طَمَّاعٌ

Merchandise *n.* بَضَائِعُ . تِجَارَةٌ

Merchant *a.* تَاجِرٌ

Merchantman *n.* سَفِينَةٌ تِجَارِيَّةٌ

Merciful *a.* رَحِيمٌ . رَؤُوفٌ

Merciless *a.* عَدِيمُ ٱلرَّحْمَةِ . صَارِمٌ

Mercurial *a.* زِئْبَقِيٌّ . حَادُّ ٱلطَّبْعِ

Mercury *n.* زِئْبَقٌ . عُطَارِدُ (سَيَّارٌ)

Mercy *n.* رَحْمَةٌ . رَأْفَةٌ

Mere *a.* مُجَرَّدٌ . خَالِصٌ

Merely *ad.* فَقَطْ . لَا غَيْرُ

Merge *v. t.* or *i.* غَطَسَ. إِخْتَفَى فِي

Meridian *n.* نِصْفُ ٱلنهارِ وَخَطُّهُ

Merit *n.* or *v. t.* فَضْلٌ. إِسْتِحْقَاقٌ. إِسْتَحَقَّ

Merited *a.* مُسْتَحِقٌ. مُسْتَوْجِبٌ

Meritorious *a.* مُسْتَحِقٌّ ٱلثَّنَاءَ أَوِ ٱلثَّوابِ

Merriment *n.* فَرَحٌ. طَرَبٌ. إِنْبِسَاط

Merry *a.* فَرِحٌ. طَرِبٌ

Mesmerism *n.* تَنْوِيمٌ إِصْطِنَاعِيٌّ

Mess *n.* طَبْخَةٌ. حِصَّةٌ. خَلْطٌ

Message *n.* رِسَالَةٌ. بَلاغٌ

Messenger *n.* رَسُولٌ. سَاعٍ

Messiah *n.* أَلْمَسِيحُ

Metal *a.* مَعْدِنٌ

Metallic *n.* مَعْدِنِيٌّ

Metallurgy *n.* عِلْمُ ٱلْمَعَادِنِ

Metaphor *n.* إِسْتِعَارَةٌ. مَجَاز

Metaphorical / Metaphoric } *a.* إِسْتِعَارِيٌّ مَجَازِيٌّ

Metaphysical *a.* مُخْتَصٌّ بِعِلْمِ ٱلْمَعْقُولَاتِ

Metaphysician *n.* عَالِمٌ بِٱلْمَعْقُولَاتِ

Metaphysics *n.* عِلْمُ مَاوَرَاءَ ٱلطبيعةِ

Mete *v. t.* قَاسَ. كَالَ ـِ

Meteor *n.* شِهَابٌ

Meteorite / Meteorolite } *n.* حَجَرٌ مِنَ ٱلْجَوِّ نيزكٌ

Meteorology *n.* علمُ ٱلظَّوَاهِرِ ٱلْجَوِّيَّة

Meter *n.* مِقْيَاسُ ٱلْمَاءِ وَٱلْغَازِ

Metre *n.* مِتْرٌ. وَزْنُ ٱلشِّعْرِ

Method *n.* طَرِيقَةٌ. اسْلُوبٌ. نِظَامٌ

Methodic / Methodical } *a.* بِتَرْتِيبٍ. بِنِظَامٍ

Metrical *a.* مَوْزُونٌ. نَظْمِيٌّ

Metropolis *n.* عَاصِمَةُ بِلَادٍ

Metropolitan *n.* مطرانٌ مُخْتَصٌّ بِقَصَبَةٍ

Mettle *n.* مُرُوءَةٌ. نَخْوَةٌ. نَشَاطٌ

Mew *v. i.* مَاءَ كَالْقِطِّ. نَوَّى

Miasma *n.* أَبْخِرَةٌ سَامَّةٌ

Mice *n.* (*pl.* of Mouse). فِيرانٌ

Microscope *n.* مِجْهَرٌ. (مِكْرُسْكُوبٌ)

Midday *n.* نِصفُ ٱلنَّهارِ. مُنتَصَفُهُ
Middle *a.* or *n.* مُنتَصَفٌ أَوسَطُ. وسَطٌ
Middling *a.* متوَسِّط. بَيْنَ بَيْن
Midnight *n.* مُنتَصَفُ ٱللَّيْلِ
Midriff *n.* الحِجابُ ٱلحاجِزُ
Midshipman *n.* ضابِطٌ صغيرٌ في بارِجةٍ
Midst *n.* وَسَطٌ
Midway *n.* مُنتَصَفُ ٱلمَسافة
Midwife *n.* قابِلَةٌ ج قَوابِلُ. (دايَةٌ)
Midwifery *n.* قِبالَة
Mien *n.* هَيئَةٌ. طَلْعَةٌ
Might *n.* قُوَّةٌ. بأسٌ. شِدَّةٌ
Mightily *ad.* بِشِدَّةٍ. جِدًّا
Mighty *a.* قَوِيٌّ. قَدِيرٌ. عزِيزٌ
Migrate *v. i.* هاجَرَ. إِنتَقَلَ
Migration *n.* مُهاجَرَةٌ. إِنتِقالٌ
Migratory *a.* راحِلٌ. مُتَنَقِّلٌ
Mild *a.* لطِيفٌ. حَليمٌ. معتَدِلٌ

Mildew *n.* عَفُونَةٌ
Mildness *n.* لطفٌ. حِلمٌ. رِقَّةٌ
Mile *n.* مِيلٌ ج أَمْيالٌ
Militant *a.* مُحارِبٌ. مُجاهِدٌ
Military *a.* حَرْبِيٌّ. عَسْكَرِيٌّ
Militia *n.* جُنْدُ ٱلرَّدِيفِ
Milk *n.* or *v. t.* حُلِيبٌ. لَبَنٌ. حَلَبَ ـُ
Milkyway *n.* المَجَرَّةُ
Mill *n.* or *v. t.* مِطْحَنَةٌ. معمَلٌ. طَحَنَ ـَ
Millennium *n.* ألفُ سَنةٍ
Miller *n.* طَحَّانٌ
Millet *n.* ذُرَةٌ
Milliner *n.* خَيَّاطَةُ لِباسِ ٱلنِّساءِ
Millinery *n.* ملبُوساتُ ٱلنِّساءِ
Million *n.* ألفُ ألفٍ. مَليُونٌ
Millionaire *n.* وافِرُ ٱلغِنَى
Millstone *n.* حجرُ طاحونٍ. رحى
Milt *n.* طِحال

Mimic *n.* or *v. t.* مُقَلِّد . قَلَّدَ هزلاً

Minaret *n.* مِأذَنة ج مآذن

Mince *v. t.* or *i.* قرَّطَ . (فرَمَ) تَخَطَّرَ

Mind *n.* عَقْل . ذِهْن . نِيَّة

Mind *v. t.* بالى بِهِ . إِكْتَرَثَ . إِعْتَنَى

Minded *a.* مُتَفَكِّر . مَائل إلى

Mindful *a.* مُبالٍ . مُكْتَرِثٌ . مُعْتَن

Mine *pron.* or *n.* لي . مَعْدِن . لُغْمٌ

Miner *n.* صَانِعٌ فِي مَنَاجِمَ

Mineral *n.* or *a.* جَمَاد . جَمَادِيٌّ

Mineralogist *n.* عَالِمٌ بِالْجَمَادَاتِ

Mineralogy *n.* عِلْمُ ٱلْجَمَادِ وَٱلْمَعَادِنِ

Mingle *v. t.* or *i.* خَلَطَ ـِ مَرَجَ ـُ . إِمْتَزَجَ

Miniature *n.* صُورَةٌ . صَغِيرَةٌ

Minimum *n.* الأَقَلُّ . أَقَلُّ مِقْدَارٍ

Mining *n.* مُعَالَجَةُ ٱلْمَعَادِنِ او ٱللغوم

Minister *v.t.* خَدَمَ ـُ . امَدَّ . قَدَّمَ لِ

Minister *n.* خَادِمٌ قِسِّيسٌ . سَفِيرٌ . وَزِيرٌ

Ministerial *a.* قُسُوسِيٌّ . وَزِيرِيٌّ

Ministration *n.* خِدْمَة

Ministry *n.* خِدْمَة . وِزَارَة

Minor *a.* اصْغَرُ عُمْراً . قَاصِرٌ . اصغر

Minority *n.* ٱلْعَدَدُ ٱلاقل . سِنُّ ٱلْقُصُورِ

Minstrel *n.* مُغَنٍّ . عَوَّاد

Mint *n.* مَضْرِبُ نُقُودٍ . نَعْنَعٌ

Minuend *n.* ٱلْمَطْرُوحُ مِنْهُ

Minus *a.* عَلامَةُ ٱلطَّرْحِ (—) . إِلاَّ

Minute *n.* دَقِيقَةٌ . تَذْكِرَةٌ

Minute *a.* دَقِيق . مُدَقَّق

Minutely *ad.* بِدِقَّةٍ . بِضَبْطٍ

Minuteness *n.* دِقَّةٌ . صِغَرٌ

Miracle *n.* آيَةٌ . مُعْجِزَةٌ . عَجِيبَةٌ

Miraculous *a.* عَجِيبٌ . خَارِقُ ٱلْعَادَةِ

Mirage *n.* سَرَابٌ . لَعْلَعٌ

Mire *n.* وَحْلٌ . حَمَاةٌ

Mirror *n.* مِرْآة ج مَرَايَا

Mirth *n.* فَرَحٌ . سُرُورٌ. طَرَبٌ

Mirthful *a.* طَرِبٌ . فَرِحٌ

Miry *a.* ذُو وَحلٍ

Misanthrope *n.* }
Misanthropic *a.* } مُبْغِضُ ٱلْبَشَرِ

Misanthropy *n.* بُغضُ ٱلْبَشَرِ .وَحْشَةٌ

Misapplication *n.* سُوءُ ٱلاِسْتِعْمَالِ

Misapply *v. t.* أَسَاءَ ٱلاِسْتِعْمَالَ

Misapprehend *v. t.* أَسَاءَ ٱلْفَهْمَ

Misapprehension *n.* سُوءُ ٱلْفَهْمِ

Misbehave *v. i.* أَسَاءَ ٱلتصرُّف

Misbehaviour *n.* سُوءُ ٱلتَّصرُّفِ

Misbelief *n.* إِعتِقَادٌ . فَاسِدٌ

Misbelieve *v. t.* أَسَاءَ ٱلاِعْتِقَادَ

Miscalculate *v. t.* أَساءَ ٱلْحِسَابَ

Miscarriage *n.* خَيبَةٌ .إِسْقَاطُ ٱلْجَنِينِ

Miscarry *v. i.* خَابَ ـِ . اسقَطَتْ

Miscellaneous *a.* مُتَنَوِّعٌ . شَتَّى

Miscellany *n.* مَجْمُوعُ أَشيَاءَ . شَتَّى

Mischance *n.* مُصِيبَةٌ

Mischief *n.* ضَرَرٌ. سُوءٌ . شَرٌّ

Mischievous *a.* مُضِرٌّ .مُسِيءٌ .مُكَدِّرٌ

Misconceive *v. t.* أَسَاءَ ٱلْفَهْمَ. غَلِطَ ـَ

Misconception *n.* سُوءُ ٱلْمَفْهُومِيَةِ . غَلَطٌ

Misconduct *n.* سُوءُ ٱلتَّصَرُّفِ

Misconstrue *v.t.* سَاءَ ٱلتَّاوِيلَ . حَرَّفَ

Miscount *v. t.* غلطَ فِي ٱلْعَدِّ

Miscreant *n.* كَافِرٌ .شِرِّيرٌ .فَاجِرٌ

Misdate *v. t.* أَرَّخَ غَلَطًا

Misdeed *n.* فِعلٌ شِرِّيرٌ .سَيِّئَةٌ

Misdemeanor *n.* سُوءُ ٱلسِّيرَةِ . ذَنْبٌ

Misdirect *v. t.* أَرْشَدَ او عَنْوَنَ خَطَأً

Misdoing *n.* إِسَاءَةٌ . خَطِيئَةٌ

Miser *n.* }
Miserly *a.* } بَخِيلٌ . شَحِيحٌ

Miserable *a.* تَعِيس شَقِيٌّ .مِسكِينٌ

Misery *n.* مَسْكَنَةٌ . شقَاءٌ . تَعَاسَةٌ

Misfortune *n.* مُصِيبَةٌ . بَلِيَّةٌ . نَكْبَةٌ

Misgiving *n.* ريبة . قلق النفس

Misgovern *v. t.* أساء السياسة

Misgovernment *n.* سوء الإدارة

Misguide *v. t.* اساء الإرشاد. اضل

Mishap *n.* مصيبة . نازلة

Misinform *v.t.* اخبر بغير الواقع

Misinterpret *v. t.* أساء التفسير

Misjudge *v. t.* اخطأ في الحكم

Mislay *v. t.* وضع في غير محله

Mislead *v. t.* أضل . اغوى

Mismanagement *n.* سوء التدبير

Misname *v. t.* اخطأ في التسمية

Misnomer *n.* إسم في غير محله

Misplace *v. t.* وضع في غير محله

Misprint *n.* غلط في الطبع

Mispronounce *v. t.* غلط في اللفظ

Mispronunciation *n.* خطا في اللفظ

Misquote *v. t.* اخطأ في الإقتباس

Misrepresent *v. t.* حرف كلامه. موه

Misrule *n.* سوء السياسة والحكم

Miss *n.* فتاة . إخطاء

Miss *v. t.* اخطأ لم يصب . اعوزه

Misshaped / **Misshapen** *a.* مشوه. قبيح الخلقة

Missile *n.* مرماة

Missing *a.* مفقود. ضائع

Mission *n.* إرسالية . جماعة مرسلة

Missionary *n.* مرسل . مبشر

Missive *n.* رسالة

Misspell *v. t.* أخطأ في التهجئة

Misspend *v. t.* صرف باطلا

Misstatement *n.* تحريف. تمويه

Mist *n.* or *v. i.* ضباب رذاذ . ارذ

Mistake *n.* or *v. t.* خطأ . سهو . اخطأ

Mistaken *a.* مخطئ

Mister *n.* سيد . افندي . خواجا

Mistranslate *v. t.* اخطأ في الترجمة

Mistress *n.* سَيِّدَةٌ . مُعَلِّمَةٌ . سرِّيةٌ
Mistrust *n.* or *v. t.* عدم ثِقَةٍ . شَكَّ في
Mistrustful *a.* عَدِيمُ ٱلثِّقَة
Misty *a.* ذُو ضَبَاب . ضَبابِيٌّ
Misunderstand *v. t.* اساءَ ٱلْفَهْمَ
Misunderstanding *n.* سُوءُ فَهْمٍ . خِلاَفٌ
Misuse *v. t.* or *n.* أَسَاءَ ٱلاَسْتِعْمَالَ
Mite *n.* شَيْءٌ يَسِيرٌ . فِلسٌ . سُوَيْسَةٌ
Mitre *n.* تَاجُ اسْقُفٍ أَوْ قَلَنْسُوَتُهُ
Mitigate *v. t.* خَفَّضَ . خَفَّفَ . لَيَّنَ
Mitten *n.* كَفٌّ بِلاَ اصَابِعٍ
Mix *v. t.* or *i.* مَزَجَ . إِمْتَزَجَ
Mixture *n.* مَزِيجٌ
Moan *v. i.* or *n.* انَّ ـِ . أَنِينٌ
Moat *n.* خَنْدَقُ تَحْصِينٍ
Mob *n.* or *v. t.* الاوْبَاشُ . قَامَ ٱلاوْبَاشُ عَلَيْهِ
Mobile *a.* سَهْلُ ٱلْحَرَكَةِ اوْ ٱلتَّغيُّر
Mobility *n.* سُهُولَةُ ٱلحَرَكَةِ . خِفَّةٌ

Mobilize *v. t.* عبَّأَ (جيْشًا) لِلْحَرْب
Mock *v. t.* or *a.* هزأ ـَ . سَخِرَ ـَ . مُصنَعٌ
Mockery *n.* هزْءٌ . سُخْرَةٌ
Mode *n.* كَيْفِيَّةٌ . أُسْلُوبٌ . عادَةٌ
Model *n.* or *v. t.* نموذَجٌ مِثَالٌ عَمِلَ على ٱلرَّسْمِ
Moderate *a.* or *v. t.* مُعْتَدِلٌ . خَفَّفَ . خَفَّضَ
Moderation *n.* إِعْتِدَالٌ . ضَبْطُ ٱلنَّفْسِ
Modern *a.* حَدِيثٌ . مُتَأَخِّرٌ
Modest *a.* مُحْتَشِمٌ . حَيِيٌّ . مُعْتَدِلٌ
Modesty *n.* حِشْمَةٌ . حَيَاءٌ
Modification *n.* تَغْيِيرٌ . نَوْعٌ
Modify *v. t.* غَيَّرَ صِفَاتِهِ . نَوَّعَ
Modulate *v. t.* اوْقَعَ عَلَى وَزْنٍ
Mohammedan *n.* or *a.* مُسْلِمٌ . إِسْلاَمِيٌّ
Moiety *n.* نِصْفٌ
Moist *a.* رطبٌ . مُنَدًّى
Moisten *v. t.* رَطَّبَ . نَدَّى . ثَرَّى
Moisture *n.* رُطُوبَةٌ . نَدًى

Molasses *n. pl.* دِبْسُ سُكَّرٍ

Mold / **Mould** *n.* or *v. i.* or *t.* عَفَنٌ. قَالِبٌ. تعَفَّنَ. صَبَّ فِي قَالِبٍ

Moldy / **Mouldy** *a.* متعفِّنٌ

Molder / **Moulder** *v.i.* إِنْحَلَّ. بَلِيَ

Mole *n.* خَالٌ. خُلْدٌ. سَدٌّ فِي ٱلْبَحْرِ

Molecule *a.* ذَرَّةٌ

Molest *v. t.* كَدَّرَ. ازْعجَ

Mollify *v. t.* لَيَّنَ. طَيَّبَ الخَاطِرِ

Molten *a.* ذَائِبٌ. مسْبُوكٌ

Moment *n.* دَقِيقَةٌ. أَهَمِّيَّةٌ

Momentary *a.* لِلَحْظَةٍ. وَقْتِيٌّ

Momentous *n.* مُهِمٌّ جِدًّا. خَطِيرٌ

Momentum *n.* قُوَّةُ ٱلإِنْدِفَاعِ

Monarch *n.* مَلِكٌ. سُلْطَانٌ

Monarchical *a.* مَلَكِيٌّ

Monarchy *n.* مَمْلَكَةٌ. مَلَكِيَّةٌ

Monastery *n.* دَيْرٌ ج أَدْيِرَةٌ

Monastic *a.* رَهْبَانِيٌّ. نَسَكِيٌّ

Monday *n.* يَوْمُ ٱلاِثْنَيْنِ

Money *n.* دَرَاهِمُ. نُقُودٌ

Moneyed *a.* ذُو مَالٍ. غَنِيٌّ

Mongrel *a.* or *n.* نَغْلٌ. خِلَاسِيٌّ

Monition *n.* إِنْذَارٌ. إِنْبَاءٌ. تَنْبِيهٌ

Monitor *n.* مُنْذِرٌ. عَرِيفٌ

Monk *n.* رَاهِبٌ. نَاسِكٌ

Monkey *n.* قِرْدٌ. (سَعْدَانٌ)

Monogamy *n.* زَوَاجٌ بِٱمْرَأَةٍ وَاحِدَةٍ

Monogram *n.* طُغْرَاءُ

Monomaniac *a.* مَجْنُونٌ فِي أَمْرٍ وَاحِدٍ

Monopolize *v. t.* إِحْتَكَرَ. خَصَّصَ لِنَفْسِهِ

Monopoly *n.* إِحْتِكَارٌ. إِمْتِيَازٌ فِي أَمْرٍ

Monosyllable *n.* لَفْظَةٌ مِنْ مَقْطَعٍ وَاحِدٍ

Monotheism *n.* التَّوْحِيدُ

Monotonous *a.* مُمِلٌّ. بَارِدٌ

Monotony *n.* عَدَمُ تغَيُّرٍ او تَنَوُّعٍ

Monster *n.* وَحْشٌ غَرِيبُ ٱلْخِلْقَةِ

Month *n.* شَهْرٌ ج اشْهُرٌ وَشُهُورٌ

Monthly *a.* شَهْرِيٌّ

Monument *a.* بِنَاءٌ لِلتَّذْكَارِ. ضَرِيحٌ

Monumental *a.* تَذْكَارِيٌّ

Mood *n.* حَالَةٌ. مِنْوَالٌ. صِيغَةُ فِعْلٍ

Moody *a.* مَهْمُومٌ. مَغْمُومٌ. نَكِدٌ

Moon *n.* قَمَرٌ ج اقْمَارٌ

Moonshine *n.* ضَوْءُ ٱلْقَمَرِ. تَظَاهُرٌ

Moor *v.t.* or *n.* رَبَطَ سَفِينَةً. مَغْرِبِيٌّ

Moorings *n. pl.* رُبُطُ ٱلسَّفِينَةِ

Mop *n.* or *v. t.* مِمْسَحَةٌ. مَسَحَ ـُ بِهَا

Mope *v. i.* مَلَّ ـَ. ضَجِرَ ـَ

Moral *a.* أَدَبِيٌّ. فَاضِلٌ. مُسْتَقِيمٌ

Moral *n.* مَغْزًى مَثَلٍ اوْ مَقْصِدُهُ

Morality *n.* إِسْتِقَامَةُ ٱلسِّيرَةِ. فَضِيلَةٌ

Moralize *v. t.* فَسَّرَ بِمَعْنًى أَدَبِيٍّ

Morally *ad.* أَدَبِيًّا

Morals *n. pl.* الآدَابُ. صِفَاتٌ ادَبِيَّةٌ

Morass *n.* مُسْتَنْقَعٌ. سَبْخَةٌ

Morbid *a.* سَقِيمٌ. وَبِيلٌ. مُغَيِّمٌ

More *a.* or *ad.* اكْثَرُ. ازْيَدُ

Moreover *ad.* ايضًا. ثُمَّ

Morn / **Morning** } *n.* صَبَاحٌ. صُبْحٌ

Morose *a.* عَبُوسٌ. نَكِدٌ

Moroseness *n.* عُبُوسَةٌ. شَرَاسَةٌ

Morrow *n.* غَدٌ. بُكْرَةٌ

Morsel *n.* لُقْمَةٌ. قِطْعَةٌ. صَغِيرَةٌ

Mortal *a.* مَائِتٌ. فَانٍ. قَاتِلٌ

Mortals *n. pl.* بَشَرٌ

Mortality *n.* مَوْتٌ. هَلَاكٌ

Mortally *ad.* لِلْمَوْتِ. مُمِيتًا

Mortar *n.* طِينٌ. هَاوُنٌ. مَدْفَعٌ قَصِيرٌ

Mortgage *n.* or *v.t.* رَهْنٌ. رَهَنَ ـَ

Mortification *n.* فَسَادٌ. قَهْرٌ. خَجَلٌ

Mortify *v. i.* or *t.* فَسَدَ ـُ. أَذَلَّ. قَمَعَ ـَ

Mosaic *n.* or *a.* فُسَيفسَاء . فُسَيفسِيٌّ

Moslem *n.* مُسلمٌ

Mosque *n.* جَامِعٌ . مسْجِدٌ

Mosquito *n.* نَامُوسَةٌ . بعوضةٌ

Moss *n.* طُحلبٌ . اشْنَةٌ

Most *a.* أَكْثَرُ . ألاكْثَرُ

Mote *n.* قَذًى . هَبْوَةٌ

Moth *n.* فَرَاشَةٌ . عُثَّةٌ

Mother *n.* امٌّ . والِدَةٌ

Mother-in-law *n.* حَمَاةٌ

Motion *n.* or *v. i.* حَرَكَةٌ . أشَارَ إِلَى

Motive *n.* بَاعِثٌ . داعٍ . مُوجِبٌ

Motley *a.* مُلَوَّنٌ . مُتَنَوِّعٌ

Motor *n.* مُحرِّكٌ

Mottled *a.* كَثِيرُ ٱلبُقَعِ ٱلمُلَوَّنَةِ

Motto *n.* عِبَارَةٌ عُنْوَانِيَّةٌ . شِعَارٌ

Mould *etc.* *see* Mold *etc.*

Mound *n.* اكَمَةٌ . تَلٌّ . مِتْرَاسٌ

Mount *n.* or *v. t.* جَبَلٌ . صَعِدَ ـَ . رَكِبَ ـَ

Mountain *n.* or *a.* جبَلٌ . جَبَلِيٌّ

Mountaineer *n.* سَاكِنُ الجَبَلِ

Mountainous *a.* كَثِيرُ ٱلجِبَالِ

Mountebank *a.* مُشَعْبِذٌ . دجالٌ

Mourn *v. i.* or *t.* نَاحَ ـُ . حَزِنَ

Mourner *n.* نَائِحٌ . نَادِبٌ . حَزِينٌ

Mournful *a.* مُحزِنٌ . مُكْرِبٌ

Mourning *n.* نَوْحٌ . حُزْنٌ . حِدَادٌ

Mouse *n.* (*pl.* Mice). فَارَةٌ ج فِيرَانٌ

Moustache *n.* شَارِبٌ ج شَوَارِبُ

Mouth *n.* فَمٌ . فُوهٌ . مَدْخَلٌ

Mouthful *n.* لُقْمَةٌ ج لُقَمٌ . اكْلَةٌ

Mouthpiece *n.* فَمُ ٱلمزمَارِ وَمَا اشْبَهَ . نَائِبٌ فِي ٱلكَلَامِ

Movable *a.* مِمَا يُحَرَّكُ اوْ يُنْقَلُ

Movables *n. pl.* بِضَائِعُ . اثَاثٌ

Move *v. t.* or *i.* نَقَلَ . حَرَّكَ . تَحَرَّكَ

Movement *n.* حَرَكَةٌ . تَحْرِيكٌ

Mow *v. t.* or *n.* حَشَّ ـِ . كُدْسٌ

Much *a.* or *ad.* كَثِيرٌ. وَافِرٌ. كَثِيرًا

Mucilage *n.* لُعَابٌ . صَمْغٌ ذَائِبٌ

Mucous *a.* مُخَاطِيٌّ

Mucus *n.* مُخَاطٌ

Mud *n.* وَحَلٌ .طِينٌ . حمأَةٌ

Muddle *v. t.* or *n.* عكَّرَ. شوَّش . إِرتِبَاكٌ

Muddy *a.* ذُوْ وَحَل

Muff *n.* فَرْوَةٌ لِلْيَدَيْنِ

Muffle *v. t.* سَتَرَ ـُ . لَفَّ ـُ . خَمرَ

Mug *n.* كُوزٌ. قَدَحٌ . إِبْرِيقٌ

Mulatto *n.* خِلاَسِيٌّ

Mulberry *n.* تُوتٌ . تُوتَة

Mule *n.* بَغْلٌ ج بِغَالٌ

Muleteer *n.* بَغَّالٌ . مُكَارٍ

Mulish *a.* عَنِيدٌ كَالبَغْلِ

Multiform *a.* مُتَعَدِّدُ ٱلْهَيْئَةِ

Multiple *n.* عَدَدٌ يُقْسَمُ عَلَى غَيْرِهِ بِلاَ بَاقٍ

Multiplicand *n.* أَلْمَضْرُوبُ (عَدَدٌ)

Multiplication *n.* أَلضَرْبُ. تَكْثِيرٌ

Multiplicity *n.* تَضَاعُفٌ . تعدُّدٌ

Multiplier *n.* أَلْمَضْرُوبُ فِيهِ

Multiply *v. t.* كَثَّرَ . ضَرب إِزْدَادَ

Multitude *n.* جُمْهُورٌ . فَوْجٌ

Mumble *v. t.* هَمَسَ ـِ دَنْدَنَ

Mummery *n.* سُخْرَةٌ . مُجُونٌ

Mummy *n.* جُثَّةٌ مُحَنطَةٌ

Mumps *n. pl.* إِلتِهَابُ ٱلْغُدَةِ ٱلنَّكفِيَةِ

Munch *v. t.* or *i.* مَضغَ ـِ لاَكَ ـُ

Municipal *a.* بَلَدِي

Municipality *n.* بَلَدِيَّةٌ . إِدَارَةُ مَدِينَةٍ

Mundane *a.* عَالَمِيٌّ . دُنْيَوِيٌّ

Munificence *n.* سَخَاءٌ . كَرَمٌ

Munificent *a.* جَوَّادٌ . كَرِيمٌ جِدًّا

Munitions *n. pl.* ذَخَائِرُ حَرْبِيَةٌ

Mural *a.* حَائِطِيٌّ . سُورِيٌّ جِدَارِيٌّ

Murder *n.* or *v. t.* قَتْلٌ . قَتَلَ ـَ

Murderer *n.* قَاتِل

Murderous *a.* مُهْلِكٌ . قَاصِد ٱلْقَتْلِ

Murky *a.* مظْلِمٌ . كَدِرٌ (هَوَآءٌ)

Murmur *v. i.* or *n.* تَذَمَّرَ . دَنْدَنَ

Murrain *n.* وَبَا ٱلْمَوَاشِي

Muscle *n.* عَضَلَةٌ . صَدَفٌ

Muscular *a.* عَضَلِيٌّ

Muse *n.* or *v. t.* إِلَاهَةُ ٱلشّعْرِ . تأَملَ

Museum *n.* مَعْرِضُ ٱلتُّحَفِ . مَتْحَفٌ

Mushroom *n.* فطر

Music *n.* صِنَاعَةُ ٱلالحَانِ . موسِيقى

Musical *a.* مُوسِيقِيٌّ . مطرِبٌ

Musician *n.* عَالِمٌ بِٱلْمُوسِيقى

Musk *n.* مِسْك

Musket *n.* بُنْدُقِيَّةٌ . بَارُودَةٌ

Muskmelon *n.* شَمَّامٌ . بِطِّيخٌ اصفَرُ

Muslin *n.* نَسِيجٌ رَقِيقٌ . شَاشٌ

Mussulman *n.* مُسْلِمٌ

Must *v. i.* (*aux.*) يَجِبُ . يَنْبَغِي

Mustard *n.* خَرْدَلٌ

Muster *v. t.* or *i.* حَشَدَ ـُ ـِ . جَمَعَ ـَ . إِجْتَمَعَ

Muster *n.* حَشْدُ ٱلْعَسَاكِرِ . دَفْتَرُهُمْ

Musty *a.* عَفِنٌ . فَاسِدٌ

Mutability *n.* عَدَمُ ثَبَاتٍ او بَقَآءٍ

Mutable *a.* مُتَغَيِّرٌ . مُتَقَلِّبٌ

Mute *a.* or *n.* صَامِتٌ . أَخْرَسُ

Mutilate *v. t.* جَدَعَ ـَ . جَذَمَ ـُ

Mutineer *n.* / Mutinous *a.* } عَاصٍ . ثَائِرٌ . مُتَمَرِّدٌ

Mutiny *n.* عِصْيَانٌ . ثَوْرَةٌ . فِتْنَةٌ

Mutter *v. t.* هَمَسَ ـِ . دَمْدَمَ

Muttering *n.* هَمْسٌ . دَمْدَمَةٌ

Mutton *n.* لَحْمُ ضَأْنٍ

Mutual *a.* مُشْتَرِكٌ . مُتَبَادِلٌ

Mutually *ad.* إِشْتِرَاكًا . تَبَادُلاً

Muzzle *v. t.* or *n.* كَمَّ ـُ . كِمَامٌ . فَمٌ

Myriad *n.*	رَبْوَةٌ . عَدَدٌ عظِيمٌ	Mystery *n.*	سِرٌّ . لُغْزٌ
Myrrh *n.*	مُرٌّ	Mystic *a.* or *n.* / Mystical *a.*	غامِض . خفيٌّ . صُوفِيٌّ
Myrtle *n.*	آسٌ	Mystify *v. t.*	حَيَّر وَخاتَل
Myself *pron.*	نفسِي . ذاتِي	Myth *n.*	خُرافةٌ . حِكايَةٌ
Mysterious *a.*	غرِيب . سِرِّيٌّ	Mythology *n.*	علمُ الخُرافاتِ . مجمُوعها

N

Nag *n.* or *v. t.*	حِصَانٌ صَغِيرٌ . نَكد	Nap *n.*	نَوْمَةٌ قَصِيرَةٌ . زَغْبَرٌ
Nail *n.* or *v. t.*	مِسمَارٌ . ظُفرٌ . سمَّرَ	Nape *n.*	قفا العُنُقِ
Naive *a.*	مُخلِصٌ . صَافِي القلْبِ	Napkin *n.*	فُوطَةٌ . مِنشَفَةٌ
Naked *a.*	عُرْيَانٌ . مَكشُوفٌ	Narcotic *a.*	مُخدِرٌ . مُنَوِّمٌ
Nakedness *n.*	عرْيٌ . عوْرَةٌ	Narrate *v. t.*	حدَّثَ . قصَّ . روى
Name *n.* or *v. t.*	إِسْمٌ . سَمَّى . ذكَرَ	Narration / Narrative *n.*	حَدِيثٌ . قِصةٌ . رِوايةٌ
Nameless *a.*	بلا اسْمٍ . مَجْهُولٌ	Narrator *n.*	مُحدِثٌ . رَاوٍ
Namely *ad.*	أَي . يعْنِي	Narrow *a.*	ضَيِّقٌ . مَحصُورٌ
Namesake *n.*	سميٌّ	Narrow *v. t.* or *i.*	ضَيَّقَ . تَضَيَّقَ

Nasal *a.* انفيٌّ . اغنُّ

Nasty *a.* وَسِخٌ . قذِرٌ . قبيحٌ

Natal *a.* وَطنيٌّ . موْلِدي

Nation *n.* أمَّةٌ . شعْبٌ

National *a.* اممي . وطنيٌّ

Nationality *n.* وَطنيةٌ . جنْسِيةٌ

Native *a.* وَطنيٌّ . أهليٌّ

Nativity *a.* موْلِدٌ . ولادَةٌ

Natural *a.* طَبيعيٌّ . فِطْريٌّ . خَلقيٌّ

Naturalist *n.* عالِمٌ بالطبيعيات

Naturalize *v. t.* ضمَّ إلى تبعية دوْلة

Naturalness *n.* طَبيعيةٌ . عدَمُ تصنعٍ

Nature *n.* ألطَّبيعةُ . خليقةٌ . ماهيةٌ

Naught *n.* لا شيءٌ . بطْلٌ . عدمٌ

Naughtiness *n.* تمرُّدٌ . رَدَاءةٌ . شرٌّ

Naughty *a.* متمرِّدٌ . فاسدٌ . شرِّيرٌ

Nausea *n.* غَثَيانٌ

Nauseate *v. t.* سبَّبَ ألغثيانَ

Nauseous *a.* مُسَبِّبُ ألغثيان . كريهٌ

Nautical *a.* موطٌ بالسفر بحراً . نوتيٌّ

Naval *a.* موطٌ بالسفن او البوارج

Nave *n.* صحنُ الكنيسة

Navel *n.* سُرَّةٌ

Navigable *a.* صالحٌ لسيْر السُفُن

Navigate *v. t.* سافر في سفينةٍ . سيَّرها

Navigation *n.* ألسيْرُ في السُفُن . عِلْمهُ

Navigator *n.* قائدُ سفينةٍ . مُديرُها

Navy *n.* أسطولٌ . مجموعُ بوارج

Nay *ad.* لا . كلا

Nazarite *n.* نذيرٌ

Near *a.* or *v.t.* قريبٌ . قرُبَ . دنا

Near / **Nearly** } *ad.* قريباً . تقريباً

Nearness *n.* قُرْبٌ

Neat *a.* نظيفٌ . مُرَتَّبٌ . بقريٌّ

Neatness *n.* نَظافةٌ . إتقانٌ

Nebula *n.* سَديمٌ

Nebular } *a.* سَدِيمِيٌّ
Nebulous }

Necessary *a.* لاَزِمٌ . ضَرُورِيٌّ . وَاجِبٌ

Necessitate *v. t.* أَلْزَمَ . احْوَجَ

Necessitous *a.* مُحْتَاجٌ . مفتقِرٌ

Necessity *n.* حَاجَةٌ . عوزٌ . ضَرُورةٌ

Neck *n.* عُنُقٌ رَقَبَةٌ

Necklace *n.* قِلاَدَةٌ . عِقْدٌ

Necromancy *n.* سِحْرٌ . خُرافَة

Necropolis *n.* مَقْبَرَةٌ . مَدْفَنٌ

Nectar *n.* شَرَابُ ٱلآلِهَةِ . شَرابٌ نَفِيسٌ

Need *n.* or *v. t.* or *i.* حَاجَةٌ . فَاقَةٌ . إِحتَاج

Needful *a.* ضَرُورِيٌّ . لازِمٌ

Needle *n.* إِبْرَةٌ . مِسَلَّةٌ

Needless *a.* لا حَاجَةَ إِلَيْهِ

Needs *ad.* لا بُدَّ من

Needy *a.* مُحْتَاجٌ . فَقِيرٌ

Nefarious *a.* شَنِيعٌ . غَايَةٌ في ٱلشرِّ

Negation *n.* نَفْيٌ . إِنكَارٌ . سَلْبٌ

Negative *a.* or *v. t.* نافٍ . سَلْبِيٌّ . أَدْحَضَ . رَفَضَ

Neglect *v. t.* or *n.* اهْمَلَ . تغافَلَ . إِهمَالٌ

Neglectful } *a.* مُهْمِلٌ . مُتَغَافِلٌ
Negligent }

Negligence *n.* إِهْمَالٌ . تَغافلٌ

Negotiate *v. t.* تَاجَرَ . فَاوَضَ . قاوَلَ

Negotiation *n.* تَدْبِيرُ امْرٍ . مُفَاوَضَةٌ

Negotiator *n.* مُدَبِّرُ امْرٍ اوْ مُعَاهَدَةٍ

Negro *n.* زِنْجِيٌّ . عَبْدٌ . أَسْوَدُ

Neigh *v. t.* صَهَلَ . حَمْحَمَ

Neighbour *n.* جَارٌ . قَرِيبٌ

Neighbouring *a.* مُجَاوِرٌ

Neighbourhood *n.* جِوَارٌ

Neither *pro.* لاَ . لا احَدَ (إِثْنَيْنِ)

Nephew *n.* إِبْنُ اخٍ اوْ اخْتٍ

Nerve *n.* or *v.t.* عَصَبٌ . قُوَّةٌ . قَوَّى

Nervous *a.* عَصَبِيٌّ . سَرِيعُ ٱلتَّأَثُّرِ

Nest *n.* عُشٌّ . وَكْرٌ

Nestle *v. t.* إِسْتَكَنَّ . (فَرْخٌ) . آوَى

Net *n.* or *a.* شَبَكَةٌ . شَرَكٌ . صَافٍ

Net *v. t.* حَبَكَ ـُ . رَبِحَ ـَ رِبْحاً خَالِصاً

Nether *a.* أَسْفَلُ . جَحِيمِيٌّ

Netting *n.* شَبَكَةٌ . شَبَكٌ

Nettle *n.* or *v. t.* قُرَّاصٌ . قَرَصَ ـُ . نَكَى

Neuralgia *n.* وَجَعُ ٱلعَصَب

Neuter *n.* لَا مُذَكَّرٌ وَلَا مُؤَنَّثٌ . لَازِمٌ

Neuter / **Neutral** } *a.* or *n.* مُحَايِدٌ

Neutrality *n.* حِيَادٌ . مُحَايَدَةٌ

Neutralize *v. t.* أَبْطَلَ فِعْلَهُ

Never *ad.* أَبَدًا . قَطُّ (مع نَفْي)

Nevertheless *ad.* مَعْ ذَلِكَ

New *a.* جَدِيدٌ . حَدِيث

Newness *n.* جِدَّةٌ

News *n.* أَخْبَارٌ . حَوَادِثُ

Newspaper *n.* جَرِيدَةٌ

Next *a.* or *ad.* أَلتَّالِي . الثَّانِي . قَادِمٌ . بَعْدُ

Nib *n.* رَأْسٌ . طَرَفٌ

Nibble *v. t.* قَرَضَ ـِ . قَضِمَ ـَ

Nice *a.* لَذِيذٌ . حَسَنٌ . مُدَقَّقٌ

Nicety *a.* دِقَّةٌ . رِقَّةٌ . تَأَنُّقٌ

Niche *n.* مِشْكَاةٌ

Nickel *n.* مَعْدِنٌ أَبْيَض

Nickname *n.* or *v. t.* لَقَبٌ . لَقَّبَ

Niece *n.* بِنْتُ أَخٍ أَو أُخْتٍ

Niggard / **Niggardly** } *n.* بَخِيلٌ . شَحِيحٌ

Nigh *a.* or *ad.* قَرِيبٌ . قَرِيباً

Nighness *n.* قُرْبٌ

Night *n.* لَيْلٌ ج لَيَالٍ

Night-fall *n.* عَشِيَّةٌ . غَسَقٌ

Nightingale *n.* بُلْبُلٌ ج بَلَابِلُ

Nightly *a.* or *ad.* لَيْلِيٌّ . كُلَّ لَيْلَةٍ

Nightmare *n.* كَابُوسٌ . ضَاغُوطٌ

Nilometer *n.* مِقْيَاسٌ لِمَاءِ النِّيلِ

Nimble *a.* خَفِيفٌ . حَرِكٌ . نَشِيطٌ

Nimbleness *n.* خِفَّةٌ نَشَاطٌ

Nine *a.*	تِسْعٌ . تِسْعَةٌ
Ninefold *a.*	تِسْعَةُ أَضْعَاف
Nineteen *a.*	تِسْعَةَ عَشَرَ . تِسْعَ عَشْرَةَ
Nineteenth *a.*	أَلتَّاسِعُ عَشَرَ
Ninetieth / **Ninety** *a.*	تِسْعُونَ
Ninth *a.*	أَلتَّاسِعُ . تُسْعٌ
Nip *v. t.* or *n.*	قَرَصَ ـُ قَرَسَ ـِ . قَرْصٌ
Nippers *n. pl.*	مِلْقَطٌ صَغِيرٌ
Nipple *n.*	حَلَمَةٌ . بِزٌّ
Nitre *n.*	مِلْحُ بَارُودٍ
No *a.* or *ad.*	لَا . لَيْسَ . كَلَّا
Nobility *n.*	شَرَفٌ . كَرَامَةٌ . الأَشْرَافُ
Noble *a.*	شَرِيفٌ . جَلِيلٌ . كَرِيمٌ
Nobleman *n.*	شَرِيفُ ٱلْأَصْلِ
Nobody *n.*	لَا أَحَدٌ . لَيْسَ أَحَدٌ
Nocturnal *a.*	لَيْلِيٌّ
Nod *n.* or *v. t.*	حَنْيَةُ ٱلرَّاسِ . حَنَاهُ
Node *n.*	عُقْدَةٌ ج عُقَدٌ
Nodose / **Nodular** *a.*	ذُو عُقَد
Noise *n.*	صَوْتٌ . ضَجَّةٌ . جَلَبَةٌ
Noiseless *n.*	بِلَا صَوْتٍ
Noisome *a.*	مُؤْذٍ . كَرِيهٌ . مُهْلِكٌ
Noisy *a.*	صَيَّاحٌ . صَوَّاتٌ
Nomad *n.* / **Nomadic** *a.*	بَدَوِيٌّ
Nomenclature *n.*	تَسْمِيَةٌ عِلْمِيَّةٌ
Nominal *a.*	إِسْمِيٌّ . بِٱلْإِسْمِ فَقَطْ
Nominate *v. t.*	سَمَّى . عَيَّنَ
Nominative *a.*	فَاعِلٌ . مُبْتَدَأ
Nominee *n.*	مُسَمًّى . مُعَيَّنٌ
Non-conductor *n.*	غَيْرُ مُوصِلٍ لِلْكَهْرَبَائِيَّةِ
None *a.*	لَا أَحَدٌ . لَيْسَ أَحَدٌ
Non-existence *n.*	عَدَمُ وُجُودٍ
Non-resident *n.*	غَيْرُ سَاكِنٍ مَحَلٌّ مُعَيَّنٌ
Nonsense *n.*	هَذَيَانٌ . هَذْرٌ
Nonsensical *a.*	بِلَا مَعْنًى . هَذِرِيٌّ

Nook *n.* زَاوِيَةٌ

Noon / Noonday *n.* أَلظُّهر . مُنْتَصَفُ ٱلنَّهَارِ

Noose *n.* أُنْشُوطَةٌ . رِبْقَةٌ

Nor *conj.* وَلاَ

Normal *a.* قَانُونِيٌّ . طَبِيعِيٌّ

North *n.* الشِّمال

North / Northern *a.* شِمَالِيٌّ

Northward *ad.* شِمَالاً

Nose *n.* أَنْفٌ . مَنْخَرٌ

Nostril *n.* مِنْخَرٌ

Not *ad.* لاَ . مَا . لَيْس . لَمْ . لَنْ

Notable *a.* شَهِيرٌ . وَجِيهٌ . عَجِيبٌ

Notary *n.* مُسَجِّلُ ٱلصُّكُوكِ

Notation *n.* تَرْتِيبُ ٱلأَرْقَامِ

Notch *n.* or *v.t.* حَزَّةٌ . فَرْضٌ . فَرَّض

Note *n.* or *v. t.* عَلاَمَةٌ . رُقْعَةٌ . كَتَبَ

Note-book *n.* دَفْتَرٌ تَذْكِرَةٍ

Noted *a.* مُقَيَّدٌ . مَشْهُورٌ . شَائِعٌ

Noteworthy *a.* مُسْتَحِقُّ ٱلذِّكْرِ

Nothing *n.* لاَ شَيْءَ

Nothingness *n.* عَدَمٌ

Notice *n.* إِعْلاَنٌ . إِلْتِفَاتٌ . تَنْبِيهٌ

Notice *v. t.* لاَحَظَ . إِلْتَفَتَ إِلَى

Noticeable *a.* مِمَّا يُلاحَظُ . مِمَّا يُذْكَرُ

Notification *n.* تَنْبِيهٌ . إِعْلاَنٌ . إِخْطَارٌ

Notify *v. t.* اخْبَرَ . أَعْلَنَ . أَعْلَمَ

Notion *n.* فِكْرٌ . تَصَوُّرٌ . رَأْيٌ

Notional *a.* وَهْمِيٌّ . خَيَالِيٌّ

Notoriety *n.* شُهْرَةٌ . صِيتٌ رَدِيءٌ

Notorious *a.* مَشْهُورٌ . سَيِّءُ ٱلصِّيتِ

Notwithstanding *conj.* مَعْ أَنْ وَلَوْ

Nought *n.* *see* Naught.

Noun *n.* إِسْمٌ ج أَسْمَاءٌ

Nourish *v. t.* قَاتَ ـُ . رَبَّى . غَذَّى

Nourishment *n.* قُوتٌ . غِذَاءٌ

Novel *a.* or *n.* جَدِيدٌ . غَرِيبٌ . رِوَايَةٌ

Novelist *n.* مُؤَلِّفُ ٱلرِّوَايَاتِ

Novelty *n.* جِدَّةٌ . نَادِرَةٌ

November *n.* تِشْرِينُ ٱلثَّانِي (نُوفَمبِرْ)

Novice *n.* مُبْتَدِئٌ . تِلْمِيذٌ جَدِيدٌ

Novitiate *n.* مُدَّةُ ٱلتَّلْمذَةِ ٱلإِبْتِدَائِيَّةِ

Now *ad.* أَلآنَ . حَالاً

Nowadays *ad.* فِي هٰذِهِ ٱلأَيَّامِ

Noway / **Nowise** } *n.* كَلَّا . لَا . ٱلْبَتَّةَ

Nowhere *ad.* غَيْرُ مَوْجُودٍ أَصْلاً

Noxious *a.* مُضِرٌّ . سَامٌّ . مُهْلِكٌ

Nozzle *n.* أَنْفٌ . خُرْطُومٌ . طَرَفٌ

Nucleus *n.* (نَوَاةٌ). مَرْكَزُ ٱلْجَوْهَرِ

Nudge *v. t.* وَكَزَ بِٱلْمِرْفَقِ

Nudity *n.* عَرَاءٌ . عُرْيٌ

Nugget *n.* كُتْلَةٌ مِنْ تِبْرٍ . شَذْرَةٌ

Nuisance *n.* مَكْرُهَةٌ . مُكَدِّرٌ

Null *a.* بَاطِلٌ . سَاقِطٌ . غَيْرُ عَامِلٍ

Nullify *v. t.* أَبْطَلَ . أَلْغَى

Nullity *n.* بُطْلَانٌ . سُقُوطٌ

Numb *a.* or *v. t.* خَدِرٌ . خَدَرَ

Number *n.* or *v. t.* عَدَدٌ . عِدَّةٌ . عَدَّ

Numberless *a.* لَا يُعَدُّ أَوْ يُحْصَى

Numbers *n.* سِفْرُ ٱلْعَدَدِ (فِي ٱلتَّوْرَاةِ)

Numbness *a.* خَدَرٌ

Numeral *n.* or *a.* عَدَدٌ . رَقْمٌ . عَدَدِيٌّ

Numerate *v. t.* عَدَّ . قَرَأَ ٱلأَرْقَامَ

Numerator *n.* صُورَةُ ٱلْكَسْرِ

Numeric / **Numerical** } *a.* عَدَدِيٌّ

Numerous *a.* كَثِيرٌ . عَدِيدٌ

Numismatics *n.* عِلْمُ ٱلنُّقُودِ

Numskull *n.* بَلِيدٌ . أَبْلَهُ

Nun *n.* رَاهِبَةٌ

Nuncio *n.* قَاصِدُ ٱلْبَابَا (نَائِبُهُ)

Nunnery *n.* دَيْرُ ٱلرَّاهِبَاتِ

Nuptial *a.* زَوَاجِيٌّ . عُرْسِيٌّ

Nuptials *n.* عُرْسٌ

Nurse *n.* مُرْضِعٌ (ة) مُمَرِّضَةٌ . مُرَبِّيَةٌ

Nurse *v. t.* أرضع . مرّض . ربّى

Nursery *n.* حجرة الأولاد .(مشتل)

Nursling *n.* رضيع

Nurture *n.* or *v. t.* تربية . ربّى

Nut *n.* جوزة . بندقة

Nutmeg *n.* جوز الطيب

Nutriment *n.* غذاء . قوت

Nutrition *n.* غذاء . قوت . تغذية

Nutritious, Nutritive *a.* مغذٍ

Nymph *n.* إلاهة الماء والجبال

O

Oak *n.* سنديان . بلوط

Oaken *a.* من سنديان

Oar *n.* مجذاف ج مجاذيف

Oarsman *n.* جذّاف

Oasis *n.* واحة ج واحات

Oats *n. pl.* (شوفان)

Oath *n.* قسم . حلف . يمين

Oatmeal *n.* دقيق شوفان

Obduracy *n.* عناد . صلابة القلب

Obdurate *a.* عنيد . متصلب القلب

Obedience *n.* طاعة . إذعان

Obedient *a.* مطيع . خاضع

Obeisance *n.* سجود . خرور

Obelisk *n.* عمود . مربع . مسلة

Obese *a.* سمين . شحيم

Obey *v. t.* أطاع . خضع ـ ل

Obituary *n.* ترجمة مختصرة لميت

Object n. شيءٌ . غايةٌ . مرامٌ . مفعولٌ بِهِ

Object v. t. إِعترَضَ . قاوَمَ

Objection n. إِعتِرَاضٌ . مانِعٌ

Objectionable a. غيرُ مقبولٍ

Objective a. خارِجٌ عَنِ ٱلعقلِ

Objector n. مُعْتَرِضٌ . مُقَاوِمٌ

Oblation n. تقدِمةٌ . قُرْبانٌ

Obligation n. فَرْضٌ . وُجوبٌ . إِمتِنانٌ

Obligatory a. مَفْرُوضٌ . وَاجِبٌ

Oblige v. t. أَوْجَبَ . عَمِلَ مَعْرُوفاً

Obliged a. ممنُونٌ . مُلتزِمٌ . شاكِرٌ

Obliging a. ذُو مَعْرُوفٍ . لَطِيفٌ

Oblique a. مُنْحَرِفٌ . مائِلٌ

Obliquity n. إِنحِرَافٌ . إِنحِناءٌ

Obliterate v. t. محا ـُ . درَسَ ـِ

Oblivion n. نِسيانٌ . عفوٌ

Oblivious a. ناسٍ . غافِلٌ

Oblong a. مُسْتَطِيلٌ

Obloquy n. طعنٌ . لُومٌ . ذمٌّ

Obnoxious a. مَكْرُوهٌ . مُعرَّضٌ لِ

Obscene a. قَبِيحٌ . فَاحِشٌ . مُفْسِدٌ

Obscenity n. قَبَاحَةٌ . كلامٌ قبيحٌ

Obscure v. t. or a. أَظْلَمَ . أَبْهَمَ . مُلتبِسٌ

Obscureness, Obscurity n. ظُلْمَةٌ . غُمُوضٌ . إِلتِبَاسٌ

Obsequies n. pl. جِنَازَةٌ

Obsequious a. خاضِعٌ . ذَلِيلٌ

Observable a. مما يلاحَظُ أَو يُرَاعَى

Observance n. مُرَاعَاةٌ . حِفظٌ . إِجراءٌ

Observant a. مُلاحِظٌ . مُنْتَبِهٌ

Observation n. مُلاحَظَةٌ . مُرَاقَبَةٌ . رَصدٌ

Observatory n. مَرْصِدٌ فلَكِيٌّ

Observe v. t. لاحَظَ . رَاعَى . رَصَدَ ـُ

Obsolete a. غيرُ مُستَعمَلٍ . مُهْمَلٌ

Obstacle n. مَانِعٌ . عائِقٌ

Obstetrics n. عِلمُ ٱلوِلادَةِ أَو ٱلتَّوْلِيدِ

Obstinacy *n.* عِنادٌ . إِصْرارٌ . مُكابَرَةٌ

Obstinate *a.* عَنِيدٌ . مُصِرٌّ . مُكابِرٌ

Obstruct *v. t.* مانَعَ . صَدَّ ـُـ . عاقَ

Obstruction *n.* مانِعٌ . سَدٌّ . عارِضٌ

Obtain *v. t.* حَصَّلَ . نالَ ـَـ . أَدْرَكَ

Obtainable *a.* مُمْكِنٌ تَحْصِيلُهُ . يُنالُ

Obtrude *v. t.* أَلَحَّ . تَداخَلَ . تَعَرَّضَ

Obtrusive *a.* فُضُولِيٌّ . مُتَداخِلٌ

Obtuse *a.* كَلِيلٌ . بَلِيدٌ . مُنْفَرِجٌ

Obtuseness *n.* كَلٌّ . بَلادَةٌ

Obverse *n.* وَجْهُ ٱلسِّكَّةِ أَوِ ٱلنُّقُودِ

Obviate *v. t.* أَزالَ . رَدَّ ـُـ . نَجا مِن

Obvious *a.* ظاهِرٌ . واضِحٌ

Occasion *n.* فُرْصَةٌ . سَبَبٌ . حاجَةٌ . مَرَّةٌ

Occasional *a.* إِتِّفاقِيٌّ . حادِثٌ أَحْياناً

Occident *n.* اَلْغَرْبُ . الاقْطارُ ٱلْغَرْبِيَّةُ

Occidental *a.* غَرْبِيٌّ . مَغْرِبِيٌّ

Occult *n.* سِرِّيٌّ . مَكْتُومٌ

Occupancy *n.* تَمَلُّكٌ . إِقامَةٌ فِي

Occupant / **Occupier** } *n.* ساكِنٌ . مُتَمَتِّعٌ

Occupation *v.* حِرْفَةٌ . إِحْتِلالٌ . تَمَتُّعٌ

Occupy *v. t.* حَلَّ فِي . شَغَلَ . إِسْتَوْلَى

Occur *v. i.* حَدَثَ . خَطَرَ بِٱلْبالِ

Occurrence *n.* حادِثَةٌ . حُدُوثٌ

Ocean *n.* اَلْبَحْرُ ٱلْمُحِيطُ . أُوقِيانُوسٌ

Oceanic *a.* بَحْرِيٌّ

Oceanica *n.* جَزائِرُ ٱلْبَحْرِ ٱلْمُحِيطِ

Octagon *n.* شَكْلٌ مُثَمَّنٌ

Octagonal *a.* ذُو ثَمانِي زَوايا

Octangular *a.* مُثَمَّنُ ٱلزَّوايا

October *n.* تِشْرِينُ ٱلأَوَّلُ (أُكْتُوبَر)

Octogenarian *n.* إِبْنُ ثَمانِينَ سَنَةً

Ocular *a.* بَصَرِيٌّ . عِيانِيٌّ

Oculist *n.* طَبِيبُ ٱلْعُيُونِ

Odd *a.* فَرْدٌ . غَرِيبٌ . زائِدٌ

Oddity / **Oddness** } *n.* غَرابَةٌ . شُذُوذٌ

Ode *n.* قَصِيدَةٌ . نَشِيدٌ

Odious *a.* مَمْقُوتٌ . كَرِيهٌ . قَبِيحٌ

Odium *n.* مَقْتٌ . كُرْهٌ . كَرَاهِيَةٌ

Odorous *a.* ذَكِيُّ ٱلرَّائِحَةِ

Odour *n.* رَائِحَةٌ

Of *prep.* مِنْ . عَنْ . عَلَامَةُ ٱلْإِضَافَةِ

Off *ad.* بَعِيدًا . عَلَى بُعْدٍ

Offal *n.* سَقَطُ ٱلذَّبِيحِ . زُبَالَةٌ

Offence / **Offense** *n.* إِغَاظَةٌ . غَيْظٌ . تَعَدٍّ

Offend *v. t.* اغَاظَ . كَدَّرَ . اخطَأَ

Offender *n.* مُذْنِبٌ . مُكَدِّرٌ . خَاطِئٌ

Offensive *a.* مُغِيظٌ . كَرِيهٌ . مُعْتَدٍ

Offer *v. t.* or *i.* قَدَّمَ . أَهْدَى . عَرَضَ

Offer *n.* إِهْدَاءٌ . عَرْضٌ . تَقْدِمَةٌ

Offering *n.* ذَبِيحَةٌ . تَقْدِمَةٌ

Office *n.* مَنْصَبٌ . خِدْمَةٌ . مَكْتَبٌ

Officer *n.* مَأْمُورٌ . ضَابِطٌ

Official *a.* or *n.* رَسْمِيٌّ . مَأْمُورٌ

Officiate *v. i.* قَامَ بِخِدْمَةٍ أَوْ وَظِيفَةٍ

Officious *a.* مُتَكَلِّفٌ . فُضُولِيٌّ

Officiousness *n.* فُضُولٌ . تَعَرُّضٌ

Offscouring *n.* سُقَاطَةٌ . نُفَايَةٌ . نَجَاسَةٌ

Offset *v. t.* or *n.* وَازَنَ . بَادَلَ . بَدَلٌ

Offshoot *n.* فَرْعٌ . عُسْلُجٌ

Offspring *n.* ذُرِّيَّةٌ . نَسْلٌ

Oft / **Often** *ad.* كَثِيرًا مَا . مِرَارًا

Ogle *v. t.* غَمَزَ عِشْقًا

Oh *inter.* آه . اوَّاه

Oh that ! يَا لَيْتَ

Oil *n.* or *v. t.* زَيْتٌ . دُهْنٌ . زَيَّتَ

Oil-cloth *n.* مُشَمَّعٌ

Oily *a.* دَهِنٌ . زَيْتِيٌّ

Ointment *n.* دِهْنٌ . مَرْهَمٌ

Old *a.* طَاعِنٌ فِي ٱلسِّنِّ . شَيْخٌ . عَتِيقٌ

Olden *a.* قَدِيمٌ

Oleander *n.* دِفْلَى . دِفْلٌ

Olive *n.* زَيْتُونَة

Omelet *n.* عُجَّة

Omen *n.* فَأْلٌ . طِيرة . عَلامَةٌ

Ominous *a.* مُنذِرٌ بِالسُّوءِ

Omission *n.* إِهمالٌ . تَرْكٌ . إِسقَاطٌ

Omit *v. t.* تَرَكَ ـُ . أَهمَلَ . أَسقَطَ

Omnibus *n.* عَجَلَةٌ كَبِيرَةٌ

Omnipotence *n.* أَلْقُدْرَة عَلَى كُلِّ شَيْءٍ

Omnipotent *a.* أَلْقَادِرُ عَلَى كُلِّ شَيْءٍ

Omnipresence *n.* أَلْحُضُورُ فِي كُلِّ مَكَانٍ

Omnipresent *a.* أَلْحَاضِرُ فِي كُلِّ مَكَانٍ

Omniscience *n.* أَلْعِلْمُ بِكُلِّ شَيْءٍ

Omniscient *a.* أَلْعَالِمُ بِكُلِّ شَيْءٍ

Omnivorous *a.* آكِلٌ مِنْ كُلِّ شَيْءٍ

On *pr.* or *ad.* عَلَى . عِنْدَ . إِلَى قُدَّامٍ

Once *ad.* مَرَّةً . قَبْلاً . وَقْتاً مَّا

One *a.* or *n.* وَاحِدٌ (ة) . أَحَدٌ . ذَات

One-eyed *a.* أَعْوَرُ

Oneness *n.* وَحْدَانِيَّةٌ

Onerous *a.* ثَقِيلٌ . شَاقٌ

Onion *n.* بَصَلَة

Only *a.* وَحِيدٌ . وَحْدَهُ . لَا غَيْرُ

Onset / **Onslaught** *n.* هُجُومٌ . حَمْلَةٌ . بَطْشٌ

Onward / **Onwards** *ad.* إِلَى قُدَّامٍ . تَقَدُّماً

Onyx *n.* جَزْعٌ (حَجَرٌ كَرِيمٌ)

Ooze *v. i.* رَشَحَ ـ . نَضَّ ـ

Opaque *a.* مُظْلِمٌ . غَيْرُ شَفَّافٍ

Open *v. t.* or *i.* or *a.* فَتَحَ ـ . إِنفَتَحَ . مَفْتُوحٌ

Opening *n.* فَتْحة . شَقٌّ . بَابٌ

Openly *ad.* عَلَانِيَةً . جِهَاراً

Openness *n.* خُلُوصٌ . مُجَاهَرَة

Opera *n.* رِوَايَةٌ مُوسِيقِيَّةٌ

Operate *v. i.* or *t.* جَرَى ـ . أَثَّرَ . عَمِلَ ـ

Operation *n.* عَمَلٌ إِجْرَاءٌ . عَمَلِيَّةٌ

Operative *a.* عَامِلٌ . مُؤَثِّرٌ . عَمَلِيٌّ

Operator *n.* عَامِلٌ . جَرَّاحٌ

Ophthalmic *a.* عَيْنِيٌّ

Ophthalmia *n.* إِلْتِهَابُ ٱلْعَيْنِ . رَمَدٌ

Opiate *n.* دَوَاءٌ أَفْيُونِيٌّ . مُنَوِّمٌ

Opinion *n.* رَأْيٌ . ظَنٌّ . إِعْتِقَادٌ

Opinionated / **Opinionative** *a.* عَنِيدُ ٱلرَّأْيِ

Opium *n.* أَفْيُونٌ

Opponent *n.* خَصْمٌ . مُقَاوِمٌ

Opportune *a.* فِي مَحَلِّهِ أَوْ حِينِهِ

Opportunity *n.* فُرْصَةٌ

Oppose *v. t.* ضَادَّ . عَارَضَ . مَانَعَ

Opposite *a.* مُقَابِلٌ . حِذَاءٌ . مُضَادٌّ

Opposition *n.* مُضَادَّةٌ . مُعَارَضَةٌ

Oppress *v. t.* ظَلَمَ . بَغَى . ضَايَقَ

Oppression *n.* ظُلْمٌ . جَوْرٌ

Oppressive *a.* / **Oppressor** *n.* ظَالِمٌ . مُضَايِقٌ . بَاغٍ

Opprobrious *a.* مَعِيبٌ . مُحَقِّرٌ . مُخْزٍ

Opprobrium *n.* عَارٌ . عَيْبٌ . خِزْيٌ

Optic / **Optical** *a.* بَصَرِيٌّ . مُخْتَصٌّ بِعِلْمِ ٱلنُّورِ

Optician *n.* صَانِعُ آلَاتٍ بَصَرِيَّةٍ

Optics *n.* عِلْمُ ٱلنُّورِ وَٱلْبَصَرِ

Optimism *n.* التَّفَاؤُلُ بِٱلْخَيْرِ

Option *n.* خِيَارٌ

Optional *a.* إِخْتِيَارِيٌّ

Opulence *n.* ثَرْوَةٌ . يُسْرٌ

Opulent *a.* غَنِيٌّ . مُوسِرٌ

Or *conj.* أَوْ . أَمْ

Oracle *n.* وَحْيٌ . رَأْيٌ حَكِيمٌ

Oracular *a.* مُتَكَلِّمٌ بِسُلْطَةٍ

Oral *a.* شِفَاهِيٌّ . لَفْظِيٌّ

Orange *n.* بُرْتُقَالٌ

Orang-outang *n.* قِرْدٌ يُشْبِهُ ٱلْإِنْسَانَ

Oration *n.* خُطْبَةٌ

Orator *n.* خَطِيبٌ

Oratorical *n.* خِطَابِيٌّ . بَلِيغٌ

Oratory *n.* عِلْمُ ٱلْخِطَابَةِ . مُصَلًّى

Orb *n.* كُرَةٌ

Orbit *n.* مَدَارُ كَوْكَبٍ. تجويفُ ٱلْعَيْنِ

Orchard *n.* بُسْتَانٌ . حَدِيقَةٌ

Orchestra *n.* جماعةعازفين موقفهم

Ordain *v. t.* أقامَ . أمرَ . رَسَمَ

Ordeal *n.* إِمْتِحَانٌ شَدِيدٌ . مِحْنَةٌ

Order *v. t.* أمرَ . رَتَّبَ . دَبَّرَ

Order *n.* امرٌ . تَرْتِيبٌ . رُتْبَةٌ

Orderly *a.* مُرَتَّبٌ. مُنْتَظِمٌ. (مراسلة)

Ordinance *n.* سُنَّةٌ . فَرْضٌ . حُكْمٌ

Ordinarily *ad.* إِعتِيَادِيًا . غَالِبًا

Ordinary *a.* إِعْتِيَادِيٌّ . مَأْلُوفٌ

Ordination *n.* إِقَامَةٌ . تَعْيِينٌ. رَسْمٌ

Ordnance *n.* مَدَافِعُ وَمُتَعَلِّقَاتِهَا

Ore *n.* خَلِيطٌ يُسْتَخْرَجُ ٱلْمَعْدِنُ مِنْهُ

Organ *n.* عُضْوٌ . وَاسِطَةٌ (ارْغُنٌ)

Organic *a.* عُضْوِيٌّ . آلِيٌّ. أَسَاسِيٌّ

Organism *n.* بِنَاءٌ . آلِيٌّ

Organist *n.* عَازِفٌ عَلَى ٱلارْغُنِ

Organization *n.* نِظَامٌ . تَرْتِيبٌ

Organize *v. t.* نَظَمَ . رَتَّبَ . جَهَّزَ

Orgies *n. pl.* بَطَرٌ مُفْرِطٌ . سُكْرٌ

Orient *n.* ٱلشَّرْقُ ٱلأَقْطَارُ ٱلشَّرْقِيَّةُ

Oriental *a.* or *n.* شَرْقِيٌّ . شَرْقِيُّ ٱلْوَطَنِ

Orientalism *n.* إِصْطِلَاحٌ شَرْقِيٌّ

Orientalist *n.* عَالِمٌ بِلُغَاتِ ٱلشَّرْقِ

Orifice *n.* مَنْفَذٌ . فَتْحَةٌ

Origin *n.* أَصْلٌ . مَبْدَأٌ . مَصْدَرٌ

Original *a.* أَصْلِيٌّ . أَوَّلِيٌّ . غَرِيبٌ

Original *n.* أَصْلٌ . صُورَةٌ أَصْلِيَّةٌ

Originality *n.* أَصْلِيَّةٌ . إِبْدَاعٌ . ذَكَاءٌ

Originate *v. t.* or *i.* أَبْدَعَ . أَوْجَدَ . نَشَأَ

Originator *n.* مُبْدِعٌ . مُخْتَرِعٌ . مُبْتَكِرٌ

Orion *n.* أَلْجَبَّارُ . أَلْجَوْزَاءُ

Ornament *n.* زِينَةٌ . زَخْرَفَةٌ

Ornament *v. t.* زَيَّنَ . زَخْرَفَ

Ornamental *a.*	زِينِيٌّ . مزيَّنٌ
Ornate *a.*	مُزخْرَفٌ . مزوَّقٌ
Ornithology *n.*	عِلْمٌ يبحَثُ فيهِ عَنِ ٱلطُّيورِ
Orphan *n.*	يَتيمٌ ج أيتامٌ . يتَامَى
Orphanage *n.*	دَارُ ٱليتَامَى
Orthodox *a.*	قَوِيمُ ٱلمَذهَبِ (ارثوذُكْس)
Orthodoxy *n.*	صحَّةُ ٱلمَذْهَبِ
Orthography *n.*	عِلْمُ ٱلتَّهجئة
Oscillate *v. i.*	ذَبْذَبَ . إرْتَجَحَ . خطَرَ
Oscillation *n.*	ذَبذَبَةٌ . إرْتِجَاجٌ
Osseous *a.*	عَظْمِيٌّ
Ossify *v. t.* or *i.*	حَوَّلَهُ أَوْ تَحوَّلَ عظْمًا
Ostensible *a.*	ظَاهِرٌ . مُدَّعًى
Ostentation *n.*	تفَاخُرٌ . مُبَاهَاةٌ
Ostentatious *a.*	متفَاخِرٌ . متبَاهٍ
Osteology *n.*	عِلْمُ ٱلعظَامِ
Ostracise *v. t.*	نَفَى ـِ . طَرَدَ ـُ
Ostrich *n.*	نعَامَةٌ
Other *a.*	آخرُ . ذَاكَ
Otherwise *ad.*	وَإلاَّ . خِلافًا لذَلِكَ
Ottar *n.*	عِطْرٌ
Otter *n.*	كلْبُ ٱلمَاءِ
Ottoman *n.*	عُثْمَانِيٌّ
Ought *v. i.*	وَجَبَ ـِ . لَزِمَ ـَ
Ounce *n.*	اوقِيَّةٌ أنكليزيَّةٌ أوْ طِبِّيَّةٌ
Our / Ours *pro.*	لَنَا . نَا
Ourselves *pro. pl.*	نَحْنُ . أنفُسُنَا
Oust *v. t.*	طَرَدَ ـُ أخْرَجَ
Out *ad.*	خَارِجًا
Outbid *v. t.*	زَايَدَ
Outbreak / Outburst *n.*	ثَوْرَةٌ . إنْفِجَارٌ
Outcast *n.*	مَطْرُودٌ . مَنْفِيٌّ
Outcry *n.*	صِيَاحٌ . صرَاخٌ
Outdo *v. t.*	فَاقَ . سَبَقَ ـُ
Outdoor *a.* / Outdoors *adv.*	خَارِجَ ٱلبَيْتِ
Outer *a.*	خَارِجِيٌّ

Outermost *a.* ألأَبْعَدُ عَنِ ٱلْمَرْكَزِ

Outfit *n.* جَهَازٌ. لَوَازِمُ

Outgrow *v. t.* سَبَقَ نُمُوًّا. زَادَ عَلَى

Outhouse *n.* بَيْتٌ خَارِجُ ٱلدَّارِ

Outlandish *a.* غَرِيبٌ. بَرْبَرِيٌّ

Outlaw *n.* فَاقِدُ ٱلْحُقُوقِ ٱلشَّرْعِيَّةِ

Outlay *n.* نَفَقَةٌ. مَصْرُوفٌ

Outlet *n.* مَخْرَجٌ. مَنْفَذٌ. مَصَبٌّ

Outline *n.* or *v. t.* رَسْمٌ مُخْتَصَرٌ. رَسَمَ ـُ

Outlive *v. t.* عَاشَ بَعْدَهُ

Outlook *n.* مَنْظَرٌ. مُرَاقَبَةٌ

Outlying *a.* بَعِيدٌ عَنِ ٱلْمَرْكَزِ. خَارِجِيٌّ

Outmost *a.* ألأَبْعَدُ عَنِ ٱلْمَرْكَزِ

Outpost *n.* مَرْكَزُ حَرَسٍ خَارِجِيٌّ

Outrage *v. t.* فَضَحَ ـَ. أَسَاءَ إِلَى

Outrage *n.* فَظِيعَةٌ. إِهَانَةٌ. بَغْيٌ

Outrageous *a.* فَظِيعٌ. مُفْرِطُ ٱلْبَغْيِ

Outrider *n.* فَارِسٌ. تَابِعٌ

Outright *ad.* حَالاً. تَمَامًا

Outrun *v. t.* سَبَقَ رَكْضًا

Outset *n.* بَدَاءَةٌ. مَطْلَعٌ

Outside *n.* أَلْخَارِجُ ظَاهِرُهُ

Outskirt *n.* ظَاهِرُ بَلَدٍ. ضَاحِيَةٌ

Outspread *v. t.* بَسَطَ ـُ. مَدَّ ـُ

Outstanding *a.* بَارِزٌ. غَيْرُ مَدْفُوعٍ

Outstrip *v. t.* سَبَقَ ـُ

Outward *a.* or *ad.* خَارِجِيٌّ. ظَاهِرٌ. إِلَى خَارِجٍ

Outweigh *v. t.* رَجَحَ ـَ. زَادَ وَزْنًا

Outwit *v. t.* فَاقَ حِيلَةً

Outwork *n.* اسْتِحْكَامٌ. خَارِجِيٌّ

Oval / **Ovate** *a.* بَيْضِيُّ ٱلشَّكْلِ. إِهْلِيلَجِيٌّ

Ovary *n.* مَبِيضٌ فِي ٱلنَّبَاتِ وَٱلْحَيَوَانِ

Ovation *n.* مَوْكِبٌ. إِكْرَامِيٌّ

Oven *n.* فُرْنٌ. تَنُّورٌ

Over *pr.* or *ad.* فَوْقَ. عَلَى. زِيَادَةً

Overbalance *v. t.* رَجَحَ ـُ. فَاقَ وَزْنًا

Overbearing *a.* مُتَجَبِّرٌ . عِطْرِيسٌ

Overboard *ad.* مِنَ ٱلسَّفِينَةِ . فِي ٱلْبَحْرِ

Overcautious *a.* زَائِدُ ٱلْحَذَرِ

Overcharge *v. t.* أَفْرَطَ فِي ٱلثَّمَنِ أَوِ ٱلْحِمْلِ

Overcoat *n.* جُبَّةٌ فَوْقَانِيَّةٌ

Overcome *v. t.* غَلَبَ بِ . قَهَرَ

Overdo *v. t.* أَفْرَطَ فِي ٱلْعَمَلِ

Overdose *n.* جُرْعَةٌ مُفْرِطَةٌ

Over-due *a.* فَائِتُ ٱلْٱسْتِحْقَاقِ (دين)

Overestimate *v. t.* أَفْرَطَ فِي ٱلتَّقْدِيرِ

Overflow *v.t.* or *n.* فَاضَ بِ . فَيَضَانٌ

Over-grown *a.* كَثِيرُ ٱلنَّبَاتِ . مُفْرِطُ ٱلنُّمُوِّ

Overhang *v. t.* أَشْرَفَ عَلَى . بَرَزَ

Overhead *ad.* فَوْقَ ٱلرَّأْسِ

Overhear *v. t.* سَمِعَ ٱتِّفَاقًا

Overland *a.* بِٱلْبَرِّ (سَفَرٌ)

Overlay *v. t.* غَشَّى بِ

Overload *v. t.* ثَقَّلَ ٱلْحِمْلَ

Overlook *v. t.* أَشْرَفَ عَلَى . أَهْمَلَ . عَفَا

Overmatch *n.* أَقْدَرُ مِنْ

Overmuch *a.* زَائِدٌ . مُفْرِطٌ

Overnight *ad.* مُدَّةَ ٱللَّيْلِ ٱلْمَاضِي

Overpay *v. t.* أَوْفَى فَوْقَ ٱلْحَقِّ

Overplus *n.* فَضْلَةٌ . بَقِيَّةٌ . زِيَادَةٌ

Overpower *v.t.* قَوِيَ عَلَى . قَهَرَ

Overrate *v. t.* أَفْرَطَ فِي ٱلتَّثْمِينِ

Overreach *v. t.* غَبَنَ بِ . جَاوَزَ

Overrule *v. t.* أَبْطَلَ تَأْثِيرَهُ أَوْحَوَّلَهُ

Overruling *a.* مُتَسَلِّطٌ . ضَابِطٌ

Overrun *v. t.* أَفْرَطَ . غَطَّى . غَزَا

Oversee *v. t.* نَاظَرَ

Overseer *n.* نَاظِرٌ . وَكِيلٌ

Overshoe *n.* جُرْمُوقٌ (كَالُوش)

Oversight *n.* إِهْمَالٌ . سَهْوٌ . مُنَاظَرَةٌ

Oversleep *v. t.* تَأَخَّرَ فِي ٱلنَّوْمِ

Overspread *v. t.* إِنْتَشَرَ عَلَى . غَطَّى

Overstep *v. t.* جَاوَزَ . تَجَاوَزَ

Overt *a.* ظَاهِرٌ . شَائِعٌ

Overtake *v. t.* لَحِقَ ـَ . أَدْرَكَ . أَلَمَّ بِ

Overtask / Overtax } *v. t.* كَلَّفَ فَوْقَ ٱلطَّاقَةِ

Overtax *v. t.* أَفْرَطَ فِي ٱلضَّرِيبَةِ

Overthrow *v. t.* قَلَبَ ـِ . هَزَمَ . هَدَمَ ـِ

Overtly *ad.* ظَاهِرًا . جِهَارًا

Overtop *v. t.* عَلَا ـُ . فَاقَ ـُ

Overture *n.* عَرْضٌ . مُفَاوَضَةٌ . فَاتِحَةٌ

Overturn *v. t.* قَلَبَ . نَكَّسَ

Overweening *a.* مُعْجَبٌ بِنَفْسِهِ . مَزْهُوٌّ

Overwhelm *v. t.* غَمَرَ ـُ . قَهَرَ ـَ

Overwork *v. t.* شَغَلَ فَوْقَ ٱلطَّاقَةِ

Oviparous *a.* بَائِضٌ . بَيُوضٌ

Ovum *n.* بَيْضَةٌ . بِزْرَةٌ . جُرْثُومَةٌ

Owe *v. t.* كَانَ مَدْيُونًا . عَلَيْهِ دَيْنٌ

Owing *a.* مَدْيُونٌ . مَطْلُوبٌ . نَاشِئٌ عَنْ

Owl *n.* بُومَةٌ ج بُومٌ

Own *a.* or *v. t.* خَاصَّتُهُ . مَلَكَ ـِ . أَقَرَّ بِ

Owner *n.* صَاحِبٌ . مَالِكٌ . رَبٌّ

Ownership *n.* مِلْكٌ

Ox (*pl.* Oxen). ثَوْرٌ

Oxalis *n.* حُمَّاضٌ (نَبَاتٌ)

Oyster *n.* نَوْعٌ مِنَ ٱلصَّدَفِ . مَحَارَةٌ

P

Pace *n.* or *v. t.* خُطْوَةٌ . خَطَا . مَشَى ـِ

Pacer *n.* رَهْوَان (فَرَسٌ)

Pacific *a.* or *n.* مُسَالِمٌ . سِلْمِيٌّ . ا لبَحْرُ ا لمحيط

Pacify *v. t.* سَالَمَ . هَدَّأَ

Pack *v. t.* رَزَمَ . حَزَمَ . كَبَسَ

Pack / **Package** *n.* رِزْمَةٌ . حُزْمَةٌ . فَرْدَةٌ

Packet *n.* حُزْمَةٌ . سَفِينَةٌ سَرِيعَةٌ

Pack-horse *n.* فَرَسٌ لِلحَمْلِ . كَدِيشٌ

Pack-saddle *n.* جَلٌّ (جِلَالٌ)

Pad *n.* or *v. t.* وِسَادَةٌ . حَشَا . بَطَّنَ

Paddle *v. i.* or *n.* جَذَفَ . مِجْذَافٌ

Padlock *n.* قُفْلٌ ج أَقْفَالٌ

Pagan *n.* وَثَنِيٌّ

Paganism *n.* عِبَادَةُ ٱلأَوْثَانِ

Page *n.* صَفْحَةٌ . غُلَامٌ

Page *v. t.* رَقَمَ ٱلأَعْدَادَ عَلَى ٱلصَّفَحَاتِ

Pageant / **Pageantry** *n.* مَوْكِبٌ . إِحْتِفَالٌ . بَهَاءٌ

Pail *n.* دَلْوٌ . سَطْلٌ

Pain *n.* or *v. t.* وَجَعٌ . أَلَمٌ . أَوْجَعَ

Painful *a.* مُوْجِعٌ . مُؤْلِمٌ . مُكَدِّرٌ

Painless *a.* بِلَا أَلَمٍ

Pains *n.* إِعْتِنَاءٌ . إِهْتِمَامٌ . دِقَّةٌ

Paint *n.* or *v. t.* دِهَانٌ . دَهَنَ . صَوَّرَ

Painter *n.* دَهَّانٌ . مُصَوِّرٌ

Painting *n.* دَهْنٌ . تَصْوِيرٌ . صُورَةٌ

Pair *n.* or *v. t.* or *i.* زَوْجٌ . زَاوَجَ . تَزَاوَجَ

Palace *n.* قَصْرٌ . بَلَاطُ ٱلمَلِكِ

Palanquin *n.* تَخْتَرَوَانٌ

Palatable *a.* مَقْبُولٌ لِلذَّوْقِ . لَذِيذٌ

Palate *n.* حَنَكٌ . سَقْفُ ٱلحَلْقِ

Palatial *a.* جَلِيلٌ . عَظِيمٌ . قَصْرِيٌّ

Pale *a.* or *v. i.* مُصْفَرٌّ . بَاهِتٌ . إِصْفَرَّ

Paleness *n.* إِصْفِرَارٌ . بَهْتُ ٱللَّوْنِ

Paleography *n.* خَطُّ ٱلقُدَمَاءِ وَعِلْمُهُ

Paleontology *n.* عِلْمُ ٱلمُتَحَجِّرَاتِ ٱلآلِيَّةِ

Palisade *n.* سِيَاجٌ مِنْ أَوْتَادٍ لِلدِّفَاعِ

Pall *n.* غِطَاءُ ٱلنَّعْشِ . رِدَاءٌ

Pallet *n.* فِرَاشٌ حَقِيرٌ . لَوْحُ مُصَوِّرٍ

Palliate *v. t.* سَتَرَ أَو خَفَّفَ بِعُذْرٍ

Palliative *n.* مُسَكِّنُ وَجَعٍ

Pallid *a.* مُصْفَرٌّ

Palm *n.* نَخْل . رَاحة آلْيَدِ

Palm-Sunday *n.* أَحَد آلشَّعَانِين

Palpable *a.* مَا يُلمَسُ . وَاضِحٌ

Palpitate *v. i.* خفقَ ـُ

Palpitation *n.* خَفَقَانٌ

Palsied *a.* مَفْوجٌ

Palsy *n.* فَالِجٌ

Paltry *n.* حَقيرٌ . خَسِيسٌ

Pamper *v. t.* أَشْبَعَ . فَتَقَ

Pamphlet *n.* كُرَّاسةٌ . رِسَالَة

Pan *n.* طَاجَنٌ . لَـكَنٌ

Panacea *n.* عِلَاجٌ لِكُلِّ دَآء

Pancreas *n.* بَنكرْيَاسٌ

Pandemonium *n.* مَجْمَعُ الشَّيَاطِين

Pander *v. i.* صَدَمَ شَهَوَات غَيْرِه

Pane *n.* لَوْحٌ . زُجَاجٍ

Panegyric *n.* مَدِيحٌ . تبْجيل

Panel *n.* لَوْحٌ . (حَشْوَة بَابٍ)

Pang *n.* أَلَمٌ وَقْتِيٌّ شَدِيدٌ . مَخَاضٌ

Panic *n.* رَوْعٌ فجَائِيٌّ بَاطِلٌ

Pannier *n.* قُفَّةٌ ، زِبيل أو زنْبيل

Panoply *n.* درعٌ كَامِلَة

Panorama *n.* مَنظرٌ . شَامِلٌ

Pant *v. i.* نَهِجَ ـَ لَهِثَ ـَ

Pantalets / **Pantaloons** *n.* سِروَالٌ ج سَرَاوِيلُ

Pantheism *n.* مَذهَبُ ألوهِيةِ الكَوْنِ

Pantheist *n.* مُعتَقِدٌ بالوهِيَّةِ الكَوْنِ

Panther *n.* نَمِرٌ ج نُمُرٌ وَنُمورَةٌ

Pantomime *n.* تَشْخيصٌ بِٱلإِشَارَات

Pantry *n.* بَيْتُ آلمونَةِ

Papa *n.* أَبٌ . بَابَا

Papacy *n.* الْبَابَويةِ (مَذْهَبٌ)

Papal *a.* بَابَوِيٌّ

Paper *n.* or *a.* وَرَق . جَرِيدَة . مِن ورَقٍ

Papist *n.* بَابَوِيٌّ تَابِع آلبَابَا

Papyrus *n.* قَصَبُ ٱلبَرْدِيّ . قِرْطَاسَةٌ

Par *n.* مُسَاوَاة . مُعَادَلَةُ ٱلقِيمَةِ

Parable *n.* مَثَلٌ ج أَمْثَالٌ

Parabola *n.* قَطْعٌ مَخْرُوطِيٌّ . شَلْجَمِيٌّ

Parade *n.* or *v. t.* مَوْكِبٌ . إِحْتَفَلَ

Paradise *n.* فِرْدَوْس . جَنَّةٌ

Paradox *n.* تَنَاقُضٌ بِٱلظَّاهِرِ فَقَطْ

Paragraph *n.* فِقْرَةٌ . فَصْلٌ . جُمْلَةٌ

Parallel *n.* or *a.* مُوَازَاةٌ . مُشَابَهَةٌ . مُوَازٍ

Parallelogram *n.* مُرَبَّعٌ مُسْتَطِيلٌ

Paralysis *n.* فَالِجٌ . شَلَلٌ

Paralytic *a.* مَفْلُوجٌ . أَشَلُّ

Paralyze *v. t.* أَشَلَّ

Paramount *a.* رَئِيسِيٌّ . أَلأَعْظَمُ . فَائِقٌ

Paramour *n.* عَاشِقٌ أو عَاشِقَةٌ

Parapet *n.* مِتْرَاسٌ . سُورٌ

Paraphrase *n.* or *v.t.* تَأْوِيل . فَسَّرَ

Parasite *n.* نَبَات أو حَيَوَان طُفَيْلِيٌّ

Parasol *n.* شَمْسِيَّةٌ صَغِيرَةٌ

Parcel *n.* or *v. t.* حُزْمَةٌ . رَبْطَةٌ . قَسَمَ ـِ

Parch *v. t.* or *i.* جَفَّفَ . لَفَحَ ـَ . تَجَفَّفَ

Parchment *n.* رِقٌّ مِنْ جِلْدٍ

Pardon *n.* or *v. t.* عَفْوٌ . غُفْرَانٌ . عَفَا ـُ

Pardonable *n.* مِمَّا يُغْفَرُ لَهُ . يُصْفَحُ عَنْه

Pare *v. t.* قَشَرَ ـِ . جَلَفَ ـُ . نَقَصَ

Parent *n.* وَالِدٌ (ة) . مَنْشَأٌ

Parentage *n.* أَصْلٌ . نَسَبٌ

Parental *a.* وَالِدِيٌّ

Parenthesis *n.* هِلاَلاَنِ وَجُمْلَةٌ بَيْنَهُمَا

Parenthetical *a.* مُعْتَرِضٌ

Paring *n.* قُشْرَةٌ . قُصَاصَةٌ

Parish *n.* أَبْرَشِيَّةٌ

Parity *n.* مُسَاوَاةٌ . مُعَادَلَةٌ . مُشَابَهَةٌ

Park *n.* مُنْتَزَهٌ . غَابَةٌ

Parley *n.* or *v. i.* مُفَاوَضَةٌ . إِئْتَمَرَ

Parliament *n.* مَجْلِسُ ٱلنُّوَّابِ

Parliamentary *a.* مَنُوط بِالْبَارْلَمَنْتِ
Parlour *n.* غُرْفَةُ الإِسْتِقْبَالِ
Parole *n.* كَلَامُ شَرَفٍ . عَهْدٌ
Paroxysm *n.* نَوْبَةُ مَرَضٍ . دَوْرٌ
Parricide *n.* قَتْلُ الْوَالِدَيْنِ أَوْ قَاتِلُهُمَا
Parrot *n.* بَبَّغَاءُ
Parry *v. t.* دَفَعَ ـ . جَانَبَ . إِجْتَنَبَ
Parse *v. t.* أَعْرَبَ
Parsimonious *n.* قَتُور . شَحِيحٌ
Parsimony *n.* قَتْرٌ . إِقْتِصَادٌ زَائِد
Parsley *n.* بَقْدُونِسٌ
Parsnip *n.* جَزَرٌ أَبْيَضُ
Parson *n.* قِسِّيسٌ . خُورِيٌّ
Parsonage *n.* بَيْتُ الْقِسِّيسِ
Part *n.* قِسْم . حِصَّة . جَانِب
Part *v. t.* or *i.* فَصَلَ ـِ . قَاسَمَ . إِفْتَرَقَ
Partake *v. t.* إِشْتَرَكَ . تَنَاوَلَ
Partial *a.* جُزْئِيٌّ . مُحَاب
Partially *ad.* جُزْئِيًّا . بِمُحَابَاةٍ
Participant *n.* مُشْتَرِكٌ . مُتَنَاوِلٌ
Participate *v. t.* إِشْتَرَكَ . أَخَذَ حِصَّةً
Participation *n.* إِشْتِرَاكٌ . إِتِّخَاذٌ
Participle *n.* إِسْمُ فَاعِلٍ أَوْ مَفْعُولٍ
Particle *n.* ذَرَّةٌ . دَقِيقَةٌ . حَرْفٌ
Particular *a.* خَاص . مُدَقِّقٌ
Particular *n.* مَادَّة . خَاصَّةٌ . تَفَاصِيل
Particularity *n.* خَاصِيَّةٌ . دِقَّةٌ . تَفْصِيل
Particularize *v. t.* خَصَّصَ . فَصَّلَ . دَقَّقَ
Parting *n.* إِنْفِتَرَاقٌ . وَدَاعٌ
Partisan *n.* حَلِيفٌ . مُتَحَزِّبٌ
Partition *n.* تَقْسِيمٌ . قِسْمَة . حَاجِزٌ
Partly *ad.* بَعْضًا . جُزْئِيًّا
Partner *n.* شَرِيكٌ . رَفِيق
Partnership *n.* شِرْكَة
Partridge *n.* حَجَلٌ
Party *n.* حِزْبٌ . جَمَاعَة . فَرِيقٌ

Paschal *a.* خَاصٌّ بعِيدِ آلْفِصْحِ
Pashalic *n.* وِلَايَةُ بَاشَا
Pass *n.* ممرٌّ . تَذْكِرَة . حَال
Pass *v. t.* or *i.* إِجتاز . عَبَرَ . عبّرَ . مرَّب
Passable *a.* ممّا يمرُّ عليهِ . جَائِزٌ
Passage *n.* ممرٌّ . مُرُورٌ . جُمْلَة
Passenger *n.* مسافرٌ . رَاكِبٌ
Passing *a.* مارٌّ . وَقتيٌّ . زَائِل
Passion *n.* انفِعَالٌ شَدِيدٌ . هوًى
Passionate *a.* سريع آلغضب . مُحتدٌّ
Passive *a.* قابل تأثيرسا . كِن . آلْمَجْهُول
Passover *n.* عِيدالفِصْحِ
Passport *n.* تَذْكِرَةُ آلْمرُورِ
Past *pr.* or *a.* or *n.* وَرَاءَ . عِبْرٌ . مَاضٍ
Paste *n.* or *v. t.* عصيدَةٌ . لاَزِقَة . أَلْزَقَ
Pasteboard *n.* وَرَقٌ سميك . كَرْتون
Pastime *n.* لعبٌ . لَهْوٌ
Pastor *n.* راعٍ . قسّيسٌ
Pastoral *a.* رَعوِيٌّ . قِسّيسيٌّ
Pastry *n.* كعكٌ . فطَائِرُ
Pasturage / **Pasture** *n.* مرْعًى . مرتعٌ
Pat *v. t.* or *n.* لَطَمَ خفيفًا وَلُطفًا
Pat *a.* في محلِّهِ . غَايَةِ آلْمُوَافَقَة
Patch *n.* or *v. t.* رُقعَة . رَقّعَ . رفأَ
Pate *n.* رَأْس . هَامَة
Patent *n.* or *v. t.* امتيَازٌ . أَعطى آمتيازاً
Patent *a.* وَاضِحٌ . جليٌّ . جِهَارِيٌّ
Paternal *a.* أَبَوِيٌّ . إِرْثيٌّ
Paternity *n.* أُبُوَّةٌ
Path *n.* سَبيل . صِرَاطٌ . سلوك
Pathetic *a.* مؤثِّرٌ في آلْعَوَاطِف
Pathless *a.* مَالاَيسلَك . لاطَرِيقَ فِيهِ
Pathology *n.* عِلمُ آلأَمْرَاض
Pathos *n.* مَا يُهيّجُ آلْعَوَاطِف
Pathway *n.* مسلكٌ . طَرِيقٌ . ممرٌّ
Patience *n.* صبرٌ . أَنَاة

Patient *a.* or *n.* صَبُورٌ . مَرِيضٌ

Patois *n.* لَغْوٌ . لَهْجَةٌ غَيْرُ فَصِيحَةٍ

Patriarch *n.* رَئِيسُ الآبَاءِ . بَطْرَكٌ

Patriarchate *a.* بَطْرَكِيَّةٌ

Patrician *n.* or *a.* نَجِيبٌ . شَرِيفٌ

Patrimony *n.* مِيرَاثٌ

Patriot *n.* / **Patriotic** *a.* } مُحِبُّ الْوَطَنِ

Patriotism *n.* مَحَبَّةُ الْوَطَنِ

Patrol *n.* or *v. i.* عَسَسٌ . دَوْرِيَّةٌ . عَسَّ ـُ

Patron *n.* وَلِيٌّ . مُحَامٍ . نَصِيرٌ

Patronage *n.* مُوَالاَةٌ . مُحَامَاةٌ

Patronize *v. t.* وَالَى . عَضَدَ ـُ . أَيَّدَ

Pattern *n.* or *v. t.* انْمُوذَجٌ . مِثَالٌ . تَمَثَّلَ بِ

Paucity *n.* قِلَّةٌ

Paunch *n.* بَطْنٌ . جَوْفٌ

Pauper *n.* فَقِيرٌ . عَائِشٌ مِنْ صَدَقَاتٍ

Pauperism *n.* فَقْرٌ . مَسْكَنَةٌ

Pauperize *v. t.* افْقَرَ

Pause *n.* or *v.i.* وَقْفٌ . فَتْرَةٌ . وَقَفَ

Pave *v. t.* بَلَّطَ . رَصَفَ ـُ . سَهَّلَ

Pavement *n.* بَلاَطٌ . رَصْفٌ . تَبْلِيطٌ

Pavillion *n.* خَيْمَةٌ . مِظَلَّةٌ

Paw *n.* or *v. i.* كَفُّ الْحَيَوَانِ . بَحَثَ بِهِ

Pawn *n.* or *v. t.* رَهِينَةٌ . رَهَنَ ـَ

Pawnbroker *n.* مُرْتَهِنٌ . مُسْتَرْهِنٌ

Pay *n.* or *v. i.* أُجْرَةٌ . أَوْفَى . ادَّى

Payable *a.* مُسْتَحِقٌّ . مَا يُوْفَى

Paymaster *n.* مُؤَدِّي الاجْرَةِ

Payment *n.* إِيفَاءٌ . دَفْعٌ . قِسْطٌ

Pea *n.* جُلْبَانٌ . بَسِلَّةٌ

Peace *n.* سَلاَمٌ . صُلْحٌ . رَاحَةٌ

Peaceable *a.* مُسَالِمٌ . مُطْمَئِنٌّ

Peaceful *a.* سِلْمِيٌّ . سَاكِنٌ

Peacemaker *n.* مُصَالِحٌ . صَانِعُ سَلاَمٍ

Peach *n.* دُرَاقِنٌ . (دُرَّاق . خَوْخ)

Peacock *n.* طَاوُوسٌ ج طَوَاوِيسُ

Peak *n.* قِمَّة . رَأْسُ جَبَلٍ
Peal *n.* or *v. i.* صَوْت قَوِيٌّ. صَوَّتَ
Pear *n.* إِنجَاص. إِجَّاصٌ. كُمَّثْرى
Pearl *n.* لُؤْلُؤَةٌ . دُرَّةٌ
Peasant *n.* فَلاحٌ
Peasantry *n.* أَلْفَلاَّحُونَ
Pebble *n.* حَصَاةٌ ج حَصَيَاتٌ وَحَصًى
Peck *n.* مِكْيَال يَسَعُ نَحْوَ مُدٍّ
Pectoral *a.* صَدْرِيٌّ
Peculation *n.* سَرْقَةٌ . إِخْتِلاَسٌ
Peculiar *a.* خَاصٌّ . نَادِرٌ
Peculiarity *n.* خَاصِّيَّةٌ . غَرَابَةٌ
Pecuniary *a.* مَالِي. مَنُوطٌ بِٱلدَّرَاهِمِ
Pedagogue *n.* مُعَلِّمُ أَوْلاَدٍ
Pedant *n.* / **Pedantic** *a.* } مُتَظَاهِرٌ بِٱلْعِلْمِ
Peddle *v. t.* دَارَ يَبِيعُ
Peddler *n.* عُنْقَاشٌ . بَيَّاعٌ
Pedestal *n.* قَاعِدَةُ عَمُودٍ
Pedestrian *n.* مَاشٍ
Pedigree *n.* نَسَبٌ
Peel *v. t.* or *n.* قَشَرَ . جَرَّدَ . قِشْرَةٌ
Peep *v. i.* or *n.* لاَصَ ـُ . سَارَقَ نَظْرَةً
Peer *n.* نَظِيرٌ . شَرِيفٌ . قَرِينٌ
Peerage *n.* رُتْبَةُ الشُّرَفَاءِ. جَمَاعَتُهُمْ
Peerless *a.* فَائِقٌ . لاَ نَظِيرَ لَهُ
Peevish *a.* نَكِدٌ
Peg *n.* or *v. t.* وَتَدٌ . مُسْمَارٌ خَشَبِيٌّ . سَمَّرَ بِهِ
Pelican *n.* بَجَعٌ (طَائِرٌ)
Pelf *n.* رِبْحٌ . مَالٌ . (خَاصَّةً) حَرَامٌ
Pellet *n.* كُرَيَّةٌ . حَبَّةٌ
Pell-mell *ad.* شَذَرَ مَذَرَ
Pelt *v. t.* رَمَى ـِ . رَجَمَ ـُ
Peltry *n.* جُلُودٌ
Pen *n.* or *v. t.* قَلَمٌ . زَرِيبَةٌ . كَتَبَ ـُ
Penal *a.* قِصَاصِيٌّ . جَزَائِيٌّ . عِقَابِيٌّ
Penalty *n.* قِصَاصٌ . عِقَابٌ

Penance *n.* كَفَّارَةٌ. عقوبةٌ. تَكْفِيرِيَّةٌ

Pencil *n.* or *v. t.* قَلَمٌ . رَسَمَ بِهِ

Pendant *n.* شَيْءٌ معلَّقٌ . قُرْطٌ

Pendent *a.* معلَّقٌ . متدَلٍّ

Pending *a.* معلَّقٌ . غيرُ مقضِيٍّ

Pendulum *n.* رَقَّاصُ ساعَةٍ

Penetrate *v. t.* خَرَقَ ـِ . تَخَلَّلَ . أَدْرَكَ

Penetration *n.* دُخولٌ. فِطْنَةٌ. ذَكاءٌ

Penetrating *a.* نافِذٌ. حادٌّ. ذَكِيٌّ

Peninsula *n.* شِبْهُ جَزِيرَةٍ

Peninsular *a.* على صُورَةِ شِبْهِ جَزِيرَةٍ

Penitence *n.* توبةٌ. إِنْسِحاقُ ٱلْقَلْبِ

Penitent *a.* تائِبٌ. نادِمٌ

Pentientiary *n.* سِجْنٌ

Penknife *n.* سِكِّينٌ صغيرٌ . (مطوى)

Penman *n.* عالِمٌ بالخَطِّ . كاتِبٌ

Penmanship *n.* صِناعةُ ٱلخَطِّ

Pennant }
Pennon } *n.* رَايَةٌ . بَيْرَقٌ صغيرٌ

Penniless *a.* فَقيرٌ . مفلِسٌ

Penny *n.* (*pl.* pence) نقودٌ أنكليزيّةٌ = ٢ بارَةً

Pension *n.* راتِبٌ . معاشٌ تقاعد

Pensioner *n.* صاحِبُ راتِبِ ٱلتَّقاعد

Pensive *n.* متفكِّرٌ . مشغولُ ٱلبالِ

Pent-up *a.* محصورٌ . محجوزٌ

Pentagon *n.* }
Pentagonal *a.* } مخمَّسُ ٱلزَّوايا

Pentateuch *n.* اسفارُ موسى ٱلخمسة

Pentecost *n.* يومُ ٱلخمسينَ. ٱلعَنْصَرَةُ

Penult *n.* مَقْطَعُ ٱلكلِمةِ قبلَ ٱلاخيرِ

Penurious *n.* بخيلٌ

Penury *a.* فقرٌ . فاقةٌ . عوزٌ

People *n.* or *v. t.* شعبٌ. أهلٌ. أناسٌ. عمَّرَ

Pepper *n.* or *v. t.* فُلْفُلٌ . فلفَلَ

Peppermint *n.* ضَرْبٌ مِنَ ٱلنَّعْنَعِ

Peradventure *ad.* لعلَّ . عسى

Perambulate *v. t.* دارَ ـُ . طافَ ـُ

Perceivable *a.* ما يُرى. ما يدرَكُ

Perceive *v. t.* رَأَى ـَ شعَرَ ـُ . أَدْرَكَ
Percent *ad.* بِٱلْمِئَة
Percentage *n.* نِسبَةٌ فِي ٱلمِئَة
Perceptible *a. see* **Perceivable.**
Perception *n.* شعورٌ . إِدْرَاكٌ
Perch *v. t.* جَثَمَ ـُ
Perchance *ad.* لَعَلَّ . رُبَّمَا
Percipient *a.* مُدرِكٌ . شَاعِرٌ
Percolate *v. i.* or *t.* رَشَحَ ـَ . صَفَّى
Percolation *n.* رَشْحٌ . تَصْفِيَة
Percussion *n.* طَرْقٌ . صَدْمٌ . قَرْعٌ
Perdition *n.* تَلَفٌ . هَلاَكٌ
Peremptory *a.* جَازِمٌ . قَطْعِيٌّ
Perennial *a.* مُستَمِرٌّ طُولَ ٱلسَّنَة
Perfect *a.* تَامٌّ . كَامِلٌ
Perfect *v. t.* كَمَّلَ . أَنْجَزَ . أَنفَذَ
Perfection *n.* كَمَالٌ . سَلاَمَة
Perfidious *n.* غَدَّارٌ . خَوَّان
Perfidy *n.* غَدْرٌ . خِيَانَة . خِدَاعٌ

Perforate *v. t.* ثَقَبَ ـُ . خَرَقَ ـُ
Perforation *n.* ثَقْبٌ . خَرْقٌ
Perforce *ad.* رغماً . جبرًا
Perform *v. t.* عَمِلَ ـَ . أَنْجَزَ . أَجْرَى
Performance *n.* عَمَلٌ . إِنجَازٌ
Performer *n.* عَامِلٌ . مُشَخِّصٌ
Perfume *n.* or *v. t.* عِطْرٌ . عَطَّرَ
Perfumery *n.* عِطْرٌ
Perhaps *ad.* رُبَّمَا . عَسَى . لَعَلَّ
Pericardium *n.* شَغَافٌ . غِلاَفُ ٱلقَلْبِ
Peril *n.* or *v. t.* خَطَرٌ . خَاطَرَ بِ
Perilous *a.* خَطِرٌ . مُخْطِرٌ
Period *n.* مُدَّة . عَصْرٌ . دَوْرٌ
Periodic / **Periodical** } *a.* دَوْرِيٌّ
Periodical *n.* نَشْرَةٌ . جَرِيدَةٌ
Periosteum *n.* سِمْحَاقٌ . غِشَاءُ ٱلْعَظْمِ
Perish *v. i.* هَلَكَ ـِ . بَادَ ـِ . فَنِيَ ـَ
Perishable *a.* سَرِيعُ ٱلزَّوَالِ أَوْ ٱلفَسَادِ

Perjure *v. t.* حَنَثَ ـ في. حلفَ ـِ زوراً

Perjury *n.* حنثٌ . يمين زورٍ

Permanence / **Permanency** } *n.* دَوَامٌ . بقاءٌ

Permanent *a.* باقٍ . ثابتٌ . مستمرٌّ

Permeable *a.* ما يتخلَّل. ما ينفذُ فيه

Permeate *v. t.* تخلَّلَ . نفذَ ـ في

Permissible *a.* مباحٌ . جائزٌ

Permission *n.* إذنٌ . رُخصةٌ

Permit *v. t.* أذنَ ـ . سمحَ ـ

Pernicious *a.* مؤذٍ . مهلِكٌ . مفسِدٌ

Perpendicular *a.* عموديٌّ . قائمٌ

Perpetrate *v. t.* فعلَ ـ . ارتكبَ

Perpetrator *n.* فاعِلٌ . مرتكِبٌ

Perpetual *a.* دائمٌ . مستمرٌّ . مؤبدٌ

Perpetuate *v. t.* أدامَ . خلَّدَ

Perpetuity *n.* دوَام . بقاءٌ

Perplex *v. t.* بهتَ ـ . حيَّرَ. شوَّشَ

Perplexing *a.* محيِّرٌ. مشوِّشٌ. مشكلٌ

Perplexity *n.* حيرةٌ . إرتباكٌ

Perquisite *n.* راتبٌ إضافيٌّ. عرضيٌّ

Persecute *v.t.* إضطهدَ. عنتَ. ظلمَ ـِ

Persecution *n.* إضطهادٌ . تعدٍ

Persecutor *n.* مضطهِدٌ

Perseverance *n.* مواظبةٌ . مداومةٌ

Persevere *v.t.* واظبَ. داومَ. لازمَ

Persian *a.* عجميٌّ . فارسيٌّ

Persist *v. i.* أصرَّ على. ثابرَ على

Persistence / **Persistency** } *n.* إصرارٌ . مثابرةٌ

Persistent / **Persisting** } *a.* مُصرٌّ . مثابرٌ

Person *n.* شخصٌ . ألذاتُ . أقنومٌ

Personal *a.* شخصيٌّ . ذاتيٌّ

Personate / **Personify** } *v. t.* شخَّصَ . مثَّلَ

Personification *n.* تشخيصٌ

Perspicacity *n.* ذكاءٌ . بصيرةٌ

Perspicuous *n.* جليٌّ . واضحٌ

Perspiration *n.* عرقٌ . رشيحٌ

Perspire *v. i.* عَرِق . رَشَحَ ـ

Persuade *v. t.* أَقْنَعَ . حَمَلَ على

Persuasion *n.* إِرْضَاءٌ . إِقْنَاعٌ . إِعتقادٌ

Persuasive *a.* مُرْضٍ . مستميل

Pert *a.* وَقِحٌ . سليط

Pertain *v. i.* إِختصَّ ب

Pertinacious *a.* مُصِرٌّ . عنيد

Pertinacity *n.* إِصْرَارٌ . عنادٌ

Pertinence / **Pertinency** *n.* مُوَافقةٌ . ملاءمة

Pertinent *a.* سديد . مناسبٌ

Perturbation *n.* قَلَقٌ . إِقلاقٌ

Perusal *n.* قِرَاءَة . مطالعة

Peruse *v. t.* قرأَ ـ . طالعَ

Pervade *v. t.* شَمَلَ ـ . عمَّ ـ . تخلَّل

Pervasion *n.* تخلُّلٌ . شمولٌ

Perverse *a.* متمرِّدٌ . شَكِسٌ

Perversion *n.* إِضلالٌ . إِفسادٌ . تحريفٌ

Perversity *n.* عِنادٌ . شَكَاسَة

Pervert *v. t.* أَضلَّ . حرَّفَ . افسدَ

Pest *a.* وَبَاءٌ . ضررٌ شديدٌ

Pester *v. t.* اقلق . أَضجرَ . ازعجَ

Pest house *n.* مستشفى لِأَمْرَاضٍ معديَة

Pestiferous / **Pestilential** *a.* وَبائِي مضِر . مفسِدٌ

Pestilence *n.* وَبَاءٌ

Pestilent *a.* مضِر . مفسدٌ

Pestle *n.* مِدَقَّة . مطرَقة

Pet *n.* or *v. t.* عَزِيز . مدلَّلٌ . دَلَّل

Petal *n.* وَرَقَة زهرَةٍ

Petiole *n.* ساق وَرَقةٍ

Petition *n.* طَلَبٌ . دعاءٌ . عريضة

Petition *v. t.* طَلَبَ ـُ . قدم عريضةً

Petrifaction *n.* تحجرٌ . محجرَةٌ

Petrify *v. t.* or *i.* حَجَّرَ . تحجَّرَ

Petroleum *n.* زَيتٌ . معدَنيٌّ . بترُولٌ

Petticoat *n.* فُستان تحتِيٌّ . تنورَةٌ

Pettish *a.* نَكِدٌ . شَكِسٌ

Petty *a.* صغير . طفيف . دني

Petulance *n.* نكد . شراسة

Petulant *a.* نكد . شرس . متذمر

Pew *n.* مقعد في كنيسة

Pewter *n.* مركب القصدير والرصاص

Phalanx *n.* كتيبة . كثيفة مربعة

Phantasm *n.* تصور . خيال

Phantom *n.* طيف . خيال

Pharaoh *n.* فرعون

Pharissee *n.* فريسي

Pharisaic *a.* مثل الفريسي . مراء

Pharisaism *n.* رياء . مذهب الفريسي

Pharmaceutic / **Pharmaceutical** *a.* صيدلي أجزائي

Pharmacist *n.* صيدلي

Pharmacopœia *n.* الأقراباذين

Pharmacy *n.* أجزائية . صيدلية .

Pharos *n.* منارة

Pharynx *n.* بلعوم

Phase *n.* منظر . صورة . حال

Phenomenon *n.* ظاهرة . حادثة

Phial *n.* قارورة . (قنينة)

Philanthropist *n.* محب البشر

Philanthropy *n.* محبة البشر

Philippic *n.* خطبة طعن

Philology *n.* علم اللغة

Philosopher *n.* فيلسوف

Philosophic / **Philosophical** *a.* فلسفي

Philsophy *n.* فلسفة

Phlegm *n.* بلغم

Phlegmatic *a.* بلغمي . بارد

Phonetic *a.* صوتي

Phosphorescent *a.* مضيء بضوء خفيف

Phosphorus *n.* فصفور

Photograph *n.* صورة شمسية

Photography *n.* التصوير الشمسي

Phrase *n.* عبارة . جملة

Phraseology *n.* صورة الكلام

Phthisis *n.* دَاءُ ٱلسِّلِّ

Physic *n.* أَلطِّبُّ. دَوَاءٌ

Physical *n.* طَبِيعِيٌّ

Physician *n.* طَبِيبٌ

Physics *n.* عِلْمُ ٱلطَّبِيعِيَّاتِ

Physiognomy *n.* هَيْئَةُ ٱلْوَجْهِ

Physiology *n.* عِلْمُ ٱلْفِسْيُولُوجِيَا

Piazza *n.* رِوَاقٌ . سَاحَةٌ

Pick *v. t.* اِلْتَقَطَ — . إِنْتَخَبَ

Pick } *n.* مِعْوَلٌ
Pick-axe }

Picket *n.* وَتِدٌ . طَلِيعَةُ حَرَسٍ

Pickle *v. t.* or *n.* كَبَسَ فِي خَلٍّ . كَبِيس

Picnic *n.* تَنَزُّهٌ

Pickpocket *n.* لِصٌّ . نَشَّالٌ

Pictorial *a.* تَصَوُّرِيٌّ . صُورِيٌّ

Picture *n.* صُورَةٌ

Picturesque *a.* جَمِيلُ ٱلْمَنْظَرِ

Pie *n.* نَوْعٌ مِنَ ٱلْحَلْوَى مَحْشُوٌّ

Piece *n.* قِطْعَةٌ . جُزْءٌ

Piecemeal *ad.* قِطْعَةً فَقِطْعَةً

Pier *n.* دِعَامَةٌ رَصِيفٌ مُمْتَدٌّ فِي ٱلْبَحْرِ

Pierce *v. t.* خَرَقَ — ُ . ثَقَبَ — ُ . طَعَنَ

Piercing *a.* خَارِقٌ . حَادٌّ

Piety *n.* تَقْوَى . تَدَيُّنٌ

Pig *n.* خِنَّوْصٌ . خِنْزِيرٌ صَغِيرٌ

Pigeon *n.* حَمَامَةٌ . يَمَامَةٌ

Pigmy *n.* قَزَمُ ٱلْجِنْسِ

Pike *n.* رُمْحٌ . حَرْبَةٌ

Pile *n.* or *v. t.* كَوْمَةٌ . وَتِدٌ . كَوَّمَ

Piles *n. pl.* بَوَاسِيرُ

Pilfer *v. t.* سَرَقَ أَشْيَاءَ طَفِيفَةً

Pilgrim *n.* حَاجٌّ . زَائِرٌ

Pilgrimage *n.* حَجٌّ

Pill *n.* حَبَّةٌ (لِلْعِلَاجِ)

Pillage *n.* or *v. t.* نَهْبٌ سَلْبٌ نَهَبَ

Pillar *n.* عَمُودٌ . اسْطُوَانَةٌ

Pillow *n.* مخدّةٌ . وِسادةٌ

Pilot *n.* or *v.t.* دَليل لِسفينةٍ . هدَى

Pimple *n.* بَثْرةٌ صغيرةٌ

Pin *n.* or *v. t.* دَبّوسٌ . ضبطَ بِهِ

Pinch *v. t.* or *n.* قبَضَ ـَ قرَصَ ـُ ضيَّقَ على

Pincers / **Pinchers** *n.* مَلقطٌ . كَمّاشةٌ

Pincushion *n.* وِسادةٌ لِلدَّبابيسِ

Pine *n.* or *v. t.* صنوبرٌ . نحَلَ ـَ . تاقَ ـُ

Pink *n.* or *a.* قرنفُلٌ وَرديُّ اللَّونِ

Pinnacle *n.* قمةٌ . شُرْفةٌ

Pint *n.* مِكيالٌ يسعُ نحوَ ٢٠٠ درهمٍ

Pioneer *n.* ممهِّدُ الطريقِ . متقدِّمٌ

Pious *a.* تقيٌّ . متديِّنٌ

Pipe *n.* قسطَلٌ . مِزمارٌ . قصبةٌ

Piper *n.* زمّارٌ

Pique *n.* or *v.t.* غيظٌ . ضجرٌ . هاجَ

Pirates *n.* لصوصُ البحرِ . قرصانٌ

Pistachio *n.* فُستُقٌ

Pistil *n.* مِدَقّةُ الزَّهرِ

Pistol *n.* فَرْدٌ . طَبَنْجةٌ

Pit *n.* حفرةٌ . هاويةٌ . نُقرةٌ

Pitch *n.* قيرٌ . درَجةُ الصَّوتِ

Pitch *v. t.* طَلَى بالقيرِ . رمَى . وقَّعَ

Pitch *v. i.* or *t.* حطَّ ـُ . نزَلَ . ضربَ

Pitcher *n.* إبريقٌ . كوزٌ

Pitfall *n.* حفرةُ صيدٍ . اغويةٌ

Pith *n.* لُبٌّ . زبدةٌ . خلاصةٌ

Pithy *a.* سديدٌ

Pitiable *a.* ما يُرثَى لهُ

Pitiful *a.* شفوقٌ . زهيدٌ . حقيرٌ

Pitiless *a.* بلا شفقةٍ . صارمٌ

Pittance *n.* مبلغٌ زهيدٌ . صدقةٌ زهيدةٌ

Pity *n.* or *v. t.* شفقةٌ . أشفقَ على

Pivot *n.* مِحوَرٌ . مَدارٌ

Placard *n.* إعلانٌ

Placate *v. t.* طيَّبَ النفسَ . سكَّنَ غيظَهُ

Place *n.* or *v. t.* مكَان . مَوْضِعٌ . وَضَعَ ـَ
Placid *a.* هَادِئٌ . سَاكِنٌ
Plagiarize *v. i.* تَنَحَّلَ . إِنتحلَ
Plague *n.* طاعون . وَبَآءٌ . بلِية
Plague *v. t.* أَزْعَجَ . عَنى . كَدَّرَ
Plain *n.* سَهْلٌ . مِهَادٌ
Plain *a.* سَهْلٌ . وَاضِحٌ . بسِيطٌ
Plainly *ad.* جليا . بإِخلاصٍ بِبَساطةٍ
Plainness *n.* وُضُوحٌ . بَسَاطة . بيَان
Plaint *n.* شَكْوَى . حَنينٌ
Plaintiff *n.* مدَّعٍ شَرْعِيٌّ
Plaintive *a.* مُحزِنٌ . حَزِينٌ
Plait *v. t.* or *n.* ضَفَرَ ـِ . ثَنى ـ . ضَفِيرَة
Plan *n.* تَدْبِيرٌ . قَصْدٌ . رَسْمٌ
Plan *v. t.* دَبَّرَ . رَسَمَ ـ هنَا
Plane *a.* or *n.* مسطَّحٌ . مسطحٌ . (فَارَة) نجارٍ
Planet *n.* سيَارٌ (نجمَة)
Planetary *a.* سَيَّارِيٌّ
Plank *n.* لَوحٌ سَمِيكٌ
Plant *n.* or *v. t.* نبتٌ . غرسَ ـِ
Plantation *n.* منبت . مزرَعَةٌ
Plaster *n.* or *v. t.* طينٌ . أزقة . طينَ
Plastering *n.* تَكلِيسٌ . وَرَقَةٌ
Plate *n.* صحنٌ . آنية فِضيَّة أَوْ ذَهَبيَّة
Plate *v. t.* لَبسَ بِمعدِنٍ
Plateau *n.* سَهلٌ مُرْتَفِعٌ . هضَبَةٌ
Platform *n.* مِنبَرٌ . سَطحٌ مُرْتَفِعٌ
Platter *n.* قَصعَةٌ ج قِصَاعٌ
Plaudit *n.* إستحسَان . مَدْحٌ
Plausible *a.* مُرْضٍ . مِمَّا يصدَّقُ
Play *v. t.* لَعبَ ـَ . شَخَّصَ . عَزَفَ ـِ
Play *n.* لَعِبٌ . تسلِيَةٌ
Playful *a.* لَعُوبٌ . دَعِبٌ
Playfellow / **Playmate** *n.* رَفيقٌ فِي اللِّعبِ
Plaything *n.* لعبة . أُلعُوبة
Plea *n.* حُجَّة . إِعتِذَارٌ . دُعاءٌ

Plead *v. i.* إحتجَّ . إبتهل . رافع

Pleasant
Pleasing } *a.* سارٌ . طيّبٌ . انيسٌ

Pleasantry *n.* مزحٌ . هزل

Please *v. t.* سرّ ـُ . أرضى . أعجبَ

Pleasure *n.* سُرورٌ . لذّةٌ . إنشراحٌ

Plebeian *a.* or *n.* عامّيٌّ . أحدُ العوامّ

Pledge *v. t.* رهنَ . تعهّد . عربنَ

Pledge *n.* رهنٌ . عهدٌ . ضمان

Plenary *a.* تامٌّ . كاملٌ . عام

Plenipotentiary *n.* سفيرٌ . مُطلق

Plenteous
Plentiful } *a.* وافرٌ . غزيرٌ . كثيرٌ

Plenty *n.* وفرٌ . كثرةٌ . غزارة

Pleurisy *n.* داءُ ذاتِ الجنب

Pliable
Pliant } *a.* ليّنٌ . مُذعِنٌ

Plight *n.* or *v. t.* عهد . حال . عهدَ ـَ

Plod *v. t.* سعى بمشقةٍ . كدّ ـُ

Plot *n.* مكيدةٌ . مؤامرة . بقعة

Plot *v. t.* or *i.* رسمَ ـُ . دبّر . إحتال

Plow
Plough } *n.* or *v. t.* محراثٌ . حرثَ ـُ

Plowshare
Ploughshare } *n.* سكّةُ محراثٍ

Pluck *v. t.* or *n.* قلعَ ـَ . قطفَ ـُ . شجاعةٌ

Plug *n.* or *v. t.* سِدادٌ . سدَّ ـُ

Plum *n.* خوخٌ . خوخةٌ (برقوق)

Plumage *n.* ريشٌ

Plume *n.* ريشةٌ . وسامُ شرفٍ

Plummet *n.* مقياسُ العمقِ . شاقولٌ

Plump *a.* or *ad.* سمينٌ . مُشحمٌ . فجأةً

Plunder *v. t.* or *n.* نهبَ ـَ . سلبَ ـُ . غنيمةٌ

Plunge *v. t.* or *i.* غمسَ ـِ . غطسَ ـِ . خاضَ ـُ

Plural *a.* or *n.* اكثرُ مِن واحدٍ . ألجمع

Plurality *n.* أكثريّةٌ . تعدّدٌ

Plus *n.* علامةُ الجمعِ (+)

Ply *v. t.* or *n.* ألحَّ . شغل . جدَّ . ثنيةٌ

Pneumatics *n. sing.* عِلمُ الهواء

Pneumonia *n.* داءُ ذات الرئةِ

Poach *v. t.* سرقَ صيدًا . نهبَ ـَ

Pocket *n.* or *v. t.* جَيْبٌ . وَضَعَ فِيهِ

Pod *n.* قُرْنَةُ نَبَاتٍ

Poem *n.* قَصِيدَةٌ

Poesy *n.* شِعْرٌ . عِلْمُ ٱلنَّظْمِ

Poet *n.* شَاعِرٌ

Poetic / **Poetical** *a.* شِعْرِيٌّ . نَظْمِيٌّ

Poetry *n.* شِعْرٌ . دِيوَانُ شِعْرٍ

Poignant *a.* شَدِيدٌ . حَادٌّ . شَاقٌّ

Point *n.* رَأْسٌ . نُقْطَةٌ . مُرَادٌ

Point *v. t.* or *i.* أَشَارَ . سَنَّ ـَ . نَقَّطَ . وَجَّهَ

Pointer *n.* دَلِيلٌ . كَلْبُ صَيْدٍ

Pointless *n.* كَلِيلٌ . بِلَا مَعْنًى

Poise *n.* ثِقْلٌ . مُوَازَنَةٌ

Poison *n.* or *v. t.* سَمٌّ . سَمَّ ـُ

Poisonous *a.* سَامٌّ

Poke *n.* or *v. t.* دَفْعٌ . دَفَعَ ـَ . وَكَزَ

Poker *n.* مِحْرَاكٌ

Polar *n.* قُطْبِيٌّ

Polarity *n.* أَلْإِتِّجَاهُ نَحْوَ ٱلْقُطْبِ

Polarize *v. t.* أَعْطَاهُ خَاصِيَةَ ٱلِاتِّجَاهِ لِلْقُطْبِ

Pole *n.* قُطْبٌ . قَضِيبٌ طَوِيلٌ

Pole-star *n.* نَجْمُ ٱلْقُطْبِ

Police *n.* ضَابِطَةُ مَدِينَةٍ . بُولِيسٌ

Policy *n.* سِيَاسَةٌ . تَدْبِيرٌ

Polish *n.* or *v. t.* صَقْلٌ . صَقَلَ ـُ

Polite *a.* أَدِيبٌ . أَنِيسٌ

Politeness *n.* أَدَبٌ . أُنْسٌ

Politic *a.* بَصِيرٌ . فَطِنٌ

Political *a.* سِيَاسِيٌّ

Politics *n. sing.* أُمُورُ ٱلسِّيَاسَةِ

Polity *n.* نِظَامُ دَوْلَةٍ أَوْ سِيَاسَةٍ

Poll *n.* or *v. t.* رَأْسٌ . إِنْتِخَابٌ . قَيَّدَ ٱلْأَسْمَاءَ

Pollen *n.* هَبَاءُ أَسْدِيَةِ ٱلنَّبَاتِ

Poll-tax *n.* ضَرِيبَةٌ عَلَى ٱلشَّخْصِ

Pollute *v. t.* أَفْسَدَ . نَجَّسَ . وَسَّخَ

Pollution *n.* نَجَاسَةٌ . رَجَاسَةٌ

Poltroon *n.* جَبَانٌ . خَسِيسٌ

Polygamy *n.* تَعَدُّدُ ٱلزَّوْجَاتِ . ضِرٌّ

Polygon *n.* كَثِيرُ ٱلاضْلاعِ

Polysyllable *n.* لَفْظَةٌ مُعَدَّدَةُ ٱلْمَقَاطِعِ

Polytheism *n.* أَلْقَوْلُ بِكَثْرَةِ ٱلآلِهَةِ

Pomade *n.* دِهَانُ ٱلشَّعْرِ

Pomegranate *n.* رُمَّانَةٌ

Pommel *v. t.* or *n.* ضَرَبَ — ِ . قَرَبُوسٌ

Pomp *n.* مُبَاهَاةٌ . مَوْكِبٌ

Pompous *a.* مُبَاهٍ . فَخُورٌ . مُتَأَبِّهٌ

Pond *n.* بِرْكَةٌ ج. بِرَك

Ponder *v. i.* تَأَمَّلَ . تَفَكَّرَ

Ponderous *a.* ثَقِيلٌ . مُهِمٌّ

Poniard *n.* or *v.t.* خَنْجَرٌ . طعن به

Pontiff *n.* حَبْرٌ . رَئِيسُ ٱلْكَهَنَةِ

Pontifical *a.* حَبْرِيٌّ . بَابَوِيٌّ

Pony *n.* فَرَسٌ صَغِيرٌ

Poodle *n.* كُلَيْبٌ

Pool *n.* بِرْكَةٌ . غَدِيرٌ

Poor *a.* فَقِيرٌ . مِسْكِينٌ . حَقِيرٌ

Poorly *ad.* بِحَالَةٍ سَيِّئَةٍ

Pop *n.* or *v.i.* صَوْتُ ٱنْفِجَارٍ . إِنْفَجَرَ

Pope *n.* بَابَا

Popery *n.* مَذْهَبُ ٱلْبَابَا

Popish *a.* بَابَوِيٌّ

Poplar *n.* شَجَرُ ٱلْحَوْزِ

Poppy *n.* خَشْخَاشٌ

Populace *n.* أَلْعَامَّةُ . رَعَاعُ ٱلنَّاسِ

Popular *a.* مقبول عِنْدَ ٱلْجُمْهُورِ

Popularity *n.* قُبُولٌ عِنْدَ ٱلنَّاسِ

Popularize *v. t.* جَعَلَ مَقْبُولاً عِنْدَ ٱلنَّاسِ

Populate *v. t.* أَعْمَرَ

Population *n.* أَهْلٌ . سُكَّانٌ

Populous *a.* كَثِيرُ ٱلسُّكَّانِ

Porcelain *n.* خَزَفٌ صِينِيٌّ

Porch *n.* رِوَاقٌ . إِيوَانٌ

Porcupine *n.* قُنْفُذ ج قنافذ

Pore *n.* مَسَمٌّ ج مسامّ

Pork *n.* لَحمُ خِنزِير

Porous *a.* ذو مسامّ

Porridge *n.* ثَرِيد. عَصِيدَة

Port *n.* ميناءٌ. يسارُ سفينةٍ. مَرْفأ

Portable *a.* خفيفٌ. يُمْكِنُ نقلُهُ

Portage *n.* نَقْلٌ. اجرتهُ

Portal *n.* بابٌ. مَدْخَلٌ

Porte *n.* الْبَابُ الْعَالي

Portend *v. t.* دلَّ على. أنبأَ بهِ

Portent *n.* علامةُ سوءٍ. شؤمٌ

Portentous *a.* مُنذِرٌ بسوءٍ

Porter *n.* حمّالٌ. بوّابٌ (عتّال. شيّال)

Port-hole *n.* كوة مدفعٍ في سفينة

Portico *n.* رواقٌ

Portion *n.* or *v. t.* جزء. حصة. قسم

Portly *a.* جسيمٌ. مهيب الهيئة

Portmanteau *n.* صندوقُ سفرٍ صغيرٌ

Portrait *n.* صورة شخص

Portray *v. t.* صوَّر. وصف —

Position *n.* مقامٌ. مركز. حال

Positive *a.* أكيدٌ. متيقنٌ. جازم

Possess *v. t.* مَلَكَ ـ حازَ ـ. إقتنى

Possession *n.* مِلْكٌ. تملّكٌ

Possessive *a.* ملكيٌّ. المضافُ إليهِ

Possessor *n.* مالِك. صاحِبٌ. ربٌّ

Possibility *n.* إمكانٌ

Possible *a.* مُمْكِنٌ. مُحتملٌ

Post *v. t.* (accounts) شطّب حساباً

Post *n.* عمودٌ. بريدٌ. منصبٌ

Postage *n.* اجرة البريد

Postal *a.* مختصٌّ بالبريدِ

Posterior *a.* خلفيٌّ. بعد. تال

Posterity *n.* ذرّية. أهل المستقبلِ

Post-haste *ad.* بغاية السّرعة

Postman *n.* سَاعِي ٱلْبَرِيدِ (بُوسْطَجِيٌّ)

Post-master *n.* مُدِيرُ ٱلْبَرِيد

Post-office *n.* مَرْكَزُ إِدَارَةِ ٱلْبَرِيدِ

Postpone *v. t.* أَخَّرَ. أَجَّلَ

Postscript *n.* ذَيْلٌ. مُلْحَق

Postulate *n.* فَرْضٌ. قَضِيَّةٌ أَوَّلِيَّة

Posture *n.* وَضْعٌ. هَيْئَةٌ. حَالَة

Posy *n.* زَهْرَةٌ. بَاقَة

Pot *n.* قِدْرٌ. مِرْجَل

Potash *n.* قِلْيٌ. قلى

Potable *a.* صَالِحٌ لِلشُّرْبِ

Potato *n.* بَطَاطِسُ

Potency *n.* عِزَّةٌ. قُوَّةٌ. صَوْلَة

Potent *a.* قَوِيٌّ. مُقْتَدِرٌ. عَزِيز

Potentate *n.* مُسَلَّط. مَلِك

Potential *a.* مُمْكِنٌ وُجُودُه

Potion *n.* جَرْعَةٌ. شَرْبَة

Pottage *n.* طَبِيخٌ مِنْ لَحْمٍ وَخُضَرٍ

Potter *n.* خَزَّافٌ. فَخَّارِيٌّ

Pottery *n.* خَزَفٌ. فَخَارٌ

Pouch *n.* كِيسٌ. جِرَابٌ. حَوْصَلَة

Poultice *n.* or *v. t.* لَزُوقٌ. عَالَجَ بِهِ

Poultry *n.* دَجَاجٌ

Pounce *v. i.* إِنْقَضَّ عَلَى

Pound *n.* رِطْلٌ أَنْكِلِيزِيٌّ. لِيرَةٌ أَنْكِلِيزِيَّة

Pound *v. t.* مَسْحُوقٌ —. دَقَّ

Pour *v.t.* or *i.* صَبَّ. سَكَبَ. تَدَفَّقَ

Poverty *n.* فَقْرٌ. فَاقَة

Powder *n.* مَسْحُوقٌ. سَفُوفٌ. بَارُودٌ

Power *n.* قُوَّةٌ. قُدْرَة. سُلْطَانٌ

Powerful *a.* قَوِيٌّ. مُقْتَدِرٌ. قَدِيرٌ

Powerless *a.* عَاجِزٌ

Pox *n.* أَلدَّاءُ الزُّهْرِيُّ

Small-pox *n.* أَلْجُدَرِيُّ

Practicability *n.* إِمْكَانُ ٱلْعَمَلِ

Practicable *a.* مُمْكِنٌ عَمَلُهُ

Practical *a.* مُوافقٌ لِلحالِ أوْ لِلعمَلِ

Practice *n.* or *v. t.* مُمارسةٌ . عادة . مارسَ

Practitioner *n.* طبيبٌ . عامِل

Prairie *n.* فلاة ذات كلأ

Praise *n.* or *v. t.* مدْحٌ . حمْد . مدحَ . سبّحَ

Praiseworthy *a.* خليقٌ بالمدح

Prance *v. i.* شبّ ـُـ (حصان)

Prate *v. i.* هذرَ ـَـ

Pratique *n.* براءة الصحّة . براتيكه

Prattle *n* or *v. i.* ثرْثرة الولد . ثرْثر

Pray *v. t.* or *i.* توسّل . تضرّع . صلّى

Prayer *n.* توسّلٌ . طلبٌ . صلاةٌ

Preach *v. i.* or *t.* كرزَ ـِـ . بشّر . وعظَ ـِـ

Preacher *n.* واعِظ . مُبشّر

Preamble *n.* دِيباجة . مقدّمة

Precarious *a.* غيرُ ثابتٍ أوْ موثوق بِهِ

Precaution *n.* حذرٌ . إحتِياط

Precautional / **Precautionary** *a.* حذرِيٌّ إحتِياطيٌّ

Precede *v. t.* سبقَ ـُـ . تقدّم

Precedence / **Precedency** *n.* تقدُّمٌ . أفضليّة

Precedent *a.* or *n.* مقدّمٌ . سابقة

Precept *n.* مبدأ . سنّة . أمْرٌ

Preceptor *n.* معلّمٌ . مهذّبٌ

Precious *a.* ثمينٌ . عزيز . نفيسٌ

Precipice *n.* جرفٌ شاهق . وهدة

Precipitance / **Precipitancy** *n.* عجلة . تهوُّرٌ

Precipitant *a.* متهوّرٌ . عجُول

Precipitate *v. t.* رسّب . اعجل

Precipitate *a.* or *n.* متهوّر . رُسوبٌ

Precipitation *n.* تهوُّرٌ . ترسيب

Precipitous *a.* شامِخ . عجُول

Precise *a.* مدقّق . مضبوطٌ . متأنّقٌ

Preciseness / **Precision** *n.* ضبْط . إتقان

Preclude *v. t.* منع . أغلق . سدّ على

Precocious *a.* بالغ قبل أوانه . مبتسر

Precociousness / **Precocity** *n.* بلوغ قبل الوقت

Preconceive *v. t.* سبق فتصور

Preconcerted *a.* متفق عليه سابقًا

Precursor *n.* سابق . علامة . بشير

Predaceous *a.* عائش بالصيد . مفترس

Predatory *n.* ناهب . خاطف . مفترس

Predecessor *n.* سابق . سالف

Predestinate / **Predestine** *v. t.* سبق فقضى قدر

Predetermine *v. t.* سبق فحتم

Predicament *n.* حال . ورطة

Predicate *n.* or *v. t.* خبر . مسند . اسند

Predict *v. t.* أنبأ به

Prediction *n.* نبوءة . إنباء

Predispose *v. t.* سبق فأمال أو هيأ

Predisposition *n.* ميل سابق

Predominant *n.* غالب . مستغل

Predominate *v. i.* فاق . غلب

Preeminence *n.* أسبقية

Preeminent *a.* فائق . سابق

Preemption *n.* حق الشفعة

Preengagement *n.* تعهد سابق

Preexistence *n.* سبق الوجود

Preexistent / **Preexisting** *a.* كائن سابقًا

Preface *n.* or *v. t.* مقدمة . صدر . فتح

Prefatory *a.* إفتتاحي . ديباجي

Prefer *v. t.* آثر . فضل . عرض —

Preferable *a.* أفضل . أولى

Preference *n.* تفضيل . إيثار

Preferment *n.* ترقية . تقديم

Prefigure *v. t.* رمز إلى . سبق فمثل

Prefix *v. t.* صدر . أدخل على

Prefix *n.* إضافة إبتدائية

Pregnancy *n.* حبل . حمل

Pregnant *a.* حبلى . متضمن كثيرًا

Prejudge *v. t.* حكم قبل الفحص

Prejudice *n.* ميل أو حكم سابق . ضرر

Prejudicial *a.* مضر . مؤذ

Prelate *n.* أُسقفٌ

Preliminary *a.* إِفتِتاحيٌّ

Prelude *n.* فاتِحَة . مقدَّمة

Premature *a.* قَبلَ وقتِهِ . مُبتَسرٌ

Premeditate *v. t.* سبَق فتأمل

Premeditated *a.* عمدِيٌّ . مقصودٌ

Premier *n.* أَوَّل . وزيرٌ أَوَّل

Premise *v. t.* or *i.* صدَّر كلامهُ ب

Premises *n. pl.* مُقدَّمات قِياس

Premium *n.* رِبًا . جزءٌ إِكراميٌّ

Preoccupy *v. t.* سبق فملك . شغل البال

Preordain *v. t.* سبَق فعين أَو أَعدَّ

Preparation *n.* إِستعداد . تهيوٌ

Preparative / Preparatory *a.* مهيِّئٌ إِستعداديٌّ

Prepare *v. t.* هيأ . أَعدَّ

Prepay *v. t.* سلَّف الاجرَة

Preponderate *v. i.* رجح ـِ . زاد على

Preposition *n.* حرفُ جرٍّ

Prepossessing *a.* مستَميِل مستَعطِفٌ

Prepossession *n.* تملُّك أَو رأيٌ سابق

Preposterous *a.* مخالفُ العقلِ . عبث

Prerequisite *a.* or *n.* لازمٌ . لزومٌ . سابِق

Prerogative *n.* إِمتِياز

Presage *n.* or *v. t.* إِنذارٌ . أَنذَر

Presbyter *n.* قسيسٌ

Presbytery *n.* مشيخَة الكنيسةِ

Prescribe *v. t.* أَمر ـُ . فرض ـِ . وصف ـِ

Prescription *n.* وصفة علاج

Presence *n.* حضور . وُجودٌ . حضرةٌ

Present *a.* or *n.* حاضِرٌ . الحاضِرُ . هدِية

Present *v. t.* أَهدَى . أَظهر . قدَّم

Presentation *n.* إِهدَاءٌ . تقديمٌ

Presentiment *n.* رأيٌ سابق . هاجسٌ

Presently *ad.* حالاً . عن قريبٍ

Preservation *n.* حِفظٌ . أَمن

Preserve *v. t.* حفِظَ ـ . صانَ

Preside *v. t.* رَأَسَ . أَدَارَ

Presidency *n.* رَآسَة

President *n.* رَئِيسٌ

Press *v. t.* ضَغَطَ ـَ كَبَسَ ـِ . حَثَّ ـُ

Press *n.* مِكْبَسٌ . مَطْبَعَة

Pressing *a.* مُهِمٌّ . ضَرُورِيٌّ

Pressure *n.* ضَغْطٌ . حَصْرٌ . إِلْحَاحٌ

Prestige *n.* نُفُوذ . جَاه

Presumable *a.* مُوَافِقُ ٱلظَّنِّ . مُحْتَمَلٌ

Presume *v. t.* or *i.* ظَنَّ . خَمَّنَ . تَجَرَّأَ

Presumption *n.* ظَنٌّ . تَجَبُّرٌ . تَرْجِيحٌ

Presumptive *a.* مَظْنُونٌ . مُرَجَّحٌ

Presumptuous *a.* مُتَجَبِّرٌ . مُعْجَبٌ

Presuppose *v.t.* سَبَقَ فَظَنَّ أَوْ فَرَضَ

Pretend *v. t.* إِدَّعَى . تَظَاهَرَ

Pretence
Pretension } *n.* إِدِّعَاء . حُجَّة

Pretentious *a.* مُبَالِغٌ فِي ٱلِادِّعَاءِ

Preternatural *a.* فَوْقَ ٱلطَّبِيعَةِ

Pretext *n.* حُجَّةٌ . إِدِّعَاء . عُذْرٌ

Pretty *a.* حَسَنٌ . جَمِيل . ظَرِيفٌ

Prevail *v. i.* غَلَبَ ـِ . فَاقَ ـُ . عَمَّ ـُ

Prevalence *n.* إِسْتِيلَاء . إِنْتِشَارٌ

Prevalent
Prevailing } *a.* مُنْتَشِرٌ . مُشْتَدٌّ

Prevaricate *v. i.* مَوَّهَ . وَارَبَ

Prevent *v. t.* مَنَعَ ـَ . صَدَّ ـُ

Preventable *a.* مِمَّا يُمْنَعُ

Preventative
Preventive } *n.* or *a.* مَانِع

Previous *a.* سَابِق . سَالِف . مَاضٍ

Prey *n.* or *v. t.* فَرِيسَةٌ . غَنِيمَةٌ . إِفْتَرَسَ

Price *n.* ثَمَنٌ . سِعْرٌ

Priceless *a.* مَا لَا يُثَمَّنُ . فَوْقَ كُلِّ ثَمَنٍ

Prick *v. t.* or *n.* نَخَسَ ـُ . نَخَزَ ـَ . نَخْسَة

Prickle *n.* شُوَيْكَةٌ

Prickly *a.* كَثِيرُ ٱلشَّوْكِ

Prickly-pear *n.* صَبِّيرٌ (تِينٌ بِشَوْكِه)

Pride *n.* كِبْرِيَاء . عِزَّةُ ٱلنَّفْسِ

Priest *n.*	كاهِنٌ . خُورِي
Priesthood *n.*	كَهَنُوتٌ
Priestly *a.*	كَهَنُوتِيٌّ
Prim *a.*	مُتَأَنِّق
Primary *a.*	أَوَّلِيٌّ . أَصْلِيٌّ
Prime *a.* or *n.*	أَوَّل . الأَعْلَى درجَةً
Primer *n.*	كِتَابُ مَبَادِئ
Primeval *a.*	مِنَ العُصُورِ الاولى
Primitive *a.*	إِبْتِدَائِيٌّ . أَصْلِيٌّ
Primness *n.*	تَأَنُّق
Prince *n.*	أَمِير . إِبْنُ مَلِكٍ
Princess *n.*	أَمِيرَة . إِبْنَةُ مَلِكٍ
Principal *a.* or *n.*	أَعْظَمُ . أَوَّلُ . رَئِيسٌ
Principality *n.*	سَلْطَنَة . إِمَارَة
Principle *n.*	مَبْدَأٌ . قَاعِدَة
Print *v. t.* or *n.*	طَبَعَ . وَسَمَ . أَثَر
Printer *n.*	طَبَّاع . صَاحِبُ مَطْبَعَةٍ
Printing *n.*	طَبْع
Prior *a.* or *n.*	سَابِق . رَئِيسُ دَيْر
Prioress *n.*	رَئِيسَةُ دَيْر
Priority *n.*	أَسْبَقِيَّة . تَقَدُّم
Prism *n.*	مَوْشُور . مَنْشُور
Prismatic *n.*	مَوْشُورِي
Prison *n.*	سِجْن . حَبْس
Prisoner *n.*	مَحْبُوس . أَسِير
Privacy *a.*	إِنْفِرَاد . عُزْلَة . سِرّ
Private *a.*	سِرِّي . مُنْفَرِد . خَاصّ
Privateer *n.*	سَفِينَة حَرْبِيَّة خَاصَّة
Privation *n.*	حِرْمَان . عَوَز . عَدَم
Privilege *n.*	إِمْتِيَاز . فَائِدَة . رُخْصَة
Privily *ad.*	سِرًّا . خِفْيَةً
Privy *a.* or *n.*	عَارِف سِرًّا . خَاصّ . خَلَاء
Prize *n.* or *v. t.*	جَائِزَة . جُعَالَة . اعز
Probability *n.*	تَرْجِيح
Probable *a.*	مُرَجَّح
Probation *n.*	إِمْتِحَان

Probe *v. t.* or *n.* سَبَرَ ـُ . مِسبارٌ

Probity *n.* إِستقامة . امانة

Problem *n.* مسألة . قضيةٌ

Problematical *a.* غيرُ ظاهرٍ . مبْهَمٌ

Proboscis *n.* خرطومٌ

Proceed *v. i.* تقدَّمَ . شرَعَ في . صدَرَ ـُ

Proceeding *n.* عمل . تصرُّفٌ

Proceeds *n. pl.* حاصِلٌ . دخْل

Process *n.* فعل . كيفية . طريقة

Procession *n.* موكِبٌ

Proclaim *v. t.* نادى ب . صرَّحَ

Proclamation *n.* مُناداة . إعلانٌ

Proclivity *n.* ميل . إنعِطاف

Procrastinate *v. t.* or *i.* أجَّلَ . تأخرَ

Procreate *v. t.* وَلَدَ ـِ . أنتجَ

Procumbent *a.* مُلقى على وجهه

Procurable *a.* ما يُحصل

Procure *v. t.* حصَّلَ . فاز بِ

Prodigal *a.* مُسرِف . مبذِّر

Prodigality *n.* تبذير . إسراف

Prodigious *a.* عظيم . عجيبٌ

Prodigy *a.* معجزة . آيةٌ

Produce *v. t.* or *n.* انتجَ . أوردَ . غلّة

Product *n.* نتيجة . حاصِل

Productive *a.* مُنتِج . مثمِر . مُسبِّبٌ

Profanation *n.* تدنيسُ مقدَّسٍ

Profane *a.* or *v. t.* دنس . دُنيوِيٌّ . دنَّسَ

Profaneness / **Profanity** *n.* دَناسة . تجديف

Profess *v. t.* أقرَّ . تظاهرَ . قال ب

Profession *n.* إقرار . عقيدة . حرفة

Professor *n.* مُقِر . استاذ

Professorship *n.* وظيفة استاذ

Proffer *v. t.* or *n.* قدَّم . أدّى . تقديم

Proficiency *n.* تقدُّم في العلوم

Proficient *a.* ماهِر . بارع

Profile *n.* رسمٌ جانبيٌّ للوجه

Profit *n.* or *v. i.* رِبْح . رَبِحَ ـَ

Profitable *a.* مُكَسِّب . مُفِيد

Profligacy *n.* خلاعَة . فجُور

Profligate *a.* خليع . فَاجِر

Profound *a.* عمِيق . خارِق . متعمّق

Profuse *a* وَافِر . مفرِط . فيَاض

Profusion *n.* وفرة . فيض . تبذِير

Progenitor *n.* جَد . سلَف

Progeny *n.* ذرّية . نَسْل

Prognosis *n.* إِنذار بنتيجة مرض

Prognosticate *v. t.* أَنبأَ أو أنبأ بهِ

Programme *n.* لائحة . تعريف

Progress *n.* تقدّم . نجاح

Progress *v. i.* تقدم . نجح ـ

Progressive *a.* مُتقدِم . متتابِع

Prohibit *v. t.* منع ـ . نهى ـ . حرَّم

Prohibition *n.* نهي . منع

Prohibitive / **Prohibitory** } *a.* مانِع . ناهٍ

Project *v. i.* or *t.* برز ـُ . قصد ـ . أَلقى

Project *n.* قصد . تدبير . مشروع

Projectile *n.* مِرْماة . قبلة

Prolific *a.* مثمر . مُنتج كثيراً

Prolix *a.* مُسهب . مُمِل

Prolixity *n.* إِسهاب . إِطناب

Prolong *v. t.* أَطال . مد ـُ

Prolongation *n.* إِطالة

Promenade *n.* تنزّه . منتزه

Prominence / **Prominency** } *n.* علوّ . بُرُوز

Prominent *a.* بارز . ظاهِر . شهير

Promiscuous *a.* مختلط . غير مُرتب

Promise *n.* or *v. t.* موعد . وعد . يعِد

Promissory *a.* وعديّ . تعهديّ

Promontory *n.* رأس عَالٍ في البحر

Promote *v. t.* ساعد . نجح . رقّي

Promotion *n.* ترْقية . تقديم

Prompt *a.* مستعد . سريعُ الفعل

Promptitude / **Promptness** *n.* إستعداد . سرعة

Promulgate *v. t.* نشر . أذاع

Prone *a.* ملقى على وجهه . مائل . منعطف

Prong *n.* شعبة

Pronoun *n.* ضمير

Pronounce *v. t.* لفظ — . صرّح ب

Pronunciation *n.* لفظ . نطق

Proof *n.* برهان . بيّنة . إمتحان

Proof *a.* ما لا يؤثّر فيه

Proof-sheet *n.* مسوّدة

Prop *n.* or *v. t.* دعامة . سند . دعم —

Propagate *v. t.* ولد . نشر — . اذاع

Propel *v. t.* دفع — . ساق —

Propensity *n.* ميل . صبو . إنعطاف

Proper *a.* لائق . موافق . خاص

Property *n.* ملك . خاصة . صفة

Prophecy *n.* نبوءة ونبوّة

Prophesy *v. i.* أنبأ . اخبر بالغيب

Prophet *n.* نبيّ ج أنبياء

Prophetic / **Prophetical** *a.* نبوي

Propitiate *v. t.* إستعطف

Propitiation *n.* إستعطاف . كفارة

Propitious *a.* منعم . موافق . مفيد

Proportion *n.* نسبة . مناسبة . حصة

Proportional / **Proportionate** *a.* نسبيّ . متناسب

Proposal *n.* عرض . قصد . رأي

Propose *v. t.* عرض — . قدم

Proposition *n.* عرض . قضيّة . مطلب

Propound *v. t.* عرض — . طرح — . قدّم

Proprietor *n.* صاحب . ربّ . مالك

Propriety *n.* لياقة . موافقة

Propulsion *n.* دفع . سوق

Prorogue *v. t.* أجل . أخر

Prosaic / **Prosaical** *a.* نثريّ . مملّ

Proscribe *v. t.* حرّم . طرد —

Prose *n.* نثر

Prosecute *v. t.* تَتَبَّعَ . إِدَّعَى عَلَى

Prosecutor *n.* مُدَّعٍ . مُوَاظِب

Proselyte *n.* or *v. t.* دَخِيل . جَلَبَ إِلَى دِين

Prosody *n.* عِلْمُ العَرُوض

Prospect *n.* مَنْظَر . أَمَل . مُنْتَظَر

Prospective *a.* مُسْتَقْبَل . مُنْتَظَر

Prosper *v. i.* نَجَحَ — أَفْلَحَ

Prosperity *n.* نَجَاحٌ . فَلَاحٌ

Prosperous *a.* نَاجِح . مُفْلِح

Prostitute *n.* عَاهِرَة . فَاجِرَة

Prostitute *v. t.* إِسْتَعْمَلَ لِغَايَةٍ رَذِيلَةٍ

Prostrate *a.* سَاجِد . مُتَمَدِّد

Prostrate *v. t.* أَلْقَى . سَجَدَ — . خَوَّرَ

Prosy *a.* مُمِلّ . مُضْجِر

Protect *v. t.* حَمَى — وَقَى — . صَانَ —

Protection *n.* حِمَايَة . وِقَايَة

Protective *a.* / **Protector** *n.* } حَامٍ . حَافِظ

Protectorate *n.* حِمَايَة

Protegé *n.* مَحْمِيّ . مَوْلِيّ

Protest *v.i.* or *t.* أَكَّدَ . صَرَّحَ بِعَدَمِ قبول

Protestation *n.* إِقَامَة الحجة . تأكيد

Protocol *n.* لَائِحَة (بروتوكول)

Protract *v. t.* أَطَالَ . أَخَّرَ

Protrude *v. t.* or *i.* أَخْرَجَ . بَرَزَ — . نَتَأَ —

Protuberance *n.* نُتُوء . بُرُوز

Proud *a.* مُتَكَبِّر . مُشَامِخ . مُعْجَب

Prove *v. t.* or *i.* بَرْهَنَ . جَرَّبَ . تَبَيَّنَ

Provender *n.* عَلِيق . عَلَف

Proverb *n.* مَثَل ج أَمْثَال

Proverbial *a.* يُضْرَبُ بِهِ المَثَل

Provide *v. t.* جَهَّزَ . قَدَّمَ . أَمَدَّ

Providence *n.* عِنَايَة . تَدْبِير

Provident *a.* ذُو عِنَايَةٍ . مُدَبِّر

Providential *a.* مِن عِنَايَةِ الله

Province *n.* إِقْلِيم . وِلَايَة

Provincial *a.* إِقْلِيمِيّ . غَيْرُ مُهَذَّب

Provison *n.* جهاز . موؤنة . شرط

Provisional / **Provisionary** *a.* وقتي . شرطي

Provocation *n.* إغاظة . تهييج

Provocative *a.* مهيّج . محرّك

Provoke *v. t.* أغاظ . هيج . أثار

Prow *n.* مقدم سفينة

Prowess *n.* بسالة . شجاعة . سطوة

Prowl *v. i.* جال ـُ . جال يفترس

Proximate *a.* ألأقرب . سابق أو تال

Proximity *n.* قرب

Proxy *n.* وكيل . وكالة

Prudence *n.* حزم . بصيرة إحتياط

Prudent *a.* حازم . فطن . حذر

Prudish *a.* متصنّع بالحشمة

Prune *n.* or *v. t.* خوخة مجففة . شذّب . قضّب

Pry *v. i.* تجسّس . رفع بمخل

Psalm *n.* مزمور ج مزامير

Psalmist *n.* موءلف آلمزامير . مرنّم

Psalter *n.* كتاب آلمزامير

Psychic / **Psychical** *a.* منوط بالنفس

Psychology *n.* ألفلسفة آلعقلية

Puberty *n.* سنّ البلوغ

Public *a.* or *n.* عمومي . شائع . آلجمهور

Publican *n.* عشار . خمار

Publication *n.* إذاعة . نشر

Publicity *n.* شيوع . إشتهار

Publish *v. t.* نشر ـُ . أشاع

Pucker *v.i.* or *n.* جعّد . جعدة . ثنية

Puddle *n.* منقع وحل

Puerile *a.* ولدي . ركيك . (صبياني)

Puff *n.* or *v. i.* نفخة . نفخ ـَ

Pugilist *n.* ملاكم

Pugnacious *a.* خصوم . محبّ آلمنازعة

Pull *v. t.* شدّ ـُ . جرّ ـُ قلع ـَ

Pulley *n.* بكرة

Pulmonary / **Pulmonic** *a.* رئوي

Pulp *n.* لُبٌّ . شَحْم

Pulpit *n.* مِنْبَرٌ

Pulsate *v. i.* نَبَضَ

Pulsation *n.* نَبْضَة . نبض

Pulse *n.* أَلنَّبْضُ . أَلْقَطَانِيُّ

Pulverize *v. t.* سحق ـَ . دق ـُ

Pump *n.* or *v.t.* طُلُمْبَةٌ . رَفَعَ مآءً بِها

Pun *n.* تَوْرِيَةٌ (فِي ٱلبَيَانِ)

Punch *v. t.* ثَقَبَ ـُ . دَفَعَ ـَ

Punch *n.* نَوْع مِنَ ٱلْمُسْكِرِ . مِثْقَب

Punctual *a.* مُرَاعِي ٱلْوَقْت . مدَقِّق

Punctuality *n* أَلتَّدْقِيقُ فِي ٱلْمِيعَادِ

Punctuate *v.t.* وَضَعَ عَلَامَاتِ ٱلْوَقْف

Puncture *n.* or *v.t.* ثَقْبَة . ثَقَبَ ـُ

Pungent *a.* حِرِّيفٌ . حَادٌّ

Punish *v. t.* عَاقَبَ . قَاصَّ

Punishment *n.* عِقَاب . قِصَاصٌ

Punitive *a.* عِقَابِيٌّ . قِصَاصِيٌّ

Punster *n.* مَاهِرٌ بِٱلتَّوْرِيَة

Puny *a.* هَزِيلٌ . ضَعِيف

Pup / **Puppy** } *n.* جَرْوُ كَلْبٍ

Pupil *n.* تِلْمِيذٌ . بُؤْبُؤُ ٱلْعَيْنِ

Puppet *n.* أُلْعُوبَةٌ

Pur or **Purr** *v. i.* or *n.* خَرْخَرَةُ ٱلْهِرِّ

Purchase *v. t.* إِبْتَاعَ . إِشْتَرَى

Purchaser *n.* مُشْتَرٍ

Pure *a.* صَافٍ . طَاهِر . صِرْفٌ

Purely *ad.* فَقَطْ

Purgative *a.* or *n.* مُطَهِّرٌ . مُسْهِل

Purgatory *n.* أَلْمَطْهَرُ

Purge *v. t.* طَهَّرَ . اسهل

Purification *n.* تَطْهِير . غَسْل

Purify *v. t.* طَهَّرَ . نَقَّى . مَحَّصَ

Purity *n.* طَهَارَةٌ . نَقَاوَةٌ . عِفَّة

Purloin *v. t.* إِخْتَلَسَ . سَرَقَ ـِ

Purple *n.* or *a.* أرْجُوَان . ارجوَانِيٌّ

Purport *n.* or *v. t.* مَضْمُون . مَعْنًى . افَادَ

Purpose *n.* or *v. t.* قصْد . نِيَّة . قَصَدَ ـِ

Purposely *ad.* عَمْدًا . قصْدًا

Purse *n.* كِيسُ دَرَاهِمَ

Pursue *v. t.* تَبِعَ ـَ طَارَدَ . سَعَى فِي

Pursuit *n.* مُطَارَدَة . إِتِّبَاع . حِرْفَة

Pursuance *n.* إِتِّبَاع

Purvey *v. t.* قَدَّمَ مَؤُنَةً . جَهَّزَ

Purveyor *n.* مُجَهِّزُ ٱلْمَؤُونَةِ

Pus *n.* صَدِيد . قَيْح . مِدَّة

Push *v. t.* or *n.* دَفَعَ ـَ . حَرَّضَ . نَشَاط

Pusillanimity *n.* جَبَانَة

Pusillanimous *a.* جَبَان صَغِيرُ ٱلنَّفْسِ

Puss / **Pussy** *n.* هِرّ . قِطّ

Pustule *n.* بَثْرَة . دُمَّل

Put *v. t.* وَضَعَ . جَعَلَ ـَ . حَرَّضَ

Putrefaction *n.* فَسَاد . عُفُونَة

Putrefy *v. i.* فَسَدَ ـُ عَفِنَ

Putrid *a.* عَفِن . فَاسِد

Puzzle *n.* or *v. t.* إِرْتِبَاك . حَيْرَة . حَيَّرَ

Pygmy *n.* قَزَم جِنْسًا

Pyramid *n.* هَرَم ج اهرَام

Pyre *n.* عُرْمَة وَقِيدٍ

Q

Quack *v. i.* or *n.* بَطْبَطَ . دَجَّال

Quackery *n.* تدجيل . مُخاتَلة

Quadrangle *n.* مُرَبَّع . دارٌ مُرَبَّعة

Quadrant *n.* رُبْعُ دائِرَةٍ

Quadratic *a.* مُرَبَّعِيٌّ

Quadrilateral *a.* ذُو أَرْبَعِ أَضْلاعٍ

Quadroon *n.* وَلَدُ أَبٍ ابيَضَ وَأُمٍّ خلاسيةٍ

Quadruped *n.* ذُو أَرْبَعِ قَوائِمَ

Quadruple *a.* أَرْبَعةُ أَضْعافٍ

Quaff *v. t.* شَرِبَ ـَ

Quagmire *n.* نَقْعٌ . حَمْأَةٌ

Quail *n.* or *v. i.* سلوى (سِمَّان) . خافَ

Quaint *a.* غَرِيبٌ . أَنِيقٌ

Quake *v. i.* إِرْتَعَدَ . رَعَشَ ـَ

Quakers *n. pl.* طائفة من المسيحيين

Qualification *n.* أَهليَّة . قَيْدٌ

Qualify *v. t.* أَهَّلَ . نَعَتَ ـَ . قَيَّدَ

Quality *n.* صِفَةٌ . خَصلَةٌ . نَبالة

Qualm *n.* غَثَيانٌ . قَلَقُ الضَمِيرِ

Quantity *n.* مِقْدار . كَمِّيَّة

Quarantine *n.* حَجْرٌ صِحِّي

Quarrel *n.* or *v. i.* خِصام . خاصَمَ

Quarrelsome *a.* خَصُوم . مِحَكٌ

Quarry *n.* مَقلَع . صَيْدٌ

Quart *n.* مكيال وَهوَ رُبعُ جالُونٍ

Quarter *n.* رُبْع . جِهَة . مَحَلّ

Quarterly *a.* or *ad.* كُلَّ ثَلاثَة أَشْهُرٍ

Quartermaster *n.* مأمورُ المُونَةِ

Quartett / Quartet } n. أَرْبَعَةٌ يغنُّون مَعاً

Quarto n. كِتابٌ مُرَبَّعُ آلشكلِ

Quartz n. ضَرْبٌ مِنَ ٱلْحَجَرِ الصلبِ

Quash v. t. سَحقَ . أَبْطَل

Quaver v. i. or n. رَجَّ (آلصَّوْتُ)

Quay n. إِسْكلَةٌ . بنْط . رَصِيف

Queen n. مَلِكَةٌ

Queer a. غَيْرُ مَأْلُوفٍ . غَرِيبٌ

Queerness n. غَرَابَةٌ

Quell v. t. أَخْمَدَ . سَكَّنَ

Quench v. t. أَطْفَأَ . أَرْوَى

Querulous a. مُتَذَمِّرٌ . مُتَشَكٍّ

Query n. or v. t. إِسْتِفْهامٌ سَأَلَ . شَكَّ

Quest n. طَلَبٌ . تفتِيشٌ

Question n. سُؤَالٌ . مَطْلَبٌ . قَضِيَّةٌ

Question v. t. سَأَلَ . إِرْتَابَ

Questionable a. فِيهِ نَظَرٌ أَوْ رَيْبٌ

Quibble n. or v. i. حِيلَةٌ . رَاوَغَ

Quibbler n. مُرَاوِغٌ فِي آلْكَلَامِ

Quick a. سَرِيعٌ . ذَكِيٌّ . حَيٌّ

Quicken v. t. أَسْرَعَ . أَحْيَا . حَرَّكَ

Quicklime n. كِلْسٌ غَيْرُ مُصَوَّلٍ

Quickness n. سُرْعَةٌ . عَجَلَةٌ

Quicksand n. رَمْلٌ يُغْرَقُ فِيهِ

Quicksilver n. زِئْبَقٌ

Quiescence n. سُكُونٌ

Quiescent a. سَاكِنٌ

Quiet v. t. هدَّأَ . سَكَّنَ . أَرَاحَ

Quiet n. or a. سُكون رَاحَةٌ سَاكِنٌ

Quietness / Quietude } a. هُدُوءٌ . سُكُونٌ

Quill n. رِيشَةٌ . قَلَمُ رِيشَةٍ

Quilt n. or v. t. لِحَافٌ . دِثَارٌ . خاطَ لِحَافاً

Quince n. سَفَرْجَلَةٌ ج سَفَارِجُ

Quinine n. كِينَا

Quinsy n. إِلْتِهَابُ آللَّوْزَتَيْنِ

Quintal n. مِئَةُ لِيبْرَا

Quire *n.*	رزمة ورق
Quit *v. t.*	ترك . قضى الواجب
Quit *a.*	محرَّر من . بريء من
Quite *ad.*	تماماً بالكلية
Quittance *n.*	تبرئة من دين . وصل
Quiver *n.* or *v. i.*	جعبة . إهتز . إرتجف
Quiz *v. t.*	خبر . سخر به
Quondam *a.*	سابق
Quorum *n.*	عدد أعضاء كاف للأشغال
Quota *n.*	حصة . نصيب
Quotation *n.*	إقتباس
Quote *v. t.*	إقتبس . ذكر (سعراً)
Quoth *v. t.*	قال
Quotient *n.*	خارج القسمة

R

Rabbi *n.*	معلم . حاخام
Rabbinic / Rabbinical *a.*	حاخامي . تلمودي
Rabbit *n.*	ارنب ج أرانب
Rabble *n.*	رعاع . أوباش
Rabid *a.*	هائج . مجنون . كلب
Race *n.*	سباق . جنس . أصل
Race *v. i.* or *t.*	سابق . جعل يسابق
Raceme *n.*	عرجون
Rack *n.*	آلة تعذيب . عذاب . رف
Racket *n.*	ضجة . جلبة
Radiance *n.*	ضياء . بهاء . لمعان
Radiant *a.*	لامع . نير
Radiate *v. i.* or *t.*	شع . أشع
Radical *a.* or *n.*	أصلي . جوهري . أصل . جذر

Radicle *n.* جذير

Radish *n.* فجلة

Radius *n.* نصف قطر. كعبرة

Raft *n.* رمث ج أرماث

Rafter *n.* رافد ج روافد

Rag *n.* خرقة. رثة

Rage *n.* or *v.i.* غيظ. غضب. إغتاظ

Ragged *a.* رث. بال

Raging *a.* هائج. ثائر. حنق

Raid *n.* غزوة. غارة

Rail *n.* قضيب حديد

Rail *v. t.* or *i.* سيّج. عيّر. إفترى

Railing *n.* تعيير. إفتراء. درابزون

Raillery *n.* هزل. مزح. مداعبة

Railroad / **Railway** *n.* سكة حديد

Raiment *n.* لباس. كسوة

Rain *n.* or *v. i.* مطر. امطر

Rainbow *n.* قوس قزح

Rainy *a.* ممطر

Raise *v. t.* رفع —. أقام. ربّى

Raisin *n.* زبيبة ج زبيب

Rake *n.* خليع. مجرفة كالمشط

Rally *v. t.* ضمّ الشاردين. داعب

Ram *n.* كبش. منجنيق. برج الحمل

Ramble *v. i.* جال. طاف —

Rambling *a.* جائل. غير سديد

Ramify *v. t.* or *i.* فرّع. تفرّع. تشعّب

Rampant *a.* مفرط. غير محصور

Rampart *n.* سور. متراس

Ramrod *n.* مدك البندقية

Rancid *a.* زنخ

Rancour *n.* حقد. غلّ. ضغينة

Rancorous *a.* مغل. حقود

Random *a.* or *n.* عاسف. غير متعمّد

Range *n.* مدى. صفّ

Range *v. t.* or *i.* صفّ —. جال. طاف —

Rank *a.* مخصب . زنخ . شديد

Rank *n.* or *v. i.* رتبة . صفّ . له رتبة

Rankle *v. i.* إشتدّ . إحتدّ

Ransack *v. t.* فتّش كثيراً . نهب ـَ

Ransom *n.* or *v. t.* فدية . إفتدى . فكّ ـُ

Rant *v. i.* أفرط بالكلام

Rap *n.* or *v. i.* لكمة . ضرب . دقّ ـُ

Rapacious *a.* طمّاع . ضار . سالب

Rapacity *n.* طمع . إختطاف

Rape *n.* إغتصاب . فضح

Rapid *a.* سريع . مسرع

Rapidity / **Rapidness** } *n.* سرعة . عجلة

Rapids *n. pl.* سيل ماء سريع

Rapier *n.* سيف خفيف ضيق النصل

Rapine *n.* نهب . إختطاف

Rapture *n.* سرور مفرط

Rapturous *a.* مفتتن . سالب العقل

Rare *a.* نادر . نفيس . لطيف

Rarefy *v. t.* or *i.* رقّق . لطّف

Rarely *ad.* نادراً

Rareness / **Rarity** } *n.* قلة الوجود . ندرة

Rascal *n.* خبيث . محتال

Rascality *n.* خبث . غبينة

Rase *v. t.* خرّب . هدم . محا ـُ

Rash *a.* هذر . مسراع . عجول

Rashness *n.* تهوّر . عدم عناية

Raspberry *n.* ثمر العليق

Rat *n.* جرذ ج جرذان

Ratan *n.* خيزران

Rate *n.* سعر . كمّية . نسبة

Rather *ad.* بالحري . أكثر

Ratify *v. t.* أمضى . أثبت . وقّع

Ratio *n.* نسبة . درجة

Ration *n.* جراية الجندي

Rational *a.* ناطق . موافق للعقل

Rationalist *n.* قائل بكفاءة العقل دون الوحي

Ratsbane *n.* سمّ الفار

Rattle *v. i.* or *t.* or *n.* صلّ ـ . صليل

Ravage *v. t.* نهب ـ . خرّب

Rave *v. i.* هذى ـ . هذر ـ

Ravel *v. t.* or *i.* فكّك . حلّ ـ . إنفكّ

Raven *n.* غرابٌ ج غربان

Ravenous *a.* لهِمٌ . نهِمٌ . كاسرٌ

Ravine *n.* وادٍ عميقٌ ضيّق

Raving *a.* هاذٍ . هائج

Ravish *v. t.* خطف ـ إغتصب . أفتن

Ravishment *n.* إغتصابٌ . ولهٌ

Raw *a.* نيّ . غير خبير . مسحوج

Rawhide *n.* سوطٌ من جلدٍ غير مدبوغ

Ray *n.* شعاعٌ . نوعٌ من السمك

Raze *v. t.* محا ـ . هدّ تماماً

Razor *n.* موسى ج مواسٍ

Reach *v. t.* or *i.* بلغ ـ . لحق . إمتدّ

React *v. t.* or *i.* ردّ الفعل

Reaction *n.* ردّ الفعل

Read *v. t.* or *i.* قرأ ـ . تلا ـ

Readable *a.* مستحق القراءة . يقرأ

Readily *ad.* بسهولة

Readiness *n.* تأهّبٌ . مبادرة

Reading *n.* قراءة . مطالعة

Readmit *v. t.* عاد فأدخل

Ready *a.* مستعدّ . حاضر . مهيّأ

Reaffirm *v. t.* كرّر . عاد فأكّد

Real *a.* حقيقيّ . فعليّ . صحيحٌ

Real-estate *n.* الأموال غير المنقولة

Reality *n.* حقيقة . وجودٌ

Realise *v. t.* أنجز . أوجد . تحقّق

Realm *n.* مملكة

Ream *n.* ماعونٌ (من الورق)

Reanimate *v. t.* أحيا . أنعش

Reap *v. t.* or *i.* حصد ـ . حصل . تمتّع

Reaper *n.* حاصد . آلة الحصاد

Reappear *v. i.* عادَ فظهر

Reappoint *v. t.* عين ثانيةً

Rear *n.* or *a.* or *v. t.* مؤخر . أقامَ . ربَّى

Rear-guard *n.* ساقةُ الجيش

Reason *v. i.* or *t.* حاجَّ . استدلَّ . أقنعَ

Reason *n.* سبب . بُرهان . عقل

Reasonable *a.* معقول . معتدِل . عاقِل

Reasoning *n.* محاجة . إستدلال

Reassure *v. t.* أكدَ ثانيةً . أمَّنَ

Rebel *n.* or *v. i.* خائِن . عاص عصى ـِ

Rebellion *n.* عِصيان

Rebellious *a.* عاص

Rebound *v. i.* or *n.* إرتدَّ . إرتداد

Rebuff *n.* or *v. t.* رد . رفض . رفضَ ـُ

Rebuke *v. t.* or *n.* وبَّخَ . توبيخ زجر

Rebut *v. t.* ردَّ دليلاً . دفعَ ـَ

Recall *v. t.* إسترجعَ . ذكرَ ـُ . نقضَ ـُ

Recant *v.t.* or *i.* إرتدَّ عن . أنكرَ

Recapitulate *v. t.* كرَّرَ ملخصاً

Recede *v. i.* رجعَ ـِ . تقهقر

Receipt *n.* or *v.t.* وصل . أعطى وصلاً

Receive *v. t.* قبِل ـَ . قبض ـِ . نالَ ـَ

Recent *a.* حديث . جديد

Receptacle *n.* وعاء . غِلاف

Reception *n.* قبول . إستقبال . أخذ

Receptive *a.* قابِل

Recess *n.* إعتزال . فراغ . فترة

Recipe *n.* وصفة دواء

Recipient *n.* مستلم . قابِل . نائِل

Reciprocal *a.* متبادِل . معاوض

Reciprocate *v. t.* or *i.* عاوضَ . تبادل

Reciprocity *n.* تبادُل الفِعلِ أو الفائدة

Recital *n.* قِراءة . رِواية . قِصة

Recitation *n.* تِلاوة عن ظهرِ القلب

Recite *v. t.* قرأَ ـَ . تلا ـُ

Reckless *a.* متهوِّر . غير مبال

Reckon *v. t.* حسب ـ . أحصى

Reckoning *n.* حساب. محاسبة

Reclaim *v. t.* إسترجع. أصلح

Recline *v. i.* إتكأ . إستند

Recluse *n.* or *a.* ناسك. معتزل

Recognisable *a.* ما يعرف أو يميز

Recognise *v. t.* عرف . قبل صريحا

Recoil *v. i.* or *n.* إرتد. نكص ـ

Recollect *v. t.* ذكر ـ . جمع ـ ثانية

Recollection *n.* ذكر وذكرى

Recommence *v. t.* بدأ ثانية

Recommend *v. t.* وصى به. مدح ـ

Recompense *v. t.* or *n.* جازى. مجازاة

Reconcile *v. t.* صالح . وفق بين

Recondite *a.* غامض . عويص

Reconnaissance *n.* إستطلاع

Reconnoiter *v. t.* إستطلع . تجسس

Reconquer *v. t.* فتح ـ . ثانية

Reconsider *v. t.* اعاد النظر في

Reconsideration *n.* مراجعة

Record *v. t.* or *n.* كتب . دون . سجل

Recount *v. t.* قص . روى بتفصيل

Recourse *n.* إلتجاء . ملجأ

Recover *v. t.* or *i.* إسترد . تعافى

Recoverable *a.* قابل الاسترداد

Recovery *n.* إسترجاع . شفاء

Recreant *a.* or *n.* خائن. جبان. نذل

Recreation *n.* تنزه . تسلية

Recriminate *v. t.* or *i.* اتهم . تعايب

Recruit *v. t.* or *i.* أمد . جدد. تعافى

Recruit *v. i.* or *n.* جند. عسكري جديد

Rectangle *n.* مربع مستطيل قائم الزوايا

Rectify *v. t.* قوم. أصلح

Rectilinear *a.* مستقيم الخطوط

Rectitude *n.* إستقامة

Rector *n.* مدير. قسيس أبرشية

كَنيسةُ أبرشيةٍ .
Rectory *n.* بيتُ آلقسيسِ

Rectum *n.* المُستقيمُ (من الأمعاء)

Recumbent *a.* مُتَّكِئٌ

Recuperate *v. i.* تعافى

Recuperative *a.* شافٍ . مُعافٍ

Recur *v. i.* عادَ . تكرَّرَ . إلتجأَ

Recurrence *n.* عَوْدٌ . تكرارٌ

Red *a.* أحمرُ

Redden *v. t.* or *i.* حَمَّرَ . إحمرَّ

Redeem *v. t.* فدَى ـِ . فكَّ ـُ

Redeemer *n.* فادٍ . مُخلِّصٌ

Redemption *n.* فِديةٌ . فداءٌ

Redness *n.* حُمرةٌ . إحمِرارٌ

Redolent *a.* فائحٌ . عَبِقٌ

Redouble *v. t.* ضاعفَ . كثَّرَ

Redoubt *n.* مِترَاسٌ . حصنٌ

Redress *v. t.* قوَّمَ . عدل . أنصفَ

Reduce *v. t.* قلَّلَ . أخضعَ . ردَّ ـُ

Reduction *n.* ردٌّ. تحويل (في آلحِساب)

Redundant *n.* زائدٌ عن آللزومِ

Reduplicate *v. t.* ضاعفَ

Re-echo *v. t.* or *i.* ردَّ آلصَّدى

Reed *n.* قصبةٌ . مِزمارٌ

Reef *n.* سلسِلةُ صُخُورٍ في آلماءِ

Reef *v. t.* طوَى ـِ (آلقُلُوعَ)

Reek *v. i.* فاحَ بُخارُهُ . بخرَ ـَ

Reel *n.* or *v. t.* or *i.* مكبٌّ . كبَّ ـُ . ترنَّحَ

Re-elect *v. t.* إنتخبَ ثانيةً

Re-embark *v. i.* or *t.* نزل ثانيةً في سفينةٍ

Re-enforce *v. t.* عزَّزَ . أمدَّ

Re-engage *v. t.* جدَّدَ آلعهدَ أو آلقِتالَ

Re-enter *v. t.* عاد فدخلَ

Re-establish *v. t.* عادَ فأقامَ أو أثبتَ

Re-examine *v. t.* عاد ففحصَ أو آمتحنَ

Refectory *n.* قاعةٌ للأكلِ

Refer *v. t.* or *i.* وجَّهَ أو أشارَ إلَى

Referee *n.* فيصل. حكم

Reference *n.* إشارة. شاهد. علاقة

Refine *v. t.* or *i.* محص. هذب. تنقى

Refinement *n.* ادب. تهذيب

Refinery *n.* معمل التمحيص أو التصفية

Refit *v. t.* عاد فجهز. أصلح

Reflect *v. i.* or *t.* تأمل. إنعكس

Reflective *a.* متأمل. عاكس

Reflector *n.* سطح عاكس. مرآة

Reflex *a.* مردود. منعكس

Reflexive *a.* مائل إلى الوراء أو الذات

Reform *v. t.* اصلح. قوم. جدد

Reform, **Reformation** *n.* إصلاح. تجديد

Reformatory *a.* or *n.* مصلح (إصلاحية)

Reformer *n.* مصلح

Refract *v. t.* كسر شعاع النور

Refraction *n.* إنكسار النور

Refractory *a.* متمرد. شكس

Refrain *v. i.* إمتنع. امسك عن

Refrangible *n.* قابل الانكسار

Refresh *v. t.* أنعش. أراح

Refreshment *n.* إنعاش. طعام

Refrigerator *n.* آلة التبريد. مبرد

Refuge *n.* ملجأ. سبيل للنجاة

Refugee *n.* ملتجئ. مهاجر. هارب

Refulgence, **Refulgency** *n.* لمعان. بهاء

Refulgent *a.* بهي. نير

Refund *v. t.* أوفى. رد

Refusal *n.* رفض. حق الأخذ دون غيره

Refuse *n.* سقاطة. نفاية

Refuse *v. t.* أبى. رفض

Refute *v.t.* أدحض. نقض. رد

Regain *v. t.* إسترد. إستعاد

Regal *a.* ملكي

Regale *v. t.* أولم وليمة فاخرة

Regard *v. t.* or *n.* لاحظ. إعتبر. إعتبار

Regardless *a.* غير مكترث. غافل

Regency *n.*	نِيابةُ ملْكٍ
Regenerate *v. t.* or *a.*	جدّد مُتجدِّد
Regent *n.*	نائبُ ٱلْمَلِكِ
Regicide *n.*	قاتِلُ ملِكٍ . قتلهُ
Regime *n.*	شكْلُ حُكُومةٍ
Regiment *n.*	كتيبة . ألاي
Region *n.*	قُطْرٌ . جِهةٌ
Register *n.* or *v. t.*	دَفْتَرٌ . سِجِلٌ . سَجل
Regress / **Regression** } *n.*	إِرْتِداد . تقهْقُر
Regret *n.* or *v. t.*	أسف تأسف عَلَى
Regular *a.*	قِياسِيٌ عَلَى تَرْتِيب
Regularity *n.*	تَرْتِيب . إِنْتِظام
Regulate *v. t.*	رتَّبَ . نظَّمَ . دبَّرَ
Regulation *n.*	قانُون . نِظَام
Regulator *n.*	مُرتِّب . آلَة ضَبْطٍ
Rehearse *v. t.*	قصَّ ـُ . تلا مُراجعةً
Reign *n.* or *v. i.*	مُلْك . ملك ـُ . إِسْتَوْلَى
Reimburse *v. t.*	أوفى كافأ
Rein *n.* or *v. t.*	عنان . عَنَّنَ . كبح ـَ
Reindeer *n.*	نوْعٌ مِنَ ٱلْإِيِلِ
Reins *n. pl.*	كِلَى
Reinstall / **Reinstate** } *v. t.*	أعادَ إِلَى منصبهِ
Reissue *v. t.* or *i.* or *n.*	عادَ فأَصْدَرَ
Reiterate *v. t.*	كرَّرَ
Reject *v. t.*	نَبذَ ـِ . رَفَضَ ـُ
Rejoice *v. i.* or *t.*	سُرَّ . فرِحَ ـَ . فرَّحَ
Rejoicing *n.*	فرَحٌ . سُرُورٌ
Rejoin *v. t.* or *i.*	لاقَى بعْدَ فِراقٍ . أجابَ
Rejoinder *n.*	مُحاوَبةٌ . جوابٌ
Rejuvenate *v. t.*	جددَ الشَّبابَ
Rekindle *v. t.*	أشعل ثانيةً
Relapse *v.i.* or *n.*	عادَ إِلَى حالتهِ . نُكِسَ نُكْسٌ
Relate *v. t.* or *i.*	قصَّ ـُ . حدَّثَ . تعلَّقَ بِ
Relation *n.*	نِسْبَةٌ . رِوَايَةٌ . نَسِيب
Relationship *n.*	قرابةٌ . نَسَب
Relative *n.* or *a.*	نسِيبٌ . مَوْصُولٌ . نِسْبِيٌ

Relax *v. t.* or *i.* أرخى. خفف. إرتخى

Relaxation *n.* إرخاء. إراحة. فرج

Relaxative / **Relaxing** } *a.* مرخ. ملين

Relay *n.* or *v. t.* بدل خيل. عاد فوضع

Release *v. t.* or *n.* أطلق. حرر. إطلاق

Relent *v. i.* رق له. سامح

Relentless *a.* بلا رحمة أو عفو

Relevant *a.* موافق. في محله

Reliable *a.* ما يركن إليه. موثوق به

Reliance *n.* ثقة. إعتماد. إتكال

Relic *n.* بقية. أثر. ذخيرة

Relief *n.* إسعاف، نجدة. إراحة

Relieve *v. t.* أراح. خفف. أمد

Religion *n.* ديانة. دين

Religious *a.* دين. ديني

Relinquish *v. t.* ترك. تنحى عن

Relinquishment *n.* ترك

Relish *n.* or *v. t.* لذة. طعم. إستلذ

Reluctance *n.* نفور. مضادة. كراهة

Reluctant *a.* نافر. غير راض

Rely *v. i.* وثق ب. إتكل على

Remain *v. i.* بقي. دام. مكث

Remainder *n.* بقية. فضلة

Remains *n. pl.* بقايا. جثة

Remand *v. t.* أعاد. رد

Remark *v. t.* or *n.* لاحظ. قال. ملاحظة

Remarkable *a.* مستحق الذكر. مشهور

Remediable *a.* قابل الإصلاح

Remedial *a.* علاجي. مصلح

Remedy *n.* or *v. t.* علاج. عالج

Remember *v. t.* تذكر. ذكر

Remembrance *n.* ذكر. ذكرى

Remind *v. t.* ذكر. (فكر)

Reminiscence *n.* ذكر. تذكار

Remiss *a.* غافل. متوان

Remission *n.* غفران. عفو

Remit *v. t.* رَدَّ ـُ . أَرْسَلَ . عَفَا ـُ

Remittance *n.* ارْسَالُ دَرَاهِم

Remittent *a.* مُنْقَطِعٌ . مُتَرَدِّدٌ

Remnant *n.* فَضْلَةٌ

Remonstrance *n.* إِعْتِرَاضٌ

Remonstrate *v. i.* إِعْتَرَضَ عَلَى . وَبَّخَ

Remorse *n.* تَوْبِيخُ ٱلضَّمِيرِ

Remorseless *a.* بِلَا رَحْمَةٍ . قَاسٍ

Remote *a.* بَعِيدٌ

Remoteness *n.* بُعْدٌ

Remount *v. t.* عَادَ فَصَعِدَ أَوْ رَكِبَ

Removal *n.* نَقْلٌ . رَحِيلٌ . عَزْلٌ

Remove *v. t.* or *i.* نَقَلَ ـُ عَزَلَ ـِ إِرْتَحَلَ

Remunerate *v. t.* جَازَى . كَافَى

Remunerative *a.* مُكَافٍ . مُرْبِحٌ

Renascence / **Renaissance** } *n.* تَجْدِيدٌ . عَوْدَةٌ

Rend *v. t.* مَزَّقَ . شَقَّ ـُ

Render *v. t.* رَدَّ ـُ . أَعْطَى . صَبَرَ

Renegade *n.* مُرْتَدٌّ . خَائِنٌ

Renew *v. t.* جَدَّدَ

Renewable *a.* قَابِلُ ٱلتَّجْدِيدِ

Renewal *n.* تَجْدِيدٌ

Renounce *v. t.* رَفَضَ ـُ . نَبَذَ ـِ

Renovate *v. t.* جَدَّدَ

Renown *n.* صِيتٌ شُهْرَةٌ ذِكْرٌ

Renowned *a.* شَهِيرٌ

Rent *v. t.* or *n.* آجَرَ . أُجْرَةٌ

Rent *n.* or *a.* شَقٌّ . فَتْقٌ . مَشْقُوقٌ

Renunciation *n.* رَفْضٌ . إِنْكَارٌ

Reorganize *v. t.* رَتَّبَ أَوْ نَظَّمَ ثَانِيَةً

Repair *v. t.* or *i.* أَصْلَحَ . رَمَّمَ . ذَهَبَ إِلَى

Reparation *n.* تَصْلِيحٌ . تَعْوِيضٌ

Repass *v. t.* or *i.* عَادَ فَاجْتَازَ أَوْ مَرَّ

Repast *n.* أَكْلَةٌ . طَعَامٌ

Repay *v. t.* وَفَى . يَفِي

Repel *v. t.* or *i.* نَسَخَ — . أَلْغَى نَسَخَ

Repeat *v. t.* كَرَّرَ . ثَنى

Repel *v. t.* دَفع ـَ . دَافَعَ

Repellent *a.* رَادٌ . منفر

Repent *v. i.* تَابَ ـُ . نَدَم ـَ

Repentance *n.* تَوْبة . نَدَامة

Repentant *a.* تائِبٌ . نَادم

Repetition *n.* تكْرار

Repine *v. i.* تَشَكَّى . تَذَمَّر

Replace *v. t.* عوَّضَ. اعاد إِلَى مَكانِهِ

Replenish *v. t.* مَلأَ أيضاً. سدَّ ٱلْعوز

Replete *a.* محْشُوٌّ . مُمْتلِئٌ . مفعم

Repletion *n.* فُعومة . إِمتلاء

Reply *n.* or *v. t.* جوابٌ .جاوَبَ . أَجَابَ

Report *v. t.* قرَّر . أَخْبَرَ

Report *n.* تَقرير . خَبر . صَوْتٌ

Reporter *a.* مُقرِّرٌ . مخبرٌ

Repose *v. i.* or *n.* إِسْتَراحَ . راحةٌ

Repository *n.* مخزنٌ . مُسْتَودعٌ

Repossess *v. t.* عاد فملك . إِسْترد

Reprehend *v. t.* وبَخ . لام ـُ

Reprehensible *a.* مُستحِقٌ ٱللَّوْم

Represent *v. t.* مثَّل .صوَّر. ناب عنْ

Representation *n.* صُورَة . نِيَابة

Representative *n.* or *a.* نائِبٌ . ممثّل

Repress *v. t.* منَع ـَ . قهر ـَ . قمع ـَ

Repressive *a.* قاهِر . مانِع

Reprieve *v. t.* or *n.* أَجّلَ ٱلقصاص

Reprimand *v. t.* or *n.* وبَّخ . توْبِيخ

Reprint *v. t.* or *n.* طَبع ثانيةً

Reprisal *n.* أَخْذ ٱلثَّأْر . إِنْتِقَام

Reproach *v. t.* or *n.* عيَّر.عار . تعيير

Reprobate *n.* مرْفُوضٌ . مرْذُول

Reproduce *v. t.* جدَّدَ . تنَاسَل

Reproduction *n.* تجْدِيد . تنَاسل

Reproductive *a.* مجدِد. مُتنَاسل

Reproof *n.* توْبيخ

Reprove *v. t.* وبخ . عزل ـُـ . لامَ ـُـ

Reptile *n.* زحافة

Republic *n.* جمهورية

Repulican *a.* جمهوري

Republicanism *n.* مذهب الجمهورية

Republish *v. t.* أصدر ثانيةً

Repudiate *v. t.* رفض ـِـ . أنكر

Repugnance / Repugnancy *n.* كراهة . نفور

Repugnant *a.* كريه . منفّر

Repulse *n.* or *v. t.* ردع . ردّ ـُـ

Repulsive *a.* رادع . قبيح . كريه

Reputable *a.* حسن الصيت . محترم

Reputation / Repute *n.* صيت . ذِكْر . شهرة

Reputed *a.* محسوب . مظنون

Request *n.* or *v. t.* طلب . طلب ـُـ . إلتمس

Requiem *n.* ترنيمة او قدّاس لأجل الموتى

Require *v. t.* إحتاج . إقتضى . ألزم

Requirement *n.* إحتياج . إقتضاء . إلزام

Requisite *a.* مطلوب . لازم

Requisition *n.* إقتضاء . إلزام

Requital *n.* مكافاة . جزاء

Requite *v. t.* كافأ . جازى . عوّض

Rescind *v. t.* نسخ ـَـ . ألغى

Rescue *v. t.* or *n.* أنقذ . خلص . نجى

Research *n.* تفتيش . بحث

Resemblance *n.* مشابهة

Resemble *v. t.* شابه . ماثل . أشبه

Resent *v. t.* إستاء . قاوم

Resentful *a.* مغتاظ . حقود

Reservation *n.* إبقاء . تقييد

Reserve *v. t.* حفظ . ابقى

Reserved *a.* محفوظ . كتوم . متحفظ

Reservoir *n.* حوض . صهريج (خزان)

Reset *v. t.* وضع ثانيةً

Reside *v. i.* سكن ـُـ . اقام

Residence *n.*	إِقَامَةٌ . سَكَنٌ
Resident *a.*	سَاكِنٌ . مُتَوَطِّنٌ
Residual *a.*	بَاقٍ . فَاضِلٌ
Residue / Residuum } *n.*	بَقِيَّةٌ . فَضْلَةٌ
Resign *v. t.*	تَخَلَّى عَنْ . سَلَّمَ
Resignation *n.*	تَسْلِيمٌ
Resigned *a.*	صَبُورٌ
Resin *n.*	رَاتِينَجٌ
Resist *v. t.*	قَاوَمَ . ضَادَّ . عَارَضَ
Resistance *n.*	مُقَاوَمَةٌ
Resistless *a.*	مَا لَا يُقَاوَمُ
Resolute *a.*	عَزُومٌ . ثَابِتُ ٱلرَّأْيِ
Resolution *n.*	عَزْمٌ . تَقْرِيرٌ . حَلٌّ
Resolve *v. t.* or *n.*	عَزَمَ . حَلَّ . عَزْمٌ
Resolvent *n.*	حَالٌّ . مُذِيبٌ
Resonance *n.*	رَدُّ ٱلصَّوْتِ . رَنِينٌ
Resort *v.i.* or *n.*	إِلْتَجَأَ إِلَى . مُجْتَمَعٌ
Resound *v. t.* or *i.*	أَذَاعَ ٱلصِّيتَ . رَنَّ
Resource *n.*	مَلْجَأٌ . وَسِيلَةٌ
Respect *v. t.* or *n.*	إِحْتَرَمَ . إِحْتِرَامٌ
Respectability *n.*	إِحْتِرَامٌ
Respecting *pr.*	بِخُصُوصِ . مِنْ جِهَةِ
Respective *a.*	كُلٌّ عَلَى حِدَةٍ . نِسْبِيٌّ
Respectable *a.*	مُحْتَرَمٌ . مُتَوَسِّطٌ
Respectful *a.*	مُحْتَرِمٌ . مُحْتَشِمٌ
Respiration *n.*	تَنَفُّسٌ . نَفَسٌ
Respiratory *a.*	تَنَفُّسِيٌّ
Respite *n.* or *v. t.*	فَتْرَةٌ . أَمْهَلَ
Resplendent *a.*	بَهِيٌّ . لَامِعٌ
Respond *v. i.*	أَجَابَ . وَافَقَ
Response *n.*	جَوَابٌ
Responsibility *n.*	مَسْئُولِيَّةٌ
Responsible *a.*	مَسْئُولٌ
Responsive *a.*	مُجِيبٌ . مُرِيدُ ٱلْجَوَابِ
Rest *v. t.* or *i.*	رَاحَ . إِسْتَرَاحَ
Rest *n.*	سُكُونٌ . رَاحَةٌ . بَقِيَّةٌ

Restaurant ***n.***	محل طعام (مَطعمٌ)
Restitution ***n.***	رَدٌّ . تعويضٌ
Restive ***a.***	قَلِقٌ . جَموحٌ
Restless ***a.***	عَدِيمُ الرَّاحةِ . جزِعٌ
Restoration ***n.***	رَدٌّ . إصلاحٌ . شفاءٌ
Restorative ***a.***	شافٍ . مقوٍّ
Restore ***v. t.***	رَدَّ . جَدَّد
Restrain ***v. t.***	مَنعَ . حجزَ
Restraint ***n.***	حَجرٌ . مانِعٌ . ضبطٌ
Restrict ***v. t.***	حصرَ . قصَرَ على
Restriction ***n.***	حصرٌ . قصرٌ
Result ***v. i.*** **or** ***n.***	نَتجَ مِنْ . نتيجةٌ
Resume ***v. t.***	إسترَدَّ . عادَ إلى
Resumé ***n.***	خُلاصَةٌ . مُلخصٌ
Resurrection ***n.***	قِيامةٌ . بعثٌ
Resuscitate ***v. t.***	أحيا . انعشَ
Retail ***v. t.*** **or** ***n.***	بَاعَ بِالمُفرَّق
Retain ***v. t.***	امسكَ . ضبطَ
Retainer ***n.***	خادِمٌ . تابِعٌ
Retaliate ***v. i.***	أخذ الثأر . إنتقمَ
Retard ***v. t.***	عَاقَ . أخَّرَ
Retention ***n.***	إمساكٌ . حجزٌ
Retentive ***a.***	حافِظٌ . ضابِطٌ
Reticent ***a.***	كتومٌ . كاظِمٌ
Retina ***n.***	شبَكِيَّةُ العَين
Retinue ***n.***	حَشمٌ . تبَعٌ
Retire ***v. i.***	تقهقرَ . إرتد
Retirement ***n.***	إعتِزالٌ . تقاعدٌ
Retort ***v. t.*** **or** ***i.***	رَد بِالمِثل
Retort ***n.***	رَدٌّ . إنبيق
Retrace ***v. t.***	رَجَعَ على الأثرِ
Retract ***v. t.***	إستَرَدَّ قولاً
Retreat ***n.*** **or** ***v. i.***	إرتِدادٌ . إرتدَّ
Retrench ***v. t.***	نقص . قلل المَصرُوف
Retribution ***n.***	مُعاقبةٌ . مُجازاة
Retributive / **Retributory** } ***a.***	عقابي

Retrieve *v. t.*	إسترد . أصلح
Retroaction *n.*	ردّ الفعل
Retrograde *a.* or *v. i.*	مرتدّ . تقهقر
Retrogression *n.*	إرتداد . إنحطاط
Retrospect / **Retrospection** } *n.*	نظر إلى الماضي
Return *v. t.* or *i.*	رجّع . رجع ـ
Return *n.*	رجوع . تعويض . ربح
Reunion *n.*	إجتماع بعد فراق
Reunite *v. t.* or *i.*	ضمّ أيضاً . إنضمّ
Reveal *v. t.*	أعلن . كشف ـ . أظهر
Revel *n.* or *v. i.*	بطر . إنهمك باللذّات
Revelation *n.*	إعلان . وحي . تنزيل
Revelry *n.*	بطر . مرح
Revenge *n.* or *v. t.*	إنتقام . إنتقم
Revengeful *v. i.*	شديد الانتقام . ضاغن
Revenue *n.*	دخل
Reverberate *v. i.*	إرتدّ الصوت وتكرّر
Revere *v. t.*	إحترم . وقّر
Reverence *n.*	إحترام
Reverend *a.*	موقّر . محترم
Reverent / **Reverential** } *a.*	محترم . إحترامي
Reverie / **Revery** } *n.*	شرود الأفكار . تأمّل
Reversal *n.*	قلب . عكس . نقض
Reverse *v. t.*	قلب . عكس ـ . أبطل
Reverse *n.*	نقيض . مصيبة . قفا
Revert *v. i.*	عاد ـ . رجع ـ
Review *n.* or *v. t.*	مراجعة . أعاد النظر
Revile *v. t.*	شتم ـ . سبّ ـ
Revisal / **Revision** } *n.*	مراجعة . تصحيح
Revise *v. t.*	راجع . نقّح . صحّح
Revisit *v. t.*	عاد فزار ـ
Revival *n.*	إنتعاش . تجديد
Revive *v. t.* or *i.*	أنعش . إنتعش
Revivify *v. t.*	أحيا . جعله ينتعش
Revocation *n.*	فسخ . إلغاء
Revoke *v. t.*	نقض ـ . ألغى . فسخ ـ

Revolt *v. i.* or *n.* عَصَى ـِ . عِصْيَانٌ

Revolution *n.* إِنْقِلَابٌ . دَوَرَانٌ

Revolutionary *a.* آيِلٌ لِلْفِتْنَةِ

Revolutionize *v. t.* غَيَّرَ كُلِّيًّا

Revolve *v. t.* or *i.* ادار . رَدَّدَ . دَارَ ـُ

Revulsion *n.* رَدٌّ . نفورٌ شَدِيدٌ

Reward *n.* or *v. t.* ثَوَابٌ . جَازَى

Rewrite *v. t.* عَادَ فَكَتَبَ

Rhetoric *n.* عِلْمُ ٱلْبَيَانِ

Rheumatism *n.* دَآءُ ٱلْمَفَاصِلِ

Rhinoceros *n.* كَرْكَدَنٌ

Rhubarb *n.* رَوَنْدٌ او رِوَنْدٌ

Rhyme *n.* سَجْعٌ . قَافِيَةٌ

Rhythm *n.* نَظْمُ ٱلشِّعْرِ

Rib *n.* ضِلْعٌ ج ضُلُوعٌ واضْلُعٌ

Ribalbry *n.* كَلَامٌ رَذِيلٌ أو فَاحِشٌ

Ribbed *a.* مُضَلَّعٌ . مُخَطَّطٌ

Ribbon *n.* شَرِيطٌ ج شُرُطٌ وشَرَائِطُ

Rice *n.* ارُزٌّ . رُزٌّ

Rich *a.* غَنِيٌّ . مُخْصِبٌ . دَسِمٌ

Riches *n. pl.* غِنًى . ثَرْوَةٌ . مَالٌ

Richness *n.* خِصْبٌ . وُفُورٌ . دَسَمٌ

Rickets *n. pl.* دَآءُ ٱلْكُسَاحِ

Rickety *a.* كَسِيحٌ . رَكِيكٌ

Rid *v. t.* أَنْقَذَ . خَلَّصَ . نَجَّى

Riddle *n.* لغزٌ . أُحْجِيَّةٌ

Ride *v. t.* or *n.* رَكِبَ ـَ . رِكْبَةٌ

Riding *n.* رُكُوبٌ

Ridge *n.* ظَهْرٌ . مرْتَفِعٌ

Ridicule *n.* or *v. t.* هزْءٌ . سَخِرَ بِ

Ridiculous *a.* مُضْحِكٌ . سُخْرِيٌّ

Rifle *n.* or *v. i.* بُنْدُقِيَّةٌ مُضَلَّعَةٌ . سَلَبَ ـُ

Rift *n.* or *v. t.* شَقٌّ . فُرْجَةٌ . شَقَّ

Rig *v. t.* جَهَّزَ ٱلسَّوَارِيَ . أَلْبَسَ

Rigging *n.* جَهَازُ سَفِينَةٍ

Right *a.* or *n.* مُصِيبٌ . مُسْتَقِيمٌ . حَقٌّ . يَمِينٌ

Right *n.* صَوَابٌ . عدلٌ . إِمتِيَازٌ

Righteous *n.* بارٌّ . تَقِيٌّ . صالِحٌ

Righteousness *n.* بِرٌّ

Rightful *a.* حقٌّ . شرْعِيٌّ . عادِلٌ

Rigid *a.* متوتِّرٌ . متَصلِّبٌ

Rigidity / **Rigidness** *n.* صلابَةٌ . عدَمُ لِيُونةٍ

Rigour *n.* عُنفٌ . شدة . صرامةٌ

Rigorous *a.* شَدِيد . عنيفٌ . صارِمٌ

Rill *n.* ساقِيَةٌ . جدْولُ ماءٍ

Rim *n.* حافَةٌ

Rind *n.* قِشْرٌ

Ring *n.* حلقةٌ . خاتِمٌ . رنين

Ring *v. t.* or *i.* دقَّ ـُ . رنَّ ـِ . طنَّ ـِ

Ringleader *n.* رئيسُ ثَوْرَةٍ

Ringlet *n.* جعيدةُ شعرٍ

Ringworm *n.* أَلقُوبَاءُ

Rinse *v. t.* شطفَ ـَ . مَضْمَضَ

Riot *n.* شَغَبٌ . فِتنةٌ . بطرٌ

Rioter *n.* / **Riotous** *a.* مُشاغِبٌ . خَلِيعٌ . بطِرٌ

Rip *v. t.* or *n.* فتق ـُ ـِ . مزق . فتقٌ

Ripe *a.* ناضِجٌ . مُسْتوٍ . كامِلٌ

Ripen *v. t.* or *i.* أنْضجَ . نضِجَ ـَ

Ripeness *n.* نُضْجٌ . كمَالٌ . بلُوغٌ

Ripple *n.* مَوْجَةٌ خفِيفَةٌ

Rise *v. i.* إرْتفعَ . قامَ ـُ . أشْرقَ

Rising *n.* قِيامٌ . طُلوعٌ . إرْتِفَاعٌ

Risk *n.* or *v. t.* خطرٌ . خاطرَ

Rite *n.* طقسٌ دِينيٌّ . سُنَّةٌ

Ritual *a.* or *n.* طقسِيٌّ . كِتابُ طُقوسٍ

Rival *n.* or *v. t.* مُناظِرٌ . سابَقَ

Rivalry *n.* مسابَقةٌ . مباراةٌ

River *n.* نَهْرٌ ج أَنْهُرٌ وأَنْهارٌ

Rivet *n.* or *v. t.* مِسْمارٌ مبجن . سَمَّرَ بِهِ

Rivulet *n.* نُهَيْرٌ . ساقِيَةٌ

Road *n.* طريقٌ . سِكَّةٌ . دَرْبٌ

Roadstead *n.* مَرْسًى . مَرْفَأٌ

Roam *v. i.* جَالَ ـُ . سَاحَ ـِ

Roan *a.* or *n.* فَرَسٌ كُمَيْتٌ مُبَقَّعٌ

Roar *v. i.* or *n.* زَمْجَرَ . زَأَرَ ـَ . زَئِيرٌ

Roast *v. t.* or *n.* شَوَى ـِ . مَشْوِيٌّ

Rob *v. t.* سَلَبَ ـُ . نَهَبَ ـَ

Robber *n.* لِصٌّ . سَرَّاقٌ

Robbery *n.* سَلْبٌ . سَرِقَةٌ

Robe *n.* or *v. t.* ثَوْبٌ . رِدَاءٌ . أَلْبَسَ

Robust *a.* ضَلِيعٌ . قَوِيُّ ٱلْجِسْمِ

Rock *n.* or *v. t.* صَخْرَةٌ . هَزَّ ـِ

Rocket *n.* سَهْمٌ نَارِيٌّ

Rocky *a.* صَخْرِيٌّ

Rod *n.* عَصًا

Roe *n.* أُنْثَى ٱلْأَيِّلِ

Rogue *n.*. مَكَّارٌ . غَدَّارٌ . خَبِيثٌ

Roguery *n.* خُبْثٌ . مَكْرٌ . حِيَلٌ

Roil *v. t.* عَكَّرَ . كَدَّرَ . هَيَّجَ

Roll *v. t.* or *i.* دَحْرَجَ . تَدَحْرَجَ . طَوَى ـِ

Roll *n.* دَرْجٌ . قَائِمَةٌ . دَحْرَجَةٌ

Roller *n.* مِحْدَلَةٌ

Romance *n.* حِكَايَةٌ . خُرَافَةٌ

Romanism *n.* عَقَائِدُ كَنِيسَةِ رُومِيَةَ

Romp *v. i.* or *n.* تَغَالَظَ فِي ٱللَّعِبِ . إِبْنَةٌ سَلِيطَةٌ

Roof *n.* سَقْفٌ . سَطْحٌ

Room *n.* مَكَانٌ . فَرَاغٌ . حُجْرَةٌ

Roomy *a.* فَسِيحٌ . رَحِيبٌ

Root *n.* or *v. i.* جِذْرٌ . أَصْلٌ . تَأَصَّلَ

Root *v. t.* نَبَشَ ـُ . إِسْتَأْصَلَ

Rope *n.* حَبْلٌ . مَرَسٌ

Rose *n.* وَرْدَةٌ

Rosette *n.* وَرْدَةٌ مِنْ شَرِيطٍ

Rosin *n.* رَاتِينَجٌ

Rosy *a.* وَرْدِيٌّ . مُحْمَرٌّ

Rot *v. i.* or *t.* or *n.* فَسَدَ ـُ . تَعَفَّنَ

Rotary / Rotatory } *a.* دَائِرٌ . دَوَّارٌ

Rotate *v. i.* or *t.* دَارَ ـُ . أَدَارَ

Rotation *n.* دَوَرَانٌ . تَنَاوُبٌ

Rotten *a.* فَاسِدٌ . عَفِنٌ

Rottenness *n.* فَسَادٌ . عُفُونَةٌ

Rotund *a.* كُرَوِيٌّ . مُسْتَدِيرٌ

Rotundity *a.* كُرَوِيَّةٌ

Rough *a.* خَشِنٌ . فَظٌّ . غَلِيظٌ

Roughness *n.* خُشُونَةٌ . غِلَاظَةٌ

Round *a.* or *n.* مُسْتَدِيرٌ . دَوْرٌ

Roundness *n.* إِسْتِدَارَةٌ . كُرَوِيهٌ

Rouse *v. t.* أَيْقَظَ . حَرَّكَ . حَرَّضَ

Rout *n.* or *v. t.* هَزِيمَةٌ . هَزَمَ ـِ

Route *n.* طَرِيق

Routine *n.* أُسْلُوبٌ . عَادَةٌ

Rove *v. i.* جَالَ ـُ . سَاحَ ـِ

Row *n.* صَفٌّ . شَغَبٌ . خِصَامٌ

Row *v. t.* جَذَفَ ـِ . قَذَفَ ـِ

Royal *a.* مَلَكِيٌّ . مُلُوكِيٌّ

Royalist *n.* مَلَكِيُّ ٱلْحِزْب

Royalty *n.* مَلَكِيهٌ . مُلْكٌ . ضَرِيبهٌ

Rub *v. t.* فَرَكَ ـُ . مَسَحَ ـَ . إِحْتَكَ

Rub *n.* فَرْكٌ . حك . صعوبهٌ

Rubbish *n.* رَدْمٌ . نُفَايَةٌ . سَقَطٌ

Ruby *n.* or *a.* يَاقُوتَةٌ . يَاقُوتِيٌّ

Rudder *n.* دَفه ٱلسَّفِينهِ

Ruddy *a.* أَحْمَرُ . أَشْقَرُ

Rude *a.* فَظٌّ

Rudeness *n.* غِلَاظَهٌ . فَظَاظَهٌ

Rudiment *n.* مَبْدَأ . اصْلٌ

Rudimental / Rudimentary } *a.* إِبْتِدَائِي

Rue *v. t.* أَسِفَ ـَ . نَدِمَ ـَ

Rue *n.* (plant) سَذَابٌ

Ruff *n.* طَوْقٌ ذُو كَشْكَشٍ

Ruffian *n.* خَبِيثٌ . غَلِيظٌ . شَرِسٌ

Ruffle *v. t.* تَنَفَّشَ . أَضْجَرَ

Rug *n.* سَجَادَةٌ . زِرْبِيَّةٌ

Rugged *a.* وَعِرٌ . خَشِنٌ

Ruin *v. t.* or *n.* خَرَبَ ـِ . خَرَابٌ

Ruinous *a.* خَرَابِيٌّ

Rule *n.* قَانُونٌ . قَاعِدَة . حُكْمٌ

Rule *v. t.* حَكَمَ ـُ . سَطَرَ

Ruler *n.* حَاكِمٌ . مُتَسَلِّطٌ . مِسْطَرَةٌ

Rumble *v. i.* خَرَّ ـُ . قَرْقَرَ

Ruminant *n.* حَيَوانٌ مُجْتَرٌّ

Ruminate *n.* or *v. i.* إِجْتَرَّ . تَأَمَّلَ

Rummage *n.* or *v. t.* قَلَّبَ . فَتَّشَ

Rumour *n.* إِشَاعَةٌ . خَبَرٌ

Rump *n.* عَجْزٌ . إِلْيَةٌ

Rumple *v. t.* جَعَّدَ . غَضَّنَ

Run *v. i.* رَكَضَ ـُ . سَالَ ـِ . جَرَى ـِ

Runaway *n.* هَارِبٌ . آبِقٌ . شَارِدٌ

Rupture *n.* فَتْقٌ . شِقَاقٌ . إِنْفِجَارٌ

Rural *a.* رِيفِيٌّ . غَيْرُ مَدَنِيٍّ

Ruse *n.* حِيلَةٌ

Rush *n.* or *v. i.* إِقْتِحَامٌ . زَحْمَةٌ . إِقْتَحَمَ

Rush *n.* بَرْدِيٌّ (نَبَاتٌ)

Rust *n.* or *v. i.* صَدَأٌ . صَدِئَ ـَ

Rustic *a.* غَيْرُ مُهَذَّبٍ . خَشِنٌ

Rustle *v. i.* جَرَّ ـُ . خَشْخَشَ

Rusty *a.* صَدِئٌ

Ruthless *a.* قَاسٍ . بِلَا رَافَةٍ

S

Sabbath *n.* سَبْتٌ . يَوْمُ ٱلأَحَدِ

Sabre *n.* سَيْفٌ ج سيوف

Sable *n.* or *a.* سَمُّورٌ (طَائِرٌ) . أَسْوَدُ

Saccharine *a.* سُكَّرِيٌّ

Sacerdotal *a.* كَهنوتِيٌّ

Sack *n.* or *v. t.* كِيسٌ . نَهَبَ ـَ

Sackcloth / Sacking } *n.* خَيشٌ . مِسْحٌ

Sacrament *n.* سِرٌّ دِينِيٌّ

Sacred *a.* مقدَّسٌ . دِينِيٌّ . مُحَرَّمٌ

Sacredness *n.* قُدْسٌ . حُرْمِيَّةٌ

Sacrifice *n.* or *v. t.* ذَبِيحَةٌ . ذَبَحَ ـَ . ضحى

Sacrificial *a.* ذَبِيحِيٌّ . قُرْبَانِيٌّ

Sacrilege *n.* تَدْنِيسُ ٱلمَقَدَسِ

Sad *a.* حَزِينٌ . كَئِيبٌ . مُحْزِنٌ

Sadden *v. t.* أَحْزَنَ

Saddle *n.* سَرْجٌ . بَرْذَعَةٌ

Saddler *n.* سَرَّاجٌ . (سُرُوجِيٌّ) بَرَاذِعِيٌّ

Sadducee *n.* صَدُوقِيٌّ

Sadness *n.* حُزْنٌ . كَآبَةٌ . غَمٌّ . لَهْفٌ

Safe *a.* or *n.* سَالِمٌ . مَصُونٌ . آمِنٌ

Safeguard *n.* or *v. t.* حِمَايَةٌ . حَمَى ـِ

Safety *n.* أَمْنٌ . سَلَامَةٌ . نَجَاةٌ

Safety-valve *n.* صِمَامُ آلَةٍ

Saffron *n.* زَعفَرَان

Sag *v. i.* حَطَّ ـُ مِنْ ثِقْلٍ

Sagacious *a.* ذَكِيٌّ . فَطِنٌ

Sagacity *n.* ذَكَاءٌ . فِطْنَةٌ

Sage *a.* or *n.* حَكِيمٌ . فَطِينٌ . قَوِيْسَةٌ

Sail *n.* or *v. i.* or *t.* قِلْعٌ . أَقْلَعَ . سَيَّرَ

Sailor *n.* نُوتِيٌّ . بَحْرِيٌّ . مَلَّاحٌ

Saint *n.* قَدِّيسٌ

Sake *n.* قَصْدٌ . غَايَةٌ . شَأْنٌ

Salad *n.* سَلَطَةٌ

Salary *n.* رَاتِبٌ . مَعَاشٌ . مَاهِيَّةٌ

Sale *n.* بَيْعٌ . رَوَاجٌ

Saleable *a.* رَائِجٌ

Salient *a.* بَارِزٌ . ظَاهِرٌ

Saline *a.* مِلْحِيٌّ . مَالِحٌ

Saliva *n.* لُعَابٌ . رِيق

Sallow *a.* مُصْفَرٌّ

Sallowness *n.* إِصفِرارٌ . صُفْرَةٌ

Sally *n.* or *v. i.* هُجومٌ . هَجمَ عَلَى

Saloon *n.* غُرْفَةُ ٱستِقبالٍ

Salt *n.* or *v. t.* مِلْحٌ . مَلَّحَ

Salt-cellar *n.* مَمْلَحَةٌ

Saltness *n.* مُلُوحَةٌ

Salt-petre *n.* مِلْحُ البارُودِ

Salubrious *a.* نافِعٌ لِلصِّحةِ

Salubrity *n.* مُلاءَمَةٌ لِلصِّحةِ

Salutary *a.* مُفِيدٌ . نافِعٌ

Salutation *n.* تَحِيَّةٌ . سَلامٌ

Salute *v. t.* or *n.* سَلَّمَ عَلَى . تَسْلِيمٌ

Salvation *n.* خَلاصٌ . نَجاةٌ . إِنقاذٌ

Salve *n.* مَرْهَمٌ . دُهْنٌ

Salver *n.* طَبَقٌ ج أَطْباقٌ

Samaritan *n.* سامِرِيٌّ

Same *n.* ذاتٌ . نَفسٌ . هُوَ هُوَ

Sameness *n.* ذاتِيَّةٌ . مُماثَلَةٌ

Sample *n.* عَيِّنَةٌ . (مَسْطَرَةٌ) . نَمُوذَجٌ

Sanative / Sanatory *a.* شافٍ . مُفِيدٌ لِلصِّحةِ

Sanctification *n.* تَقدِيسٌ . تَطْهِيرٌ

Sanctify *v. t.* قَدَّسَ . طَهَّرَ

Sanctimonious *a.* مُتَظاهِرٌ بِالتَّقوَى

Sanction *n.* or *v. t.* مُصادَقَةٌ . أَثْبَتَ

Sanctity *n.* قَداسَةٌ . قُدْسٌ

Sanctuary *n.* مَقْدِسٌ . مَعْبَدٌ . مَلاذٌ

Sand *n.* رَمْلٌ ج رِمالٌ

Sandal *n.* حِذاءٌ . نَعْلٌ

Sandal wood *n.* صَنْدَلٌ

Sandal-fly *n.* بَعوضَةٌ (سُكَيْت)

Sandstone *n.* حَجَرٌ رَمْلِيٌّ

Sandwich *n.* لَحْمٌ بَيْنَ قِطْعَتَي خُبْزٍ

Sandy *a.* رَمْلِيٌّ

Sane *a.* سَلِيمُ العَقْلِ

Sanguinary *a.* دَمَوِيٌّ . سَفَّاكُ الدَّمِ

Sanguine *a.* واثِقٌ . كَثِيرُ الرَّجاءِ

Sanitary *a.*	صحيٌّ. مفيد لِلصِحةِ
Sanity *n.*	سلامةُ ٱلْعقلِ. صِحتهُ
Sap *n.* or *v. t.*	عصيرُ ٱلنباتِ. هدمَ ٱلاساسَ
Sapient *a.*	حكيمٌ. متصنعُ ٱلْحِكمةِ
Sapling *n.*	شجيرةٌ
Sapphire *n.*	ياقوتٌ ازرقُ
Saracen *n.*	شرقيٌّ. عربيٌّ
Sarcasm *n.*	تهكمٌ. إِستهزآء
Sarcastic / Sarcastical *a.*	تهكميٌّ
Sarcophagus *n.*	ناووسٌ (تابوت قديم)
Sardonic *a.*	(ضحكٌ). تهكميٌّ
Sash *n.*	زنارٌ. برواز نافذةٍ
Satan *n.*	إِبليسُ. ٱلشيطانُ
Satanic / Satanical *a.*	إِبليسيٌّ. شيطانيٌّ
Satchel *n.*	كيسٌ صغيرٌ
Satellite *n.*	تابعٌ. قمرٌ
Sate / Satiate *v. t.*	شبَّعَ. أرضى. أفعمَ
Satiety *n.*	شبعٌ
Satin *n.*	أطلسُ حريرٍ
Satire *n.*	هجآء
Satiric / Satirical *a.*	هجائيٌّ
Satirize *v. t.*	هجا
Satisfaction *n.*	رضى. إرضآء
Satisfactory *a.*	مرضٍ. كافٍ
Satisfy *v. t.*	أرضى. أقنعَ
Saturate *v. t.*	أشربَ. أشبعَ
Saturday *n.*	يومُ ٱلسبتِ
Saturn *n.*	زحلُ
Sauce *n.*	مرقةٌ
Saucer *n.*	صحنٌ صغيرٌ. سكرجةٌ
Saucy *a.*	وقحٌ. سليط
Saunter *v. i.*	مشى متكاسلا
Sausage *n.*	مقانقُ. سجقٌ
Savage *n.* or *a.*	همجٌ. وحشيٌّ. جافٍ
Savageness *n.*	توحشٌ. قساوةٌ. همجيةٌ
Savant *n.*	علامةٌ

Save *v.t.* or *pr.* خلَّص . إِقْتَصَدَ . إِلا

Saving *a.* or *n.* مُقْتَصد . إِقْتِصَادٌ . إِسْتِثْنَاءٌ

Saviour *n.* مُخَلِّصٌ . فَادٍ

Savour *n.* or *v. i.* طَعْمٌ . إِتَّصَفَ ب

Savoury *a.* لَذِيذٌ . طَيِّبٌ . زَكِيٌّ

Saw *n.* or *v. t.* مِنْشَارٌ . نَشَرَ ـِ

Sawyer *n.* نَشَّارٌ

Say *v. t.* قَالَ ـُ . أَخْبَرَ

Saying *n.* قَوْلٌ . مَثَلٌ

Scab *n.* جُلْبَةٌ

Scabbard *n.* غِمْدٌ . قِرَابٌ

Scaffold *n.* صَقَالَة

Scaffolding *n.* صَقَالَات

Scald *v. t.* سَلَقَ ـُ . سمطَ ـِ

Scale *n.* كِفَّةُ مِيزَانٍ . حَرْشَفٌ

Scalé *v. t.* قَشَّرَ . تسوَّرَ . تَسلَق

Scalp *n.* or *v. t.* فَرْوَةُ ٱلرَّأْسِ . نَزَعَهَا

Scalpel *n.* مِشْرَطٌ ج مَشَارِطُ

Scaly *a.* ذُو حَرَاشِفَ . حَرْشَفِيٌّ

Scamp *n.* خَبِيثٌ . شِرِّيرٌ

Scamper *v. i.* رَكَضَ ـُ . فَرَّ ـِ

Scan *v. t.* تَفَرَّسَ . وَزَنَ ٱلشِّعْرَ

Scandal *n.* عَارٌ . إِفْتِرَآءٌ . فَضِيحَةٌ

Scandalize *v. t.* فَضَحَ . إِفْتَرَى . اخْجَلَ

Scandalous *a.* مَعِيبٌ . فَاضِحٌ . افْتِرَآئِيٌّ

Scant / **Scanty** *a.* نَاقِصٌ . قَلِيلٌ

Scantiness / **Scantness** *n.* نَقْصٌ . قِلَّةٌ

Scape-goat *n.* حَامِلُ ذُنُوبِ غَيْرِهِ

Scar *n.* نَدْبَةٌ . أَثَرُ جُرْحٍ

Scarce *a.* نَادِرٌ . قَلِيلُ ٱلْوُجُودِ

Scarcely *ad.* بِالْجَهْدِ . نَادِراً

Scarcity *n.* قِلَّةُ ٱلْوُجُودِ . نُدْرَةٌ

Scare *v. t.* خَوَّفَ . أَفْزَعَ . أَرْهَبَ

Scarecrow *n.* شَبَحٌ لِلتَّخْوِيفِ

Scarf *n.* وِشَاحٌ . حِمَالَةٌ

Scarify *v. t.* شَرَطَ ـِ . حَجَمَ ـُ

Scarlatina / Scarlet-fever } n. اَلْحُمَّى اَلْقِرْمِزِيَّة

Scarlet a. or n. قِرْمِزِيٌّ . قِرْمِز

Scath / Scathe } v. t. آذَى . أَهْلَكَ

Scathless a. غَيْرُ مُؤْذًى . سالمٌ

Scatter v. t. فَرَّقَ . بَدَّدَ

Scavenger n. زَبَّالٌ

Scene n. مَنْظَرٌ . فَصْلُ رِوَايَةٍ

Scenery n. مَنْظَرٌ

Scent n. or v. t. رَائِحَة . إِشْتَمَّ . عَطَّرَ

Sceptre n. صَوْلَجَانٌ . مُلْكٌ

Sceptic n. / Sceptical a. } مُرْتَابٌ

Scepticism n. إِرْتِيَابٌ . شَكٌّ

Schedule n. قَائِمَةٌ . جَدْوَلٌ

Scheme n. تَدْبِيرٌ . مَقْصَدٌ . اسْلُوبٌ

Scheme v. t. دَبَّرَ . إِخْتَرَعَ . رَسَمَ ـَ

Schism n. شِقَاقٌ . إِخْتِلَافٌ

Schismatic n. or a. رَافِضِيٌّ خَارِجِيٌّ

Scholar n. تِلْمِيذٌ . طَالِبٌ . عَالِمٌ

Scholarly a. عَالِمٌ . عِلْمِيٌّ

Scholarship n. عِلْمٌ مَالٌ وَقْفٌ لِتِلْمِيذٍ

Scholastic a. مَدْرَسِيٌّ

School n. مَدْرَسَةٌ . مَذْهَبٌ

Schooling n. تَدْرِيسٌ . تَعْلِيمٌ

School-master n. مُعَلِّمُ مَدْرَسَةٍ

Schooner n. سَفِينَةٌ ذَاتُ سَارِيَتَيْنِ

Science n. عِلْمٌ . فَنٌّ

Scientific / Scientifical } a. عِلْمِيٌّ

Scintillate v. i. تَلَأْلَأَ . بَرَقَ ـُ

Scissors n. pl. مِقَصٌّ . مِقْرَاضٌ

Scoff n. or v. i. هُزْءٌ . هَزَأَ ـَ

Scold v. t. or i. وَبَّخَ . عَنَّفَ . زَجَرَ ـُ

Scolding n. تَعْنِيفٌ . زَجْرٌ

Scoop n. or v. t. مِغْرَفَةٌ . غَرَفَ ـِ . حَفَرَ ـِ

Scope n. مَدًى . مَجَالٌ . غَايَةٌ

Scorch v. t. حَرَقَ ـِ . كَوَى ـ شَوَّطَ

Score n. عِشْرُونَ . حِسَابٌ . شَأْنٌ

Score *v. t.* خَطَّطَ . قَيَّدَ في حِسَابٍ

Scorn *n.* or *v.t.* إِحْتِقَارٌ . إِزْدَرَى بِ

Scorner / **Scornful** مُزْدَرٍ . مُحْتَقِرٌ

Scorpion *n.* عَقْرَبٌ

Scoundrel *n.* خَبِيثٌ . شِرِّيرٌ . قَبِيحٌ

Scour *v. t.* جَلَى ـِ . طَافَ عَاجِلًا

Scourge *n.* or *v. t.* سَوْطٌ . بَلِيَّةٌ . جَلَدَ ـُ

Scot-free *a.* مَعْفِيٌّ مِنْ . سَالِمٌ

Scout *n.* or *v. t.* جَاسُوسٌ . إِسْتَخَفَّ بِ

Scowl *n.* or *v. i.* عُبُوسَةٌ . عَبَّسَ . كَلَحَ ـَ

Scragged / **Scraggy** خَشِنٌ . نَحِيفٌ

Scramble *n.* or *v. i.* مُنَاوَشَةٌ . تَسَلَّقَ

Scrap *n.* قِطْعَةٌ صَغِيرَةٌ . حِتَّةٌ

Scrape *v. t.* حَتَّ ـُ . كَشَطَ ـِ . حَكَّ ـُ

Scraper *n.* مِكْشَطٌ . مِحَتٌّ

Scratch *v. t.* or *i.* خَدَشَ ـِ . حَكَّ ـُ

Scratch *n.* خَمْشٌ . خَدْشَةٌ

Scrawl *n.* خطٌ رَدِيءٌ

Scream / **Screech** *v. i.* or *n.* صَاحَ ـِ . صَيْحَةٌ

Screen *n.* or *v. t.* سِتْرٌ . سَتَرَ ـُ

Screw *n.* or *v. t.* (برمه) . شَدَّ بِهَا

Scribble *v.i.* or *t.* أَسَاءَ خَطًّا وَمَعْنًى

Scribbler *n.* مُؤَلِّفٌ رَكِيكٌ

Scribe *n.* كَاتِبٌ

Scrimp *v. t.* ضَيَّقَ . قَصَّرَ

Script *n.* أَحْرُفُ طَبْعٍ شَبِيهَةٌ بِالْخَطِّ

Scriptural *a.* مُطَابِقٌ لِلْكِتَابِ ٱلْمُقَدَّسِ

Scripture *n.* الْكِتَابُ ٱلْمُقَدَّسُ

Scrofula *n.* دَاءُ ٱلْخَنَازِيرِ

Scrofulous *a.* مُصَابٌ بِدَاءِ ٱلْخَنَازِيرِ

Scroll *n.* دَرْجٌ

Scrub *n.* or *v. t.* خَسِيسٌ . جَلَى ـِ . مَسَحَ

Scruple *n.* or *v. i.* شَكٌّ . إِرْتِيَابٌ . تَرَدَّدَ

Scrupulous *a.* مُتَرَدِّدٌ . مُحْتَرِسٌ

Scrutinize *v. t.* دَقَّقَ ٱلنَّظَرَ . تَفَحَّصَ

Scrutiny *n.* فَحْصٌ مُدَقِّقٌ . إِنْعَامُ نَظَرٍ

Scuffle *n.* or *v. t.* مُصَارَعَةٌ . نَاوَشَ

Sculptor *n.* نَحَاتٌ . نَقَّاشٌ

Sculpture *n.* صِنَاعَةُ ٱلنَّحْتِ

Scum *n.* or *v. t.* رَغْوَةٌ . زَبَدٌ . نَزَعَهَا

Scurf *n.* هِبْرِيَةٌ . قِشْرَةُ ٱلرَّأْسِ

Scurrilous *a.* قَبِيحٌ . رَذِيلٌ . سَفِيهٌ

Scurvy *n.* or *a.* دَاءُ ٱلإِسْكَرْبُوطِ . خَسِيسٌ

Scuttle *n.* or *v.t.* سَطْلُ فَحْمٍ . ثَقَبَ سَفِينَةً لِتَغْرَقَ

Scythe *n.* مِحْصَدٌ . مِنْجَلٌ

Sea *a.* بَحْرٌ

Seaboard, Seacoast *n.* شَطُّ ٱلْبَحْرِ . رِيفٌ

Seafarer, Seafaring *n.* مَلَّاحٌ . بَحْرِيٌّ

n. or *v.* خَتْمٌ . خَاتَمٌ خَتَمَ . عِجْلُ ٱلْبَحْرِ

Seam *n.* دَرْزٌ . نَدْبَةٌ . طَبَقَةٌ

Seaman *n.* بَحْرِيٌّ

Seamanship *n.* مِلَاحَه

Seamstress *a.* خَيَاطَةٌ

Seaport *n.* مِينَاءٌ . فُرْضَةٌ

Sear *v. t.* كَوَى ـِ . جَفَّفَ . صَلَّبَ

Search *v. t.* or *n.* فَتَّشَ . تَفَحَّصَ . تَفْتِيشٌ

Searching *a.* مُسْتَقْصٍ . مُدَقِّقٌ . نَافِذٌ

Seasick *a.* مُصَابٌ بِدُوَارِ ٱلْبَحْرِ

Seaside *n.* سَاحِلُ ٱلْبَحْرِ . رِيفُهُ

Season *n.* فَصْلٌ . وَقْتٌ . مُدَّةٌ

Seasonable *a.* فِي وَقْتِهِ . فِي مَحَلِّهِ

Seasoning *n.* تَابَلٌ . تَتْبِيلٌ . تَجْفِيفٌ

Seat *n.* or *v. t.* مَقْعَدٌ . مَجْلِسٌ . أَجْلَسَ

Seaward *ad.* إِلَى جِهَةِ ٱلْبَحْرِ

Secede *v.i.* إِنْفَصَلَ . إِعْتَزَلَ . خَرَجَ ـُ

Secession *n.* اِنْفِصَالٌ . خُرُوجٌ

Seclude *v. t.* حَجَبَ ـُ . جَعَلَ بِعُزْلَةٍ

Seclusion *n.* عُزْلَةٌ . خُلُوٌّ

Second *n.* ثَانِيَةٌ ج ثَوَانٍ

Second *a.* or *n.* or *v. t.* الثَّانِي . أَيَّدَ

Secondary *a.* ثَانَوِيٌّ . غَيْرُ مُهِمٍّ

Second-hand *a.* مُسْتَعْمَلٌ

Second-rate *a.* مِنَ ٱلدَّرَجَةِ ٱلثَّانِيَةِ

Secrecy *n.*	سر . كِتمَان
Secret *a.* or *n.*	سِرِّيٌّ . مَكتُومٌ . سِرٌّ
Secretary *n.*	كَاتِبٌ . نَاظِرُ دَائِرَةٍ
Secrete *v. t.*	اخفى . خبأ . أفرز
Secretion *n.*	إخفاء . إفراز
Sect *n.*	طَائِفَةٌ . شيعة . مَذْهَبٌ
Sectarian *a.* / **Sectary** *n.*	طَائِفِيٌّ . تحزبي
Section *n.*	قِطعة . قِسمٌ . فَصلٌ
Secular *a.*	غير دِينِيٍّ . عَالَمِيٌّ
Secularize *v. t.*	حوّل إلى غاية عالَمِيّة
Secure *a.* or *v. t.*	مُطمَئِنٌّ . حَصل . أحرز
Security *n.*	أمن طمأنينة . ضمَانٌ
Sedate *a.*	رزين . هادِئ
Sedative *a.* or *n.*	مُسَكِّنٌ
Sedentary *a.*	قاعِد . ملازِمُ الجلوس
Sediment *n.*	رَاسِبٌ . ثُقْلٌ
Sedition *n.*	فِتنة . ثورة . شغب
Seditious *a.*	مشاغِبٌ . مهيِّج . . مثير
Seduce *v. t.*	أغوى . أضلّ
Seductive *a.*	مغوٍ مُفتِنٌ . مضِل
Sedulous *a.*	كَدود . مجتهِد
See *v. t.* or *n.*	رَأى ـَ . نظر ـُ . ابرشية
Seed *n.*	بِزرٌ . زَرعٌ . نسل
Seedling *n.*	نبات مِن بِزرة
Seed-time *n.*	أبان الزرع
Seedy *a.*	كثير البزر . بَال
Seek *v. t.*	طَلَبَ ـُ . فتّش . جدّ ـِ
Seeing *con.*	بما أنْ
Seem *v. i.*	ظهر ـَ . بان ـِ
Seemingly *ad.*	بحسَبِ الظاهِر
Seemly *a.*	لائِق . حسَنٌ
Seer *n.*	رائي . نبي
Seethe *v. t.*	طبخ ـُ . غلى
Segment *n.*	قِطعة
Segregate *v. t.*	فصل ـ . أفرز
Seize *v.t.*	قبض ـِ . خطف ـَ . إعترى

Seizure *n.* قَبْضٌ . ضَبْطٌ

Seldom *ad.* نَادِراً . قَلَّمَا

Select *v. t.* or *a.* إِخْتَارَ . إِصْطَفَى . صَفِيٌّ

Self *n.* ذَاتٌ . نَفْسٌ

Self-conceit *n.* عُجْبٌ

Self-denial *n.* إِنْكَارُ ٱلذَّاتِ

Self-evident *a.* غَنِيٌّ عَنِ ٱلْبَيَانِ

Selfish *a.* مُحِبُّ ٱلذَّاتِ

Selfishness *n.* مَحَبَّةُ ٱلذَّاتِ

Self-respect *n.* إِحْتِرَامُ ٱلذَّاتِ

Self-same *a.* ذَاتٌ . بِعَيْنِهِ

Self-will *n.* عِنَادٌ

Sell *v. t.* بَاعَ ـِ

Semblance *n.* شِبْهٌ . شَكْلٌ . صُورَةٌ

Semi *n.* نِصْفٌ (فِي ٱلتَّرْكِيبِ)

Semi-annual *a.* كُلَّ نِصْفِ سَنَةٍ

Semi-circle *n.* نِصْفُ دَائِرَةٍ

Semicolon *n.* (;) عَلَامَةُ وَقْفٍ كَذَا

Seminary *n.* مَدْرَسَةٌ

Semitic *a.* سَامِيٌّ

Senate *n.* مَشْيَخَةٌ . مَجْلِسُ اعْيَانٍ

Senator *n.* عُضْوُ مَجْلِسِ ٱلْأَعْيَانِ

Send *v. t.* أَرْسَلَ . بَعَثَ ـَ

Senility *n.* شَيْخُوخَةٌ . كِبَرٌ

Senior *n.* or *a.* أَكْبَرُ عُمْراً . أَلْمُتَقَدِّمُ

Seniority *n.* أَسْبَقِيَّةٌ سِنّاً أَوْ مَنْصِباً

Sensation *n.* حِسٌّ . شُعُورٌ . تَأْثِيرٌ

Sensational *a.* مُهَيِّجُ ٱلْعَوَاطِفِ

Sense *n.* حِسٌّ . حَاسَّةٌ . مَعْنًى

Senseless *a.* بِلَا حِسٍّ أَوْ مَعْنًى . مَغْشِيٌّ عَلَيْهِ

Sensibility *n.* حَاسِيَّةٌ . رِقَّةُ ٱلنَّفْسِ

Sensible *a.* حَسَّاسٌ . عَاقِلٌ . مَحْسُوسٌ

Sensitive *a.* دَقِيقُ ٱلْحِسِّ وَٱلْاِنْفِعَالِ

Sensual *a.* }
Sensualist *n.* } حَيَوَانِيٌّ . شَهْوَانِيٌّ

Sensualism }
Sensuality } *n.* شَهْوَانِيَّةٌ

Sentence *n.* جُمْلَةٌ . قَضَاءٌ . حُكْمٌ

Sentient *n.*	حَسّاس. مُدرِكٌ بِالحِسِّ
Sentiment *n.*	حِس. عاطِفَة. مَعنًى
Sentinel / Sentry *n.*	حارِسٌ. خَفَر
Separable *a.*	قابِل الفَصلِ
Separate *v. t.* or *a.*	فَصَل ـِ مُنفَصِلٌ
Separation *n.*	فَصلٌ. إِنفِصالٌ. مُفارَقة
Separatist *n.*	مُعتَزِلٌ. مُنشَقٌّ
September *n.*	شَهرُ أَيلول. (سبتمبر)
Septennial *a.*	كُلَّ سَبعِ سِنين
Septentrional *a.*	شِمالِيٌّ
Septuagenarian *n.*	إِبنُ ٧٠ سَنَةً
Septuagint *n.*	أَلتَّرجَمَةُ السَّبعِينِيَّة
Sepulchre *n.*	قَبرٌ. ضَرِيح
Sepulture *n.*	دَفنٌ
Sequel *n.*	تابِعٌ. تالٍ. نَتِيجَةٌ
Sequence *n.*	تَتابُعٌ. تالٍ
Sequester / Sequestrate *v. t.*	ضَبَطَ ـُ حَجَزَ ـُ
Serdphic *a.*	مَلائِكِيٌّ. بَهِيٌّ
Serenade *n.* or *v. t.*	عَزفُ المُوسِيقَى بِاللَّيلِ
Serene *a.*	هادِئٌ. صافٍ. رَصِينٌ
Serenity *n.*	صَفاءٌ. هُدُوءٌ
Serf *n.*	عَبدٌ
Sergeant *n.*	جاوِيشٌ. شاوِيشٌ
Serial *a.* or *n.*	مُتَتابِعٌ. رِوايَةٌ تُطبَعُ أَجزاءً مُتَتابِعَةً
Series *n.*	نَسَقٌ. سِلسِلَةٌ
Serious *a.*	رَزِينٌ. جادٌّ. عَظِيمٌ
Sermon *n.*	مَوعِظَةٌ
Serpent *n.*	حَيَّةٌ. ثُعبانٌ
Serpentine *a.*	مُلتَفٌّ كَالحَيَّةِ
Servant *n.*	خادِمٌ. أَجِيرٌ
Serve *v. t.*	خَدَمَ ـُ. عَبَدَ ـُ. صَلَحَ لِ
Service *n.*	خِدمَةٌ. عِبادَةٌ. مَعرُوفٌ
Serviceable *a.*	مُفِيدٌ. صالِحٌ لِ
Servile *a.*	ذَلِيلٌ. خاضِعٌ
Servility *n.*	تَذَلُّلٌ. عُبُودِيَّةٌ

Servitor *n.*	خَادِمٌ . تَابِعٌ
Servitude *n.*	عُبُودِيَّةٌ . رِقٌّ
Sesame *n.*	سِمْسِمٌ
Session *n.*	جَلْسَةٌ
Sesspool *n.*	بَالوعَة أَوْسَاخٍ
Set *v.t.* or *i.*	وَضَعَ ـَـ . جَبَرَ ـُـ . غَابَ ـِـ
Set *n.*	طَقْمٌ . قَوْمٌ . حِزْبٌ
Settle *v. i.*	سَكَنَ ـُـ . أَثْقَلَ . هَدَأَ
Settle *v. t.*	أَسْكَنَ . دَبَّرَ . أَنْجَزَ
Settlement *n.*	مَسْكَنٌ . تَسْوِيَةٌ
Settlings *n. pl.*	دُرْدِيٌّ . رُسُوبٌ
Seven *a.*	سَبْعٌ أَوْ سَبْعَةٌ
Seventh *a.*	سَابِعٌ
Seventeen *a.*	سَبْعَةَ عَشَرَ
Seventieth / **Seventy** } *a.*	سَبْعُونَ
Sever *v. t.*	فَصَلَ ـِـ . قَطَعَ ـِـ
Several *a.*	بَعْضٌ . بِضْعَةٌ . فَرْدٌ
Severally *ad.*	أَفْرَادًا . عَلَى حِدَةٍ
Severance *n.*	فَصْلٌ . قَطْعٌ
Severe *a.*	قَاسٍ . صَارِمٌ . شَدِيدٌ
Severity *n.*	صَرَامَةٌ . شِدَّةٌ . عُنْفٌ
Sew *v. t.*	خَاطَ ـِـ . خَيَّطَ
Sewer *n.*	خَيَّاطٌ . بَالُوعَةٌ . سَرَبٌ
Sex *n.*	جِنْسٌ
Sextant *n.*	آلَةٌ لِقِيَاسِ ٱلزَّوَايَا
Sexton *n.*	قَنْدَلَفْتٌ . حَفَّارُ ٱلْقُبُورِ
Sexual *a.*	جِنْسِيٌّ . مُمَيِّزُ ٱلْجِنْسِ
Shabby *a.*	رَثِيثٌ . خَسِيسٌ
Shackle *v. t.*	قَيَّدَ . عَاقَ
Shackles *n. pl.*	قُيُودٌ . أَغْلَالٌ
Shade *n.* or *v. t.*	ظِلٌّ . خَيَالٌ . ظَلَّلَ
Shadow *n.*	ظِلٌّ . رَمْزٌ
Shadowy *a.*	مُظَلِّلٌ . وَهْمِيٌّ . مُبْهَمٌ
Shady *a.*	مُظَلَّلٌ . كَثِيرُ ٱلظِّلِّ
Shaft *n.*	سَهْمٌ . بِئْرٌ . عَرِيشٌ
Shagged / **Shaggy** } *a.*	اشْعَرُ . كَثٌّ

Shake *v. t.* or *i.* or *n.* هَزَّ ـِ . آهْتزَ . هزة

Shall *aux. v.* فِعلٌ إِضَافي يَدلُّ عَلَى ٱلاِسْتِقْبَالِ

Shallow *a.* قَلِيلُ ٱلْغوْرِ . ضعِيفٌ

Sham *n.* or *a.* or *v. i.* تصنعٌ . غِشٌّ

Shambles *n. pl.* مسلخٌ . مَجْزَرٌ

Shame *n.* خزْيٌ . عَارٌ . خجلٌ

Shamefaced *a.* مستحٍ . خَجِل

Shameful *a.* مُخزٍ . مُعيبٌ . قبيحٌ

Shameless *a.* بِلاَ حيَاَءٍ

Shank *n.* سَاقٌ . يدُ آلَةٍ

Shanty *n.* كوخ

Shape *v.t.* or *n.* كَوَّنَ . صُورَةٌ . هيئَةٌ

Shapeless *a.* بِلاَ شَكْلٍ أَوْ ترتِيبٍ

Shapely *a.* جَمِيلُ ٱلشَّكْلِ

Share *v. t.* or *i.* قَاسَمَ . شَارَكَ

Share *n.* حِصَّة . سهمٌ . سِكة

Share-holder *n.* صَاحِبُ سهمٍ

Shark *a.* كَلْبُ ٱلْبَحْرِ

Sharp *a.* حَادٌّ . حِرِّيفٌ . خَارِقٌ . ذَكِي

Sharpen *v. t.* سنَّ . انْهَضَ

Sharpness *n.* حِدَّةٌ . حِذْقٌ . شِدَّةٌ

Shatter *v. t.* كَسَّرَ . قَصفَ . ابَادَ

Shave *v. t.* حَلَقَ ـِ . غَبَنَ ـِ

Shaving *n.* نُجَارَة . شَرِيحَة رَقِيقَةٌ

Shawl *n.* شَالٌ

She *pron.* هِيَ

Sheaf *n.* حزمَةُ قَمْحٍ

Shear *v. t.* جَزَّ ـُ

Shears *n. pl.* مجز . مِقَصٌّ

Sheath *n.* غِلاَفٌ . غِمْدٌ

Sheathe *v. t.* غَلفَ ـِ . غمَدَ ـُ

Shed *v.t.* سَفكَ ـُ . ذَرفَ ـِ . خلَعَ ـَ

Sheep *n.* غَنَمٌ . ضَأن . شَاة

Sheep-fold *n.* حظِيرَةٌ . صِيرَة

Sheepish *a.* مستحٍ . خَجِل

Sheer *a.* مَحْضٌ . خَالِصٌ

Sheet *n.* مُلَاءَةٌ . شَرْشَفٌ . طَلْحِيَّةٌ

Shelf *n.* رَفٌّ ج رُفُوفٌ

Shell *n.* قِشْرَةٌ . صَدَفَةٌ . قُنْبُلَةٌ

Shell *v. t.* قَشَرَ ـُ . رَمَى بِالْقَنَابِلِ

Shell-fish *n.* صَدَفٌ

Shelter *n.* or *v. t.* مَأْوًى . آوَى . حَمَى ـِ

Shepherd *n.* رَاعٍ ج رُعَاةٌ

Sherbet *n.* شَرَابٌ

Sheriff *n.* مَأْمُورٌ يُجْرِي ٱلْأَحْكَامَ

Shield *n.* or *v. t.* تُرْسٌ . حَمَى ـِ . صَانَ

Shift *v. t.* or *n.* نَقَلَ . غَيَّرَ . حِيلَةٌ

Shiftless *a.* عَدِيمُ ٱلتَّدْبِيرِ . قَاصِرٌ

Shilling *n.* ١/٢٠ مِنَ ٱللِّيرَا ٱلْإِنْكِلِيزِيَّةِ

Shin *n.* مُقَدَّمُ ٱلسَّاقِ

Shine *v. i.* أَضَاءَ . أَشْرَقَ

Shingle *n.* or *v. t.* لَوْحٌ رَقِيقٌ . غَطَّى بِهِ

Shining, Shiny *a.* مُضِيءٌ لَامِعٌ

Ship *n.* or *v. t.* سَفِينَةٌ . أَنْزَلَ فِيهَا

Shipment *n.* إِرْسَالِيَّةُ بِضَاعَةٍ

Shipping *n.* مُجْتَمَعُ سُفُنٍ

Shipwreck *n.* ٱنْكِسَارُ سَفِينَةٍ

Shire *n.* مُقَاطَعَةٌ . لِوَاءٌ

Shirk *v. t.* تَجَنَّبَ (ٱلْوَاجِبَ)

Shirt *n.* or *v. t.* قَمِيصٌ ج قُمْصَانٌ . أَلْبَسَهُ

Shiver *v. i.* or *t.* اقْشَعَرَّ . حَطَّمَ

Shoal *n.* سِرْبُ (سَمَكٍ) . ضَحْلٌ

Shock *n.* or *v. t.* صَدْمَةٌ . رَجَّةٌ . ازْعَبَ

Shocking *a.* هَائِلٌ . مُكَدِّرٌ

Shoe *n.* or *v. t.* حِذَاءٌ . نَعْلٌ . نَعَلَ ـَ

Shoemaker *n.* سَكَّافٌ . إِسْكَافٌ

Shoot *v. t.* or *i.* أَطْلَقَ . رَمَى ـِ . فَرَّخَ

Shoot *n.* فَرْخٌ . عُسْلُجٌ

Shop *n.* دُكَّانٌ . حَانُوتٌ

Shop-keeper *n.* صَاحِبُ دُكَّانٍ

Shopping *n.* شِرَاءٌ . مِسْوَاقٌ

Shore *n.* شَطٌّ . شَاطِئٌ

Short *a.* قَصِيرٌ . نَاقِصٌ

Shorten *v. t.* or *i.* قَصَّرَ . تَقَصَّرَ

Short-lived *a.* قَصِيرُ ٱلْعُمْرِ

Shortness *n.* قِصَرٌ . إِيجَازٌ

Short-sighted *a.* قَصِيرُ ٱلْبَصَرِ

Shot *n.* رَمْيَةٌ . خُرْدُقٌ . رَامٍ

Should *pret.* of shall

Shoulder *n.* كَتِفٌ . مَنْكِبٌ

Shout *v. t.* or *n.* زَعَقَ ـَ . صَاحَ . هُتَافٌ

Shove *v. t.* or *n.* دَفَعَ ـَ . دَفْعَةٌ

Shovel *n.* or *v. t.* مِجْرَفَةٌ . جَرَفَ ـُ

Show *v. t.* أَظْهَرَ . بَيَّنَ . هَدَى ـِ

Show *n.* مَعْرِضٌ . مَنْظَرٌ . تَظَاهُرٌ

Shower *n.* مَطْرَةٌ

Showy *a.* زَاهٍ . مُزَخْرَفٌ

Shred *n.* or *v. t.* شِقَّةٌ . قِطْعَةٌ رَقِيقَةٌ . قَطَّعَ

Shrew *n.* سَلِيطَةٌ . صَخَّابَةٌ

Shrewd *a.* حَاذِقٌ . دَاهٍ

Shriek *v. i.* or *n.* صَرَخَ ـُ . صُرَاخٌ

Shrill *a.* حَادُّ ٱلصَّوْتِ

Shrine *n.* مَقَامٌ مُقَدَّسٌ . مَعْبَدٌ

Shrink *v. i.* تَقَلَّصَ . نَقَصَ . ٱشْمَأَزَّ

Shrivel *v. t.* or *i.* غَضَّنَ . تَغَضَّنَ

Shroud *n.* or *v.t.* كَفَنٌ . سَتْرٌ . سَتَرَ

Shrub *n.* نَجْمُ ٱلْأَشْجَارِ . شُجَيْرَةٌ

Shrubbery *n.* مُجْتَمَعُ أَنْجُمٍ

Shrubby *a.* نَجْمِيٌّ . كَثِيرُ ٱلْأَنْجُمِ

Shrug *v. t.* or *n.* هَزَّ (ٱلْأَكْتَافَ)

Shudder *n.* or *v. i.* ٱرْتِعَاشٌ . ٱرْتَجَفَ

Shuffle *v. t.* خَلَطَ . ٱحْتَالَ

Shun *v. t.* أَعْرَضَ عَنْ . ٱجْتَنَبَ

Shut *v. t.* or *i.* أَغْلَقَ . انْغَلَقَ

Shutter *n.* دَرْفَةٌ

Shuttle *n.* مَكُّوكٌ

Shy *a.* or *v.i.* مُسْتَحٍ . وَجِلٌ . أَجْفَلَ

Shyness *n.* حَيَاءٌ . وَجَلٌ

Sibyl *n.* كَاهِنَةٌ . وَثَنِيَّةٌ . عَرَّافَةٌ

Sick *a.* مَرِيضٌ . عَلِيلٌ

Sicken *v. t.* or *i.* قَزَّزَ . مَرِضَ

Sickish *a.* مُقَزِّزٌ

Sickle *n.* مِنْجَلٌ

Sickly *a.* وَخِيمٌ . سَقِيمٌ . ضَعِيفٌ

Sickness *n.* مَرَضٌ . عِلَّةٌ

Side *n.* جَانِبٌ . نَاحِيَةٌ . حِزْبٌ

Sideboard *n.* خِزَانَةُ ٱلسُّفْرَةِ

Sidelong *a.* جَانِبِيٌّ . مُنْحَرِفٌ

Sidereal *a.* كَوْكَبِيٌّ . نَجْمِيٌّ

Side-saddle *n.* سَرْجٌ لِلنِّسَاءِ

Sidewise *ad.* بِالْعَرْضِ . جَانِباً

Siege *n.* مُحَاصَرَةٌ . حِصَارٌ

Siesta *n.* قَيْلُولَةٌ

Sieve *n.* مُنْخُلٌ . غِرْبَالٌ

Sift *v. t.* غَرْبَلَ . تَفَحَّصَ

Sigh *v. i.* or *n.* تَنَهَّدَ . زَفَرَ ـِ . زَفِيرٌ

Sight *n.* نَظَرٌ . بَصَرٌ . مَنْظَرٌ

Sightless *a.* أَعْمَى

Sightly *a.* ظَاهِرٌ . شَهِيٌّ لِلنظَرِ

Sign *n.* عَلَامَةٌ . إِشَارَةٌ . آيَةٌ

Sign *v. t.* or *i.* أَمْضَى . أَشَارَ إِلَى

Signal *n.* or *a.* إِشَارَةٌ . مُمْتَازٌ

Signalize *v. t.* مَيَّزَ . شَهَرَ

Signature *n.* إِمْضَا

Signet *n.* خَتْمٌ . خَاتَمٌ

Significance, Significance *n.* مَعْنًى . اهَمِيَّةٌ

Significant *a.* دَالٌ . مُهِمٌّ

Signification *n.* مَعْنًى . فَحْوَى

Signify *v. t.* افَادَ . عَنَى ـِ

Silence *n.* سُكُوتٌ . هُدُوٌّ . سُكُونٌ

Silence *v. t.* أَسْكَتَ . أَفْحَمَ

Silent *a.* سَاكِتٌ . سَاكِنٌ

Silk *n.* حَرِيرٌ . سُنْدُسٌ

Silk, Silken *a.* حَرِيرِيٌّ

Silk-worm *n.*	دُودُ ٱلْقَزِّ
Silky *a.*	نَاعِمٌ . أَمْلَسُ
Sill *n.*	اُسْكُفَّةٌ (اسفلُ ٱلبابِ أَوْ ٱلشُّبَّاكِ)
Silliness *n.*	غَبَاوَةٌ . رُعُونَةٌ
Silly *a.*	أَرْعَنُ . غَبِيٌّ
Silver *n.* or *a.*	فِضَّةٌ . فِضِّيٌّ
Silversmith *n.*	صَائِغٌ ج صَاغَةٌ
Silvery *a.*	فِضِّيٌّ . كَالْفِضَّةِ
Similar *a.*	شَبِيهٌ . مِثْلٌ . مُشَاكِلٌ
Similarity / Similitude } *n.*	مُشَابَهَةٌ
Simile *n.*	تَشْبِيهٌ
Simmer *v. t.*	غَلَى بِخِفَّةٍ
Simony *n.*	شِرَاءُ رُتَبِ الْكَنِيسَةِ
Simoom *n.*	سَمُومٌ (رِيحٌ)
Simper *v. i.*	تَبَسَّمَ كَالأَبْلَهِ
Simple *a.*	بَسِيطٌ . هَيِّنٌ . وَاضِحٌ
Simpleton *n.*	غَبِيٌّ . أَبْلَهُ
Simplicity *n.*	بَسَاطَةٌ . سَذَاجَةٌ
Simplify *v. t.*	جَعَلَهُ بَسِيطًا . سَهَّلَ
Simply *ad.*	بِبَسَاطَةٍ . فَقَطْ
Simulate *v. t.*	تَشَبَّهَ . تَظَاهَرَ بِ
Simultaneous *a.*	فِي وَقْتٍ وَاحِدٍ
Sin *n.* or *v. i.*	خَطِيَّةٌ . أَخْطَأَ
Since *ad.* or *pr.* or *con.*	بَعْدُ . مُنْذُ . لِأَنَّ
Sincere *a.*	مُخْلِصٌ . نَصُوحٌ
Sincerity *n.*	إِخْلَاصٌ . صَفَاءُ ٱلنِّيَّةِ
Sine *n.*	جَيْبٌ فِي (ٱلْهَنْدَسَةِ)
Sinew *n.*	وَتَرٌ . أَصْلٌ قُوَّةٌ
Sinewy *a.*	قَوِيٌّ . ضَلِيعٌ . عَضِلٌ
Sinful *a.*	خَاطِئٌ . أَثِيمٌ
Sinfulness *n.*	خَطِيَّةٌ . حَالَةُ ٱلإِثْمِ
Sing *v. t.*	رَنَّمَ . غَنَّى . رَتَّلَ
Singe *v. t.*	مَسَّتْهُ ٱلنَّارُ قَلِيلاً
Singing *n.*	غِنَاءٌ . تَرْنِيمٌ
Single *a.*	فَرْدٌ . وَاحِدٌ . عَازِبٌ
Singleness *n.*	وَحْدَةٌ . بَسَاطَةٌ

Singular *n.* مُفْرَدٌ . غَرِيبٌ . عَجِيبٌ

Singularity *n.* وَحْدَةٌ . غَرَابَةٌ

Sinister *a.* يَسَارٌ . مَشُومٌ

Sink *v. i.* or *t.* غَرِقَ ـَ . انْحَطَ . أَغْرَق

Sink *n.* مَصَبٌّ . بَالوعَةٌ

Sinking-fund *n.* مَال لاَستِهلاَكِ دَيْنٍ

Sinless *a.* بِلاَ خَطِيئةٍ . بَارٌّ

Sinner *n.* خَاطِئٌ

Sinuosity *n.* تَعَرُّجٌ

Sinuous *a.* مُتَعَرِّجٌ

Sip *n.* or *v. t.* مَصَّةٌ . تَمَصَّص

Sir *n.* سَيِّد

Sire *n.* أَبٌ . مَوْلَى (لِلْمُلوك)

Siren *n.* or *a.* جِنِّيَّةُ البَحرِ . فَتَّانٌ

Sirocco *n.* رِيحٌ . شَرْقِيَّةٌ . سَمُومٌ

Sirup *n.* عَصِيرٌ مُحَلًّى . شَرَابٌ

Sister *n.* اخت . شَقِيقَةٌ

Sister-in law *n.* سِلْفَةٌ . اخت الزَّوْج أَوْ الزَّوْجَة

Sister-hood *n.* جَمْعِيَّةُ نِسَاءٍ أَو رَاهِبَات

Sit *v. t.* جَلَسَ ـِ . اسْتَقَرَّ . حَضَنَ ـُ

Site *n.* مَوْقِعٌ . مَوْضِعٌ

Sitting *n.* جُلوسٌ . جَلْسَةٌ

Situate / Situated *a.* وَاقِعٌ

Situation *n.* مَوْقِعٌ . مَنْصِبٌ . حَالٌ

Six *a.* سِتَّةٌ أَو سِتٌّ

Sixpence *n.* نِصْفُ شِلِينٍ

Sixteen *a.* سِتَّة عَشَر

Sixteenth *a.* السَّادِسُ عَشَر

Sixth *a.* سَادِسٌ

Sixty *a.* سِتُّون

Size *n.* حَجْمٌ . قَدْرٌ . قَدٌّ

Skate *n.* نَعل لِلسَّيْرِ عَلَى الجَلِيدِ

Skein *n.* شَلَّةُ خِيطَانٍ . خُصْلَة

Skeleton *n.* هَيْكَل حَيَوَانٍ

Skeptic *etc.* see Sceptic *etc.* مُرْتَابٌ

Sketch *n.* or *v. t.* رَسْمٌ . رَسَمَ ـُ

Skiff *n.* قَارِبٌ . زَوْرَق

Skilfulness / **Skill** *n.* مَهَارَةٌ

Skilful / **Skilled** *a.* مَاهِرٌ . خَبِيرٌ

Skim *v. t.* or *i.* نَزَعَ ـَ ٱلرَّغْوَةَ . سَفَّ ـَ

Skin *n.* or *v. t.* جِلْدٌ . قِشْرٌ . سَلَخَ ـَ

Skinny *a.* هَزِيلٌ . جِلْدِيٌّ

Skip *v. i.* or *t.* قَفَزَ ـِ . فَاتَ . تَرَكَ

Skipper *n.* رُبَّان سَفِينَةٍ صَغِيرَةٍ

Skirmish *n.* قِتَالٌ خَفِيفٌ

Skirt *n.* هُدْبٌ . تُخْمٌ

Skittish *a.* جَفُول

Skulk *v. i.* ٱخْتَبَأَ دَهَاءً

Skull *n.* جُمْجُمَةٌ

Sky *n.* جَوٌّ . جَلَدٌ . سَمَاءٌ

Sky-lark *n.* قُنْبُرَةٌ ج قَنَابِرُ

Sky-light *n.* كُوَّةٌ فِي ٱلسَّقْفِ

Slab *n.* لَوْحُ حَجَرٍ أَوْ خَشَبٍ

Slack *a.* مُسْتَرْخٍ . مُتَغَافِل

Slack / **Slacken** *v. t.* or *i.* أَرْخَى . خَفَّ ـِ

Slackness *n.* رَخَاءٌ . تَوَانٍ

Slain *pp.* of slay مَذْبُوحٌ

Slake *v. t.* رَوِيَ ـَ . صَوَّلَ

Slam *v. t.* أَغْلَقَ بِعُنْفٍ

Slander *v. t.* or *n.* نَمَّ ـِ . نَمِيمَةٌ

Slanderer *n.* / **Slanderous** *a.* نَمَّامٌ . مُفْتَرٍ

Slang *a.* كَلَامٌ عَامِّيٌّ

Slant *v. i.* or *t.* مَالَ ـُ . أَمَالَ

Slanting *a.* مَائِلٌ . غَيْرُ عَمُودِيٍّ

Slap *v. t.* or *n.* لَطَمَ ـِ . لَطْمَةٌ

Slash *v. t.* or *n.* شَقَّ ـُ . جَرَحَ ـَ

Slate *n.* or *v. t.* لَوْحُ حَجَرٍ . غَطَّى بِهِ

Slate-pencil *n.* قَلَمُ حَجَرٍ

Slaughter *n.* or *v. t.* ذَبْحٌ . ذَبَحَ ـَ

Slave *n.* عَبْدٌ . رَقِيقٌ . مَمْلُوك

Slaver *n.* سَفِينَةٌ لِجَلْبِ ٱلْعَبِيدِ

Slavery *n.* عُبُودِيَّةٌ . رِقّ

Slavish *a.* عَبْدِيٌّ . ذَلِيلٌ

Slay *v. t.* (*pp.* Slain) قَتَلَ ـ . ذَبَحَ

Sled / Sledge } *n.* مَرْكَبَةٌ لِلثَّلْجِ

Sledge *n.* مِهَدَّةٌ

Sleek *a.* أَمْلَسُ . لَيِّنٌ

Sleep *n.* or *v. i.* نَوْمٌ . رُقَادٌ . نَامَ ـَ

Sleepiness *n.* نُعَاسٌ

Sleepless *a.* بِلاَ نَوْمٍ

Sleepy *a.* نَعْسَانُ

Sleet *n.* ثَلْجٌ وَمَطَرٌ مَعاً

Sleeve *n.* كُمٌّ ج أَكْمَامٌ

Sleigh *n.* مَرْكَبَةٌ لِلثَّلْجِ

Sleight *n.* خِفَّةُ يَدٍ . حِيلَةٌ

Slender *a.* أَهْيَفُ . دَقِيقٌ . ضَعِيفٌ

Slenderness *n.* رِقَّةٌ . ضُعْفٌ

Slice *n.* or *v. t.* شَرِيحَةُ لَحْمٍ . شَرَّحَ

Slide *v. i.* or *t.* زَلَجَ ـِ . زَلَقَ ـَ . أَزْلَقَ

Slight *a.* or *n.* زَهِيدٌ . آسْتِخْفَافٌ

Slight *v. t.* أَهَانَ . آسْتَخَفَّ بِهِ

Slily *ad.* بِحِيلَةٍ . إِخْتِلاَساً . خَفِيَّةً

Slim *a.* رَقِيقٌ . أَهْيَفُ

Slime *n.* رَدْغَةٌ . وَحْلٌ خَفِيفٌ

Sling *n.* or *v. t.* مِقْلاَعٌ . قَذَفَ بِهِ ـِ

Slink *v. i.* آنْسَلَّ

Slip *v. i.* or *n.* زَلَقَ . زَلْقَةٌ ـَ . زَلَّةٌ

Slipper *n.* أَشْفٌ . بَابُوجٌ

Slippery *a.* زَلِقٌ . زَلْجٌ . مُتَقَلِّبٌ

Slit *n.* or *v. t.* شَرْمٌ . شَرَمَ ـِ

Sliver *n.* or *v. t.* شَظِيَّةٌ . شَقَّةٌ . شَظَّيَا

Sloop *n.* سَفِينَةٌ لَهَا سَارِيَةٌ وَاحِدَةٌ

Slope *n.* اِحْدُورٌ . حُدُورٌ

Sloppy *a.* قَذِرٌ . وَحْلٌ

Sloth *n.* كَسَلٌ . كَسْلاَنٌ (حيوان)

Slothful *a.* كَسْلاَنُ . بَطِيٌّ

Slough *n.* مَحَلٌّ كَثِيرُ ٱلْوَحْلِ

Sloven *a.* غَيْرُ مُهَنْدَمٍ

Slovenly *ad.* بِلاَ إِتْقَان

Slow *a.* بَطِيءٌ

Slowness *n.* بُطْءٌ . تَأَخُّرٌ

Slug *n.* كَسْلاَنٌ . بَزَّاقَة . عُرْيَانَةٌ

Sluggard *n.* / **Sluggish** *a.* كَسْلاَنٌ . بَلِيد

Sluice *n.* مَنْفَذ مَاءٍ في سَدٍّ

Slumber *v. i.* or *n.* نَعَسَ ـَ . نَامَ ـَ . نَوْمٌ

Slur *v. t.* or *n.* آسْتَخَفَّ . لَوَّثَ

Sut *n.* بَذَّةٌ

Sly *a.* مُحْتَالٌ . إِدَاهٍ

Slyly *ad.* حِيلَةً . خُفْيَةً

Slyness *n.* دَهَاءٌ . دَسٌّ . آسْتِخْفَاءٌ

Smack *n.* سَفِينَةٌ صَغِيرَةٌ . قُبْلَةٌ قَوِيَّةٌ

Small *a.* صَغِيرٌ . دَقِيقٌ

Small-pox *n.* جُدَرِيٌّ

Smart *a.* نَشِيطٌ . نَبِيهٌ . حَاذِقٌ

Smart *v. i.* or *n.* تَأَلَّمَ شَدِيدًا . أَلَمٌ

Smartness *n.* حَذَاقَةٌ . حِدَّةٌ

Smash *v. t.* or *n.* كَسَّرَ . حَطَّمَ

Smattering *n.* رُكَاكَةُ عِلْمٍ

Smear *v. t.* لَطَخَ ـَ . وَسَّخَ

Smell *n.* رَائِحَةٌ . شَمٌّ . حَاسَّةُ

Smell *v. t.* or *i.* شَمَّ ـُ . فَاحَ ـَ

Smelt *v. t.* أَذَابَ . أَمَاعَ

Smile *v. i.* or *n.* تَبَسَّمَ . تَبَسُّمٌ

Smirch *v. t.* وَسَّخَ . سَوَّدَ

Smite *v. t.* ضَرَبَ ـُ . قَتَلَ ـِ . لَفَحَ ـَ

Smith *n.* حَدَّادٌ . نَحَّاسٌ . صَائِغ

Smoke *n.* or *v. t.* دُخَانٌ . دَخَنَ

Smoker *n.* شَارِبُ تُتُنٍ أَوْ دُخَانٍ

Smoky *a.* مُدَخِّنٌ . مُتَدَخِّنٌ

Smooth *a.* or *v. t.* مَلِسٌ . مُسْتَوٍ . مَلَّسَ

Smoothness *n.* مَلاَسَةٌ . آسْتِوَاءٌ

Smother *v. t.* خَنَقَ ـُ . أَطْفَأَ

Smoulder *v. i.* آحْتَرَقَ بِدُونِ لَهِيبٍ

Smuggle *v. t.* هَرَّبَ . أَدْخَلَ خُلْسَةً

Smutty *a.* كَتِنٌ . وَسِخٌ

Snag *n.* خَشَبَةٌ تُصَادِمُهَا سَفِينَةٌ . مَانِعٌ

Snail *n.* بَزَّاقَةٌ . حَلَزُونَة

Snake *n.* حَيَّةٌ . أَفْعَى

Snap *v. t.* or *i.* قَصَفَ ـِ . اَنْقَسَمَ بِصَوْتٍ

Snappish *a.* نَكِدٌ . حَادُّ ٱلْكَلَامِ

Snare *n.* شَرَكٌ . مَكِيدَة

Snarl *v. i.* هَرَّ ـِ . هَمْهَمَ

Snatch *v. t.* خَطِفَ ـَ

Sneak *v. i.* اَنْسَلَّ . اَنْدَسَّ

Sneak *n.* **Sneaking** *n.* } ذَلِيلٌ . دَسِيسٌ

Sneer *v. i.* or *n.* هَزَأَ . اَسْتَخَفَّ . هُزْءٌ

Sneeze *v. i.* عَطَسَ ـُ

Sniff *v. t.* اشْتَمَّ . اَسْتَنْشَقَ

Snip *v. t.* قَطَعَ ـَ . قَرَضَ ـِ

Snipe *n.* نَوْعٌ مِنَ ٱلْقَطَا

Snob *n.* **Snobbish** *a.* مُتَظَرِّفٌ . مُتَظَاهِرٌ بِالشَّرَفِ

Snooze *v. i.* نَامَ نَوْمًا خَفِيفًا

Snore *v. i.* شَخَرَ ـُ خَرْخَرَ

Snort *v. i.* نَخَرَ ـِ

Snout *n.* خُرْطُومٌ . ج خَرَاطِيم

Snow *n.* or *v. i.* ثَلْجٌ . ثَلَجَ ـُ

Snow-drift *n.* كَوْمَةُ ثَلْجٍ

Snowy *a.* مُثْلِجٌ . أَبْيَضُ

Snub *v. t.* عَامَلَ بِفَظَاظَةٍ . خَجَّلَ

Snuff *n.* or *v. i.* سَعُوطٌ . نَزَعَ ٱلذُّبَالَةَ

Snuff-box *n.* عِلْبَةُ ٱلسَّعُوطِ

Snuffers *n. pl.* مِقْرَاضُ ٱلْفَتِيلَةِ

Snuffle *v. i.* نَخَرَ ـِ

Snug *a.* مُتَلَبِّدٌ . يُنَاسِبُ مَحَلَّهُ

Snuggle *v. i.* اَسْتَكَنَّ

So *ad.* كَذَا . هٰكَذَا . كَذٰلِكَ

Soak *v. t.* or *i.* نَقَعَ ـَ . تَشَرَّبَ

Soap *n.* or *v. t.* صَابُونٌ . عَامَلَ بِهِ

Soapsuds *n.* رَغْوَةُ ٱلصَّابُونِ

Soar *v. i.* اَسْتَعْلَى (طَيْرٌ)

Sob *v. i.* or *n.*	بَكَى مَعَ تَنَهُّدٍ
Sober / **Soberminded** } *a.*	رَزِينٌ. صاحٍ
Soberness / **Sobriety** } *n.*	رَزَانَةٌ. تَعَفُّفٌ
Sociability *n.*	انسٌ. عِشْرَةٌ
Sociable *a.*	انِيسٌ. أَلِيفٌ
Social *a.*	أَلِيفٌ. جُمْهُورِي
Socialism *n.*	مَذْهَبُ ٱلإِشْتِرَاكِيِّين
Society *n.*	ٱلْهَيْئَةُ ٱلاجْتِمَاعِيَّة
Sock *n.*	جَوْرَبٌ
Socket *n.*	نُقْرَةٌ. تَجْوِيفٌ
Sod *n.*	مدَرٌ فيهِ جذورُ كَلاَءٍ
Soda *n.*	ٱلْقِلَى. نطْرُونٌ
Sodden *a.*	مَسْلُوقٌ. مَنْقُوعٌ
Sofa *n.*	مَقْعَدٌ. دِيوَانٌ
Soft *a.*	نَاعِمٌ. لَيِّنٌ. طِفْلٌ
Soften *v. t.* or *i.*	لَيَّنَ. لاَنَ ـِ
Softness *n.*	لِينٌ. نعومَة
Soil *v. t.* or *n.*	لَطخ ـَ وَسَّخَ. تُرْبَةٌ
Sojourn *v.i.* or *n.*	تَغَرَّبَ. غُرْبَةٌ
Sojourner *n.*	مُتَغَرِّبٌ
Solace *v. t.* or *n.*	سَلَّى عَزَّى. سلْوَى
Solar *a.*	شَمْسِيٌّ
Solder *n.* or *v. t.*	لِحَامٌ. لَحَمَ ـُ
Soldier *n.*	عَسْكَرِيٌّ. جنْدِيٌّ
Soldiery *n.*	عَسَاكِرُ
Sole *n.*	نعلٌ. أَسْفَلُ ٱلْقَدَمِ
Sole *v. t.* or *a.*	خَصَفَ ٱلنَّعْلَ. وحيدٌ
Solely *ad.*	فقط
Solemn *n.*	مُوَقَّرٌ. خَطِيرٌ
Solemnity *n.*	ٱحتِفَالٌ. وَقَارٌ
Solemnize *v. t.*	احتَفَلَ. مَارَسَ سِرًّا
Solicit *v. t.*	تَوَسَّلَ. طَلَبَ ـُ
Solicitation *n.*	تَوَسُّلٌ. ٱلْتِمَاسٌ
Solicitor *n.*	وَكِيلُ دَعَاوٍ
Solicitous *a.*	مُهْتَمٌّ. رَاغِبٌ في
Solicitude *n.*	هَمٌّ. رَغْبَةٌ

Solid *a.*	جَامِدٌ . مَتِينٌ . مُجَسَّمٌ
Solidify *v. t.* or *i.*	جَمَدَ . تَجَمَّدَ
Solidity *n.*	جُمُودٌ . مَتَانَةٌ
Soliloquize *v. t.*	كَلَّمَ نَفْسَهُ
Soliloquy *n.*	مُخَاطَبَةُ ٱلذَّاتِ
Solitariness *n.*	تَوَحُّدٌ . ٱنْفِرَادٌ
Solitary *a.*	مُنْفَرِدٌ . مُعْتَزِلٌ
Solitude *n.*	وَحْدَةٌ . عُزْلَةٌ
Solo *n.*	غِنَاءُ شَخْصٍ وَحْدَهُ
Solstice *n.*	نُقْطَةُ ٱنْقِلَابِ ٱلشَّمْسِ
Soluble *a.*	قَابِلُ ٱلذَوَبَانِ أَوِ ٱلْحَلِّ
Solution *n.*	حَلٌّ . مَحْلُولٌ
Solvable *a.*	قَابِلُ ٱلْحَلِّ أَوِ ٱلْوَفَاءِ
Solve *v. t.*	حَلَّ ـُ أَوْضَحَ
Solvency *n.*	قُدْرَةٌ عَلَى ٱلْوَفَاءِ
Solvent *a.*	قَادِرٌ عَلَى ٱلْوَفَاءِ
Solvent *n.*	سَائِلٌ مُحَلِّلٌ أَوْ مُذَوِّبٌ
Sombre *a.*	مُظْلِمٌ . مُغِيمٌ
Some *a.*	بَعْضٌ
Somebody *n.*	وَاحِدٌ . أَحَدٌ مَّا
Somehow *ad.*	كَيْفَمَا كَانَ
Somersault, Somerest *n.*	وَثْبَةُ ٱنْقِلَابٍ
Something *n.*	شَيْءٌ مَا
Sometime *ad.*	وَقْتًا مَّا
Sometimes *ad.*	أَحْيَانًا
Somewhat *ad.* or *n.*	نَوْعًا . شَيْءٌ مَا
Somewhere *ad.*	فِي مَكَانٍ مَّا
Somnambulism *n.*	مَشْيٌ فِي ٱلنَّوْمِ
Somnambulist *n.*	مَاشٍ فِي ٱلنَّوْمِ
Somnolence *n.*	نُعَاسٌ
Son *n.*	ٱبْنٌ ج أَبْنَاءٌ وَبَنُونَ
Son-in-law *n.*	زَوْجُ ٱبْنَتِهِ . صِهْرٌ
Song *n.*	أُغْنِيَّةٌ . نَشِيدٌ
Songster *n.*	مُغَنٍّ . مُغَرِّدٌ
Sonnet *n.*	قَصِيدَةٌ قَصِيرَةٌ
Sonorous *a.*	صَائِتٌ . رَنَّانٌ

Sonship *n.*	بُنُوَّةٌ
Soon *ad.*	عَنْ قَرِيبٍ . سَرِيعًا
Soot *n.*	كَتَنٌ . سُخَامٌ
Soothe *v. t.*	خَفَّفَ . لَاطَفَ . سكَّنَ
Soothsayer *n.*	عَرَّافٌ . مُنَجِّمٌ
Sooty *a.*	كَتَنِيٌّ . سُخَامِيٌّ
Sophism / **Sophistry** } *n.*	سَفْسَطَةٌ
Sophist *n.* / **Sophistical** *a.* }	سَفْسَطِيٌّ
Soporific *n.* or *a.*	مُنَوِّمٌ
Sorcerer / **Sorceress** } *n.*	سَاحِرٌ . سَاحِرَةٌ
Sorcery *n.*	سِحْرٌ
Sordid *a.*	خَسِيسٌ . طَمَّاعٌ
Sore *a.* or *n.*	مُؤْلِمٌ . شَدِيدٌ . قَرْحَةٌ
Sorely *ad.*	جِدًّا
Sorrel *a.* or *n.*	أَشْقَرُ . حُمَاضٌ
Sorrow *n.* or *v. i.*	حُزْنٌ . حَزِنَ
Sorrowful *a.*	حَزِينٌ . كَئِيبٌ
Sorry *a.*	مُكَدَّرٌ . آسِفٌ . مُتَحَسِّرٌ
Sort *n.*	نَوْعٌ . صِنْفٌ . شَكْلٌ
Sort *v. t.*	رَتَّبَهُ عَلَى أَشْكَالِهِ
Sot *n.* / **Sottish** *a.* }	سِكِّيرٌ . أَبْلَهُ
Sought *pp.* (Seek)	مَطْلُوبٌ
Soul *n.*	نَفْسٌ . رُوحٌ . حَيَاةٌ
Soulless *a.*	بِلَا نَفْسٍ . خَسِيسٌ
Sound *a.* or *n.*	صَحِيحٌ . صَوْتٌ . مَضِيقٌ
Sound *v.t.* or *i.*	سَبَرَ . صَاتَ
Soundings *n. pl.*	قِيَاسُ عُمْقِ ٱلْبَحْرِ
Soundly *ad.*	جَيِّدًا بِصَوَابٍ
Soundness *n.*	صِحَّةٌ . مَتَانَةٌ
Soup *n.*	شَوْرَبَةٌ
Sour *a.*	حَامِضٌ . شَكِسٌ
Source *n.*	أَصْلٌ . مَصْدَرٌ . يَنْبُوعٌ
Sourness *n.*	حُمُوضَةٌ . شَكَاسَةٌ
Souse *v. t.*	غَطَّسَ . غَمَسَ
South *n.* or *a.*	جَنُوبٌ . جَنُوبِيٌّ
South-east *n.*	ٱلْجَنُوبُ ٱلشَّرْقِيُّ

Southerly / Southern } *a.* جُنُوبِيٌّ

Southward *ad.* جَنُوبًا . إِلَى ٱلْجَنُوب

South-west *n.* ٱلْجَنُوبُ ٱلْغَرْبِيُّ

Souvenir *n.* تَذْكَارٌ . تَذْكِرَةٌ

Souvereign *n.* or *a.* مَلِكٌ . سُلْطَانِيٌّ

Souvereignty *n.* مُلْكٌ . سَلْطَنَة

Sow *n.* or *v. t.* خِنْزِيرَةٌ . زَرَعَ ـ أَذَاعَ

Space *n.* خَلَاءٌ . مَسَافَةٌ . مُدَّةٌ

Spacious *a.* فَسِيحٌ . رَحِيبٌ

Spade *n.* مِجْرَفَةٌ . مَرٌّ . لَوْحٌ

Span *n.* or *v. t.* شِبْرٌ . قَاسَ بِهِ

Spaniard *n.* / Spanish *a.* } إِسْبَنْيُولِيٌّ

Spaniel *n.* نَوْعٌ مِنَ ٱلْكَلْبِ

Spank *v. t.* لَطَمَ عَلَى ٱلْعَجْزِ

Spar *n.* سَارِيَةٌ . حَجَرٌ مُتَبَلْوِرٌ

Spare *a.* يَسِيرٌ . نَحِيفٌ . فَارِغٌ

Spare *v. t.* عَفَا عَنْ . ٱسْتَحْيَا . ٱقْتَصَدَ

Spark *n.* شَرَارَة . جُزْءٌ يَسِيرٌ

Sparkle *v. i.* أَخْرَجَ شَرَرًا . تَلَأْلَأَ

Sparrow *n.* عُصْفُورٌ دُورِيٌّ

Sparse *a.* مُتَشَتِّتٌ مُتَفَرِّق

Spasm *n.* تَشَنُّجٌ

Spasmodic *a.* تَشَنُّجِيٌّ . مُتَقَطِّعٌ

Spatter *v. t.* لَطَخَ ـَ

Spawn *n.* or *v. i.* بَيْضُ ٱلسَّمَكِ . بَاضَ ـِ

Speak *v. i.* تَكَلَّمَ . نَطَقَ ـِ

Speaker *v.* مُتَكَلِّمٌ . رَئِيسُ مَجْلِسٍ

Spear *n.* رُمْحٌ . حَرْبَةٌ

Special *v.* خَاصٌّ . خُصُوصِيٌّ

Speciality *n.* خُصُوصِيَّةٌ

Specie *n.* نُقُودٌ . مَسْكُوكَات

Species *n.* نَوْعٌ ج أَنْوَاعٌ

Specific *a.* نَوْعِيٌّ . خُصُوصِيٌّ . جَازِمٌ

Specification *n.* تَخْصِيصٌ . تَعْرِيفٌ

Specify *v. t.* خَصَّصَ . صَرَّحَ . عَرَّفَ

Specimen *n.* مِثَال . مَسْطَرَة . عَيِّنَةٌ

Specious *a.* حَسَنٌ أَوْحَقٌّ بالظاهِرِ

Speck *n.* نُقطَةٌ . لَطْخَة

Speckled *n.* مُنَقَّطٌ . أرقط

Spectacle *n.* مَنْظَرٌ. مَشْهد

Spectacles *n. pl.* مِنْظَرٌ (عُوَيْنات)

Spectator *n.* شاهِدٌ . مُتَفَرِّجٌ

Spectre *n.* خَيالٌ . طَيْفٌ

Speculate *v. i.* تَأَمَّلَ . تَفَلْسَفَ

ابْتَاعَ بِانْتِظَارِ زِيادَةِ الثمَنِ. ضَارَبَ

Speculative *a.* نَظَرِيٌّ . فَلْسَفِيٌّ

Speculum *n.* مرآةٌ . مِنظارٌ

Speech *n.* كَلامٌ . خِطَابٌ . لغَةٌ

Speechless *a.* صامِتٌ . أَخرَسُ

Speed *n.* سُرعَةٌ . فَلاحٌ . توفيقٌ

Speedy *a.* سَرِيعٌ

Spell *n.* دَوْرٌ . بُرْهةٌ

Spell *v. t.* هَجّى . تَهجى

Speller *n.* مُتَهَجٍّ . كِتابُ تَهْجِيَةٍ

Spend *v. t.* صرَفَ . أَنْفَقَ . أَفْرَغَ

Spendthrift *n.* مُسْرِفٌ . مُبَذِّرٌ

Spew *v. t.* or *i.* اسْتَفْرَغَ . قاءَ

Sphere *n.* كُرَةٌ . دائِرَةٌ . مَقامٌ

Spheric / **Spherical** *a.* كُرَوِيٌّ

Spheroid *n.* شِبْهُ كُرَةٍ

Sphinx *n.* أبو الهَوْلِ

Spice *n.* طِيبٌ . تابِلٌ

Spicy *a.* تابِلِيٌّ . حَرِّيفٌ . مُطَيَّبٌ

Spider *n.* عنكبوتٌ . رُتَيْلاء

Spike *n.* or *v. t.* سُنبلَةٌ . مِسمارٌ كَبيرٌ . سمَّرَ بِهِ

Spikenard *n.* نارِدِينٌ

Spill *v. t.* or *i.* أَراقَ . كبَّ ـُ . انْكَبَّ

Spin *v. t.* or *i.* غَزَلَ ـِ . بَرَمَ ـُ

Spinach / **Spinage** *n.* إِسْبانَخٌ

Spinal *a.* فَقَرِيٌّ

Spindle *n.* or *v. i.* مِغْزَلٌ . طالَ . استَدَقَّ

Spine *n.* العَمُودُ الفَقَرِيُّ . شَوْكَةٌ

Spinster *n.*	امرأة . غير متزوجة
Spiral *a.*	لولبي
Spire *n.*	برج بهيئة مسلّة
Spirit *n.*	روح . نشاط . طبع
Spirited *a.*	نشيط
Spiritless *a.*	خائر . متراخ
Spiritual *a.*	روحي . ديني
Spirituality *a.*	روحانية
Spirituous *a.*	روحي . مسكر
Spit *n.* or *v. t.*	سفود . بصاق بصق
Spite *n.* or *v. t.*	ضغينة . غل . ضغن حقد
Spiteful *a*	ضغن . مغل . حقود
Spittle *n.*	بصاق . لعاب . تفل
Spittoon *n.*	مبصقة
Splash *v. t.*	لطم السائل فرشه
Spleen *n.*	طحال . حقد
Splendid *a.*	فاخر . باهر . بهي
Splendour *n.*	بهاء . رونق . جلال
Splice *v. t.* or *n.*	أوصل الطرفين
Splint / Splinter *n.*	شظية . جبرة
Split *v. t.*	شق . فلق
Spoil *v. t.* or *i.*	نهب . أفسد . فسد
Spoil *n.*	نهب . غنيمة
Spokesman *n.*	نائب في التكلم
Spoliation *n.*	نهب . تشليح
Sponge *n.* or *v. t.*	إسفنجة . سفنج . مسح بها
Spongy *a.*	إسفنجي
Sponsor *n.*	كفيل . إشبين
Spontaniety *n.*	فعل من تلقاء النفس
Spontaneous *a.*	من النفس رأسا
Spool *n.*	ميلكة (بكرة)
Spoon *n.*	ملعقة ج ملاعق
Spoonful *n.*	ملء ملعقة
Sporadic *a.*	متوحد . متفرق
Spore *n.*	بزيرة دقيقة جدا
Sport *n.*	لعب . طرب . صيد

Sportsman *n.* صَيَّادٌ

Spot *n.* مَوْضِعٌ . بقعةٌ . لَطْخَةٌ

Spotless *a.* طاهِرٌ . بِلاَعَيْب

Spotted *a.* مُلَطَّخٌ . أَرْقَط

Spouse *n.* زَوْجٌ . زَوْجَةٌ

Spout *n.* or *v. i.* صُنْبُورٌ . تَفَجَّرَ

Sprain *n.* or *v. t.* وَثْيٌ . وَثِيَ

Sprawl *v. i.* اسْتَلْقَى

Spray *n.* رِشَاشُ الْمَاءِ

Spread *v. t.* or *i.* نَشَرَ . انْتَشَرَ

Spree *n.* سَكْرَةٌ

Sprig *n.* شعبةٌ . عُسْلُجٌ

Sprightful / Sprightly } *a.* نَشِيطُ الجَسَدِ وَالْعَقْلِ

Spring *v. i.* وَثَبَ . صَدَرَ . انْفَجَر

Spring *n.* وَثْبَةٌ . نَبْعٌ . رَبِيعٌ . زُنْبُرُكٌ

Sprinkle *v.t.* or *i.* رَشَّ . نَضَحَ

Sprite *n.* خَيَالٌ . طَيْفٌ

Sprout *v. i.* or *n.* نَبَتَ . فَرَّخَ . فرخ

Spry *a.* خَفِيفُ الْحَرَكَةِ . نَشِيطٌ

Spue *v. i.* اسْتَفْرَغَ . تَقَيَّأَ

Spur *n.* مِهْمَازٌ . ظَهْرٌ بَارِزٌ

Spur *v. t.* حَثَّ . أَنْهَضَ . نَخَسَ

Spurious *a.* كَاذِبٌ . مزوَّرٌ

Spurn *v. t.* رَفَضَ . أَنِفَ مِنْ

Spurt *v. t.* or *i.* فجرَ . انْفَجَرَ

Spy *n.* or *v. t.* جاسُوسٌ . نَظَرَ

Spyglass *n.* نظَّارَةٌ صَغِيرَةٌ

Squabble *v. i.* شَاجَرَ . نَازَعَ

Squad *n.* شِرْذِمَةٌ

Squadron *n.* كُرْدُوسَة . جَمَاعَةُ سُفُنٍ

Squalid *a.* قَذِرٌ . وَسِخٌ

Squall *n.* or *v. t.* هَبَّةٌ قَوِيَّةٌ . صَرَخَ

Squalor *n.* قَذَرٌ . وَسَخٌ

Squander *v. t.* بَذَّرَ . أَسْرَفَ

Square *a.* or *n.* مُرَبَّعٌ . عَادِلٌ . سَاحةٌ

Square *v. t.* رَبَّعَ . كَعَّبَ . سَدد

Squash *n.*	كُوسَى . لَقْطِين
Squat *v. t.*	قَعَدَ القرفصى
Squeak *n.* or *v. i.*	صَرِير . صَرَّ ـ
Squeal *v. i.*	صَاحَ كَالْخِنْزِير
Squeeze *v. t.*	ضَغَطَ ـ . عَصَرَ ـ
Squint *v. i.* or *n.*	حَوِلَ ـ . حَوَل
Squint-eyed *a.*	أَحْوَل
Squirrel *n.*	سِنْجَاب
Stab *v. t.* or *n.*	طَعَنَ ـ . طَعْنَة
Stability *n.*	ثَبَات . رُسُوخ
Stable *n.* or *a.*	إِصْطَبْل . أَخُور . ثَابِت
Stack *n.* or *v. t.*	كَوْمَة . كَوَّم
Staff *n.*	عُكَّاز . رُكْن ج أَرْكَان
Stag *n.*	ذَكَرُ الْإِيِل
Stage *n.*	دَكَّة . دَرَجَة . مَرْحَلَة
Stagger *v. i.* or *t.*	تَرَنَّحَ . تَمَايَلَ . أَرَابَ
Stagnant *a.*	سَاكِن . فَاسِد . كَاسِد
Stagnate *v.i.*	سَكَنَ ـ . فَسَدَ ـ . كَسَدَ
Staid *a.*	رَزِين . رَصِين
Stain *v. t.* or *n.*	صَبَغَ ـ . لَطَخَ ـ . لَطْخَة
Stainless *a.*	بِلَا عَيْب . نَقِيّ
Stairs / Stair-case } *n.*	مِعْرَج . سُلَّم
Stake *n.*	وَتَد . رَهْن . إِسْتِشْهَاد
Stake *v. t.*	خَاطَرَ بِـ . رَاهَنَ
Stale *a.*	تَافِه . عَتِيق
Stalk *n.*	سَاق نَبَات . رُجَيْلَة
Stall *n.*	مَعْلَف . دُكَّان
Stallion *n.*	فَحْل ج فُحُول
Stalwart *a.*	قَوِيّ . شُجَاع
Stamen *n.*	سَدَاة ج أَسْدِيَة
Stammer *v. i.*	تَمْتَمَ . لَجْلَجَ
Stamp *v. t.*	خَبَطَ بِـ . طَبَعَ ـ . رَسَمَ ـ
Stamp *n.*	طَبْع . رَسْم . دَمْغَة
Stampede *n.*	هَزِيمَة
Stanch *a.* or *v. t.*	ثَابِت . وَقَّفَ نَزَفًا
Stand *v. i*	وَقَفَ ـ . ثَبَتَ ـ . بَقِيَ

Stand *n.* مَوْقِفٌ . قاعِدَةٌ . ثُبُوتٌ

Standard *n.* عَلَمٌ . مِقْيَاسٌ . قَاعِدَةٌ

Standing *a.* قائِمٌ . ثَابِتٌ . دَائِمٌ

Stanza *n.* دَوْرُ شِعْرٍ

Stable *n.* or *a.* زرِيبَةٌ . حَاصِلٌ . رَئِيسِيٌّ

Star *n.* نَجْمَةٌ . كَوْكَبٌ

Starboard *n.* يَمِينُ السَّفِينَةِ

Starch *n.* or *v. t.* نَشَا . نَشَّى

Stare *v. i.* تَفَرَّسَ . حَمْلَقَ

Stark *a.* مَحْضٌ . كُلِّيٌّ . جَامِدٌ

Starlight *n.* نُورُ النُّجُومِ

Starry *a.* ذُو نُجُومٍ أو كَثِيرُهَا

Start *v. i.* or *t.* بَدَا . أَجْفَلَ . حرَّكَ

Startle *v. t.* جَفَلَ . أَرْعَشَ

Starvation *n.* أَلْمَوْتُ جُوعاً

Starve *v. i.* or *t.* مَاتَ أوْ أَمَاتَ جُوعاً

State *n.* حَالٌ . وِلَايَةٌ . حُكُومَةٌ

State *v. t.* قَالَ . قَصَّ . قَرَّرَ

Stateliness *n.* أُبَّهَةٌ . جَلَالَةٌ

Stately *a.* جَلِيلٌ . عَظِيمٌ . مُوَقَّرٌ

Statement *n.* قَوْلٌ . تَقْرِيرٌ

Statesman *n.* عَالِمٌ بِالسِّيَاسَةِ

Statesmanship *n.* عِلْمُ السِّيَاسَةِ

Station *n.* مَنْصِبٌ . رُتْبَةٌ . مَحَطَّةٌ

Station *v. t.* وَضَعَ . نَصَبَ

Stationary *a.* وَاقِفٌ . ثَابِتٌ

Stationery *n.* أَدَوَاتُ الْكِتَابَةِ

Statistics *n.* عِلْمُ الإِحْصَاءِ أوِ التَّعْدَادِ

Statuary *n.* مُجْتَمَعُ تَمَاثِيلَ

Statue *n.* تِمْثَالٌ

Stature *n.* قَدٌّ . قَامَةٌ

Statute *n.* سُنَّةٌ . نِظَامٌ

Stave *v. t.* كَسَرَ . أَخَّرَ

Stave *n.* لَوْحٌ . ضَيِّقٌ لِبَرْمِيلٍ

Stay *v. i.* or *t.* اسْتَمَرَّ . وَقَفَ . دَعَمَ

Stead *n.* عوضٌ . بَدَل

Steadfast *a.* ثَابِتٌ . رَاسِخٌ

Steadfastness / Steadiness *n.* حزمٌ . ثبَاتٌ

Steady *a.* ثَابِتٌ . غيرُ متقلِّب

Steak *n.* شرِيحةُ لحمٍ

Steel *v. t.* or *i.* سَرقَ . انسلَّ

Stealth *n.* انسلالٌ . اختلاسٌ

Stealthy *a.* منسلٌّ . مُختلِسٌ

Steam *n.* or *v. i.* بخارٌ . بخرَ

Steam-boat / Steamer *n.* بَاخِرةٌ . وابورٌ

Steam-engine *n.* آلةٌ بخاريّةٌ

Steed *n.* جوادٌ ج جيادٌ

Steel *n.* or *v. t.* فُولاذٌ . قسّى

Steelyard *n.* قبّانٌ

Steep *a.* or *v. t* منحدرٌ جدّاً . نقعَ

Steeple *n.* منارةُ كنيسةٍ

Steepness *n.* شِدّةُ تحدُّرٍ

Steer *v. t.* أدارَ سفينةً

Stellar *a.* نجمي

Stem *v. t.* وقفَ . دفعَ

Stem *n.* سَاقٌ . مقدَّمُ سفينةٍ

Stench *n.* رائحةٌ قبيحةٌ

Step *n.* or *v. i.* خُطوةٌ . خطا

Step-child *n.* ولدُ الزوجِ أو الزوجةِ

Step-father *n.* زوجُ الأمِّ . رابٌّ

Step-mother *n.* زوجةُ الأبِ . رابّةٌ

Stepping-stone *n.* وسيلةٌ . مرقاةٌ

Sterile *a.* عقيمٌ . أجذبُ

Sterility *n.* جذبٌ . عقمٌ

Sterling *n.* or *a.* دراهمُ إنكليزيّةٌ . حقيقيٌّ

Stern *n.* or *a.* مؤخَّرٌ . عبوسٌ

Sternness *n.* عبوسٌ

Stethoscope *a.* مستقصيةٌ . صدريّةٌ

Stew *v. t.* or *n.* سلقَ رُويداً . يخنةٌ

Steward *n.* وكيلٌ . قهرمانٌ

Stewardship *n.* وكالةٌ قهرمةٌ

Stick *n.* or *v.t.* قَضِيبٌ . اِلْزَق . طَعَن

Stickiness *n.* لُزُوجَةٌ

Stickle *v. i.* نَازَعَ مُكَابَرَةً

Sticky *a.* لَزِجٌ . دَبِق

Stiff *a.* جَامِدٌ . صُلْبٌ . مُتَيَبِّسٌ

Stiffen *v. t.* or *i.* جَمَّدَ . جَمَدَ ـُ

Stiffness *n.* جُمُودٌ . اِشْتِدَادٌ . صَلَابَةٌ

Stiff-necked *a.* صُلْبُ الرَّقَبَةِ

Stifle *v.* أَطْفَأَ . سَكَّنَ . خنق ـُ

Stigma *n.* عَيْبٌ . سِمَةٌ

Stigmatize *v.* عَيَّبَ . وَسَمَ ـِ

Still *v.t.* or *a.* سَكَّنَ . سَاكِنٌ . سَاكِت

Still *ad.* إِلَى الآنَ . مَعَ ذَلِكَ

Still-born *a.* (وَلَدٌ) سِقْطٌ

Stillness *n.* سُكُونٌ . هُدُوٌّ

Stimulant *a.* or *n.* / Stimulative *a.* } مُنَبِّهٌ . مُنَشِّطٌ

Stimulate *v. t.* نَبَّهَ . حَرَّضَ

Stimulation *n.* تَحْرِيضٌ . تَهْيِيجٌ

Stimulus *n.* مُنَبِّهٌ . مُحَرِّكٌ

Sting *n.* or *v. t.* لَسْعَةٌ . لَسَعَ ـَ

Stinginess *n.* بُخْلٌ . شُحٌّ

Stingy *a.* بَخِيلٌ . شَحِيحٌ

Stink *n.* or *v. i.* نَتَانَةٌ . نَتَنَ ـِ

Stint *v. t.* or *a.* حَدَّدَ . حَدٌّ . عَمَلٌ مَحْدُودٌ

Stipend *v.* رَاتِبٌ . مَعَاشٌ

Stipulate *v. i.* اِشْتَرَطَ

Stipulation *n.* شَرْطٌ . اِتِّفَاقٌ

Stir *v. i.* or *t.* تَحَرَّكَ . حَرَّكَ . هَزَّ ـِ

Stirrup *n.* رِكَابٌ ج رُكُبٌ

Stitch *v. t.* خَاطَ ـِ . دَرَزَ ـُ

Stock *n.* أَصْلٌ . مَالٌ . سِلَعٌ

Stock *v. t.* جَهَّزَ . ذَخَرَ

Stockade *n.* سِيَاجٌ لِلتَّحْصِينِ

Stock-holder *n.* صَاحِبُ أَسْهُمٍ

Stocking *n.* جَوْرَبٌ

Stocks *n. pl.* أَسْهُمٌ مَالِيَّةٌ . مِقْطَرَةٌ

Stocky *a.* ضَخْمٌ . قويُّ الجِسْمِ

Stoic *a.* or *n.* غيرُ مبالٍ بما يَحْدُثُ

Stoicism *n.* مَذْهَبُ غيرِالمُكْتَرِثِين بِالدهرِ

Stole, Stolen, *see* Steal. سَرَقَ

Stolid *a.* بليد. أبلهُ

Stolidity *n.* بلادَةٌ . بلاهَةٌ

Stomach *n.* or *v. t.* مَعِدَةٌ . احتملَ

Stone *n.* حجرٌ. نواةٌ. رَجَمَ
or *v. t.* أخْرَجَ البِزْرَةَ أو النواةَ

Stone-cutter *n.* نحّاتٌ

Stone-ware *n.* آنِيةٌ. حجرِية

Stony *a.* مُحْجِرٌ

Stool *n.* كُرْسِيٌّ لِلرِّجْلَيْنِ . إِسْكَمْلَةٌ

Stoop *v. i.* انحنَى . خضع ـَ

Stop *v. t.* or *i.* وَقَّفَ . وَقَفَ ـِ

Stop *n.* وَقْفٌ . وُقُوفٌ . سَدٌّ

Stoppage *n.* وَقْفٌ . تَوْقِيفٌ

Stopper
Stopple } *n.* سِدَادٌ . صِمَامٌ

Storage *n.* خزنٌ . إِدّخارٌ

Store *n.* or *v. t.* كَمِّيَّةٌ . مُؤْنَةٌ . مَخْزَن. ذخر

Storied *a.* مَقُولٌ فِي رِوايَةٍ . ذُوطَبقَاتٍ

Stork *n.* بجَعٌ

Storm *n.* نوءٌ. عاصفٌ . هُجُومٌ

Storm *v. t.* or *i.* هجَمَ عَلَى . عصَفَ

Stormy *a.* عَاصفٌ . كثِيرِ الأَنْوَاءِ

Story *n.* قصةٌ . طَبَقَةٌ بَيْتٍ

Stout *a.* قويٌّ . جَسُورٌ . سَمِينٌ

Stoutness *n.* قوَّةٌ . شِدَّةٌ . سِمنٌ

Stove *n.* وُجَاقٌ . موقِدٌ

Stow *v. t.* خَزَنَ ـِ . عَبَّى

Straddle *v. i.* or *t.* فَجَّ ـُ . رَكِبَ ـَ

Straggle *v. i.* شَرِدَ ـُ . عَنْ . هامَ ـِ

Straggler *n.* شَارِدٌ

Straight *a.* or *ad.* مستقِيمٌ . رَأْساً

Straighten *v. t.* قوَّمَ . سوَّى

Straightforwad *a.* مُسْتَقِيمٌ . عَادِلٌ

Straightway *ad.* حالاً . على الفور

Strain *v. t.* شدّ ـِ . وثى ـِ . صفى

Strain *n.* جهد . اسلوب

Strainer *n.* مِصفاة

Strait *a.* or *n.* ضيق . ضيقة . مضيق

Straiten *v. t.* ضيّق . شدّ ـُ

Strand *n.* شطّ . طاق حبل

Strange *a.* غريب . عجيب

Strangeness *n.* غرابة

Stranger *n.* غريب . أجنبيّ

Strangle *v. t.* خنق ـُ

Strangulation *n.* خنق . اختناق

Strap *n.* or *v. t.* سير . شدّ به

Strapping *a.* طويل . خليع

Strata *n. pl.* طبقات . صفوف

Stratagem *n.* حيلة . مكيدة

Strategy *n.* علم إدارة الحرب

Stratification *n.* نضد الطبقات

Stratum *n.* طبقة

Straw *n.* قش . تبن

Strawberry *n.* ثمر كالتوت . فراولا

Stray *v. i.* ضلّ ـِ . شرد ـُ . تاه ـِ

Streak *n.* خطّ

Streaked / Streaky *a.* مخطط

Stream *n.* or *v. i.* مجرى . نهر . سال ـِ

Streamlet *n.* نهير . ساقية

Street *n.* طريق . زقاق . شارع

Strength *n.* قوة . متانة

Strengthen *v. t.* قوّى . شدّد

Strenuous *a.* عزوم . مجدّ

Stress *n.* ضغط . شدة

Stretch *v. t.* or *i.* مدّ ـُ . وسّع . إمتد

Stretch *n.* امتداد . اتساع

Strew *v. t.* بذر . فرّق . نشر

Stricken *a.* مصاب . متضايق

Strict *a.* مدقق . مشدد . صارم

Strictly *ad.* بضبطٍ بصرامةٍ بالتمامِ

Strictness *n.* تدقيقٌ . تشديدٌ

Stricture *n.* تنكيت . تضيق

Stride *n.* or *v. i.* خطوةٌ طويلةٌ

Strife *n.* نزاعٌ . مناظرةٌ

Strike *v. t.* ضربَ ـِ . أثَّرَ . اصابَ

Striking *a.* مؤثِّرٌ . غريبٌ

String *n.* خيطٌ . وترٌ . سلسلةٌ

String *v. t.* جهّز بوترٍ . صفَّ

Stringent *a.* مشدِّدٌ . خطيرٌ . مهمٌّ

Stringy *a.* ليفي . خيطيٌّ

Strip *v. t.* عرّى . قشرَ . نزعَ ـِ

Strip *n.* قطعةٌ ضيقةٌ . سيرٌ

Stripe *n.* قلمٌ . خطٌّ . ضربةُ سوطٍ

Striped *a.* مخطط

Stripling *n.* ولدٌ . غلامٌ

Strive *v. i.* جدَّ ـِ . كدَّ ـُ . إجتهد

Stroke *n.* ضربةٌ . مصيبةٌ . إصابةٌ

Stroke *v. t.* دلكَ ـُ . لاطفَ

Stroll *v. i.* جالَ ـُ . عارَ ـِ

Strong *a.* قويٌّ . متينٌ . شديدٌ

Stronghold *n.* حصنٌ . معقل

Structure *n.* هيئةٌ . بنيةٌ . بناءٌ

Struggle *v. i.* جدّ . عارك

Struggle *n.* عراكٌ

Strumpet *n.* عاهرةٌ . فاجرةٌ

Strut *v. i.* تبخترَ . تخطرَ

Stubble *n.* هشيمٌ

Stubborn *a.* عنيد . ماردٌ

Stucco *n.* or *v. i.* جصٌّ . طلى بهِ

Stud *n.* طوالة خيلٍ . زرٌّ

Studded *a.* مرصَّعٌ

Student *n.* تلميذٌ . طالبُ علمٍ

Studied *a.* مدروسٌ . مهيأً . مدبَّرٌ

Studious *a.* مجدٌّ في الدرسِ

Study *n.* or *v. t.* درسٌ . درسَ ـُ

Stuff *n.*	مادةٌ . متَاعٌ . قُمَاشٌ
Stuff *v. t.*	حَشَا . أَفْعَمَ
Stuffing *n.*	حَشْوٌ
Stultify *v. t.*	جهَّلَ . حَمَّقَ
Stumble *v. i.*	عَثَرَ ـُ . زَلَّ ـَ . كَبَا ـُ
Stumbling-block *n.*	حَجَرُ عَثْرَةٍ
Stump *n.*	قَرْمِيةٌ ج قَرَامِيُّ
Stun *v. t.*	دَوَّخَ . حَيَّرَ . بَهَّتَ
Stunt *v. t.*	وَقَّفَ عَنِ ٱلنموِّ
Stupefy *v. t.*	أَدْخَلَ . بَهَّتَ . خدر
Stupendous *a.*	عَظِيمٌ جدًّا . عَجِيبٌ
Stupid *a.*	بَلِيدٌ . أَبْلَهُ . أَخْرَقُ
Stupidity *n.*	خُرْقٌ . بلَاهَةٌ
Stupor *n.*	سُبَاتٌ . خَدَرٌ
Sturdy *a.*	قَوِيٌّ . عزومٌ
Stutter *v. i.*	تَمْتَمَ . لَجْلَجَ
Sty *n.*	زَرِيبَةُ ٱلْخَنَازِيرِ . شحَاذُ ٱلْعَيْنِ
Style *n.*	اسْلُوبٌ . عِبَارَةٌ . زِيٌّ
Stylish *a.*	بحَسبِ ٱلزِّيِّ . انيق
Suasive *a.*	مُقْنِعٌ
Suavity *n.*	لَطَافَةٌ . أَدَبٌ . عُذُوبَةٌ
Subdivide *v. t.*	جزَّأ ايضًا
Subdivision *n.*	تَجْزِئَةُ ٱلْمُجزإِ
Subdue *v. t.*	أَخْضَعَ . غَلَبَ ـِ
Subject *n.*	تابِعٌ . مَوضوعٌ . فَاعِلٌ
Subject *v. t.* or *a.*	خَضَعَ . خَاضِعٌ . تَحتَ
Subjection *n.*	إِخضَاعٌ . خضوع
Subjective *a.*	باطِنِيٌّ . ذِهْنِيٌّ
Subjoin *v. t.*	لَحِقَ بِهِ . ذَيَّلَ
Subjugate *v. t.*	أَخْضَعَ . قَهَرَ ـَ
Subjunctive *a.*	مُلْحق . مَوْصُوْلٌ بِهِ
Sublime *a.*	سَامٍ . جَلِيلٌ . رَفِيعٌ
Sublimity *n.*	سُمُوٌّ . جلَالَةٌ . رِفْعَةٌ
Submerge *v. t.*	أَغرَقَ . غَطَّسَ
Submersion *n.*	تغطِيسٌ
Submission *n.*	خُضُوعٌ . تسْلِيمٌ

Submissive *a.* خاضِعٌ. طائِعٌ

Submit *v. i.* or *t.* خَضَعَ ـَ. سَلَّمَ

Subordinate *a.* تابِعٌ. دُونٌ. ثانَوِي

Subordination *n.* خُضُوعٌ. تَبَعِيَّةٌ

Suborn *v. t.* حَمَلَ عَلى حَلْفِ زُورٍ

Subscribe *v.t.* or *i.* أَمْضَى. رَضِيَ بِهِ. اشْتَرَكَ فِي

Subscriber *n.* مُشْتَرِكٌ

Subscription *n.* قِيمَةُ اشْتِرَاكٍ

Subsequent *a.* تالٍ. تابِعٌ

Subsequently *ad.* بَعْدُ. مِنْ بَعْدُ

Subserve *v. t.* خَدَمَ ـُ. أَفادَ

Subservient *a.* مُفيدٌ لَهُ. خاضِعٌ

Subside *v. i.* خَمَدَ ـُ. سَكَنَ ـُ

Subsidence *n.* سُكُونٌ. هُبُوطٌ

Subsidiary *a.* مُعاوِنٌ. إِضافِيٌّ

Subsidize *v. t.* أَعانَ بِدَراهِمَ لِخِدْمَةٍ

Subsidy *n.* إِعانَةٌ مالِيَّةٌ

Subsist *v. i.* اقْتاتَ. بَقِيَ ـَ. وُجِدَ

Subsistence *n.* مَعِيشَةٌ. وُجُودٌ

Substance *n.* مادَّةٌ. جَوْهَرٌ. خُلاصَةٌ

Substantial *a.* حَقِيقِيٌّ. جَوْهَرِيٌّ

Substantiate *v. t.* أَثْبَتَ. حَقَّقَ

Substantive *n.* or *a.* اسْمٌ. حَقِيقِيٌّ

Substitute *n.* or *v. t.* عِوَضٌ. أَبْدَلَ

Substitution *n.* إِبْدالٌ

Substruction / Substructure *n.* بِنَاءٌ تَحْتِي. أَساسٌ

Subtend *v. t.* قاطَعَ مِنْ أَسْفَلَ أَوْ مُقابِلاً

Subterfuge *n.* مُوارَبَةٌ. حِيلَةٌ

Subterranean / Subterraneous *a.* تَحْتَ الأَرْضِ

Subtle *a.* داهٍ. مُحْتالٌ. مَكّارٌ

Subtilty / Subtlety *n.* حِيلَةٌ. دَهاءٌ

Subtract *v. t.* طَرَحَ ـَ. أَسْقَطَ مِنْ

Subtraction *n.* طَرْحٌ

Subtrahend *n.* اَلْمَطْرُوح

Suburban *a.* مِنْ سَوادِ مَدِينَةٍ

Suburbs *n. pl.* سَوادُ مَدِينَةٍ

Subversion *n.* قلبٌ. هدمٌ. تحريفٌ

Subversive *a.* مُخرّبٌ. مُحرّفٌ

Subvert *v. t.* قَلَبَ. خرَّبَ. حرّفَ

Succeed *v. t.* or *i.* تَبِعَ. حلَّ محلّهُ. نَجَحَ

Success *n.* نجاحٌ. فوزٌ

Successful *a.* ناجحٌ. ظافرٌ

Succession *n.* تَتَابُعٌ. خِلافةٌ

Successive *a.* مُتتابعٌ. متعاقِبٌ

Successor *n.* تابِعٌ. خلفٌ. خليفةٌ

Succinct *a.* مُوجزٌ. مُلخَّصٌ

Succour *n.* or *v. t.* إِغاثةٌ. أغاثَ. أعانَ

Succulent *a.* غَضٌّ

Succumb *v. i.* خَضَعَ. ماتَ

Such *a.* كَذا. كهذا. مِثْلُ هذا

Suck *v. t.* رَضِعَ. امتصَّ

Sucker *n.* فرخٌ. عُسلجٌ. نوعٌ من السَّمكِ

Suckle *v. t.* أرْضَعَ

Suckling *n.* رَضيعٌ ج رضعٌ

Suction *n.* مَصٌّ

Sudden *a.* فجائيٌّ. باغتٌ

Suddenly *ad.* بَغتةً

Sue *v. t.* ادَّعى عليهِ. حاكم. طَلَبَ

Suet *n.* شَحْمٌ

Suffer *v. t.* or *i.* احتَمَلَ. قاسى. رَخَّصَ

Sufferable *a.* ما يُحتمل

Sufferance *n.* رُخصةٌ. احتمالٌ

Sufferer *n.* مُصابٌ. مُكابدٌ. مُتألمٌ

Suffering *n.* ألمٌ. ضيقٌ. عذابٌ

Suffice *v. i.* or *t.* كَفى. أغنى

Sufficiency *n.* كِفايةٌ. مُكنةٌ

Sufficient *a.* كافٍ. مغنٍ

Suffix *n.* مُضافٌ إلى آخرهِ

Suffocate *v. t.* خنقَ. فطّس

Suffocation *n.* خنقٌ. اختناق

Suffrage *n.* حقُّ صوتِ الانتخابِ

Suffuse *v. t.* نشرَ . أفشى
Sugar *n.* سُكَّرٌ
Sugar-basin, **Sugar bowl** *n.* سُكَّرِيَّةٌ
Sugar-cane *n.* قَصَبُ ٱلسُّكرِ
Sugar-loaf *n.* رَأْسُ سُكرٍ
Sugar-plum *n.* مُلَبَّسٌ
Suggest *v. t* أوعز . قدَّم رأياً
Suggestion *n.* تَقْدِيمُ رَأْيٍ . تَلْمِيحٌ
Suggestive *a.* مُلَمِّحٌ . مُشِيرٌ إلى
Suicidal *n.* آئِلٌ لِقَتْلِ ٱلنفسِ
Suicide *n* قَتْلُ ٱلنَّفْسِ . ٱنْتحارٌ
Suit *n.* or *v. t.* حُلَّةٌ . ثِيَابٌ . دَعْوَى . نَاسَبَ
Suitable *a.* مُوَافِقٌ . مُنَاسِبٌ
Suitableness *n.* مُنَاسَبَةٌ
Suite *n.* حَشَمٌ . طَقْمٌ
Suitor *n.* طَالِبٌ . مُحِبٌّ . صَاحِبُ دَعْوَى
Sulky, **Sullen** *a.* عَبُوسٌ . حَرِيدٌ
Sully *v. t.* لَطَخَ . ثَلَمَ ٱلصِّيتَ

Sulphur *n.* كِبْرِيتٌ
Sulphureous, **Sulphurous** *a.* كِبْرِيتِيٌّ
Sultriness *n.*, **Sultry** *a.* عَكٌّ
Sum *n.* مَجْمُوعٌ . حاصِلٌ
Sumach *n.* سُمَّاقٌ (شَجَرَةٌ)
Summarily *ad.* مُلَخَّصاً . حَالاً
Summary *n.* or *a.* مُلَخَّصٌ
Summer *n.* صَيْفٌ . قَيْظٌ
Summit *n.* قِمَّةٌ . رَأْسٌ
Summon *v. t.* اسْتَدْعَى . ٱسْتَحْضَرَ
Summons *n. sing.* ٱسْتِحْضَارٌ
Sumptuous *a.* فَاخِرٌ . بَهِيٌّ . ثَمِينٌ
Sun *n.* or *v. t.* شَمْسٌ . شَمَّسَ
Sun-beam *n.* شُعَاعُ ٱلشَّمْسِ
Sunday *n.* يَوْمُ ٱلأَحَدِ
Sunder *v. t.* فَصَلَ ـــِ
Sun-dial *n.* سَاعَةٌ شَمْسِيَّةٌ
Sundries *n. pl.* أَشْيَاءُ شَتَّى

Sundry *a.* شَتَّى

Sunken *a.* غارِق. تحتَ ٱلْماء

Sunlight *n.* نُورُ ٱلشَّمْسِ

Sunlit *a.* مُنوَّرٌ مِنَ ٱلشمْسِ

Sunny *a.* شَمْسٌ. مُعَرَّضٌ المشَّمْسِ

Sunrise *n.* شُرُوقُ ٱلشَّمْسِ

Sunset *n.* غُرُوبُ ٱلشَّمْس

Sunshine *n.* ضَوْءُ ٱلشَّمْسِ

Sun-stroke *n.* رعْنٌ

Sup *v. i.* تَعَشَّى

Superabundance *n.* وَفْرَةٌ. فَرْطٌ

Superabundant *a.* مُفْرِطٌ. وَافِر

Superannuated *a.* عاجِزٌ مِنَ ٱلْكِبَرِ

Superb *a.* فَاخِرٌ. نَفِيسٌ. بَهِيٌّ

Supercilious *a.* مُتَغَطْرِسٌ. مُتَجَبِّر

Supereminent *a.* فَائِقٌ جِدًّا

Supererogatory *a.* نَافِلِيٌّ

Superficial *a.* سَطْحِي. ظاهِرِي

Superfine *a.* نفِيسٌ جِدًّا. سَامٍ

Superfluity *n.* زِيَادَةٌ. فضْل

Superfluous *a.* زَائِد. فَوْق اللازِمِ

Superintend *v. t.* نَاظَرَ. تَوَكَّلَ على

Superintendence *n.* مُناظَرَةٌ

Superintendent *n.* نَاظِرٌ. وَكِيلٌ

Superior *a.* or *n.* فَائِقٌ. أَعْظَمُ. رَئِيسٌ

Superiority *n.* سَبْقٌ. أَفْضَلِيَّةٌ

Superlative *a.* الأَفْضَلُ. أَفْعَلُ ٱلتَفْضِيلِ

Supernatural *a.* فَوْقَ ٱلطَّبِيعَةِ

Superscribe *v t.* عَنْوَنَ

Superscription *n.* عُنْوَانٌ

Supersede *v. t.* عَزَّلَ ـــِ. الْغَى

Supernal *n.* عَلَوِي. سَمَاوِي

Superstition *n.* وَهْمٌ. خُرَافَةٌ

Superstitious *n.* مُتَوَهِّمٌ. خُرَافِيٌّ

Superstructure *n.* بِنَاءٌ فَوْقَ غَيْرِهِ

Supervene *v. i.* حَدَثَ عَرَضاً

Supervise *v. t.*	ناظر . راقب
Supervisor *n.*	ناظر . مناظر
Supine *a.*	متكاسل . غير مكترث
Supineness *n.*	توان . تهامل
Supper *n.*	عشاء
Supplant *v. t.*	استبدل حيلة
Supple *a.*	مرن . لين . منقاد
Supplement *n.*	ملحق . إضافة
Supplemental / Supplementary *a.*	إضافي
Suppleness *n.*	مرونة . ليونة
Suppliant / Supplicant *a.*	متوسل . متضرع
Supplicate *v. t.*	توسل . تضرع إلى
Supplication *n.*	توسل . التماس
Supplies *n. pl.* / Supply *n.*	مؤونة . ذخيرة . كفاءة
Supply *v. t.*	جهز . قدم . أورد
Support *v. t.*	عضد . عال . امد
Support *n.*	سند . عول . عضد
Supportable *a.*	يحتمل . يطاق
Supposable *a.*	مظنون . محتمل
Suppose *v. t.*	ظن ـ فرض ـ
Supposition *n.*	ظن . فرض
Suppositious *a.*	غير حقيقي . مظنون
Suppress *v. t.*	أخمد . أبطل . منع ـ
Suppression *n.*	ابطال . إخماد
Suppurate *v. i.*	قاح ـ تقيح
Suppremacy *n.*	سلطة . رياسة تفوق
Suppreme *a.*	الأعظم . مطلق التسلط
Sure *a.*	اكيد . يقين . محقق
Surety *n.*	أمن . كفالة . يقين
Surf *n.*	أمواج على الشط
Surface *n.*	سطح . وجه
Surfeit *n.* or *v. t.*	كظة . كظ ـ
Surge *n.* or *v. i.*	موج عظيم . تموج
Surgeon *n.*	جراح
Surgery *n.*	علم الجراحة
Surgical *a.*	جراحي

Surly *a.* شَكِسٌ . فَظٌّ

Surmise *n.* or *v. t.* حَدْسٌ . خَمَّنَ

Surmount *v. t.* عَلَا عَلَيْهِ او . غَلَبَ بِ

Surname *n.* اَسْمُ الْعَائِلَةِ . لَقَبٌ

Surpass *v. t.* سبق ــِ . فَاقَ ــُ

Surpassing *a.* فَائِقٌ . جَيِّد جدًّا

Surplus *n.* فَضْلَةٌ . بَقِيَة

Surprise *n.* or *v. t.* تَعَجُّبٌ . جا . ادْهَشَ

Surrender *v. t.* or *n.* سَلَّمَ . تَسْلِيمٌ

Surreptitions *a.* مَا يفعَل خُلْسةً أَوْ غدراً

Surround *v. t.* احاط بِهِ . أَحْدَقَ

Survey *v. t.* عَايَنَ. فحصَ ــَ . مَسَحَ ــَ

Survey / Surveying *n.* مَسْحٌ . مِسَاحة

Surveyor *n.* مَسَّاحٌ

Survival *n.* بَقَاءٌ بعدَ آخرَ

Survive *v. t.* عَاشَ بعدَهُ

Susceptibility *n.* حِسٌّ . تأثُّر

Susceptible *a.* مُحِسٌّ . متأثِّرٌ . قَابِلٌ

Suspect *v. t.* اتَّهَمَ . اشْتَبَهَ

Suspend *v. t.* وَقَّفَ . أَجَّلَ . علق

Suspense *n.* تَرَدُّدٌ . حِيرَةٌ

Suspension *n.* توقيفٌ . تعطيل

Suspension *n.* تُهْمَةٌ . شُبْهَةٌ

Suspicious *a.* ظَنَّان . مُشْتَبِهٌ

Sustain *v. t.* احتَمَلَ . سَنَدَ ــُ . عَضَدَ ــُ

Sustenance *n.* قُوتٌ . عَضد

Suture *n.* درز

Suzerain *n.* مَوْلًى

Swab *n.* or *v. t.* مِسْحَةٌ . مَسَحَ بِهَا

Swaddle *v. t.* or *n.* قَمَطَ . قِمَاط

Swagger *v. i.* or *n.* تَغَطْرَسَ . غَطْرَسَةٌ

Swain *n.* فلاحٌ . فلاحٌ عاشِقٌ

Swallow *v. t.* or *n.* ازْدَرَدَ . سنونو

Swamp *n.* مستنقعٌ . سَبَخَةٌ . غَمْقَةٌ

Swan *n.* نوعٌ مِنَ الاوزِ

Sward *n.* جَزْمَةٌ . أَرْضٌ كَثِيرَةُ الْكَلَإِ

Swarm *n.* or *v. i.* ثَوْل . ازْدَحَمَ

Swarthy *a.* أَسمَرُ

Sway *v. t.* or *i.* مَلَكَ . أَمالَ . تَمَايَلَ

Swear *v. i.* حَلَفَ ـ . اقْسَمَ . شَتَمَ ـُ

Swearing *n.* حلف. تجديفٌ

Sweat *n.* or *v. i.* عَرَقٌ . عَرِقَ ـ

Sweep *v. t.* كَنَسَ . جَرَفَ ـ

Sweepings *n. pl.* كُنَاسَةٌ . زُبَالَةٌ

Sweet *a.* or *n.* حَلْوٌ . عَذْبٌ . حَلْوَى

Sweeten *v.t.* or *i.* حَلَّى . حَلا ـ

Sweetheart *n.* عَاشِقٌ (ة) مَعْشوق (ة)

Sweetmeat *n.* حلوَى ج حَلاَوَى

Sweetness *n.* حَلاَوَةٌ . عذوبة

Swell *v. i.* or *n.* انْتَفَخَ . وَرِمَ ـِ . عُبابٌ

Swelling *n.* وَرَمٌ

Swelter *v. i.* تضايَق مِنَ الحَرِّ

Swerve *v.* مَالَ ـِ انْحَرَفَ

Swift *a.* سَرِيعٌ

Swiftness *n.* سُرْعَةٌ

Swim *v. i.* سَبَحَ ـ

Swimming *n.* سِبَاحَةٌ

Swimmingly *ad.* جَيِّدًا . بتوْفيقٍ

Swindle *v. t.* or *n.* غَبَن ـِ . غدرَ ـُ

Swine *n.* خِنزيرٌ ج خنازِيرُ

Swing *v. t.* or *i.* ارْجَحَ . ارْتَجَحَ . تَمَايَلَ

Swing *n.* أُرْجُوحَةٌ . مَرْجُوحَةٌ

Switch *n.* قَضِيبٌ لَيِّنٌ

Swoon *v. i.* or *n.* غُشِيَ عَلَيْهِ . غَشْيَةٌ

Swoop *v. i.* انْقَضَّ عَلَى

Sword *n.* سَيْفٌ . ج سُيُوفٌ . حُسَامٌ

Sycamore *n.* جُمَّيْزٌ . جُمَّيْزَةٌ

Sycophant *n.* مُدَاهِنٌ

Syllable *n.* مَقْطَعُ كَلِمَةٍ

Syllabus *n.* خُلاَصَةٌ . مُخْتَصَرٌ

Syllogism *n.* قِيَاسٌ مَنطِقِي

Sylvant *a.* غَابِيٌّ

Symbol *n.* رَمزٌ . مِثَالٌ . عَلَامَةٌ

Symbolic / **Symbolical** *a.* رَمزِي . اِستعارِيٌّ

Symmetrical *a.* متَنَاسِبُ الأَجزَاءِ

Symmetry *n.* تَنَاسبُ الأَجزَاءِ

Sympathetic مُشتَرِكٌ فِي شعورِ غَيرِهِ

Sympathize *v. i.* اِشترَكَ فِي شعورِهِ

Sympathy *n.* إِشتِراكٌ فِي شعورِهِ

Symptom *n.* عَلَامَةٌ . عَرَض مرَضٍ

Synagogue *n.* مجمَعُ اليَهُود

Synchronism *n.* اِتِّفَاقٌ فِي الوَقتِ

Syndicate *n.* وِكَالَةٌ أَو شِرِكَةٌ لإِجرَاءِ أَشغَال

Synonym / **Synonyme** *a.* كَلِمَةٌ مُترَادِفة

Synonymous *a.* مُترَادِفٌ

Synopsis *n.* ملَخَّصٌ . خُلَاصَةٌ

Synoptic / **Synoptical** *a.* مُلَخَّصِيٌّ . شَامِلٌ

Syntax *n.* عِلمُ النحوِ

Synthesis *n.* تَركِيبٌ . تَأْلِيفُ الأَفكَارِ

Syriac *a.* سِريَانِيٌّ

Syringe *n.* or *v. i.* مِحقَنَةٌ . عَالَجَ بِهَا

Syrup *n.* عَصِيرٌ مُحلًّى . شَرَابٌ

System *n.* تَرتِيبٌ . نِظَامٌ . مَذهَبٌ

Systematic / **Systematical** *a.* نِظَامِيٌّ . تَرتِيبِيٌّ

Systematize *v. t.* نَظَمَ . رَتَّبَ

T

Tabernacle *n.* خَيمٌ . مَظَلَّمٌ

Table *n.* مَائِدَةٌ . سُفرَةٌ . جَدوَلٌ

Tableau *n.* صُورَةٌ . تَشخِيصٌ

Table-land *n.* نَجدٌ . هَضبَةٌ . صَعِيدٌ

Tablet *n.* لَوحٌ لِلكِتَابَةِ

Tabular *a.* مُسَطَّحٌ . جَدوَلِيٌّ

Tacit *a.* سَاكِتٌ . مُضَمَّنٌ . مفهُومٌ

Taciturn *a.* سَكُوتٌ . كَتومٌ

Taciturnity *n.* سُكُوت

Tack *n.* مسمَارٌ صَغِيرٌ . مَجرَى ٱلسَّفِينة

Tack *v. t.* سَمَّرَ خفيفاً . غَيَّرَ مَجرَى السفِينةِ

Tackle *n.* **or** *v. t.* جِهازٌ . آلاتٌ . قَبَضَ . شَدَّ

Tackling *n.* جِهازُ ٱلسَّوَارِي والقُلوعِ

Tact *n.* مَهَارَةٌ . لَبَاقَةٌ . فِرَاسَةٌ

Tactical *a.* مُختَصٌّ بِتَنظِيمِ ٱلجُيُوشِ

Tactics *n. sing.* عِلمُ تَنظِيمِ ٱلجُيُوشِ

Tadpole *n.* وَلَدُ ٱلضِّفْدَعِ

Tail *n.* ذَنَبٌ . ذَيلٌ . مُؤَخَّر

Tailor *n.* خَيَّاطٌ

Taint *v. t.* **or** *n.* شَابَ ـُ لَطْخَة

Take *v. t.* اخَذَ ـُ تَنَاوَلَ

Taking *a.* **or** *n.* جَاذِبٌ . أَخْذٌ

Tale *n.* قِصَّةٌ . حِكَايَةٌ . رِوَايَةٌ

Tale-bearer *n.* نَمَّامٌ . وَاشٍ

Talent *n.* وَزْنَةٌ . مَوْهِبَةٌ

Talented *a.* ذَكِيٌّ . لَوْذَعِيٌّ

Talisman *n.* طِلَسْمٌ ج طَلَاسِمُ

Talk *n.* **or** *v. i.* كَلَامٌ . تَكَلَّمَ

Talkative *a.* كَثِيرُ ٱلكَلَامِ

Tall *a.* طَوِيلُ ٱلقَامَةِ . عَالٍ

Talness *n.* طُولٌ . عُلُوٌّ

Tallow *n.* شَحْمٌ

Tally *v. i.* طَابَقَ . اتَّفَقَ

Tallon *n.* مِخْلَبٌ . ظِفْرٌ

Tamable *a.* ما يُؤْنَسُ . يُطَبَّعُ . يُذَلَّلُ

Tame *a.* **or** *v. t.* دَاجِنٌ . ذَلُولٌ . ذَلَّلَ

Tamely *ad.* تَذَلُّلاً

Tamper *v. i.* تَدَاخَلَ فِي . لَعِبَ فِي

Tan *n.* **or** *v. t.* دِبْغَةٌ . دَبَغَ ـَ

Tangent *n.* خَطٌّ مُمَاسٌّ لِقَوْسٍ

Tangible *a.* مَا يُمَسُّ أَو يُلْمَسُ . مَحسُوسٌ

Tangle *v. t.* **or** *n.* شَبَّكَ . عُقْدَةٌ

Tank *n.* حَوْضٌ . بِرْكَةٌ

Tanner *n.* دَبَّاغٌ

Tannery *n.* مَدْبَغَةٌ . دَبَّاغَةٌ

Tantalize *v. t.* عَذَّبَ بِرَجَاءِ ٱلْمُسْتَحِيلِ

Tantamount *a.* مُسَاوٍ

Tap *n.* دَقَّ ـُ خَفِيفاً . بَزَلَ ـُ

Tape *n.* شَرِيطٌ

Taper *n.* or *v. i.* شَمْعَةٌ . إِسْتَدَقَّ

Tap-root *n.* ٱلْجِذْرُ ٱلْأَصْلِيُّ ٱلْمُسْتَقِيمُ

Tapestry *n.* أَنْسِجَةٌ مُوَشَّاةٌ لِلتَّعْلِيقِ

Tapeworm *n.* الدودَةُ ٱلْعَرِيضَةُ

Tar *n.* or *v. t.* قَطْرَانٌ طَلَى بِهِ . نُورِتِي

Tardiness *n.* تَأَخُّرٌ . بُطْوءٌ

Tardy *a.* مُتَأَخِّرٌ . بَطِيءٌ

Tare *n.* زُوَانٌ

Target *n.* هَدَفٌ . تُرْسٌ صَغِيرٌ

Tariff *n.* تَعْرِيفٌ . جَدْوَلُ جَمَارِكَ

Tarnish *v. t.* كَدَّرَ ٱللَّوْنَ . لَطَّخَ

Tarry *v. i.* مَكَثَ ـُ . أَبْطَأَ

Tart *a.* or *n.* حَامِضٌ . حَادٌّ . فَطِيرَةٌ

Tartar *n.* طَرْطِيرٌ . تَتَرِي

Tartness *n.* حُمُوضَةٌ . حِدَّةٌ

Task *n.* شُغْلٌ مَفْرُوضٌ . عَمَلٌ شَاقٌّ

Tassel *n.* شَرَّابَةٌ . زِرٌّ

Taste *v. t.* or *n.* ذَاقَ ـُ . ذَوْقٌ . مَشْرَبٌ

Tasteful, Tasty } *a.* بِحَسَبِ ٱلذَّوْقِ . أَنِيقٌ

Tasteless *a.* بِلَا طَعْمٍ . تَافِهٌ

Tatter *v. t.* or *n.* مَزَّقَ . خِرْقَةٌ . رِثَّةٌ

Tattle *v. i.* هَذَرَ ـِ . فَضَحَ ٱلسِّرَّ

Taunt *v. t.* عَيَّرَ عَنَّفَ

Tavern *n.* فُنْدُقٌ . حَانَةٌ

Tawdry *a.* مُتَظَرِّفٌ بِلَا ذَوْقٍ

Tawny *a.* أَسْمَرُ

Tax *n.* ضَرِيبَةٌ . رَسْمٌ

Taxable *a.* تَحْتَ ضَرِيبَةٍ أَوْ رَسْمٍ

Taxation *n.* الضَّرَائِبُ بِجُمْلَتِهَا

Tea *n.* شَايٌ

Teach *v. t.* عَلَّمَ . دَرَّسَ

Teachable *a.* قَابِلُ ٱلتَّعْلِيمِ . طَوْعٌ

Teacher *n.* مُعَلِّمٌ . مُدَرِّسٌ

Team *n.* ثَوْرُ ٱلْحِرَاثَةِ . قِطَارُ دَوَابَّ

Tea-pot *n.* إِبْرِيقُ شَايٍ

Tear *n.* دَمْعَةٌ . شَرْمٌ . مَزْقَةٌ

Tear *v. t.* مَزَّقَ . شَقَّ ـُـ

Tearful *a.* دَمِيعٌ

Tease *v. t.* نَكَّدَ . أَضْجَرَ

Teat *n.* حَلَمَةُ حَيَوَانٍ . بِزٌّ

Technical *a.* صِنَاعِيٌّ . اِصْطِلَاحِيٌّ

Technology *n.* ٱلْبَحْثُ عَنِ ٱلصِّنَاعَاتِ وَحُدُودِهَا

Tedious *a.* مُتْعِبٌ . مُمِلٌّ . مُطَوَّلٌ

Tediousness, **Tedium** } *n.* مَلَلٌ . ضَجَرٌ

Teem *v. i.* غَصَّ ـُـ . أَنْتَجَ كَثِيرًا

Teens *n. pl.* ٱلْعُمْرُ بَيْنَ ١٣ و ١٩ سَنَةً

Teeth *n. pl. of* Tooth أَسْنَانٌ

Teetotal-ism *n.* ٱلِامْتِنَاعُ عَنِ ٱلْمُسْكِرَاتِ

Telegram *n.* رِسَالَةٌ بَرْقِيَّةٌ

Telegraph *n.* سِلْكٌ بَرْقِيٌّ

Telephone *n.* آلَةٌ لِلتَّكَلُّمِ عَلَى بُعْدٍ

Telescope *n.* نَظَّارَةٌ . مِنْظَرٌ

Tell *v. t.* or *i.* خَبَّرَ . حَدَّثَ . قَالَ

Tell-tale *n.* وَاشٍ

Temerity *n.* تَهَوُّرٌ . اِعْتِسَافٌ

Temper *n.* طَبْعٌ . خُلْقٌ

Temper *v. t.* مَزَجَ ـُـ . لَطَّفَ . عَدَّلَ

Temperament *n.* مِزَاجٌ

Temperance *n.* اِعْتِدَالٌ . عِفَّةٌ

Temperate *a.* مُعْتَدِلٌ . عَفِيفٌ

Temperature *n.* دَرَجَةُ ٱلْحَرَارَةِ

Tempest *n.* عَاصِفَةٌ . نَوْءٌ

Tempestuous *a.* عَاصِفٌ . زَوْبَعِيٌّ

Temple *n.* هَيْكَلٌ . صُدْغٌ

Temporal *a.* زَمَنِيٌّ . صُدْغِيٌّ

Temporarily *ad.* وَقْتِيًّا

Temporary *a.* وَقْتِيٌّ . إِلَى حِينٍ

Temporise *v. i.* دَارَ مَعَ ٱلْأَحْوَالِ

Tempt *v. t.* جَرَّبَ . أَغْوَى

Temptation *n.* تَجْرِبَةٌ

Tempter *n.* مُجَرِّبٌ

Ten *a.* عَشَرَةٌ . عَشْرٌ

Tenable *a.* قَابِلُ ٱلتَّمَسُّكِ بِهِ أَوْ ٱلْإِثْبَاتِ

Tenacity *n.* تَمَسُّكٌ . تَشَبُّثٌ

Tenant *n.* مُسْتَأْجِرٌ

Tenantry *n.* مُسْتَأْجِرُو أَمْلَاكٍ

Tend *v. t.* or *i.* آلَ . مَالَ إِلَى . إِعْتَنَى بِ

Tendency *n.* مَيْلٌ . ٱنْعِطَافٌ

Tender *a.* غَضٌّ . طَرِيٌّ . حَنُونٌ

Tender *n.* or *v. t.* عَرْضُ سِعْرٍ . عَرَضَ

Tenderness *n.* حُنُوٌّ . رِقَّةٌ

Tendon *n.* وَتَرٌ

Tendril *n.* عُسْلُجٌ لَوْلَبِيٌّ لِلتَّعَلُّقِ

Tenement *n.* مَسْكَنٌ مُسْتَأْجَرٌ

Tenet *n.* عَقِيدَةٌ . مَذْهَبٌ

Tenfold *n.* عَشَرَةُ أَضْعَافٍ

Tennis *n.* نَوْعٌ مِنْ لِعْبِ ٱلْكُرَةِ

Tenor *n.* فَحْوَى . سِيَاق

Tense *a.* or *n.* مَشْدُودٌ . زَمَانُ ٱلْفِعْلِ

Tension *n.* شَدٌّ . ٱشْتِدَادٌ

Tent *n.* خَيْمَةٌ . صِيوَانٌ . فُسْطَاطٌ

Tentacle *n.* قَرْنُ ٱلْحَشَرَاتِ

Tentative *a.* تَجْرِيبِيٌّ

Tenth *a.* عَاشِرٌ

Tenuity *n.* رِقَّةٌ . لَطَافَةٌ

Tenure *n.* ٱسْتِئْجَارٌ

Tepid *a.* فَاتِرٌ

Terebinth *n.* شَجَرُ ٱلْبُطْمِ

Term *n.* عِبَارَةٌ . مُدَّةٌ . شَرْط . حَدٌّ

Term *v. t.* سَمَّى . دَعَا

Terminal *a.*	فِي ٱلطَّرَفِ . آخِرٌ
Terminate *v. t.*	أَنْهَى . إِنْتَهَى
Termination *n.*	إِنْهَآءٌ . نِهَايَةٌ
Terminus *n.*	تَخْمٌ . طَرَفٌ . حَدٌّ
Terrace *n.*	سَطْحُ بَيْتٍ . دَكَّةٌ
Terra-Cotta *n.*	فَخَّارٌ
Terrestrial *a.*	ارضِيٌّ
Terrible *a.*	مُخِيفٌ . هَائِلٌ
Terrier *n.*	ضَرْبٌ مِنْ كِلَابِ ٱلصَّيْدِ
Terrific *a.*	مُسَبِّبُ خَوْفٍ شَدِيدٍ
Terrify *v. t.*	خَوَّفَ . فَزَّعَ
Territory *n.*	إِقْلِيمٌ . ارْضٌ مَمْلَكَةٍ
Terror *n.*	هَوْلٌ . فَزَعٌ
Terse *a.*	أَنِيقُ ٱلعِبَارَةِ . مُوْجَزُهَا
Terseness *n.*	إِيجَازٌ
Test *n.* or *v. t.*	اِمْتِحَانٌ . جَرَّبَ
Testament *n.*	عَهْدٌ . وَصِيَّةٌ
Testamentary *a.*	مَنُوطٌ بِوَصِيَّةٍ
Testator *n.*	مُوصٍ
Testicle *n.*	خُصْيَةٌ ج خُصًى
Testify *v. t.*	شَهِدَ ـَ
Testimonial *a.* / **Testimony** *n.*	شَهَادَةٌ
Testiness *n.*	حِدَّةٌ . شَكَاسَةٌ
Tetanus *n.*	دَآءُ ٱلكُزَازِ
Tether *v. t.*	شَكَلَ ـُ . شَكَّلَ
Teutonic *a.*	جَرْمَانِيٌّ
Text *n.*	مَتْنٌ . مَوضُوعٌ
Text-book *n.*	كِتَابُ دَرْسٍ
Textile *a.*	مَنْسُوجٌ . نَسِيجِيٌّ
Texture *n.*	نَسِيجٌ
Than *conj.*	مِنْ (بَعْدَ أَفْعَلِ ٱلتَّفْضِيلِ)
Thank *v. t.*	شَكَرَ ـُ . أَثْنَى عَلَى
Thankful *a.*	شَاكِرٌ . شَكُورٌ
Thankfulness *n.*	شُكْرَانٌ . شُكْرٌ
Thankless *a.*	عَدِيمُ ٱلشُّكْرِ
Thanks *n.*	(تَشَكُّرَات)

Thanksgiving *n.*	شُكْرٌ . حَمْدٌ
That *pron.* or *conj.*	ذَلِكَ . أَنْ
Thatch *n.* or *v. t.*	غِمَاءٌ . غَمَى ـُ
Thaw *v. i.* or *t.*	ذَابَ ـُ . أَذَابَ
The *def. article.*	اَلْ اَلتَّعْرِيفِ
Theatre *n.*	مَسْرَحٌ . مَلْعَبٌ
Theatric / **Theatrical** *a.*	مَسْرَحِيٌّ
Thee *p. pron.*	لِكَ (ضَمِيرُ اَلْمُخَاطَبِ)
Theft *n.*	سَرِقَةٌ
Theirs *a. pron.*	الذي لَهُمْ
Theism *n.*	اَلْإِعْتِقَادُ بِوُجُودِ اللهِ
Theist *n.*	مُعْتَقِدٌ بِاللهِ
Them *p. pron.*	هُمْ . هُنَّ (مَنْصُوبٌ اومَجْرورٌ)
Theme *n.*	مَوْضُوعٌ . جُمْلَةٌ . مَقَالَةٌ
Themselves *pron. pl.*	هُمْ أَنْفُسُهُمْ
Then *ad.*	عِنْدَ ذَلِكَ . حِينَئِذٍ . إِذًا
Thence *ad.*	مِنْ هُنَاكَ
Thenceforth / **Thenceforward** *ad.*	مِنْ ذلكَ ٱلوَقْتِ

Theodolite *n.*	آلَةٌ لِلسِّبَاحَة
Theologian *n.*	عَالِمٌ بِاللاَّهُوتِ
Theologic / **Theological** *a.*	لاَهُوتِيٌّ
Theology *n.*	عِلْمُ اَللاهُوْتِ
Theorem *n.*	قَضِيَّةٌ هَنْدَسِيَّةٌ
Theoretic / **Theorotical** *a.*	نَظَرِيٌّ . تَصَوُّرِيٌّ
Theorise *v. i.*	نَظَرَ فِي . إِرْتَأَى
Theory *n.*	نَظَرِيَّةٌ . رَأْيٌ
Therapeutic *a.*	عِلاَجِيٌّ . شِفَائِيٌّ
There *ad.*	هُنَاكَ . حَرْفٌ لِلإِبْتِدَاءِ
Thereabout *ad.*	تَقْرِيبًا
Thereafter *ad.*	بَعْدَ ذَلِكَ . ثُمَّ
Thereby *ad.*	بِذَلِكَ . لِذَلِكَ
Therefore *ad.*	لِذَلِكَ . لِأَجْلِ ذَلِكَ
Therein *ad.*	فِي ذَلِكَ . هُنَاكَ
Thereof *ad.*	مِنْ ذَلِكَ . مِنْهُ
Thereupon *ad.*	حِينَئِذٍ . عِنْدَ ذَلكَ
Therewith *ad.*	لِذَلِكَ . بِهِ

Thermal *a.* مَنُوطٌ بِالْحَرِّ

Thermometer *n.* مِيزَانُ ٱلْحَرَارَةِ

Thesaurus *n.* خَزْنَةٌ . قَامُوسٌ جَامِعٌ

These *pron. pl. of* **this** هٰؤُلَاءِ

Thesis *n.* مَوْضُوعٌ . مَبْحَثٌ . مقالَةٌ

They *pl. pron.* هُمْ هُنَّ (مرفوعٌ)

Thick *a.* سميكٌ . كثيفٌ . ثخينٌ

Thicken *v. t.* or *i.* سَمُكَ . كَثُفَ

Thicket *n.* أَجَمَةٌ . دَغَلٌ

Thickness *n.* سَمْكٌ . كَثَافَةٌ

Thick-set *a.* ضَخْمٌ

Thief *n.* سَارِقٌ . لِصٌّ

Thieve *v. i.* لَصَّ ـَ

Thievish *a.* مُتَلَصِّصٌ

Thigh *n.* فَخِذٌ ج أَفْخَاذٌ

Thimble *n.* قِمْعٌ . كِشْتُبَانٌ

Thin *a.* رقيقٌ . نَحِيفٌ .

Thine *a. pron.* لَكَ . ٱلَّذِي لَكَ

Thing *n.* شَيْءٌ . أَمْرٌ

Think *v. i.* or *t.* ٱفْتَكَرَ . ظَنَّ

Third *a.* or *n.* ثَالِثٌ . ثُلْثٌ

Thirst *n.* or *v. i.* عَطِشَ عَطَشٌ ـَ

Thirsty *a.* عَطْشَانُ م عَطْشَى

Thirteen *a.* ثَلٰثَةَ عَشَرَ

Thirteenth *a.* الثَالِثُ عَشَرَ

Thirtieth *a.* ٱلثَلَاثُونَ

Thirty *a.* ثَلَاثُونَ

This *pron.* هٰذَا . هٰذِهِ

Thistle *n.* شَوْكٌ . حَسَكٌ

Thither *ad.* إِلَى هُنَالِكَ

Thong *n.* سَيْرٌ . شِرَاكٌ

Thorax *n.* ٱلصَّدْرُ

Thorn *n.* شَوْكٌ . أَشْوَاكٌ

Thorny *a.* كَثِيرُ ٱلشَوْكِ . عَسِرٌ

Thorough *a.* كَامِلٌ . شَامِلٌ

Thoroughfare *n.* سِكَّةٌ . شَارِعٌ

Those *pl. of* that اولئِكَ

Thou *pron.* أَنْتَ

Though *conj.* مَعْ ان . وَلَوْ . وَان

Thought *n.* فِكْرٌ . رَأْيٌ

Thoughtful *a.* مُتَفَكِّرٌ . رَزِينٌ . مُهْتَمّ

Thoughtless *a.* طائِشٌ . غافِلٌ

Thousand *a.* or *n.* أَلْفٌ

Thousandth *n.* أَلالْفُ

Thraldom / **Thralldom** *n.* عُبُودِيَّةٌ . رِقٌّ

Thrash *v. t.* دَرَسَ ٱلْحُبُوبَ . ضَرَبَ

Thread *n.* or *v. t.* خَيْطٌ . أَدْخَلَهُ فِي إِبْرَةٍ

Threadbare *a.* بالٍ

Threat *n.* تَهْدِيدٌ . وعِيد

Threaten *v. t.* or *i.* هدَّدَ . اوْعَدَ . هَمَّ بِ

Threatening *a.* مُهَدِّدٌ . مُوشِكٌ

Three *a.* ثَلٰثَة . ثلاثَة . ثلاثٌ

Threefold *a.* ثَلاثَة أَضْعافٍ

Threescore *a.* سِتُونَ

Thresh *v. t.* دَرَسَ ٱلْحُبُوبَ

Threshold *n.* أُسْكُفَّة . مدْخَلٌ

Thrice *ad.* ثَلاثَ مَرَّاتٍ

Thrift *n.* نجاحٌ . اقتِصادٌ

Thriftless *a.* عَدِيمُ ٱلتَّدْبِيرِ وَالنَّجاح

Thrifty *a.* نَاجِحٌ . مقتَصِد

Thrill *v. t.* or *n.* حَرَّكَ . هاجَ . اهْتِزازٌ

Thrilling *a.* مُهَيِّجٌ . مُؤَثِّرٌ جِدًّا

Thrive *v. i.* نَجَحَ . أَفْلَحَ

Throat *n.* حلْقومٌ . بلْعومٌ حلْق

Throb *v. i.* خَفَقَ . اخْتَلَجَ

Throe *n.* أَلمٌ شَدِيد . مَخاضٌ

Throne *n.* عَرْش

Throng *n.* or *v. t.* or *i.* زحمة . تقاطَرَ

Throttle *v. t.* خَنَقَ

Through *pr.* مِنَ ٱلْأَوَّلِ إِلَى ٱلآخِرِ . بِوَاسِطَةِ

Throughout *pr.* or *ad.* فِي كُلِّهِ

Throw *v. t.* or *n.* رَمَى . رَمْيَة

Thrust *v. t.* or *n.* دَفَعَ . طَعَنَ ـُ دَفْعَةٌ

Thumb *n.* or *v. t.* إِبْهَامٌ ج أَبَاهِمُ . وَسَّخَ بِهَا

Thump *n.* or *v. t.* ضَرَبَ . وَكَزَ . ضَرْبَةٌ

Thunder *n.* or *v. i.* رَعْدٌ . رَعَدَ ـُ

Thunder-bolt *n.* صَاعِقَةٌ

Thunder-struck *a.* صَعِقٌ . مَذْهُوشٌ

Thursday *n.* يَوْمُ ٱلْخَمِيسِ

Thus *ad.* هٰكَذَا . كَذَا

Thwart *v. t.* عَارَضَ . عَطَّلَ

Thy *poss. pron.* لَكَ

Thyme *n.* سَعْتَرٌ

Thyself *pron.* أَنْتَ نَفْسُكَ

Tick *n.* or *v. i.* قَرَّاضَةٌ . تَكْتَكَ

Ticket *n.* تَذْكِرَةٌ إِجَازَةٌ

Tickle *v. t.* دَغْدَغَ

Tide *n.* مَدُّ ٱلْبَحْرِ وَجَزْرُهُ

Tidings *n. pl.* أَخْبَارٌ

Tidy *a.* نَظِيفٌ . مُرَتَّبٌ

Tie *v. t.* رَبَطَ ـِ . عَقَدَ ـِ . قَيَّدَ

Tier *n.* طَبَقَةٌ . صَفٌّ

Tiger *mas.* / **Tigress** *fem.* } *n.* نَمِرٌ . نَمِرَةٌ ج نُمُورٌ

Tight *a.* شَدِيدٌ . مَشْدُودٌ

Tighten *v. t.* شَدَّ ـُ أَحْكَمَ . مَكَّنَ

Tile *n.* or *v. t.* قَرْمِيدَةٌ . غَطَّى بِهَا

Till *ad.* or *n.* حَتَّى . إِلَى . صُنْدُوق دَرَاهِمَ

Till *v. t.* حَرَثَ ـُ . فَلَحَ ـَ

Tillage *n.* حِرَاثَةٌ . فِلَاحَةٌ

Tilt *v. t.* أَمَالَ . طَعَنَ ـَ

Timber *n.* خَشَبٌ

Time *n.* زَمَانٌ . وَقْتٌ مَرَّةٌ

Timely *ad.* فِي وَقْتِهِ . فِي مَحَلِّهِ

Time-piece *n.* سَاعَةٌ

Timid / **Timorous** } *a.* خَائِفٌ . جَبَانٌ

Timidity *n.* جَبَانَةٌ . حَيَاءٌ

Tin *n.* قَصْدِيرٌ . تَنَكٌ . صَفِيحٌ

Tiucture *n.* صِبْغَةٌ . لَوْنٌ

Tinder *n.* صُوفَانٌ

Tinge *v. t.* لَوَّنَ خَفِيفاً

Tingle *v. i.* تأَلَّمَ شَدِيداً

Tinker *n.* or *v. t.* سَنْكَرِيٌّ . اصْلَحَ أَوْعِيَة

Tinkle *v. i.* طَنَّ ـِ

Tinkling *n.* طَنِينٌ

Tinman / **Tinner** *n.* تَنْكَارِيٌّ

Tinsel *n.* or *a.* بَهْرَجٌ . لَامِعٌ

Tint *n.* لَوْنٌ خَفِيفٌ

Tiny *a.* صَغِيرٌ جِدًّا . زَهِيدٌ

Tip *n.* or *v. t.* طَرَفٌ . رَاسٌ . أَمَالَ

Tippler *n.* سِكِّيرٌ

Tipsy *a.* سَكْرَانُ

Tiptoe *n.* أَطْرَافُ أَصَابِعِ ٱلْقَدَمِ

Tiptop *n.* اعْلَاهُ . سَامٍ . غَايَةٌ فِي ٱلْجُودَةِ

Tirade *n.* شَتْمٌ

Tire *v. t.* or *n.* اتْعَبَ . طَبَانٌ

Tired *a.* مُتْعَبٌ

Tiresome *a.* مُتْعِبٌ . مُمِلٌّ

Tissue *n.* نَسِيجٌ

Tithe *v. t.* or *n.* عَشَّرَ . عشر

Title *n.* لَقَبٌ . عِنْوَانٌ . حَقٌّ

Titular *a.* بِٱلِاسْمِ فَقَطْ . اسْمِيٌّ

To *pr.* إِلَى . نَحْوَ . لِ

Toad *n.* نَوْعٌ مِنَ ٱلضِّفْدَعِ

Toadstool *n.* فُطْرٌ

Toast *v. t.* or *n.* حَمَّصَ . خُبْزٌ مُحَمَّصٌ

Tobacco *n.* تَبْغٌ . تُتُن . دُخَانٌ

To-day *n.* الْيَوْمُ

Toddle *v. i.* دَبَّ ـُ

Toddy *n.* شَرَابٌ مُسْكِرٌ

Toe *n.* اصْبَعُ ٱلْقَدَمِ

Together *ad.* مَعاً

Toil *v. i.* or *n.* تَعِبَ ـَ . تَعَبٌ . كَدٌّ

Toilet *n.* زِينَةٌ . لِبَاسٌ . مَائِدَةٌ لِلُّبْسِ

Toilsome *a.* مُتْعِبٌ . شَاقٌّ

Token *n.* تَذْكِرَةٌ . عَلَامَةٌ

Tolerable *a.* مُحْتَمَلٌ . مُعْتَدِلٌ

Tolerance / **Toleration** *n.* اِحْتِمَالٌ . تَسَامُحٌ

Tolerate *v. t.* أَبَاحَ . اِحْتَمَلَ

Toll *n.* or *v. t.* رَسْمٌ . دَقَّ

Tomahawk *n.* فَاسٌ حَرْبِيَّةٌ لِلْهُنُودِ

Tomato *n.* (بَنَدُورَةٌ . طَمَاطِمُ)

Tomb *n.* قَبْرٌ . ضَرِيحٌ

Tombstone *n.* حَجَرُ قَبْرٍ

Tome *n.* كِتَابٌ . مُجَلَّدٌ

To-morrow *n.* اَلْغَدُ

Ton *n.* وَزْنٌ = ٢٠٠٠ لِيبْرَا

Tone *n.* صَوْتٌ . نَغْمَةٌ

Tongs *n. pl.* مِلْقَطٌ

Tongue *n.* لِسَانٌ . لُغَةٌ

Tongue-tied *a.* مَعْقُودُ اللِّسَانِ

Tonic *a.* or *n.* مُقَوٍّ

To-night *n.* هٰذِهِ اللَّيْلَةَ

Tonnage *n.* وَزْنُ مَا تَسَعُهُ سَفِينَةٌ

Tonsil *n.* لَوْزَةُ الْحَلْقِ

Tonsure *n.* حَلْقُ قِمَّةِ الرَّأْسِ

Too *ad.* بِزِيَادَةٍ . أَيْضًا

Tool *n.* آلَةٌ . أَدَاةٌ

Tooth *n.* سِنٌّ . نَابٌ . ضِرْسٌ

Toothache *n.* وَجَعُ الأَسْنَانِ

Toothless *a.* بِلَا أَسْنَانٍ

Tooth-pick *n.* سِوَاكٌ

Toothsome *a.* لَذِيذٌ

Top *n.* قِمَّةٌ . سَطْحٌ . دُوَّامَةٌ . (نَحْلَةٌ)

Toper *n.* سِكِّيرٌ

Tophet *n.* اَلْجَحِيمُ

Topic *n.* مَوْضُوعٌ . مَبْحَثٌ

Topical *a.* مَحَلِّيٌّ . مَوْضُوعِيٌّ

Topmost *a.* اَلْأَعْلَى

Topography *n.* تَخْطِيطٌ . وَصْفٌ

Topple *v. i.* اِهْتَزَّ . اِنْقَلَبَ

Torch *n.* مِشْعَلٌ

Torment *n.* or *v. t.* عَذَابٌ . عَذَّبَ

Tormenter
Tormentor } *n.* مُعَذِّبٌ

Tornado *n.* زَوْبَعَةٌ

Torpedo *n.* لَغَمٌ بَحْرِيٌّ . فَتْرَةٌ (سَمَكَةٌ)

Torpid *a.* ثَقِيلُ الْحَرَكَةِ

Torpidity
Torpor } *n.* سُبَاتٌ . ثِقَلٌ

Torrent *n.* سَيْلٌ

Torrid *a.* حارٌّ جدا

Tortoise *n.* سُلَحْفَاةٌ ج سلاحف

Tortuous *a.* مُعَوَّجٌ

Torture *n.* عذابٌ . تَعْذِيبٌ

Toss *v. t.* or *i.* طرحَ ـ . انقلبَ

Total *a.* or *n.* كُلِّيٌّ . جُمْلَةٌ . مَجْمُوعٌ

Totality *n.* كُلِّيَّةٌ . جُمْلَةٌ

Totally *ad.* بِأَسْرِهِ . جُمْلَةً

Totter *v. i.* اهتزَّ . همَّ بالسقوطِ

Touch *v. i.* مسَّ ـ . لمسَ ـ

Touching *a.* لامِسٌ . مؤثِّرٌ

Touchy *a.* سَرِيعُ الْغَيْظِ

Tough *a.* صُلْبٌ . قاسٍ

Toughen *v. t.* صلَّبَ . قسَّى

Tour *n.* سِيَاحَةٌ . سَفْرَةٌ

Tourist *n.* سائحٌ . مُسافِرٌ

Tournament *n.* تَطَاعُنٌ لعِبِيٌّ

Tow *n.* or *v. t.* مُشَاقَةُ الْكَتَّانِ . جرَّ

Toward
Towards } *prep.* إِلَى . نَحْوَ

Towel *n.* مِنْشَفَةٌ

Tower *n.* or *v. t.* بُرْجٌ . ارتفعَ

Towering *a.* عالٍ . مُرْتَفِعٌ

Tow-line *n.* حَبْلُ الْجَرِّ (لسفينةٍ)

Town *n.* بَلْدَةٌ . مدينةٌ

Township *n.* بَلْدَةٌ مَعَ ضواحيها

Toxicology *n.* عِلْمُ السُّمُومِ

Toy *n.* or *v. t.* لُعْبَةٌ . لاعبَ . عَبِثَ

Trace *v. t.* رَسَمَ ـ . استقصى

Trace *n.*	أثرٌ. علامةٌ. رَسمٌ
Traces *n. pl.*	سُيُورُ الخَيلِ
Traceable *a.*	مايُستَدلُّ عليهِ
Track *v. t.*	تأثَّرَ. اقتفى
Track *n.*	مَسْلَكٌ. اثرٌ. اثرُ قدمٍ
Trackless *a.*	لا مَسْلَكَ فيهِ ولا أَثَرَ
Tract *n.*	إقليمٌ. مقالةٌ
Tractable *a.*	طوعٌ. طائعٌ
Tractability *n.*	طَوعيَّةٌ. انقيادٌ
Traction *n.*	جذبٌ. مدٌّ. جرٌّ
Trade *n.* or *v. i.*	تجارةٌ. حرفةٌ. تاجرَ
Trade-mark *n.*	علامةُ بضائعٍ
Trader / **Tradesman** *n.*	تاجرٌ ج تُجارٌ
Tradition *n.*	تقليدٌ. حديثٌ
Traditional / **Traditionary** *n.*	تقليديٌّ
Traduce *v. t.*	نمَّ ـُـ عابَ ـِـ
Traffic *n.*	تجارةٌ. مُعاملةٌ
Tragedy *n.*	رِوايةٌ او حادثةٌ هائلةٌ
Tragic / **Tragical** *a.*	هائلٌ. فظيعٌ
Trail *v. t.* or *i.*	جرَّ ـُـ انسحبَ
Train *v. t.*	هذَّبَ. ادَّبَ
Trait *n.*	صِفةٌ. علامةُ خُلقٍ
Traitor *n.* / **Traitorous** *a.*	خائنٌ
Trammel *v. t.* or *n.*	عاقَ. أوثقَ. عائقٌ
Trample *v. t.*	داسَ ـُـ ازدرى بِ
Trance *n.*	غيبةٌ
Tranquil *a.*	هادئٌ. مُستريحٌ
Tranquilize / **Tranquillize** *v. t.*	هدَّأ. أمَّنَ
Tranquillity *n.*	هدوءٌ
Transact *v. t.*	قضى ـِـ. أجرى
Transaction *n.*	عملٌ. امرٌ
Transcend *v. t.*	فاقَ ـُـ. جاوزَ
Transcendent *a.*	فائقٌ
Transcribe *v. t.*	نسخَ ـَـ. نقلَ ـُـ
Transcript *n.*	نسخةٌ
Transcription *n.*	نسخٌ

Transfer *v. t.* or *n.* نَقَلَ ـُ . نَقْلٌ

Transferable *a.* قَابِلُ ٱلنَّقْلِ أَوِ ٱلتَّحْوِيلِ

Transference *n.* نَقْلٌ. تَحْوِيلٌ

Transfigure *v. t.* جَلَّى. غَيَّرَ ٱلشَّكْلَ

Transfix *v. t.* خَرَقَ ـِ . انْفَذَ فِي

Transform *v. t.* غَيَّرَ . حَوَّلَ

Transformation *n.* تَغْيِيرٌ

Transgress *v. t.* خَالَفَ . تَعَدَّى

Transgression *n.* تَعَدٍّ . خَطِيَّةٌ

Transgressor *n.* خَاطِئٌ . مُخَالِفٌ

Tranship *v. t.* نَقَلَ مِنْ سَفِينَةٍ إِلَى اخْرَى

Transient *a.* وَقْتِيٌّ . زَائِلٌ

Transit *n.* عُبُورٌ . إِجْتِيَازٌ

Transition *n.* عُبُورٌ . انْتِقَالٌ

Transitive *a.* مُتَعَدٍّ (فعل)

Transitory *a.* وَقْتِيٌّ . زَائِلٌ

Translatable *a.* قَابِلُ ٱلتَّرْجَمَةِ

Translate *v.* تَرْجَمَ . نَقَلَ ـُ

Translation *n.* تَرْجَمَةٌ . نَقْلٌ

Translator *n.* مُتَرْجِمٌ

Translucent *a.* شَفَّافٌ بَعْضَ ٱلشُّفُوفِ

Transmarine *a.* مَا وَرَاءَ ٱلْبَحْرِ

Transmigrate *v. t.* هَاجَرَ . انْتَقَلَ

Transmigration *n.* مُهَاجَرَةٌ . تَنَاسُخٌ

Transmission *n.* إِرْسَالٌ . انْفَاذٌ

Transmit *v. t.* أَرْسَلَ . أَنْفَذَ إِلَى

Transmutation *n.* تَحْوِيلٌ . تَحَوُّلٌ

Transparency *n.* شُفُوفٌ

Transparent *a.* شَفَّافٌ . وَاضِحٌ

Transpire *v. i.* حَدَثَ ـُ . ذَاعَ ـِ

Transplant *v. t.* نَقَلَ ـُ غَرْسًا

Transport *n.* نَقْلٌ . سَفِينَةُ نَقْلٍ . طَرَبٌ

Transport *v. t.* نَقَلَ ـُ . أَبْهَجَ

Transportation *n.* نَقْلٌ . نَفْيٌ

Transpose *v. t.* بَدَّلَ . عَكَسَ ـِ

Transposition *n.* تَبْدِيلُ ٱلْمَكَانِ

Transverse *a.*	مُعارِضٌ
Trap *n.* or *v. t.*	مَصِيدَةٌ . صادَ بها
Trapdoor *n.*	بابٌ مَخْفِيٌّ
Trapezium *n.*	مُربعٌ منحَرِفٌ
Trappings *n. pl.*	عدة زِينَةٍ لِلْخَيْلِ خاصةً
Trash *n.*	نُفَايَةٌ . سَقَط
Trashy *a.*	باطلٌ . خَسِيسٌ
Travail *v.i.* or *n.*	تَعِبَ ـَ . تمَخَّضَ مَخَاضٌ
Travel *v. i.*	سافَرَ . سَاحَ ـ
Traveller *n.*	مُسافِرٌ . سائِحٌ
Traverse *v. t.*	قَطَعَ ـ . عارَض
Tray *n.*	طبقٌ . صِينِيةٌ
Treacherous *a.*	خائِنٌ . غادِرٌ
Treachery *n.*	خيانَةٌ ، غَدْرٌ
Treacle *n.*	دُبْسٌ
Tread *v. i.* (trod)	دَاسَ ـ
Treason *n.*	خِيانَةٌ
Treasonable *a.*	ذُو خِيانَةٍ
Treasure *n.* or *v. t.*	كَنْزٌ . ذَخرَ ـَ
Treasurer *n.*	أَمِينُ الصُنْدُوقِ . خازِنٌ
Treasury *n.*	خزنة . بيْتُ المَالِ
Treat *v. t.* or *i.*	عَامَلَ. بَحَثَ ـَ. عالَجَ
Treatise *n.*	مقالةٌ . رِسَالَة
Treatment *n.*	معامَلَةٌ . معَالجَةٌ
Treaty *n.*	معَاهَدَةٌ
Treble *a.* or *v. t.* or *i.*	مثلَّثٌ . ثَلث َ. تثَلَّثَ
Tree *n.*	شَجَرَةٌ
Trellis *n.*	عَرِيشٌ . شُبَاكٌ
Tremble *v. i.*	إرتجفَ . إرْتعدَ
Tremendous *a.*	عظِيمٌ . هائِلٌ
Tremor *n.*	قشعرِيرَةٌ . رَجفَةٌ
Tremulous *a.*	مُرتجِفٌ . مُرْتعشٌ
Trench *n.*	خندق ج خنَادِقُ
Trepidation *n.*	إرتجافٌ . فزَعٌ
Trespass *v. i.* or *n.*	تعدى . أخطأ . تَعَدٍّ
Tress *n.*	خُصْلَةٌ . ضفيرَةٌ

Triad *n.* إتحاد ثلثة في واحد

Trial *n.* تجربة . محاكمة . بلية

Triangle *n.* مثلث

Triangular *a.* مثلث الشكل

Tribe *n.* قبيلة . سبط . جنس

Tribulation *n.* ضيق . شدة

Tribunal *n.* محكمة . مجلس . ديوان

Tribune *n.* حاكم روماني . منبر

Tributary *a.* تحت الجزية . فرع نهر

Tribute *n.* جزية . خراج

Trice *n.* لحظة . لمحة

Trick *n.* حيلة . مكيدة

Trickery *n.* إحتيال . خداع

Trickish *a.* محتال . غشاش

Trickle *v. i.* نض . نز

Tri-coloured *a.* ذو ثلاثة ألوان

Trident *n.* صولجان ذو ثلث شوكات

Tridunnial *a.* كل ثلاث سنين

Trifle *n.* or *v. t.* شيء زهيد . عبث

Trifling *n.* زهيد ما لا يعتبر . عبث

Triform *a.* مثلث الشكل

Trigger *n.* زناد البندقية

Trigonometry *n.* علم المثلثات

Trilateral *a.* ذو ثلثة جوانب

Triliteral *a.* ذو ثلثة أحرف

Trill *n.* or *v. t.* تطريب . طرب

Trim *a.* or *v. t.* أنيق . قص . زين

Trimming *n.* زينة (خرج)

Trinity *n.* ثالوث

Trinket *n.* حلية . شيء زهيد

Trio *n.* ثلثة متحدون

Trip *v. i.* مشى بخفة . عثر . كبا

Trip *n.* عثرة . سفرة

Triple *a.* مثلث . ثلاثي

Triplet *n.* ثلثة أبيات شعر على قافية واحدة

Tripod *n.* ذو ثلاث قوائم

Trisyllabic *a.* / **Trisyllable** *n.* } ذات ثلثة مقاطع

Trite *a.* كثير الاستعمال. مبتذل

Triumph *n.* or *v. i.* نصرة. إنتصر

Triumphal / **Triumphant** } *a.* منصور. نصري

Triumvirate *n.* حكم ثلثة

Triune *n.* مثلث الأقانيم. ثالوثي

Trivial *a.* زهيد. حقير

Trodden *pp. of* **tread.** مدوس

Troop *n.* جماعة. كتيبة

Trooper *n.* جندي. فارس

Trophy *n.* علامة نصرة

Tropic *n.* منطقة حارة

Tropical *a.* مختص بالمنطقة الحارة

Trot *v. i.* or *n.* خب ـُ . خبب

Trouble *v. t.* or *n.* كدر. أزعج. ضيق

Troublesome *a.* مكدر. شاق

Troublous *a.* مضطرب. شاق

Trough *n.* حوض

Trousers / **Trowsers** } *n.* سراويل

Trousseau *n.* جهاز عروس

Trowel *n.* ملعقة البناء

Truant *a.* or *n.* كسلان. مهمل الواجبات

Truce *n.* هدنة

Trudge *v. i.* مشى ـِ تعب في المشي

True *a.* حقيقي. أكيد. امين. صحيح

Truly *ad.* حقا

Trump / **Trumpet** } *n.* بوق

Trumpery *n.* خداع. عبث

Trumpeter *n.* بواق

Truncate / **Truncated** } *a.* أقطع مجزوم

Trunk *n.* صندوق. ساق. خرطوم

Trust *n.* ثقة. وديعة. إئتمان

Trust *v. i.* or *t.* وثق ـِ صدق

Trustee *n.* وكيل. أمين

Trustful *a.* واثق

Trustiness *n.* أمانة

Trusty / **Trustworthy** *a.* أمين. موثوق به

Truth *n.* حق. صدق. صواب

Truthful *a.* صادق

Try *v. t.* or *i.* جرب. حاول

Trying *a.* مجرب. شاق. مكدر

Tub *n.* مرجل

Tube *n.* انبوبة

Tubercle *n.* عجرة. درنة

Tubercular / **Tuberculous** *a.* درني

Tuck *n.* or *v. t.* ثنية. طية. طوى ـ

Tuesday *n.* يوم الثلاثاء

Tuft *n.* خصلة. قنبرة

Tug *v. t.* or *i.* شد ـ. جذب ـ

Tug-boat *n.* وابور جرار

Tuition *n.* اجرة تعليم

Tulip *n.* ضرب من الزنبق

Tumble *v. i.* سقط ـ هبط ـ تقلب

Tumbler *n.* قدح ج اقداح

Tumid *a.* منتفخ. وارم

Tumour *n.* ورم. خراج

Tumult *n.* شغب. ضجة. جلبة

Tumultuary / **Tumultuous** *a.* شاغب

Tune *n.* or *v. t.* نغمة. لحن. أوقع

Tunnel *n.* or *v. t.* سرداب. سرب. حفره

Turban *n.* عمامة. لفة

Turbid *a.* عكر. كدر

Turbulence / **Turbulency** *n.* تشويش. شغب

Turbulent *a.* مشاغب. مهيج

Turf *n.* ارض كثيرة الكلإ

Turgid *a.* وارم. منتفخ

Turkey *n.* تركيا. ديك رومي

Turquoise *n.* فيروز

Turmoil *n.* اضطراب. شغب

Turn *v. t.* or *i.* خرط ـ. أدار. دار ـ

Turn *n.* دورة. برمة

Turner *n.* خراط

Turnip *n.*	لِفْتٌ
Turnkey *n.*	بَوَّابُ سِجْنٍ
Turpentine *n.*	رَاتِينَجُ ٱلصَّنَوْبَرِ
Turpitude *n.*	قَبَاحَةٌ
Turret *n.*	بُرْجٌ
Turreted *a.*	ذُو أَبْرَاجٍ
Turtle *n.*	سُلَحْفَاةٌ
Turtledove *n.*	حَمَامَةٌ . يَمَامَةٌ
Tusk *n.*	نَابٌ ج أَنْيَابٌ
Tussle *n.*	مُصَارَعَةٌ
Tutelage *n.*	حِمَايَةٌ . وَكَالَةٌ
Tutelar / Tutelary } *a.*	حَافِظٌ . مُحَامٍ
Tutor *n.*	مُعَلِّمٌ . مُهَذِّبٌ
Twain *n.*	إِثْنَانِ م إِثْنَتَانِ
Twang *v. i.* or *n.*	رَنَّ ـِ . رَنِينٌ
Tweezers *n. pl.*	مِلْقَطٌ صَغِيرٌ
Twelfth *a.*	أَلثَّانِي عَشَرَ
Twelve *a.*	إِثْنَا عَشَرَ وَٱثْنَتَا عَشْرَةَ
Twentieth *a.*	ٱلْعِشْرُونَ
Twenty *a.*	عِشْرُونَ
Twice *ad.*	مَرَّتَيْنِ
Twig *n.*	عُسْلُوجٌ ج عَسَالِيجُ
Twilight *n.*	شَفَقٌ
Twin *n.*	تَوْأَمٌ
Twine *n.* or *v. i.*	خَيْطُ دَوْبَارَةٍ . فَتَلَ ـِ
Twinge *v. i.* or *n.*	تَأَلَّمَ . أَلَمٌ
Twinkle *v. i.*	تَلَأْلَأَ . لَمَعَ ـَ
Twinkle / Twinkling } *n.*	لَأْلَأَةٌ . لَمَعَانٌ
Twirl *v. t.* or *i.*	بَرَمَ ـُ دَوَّرَ . دَارَ
Twist *v. t.*	فَتَلَ ـِ . جَدَلَ ـُ ـِ . حَرَّفَ
Twitch *v. t.* or *n.*	شَدَّ بِهِ بَغْتَةً
Twitter *v. i.*	غَرَّدَ
Two *a.*	إِثْنَانِ م إِثْنَتَانِ
Two-edged *a.*	ذُو حَدَّيْنِ
Twofold *a.*	مُثَنًّى . مُضَاعَفٌ
Tympanum *n.*	طَبْلَةُ ٱلْأُذُنِ

Type *n.* رَمْزٌ . صُورَةٌ . حَرْفُ طَبْعٍ

Typhoid *a.* or *n.* اَلْحُمَّى ٱلتِّيفُودِيَّةُ

Typhus *a.* or *n.* اَلْحُمَّى ٱلتِّيفُوسِيَةُ

Typical *a.* رَمْزِيٌّ . مِثَالِيٌّ

Typify *v. t.* رَمَزَ . اشَارَ إِلى

Typographical *a.* منوطٌ بِالطَّبْعِ

Typography *n.* صِنَاعَة ٱلطَّبْعِ

Tyrannical, Tyrannic *a.* ظَالِمٌ . طَاغٍ

Tyrannize *v. t.* ظَلَمَ

Tyranny *n.* ظُلْمٌ . بَغْي

Tyrant *n.* ظَالِمٌ . طَاغٍ . بَاغٍ

U

Ubiquity *n.* حُضُورٌ فِي كُلِّ مَكَان

Udder *n.* ضَرْعٌ ج ضُرُوعٌ

Ugliness *n.* بَشَاعَةٌ . قَبَاحَةُ ٱلْمَنْظَرِ

Ugly *a.* قَبِيحُ ٱلْمَنْظَرِ

Ulcer *n.* قُرْحَةٌ

Ulcerate *v. i.* تَقَرَّحَ

Ulceration *n.* تَقَرُّحٌ

Ulna *n.* زَنْدٌ

Ulterior *a.* أَبْعَدُ . وَرَآءَ

Ultimate *a.* الأَبْعَدُ . نِهَائِيٌّ

Ultimatum *n.* قَرَارٌ نِهَائِيٌّ

Ultra *a.* مُفْرِطٌ . مُتَجَاوِزُ ٱلْحَدِّ

Umbel *n.* صِيوَانُ أَزْهَارٍ

Umbelliferous *a.* صِيوَانِيٌّ

Umbrage *n.* غَيْظٌ . حِقْدٌ

Umbrageous *a.* ظَلِيلٌ

Umbrella *n.* شَمْسِيَّةٌ

Umpire *n.* فَيْصَلٌ . حَكَمٌ

Un حرف نفي في التركيب

Unable *a.* غير قادر

Unabridged *a.* غير مختصر . مطوّل

Unacceptable *a.* غير مقبول

Unaccommodating *a.* غير مساهل

Unaccompanied *a.* غير مرافق

Unaccountable *a.* غير مسؤول . غير مفهوم

Unaccustomed *a.* غير معتاد

Unacknowledged *a.* غير مسلم به

Unacquainted *a.* غير عارف به

Unadvisable *a.* غير موافق

Unaffected *a.* غير مؤثر

Unaided *a.* غير مساعد . وحده

Unalterable *a.* مالا يتغير . ثابت

Unamiable *a.* غير لطيف . شرس

Unanimity *n.* إجماع الرأي

Unanimou *a.* مجمع الرأي

Unanswerable *a.* مالا يرد عليه

Unappreciated *a.* غير معتبر

Unapproachable *a.* مالا يدنى منه

Unappropriated *a.* غير مخصص

Unarmed *a.* غير متسلح

Unasked *a.* غير مطلوب

Unaspiring *a.* غير طالب الرفعة

Unassailable *a.* لا يهاجم . منيع

Unassisted *a.* غير مساعد . وحده

Unassuming *a.* غير معجب . متواضع

Unattainable *a.* لا يحصل

Unattended *a.* غير مرافق . وحده

Unauthorised *a.* غير مباح

Unavailing *a.* غير مفيد . عبث

Unavoidable *a.* مالا بد منه

Unaware *a.* غير عارف

Unawares *ad.* على غفلة

Unbar *v. t.* رفع المغلاق . فتح

Unbecoming *a.* غيرُ لائقٍ

Unbelief *n.* عدمُ إيمانٍ أوْ تصديقٍ

Unbeliever *n.* / **Unbelieving** *a.* غيرُ مؤمنٍ

Unbending *a.* متصلِّبٌ

Unbiassed *a.* غيرُ متحاملٍ أوْ متحزّبٍ

Unbind *a.* حلَّ . فكَّ

Unblemished *a.* بلا عيبٍ

Unblushing *a.* بلا حياءٍ . وقحٌ

Unbolt *v. t.* فتحَ المغلاقَ

Unborn *a.* غيرُ مولودٍ

Unbosom *v. t.* صرّحَ بهِ . أقرَّ

Unbounded *a.* غيرُ محدودٍ

Unbridle *v. i.* فكَّ اللجامَ . أطلقَ

Unbroken *a.* غيرُ منقطعٍ

Unbuckle *v. t.* فكَّ الإبزيمَ

Unburden *v. t.* نزعَ حملاً . أراحَ

Unburied *a.* غيرُ مدفونٍ

Unbutton *v. t.* فكَّ الأزرارَ

Uncanonical *a.* غيرُ قانونيّ

Unceasing *a.* غيرُ منقطعٍ . دائمٌ

Unceremonious *a.* عديمُ التكليفِ

Uncertain *a.* غيرُ مؤكدٍ . مشكوكٌ فيهِ

Uncertainty *n.* عدمُ يقينٍ . شكٌّ

Unchain *v. t.* فكَّ القيدَ أوْ الزنجيرَ

Unchangeable / **Unchanging** *a.* غيرُ متغيّرٍ

Uncharitable *a.* عديمُ المحبّةِ

Unchaste *a.* غيرُ عفيفٍ . نجسٌ

Unchristian *a.* مخالفُ المسيحيّةِ

Uncivil *a.* غيرُ أنيسٍ . فظٌّ

Uncivilized *a.* غيرُ متمدّنٍ

Uncle *n.* عمٌّ . خالٌ

Unclean *a.* غيرُ طاهرٍ . نجسٌ

Uncleanness *n.* نجاسة

Unclose *v. t.* فتحَ . كشفَ

Uncoil *v. t.* فكَّ الملتفَّ . أرخى

Uncomely *a.* غيرُ كيّسٍ أوْ ظريفٍ

Uncomfortable *a.* غيرُ مستريحٍ . شاقٌّ

Uncommon *a.* غيرُ معهودٍ . نادِرٌ

Uncomplaining *a.* غيرُ شاكٍ

Uncompromising *a.* غيرُ متراضٍ . عنيدٌ

Unconcern *n.* عدمُ اكتراثٍ

Unconditional *a.* بلا شرطٍ . مطلقٌ

Uncongenial *a.* غيرُ مؤانِسٍ

Unconqurable *a.* لا يغلبُ

Unconscious *a.* غيرُ شاعرٍ او عالمٍ

Unconsciousness *n.* غيبةٌ

Unconstitutional *a.* مخالِفُ النِّظام

Uncontrollable / **Uncontrolled** } *a.* لا يضبط

Unconverted *a.* غيرُ تائبٍ أوْ متغيّرٍ

Uncork *v. t.* أخرجَ السِّدادَ

Uncorrupt / **Uncorrupted** } *a.* غيرُ فاسِدٍ . غيرُ مرتشٍ

Uncounted *a.* غيرُ معدودٍ

Uncourteous *a.* عديمُ الانس . فظ

Uncouth *a.* غيرُ مألوفٍ . أخرقُ

Uncover *v. t.* كشفَ ـِ . فتحَ ـَ

Unction *n.* مَسْحةٌ

Unctuous *a.* دِهنٌ . ذو زيتٍ

Uncultivated *a.* غيرُ محروثٍ . غيرُ مهذَّب

Uncut *a.* غيرُ مقصوصٍ أوْ مقطوعٍ

Undaunted *a.* جسورٌ . غيرُ خائفٍ

Undeceive *v. t.* أزالَ الغرورَ والغلط

Undecided *a.* مترددٌ

Undefiled *a.* غيرُ مدنسٍ . طاهرٌ

Undefined *a.* غيرُ محدودٍ

Undeniable *a.* لا يُنكَرُ

Under *prep.* تحتَ

Underbid *v. i.* عرضَ أقلّ

Underbrush *n.* أنجمٌ تحتَ شجرٍ

Undercurrent *n.* مجرى تحتَ الماء

Undergo *v. i.* إحتملَ . قاسى

Undergraduate *n.* تلميذ مدرسةٍ

Underground *v.* تحتَ الارض

Undergrowth *n.* شجيرات تحت شجر

Underhand / Underhanded *a.* مستور. غادر

Underlie *v. t.* وجد تحت

Underline *v. t.* خطّ تحت السطر

Underling *n.* شخص دون. أجير

Undermine *v. t.* حفر تحت. نقض

Underneath *ad.* تحت

Underpinning *n.* حجارة الأساس

Underrate *v. t.* إستصغر. إستخفّ

Underscore *v. t.* رسم تحته خطًّا

Undersell *v. t.* باع بأقلّ ثمن

Understand *v. t.* فهم. أدرك

Understanding *n.* ذهن. إدراك

Undertake *v. t.* تعاطى. إلتزم

Undertaker *n.* مدبّر الدفن

Undertaking *n.* مسعى. مشروع

Undertone *n.* صوت منخفض

Undervalue *v. t.* بخس. إستخفّ به

Undeserved *a.* غير مستحقّ

Undeserving *a.* غير مستحقّ

Undesigned *a.* غير مقصود. إتّفاقيّ

Undesirable *a.* غير شهيّ أو مرغوب فيه

Undeviating *a.* غير منحرف. مستقيم

Undignified *a.* غير لائق الشأن

Undisguisied *a.* غير مستتر. ظاهر

Undismayed *a.* غير خائف

Undivided *a.* غير منقسم. متحد

Undo *v. t.* حلّ. أبطل. عكس

Undone *a.* معطّل. هالك

Undoubted *a.* لا ريب فيه. مقرّر

Undress *v. t.* نزع الثياب. خلع

Undue *a.* مفرط. زائد

Undulated *a.* متموّج. غير مستوٍ

Undulation *n.* تموّج

Unduly *ad.* بزيادة. في غير محلّه

Undutiful *a.* غير مطيع

Undying *a.* غير مائت . خالد

Unearth *v. t.* نبش ـُ . كشف ـِ

Unearthly *n.* غير طبيعي

Uneasiness *n.* إضطراب . همّ . قلق

Uneasy *a.* غير مستريح . مهتمّ

Uneducated *a.* غير مهذب . أُمّي

Unembarrassed *a.* غير مرتبك

Unending *a.* غير متناهٍ

Unengaged *a.* غير مربوط . متفرّغ

Unenlightened *a.* جاهل

Unenviable *a.* غير شهيّ . مكروه

Unequal *a.* غير متساوٍ . عاجز

Unequalled *a.* فريد . فائق

Unequivocal *a.* غير مبهم . صريح

Unerring *a.* غير مخطىء . مصيب

Uneven *a.* غير مستوٍ

Unevenness *n.* عدم استواء

Unexpected *a.* غير منتظر

Unexpressed *a.* غير منطوق به

Unfaded / **Unfading** *a.* غير ذابل

Unfailing *a.* غير منقضٍ . باقٍ

Unfair *a.* غير عادل

Unfairness *n.* عدم إنصاف

Unfaithful *n.* غير أمين

Unfaithfulness *n.* عدم امانة

Unfashionable *a.* خلاف الزيّ

Unfasten *v. t.* فكّ ـُ . حلّ ـُ

Unfathomable *a.* ما لا يُسبَر

Unfavourable *a.* مخالف المطلوب

Unfeeling *a.* غير متأثر . بلا رحمة

Unfeigned *a.* بلا رياء . مخلص

Unfelt *a.* غير مشعور به

Unfilial *a.* غير لائق بالبنين

Unfinished *a.* غير متمم أو منجز

Unfit *a.* غير لائق . غير أهل

Unfold *v. t.* نشر ـُ كشف ـِ فسّر

Unforeseen *a.* غيرُ منتظَرٍ

Unforetold *a.* غيرُ مُخبَرٍ بهِ

Unforgiven *a.* غيرُ مغفور

Unfortunate *a.* بخِسٌ . منكودُ الحظِ

Unfounded *a.* بلا اساسٍ

Unfrequent *a.* نادِرٌ

Unfrequented *a.* غيرُ مُترَدَّدٍ إليْهِ

Unfriendly *a.* غيرُ ودُودٍ . خَصِيمٌ

Unfruitful *a.* غيرُ مثمِرٍ

Unfurl *v. t.* نَشَرَ ـُ

Ungainly *a.* أخرق

Ungenerous *a.* غيرُ كريمٍ . شَحِيحٌ

Ungentlemanly *a.* غيرُ أديبٍ

Ungodliness *n.* عدمُ تقوى . شَرٌّ

Ungodly *a.* عدِيمُ التقوى . شِرِّيرٌ

Ungovernable *a.* ما لا يُضبَطُ

Ungraceful *a.* غيرُ ظريفٍ. أخرَق

Ungracious *a.* غير لطيفٍ .سَيِّئٌ

Ungrammatical *a.* مُخالِفٌ لِعِلمِ النَّحْوِ

Ungrateful *a.* غيرُ شكورٍ. كنودٌ

Ungratefulness *n.* عدمُ الشكرِ

Ungrounded *a.* ما لا أصلَ لهُ

Unguarded *a.* غيرُ مصونٍ . متغافِلٌ

Unguent *n.* دهنٌ. مرهمٌ

Unhallowed *a.* غيرُ مقدَسٍ. مُحرَّمٌ

Unhappiness *n.* غمٌّ . كدَرٌ

Unhappy *a.* مغمومٌ . تعيسٌ

Unharness *v. i.* نزعَ عدَّةَ الخيلِ

Unhealthful, **Unhealthy** *a.* غيرُ موافِقٍ الصحةَ . وَخِيمٌ

Unheard *a.* غيرُ مسموعٍ

Unheeded *a.* غيرُ مُكترَثٍ لهُ

Unhesitating *a.* غيرُ مترَدِّدٍ

Unhinge *v. t.* خلَعَ ـَ

Unhitch *v. t.* فكَّ ـُ حلَّ ـُ

Unholy *a.* غيرُ مقدسٍ . دَنِسٌ

Unhonoured *a.* غَيْرُ مُكَرَّمٍ
Unhook *v. t.* فَكَّ ـُ
Unhorse *v. t.* رَمَى عَنِ ٱلْفَرَسِ
Unhurt *a.* غَيْرُ مُؤْذًى. سَلِيمٌ
Unicorn *n.* وَحِيدُ ٱلْقَرْنِ
Uniform *a.*, عَلَى نَسَقٍ وَاحِدٍ
Uniform *n.* بِذْلَةٌ رَسْمِيَّةٌ
Uniformity *n.* وَحْدَةُ ٱلشَّكْلِ أَوِ ٱلنِّظَامِ
Unimpeachable *a.* مَا لَا يُعَابُ
Unimportant *a.* غَيْرُ مُهِمٍّ
Unimproving *a.* غَيْرُ مُتَقَدِّمٍ
Uninhabitable *a.* مَالَا يُسْكَنُ
Unintelligible *a.* مَالَا يُفْهَمُ
Unintended / **Unintentional** *a.* غَيْرُ مَقْصُودٍ
Uninteresting *a.* غَيْرُ لَذِيذٍ. مُمِلٌّ
Uninterrupted *a.* غَيْرُ مُنْقَطِعٍ
Uninvited *a.* غَيْرُ مَدْعُوٍّ. طُفَيْلِي
Union *n.* إِتِّحَادٌ. ضَمٌّ صِلَة
Unionist *n.* مُرِيدُ ٱلِٱتِّحَادِ
Unique *a.* فَرِيدٌ. وَحِيدٌ
Unison *n.* إِتِّفَاقُ ٱلْأَصْوَاتِ
Unit *n.* فَرْدٌ. وَاحِدٌ
Unitarian *n.* مُوَحِّدٌ. مُنْكِرُ ٱلثَّالُوثِ
Unite *v.t.* or *i.* ضَمَّ ـُ. وَصَلَ. إِتَّحَدَ
United *a.* مُتَّحِدٌ. مُتَّصِلٌ
Unity *n.* وَحْدَانِيَّةٌ. وَحْدَةٌ
Univalve *n.* / **Univalvular** *a.* ذُو مِصْرَاعٍ وَاحِدٍ
Universal *a.* عَامٌّ. شَامِلٌ
Universalist *n.* ٱلْقَائِلُ بِخَلَاصِ ٱلْجَمِيعِ
Universality *n.* عُمُومِيَّةٌ. كُلِّيَّةٌ
Universe *n.* ٱلْكَوْنُ
University *n.* مَدْرَسَةٌ جَامِعَةٌ
Unjust *a.* غَيْرُ عَادِلٍ. ظَالِمٌ
Unjustifiable *a.* مَالَا يُبَرَّرُ وَيُعْذَرُ
Unkind *a.* عَدِيمُ ٱلْمَعْرُوفِ. مُسِيءٌ
Unkindness *n.* إِسَاءَةٌ

Unknowingly *ad.* سهواً . غفلةً

Unknown *a.* غير معروفٍ . مجهولٌ

Unlace *v. t.* حلّ الشريط

Uniade *v. i.* فرّغ مركباً

Unlawful *a.* غير شرعيٍّ أو جائزٍ

Unlearn *v. t.* تعلّم خلافه . نسي

Unlearned *a.* أُمّيٌّ . مَنْسِيٌّ

Unleavened *a.* غير مختمرٍ . فطيرٌ

Unless *cong.* مالم . لولم . إن لم

Unlettered *a.* أُمّي

Unlike *a.* غير مشابهٍ . مخالفٌ

Unlikely *ad.* بعيد الوقوع

Unlikeness *n.* عدم مشابهةٍ

Unlimited *a.* غير محدودٍ

Unload *v. t.* حطّ الحمل . فرّغه

Unlock *v. t.* فتح قفلاً

Unloveliness *n.* عدم جمالٍ أو لطفٍ

Unlovely *a.* غير جميلٍ . غير محبوبٍ

Unlucky *a.* نحسٌ . مشؤومٌ

Unman *v. t.* أوهن . خوّف

Unmanageable *a.* مالا يُضبط

Unmanly *a.* قليل المروءة . خنثٌ

Unmannered / Unmannerly *a.* قليل الأدب

Unmarried *a.* عازبٌ

Unmask *v. t.* كشف الستار

Unmeaning *a.* بلا معنًى

Unmerciful *a.* بلا شفقةٍ

Unmerited *a.* غير مستوجبٍ

Unmindful *a.* متغافلٌ

Unmingled *a.* غير ممزوجٍ . صرفٌ

Unmitigated *a.* غير ملطفٍ . محضٌ

Unmotherly *a.* مخالفٌ لصفة الأمّ

Unmurmuring *a.* غير متذمّرٍ

Unmusical *a.* غير مطربٍ

Unnatural *a.* غير طبيعيٍّ

Unnecessary *a.* غير لازمٍ

Unneighbourly a. مخالِفُ حقِ القَرِيب

Unnerve v. t. أوْهَنَ

Unnumbered a. غيرُ معدودٍ

Unobjectionable a. ما لا يُعتَرَضُ عليهِ

Unobservable a. ما لا يُلاحَظ

Unobserving a. غيرُ ملاحِظٍ أو منتبهٍ

Unobtrusive a. غيرُ فضوليّ

Unoccupied a. غيرُ مشغولٍ . فارغٌ

Unoffending a. غيرُ مُكدِرٍ

Unofficial a. غيرُ رسميّ

Unostentatious a. غيرُ متفاخرٍ

Unpack v. i. فكَّ المحزومَ أو المعبَّى

Unpaid a. غيرُ مدفوعٍ

Unpalatable a. غيرُ لذيذٍ

Unparalleled a. لا مثيلَ لهُ

Unpardonable a. لا يُغفَرُ

Unparliamentary a. مخالِفُ قانونِ مجلسٍ

Unphilosophical a. مخالِفُ الفلسفةِ

Unpitied a. غيرُ مشفوقٍ عليهِ

Unpitying a. غيرُ شفوقٍ

Unpleasant a. غيرُ مرْضٍ . كريهٌ

Unpleasantness a. كدَرٌ

Unpoetical a. عديمُ روحِ الشعرِ

Unpolished a. غيرُ مصقولٍ أو مهذَّبٍ

Unpolite a. غيرُ أديبٍ

Unpolluted a. غيرُ مفسدٍ . طاهرٌ

Unpopular a. غيرُ مقبولٍ عندَ الناسِ

Unprecedented a. لا سابقَ لهُ

Unprejudiced a. خالٍ من الغَرَضِ

Unpremeditated a. غيرُ مقصودٍ

Unprepared a. غيرُ مُستعِدٍ

Unpretending a. متواضِعٌ . بسيطٌ

Unprincipled a. غيرُ مُراعي الحَقِّ

Unprinted a. غيرُ مطبوعٍ

Unproductive a. غيرُ مثمرٍ . عقيمٌ

Unprofitable a. غيرُ مربحٍ أو مفيدٍ

Unpromising *a.* مالا أمَلَ فيهِ

Unpropitious *a.* غَيْرُ مُوَافِقٍ

Unprotected *a.* غَيْرُ مَصُونٍ

Unpublished *a.* غَيْرُ مَنْشُورٍ أوْ مُذَاعٍ

Unqualified *a.* غَيْرُ أَهْلٍ لَه

Unquenchable *a.* مَا لَا يُطْفَا

Unquestionable *a.* مَا لَا رَيْبَ فِيهِ

Unravel *v. t.* حَلَّ ـُ . فَكَّ ـُ

Unreal *a.* غَيْرُ حَقِيقِيٍّ . وَهْمِيٌّ

Unreasonable *a.* لَا يُوَافِقُ ٱلْعَقْلَ . غَيْرُ عَادِلٍ

Unredemeed *a.* غَيْرُ مَفْدِيٍّ أو مُوفًى

Unregenerate *a.* غَيْرُ مُتَجَدِّدِ ٱلْقَلْبِ

Unregistered *a.* غَيْرُ مُسَجَّلٍ

Unrelenting *a.* غَيْرُ مُسَامِحٍ . مُصِرٌّ

Unremitting *a.* مُسْتَمِرٌّ

Unrepenting *a.* غَيْرُ تَائِبٍ

Unrequited *a.* غَيْرُ مُكَافَإٍ

Unreserved *a.* غَيْرُ كَتُومٍ . مُخْلِصٌ

Unresisting *a.* غَيْرُ مُقَاوِمٍ

Unrestrained *a.* غَيْرُ مَحْصُورٍ

Unrewarded *a.* غَيْرُ مُجَازًى

Unrighteous *a.* غَيْرُ بَارٍّ . أَثِيمٌ

Unrighteousness *n.* إِثْمٌ

Unripe *a.* غَيْرُ نَاضِجٍ . فِجٌّ

Unrivalled *a.* لَا مَثِيلَ لَهُ

Unrobe *v. t.* خَلَعَ ٱلثِّيَابَ

Unroll *v. t.* فَتَحَ دَرْجًا . نَشَرَهُ

Unroof *v. t.* رَفَعَ ٱلسَّطْحَ عن

Unruffled *a.* غَيْرُ مُهَيَّجٍ . هَادِئٌ

Unruly *a.* مَا لَا يُضْبَطُ . عَنِيد

Unsaddle *v. t.* رَفَعَ ٱلسَّرْجَ عَنْهُ

Unsafe *a.* غَيْرُ أَمِينٍ . مُخْطِرٌ

Unsaid *a.* غَيْرُ مَقُول

Unsaleable *a.* مَا لَا يُبَاعُ . كَاسِدٌ

Unsanctified *a.* غَيْرُ مُقَدَّسٍ أو مُطَهَّرٍ

Unsatisfactory / **Unsatisfying** *a.* غَيْرُ مُرْضٍ

Unsavoury *a.* غَيْرُ مقبُولٍ لِلذَّوْقِ

Unsay *v. t.* أَبْطَلَ ٱلْقَوْلَ

Unscrew *v. t.* فَكَّ ٱللَّوْلَبَ

Unscriptural *a.* ضِدُّ ٱلكِتَابِ ٱلمقدَّسِ

Unseal *v. t.* فَكَّ ٱلْخَتْمَ

Unsearchable *a.* مَالاَ يُفْحَصُ أوْ يُسْتَقْصَى

Unseasonable *a.* فِي غَيْرِ آنِهِ

Unseemly *a.* غَيْرُ لاَئِقٍ

Unseen *a.* غَيْرُ مَنْظُورٍ

Unselfish *a.* غَيْرُ مُحِبِّ ٱلذَّاتِ

Unserviceable *a.* غَيْرُ نَافِعٍ

Unsettle *v. t.* أَزْعَجَ . شَوَّشَ

Unshaken *a.* غَيْرُ مُزَعْزَعٍ

Unsheathe *v. t.* إِسْتَلَّ مِن غِمْدِهِ

Unshod *a.* حَافٍ

Unshrinking *a.* غَيْرُ مُرْتَدٍّ . جَسُورٌ

Unsightliness *n.* قَبَاحَةُ ٱلْمَنْظَرِ . بَشَاعَةٌ

Unsightly *a.* قَبِيحُ ٱلْمَنْظَرِ . بَشِعٌ

Unskillfull / Unskilful *n.* غَيْرُ مَاهِرٍ

Unsociable *a.* غَيْرُ أَلِيفٍ

Unsocial *a.* غَيْرُ أَلِيفٍ . آبِدٌ

Unsold *a.* مَا لَمْ يُبَعْ

Unsolicited *a.* غَيْرُ مَطْلُوبٍ

Unsophisticated *a.* بَسِيطٌ . سَاذِجٌ

Unsought *a.* غَيْرُ مَطْلُوبٍ

Unsound *a.* غَيْرُ صَحِيحٍ أوْ سَالِمٍ

Unsoundness *n.* إِخْتِلاَلٌ . إِعْتِلاَلٌ

Unsparing *a.* غَيْرُ مُقْتَصِدٍ . قَاسٍ

Unspeakable *a.* مَالاَ يُنْطَقُ بِهِ

Unspent *a.* غَيْرُ مَصْرُوفٍ . بَاقٍ

Unspotted *a.* غَيْرُ مُلَطَّخٍ . طَاهِرٌ

Unstable *a.* غَيْرُ ثَابِتٍ . مُتَرَدِّدٌ

Unstained *a.* غَيْرُ مُلَوَّثٍ . بِلاَ عَيْبٍ

Unsteady *a.* غَيْرُ ثَابِتٍ . مُتَقَلِّبٌ

Unstinted *a.* غَيْرُ مَحْدُودٍ

Unstrung *a.* مَحْلُولٌ : مُرْتَخٍ

Unsubstantial *a.*	غيرُ حقيقيّ أَوْ متينٍ
Unsuccessful *a.*	غيرُ ناجحٍ
Unsuitable / **Unsuited** } *a.*	غيرُ ملائمٍ
Unsullied *a.*	غيرُ معيبٍ
Unsupported *a.*	غيرُ مسندٍ
Unsurpassed *a.*	مالم يفقهُ شيءٌ
Unsusceptible *a.*	غيرُ حاسٍّ
Unsuspicious *a.*	غيرُ ظنّانٍ . واثقٌ
Unsystematic *a.*	غيرُ منتظمٍ
Unstained *a*	غيرُ فاسدٍ
Untasted *a.*	غيرُ مذوقٍ
Untaught *a.*	غيرُ معلَّمٍ . أُمّيٌّ
Untenable *a.*	مالا يؤيَّد . باطلٌ
Unthankful *a.*	غيرُ شكورٍ
Unthankfulness *a.*	عدمُ شكرٍ
Unthinking / **Unthoughtful** } *a.*	غيرُ منتبهٍ . غافلٌ
Unthrifty *a.*	غيرُ مقتصدٍ
Untidy *a.*	غيرُ نظيفٍ او مرتَّبٍ
Untie *v. t.*	حلّ عقدةً
Until *prep.*	حتّى . إلى . أنْ . إلى
Untimely *a.*	في غيرِ وقتهِ
Untiring *a.*	مالا يتعبُ أو يكلُّ
Unto *prep.*	حتّى . إلى
Untold *a.*	غيرُ مذكورٍ . غيرُ محصًى
Untoward *a.*	مشؤومٌ . شاقٌّ
Untractable *a.*	مالا يُضبطُ . عنيدٌ
Untried *a.*	غيرُ مختبرٍ
Untrodden *a.*	غيرُ مسلوكٍ
Untrue *a.*	كاذبٌ . غيرُ امينٍ
Untruth *n.*	كذبٌ
Untruthful *a.*	كاذبٌ
Untwist *v. t.*	حلّ المفتولَ
Unused *a.*	غيرُ مستعملٍ
Unusual *a.*	نادرٌ . شاذٌّ
Unutterable *a.*	مالا ينطقُ بهِ
Unveil *v. t.*	كشفَ البرقعَ . بيّنَ

Unvarnished *a.* غَيْرُ مَدْهُونٍ. بَسِيطٌ

Unvaried / **Unvarying** *a.* غَيْرُ مُتَغَيِّرٍ

Unwarlike *a.* غَيْرُ جَدِيرٍ بِالْحَرْبِ

Unwarrantable / **Unwarranted** *a.* غَيْرُ جَائِزٍ

Unwary *a.* غَيْرُ مُتَحَذِّرٍ . عَاقِلٌ

Unwearied *a.* غَيْرُ مُتْعَبٍ

Unwelcome *a.* غَيْرُ مُرَحَّبٍ بِهِ

Unwell *a.* مَرِيضٌ

Unwept *a.* غَيْرُ مَأْسُوفٍ عَلَيْهِ

Unwholesome *a.* ضَارٌّ بِالصِّحَّةِ

Unwieldy *a.* ضَخْمٌ . ثَقِيلٌ

Unwilling *a.* غَيْرُ رَاضٍ

Unwind *v. t.* حَلَّ الْمَلْفُوفَ

Unwise *a.* غَيْرُ حَكِيمٍ

Unwittingly *ad.* بِلَا مَعْرِفَةٍ أَوْ قَصْدٍ

Unwomanly *a.* غَيْرُ لَائِقٍ بِالْمَرْأَةِ

Unwonted *a.* غَيْرُ مُعْتَادٍ . نَادِرٌ

Unworn *a.* غَيْرُ مَلْبُوسٍ

Unworthily *ad.* بِلَا ٱسْتِحْقَاقٍ

Unworthiness *n.* عَدَمُ ٱسْتِحْقَاقٍ

Unworthy *a.* غَيْرُ لَائِقٍ أَوْ مُسْتَحِقٍّ

Unwritten *a.* غَيْرُ مَكْتُوبٍ . شَفَهِيٌّ

Unyielding *a.* غَيْرُ مُذْعِنٍ . ثَابِتٌ

Unyoke *v. t.* رَفَعَ ٱلنِّيرَ

Up *ad.* إِلَى فَوْقٍ . فَوْقُ

Upbraid *v. t.* وَبَّخَ . لَامَ ـُ

Upheaval *n.* إِرْتِفَاعٌ . إِنْدِفَاعٌ

Upheave *v. t.* رَفَعَ ـَ

Uphill *a.* عَسِرٌ . شَاقٌّ

Uphold *v. t.* سَنَدَ . أَيَّدَ . عَضَدَ ـُ

Upholder *n.* مُؤَيِّدٌ . عَاضِدٌ . ظَهِيرٌ

Upholsterer *n.* مُنَجِّدٌ

Upholstery *n.* مَفْرُوشَاتٌ

Upland *n.* نَجْدٌ . صَعِيدٌ

Uplift *v. t.* رَفَعَ . رَقَّى

Upon *prep.* عَلَى . عِنْدَ . حِينَ

Upper *a.* أَعْلَى . عَلَوِيٌّ . فَوْقَانِيٌّ
Upperhand *n.* أَسْبَقِيَّةٌ . غَلَبَةٌ
Uppermost *a.* أَلْأَعْلَى
Upright *a.* مُسْتَقِيمٌ . قَائِمٌ
Uprightness *n.* إِسْتِقَامَةٌ
Uproar *n.* شَغَبٌ . ضَجَّةٌ . ضَوْضَاءٌ
Uproot *v. t.* قَلَعَ ـَ . إِسْتَأْصَلَ
Upset *v. t.* قَلَبَ ـِ . نَكَسَ ـُ
Upshot *n.* نَتِيجَةٌ . عَاقِبَةٌ
Upside-down *a.* مَقْلُوبٌ
Upstart *n.* or *a.* حَدِيثُ النِّعْمَةِ
Upward / **Upwards** *ad.* إِلَى فَوْق
Urban *a.* مَدَنِيٌّ
Urbane *a.* مُهَذَّبٌ . لَطِيفٌ . أَنِيسٌ
Urbanity *n.* أَدَبٌ . أُنْسٌ
Urchin *n.* وَلَدٌ خَبِيث . قُنْفُذٌ
Urge *v. t.* حَرَّضَ . حَثَّ ـُ
Urgency *n.* لَجَاجَةٌ . ضَرُورَةٌ
Urgent *a.* مُلِحٌّ . ضَرُورِيٌّ
Urinary *a.* بَوْلِيٌّ
Urine *n.* بَوْلٌ
Urn *n.* جَرَّةٌ . قَارُورَةٌ
Us *pron.* ضَمِيرٌ مُتَّصِلٌ (نا)
Usage *n.* اسْتِعْمَال . عَادَةٌ
Use *n.* or *v. t.* إِسْتِعْمَالٌ . إِسْتَعْمَلَ
Useful *a.* مُفِيدٌ . نَافِعٌ
Usefulness *n.* مَنْفَعَةٌ . فَائِدَةٌ
Useless *a.* بِلَا فَائِدَةٍ
Usher *n.* or *v. t.* عَرِيفٌ . أَدْخَلَ
Usual *a.* إِعْتِيَادِيٌّ . دَارِجٌ . جَارٍ
Usurer *n.* مُرَابٍ
Usurp *v. t.* إِغْتَصَبَ
Usurpation *n.* إِغْتِصَابٌ
Usurper *n.* مُغْتَصِبٌ
Usury *n.* رِبًا
Utensil *n.* آلَةٌ . وِعَاءٌ

Utility *n.* فَائِدَةٌ . نفعٌ

Utmost *a.* الأَقْصَى

Utter *v. t.* نَطَقَ . فَاهَ بِهِ

Utterance *n.* نطْقٌ

Utterly *ad.* تَمَامًا بِالكلّيةِ

Uttermost *a.* الأقصى . الأَبْعَدُ

Uxorious *a.* مفرط الحُبِّ لِزَوْجَتِهِ

V

Vacancy *n.* فراغ . مَنْصِبٌ خالٍ

Vacant *a.* فارغ . خالٍ

Vacate *a.* اخلى . تركَ

Vacation *n.* فَرَاغٌ . بِطَالَةٌ . فُرْصَة

Vaccinate *v. t.* طعَّمَ

Vaccination *n.* تطْعيم

Vaccine *n.* مادة لِلتَّطْعيم

Vacillate *v. i.* تَرَدَّدَ

Vacillation *n.* تَرَدُّدٌ

Vacuity } *n.* فَرَاغٌ . خَلاَءٌ
Vacuum }

Vagabond *n.* طَوَّافٌ . بَطَّالٌ . (مُتَشَرِّدٌ)

Vagabondage *n.* بطالةٌ

Vagary *n.* تَصَوُّرٌ بَاطِلٌ . وَهْمٌ

Vagrancy *n.* جَوَلاَنٌ للتَسوُّل

Vagrant *n.* تَائِهٌ . بطّالٌ . (مُعَتَرٌّ)

Vague *a.* مُبْهَمٌ . غَيْرُ وَاضِحٍ

Vail *n.* بُرْقُعٌ . قِنَاعٌ

Vain *a.* باطلٌ . مُعْجَبٌ

Vainglorious *a.* متصلِّفٌ

Vale *n.* وَادٍ . وَهْدٌ

Valedictory *n.* خِطَابٌ وِدَاعِيٌّ

Valet *n.* خادِمٌ شَخْصِيٌّ

Valiant *a.* بَاسِلٌ . شُجَاعٌ
Valid *a.* ثَابِتٌ . شَرْعِيٌّ . حَقِيقِيٌّ
Validity *n.* ثُبُوتٌ . شَرْعِيَّةٌ
Valise *n.* صَنْدُوقُ سَفَرٍ صَغِيرٌ
Valley *n.* وَادٍ ج أَوْدِيَةٌ
Valorous *a.* بَاسِلٌ . شُجَاعٌ
Valour *n.* شَجَاعَةٌ . بَسَالَةٌ إِقْدَامٌ
Valuable *a.* ثَمِينٌ
Valuation *n.* تَثْمِينٌ . تَقْدِيرٌ
Value *n.* ثَمَنٌ . قِيمَةٌ أَهَمِّيَّةٌ
Value *v. t.* ثَمَّنَ . إِعْتَبَرَ
Valve *n.* صِمَامٌ
Vampire *n.* وَطْوَاطٌ كَبِيرٌ
Van *n.* طَلِيعَةُ ٱلْجَيْشِ . عَرَبَةٌ
Vandal *n.* بَرْبَرِيٌّ مُخَرِّبٌ
Vandalism *n.* تَخْرِيبٌ بَرْبَرِيٌّ
Vane *n.* دَوَّارَةٌ تَدُلُّ عَلَى جِهَةِ ٱلرِّيحِ
Vanguard *n.* طَلِيعَةُ جَيْشٍ
Vanish *v. i.* إِخْتَفَى . زَالَ ـ
Vanity *n.* عُجْبٌ . تَكَبُّرٌ بُطْلٌ
Vanquish *v. t.* قَهَرَ ـ غَلَبَ ـ
Vantage-ground *n.* مَقَامٌ أَفْضَلُ
Vapid *a.* تَافِهٌ نَاشِفٌ بِلَا طَعْمٍ
Vapour *n.* بُخَارٌ
Vapour-bath *n.* حَمَّامٌ بُخَارِي
Vaporize *v. t.* حَوَّلَ إِلَى بُخَارٍ
Variable *a.* مُتَغَيِّرٌ . مُتَقَلِّبٌ
Variableness *n.* تَغَيُّرٌ . تَقَلُّبٌ
Variance *n.* إِخْتِلَافٌ . خِلَافٌ
Variation *n.* تَغَيُّرٌ . إِخْتِلَافٌ . فَرْق
Variegate *v. t.* لَوَّنَ . رَقَشَ ـ
Variety *n.* نَوْعٌ . شَكْلٌ . تَنَوُّعٌ
Varioloid *n.* جُدَرِيٌّ خَفِيفٌ
Various *n.* مُتَنَوِّعٌ . شَتَّى .
Varlet *a.* دَنِيٌّ . خَبِيثٌ
Varnish *n.* نَوْعٌ مِنَ ٱلصَّبْغِ (فرنيش)

Vary *v. t.* or *i.* غَيَّرَ . نَوَّعَ . تَغَيَّرَ

Vase *n.* إِنَاءٌ . ظَرْفٌ

Vassal *n.* تَابِعٌ . مُزَارِعٌ تَابِعٌ

Vassalage *n.* خُضُوعٌ . عُبُودِيَّةٌ

Vast *a.* عَظِيمٌ . فَسِيحٌ . عَدِيدٌ

Vastness *n.* عَظَمَةٌ . إِتِّسَاعٌ

Vat *n.* حَوْضٌ ج أَحْوَاضٌ

Vault *n.* قَبْوٌ . قُبَّةٌ . خَشْخَاشَةٌ

Vault *v. t.* or *i.* عَقَدَ ـِ . قَفَزَ ـِ

Vaulted *n.* مُقَبَّبٌ . مَقْبُوٌّ

Vaunt *v. i.* إِفْتَخَرَ . تَصَلَّبَ

Veal *n.* لَحْمُ عِجْلٍ

Veer *v. t.* or *i.* أَدَارَ . دَارَ ـُ

Vegetable *n.* نَبَاتٌ . خُضْرَةٌ . بَقْلٌ

Vegetate *v. t.* نَبَتَ ـُ . نَمَا كَالْبُقُولِ

Vegetation *n.* عُشْبٌ . نَبَات

Vehemence *n.* شِدَّةٌ . عُنْفٌ

Vehement *a.* عَنِيفٌ . مُشَدِّدٌ

Vehicle *n.* مَرْكَبَةٌ . عَرَبَةٌ

Veil *n.* بُرْقُعٌ . نِقَابٌ . قِنَاعٌ

Veil *v. t.* تَنَقَّبَتْ . حَجَبَ ـُ

Vein *n.* عِرْقٌ . وَرِيدٌ

Veined } *a.* ذُو عُرُوقٍ أَو أَوْرِدَةٍ
Veiny

Vellum *n.* رَقٌّ لِلْكِتَابَةِ

Velocity *n.* سُرْعَةُ السَّيْرِ

Velvet *n.* مُخْمَلٌ . قَطِيفَةٌ

Velvety *a.* مُخْمَلِيٌّ . أَمْلَسُ

Venality *n.* إِرْتِشَاءٌ . أَلْمَيْلُ إِلَيْهِ

Vend *v. t.* بَاعَ ـِ

Vender } *n.* بَائِعٌ
Vendor

Veneer *v. t.* لَبَّسَ . غَشَّى

Venerable *a.* مُحْتَرَمٌ . وَقُورٌ

Venerate *v. t.* إِحْتَرَمَ . وَقَّرَ

Veneration *n.* إِحْتِرَامٌ . تَوْقِيرٌ

Venereal *a.* زُهَرِيٌّ

Vengeance *n.* نِقْمَةٌ . ثَأْرٌ

Vengeful *n.* مُنْتَقِمٌ . حَقُودٌ

Venial *n.* مِمَّا يغفَرُ أو يعذَرُ . زَهِيدٌ

Venison *n.* لَحْمُ ٱلصَّيْدِ

Venom *n.* سُمٌّ . حِقْدٌ

Venomous *a.* سَامٌ . حَقُودٌ

Venous *a.* وريديٌّ (لِلدمِ)

Vent *n.* مَنفَذٌ . إظهَارٌ . نُطْقٌ

Vent *v. t.* نَفَثَ ـُ . أَظْهَرَ (حِقدًا)

Ventilate *v. t.* هوَّى عَرَضَ لِلْهَوَاءِ

Ventilation *n.* تَهْوِيَةٌ

Ventilator *n.* مَنْفَذٌ لِلْهَوَاءِ

Ventriloquism *n.* أَلتَّكَلُّمُ مِنَ ٱلْجَوْفِ

Ventriloquist *n.* متَكَلِّمٌ مِنَ ٱلْجَوْفِ

Venture *n.* or *v. t.* مُخاطَرَةٌ تجَرَّأَ

Venturesome / **Venturous** *a.* مُخاطِرٌ . جَسُورٌ

Venus *a.* أَلزهرَةُ . إِلَاهَةُ ٱلعِشقِ

Veracious *a.* صَادِقٌ

Veracity *n.* صِدْقٌ

Veranda *n.* رِوَاقٌ ج أَروِقَةٌ

Verb *n.* فِعْلٌ ج أَفْعَالٌ

Verbal *a.* فِعلِيٌّ . لَفْظِيٌّ

Verbally *ad.* شِفَاهاً . لَفظاً

Verbatim *ad.* حَرْفِيًّا

Verbosity *n.* كَثْرَةُ ٱلْكَلَامِ

Verdant *a.* أخضَرُ . غَنِيٌّ . نَضِرٌ

Verdict *n.* حُكْمٌ . قَضَاءٌ . فتوَى

Verdigris *n.* زِنجارٌ

Verdure *n.* خُضْرَةٌ

Verge *n.* حَافَّةٌ . حرفٌ . حَدٌّ

Verge *v. i.* إِقْتَرَبَ . مَالَ ـِ

Verification *n.* تَحْقِيقٌ . إِثْبَاتٌ

Verify *v. t.* حَقَّقَ

Verily *ad.* حَقًّا

Verisimilitude *n.* مُشَابَهَةٌ إِمْكَانِيَّةٌ

Veritable *a.* حَقِيقِيٌّ . وَاقِعٌ

Verity *n.* حَقٌّ . حقِيقَةٌ . صِدقٌ

Vermillion *n.*	زُنْجُفْر . حُمْرَة
Vermin *n.*	حشرات خبيثة
Vernacular *a.*	وَطَنِيّ (لُغَة)
Vernal *a.*	رَبِيعِيّ
Versatile *a.*	مُتَقَلِّب . مَاهِر
Versatility *n.*	مَهَارَة
Verse *n.*	بَيت شِعْرٍ . دَوْر
Versed *a.*	حَاذِق . خَبِير . عَالِم
Versification *n.*	نَظْم
Versify *v. i.* or *t.*	نَظَمَ ـِ . شعرَ ـُ
Version *n.*	تَرْجَمَة
Vertebra *n.*	فَقْرَة ج فَقَار
Vertebral *a.*	فِقْرِيّ
Vertebrate *a.*	ذُو فِقْرَاتٍ أَوْ فِقَارٍ
Vertex *n.*	قِمَّة . رَأْس
Vertical *a.*	عَمُودِيّ
Vertigo *n.*	دُوَار
Very *a.* or *ad.*	حَقِيقِيّ . ذَات . جدًّا
Vespers *n. pl.*	صَلَاة ٱلْمَسَاء
Vessel *n.*	مَرْكَب . سَفِينَة . وِعَاء
Vest *n.*	صَدْرِيَّة . صَدْرَة
Vestal *a.* or *n.*	عَفِيف . عَذْرَاء
Vested *a.*	ثَابِت . مُعَيَّن . مُقَلَّد
Vestibule *n.*	دِهْلِيز
Vestige *n.*	أَثَر . رَسْم
Vestment *n.*	لِبَاس . حُلَّة
Vesture *n.*	ثَوْب . لِبَاس
Veteran *a.*	مُجَرَّب . مُتَمَرِّن
Veterinary *a.*	مَنُوط بِطِبِّ ٱلْحَيَوَانَاتِ
Veto *n.* or *v. t.*	نَهْي . مَنْع . رَفْض . رَفَضَ
Vex *v. t.*	أَضْجَرَ . كَدَّرَ . أَغَاظَ
Vexation *n.*	كَدَر . مُضَايَقَة
Vexatious *n.*	مُضَايِق . مُكَدِّر
Viaduct *n.*	سِكَّة مُرْتَفِعَة . جِسْر
Vial *n.*	قَارُورَة . جَام
Viands *n. pl.*	أَطْعِمَة

Vibrate v. t. or i. رَجّ ـ . إِرْتَجّ . إِهْتَزّ
Vibration n. إِهْتِزَازٌ
Vicar n. نَائِبٌ . خُورِيٌّ . قِسِّيسٌ
Vicarious n. نَائِبٌ . مُوَكَّلٌ
Vice n. رَذِيلَةٌ . شَرٌّ . مِلْزَمَةٌ . عِوَضٌ
Vice-admiral n. نَائِبُ رَئِيسِ أُسْطُولٍ
Vicegerent n. نَائِبٌ
Viceroy n. نَائِبُ مَلِكٍ
Vicinage / Vicinity n. جُوَارٌ
Vicious a. فَاسِدٌ . شِرِّيرٌ . خَلِيعٌ
Vicissitude n. تَقَلُّبٌ
Victim n. قَتِيلٌ . ذَبِيحٌ
Victor n. / Victorious a. قَاهِرٌ . غَالِبٌ . مَنْصُورٌ
Victory n. نَصْرٌ . غَلَبَةٌ . فَوْزٌ
Victual v. t. زَوَّدَ . مَوَّنَ
Victuals n. pl. طَعَامٌ . مَأْكُولَاتٌ
Vie v. i. بَارَى . سَابَقَ . نَافَسَ
View v. t. نَظَرَ ـُ . رَأَى ـَ . تَطَلَّعَ
View n. مَنْظَرٌ . رَأْيٌ
Vigil n. سَهَرٌ . صَلَاةٌ سَهَرِيَّةٌ
Vigilance n. مُرَاقَبَةٌ . سَهَرٌ
Vigilant a. سَاهِرٌ . حَذِرٌ . مُنْتَبِهٌ
Vigorous a. قَوِيٌّ . نَشِيطٌ . شَدِيدٌ
Vigour n. شِدَّةٌ . قُوَّةٌ . نَشَاطٌ
Vile a. رَذِيلٌ . نَجِسٌ . قَبِيحٌ
Vileness n. قَبَاحَةٌ . خَسَاسَةٌ
Vilify v. t. عَابَ ـِ . شَتَمَ ـِ
Villa n. دَارُ سَكَنٍ خَارِجَ ٱلْمَدِينَةِ
Village n. قَرْيَةٌ . ضَيْعَةٌ
Villager n. قَرَوِيٌّ
Villain n. / Villainous a. خَبِيثٌ . شِرِّيرٌ
Villainy / Villany n. خُبْثٌ . شَرٌّ
Vindicate v. t. بَرَّأَ . بَرَّرَ . ثَبَّتَ
Vindication n. تَبْرِئَةٌ . إِثْبَاتٌ
Vindictive a. ضَغِنٌ . طَالِبُ ٱلْاِنْتِقَامِ
Vine n. كَرْمَةٌ . زَرَجُونٌ . دَالِيَةٌ

Vinegar *n.* خَل

Vineyard *n.* كَرْمٌ

Vintage *n.* قِطَافٌ. حاصِلُ ٱلْكرْمِ

Viol / Viola } *n.* كَمَنْجَةٌ كبيرَة

Violate *v. i.* خَالَفَ. نكَثَ ـُ اغْتَصَبَ

Violation *n.* مُخَالَفَةٌ. نَكْثٌ

Violence *n.* عَنْفٌ. قوَّةٌ. غصْبٌ

Violent *a.* عَنِيفٌ. شَدِيدٌ. ظَلُومٌ

Violet *n.* or *a.* بَنَفْسَجة. بَنَفْسَجِيٌّ

Violin *n.* كَمَنْجَةٌ

Viper *n.* أَفْعَى. صِل

Virago *n.* سَلِيطَةٌ

Virgin *n.* عَذْرَآءُ

Virginity *n.* عذْرَةٌ

Virile *a.* رَجُلِيٌّ. مَرْئِيٌّ

Virility *n.* رُجُولِيَّة

Virtual *a.* حَقِيقِي. بِالْحَقِيقَة

Virtue *n.* فَضِيلَة. جُودَة. قوَّة

Virtuous *a.* عفيفٌ. نَقِيٌّ. صَالِحٌ

Virulence *n.* شِدَّة. عنفٌ. سَلاَقَةٌ

Virulent *a.* شَدِيدٌ. عَنِيفٌ. سَامٌّ

Virus *n.* سَمٌّ. صَدِيدٌ

Visage *n.* مُحَيًّا. وَجْهٌ. طَلْعَة

Viscera *n. pl.* أَحْشَاءٌ

Viscid / Viscous } *a.* لَزِجٌ. دَبِقٌ

Viscount *n.* أَمِيرٌ. رتْبَةٌ أَمِيرِيَّةٌ

Visibility *n.* امكانِيَّة نَظَرِهِ. ظهُورٌ

Visible *v. t.* ما ينظَرُ. ظَاهِرٌ

Vision *n.* نَظَرٌ. رُؤْيَةٌ. رُؤْيَا

Visionary *a.* خيَالِيٌّ. وَهْمِيٌّ

Visit *n.* or *v. t.* زِيَارَةٌ. زَارَ ـُ. إِفْتَقَدَ

Visitation *n.* إِفْتِقَادٌ. مُصِيبَةٌ

Visitor *n.* زَائِرٌ. ضَيْفٌ. مُفَتِّشٌ

Vista *n.* مَنْظَرٌ (إِلى بَعِيدٍ)

Visual *a.* مرْئِيٌّ. نَظَرِيٌّ. بَصَرِيٌّ

Vital *a.* حَيَوِيٌّ. ضَرورِيٌّ

Vitality *n.* حَيَوِيَّةٌ رُوحُ ٱلْحَيَاةِ

Vitals *n. pl.* ألأَحْشَاءُ ٱلرَّئِيسِيَّةُ

Vitiate *v. t.* أَفْسَدَ . أَبْطَلَ

Vitreous *a.* زُجَاجِيٌّ

Vitriol *n.* زَاجٌ . شَبٌّ

Vituperate *v. t.* شَتَمَ ـُ . طَعَنَ ـَ

Vivacious *a.* خَفِيفٌ . مَرِحٌ . ذَكِيٌّ

Vivacity *n.* خِفَّةٌ . مَرَحٌ . نَشَاطٌ

Vivid *a.* بَرَّاقٌ . مُؤَثِّرٌ

Vividness *n.* وُضُوحٌ . لَمَعَانٌ

Vivify *v. t.* أَحْيَا . أَنْعَشَ

Vivisection *n.* تَشْرِيحُ ٱلْجِسْمِ ٱلْحَيِّ

Vixen *n.* سَلِيطَةٌ . وَقِحَةٌ

Viz *ad.* أَيْ . يَعْنِي

Vizier *n.* وَزِيرٌ

Vocabulary *n.* قَامُوسٌ مُوجَزٌ

Vocal *a.* صَوْتِيٌّ . مَلْفُوظٌ

Vocalize *v. t.* لَفَظَ ـِ . حَرَّكَ (الحروف)

Vocation *n.* دَعْوَةٌ . وَظِيفَةٌ . حِرْفَةٌ

Vociferate *v. t.* صَاحَ ـِ . صَرَخَ ـُ

Vociferous *a.* صَائِحٌ . هَاتِفٌ

Voice *n.* صَوْتٌ . صِيغَةُ ٱلْمَعْلُومِ أَوِ ٱلْمَجْهُولِ

Void *a.* or *n.* فَارِغٌ . خَالٍ . بَاطِلٌ . خَلَاءٌ

Volatile *a.* طَيَّارٌ . مُتَقَلِّبٌ

Volcanic *a.* بُرْكَانِيٌّ

Volcano *a.* بُرْكَانٌ . جَبَلُ نَارٍ

Volition *n.* إِرَادَةٌ . إِخْتِيَارٌ

Volley *n.* إِطْلَاقُ أَسْلِحَةٍ كَثِيرَةٍ مَعًا

Volublity *n.* كَثْرَةُ ٱلْكَلَامِ

Voluble *a.* كَثِيرُ ٱلْكَلَامِ

Volume *n.* مُجَلَّدٌ . جِرْمٌ . سَعَةٌ

Voluminous *a.* كَثِيرٌ . مُطَوَّلٌ

Voluntary *a.* إِخْتِيَارِيٌّ . طَوْعِيٌّ

Volunteer *n.* مُتَطَوِّعٌ . مُتَبَرِّعٌ

Voluptuary *n.* / **Voluptuous** *a.* } شَهْوَانِيٌّ . مُتَنَعِّمٌ

Vomit *v. t.* or *n.* إِسْتَفْرَغَ . قَيْءٌ

Voracious *a.* نَهِمٌ . أَهْيَمُ . شَرِهٌ

Voracity *n.* نَهْمَةٌ . شَرَهٌ

Vortex *n.* دُرْدُورٌ

Votary *n.* مُتَعَبِّدٌ . نَذِيرٌ

Vote *n.* or *v. i.* صَوْتٌ فِي ٱلاَنْتِخَابِ

Voter *n.* مَنْ لَهُ حقٌّ فِي ٱلانْتِخَابِ

Votive *a.* نَذْرِيٌّ

Vouch *v. t.* or *i.* أَثْبَتَ . شَهِدَ

Voucher *n.* شَاهِدٌ . بَيِّنَةٌ

Vouchsafe *v. t.* مَنَحَ . أَنْعَمَ عَلَى . وَهَبَ

Vow *n.* or *v. t.* نَذْرٌ . نَذَرَ ـُ

Vowel *n.* حَرْفُ عِلَّةٍ

Voyage *n.* or *v. i.* سَفَرٌ . سَافَرَ

Voyager *n.* مُسَافِرٌ

Vulgar *a.* دَارِجٌ . دَنِيٌّ . خَسِيسٌ

Vulgarism *n.* إِصْطِلاَحٌ . دَارِجٌ

Vulgarity *n.* دَنَاءَةٌ . قِلَّةُ أَدَبٍ

Vulnerable *a.* قَابِلُ ٱلْجَرْحِ اَوْ ٱلطَّعْنِ.

Vulture *n.* نَسْرٌ . شُوحَةٌ

Vying *See* Vie مُنَافِسٌ

Vulgate *n.* تَرْجَمَةُ ٱلْكِتَابِ ٱلْمُقَدَّسِ ٱللاَّتِينِيَّةُ

W

Wabble *v. i.* تَرَنَّحَ . تَمَايَلَ

Wad *n.* or *v. t.* حَشْوَةٌ . حشَا ـُ

Wadded *a.* مَحْشُوٌّ

Waddle *v. i.* تَمَايَلَ فِي ٱلْمَشْيِ

Wade *v. i.* خَاضَ ـُ

Wafer *n.* بُرْشَانَةٌ

Waft *v. t.* حَمَلَ ـِ (ٱلرِّيحُ)

Wage *n.* or *v. t.* مَازِحٌ . هَزَّ ـ بَصْبَصَ

Wage *v. t.* رَاهَنَ . إِسْتَأْجَرَ . حَارَبَ

Wager *n.* or *v. t.* رَهْنٌ . رَاهَنَ

Wages *n. pl.* أُجْرٌ . كِرَاءٌ

Waggish *a.* مَازِحٌ . مَاجِنٌ

Waggon *n.* مَرْكَبَةٌ . عَرَبَةٌ

Waif *n.* لَقِيطٌ

Wail *v. i.* or *n.* وَلْوَلَ . عَوَّلَ . عَوِيلٌ

Waist *n.* خَصْرٌ . حَقْوٌ

Waistcoat *n.* صُدْرَةٌ . صَدْرِيَّةٌ

Wait *v. i.* إِنْتَظَرَ . إِسْتَأْنَى . تَرَبَّصَ

Waiter *n.* خَادِمٌ . طَبَقٌ

Waiting-maid *n.* خَادِمَةٌ . جَارِيَةٌ

Waive *v. t.* تَرَكَ ـُ . خَلَّى . تَنَحَّى عَنْ

Wake *v. i.* إِسْتَيْقَظَ . إِنْتَبَهَ

Wake *n.* حِرَاسَةُ مَيْتٍ . أَثَرُ سَفِينَةٍ

Wakeful *a.* يَقِظٌ . سَاهِرٌ

Waken *v. i.* or *t.* تَيَقَّظَ . أَيْقَظَ . نَبَّهَ

Walk *v. t.* or *n.* مَشَى ـِ مَشْيٌ . مَمْشًى

Wall *n.* or *v. t.* حَائِطٌ . سُورٌ . حَوَّطَ

Wallet *n.* جِرَابٌ . كِيسٌ . قَلْعٌ

Wallow *v. i.* تَمَرَّغَ

Walnut *n.* جَوْزَةٌ . شَجَرُ ٱلْجَوْزِ

Waltz *n.* نَوْعٌ مِنَ ٱلرَّقْصِ

Wan *n.* أَصْفَرُ . مُصْفَرٌّ

Wand *n.* قَضِيبٌ . صَوْلَجَانٌ

Wander *v. i.* تَاهَ ـِ . ضَلَّ ـِ . حَادَ ـِ

Wanderer *n.* تَائِهٌ . ضَالٌ . جَائِلٌ

Wane *v. i.* تَنَاقَصَ . إِنْحَطَّ

Want *v. t.* or *i.* } إِحْتَاجَ . ارَادَ . نَقَصَ ـُ

Want *n.* حَاجَةٌ . فَاقَةٌ . نَقْصٌ

Wanting *a.* نَاقِصٌ . مَفْقُودٌ

Wanton *a.* فَاجِرٌ . بَطِرٌ . لَاهٍ

War *n.* or *v. i.* حَرْبٌ . حَارَبَ

Warble *v. i.* غَرَّدَ

Warbler / Warbling } *n.*	مُغَرِّدٌ
Ward *n.*	حِرَاسَةٌ . قاصِرٌ لهُ وَصِيٌّ
Warden *n.*	حَافِظٌ . وَكِيلٌ
Wardrobe *n.*	خِزَانَةُ ثِيَابٍ . لِبَاسٌ
Wares *n. pl.*	سِلَعٌ . بَضَائِعُ
Warehouse *n.*	مَخْزَنٌ
Warfare *n.*	مُحَارَبَةٌ . مُجَاهَدَةٌ
Warily *ad.*	بِحَذَرٍ . مُتَحَذِّراً
Wariness *n.*	حَذَرٌ . إِحْتِيَاطٌ
Warlike *a.*	حَرْبِيٌّ . مُحِبٌّ الْحَرْبِ
Warm *a.* or *v. t.*	دَافِئٌ . حَارٌّ . سَخَّنَ
Warmly *ad.*	بِحَمَاسَةٍ . بِغَيْرَةٍ
Warmth *n.*	دِفْءٌ . حَرَارَةٌ
Warn *v. t.*	حَذَّرَ . أَنْذَرَ
Warning *n.*	إِنْذَارٌ . إِخْطَارٌ
Warp *n.* or *v. t.*	سَدَاةٌ . حَرَّفَ
Warrant *n.*	تَفْوِيضٌ . إِجَازَةٌ . أَمْرٌ
Warrant *v. t.*	كَفَلَ . ضَمِنَ . بَرَّرَ
Warrantable *a.*	جَائِزٌ
Warrior *n.*	مُحَارِبٌ . جُنْدِيٌّ
Wart *n.*	ثُؤْلُولٌ ج ثَآلِيل
Wary *a.*	مُتَحَذِّرٌ . مُحْتَرِسٌ . بَصِيرٌ
Was *see* Be.	كَانَ يَكُونُ
Wash *v. t.* or *i.*	غَسَلَ ـِ . إِغْتَسَلَ
Wash *n.*	غَسْلٌ . غَسْلَةٌ
Washer-woman *n.*	غَسَّالَةٌ
Washing *n.*	غَسْلٌ . غَسَالَةٌ . غَسِيلٌ
Wasp *n.*	زُنْبُورٌ ج زَنَابِيرُ
Waspish *a.*	نَكِدٌ . سَرِيعُ الْغَيْظِ
Waste *v. t.* or *i.*	أَسْرَفَ . بَذَّرَ . ضَنِيَ ـَ
Waste *n.*	إِسْرَافٌ . خَرَابٌ . صَحْرَاءُ
Wasteful *a.*	مُسْرِفٌ . مُبَذِّرٌ
Watch *n.*	خَفِيرٌ . هَزِيعٌ . سَاعَةٌ
Watch *v. t.* or *i.*	حَرَسَ ـِ . رَاقَبَ . سَهِرَ ـَ
Watchful *v.*	مُرَاقِبٌ . حَذِرٌ . مُنْتَبِهٌ
Watch-maker *n.*	سَاعَاتِيٌّ

Watchman *n.* حَارِسٌ . رَقِيبٌ

Watch-tower *n.* بُرْجُ ٱلرَّقِيبِ

Watchword *n.* شِعَارٌ

Water *n.* or *v. i.* مَآءٌ . سَقَى ـِ

Water-course *n.* مَجْرَى مَآءٍ

Water-cress *n.* قُرَّةُ ٱلْعَيْنِ (نبات)

Waterfall *n.* شَلَّالٌ

Water-melon *n.* بَطِّيخٌ أَحْمَرُ

Waterproof *n.* مُشَمَّعٌ

Water-spout *n.* عَمُودُ مَاءٍ

Watery *a.* مَائِيٌّ . خَفِيفٌ . تَافِهٌ

Wave *n.* or *v.t.* or *i.* مَوْجٌ . هَزَّ . هَاجَ ـُ

Waver *v. i.* تَرَدَّدَ . إِرْتَابَ . تَمَايَلَ

Wavy *a.* مُتَمَوِّجٌ

Wax *n.* or *v.t.* or *i.* شَمْعٌ . أَشْمَعَ . زَادَ ـِ

Waxen *a.* شَمْعِيٌّ

Waxwork *n.* صُوَرٌ أَوْ شُخُوصٌ شَمْعِيَّةٌ

Way *n.* طَرِيقٌ . مِنْوَالٌ . وَسِيلَةٌ

Wayfarer / Wayfaring *n.* مُسَافِرٌ . إِبْنُ ٱلسَّبِيلِ

Waylay *v. t.* اكْمَنَ لَهُ

Wayward *a.* جَامِحٌ غَيْرُ مُطِيعٍ

We *pron. pl.* نَحْنُ

Weak *a.* ضَعِيفٌ . وَاهِنٌ . ومُرْتَخٍ

Weaken *v. t.* أَضْعَفَ . أَوْهَنَ

Weakness *n.* ضَعْفٌ . وَهْنٌ . سُقْمٌ

Weal *n.* خَيْرٌ . سَعَادَةٌ

Wealth *n.* ثَرْوَةٌ . غِنًى . وَفْرَةٌ

Wealthy *a.* غَنِيٌّ . ذُو ثَرْوَةٍ

Wean *v. t.* فَطَمَ ـِ

Weapon *n.* سِلَاحٌ

Wear *v. t.* لَبِسَ ـَ . أَبْلَى

Weariness *n.* تَعَبٌ . ضَنْكٌ . إِعْيَآءٌ

Wearisome *a.* مُتْعِبٌ . مُمِلٌّ

Weary *a.* or *v. t.* تَعِبٌ . أَتْعَبَ . ازعج

Weasel *n.* إِبْنُ عِرْسٍ . نِمْسٌ

Weather *n.* حَالَةُ ٱلْجَوِّ . طَقْسٌ

Weather-cock *n.*	دَوَّارَةُ ٱلرِّيحِ
Weave *v. t.*	حَاكَ . نَسَجَ ـُ
Weaver *n.*	حَائِكٌ . نَسَّاجٌ
Web *n.*	نَسِيجٌ
Wed *v. t.* or *i.*	تَزَوَّجَ
Wedding *n.*	عُرْسٌ
Wedge *n.*	سَفِينٌ
Wedlock *n.*	زِيجَةٌ . زَوَاجٌ
Wednesday *n.*	يَوْمُ ٱلأَرْبِعَاءِ
Weld *n.* or *v. t.*	عُشْبٌ بَرِّي . قَلَعَهُ
Week *n.*	أُسْبُوعٌ
Weekday *a.*	غَيْرُ يَوْمِ ٱلاحد
Weekly *a.* or *ad.*	اسْبُوعِيٌّ . أسْبوعِيًّا
Weep *v. i.*	بَكَى
Weevil *n.*	سُوسٌ
Weigh *v. t.*	وَزَنَ ـِ . تامَّل . ثَقُلَ ـُ
Weight *n.*	وَزْنٌ . ثِقْلٌ . أَهَمِيَّةٌ
Weighty *a.*	ثَقِيلٌ . مُهِمٌّ
Weir *n.*	سَدُّ نَهْرٍ
Weird *a.*	غَيْرُ طَبِيعِيٍّ . غَرِيبٌ
Welcome *n.* or *a.*	تَأْهِيلٌ . مُرَحَّبٌ بِهِ
Weld *v. t.*	لَحَمَ ـُ
Welfare / Well-being *n.*	خَيْرٌ . حظ . سَلَامَةٌ
Well *a.* or *ad.*	مُعَافًى . جَيِّدٌ . حَسَنًا
Well *n.* or *v. i.*	بِئْرٌ . نَبَعَ ـَ
Well-bred *a.*	مُهَذَّبٌ . حسن ٱلتَّرْبِيَةِ
Well-nigh *ad.*	تقريباً
Well-spring *n.*	نَبْعٌ
Welter *v. i.*	تمرَّغ . تَقَلَّبَ
Wen *n.*	سِلْعَةٌ . غُدَّةٌ
Wench *n.*	جَارِيَةٌ
Went *See* Go.	ذَهَبَ ـَ
Were *See* Be.	كانُوا
West *n.*	مَغْرِبٌ . غَرْبٌ
Western *a.*	غَرْبِيٌّ
Westward *ad.*	غرْباً . نَحْوَ ٱلغَرْبِ

Wet *a.* مَبْلُول . رَطْبٌ . مَاطِرٌ

Wether *n.* كَبْشٌ خَصِيٌّ

Whale *n.* حُوتٌ

Wharf *n.* إِسْكِلَة . (رَصِيفٌ)

What *pron.* مَا . مَاذَا

Whatever / Whatsoever } *pron.* مَهْمَا . كُلَّمَا

Wheat *n.* قَمْحٌ . بِرٌّ . حِنْطَةٌ

Wheedle *v. t.* دَاهَنَ . دَارَى . تَمَلَّقَ

Wheel *n.* دُولَابٌ (عَجَلَةٌ)

Wheel-barrow *n.* عَجَلَةُ ٱلْيَدِ

Whelp *n.* شِبْلٌ . جَرْوٌ

When *ad.* مَتَى . لما . عِنْدِ ما

Whence *ad.* مِنْ أَيْنَ . مِنْ حَيْثُ

Whenever / Whensoever } *ad.* كُلَّمَا . مَتَى مَا

Where *ad.* أَيْنَ . إِلَى أَيْنَ . حَيْثُ

Whereabouts *ad.* or *n.* أَيْنَ . مَكَانٌ

Whereas *conj.* بِمَا أَنْ . عَلَى أَنَّ

Whereat *ad.* عِنْدَ ذَلِكَ

Whereby *ad.* أَلَّذِي بِهِ . مِنْ حَيْثُ

Wherefore *ad.* لِذَلِكَ . مِنْ ثَمَّ . لِمَاذَا

Wherein *ad.* حَيْثُ أَيْنَ

Whereof *ad.* أَلَّذِي مِنْهُ

Whereon / Whereupon } *ad.* إِذْ ذَاكَ . عِنْدَ ذَلِكَ

Wheresoever / Wherever } *ad.* حَيْثُمَا . أَيْنَمَا

Whereto / Whereunto } *ad.* إِلَى حَيْثُ

Wherewith / Wherewithal } *ad.* مَا بِهِ . بِمَا

Whet *v. t.* سَنَّ . هَيَّجَ . شَوَّقَ

Whether *pron.* or *conj.* أَيُّهُمَا . إِنْ كَانَ

Whetstone *n.* مِسَنٌّ . مِشْحَذٌ . صُلَّبٌ

Whey *n.* مَصْلٌ

Which *pron.* مَا . مَنْ . أَلَّذِي

Which-ever / Which-so-ever } *pron.* أَيُّمَا . هٰذَا أَوْ ذَاكَ

Whiff *n.* نَفْحَةٌ . نَفَسٌ

Whig *n.* مِنْ حِزْبِ ٱلْأَحْرَارِ ٱلْإِنْكِلِيز

While *n.* مُدَّة . وَقْتٌ . حِينٌ

While / Whilst } *ad.*	بينما . حينما . لمَّا . إذْ
Whim *n.*	وَهْمٌ . تصوُّرٌ باطِلٌ
Whimper *v. i.*	بَكى خفيفاً كالْوَلَدِ
Whimsical *a.*	وَهْمِيٌّ . غريبٌ
Whine *v. i.* or *n.*	هرَّ ـِ . هرِيرٌ
Whip *n.* or *v. t.*	سَوْطٌ . ساطَ ـُ
Whir *v. i.*	دَارَ بِصَوْتٍ . خرَّ
Whirl *v. t.* or *i.*	دوَّرَ ـُ دار
Whirlpool *n.*	دُرْدُورٌ
Whirlwind *n.*	زَوْبَعَةٌ
Whisker *n.*	لِحْيَةُ ٱلْعَارِضِ
Whisk *v. t.*	حرَّكَ . جَرَفَ بِسُرْعَةٍ
Whisky *n.*	نوْعٌ منَ ٱلْعَرَقِ . وِسكِي
Whisper *n.* or *v. i.*	وَسْوَسَةٌ . سارَّ
Whistle *v. i.* or *n.*	صفرَ ـِ . صافُورَةٌ
Whit *n.*	نُقْطَةٌ . ذَرَّةٌ . بَتَّةٌ
White *a.* or *n.*	أَبْيَضُ . بياضٌ
Whiten *v. t.* or *i.*	بَيَّضَ . إِبْيَضَّ
Whiteness *n.*	بَيَاضٌ
Whitewash *n.*	بَيَاضُ ٱلْجِيرِ
Whither *ad.*	إِلى أَيْنَ
Whithersoever *ad.*	أَيْنَمَا . حَيْثُمَا
Whitish *a.*	ضَارِبٌ إِلى ٱلْبَيَاضِ
Whittle *v. t.*	قَشَرَ بِسِكِّينٍ . بَرَى ـِ
Whiz *n.* or *v. i.*	صَفِيرُ ٱلسَّهْمِ . صَفَرَ ـِ
Who *rel.* or *int. pron.*	الَّذِي . أَيُّ . مَنْ
Whoever *rel. pron.*	مَنْ . كُلُّ مَنْ
Whole *a.*	كُلٌّ . صَحِيحٌ . كامِلٌ
Wholesale *n.* or *a.*	بَيْعٌ بِالْجُمْلَةِ
Wholesome *a.*	سَلِيمٌ . مُوَافِقُ ٱلصِّحَّةِ
Wholly *ad.*	جُمْلَةً . كافَّةً . تَمَاماً
Whom *pron.* See Who.	ٱلَّذِي
Whoop *n.* or *v. i.*	صِيَاحٌ . صَاحَ ـِ . زَعَق
Whooping-cough *n.*	دَاءُ ٱلشَّهْقَةِ
Whore *n.*	زَانِيَةٌ . عَاهِرَةٌ . فَاجِرَةٌ
Whoredom *n.*	عَهْرٌ . فُجُورٌ

Whose *poss. pron. See* Who [er.
Whosoever *rel. pron. See* Whoev-
Why *ad.* لماذا . لِمَ
Wick *n.* فتيلة . شعيلة
Wicked *a.* شرير . اثيم . طالح
Wickedness *n.* شر . إثم
Wicket *n.* باب صغير
Wide *a.* واسع . فسيح . عريض
Widely *ad.* جدا . شائعا . إتساعا
Widen *v. t.* or *i.* وسع . إتسع
Widow *n.* أرملة ج أرامل
Widower *n.* ارمل
Widowhood *n.* ترمل
Width *n.* عرض . إتساع
Wield *v. t.* إستعمل . أدار . دبر
Wife *n.* زوجة . قرينة . إمرأة
Wig *n.* شعر مستعار
Wigwam *n.* كوخ الهنود
Wild *a.* بري . وحشي . فالت

Wilderness *n.* برية . بادية
Wildly *ad.* بجنون . طيشا
Wile *n.* حيلة . . مكيدة . خدعة
Wilful *a.* عنيد
Wilfulness *n.* عناد
Will *v. i.* سوف
Will *v. t.* or *n.* أراد . أوصى . إرادة . وصية
Willing *a.* راض . مريد
Willingness *n.* رضى . قبول
Willow *n.* صفصاف
Wilt *v. i.* ذمل ـ
Wily *a.* بكار . مختال . خداع
Win *v. t.* ربح ـ . فاز ـ . أرضى
Wince *v. i.* جفل عن
Wind *n.* ريح
Wind *v. t.* or *i.* فتل ـ . دار ـ
Winding-sheet *n.* كفن ج اكفان
Windlass *n.* آلة لرفع الأثقال

Windmill *n.* طَاحُون تُدِيرهُ ٱلرِّيحُ

Window *n.* طَاقَةٌ . كُوَّةٌ . شُبَّاكٌ

Windpipe *n.* قصبة آلرِّئَةِ

Windward *ad.* إِلَى جِهَةِ ٱلرِّيحِ

Windy *a.* كَثِيرُ ٱلرِّيحِ . بَاطِلٌ

Wine *n.* خمرٌ . نبيذٌ

Wine-bibber *n.* شرِّيبُ خَمْرٍ

Wine-glass *n.* قَدَحٌ . كَاسٌ

Wing *n.* جَنَاحٌ . كَنَفٌ

Wink *v. i.* طَرَفَ ـِ . تَغَاضى عَنْ

Winner *n.* فَائِزٌ . غَالِبٌ

Winning *a.* مُرْضٍ . مُسْتَمِيلُ ٱلْقَلْبِ

Winnow *v. t.* ذَرَّى

Winter *n.* فصلُ ٱلشِّتَاءِ

Wintery / Wintry } *a.* شَتَوِيٌّ . شَاتٍ . بَارِدٌ

Wipe *v. t.* مَسَحَ ـَ . نَظَفَ . مَحَا ـُ

Wire *n.* or *v. t.* شَرِيطٌ . سِلْكٌ . رَاسَلَ بِهِ

Wiry *a.* شَرِيطِيٌّ . ضَلِيعٌ . قَوِيٌّ

Wisdom *n.* حِكْمَةٌ . فِطْنَةٌ

Wise *a.* حَكِيمٌ . عَاقِلٌ

Wish *v. t.* or *n.* اراد . تَمَنَّى . إِرَادَةٌ . بُغْيَةٌ

Wistful *a.* تَائِقٌ . رَاغِبٌ

Wit *n.* ذَكَاءٌ . حِذْقٌ . بَصِيرَةٌ

Witch *n.* سَاحِرَةٌ

Witchcraft *n.* سِحْرٌ . كَهَانَةٌ

Wichery *n.* سِحْرٌ . فُتُونٌ

With *prep.* مَعْ . بِ . عِنْدَ . مِنْ

Withal *ad.* أَيْضاً . مَعْ كلِّهِ

Withdraw *v. t.* or *i.* إِسْتَرَدَّ . إِرْتَدَّ

Withdrawal *n.* إِسْتِرْجَاعٌ . إِرْتِدَادٌ

Wither *v. t.* or *i.* أَذْبَلَ . ذَبَلَ ـُ

Withers *n. pl.* حَارِكٌ (عَظْمٌ بِأَعْلَى ٱلظَّهْرِ)

Withhold *v. t.* أَمسَكَ عَنْ

Within *prep.* دَاخِلَ . فِي . ضِمْنَ

Without *prep.* خَارِجٌ . بِدُونِ . مَالَمْ

Withstand *v. t.* قَاوَمَ . ثَبَتَ ضِدَّ

Witless *a.* غَبِيٌّ . أَخْرَقُ

Witness *n.* or *v. i.* شَاهِدٌ . شَهَادَةٌ . شَاهَدَ

Witticism *n.* مُلْحَةٌ

Wittingly *ad.* قَصْداً . بِعِلْمٍ

Witty *a.* ذَكِيٌّ . ظَرِيفٌ

Wives *n. pl. See* Wife زَوْجَاتٌ

Wizard *n.* سَاحِرٌ

Woe *n.* وَيْلٌ . بَلِيَّةٌ . حُزْنٌ

Woe-begone *a.* حَزِينٌ . مَغْمُومٌ

Woeful / **Woful** } *a.* حَزِينٌ . مُحْزِنٌ

Wolf *n.* ذِئْبٌ ج ذِئَابٌ

Woman *n.* (*pl.* Women). مَرْأَةٌ . إِمْرَأَةٌ

Womanhood *n.* حَالَةُ ٱلْمَرْأَةِ. ٱلنِّسَاءُ

Woman-kind *n.* جِنْسُ ٱلنِّسَاءِ

Womb *n.* رَحِمٌ ج أَرْحَامٌ

Wonder *n.* تَعَجُّبٌ. غَرِيبَةٌ . مُعْجِزَةٌ

Wonderful / **Wondrous** } *a.* عَجِيبٌ . مُدْهِشٌ

Wont *a.* or *n.* مُعْتَادٌ . عَادَةٌ

Wonted *a.* مُعْتَادٌ

Woo *v. t.* تَوَدَّدَ إِلَى . إِسْتَعْطَفَ

Wood *n.* خَشَبٌ . حَطَبٌ . غَابَةٌ

Woodcock *n.* دُجَاجُ ٱلأَرْضِ

Woodcut *n.* نَقْشٌ عَلَى خَشَبٍ

Wooded *a.* ذُو أَشْجَارٍ

Wooden *a.* خَشَبِيٌّ . مِنْ خَشَبٍ

Woodman *n.* حَطَّابٌ

Woody *a.* خَشَبِيٌّ . كَثِيرُ ٱلأَشْجَارِ

Woof *n.* لُحْمَةٌ

Wool *n.* صُوفٌ

Woollen *a.* صُوفِيٌّ . مِنْ صُوفٍ

Woolly *a.* صُوفِيٌّ . ذُو صُوفٍ

Word *n.* كَلِمَةٌ . وَعْدٌ . أَمْرٌ

Wording *n.* عِبَارَةٌ . تَرْكِيبُ عِبَارَةٍ

Wordy *a.* كَثِيرُ ٱلْكَلَامِ

Work *n.* or *v. i.* شُغْلٌ . عَمَلٌ . إِشْتَغَلَ

Worker / **Workman** } *a.* صَانِعٌ . فَاعِلٌ

Workmanship n. صَنْعَةٌ . عَمَلٌ

Workshop n. مَعْمَلٌ . دُكَّانُ شُغْلٍ

World n. عَالَمٌ . دُنْيَا

Worldliness n. مَحَبَّةُ ٱلدُّنْيَا

Worldly n. مُحِبُّ ٱلدُّنْيَا . دُنْيَوِيٌّ

Worm n. دُودَةٌ ج دُودٌ . دِيدَان

Worm-eaten a. مُسَوَّسٌ

Wormy a. مُدَوِّدٌ . كَثِيرُ ٱلدُّودِ

Worn pp. مَلْبُوسٌ . تَعِبٌ . مَنْهُوكٌ

Worry v. t. or i. كَدَّرَ . أَهَمَّ . إِهْتَمَّ

Worse a. or ad. أَرْدَأُ . شَرٌّ

Worship n. or v. t. عِبَادَةٌ . عَبَدَ ـُ

Worshipper n. عَابِدٌ . سَاجِدٌ

Worst a. or v. t. اَلْأَرْدَأُ . غَلَبَ ـِ

Worsted n. or a. غَزْلٌ صُوفِيٌّ

Worth n. or a. قِيمَةٌ . مُعَادِلٌ . مُسْتَحِقٌ

Worthily ad. بِٱسْتِحْقَاقٍ . بِلِيَاقَةٍ

Worthless a. بِلَا قِيمَةٍ . غَيْرُ نَافِعٍ

Worthy a. مُسْتَحِقٌ . أَهْلٌ . فَاضِلٌ

Would (See Will.) سَوْفَ . يَالَيْتَ

Wound n. or v. t. جُرْحٌ . جَرَحَ ـَ

Wound pp. of Wind. مَفْتُولٌ . مَلْفُوفٌ

Wove / Woven } See Weave. مَنْسُوجٌ

Wrangle v. i. نَازَعَ . شَاجَرَ

Wrap v. t. لَفَّ ـُ

Wrapper / Wrapping } n. لِفَافَةٌ . غِلَافٌ

Wrath n. غَيْظٌ . سُخْطٌ . غَضَبٌ

Wrathful a. غَضُوبٌ . سَاخِطٌ . مُغْتَاظٌ

Wreak v. أَنْزَلَ عَلَى . أَحَلَّ بِهِ

Wreathe n. اكْلِيلُ أَزْهَارٍ . ضَفِيرَةٌ

Wreathe v. t. ضَفَرَ ـِ لَفَّ ـُ

Wreck v. t. or n. كَسَّرَ . خَرَّبَ . كَسْرٌ

Wren n. ضَرْبٌ مِنَ ٱلْعَصَافِيرِ

Wrench v. t. لَوَّى . إِغْتَصَبَ

Wrest v. t. إِغْتَصَبَ . خَطَفَ ـَ . حَرَّفَ

Wrestle v. i. صَارَعَ

Wrestling *n.* مُصَارَعَةٌ
Wretch *n.* شَقِيٌّ . خَبِيثٌ . حَقِيرٌ
Wretched *a.* شَقِيٌّ . تَعِسٌ . بَائِسٌ
Wriggle *v. i.* تَلَوَّى
Wright *n.* صَانِعٌ
Wring *v. t.* عَصَرَ ـِ . إِغْتَصَبَ
Wrinkle *n.* or *v. t.* جَعْدَةٌ . تَجَعَّدَ
Wrist *n.* مِعْصَمٌ . رُسْغٌ
Write *n.* كَتَبَ ـُ . حَرَّرَ . أَلَّفَ
Writer *n.* كَاتِبٌ . مُؤَلِّفٌ
Writhe *v. t.* تَلَوَّى
Writing *n.* كِتَابٌ . كِتَابَةٌ
Written *a.* مَكْتُوبٌ . خَطِّيٌّ
Wrong *n.* ظُلْمٌ . ضَرَرٌ . خَطَأٌ
Wrong *n.* غَيْرُ صَحِيحٍ . مُخْطِئٌ
Wrong *v. t.* ظَلَمَ ـِ . أَضَرَّ . أَسَاءَ إِلَى
Wrongful *a.* مُضِرٌّ . ظَالِمٌ . غَيْرُ عَادِلٍ
Wroth *a.* مُغْتَاظٌ . غَضْبَانُ
Wrought *a.* مَصْنُوعٌ
Wrung *See* Wring. مَعْصُورٌ
Wry *a.* أَزْوَرُ . مُعَوَّجٌ

Y

Yacht *n.* سَفِينَةٌ صَغِيرَةٌ لِلتَّنَزُّهِ . يَخْتٌ
Yard *n.* ذِرَاعٌ إِنْكِلِيزِيٌّ
Yarn *n.* غَزْلٌ . قِصَّةٌ . طَوِيلَةٌ
Yawl *n.* زَوْرَقٌ
Yawn *v. i.* or *n.* تَثَاءَبَ . تَثَاؤُبٌ
Ye *p. pron.* أَنْتُمْ . أَنْتُنَّ
Yea *ad.* نَعَمْ
Year *n.* سَنَةٌ . عَامٌ

Yearling *n.*	حوْلِيٌّ . إِبْنُ سَنَةٍ
Yearly *a.*	سَنَوِيٌّ
Yearn *v. i.*	إِشْتَاقَ إِلَى . حنَّ ـِ
Yearning *n.*	حَنِينٌ . شَوْقٌ
Yeast *n.*	خَمِيرٌ
Yell *v. i.* or *n.*	صَاحَ ـِ . صَيْحَةٌ
Yellow *a.*	أَصْفَرُ
Yellowish *a.*	ضَارِبٌ إِلَى ٱلصُّفْرَةِ
Yelp *v. i.*	هَرَّ ـِ . نَبَحَ ـَ
Yeoman *n.*	فَلاحٌ . صَاحِبُ مُلْكٍ
Yes *ad.*	نَعمْ . بَلَى
Yesterday *ad.*	أَلْبَارِحَةَ . أَمْسِ
Yet *conj.*	مَعْ ذَلِكَ . بَعْدُ
Yield *v. t.* or *i.*	أَنْتَجَ . سَلَّمَ . أَذْعَنَ
Yielding *a.* or *p. pr.*	مذْعِنٌ . لَيِّنٌ . مُنْتِجٌ
Yoke *n.* or *v. t.*	نِيرٌ . وَضَعَ ٱلنِّيرَ
Yoke-fellow *n.*	أَلِيفٌ . شَرِيكٌ
Yolk / **Yelk** } *n.*	محُّ ٱلْبَيْضِ (الصفار)
Yon *a.* / **Yonder** *ad.* }	هنَاكَ . ذَاكَ
Yore *ad.*	قَدِيماً
You *p. pron.*	أَنْتمْ . أَنْتنَّ
Young *a.* or *n.*	صَغِيرُ ٱلعمرِ . طِفْلٌ
Younger *a.*	أَصْغَرُ عُمْراً
Youngest *n.*	الأَصْغَرُ عُمراً
Youngster *n.*	صَبِيٌّ . فَتًى
Your *poss. pron.*	كَ . كمْ . كنَّ . كمَا
Yours *pross. pron.*	لَكَ . لَكُمْ . لَكُنَّ
Yourself *p. pron.*	أَنْتَ نَفْسكَ
Youth *n.*	حَدَاثَة صَبْوَةٌ
Youthful *a.*	حَدِيث ٱلسِّنِّ . شَابٌّ

Z

Zeal *n.*	غيرة . مروءة. إقدام
Zealot *n.* / **Zealous** *a*	غيور
Zebra *n.*	فرس وحشي مخطط
Zenith *n.*	سمت الرأس
Zephyr *n.*	نسيم
Zero *n.*	صفر
Zest *n.*	شهية . لذة
Zigzag *a.* or *n.*	متعرج . تعريج
Zinc *n.*	توتيا
Zion *n.*	صهيون
Zodiac *n.*	منطقة البروج
Zone *n.*	منطقة
Zoological *a.*	منوط بعلم الحيوان
Zoologist *n.*	عالم بالحيوان
Zoology *n.*	علم الحيوان

English-Arabic

SUPPLEMENT

of Modern Science Terminology

A

abdomen بَطْن ، جوف
aberration زَيغ ، انحِراف
absolute alcohol كُحُولٌ صِرف
absolute temperature دَرجةُ الحرارة المُطلَقَة
absolute zero دَرجةُ ٱلصِّفر المُطلَق
absorption امتِصاص ، مَصّ
acceleration تَسارُع ، تَعجيل
accommodation تكَيُّف ، تَكييف
accumulator مِرْكَم ، مُرَكِّم ، حاشِدة أو مُدَّخِرة كَهربائيّة
acetic acid حامِضُ الخَلّيك ، حامضُ الخَلّ
acetone خَلُّون ، أسِيتون
acetylene أسِيتيلين ، غاز الأسِيتيلين (إيثاين)
achene اخينيوم ، ثمرة فقيرة
Achilles tendon وَتَرُ أخِلّس ، وَتَرُ ٱلعُرقُوب
achromatic lens عَدَسة لالونيّة ، عَدَسة أكروماتيّة
acidic حامِضيّ ، حَمْضِيّ
acid radical شِقٌّ حامِضِيّ
acid salt مِلْحٌ حامِضِيّ
acids ألحوامِض
acoustics السَّمعيّات ، ألصَّوتيّات ، عِلم الصَّوت
activated carbon كَربونٌ مُنَشَّط
adhesion التِصاق ، تلاصُق ،جاذِبيّةُ الآلتِصاق
adrenal body غُدَّةُ الكُظْر ، ألكُظر
adrenalin أدرينالين ، كُظْرين
adsorption امتِزاز ، لُزوب
adventitious عَرَضيّ
aerobic respiration تنفُّسٌ هَوائِيّ
aerosol هباءٌ جَوِّيّ • مِرذاذٌ بالغاز المَضغوط
afferent وارِد ، مُوَرِّد ، ناقِلٌ من الطرف الى ٱلمركز
affinity أُلفَـة
afterbirth ألسُّخُد وأغشيته ، ألخَلاص
agar agar آغار ، أغار آغار
aggregate fruit ثَمرة مُتَجمِّعة ، ثمرة مُتضاعِفة
agonic line خطُّ آللاّإنحراف (المَغنطِيسيّ)
air bladder مَثانَةٌ هَوائِيّة
air sac كِيسٌ هَوائِيّ
albumen زُلال ، آح (بياضُ البَيض) ، سُوَيداءُ آلبزرة
alchemist مُمارِسُ الكيمياءِ آلقديمة
alchemy ألكِيمياءُ القَديمة
algae أُشْنات ، طحالِب
alimentary canal قَناةُ آلهَضْم
alkali قِلْي ، ألقَالي
alkali metals فِلِزّاتٌ قِلْويّة
alkaline (مَحلولٌ) قِلْويّ
allotrope شَكلٌ مُتآصِل
allotropy تآصُل ، تَعَدُّدُ الأشكال آلمُتآصلة
alloy سَبِيكَة ، أُشابَة ، خَليط مَعدِنيّ
alpha particle دقيقة ألفا ، جُسَيْمٌ ألفيّ
alternating current تَيّارٌ مُتناوِب ، تَيّار مُتَرَدِّد
alternation of generations تَناوُبُ الأجيال ، تعاقُبُ الأجيال
alternator مُنَوِّب ، مُوَلِّدُ التيّار المُتناوِب
altimeter ألتيمتر ، مقياسُ الارتِفاع
aluminium ألومِنيوم
alveolus حُجَيرة ، حُوَيْصِلَة

amalgam	مُلْغَم
amber	راتينجٌ أصفر ، كَهْرَمان
amino acids	حَوامِضُ أمينيّة
ammeter	أمّيتر ، أمبير مِتر ، مِقياس الأمبير
ammonia	أمُونيا ، غازُ النُّشادِر
amnion	ألسَّلَى ، الصَّاءَة
amorphous	لاشكليّ ، غير مُتَبلْوِر ، لابِلّوري
ampere	أمبير
ampere-hour	أمبير ساعَة ، أمْبير ساعيّ
amphibia	بَرمائيّات ، قَوازِب
amphibious	بَرْمائي ، قازِب
amphoteric	أمفوتَري ، حَمْضيٌّ قِلْويّ
amplifier	مُضَخِّم
amplitude	سَعَة ، قِمةُ ٱلذُّرْوَة
ampulla	أمبولَة ، مَجَلَة
anabolism	أيضٌ بِنائي ، ابْتِناء ، بِناء
anaemia	أنيمية ، فَقْرُ ٱلدَّم
anaerobic respiration	تنفّسٌ لاهوائيّ
anaesthetic	مُخَدِّر ، بَنْج
analysis	تحليل
anatomy	تشريح ، عِلمُ التشريح
aneroid	لامائِليّ
Angiospermae	كاسِيات ٱلبزر ، وعائيات البُزور
angular velocity	سُرعة زاويّة
anhydride	أنْهيدريد ، أندريد ، بِلا ماء
anhydrous	لامائيّ ، خالٍ من ٱلماء
animal	حَيَوان ،
animal charcoal	ألفحم ٱلحَيَواني
anion	آنيُون ، أيونٌ سالِب الشّحنة
annuals	الحَوْليّات ، النباتات الحَوليّة
annual rings	حلقات حَوليّة ، حلقات سَنَويّة
annulus	حَلْقَة ، طَوق
anode	أنُود ، مَصْعَد
antenna	زُبانَى ، قَرنُ استِشعار
anterior	أماميّ ، قَبْليّ
anther	مِئبَر
anthracite	فحم الأنثراسيت
anthrax	ألجَمْرة
antibiotic	مُضادٌّ حَيَويّ ، مُردٍ
antibody	جِسْمٌ مُضادّ
antifreeze	مُقاوِمُ التجمُّد ، مُعيقُ التجَمُّد
antigen	مُوَلِّدُ المُضادّ
antiseptic	مُطَهِّر ، مانِعٌ لِلعُفونة
anus	شَرَج ، إسْت
anvil	سَنْدان ، العَلاة
aorta	وَتين ، شِريانُ الوَتين
aperture	كُوَّة ، فُتْحَة
appendix	زائدة ، الزائدة الدُّوديّة
aquatic	مائيّ ، يألَف ٱلماء
aqueous	مائي ، ذو ماء
aqueous humour	خِلْطٌ مائي ، الرُّطوبة المائية (في العَيْن)
arable	مُفتلَحٌ ، صالح لِلزِّراعة
arboreal	شجريّ
arc light	مِصباحٌ قوسيّ
area	مِساحَة
argon	أرغون ، أرجون
armature	مُتحرِّض ، عُضو الإنتاج
arteriole	شُرَيِّن ، شريان دقيق
artery	شِريان
articulation	اتّصال مَفصِليّ ، تَمَفْصُل
asbestos	أميَنْتُوس ، حَرير صَخْري
aseptic	مُعَقَّم ، مُطَهَّر
asexual	لاجِنْسيّ ، لاتزاوُجيّ

aspirator سَفّاطة ، مَصّاصة ، شَفّاطة

assemblage مَجموعة ، تركيبة

assimilation تَمثيل ، تمثُّل ، ابتِناء

association تَرابُط ، ارتباط ، ترابُط ، تَداعٍ

astronomical telescope مِقرابٌ فَلكي ، تِلِسكوب فلكيّ

atlas فَهقة ، فِقرَةُ العُنق الأولى

atmosphere جَوٌّ • وَحدَةُ الضَغط الجوّي

atmospheric pressure ضَغطٌ جَوّي

atom ذَرّة ، جَوهَرٌ فَرد

atomic ذَرّي

atomic energy الطّاقة الذَرّية

atomic mass unit وَحدةُ الكُتلة الذرّية

atomic number العَدَدُ الذرّي

atomic pile قَمين ذريّ ، مُفاعِلٌ ذَرّي

atomic weight وزنٌ ذَرّي

atrium أُذينُ القَلب

auditory سَمعيّ

auricle أُذَينُ القَلب

axil إبْط

axis مِحور ، خطُّ المِحوَر • ألفايق ، فقرة العنق الثانية

axon مِحور اللّيفة العصبيّة ، مِحورُ العَصَبة

B

backbone صُلب ، عَمود فَقَري

bacteria بكتريا ، بكتيريا ، جراثيم ، راجبيّات

bakelite باكَليت

baking powder مَسحوقُ الخَبيز ، خميرة اصطِناعيّة

baking soda صودا الخَبيز ، بيكربونات الصودا

balance مِيزان

barb أسَلة

bark لحاء ، قِلف ، قِشر

barometer بارومِتر ، مِرواز ، مِقياسُ الضغط الجوّي

base قاعِدة

basic قاعِدِيّ

basicity قاعِديّة

basic oxide أُكسيد قاعِديّ

basic salt مِلح قاعِدي

bast لحاءٌ داخليّ

battery بطّارية ، حاشِدة

beaker كأس ، كُوب

beam عاتِق (الميزان) • حُزمَة أشِعة

beet sugar سُكّرُ البَنجر

benzene بِنزين

beriberi رُزام ، ألبري بَري

berry ثمرة لُبيّة ، ثمرة عِنَبيّة

beta particle جُسَيمٌ بائي ، دقيقةُ بيتا

bi- ثُنائي ، ثاني

biceps ذاتُ الرأسَين ، العضلة ذاتُ الرأسين

biconcave ثُنائيُّ التقعُّر ، مُقعَّرُ الوَجهَين

biconvex مُحدَّب الوجهين ، ثنائي التحدُّب

bicuspid ذو شُرفَتَين • صِمام ذو شُرفتين

biennial مُحول ، نبات ثُنائي الحَوْل

bile مِرّة ، الصَّفراء

bile duct قَناةُ الصَّفراء

billion بِلْيُون

bimetallic strip شَريحة ثُنائيّة المَعدِن

binary ثُنائي العُنصُر ، ثنائي

binoculars مِنْظارٌ ثُنائي ٱلعَيْنِيَّة ، ذو العينيتَيْن
biology بَيُولوجية • علم الأحياء
bivalve ذُو صِمامين
black lead غرافيت تجاري
bladder مَثَانَة
bladderworm يَرَقانَةُ الشّريطية ، يرقَانَةُ الدودة الوحيدة
blast furnace فِرنُ الصَّهر ، الفُرنُ العَالي
bleaching قَصْر ، تَقْصير (الألوان) ، تَبْييض
bleaching powder مَسْحُوقُ ٱلقَصْر ، مسحوق تقصير الألوان
blend مَزيج ، تَوْليفة
blight آفة
block and tackle بَكَّارة ، بكَرةٌ وحَبْل
blood دَم
blood group فِئَةُ الدّم ، زُمْرَةُ الدم
blowpipe قَصَبَةُ نَفْخ ، بُوري ، حِملاج
blubber شَحمُ ٱلحُوت
boat قارِب ، زَورق
bob ثِقَل ٱلبندول
boiling غَلَيان
boiling point نُقطةُ ٱلغَلَيان ، درجة الغليان
bond وَصْلة ، رابطٌ كِيميائي
bone عَظْم
bone ash رَمادُ العَظْم
bone black ألفحمُ العَظْمِيّ
borax بَوْرَق ، بُورات الصوديوم المائية
bosshead قامِطةُ شَبْك ، صُرَّة قَمطٍ بٱلحامِل
botany عِلمُ النَّبات
bract قِنابَة ، قُنابَة
brain دِماغ
brass نُحاسٌ أصفَر
breastbone قَصّ ، عَظمُ الصَّدْر
breathing تنفُّس
brimstone كِبْريتُ ٱلعمُود
brine مَحلولٌ مِلحيّ
brittle قَصِفٌ ، قصِم
bronchus شُعْبَة هوائيّة
bronze ألبرونز
bud بُرعُم ، بُرَيْعِمَة
bulb بَصَلَة ، بُصَيْلَة
buoyancy طَفْويَّة ، دَفْعٌ تَعويميّ
burette سَحّاحَة
burning احتِراق ، إحراق
butane بيُوتان ، غازُ ٱلبيُوتان
by-product مُنتَجٌ ثانَوِيّ ، نِتاجٌ جانِبيّ

C

calcium ألكالسيوم • الكَلْسيُوم
calcium oxide أُكسيد ٱلكالسيُوم ، جِيرٌ حَيّ
calcium phosphate فُسفات الكالسيُوم
calcium sulphate كِبريتات الكالسيُوم
calibrate يُدَرِّج ، يُعايِر ، يُقَوِّم
callipers قَدَمة ، فِرجار ٱلثُّخن
calorie كالُوري ، سُعْر
calorimeter مِسْعَر ، كالُوريمتر
calyx كِمٌّ ، كأسُ الزَّهرة
cambium كمبيُوم ، قُلْب
camera كامِيرا ، آلةُ تَصوير
camouflage تَمويه ، تَعْمِيَة
camphor كافُور
canal قَناة

cane sugar	سُكَّرُ القَصَب
canine	كَلبِيّ · نابِيّ ، ناب
capacitor	مُكَثِّف
capillarity	ألخاصّة الشَّعريَّة
capillary	شَعْرِيّ
capillary tube	أُنبوبٌ شَعرِيّ
capsule	جِرْوٌ ، عُلَيْبَة
carapace	ذَبْل
carbohydrates	كَربُوهِيدرات
carbon	كَربُون
carbon cycle	دَورةُ الكَربون (في الكَون)
carbon dioxide	ثاني أُكسيد الكَربُون
carbonates	كَربُونات ، أملاحُ حامِض الكربونيك
carbonic acid	حامِضُ الكربونيك
carnivore	لاحِم ، آكِلُ اللَّحْم
carpel	خِباء ، كَرْبَلَة ، مِدَقَّة
cartillage	غُضْروف
cast iron	حَديدُ الزَّهر ، حَديدُ الصَّبّ
catabolism	أيضٌ هَدْمِيّ ، اِنتِقاض
catalyst	حَفّاز ، مادّة حفّازَة
caterpillar	أُسروع ، سُرفَة ، يَرقانة العُثّ والفراش
cathode	كاثود ، مَهْبِط
cathode-ray tube	أُنبوب أشِعَّةِ الكاثود ، أنبوب الأشعة الكاثوديّة
caudal	ذَيْليّ ، ذَنَبِيّ
caustic	كـاوٍ ، أكّـال
caustic potash	ألبوتاسا الكاوِيَة
caustic soda	الصودا الكاوية
cell	خَلِيَّة ، عَمُود · خليّة ، وَحدةُ الأجسام الحيّة
cell division	انقِسام الخَلِيّة ، انشِطارٌ خَلَوِيّ
cell sap	عَصير خَلَوِيّ
cellulose	سِلْيُولوز ، خَلِيُّوز
cement	إسْمَنْت ، مِلاط · إسْمَنْتُ السِّنّ
centi-	سَنْتي ، جُزْءٌ من مِئة
centigrade temperature	درجةُ الحرارة بالميزان المئوي (السنتيغراد)
centre of gravity	مَرْكَزُ الثِّقَل
centrifugal force	قُوَّة نابِذَة ، قُوَّةُ الطَّرْد المركزيّ
centrifuge	نابِذَة ، فَرّازة ، جِهازُ طَرْدٍ مَرْكزيّ
cerebellum	مُخَيْخ ، رَنْح
cerebrum	مُخّ
chain	سِلْسِلة
chain reaction	تَفاعُل مُتَسلسِل
chalk	طَباشير ، حَجر كِلسيّ طباشيري
change of state	تَغيُّر الحالَة ، استِحالة
character	صِفـة
characteristic	مُمَيِّز ، خاصّ
chemical compound	مُرَكَّبٌ كيماوِيّ
chemical reaction	تفاعُل كيماوِيّ
chloride	كلُوريد ، كلورور
chlorine	كلُور ، غاز الكلُور
chlorophyll	يَخْضُور ، كلُوروفيل
choke	خانِقٌ ، مِلَفٌّ خانِق
chromosome	كروموسُوم ، صِبْغِيّ
cilia	هُدْب
circuit	دارَة ، دائرة
citric acid	حامِض الليمون
class	طـائفة
classification	تَصنيف

clavicle ترقوة

clay طِين ، طُفَال

cleavage تفلّج ، انشِقاق

clinical thermometer ترمومِتر طِبّي

clinker خَبَثُ الفحم ، مُخلّفات الاحتِراق

cloud سَحابَة ، غَيْمَة

coagulate خثّر ، جلّط ، تخثّر

coal فحم (حجري)

coal gas غاز الفحم ، غازُ الاستِصباح

coal tar قطِران الفحم ، قارُ الفحم الحجريّ

cocaine كُوكايين

coccyx عُصْعُص

cochlea قَوقَعة (الأذُن) ، حَلَزُون الأذُن الباطِنة

cocoon فَيْلجة ، صُلَّجة ، شَرْنَقَة

coelom جَوف

cohesion تماسُك ، جاذِبيةُ التماسُك

coition جماع ، اتّصالٌ جِنْسِيّ

coke كُوك ، فحمُ الكُوك

cold-blooded باردُ الدّم ، مُتغيّرُ درجة الحرارة

collarbone ترقُوة

colloid مادة غَروانيّة ، غَروانيّ

colon قُولُون

colonization استِعْمار ، انشاءُ المُستَوطنات

colony عَمِيرة ، مُستَعْمَرة

colour لون

colour blindness عَمى الألوان ، العَمى اللّونيّ

colour filter مُرشّحُ ألوان

combination إتّحاد (كيماوي)

combustion احتِراق

commutator مُبَدّل ، عضوُ تبديل ، عُضو توحيد

compass بُوصَلَة ، حُكّ

complementary colours ألوانٌ مُتَتامّة

complex مُركّب ، مُعقّدُ التركيب

component مُركّب ، مُكوّن ، عُنصرٌ مُكوّن

composition تَركيب ، تأليف ، تكوين

compound مُركّب (كيماوي)

concave مُقعّر

concentrate ركّز

concentrated مُركّز

concentration تَركيز

concentric مُتمركِز ، مُتّحِدُ المركز

concrete خرسانة ، إسْمنت ، أبْرَق

condensation تكاثُف ، تكثيف ، تكثّف

condense كثّف

condenser مُكثِّف (كهربائيّ) ، مُكثّفة (بصريّة) ، مُكثّف ، جِهاز تكثيف

conduction توصيل ، ايصال ، نَقْل

conductor مُوصّل ، ناقِل

cone كُوزٌ صنوبريّ ، مَخروط ، خلية مَخروطيّة

conjugation تزاوُج ، اقتِران

conjunctiva مُلتحمة ، غشاءُ الجَفن الباطنُ

consciousness وعْي ، إدراك

constant ثابِت ، كمّيّة ثابِتة

constituent مُقوّم ، جُزءٌ قِوامِيّ

control experiment تَجْربة حاكِمة ، تجربة مُقارِنَة

convection ألحَمْل (الحراري) ، ألتصعُّد (الحراريّ)

converging lens عدسةٌ لامّة ، عدسة مُجمِّعة

convex مُحدّب

coolant مُبرّد ، مَحلولٌ مُبرّد ، سائِلُ تَبريد

coordination	انسجام ، تَنسيق
copious	وافِر ، غزير
copper	نُحاس
copper sulphate	كِبريتات النُّحاس ، الزّاجُ الأزرق
coral	مَرجان ، بُسَّذ
cork	فِلّين ، لِحاء
corm	قُرمَة ، كَعبٌ بصَلِيّ
cornea	قَرنيَّة (العين) ، ألقرنيَّة
corolla	تُوَيج (الزهرة) ، إكليل
corpuscle	كُرَيّة ، جُسَيمٌ خَلَوِيّ
corrode	بَلِيَ ، صَدِيء ، تَحاتٌ ، حَتّ
corrosion	حتٌّ كيميائي ، تآكُل ، تَحاتّ
corrosive	أكّال ، حـاتّ
cortex	لِحاء ، قِشر
cosmic radiation	الإشعاعُ الكَونيّ
cotyledon	فِلقـة
couple	مُزدَوِجَة
covalent	إسهاميّ الترابُط
covalent compound	مُرَكَّبٌ إسهاميُّ التّرابُط
cowpox	جُدَريّ ألبَقَر
cracking	ألتّكسير ، ألتّقطير الهَدّام
cramp	تَشَنُّج ، عُقّال ، مَعَص
cranium	قِحف ، جُمْجُمة
critical temperature	دَرجَةُ الحرارة ألحَرِجَة
crop rotation	تَعاقُب ألزُّروع
cross-pollination	تَلقيح مُختَلِط ، إلقاحٌ تَهجينيّ
crucible	بُوتَقَة ، بُودَقَة
crystal	بِلَّورَة ، بَلّورة
crystalline	بِلَّوريّ ، مُتبلور ، مُتَبَلِّر
crystallize	تَبَلْوَر ، بَلوَر ، تَبَلّر
cubic	مُكعَّب ، تَكعيبيّ
culture	مُستَنبَت ، استِنبات
current	تَيّـار
cutting	فَسيلَة
cycle	دَورَة ، دَوْر
cyst	كُيَيسٌ غِشائيّ • كيس مَثانيّ
cytoplasm	سيتوبلازم ، حَشْوَة

D

damping-off	ذُبولٌ فطريّ
deca-	عشرة ، دِيكا
decant	صَفَّق (السائِلَ)
decay	تَضاؤل ، وَهَن • اضمِحلال ، انحِلال
deceleration	تَباطُؤ
deci-	عُشر ، دِيسي
deciduous	مُصِل ، سَلِيب ، نَفَضِيّ
declination	انحِراف ، حُدور (مِغنطيسي)
decolorize	أنصلَ ، نصَّل (اللّون) ، أزال اللون
decomposition	تحَلُّل • انحِلال
defecation	تبرُّز ، تغوُّط
degradation	انحِلال ، إدناء
dehydration	نَزعُ ألماء ، إزالةُ ألماء
deliquescence	تَمَيُّع ، تَسيُّل ، انمِياع
deliquescent	مائع ، مُتَمَيِّع ، مُتَسَيِّل
dendrite	زائِدة شَجَريّة
dendron	تَشَعُّب عَصَبِيّ ، غُصينٌ عَصَبيّ
density	كَثـافة
deodorant	مُزيلُ الرّائحة
deposit	رُسابَة ، قَرارة ، راسِب
dermis	أدَمـة

desiccator مُجفِّفة ، وِعاءُ تَجفيف
destructive distillation تَقطير هدّام ، تقطير إتلافيّ
detect كَشَف ، اكتَشَف ، استَبان
detergent مُنظِّف ، مُزيلٌ للأوساخ
deuterium ديُوتِريوم ، الهيدروجين الثقيل
deviation انحِراف ، انعطاف ، حَيَدان
dew point نُقطَة النَّدى
di- ثُنـائيّ
diabetes ألداءُ السُّكَّري ، ألزَّرب
diamond ماس ، ألماس
dicotyledon ذُو فِلقَتَين ، نباتٌ من ذوات الفِلقَتين
dielectric عازِلٌ كهربائي
diesel oil زيتُ الدِّيزل
differentiation تَمايُز ، تخلُّق
diffuse نَشَر ، اِنتَشَر
diffusion انتِشار ، نَشْر • انتِشارُ الضَوء
digestion هَضْم ، اهتِضام
digit إصبَع
diluent مُخفِّف
dilute مُخفَّف
diode دايُود ، صِمامٌ ثُنائي
dip مَيْل ، المَيْلُ (المغنطيسي)
direct current تيّار مُستَمِرّ ، تيّار مُطَّرِد
discrete مُنفَصِل ، مُتَميِّز ، مُتَفرِّد
disease مَرَض ، داء ، سَقَم
disinfectant مُطَهِّر ، مُبيدُ الجَراثيم
disintegration تَفتُّت ، إنحِلال
dispersion تَشَتُّت ، تَفَرُّج
displacement إزاحـة
dissociate تَفكَّك (بالحرارة) ، انحَلَّ (بالذوبان)
dissociation انحِلال (بالحرارة) ، تفكُّك ، حَـلّ
dissolve ذاب ، أذاب
distal قَصِيّ ، أقصى
distil قَطَّر ، تقطَّر ، فَصَلَ بالتقطير
distillate قُطـارة
distilled water مـاءٌ مُقطَّر
diverging lens عَدسة مُفرِّقة ، عدسَة مُقعَّرة
dominance سِيادة ، تسلُّط
dormancy هُجوع ، سُبات ، رُقاد
dorsal ظَهريّ
dough عَجين
drone ذكرُ النَّحل ، يَعسُوب
dropping funnel قِمعٌ قطّار ، قِمعُ القَطْر
drug عَقّار ، دَواء • مُخَدِّر
dry cell خلِيَّة جافّة
dry ice جليدٌ جافٌّ ، ثاني اكسيد الكربون الجليديّ
drying agent عامل تجفيف ، مُجفِّف
ductless gland غُدّة صَمّاء ، غدّة لا قنويّة
duodenum الإثنا عَشَري ، ألعَفج
dye صِبْغ ، صِباغ ، صِبْغَة
dynamo دِينامو ، دِنَمو ، مُوَلِّد كهربائي

E

ear أُذُن
ear drum طَبلَة الأُذُن
earpiece أُذُنيَّة ، أُذُنيَّةُ السمّاعة
earth أرض ، أرضيّ
earthenware فخّاريات ، أواني خَزفيَّة

earth's magnetism	مغنطيسيّة الأرض
echo	صدًى
eclipse	كُسوف (الشمس) ، خُسوف (القمَر)
ecology	عِلمُ البيئة
ectoplasm	جِبْلَة خارِجيّة ، بلازْمَا خارجيّة
effector	مُسْتَجيبَة
efferent	صادِر ، مُصْدِر ، ناقل من المركز إلى الأطراف
effervescent	فوّار ، مُصْدِرٌ الفقاقيع
efficiency	فَعّالية ، كِفاية ، مَردُود
efflorescence	تزهُّر
effort	جُهد ، مَجْهُود
effusion	إندِفاق ، انبجاس
egestion	طَرْحُ الفَضَلات ، إخراجُ الفضلات ، قـذف
egg	بَيْضَة
elasticity	مُرونَة
electric bell	جَرسٌ كهربائي
electric charge	شِحْنَة كهربائيّة
electric current	تيّار كهربائي
electric field	مَجال كهربائي
electric motor	مُحَرِّكٌ كهربائيّ ، مُوتور كهربائي
electric power	قُدرةٌ كهربائيّة
electrode	إلِكترود ، قُطْب
electrolysis	ألتَّحليل الكهربائي ، ألتحَلُّل بالكهرباء
electrolyte	الِكتروليت ، مَحلول كهربائي ، مُنْحَلٌّ كهربائي
electrolyze	حَلَّل بالكهرباء
electromagnet	مِغنطيس كهربائي
electromotive force	قُوّة دافِعة كهربائيّة
electron	إلِكترون ، كُهَيْرِب
electroplating	الطِّلاءُ بالكهرباء ، ألتَّصفيح الـكهربائي
electroscope	مِكشاف كهربائي ، إلِكتروسكوب
element	عُنْصُر
embryo	جَنين
embryology	عِلمُ الأجِنّة
emulsion	مُسْتَحْلَب
endoplasm	جِبلَة داخليّة ، بلازما داخليّة
endosperm	إندوسِبرم ، سُويداءُ البِزْرة
energy	طـاقة
environment	بيئة ، مُحيط ، وَسَط
enzyme	أنزيم ، خَميرة
epigeal	فَوق سَطحيّ ، فَوق تُربيّ ، نامٍ فوق سطح الأرض
epiglottis	غَلْصَمة ، لِسانُ المِزمار
equation	مُعـادَلة
equilibrium	تَوازن ، إتّزان ، تعادُل ، توازُن (كيماوي)
erythrocyte	كُرَيّةٌ (دم) حمراء
ethanol	إيثانول ، كُحول أثيلي
ether	إثير
ethylene	إيثيلين
evaporate	بَخَّر ، تبخَّر
evaporation	تَبَخُّر ، تَبخير ، تركيز بالتبخير ، تجفيفٌ بالتبخير
evergreen	دائم الخُضرة ، نبات دائمُ الخُضْرة
evolution	نظريةُ النُّشوء والارتقاء ، تَطوُّر ، انبعاث ، إطلاق ، انطِلاق (الغاز)
evolve	بَعث ، انبَعث ، انطلَق
excretion	إفراز ، ابراز ، إطراحُ (الفضلات)

experiment تجربة ، إختبار

expiration زفير ، زفر

explosion انفجار ، تفجُّر

explosive مُتفجِّر ، مادّة متفجِّرة • مُتفجِّر ، قابِلٌ للانفجار

extinguish أطفأ ، أخمَدَ

extract استخلص ، استَخرج

extraction استِخلاص ، استخراج

eye عَيْن

eyepiece عَينيّة ، عدسة عَينيّة

F

face وَجه ، سطح

facet وُجَيه ، سُطَيح

faeces غائط ، بِراز

fatigue تعب ، كلال

fats دُهون ، شُحوم

feather ريشة

femur عظمُ الفخِذ ، فَخِذ

fenestra كُوَّة ، نافِذة

fermentation اختِمار ، تخمُّر ، تَخْمير

fertilization إخصاب ، تلقيح ، إلقاح

fertilizer سَماد ، مُخصِب

fibre لِيفة ، تيلَة ، فِبْر

fibula شظِيّة ، القصبة الصُّغرى

field مَجال ، حَقْـل

filament فَتيلَة • لُيَيفة ، شُعَيرة • خُيَيط ، خيطُ السَّداة

filter مُرشِّح • رشَّح ، ترشَّح

filter paper وَرقُ ترشيح

filtrate رُشاحة ، راشِح

filtration ترشيح ، ارتشاح ، تَرشُّح

fins زَعانِف

fireclay طِينٌ حراريّ ، طُفال ، صَلصال ناريّ

fire extinguisher مِطفأة حريق ، مُطفِئة حريق

fissile انشِطاريّ ، قابِلٌ للانشِطار

fission انشِطار ، انفلاق

flame لَهَب ، شُعلة

flammable لَهُوب ، مُلتهِب ، سريعُ الالتِهاب

flocculation تندُّف ، تَدمُّج ، اندِماج

flower زَهرة ، نَوْرة

fluid مائع ، سَيَّال

fluke دُوَيدة شريطيّة • وُرَيقة

fluorescence تفلوُر ، فَلوَرِيّة ، ألَق

flux صَهور ، مُساعِدُ صَهر • دَفْق ، تَدفُّق

foam fire extinguisher مِطفأةُ حريقٍ رغويّة

focal length طُولٌ بُؤريّ ، بُعدٌ بُؤريّ

focal plane مستوىً بُؤريّ

focus بُؤرة ، مِحرق

foetus حَميل ، جَنين

fog ضَباب

force قُوّة

force pump مِضخّة دفْقٍ قَسْريّ ، مِضخّة دافِعة

forceps مِلقط ، جِفت

formula صِيغة

fossil أُحفورة ، مُستحاثة ، مُستحجِرة

freezing point نُقطةُ التجمُّد

frequency تردُّد ، تَواتُر

friction احتِكاك

fruit ثَمرة

fuel	وَقود
fuel oil	زيت الوقود ، مازوت
fulcrum	نُقطة ارتكاز ، مرتكَز
function	وَظيفة
fungus	فُطر
funnel	قِمْع
fur	قِشر ، حَرشَف . فَرْو
furnace	فُرْن
fuse	مِصْهَر ، صهيرة ، فاصِمة انصهاريّة
fusion	صَهر ، انصهار ، إندماج ، إتّحاد

G

gall bladder	المَرارة ، الحُوَيصلة الصفراويّة
galvanize	غَلْفن ، طلَى بالزِّنك
galvanometer	غلفانومِتر
gamma rays	أشِعّة غاما ، الأشِعّة الجيميّة
ganglion	عقدة عَصَبيّة ، ضَواة
gas	غاز ، غازولين ، بِنزين
gaseous	غـازِيّ
gas oil	زيتُ الغاز ، السُّولار
gasoline	غازولين ، بِنْزين
gastric	مَعِديّ
gauze	بِتّ ، نسيج شبكيّ
gel	جِل ، غروانيّ هُلاميّ القَوام
gene	جِينة ، مُوَرِّثة
generator	مُوَلِّد ، مُولِّد كهربائيّ
genetics	علم الوِراثة
genus	جِنْس
germ	مِكْروب ، جُرثُومة
germination	إنتاش ، إنْبات
gill	خَيشوم ، غَلصَم
girdle	حِزام ، نِطاق ، زُنّار
gland	غُدّة
glass	زُجـاج
glottis	مِزمار (الحَنجَرة) ، زَرْدَمة
glucose	غلوكوز ، سُكَّرُ ٱلعِنَب
goitre	سَلْعَة ، تضخُّم الغُدّة ٱلدّرَقيّة
gold	الذَهَب
gradient	مَمـال ، تدرُّج
graduate	دَرَّج
graduated cylinder	مِخبار مُدرَّج
graft	طُعْم ، تطعيم ، رُقعة
gram	غرام
grape sugar	سُكَّر العنب ، غلوكوز
graph	رَسْمٌ بيانيّ ، خَطٌّ بيانيّ ، مُخَطَّطٌ بيانيّ
graphite	غرافيت ، جرافيت
gravity	جاذبيّة ، ثِقَل
grid	شبكة (الكترود) ، شبكةُ توزيع ٱلقُدرة
gristle	غُضروف
group	مجموعة ، طائفة ، فئة
growth	نُمُوّ ، نَماء
gunpowder	مَسحوقُ البارود ، بارود
gut	قَناةُ الهَضْم
gypsum	جِبْس ، جِصّ ، كبريتات الكالسيوم المـائيّة

H

habitat	مَنْبِت ، مَوطِن ، بيئة طَبيعيّة
haemoglobin	هيموغلوبين ، يَحمور
hair	شَعر

hammer مِطرقة ، العظمُ المِطْرَقيّ
hard water ماءٌ عَسِر
heart قَلْب
heat سَخَّن ، حَمَّى ، أحْمَى • حَرارة ، كمية الحرارة
heat energy طاقة حرارية
heavy water الماءُ الثَّقيل
helium هِلْيُوم ، غازُ الهِلْيُوم
hepatic كَبِديّ
herbaceous عُشْبِيّ
herbivorous عاشِب ، آكِلُ العُشب
heredity وِراثة
hermaphrodite خُنْثَى ، خُنْثِيّ
hexagonal سُداسِيّ ، سُداسِيُّ الأضلاع
honey عَسَل ، شَهْد
hormone هُرْمون ، حاثَّة
horsepower قدرة حِصانِيّة
humerus عَضُد ، عَظْمُ العَضُد
humid رَطْب
humidity رُطوبَة ، رُطوبةُ الجَوّ
humus دُبَــال
hybrid هَجين ، نَغْل ، مُوَلَّد
hydrated مُمَيَّأ ، مُتَمَوِّه • مَيِه ، مُمَيَّه
hydraulic press مِكْبَسٌ مائيّ ، مِكبس هَيدروليّ
hydrocarbons هَيْدروكَربونات
hydrogen هَيدرُوجين ، إيدرُوجين ، غازُ الهَيدروجين
hydrogenation هَدْرَجة ، أَدْرَجَة
hydrolysis حَلْمأة ، التحلُّل بالماء ، انحِلال مائيّ
hydrometer هَيدرومِتْر ، ايدرومتر ، مِنْيَل ، مِكْثاف السوائِل
hydrophyte نبات مائيّ
hydroponics الزِّراعة المائيّة
hydroxide هَيدروكسيد ، أكسيد مائي
hygrometer هَيْجرومِتْر ، مِرطاب ، مقياس الرُّطوبة النسبيّة
hygroscopic مُستَرطِب ، استرطابيّ ، ماصٌّ الرُّطوبة
hypermetropia مَدُّ البَصر ، طُول البَصر ، الطَّرْح

I

ice جليد ، جَمَد
ignition إشعال ، إيقاد • إيراء ، إضرام • اشتعــال
illumination إنارة ، إضاءَة ، استِضاءَة
image صُورة ، خَيال
immiscible لاخَلُوط ، لاامتزاجيّ
immunity مَناعة ، حَصانة
impervious كَتيم ، غير مُنْفِذ
impulse دَفْع ، دَفْعة • حافِز ، دافِع
incidence سُقوط ، وُرود
incisor قاطِعة ، ثَنِيَّة
inclined plane سَطحٌ مائل
incubation حَضانة ، حِضان • فترةُ الحَضانة
indicator كاشِف • دَليل ، مُبَيِّن
inert خامِل ، غَيْرُ فَعَّال
inertia القُصورُ الذاتي ، ألعَطالة ، قوة الاستِمرار
inflammable لَهُوب ، سَريعُ الالتهاب

inflorescence إزهرار ، إزْهار
influenza إنفلُونزا ، النَّزْلة الوافِدة
ingestion ابتلاع ، إزْدِراد
ingot صُبَّة ، كتلة مَعدِنيّة مَصبوبَة
inoculation تطعيم ، تَلقيح
inorganic لاعُضويّ ، غَيْرُ عُضويّ
insecticide مُبيدٌ حَشريّ
insoluble غَيْرُ ذوَّاب ، عَديمُ ٱلذَّوَبان
inspiration شَهيق
instinct غَريزة
insulator عازِل ، مادةٌ عازِلَة
intelligence ذَكاء ، فِطْنَة
interference تَداخُـل
intestine مِعًى ، مِعِيٌّ ، مَصير
inversely proportional مُتَناسِبٌ عَكسياً
invertebrate لافَقاريّ ، لافَقريّ ، حيوان من اللافقاريّات
investigate استَقْصى ، حَقَّق في
iodine ألْيُود
iris قُزَحِيَّة (ٱلعَيْن)
iron ألحديد
irritability قابِليَّة ٱلاستِثارة ، تهيُّجيَّة ، حَساسِية
isotopes نَظائِر ، مُتماكِنات

J

jaw فَكّ ، حَنَك
joint مَفصِل

K

keel زَورقُ التُّوَيج · رافِدةُ القَصّ ، صَالِبُ العظم الزورقي
keeper حافظة ، حافظة المغنطيس
kidney كُلْوَة ، كُلْيَة
kilogram كِيلُوغرام
kinetic energy طاقة حَرَكيّة ، طاقةُ ٱلحركة
knocking خَبْط ، دَقّ ، طَقْطَقَة

L

lamina رَقيقة ، صَفيحة رَقيقة ، نَصْلُ (الورقة)
lard شَحْم ، دُهن حيَوانيّ
larva يَرقانة ، يَرقة ، دُعْموص
larynx حَنْجَرة
lather رَغْوَة
lattice شَبَكة ، نَسَق
laxative مُسهِل ، مُلَيِّن
lead ألرَّصاص
leaf ورقَةُ نبات
leaflet وُرَيقَة
legume قَرْنُ (البَقْل) ، سِنْفَة
lens عَدَسَة
leucocyte كُرَيَّة (دم) بَيْضاء ، كُرَيْضَة
lever عَتَلَة ، مُخْل
lichen أُشْنَة ، حَزاز
life history سِيرة ، تاريخُ ٱلحياة

lift pump	مِضخَّة رافِعة
ligament	رِبـاط
light	ضَوء ، نُور ، طاقَة شمسيَّة
lightning	بَرق ، صاعِقَة
lime	كِلْس ، جِير ، أُكسيد الكالسيوم
limestone	حَجَرُ الكِلْس ، حَجَرٌ جيريّ
linkage	تَرابُط
liquefy	سَيَّل ، تسيَّل ، أسال
liquid	سائِل ، مائِع
litmus	صِبْغُ عَبَّاد الشَّمس
litre	لِتْر
liver	كَبِـد
load	ثِقْل ، حِمْل
loam	طُفَالٌ رَمْلِيّ ، تُربة رَمْليَّة طينيَّة
locomotion	تَحرُّك ، تَنَقُّل
long sight	مَدُّ البَصَر
loudspeaker	مِجْهار ، مُكَبِّرُ الصَّوت
lubricant	مُزَلِّق ، مادَّةُ تَزليق
lung	رِئَــة
lymph	لِمْف ، لَنْف

M

machine	مَكِنَة ، آلَة
maggot	يَرقَةُ ذُبابيَّة
magnesium	المَغْنِيسيوم
magnetic compass	بُوصلة مغنطيسيّة
magnetic field	مَجالٌ مِغنطيسي
magnetic pole	قُطبٌ مِغنطيسيّ
magnification	تكبير ، تضخيم
magnifying glass	عَدَسَة مُكَبِّرة

malaria	مَلاريا ، بُرَداء
malleable	طَرُوق ، قابلٌ لِلطَّرق
mammal	لَبُون ، ثَدييّ ، حَيوان من اللَّبُونات
marble	رُخام ، مَرْمَر
marrow	نِقْي ، نُخاعُ العَظْم
mass	كُتلَة
mastication	مَضغ
mate	تَزاوَج
mechanical energy	طاقة ميكانيكيَّة
mechanism	آليَّة ، مَسلك (التفاعُل)
median	مُتوسِّط ، مستقيم مُتوسِّط
melt	صَهَر ، أذاب ، ذاب • صُهارة ، ذَوب
melting point	نُقطةُ الانصِهار
membrane	غِشاء
meniscus	هِلاليَّة ، سَطحٌ هِلالي
menstruation	الحَيْض ، الطَّمْث
mercury	الزئبق
meridian	خطُّ الزَّوال ، خَطُّ الطُّول
metabolism	أَيْض
metal	فِلِزّ ، مَعدِن فِلِزّي
metamorphosis	تَحوُّل ، استِحالة
metre	مِتْر
milk	حَليب ، لَبَن
millilitre	مِلِيلِتْر ، سَنْتيمتر مُكَعَّب
mineral	مَعْـدِن
mineral oil	زَيتٌ مَعدِني
mirage	سَراب
mirror	مِرآة
mist	ضَبـاب
mixture	مَزيج ، مَخلُوط
mobile	مُتَحَرِّك ، سَيّار ، مُتَنَقِّل
moderator	مُهَدِّىء (النيوترونات)

moisture رُطوبة
molars الطواحِن ، الأضراس
molecule جُزَيء
momentum كَمِّيّة التحرُّك ، زَخْم
mordant مُرَسِّخ ، مُرَسِّخ الصِّبغة
mortar مِلاط • هاون
moss طُحْلُب ، حَزاز
motor spirit بِنزين مُحَرِّكات
mould عَفَن ، فُطْر صَغير
moulting انسلاخ • طَرْحُ الرِّيش
mucilage صَمْغٌ نَباتيّ
mucus مُخاط
muscle عَضَلَة
mutation طَفْرة ، تَحَوُّلٌ طارىء
myopia ألحَسَر ، قِصَرُ البَصَر

N

nasal أنفيّ
natural gas ألغازُ الطبيعيّ
nectar رَحيق ، مِغْثَر (الزَّهر)
neon النِّيون ، غاز النِّيون
nerve عَصَب
nervous system جِهاز عَصَبيّ
neuron خَلِيّة عصبيّة ، عَصَبَة
neutral مُتَعادِل ، مُحايِد
neutralization تعادُل • مُعادَلة ، تَفاعُل تعادُليّ
nickel النِّيكِل
nitrogen ألنّتروجين ، ألازوت
nuclear power القُدرة النوويّة
nucleus نَواة (الذرّة) ، نَواة (الخليّة)

O

objective شَيئيّة ، عدسة شَيئيّة
oesophagus ألمَريء
oil زَيت ، نِفط • زَيت
omnivorous قارِت ، عاشِبٌ لاحِم
opaque غيرُ شفّاف ، غيرُ مُنفِذ ، أكْمَدُ
optic بَصَريّ
orbit حِجاج ، وَقب ، مَحْجَر (العين) ، مَدار ، فَلَك • مَسارٌ مَداريّ
ore خام ، رِكاز ، خامَة
organ عُضو
organic عُضويّ
organism مُتَعَضٍّ ، كائنٌ حيّ
origin أصل ، مَصدر ، مَنْشأ
oscillation ذَبذَبة ، نَوَسان ، تذبذُب ، ترجُّح
osmosis التناضُح ، الانتشار الغشائي
ovary مَبيض
oviparous بَيوض ، حيوانٌ بَيُوض
ovum بَيْضَة ، بُيَيْضَة
oxidant مُؤكسِد ، عامِلٌ مُؤكسِد
oxidation أكسَدَة ، تأكسُد
oxide أُكسيد
oxidize أكسد ، تأكسد
oxygen أُكسجين
ozone الأوزون ، غازُ الأوزون

P

paint	دِهان ، طِلاء ، بُوية
palate	حَنَك ، سقفُ الحَلْق
pancreas	المِعْقَد ، البَنْكرياس
paper	وَرَق
paraffin oil	الكيروسين ، زيت البرافين
paraffin wax	شَمْعُ ٱلبَرافين
parallax	اختِلافُ المَنْظَر
parallelogram	مُتوازِي أَضلاع
parasite	طُفَيل ، طُفَيليّ
parotid gland	الغُدَّة النكفيَّة
pasteurization	تَعقيم ، بَسْتَرة
pasture	مَرعَى
patella	رَضَفَة
pathogen	مُمرِض ، كائنٌ مُمرِض
peak value	القيمة الذُّرويَّة ، قيمة الذُّروة
peat	ألخُثّ
pelvis	الحَوْض ، تجويف الحَوض
pendulum	بَندول ، رَقّاص ، نَوّاس
penis	قَضيب (الذَّكَر)
penumbra	شِبهُ الظِّلّ
percolate	ترشَّحَ ، وَشَل ، تخلَّل
perennial	مُعَمِّر ، دائم
perianth	كِمّ ، كِمُّ الزَّهْرة
pericardium	تأمُور ، شِغاف القَلْب
pericarp	غِلافُ الثمرة ، غِلافُ البِذْرة
period	فَترة ، دَور
periscope	مِثفاق ، بريسكوب
peritoneum	صِفاق ، بَريتون ، هُرْب
permeable membrane	غشاءٌ مُنفِذ ، غِشاءٌ نَفيذ
perspiration	عَرَق
pestle	مِدَقَّة ، يَدُ الهاوَن
petal	تُويجيَّة ، ورقة تُويجيَّة ، بَتَلَة
petrify	حَجَّر ، تحجَّر ، استَحْجَر
petrol	بِنْزين ، غازُولين
petroleum	البترول ، النِّفط ، زَيتُ البِترول
pharynx	بُلْعُوم
phase	شَكْل ، طَور
phenomenon	ظـاهِرَة
philosopher	فيلسوف
phloem	لِحـاء
phosphorus	ألفُسفور ، ألفُوسفور
photosynthesis	ألتمثيلُ الضَّوئي ، ألتخليقُ الضوئي
phylum	شُعبَـة
physical changes	تَغَيُّرات طَبيعيَّة
physiology	الفِسيولوجيَة ، عِلمُ وَظائف الأعضاء
pigment	صِبْغ ، صِباغ ، خِضب ، خِضاب ، لَونٌ صِبغِيّ
pinnate	ريشيّ
pipette	ماصَّة ، ماصَّة مُدَرَّجَة
pistil	مِدَقَّـة
pitch	قار ، زِفْت ، قِير
pituitary gland	الغُدّة النُّخاميَّة
placenta	ألسُّخْد ، المَشيمَة
plane	مُستوٍ ، مُنْبَسِط
plankton	عَوالِق
plasma	مَصْلُ الدم ، بلازْما ، جِبْلَة
plastic	لَدْن ، لَدائنيّ
plastics	أللدائن ، ألبلاستيك ، المواد اللدائنية

plating	ألتصفيح ، الطِّلاءُ (الكهربائيُّ) ٱلمَعدِنيّ
platinum	ألبلاتين
polarization	استِقطاب ، استِقطاب الخَلايا
pole	قُطب (المغنطيس) ٠ قُطب (المرآة)
pollen	لَقاح ، غُبار الطَّلْع
pollination	تلقيح ، تأبير
porcelain	صِينيّ ، خَزَف صِينيّ
porous	مَسامِيّ
porous pot	وعاءٌ مَسامِيّ
posterior	خَلفِيّ
potassium	البُوتاسيوم
potential	جُهد ، جُهدٌ كَهربائيّ
potential energy	طاقةُ الوَضْع ، طاقةٌ كامِنة
power	قُدرة (كهربائية) ٠ قُوّة (العدسة) ٠ قُدرة (مِيكانيكيّة)
precipitate	تَرسُّب
precipitation	تَرسُّب ، ترسيب ، إرساب
predator	ضارٍ ، حيوانٌ مُفترِس
pregnancy	حَمْل ، حَبَل
premolar	طاحِنٌ أماميّ
pressure	ضَغط
prism	مَوشور ، مَنشور
proboscis	خُرطوم
process	عَمَليّة ، أُسلوب
propagate	تـكاثَر
property	خاصَّة ، خاصِّيّة ، مِيزة
proportional	نِسبيّ ، تناسبيّ ، مُتناسب
proton	برُوتون ، أوَيْل
protoplasm	الجِبْلَة الأولى ، الهَيُولى ، البروتوبلازم
protozoans	الأوالي ، الأوليّات
pruning	تقليم ، تشذيب
puberty	بُلوغ ، حُلْم
pubis	عانَة ٠ عَظمُ ٱلعانة
pulley	بَكَرة
pulmonary	رئويّ
pulse	نَبْضَة ، نَبض
pungent	حادّ ، لاذِع
pupa	خـادِرة
pupil	بُؤبؤ ، إنسانُ العين
pus	صَديد ، قيح
pump	مِضَخَّة

Q

quadruped	ذو أربع ، حيوان من ذواتِ ٱلأربَع
qualitative analysis	التحليل النوعيّ
quantitative analysis	ألتحليلُ الكَمّي
quartz	المَرْو ، كوارتز
queen	مَلِـكة
quicklime	الجيرُ الحيّ ، اكسيد الكالسيوم
quill	قَلَم ، سَهمُ الريشة

R

radiation	إشعاع (طاقيّ) ، إشعاع
radicle	جُذَير
radioactive	إشعاعيّ ، مُشِعّ ، ذو نشاطٍ اشعاعيّ
rarefaction	تَخلخُل
rayon	رايُون ، حَرير اصطِناعيّ
react	تفـاعَلَ

reactive	مُتَفاعِل ، تفاعُليّ ، فَعَّال
reactor	مُفاعِل (نوويّ)
reagent	كاشِف ، مُفاعِل (كيماويّ)
receiver	مُستَقبِل • وعاءُ استِقبال
receptacle	كُرسِيّ الزهرة ، قُرصُ النَّورة
receptor	مُتَقبِّل
recessive	مُتَنَحٍّ ، مُنْحَسِر
rectum	المستقيم ، المِعى المُستقيم
red blood cells	كريات الدم الحمراء
reduction	اختِزال ، خَفْضُ الأكسدة
refine	كَرَّر ، نَقّى
reflection	انعِكاس
refraction	إنكِسار
refractive index	مُعامِلُ الانكسار ، دَليلُ الانكِسار
refrigerator	بَرّاد ، وَحدةُ تبريد
regeneration	إعادةُ توليد • تجديد ، تجدُّد
relative density	الكثافة النِّسبيَّة
relay	مُرَحِّل ، مُتابِع ، مُرَحِّلة
reproduction	تكاثر ، توالُد ، تناسُل
reptile	زاحِف
residue	ثُمالة ، فُضالة ، بقيَّة ، فضلة
resins	راتِينجات ، راتِينات
resistance	مُقاوَمة
respiration	تَنَفُّس
response	استِجابة ، تجاوُب
resultant	مُحَصِّلة
retardation	تَقاصُر
retina	شبكيّة (العين)
retort	إنبيق • مُعوَجَّة
reversible	عكوس ، انعكاسي ، قابِلٌ للانعِكاس
rhombic	مُعَيَّني
rib	ضِلع
rickets	ألكُساح ، كساح الأطفال
rodent	قارِض ، حَيوان قارض ، قاضم
root	جَذر
root hair	جذر شَعريّ
rotation of crops	تعاقُب الزُّروع ، مُناوَبة المَحاصيل
ruminant	مُجتَرّ ، حيوانٌ مُجتَرّ
rust	صَدَأ
rusting	صَدَأ ، تآكُلٌ بالصدأ

S

saliva	لُعاب ، ريق
salt	مِلح • مِلح الطعام
sand	رَمْل
sand bath	مَغطَس رمليّ ، حمّام رَمليّ
sap	نُسْغ ، عُصارة
scale	قِشرة كِلسيَّة • حَرْشَفة ، فَلْس ، قِشرة • قِشرة بُرعُميَّة
scar	نَدَبة ، نَدَب
scavenger	قَمّام
scrap metal	خُردَة ، نُفايَةُ الحَدائِد
screw jack	مِرفاع لَولَبيّ
scum	زَبَد ، غُثاء
scurvy	الحَفَر ، الإسقربوط
second	ثانية
secretion	مُفرَز ، إفراز
sedative	مُسَكِّن ، عَقّار مُسَكِّن
sediment	رُسابة ، قُرارة ، رُسوب

seed	بِذرة ، بِزْرة ، حَبَّة
segment	شُدْفَة ، قطعة دائرية ، فِلْقة
semen	اَلْمَنِيّ
sensitivity	حسّاسِيّة
sepals	كأسيّات ، اوراق كأسيّة ، تَبلات
sepsis	خَمَج ، إنتان
serum	مَصْـل
sex	جِنْس
sexual reproduction	أَلتناسُل الجِنْسي ، التكاثُر الشَّقِيّ
shadow	ظِـلّ
shellac	صَمغُ آللّك ، أَلشّيلاك
shivering	ارتجاف ، ارتعاش ، رُعاش
short circuit	دائرةُ قِصَر
short sight	حَسَر ، قِصَرُ البَصَر
shunt	مُفَرِّعُ التيّار ، تحويلة
silage	عَلَفٌ مطمور ، عَلَف سَلَوِيّ
silt	غِرْيَن ، طَمْي
silver	ألفِضّة
sinus	جَيب ، تَجويف عظميّ
siphon	مِمَصّ ، مَثعَب ، سيفون
siren	سَرينة ، صَفّارةُ إنذار
skeleton	هيكل عظميّ
skin	جِلْـد
skull	جُمْجُمة
slag	جُفاء ، خَبَث
slaked lime	جِيرٌ مُطفأ
smallpox	ألجُدَري
smelting	صَهر ، تَنقِيةٌ بالصَّهر
smog	ضَباب دُخانيّ ، ضَخـان
smoke	دُخـان
socket	وَقْبَة ، وَقْب ، مَغرِز

soda water	ماء الصودا ، ماءٌ غازيّ
sodium	ألصُّوديُوم
soft water	ماءٌ يَسِر
soil	تُربَـة
solder	سَبيكةُ لِحام ، لِحام
solenoid	مِلَفٌّ لَوْلَبِيّ
solid	صُلْب ، جامِد
soluble	ذَوّاب ، قابِلٌ للذَّوَبان
solute	مُذاب ، ذائِب ، مادَّة مُذابة
solution	مَحلُول
solvent	مُذيب ، مادة مُذيبَة
soot	سِناج ، سُخام
spatula	مِلْوَق
spawn	سَرْءٌ
specialization	تَخَصُّص ، تَهايُؤ
species	نَوع
specific	نوعِيّ
specific gravity	الوزنُ النوعي ، الثِّقل النوعي ، الكثافة النسبيّة
spectrum	طيف
speed	سُرعَـة
sperm	نُطفة ، مَنيّ ، حُيَيٌّ مَنَوِيّ
spinal cord	نُخاعٌ شَوكيّ
spindle	وَشيعة ، مِغْزَل
spleen	طِحـال
spontaneously	تِلقائيّاً ، عفويّاً
spore	بَوغ ، بَوْغَة
spring balance	ميزان زُنبركيّ
stainless steel	فُولاذٌ لا يَصْدأ
stalactites and stalagmites	ألهوابِطُ والصَّواعِد
stalk	ساق ، جِذع ، سُوَيقة ، عُنُق
stamen	سَـداة

standard solution	مَحلولٌ عياريّ
starch	ألنَّشا
state	حالَة ، حال ، وَضْع
static electricity	الكهربائيّة الساكنة
steam	بُخارُ آلماء
steel	الفُولاذ ، ألصُّلْب
steelyard	مِيزَان قَبانيّ
stem	ساق (نباتيّة)
sterilization	تَعقيم ، إعقام
stigma	مِيْسَم ، سِمَة
still	مِقْطَر ، إنْبيق
stimulus	مُنَبِّه ، حافِز ، مُثير
stock	أَرومة ، جِذع ، ساق
stomach	مَعِــدَة
style	قلم ، حامِلُ السِّمَة
subcutaneous	تحت الجلد ، تحت جلديّ
sublimation	التسامي ، التصعيد
sublime	صعَّد ، تَصعَّد ، تسَامَى
succulent fruit	ثمرة عُصاريّة ، ثمرة لِحيمة
sucrose	السُّكْروز ، سُكَّرُ القَصَب
sugar	ألسُّكَّر ، ألقَنْد
sulphur	الكِبريت
sunlight	ضَوءُ آلشَّمس
supercooling	فَرطُ التبريد
surface tension	ألتوتُّر السطحيّ
suspension	مُسْتَعْلَق ، مَزيجٌ مُعلَّق
sweat	عَرَق
sweat gland	غُدّة عَرَقيّة
symbiosis	ألتعايُش ، التكافُل المَعيشي
symbol	رَمز (كيماوي) ، رَمز
synapse	اتِّصال عَصَبيّ ، تَشابُكٌ عصبيّ
synthesis	تَركيب ، تَوليف
synthesize	رَكَّب ، ألَّف ، اصطَنع
synthetic	اصطناعي ، تركيبي ، صُنْعيّ ، تَخليقي ، مُصطَنع
syringe	مِحقَنَــة

T

tadpole	شُرغوف ، فَرخُ الضفدع
tail	ذَيل ، ذَنَب
taproot	جِنْث ، جذرٌ وَتديّ رئيسيّ
tar	قِطران ، قار ، قِير
tarnish	تكَدَّر ، فقد اللَّمْعَة ، أطفأ اللّمْعَة
teat	حَلَمة ، حَلَمة الثّدي ، طِبْي
telephone	تِلفون ، هاتِف
temperature	درجة الحرارة
tendon	وَتَر
tendril	عَنَمة ، حالِق ، مِعلاق
tension	شَدّ ، توَتُّر
terminal bud	بُرعُم انتهائي ، بُرعُمٌ طَرَفيّ
testis	خُصْيَــة
test tube	أُنبوب اختِبار
tetanus	ألكُزاز
tetrahedron	رُباعيّ السطوح المُثَلَّثيّة
textiles	مَنسوجات ، أنسِجة
theory	نَظَريّــة
thermocouple	مُزْدَوجة حراريّة
thermometer	تِرمُومِتر، مِحرار، مقياسُ الحرارة
thermos flask	تِرموس ، كَظيمة
thermostat	تِرموستات ، مُثبِّتة درجة الحرارة
thorax	صَــدر
thrust	دَفع ، دَفْعَة ، دَسْر

thymus التّوتة ، ألغُدَّة الصعْتَريّة
thyroid الدّرَقِية ، ألغُدَّة الدرقيّة
timbre جرْس (الصوت)
tin ألقصدير ، التّنْك
tincture صِبْغَة ، محلولٌ كُحوليّ
tissue نَسيج
titration المُعايَرة بالتحليل الحجمي
tongue لِسـان
tonsils اللوزتان ، لَوزتا الحَلْق
tooth سِنّ ، ضِرس
touch لَمْس ، حاسّة اللّمْس
toxic سامّ ، سُمّي
tracer مُقتَفٍ ، مادة تَتبّع ، مادّة استشفافيّة
trachea ألرّغامَى ، القَصَبة الهوائيّة
trajectory مَسارُ المَقذوف ، مَسير المَقذوف
transformer مُحَوّل
transfusion نَقْلُ آلدّم
translucent شَفّ ، نِصْفُ شَفّاف
transparent شَفّاف ، شَفيف
transpiration ألنّتْح
tripod حامِلٌ ثُلاثيّ
tropism انتِحاء ، تأوُّد
trough طَسْت ، حَوض
tuber عُسقول ، دَرَنَة
tuberculosis ألسُّل ، ألتدرُّن آلرّئوي
tuning fork شوكةٌ رنّانة
turbid عَكِر ، كَدِر ، مُتَعكّر
turgor اكْتِناز ، تَنَفُّخ
twig غُصَين ، عُسلوج
twins تَوْأمـان
typhoid fever التيفوئيد ، حُمّى التيفوئيد
typhus التّيفوس ، حُمّى آلتّيفوس

U

ultraviolet radiation الإشعاعُ فَوقَ البَنَفْسَجي
umbilical cord حَبلٌ سُرّي
umbra ظِلّ ، سُويداءُ الظّلّ
unicellular أُحاديُّ الخليّة
unit وَحْدَة (قياس) • وَحدة (طاقِيّة)
unstable غير ثابِت ، غيرُ مُستَقِرّ
upthrust دَفْعٌ عُلْويّ
urinary bladder المثـانة
urine بَول

V

vaccination تَلْقيح ، تَطعيم ، حَقنٌ باللّقاح
vaccine لَقاح ، طُعْم
vacuole حُوَيصلة ، تَجويف خلَويّ
vacuum فراغ ، خَواء
vagina مَهْبِـل
valency تكافؤ • تكافُئيّة ، قوة التكافؤ
valve صِمام ، مِصراع
vane نَصْلُ الريشة ، صفحة الريشة
vapour بُخـار
vapour pressure ضغطُ البُخار
variation تغيُّر ، تبَدُّل ، اختِلاف ، تبايُن
varnish وَرنيش ، بَرنيق
vascular وِعائيّ
vector مُتّجه ، كَميّة مُوَجّهة • ناقِل
vegetable oil زيتٌ نباتيّ

vegetative reproduction	ألتكاثُر الخُضَري
vein	وَريد ، عِرق
velocity	سُرعَة ، سُرعَة اتجاهيّة
vena cava	ألوريدُ الأجوَف
venation	تعَرُّق ، تعريق
ventricle	بُطَيْن
vertebra	فِقْرة ، فَقارَة
vessel	وِعـاء
vestibule	دِهليز ، دهليزُ الأذُن
vestigial organ	عُضْوٌ لاوظيفيّ ، عُضو أثريّ
villus	زغْبَة ، خَمْلَة
vinegar	خَـلّ
virus	حُمَة ، فيرُوس
viscera	أحشاء
viscous	لَزِج ، دَبِق
vision	رُؤية ، إبْصار
vitamins	الفيتامينات ، ألحَيَمينات
vitriol	الزّاج ، زيتُ الزّاج
viviparous	وَلُود
vocal cord	وَتَرٌ صَوتيّ
volatile	سَريع التبخُّر ، طيَّار ، مُتَطاير
volt	فُولط ، فُلْط
voltage	فلطيّة ، جُهدٌ كهربائيّ
voltmeter	فُلْطِمتر ، مقياسُ الفلطيّة
volume	حَجم
volumetric analysis	التحليل ألحَجْمي
vulva	ألفَرْج

W

warm-blooded	ثابِتُ الحرارة ، ذُو دمٍ حار
waste product	فَضْلَة ، مُنتَجٌ فضَاليّ
water	ماء ، ألماء
water bath	مَغْطَسٌ مائيّ ، حَمَّام مائيّ
watt	وَاط
wave	مَوجَة ، تمَوُّج
wavelength	طُولٌ مَوجيّ
wean	فَطَم
weed	عُشب ، عُشْبَة ضارَّة
weight	وَزن ، ثِقْل
weightlessness	انعِدام الوَزن
welding	لِحام ، تلحيم
white blood cells	كرياتُ الدمِ البَيضاء
wilting	ذُبُول
windpipe	القَصَبة الهوائيّة
wing	جَناح
wire gauze	شبكة سلكيّة
womb	رَحِم
wool	صُوف
work	شُغْـل
wrist	رسْغُ اليَد ، مِعْصَم

X Y Z

X-rays	اشِعّة إكس ، الاشعة السِّينيّة
xylem	خَشَب ، نسيجُ الخشَب
yeast	خميرة
yellow	أصفَر
yolk	مُحّ ، صَفارُ البيض
zinc	ألزِّنك ، ألخَارصين
zone	نِطاق ، مِنْطقة
zoology	عِلْمُ ألحَيوان